Fodor's upCLOSE

MEXICO

the complete guide, thoroughly up-to-date

SAVVY TRAVELING: WHERE TO SPEND, HOW TO SAVE

packed with details that will make your trip

CULTURAL TIPS: ESSENTIAL LOCAL DO'S AND TABOOS

must-see sights, on and off the beaten path

INSIDER SECRETS: WHAT'S HIP AND WHAT TO SKIP

the buzz on restaurants, the lowdown on lodgings

FIND YOUR WAY WITH CLEAR AND EASY-TO-USE MAPS

Previously published as *The Berkeley Guide to Mexico*

FODOR'S TRAVEL PUBLICATIONS, INC.

NEW YORK • TORONTO • LONDON • SYDNEY • AUCKLAND

www.fodors.com/

FODOR'S UPCLOSE™ MEXICO

Editor: Jennifer L. Brewer

Editorial Contributors: Patricia Alisau, Trudy Balch, Jennifer Bartlett, Kate Deely, David Henschel, Wendy Luft, Dan Millington, Jane Onstott, Heidi Sarna

Editorial Production: Laura M. Kidder, Linda K. Schmidt

Maps: David Lindroth, *cartographer*; Robert Blake, *map editor*

Design: Fabrizio La Rocca, *creative director*; Allison Saltzman, *cover and text design*; Jolie Novak, *photo editor*

Production/Manufacturing: Mike Costa

Cover Art: Randy Wells/Tony Stone Images

SPECIAL SALES

CONTENTS

I. BASICS 1

2. MEXICO CITY AND ENVIRONS 25

3. BAJA CALIFORNIA 69

4. SONORA AND LOS MOCHIS 106

5. NORTH CENTRAL MEXICO AND THE COPPER CANYON 123

6. NORTHEASTERN MEXICO 145

7. EL BAJIO 164

TRAVELING UPCLOSE

Swim in the Caribbean. Stay in a cabaña. Try a hostel. Shop for a picnic. Have lunch next to a Maya ruin. Prowl the city markets. Go to a festival. Commune with nature. Memorize the symphony of the streets. And if you want to experience the heart and soul of Mexico, whatever you do, don't spend too much money. The deep and rich experience of Mexico that every true traveler yearns for is one of the things in life that money can't buy. In fact, if you have it, don't use it. Traveling lavishly is the surest way to turn yourself into a sideline traveler. Restaurants with white-glove service are great—sometimes—but they're usually not the best place to find the perfect mole poblano. Doormen at plush hotels have their place, but not when your look-alike room could be anywhere from Dusseldorf to Detroit. Better to stay in a more intimate place that truly gives you the atmosphere you traveled so far to experience. Don't just stand and watch—jump into the spirit of what's around you.

If you want to see Mexico up close and savor the essence of the country and its people in all their colorful, exuberant, sometimes infuriatingly chaotic glory, this book is for you. We'll show you the local culture, the offbeat sights, the bars and cafés where tourists rarely tread, and the family-run hotels and other hostelries where you'll meet fellow travelers—places where the locals would send their friends. And because you'll probably want to see the famous places if you haven't already been there, we give you tips on losing the crowds, plus the quirky and obscure facts you want as well as the basics everyone needs.

OUR GANG

Who are we? We're artists and poets, slackers and straight arrows, and travel writers and journalists, who in our less hedonistic moments report on local news and spin out an occasional opinion piece. What we share is a certain footloose spirit and a passion for magical Mexico, which we celebrate in this guidebook. Shamelessly, we've revealed all of our favorite places and our deepest, darkest travel secrets, all so that you can learn from our past mistakes and experience the best part of Mexico to the fullest. If you can't take your best friend on the road, or if your best friend is hopeless with directions, stick with us.

A psychologist turned journalist, **Patricia Alisau** was so drawn to the surrealism of Mexico that she moved to the capital some 20 years ago. She was a staff writer for the *News,* Mexico's English-language daily, cut her teeth as a war correspondent for the Associated Press during the Nicaragua Revolution, and now writes travel and business features for international publications. For this book she updated the Mexico City and Environs, Northeastern Mexico, Central Cities, Veracruz, Chiapas and Tabasco, and Yucatán Peninsula chapters.

Trudy Balch, who updated the Central Highlands chapter, has been a *Tapatía* (as residents of Guadalajara are called) in absentia since the early 1990s, when a stint as a newspaper reporter there sent her scouring for local stories. Now based in New York City, she writes about travel and business in Mexico and other Latin American countries and spends her spare time searching for good *birria* and mariachi music.

Since graduating from college two years ago, **Jennifer Bartlett** has been traveling nonstop. She has visited more than 15 countries and collaborated on several guidebooks. Her interest in Mexico is fairly recent, her first love being Southeast Asia. However, after updating the North Central Mexico and the Copper Canyon chapter she became so enchanted with the country she has decided to stay. Currently, Jennifer resides in Mexico City, where she is freelancing and continuing to improve her Spanish.

Kate Deely is a freelance writer living in San Diego, California. Mexico's Baja Peninsula was Kate's weekend home away from home as she grew up in Southern California. She spent many spring breaks and holiday weekends in San Carlos, Guaymas, and Puerto Peñasco. For this book she updated chapters on Baja California and Sonora and Los Mochis.

After obtaining his degree in political science with a minor in Spanish literature from the University of California at Berkeley, **David Henschel,** who updated the introduction to this book, decided there'd be no better way to become acquainted with Mexico than to be employed by its government. He worked for a year and a half at the Consulate General of Mexico in San Francisco and is now a student in the Graduate School of Foreign Service at Georgetown University.

When she was fresh out of college, **Wendy Luft** jumped at the chance to take a job with the Mexican tourist office—for a year or two at most, she figured. Some 25 years later, she and her Mexican husband and their adolescent sons, inveterate travelers all, traverse the country together from their home base in Mexico City. As a writer, editor, and public relations representative, Wendy has written and collaborated on many travel books and articles about her adopted country. In 1997 she won the *Pluma de Plata,* an award given by the Mexican government for travel writing, for an article on Oaxaca. Wendy updated the El Bajio and Pacific Coast chapters.

Dan Millington is a freelance writer and photographer based in Laguna Beach, California. Dan has traveled extensively throughout Mexico to write about and photograph its diverse cultures and distinct people. He's also explored Europe, the Mediterranean, the Pacific Rim, and the Americas in search of enlightening stories and unique photographs. For this book he covered Cancún, Cozumel and Isla Mujeres.

Jane Onstott, who updated the chapter on Oaxaca, was primed for adventure travel in her late teens, when she wandered Honduras for six months after being stood up at the airport by an inattentive suitor. A stoic if inefficient traveler, she has since survived a near plunge into a gorge in the highlands of Mexico, a knife-wielding robber in Madrid, and a financial shipwreck on one of the more remote Galápagos islands. The last, happily, led to a position as director of communications and Information at the Darwin Research Station on Santa Cruz Island. In between trips all over Latin America, she lives in Oaxaca, where she studies painting.

Heidi Sarna has been writing about travel nonstop since she took six months off to see the world a few years back, hitting 35 countries on six continents. Well acquainted with preparing for journeys abroad, she updated the Basics chapter. Heidi contributes to *Bride's,* countless newspapers, and numerous Fodor's guides.

A SEND-OFF

Always call ahead. We knock ourselves out to check all the facts, but everything changes all the time, in ways that none of us can ever fully anticipate. Whenever you're making a special trip to a special place, as opposed to merely wandering, always call ahead. Trust us on this.

And then, if something doesn't go quite right, as inevitably happens with even the best-laid plans, stay cool. Missed your train? Stuck in the airport? Use the time to study the people. Strike up a conversation with a stranger. Study the newsstands or flip through the local press. Take a walk. Find the silver lining in the clouds, whatever it is. And do send us a postcard to tell us what went wrong and what went right. You can e-mail us at: editors@fodors.com (specify the name of the book on the subject line) or write the Mexico editor at Fodor's upClose, 201 East 50th Street, New York, NY 10022. We'll put your ideas to good use and let other travelers benefit from your experiences. In the meantime, bon voyage!

INTRODUCTION

UPDATED BY DAVID HENSCHEL

When you enter Mexico, you step into a landscape of smoldering volcanoes, rugged plateaus, azure seas, and whispering cornfields. In a land so rich and varied, it's easy to lose yourself. And in a sense, that's what a visit to Mexico is about—wandering the twisting streets of colonial *barrios* (neighborhoods), stumbling upon ancient ruins in dense tropical jungle, or floating in the bathtub waters of the Caribbean. But while a trip to Mexico is about leaving the complications and stresses of home behind, it's also about finding and appreciating a way of life that has nothing to do with beach-side reveries and adrenaline-driven adventure treks. Discovering the real Mexico isn't an effortless process, though: To catch more than a glimpse of Mexican life, you need to travel to untouristed sites, engage in conversation with vendors at the local market, or volunteer for a nonprofit organization. Anywhere you go, if you make the effort to speak even a few words of Spanish, you will no doubt be greeted like an old friend, invited to share meals and perhaps even to spend the night. These encounters will allow you to discover a people that are as warm and open as the country itself. And hopefully, along with those tacky souvenirs and stunning photographs, you'll take home a solid understanding of what it means to live in Mexico today.

This country is home to almost 100 million people, a diverse population consisting of *mestizos* (those of mixed Spanish and Indian descent), *indígenas* (indigenous people, those who speak one or more of the 50 distinct Indian languages), and lesser numbers of those of European, African, or Asian descent. A race- and class-based hierarchy is still prevalent, with lighter-skinned mestizos and those of European descent at the top of the social scale, and indígenas at the bottom. However, this stratification doesn't encompass all aspects of society; Catholicism, for one, plays a central role in the lives of most Mexicans and acts as a unifying force. Since many folk religions and traditions were assimilated into the Catholic liturgy during Spanish rule, a unique blend of Spanish and indigenous culture flourishes today. This syncretism can be seen in nationwide fiestas such as the *Día de los Muertos* (Day of the Dead), created from the merging of All Souls Day (a Catholic holiday commemorating the dead) and an Aztec festival in honor of the glorious deaths of warriors and children.

Festivals may unite entire cities in a spirit of celebration, but once the music has died down and the fireworks are over, Mexico's grim economic, social, and political situation is all the more apparent: Corrugated-tin shacks line the roads to luxury tourist resorts, indigenous children peddle trinkets for their families' only income, and eager laborers line the treacherous U.S.-Mexico border, angling for a chance to reach the other side. The presence of a large, cheap workforce along the border, combined with virtually nonexistent environmental restrictions, have resulted in an influx of foreign-owned factories, known as *maquiladoras,* in the last few decades. These factories, most of which are associated with the electronics or garment industry, promise steady employment and above-average pay, but the vast majority of workers receive a paltry 30¢–$1.50 per hour and face appalling health conditions. Many laborers (mostly women) lose their jobs after six years, when eye strain prevents them from threading a needle, or when industrial dust fills their lungs.

Mexico's sweatshop nightmare is largely a product of its faltering economy. In December 1994, following a period of chronic borrowing from the World Bank, erratic United States investment in Mexican bonds, and a general undercutting of national business, the Mexican government devalued the peso by 50%, sending the country's already depressed economy into a tailspin. The gross domestic product dropped by 7%, causing 2 million people to lose their jobs and leaving one in two Mexicans living in poverty. Even without such hardship, an estimated 1 million new jobs must be created annually to keep pace with the country's burgeoning population, though it's unlikely that these much-needed jobs will ever materialize. And when growth does take place in industry and agro-exports it is often at the expense of Mexico's valuable natural resources—air, water, land, and wildlife. Half of the country's land is too eroded or exhausted to support farming, forcing *campesinos* (rural dwellers) to plunder virgin forests.

Look for the real Mexico in the jovial marimba music of Veracruz, the Spanish-influenced jarabe tapatío (Mexican hat dance) of Guadalajara, and in Puebla's culinary delicacy, mole poblano.

With its economy in chaos, modern Mexico has been rocked by political upheaval and popular revolt. On January 1, 1994 a poorly armed but well-organized group calling itself the Zapatista National Liberation Army (EZLN) attacked four Chiapan towns, demanding land redistribution, improved education and health care, and democratic reform for southern Mexico's indigenous population. This uprising led to peace talks between the Zapatistas and the Mexican government, talks that soon stalled due the Zapatistas' claims of government abuses. Accusations of the torture of indigenous leaders, ineffectual and fraudulent land redistribution, and persecution of foreign volunteers in Chiapas are just a few of the charges to which the current Mexican president, Ernesto Zedillo, must respond. His monolithic, quasi-centrist PRI (Institutional Revolutionary Party) has had a stronghold on Mexican politics for the last 6½ decades and carries the burden of Mexico's social, political, and economic woes.

Fortunately, recent events suggest that the PRI may finally be losing its grip. The conservative PAN (National Action Party) and left-of-center PRD (Party of the Democratic Revolution) have gained popularity in the last decade. Cuauhtémoc Cárdenas, winner of 1997's first-ever elections for *regente* (mayor) of Mexico City—historically a presidentially appointed position and the second most powerful post in the country—is a member of the PRD. Indeed, the July elections marked the first time in history that the ruling PRI failed to secure a majority in Congress.

However, despite promising electoral reforms, the hottest topic of conversation in Mexico today continues to be political scandal. In recent years Mexican leaders have been caught up in an embarassing string of corruption, extortion, and murder cases; in the most noteworthy, Raúl Salinas, brother of former president Carlos Salinas, landed in jail for masterminding a plot to kill the secretary general of the PRI. In February 1997 Mexican drug czar Jesús Rebollo Gutiérrez, an ex-army general whose appointment received international praise, was found to be in league with Mexico's most notorious drug traffickers. And Carlos Salinas, once championed as the man who would take Mexico into the 21st century, has fled to Ireland. In a nod to the national obsession, Mexico's most popular soap opera, *Nada Personal,* now bases its story line on the latest real-life political scandals.

A look at the nation's history shows that the disappointments and complexities of modern Mexican politics may have deep historical roots. The Olmec culture, considered the "mother culture" of Mesoamerica, appeared around 1000 BC and created a flourishing society adept in artistry, technology, and agriculture. By 400 BC the Olmec civilization had essentially disappeared. During the next few centuries several sophisticated cultures emerged almost concurrently: the Zapotec and Mixtec of southern Mexico, the Huastec and Totonac of Veracruz, the Tarascans of Michoacán, the Maya of the Yucatán and northern Central America, and the nameless founders of Teotihuacán. Of all these early civilizations, the Maya were perhaps the most influential and advanced, constructing pyramids and developing a writing system that included more than 300 glyphs. Despite these achievements, most Mayan cities were abandoned sometime in the 10th century, for reasons still unclear to archaeologists.

One final pre-Columbian power waited in the wings. Claiming to come from a mystical heaven known as Aztlán, the Aztec people migrated from the present-day U.S. Southwest to central Mexico in the 12th century, founding their impressive capital Tenochtitlán on the ruins of Teotihuacán near modern Mexico City. Within a century, the Aztec earned a reputation for fearlessness in battle and for gruesome human sacrifice. In their rapid rise to power they conquered almost all of the other Mesoamerican civilizations. By the time the Spaniards arrived in 1519, the Aztec empire was roughly the size of modern-day France. In the end, the last great indigenous empire in Mexico was overthrown by the Spanish: After a meeting between Hernan Cortés and the Aztec *cacique* (chief) Moctezuma, the politically savvy Cortés formed alliances with vanquished tribes that were eager to throw off the yoke of Aztec rule. Over the next 20 years, Mexico's indigenous population, decimated by battle and European diseases, fell from 22 million to just 1.5 million, while inhabitants of Spanish extraction consolidated their power.

The effort to throw off Spanish rule began in earnest three centuries after the arrival of the conquistadors. However, ousting the Spanish was only one facet of the struggle for Mexican independence. In 1848 Mexico suffered the tremendous loss of half its territory—comprising modern-day California, Arizona, New Mexico, and Texas—to the land-hungry United States. France also had its eye on Mexico, sending troops in 1861 to clear the way for a new emperor, Maximilian, Archduke of Austria. Even after the French army's defeat at Puebla on May 5, 1862 (now celebrated annually as Cinco de Mayo), France did not completely withdraw from the country until five years later, when Maximilian was executed.

By the turn of the 20th century, many of the problems that exist today were already well in place: Wealth was concentrated in the hands of a few *hacendados* (landowners) and foreign investors; indigenous people had been driven from their ancestral lands; and a vast network of patronage controlled government processes. When dictator Porfirio Díaz took control in 1884, it appeared that Mexico was headed in the right direction, moving toward modernization with public services such as rail and telegraph lines. However, the costs far outweighed the gains: Rigged elections, a stifled press, and a deeply impoverished majority soon followed. In 1910, these problems spurred the 10-year Mexican Revolution, a series of civil wars fought by Mexico's bourgeoisie. The revolutionary movement against Díaz was led by Francisco I. Madero, was joined by a number of rebel armies, including those led by "Pancho" Villa to the north and by Emiliano Zapata in central Mexico. Together these forces were successful in bringing Díaz's resignation, and Madero was the almost unanimous winner in the free elections that followed. Sadly, many high-minded goals fell by the wayside during Madero's regime.

Though the middle class and the elite were the real winners of the Mexican Revolution, the struggle's populist legacy remains—both superficially in the PRI's rhetoric and more profoundly in contemporary leftist revolutionary movements. Mexico's tradition of strength in the face of adversity continues today, and examples of determination and hope abound: In the Lacandón jungle, the Zapatistas have joined forces with other indígenas, creating cooperative "centers of resistance" in communities that were destroyed by the Mexican army during the uprising. In Guerrero, months of protests by human rights groups over the police killings of at least 25 peasants led to the resignation in March 1996 of the state's governor, who had attempted to cover up the murders. The civic organization El Barzón, formed after the peso's devaluation in December 1994, now has 600,000 members and continues to fight for the rights of the newly impoverished middle class. All of these popular movements indicate that political activism is reaching a wider segment of Mexico's people, and Mexicans are optimistic that their continued struggle will effect positive change.

Despite its ongoing crises, or perhaps because of them, Mexico continues to fascinate visitors. But a trip to Mexico is what you make of it, and those who never look any deeper into the country than the bottom of their margarita glass will come away with nothing more than a lot of sand in their luggage and hazy memories of nights spent dancing in Cancún discos. Hedonistic indulgences set to a soundtrack of strumming mariachis and crashing waves are all fine and good, but those in search of more intelligent escapes should look beyond the resort towns. You'll encounter places and people who can tell you wonders about the Mexican reality: The elderly woman sitting next to you on the bus may have had firsthand experience of the revolution, and your hotel owner may be eager to engage you in a lengthy discussion of NAFTA. All you need to experience Mexico to its fullest is a little travel savvy, some basic conversational skills, and a desire for adventure. Getting lost in this country's land, politics, and history could be the most rewarding thing you've ever done.

MEXICO

CALIFORNIA

Tijuana
Mexicali
Ensenada

ARIZONA

NEW MEXICO

BAJA
CALIFORNIA
NORTE

Golfo

Nogales

Ciudad Juárez

Nuevo Casas Grandes

Guerrero Negro

de

Hermosillo

SONORA

CHIHUAHUA

Santa Rosalía

Chihuahua

California

Cuidad Obregón

BAJA
CALIFORNIA
SUR

Los Mochis

SINALOA

COAHUILA

DURANGO

La Paz

Culiacán

Saltillo

Mazatlán

Durango

ZACATECAS

SIERRA MADRE OCCIDENTAL

Zacatecas

Tepic

AGUASCALIENTES

Sa
Po

NAYARIT

Aguascalientes

Puerto Vallarta

Guanajuato

S

Guadalajara

GUANAJUATO

JALISCO

Querétaro

Manzanillo

Colima

Morelia

Toluc

COLIMA

MICHOACÁN

SIERRA MA

MORE

PACIFIC OCEAN

GUERRERO

Ixtapa/Zihuatanejo

Chilpancing
Acapulco

N

0   200 miles

0   300 km

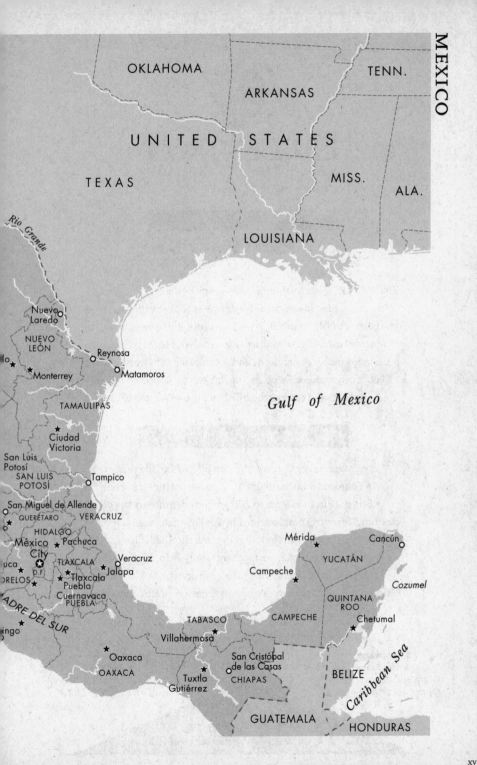

OKLAHOMA

ARKANSAS

TENN.

UNITED STATES

TEXAS

MISS.

ALA.

LOUISIANA

Rio Grande

Nuevo
Laredo

NUEVO
LEÓN

Reynosa

Monterrey

Matamoros

TAMAULIPAS

Gulf of Mexico

Ciudad
Victoria

San Luis
Potosí

SAN LUIS
POTOSÍ

Tampico

San Miguel de Allende

QUERÉTARO

VERACRUZ

HIDALGO

México
City

Pachuca

Mérida

Cancún

YUCATÁN

TLAXCALA

uca

D.F.

Veracruz

Tlaxcala

Campeche

Cozumel

RELOS

Puebla

Jalapa

QUINTANA
ROO

Cuernavaca

PUEBLA

CAMPECHE

Chetumal

ADRE DEL SUR

TABASCO

ingo

Villahermosa

Oaxaca

San Cristóbal
de las Casas

BELIZE

Caribbean Sea

OAXACA

Tuxtla
Gutiérrez

CHIAPAS

GUATEMALA

HONDURAS

ENCUENTROS
SPANISH ▼ LANGUAGE

BASICS

contacts and savvy tips to make your trip hassle-free

I f you've ever traveled with anyone before, you know that there are two types of people in the world, the planners and the nonplanners, and that travel brings out the worst in both groups. Left to their own devices, the planners will have you goose-stepping from attraction to attraction on a cultural blitzkrieg, while the nonplanners will invariably miss the flight, the bus, and maybe even the point. This chapter offers you a middle ground: enough information to help you plan your trip to Mexico without forcing you to follow a specific itinerary. One final bit of advice: once you're on the road, remain flexible; the most hair-pulling situations often turn into the best travel stories back home.

AIR TRAVEL

MAJOR AIRLINE OR LOW-COST CARRIER?

Most people choose a flight based on price. Yet there are other issues to consider. Major airlines offer the greatest number of departures; smaller airlines—including regional, low-cost, and no-frill airlines—usually have a more limited number of flights daily. Major airlines have frequent-flyer partners, which allow you to credit mileage earned on one airline to your account with another. Low-cost airlines offer a definite price advantage and fewer restrictions, such as advance-purchase requirements. Safety-wise, low-cost carriers as a group have a good history, but **check the safety record before booking** any low-cost carrier; call the Federal Aviation Administration's Consumer Hotline (*see* Airline Complaints, *below*).

MAJOR AIRLINES • American (tel. 800/433–7300) to Mexico City, Cancún. **Continental** (tel. 800/525–0280) to Mexico City, Cancún. **Delta** (tel. 800/241–4141) to Mexico City, Cancún. **Northwest** (tel. 800/447–4747) to Mexico City. **United** (tel. 800/538–2929) to Mexico City. **USAirways** (tel. 800/428–4322) to Cancún. U.K.: **British Airways** (tel. 0345/222–111) has a direct flight from the United Kingdom to Mexico City. Other airlines flying to Mexico, with brief stops en route, include **Continental** (tel. 0800/776–464), from Gatwick via Houston, from Birmingham and Manchester via Newark; **American** (tel. 0345/789–789), via Dallas or Miami; **KLM** (tel. 0990/750–900), via Amsterdam; **Air France** (tel. 0181/742–6600), via Paris; **Delta** (tel. 0800/414–767), via Atlanta; **United** (tel. 0800/888–555), via Chicago or Washington, Dulles; **Lufthansa** (tel. 0345/737–747) via Frankfurt; and **Iberia** (tel. 0171/830–0011) via Madrid.

SMALLER AIRLINES • **Aero California** (tel. 800/237–6225) to Mexico City. **Aeromexico** (tel. 800/237–6639) to Mexico City, Cancún. **America West** (tel. 800/235–9292) to Mexico City. Mexicana (tel. 800/531–7921) to Mexico City, Cancún.

DON'T STOP UNLESS YOU MUST

When you book, **look for nonstop flights** and **remember that "direct" flights stop at least once.** International flights on a country's flag carrier are almost always nonstop; U.S. airlines often fly direct. Try to **avoid connecting flights,** which require a change of plane. Two airlines may jointly operate a connecting flight, so ask if your airline operates every segment—you may find that your preferred carrier flies you only part of the way.

USE AN AGENT

Travel agents, especially those who specialize in finding the lowest fares (*see* Discounts & Deals, *below*), can be especially helpful when booking a plane ticket. When you're quoted a price, **ask your agent if the price is likely to get any lower.** Good agents know the seasonal fluctuations of airfares and can usually anticipate a sale or fare war. However, waiting can be risky: The fare could go *up* as seats become scarce, and you may wait so long that your preferred flight sells out. A wait-and-see strategy works best if your plans are flexible, but if you must arrive and depart on certain dates, don't delay.

GET THE LOWEST FARE

The least-expensive airfares to Mexico are priced for round-trip travel. Major airlines usually require that you **book in advance and buy the ticket within 24 hours,** and you may have to stay over a Saturday night. It's smart to **call a number of airlines, and when you are quoted a good price, book it on the spot**—the same fare may not be available on the same flight the next day. Airlines generally allow you to change your return date for a fee of $25–$50. If you don't use your ticket you can apply the cost toward the purchase of a new ticket, again for a small charge. However, most low-fare tickets are nonrefundable. To get the lowest airfare, **check different routings.** If your destination or home city has more than one gateway, compare prices to and from different airports. Flexibility is the key to getting a serious bargain on airfare. If you can play around with your departure date, destination, and return date, you will probably save money. Ask which days of the week are the cheapest to fly on—weekends are often the most expensive. Even the time of day you fly can make a big difference in the cost of your ticket. Also look into discounts available through student- and budget-travel organizations (*see* Students, *below*).

To save money on round-trip flights originating in the United Kingdom, **look into an APEX or Super-PEX ticket.** APEX tickets must be booked in advance and have certain restrictions. Super-PEX tickets can be purchased at the airport on the day of departure—subject to availability.

CHECK WITH CONSOLIDATORS

Consolidators, also sometimes known as bucket shops, buy tickets for scheduled flights at reduced rates from the airlines then sell them at prices that beat the best fare available directly from the airlines, usually without advance restrictions. Sometimes you can even get your money back if you need to return the ticket. Carefully read the fine print detailing penalties for changes and cancellations, **confirm your consolidator reservation with the airline,** and be sure to check restrictions, refund possibilities, and payment conditions

CONSOLIDATORS • **Airfare Busters** (5100 Westheimer Ave., Suite 550, Houston, TX 77056, tel. 713/961–5109 or 800/232–8783, fax 713/961–3385). **Globe Travel** (507 5th Ave., Suite 606, New York, NY 10017, tel. 212/843–9885 or 800/969–4562, fax 212/843–9889). **United States Air Consolidators Association** (925 L St., Suite 220, Sacramento, CA 95814, tel. 916/441–4166, fax 916/441–3520). **UniTravel** (1177 N. Warson Rd., St. Louis, MO 63132, tel. 314/569–2501 or 800/325–2222, fax 314/569–2503). **Up & Away Travel** (347 5th Ave., Suite 202, New York, NY 10016, tel. 212/889–2345 or 800/275–8001, fax 212/889–2350).

CONSIDER A CHARTER

Charters usually have the lowest fares but are not dependable. Departures are infrequent and seldom on time, check-in can be chaos, schedules are often weird, and flights can be delayed for up to 48 hours or can be canceled for any reason up to 10 days before you're scheduled to leave. Moreover, itineraries and prices can change after you've booked your flight, so you must **be very careful to choose a legitimate charter carrier.** Don't commit to a charter operator that doesn't follow proper booking procedures. Be especially careful when buying a charter ticket, and read the fine print regarding refund policies. If you can't pay with a credit card, **make your check payable to a charter carrier's escrow account** (unless you're dealing with a travel agent, in which case his or her check should be made payable to the escrow account). The name of the bank should be in the charter contract.

CHARTER CARRIERS • SunTrips (2350 Paragon Dr., San Jose, CA 95131, tel. 408/432–1101 or 800/786–8747). **Travel Time** (1 Halladie Plaza, Suite 406, San Francisco, CA 94102, tel. 415/677–0799 or 800/956–9327, fax 415/391–1856).

GO AS A COURIER

Courier flights are simple: You sign a contract with a courier service to baby-sit their packages (often without ever laying eyes on them, let alone hands), and the courier company pays half or more of your airfare. On the day of departure, you arrive at the airport a few hours early, meet someone who hands you a ticket and customs forms, and off you go. After you land, you simply clear customs with the courier luggage, and deliver it to a waiting agent.

It's cheap and easy, but there are restrictions: Flights are usually booked only a week or two in advance—often only a few days in advance—and you are allowed carry-on luggage only, because the courier uses your checked luggage allowance to transport the shipment. You must return within one to four weeks, and times and destinations are limited. If you plan to travel with a companion, you'll probably have to travel a day apart. And you may be asked to pay a deposit, to be refunded after you have completed your assignment.

COURIER CONTACTS • Discount Travel International (169 W. 81st St., New York, NY 10024, tel. 212/362–3636, fax 212/362–3236). **Now Voyager** (tel. 212/431–1616, fax 212/334–5243). **Air Facility** (153-40 Rockaway Blvd., Jamaica, NY 11434, tel. 718/712–1769, fax 718/712–1574).

AVOID GETTING BUMPED

Airlines routinely overbook planes, knowing that not everyone with a ticket will show up, but sometimes everyone does. When that happens, airlines ask for volunteers to give up their seats. In return these volunteers usually get a certificate for a free flight and are rebooked on the next flight out. If there are not enough volunteers the airline must choose who will be denied boarding. The first to get bumped are passengers who checked in late and those flying on discounted tickets, **so get to the gate and check in as early as possible,** especially during peak periods.

Always **bring a photo ID to the airport.** You may be asked to show it before you are allowed to check in.

ENJOY THE FLIGHT

For better service, **fly smaller or regional carriers,** which often have higher passenger-satisfaction ratings. Sometimes you'll find more legroom and better food.

For more legroom, **request an emergency-aisle seat**; don't however, sit in the row in front of the emergency aisle or in front of a bulkhead, where seats may not recline.

If you don't like airline food, **ask for special meals when booking.** These can be vegetarian, low-cholesterol, or kosher, for example.

Some carriers have prohibited smoking throughout their systems; others allow smoking only on certain routes or even certain departures from that route, so **contact your carrier regarding its smoking policy.**

COMPLAIN IF NECESSARY

If your baggage goes astray or your flight goes awry, complain right away. Most carriers require that you file a claim immediately.

AIRLINE COMPLAINTS • U.S. Department of Transportation **Aviation Consumer Protection Division** (C-75, Washington, DC 20590, tel. 202/366–2220). **Federal Aviation Administration (FAA) Consumer Hotline** (tel. 800/322–7873).

FLYING WITHIN MEXICO

Domestic plane travel cost about four times as much as a first-class bus ticket, but it will save you travel time. **Mexicana** and **Aeroméxico** are government-subsidized and offer similar fares. **Aero California** flies between Baja California cities and some places in northwestern Mexico. **Aerocaribe** and **Aviacsa** operate in southeast Mexico.

DOMESTIC AIRLINES • All of the following phone numbers can only be dialed from Mexico: **Mexicana** (tel. 800/52–220). **Aeroméxico** (tel. 800/90–999). **Aero California** (tel. 5/20–713–92 from Mexico City). **Aerocaribe** (tel. 800/70–579). **Aviacsa** (tel. 800/62–126).

AIRPORTS

Major airports are: Acapulco (**General Juan Alvarez airport**), Cancún (**Cancún airport**), Cozumel (**Cozumel airport**), Guadalajara (**Don Miguel Hidalgo airport**), Ixtapa (**Ixtapa/Zihuatanejo airport**), Mazatlán (**General Rafael Buena airport**), Mérida (**Licenciado Manuel Crescencio Rejon airport**), Mexico City (**Benito Juarez airport**), Puerto Vallarta (**Puerto Vallarta airport**), and **Los Cabos airport** in Los Cabos.

By plane, Mexico City is 4½ hours from New York, 4 hours from Chicago, and 3½ hours from Los Angeles. Cancún is 3½ hours from New York and from Chicago, 4½ hours from Los Angeles. Acapulco is 6 hours from New York, 4 hours from Chicago, and 3½ hours from Los Angeles.

AIRPORT INFORMATION • General Juan Alvarez airport (tel. 011–52–748/4–08–87). **Cancún airport** (tel. 011–52–98/86–00–49). **Cozumel airport** (tel. 011–52–98/72–04–85). **Don Miguel Hidalgo airport** (tel. 011–52–3/688–51–20). **Ixtapa/Zihuatanejo airport** (tel. 011–52–755/4–20–70). **General Rafael Buena airport** (tel. 011–52–69/82–21–77). **Licenciado Manuel Crescencio Rejon airport** (tel. 011–52–99/24–87–42). **Benito Juarez airport** (tel. 011–52–16/33–07–34). **Puerto Vallarta** (tel. 011–52–322/11–2–98). **Los Cabos airport** (tel. 011–52–684/3–03–41).

BICYCLING

Bike travel in Mexico is for the hardy and experienced rider. Some roads have never seen a bicycle, and drivers are not accustomed to cyclists. In addition, most Mexican roads lack shoulders and are often pitted. Despite these drawbacks, traveling by bike in Mexico can be fun if you plan ahead, and bikes are especially useful for travel to places where there are only dirt roads or tracks, or where public transportation is scant. In the Yucatán, for example, bikes are a primary form of transportation for locals, and bike-repair shops are common even in smaller towns. When planning your trip, consult an up-to-date AAA, Pemex, or Guía Roji map. Be sure to carry plenty of water and everything you might need to repair your bike. Pack extra patch kits, as shards of glass often litter the roads. If you can take your bike apart and fold it up, buses will allow you to store it in the cargo space; bikers in the Copper Canyon can transport their bikes on the trains. If you go on your own and plan on pedaling only part of the way, Amtrak will transport your bike to the border. They provide the bike box, but require you to disassemble the bike.

RESOURCES • _Latin America by Bike_ (Mountaineer Books; 306 2nd Ave. W., Seattle, WA 98119, tel. 206/223–6303; $14.95), by Walter Sienko, provides information on biking opportunities in Mexico as well as Central and South America. **_Bicycling Mexico_** (Hunter Publishing Inc.; 300 Raritan Center Pkwy., Edison, NJ 08818, tel. 201/225–1900, fax 201/417–0482; $16.95), by Ericka Weisbroth and Eric Ellman, is the bible of bicyclists, complete with maps, color photos, historical information, and a kilometer-by-kilometer breakdown of every route possible. For a list of companies that run organized bike tours of Mexico, _see_ Tour Operators, _below_.

BIKES IN FLIGHT

Most airlines will ship bikes as luggage, provided they are dismantled and put into a box. Call to see if your airline sells bike boxes (around $10). International travelers departing from the United States can substitute a bike for their second piece of checked luggage at no extra charge, or pay $100 to bring the bike along as an additional piece of luggage.

BUS TRAVEL

There aren't many direct buses into Mexico. Usually, you must trundle down to the border, cross, and then change to a Mexican bus on the other side to continue your journey. At the El Paso–Ciudad Juárez border crossing, **Greyhound** has a bus that will take you from El Paso to the Ciudad Juárez bus terminal, stopping at border customs along the way. San Diego–Tijuana has a similar system, called **Mexi-Coach** (_see_ Chapter 3) which runs from San Ysidro, on the U.S. side, to downtown Tijuana. Otherwise, Greyhound will get you to, but not across, the border; the company serves El Paso, Del Río, Laredo, McAllen, Eagle Pass, and Brownsville, Texas; Nogales, Arizona; and Calexico and San Diego, California.

Another option is to book a tour with **Green Tortoise,** the cheap alternative to humdrum bus travel. From November through April, Green Tortoise buses—equipped with sleeping pads, kitchens, and stereos—offer 9- and 14-day trips from the West Coast of the United States to Baja California. In November and December, limited space is available for longer trips to Mexico City, Mérida, and Guatemala.

RESOURCES • Greyhound (tel. 800/231–2222). **Green Tortoise Adventure Travel** (494 Broadway, San Francisco, CA 94133, tel. 415/956–7500, or 800/867–8647 outside CA).

WITHIN MEXICO

Bus travel throughout Mexico is cheap and easy. Buses are basically divided into first and second class, but in reality they run the gamut from dilapidated school buses with shrines to the Virgin of Guadalupe attached to the grill and blasting ranchera music, to luxury liners with air-conditioning, bathrooms, onboard movies, and free refreshments. Most of the time, however, second-class means a comfortable bus with no air-conditioning that makes a number of stops, while first-class service consists of a cleaner bus, chilled beyond reason, and (usually) a direct ride. Super-deluxe buses are usually designated *plus* or *especial*. The largest second-class bus line in Mexico is **Flecha Amarilla**; first-class lines include **Omnibús de Mexico, Futura, Transportes del Norte,** and **Élite.**

CAMPING

A host of camping opportunities exist in Mexico, but don't expect the typical U.S.-style campground. Mexico's campgrounds are usually nothing more than trailer parks with running water, cooking areas, and room to pitch tents; sites can cost $1–$8. To enjoy more rustic surroundings, you can set up camp off the road or on the beach in relative safety, and save loads of money. Usually, you can camp at an *ejido* (farming community) or on someone's land for free as long as you ask permission first; ask locals about the safest and best spots. Do not camp, however, at archaeological sites. For more detailed camping information and humorous camping anecdotes, look to *The People's Guide to Mexico* (John Muir Publications, Box 613, Sante Fe, NM 87504, tel. 800/285–4087; $17.95) by Carl Franz.

Camping supplies are scarce in Mexico. Before you begin packing loads of camping gear, however, consider how much camping you will actually do versus how much trouble it will be to haul around your tent, sleeping bag, stove, and accoutrements. Even finding a place to store your gear can be difficult, as storage lockers tend to be small.

In many towns along the Pacific and Caribbean coasts, beachside *palapas* (thatched huts) are an excellent alternative to tent camping. All you'll need for a night in a palapa is a hammock (which you can purchase cheaply in Mexico), some mosquito netting, and a padlock for stashing your belongings in a locker.

CAR RENTAL

If you want to rent in the United States and drive down to Mexico, you'll find rental companies less than obliging. You can rent a car from **Avis** in Yuma, Arizona, or San Diego, California, and drive it into Mexico, but only for a maximum of 714 km (450 mi) one-way. **Dollar** will allow you to drive 241 km (150 mi) into Mexico from San Diego or from McAllen, Texas, as far as Monterrey. Finally, **Thrifty** allows you to drive from San Diego into Mexico, but only for 80 km (50 mi).

Rates in Mexico City begin at $35 a day and $189 a week for an economy car with air conditioning, manual transmission, and unlimited mileage. Rates in Acapulco begin at $35 a day and $189 a week. This does not include tax on car rentals, which is 15%. The companies that rent for Baja have different prices and sometimes different rules than mainland Mexico.

CUT COSTS

To get the best deal, **book through a travel agent who is willing to shop around.**

Be sure to **look into wholesalers,** companies that do not own fleets but rent in bulk from those that do and often offer better rates than traditional car-rental operations. Prices are best during off-peak periods. Rentals booked through wholesalers must be paid for before you leave the United States.

Also **ask your travel agent about a company's customer-service record.** How has it responded to late plane arrivals and vehicle mishaps? Are there often lines at the rental counter, and, if you're traveling during a holiday period, does a confirmed reservation guarantee you a car?

No matter who you rent from, remember to ask about required deposits, cancellation penalties, and drop-off charges if you're planning to pick up the car in one city and leave it in another.

MAJOR AGENCIES • Budget (tel. 800/527–0700, 0800/18–11–81 in the U.K.). **Dollar** (tel. 800/800–4000; 0990/56–56–56 in the U.K., where it is known as Eurodollar). **Hertz** (tel. 800/654–3001, 800/263–0600 in Canada, 0345/55–58–88 in the U.K.). **National InterRent** (tel. 800/227–3876; 0345/22–25–25 in the U.K., where it is known as Europcar InterRent). **Thrifty** (tel. 800/367–2277).

RENTAL WHOLESALERS • Auto Europe (tel. 207/842–2000 or 800/223–5555, fax 800/235–6321). The **Kemwel Group** (tel. 914/835–5555 or 800/678–0678, fax 914/835–5126).

INSURANCE

When driving a rented car you are generally responsible for any damage to or loss of the vehicle. You also are liable for any property damage or personal injury that you may cause while driving. **All major rental agencies require that you purchase Mexican insurance,** usually about $15–$20 per day.

BEWARE SURCHARGES

Before you pick up a car in one city and leave it in another, **ask about drop-off charges or one-way service fees,** which can be substantial. Note, too, that some rental agencies charge extra if you return the car before the time specified on your contract. To avoid a hefty refueling fee, **fill the tank just before you turn in the car,** but be aware that gas stations near the rental outlet may overcharge.

MEET THE REQUIREMENTS

In Mexico your own driver's license is acceptable identification. However, an International Driver's Permit is a good idea; it's available from the American or Canadian automobile association, or, in the United Kingdom, from the Automobile Association or Royal Automobile Club.

CONSUMER PROTECTION

Whenever possible, **pay with a major credit card** so you can cancel payment if there's a problem, provided that you can provide documentation. This is a good idea whether you're buying travel arrangements before your trip or shopping at your destination.

If you're doing business with a particular company for the first time, **contact your local Better Business Bureau and the attorney general's offices** in your state and the company's home state, as well. Have any complaints been filed?

Finally, if you're buying a package, always **consider travel insurance** that includes default coverage (*see* Insurance, *above*).

LOCAL BBBS • Council of Better Business Bureaus (4200 Wilson Blvd., Suite 800, Arlington, VA 22203, tel. 703/276–0100, fax 703/525–8277).

CUSTOMS & DUTIES

When shopping, **keep receipts** for all of your purchases. Upon reentering the country, **be ready to show customs officials what you've bought.** It's best to have everything in one easily accessible place—and don't wrap gifts. If you feel a duty is incorrect, appeal the assessment. If you object to the way your clearance was handled, get the inspector's badge number. In either case, first ask to see a supervisor, then write to the port director at the address listed on your receipt. Send a copy of the receipt and other appropriate documentation. If you still don't get satisfaction you can take your case to customs headquarters in Washington.

ENTERING AUSTRALIA

If you're 18 or older, you may bring back A$400 worth of souvenirs and gifts, including jewelry. Your duty-free allowance also includes 250 cigarettes or 250 grams of tobacco and 1,125ml of alcohol, including wine, beer, or spirits. Residents under 18 may bring back A$200 worth of goods.

INFORMATION • Australian Customs Service (Regional Director, Box 8, Sydney, NSW 2001, tel. 02/9213–2000, fax 02/9213–4000).

ENTERING CANADA

If you've been out of Canada for at least seven days you may bring in C$500 worth of goods duty-free. If you've been away for fewer than seven days but more than 48 hours, the duty-free allowance drops to C$200; if your trip lasts 24–48 hours, the allowance is C$50. You may not pool allowances with family members. Goods claimed under the C$500 exemption may follow you by mail; those claimed under the lesser exemptions must accompany you.

Alcohol and tobacco products may be included in the seven-day and 48-hour exemptions but not in the 24-hour exemption. If you meet the age requirements of the province or territory through which you reenter Canada you may bring in, duty-free, 1.14 liters (40 imperial ounces) of wine or liquor *or* 24 12-ounce cans or bottles of beer or ale. If you are 16 or older you may bring in, duty-free, 200 cigarettes and 50 cigars; these items must accompany you.

You may send an unlimited number of gifts worth up to C$60 each duty-free to Canada. Label the package UNSOLICITED GIFT—VALUE UNDER $60. Alcohol and tobacco are excluded.

INFORMATION • Revenue Canada (2265 St. Laurent Blvd. S, Ottawa, Ontario K1G 4K3, tel. 613/993–0534, 800/461–9999 in Canada).

ENTERING MEXICO

If you're arriving in Mexico City, you may be one of the one in 10 people whose luggage is searched. Before passing through customs you'll press a button in front of a small stoplight apparatus. If the resulting light is green, you can pass go; if it's red, officials search your baggage. You will be given a baggage-declaration form to itemize what you're bringing into the country. You're allowed to bring in 3 liters of spirits or wine for personal use, 400 cigarettes, two boxes of cigars, a reasonable amount of perfume for personal use, one movie camera and one regular camera, eight rolls of film for each, and gift items not to exceed a total of $120.

ENTERING NEW ZEALAND

Although greeted with a "Haere Mai" ("Welcome to New Zealand"), homeward-bound travelers with goods to declare must present themselves for inspection. If you're 17 or older, you may bring back NZ$700 worth of souvenirs and gifts. Your duty-free allowance also includes 200 cigarettes or 250 grams of tobacco or 50 cigars or a combo of all three up to 250 grams; 4.5 liters of wine or beer and one 1,125-ml bottle of spirits.

INFORMATION • New Zealand Customs (Custom House, 50 Anzac Ave., Box 29, Auckland, New Zealand, tel. 09/359–6655, fax 09/309–2978).

ENTERING THE U.K.

From countries outside the EU, including Mexico, you may import, duty-free, 200 cigarettes or 50 cigars; 1 liter of spirits or 2 liters of fortified or sparkling wine or liqueurs; 2 liters of still table wine; 60 milliliters of perfume; and 250 milliliters of toilet water; plus £136 worth of other goods, including gifts and souvenirs.

INFORMATION • HM Customs and Excise (Dorset House, Stamford St., London SE1 9NG, tel. 0171/202–4227).

ENTERING THE U.S.

Like most government organizations, the U.S. Customs Service enforces a number of mysterious rules. These are the rules: When you return to the United States, you have to declare all items you bought abroad, but you won't have to pay duty unless you come home with more than $400 worth of foreign goods—as long as you've been out of the country for at least 48 hours and haven't already used the $400 allowance or any part of it in the past 30 days. For purchases between $400 and $1,000, you have to pay a 10% duty. You also have to pay tax if you exceed your duty-free allowances: one liter of alcohol or wine, 100 non-Cuban cigars or 200 cigarettes or 2 kilograms of tobacco, and one bottle of perfume. Antiques, which the U.S. Customs Service defines as objects more than 100 years old, enter duty-free, as do original works of art done entirely by hand, including paintings, drawings, and sculptures. Prohibited at all times: meat products, seeds, plants, and fruits.

You may also send packages home duty-free: up to $200 worth of goods for your own use, with a limit of one parcel per addressee per day (and no alcohol or tobacco products or perfume worth more than $5); label the package PERSONAL USE, and attach a list of its contents and their retail value. Do not label the package UNSOLICITED GIFT, or your duty-free exemption will drop to $100. Mailed items do not affect your duty-free allowance on your return.

INFORMATION • U.S. Customs Service (Inquiries, Box 7407, Washington, DC 20044, tel. 202/927–6724; complaints, Commissioner's Office, 1301 Constitution Ave. NW, Washington, DC 20229; registration of equipment, Resource Management, 1301 Constitution Ave. NW, Washington DC, 20229, tel. 202/927–0540).

DINING

Dining in Mexican restaurants can be a disconcerting experience at first. When you sit down, a waiter brings you a menu, then returns after about 30 seconds to take your order. He or she expects you to be ready; if you need more time, you'll have to ask for it and you might get a look of surprise. This speediness is balanced by the length of time it takes to actually receive your food—sometimes decades.

Choosing a dish gets even more complicated when you try to order and find out that maybe 5% of the items on the menu are actually available. Standard practice in Mexico is to tip 10% or a bit higher at sit-down restaurants and bars—there's no need to tip at food stands.

Mexicans make good use of their natural resources, which means that corn and the tortillas made from them are plentiful. Other staple elements include chile peppers, refried pinto (or black) beans, grilled and stewed meats, rice, cheese, and salsa. *Desayuno* (breakfast) often consists of a slab of meat or spicy *huevos rancheros* (fried eggs with salsa, served on tortillas), tropical fruit salads, fresh-squeezed juices, and an array of sugary sweetbreads. Lunch, or *comida,* is the big meal of the day, served between 1 and 3. Most restaurants offer some sort of *comida corrida*; these four-course, fixed-price lunch specials won't set you back more than $3. A lighter *cena* (dinner) is served between 6 and 8 PM.

Tortas (Mexican sandwiches served in a roll) are especially popular at food stands. Other delectable delights include *pozole* (a corn stew with meat or vegetables), mole (a sauce made out of chocolate and chiles, served over meats), and *chiles rellenos* (chiles stuffed with cheese or meat, deep-fried, and served in a red sauce). Vegetarian restaurants are difficult to find in all but the largest cities, but with the abundance of beans, fresh fruit, vegetables, and nuts, herbivores should do just fine. Be aware that lard is often used in the preparation of tortillas and refried beans.

The **price categories in this book** are based on the assumption that your meal consists of a main course, a drink, and a cup of coffee.

DISABILITIES & ACCESSIBILITY

ACCESS IN MEXICO

Mexico is poorly equipped for travelers with disabilities. There are no special discounts or passes for disabled travelers in Mexico, nor is public transportation, including the Mexico City Metro, wheelchair accessible. Roads and sidewalks are often crowded, in poor condition, and without ramps, and people on the street will not usually assist you unless expressly asked. Renting or bringing a car or van is your best bet for exploring the country comfortably.

Most hotels and restaurants have at least a few steps, and while rooms considered "wheelchair accessible" by hotel owners are usually on the ground floor, the doorways and bathroom may not be maneuverable. It's a good idea to call ahead to find out what a hotel or restaurant can offer. Despite these barriers, Mexicans with disabilities manage to negotiate places that most travelers outside Mexico would not consider accessible. The best choice of accessible lodging is found in major resort towns like Acapulco and Mazatlán.

TIPS & HINTS

When discussing accessibility with an operator or reservationist, **ask hard questions.** Are there any stairs, inside *or* out? Are there grab bars next to the toilet *and* in the shower/tub? How wide is the doorway to the room? To the bathroom? When possible, **opt for newer accommodations,** which are more likely to have been designed with access in mind. Older buildings may offer more limited facilities. Be sure to **discuss your needs before booking.**

COMPLAINTS • **Aviation Consumer Protection Division** (*see* Air Travel, *above*) for airline-related problems.

TRAVEL AGENCIES

Some agencies specialize in travel arrangements for individuals with disabilities.

RESOURCES • **Access Adventures** (206 Chestnut Ridge Rd., Rochester, NY 14624, tel. 716/889–9096), run by a former physical-rehabilitation counselor. **Hinsdale Travel Service** (201 E. Ogden Ave., Suite 100, Hinsdale, IL 60521, tel. 630/325–1335), which offers advice from wheelchair traveler Janice Perkins. **Wheelchair Journeys** (16979 Redmond Way, Redmond, WA 98052, tel. 206/885–2210 or 800/313–4751), for general travel arrangements.

DISCOUNTS & DEALS

While your travel plans are still in the fantasy stage, start studying the travel sections of major Sunday newspapers: You'll often find listings for good packages and incredibly cheap flights. Surfing the Internet can also give you some good ideas. Travel agents are another obvious resource; the computer networks to which they have access show the lowest fares before they're even advertised. Agencies on or near college campuses, accustomed to dealing with budget travelers, can be especially helpful.

Always **compare all your options before making a choice.** A plane ticket bought with a promotional coupon may not be cheaper than the least expensive fare from a discount ticket agency. (For more on getting a deal on airfares, *see* Air Travel, *above*.) When evaluating a package, keep in mind that what you get is just as important as what you save. Just because something is cheap doesn't mean it's a bargain.

CREDIT CARDS & AUTO CLUBS

When you use your credit card to make travel purchases you may get free travel-accident insurance, collision-damage insurance, and medical or legal help, depending on the card and the bank that issued it. So **get a copy of your credit card's travel-benefits policy.** If you are a member of the American Automobile Association (AAA) or an oil-company-sponsored road-assistance plan, always **ask hotel or car-rental reservationists about auto-club discounts.** Some clubs offer additional discounts on admission to attractions. And don't forget that auto-club membership entitles you to free maps and trip-planning services.

DISCOUNTS BY PHONE

Don't be afraid to **check out "1-800" discount reservations services,** which use their buying power to get a better price on hotels, airline tickets, even car rentals. When booking a room, always **call the hotel's local toll-free number** (if one is available) rather than the central reservations number—you'll often get a better price. Always ask about special packages. When shopping for the best deal on car rentals, **look for guaranteed exchange rates,** which protect you against a falling dollar. With your rate locked in, you won't pay more even if the price goes up in the local currency.

CHEAP AIRLINE TICKETS • Try tel. **800/FLY–4–LESS** or tel. **800/FLY–ASAP.**

CHEAP HOTEL ROOMS • Players Express Vacations (tel. 800/458–6161) offers bookings in major Mexican cities, as does **Steigenberger Reservation Service** (tel. 800/223–5652).

PACKAGE TOURS

Packages and guided tours can both save you money, but don't confuse the two. When you buy a package your travel remains independent, just as though you had planned and booked the trip yourself. Fly/drive packages, which combine airfare and car rental, are often a good deal.

DRIVING

Driving in a foreign country is always an adventure, and the quality of Mexican roads varies substantially from region to region. Drivers need a current license and registration, as well as a vehicle permit from border officials for cars not registered in Mexico. For the lowdown on permit procedures, *see* Entering Mexico, *below*.

The maximum speed on most Mexican highways is 100 km (62 mi) per hour (120 km/74 mi on some expressways). On many state and local roads, however, you'll be lucky to do half that, as many roads, even those connecting major towns, are single-lane routes clogged with smoke-belching trucks. Trucks will often help you out by flashing their turn signals to let you know that it is safe to pass. Toll roads, or *autopistas,* connect some major cities, charging random prices at randomly dispersed toll booths. However, it may be worth the added expense: Emergency phones and water pumps are available about every 15 km (9 mi), the fees keep traffic to a minimum, and road conditions are generally excellent. Driving at night is discouraged, as roads are often poorly marked and, in rural areas, animals wandering onto roadways can be a major hazard. If you are involved in an accident, notify the police immediately; take pictures of all cars involved; and collect information from the other driver if possible. Even if the accident wasn't your fault, the rule in Mexico is "guilty until proven innocent," and the police will not necessarily take your word as gospel if the other driver blames you. Photos will strengthen your case.

You are required to stop and show your personal and vehicle documents at all roadside customs checkpoints. You are also required to stop anytime a police officer waves you over, but be cautious: Travelers are prime targets for robbers who pose as the police. Highways 1 and 15 in Sinaloa have become infamous for this sort of robbery. If you are pulled over, keep calm, look important (if possible), and behave politely. A 50–100 peso ($6–$13) *mordida* (bribe; literally, "bite") might speed the process along, though don't volunteer this unless it looks like there's no other option. As for fuel, all the gas you buy will be from Pemex, Mexico's state-owned oil monopoly. Quality is low, so you may hear some unfamiliar engine knocks. Pemex's unleaded Magna Sin gas should be safe for most vehicles requiring unleaded gasoline. Fill up when you see a station, since the next one may have a broken pump.

Free roadside emergency service is available in much of the country from the *Ángeles Verdes* (Green Angels), a group of radio-dispatched, English-speaking mechanics. If you break down, pull over and pop your hood up; one will come cruising along if you wait long enough. It's a good idea to keep their 24-hour toll-free emergency number on hand (tel. 800/903–92). The **Asociación Mexicana Automovi-lística** (AMA; Orizaba 7, Col. Roma, Distrito Federal, CP 06700, México, tel. 5/511–62–85. Emergency tel. 5/588–70–40 or 5/761–60–22), Mexico's motoring club, gives discounted services to AAA members. For a $50 registration fee, they'll provide roadside repairs, fuel and tire service, plus free towing (up to 10 km) in Mexico City, Puebla, and other central Mexican towns. Parts and knowledgeable mechanics can be extremely hard to find for European cars such as BMWs, Saabs, Volvos, and Citroëns, and high-priced American models.

AUTO CLUBS • In the United States, **American Automobile Association** (tel. 800/564–6222). In the United Kingdom, **Automobile Association** (AA, tel. 0990/500–600), **Royal Automobile Club** (RAC, membership tel. 0990/722–722; insurance 0345/121–345).

ROAD GUIDES • Guía Roji publishes an excellent road atlas. Pemex's *Atlas de Carreteras y Ciudades Turísticas* is also good. Both of these are widely available in bookstores and at newsstands in Mexico.

MOTORCYCLES

Motorcycling conditions in Mexico are not ideal, as roads are not always in the best condition. You should know how to do your own repairs and bring plenty of supplies. As with any vehicle in Mexico, avoid driving at night. The same rules apply to bringing a motorcycle into Mexico as bringing a car in (*see below*). Rentals in Mexico are very expensive so you're best off bringing your own bike.

ENTERING MEXICO

Bringing a car into Mexico is a complicated afffair. The owner of the vehicle must provide proof of ownership, state registration, and a valid driver's license issued outside Mexico. The owner must also provide a credit card number (American Express, Visa, Diner's Club, or MasterCard) or a bond as security against selling the car while in Mexico. All documents and credit cards must be in the name of the owner, who must be driving the car.

All of this information must be presented to Mexican customs officials upon entrance in Mexico. Usually, their office is adjacent to the border crossing station. If your permit runs out or you are found without the proper documents, your car can be immediately confiscated. However, these restrictions only apply for bringing a car into mainland Mexico—Baja is trouble-free motoring as long as you don't go past Ensenada, 100 km (62 mi) south of Tijuana. The government of the state of Sonora, which borders Arizona, has a new car registration program called **Only Sonora**; *see* Chapter 4 for details.

Foreign insurance on your car is not valid in Mexico. Mexican insurance is sold by the day near border crossings; rates are approximately $10 per day with liability only, $14 for full coverage. Prices will vary with the value of the car, and rates get cheaper the longer the period of coverage. It doesn't matter which of the border agencies you use—they all provide the same coverage for the same price.

ELECTRICITY

Electrical converters are not necessary because Mexico operates on the 60-cycle, 120-volt system; however, many Mexican outlets have not been updated to accommodate three-prong and polarized plugs (those with one larger prong), so you may need an adapter. Hotels sometimes have 110-volt outlets for low-wattage appliances marked "For Shavers Only" near the sink; don't use them for high-wattage appliances like blow dryers.

GAY & LESBIAN TRAVEL

Gender roles in Mexico are pretty rigidly defined, especially in rural areas. Openly gay couples are a rare sight, and two people of the same gender may have trouble getting a *cama matrimonial* (double bed) at hotels. Alternative lifestyles (whether they be homosexuality or any other bending of conventional roles) are more easily encountered and accepted in such metropolitan centers as Acapulco, Guadalajara, and Mexico City. However, all travelers, regardless of sexual orientation, should be extra cautious when frequenting gay-friendly venues, as police sometimes crash these clubs and assault whomever they please. The victims receive little sympathy from the public.

GAY- AND LESBIAN-FRIENDLY TRAVEL AGENCIES • **Advance Damron** (1 Greenway Plaza, Suite 800, Houston, TX 77046, tel. 713/682–2002 or 800/695–0880, fax 713/888–1010). **Club Travel** (8739 Santa Monica Blvd., West Hollywood, CA 90069, tel. 310/358–2200 or 800/429–8747, fax 310/358–2222). **Islanders/Kennedy Travel** (183 W. 10th St., New York, NY 10014, tel. 212/242–3222 or

800/988–1181, fax 212/929–8530). **Now Voyager** (4406 18th St., San Francisco, CA 94114, tel. 415/626–1169 or 800/255–6951, fax 415/626–8626). **Yellowbrick Road** (1500 W. Balmoral Ave., Chicago, IL 60640, tel. 773/561–1800 or 800/642–2488, fax 773/561–4497). **Skylink Women's Travel** (3577 Moorland Ave., Santa Rosa, CA 95407, tel. 707/585–8355 or 800/225–5759, fax 707/584–5637) for lesbian travelers.

HEALTH

Although Mexico does not require a vaccine certificate of its visitors, you may want to use your upcoming trip as an excuse to update routine immunizations. These include measles, mumps, rubella, diphtheria, tetanus, polio, and hepatitis B. Also consider updating your influenza and pneumococcal vaccines. Immune globulin (IG), or the longer-lasting Havrix Hepatitis A vaccine—both used to prevent Hepatitis A—are suggested if you are traveling to underdeveloped areas that may have dubious sanitation. Beyond that, the vaccines you should get are determined by your specific destination and a careful consideration of the vaccines' effectiveness and side effects. Consult with your physician to be sure you get all of the shots you need before you go. If your doctor isn't familiar with the risks associated with travel in your destination, you might be better off at a travel clinic (sometimes located in international airports). Ask your doctor to suggest one.

Finally, compared to the risks of malaria and dengue fever, sunburn may not seem very important, but you're much more likely to suffer from a painful sunburn than any exotic disease during your vacation in Mexico. Even if you have a dark complexion, **bring plenty of powerful sunscreen,** and slather it on at every opportunity.

STAYING WELL

According to the Centers for Disease Control and Prevention (CDC), there is a limited risk of malaria and dengue fever in certain rural areas of Mexico. Travelers in most urban or easily accessible areas need not worry. However, if you plan to visit remote regions or stay for more than six weeks, **check with the CDC's International Travelers Hotline** (*see* Health Warnings, *below*). In areas with malaria and dengue, which are both carried by mosquitoes, take mosquito nets, wear clothing that covers the body, apply repellent containing DEET, and use a spray against flying insects in living and sleeping areas. The CDC hot line recommends chloroquine (analen) as an antimalarial agent; no vaccine exists against dengue.

The major health risk in Mexico is posed by the contamination of drinking water, fresh fruit, and vegetables by fecal matter, which causes the intestinal ailment known as traveler's diarrhea. To prevent it, **watch what you eat and drink.** Stay away from uncooked food and unpasteurized milk and milk products, and **drink only bottled water or water that has been boiled** for at least 20 minutes. When ordering cold drinks at untouristed establishments, skip the ice: *sin hielo*. (You can usually identify ice made commercially using purified water by its uniform shape and the hole in the center.) Hotels with water purification systems will post signs to that effect in the rooms. *Tacos al pastor*—thin pork slices grilled on a spit and garnished with the usual cilantro, onions, and chile—are delicious but dangerous. Be wary of Mexican hamburgers, because you can never be certain what meat they are made with (horsemeat is very common).

If these measures fail, try paregoric, a good antidiarrheal agent that dulls or eliminates abdominal cramps, which requires a doctor's prescription in Mexico; or in mild cases, Pepto-Bismol or Imodium (loperamide), which can be purchased over the counter. Get plenty of purified water or tea—chamomile is a good folk remedy for diarrhea. In severe cases, rehydrate yourself with a salt-sugar solution (½ tsp. salt and 4 Tbsp. sugar per quart/liter of water).

HEALTH WARNINGS • National Centers for Disease Control (CDC, National Center for Infectious Diseases, Division of Quarantine, Traveler's Health Section, 1600 Clifton Rd., M/S E-03, Atlanta, GA 30333, tel. 404/332–4559, fax 404/332–4565).

DIVERS' ALERT
Do not fly within 24 hours of scuba diving.

HOLIDAYS

On public holidays, expect lively celebrations that consume whole towns and close most businesses. The following are some of the most important holidays celebrated throughout the country. Regional festivals are listed in individual chapters.

January 1: The **New Year** is celebrated with mariachi music, midnight church bells, and an early morning *misa de gallo* (rooster mass). Many agricultural and livestock fairs are also held around this date.

January 6: **El Día de los Reyes** (Feast of the Epiphany or Three Kings Day) is a traditional day of gift-giving.

February 5: **Día de la Constitución,** or Constitution Day, is a national holiday during which official speeches and ceremonies are conducted nationwide.

Late February or early March: "Eat, drink, and be merry, for tomorrow we shall fast" is the idea behind the raucous **Carnaval**—the last chance to gorge on food and fun before the 40 somber days of Lent. It's primarily celebrated in Mazatlán and Veracruz.

March 21: **Natalicio de Benito Juárez** and **Día de la Primavera** celebrate the birthday of Mexico's reformist president, Benito Juárez, and also mark the date of the spring equinox.

March or April: **Semana Santa** (Holy Week) arrives the week preceding Easter. The holiday is basically an excuse for Mexican families to hit the beach for a week.

May 1: All businesses close for **Día del Trabajo** (Labor Day), which is celebrated with workers' parades and speeches.

May 5: **Cinco de Mayo** is a national holiday that tributes the Mexican defeat of the French at the Battle of Puebla in 1862.

September 15–16: **Día de la Independencia** (Independence Day) commemorates the speech, or *grito,* by Father Miguel Hidalgo that called for rebellion against the Spanish in 1810.

November 1–2: **Día de los Muertos** (Day of the Dead) honors dearly departed friends, relatives, and ancestors. Mexicans visit grave sites, eat an honorary meal in a candlelit cemetery at midnight, and build altars in their homes with offerings of food, flowers, fruits, and sweets.

November 20: The **Aniversario de la Revolución** recalls the Mexican Revolution with parades, speeches, and patriotic events.

December 12: **Día de la Virgen de Guadalupe** (Day of the Virgin of Guadalupe) honors the patron saint of Mexico with religious rites, processions, and pilgrimages.

December 24–25: **Navidad** (Christmas) is a family celebration with dinner and midnight mass on Christmas Eve, followed by mass on Christmas Day.

INSURANCE

Many private health-insurance policies do not cover you outside the United States. If yours is among them, consider buying supplemental medical coverage, available through several private organizations. It's worth noting that such organizations as STA Travel and the Council on International Educational Exchange (*see* Students, *below*) include health-and-accident coverage when you acquire a student ID.

Citizens of the United Kingdom can buy an annual travel-insurance policy valid for most vacations during the year in which it's purchased. If you are pregnant or have a preexisting medical condition, make sure you're covered.

TRAVEL INSURERS • In the U.S., **Access America** (6600 W. Broad St., Richmond, VA 23230, tel. 804/285–3300 or 800/284–8300), **Carefree Travel Insurance** (Box 9366, 100 Garden City Plaza, Garden City, NY 11530, tel. 516/294–0220 or 800/323–3149), **Travel Guard International** (1145 Clark St., Stevens Point, WI 54481, tel. 715/345–0505 or 800/826–1300), **Travel Insured International** (Box 280568, East Hartford, CT 06128–0568, tel. 860/528–7663 or 800/243–3174). In Canada, **Mutual of Omaha** (Travel Division, 500 University Ave., Toronto, Ontario M5G 1V8, tel. 416/598–4083, 800/268–8825 in Canada). In the U.K., **Association of British Insurers** (51 Gresham St., London EC2V 7HQ, tel. 0171/600–3333).

LANGUAGE

Although Spanish is the official language of Mexico, 50 different Indian languages are spoken by more than 5 million people in Mexico. In fact, about 15% of the population does not speak Spanish. Different Maya dialects are spoken as a first language in a few places, especially in the south, and variants of Nahuatl, the Aztec language, are also common. Knowing even a little Spanish, though, will make your trip more enjoyable, and Mexicans generally appreciate the fact that you're trying. For a list of helpful Spanish phrases (with English translations) *see* the glossary at the end of this book.

Study Spanish in a small, internationally-acclaimed school emphasizing quality and individual attention.

SPANISH LANGUAGE INSTITUTE
of Cuernavaca, Morelos, Mexico

- All levels of Spanish in classes of five students maximum
- Family stays and full excursion program
- All adult ages (17 min.) and levels — college, professionals, retirees
- College credit available through U.S. university
- Begin on any Monday year-round, courses from 2-12 weeks

Call Language Link toll free at 800-552-2051 or visit our web site at http://www.langlink.com
It adds no additional cost to register through Language Link than directly with the school. We make it easy, convenient, and give you complimentary insurance. Programs also in Costa Rica, Ecuador, Peru, and Guatemala.

LAUNDRY

Lavanderías (laundromats) exist in all parts of Mexico and usually charge about $1–$3 per kilo. You can save money by putting together a do-it-yourself laundry kit: a plastic bottle of liquid detergent or soap, 3 or more feet of clothesline, some plastic clips (bobby pins or paper clips can substitute), and a universal sink plug. All of these items are available in stores in Mexico.

LODGING

Mexico offers nearly every type of hotel imaginable, from spotless, sterile rooms, to cozy, colonial houses, to cubicles with bare concrete floors and saggy beds. In general the more you pay for a room, the better quality you'll receive, though this—like everything in Mexico—varies. Checkout time at most hotels is 1 PM, and you can usually leave your valuables behind the desk while you roam about during the day. Many places will watch your backpack for several days, usually at no charge, if you ask.

Hotel/motel chains are not in the budget range in Mexico. What most people understand as bed-and-breakfasts are very rare, though some budget establishments will include breakfast with the price of a room. Mexico does, however, have a network of about 16 youth hostels, called *villas juveniles.* No sort of membership card is necessary to stay in the hostels, which are usually located on a town's outskirts and cost less than $5 a night.

The **price categories in this book** typically refer to the off-season cost of the least expensive double room available, plus tax.

LODGING ALTERNATIVES

Formed in the aftermath of World War II, **Servas** (11 John St., Suite 407, New York, NY 10038, tel. 212/267–0252) is a membership organization dedicated to promoting peace and understanding around the globe. Becoming a member makes you eligible to receive their international directory, which you may use to arrange two-night stays with participating host families (longer visits must be arranged privately with the family). Servas has 204 hosts scattered throughout Mexico, though some regions have only one or two per state. Membership is $55 per year, and a deposit of $25 is required for each five host lists you receive.

MAIL

Mail to points beyond Mexico takes anywhere from one to six weeks to arrive, depending on your luck and the size of the city from which you mail the missive. If you're in a hurry, you can send a letter via registered mail, which takes about five to seven days, or by Mexpost, the fastest (about two days) and most expensive method. Mailing a package from Mexico can be a hassle: It involves buying the necessary paper, tape, box, and string, then visiting the post office and the customs office. Go to the post office first for instructions, as the procedure varies from city to city. Do not attempt to pack up and wrap the goods yourself; the post office worker will rip everything apart, inspect the contents, and charge you to rewrap it Mexican-style. They will also charge you duty tax if your package contains anything of value (the person who receives the package will probably have to pay a tax as well).

RECEIVING MAIL

You can receive mail in Mexico via *Lista de Correos* (poste restante). Mail is held for up to 10 days, after which it is returned to sender. You must present a picture ID to retrieve your mail. For the Lista de Correos address in any given town, look under the heading "Mail" for that town.

MONEY

"Nuevos pesos," or new peso notes, come in denominations of 10, 20, 50, and 100 pesos. Old bills still circulate in some areas; they come with three zeroes attached (i.e., 10,000 = 10; 50,000 = 50). Do not accept old pesos as change from anyone, as it will be impossible to spend them elsewhere.

Many shop and restaurant owners are unable to make change for large bills. Enough of these encounters may compel you to request *billetes chicos* (small bills) when you exchange money. Prices quoted in this book are in dollars and are based on an exchange rate of 7.25 pesos to the dollar.

ATMS

The networks most commonly found in Mexico are Cirrus and Plus. Major banks with 24-hour ATMs can be found in all but the smallest Mexican towns. If your transaction cannot be completed—an annoyingly common occurrence—chances are that the computer lines are busy and you'll just have to try again later. Another problem is that many **Mexican ATMs only accept PINs of four or fewer digits**; if your PIN is longer, ask your bank about changing it. Visa and MasterCard work in many Mexican ATMs, but American Express does not. The ATMs at Banamex, one of the oldest and perhaps the strongest nation-wide banks, tend to be the most reliable, and generally give you an excellent exchange rate. Bancomer is another bank with many *cajero automatico* (ATM) locations, but generally they don't accept Plus or Cirrus cards and you can receive money only with Visa or MasterCard. The newer Serfín banks have reliable ATMs that accept credit cards as well as Plus and Cirrus cards.

ATM LOCATIONS • Cirrus (tel. 800/424–7787). A list of **Plus** locations is available at your local bank.

COSTS

The Mexican economy has steadily improved in the past two years, and financial wizards expect moderate growth to continue into 1998. Still, devaluation plus steady inflation mean that the dollar (and most other foreign currencies) buys a lot more in Mexico than it does in Western Europe and the United States. Prices vary according to the universal rule, however—the more cosmopolitan the city, the more expensive the taco. Your travel to and from Mexico will probably be your biggest expense, followed by lodging and transport.

LODGING • Most travelers bed down in hotels, though camping is a safe option in designated spots. Hotel prices start at around $8 per person. In a typical city, expect to pay $10–$15 for a double; add a few dollars if you want air-conditioning. Rooms with a double bed often cost a dollar or two less than those with two singles. Mexico's few hostels average $5 a night.

FOOD • If you're willing to forgo tourist fare, you'll be able to spend very little money on food. One sure cost-cutting strategy is to buy fresh fruits and vegetables in the local market—every city, town, and village has a daily market. Most markets also have small *fondas* (covered food stands) offering *comidas corridas* (fixed-price lunch specials) for less than $3. *Panaderías* (bakeries) sell breads and pastries.

TRANSPORTATION • Buses are widely used in Mexico, so fares remain very low. Buses range from antiquated second-class school buses to first-class coaches. Prices correlate less with the number of hours traveled than with the popularity of the route—heavily traveled routes are served by more classes of service at lower prices. Local city buses and transportation between rural towns cost 50¢, while a 9- to 12-hour ride on a first-class bus costs around $10. Trains (especially second class) are considerably cheaper than buses, but much slower and often less comfortable. During peak travel times such as Semana Santa, trains fill up with locals and their livestock. Driving your own car in Mexico gives you flexibility, but toll fees and poor road conditions can make driving an expensive hassle. Domestic plane fares will flatten your wallet considerably.

ENTERTAINMENT • Entertainment costs can be very high in big cities, where getting a foot in the door of an average club means coughing up anywhere from $5 to $30. Drink prices at an average bar are comparable to those north of the border: Beers run $1–$2 at popular watering holes. Movie tickets, at least, are a reasonable $2–$3. In many cities, thanks to government subsidies, entrance to some theater, dance, and musical events is free (these bargains are usually cultural events featuring traditional music or dance). Most museums and historical sites charge a $1–$2 admission.

CURRENCY EXCHANGE

You'll get a better deal buying pesos in Mexico than at home. Nonetheless, it's a good idea to exchange a bit of money into pesos before you arrive in Mexico in case the exchange booth at the train station or airport at which you arrive is closed or has a long line. At other times, for the most favorable rates, **change money at banks.** Although fees charged for ATM transactions may be higher abroad than at home, Cirrus and Plus exchange rates are excellent, because they are based on wholesale rates offered only by major banks. You won't do as well at exchange booths in airports or rail and bus stations, in hotels, in restaurants, or in stores, although you may find their hours more convenient.

Most banks only change money on weekdays until 1 (though they stay open until 5), while *casas de cambio* (private exchange offices) generally stay open until 6 and often operate on weekends. Bank rates are regulated by the federal government and are therefore invariable, while casas de cambio have slightly more variable rates. Some hotels also exchange money, but they usually do it at extortionate rates. It helps to exchange money before the banks close, when everybody else's rates tend to worsen.

When changing money, do not accept any partially torn or taped-together bills; they will not be accepted anywhere.

EXCHANGE SERVICES • **International Currency Express** (tel. 888/842–0880 on the East Coast or 888/278–6628 on the West Coast for telephone orders). **Thomas Cook Currency Services** (tel. 800/287–7362 for telephone orders and retail locations).

TRAVELER'S CHECKS

Whether or not to buy traveler's checks depends on where you are headed. You should **take cash if your trip includes rural areas** and small towns; traveler's checks if you're visiting cities. If a thief makes off with your checks, they can usually be replaced within 24 hours. Always pay for your checks yourself—don't delegate—or there may be problems if you need a refund later on.

Budget establishments in Mexico are extremely unlikely to accept traveler's checks of any sort. They are, however, accepted at most banks, casas de cambio, and some fancy hotels. Some banks and credit unions will issue checks free to established customers, but most charge a 1%–2% commission fee. Buy the bulk of your traveler's checks in small denominations (a pack of five $20 checks is the smallest), as many establishments won't accept large bills.

PACKING FOR MEXICO

Backpacks are the most manageable way to lug belongings around, but they instantly brand you a foreign tourist. Also, outside pockets on backpacks are especially vulnerable to pickpockets, so don't store any valuables there. If you want to blend in with the local population, bring a duffel or a large shoulder bag. Like new shoes, fully packed luggage should be broken in: If you can't tote your bag all the way around the block at home, it's going to be worse than a ball and chain in Mexico. Leaving some room for gifts and souvenirs is also wise.

Smart—and not terribly fashion-conscious—travelers will bring two outfits and learn to wash clothes by hand regularly. Packing light does not mean relying on a pair of cut-off shorts and a tank top to get you through any situation, though. Shorts, along with other skin-exposing vestments, will make you awfully conspicuous in small Mexican towns, and women wearing them will attract attention they could probably live without. At resorts and most beach areas, however, shorts are fairly common and locals have become accustomed to seeing lots of foreign flesh. In general, though, you'll find that Mexicans dress more formally than gringos, and Mexican women stay more covered than their northern *compañeras*.

For maximum comfort, bring about two pairs of cotton pants; these will also dry more quickly than jeans. Bring several T-shirts and one sweatshirt or sweater for cooler nights. Socks and undies don't take up too much room, so throw in a couple extra pairs. In jungle areas, you'll need to wear socks and long pants to prevent bug bites and scratches from possibly toxic plants. You'll probably want a swimsuit even if you're not headed for the beach—you never know when you'll stumble across a swimming hole, river, or public pool. Rain gear is a must if you're traveling during rainy season. If you sunburn easily—and you're going to burn more easily than you think in Mexico—definitely bring or buy a large-brimmed hat to keep the sun off your face and ears (baseball caps don't work).

Recommended footware: a sturdy pair of walking shoes or hiking boots (broken in before your trip), a spare pair of shoes (preferably sandals) to give your tootsies a rest, and plastic sandals or thongs to protect feet on shower floors and for camping or beach-hopping. Since many Mexican shoe stores don't carry sizes larger than seven for either men or women, you may be in serious trouble if you have big feet and your shoes give out. Your only option may be to ask a marketplace artisan to customize a pair of leather sandals.

Bring an extra pair of eyeglasses or contact lenses in your carry-on luggage, and if you have a health problem, **pack enough medication** to last the entire trip or have your doctor write you a prescription using the drug's generic name, because brand names vary from country to country. It's important that you **don't put prescription drugs, your passport, or other valuables in luggage to be checked**: It might go astray. To avoid problems with customs officials, carry medications in the original packaging. Use containers that seal tightly and pack them in a separate waterproof bag; the pressure on airplanes can cause lids to pop off and create instant moisturizer slicks inside your luggage. Also, don't forget the addresses of offices that handle refunds of lost traveler's checks.

In case you want to be welcomed there.

We're here to see that you're always welcomed at establishments everywhere. That's why millions of people carry the American Express® Card – for peace of mind, confidence, and security, around the world or just around the corner.

do more ®

Other stuff you might not think to pack but will be glad to have: a miniature flashlight; a pocket knife; a water bottle; sunglasses; several large zip-type plastic bags; a travel alarm clock; a needle and a small spool of thread; extra batteries; a good book; and a day pack.

MAIL-ORDER TRAVEL GEAR CATALOGS • Magellan's (tel. 800/962–4943, fax 805/568–5406). **Orvis Travel** (tel. 800/541–3541, fax 540/343–7053). **TravelSmith** (tel. 800/950–1600, fax 800/950–1656).

TAKING LUGGAGE ON THE PLANE

In general, you are entitled to check two bags on flights within the United States and on international flights leaving the United States. A third piece may be brought on board, but it must fit easily under the seat in front of you or in the overhead compartment.

If you are flying between two foreign destinations, note that baggage allowances may be determined not by piece but by weight—generally 88 pounds (40 kilograms) in first class, 66 pounds (30 kilograms) in business class, and 44 pounds (20 kilograms) in economy. If your flight between two cities abroad *connects* with your transatlantic or transpacific flight, the piece method still applies.

Airline liability for baggage is limited to $1,250 per person on flights within the United States. On international flights it amounts to $9.07 per pound or $20 per kilogram for checked baggage (roughly $640 per 70-pound bag) and $400 per passenger for unchecked baggage. Insurance for losses exceeding these amounts can be bought from the airline at check-in for about $10 per $1,000 of coverage; note that this coverage excludes a rather extensive list of items, which is shown on your airline ticket.

At check-in, **make sure that each bag is correctly tagged** with the destination airport's three-letter code. If your bags arrive damaged or not at all, file a written report with the airline before leaving the airport. If you're traveling with a backpack, tie all loose straps to each other or onto the pack itself, so that they don't get caught in luggage conveyer belts.

PASSPORTS & VISAS

Once your travel plans are confirmed, **get a passport even if you don't need one to enter Mexico**—it's always the best form of ID. **Make photocopies of the data page**; leave one copy with someone at home and keep another with you, separate from your passport. If you lose your passport, promptly call the nearest embassy or consulate and the local police; having a copy of the data page can speed replacement. All foreigners traveling for more than 72 hours in Mexico must obtain a tourist card (called an F.M.T.).

TOURIST CARDS

If you intend to visit border towns only, you can do so without a tourist card for up to 72 hours. Otherwise you must show proof of citizenship (either an original birth certificate and a photo ID, or a passport) and obtain a tourist card. Driver's licenses, credit cards, and military papers will not suffice. A naturalized citizen must carry at least one of the following documents: naturalization papers, a U.S. passport, or an affidavit of citizenship. F.M.T.s are available at Mexican government border offices at any port of entry, on flights into Mexico, and at any Mexican Ministry of Tourism or consulate in the United States. No matter where you get it, when crossing the border you must sign the card in the presence of the Mexican immigration official, who may also ask to see proof of citizenship. Be sure to hold on to your receipt, because you are required to fork it over on departure. If you lose it, expect to visit with the border officials for a while.

Tourist cards last up to 180 days for U.S. citizens (90 days for citizens of most other countries), after which time you must go to the local Delegación de Servicios Migratorios to apply for a visa. Upon leaving Mexico, your card is taken and a new one is issued if and when you return. If you lose your card, you must also go to the Delegación de Servicios Migratorios. To cut through at least a portion of the red tape involved, it's a good idea to make a photocopy of your card and keep it in a separate place. Carry the original with you at all times; it's required by law.

AUSTRALIAN CITIZENS

Citizens of Australia need only a valid passport to enter Mexico for stays of up to 90 days.
INFORMATION • Australian Passport Office (tel. 008/131–232).

CANADIANS

You need only a valid passport to enter Mexico for stays of up to 90 days.
INFORMATION • Canadian Passport Office (tel. 819/994–3500 or 800/567–6868).

NEW ZEALAND CITIZENS

Citizens of New Zealand need only a valid passport to enter Mexico for stays of up to 90 days.

INFORMATION • New Zealand Passport Office (tel. 04/494–0700 for information on how to apply, 0800/727–776 for information on applications already submitted.

U.K. CITIZENS

Citizens of the United Kingdom need only a valid passport to enter Mexico for stays of up to 90 days.

INFORMATION • London Passport Office (tel. 0990/21010) for fees and documentation requirements and to request an emergency passport.

U.S. CITIZENS

For stays of up to 180 days, any proof of citizenship is sufficient for entry into Mexico. Minors also need parental permission.

SAFETY

Money belts may be bulky to wear and unsightly to look at, but it's better to be embarrassed than broke. You'd be wise to carry your cash, traveler's checks, credit cards, and passport there or in some other inaccessible place such as a front or inner pocket, or a bag that fits underneath your clothes. Keep a copy of your passport somewhere else. Waist packs are safe if you keep the pack part in front of your body. And never leave your belongings unguarded, even if you're only planning to be gone for a minute.

Police rarely hassle travelers unless they are excessively loud, drunk, or involved in a brawl, in which case the police can incarcerate you overnight in jail and confiscate your money. Since you are not protected by the laws of your native land once you're on Mexican soil, your embassy can do little for you.

RESOURCES • If you do get into a scrape with the law, you can call the **Citizens' Emergency Center** (tel. 202/647–5225) in the United States, weekdays 8:15 AM–10 PM, Saturday 9 AM–3 PM, EST. After hours and on Sunday, call the emergency duty officer (tel. 202/634–3600). In Mexico you can also call the English-speaking **Procuraduría de Protección al Turista** (Attorney General for the Protection of Tourists). The 24-hour hotline in Mexico City is 5/14–21–66 or 5/14–01–55.

PRECAUTIONS FOR WOMEN

Travel guides often refer to the chauvinism and sexual aggressiveness of Mexican men. And although this is largely a caricature, it's clear that Mexican machismo is not completely dismissable as a stereotype. Foreign women traveling alone in Mexico do tend to receive plenty of *piropos* (compliments) from total strangers, but there are few places in the world where they don't. The hard part is dealing with the persistence of Mexican men. What may have started out as a request for directions or a friendly conversation can suddenly become a springboard for something more. Polite excuses won't do any good: You can't meet them for a drink because you're changing your plane ticket? No problem—they'll be glad to accompany you. The best strategy is a firm "No, gracias," or "Mi novio me está esperando en el hotel" (My boyfriend is waiting for me back at the hotel). In general, exercise the same caution you would traveling anywhere— be alert, be cautious about who you are alone with, appear confident—and you should minimize problems. If you are traveling alone, don't let your gender prevent you from adventuring, but think twice about hitchhiking or camping solo. Needless to say, you'll attract less attention if less of your skin is showing: The "good girl/bad girl, Madonna/whore" dichotomies still have a secure place in Mexico's consciousness.

RESOURCES • Movimiento Nacional Para Mujeres (San Juan de Letrán 11-411, México, D.F., tel. 5/512–58–41) can put you in contact with women's organizations all over Mexico.

STUDENTS

DEALS

To save money, **look into deals available through student-oriented travel agencies** and the various other organizations involved in helping out student and budget travelers. Typically, you'll find discounted airfares, rail passes, tours, lodgings, or other travel arrangements, and you don't necessarily have to be a student to qualify.

The big names in the field are STA Travel, with some 100 offices worldwide, and the Council on International Educational Exchange (CIEE or "Council" for short), a private, nonprofit organization that administers work, volunteer, academic, and professional programs worldwide and sells travel arrangements through its own specialist travel agency, Council Travel. Travel CUTS, strictly a travel agency, sells discounted airline tickets to Canadian students from offices on or near college campuses. The Educational Travel Center (ETC) books low-cost flights to destinations within the continental United States and around the world. And Student Flights, Inc., specializes in student and faculty airfares.

Most of these organizations also issue student identity cards, which entitle their bearers to special fares on local transportation and discounts at museums, theaters, sports events, and other attractions, as well as a handful of other benefits, which are listed in the handbook that most provide to their cardholders. Major cards include the International Student Identity Card (ISIC) and GO25: International Youth Travel Card (GO25), available to non-students as well as students age 25 and under; the ISIC, when purchased in the United States, comes with $3,000 in emergency medical coverage and a few related benefits. Both the ISIC and GO25 are issued by Council Travel or STA in the United States, Travel CUTS in Canada, at student unions and student-travel companies in the United Kingdom, and by STA in Australia. The International Student Exchange Card (ISE), issued by Student Flights, Inc., is available to faculty members as well as students, and the International Teacher Identity Card (ITIC), issued by Travel CUTS, provides similar benefits to teachers in all grade levels, from kindergarten through graduate school. All student ID cards cost between $10 and $20.

Foreign student ID cards are not universally accepted in Mexico; discounts for museum and theater admission usually apply exclusively to students at Mexican universities. Don't leave your student ID at home, though, because discounts are often left to the discretion of the person working the door. While an ID card issued by a home university or college may be sufficient to prove student status for admission discounts, the ISIC and GO25 have the extra feature of providing insurance in case of accident or other catastrophes.

STUDENT I.D.S AND SERVICES • Council on International Educational Exchange (CIEE): 205 E. 42nd St., 14th floor, New York, NY 10017, tel. 212/822–2600 or 888/268–6245. **Council Travel in the U.S.:** tel. 800/226–8624. **Council Travel in Europe:** in London, 28A Poland St., Oxford Circle, tel. 171/287–3337; in Paris, 66 av. des Champs-Elysées, tel. 01–46–55–55–65; in Dusseldorf, Graf Adolf Strasse 64, tel. 089/395022. **Educational Travel Center:** 438 N. Frances St., Madison, WI 53703, tel. 608/256–5551 or 800/747–5551. **STA in the U.S.:** tel. 800/777–0112. **STA elsewhere:** in London, tel. 171/361–6262; in Frankfurt, tel. 69/979–07460; in Auckland, tel. 0800/100–677; in Melbourne, 3/9349–2411; in Johannesburg, 11/447–5551. **Student Flights:** 5010 E. Shea Blvd., Suite A104, Scottsdale, AZ 85254, tel. 602/951–1177 or 800/255–8000. **Travel CUTS:** 187 College St., Toronto, Ontario M5T 1P7, tel. 416/979–2406 or, in Canada, 800/667–2887.

Many Mexican universities are open to foreigners for Spanish-language programs and for general enrollment. Language schools are listed in the Basics sections for the cities where they exist, but the most popular places to study (and consequently the most packed with English speakers) are Cuernavaca and San Miguel de Allende, as well as the more cosmopolitan Mexico City and Guadalajara.

RESOURCES • American Institute for Foreign Study (102 Greenwich Ave., Greenwich, CT 06830, tel. 203/869–9090 or 800/727–2437, fax 203/869–9615). **American Council of International Studies (ACIS)** (19 Bay St., Boston, MA 02215, tel. 617/236–2051 or 800/888–2247). **Council on International Educational Exchange** (*see above*). **Institute of International Education (IIE)** (809 U.N. Plaza, New York, NY 10017, tel. 212/984–5413). **World Learning** (Kipling Rd., Box 676, Brattleboro, VT 05302, tel. 802/257–7751 or 800/451–4465, fax 802/258–3248).

The **Center for Global Education at Augsburg College** (2211 Riverside Ave., Minneapolis, MN 55454, tel. 612/330–1159, fax 612/330–1695) offers informative, alternative travel seminars in Mexico and elsewhere in Central America that bring travelers in direct contact with grassroots organizations in the developing world. Call for a copy of their newsletter, *Global News and Notes,* and brochures on current travel seminars.

TELEPHONES

Many different options for making phone calls exist, but none are completely reliable everywhere. Simply put: Calling out of Mexico can be a challenging, frustrating, and expensive experience.

The country code for Mexico is 52. When dialing a Mexican number from abroad, drop the initial 0 from the local area code. The city code for Mexico City is 5. Dial 02 for the domestic operator in Mexico; 09 for the international operator (who should speak English or be able to find someone who does); 04 for local information; and 01 for long-distance information. You can dial long-distance calls directly: to the

United States, dial 95 + area code + number; direct to the rest of the world, dial 98 + country code + city code + number; direct to other parts of Mexico, dial 91 + number.

CASETAS DE LARGA DISTANCIA

For local or long-distance calls, one option is to find a *caseta de larga distancia,* a telephone service usually operated out of a store such as a *papelería* (stationery store), pharmacy, restaurant, or other small business; look for the phone symbol on the door. Casetas may cost more to use than pay phones, but you have a better chance of immediate success. To make a direct long-distance call, tell the person on duty the number you'd like to call, and he or she will give you a rate and dial for you. Rates seem to vary widely, so shop around. Sometimes you can make collect calls from casetas, and sometimes you cannot, depending on the individual operator and possibly your degree of visible desperation. Casetas will generally charge 50¢–$1.50 to place a collect call (some charge by the minute); it's usually better to call *por cobrar* (collect) from a pay phone.

PHONE CARDS

In some areas, pay phones accept prepaid cards, called **Ladatel** cards, sold in 10-, 30-, or 50-peso denominations (approximately $1.75, $5, or $8.25) at newsstands or pharmacies. Many pay phones in Mexico only accept these cards; coin-only pay phones are usually broken. To use a Ladatel card, simply insert it in the slot of a silver Multitarjetas phone, dial 95 (for calls to the States), and the area code and number you're trying to reach. Credit is deleted from the card as you use it, and your balance is displayed on a small screen on the phone so you can keep tabs on how much you've got left.

COLLECT CALLS & CALLING CARDS

For an international collect or calling-card call, dial the long-distance operator (09), wait as long as 30 minutes for the bilingual long-distance operator to pick up the line, and give him or her the number you want to call and your name or card number, as appropriate. You can also use a Ladatel card (*see above*) to make an international call. Collect calls can also sometimes be placed from casetas de larga distancia (*see above*) for a fee.

CALLING THE U.S.

Before you go, **find out the local access codes** for your destinations. AT&T, MCI, and Sprint long-distance services make calling home relatively convenient, but you may find the local access number blocked in many hotel rooms. First ask the hotel operator to connect you. If the hotel operator balks, ask for an international operator, or dial the international operator yourself. One way to improve your odds of getting connected to your long-distance carrier is to travel with more than one company's calling card (a hotel may block Sprint, for example, but not MCI). If all else fails, call your phone company in the United States collect, or make your call from a pay phone in the hotel lobby.

TO OBTAIN ACCESS CODES • AT&T USADirect (tel. 800/874–4000). **MCI** Call USA (tel. 800/444–4444). **Sprint** Express (tel. 800/793–1153).

TOUR OPERATORS

Buying a vacation package can make your trip to Mexico less expensive. The tour operators who put them together may handle several hundred thousand travelers per year and can use their purchasing power to give you a good price. Their high volume may also indicate financial stability. But some small companies provide more personalized service; because they tend to specialize, they may also be more knowledgeable about a given area.

A GOOD DEAL?

The more your package includes, the better you can predict the ultimate cost of your vacation. Make sure you know exactly what is covered, and **beware of hidden costs.** Are taxes, tips, and service charges included? Transfers and baggage handling? Entertainment and excursions? These add up.

If the package you are considering is priced lower than in your wildest dreams, **be skeptical.** Ask about the hotel's location, room size, beds, and whether it has a pool, room service, or programs for children, if you care.

BUYER BEWARE

Each year consumers are stranded or lose their money when tour operators—even large ones with excellent reputations—go out of business. So **check out the operator.** Find out how long the company has been in business, and ask for references that you can check. And **don't book unless the firm has a consumer-protection program.**

Members of the National Tour Association and United States Tour Operators Association are required to set aside funds to cover your payments and travel arrangements in case the company defaults. Non-members may carry insurance instead. Look for the details, and for the name of an underwriter with a solid reputation, in the operator's brochure. And when it comes to tour operators, **don't trust escrow accounts.** Although there are laws governing charter-flight operators, no governmental body prevents tour operators from raiding the till. For more information, *see* Consumer Protection, *above.*

TOUR-OPERATOR RECOMMENDATIONS • **National Tour Association** (NTA, 546 E. Main St., Lexington, KY 40508, tel. 606/226–4444 or 800/755–8687). **United States Tour Operators Association** (USTOA, 342 Madison Ave., Suite 1522, New York, NY 10173, tel. 212/599–6599, fax 212/599–6744).

USING AN AGENT

A good travel agent is an excellent resource. When shopping for one, **collect brochures from several sources** and remember that some agents' suggestions may be skewed by promotional relationships with tour and package firms that reward them for volume sales. If you have a special interest, **find an agent with expertise in that area.**

SINGLE TRAVELERS

Remember that prices for vacation packages are usually quoted per person, based on two sharing a room. If traveling solo, you may be required to pay the full double-occupancy rate.

PACKAGES

The companies listed below offer vacation packages in a broad price range.

AIR/HOTEL • **Aeromexico Vacation** (tel. 800/245–8585). **American Airlines Fly AAway Vacations** (tel. 800/321–2121). **Certified Vacations** (110 E. Broward Blvd., Fort Lauderdale, FL 33302, tel. 954/522–1440 or 800/233–7260). **Continental Vacations** (tel. 800/634–5555). **Delta Dream Vacations** (tel. 800/872–7786). **United Vacations** (tel. 800/328–6877). **USAirways Vacations** (tel. 800/455–0123).

FROM THE U.K. • **Bales Tours** (Bales House, Junction Rd., Dorking, Surrey RH4 3HL, tel. 01306/876–881 or 01306/885–991). **British Airways Holidays** (Astral Towers, Betts Way, London Rd., Crawley, West Sussex RH10 2XA, tel. 01293/723–181). **Journey Latin America** (14–16 Devonshire Rd., Chiswick, London W4 2HD, tel. 0181/747–8315). **Kuoni Travel** (Kuoni House, Dorking, Surrey RH5 4AZ, tel. 01306/742–222). For a custom-designed holiday contact **Steamond Travel** (23 Eccleston St., London SW1 9LX, tel. 0171/286–4449) or **Trailfinders** (42–50 Earls Court Rd., London W8 6FT, tel. 0171/937–5400).

THEME TRIPS

ADVENTURE • **Adventure Center** (1311 63rd St., #200, Emeryville, CA 94608, tel. 510/654–1879 or 800/227–8747, fax 510/654–4200). **Baja Expeditions** (2625 Garnet Ave., San Diego, CA 92109, tel. 619/581–3311 or 800/843–6967, fax 619/581–6542). **Himalayan Travel** (110 Prospect St., Stamford, CT 06901, tel. 203/359–3711 or 800/225–2380, fax 203/359–3669). **Mountain Travel-Sobek** (6420 Fairmount Ave., El Cerrito, CA 94530, tel. 510/527–8100 or 800/227–2384, fax 510/525–7710). **OARS** (Box 67, Angels Camp, CA 95222, tel. 209/736–4677 or 800/346–6277, fax 209/736–2902). **Trek America** (Box 189, Rockaway, NJ 07866, tel. 201/983–1144 or 800/221–0596, fax 201/983–8551).

ART & ARCHAEOLOGY • **Archaeological Conservancy** (5301 Central Ave. NE, #1218, Albuquerque, NM 87108-1517, tel. 505/266–1540). **Armadillo Tours International** (4301 Westbank Dr., #B360, Austin, TX 78746, tel. 512/328–7800 or 800/284–5678). **Far Horizons Archaeological & Cultural Trips** (Box 91900, Albuquerque, NM 87199-1900, tel. 505/343–9400 or 800/552–4575, fax 505/343–8076). **Maya-Carib Travel** (7 Davenport Ave., #3F, New Rochelle, NY 10805, tel. 914/354–9824 or 800/223–4084, fax 914/353–7539). **M.I.L.A.** (100 S. Greenleaf Ave., Gurnee, IL 60031-3378, tel. 847/249–2111 or 800/367–7378, fax 847/249–2772). **Sanborn's Viva Tours** (2015 S. 10th St., Box 519, McAllen, TX 78505-0519, tel. 210/682–9872 or 800/395–8482, fax 210/682–0016).

BICYCLING • **Backroads** (801 Cedar St., Berkeley, CA 94710-1800, tel. 510/527–1555 or 800/462–2848, fax 510/527–1444). **Expedition Touring** (300 3rd Ave. W, Seattle, WA 98119, tel. 206/463–4081).

FISHING • **Anglers Travel** (3100 Mill St., #206, Reno, NV 89502, tel. and fax 702/853–9132). **Cutting Loose Expeditions** (Box 447, Winter Park, FL 32790, tel. 407/629–4700 or 800/533–4746). **Fishing International** (Box 2132, Santa Rosa, CA 95405, 707/539–3366 or 800/950–4242, fax 707/539–1320). **Mexico Sportsman** (100-115 Travis St., San Antonio, TX 78205, tel. 210/212–4566 or 800/633–

3085, fax 210/212–4568). **Rod and Reel Adventures** (3507 Tully Rd., #B6, Modesto, CA 95356-1052, tel. 209/524–7775 or 800/356–6982, fax 209/524–1220).

NATURAL HISTORY • Earthwatch (Box 9104, 680 Mount Auburn St., Watertown, MA 02272, tel. 617/926–8200 or 800/776–0188, fax 617/926–8532) for research expeditions. **Forum Travel International** (91 Gregory La., #21, Pleasant Hill, CA 94523, tel. 510/671–2900, fax 510/671–2993). **National Audubon Society** (700 Broadway, New York, NY 10003, tel. 212/979–3066, fax 212/353–0190). **Natural Habitat Adventures** (2945 Center Green Ct., Boulder, CO 80301, tel. 303/449–3711 or 800/543–8917, fax 303/449–3712). **Oceanic Society Expeditions** (Fort Mason Center, Bldg. E, San Francisco, CA 94123-1394, tel. 415/441–1106 or 800/326–7491, fax 415/474–3395). **Pacific Sea-Fari Tours** (2803 Emerson St., San Diego, CA 92106, tel. 619/226–8224).

RIVER RAFTING • Far Flung Adventures (Box 377, Terlingua, TX 79852, tel. 915/371–2489 or 800/359–4138, fax 915/371–2325).

SCUBA DIVING • Rothschild Dive Safaris (900 West End Ave., #1B, New York, NY 10025-3525, tel. 800/359–0747, fax 212/749–6172). **Tropical Adventures** (111 2nd Ave. N, Seattle, WA 98109, tel. 206/441–3483 or 800/247–3483, fax 206/441–5431).

SPAS • Spa-Finders (91 Fifth Ave., #301, New York, NY 10003-3039, tel. 212/924–6800 or 800/255–7727).

TRAIN TOURS • Mexico by Train (Box 2782, Laredo, TX 78044-2782, tel. and fax 210/725–3659 or 800/321–1699).

VILLA RENTALS • Villas International (605 Market St., San Francisco, CA 94105, tel. 415/281–0910 or 800/221–2260, fax 415/281–0919).

WALKING • Backroads (*see* Bicycling, *above*).

YACHT CHARTERS • Ocean Voyages (1709 Bridgeway, Sausalito, CA 94965, tel. 415/332–4681 or 800/299–4444, fax 415/332–7460). **The Moorings** (19345 U.S. Hwy. 19 N, 4th floor, Clearwater, FL 34624-3193, tel. 813/530–5424 or 800/535–7289, fax 813/530–9474).

RESPONSIBLE TOURISM

The **North America Coordinating Center for Responsible Tourism** (2 Kensington Rd., San Anselmo, CA 94690–2905, tel. 415/258–6594) is a private, nonprofit organization that works on several levels to change the way that North Americans travel. The staff will gladly tell you how to travel in Mexico and other developing countries without having a negative impact on the country's economy or society. Aside from conducting workshops and seminars, they publish a quarterly newsletter called "Responsible Traveling," which states their goals and gives information on workshops around the United States.

TRAIN TRAVEL

Amtrak (tel. 800/872–7245) will get you as far as San Diego, El Paso, or San Antonio. From San Antonio, you'll have to catch another bus to Laredo, on the border. From El Paso or Laredo, you'll be able to walk across the border. The **San Diego Trolley** (tel. 619/231–8549) will get you from the train station to downtown San Diego, where another trolley departs every 15 minutes for the San Ysidro border crossing (*see* Tijuana *in* Chapter 3).

WITHIN MEXICO

Of all the forms of transport in Mexico, trains have the worst reputation: notoriously run-down, slow, late, and a haven for thieves. Depending on the type of train and route, they can arrive absurdly late or leave absurdly early, but they are always slower than buses. Buying a ticket is also a uniquely frustrating experience, as ticket offices are often closed most of the day, generally until trains actually roll in; it's a good idea to call the train station in advance whenever possible. There are several classes of service, not all of which are available for any given route. Special first class usually has air-conditioning and functioning bathrooms with water. A limited number of expensive sleeper cars are available on some trains offering special first class. Advantages to train travel include great scenery, a certain romantic air, and a leisurely pace. If you're going to ride any train, your best bet is the **Chihuahua al Pacífico** (the Copper Canyon train), which is tourist-friendly and has an on-time, safe, and easily accessible first-class line.

TRAVEL AGENCIES

A good travel agent puts your needs first. **Look for an agency that specializes in your destination, has been in business at least five years, and emphasizes customer service.** If you're looking for an agency-organized package, choose an agency that's a member of the National Tour Association or the United States Tour Operator's Association (*see* Tour Operators, *above*).

LOCAL AGENT REFERRALS • American Society of Travel Agents (ASTA; 1101 King St., Suite 200, Alexandria, VA 22314, tel. 703/739–2782, fax 703/684–8319). **Alliance of Canadian Travel Associations** (Suite 201, 1729 Bank St., Ottawa, Ontario K1V 7Z5, tel. 613/521–0474, fax 613/521–0805). **Association of British Travel Agents** (55–57 Newman St., London W1P 4AH, tel. 0171/637–2444, fax 0171/637–0713).

U.S. GOVERNMENT

The U.S. government can be an excellent source of inexpensive travel information. When planning your trip, **find out what government materials are available.**

ADVISORIES • U.S. Department of State American Citizens Services Office (Room 4811, Washington, DC 20520); enclose a self-addressed, stamped envelope. Interactive hot line (tel. 202/647–5225, fax 202/647–3000). Computer bulletin board (tel. 202/647–9225).

PAMPHLETS • Consumer Information Center (Consumer Information Catalogue, Pueblo, CO 81009, tel. 719/948–3334) for a free catalog that includes travel titles.

VISITOR INFORMATION

For general information contact the government tourist offices below.

MEXICAN GOVERNMENT TOURIST OFFICES (MGTO) • In the United States: U.S. nationwide (tel. 800/446–3942). New York City (405 Park Ave., Suite 1402, New York, NY 10022, tel. 212/838–2949 or 212/421–6655, fax 212/753–2874). Chicago (70 E. Lake St., Suite 1413, Chicago, IL 60601, tel. 312/606–9252, fax 312/606–9012). Los Angeles (1801 Century Pk. E, Suite 1080, Los Angeles, CA 90067, tel. 310/203–8191, fax 310/203–8316). Houston (5075 Westheimer, Suite 975W, Houston, TX 77056, tel. 713/629–1611, fax 713/629–1837). Coral Gables (2333 Ponce de Leon Blvd., Suite 710, Coral Gables, FL 33134, tel. 305/443–9160, fax 305/443–1186). **In Canada:** Montréal (1 Place Ville Marie, Suite 1626, Montréal, Québec H3B 2B5, tel. 514/871–1052, fax 514/871–3825). Toronto (2 Bloor St. W, Suite 1801, Toronto, Ontario M4W 3E2, tel. 416/925–0704, fax 416/925–6061). Vancouver (999 W. Hastings St., Suite 1610, Vancouver, British Columbia V6C 2WC, tel. 604/669–2845, fax 604/669–3498). **In the United Kingdom:** London (60 Trafalgar Sq., London WC2N 5DS, tel. 0171/734–1058, fax 0171/930–9202).

VOLUNTEERING

For those who have some extra time and money, volunteer positions provide a great opportunity to get to know Mexican culture from more than a tourist's perspective. Council (*see* Students, *above*) is a key player, running its own roster of projects and publishing a directory that lists other sponsor organizations, *Volunteer! The Comprehensive Guide to Voluntary Service in the U.S. and Abroad* ($12.95 plus $1.50 postage). Service Civil International (SCI), International Voluntary Service (IVS), and Volunteers for Peace (VFP) run two- and three-week short workcamps; VFP also publishes the *International Workcamp Directory* ($12). WorldTeach programs, run by Harvard University, require that you commit a year to teaching on subjects ranging from English and science to carpentry, forestry, or sports.

RESOURCES • SCI/IVS (5474 Walnut Level Rd., Crozet, VA 22932, tel. 804/823–1826). **VFP** (43 Tiffany Rd., Belmont, VT 05730, tel. 802/259–2759, fax 802/259–2922). **WorldTeach** (1 Eliot St., Cambridge, MA 02138–5705, tel. 617/495–5527 or 800/483–2240, fax 617/495–1599).

WHEN TO GO

The most popular vacation times in Mexico are Semana Santa (Holy Week, the week before Easter) and the weeks from Christmas through New Year's. During these holidays, hotels in most communities, even small ones, are usually booked well in advance, prices may be jacked up, and armies of tourists swarm

THE HIGHS
AND THE LOWS

Average daily high and low temperatures stack up as follows:

CITY	JANUARY: HIGH/LOW	JUNE: HIGH/LOW
ACAPULCO	88°F/72°F (31°C/22°C)	91°F/77°F (33°C/25°C)
COZUMEL	82°F/68°F (28°C/20°C)	89°F/75°F (32°C/24°C)
ENSENADA	64°F/45°F (18°C/7°C)	75°F/61°F (32°C/24°C)
GUADALAJARA	75°F/45°F (24°C/7°C)	79°F/59°F (25°C/15°C)
LA PAZ	72°F/57°F (22°C/14°C)	95°F/75°F (35°C/24°C)
MEXICO CITY	70°F/41°F (21°C/5°C)	73°F/52°F (23°C/11°C)
MONTERREY	68°F/48°F (20°C/9°C)	91°F/72°F (34°C/22°C)
OAXACA	82°F/46°F (28°C/8°C)	84°F/60°F (29°C/16°C)
VERACRUZ	77°F/64°F (25°C/18°C)	87°F/77°F (31°C/25°C)

popular attractions. Resorts popular with college students (i.e., any place with a beach) tend to fill up in the summer months, when schools are out. To avoid hordes of foreign and local tourists, heavy rains, and high prices, the best times to go are October and March–May.

CLIMATE

Temperate is the word in central Mexico, where the high elevation keeps the area mild year-round. Northern Mexico and Baja are dry and scorching, while the south lapses into cool, stormy, and hot cycles. The coastal regions are graced by cool ocean breezes, which provide a welcome respite from simmering inland temperatures. As you meander through mountains and desert, beach and jungle, be ready for distinct climate changes. From December though February, the air tends to cool down and dry up; in inland northern Mexico, temperatures can approach freezing. Mexico's long rainy season extends from June until mid-October.

MEXICO CITY AND ENVIRONS 2

UPDATED BY PATRICIA ALISAU

The first thing that strikes you about Mexico City is the sheer number of inhabitants. It's simply mind-boggling to think that 16 million people share this city, especially given the statistics: Approximately 20% of Mexico's population lives on the 1% of Mexican land known as El Distrito Federal, or Mexico City. The challenge of cohabitation in such a dense urban area—it's just a tiny district sandwiched between the states of Mexico and Morelos—is what gives this city and its residents such vitality.

Overpopulation is only one of the factors that defines D.F. life; another is a tangible connection with the past, made possible by the fact that this site has served as a capital ever since the Aztec people founded the city of Tenochtitlán here in 1325. In 1521 Hernán Cortés began constructing what would become present-day Mexico, leveling most of the ancient Aztec city and building directly on top of the ruins. Today, the routines of cosmopolitan life takes place amid the remnants of this ancient city, parts of which lay partially excavated several meters below the level of the modern D.F. Thus, historical space ceases to be a fenced-off site, becoming, instead, a familiar neighbor that lends a supportive hand to the present: Colonial churches share room with modern high-rises, children roller-skate on Sunday past the ruins of the precolonial ceremonial center in the Plaza Tlatelolco, and street vendors hawk their wares in the shadow of the 400-year-old Templo Mayor.

Chilangos, as Mexico City's residents are called, come from every state in the country. Rural migrants pour into the city daily, looking for work and a better standard of living after resources from the countryside have dried up. Although Mexico has paid lip service to *indígenas* (indigenous people) since the Revolution, indigenous migrants—mostly from the Zapotec, Mixtec, and Otomí tribes—actually end up as the lowest classes in Mexico City, living in slums and selling chewing gum or shining shoes to survive. Residents call them *paracaidistas* (parachuters), because they come out of nowhere and seize any scrap of land available, from abandoned lots to the meager strips of land beside railroad tracks. Such poverty is well hidden from the privileged eyes of those who occupy the more posh districts of town, such as Polanco, Lomas, and Coyoacán. Any meeting between the two classes reveals an unsettling and somewhat depressing contrast: Poor children peddle roses and put on street shows late at night for the crowds of trendy *niños popis* (wealthy Mexico City teenagers) who club-hop in their shiny, expensive imported cars.

Even the environment in Mexico City is experiencing turbulent changes. Famed for its clean mountain air at the beginning of the century, the city is now notorious for its smog—brought about by rapid industrialization and explosive population growth. The problem is exacerbated by the uninterrupted range of

volcanic mountains that encircles the city, trapping in the pollution. Smog isn't the capital's only problem: The marshy soil upon which the city is built (the site was a lake but has been gradually filled in by successive civilizations) has caused many buildings to sink several inches per year.

But despite all its environmental and economic problems, the oldest capital in the Americas is worth a visit for its excellent museums, impressive ruins, and fine arts. Though you may be reluctant to embrace this unwieldly city of staggering pollution and obvious overcrowding, come with your arms open and your preconceptions in check.

BASICS

AMERICAN EXPRESS

This main branch replaces and sells traveler's checks, cashes cardholders' personal checks, and provides travel services. Avoid changing money here, since the rates are poor. Cardholders' mail will be held if sent to the following address: Paseo de la Reforma 234, esq. Havre, Col. Juárez, México, D.F., CP 06600, México. *Tel. 5/514–06–29 or 5/207–72–82. Open weekdays 9–6, Sat. 9–1. From Metro Insurgentes, take Génova north to Reforma, turn right and go 2 blocks. Hotel Nikko office: Campos Eliseos 204, tel. 5/282–21–47; Metro: Auditorio. Hotel Camino Real office: Mariano Escobedo 700, Col. Anzures, tel. 5/203–11–48; Metro: Chapultepec.*

BOOKSTORES

The American Bookstore offers a large selection of books and magazines in English, as well as the *Guía Pronto,* which has a good map of Mexico City. *Madero 25, tel. 5/512–03–06. 4½ blocks west of Zócalo. Open Mon.–Sat. 9:30–7, Sun. 10–3.*

The **Benjamin Franklin Library,** affiliated with the U.S. Embassy, was designed to nurture understanding between the United States and Mexico. Even mutual understanding has its limits, however: Although anyone can peruse the shelves, only Mexico City residents and foreigners who can prove they're working in Mexico can check out books. The library has a good reference section, plus numerous U.S. novels, periodicals, and magazines. On the second floor, the office of the **English Language Program** lists institutions looking for English teachers. *Londres 16, tel. 5/211–00–42. Open Mon. and Fri. 3–7:30, Tues.–Thurs. 10–3.*

Gandhi, a coffeeshop/bookstore in Coyoacán, supplies a noteworthy selection of Spanish tiles, supplemented by gorgeous art books and a handful of English books. For those who make a hobby of spotting famous literati, Mario Vargas Llosa has been known to browse here alongside the UNAM students. Also in Coyoacán, **El Parnaso** (corner of Carrillo Puerto and Jardín Centenario) features the same books as Gandhi, as well as the same hours of operation. *Gandhi: M. A. de Quevedo 134, tel. 5/662–09–76 or 5/661–09–11. ½ block west of Metro M. A. de Quevedo. Open weekdays 9 AM–11 PM, weekends 10–10.*

CASAS DE CAMBIO

All banks offer the same government-set *tipo de cambio* (exchange rate), but they often change money only until noon or 1:30. Even worse, banks usually require you to run through a lengthy set of bureaucratic hurdles, gathering signatures and receipts in triplicate, before the financial alchemists will turn your foreign currency into pesos. **Banamex** (tel. 5/709–98–85 or 5/542–42–61) is the most accessible bank, with branches on practically every block in the downtown area.

If time is of the essence, you'll find several **casas de cambio** willing to do the job faster—and, if you're lucky, at better rates than banks. The best rates can usually be found in the Zona Rosa. **Casa de Cambio Consultoria Internacional** (Río Tíber 110, tel. 5/207–99–20) and **Casa de Cambio Amberes** (Amberes 40, tel. 5/207–05–97) are both open weekdays 8:30–5:30.

DISCOUNT TRAVEL AGENCIES

Agencia de Viajes Tony Pérez does a lot of business with the U.S. Embassy across the street and knows about the latest airline promotions. *Río Volga 1, at Río Danubio, tel. 5/533–11–48 or 5/533–11–49. Near Ángel de la Independencia monument, across from Zona Rosa. Open weekdays 8:30–6:30, Sat. 9–1.*

Turismo Mirey wins the prize for most honest travel agency in the D.F., and the staff goes out of their way to find you the best travel deals. They also offer great half-day trips from Mexico City: $25 per person will buy you a tour of the Teotihuacán pyramids, transportation included. *Liverpool 162 A, in Zona Rosa, tel. 5/208–09–43. Open weekdays 9:30–7, Sat. 11–2.*

EMBASSIES

Australia. *925 Rubén Darío 55, Col. Polanco, tel. 5/531–52–25 (information) or 5/905–407–1698 (emergencies). Metro: Polanco. Open Mon.–Wed. 8–2 and 3–5, Thurs. and Fri. 8–2.*

Canada. The embassy also has a lending library. *Schiller 529, at Tres Picos, Col. Polanco, tel. 5/724–79–00. Metro: Polanco. Open weekdays 9–1 and 2–5; library open weekdays 9–12:30. Closed Canadian and Mexican holidays.*

New Zealand. *José Luis LaGrange 103, 10th floor, Col. Polanco, tel. 5/281–54–86, fax 5/281–52–12. Metro: Polanco. Open Mon.–Thurs. 9–2 and 4–5, Fri. 9–1. Closed Mexican holidays.*

United Kingdom. *Río Lerma 71, Col. Cuauhtémoc, tel. 5/207–24–49 or 5/207–20–89. Metro: Insurgentes. Open weekdays 8:30–3:30; weekdays 9–2 for visas and registration. Closed some Mexican and all British holidays.*

United States. *Paseo de la Reforma 305, Col. Cuauhtémoc, near Ángel de la Independencia monument, tel. 5/211–00–42, fax 5/511–99–80. Metro: Insurgentes. Open weekdays 8:30–5. Closed Mexican and U.S. holidays.*

Mexico City is also known as México D.F. (Distrito Federal), or just D.F. Less flattering nicknames include "Chilangolandia," a fusion of "chilango" and "Disneylandia," as well as "DFectuoso."

EMERGENCIES

In an emergency, dial **08** from any phone in Mexico City. Or call directly to the **fire** department (tel. 5/768–37–00), the **police** (tel. 5/588–51–00), or for **ambulance** service, the Cruz Roja (Red Cross; tel. 5/557–57–57).

The **Procuraduría General de Justicia** (Public Prosecutor) offers emergency assistance to tourists in Mexico City. Police, lawyers, and a doctor staff the two offices 24 hours a day. If you lose your passport or are a victim of a serious crime, you can make a report in English and the staff will translate it into Spanish for you. *Zona Rosa: Florencia 20, tel. 5/625–70–20 or 5/625–87–61; Metro: Insurgentes. Centro: Argentina, at San Ildefonso, tel. 5/625–87–62; Metro: Zócalo.*

The government-funded AIDS awareness group, **CONASIDA,** provides crisis counseling, medical referrals, lab testing, and support groups. The organization also sponsors the AIDS hotline, **TELSIDA** (tel. 5/207–40–77; phones open weekdays 9 AM–9:30 PM). All services are free and available in English. *Flora 8, Col. Roma, tel. 5/207–44–43. Metro: Cuahtémoc. Open weekdays 8–2 and 3–7.*

The **Locatel** (tel. 5/658–11–11) information and referral service offers bilingual information and assistance for almost any situation: lost persons or vehicles, medical emergencies, public transportation, and mental illness, among others. It's one of the most efficient public services offered by the city.

LAUNDRY

Laundromats are scarce in the city's center, which means you'll either have do the dirty work yourself or lug the load to another part of town. Your best bet is to find a hotel that offers laundry service. **Lavandería Edison** (Edison 91, near Monumento de la Revolución, no phone; open weekdays 10–7, Sat. until 6) is the only *lavandería* near the hotels in the Metro Revolución area. Once you get a look at their prices, you'll realize your clothes aren't so dirty after all: Doing your own load costs $1.75 to wash or dry; letting someone else handle it (one-hour service) costs $6. From Metro Revolución, walk toward the monument on Buenavista and then turn right on Edison. At **Lavandería Kiko** (Misioneros 9, Local B, no phone; open Mon.–Sat. 10–6) 3 kilos (6½ pounds) of dirty laundry cost $2 to wash and dry if you do it yourself, or $3.25 if someone else does it. From Metro Pino Suárez, walk east six blocks on Misioneros.

LUGGAGE STORAGE

If your hotel won't take your bags, the airport, train station, and all four bus stations have luggage storage (*see* Coming and Going, *below*). If you'll be gone more than a few days, use the service at the airport or at TAPO (the eastern bus station), where you can keep the key to your locker.

MAIL

The **Dirección General de Correos** (main post office), in a neo-Renaissance building across from Bellas Artes, sells stamps at the *estampillas* windows and distributes mail at the *lista y poste restante* window. Mail sent to you at the following address will be held for up to 10 days: Lista de Correos, Administración

1, Palacio Postal, México, D.F., CP 06002, México. Smaller branches are at the Central Poniente and Central Sur bus stations, and at the UNAM campus next to the main library. *Main branch: Lázaro Cárdenas, at Tacuba, tel. 5/512–98–20. 1 block from Alameda Central. Open weekdays 8 AM–10 PM, Sat. 8–8, Sun. 8–4.*

Cetel, in the heart of the Zona Rosa, offers the best deal on faxes ($2 per page). *Liverpool 162-A, between Florencia and Amberes, tel. and fax 5/533–64–21.*

MEDICAL AID

Two private hospitals with English-speaking staff are: **Hospital Español** (Ejercito Nacional 613, Col. Granada, tel. 5/203–37–35) and **American British Cowdray Hospital (ABC)** (Sur 138, at Observatorio, tel. 5/230–80–00). To reach the latter from Metro Tacubaya, take a *pesero* (collective taxi) marked CUAJIMALTA or NAVIDAD to Colonia Las Américas.

If you need free or inexpensive medical care, the following hospitals also have some English-speaking staff: **Hospital General Balbuena (DDF)** (Cecilio Robelo y Sur 103, Col. Jardín Balbuena, tel. 5/764–03–39; Metro: Moctezuma) and **Hospital Santa Fé** (San Luis Potosí 143, tel. 5/574–10–11; Metro: Chilpancingo). **Hospital de la Mujer** (Díaz Mirón 375, Col. Santo Tomás, tel. 5/341–43–09 or 5/341–19–52; Metro: Colegio Militar) offers 24-hour emergency services for women, and a drop-in, low-cost gynecological clinic (about $3 for an office visit) weekdays, 8–noon.

For late-night pharmaceuticals, the chain **Sanborns** (open daily 7:30 AM–1 AM) is your best bet, with locations throughout the city. The pharmacy chain **El Fénix** also has several stores throughout the city, including one at Madero 39 (tel. 5/521–98–02; open Mon.–Sat. 8 AM–9 PM, Sun. 10–7). For 24-hour service, try the **Mocel Hospital** (Gelati 27, tel. 5/277–31–11) in San Miguel Chapultepec, near Chapultepec Park. Each of the bus stations (*see* Coming and Going, *below*) also has a 24-hour pharmacy.

NEWSPAPERS AND PERIODICALS

In a city with more than 30,000 English-speaking expatriates, you'll have very little trouble locating English-language publications. Be on the lookout for *The Mexico City News* and *The Mexico City Times*, available at most Sanborns stores, newsstands, and some bookstores. These contain summaries of national and international news, entertainment, classifieds, and, most importantly, horoscopes and Ann Landers. *The Mexico City Daily Bulletin* is full of ads and handy sections like "Bible Digest" and "The World of Science." Published Tuesday–Sunday, it's available free at many hotels and at tourist offices. Look beyond the propaganda for helpful suggestions about hotels, restaurants, and places to shop; also cut out the great city map to carry around with you. *Tiempo Libre* is a Spanish weekly that lists entertainment information on almost everything, including gay clubs and events. Pick one up at Sanborns or a news kiosk for less than $1.

PHONES

Place local calls (13¢) at any orange public phone or from either the blue or gray **Ladatel Multitarjetas** phones. Phones that actually work can be identified by the long line of folks waiting to use them. If you'd rather avoid the wait, many establishments will let you use their phone, but at a higher cost. For local directory assistance, dial an operator at **04.**

The easiest way to make a long-distance call is with a prepaid LADA card on a Ladatel phone. You can buy LADA phone cards at any newsstand, lottery booth, or Sanborns in 20- or 50-peso denominations. A more expensive option is to place long-distance calls at a *caseta de larga distancia* (long-distance telephone office), generally marked with a large, blue sign. They're in all bus stations, the airport, and the train station; some (airport, Central Poniente, Tasqueña) are open 24 hours. At all casetas, you place the call and pay when you're done.

SCHOOLS

The **Centro de Enseñanza para Extranjeros** (School for Foreign Students) at **UNAM** (Universidad Nacional Autónoma de México) offers classes for visitors. Intensive and regular semester courses covering Spanish; Chicano studies; and Mexican art, history, and literature are open to anyone with a high-school degree. Each intensive course costs about $240; most classes are taught in Spanish. Registered students have access to the university's facilities, such as gyms, swimming pools, libraries, and the campus medical center. *Mailing address: CEPE, AP 70-391, C.U. Delegación Coyoacán, México, D.F., CP 04510, México, tel. 5/622–24–70, fax 5/616–26–72.*

TOURS

For inexpensive, city-sponsored tours, contact **Paseos Por Centro Historico** (tel. 5/512–10–12). For $3 you'll get to hop on a streetcar and cruise around downtown while a guide rambles on about the historical significance of each building or site. The only catch is that you can't disembark at any of the sites. The 50-minute tours leave daily, every hour on the hour 10–5, from the Museo de la Ciudad de México and the Palacio de Bellas Artes. To reserve an English-speaking guide, you must have a group of at least 20 people and call a day in advance.

For a more involved tour, contact **Paseos Culturales de INAH** (Instituto Nacional de Antropología e Historia; Frontera 53, Col. San Ángel, tel. 5/616–52–28) for a program of prescheduled thematic tours. These unique tours, usually taking place on the weekends, head for outlying historical areas, such as Teotihuacán and Meztitlán, or may cover the footsteps of important people like Sor Juana. The Spanish-only tours last from 8 to 8, cost $17, and leave from Córdoba 45, Colonia Roma, at 8 AM. Overnight tours cost $32–$50.

VISITOR INFORMATION

Tourist offices in both the international and domestic terminals of the **airport** and in the **TAPO** (*see* Coming and Going, *below*) offer help with directions and hotel reservations. The **Asociación Méxicana de Hoteles y Moteles** (tel. 5/203–04–66) also has offices at the airport and will make reservations for you. They're next to the baggage claims at the domestic and international terminals, before the immigration booths.

Wander Mexico City for a day, and you'll notice dozens of Sanborns stores. The chain is rumored to have connections to former president Carlos Salinas de Gortari, who many claim is the real owner.

Another good source of information is the **Secretaría de Turismo (SECTUR)**, whose competent and friendly English-speaking staff distributes brochures and maps, assists in trip planning, and makes hotel reservations anywhere in Mexico. Choose from their array of phone numbers: 5/250–01–23 for 24-hour complaints and emergencies, 5/250–01–51 for 24-hour multilingual tourist information, and toll-free 91–800/9–03–92 (from Mexico) or 800/482–9832 (from the U.S. and other countries) for general information. *Presidente Mazarik 172, Col. Polanco, tel. 5/250–85–55 ext. 168 or 5/255–22–95. From Metro Polanco, walk south on Horacio and 2 blocks west on Hegel. Open weekdays 8 AM–9 PM.*

COMING AND GOING

BY BUS

Each of Mexico City's four main bus terminals is at a different cardinal point of the city, and *generally* services the corresponding section of the country. If you're traveling during Christmas, Easter, or during the peak tourist months of July and August, buy your tickets well in advance and be prepared for a mob scene. Tickets for most buses go on sale about three weeks before the departure date. It's best to check your baggage about half an hour before departure and board 20 minutes in advance. Find out the departure point for your bus and don't stray from it; the boarding announcements are virtually unintelligible, even to Spanish-speakers. Unless otherwise noted, the prices listed below are the lowest available, generally on CLASE ECONÓMICO (second-class) buses. However, for long-distance trips you may wish to pay a bit more for one of the deluxe buses, which feature air-conditioning, TV, toilets, and reclining seats.

If you plan to cross the United States–Mexico border by bus, you can purchase connecting tickets for U.S.-bound buses at **Agencía de Viajes Reforma** (Paseo de la Reforma 29, tel. 5/592–37–76 or 5/546–87–59), a a travel agency affiliated with the Greyhound bus line. Another option is **Estrella Blanca** (Terminal Central del Norte, tel. 5/729–07–25), which lets you purchase Greyhound bus tickets for trips across the Texas and New Mexico borders.

TERMINAL CENTRAL DE AUTOBUSES DEL NORTE • The northern terminal is a massive semicircular building across the street from Metro Autobuses del Norte. This bus station is large and intimidating, but if you want to go anywhere north of Mexico City, you'll have to come here. Companies serving this station include: **Estrella Blanca** (tel. 5/729–07–62 or 5/729–07–25), with service to Guadalajara (7½ hrs, $18), Hermosillo (30 hrs, $59), Mazatlán (17 hrs, $34), Monterrey (12 hrs, $25), Nuevo Laredo (15 hrs, $33), Puerto Vallarta (14 hrs, $36), Querétaro (3 hrs, $7), and Tijuana (44 hrs, $63); **Flecha Amarilla** (tel. 5/567–80–33), which serves Aguascalientes (7 hrs, $14), Guadalajara (8 hrs, $18), Morelia (6 hrs, $10), and San Miguel de Allende (4 hrs, $7.50); **Omnibús de México** (tel. 5/567–67–96), which serves Chihuahua (20 hrs, $53), Durango (12 hrs, $33), and Guanajuato (5 hrs, $13); and **Autobuses del Oriente (ADO)** (tel. 5/567–62–47), with buses to Jalapa (5 hrs, $10.50).

Autobuses del Norte is the biggest and best-equipped station in the city, furnished with a **casa de cambio** (open weekdays 8–8 and weekends 9–4), a Banamex **ATM,** a 24-hour **caseta de larga distancia,** and **luggage lockers** ($1.50–$2.50 for 24 hrs). A small booth marked HOTELES ASOCIADOS (tel. 5/587–85–51; open weekdays 2–9) offers free help with hotel reservations. *Av. de los 100 Metros 4907, tel. 5/587-59–67 or 5/587–59–73.*

There are no budget hotels near the terminal, but you can easily reach the centro by public transportation. For a pesero, go down into the Metro and cross under the street: The RUTA 1 BELLAS ARTES pesero runs to the Bellas Artes/Alameda Central area and the RUTA 88 METRO REVOLUCION goes to the hotels near Metro Revolución. If you can't wait to take your first Metro ride, jump on Line 5 toward Pantitlán, change at Metro La Raza to Line 3 toward Universidad (inconvenient if you have a lot of luggage, since the "Tunnel of Science" connecting the two lines seems a million miles long), and get off at Metro Juárez or Metro Hidalgo, where many budget hotels are clustered. A regulated taxi to a hotel in the centro will cost you about $4; buy a ticket at the taxi booth next to the Banamex ATM. Collective taxis are about half that price, but you may have to wait for half an hour and then tip whoever found the cab for you.

TERMINAL CENTRAL DEL SUR/TASQUENA • Tasqueña, as this station is usually called, is easily reached from the Metro station of the same name on Line 2. This terminal is almost always a madhouse and serves mostly southern and southwestern Mexico. **Estrella de Oro** (tel. 5/549–85–20) serves Acapulco ($25 express; $15 with stops) and Ixtapa/Zihuatanejo ($35 express; $20 with stops). The first-class **Autopullman de Morelos** (tel. 5/549–35–05) line heads for Cuernavaca (1 hr, $3), Cuautla (1½ hrs, $3.50), and Tepoztlán (1 hr, $2.50). **Cristóbal Colón** (tel. 5/544–24–14), another first-class line, offers buses to Oaxaca city (6 hrs, $17), Huatulco (16 hrs, $24), Puebla (2 hrs, $4), and Puerto Escondido (18 hrs, $27). Tasqueña lacks a casa de cambio or ATM, but has a 24-hour **caseta de larga distancia** that accepts both Visa and MasterCard. The caseta also has a fax, photocopying machine, and doubles as a travel agency offering cheap packages to the beach. There's also a **pharmacy** and **luggage storage** (opposite door 3; $1.50–$2.50 per day), both open 24 hours. *Tasqueña 1320, tel. 5/544–21–01 or 5/689–97–95.*

The Metro is by far the cheapest transport from Tasqueña to the budget hotels in the centro: Hop on at Metro Tasqueña and take Line 2 toward Cuatro Caminos and get off at Metro Allende. Taxis provide a more comfortable alternative. The ticket system mandates a rate of about $5 to the downtown area and $6 to the airport; purchase tickets at the taxi booth in front of door 3.

TERMINAL AUTOBUSES DE PASAJEROS DE ORIENTE (TAPO) • TAPO is in a working-class area just east of the city center and is easily reached from the adjacent San Lázaro Metro station (Line 1). Buses depart this large, clean terminal for eastern destinations, although you can also catch the odd southbound bus from here. **ADO** (tel. 5/542–71–92 or 5/542–71–97) serves Cancún (24 hrs, $47), Jalapa (5 hrs, $10.50), Oaxaca city (6 hrs, $17), and Veracruz city (9 hrs, $14). The first-class **Cristóbal Colón** (tel. 5/542–72–63) line travels to Oaxaca city (6 hrs, $17), San Cristóbal de las Casas (21 hrs, $32), and Tuxtla Gutiérrez (12 hrs, $31.50). **Luggage storage** ($2.50 for 24 hrs), a **caseta de larga distancia** (open daily 7 AM–11 PM), a Banamex **ATM,** and the friendly, bilingual staff at the **tourist information desk** (near the Metro exit; open daily 9–9) make this one of the more pleasant terminals to be stranded in. The boarding announcements at TAPO are audible but not necessarily intelligible, especially if you've fallen prey to the music videos playing here on large monitors. *Zaragoza 200, tel. 5/762-59–77.*

There are several ways to reach the cheap hotels in the centro: The RUTA 22 ZÓCALO/BELLAS ARTES pesero or the ALAMEDA bus will pick you up right in front of the terminal; or take the Metro toward Observatorio, get off at Balderas, change to Line 3, head toward Indios Verdes, and get off at Juárez. You can also take a taxi for $2.50 to the downtown area, $3.50 to the airport.

TERMINAL CENTRAL PONIENTE • This recently remodeled terminal has a 24-hour **luggage storage** in room E ($1 for 24 hrs), a 24-hour **caseta de larga distancia,** and a **post office** (open weekdays 8 –7). Most destinations from this station are also served by the three other, more convenient stations. **Tres Estrellas de Oro** (tel. 5/271–03–33) runs only from this terminal, serving Tijuana (48 hrs, $64), Mazatlán (18 hrs, $34), and Guadalajara (8 hrs, $18). To reach the centro from the station, take Line 1 to Pino Suárez, switch to Line 2, and get off at Zócalo. Otherwise, purchase a regulated taxi ticket to the downtown area (about $5) in the station. *Corner of Sur 122 and Río Tacubaya, tel. 5/271–45–19.*

BY CAR

A quick count of the memorial crosses on the sides of the roads will help you understand why many Mexicans keep religious figurines on their dashboards or hanging from their rearview mirrors—use your finest defensive driving skills if you wish to survive. The main highways approaching Mexico City are 85 from the north, 136 and 150 from the east, 95 from the south, and 15 from the west. These main highways are generally well maintained; just be careful driving at night, as occasional steep shoulders and deep gutters can cause your car to roll over. However, tolls for *carreteras de quota*, the new super highways with better road conditions, can be outrageous. **Auxilio Turístico Ángeles Verdes** (Green Angels; tel. 5/250–82–21 or 5/250–01–23) is a group of radio-dispatched mechanics who offer free roadside assistance for minor car problems.

BY PLANE

The **Aeropuerto Internacional de la Ciudad de México** is big but manageable and always buzzing with activity. Most major carriers, including Mexicana, American, Delta, Air France, and Iberia, operate from this airport, which connects Mexico with just about every destination in the world.

At the airport, **Bancomer** (open daily 9–9) and **Banamex** (open daily 9–8) have the same exchange rates, and the latter has a 24-hour ATM that accepts Cirrus and Plus cards. **Storage lockers** ($3 for 24 hrs) in both the domestic and the international terminals are always open; the lockers are in terminal E, right across from customs, and in terminal A, behind the stairs to the restaurants. There are two **tourist information offices** (tel. 5/762–67–63 or 5/762–67–73; open daily 9–9), one in domestic terminal A and the other in international terminal F. Their friendly and well-informed staff makes hotel reservations, provides directions and maps, and dispenses advice. The office of the **Asociación Méxicana de Hoteles y Moteles** (*see* Visitor Information, *above*), which can recommend accommodations for every budget, also has

In Mexico City, keep your purse, daypack, or camera in front of you, especially at rush hour and in Metro stations; thieves have been known to slit backpacks and purse straps before you can say "¡Socorro!"

offices in terminals A and F and purports to be open 24 hours a day. The **Caseta Pública** in terminal F is open 24 hours. You can call long distance and send faxes, but you cannot make collect calls. Several **pharmacies** (open daily 7 AM–10 PM) are scattered throughout terminals A and F.

AIRPORT TRANSIT • The only realistic airport transportation for budget travelers is the Metro. It's a cheap but fairly time-consuming (one hour to the centro) way to travel and probably not the safest after dark, especially since you'll have to make at least one line change to get to or from downtown. From the international exit at the airport, turn left, and walk for about 1 km (½ mi) (think twice about doing this with heavy luggage). Get on Line 5 at the Terminal Aérea station and follow the signs reading PANTITLAN. When you reach Pantitlán, change to Line 9, and follow the signs reading TACUBAYA. At the Chabacano stop, transfer to Line 2 and follow signs reading CUATRO CAMINOS. You can get off at the Allende, Zócalo, or Bellas Artes stops for the budget hotels in the centro. Just remember that the Metro does not run after 12:30 AM. If you have a late flight, your only option is to take a taxi. Taxi service from the airport is regulated and you must purchase a ticket at the office in the far end of the domestic terminal or at the international terminal next to the baggage claim, where prices are set according to destination and number of passengers. Rates for downtown-bound taxis start at about $6 for one to four passengers. If you have an early flight or just plain want to make it there on time, a radio taxi is your best bet (*see* Getting Around, *below*), at about $8. If you want to rent a car, visit the few rental agencies in Sala E.

BY TRAIN

The train is slow, and it's not fun. Any illusions you may have had about rushing through the countryside by night (thereby saving money on hotels) should be quickly forgotten. Of course you can't ignore the fact that second-class train tickets are 60% (first-class 20%) cheaper than bus prices. **Estación Central Buenavista** is in a rather run-down area of the city—not the best place to be caught lugging your suitcase around late at night. From the station, reach the budget lodging near Metro Revolución by walking south on Insurgentes Sur to Reforma, turn left and walk to La Fragua, turn left one block and you're there. To reach hotels south of the Alameda by minibus, take a RUTA 99 ALAMEDA/BELLAS ARTES pesero from Metro Revolución; to reach lodging near the Zócalo, take RUTA 99 TACUBA.

The friendly folks at the **information booth** (left of ticket window, tel. 5/547–65–93 or 5/547–10–84) field queries about rail travel daily 6:30 AM–9:30 PM. For help in English, stop by the **Oficina Comercial**

de Pasajeros (next to the caseta de larga distancia, tel. 5/547–86–55; open weekdays 10–3 and 5:30–8). **Luggage storage** (down the ramp across from the second-class ticket booth) costs 75¢ per hour per bag, but it's only open 6:30 AM–9:30 PM. There is no ATM near the station, but you can visit Banamex or Bancomer near Metro Revolución on Alvarado.

First-class and **sleeper-car** tickets can be purchased from any one of the *boletos* windows. They're almost twice as expensive as second-class tickets, but at least you're guaranteed a seat and won't run the risk of having to stand for 36 hours. Likewise, if you're going on a long trip, the sleeper cars (available only on some routes) are indispensable and well worth the money. Trains are packed during the Christmas season, Semana Santa (Holy Week, the week preceding Easter), and summer months, so make reservations in advance if possible. **Second-class** tickets (same-day cash purchases only) are sold from a line of windows hidden in the back of the building: Go down the ramp at either side of the main building to find the second-class *taquillas* (ticket booths), open from 6 AM until the last train leaves. Seats are not reserved, so it's best to arrive at least one–four hours before departure; the earlier you get here, the better your chance of getting a seat.

The first-class **Tren División del Norte** leaves daily at 8 PM for Ciudad Juárez (27 hrs, $36), stopping along the way in Querétaro, Aguascalientes, Zacatecas, and Chihuahua, as well as many other cities. **Tren Tapatío** leaves daily at 8:30 PM for Guadalajara; first-class fare is $13, and $32 will get you a sleeping berth (only available on the weekends). **Tren Regiomontano** departs at 7 PM for Monterrey (14 hrs; 1st class $23, 2nd class $13, $47 for weekend-only sleeping berth) stopping in San Luis Potosí and Saltillo. The **Tren Oaxaqueño** to Oaxaca city (15 hrs; $13.50 1st class, $7.75 2nd class) leaves daily at 7:10 PM. The **Tren Jarocho** departs daily for Veracruz city (10 hrs; $10.50 1st class, $7 2nd class, $25 for weekend-only sleeping berths) at 9:15 PM.

GETTING AROUND

Mexico City's size can easily confuse and intimidate travelers. The streets are not all neatly set out in a grid, and their names can change as often as five times as they pass through some of the 350 *colonias* (neighborhoods). You can orient yourself in the downtown area by using the two major arteries, **Paseo de la Reforma** and **Avenida Insurgentes,** as guides. Insurgentes runs north–south, intersecting Reforma in the busy downtown area and continuing south through the trendy Zona Rosa. Reforma passes through Chapultepec Park in the southwest of the city and continues north through the downtown, just missing the northwest corner of the Alameda Central. Just south of Alameda Central, Reforma intersects another important street, **Avenida Juárez.** West of Reforma, Juárez ends in the Plaza de la República and the Monumento a la Revolución; east of Reforma, Juárez runs from the Alameda Central to the Zócalo, becoming Avenida Madero as it runs through the *centro histórico* (historic center) of the D.F.

BY BUS

Every day, hundreds of thousands of passengers ride Mexico City's buses. Although the system serves the entire city (destinations are marked on the windshields), two routes are particularly useful and run all night long: RUTA 55, the principal route between the Zócalo and Chapultepec Park, travels along the Paseo de la Reforma, Juárez, and Madero; and RUTA 17, the route connecting Metro Indios Verdes to Ciudad Universitaria (University City, or UNAM), passing along Insurgentes through San Ángel. Most other buses run daily 5 AM–midnight. While service is generally reliable and always cheap (about 12¢), the lumbering vehicles absolutely crawl during rush hours (7–10 AM and 5–9 PM). Buses are also extremely crowded during these peak hours. If you can't make out the tangle of bus lines on your own, any of the friendly tourist agencies in the Zona Rosa will help you get where you're going.

BY CAR

Only the very brave or very foolish attempt to drive in Mexico City. Parking is nearly impossible to find, roads are confusing, traffic is eternally congested, and most other drivers are *totalmente locos*. Plus, all cars are prohibited from driving one to two days a week, depending on the pollution level. The days are determined either by a colored sticker on the car or the last digit of the vehicle's license plate number. This law does not apply to vehicles with foreign license plates or to rental cars (your rental car should have a special plate that exempts it from the restriction). If you are driving, invest in a good street map like the *Guía Roji* or the *Guía Pronto* and try to drive like a chilango—fearlessly and with death as your backseat driver.

To rent a car you must have a credit card and a driver's license. Be prepared to spend plenty of money: The most affordable rentals go for about $45 a day, mileage and insurance included. Though the minimum age requirement differs from company to company, one thing remains constant: All companies charge a 15% government tax. Rental company offices at the airport are open 24 hours, and there are dozens of branches in the Zona Rosa. Major companies include **Avis** (tel. 5/588–88–88 or toll free 91–800/7–07–77), **Budget** (tel. 5/271–43–22), **Dollar** (tel. 5/328–62–23), and **National** (tel. 5/575–22–79 or toll free 91–800/9–01–86). **Hertz** (tel. 5/592–60–82 or toll-free 91–800/7–00–16) is one of only a few companies that rents to drivers ages 18–25.

BY METRO

The Metro is by far the fastest and cheapest way to explore Mexico City, and it is simple to use: Each of the nine lines is color coded, and stations are named for major sights nearby. Route maps are posted throughout every station, and free *Red del Metro* maps are available at the information booths of the principal stations. To avoid accumulating a pocketful of change every time you buy a ticket (15¢), you can purchase 10 at a time (there is no expiration date). Tickets are sold at the windows labeled TAQUILLA, near the main entrances to the metro lines. Transfers don't cost extra, but make sure not to follow the crowds out of the station; once you pass through the *salida* (exit), you'll need a new ticket to reenter.

Large backpacks or luggage are technically not allowed on the Metro, though it's unlikely anyone will stop you. Because of crowds, however, it's actually difficult to fit into the Metro with a large bag during peak hours, when the trains become a claustrophobic's nightmare. When it's crowded, get close to the door well before your stop—the rush of incoming passengers gives you little time to exit. During rush hours (7–10 and 5–9), the first cars on Lines 1, 2, and 3 are reserved for women and children, and guards posted at the gates strictly enforce the rule. Lines 1–9 run weekdays 5 AM–12:30 AM, Saturday 6 AM–1 AM, and Sunday 7 AM–12:30 AM.

> *Use of the word pesero to describe a collective taxi or city minibus dates from the good old days when a ride actually cost one peso.*

BY PESERO

Throughout the D.F., peseros, which include *combis* (old VW vans) and *micros* (a slightly larger version of the combi), squeeze through impossible spaces, turn left from the far right lane, go from full throttle to a dead stop in seconds, and manage to deliver people alive to thousands of street corners all over the city. Peseros cover general zones marked by a number, preceded by the words RUTA NO. painted on the side of the minibus. Individual routes within the zones vary, though, so it's a good idea to ignore the ruta numbers and concentrate on reading the destination posted in the window. Corners with stoplights and bus stops are the easiest places to catch peseros, but they generally stop wherever you hail them. Designated stops along Insurgentes and Reforma, however, are indicated by a white-and-green sign. The fare is based upon how far you go: about 15¢ for up to 5 km (3 mi), 25¢ for 5 km–12 km (3 mi–7 mi), and 30¢ for 12 km (7 mi) or more. For more information or to file a complaint, call 5/605–66–67 or 5/605–59–22 between 9 AM and 3 PM or between 6 PM and 8 PM.

BY TAXI

Taxis are easy to come by all over the D.F., especially in the downtown area. The big American sedans parked outside major hotels and museums (and all around the Zona Rosa), called *sitio* cabs, are tourist taxis whose English-speaking drivers will gladly take you on shopping tours or off to see the sites. Of course, at the end of your leisurely drive through the city they'll also charge you a small fortune—generally twice as much as the metered taxis. Your best bet is to stick to the "real" taxis—usually green or yellow VW Bugs and small sedans available when the sign on the dash says LIBRE. The green ones use only unleaded gasoline so they're more environmentally sound (a big consideration in this smoggy city). If the meter works, the standard, nonnegotiable rate will be used. However, if the meter is "broken," you'll have a chance to bargain for your ride before you get in. You'll be glad you did, when, after a series of convoluted circles and backtracking, you finally reach your hotel and the meter has skyrocketed. After all, the D.F. is a huge city, and most drivers only have a general idea of a particular museum or hotel's whereabouts. After 10 PM, fares go up officially by about one-tenth and drivers tend to be reluctant to venture very far out of the city. Also beware of crossing the line between the D.F. and the Estado de México. Although there is no visible difference between these two areas, taxi drivers automatically double their rates once they cross the border. Tipping is necessary only when the driver helps you with your bags, drives in a non-life-threatening manner, or otherwise goes out of his way to make your journey somewhat pleasurable.

Radio-dispatched taxis will fetch you wherever you are, although finding a cab downtown isn't a problem at any hour. If you've made an appointment the night before, it's best to call and remind them half

MEXICO CITY BUS ROUTES

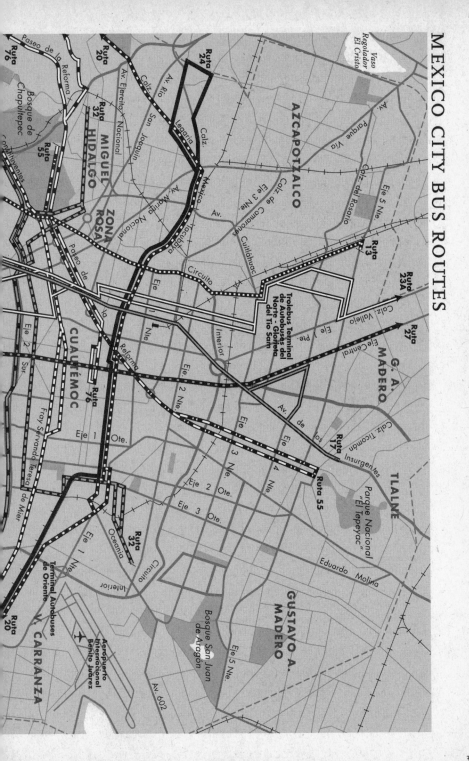

MEXICO CITY BUS ROUTES

Vaso
Regulador
El Cristo

AZCAPOTZALCO

Ruta 24

Ruta 20

Ruta 32

Ruta 76

Ruta 55

MIGUEL HIDALGO

Av. Ejército Nacional

Av. Río San Joaquin

Calz. Legaria

Calz. México

Av. Marina Nacional

Calz. Camarones

Cuitláhuac

Av. Vallejo

ZONA ROSA

Paseo de la Reforma

Bosque de Chapultepec

Constituyentes

Circuito

Interior

Trolebus Terminal de Autobuses del Norte - Glorieta del Tío Sam

Eje 1 Pte.

Eje 1 Pte.

Calz. Vallejo

Eje 3 Nte.

Eje 5 Nte.

Calz. del Rosario

Parque Vía

Ruta 13

Ruta 23A

Ruta 27

G. A. MADERO

Eje Central

CUAUHTÉMOC

Ruta 76

Eje 2 Sur

Eje 1 Ote.

Fray Servando Teresa de Mier

Reforma

Eje 2 Nte.

Eje 2 Nte.

Eje 3 Nte.

Eje 4 Nte.

Ruta 55

Ruta 17

Insurgentes

Calz. Ticomán

Av. de los

TLALNE

Parque Nacional "El Tepeyac"

Ruta 32

Oceanía

Circuito Interior

Eje 3 Ote.

Eje 2 Ote.

Eje 1 Nte.

Terminal Autobuses de Oriente

Ruta 20

V. CARRANZA

Aeropuerto Internacional Benito Juárez

Bosque San Juan de Aragón

Eduardo Molina

GUSTAVO A. MADERO

Eje 5 Nte.

Av. 602

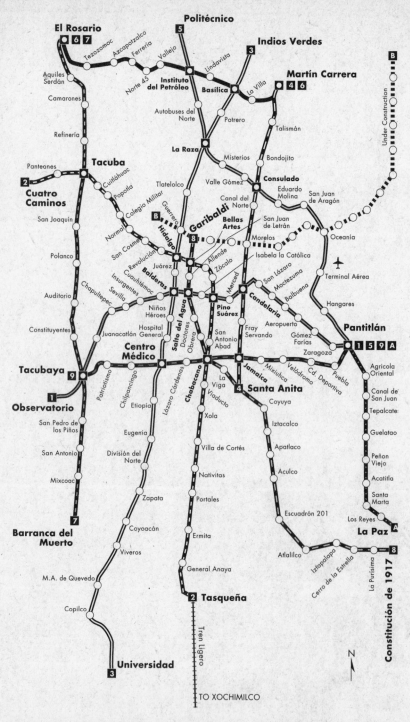

an hour before they're supposed to arrive. Several companies are listed in the phone book under *Sitios de Automóviles,* or try **Servi Taxis** (tel. 5/271–2560 or 5/519–7690).

Keep in mind that tourists have recently been mugged and robbed by gypsy (unlicensed) VW cab drivers, usually at night. The drivers work in tandem with another car following behind; when the cab gets to a darkened street, it pulls over to allow the thugs in the other car to rob the passengers. The thieves always take credit cards and force victims to withdraw cash with their bank cards at the nearest ATM machine. The illegal cabs prowl all the usual tourist spots: bus terminals, restaurants, nightclubs, and the Zona Rosa. The best preventitive measure is to use radio or sitio cabs at night. And as always, keep a low profile; jewelry and other ostentatious displays of wealth will only make you look like a more attractive target.

WHERE TO SLEEP

Cheap hotels in Mexico City are filled by traveling Mexicans, be they vacationing families or suited businessmen. The budget hotel areas listed here are conveniently clustered around Metro stops Pino Suárez, Zócalo, Bellas Artes, and Revolución. Reservations are always a good idea, especially during the major holidays of Christmas and Semana Santa (Holy Week, the week preceding Easter) and the summer months. If you don't have reservations, at least try to arrive close to check-out time (noon–2), when other guests will be vacating the rooms. Tax is usually included in the government-controlled room price.

NEAR THE ZOCALO

The huge colonial buildings in the area near the Zócalo have been subdivided over time to create a densely populated commercial and residential area. The busy downtown area is heavily traveled by day and virtually empty by night. Be cautious when wandering the deserted night streets, especially alone.

UNDER $10 • Hotel Habana. Sleek and decorated in pastels, this is the place to pamper yourself for the fewest pesos. The rooms (and beds) are decadently over-size, the bathrooms are clean and modern, and there's steaming hot water. Rooms all have TVs and cost $9.50 for a single or one-bed double, $14 for a double with two beds. *República de Cuba 77, between Palma and República de Chile, tel. 5/518–15–89 or 5/518–15–90. 50 rooms, all with bath. Snack bar, luggage storage, safe-deposit boxes. Reservations advised. Cash only.*

Hotel Isabel. The Isabel's business card proudly trumps itself up as being "an ideal place for tourists," and German travelers in particular seem to heed the call. The place is gorgeous, with a slight Spanish-Inquisition theme: Dangerous-looking iron relics and numerous portraits of "La Isabel" overlook a huge, but cozy, lobby perfect for socializing with other international travelers. Try for one of the quiet fourth-floor rooms with outdoor patios facing away from the street. Singles or doubles with a clean communal bathroom cost $8; doubles with bath cost $14 *Isabel la Católica 63, tel. 5/518–12–13, fax 5/521–12–33. 72 rooms, 63 with bath. Restaurant, bar. Cash only.*

Hotel Juárez. On a small side street off bustling 5 de Mayo, this budget hotel is hard to find but worth the effort. The cool, trickling fountain in the Moorish-style lobby sets the tone, although the dim corridors might make you wonder if the colonial theme is being stretched a bit too far. Paneled double rooms with TV, phone, and piped-in Muzak are a great deal at $9.50 for one bed, $11 for two. *Cerrada de 5 de Mayo 17, on a side street between Isabel la Católica and Palma, tel. 5/512–69–29 or 5/518–47–18. From Metro Allende, 1 block south on Isabel la Católica, left on 5 de Mayo. 39 rooms, all with bath. Luggage storage. Reservations advised. Cash only.*

Hotel San Antonio. This quiet hotel on a dead-end alley usually has vacancies even in the afternoon. It's only a block from the Zócalo though difficult to find. The small, bright rooms (double $10), have green bedspreads and impeccably clean bathrooms with water that takes a while to get hot. All rooms have TVs, phones, soap, and towels. Avoid the noisy rooms on the ground floor. *Callejón 5 de Mayo 29, tel. 5/512–99–06. From Zócalo, west on 5 de Mayo, left on Palma, right on Cerrada de 5 de Mayo until it turns into Callejón 5 de Mayo. 44 rooms, 40 with bath. Cash only.*

UNDER $15 • Hotel La Marina. The lobby, with a ship's steering wheel commanding a place of honor on the turquoise walls, is the only thing "marine" about this hotel. Rooms ($14.50 doubles) have valentine-red carpets and pink bedspreads that are comfortable, if worn. The bathrooms are clean and modern. *Allende 30, at Domíguez, tel 5/518–24–45. 47 rooms, all with bath. Luggage storage. Reservations advised.*

Hotel Principal. The management at this nunnery-turned-hotel has done wonders to liven up the place—plants and natural light make it look like a giant greenhouse. Clean and comfortable doubles with baths (soap and towels included) cost $14 for a *cama matrimonial* (double bed), or $15 for two beds. *Bolívar 29, between 16 de Septiembre and Madero, tel. 5/521–13–33 or 5/521–20–32. 100 rooms, 60 with bath. Restaurant, luggage storage. Cash only.*

UNDER $25 • Hotel Canadá. This hotel tries to make you feel important from the moment you walk in. A uniformed bellboy greets you at the door, the reception staff is always on its best behavior, and the rooms, although small, possess TVs and telephones. Doubles with one bed go for $23 (two beds $25). *5 de Mayo 47, tel. 5/518–21–06, fax 5/512–93–10. 85 rooms, all with bath. Laundry, safe-deposit box.*

UNDER $35 • Hotel Catedral. The only noise you'll hear in this extremely comfortable hotel is the toll of the cathedral's bells (which unfortunately continue throughout the night). Rooms are decorated in soothing pastels, and the beds and mirrors are tastefully trimmed in oak. Doubles cost $32, and all rooms have TVs, phones, and spacious closets. For a real treat, get the junior suite with a Jacuzzi bathtub (an additional $9). The large, clean bathrooms have huge showers and plenty of hot water. *Donceles 95, tel. 5/518–52–32, fax 5/512–43–44. 120 rooms, all with bath. Restaurant, bar, laundry, luggage storage, parking, room service, safe-deposit box, travel agency. Reservations advised.*

Hotel Gillow. A short walk from the Zócalo, this luxury hotel has huge rooms with all the trimmings, such as room service, TVs, and phones. Bathrooms have a tub and a wood-trim mirror. One-bed doubles cost $26, two-bed doubles $32. *Isabel la Católica 17, between Madero and 5 de Mayo, tel. 5/518–14–40. 103 rooms, all with bath. Restaurant, laundry, luggage storage, safe-deposit box, travel agency.*

SOUTH OF THE ALAMEDA CENTRAL

The area just south of the Alameda Central is packed with hotels, cheap *taquerías* (taco stands), and shops selling bric-a-brac. Most hotels are just a short walk from the Palacio de Bellas Artes and the Museo Mural de Diego Rivera. The small *barrio chino* (Chinatown) on Dolores is also nearby. Although the area is fairly safe and a bit more lively at night than the neighborhoods around the Zócalo, take normal precautions when out after dark.

UNDER $15 • Hotel del Valle. Don't be put off by the nondescript lobby or bland rooms. The location and price ($9 for one bed, $11 for two) are good, and the bathrooms are as clean as they come. Plus, each room is equipped with a phone and TV. The reliable but somewhat dilapidated elevator is a pleasure if you're toting heavy baggage. *Independencia 35, tel. 5/521–80–67. 50 rooms, all with bath. Restaurant, laundry, luggage storage. Reservations advised. Cash only.*

Hotel Toledo. The lobby is cozy and welcoming despite the *telenovelas* (soap operas) flickering on the TV. A mint-green stairway winds up to spacious and airy rooms with worn carpet and thinning bedspreads. Noise is minimal, unless you're in a room facing the street. The bathrooms are old but clean and have reliable hot water. Doubles are $13. *López 22, tel. 5/521–32–49, fax 5/518–56–31. From Metro Bellas Artes, south on Cárdenas (Eje Central), right on Independencia, left on López. 35 rooms, all with bath. Snack bar, luggage storage. Reservations advised. Cash only.*

UNDER $25 • Hotel Fleming. Don't let the vinyl in the '50s-style lobby fool you—this is a posh hotel. The spacious rooms have mirrors, TVs, phones, and matching pastel curtains and comforters. Doubles are $24. For an additional $10 you can get a room with a Jacuzzi bathtub. *Revillagigedo 35, tel. 5/510–45–30. From Metro Juárez, 2 blocks east on Juárez, right on Revillagigedo. 75 rooms, all with bath. Restaurant, laundry, luggage storage, parking. Reserve at least 2 days in advance.*

UNDER $30 • Hotel Marlowe. The beautiful, fully carpeted rooms here have large desks, TVs, and touch-tone phones, while the impeccable bathrooms have enough hot water to fog their full-length mirrors. Doubles cost $28. *Independencia 17, between López and Dolores, tel. 5/521–95–40. 107 rooms, all with bath. Restaurant, laundry, luggage storage, parking, travel agency.*

NEAR METRO REVOLUCION

The budget hotels near the Metro Revolución are all within a one-block radius of each other, so try two or three to find the best deal. Despite the peaceful atmosphere on the tree-lined streets, it's only a five-minute Metro ride to the hustle and bustle of the city center. The area is also bordered by major thoroughfares—Insurgentes Norte, Puente de Alvarado, and Reforma—which provide easy access to all points in the city.

UNDER $10 • Casa de los Amigos. The friendly, English-speaking staff at this Quaker house won't make you pass a test to stay here, but you must abide by some of the Casa's rules: No alcohol or drugs allowed and smoking permitted only on the patio. In return you'll get the lowdown on volunteer opportunities and Spanish language classes in Mexico and Guatemala, as well as use of their library. The Casa serves huge, healthy breakfasts ($1.50) weekdays 8–9 AM, the perfect time to socialize with other international travelers. Single-sex dorm beds are $5.50 and private doubles $11 ($12.50 with bath). Apartments with kitchen and bathroom costs $14–$18. Make a reservation by fax. *Ignacio Mariscal 132, tel. 5/705–06–46 or 5/705–05–21, fax 5/705–07–71. 24 dorm beds, 3 singles and 3 doubles without bath, 2 doubles with bath, 1 apartment. Kitchen, laundry, luggage storage. Cash only.*

Hotel Ibiza. This remodeled hotel struggles to be elegant (but doesn't quite succeed) with its pink and gray marble. At least it's refurbished, clean, and has an elevator. Plus you get all the amenities that accompany modernity: a phone, TV, hot water, and piped-in music. Doubles are $10. *Ponciano Arriaga 22, tel. 5/566–81–55. 29 rooms, 22 with bath. Limited luggage storage. Cash only.*

Hotel Pennsylvania. The Pennsylvania's renovated "king-size" rooms (doubles $11) are done in light peach and baby blue, while the older, cheaper, and mustier rooms (doubles $8.50) tend to have a more motley decor. Showering should be considered a lesson in patience: The hot water will come, eventually. *Ignacio Mariscal 101, tel. 5/703–13–84. 80 rooms, all with bath. Cash only.*

UNDER $15 • Hotel Carlton. Across the street from a tree-filled plaza, this hotel features spacious, clean rooms and bathrooms. The management fumigates the place once a month—the odor is unpleasant, but at least you can rest assured that nothing will slither, crawl, or creep its way into your bed. Rooms come in two prices: nonrenovated ($10 doubles) and renovated ($11.50 doubles). *Ignacio Mariscal 32-B15, tel. 5/566–29–11 or 5/566–29–14. From Metro Revolución, east on Puente de Alvarado to Ramos Arizpe and right 1 block. 41 rooms, all with bath. Restaurant, luggage storage, safe-deposit box. Reservations advised. Cash only.*

Hotel Oxford. Wood-panel walls and gray-marble floors in the entryway are a nod to this hotel's British namesake. Rooms are huge, clean, and decorated with clashing patterns; the best overlook the plaza. Doubles are $10–$11.50. The bar next door offers room service from noon to midnight. *Ignacio Mariscal 67, tel. 5/566–05–00. 48 rooms, all with bath. Luggage storage, safe-deposit boxes. Reservations advised. Cash only.*

UNDER $20 • Gran Hotel Texas. At this hotel with an American name and a Spanish owner, the rooms aren't as nice as the gracious lobby would have you believe, but they do include a phone, cable TV, and purified drinking water. Doubles cost $18. *Ignacio Mariscal 129, tel. 5/705–57–82, fax 5/566–97–24. 52 rooms, all with bath. Laundry, luggage storage, parking, safe-deposit box.*

Hotel Frimont. Spacious rooms decked out in a light-brown color scheme come with TV and phones, and almost-scalding water streams out of the shower. There are Ladatel phones in the lobby, and the friendly staff offers currency exchange. Many business travelers take advantage of the reasonable prices: doubles $16–$18. *Jesús Terán 35, tel. 5/705–41–69. From Metro Revolución, east on Puente de Alvarado, right on Jesús Terán. 85 rooms, all with bath. Restaurant, laundry, luggage storage, parking, travel agency. Reservations advised.*

NEAR METRO PINO SUAREZ

The hotels here appeal to traveling salespeople and tourists willing to stay in a neighborhood that's not quite so central or convenient. There isn't much to see in these few blocks south of the Zócalo, but the hotels are cheap, you're likely to find vacancies year-round, and getting to the major sights is a breeze, thanks to the Metro. During the day the streets are crowded with shoppers looking for bargains on everything from clothing to cashews. At night, however, it's spookily quiet.

UNDER $10 • Hotel Latino. This modern, pastel-decor hotel has its advantages: TVs, cleanliness, great water pressure, and incredibly quiet rooms (perhaps because they have no windows). On the downside, you may have to wade through hordes of people waiting for the bus right in front of the hotel's only entrance. Doubles cost $8. *Netzahualcóyotl 201, tel. 5/522–36–47. 40 rooms, all with bath. Luggage storage. Reservations advised. Cash only.*

Hotel Monte Carlo. This beautiful, quiet hotel is by far the nicest in its price range. A large, marble staircase rises from the lobby to the black-and-white-tile second floor. The huge rooms, complete with kitschy decorations, phones, and French doors, are spotless, and the bathrooms have hot water. Dou-

MEXICO CITY LODGING

Casa de los Amigos, **1**
Casa González, **9**
Gran Hotel Texas, **2**
Hotel Calvin, **11**
Hotel Canadá, **23**
Hotel Carlton, **7**
Hotel Catedral, **19**
Hotel del Valle, **13**
Hotel Edison, **3**
Hotel Fleming, **12**
Hotel Frimont, **8**
Hotel Gillow, **22**
Hotel Habana, **18**
Hotel Ibiza, **4**
Hotel Isabel, **25**
Hotel Juárez, **20**
Hotel Latino, **28**
Hotel La Marina, **17**
Hotel Marlowe, **14**
Hotel Monte Carlo, **26**
Hotel Oxford, **6**
Hotel Parador Washington, **10**
Hotel San Antonio, **24**
Hotel Toledo, **15**
Hotel Pennsylvania, **5**
Hotel Principal, **16**
Hotel Roble, **27**
Hotel Zamora, **21**

bles cost $10 ($14 with bath). *República de Uruguay 69, tel. 5/518–14–18 or 5/521–25–59. 70 rooms, 35 with bath. Luggage storage, parking. Reservations advised. Cash only.*

UNDER $20 • Hotel Roble. The Hotel Roble is on the A list for comfort: Rooms are clean and modern, plus there's an excellent restaurant conveniently located next door. Gray carpets go quite charmingly with the pastel decor, and the water in the clean bathrooms gets hot if you give it time. The cost is $15–$17 for doubles. *República de Uruguay 109, tel. 5/522–78–30 or 5/522–80–83. 61 rooms, all with bath. Restaurant, room service, luggage storage.*

ZONA ROSA

Hotels in the Zona Rosa are as posh and expensive as the bars and restaurants that surround them. Still, you can find comfortable and affordable lodging in the residential areas bordering the tourist zone. Insurgentes and Paseo de la Reforma run right through the area, and the greenery of Parque Chapultepec is a hop, skip, and a jump away.

UNDER $15 • Hotel Parador Washington. This sprawling pink building on a tree-lined plaza boasts Sevillian architecture, large but worn rooms, and one of the friendliest staffs around. If the manager happens to be in, he's always willing to offer free Spanish lessons and will tell you all about his experiences with the KGB. Doubles cost $13–$14. *Dinamarca 42, at Londres, tel. 5/546–44–00 or 5/566–86–48. From Metro Insurgentes, 4 blocks east on Chapultepec, left on Dinamarca. 25 rooms, all with bath. Laundry, luggage storage. Cash only.*

UNDER $35 • Casa González. The stately Casa will make you feel like you've accidentally stumbled into a rambling 19th-century home, while its tastefully decorated living room looks as if it has been anticipating your arrival. Cozy, old-fashioned rooms are immaculate, graced with wood furniture; the spotless bathrooms, complete with tubs, are lined with traditional *azulejos* (tiles). Doubles cost $31. Señor González, who speaks fluent English, cooks delicious meals to order (breakfast $4.25, dinner $12). *Río Sena 69, tel. 5/514–33–02. From Metro Insurgentes, take Génova across Reforma and Río Lerma. 20 rooms, all with bath. Luggage storage. Cash only.*

FOOD

You can spend plenty of pesos eating your way through Mexico City's wide range of restaurants. All over the city, but particularly in the Zona Rosa, you can find just about anything to suit your tastes—from snazzy sushi bars to that ubiquitous American chain, Taco Bell.

It's also possible to eat for very little money in Mexico City, but only if you're not scared by the myth that eating at tiny mom-and-pop operations or at street stands will send you running for the bathroom. The food at these places is usually cooked to order, so you can tell if it has been sitting out too long or hasn't been cooked well enough. If there's a crowd of local folk at a certain place, you can bet the food there is good, fresh, and well-cooked. A few healthy goodies to look for at street stands citywide include *alegrías,* large cookies made with amaranth (a whitish grain) and honey; *empanadas,* fried tortilla turnovers filled with cheese; and fresh-roasted chestnuts. Another budget survival tactic is the *comida corrida* (preprepared lunch special), usually beans and rice with a meat entrée, plus coffee and sometimes soup or salad, usually for less than $4. Try the restaurants along Isabel la Católica in the downtown area: They usually post their daily comida corrida conspicuously. If you don't mind standing, *puestecitos* (food stands) almost always surround Metro stations, selling everything from *tacos de cabeza* (tacos made with head meat) to *tamarindo* (tamarind) candy. Stalls selling fruits and vegetables as well as taco stands flourish at the city's markets (*see* Shopping, *below*). For those with sudden, uncontrollable hankerings for a hamburger, there is always **Sanborns** or **Vips,** chain restaurants with hybrid menus offering both American and Mexican cuisines. The supermarket closest to the downtown area is **Aurrera,** on Calle Tlalpán, near Metro Nativitas.

ZOCALO/BELLAS ARTES

Plenty of restaurants crowd the center of the city, from humble *fondas* (covered food stands) to elegant tourist-oriented places. The 24-hour **Café El Popular** (5 de Mayo 52, tel. 5/518–60–81) dishes up basics like pancakes and tamales. Satisfy your sugar cravings at **Dulcería Celaya** (5 de Mayo 39, no phone), still in the same beautiful 19th-century building in which it was founded in 1874. Fans of *churros* (a long, twisted, sugar-coated donut) crowd the 24-hour **Churrería El Moro** (Lázaro Cárdenas 42, tel. 5/512–08–96). **La Michoacana,** an ice cream and *agua fresca* (fresh fruit drink) chain, has shops throughout the city. Forgo the usual vanilla ice cream and go for more adventurous flavors—such as guanábana, mamey, or alfalfa.

UNDER $5 • Café Cinco de Mayo. Come here to slurp delicious soup in an authentic lunch-counter atmosphere, complete with twirling stools. A full menu of Mexican dishes is also featured, but the soups are the real draw: Among the best are cream of mushroom and *caldo xochimilco* (chicken-rice stew with cilantro and avocado), both for $1.75. *5 de Mayo 57, tel. 5/510–19–95. 1 block west of Zócalo. Cash only.*

Le Rendez-Vous. The tile-and-mirror, ballroomlike ambience here makes this joint a special place for any meal. A decadently large plate of thick hotcakes or *huevos rancheros* (ranch-style eggs, with spicy tomato sauce, tortillas, and beans), served with coffee and fresh orange juice, is a mere $2. A generous order of enchiladas, with soup, coffee, and dessert is $3. *Madero 29, no phone. From Metro Allende, south on Isabel la Católica, right on Madero. Cash only.*

Super Soya. Everything in this bright little health food store and vegetarian restaurant is orange: the floor, counters, and even the waitresses' uniforms. At lunchtime you'll have to fight for a seat to enjoy your soyburger, vegetarian taco (40¢), or fruit salad with yogurt. If you crave ice cream, don't miss the fragrant, homemade waffle cones. *Tacuba 40, at Motolinia, no phone. Near Metro Allende. Cash only.*

Vegetariano y Dietético. You'll have to hunt carefully to find this vegetarian eatery. It's up a long, narrow stairway squeezed between two jewelry shops (look for the doormat in the entryway). The filling vegetarian *menú del día* (daily special; served daily 1–7 PM) with fruit or vegetable salad, hot or cold soup, two main dishes, dessert, and agua fresca, costs only $2.75. A variety of à la carte dishes, such as mushrooms in *salsa verde* (green sauce), are also reasonably priced. With any luck, you'll catch the occasional piano player who'll liven up your meal with an off-tune version of *The William Tell Overture. Madero 56, 1st floor, tel. 5/521–68–80. 1 block west of Zócalo. Closed Sun. Cash only.*

UNDER $10 • Café de Tacuba. Founded in 1912, this chandelier-lit restaurant is a perfect treat. Waitresses adorned with ridiculously large bows on their heads serve traditional dishes like *pozole* (hominy soup) and spinach-topped *enchiladas tacuba.* Some lighter dishes are less than $3. The café usually gets fairly crowded for lunch and dinner, especially Thursday–Sunday 6–10, when there's live music. *Tacuba 28, near Metro Allende, tel. 5/512–84–82.*

La Ópera. This former men-only cantina boasts a colorful history. Porfirio Díaz and his decadent crowd drank here, and Pancho Villa once stormed in and shot holes in the ceiling. Women weren't allowed through the doors until antidiscrimination laws passed in 1975. Today the old-fashioned, carved wood booths and gilded, ornate ceiling (look for bullet holes) make this an elegant escape from the hectic rhythm of the Zócalo. Enjoy delicious paella ($7) or the avocado stuffed with shrimp. If you're feeling adventurous, ask for the Pancho Villa cocktail ($2.50–$3.75): tequila served in a hollowed cucumber, accompanied by *sangrita* (tomato juice) in a fresh tomato. *5 de Mayo 10, at Filomeno Mata, tel. 5/512–89–59. 5 blocks from Zócalo. No breakfast.*

Restaurant Emir. If you're tired of the same old enchiladas, make your taste buds tingle again at this airy Lebanese restaurant. The *plató libanés* (Lebanese plate; $7.50), with spinach *empanadas* (turnovers) and lentil rice, is a delectable edible, as is the *tortita de falafel* (falafel sandwich) with a side of hummus. *República de Salvador 146, 1st floor, tel. 5/510–15–90. Between Correo Mayor and Pino Suárez. Cash only.*

ZONA ROSA

The Zona Rosa brims with restaurants, bars, and nightspots, most of them priced beyond a budget traveler's means. Some streets are closed to vehicular traffic, and pedestrians stroll leisurely past street performers and beggars. Copenhague, a tiny block-long street just south of Paseo de la Reforma, has a great variety of restaurants and boutiques, but this area tends to be pricey. There are cheaper joints on Chapultepec near Amberes, right outside Metro Insurgentes. To dine outside of the tourist zone, cross Reforma and continue beyond the U.S. Embassy to Río Lerma (or any other street whose name begins with Río), where you'll find small restaurants offering cheap but tasty comidas corridas.

UNDER $5 • El Gallito Taquería. This taquería serves a variety of hot, delicious snacks sure to satisfy most late-night cravings. The restaurant fills up by 3 AM, when the clubs in the Zona close down for the night. The tacos *poblanos con queso* (with pork and cheese) are filling. Vegetarians can broaden their culinary horizons with the *nopal con queso* (diced cactus leaves and melted cheese). *Liverpool 115, tel. 5/511–14–36. ½ block north of Génova. Cash only.*

Kobá-Ich. This small, clean restaurant seems to attract a largely foreign clientele, perhaps because of the posted sign claiming in English to provide ALL THE FLAVOR OF YUCATÁN AT YOUR TABLE. One taste of the *pollo pibil* (chicken baked in banana leaves)—so tender it falls off the bone—will get you hooked. For the more adventurous, try tacos *de cazón* (baby shark). *Londres 136-A, between Génova and Amberes, tel. 5/208–57–91. From Metro Insurgentes, take Génova to Londres and turn left. Closed Sun. Cash only.*

UNDER $10 • Fonda El Refugio. Gleaming white walls, shiny copper pots, and small wooden tables handsomely furnish this elegant restaurant. The *sopa de hongos* (mushroom soup) and the *pescado a la veracruzana* (red snapper cooked with tomatoes, onions, capers, peppers, and herbs) both go well with the $3.50 powerhouse margaritas. *Liverpool 166, at Génova, tel. 5/207–27–32. No breakfast.*

UNDER $15 • Bellinghausen. Don't let the German name deceive you—this posh restaurant in the center of Zona Rosa specializes in Mexican food. The wood-panel interior and the outdoor garden create a cozy, upscale atmosphere, and the food is delicious. Try fried *huachinango* (red snapper) or the *filete chemita* (beef) for $10. Especially good are *chiles en nogada* (chiles stuffed with beef and covered in a walnut sauce and pomegranate seeds), a Puebla specialty available only in September. *Londres 95, at Niza, tel. 5/207–49–78 or 5/207–40–49. No breakfast.*

COYOACAN

Although people come to Coyoacán from all over the D.F., the area retains the atmosphere of a small neighborhood, where cozy family establishments and tiny taquerías cluster around charming plazas. About one and a half blocks south of the plazas on Carrillo Puerto is a particularly inviting collection of fondas and taquerías. Or walk four blocks north on Allende to the **Mercado,** where you can purchase fresh fruit and vegetables, or snack on delicious chicken, shrimp, or beef tostadas ($3).

UNDER $5 • Merendero "Las Lupitas." This restaurant lies on a narrow cobblestone street just off sleepy Plaza Santa Catarina. The dining area is suffused with natural light, earth-tone tiles cover the floor, and sturdy wooden beams support the ceiling. The food has a *norteño* (northern Mexican) influence, so flour rather than corn tortillas are used; try the *gorditas norteñas* (flour tortillas stuffed with potatos and chorizo). The lightly fried cheese or meat empanadas are practically greaseless and cost less than $3. *Jardín de Santa Catarina 4, at Francisco Sosa, tel. 5/554–33–53. From Jardín Centenario, west on Francisco Sosa for a few blocks. Cash only.*

Taco Inn. As the name suggests, this clean and colorful taquería caters to gringos. The food, however, is as authentic as it gets. The beef tacos with cilantro and onions and the ignominiously named *gringas* (pork and cheese sandwiched between two flour tortillas) both go for $1.50. *Presidente Carranza 106, at Carrillo Puerto, tel. 5/659–88–62. From Jardín Centenario, left on Carrillo Puerto. No breakfast. Closed Sun.*

UNDER $10 • Fonda El Morral. This bright, Spanish-style fonda is framed by beautiful wrought-iron windows and blue-and-white-tile doorways. The comida corrida here is a reasonable $3, while a generous and sizzling *carne tampiqueña* (grilled meat) goes for $7. *Allende 2, tel. 5/554–02–98. From Metro Coyoacán, take* VILLA COAPA *pesero to Jardín Centenario. Open daily. Cash only.*

SAN ANGEL

Most visitors avoid the busy avenidas Insurgentes and Revolución and head up to the quiet cobblestone streets of Plaza San Jacinto to relax and enjoy the serenity of this small, charmingly colonial neighborhood. There's a good selection of restaurants along Madero, but even cheaper fare can be found on the side streets near the Pemex station (at the base of the Plaza del Carmen). The intersection of Quevedo and Universidad (near Metro M. A. de Quevedo) is another great place to find fast, cheap food in small hectic restaurants or *puestecitos.*

UNDER $5 • Fechoria. This Argentine restaurant has a huge upstairs window through which you can look down upon sweaty pedestrians—if only they knew you were relaxing in front of a plate of ricotta ravioli and a cool glass of wine ($1.50). Expect a youthful, hungry crowd on weekends. *La Paz 58-A, tel. 5/550–18–34. From Metro M. A. de Quevedo, west on Quevedo to La Paz. No breakfast.*

Parrilla El Tecolote. This taquería is a standout for its incredibly inexpensive food. The waiters are in a constant, frantic rush, and by early afternoon the place is packed. Enjoy a bowl of *sopa de verduras con pollo* (vegetable soup with chicken) for 50¢, or the filling comida corrida ($1.50). The Tecolote's innocuous-looking green salsa will have you begging for a glass of water. *M. A. de Quevedo 75, no phone. 1½ blocks from Metro M. A. de Quevedo. Cash only.*

UNDER $10 • La Casona del Elefante. This sophisticated and relatively inexpensive Indian restaurant, next to the Bazar Sábado has an entryway hidden behind a group of tall potted plants. Inside, you'll find delicious food served by frenzied waiters in spangled, glittering vests. A tray of spicy salsas arrives at your table before you know what to order, although service slows considerably after that. All of the meat and fish curries are recommended, and the curried vegetables make a good meal for about $4. *Plaza San Jacinto 9, tel. 5/616–16–01 or 5/616–22–08. From Metro M. A. de Quevedo, west on Quevedo, left on La Paz; when it forks, take Madero to Plaza San Jacinto. No breakfast. Closed Mon.*

CAFES

Luna Café. This tiny café on the western edge of the Zona Rosa is a great place to escape from the hectic pace of the surrounding area. Its small wooden tables are perfect for writing letters, and the strong cappuccino is only $1. *Florencia 36, between Londres and Hamburgo, tel. 5/511–27–77. Metro: Insurgentes. Closed Sun. Cash only.*

Café Gandhi. If you packed a beret, whip it out for a visit to this well-known gallery/bookstore/coffeehouse. Strong cappuccino can be ordered with Kahlúa or Amaretto ($2) for an added kick. Service is about as slow as the chess players, who pass entire afternoons brooding over moves while their cigarettes burn low. Nonsmokers can rejoice, however; the enlightened management provides a tiny no-smoking section. *M. A. de Quevedo 128, tel. 5/550–25–24. Metro: M. A. de Quevedo.*

El Parnaso Café. To pass a quiet afternoon, settle comfortably beneath the shady awnings of this popular café/bookstore in the eastern corner of Coyoacán's Jardín Centenario. Table-sharing is encouraged on the weekends when it's crowded. The waiters are always on the run, so they don't pay much attention to you—but once you get your coffee, the afternoon is yours. *Carrillo Puerto 2, tel. 5/554–22–25. From Metro M. A. de Quevedo, take VILLA COAPA pesero to Jardín Centenario. Cash only.*

La Vienet Café. After a visit to the Frida Kahlo museum, be sure to stop by this little café for some of the sweetest desserts around. Its balcony and beautiful wrought-iron chairs almost make you forget that "The Best of Barry Manilow" is playing in the background. Just close your eyes and have another bite of mocha cake ($1.50). *Viena, at Abasolo, tel. 5/554–45–23. 2 blocks north and 1 block east of Frida Kahlo museum. Closed Mon. Cash only.*

EXPLORING MEXICO CITY

You could live in Mexico City for years and still never see all there is to see, so your best bet for tackling this sprawling metropolis is to see the sights district by district. Keep in mind that each area has a distinct flavor and atmosphere that goes beyond the tourist attractions; you'll understand life in Mexico City better by taking things one at a time than by storming through the sights on automatic pilot. Start your tour at the excavated site of the Templo Mayor, on the northeast end of the **Zócalo.** A view from its museum gives a good introduction to Mexico City's multilayered history: Stare past the pre-Columbian ruin and colonial Catedral Metropolitana, to the modern high-rises of the **Zona Rosa.** Next, head for the **Alameda Central,** home to a cluster of excellent museums that allow you to submerge yourself in the country's dramatic art. Once bedroom communities for Mexico City's elite, **San Ángel** and **Coyoacán** brim with quaint cobblestone streets and colonial mansions. Also an easy metro ride from the centro is the **Basílica de Guadalupe,** fundamental in understanding the religious fervor surrounding the Virgin of Guadalupe. Finally, end up where it all began—at the ancient city of **Teotihuacán** (*see* Near Mexico City, *below*), where you can stand on top of the Píramide del Sol as the Teotihuacán priests did, 500 years before the Aztec people arrived. When planning your week of sightseeing remember that all museums in Mexico City are free on Sunday.

ZOCALO

The spot presently occupied by Mexico City's Zócalo used to function as the center of Tenochtitlán, the Aztec capital. Sadly, hardly anything from this majestic era remains: The Spanish, arrogant and anxious to secure a hold on the New World, built directly on top of the Aztec structures. Beginning in the 16th century, ornate churches and convents, fancy mansions, and other stately edifices were constructed around the plaza, sometimes incorporating the volcanic stone pilfered from Aztec buildings. Toward the end of the 19th century, the upper classes began moving out of the crowded downtown, leaving their mansions to be partitioned and occupied by the working class and the poor. Today the Zócalo, bordered by some of the most beautiful buildings of the colonial era, is a constant buzz of activity. Men in search of employment line up by the cathedral gate and busloads of school children on field trips periodically mob the plaza. The Zócalo is also the city's forum for political activity. Most protest marches end here, and many anti-PRI groups distribute flyers or sell newsletters on the plaza. This is also the place to stock up on Carlos Salinas de Gortari puppets or Subcomandante Marcos T-shirts.

LA CATEDRAL METROPOLITANA

This enormous cathedral on the north side of the Zócalo was built between 1573 and 1861. The first large altar in the center of the cathedral, the **Altar de Perdón,** is a copy of the original that burned in a 1967 fire. Smaller chapels line both sides of the cathedral; all are beautiful, but a few deserve special attention. The first chapel on the left contains a display with sculpted flowers, each with four petals—an example of the indigenous influence on the church's architecture. The petals represent the Aztec view of the universe, each petal symbolizing one of the four principal gods. The third chapel (also on the left, toward the back of the church) contains **El Señor del Cacao,** an image of Christ fashioned from corn paste, human nails, and hair. The paintings in the seventh chapel are dedicated to Felipe de Jesús, a martyred saint, and illustrate the story of his journey to Mexico from the Philippines. Apparently his ship was blown off course and wrecked in Japan, where he was condemned to death by the emperor. Legend has it that before his execution he predicted that the city in which he died (Nagasaki) would go up in flames. The **Sagrario Metropolitano,** a chapel on the east side of the cathedral, was built in 1749 to hold the church's most sacred relics. The cathedral is a perfect example of the ultra-baroque architecture known as *Churrigueresque,* which was introduced in the Americas by José Churriguera of Spain. The cathedral's ornate columns actually don't support the ceiling at all—they were designed purely for decorative purposes.

For more information on the history and architecture of the cathedral, ask at the information booth for Martín Castellanos. For $10 this artist-turned-tour-guide will tell you (in English or Spanish) everything there is to know about La Catedral—or any other place in Mexico City for that matter. Official guides, sporting green "Secretaria del Turismo" badges, are also available for $3.50. *Zócalo, across from Palacio Nacional. Mass held daily at 9:30 AM.*

MUSEO DE LA CARICATURA

Formerly the Colegio de Cristo (College of Christ), this beautiful building now houses the Latin American Cartoon Museum. The drawings run the gamut from sophisticated political commentary and satire to simple jokes that don't demand any knowledge of Spanish. During restoration of the building after the 1985 earthquake, pre-Columbian artifacts, including the sculpted head of a serpent, were unearthed here. The serpent's head was left as it was found and lies at the back of the museum. *Donceles 99-A, tel. 5/615–24–23. 2 blocks north of Zócalo. Admission: 75¢. Open weekdays 10–6, weekends 10–5.*

MUSEO JOSE LUIS CUEVAS

Housed in a former convent, this museum caused quite a stir when it was opened in 1992 by famous Mexican artist José Luis Cuevas. The biggest controversy was over inauguration of Cuevas's "Sala de Erotica," a permanent collection of paintings with erotic themes. Before entering the Sala, you can watch a video of Cuevas (lying languidly in bed) explain his paintings and his sexuality. Temporary exhibits feature contemporary Latin American artists and change every six weeks. Performance art pieces are held in the main room of the museum, and change weekly. *Academia 13, between Moneda and República de Guatemala, tel. 5/542–89–59. Admission: 75¢, free on Sun. Open Tues.–Sun. 10–6. Performance art held Sat. at noon, Sun. at noon, 2, and 6.*

PALACIO NACIONAL

The National Palace was built under the direction of Hernán Cortés, on the site where Montezuma's Grand Palace once stood. In fact, the *tezontle* (volcanic rock) now in its facade was taken piece by piece from Montezuma's palace and incorporated into the Spanish design. It was in the courtyard of this impressive edifice that Cortés entertained guests with Mexico's first bullfights. The bullfights are no

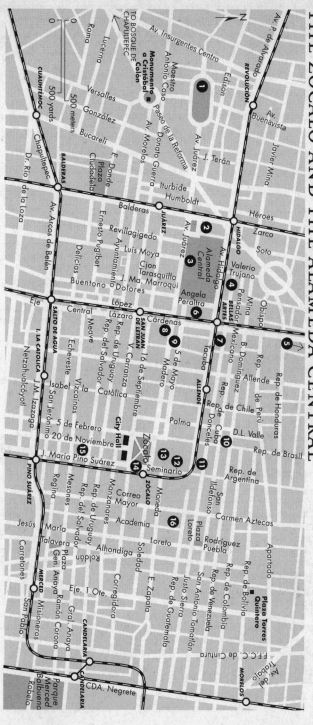

MEXICO'S ORIGINAL ZOCALO

The Zócalo, officially called Plaza de la Constitución, is the largest plaza in the Western Hemisphere.

Its name, zócalo, which actually means "pedestal," came about by accident: In the 19th century there were plans to build a monument to Mexican independence in Mexico City's main plaza. Though these grand plans were never realized, workers did construct the base, or pedestal, for the monument that never was.

The misnomer stuck and is now the term applied to the main plazas of most Mexican cities.

longer, but the bell rung by Padre Hidalgo to proclaim Mexico's independence in 1810 hangs on the palace's central facade; inside the palace you'll find the offices of the president, the Federal Treasury, and the National Archive.

The second story of the Palace's main courtyard is covered with more than 1,200 square ft of murals that took Diego Rivera and his assistants more than 16 years to paint (1929–45). The series, called *Epic of the Mexican People in Their Struggle for Freedom and Independence,* portrays two millennia of Mexican history. The hero of the pre-Hispanic panels is the plumed serpent god, Quetzalcoatl, whose prophesied return supposedly facilitated Cortés's conquest. Also prominently portrayed in the murals are a man offering a human arm for sale; Spanish soldiers arriving in the not-so-New World; Hidalgo ringing the independence bell; revolutionaries Zapata and Pancho Villa; and even Karl Marx, smiling amid scenes of class struggle. Today a visit to the Palacio speaks volumes about the country's political uneasiness: Heavily armed guards flank the door and patrol the interior. To get in, you have to leave an ID at the door—but a visit is definitely worth the extra hassle. *East side of Zócalo, tel. 5/512–20–60. Admission free. Open daily 9–5.*

TEMPLO MAYOR

The Templo Mayor (Great Temple) was the political and spiritual center of the Aztec empire. For more than 400 years it remained buried beneath the Zócalo until, in February 1978, telephone-company workers struck a small section of stone that turned out to be a portion of an 8-ton carving of Coyolxauhqui, goddess of the moon.

The temple itself was a massive structure, improved and enlarged on at least five separate occasions. Each renovation was a symbolic affirmation of the reigning Aztec's supremacy in the conquered Valley of Mexico. Most temples are typically dedicated to one major deity, and indeed Templo Mayor was dedicated to Huitzilopochtli (hummingbird god of the sun, and of war). Here the Aztec sacrificed as many as 10,000 persons every year (most of them either human tithes selected from conquered tribes, or captured rival warriors) in an effort to appease the gods and scare the daylights out of any tribes who dared defy Aztec hegemony. According to Aztec religion, without this sort of divine nourishment, the sun god would refuse to move across the sky.

Artifacts found during the excavation of Templo Mayor are displayed in the **Museo del Templo Mayor.** Exhibited items include ceramic warriors, stone knives, skulls of sacrificial victims, the massive stone disk of moon goddess Coyolxauhqui, and a miniature model of Tenochtitlán. Free tours are available in English and Spanish, but you must reserve two weeks in advance. Guides certified by the tourist office are available at the door and charge about $7 for a group tour. *Seminario 8, at República de Guatemala, tel. 5/542–47–84, fax 5/542–17–17. Admission: $2.25, free Sun. Open Tues.–Sun. 9–5.*

ALAMEDA CENTRAL

The Alameda Central was the site of a *tianguis* (open-air market) during the reign of the Aztecs, and the spot where heretics were burned during the Inquisition. By the mid-19th century it had become a park where the rich strolled under the trees, while the poor (who were kept out) looked on. Now everybody meanders its grounds, lingering over lunch, playing chess, sleeping on the grass, or gossiping on the benches. The white marble semicircle on the south side of the park, opposite Metro Bellas Artes, is the monument **Hemiciclo de Juárez,** which commemorates Benito Juárez, one of Mexico's greatest presidents. On the eastern edge of the park lies the baroque **Casa de Los Azulejos** (Madero 4). Originally the residence of aristocrats, it later became the elite Mexico City Jockey Club, and then, during the revolutionary turmoil, served as the headquarters for anarchist groups. Today it houses a Sanborns chain store.

MUSEO FRANZ MAYER

Originally built in the 16th century and used since as a hospital, an orphanage, and a convent, this structure now serves as an art museum. The displays feature an impressive collection of 16th- to 19th-century Mexican and European sculpture, furniture, and paintings, amassed by Franz Mayer (a.k.a. Don Pancho), a German-born farmer who lived in Mexico nearly his entire life. The shady, colonial courtyard and fountain are the perfect place to take a breather from the flurry of traffic on Avenida Hidalgo. Tours cost $1; call at least 72 hours in advance if you'd like one in English. *Hidalgo 45, in front of Metro Bellas Artes, tel. 5/518–22–66. Admission: $1.25. Open Tues.–Sun. 10–5. Guided tours Tues.–Fri. at 10:30, 11:30, 12:30, 1:30, Sat. at 10:30, 11:30, and 12:30.*

MUSEO MURAL DE DIEGO RIVERA

The Hospital de Jesús, on Pino Suárez, stands where Hernán Cortés first met Aztec emperor Montezuma II. Cortés founded the hospital in 1524, and his bones were later interred in its chapel.

Diego Rivera's mural *Sueño de una Tarde Dominical en la Alameda Central* (Dream of a Sunday Afternoon in the Alameda Central) used to hang in the lobby of the Del Prado hotel until the hotel was damaged by a 1985 earthquake. It's now showcased in its own museum. Despite its seemingly benign subject matter, the work initially caused a stir when Rivera captioned it "Dios no existe" (God doesn't exist). After several incidents of vandalism, Rivera painted over the offending words with "Conferencia de Letrán, año de 1836," a reference to a speech given by the mid-19th century radical congressman Ignacio Ramírez, in which he declared God to be "nonexistent." Intriguing temporary exhibits of modern art and photography by Mexican as well as international artists are also featured. When you're done with the museum, stroll through the Alameda Central and notice that the vendors and other characters portrayed in Rivera's work are still out in full force. *Plaza Solidaridad, tel. 5/510–23–29 or 5/512–07–54. From Metro Balderas, cross street to Plaza Solidarida. From Metro Juárez, north on Balderas to plaza. Admission: $2, free on Sun. Open Tues.–Sun. 10–6.*

MUSEO NACIONAL DE ARTE

This imposing stone building, once home to the *Palacio de Communicación* (Communications Palace), now houses an impressive collection of artwork on two floors. The 20th-century exhibits on the first floor include some of the more famous works in post-revolutionary *indigenismo* (indigenous style). Indigenismo painters, including Rivera, Orozco, and Siqueiros, glorified rural life, the *indígena* (indigenous person), and the *campesino* (rural dweller), finding in these figures a new understanding of *lo mexicano* (Mexicanness) and a basis for a national, non-anglocentric style. Nineteenth-century works, like those of José María Velasco (famous for his innovative landscapes), are on the second floor, along with occasional temporary exhibits. *Tacuba 8, tel. 5/521–73–20. Admission: $1.25, free Sun. Open Tues.–Sun. 10–6.*

MUSEO NACIONAL DE LA REVOLUCION

Housed in the basement of the **Monumento a la Revolución,** this museum is well worth a several-blocks detour from the Alameda. Newspapers, films, and dioramas carefully document more than half a century of Mexican history, from the presidency of Benito Juárez to the signing of the constitution in 1917. *Plaza de la República, tel. 5/546–21–15. From Alameda Central, west on Juárez. Admission free. Open Tues.–Sat. 9–5, Sun. 10–3.*

PALACIO DE BELLAS ARTES

The two attractions here are the theater and museum. Construction of the neoclassical, Carrera marble Palace of Fine Arts began in 1904 under President Porfirio Díaz. It was scheduled for completion in 1910, the centennial of Mexican independence, but neither Díaz nor Italian architect Adamo Boari took the area's porous subsoil into account (indeed, the building is still sinking today). Technical difficulties coupled with the upheaval of the Mexican Revolution delayed completion of the building until July, 1932.

RIVERA VS.
THE ROCKEFELLERS

Despite Diego Rivera's outspoken opposition to capitalism, in 1933 the Rocke-feller Foundation of New York City commissioned the acclaimed artist to paint a mural, called "Man at the Crossroads," for the RCA Building in Manhattan, New York. As Rivera's work began to take shape, his patrons were shocked to find that the artist had secretly added Lenin's visage to the original design. When Diego refused to to paint over Lenin's face the mural was destroyed—but a repro-duction of this masterpiece now hangs in Mexico City's Palacio de Bellas Artes.

By then architectural styles had changed, and the building was given an art deco interior by architect Federico Mariscal, who combined geometric shapes, straight lines, and traditional Mexican forms.

The theater has a glass stage curtain (lowered only during Sunday morning performances) that depicts the two volcanoes to the south of the D.F.; it was designed by Gerardo Murillo (a.k.a. Dr. Atl) and assem-bled by Tiffany's of New York City. This is the place to see performances of the **Ballet Folklórico,** the **Compañía Nacional de Danza** (National Ballet), and the **Orquesta Sinfónica Nacional** (National Sym-phony Orchestra). Tickets for performances (*see* After Dark, *below*) can be purchased at taquillas (open Mon.–Sat. 11–7 and Sun. 9–7) on the first floor of the palace, next to the main entrance.

The top floor of the palace houses the **Museo Nacional de Arquitectura** (National Architecture Museum); its permanent collection includes murals by Diego Rivera, Siqueiros, Orozco, and Tamayo, as well as the original architectural plans for the Palacio de Bellas Artes (*see above*). Temporary exhibits are also showcased here. *Lázaro Cárdenas, at Juárez, across from Alameda Central, tel. 5/521–92–55 and 5/512–36–22. Museum admission: $1.50, free Sun. Museum open Tues.–Sun. 10–6.*

PLAZA DE LAS TRES CULTURAS/TLATELOLCO

At the center of the Tlatelolco District, this plaza is best known for the events that took place here on October 2, 1968. On that fateful evening, about 5,000 people gathered on Plaza de las Tres Culturas in a peaceful demonstration to decry the government's failure to meet student demands. Discontent focused on President Díaz Ordaz's anti-activist laws, the use of *grenaderos* (paramilitary riot squads) against students, and the huge expenses incurred by Mexico's preparations for hosting the 1968 sum-mer Olympics. The protesters were met by army and police units in tanks and armored cars. The gov-ernment claims to this day that snipers in surrounding apartment buildings then opened fire, which police returned. Others claim that the army shot first. At any rate, few today doubt that the death toll was well into the hundreds.

The plaza is named for the three main cultures of Mexico—indigenous, Spanish, and mestizo—and ele-ments of all three exist here. The indigenous element is present in the massive ruins of a pre-Hispanic ceremonial center that surround **Iglesia de Santiago Tlatelolco.** The church is representative of the Spanish, and houses the baptismal font of Juan Diego, the Indian convert to whom the Virgin of Guadalupe famously appeared in 1531. A battle monument on the plaza translates as: "This was neither victory nor defeat. It was the sad birth of the mestizo people, who are Mexico today." It refers to the defeat of Tlatelolco's Aztec by Cortés. Mestizo culture is also represented on the plaza by the ultramodern Min-istry of Foreign Affairs. *From Metro Tlatelolco, east on Manuel González, right on Lázaro Cárdenas.*

TORRE LATINOAMERICANA

This 44-story tower stands surrounded by downtown's colonial buildings. The view from the *mirador* (observation deck) will leave you breathless, especially if you decide to forgo the elevator. The **Fantás-tico Mundo del Mar** (Fantastic World of the Sea), the highest aquarium in the world, is on the tower's 38th floor. *Lázaro Cárdenas 43, corner Madero, no phone. 3 blocks from Metro Bellas Artes. Tower/aquarium admission: $2.50. Open daily 9 AM–11 PM.*

BOSQUE DE CHAPULTEPEC

Known simply as "Chapultepec," this park is a green haven for families, joggers, cyclists, and young lovers looking to escape all things urban. Unfortunately, all these people usually want to escape city life at the exact same time, making the park quite crowded on weekends. Guarding the entrance to the park is the **Monumento a los Niños Héroes,** which honors six young military cadets who died defending *la patria* (the fatherland) during the U.S. invasion in 1847. The invasion cost Mexico almost half its national territory, including what are now the states of Texas, California, Arizona, New Mexico, and Nevada. Tuesday–Sunday you can boat ($1.25 per hr; maximum five people) on the bright green **Lago Chapultepec.** Any day of the week you can enjoy the thrills of **La Feria** amusement park (admission $3), which boasts rides that spin, loop, and whirl. All of the museums described *below* are clustered along Paseo de la Reforma, so if you only have a few hours to spare, stick to this main thoroughfare. Metros Chapultepec and Auditorio are inside the park, and buses and peseros to the park run west along Paseo de la Reforma from the centro.

CASTILLO DE CHAPULTEPEC

The neoclassical Chapultepec Castle sits perched atop Cerro Chapulín (Grasshopper Hill), overlooking the entire Valley of Mexico. The oldest portions of the castle date to 1785, when Viceroy Bernardo de Galvez built the first fort here. In 1841 the castle was converted into a military academy. Shortly after, at the end of the bloody battle for Mexico City during the U.S. invasion, a young cadet named Juan Escutia, realizing the battle was lost, climbed to the top of the northern tower, wrapped himself in the Mexican flag, and jumped to his glorious death. A tomb at the foot of the hill marks the place where he landed. Almost 20 years later, Emperor Maximilian, installed by the French, remodeled the castle and moved in. It remained the official residence of the Mexican head of state until 1944, when President Lázaro Cárdenas moved his headquarters to Los Pinos, the current presidential residence, and returned the castle to the Mexican people as the **Museo Nacional de Historia.** The fascinating museum uses artifacts like teacups, jewelry, and clothing from different social classes and various time periods to tell Mexico's economic, cultural, and political history. Your museum admission ticket also give you a peek at the

VIVA LA VIDA, FRIDA KAHLO

Frida Kahlo, Mexico's most famous female artist, was born and died in La Casa Azul in the Coyoacán district of Mexico City. Though she traveled little during her lifetime, her image now adorns T-shirts and postcards all over the world, and she has become something of a feminist icon both in Mexico and abroad.

Kahlo was born to a Hungarian Jewish father and a Mexican mother in 1907 (though she often claimed that her birth date was 1910, the year the Revolution began). She was almost killed in a bus accident when she was a teenager, which left her in almost constant pain for the rest of her life. She died in 1954, at the age of 47.

Kahlo's art is as colorful and flamboyant as its main subject, which was usually Frida herself. She often depicted her suffering in her paintings, which represented her bleeding, cracked open, or torn apart and sewn back together. Other themes are political (she was a Communist and a revolutionary, sustaining a deep and multifaceted relationship with Leon Trotsky when he lived in Mexico) or concern aspects of her personal life, such as her stormy marriage to muralist Diego Rivera.

Her frank, unapologetic portrayal of her own physical and emotional pain illustrates her very public refusal to be a "typical" Mexican woman, a sufrida (long-suffering woman) who bears her sorrows in silence. Her last painting, completed eight days before she died, shows juicy melons, cut open and waiting to be eaten. It is titled Viva la Vida (Live Life).

castle's interior: Tours show some castle rooms with original furnishings, including the bedroom of the fiery Porfirio Díaz. It's all complemented by murals by José Clemente Orozco and Diego Rivera. You can walk up Grasshopper Hill to the castle, or take a train (60¢) that runs sporadically from the hill's base. *Uphill, beyond Monumento a Los Niños Héroes, tel. 5/286–07–00. Admission: $2; free Sun.; free Tues.–Sat. after 4 PM. Open Tues.–Sun. 9–5.*

MUSEO DE ARTE MODERNO

This Chapultepec Park museum is dedicated to modern painting, photography, and sculpture; the permanent collection includes works by Frida Kahlo, Dr. Atl, Rufino Tamayo, and Diego Rivera. The annex to the main building houses temporary exhibits of contemporary Mexican and international painting, lithography, sculpture, and photography. The museum's gardens are dotted with strange and wonderful sculptures. *South side of Reforma, at Gandhi, tel. 5/553–62–33 or 5/211–83–31. Admission: $1.75, free Sun. Open Sun.–Fri. 10–5:30.*

MUSEO NACIONAL DE ANTROPOLOGIA

Mexico's complex anthropological heritage demands a museum as grand as this one. It's by far the best in the country, with perhaps the finest archaeological collection in the world: Each room displays artifacts from a different geographic region and/or culture. Don't try to see it all at once—you'll only end up tired and loathing antiquities. However, don't miss the display of stelae from Tula (*see* Near Mexico City, *below*), with bas-reliefs carvings that indicate a heavy Maya influence. The museum also houses the original *Piedra del Sol,* the famous Aztec calendar. **Cafeteria Museo,** downstairs, offers an outdoor patio where you can relax, sip a cappucino, and eat for less than $6. *Paseo de la Reforma, at Gandhi, tel. 5/553–19–02. Admission: $2.50, free Sun. Open Tues.–Sat. 9–7, Sun. 10–6.*

MUSEO TAMAYO DE ARTE CONTEMPORANEO INTERNACIONAL

You may have difficulty finding this museum, as it's tucked within the dense foliage of Chapultepec Park. Don't give up—just look for the whimsical, fire engine–red sculpture that marks the museum's main entrance. In 1981, artist Rufino Tamayo and his wife, Olga, established this sleek, granite museum as a repository for their personal collection of paintings and sculpture. It contains pieces by Lilia Carillo, René Magritte, Joan Miró, and quite a few of Tamayo's own works. The aquatic sculptures at the front of the museum were once immersed for months at a time in the Atlantic Ocean to achieve that rustic, oxidized look. *Just off Paseo de la Reforma, at Gandhi, tel. 5/286–65–19. Admission: $1.50, free Sun. Open Tues.–Sun. 10–6.*

EL PAPALOTE/MUSEO DEL NINO

Established in 1995 with money from the Mexican government and the Lotería Nacional (National Lottery), El Papalote is an interactive children's museum reminiscent of an indoor amusement park, with more than 360 unusual science demonstrations. Here you can lounge on a bed of nails, experience momentum on a spinning machine, blow bubbles bigger than your body, or stomp out the Mexican national anthem on a musical carpet. An IMAX theater shows nature and science films. *Constituyentes 268, at Periférico, tel. 5/237–11–78. Admission: $5. Open daily 9–1 and 2–6 (additional hrs Thurs. 7 PM–11 PM).*

SALA DE ARTE PUBLICO SIQUEIROS

Just before his death, muralist David Alfaro Siqueiros (a supporter of Stalin who had been involved once in an unsuccessful attempt to assassinate Trotsky) bequeathed his home and studio to the people of Mexico. The walls of his workshop are covered with murals, and the house is cluttered with paintings, photographs, and some of the sketches he made for his most famous works, such as *New Democracy* (the painting itself is currently on display in the Palacio de Bellas Artes; *see* Alameda Central, *above*). *Tres Picos 29, between Schiller and Hegel, Col. Polanco, tel. 5/531–33–94 or 5/545–59–52. From Metro Auditorio, north on Arquimedes, right on Rubén Darío, left on Hegel, and right on Tres Picos. Admission: $1.25. Open Tues.–Sun. 10–6.*

ZOOLOGICO DE CHAPULTEPEC

In its recent remodeling campaign, the zoo did away with cages and fences in an attempt to present wildlife in a setting similar to its natural habitat. The big drawback to all these natural surroundings is that the animals can now camouflage themselves from you, the camera-toting visitor. A glimpse of the panda bears, however, is well worth the trip: This is the zoo in which the panda has best survived in captivity. *Reforma, next to the lake, tel. 5/553–69–29. First entrance to park from Metro Auditorio. Admission free. Open Tues.–Sun. 9–4:15; Panda House open Tues.–Sun. 9–11 and 3–4.*

SAN ANGEL

The past 50 years have seen this *pueblito* (village) develop into a bedroom community catering exclusively to Mexico City's rich. The sprawl of the city, however, cannot be forever held at bay: Avenidas Insurgentes and Revolución cross the suburb, bringing traffic, noise, and dusk-til-dawn nightlife. Still, this neighborhood has its share of quiet, cobblestone streets and well-preserved colonial architecture (sometimes hidden behind gates and high walls). In the center of San Ángel is **Plaza San Jacinto,** where artists peddle their wares on Saturday during the **Bazar del Sábado** (open 10–8). Gawking tourists and niños popis buy fashionable handicrafts from vendors who don't balk when they see credit cards. Despite the commercialism, the market is well worth a visit. East of the plaza sits the **Ex-Convento de Carmen** (Former Carmelite convent; corner Revolución and Monasterio, tel. 5/616–28–16; open Tues.–Sun. 10–5), now a museum that displays religious artifacts, a few mummified corpses, and occasional art exhibits. Admission is $2.50, free Sunday. East of Revolución, the **Monumento a Obregón,** in honor of the general of the Mexican Revolution, dominates the corner of La Paz and Insurgentes.

MUSEO ALVAR Y CARMEN T. DE CARRILLO GIL

Alvar de Carrillo Gil, a doctor and pharmaceuticals producer, together with wife Carmen set up this spacious museum to house their private art collection, which features works by Wolfgang Paalen, David Alfaro Siqueiros, Gunther Gerzso, and José Clemente Orozco. For muralist buffs, this is a chance to see many of

SAN ÁNGEL AND COYOCÁN

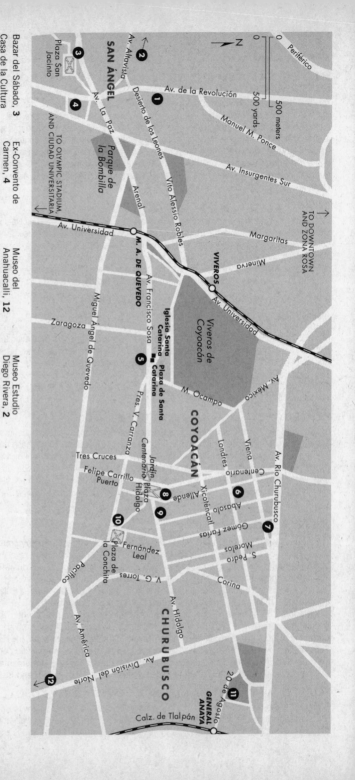

the important, smaller paintings composed by Siqueiros and Orozco. Dr. Gil liked slapping paint on canvas as well, and some of his own creations hang on the gleaming white walls. The museum also hosts rotating exhibits by contemporary Mexican artists. *Revolución 1608, at Desierto de los Leones, tel. 5/550–12–54 or 5/550–39–83. From Metro Barranca del Muerto, catch a SAN ANGEL bus from Avenida Revolucín; get off at corner Altavista and Revolución. Admission: $1.25, free Sun. Open Tues.–Sun. 10–6.*

MUSEO ESTUDIO DIEGO RIVERA

Some of Diego's last paintings are still resting here on ready easels, and his denim jacket and shoes sit on a wicker chair, waiting: The museum that once was home to Diego Rivera and his artist wife, Frida Kahlo, appears as if the two could return at any moment to continue work or share some tequila with Rivera's cronies Leon Trotsky, Lázaro Cárdenas, or John Dos Passos. Juan O'Gorman, a famous architect and close friend of Rivera's, designed the house in the functionalist spirit, with an intent to economize space: Diego's bedroom also served as a place to store pigeon food and as a model's changing room. Papier mâché skeletons draped around the bed suggest that Rivera shared the Mexican penchant for black humor. *Diego Rivera 2, at Altavista, tel. 5/616–09–96 or 5/550–11–89. Take RUTA 43 ALTAVISTA pesero from corner of Revolución and La Paz (in front of Pemex station). Or walk 15 min along Altavista. Admission: $1.50, free Sun. Open Tues.–Sun. 10–6.*

COYOACAN

Coyoacán was a rural village until the 1940s, when wealthy chilangos began moving out here to escape the urban madness of Mexico City. Now it's just half an hour by Metro from the center of town and has evolved into one of the many suburbs swallowed by D.F.'s sprawl. Centuries-old homes, narrow cobblestone streets, an abundance of bohemian markets and restaurants, and proximity to the Universidad Nacional Autónoma de México (*see below*) attract an affluent and academic elite. Although Coyoacán and San Ángel are often paired together, Coyoacán attracts a more artsy, politically conscious group.

In 1847, 50 Irish soldiers were excuted at Plaza San Jacinto in San Ángel. They had come to fight with the Americans in the Mexican-American War, but later deserted and joined the Catholic Mexicans.

On weekends, musicians and handicraft vendors fill the **Jardín Centenario** between Carrillo Puerto and Tres Cruces. Families wander the adjacent **Plaza Hidalgo,** enjoying the open-air karate demonstrations or exercise classes. The red building on the plaza's north side is the **Palacio de Cortés,** once the conquistador's home and now Coyoacán's administrative center. In the back portion of the palace are the offices of the **Foro Cultural Coyoacanense** (tel. 5/658–48–91), whose friendly staff provides loads of tourist information (ask them to tell you about Cortés's secret tunnel), as well as the scoop on free concerts. The **Museo Nacional de las Intervenciones** (tel. 5/604–06–09; admission $2, free Sun.; open Tues.–Sun. 9–6) chronicles Mexico's foreign interventions through displays of guns, flags, documents, maps, and other artifacts. The museum is inside the beautiful **Ex-Convento de Churubusco,** on the corner of Agosto and General Anaya.

The **Casa de la Cultura Jesús Reyes Héroes** (Francisco Sosa 202, tel. 5/658–55–19) publishes an indispensable monthly calendar of cultural activities in Coyoacán. For a free guided tour of Coyoacán's main attractions, call the **Delegación de Coyoacán** (tel. 5/659–22–56). The tour leaves from the kiosk in Plaza Hidalgo at 10 AM on weekends and wanders through some of the most beautiful sections of Coyoacán: the beautiful tree-filled **Víveros de Coyoacán** park; part of the UNAM campus; and the **Plaza de la Concepción** (popularly known as Plaza de la Conchita), where you'll see the **Casa de la Malinche,** the house Cortés supposedly built for his Aztec translator and lover. *From Metro Coyoacán, take PLAZA VILLA COAPA pesero.*

MUSEO CASA DE LEON TROTSKY

This dark, fortresslike house was the home of one of the most important figures of the Russian Revolution, and its history reads like a soap opera. In 1937, after being exiled from the Soviet Union, Leon Trotsky was granted asylum in Mexico by President Lázaro Cárdenas at the urging of muralist Diego Rivera, whom Trotsky had met in Paris. Upon their arrival, Trotsky and his wife moved to this unpleasant-looking dwelling. The first attempt to assassinate Trotsky left bullet holes that are still visible in Trotsky's bedroom. Unfortunately for Leon, the second attempt was successful. The study where Trotsky was fatally stabbed remains untouched: On the desk lies an article he was reading when Ramón Mercader, his secretary's boyfriend, stabbed him with an ice pick on August 29, 1940. If you speak Spanish, the guards will tell you, among other things, how Trotsky's teeth left a permanent scar on Mercader's hand; how he clung to life for 26 hours; what his last words were; and where his ashes are interred in the garden. *Río Churubusco 410, between Gómez Farías and Morelos, tel. 5/658–87–32. From Plaza Hidalgo, north on Allende 6 blocks, then right. Admission: $1.50. Open Tues.–Sun. 10–5.*

MUSEO DE CULTURAS POPULARES

Rotating exhibits of folk art from Mexico and elsewhere are beautifully displayed here, accompanied by plentiful information (in Spanish). More than just a museum, this solid colonial building has become a center for community activities, hosting frequent art and dance workshops (flyers for upcoming activities are posted on the front door). The monthly newsletter *El Canario de Coyoacán* is distributed here and provides the latest on music and dance shows throughout Coyoacán. *Hidalgo 289, between Allende and Abasolo, tel. 5/658–12–65. From Metro Coyoacán, take PLAZA VILLA COAPA pesero to Jardín Centenario and walk a few blocks along Hidalgo. Admission free. Open Tues.–Fri. 9:30–6, weekends until 8.*

MUSEO DE FRIDA KAHLO

This blue house in Coyoacán is where painter Frida Kahlo (*see box, above*) was born, grew up, and lived briefly with husband Diego Rivera until she died in 1954. Now a museum, the building is filled with colorful yet sad remnants of Kahlo's life: self-portraits; illustrated journals; love notes; pictures of Mao Tsetung, Lenin, and Stalin; clunky clay jewelry; and the beautifully embroidered Tehuana skirts that Kahlo favored. Life-size papier-mâché statues and other folk art collected by Kahlo and Rivera adorn the house and lush garden. As a result of childhood polio and a bus accident when she was a teenager, Kahlo endured more than 30 difficult operations; her decorated body cast and her startling paintings convey both her intense emotional and physical suffering, as well as her pride in and passion for Mexican culture. *Londres 247, at Allende, tel. 5/554–59–99. From Metro Coyoacán, take PLAZA VILLA COAPA pesero to the plaza, and walk 5 blocks north on Allende. Admission: $1.50. Open Tues.–Sun. 10–5:45.*

MUSEO DEL ANAHUACALLI

What *do* you do with all those pre-Columbian artifacts you've collected over the years? If you're Diego Rivera, you design your own museum. The huge black building that houses Rivera's collection was constructed in the 1960s from volcanic rock. Even if you're tired of archaeological treasures, visit the building just because it's so strange, like an aboveground tomb that promises (and delivers) echoing footfalls and eerie silence. The third floor displays sketches for some of Rivera's murals, including *Man at the Crossroads*, now in the Palacio de Bellas Artes (*see box, above*). *Calle del Museo 150, tel. 5/617–43–10 or 5/617–37–97. From Metro Tasqueña, take trolley to Xotepingo stop; exit to right at CALLE DEL MUSEO sign, backtrack to intersection, and turn left. Admission $1.25, free Sun. Open Tues.–Sun. 10–6.*

UNIVERSIDAD NACIONAL AUTONOMA DE MEXICO (UNAM)

The National Autonomous University of Mexico, one of the oldest universities in the Americas, rests upon a lava bed in a residential district in the southern part of the city. Originally made up of various *facultades* (schools) scattered throughout the city, the UNAM was consolidated into one huge campus in the 1950s and now has more than 100,000 students. The vast campus is generally known as the *Ciudad Universitaria* (University City), or simply C.U., a fitting title since you have to take a bus just to cross campus.

Over the past several years the campus has served as a center of political activity. In sympathy with the Zapatista movement in Chiapas, students have staged marches and hunger strikes in protest of the government. Many believe that while the government pretends to tolerate UNAM's high level of political activity, it does so only to identify its adversary. The massacre at Tlatelolco in 1968 (*see* Plaza de las Tres Cultures/Tlatelolco, *above*) brutally exemplifies the opposition between student and state.

The university's architects sought to incorporate here the best of traditional and modern design while striving to create buildings that would harmonize with the natural landscape of cactus and black volcanic rock. They succeeded with the huge volcano-shape **Estadio Olímpico** (Olympic Stadium), site of the 1968 Olympics. The outer ramps of the stadium are decorated with yet another Diego Rivera mural, this one titled *La Universidad, la familia mexicana, la paz y la juventud deportista* (University, Mexican Family, Peace, and Athletic Youth). Murals by Carlos Mérida, David Alfaro Siqueiros, and Juan O'Gorman are just about everywhere on the campus, from the **Torre de la Rectoría** (Tower of the Rectory) on the northwest side of campus to the **Vestíbulo de la Sala Nezahualcóyotl** in the south.

The **Espacio Escultórico** (Sculpture Space), an ecological reserve at the southern end of the campus, is home to numerous sculptures by Mexican artists. The reserve is easily accessible via a long, winding lava-paved path, and is popular for climbing and picnicking on sunny afternoons. Just down the street, behind the **Biblioteca Nacional** (National Library; open weekdays 9–7) is a sculpture, *Las Serpientes del Pedregal*, which "slithers" around the library. Transportation on campus is free, so exploring is easy once you figure out the intricate

UNAM tuition costs about as much as a couple of metro tickets (about 20 centavos, which is less than a peso). Any attempts to raise it are met with angry protests by students.

web of peseros needed to cross the campus (try asking a friendly student). *Tel. 5/662–05–32 for general campus information. Take* TLALPAN JOYA *pesero south on Insurgentes to 3rd pedestrian overpass on campus; cross street, and head north past Biblioteca Nacional. Or from Metro Universidad, exit through Salida E and take* ZONA CULTURAL *pesero to Espacio Escultórico.*

LA VILLA DE GUADALUPE

La Villa's two basilicas dedicated to the Virgen de Guadalupe make it the most revered Christian site in Mexico. To this day, millions flock to the site where the Virgen is said to have appeared to Juan Diego, an indigenous convert to Christianity, in 1531. Unlike the fair Mary of the Roman Catholic tradition, the Virgen de Guadalupe had a brown complexion and spoke Nahuatl, Diego's native tongue. The Virgen instructed Diego to gather a bunch of roses—a seemingly impossible task in winter—as a testament of the truthfulness of his vision. When Diego told his story to a priest, the father scoffed, calling him a heretic and claiming that the story was pure fantasy. Yet when Juan Diego opened his cloak, out fell the roses the Virgen had told him to gather, leaving an image of the Virgen imprinted on the inside of the cloak.

The baroque **Antigua Basílica** dates to 1536. Unfortunately, it was built on soft, unstable soil, and is slowly sinking; it is no longer open to the public. Nearby, the hulking, modern mass that is the **Basílica Nueva** operates as a full-service church. Juan Diego's cloak is on view here, and you can drink Holy Water out of Virgen de Guadalupe-shape bottles sold at the stands outside. At the top of Tepeyac hill, inside the **Capilla del Posito**, pilgrims stand in line to file past a replica of Juan Diego. Many rub their hands on the glass that encloses him, then proceed to pass the holiness along onto their clothes, their children, and their spouses. Coming down the steps from the Capilla, have your picture taken on a plastic burro in front of a shrine to the Virgen; the photographers will make it into a keychain for you. *Calzada de Guadalupe, between Juan de Zumárraga and Hidalgo, near Metro La Villa. Admission free. Open daily 6 AM–10 PM.*

CHEAP THRILLS

In colonial times, when literacy rates were low, scribes would gather in the plazas to write or read letters for a nominal fee. Today the tradition continues (although in a slightly modernized form) on the **Plaza Santo Domingo.** Modern-day scribes can be found in the local plaza with their typewriters, transcribing everything from term papers to love letters; they'll even help you compose the latter if your passion doesn't transfer too gracefully to paper. In a row across from the typists are the printers, who churn out everything from business cards to wedding invitations. Both printers and typists work the plaza daily from about 9 to 6. *3 blocks north of Zócalo on Monte de Piedad, which becomes República de Brasil.*

FESTIVALS

Easter. Like everywhere else in Mexico, **Semana Santa** is a cause for joyous celebrations and religious processions throughout the city. In Iztapalapa, in the southeastern part of the city, devotees reenact the Stations of the Cross, complete with a dramatization of the crucifixion. On **Sábado de Gloria** (the Saturday before Easter Sunday), people often run around throwing water at each other. Although this act originally had religious significance, any such meaning is often lost amid the chaos. *Late Mar./early Apr.*

Independence celebrations. Weeks ahead of time, the city is festooned in the national colors of red, green, and white. The celebrations commence on the evening of September 15, when the president steps onto the balcony at the Palacio Nacional to read Hidalgo's "Grito de Dolores," the call for independence that provoked 10 years of struggle against the Spanish. The Zócalo is so packed with people that you could faint and still not hit the ground; confetti lies inches thick throughout the centro; and fireworks explode all night long. *Sept. 15 and 16.*

Feast Day of the Virgin of Guadalupe. The celebration of the patron saint of Mexico fills the elaborately decorated city with processions and dances. Days beforehand, pilgrims from all over the country arrive at the Basílica de Guadalupe (*see* La Villa de Guadalupe, *above*) by bus or on foot, many placing large cactuses on their backs and crawling on their knees in the final steps of the pilgrimage. Have someone teach you the words to "Las Mañanitas," the birthday song, or you'll feel left out when the entire city begins singing it in honor of "the birth" of the Virgin. If you have a son, dress him up like Juan Diego; this is the way legions of Mexican children pay homage to the indígena to whom the Virgin first appeared. *Dec. 12.*

Christmas Day. The festivities begin about two weeks before *Navidad* (Christmas), with the entire city being draped in lights. Take a tour through the city's more residential neighborhoods to see *los nacimientos*: life-size replicas of the nativity scene set up in people's gardens and yards. They're usually made of wood or stone, but the most elaborate ones include actual, bleating livestock. *Dec. 25.*

SHOPPING

Handicrafts are generally more expensive in Mexico City than elsewhere in the country. During the winter (mid-December through early January) and summer (July and August) tourist seasons, stalls with all sorts of goodies are set up on the Zócalo, just west of the cathedral. Even more expensive wares are sold year-round in the Zona Rosa. Except where noted below, shops and markets are generally open daily 10–7.

Bazar de Velas. This small shop, about a block from the Museo de León Trotsky, specializes in candles of every sort. Some are sculpted to look like a small pillar or colored to resemble an elaborately painted fresco. Still others are carved to resemble flowers, waterfalls, bees, and dolls. All are handcrafted works of art, used primarily during Navidad and other religious holidays. Prices range from less than a dollar to $50. They'll fit in your suitcase; just make sure they don't get too hot and melt. *Río Churubusco 306, tel. 5/554–45–96. Metro: Coyoacán. Closed Sun.*

La Ciudadela. Tucked away behind a doorless iron entry, this market consists of wall-to-wall handicraft stores offering some of the best prices in the city. Mounds of beautiful silver jewelry from Taxco, bags and jackets from Chiapas, and even those "My parents went to Mexico City. . ." T-shirts can be found if you look hard enough. The merchants are tourist-wise—many accept credit cards, but bargaining is still expected. *Balderas and Ayuntamiento, at Plaza La Ciudadela. 5 blocks south of Metro Juárez, or 1 long block north of Metro Balderas.*

Fonart. High-quality, government-approved folk art is available in any one of the several Fonart (National Fund for the Promotion of Arts and Crafts) outlets in the city. The pieces come from all over Mexico, so you can get just about anything here, though it will probably cost you at least twice as much as it would in that remote highland village. Plus, only a small percentage of your purchase trickles down to the artisans themselves. *Juárez 89, tel. 5/521–01–71. Other locations: Patriotismo 691, Metro Mixcoac, tel. 5/563–40–60; Carranza 115, Coyoacán, tel. 5/254–62–70. All stores closed Sun.*

La Lagunilla. Once known as the Thieves' Market, La Lagunilla consists of three main markets: The **Mercado de Ropa** (Eje 1 Norte, between Allende and Chile) sells shimmery dresses à la Saturday Night Fever, while the **Mercado de Comestibles** (Eje 1 Norte, at Comonfort) sells fruit and vegetables. The **Mercado de Artesanía** (Allende, between República de Honduras and Ecuador) overflows with furniture, coins, tacky paintings of the Last Supper, and a smattering of nice antiques. This market is at its liveliest on Sunday, when curio stalls are set up outside the main building.

Mercado San Juan. Officially the *Mercado de Curiosidades Centro Artesanal,* this conglomeration of tiny shops in a pink-and-white concrete building feels more like a shopping mall than a crafts market. However, good-quality artesanía, blankets, hammocks, silver, and mounds of tourist trinkets are yours for the asking here. Don't expect too much leeway in the prices—anything short of throwing yourself on the market floor and weeping uncontrollably will probably not move the gringo-wise vendors. *Ayuntamiento, at Dolores, 4 blocks south of Metro Juárez and Alameda Central.*

La Merced and **Sonora** are separate markets connected by a small side street, Cabaña. Edible goods are sold in the huge warehouse of La Merced, pervaded by the sweet smell of fresh fruits and vegetables. Also inside is the **Mercado de Dulces** (candy market), with more sweets than you've ever seen in your life. Outside you can buy useful items like umbrellas, pots, pans, clothes, and toiletries. At the Sonora market, just across the way, you'll find herbal potions that guarantee effectiveness against everything from evil spirits to impotence. At the very back, tropical birds, goats, puppies, and other sad-looking caged animals are also for sale: some for pets and some for food. *Mercado de La Merced: Circunvalación, at San Pablo. Metro: Merced. Mercado Sonora: 2 blocks south of La Merced on Fray Servando Teresa de Mier.*

Vendors at Mercado Sonora claim that their magic potions can soothe a troubled marriage. For one peso, buy a sachet of magic with a title such as Sígueme y obedéceme (Follow and obey me).

The **Portales de los Mercaderes** (Merchant's Arcade) market has been around in one form or another since 1524. These days, it's lined with jewelry shops that sell gold by the gram as well as authentic Taxco silver at prices lower than those in Taxco itself. *West side of Zócalo, between Madero and 16 de Septiembre.*

Tianguis del Libro. At this shop, stock up on Mexican pop culture; videotapes of elusive Mexican films are an especially good bargain here. The complete, three-tape collection of María Félix (Mexico's most revered movie star of the '30s and '40s) is $17. Individual videotapes, featuring the popular comedian Cantínflas, or modern documentaries such as *Los Niños de Chiapas,* will run you about $5–$7. Jazz, blues, classical, rumba, salsa, and Mexican pop cassettes are $2 each. If you read Spanish, a wide selection of classic and modern Latin American and Spanish literature runs 75¢–$3. *128 M. A. Quevedo, near La Paz. Metro: M. A. Quevedo.*

AFTER DARK

El reventón (the party) starts late in Mexico City and keeps going until the early hours of the morning; even after the clubs close at 3 AM, people grab a taco and beer and wait until the more respectable hour of 4 to mosey off to bed. The most lively areas at night are the Zona Rosa and Insurgentes Sur in Colonia Juárez, where snazzy clubgoers in black evening wear, "cool" teenagers in ripped jeans, and camera-toting tourists all mingle until dawn. Clubs are the places to be, whether they play disco or *música tropical* (a mix of salsa, merengue, and cumbia). Dance club covers are usually quite high, but women often get in free or at a reduced price. If you'd rather let someone else have the spotlight while you relax and soak in the culture, there's always Mexico City's theater scene. A wide variety of performances, from musicals to works by Mexican and international playwrights, ensure something for everyone. Check *Tiempo Libre* (75¢ at most newsstands) for theater listings and other entertainment information. One final note: Virtually all bars and clubs in Mexico City accept credit cards.

A favorite among locals and tourists alike, **Plaza Garibaldi** (Eje Central, at República de Perú) heats up weekend nights with competing mariachi bands in full regalia, who sing of lost love and cheatin' women. Couples come to be serenaded, and foreigners come to experience "traditional" Mexico. Buying a song can be a bit pricey ($10), but it's simple enough to walk around and listen in on other people's favorite mariachi tunes. Additionally, many no-cover cantinas and dance clubs line Plaza Garibaldi.

BARS

Bar Jorongo. This chic local institution features romantic trios playing hits from the 1940s and '50s. The bar is dark and cozy, popular with an all-ages crowd. *Maria Isabel Sheraton Hotel, Reforma 325, tel. 5/207–39–33. Across from Zona Rosa. Cover: $7. Open daily until 2 AM.*

La Casa del Inquisidor. Just like the name (The Inquisitor's House) says, this huge, two-story bar is decorated like someone's home: You might start off by having a drink in the garden, and by the end of the evening you may be dancing in the bedroom. Adventuresome drinks, such as *medias de seda* (silk stockings) and *semen de burro* (donkey semen), cost $2–$4. *Durango 181, 2 blocks from Metro Insurgentes, tel. 5/511–673–15. No cover. Open Tues.–Sun. until 2:30 AM.*

La Guadalupana. This famous Coyoacán cantina, dating from 1932, is always packed and heavy on the local color. The crowd is overwhelmingly male, so unaccompanied women will be showered with attention (however, if you feel harassed, the waiters will politely remove the offender from your area and, if necessary, from the establishment). On the plus side there are eight tequilas to choose from here. *Higuera 14, tel. 5/554–62–53. From Metro Coyoacán, take* VILLA COAPA *pesero to Plaza Hidalgo. No cover. Open Mon.–Sat. until midnight, Sun. until 6.*

CINEMAS

Most U.S. movies show in Mexico City within a few months of their release, so finding a film in English is easy. However, films are sometimes in poor condition, full of scratches and squiggly lines, and the volume tends to be low, since most of the audience depends on the subtitles, but for $3 ($1.50 on Wednesday) it's not so bad. Paseo de la Reforma in the Zona Rosa has quite a few big screens showing recent American and European films; look for **Diana** (Reforma 423, near Metro Sevilla, tel. 5/511–32–36), **Latino I** (Reforma 296, near Metro Insurgentes, tel. 5/525–87–57), **París** (Reforma 92, near Metro Hidalgo, tel. 5/535–32–71), and **Paseo** (Reforma 35, tel. 5/546–58–43). For artsier films, check out the government-run **Cineteca** (México-Coyoacán 389, near Metro Coyoacán, tel. 5/688–32–72). *Tiempo Libre* (75¢) prints current movie listings by title and theater.

DANCE

The **Ballet Folklórico de México,** which performs in the Palacio de Bellas Artes (*see* Exploring, *above*), is world-renowned for its stunning presentations of Mexican regional folk dances. Performances are held Wednesday evening at 8:30 PM and Sunday at 9:30 AM and 8:30 PM. You can buy tickets ($12–$28) on the first floor of the Palacio (tel. 5/512–36–33; open Mon.–Sat. 11–7, Sun. 9–7) or through Ticketmaster (tel. 5/325–90–00). The **Ballet Folklórico Nacional Aztlán** performs the same stellar dancing for half the price at the newly renovated Teatro de la Cuidad (Donceles 36, between Bolívar and Chile, tel. 5/510–21–97). Check the current performance schedule and purchase tickets either through Ticketmaster or at the theater lobby.

GAY CLUBS

The days when clubs were raided and homosexuals were menaced are not a thing of the past. However, as one club worker stated, there usually aren't problems with the police as long as there isn't too much "display" outside the club. Still, once a year the Operativos de Seguridad will make a preannounced visit to check out a place. This is supposedly a normal procedure, and done at all the discos. Nevertheless, be careful.

Bota's Bar. One of the most happening gay bars in the D.F., Bota's has mirrored walls and bright neon lights. The transvestite shows (Thurs.–Sat.) and frequent striptease competitions are extravagant, to say the least. The gay bar is upstairs from a straight (and unhip) bar of the same name. *Niza 45, tel. 5/514–46–00. Metro: Insurgentes. Cover: $5 (includes 2 drinks). Open Thurs.–Sun. until 4 AM.*

Butterfly. This techno club looks more like a bus terminal than a disco. With five bars, two snack shacks, about 50 tables, and a huge dance floor that's packed to capacity, it's by far the largest gay (and to a lesser degree, lesbian) club in town. The transvestite show (11:30 PM and 2 AM on Friday and Saturday, midnight the rest of the week) is widely regarded as the best around. Butterfly is rather tricky to find since there is no sign, but it's a block and a half from Metro San Juan de Letrán. *Izazaga 9, tel. 5/761–18–61. Cover: $5 (includes 2 drinks). Open daily until 5:30 AM.*

El Don. Despite the name, this casual discotheque does not cater to Spanish noblemen. To the contrary, it attracts jean-clad lesbians, who dance to everything from Elvis Presley to techno. Transvestite shows are held on Saturday night at 1:30 AM. *Tonalá 79, Col. Roma, tel. 5/207–08–72. Metro: Insurgentes. Cover: $3 (includes 1 drink). Open Wed.–Sat. until 5 AM.*

El Taller. This popular gay bar in the Zona Rosa prides itself on its longevity (10 years and running) and low profile: There's no sign on the small, inconspicuous entrance door. Stairs lead down to a dark, grooving men-only disco (women are not allowed). The dress code is mostly black, leather, and chains. *Florencia 37, Zona Rosa, tel. 5/533–49–70. 1½ blocks from Ángel de la Independencia monument. Metro: Insurgentes. Cover: $4–9; free on Tues. and Wed. Open daily until 3:30 AM.*

MUSIC AND DANCING

Mexico City's music scene has something for everyone. The latest craze is the *Rock en Español* (Rock in Spanish) movement; new bands abound, playing everything from mainstream pop to obscure punk. For the scoop on Mexico City's underground scene, ask patrons at Rockotitlán (*see below*).

JAZZ • New Orleans. This restaurant/bar delivers the best jazz bands in Mexico City, with Ezequial Miranda performing his popular blend of Latin jazz on Friday and Saturday nights. Watch out: You'll be expected to order something, and the $3.50 cover charge will slyly be added to your bill before you leave. *Revolución 1655, San Ángel, tel. 5/550–19–08. Metro: M. A. de Quevedo. Open Tues.–Sat. until 2 AM, Sun. until 1:30 AM.*

ROCK, RAP, AND ALTERNATIVE MUSIC • El Hijo del Cuervo. Students and hip intellectuals of all ages pack into this cool art deco bar for an interesting mix of rock and nueva canción and the occasional theater show. Check *Tiempo Libre* under "bares con variedad" for schedules. Cover varies (up to $7), depending on the show. *Jardín Centenario 17, Coyoacán, tel. 5/658–53–06. From Metro Coyoacán, take VILLA COAPA pesero to Jardín Centenario. Open daily until midnight.*

The five best tequilas, according to a bartender at La Guadalupana: Herradura Blanco, Reposado; Sauza, Generaciones; Sauza, Conmemorativo; Cuervo, 1800; Sauza, Hornitos.

Rockotitlán. After jamming nonstop for more than 10 years, this bar deserves a medal for longevity. Come listen to Mexico's best rock, alternative, and funk bands in an unpretentious setting that manages to look simultaneously like a garage and an outdoor terrace. *Insurgentes Sur 953, Col. Nápoles, tel. 5/687–78–93. Take SAN ANGEL pesero south on Insurgentes; it's on the 3rd floor of a small commercial building on a traffic circle. Cover: $5–$15. Open daily until 2 AM.*

Rockstock. This is considered by many to be the best club in Mexico City. Arrive before 10:30 PM or you'll have to brave the black-clad masses that jam the entryway, hoping to get the nod from Rockstock's young bouncers. The crowd is young, casually dressed, and party-minded. *Reforma 260, Zona Rosa, tel. 5/533–09–06. From Metro Insurgentes, take Génova north to Reforma and turn right. Cover: $11.50–$17; free Sat. to women. Open Thurs.–Sat. until 3 AM.*

MÚSICA TROPICAL • Música tropical refers mostly to rumba, which has Cuban roots. During the past 20 years, a new style of rumba—called either *rumba urbana* or *rumba chilanga*—has emerged, with a faster, more aggressive rhythm and lyrics that touch on social and urban themes more often than romantic ones. Two rumba chilanga bands to keep an eye out for are "Caliente" and "La Nueva Familia."

Bar León. The live music at this swanky club lures the cool and goofy alike. Patrons are a mix of students, foreigners from the hotel upstairs, and regulars stepping to rumba chilanga. *República de Brasil 5, Col. Centro, tel. 5/510–30–93. North of cathedral. Metro: Allende. Cover: $4.25, plus 1-drink minimum. Open Wed.–Sat. until 3 AM.*

Mama Rumba. By day, this is a small, nondescript Cuban restaurant. Weekend nights it explodes with the beat of salsa, danzón, cha-cha-cha, and conga, led by live Cuban bands. Cuban concoctions like *mojito* (Cuban rum, mint leaves, Angostura bitters, and sugar) are under $3. Tukio, the manager, is pura *corazón* (a good guy). *Corner Medellín and Querétaro, Col. Roma, tel. 5/564–69–20. Take INSURGENTES pesero to Querétaro, or catch a cab (10 min, $2) from Zona Rosa. No cover. Open Thurs.–Sat. until 2:30 AM. Reservations advised.*

Salón Q. This huge salsa club is one of the more popular places to come and shake your booty. The crowd is young, the music loud, and the drinks are expensive but strong. A *muppet* (Hornitos tequila and grapefruit juice) costs $3. *Reforma 169, Col. Guerrero, tel. 5/529–34–95. Metro: Insurgentes. Cover: $5.50. Open Thurs.–Sat. until 2 AM.*

DANCE HALLS • *Salones de baile* (dance halls) are the essence of working-class popular culture in Mexico City. The dance-hall craze, which began in the late 1920s, reached a peak during World War II, when live bands played mambo, swing, fox-trot, and the ever-popular danzón to crowds of eager young dancers. The youth of today prefer the downtown discos, and salones are slowly fading away. The two dance halls listed below attract a crowd of 20- to 80-year-olds whose common denominator is their love of dancing and dressing up.

Salón Colonia. Opened in 1922, Colonia is Mexico City's original dance hall and a favorite with the older crowd. The atmosphere is low key, and the folks on the dance floor are friendly—it's the perfect place to practice your moves. *Manuel M. Flores 33, Col. Obrera, tel. 5/578–06–19. 3½ blocks east of Metro San Antonio Abad. Cover: $3. Open Wed. 6–11:30 PM and Sun. 4–10 PM.*

Salón Los Ángeles. This vast dance hall (capacity 3,000) attracts an all-ages crowd that sways to salsa rather than the slower danzón. The 1930s decor looks as if it came right from an old Mexican movie, with a soda fountain and a huge, open dance floor. Various internationally known musicians make once-monthly appearances. *Lerdo 206, near Flores Magon, Col. Guerrero, tel. 5/597–51–81. Metro: Tlatelolco. Cover: $4; $8–$11 for headline acts. Open Mon.–Sat. 6 PM–3 AM, Sun. 6 PM–11 PM.*

PEÑAS • *Peñas* (musical gatherings) first began in the mid-'60s when leftists gathered to sing songs of revolution, using the music of rural Latin America then ignored by commercial radio. When dictatorships throughout the Americas imposed *apagones culturales* (cultural blackouts), artists were forced into exile, prompting thousands of Chileans, Uruguayans, and Brazilians, among others, to make their way to Mexico City. They brought with them nueva canción, the folk music that is still an important element of peña atmosphere. Although these days peñas are less ardently revolutionary, with a feel somewhere between a café and a bar, they function as cultural centers where people 18 and up relax, listen to music or poetry, or just spend time chatting with friends.

Hostería El Trobador. Walk into this bar and you'll think you walked into an old ranch house from the northern territories of Coahuila, complete with a stuffed, mounted antelope head staring down from the wall. El Trobador offers live Latin American folk music, nueva canción, and sappy romantic music six days a week—no cover charge or drink minimum. *Presidente Carranza 82, at 5 de Febrero, Col. Coyoacán, tel. 5/554–72–47. From Metro Coyoacán, take* VILLA COAPA *pesero to the Jardín Centenario; the peña is 3 blocks away. Peña performed Tues.–Sun. 7 PM–1 AM.*

Mesón de la Guitarra. One look at the decked-out crowd at this fancy peña and it becomes obvious that la Guitarra is for having a good time, not planning revolutions. Under the same management, **Peña Gallos** (Revolución 736, near Metro Mixcoac, tel. 5/563–09–63) is larger, but identical in every other respect. Cover is $4 in both peñas, although women get in free on Thursday, and everyone gets in free after midnight on Friday and Saturday. Reservations are a good idea if you plan to arrive after 9:30 PM. Beers run $1.50, mixed drinks $2.50. Music consists of Andean pipe music, traditional Mexican ranchera songs, indigenous music from Oaxaca, and tropical music from Veracruz. No American music allowed! *Félix Cuevas 332, between Patricio Sainz and Moratel, tel. 5/559–15–35 or 5/559–24–35. Take a bus down Insurgentes Sur to Félix Cuevas, and ask to be let off at the Liverpool department store; walk east 5 blocks. Open Thurs. 7 PM–1 AM, Fri. and Sat. 7 PM–3 AM.*

SPECTATOR SPORTS

Bullfighting and *fútbol* (soccer) are the most popular spectator sports in Mexico City. The *corrida* (bullfight) itself resembles a play, divided up into three acts called *tercios*. The objective is to kill the bull, which takes place in the third act, the act of death. The corrida is attended mainly by men, who would look equally at home at a *charreada* (rodeo) in their cowboy hats and boots. Fútbol matches tend to draw a more motley bunch, with everyone from college kids to grandmothers shouting support from the stands. During *clásico* fútbol matches between rivals Las Águilas (Mexico City) and Las Chivas (Guadalajara), each team's audience goads the other with chants and songs.

BULLFIGHTING

Plaza México is the largest bullfighting arena in the world (capacity 50,000), and corridas are held here Sunday at 4 PM. Tickets ($2–$25) for seats on the sunny side (*sol*) tend to be cheaper and rowdier than the seats on the shady side (*sombra*). The ticket window is open weekends 11 AM–2 PM; arrive an hour before the corrida to purchase tickets. *Augusto Rodín 241, Ciudad de los Deportes, tel. 5/563–39–61. Take INSURGENTES SUR/SAN ANGEL pesero south on Insurgentes Sur.*

JAI ALAI

The skill and coordination required to play *frontón* (jai alai), a lightning-fast Basque handball game (the fist-size balls have been clocked at more than 110 mph), draws crowds of spectators. Of course, they aren't so awestruck that they forget to place bets, which—at about a dollar a match—are as innocuous as they come. You can check out the action at **Frontón México** (NW corner of Plaza de la República) Monday–Thursday and Saturday from 6 PM to 1 AM. Women's matches are played at **Frontón Metropolitano** (Bahía de Todos los Santos 190) Monday–Saturday 4–10.

RODEOS

Charreadas (rodeos) are held Sunday at noon at **Lienzo Charro de la Villa** (Metro: Indios Verdes) and occasionally at **Lienzo del Charro** (Constituyentes 500; take any pesero from Metro Chapultepec). A show usually costs about $1.25. Check in the newspaper *Ovaciones* for any announcements regarding prospective rodeos or call 5/277–87–10, weekdays 9–5.

SOCCER

Fútbol is the passion of the republic, and during important matches Mexico City is practially paralyzed. Most games take place in the gigantic **Estadio Azteca,** in the southern part of the city, where the World Cup Finals were held in 1970 and 1986. The professional season lasts from September to June. Tickets ($8–$15) for the games are sold at the *taquillas* (ticket counters) outside the stadium; you can buy them the day of the game, but arrive at least an hour before kickoff. From Metro Tasqueña, catch a *tren ligero* (light-rail train) or *trolebus* (electric bus) straight to the stadium. The daily sports newspaper *Ovaciones* (50¢) lists game schedules.

Many Mexican families hold birthday fiestas aboard the lanchas (motorboats) that ply Xochimilco's canals. Somehow, they'll even squeeze a mariachi band on board to play "Las Mañanitas" (the birthday song).

NEAR MEXICO CITY

XOCHIMILCO

More than 700 years ago the Valley of Mexico was almost entirely underwater. This shortage of terra firma prompted the indigenous Xochimilco, the first tribe to inhabit the area, to build a series of *chinampas* (floating "islands" constructed of mud, reeds, and grasses) and anchor them to the lake bed with long poles. As the natural grasses and reeds on the islands began to grow, their roots extended into the water, becoming permanently affixed to the lake bed. As more and more of these floating islands took root, the lake was slowly transformed into a maze of canals. The Xochimilco's vast agricultural knowledge—which enabled them to harvest four crops annually from the fertile chinampas—was picked up by the Aztecs 300 years later, providing a sound economical base for the empire. Even now, after six centuries of conquest and colonialism, the floating gardens of Xochimilco, 21 km (13 mi) south of Mexico City's Zócalo, remain a testament to this ingenious innovation.

Xochimilco, with its central plaza and market, feels like a small village rather than a group of impermanent islands. The gardens are a favorite picnic spot for middle-class families, but visitors are rare during the week. Sunday is the busiest day, when you'll be penned in by boats on all sides. Enterprising boat owners pick out tourists and try to persuade them to commit to their *trajinera* (flat-bottom boat; $7–$8 per hr depending on size) before they've even seen the water. Although the government sets prices, you can usually negotiate. A ride in a more touristy *chalupa* (small canoe) lasts about two hours and costs around $5 for two or more people. You can bring your own lunch to Xochimilco, or buy warm tamales from the smaller boats that circulate on the lake. Xochimilco is open daily 7–7. For further information, call their tourist hotline at 5/676–88–79 or 5/676–08–10.

Many of the flowers grown on the Xochimilco floating gardens are sold at the **Mercado de Flores de Pedregal de San Ángel,** a 24-hour flower market in Mexico City. It costs $1 for a dozen long-stemmed

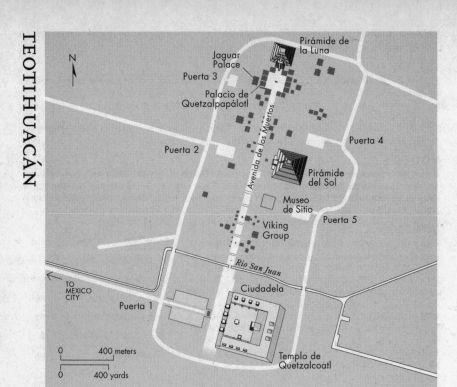

N

Pirámide de la Luna

Jaguar Palace

Puerta 3

Palacio de Quetzalpapálotl

Avenida de los Muertos

Puerta 2

Puerta 4

Pirámide del Sol

Museo de Sitio

Puerta 5

Viking Group

Río San Juan

TO MEXICO CITY

Ciudadela

Puerta 1

0   400 meters

0   400 yards

Templo de Quetzalcoatl

red roses. *Flower market: Av. Revolución, near Iglesia del Cármen, no phone. From Metro Tasqueña, take Line 2 toward Cuatro Caminos, get off at Pino Suárez and change to Line 1; head toward Observatoria and exit at Insurgentes. Take* AVENIDA REVOLUCION *pesero and get off near Iglesia del Carmen.*

COMING AND GOING

The easiest way to reach Xochimilco is to take the Metro to Tasqueña, hop on the *tren ligero* (light-rail train), and get off at the last station. From here, walk south on Cuauhtémoc to Morelos, make a left, and you'll be in the town center. The trip to Xochimilco takes less than an hour. If you're driving, take highway Periférico Sur and get off at the Cuemalco/Xochimilco exit. From here, take Avenida Prologación División Del Norte until you reach the EMBARACADERO sign, then take the Manantiales exit, which will take you to the lancha docks.

TEOTIHUACAN

By the 12th century, when the Aztec migrated to the Valley of Mexico, Teotihuacán had already been abandoned for more than 500 years. Awestruck by the massive stone temples jutting high above the lush valley floor, the Aztec named the mysterious ruins "Place Where Men Become Gods."

More than a millennium has passed since the Teotihuacán people inhabited the beautiful stone city, and information about the ancient civilization remains scant. Archaeologists have managed only to divide the history of the site into four distinct stages: What was to become the greatest city of Mesoamerica began in a rather humble way, as a few farming villages in the center of the Valle de Teotihuacán around 900 BC. Gradually the villages grew into larger settlements, increasing their wealth through mining and trading obsidian with neighboring towns. By 100 BC, Teotihuacán was a prosperous society controlled by an ecclesiastic oligarchy.

The powerful union of religious and political authorities made it possible to mobilize a labor force capable of building two massive pyramids: the **Pirámide del Sol** (Pyramid of the Sun) and the **Pirámide de la Luna** (Pyramid of the Moon). By around AD 300 Teotihuacán had reached the height of its power; its empire spread outward from the valley across Mesoamerica. Having conquered so much territory, the people turned their attention to beautifying their capital city—it is from this period that the most impressive artwork dates. Around AD 650, the city began to wane, although no one is quite sure why. Buildings eroded and, slowly, the city was abandoned. Eventually, Teotihuacán was pillaged by outsiders, forcing the remaining residents to migrate elsewhere. The once-great city was soon enveloped by surrounding vegetation.

These days, the ruins have been cleared of foilage and groomed for easy tourist access. After you enter the archaeological zone and cross the main thoroughfare, **Avenida de los Muertos** (Avenue of the Dead), you come to the **Ciudadela** (Citadel), a huge square with apartment complexes and temples. The detail and workmanship of the artwork here have led archaeologists to speculate that they were once the living quarters of ruling priests. At the far end of the citadel is the **Templo de Quetzalcoatl,** made up of two pyramids; the one on top is a reconstruction of the older pyramid below. The facade of the older one bears bas-reliefs of the plumed serpent god Quetzalcoatl (with a mane of feathers around his head) and the square-faced rain god Tlaloc. For a better view of the sculptures, go around to the walkway between the two buildings. Halfway down the Avenida de los Muertos is the enormous, unmistakable **Pirámide del Sol**; rising more than 215 ft high, it's the third-largest pyramid in the world. After 248 extremely steep steps, the view of lush green mountains and white fluffy clouds is equally breathtaking. Discovered in 1962, the **Palacio de Quetzalpapálotl** was probably the home of the Teotihuacán power class, and is now almost fully reconstructed. Some of the butterflies carved into the columns still have their original beady obsidian eyes, that gaze, as they have for centuries, over the beautiful open plazas of the city. Just west of the palacio is the **Jaguar Palace,** with reconditioned red-and-green murals showing jaguars dressed in feathers and performing various human activities. These same brilliant reds and greens, as well as blacks and yellows, once covered much of the city. A thorough tour of the ruins would take an entire day, but you

When packing for a trip to Teotihuacán, bring a hat, sunscreen, layered clothing, and a water bottle. Climbing around the ruins is hard work, especially as they're 7,482 ft above sea level.

can see a lot, if not every pyramid, in three or four hours. *Admission: $2.50; includes admission to Museo de Sitio de Teotihuacán (see below). Ruins open Tues.–Sun. 8–5.*

With clear explanations in both Spanish and English, **Museo de Sitio de Teotihuacán** gives an excellent overview of the Teotihuacán empire. Through artifacts found on site, it details Teotihuacán's technological and religious development; particularly interesting are the mass burials of human "offerings" (the museum tastefully avoids using the word "sacrifices") to the temple, with all their jewelry intact. One room of the museum has a huge scale model of the original city beneath a glass floor. Your $2.50 museum admission also gets you into the ruins. *At Puerta 5, tel. 595/6–00–52. Open daily 8–5.*

COMING AND GOING

Autobuses Teotihuacán (tel. 5/587–05–01) buses depart from the far north end of the Autobuses del Norte terminal (*see* Coming and Going *in* Basics, *above*) in Mexico City about every 20 minutes 6 AM–3 PM. The bus (1 hr, $1.25) drops you off at the main entrance, Puerta 1. The last bus back to Mexico City leaves Teotihuacán at 6 PM.

FOOD

Just outside Puerta 1, a series of fondas sell comidas corridas for about $2, in addition to the usual cheap tacos. No food or drink is officially permitted in the archaeological zone (except in the overpriced restaurant inside the complex), though the garbage cans on the site are filled with food wrappers and bottles. It's doubtful anyone will complain if you pull out your lunch, as long as you take your trash with you.

If you're dying to spend a day on the lake, rent a *lancha rápida* (speedboat) for $40 per half day (equipment included; maximum five people), or just take a leisurely boat ride for $4. To explore the village, rent a bike ($3.25 per hr) from the shop on 17 de Septiembre 200 (open daily 9–8). When it comes to hiking, the courageous attack the steep **Cerro de la Peña,** a half-hour walk northwest of town. You won't need rock-climbing equipment—just a lot of stamina to reach the top of the hill, where you'll be treated to a stunning view of the lake and the town. The less active can take a collective taxi from the center (60¢) to the nearby town of **Avándaro** and walk the 3-km (2-mi) **Velo de Novia** trail, which borders a small cascade and follows the stream into the surrounding hills. The trailhead for Velo de Novia begins at the bridge on the river. If you'd rather that someone with four legs do the walking for you, rent horses ($8 an hour) from the stables on the corner of Avándaro and Glorieta.

BASICS

Centro de Cambio Valle (Benito Juárez 103, at Porfirio Díaz, tel. 726/2–40–05) exchanges money daily 9–3. The **post office** (Joaquín Pagaza 200, tel. 726/2–03–73) is open weekdays 9–4 and Saturday 9–1. Ladatel phones abound, and the **caseta de larga distancia y fax** (Plaza de la Independencia 6, tel. 726/2–09–00) is open 7 AM–9 PM. The main plaza is lined with pharmacies, including **Farmacia y Perfumería Paty** (Villa Gran 200, tel. 726/2–01–62; open daily 9–3 and 4–9).

COMING AND GOING

México–Zinacantepec buses depart Mexico City's Central Poniente for Valle de Bravo (3 hrs, $4.50) every 20 minutes 5 AM–7:30 PM. The last bus from Valle de Bravo back to Mexico City leaves at 7 PM from the Central Camionera (corner of 16 de Septiembre and Zaragoza).

WHERE TO SLEEP AND EAT

Hotel Mary (Jardín Central, facing the plaza, tel. 726/2–29–67) rents decent rooms at $13 for doubles. **Posada María Isabel** (Vergel 104, tel. 726/2–30–36) has a well-kept patio garden and medium-size double rooms for $15. Both of the above accept cash only. You can camp for free just outside town: From the plaza, walk down Joaquín Pagaza, turn right on Calle de la Cruz, and continue to the piers; from here take a boat ($3.25) across the lake to the campgrounds.

Filling your tummy can be expensive (especially if you come on a weekday when most places are closed). **El Bocaito** (Vergel 202, tel. 726/2–01–33; closed Mon.–Thurs.) serves incredible homemade pizzas for about $4. **La Cueva del León** (Plaza de la Independencia 2, tel. 726/2–40–62) has colorful tables overlooking the plaza. Their grilled trout ($5) is fresh from Lake Avándaro. For cheap tacos and such, head to the town's daily **market** (corner Hidalgo and Independencia).

BAJA CALIFORNIA

UPDATED BY KATE DEELY

T he image of a tall, spiny saguaro cactus framed against the cool blue of the Pacific typifies the rugged landscape of Baja. Throw in mellow, out-of-the-way towns, immaculate beachside resorts, and bustling, northern cities renowned for wild nightlife and you'll have an idea of the peninsula's diversity. This variety attracts very different types of travelers—from sports enthusiasts who come for the windsurfing, fishing, and scuba diving to those who do nothing except fry their skin by day and their brain cells by night.

Only in recent years, with the influx of people from all over the country, has Baja become genuinely integrated into mainstream Mexican culture and consciousness. Before then, the peninsula was largely considered frontier territory. Although Hernán Cortés officially "discovered" Baja while looking for pearls and Amazon queens, Jesuit missionaries in the late 17th century were the first Europeans to settle successfully on the peninsula. From their original outpost in Loreto, the Spaniards extended the Spanish frontier into what is now Northern California. However, with Mexico's independence and the demise of the mission system, Baja withered, leaving a few scattered ranches and mining towns that stood untouched until tourism briefly boomed in the 1930s. It wasn't until the early 1970s, with the completion of the trans-peninsular highway (Highway 1), that Baja's isolation finally ended and the region became a popular tourist destination.

Today, Baja California Norte (Northern Baja California) is characterized by border towns, where tourists (primarily American college students) come to take advantage of the low drinking age, and beach towns, filled with similarly minded tourists who've come to frolic on the sand. Baja California Sur (Southern Baja California) is much more mellow, with a tourist industry centered around sailing, fishing, and whale-watching. If you've got access to a four-wheel-drive vehicle, you can also venture to the isolated Sierra la Gigante mountains. La Paz, the Baja California Sur state capital , offers the same spectacular beaches as the rest of the peninsula, but the city is unique in its friendly, authentic Mexican ambience and culture. At the southernmost tip of the peninsula is Los Cabos, a region famous for white sandy beaches and turquoise-hue waters. Cabo San Lucas is the major resort town here, where self-pampering reigns supreme and sport fishing ranks a close second. San José del Cabo, just to the east, is a quieter city that attracts a less rowdy type of traveler. Although these and other towns are rapidly being built up, Baja still offers miles of rarely visited coastline and remote mountain hideaways. Sadly, these idyllic regions are nearly inaccessible to the budget traveler: If you're determined to get off the beaten path, you can either bring a sturdy vehicle, blow your life savings on taxi drivers and guides, or start exercising your thumb.

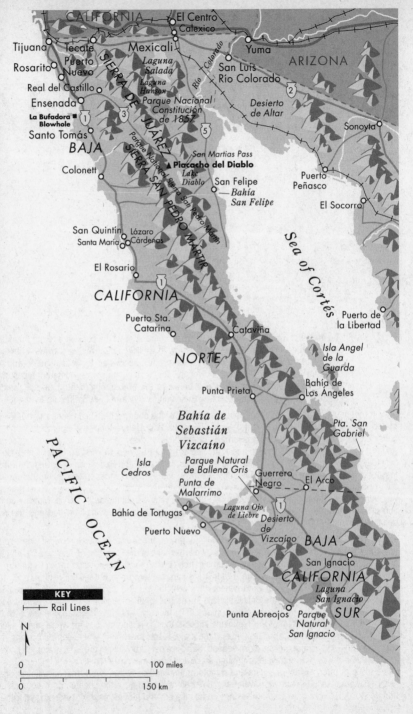

CALIFORNIA

El Centro
Calexico

Tijuana
Tecate
Mexicali
Yuma
ARIZONA

Rosarito
Puerto
Nuevo
San Luis
Río Colorado

Real del Castillo

Ensenada
SIERRA DE JUÁREZ
Laguna
Salada
Río Colorado
Desierto
de Altar

La Bufadora ■
Blowhole

Laguna
Hanson

Santo Tomás
Parque Nacional
Constitución
de 1857

Sonoyta

BAJA

Colonett
Parque Nacional Sierra San Pedro Mártir
San Martias Pass
▲ Piacacho del Diablo
Lake
Diablo

Puerto
Peñasco

San Felipe
Bahía
San Felipe

El Socorro

San Quintín
Lázaro
Cárdeñas

SIERRA SAN PEDRO MÁRTIR

Santa María

El Rosario

CALIFORNIA

Sea of
Cortés

Puerto Sta.
Catarina

Cataviña

Puerto de
la Libertad

NORTE

Isla Angel
de la
Guarda

Punta Prieta

Bahía de
Los Angeles

Pta. San
Gabriel

Bahía de
Sebastián
Vizcaíno

PACIFIC

Isla
Cedros

Parque Natural
de Ballena Gris

Guerrero
Negro
El Arco

Punta de
Malarrimo

Bahía de Tortugas

Laguna Ojo
de Liebre

Desierto
de
Vizcaíno

BAJA

OCEAN

Puerto Nuevo

CALIFORNIA

San Ignacio

Laguna
San Ignacio

SUR

Punta Abreojos
Parque
Natural
San Ignacio

KEY
├──┤ Rail Lines

N

0   100 miles

0   150 km

BAJA CALIFORNIA NORTE

Baja California Norte is a favorite with tourists, thousands of whom cross the border in search of exotic Mexico; most just end up buying mass-produced trinkets and partying in Tijuana until they drop. Farther south, the beach towns of Rosarito, Ensenada, and San Felipe attract similar weekend crowds seeking daytime fun and nighttime parties. Because of the region's reputation, those travelers interested in an authentic Mexican experience often skip Tijuana and its environs altogether. That said, those who are willing to wander off northern Baja's tourist track will find some surprises. The rise of the *maquiladoras* (*see box, below*) has caused hordes of migrant workers, mostly from the poorer southern states, to settle in Tijuana looking for work; they bring with them the food, arts, and customs of their far-off home villages.

TIJUANA

Sprawled alongside what is probably the most heavily crossed border in the world, Tijuana mainly attracts tourists with a single goal in mind: to party. Popular wisdom among foreigners and Mexicans contends that Tijuana is more an amalgamation of Mexican and gringo cultures than a "real" Mexican city, and it's a lawless den of hedonism at that. In certain respects, these impressions are accurate, and those who disdain made-for-export *artesanía* (handicrafts), dollar beers, and eyebrow-raising sex shows may wish to avoid this city altogether. The

The Baja peninsula's isolation from mainland Mexico and close proximity to the United States means that prices are often higher here than in other parts of the country.

main drag, Avenida Revolución, is by day a magnet for the middle-age, trinket-buying crowd; by night it attracts U.S. partyers (most under 21) who come to drink and dance. Just one block west of Revolución, however, is Tijuana's principal commercial street, Avenida Constitución, which bustles with hardware stores, pharmacies, microphone-wielding salesmen, and strolling Mexican families. Here you'll find restaurants and shops representing almost every state in Mexico—evidence of the plurality of Mexican cultures that exists here, though all are inevitably influenced by the *gigante al norte* (giant to the north). As you would expect from a city that's home to residents from all over the country, Tijuana is also an important departure point for numerous destinations throughout Mexico.

BASICS

AMERICAN EXPRESS

The AmEx office is in the **Viajes Carrousel** travel agency. In addition to the usual cardholder services, even nonmembers can change up to $100 in cash or traveler's checks or have their mail held at the following address: Boulevard Sánchez Taboada y Clemente Orozco, Edificio Husa, Zona Río, Tijuana, Baja California Norte, CP 22320, México. *Sánchez Taboada, at Clemente Orozco, tel. 66/34–36–60. Open weekdays 9–5, Sat. 9–1.*

AUTO PARTS/SERVICE

Serviautos and Servipartes (Revolución 216, at Coahuila, tel. 66/85–97–22) can help you out Monday–Saturday 8:30–7:30. The **Green Angels** (tel. 66/24–83–93), a government service, offers free 24-hour assistance to drivers with car trouble, including gas and limited repair work. Call them and they'll come to the rescue.

CASAS DE CAMBIO

American dollars are accepted in Tijuana, Mexicali, Ensenada, and Rosarito, but you'll get a poor exchange rate. Money changers abound in Tijuana's tourist district but only deal in cash. For changing pesos to dollars, you'll find the best rates from money changers on San Ysidro Boulevard in San Ysidro, just before you cross the border. To purchase or change traveler's checks, try the AmEx office (*see above*) or **Banamex** (La Juventud, just across the pedestrian bridge, tel. 66/83–52–48; open weekdays 9–5). ATMs accepting Visa, MasterCard, Plus, and Cirrus cards can be found at most banks; try **Serfín** at Constitución and Calle 6.

MANUFACTURERS OF MISERY

Maquiladoras (also called maquilas) are foreign-owned factories that use developing countries' cheap labor and tariff-free zones to produce cars, electronics, and other consumer goods for export to the First World.

In Mexico, the government's Border Industrialization Program opened the northern border to maquilas in 1965. After the 1982 peso devaluation, Mexican labor became some of the cheapest in the world, and multinational companies raced to Tijuana, Mexicali, Nogales, Ciudad Juárez, and Matamoros. There are now some 3,000 of these plants in Mexico, employing more than 750,000 Mexicans.

Though the maquilas have created jobs, there has been no parallel development of housing, health services, or basic sanitation for workers. Instead, maquila owners turn a blind eye to surrounding communities of cardboard shacks, where residents suffer from malnutrition, poverty, and disease. And Mexico's lax environmental laws allow toxic wastes from the maquilas to contaminate the groundwater that these communities use for cooking and drinking.

CONSULATES

Canada. Citizens of Australia can also find help at the Canadian consulate. *Germán Gedovius 10411–201, Zona Río, tel. 66/84–04–61. Open weekdays 9–1.*

United Kingdom. *Salinas 1500, tel. 66/86–53–20. Open weekdays 9–3.*

United States. In an after-hours emergency, call the San Diego office at 619/231–8414 and an agent in Tijuana will be contacted. *Tapachula 96, Col. Hipódromo, tel. 66/81–74–00. Open weekdays 8–4:30.*

CROSSING THE BORDER

U.S. and Canadian citizens don't need tourist cards to travel south as far as Ensenada or to Mazatlán farther down the mainland. Other destinations require tourist cards, available from the **Oficina de Migración** (immigration office, tel. 66/82–49–47; open 24 hrs) just across the border, under the bridge that passes over the freeway. When entering or leaving Baja by land, a driver's license or birth certificate is sufficient identification, although it's a good idea to bring your passport if you plan to travel elsewhere in the country. For more information on tourist cards, *see* Chapter 1.

EMERGENCIES

In Tijuana, contact the **police** at 134; the **fire** department at 136; and **Cruz Roja** (ambulance service) at 132.

LAUNDRY

Tijuana's laundromats are inconveniently located far from budget lodging areas, but if you're desperate try **Lavamática La Burbuja.** Washing and drying your own clothes costs about $2.50 and giving the honor to someone else is $3.50. *Calle 2 No. 1443, between Calles F and G, Centro Tijuana. Open 24 hrs.*

MAIL

It's cheaper and faster to send international mail from the United States than from Mexico. If that's impractical, Tijuana's **post office** is close to the center of town, east of Revolución. They'll hold mail for you at the following address for up to 10 days: Lista de Correos, Avenida Negrete y Calle 11, Tijuana, Baja California Norte, CP 22000, México. Head next door to Telecomm to send telegrams and faxes.

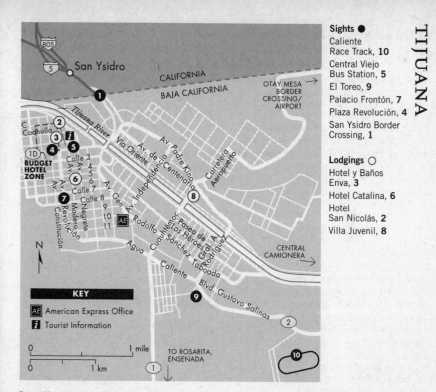

Sights ●

Caliente
Race Track, **10**

Central Viejo
Bus Station, **5**

El Toreo, **9**

Palacio Frontón, **7**

Plaza Revolución, **4**

San Ysidro Border
Crossing, **1**

Lodgings ○

Hotel y Baños
Enva, **3**

Hotel Catalina, **6**

Hotel
San Nicolás, **2**

Villa Juvenil, **8**

KEY

AE American Express Office

ℹ Tourist Information

0 ———————— 1 mile

0 ———————— 1 km

Post office: Avenida Negrete and Calle 11, tel. 66/84–79–50. Open weekdays 8–5, Sat. 9–1. Telecomm open weekdays 8–8, weekends 8–1.

MEDICAL AID

Dr. Manuel R. Laza at the **Centro Médico España** (Calle 2 No. 1844, near Constitución, tel. 66/85–24–50) speaks English and is available Monday–Saturday 8:30–8 and Sunday until 2 PM. Plenty of 24-hour pharmacies lie along Constitución, including **Farmacia Regis** (Calle 5 and Constitución, tel. 66/85–13–49), where someone can usually help you in English.

PHONES

Collect calls are easy to place from Tijuana's pay phones, but it's more expensive to make international calls from Mexico than from the United States. If you want to call from a *caseta de larga distancia* (long-distance telephone office), go to **Copias Rubi,** where calls to the States are discounted 50% weekdays after 8 PM, all day on Saturday, and Sunday until 5 PM. *Calle 7 No. 1906, near Constitución, tel. 66/85–03–11. Open daily 9 AM–10 PM.*

VISITOR INFORMATION

Tijuana has a number of tourist offices. The most centrally located, **CANACO** (Revolución, at Calle 1, tel. 66/88–16–85, fax 66/85–84–72; open daily 9–7), is run by Tijuana's chamber of commerce and has an English-speaking staff and decent maps. A less busy bureau is the **Tourism and Convention Bureau** (tel. 66/83–14–05; open daily 9–7), just across the border past the taxi stand, in the small, white building shared with Smokin' Joe's liquor. The English-speaking staff here is very knowledgeable and friendly. They sell auto insurance, give directions to sights in Baja, and provide maps of Tijuana—but despite the location they do not offer tequila shots.

For information on Tijuana's gay scene, check out **Café Emilio's** (Calle 3, between Constitución and Niños Héroes, no phone). This café/club is also a resource center for gay groups and boasts a makeshift AIDS clinic, the newspaper *Frontera Gay,* and other resources. The club keeps a low profile, so hours are sporadic.

COMING AND GOING

BY BUS

Tijuana has two bus stations: The **Central Camionera,** which is served by major mainland companies, and the **Central Viejo,** for buses to Tecate. **Greyhound** (tel. 66/21–29–48, or 800/231–2222 in the U.S.) buses to the United States depart from both stations, as well as from the station on the San Ysidro side of the border (799 E. San Ysidro Blvd., tel. 619/428–1194). They leave every hour 5 AM–6 PM for San Diego (50 min, $6) and Los Angeles (3½ hrs, $11), and you can change in Los Angeles to continue on to San Francisco (12–13 hrs, $36). The San Ysidro Greyhound station offers lockers ($2 for 6 hrs, quarters only) and luggage storage ($3 per bag per day).

CENTRAL CAMIONERA • Three bus companies share the Central Camionera (tel. 66/21–29–85) on the eastern edge of Tijuana, far from the budget-hotel area and most tourist activities. **Transportes Norte de Sonora** operates buses throughout the country, with frequent first- and second-class service to Guadalajara (36 hrs; $97 1st class, $80 2nd class) and Mexico City (48 hrs; $98 1st class, $82 2nd class). **Transportes Pacífico** (tel. 66/21–26–06) also has express buses down the mainland coast to Guadalajara and Mexico City. **Autotransportes de Baja California (ABC)** (tel. 66/21–24–58 or 66/21–24–61) serves Baja with hourly first- and second-class buses 6 AM–8 PM to Mexicali (3 hrs, $12), San Felipe (6 hrs, $17), and Ensenada (1½ hrs, $5). La Paz (22 hrs, $47) is served only by first-class buses, with departures at 8 AM, noon, 6 PM, and 9 PM.

From downtown Tijuana, a taxi will take you down Revolución to the Central Camionera for $7–$10, but your best option is to catch a brown-and-white CENTRAL CAMIONERA *colectivo* (communal taxi; 15 min, $1.25) from the stop on Madero, between Calles 2 and 3. To get from the bus station to the budget-hotel area, find a bus marked CENTRO. The station offers luggage storage (open daily 6:30 AM–10:30 PM) for 65¢ an hour. You can also place long-distance calls (cash only) from the station's **Sendetel** booth (tel. 66/21–23–04), open daily 4 AM–11 PM. Money exchange is available daily 6 AM–10 PM.

CENTRAL VIEJO • Buses to Tecate (1½ hrs, $2) leave regularly from the Central Viejo (Madero, at Calle 1, tel. 66/88–07–52) from 5:30 AM to 9 PM. The station is within walking distance of both the border and the budget-hotel area. To reach the station from the border, cross over the Río Tijuana pedestrian bridge and continue straight on Calle 1. To reach the budget-hotel area from the bus station, continue on Calle 1 to Coahuila.

BY CAR

There are two border crossings in Tijuana. The San Ysidro–Tijuana crossing is the busiest; on weekends and holidays, the wait to enter the United States by car can be two hours. Lines are shorter at the less central **Otay Mesa** border (near Tijuana airport, 10 min east of San Diego), but it's only open 6 AM–10 PM. If you're in Mexico and want to check on border traffic, call 66/83–14–05 for information in English.

If you're going to TJ (as Tijuana is commonly called by gringos) and you opt not to take the trolley, you should park on the U.S. side at one of the many well-lit, 24-hour lots within walking distance of the border ($6 per 24 hours). If you want to rent a car, try **AVIS** (tel. 800/852–4617), which has an office in San Diego and will let you take a car 714 km (450 mi) south into Baja for up to 30 days. For more details about the legal and financial formalities involved with taking a car into Mexico, *see* Chapter 1.

BY PLANE

The airport is on the eastern edge of the city, by the Otay Mesa border crossing; from the San Ysidro border or downtown, a taxi out here costs $7–$10. The city bus marked AEROPUERTO (30–40 min, 30¢) also makes the trip to the airport—catch it at the traffic circle near the border. Domestic plane fares in Mexico are no bargain, but they're usually substantially cheaper than international flights into Mexico. If you're in Southern California, you're better off crossing into Tijuana and buying your plane ticket there. When you leave Mexico, don't forget the $12 departure tax, payable in dollars or pesos. The **Aero California** office (Plazería Commercial Center, across from Cultural Center, tel. 66/84–21–00, or 800/237–6225 in the U.S.) is open weekdays 8–7. They serve Los Angeles and Tucson in the United States, and also fly daily to La Paz and four times per day to Mexico City ($150 one-way). **Aeroméxico** (Revolución, at Calle 8, tel. 66/85–44–01, or 800/237–6639 in the U.S.) and **Mexicana** (Paseo de los Héroes 1511, tel. 66/34-65-66, or 800/531–7921 in the U.S.) both offer flights to cities throughout Mexico at competitive prices.

BY TROLLEY

The **San Diego Trolley** (tel. 619/231–8549) runs from the America Plaza Transfer Station (C St., between Kettner and India Sts.) in downtown San Diego to San Ysidro, stopping right at the border. Trolleys make the 45-minute trip about every 15 minutes 5 AM–12:15 AM, except on Saturday night, when hourly service continues from midnight until 5 AM Sunday. Many trolley stations along the line provide free parking, which can save you $6 in parking expenses at San Ysidro. Be sure to park in a guarded and well-lit parking lot.

GETTING AROUND

Tijuana, unlike most Mexican cities, lacks a definite center; there's no principal church or square by which to orient yourself. Avenidas Revolución and Constitución—where most of the city's bars and clubs are—lie in the most "central" part of town. The jai alai arena and dozens of street vendors are also in this area, which is best explored on foot. To reach the bullring or racetrack, both on the outskirts of town, take a minibus from the bus stop on Madero between Calles 2 and 4. *Avenidas* in Tijuana run north–south and *calles* run east–west. Address numbers were changed in 1993, so many buildings have two numbers—those written in blue are the current ones.

BY BUS

Buses marked 5 or 10 CENTRO go down Boulevard Agua Caliente, but *peseros* (minibuses) are faster and offer more frequent service. Both cost less than $1. The peseros on the Agua Caliente route are red-and-black station wagons; catch them on Calle 2 near Avenida Revolución. Tan-and-white station wagons go to the Glorieta Cuauhtémoc and the shopping centers along the Río Tijuana; catch them on Calle 3. Buses to the airport and the bus station stop at the traffic circle across from the border crossing, and on Calle 4 at Niños Héroes. The easiest way to reach the border from downtown is to catch a **Mexi-Coach** bus ($1), which leaves Revolución (between Calles 6 and 7) every half hour 9–9, making stops along Revolución on the way.

> *"Poor Mexico, so far from God, so close to the United States."*— Porifirio Díaz, Mexican president *from 1877 to 1880 and 1884 to 1911.*

BY TAXI

Cabs don't have meters, so be sure to negotiate the fare before boarding. A trip between the border and downtown should cost about $5, while a ride from the border or city center to the Central Camionera or airport should run $7–$10.

WHERE TO SLEEP

Tijuana's really cheap hotels are northwest of Revolución and around Coahuila. They're only a little darker, dingier, and noisier than those on Revolución itself, and they cost $5–$10 less. Women, however, may find the attention they get in the red-light district bothersome and should think twice before staying here. All the hotels listed below have hot water 24 hours a day.

UNDER $10 • Hotel y Baños Enva. The small, dark rooms at this hotel face a newly painted courtyard, and though a bit worn, they each have a fairly clean private bathroom. Next door is a bath where men may use the sauna, whirlpool, and steam room for $3 (women are not allowed at the bath). Doubles cost $9 with a $1.50 key deposit. *Artículo 123 (Calle 1) No. 1918, near Constitución, tel. 66/85-22–41. 38 rooms, all with bath. Luggage storage. Cash only.*

UNDER $25 • Hotel Catalina. Clean, quiet, and comfortable, this is the best deal in the tourist area. Doubles cost $15, more if you want a TV. All rooms have phones from which you can make free local or collect international calls. Reservations are recommended on weekends. *Calle 5, at Madero, tel. 66/85-97–48. 38 rooms, all with bath. Luggage storage. Reservations by mail: P.O. Box 3544, San Ysidro, CA 92073, U.S.A. Cash only.*

Hotel San Nicolás. This quiet, safe hotel has a pleasant lobby with couches and a TV; doubles are $24. You can enjoy a picnic on the tables in the rear lot, or take advantage of the secure parking area. The front desk changes money and assists with long-distance collect calls. *Madero 538, between Calles 1 and 2, tel. 66/85-98–93. 28 rooms, all with bath.*

HOSTELS

Villa Juvenil (CREA). If by some odd chance you're in Tijuana to sleep rather than to hit the nightclubs, stay at this small, clean youth hostel in a peaceful neighborhood southeast of downtown. The five-person, single-sex dorm rooms are $5 per bed. *Padre Kino 22320, tel. 66/84–25–23. 66 beds. Take* *colectivo* marked EL POSTAL from Calle 3 and Revolución, and ask driver to stop at CREA. Curfew 10 PM. Air-conditioning. No age restrictions. Cash only.

FOOD

Because people from all over the country have settled here, Tijuana is a great place to sample the diversity of Mexican cuisine. Food stalls at the daily **mercado municipal** (Niños Héroes, between Calles 1 and 2) serve dishes from Jalisco, Guanajuato, Michoacán, Guaymas, and other areas for less than $5. Arrive between 1 and 2 PM for the best food selection. Along Calle 2, between Revolución and Constitución, there's a good selection of inexpensive eateries that cater primarily to a working-class clientele. Prices on Revolución tend to be higher than on surrounding streets, and restaurants on Agua Caliente tend to be even more expensive.

UNDER $5 • Café Pekín. This family-style Chinese restaurant is popular with locals for its shrimp curry and other delicious entrées. It serves terrific lunch combos (consisting of an egg roll, almond veggies, two super-hot chiles, and either a huge pile of fried rice or pineapple chicken; $3–$5), and you can get food to go. *Constitución 1435, at Calle 7, tel. 66/85–24–30. No breakfast.*

Restaurant Los Norteños. Tables outside this small restaurant are great for watching the action on Plaza Revolución. If you've hit taco overload, try the meat or veggie sandwiches. Breakfast costs less than $2. *Constitución 530, near Calle 2, tel. 66/85–68–55. Cash only.*

UNDER $10 • Tortas Ricardo's. Looking somewhat like a '50s diner, this 24-hour restaurant has an extensive menu and serves breakfast at all hours. They also have traditional Mexican *tortas* (sandwiches) and fish or meat dishes. *Corner of Calle 7 and Madero, tel. 66/85–40–31. Cash only.*

La Vuelta. This fabulous 24-hour restaurant doubles as a nightclub with live mariachi music (Mon.–Thurs. 8 PM, Sat. 8:30 PM, and Sun. 6:30 PM). The grilled meats ($7–$10) and *antojitos* (appetizers) are delicious. Two-for-one margaritas (weekdays 7 AM–10 PM) go splendidly with La Vuelta's free chips and salsa. *Revolución No. 8210, at Calle 11, tel. 66/85–73–09. At curve where Revolución changes to Agua Caliente.*

AFTER DARK

If you like all-night parties, it's easy to find something to do in Tijuana. Barkers along Revolución (between Calles 1 and 2) lure young, minimally clad revelers into neon-lit dance halls with offers of free tequila and the latest American music craze. Most places are cover-free; margaritas typically costs $3–$4 and beers $2.50. If you plan on crossing back over the border at the end of your wild night, sober up first: U.S. customs has been known to give fines for public drunkenness to those who are on the verge of *manejando la camioneta porcelana* (driving the porcelain bus).

Tilly's Fifth Avenue (Calle 5 No. 1109, at Revolución, tel. 66/85–72–45) and **People's** (Calle 2, at Revolución, tel. 66/85–45–72) are both open weekdays until 2 AM and weekends until dawn. Saturday nights are the most popular—so popular that men get charged a $3–$5 cover on holiday weekends. (If your party has a majority of women, you can often let machismo work for you and negotiate a deal on the cover charge.) **Red Square** (Revolución, near Calle 6, tel. 66/88–27–82) has a swank interior with a red spiral staircase and wide balcony, and it stays open until 3 AM.

The restaurant/nightclub **La Vuelta** (*see* Food, *above*) draws a jovial, primarily local crowd. **Disco Salsa** (Revolución 751, between Calles 1 and 2a) plays salsa and merengue weekend nights until 3 AM, while **La Loa** (Revolución, at Calle 2) is the place to catch live bands. **El Ranchero** (Plaza Santa Cecilia 769, tel. 66/85–28–00; weekdays until 3 AM, weekends until dawn) is a no-games gay bar, frequented by both tourists and locals. Women are welcome but are an obvious minority.

CLUBS

La Estrella. Packed with locals, this is the place to dance to cumbia and salsa tunes. Hard-working *tijuanenses* come here to let loose, and women without men in tow should be prepared to dance a lot. The $2 cover (men only) includes a free Tecate, but those without an attitude may want to skip this club—La Estrella occasionally gets rough. *Calle 6, just east of Revolución, tel. 66/88–13–49. Open daily until 5 AM.*

Mike's Disco. If you're looking for a way into the gay scene in Tijuana, this is a good place to start. Drag shows with men dressed up like famous Mexican actresses are the main draw at this alternative nightclub. Performances happen nightly at midnight and 3 AM. The cover on Friday and Saturday nights is $4, regardless of gender. Pick up the newspaper *Frontera Gay* for information on what else is going on around town. *Revolución 1220, near Calle 6, tel. 66/85–35–34. Open weekdays (except Wed.) until 3 AM, weekends until 7 AM.*

SPECTATOR SPORTS

BULLFIGHTING

Tijuana has two bullrings: **El Toreo de Tijuana,** which is downtown on Agua Caliente, and **Plaza de Toros Monumental,** the second-largest bullring in the world, by the beach and nicknamed the "Bullring by the Sea." Fights take place from May until late September, Sunday at 4 PM. Tickets start at $7 for seats in the sun and $11.50 for seats in the shade. The bloodthirsty can purchase $50 seats that will put them close enough to get splattered. Buy tickets at the caseta on Revolución (between Calles 3 and 4, tel. 66/85–22–10), open weekends 10 AM–7 PM, or at the ring (Highway 1-D, by the ocean); arrive early to guarantee yourself a ticket. The easiest way to reach the Plaza de Toros is to take the Mexi-Coach bus (½ hr, $2) that leaves at 3:30 PM from Revolución (between Calles 6 and 7). Otherwise, take a blue-and-white PLAYAS bus (40¢) from Calle 3 and Niños Héroes.

DOG RACES

Greyhound races are held at **Caliente Race Track,** a few kilometers east of town, daily at 8 PM. There are matinees on weekends. *Tel. 66/81–78–11. From Calle 2, take bus marked BLVD AGUA CALIENTE (10 min, 40¢).*

Tijuana's budget hotels fill up quickly on weekends, so either arrive early on Friday to stake out your room or make reservations several days in advance.

JAI ALAI

This Basque game, known as *frontón* in Spanish, is played at a dramatic Moorish-style palace, **El Palacio Frontón** (Revolución, near Calle 8, tel. 66/38–43–07). The game is similar to racquetball: It's played with a curved, wicker basket, three walls, and a balsa-wood, goatskin-wrapped ball that travels at speeds of up to 110 mph. Jai alai is popular with bettors—next door, you can wager on football, baseball, and horse races. For game times call 66/85–25–24 or 66/38–43–08.

NEAR TIJUANA

ROSARITO

About 45 km (27 mi) south of the border, Rosarito is one expansive, expensive beach party. It's the first popular beach south of Tijuana—not because it's beautiful, but because it's convenient to the United States. The best time to show up in town is May 14, when parades, traditional dances, and the crowning of an annually selected queen celebrate the founding of Rosarito. Other times of the year, drunk American college students are plentiful here, particularly on weekends and during summer months; most can be found in **Papas and Beer on the Beach** (Coronado, at Eucalipto 400, tel. 661/2–04–44), a popular dance club/volleyball court/outdoor bar/restaurant where a tiny fish taco costs $1. The cover charge is $3–$10 (depending on how busy it is), and a margarita costs $4.50. Thursday is ladies' night—meaning no cover and two-for-one drink specials for the fairer sex. The Rosarito **tourist office** (Benito Juárez 8, at the north end of town, tel. 661/2–02–00; open Mon.–Sat. 9–7, Sun. 10–4) has a friendly, English-speaking staff and good maps of Baja California.

Around 20 minutes south of Rosarito by car, **Puerto Nuevo** (or Lobster Village, as it is commonly called) consists of a cluster of restaurants, each trying to sell you the lobster for which the town is famous. The town has become so popular that some restaurants now charge $15 for a plate of crustaceans—although you might luck out and get a lobster with fixin's and a margarita for $11. Puerto Nuevo is also a great surf spot, with better waves and fewer swimmers than Rosarito.

COMING AND GOING • Buses don't serve Rosarito; colectivos do. To reach Rosarito from downtown Tijuana (1 hr, 50¢), catch a yellow-and-white colectivo on Revolución—these run 24 hours a day. You can catch the colectivo back to Tijuana half a block north of the Rosarito Beach Hotel. To reach Puerto Nuevo from Rosarito (15 min, $1), take the white taxi with burgundy and blue stripes that runs from the Brisas del Mar Hotel (Benito Juárez 22), daily 5 AM–11 PM.

WHERE TO SLEEP • The popularity of Rosarito beach, especially on weekends and holidays, makes it hard to find a cheap place to crash; you might be better off making this a day trip from TJ. Large, expensive, American-owned hotels and resorts have taken over, but cosy **Cupalas del Marís** (Guadalupe Victoria 9, tel. 661/2–24–90) provides small, neat rooms for about $25. It's a quiet haven in this noisy beach town, with satellite TV, pool, and hot tub. Another option is to rent a tiny cabin ($10 for up to two people) one block from the beach (corner of Sánchez Taboada and Cárdenas, tel. 661/2–09–76). To get here, walk two blocks toward the beach from the red CALIMAX sign on Benito Juárez; the office is open Monday–Saturday only, and accepts cash only.

TECATE

If you want a break from the hectic pace of Tijuana, head one hour east by bus to Tecate. Nestled at the base of the Sierra de Juárez mountains, this small town lies right on the United States–Mexico border. No city sits across from Tecate on the American side, and the Mexican government has not developed the town for tourism, which accounts for its genuine, friendly feel. There's not much to do in Tecate except enjoy the shady plaza and pleasant atmosphere, but if you plan a couple of days in advance, you can take a free tour of the huge **Tecate Brewing Company** (Guerra 70, tel. 665/4–20–11, ext. 123 or 291; open daily 8–noon and 1–5). Tour times vary, depending on the production schedule. There's also a beer garden, **Jardín de Cerveza** (Hidalgo, tel. 665/4–20–11, ext. 123; open Tues.–Sat. 10–5, Sun. 10–4), where you can enjoy Tecate's brews. The free **Instituto de Cultura** (next to the tourist office, tel. 665/4–14–83; open weekdays 9–6) changes its exhibits of paintings and sculpture monthly. People from surrounding ranches and northern Baja descend upon Tecate July 8–25 for a traditional *fiesta ranchera* (country fair), including food, crafts, music, and dancing.

BASICS • Change cash and traveler's checks at **Bancomer** (Juárez, at Presidente Cárdenas; open weekdays 9–1:30); it also has an ATM that accepts Plus and Cirrus cards. To make collect and credit card calls, try the **Computel** phone office (open daily 7 AM–9 PM) in the bus station on Juárez. For medical aid, English-speaking **Dr. Nestor López Arellano** (Presidente E. Calles 56, tel. 665/4–07–39) is available weekdays 10–2 and 3–8, Saturday 7:30 AM–5 PM. **Farmacia San Carlos** (Juárez 106, tel. 665/4–12–06) is a pharmacy open daily 8 AM–10 PM. The **tourist office** (tel. 665/4–10–95; open weekdays 8–7, weekends 10–3) on the *zócalo* (main square) has lots of helpful maps and brochures.

COMING AND GOING • Buses to Tecate (1½ hrs, $2) leave every half hour 5:30 AM–9 PM from Tijuana's Central Viejo (*see above*). From Tecate, seven buses go to Ensenada (2 hrs, $3) daily 8 AM–10 PM. Buses also leave for Mexicali (2 hrs, $5.50) every hour 7 AM–10 PM. Tecate's **bus station** (tel. 665/4–12–20) is on Benito Juárez, toward the east side of town. As you leave the station, turn left on Juárez and walk one block to the zócalo.

WHERE TO SLEEP AND EAT • The cheapest lodging in Tecate is at **Hotel Colonial** (Juárez 230, near the bus station, tel. 665/4–15–04). Newly painted and refurbished, this hotel has dinky little rooms with relatively clean bathrooms ($20). Call first, however, as it's sometimes closed. **Motel Paraíso** (Alderete 83, at Juárez, tel. 665/4–17–16) has comfortable, clean rooms ($20), each with a fan and private bath. To get here, walk about five blocks west of the zócalo on Juárez. The rooms are basically the same at **Hotel Tecate** (SW corner of zócalo, at Libertad and Presidente Cárdenas, tel. 665/4–11–16). You pay a bit extra for the convenient location: Doubles with private bath are $16, or $20 with TV.

For good food served on a shady patio, try **Jardín Tecate** (south side of the zócalo, tel. 665/4–34–53) with a menu featuring chef salads, onion soup, and garlic fish, all less than $3. **Restaurant Íntimo** (Juárez 181, tel. 665/4–48–19) has picnic tables in its front garden and is a nice place for breakfast; omelets and hotcakes cost $2. A house specialty is the *pescado veracruzano* (red snapper cooked in tomatoes, onions, capers, peppers, and herbs).

MEXICALI

Poor, urban, and seemingly endless, Mexicali easily fits the description of the stereotypical border town. Indeed, the capital city of Baja California Norte is similar in character to Tijuana, but because of its relative isolation (160 km/96 mi east of Tijuana), awful summer heat, and lack of tourist attractions, it's much less frequently visited. Recently Mexicali has made aggressive attempts to shed its tawdry image and recruit more respectable tourists, as the downtown shopping district and the new **Centro Cívico-Comercial** (commercial and civic center) attest. Despite these improvements, most tourists still spend only as much time here as is necessary to fill the gas tank. Immigrants from rural Mexico, however, flock here seeking work in the maquiladoras that have sprung up all along the border.

Mexicali's most unique feature is its large Chinese population, descendants of immigrants brought to Mexico in 1902 to build the Imperial Canal to the north. The city has numerous Chinese restaurants and shops and even a small Chinese-language newspaper. To learn more about the colonial history of Baja California, visit the free **Museo Regional de la Universidad de Baja California** (Reforma, at Calle L, tel. 65/54–19–77), which also includes exhibits on human evolution, geology, and paleontology. At least one Sunday a month between October and May, Mexicali's **Plaza de Toros Calafia** hosts some of the best matadors and bulls in all of Mexico; the cheapest tickets, available at the Centro Cívico-Comercial (Calafia, at Av. de los Héroes, no phone), cost about $10. If you're in Mexicali during the beginning of October, check out the city's biggest bash, the 15-day **Fiesta del Sol** (Sun Festival), which features live music, drinking, dancing, cockfights, and cultural exhibits. The festival is held at the **Parque Vicente Guerrero** on López Mateos.

BASICS

The **post office** (Madero 491, tel. 65/52–25–08; open weekdays 8–6:30, Sat. 9–1) is a few blocks from the border, but it's much cheaper and quicker to send international mail from the United States: **Casa de Cambio Lin** (236 1st St., tel. 619/357–5304), on the same block as the Greyhound station in Calexico (*see below*), is a money exchange office that sells stamps and has mailboxes out front. **Bancomer** (Madero, 1 block from the border, tel. 65/54–26–00; open weekdays 9–1) changes money and has an ATM. You can make cash but not collect calls until around 7:30 PM from the caseta across from Hotel 16 de Septiembre (*see* Where to Sleep, *below*). **Dr. Juan David Molina Velasco** (Madero 420, Suite 102, tel. 65/52–65–60 or 65/65–32–67 after hours) provides 24-hour emergency service, although his office is only open weekdays 10–3 and 5–8, Saturday 10–3 (June–Sept., Mon.–Sat. 10–3 only). The friendly staff at **Farmacia Benavides** (Reforma, at José Azueta, tel. 65/52–29–18; open daily 8 AM–10 PM) can help with nonemergencies.

The **tourist office** (López Mateos, at Carmelia, about 2 km/1 mi from border, tel. 65/57–23–76; open weekdays 9–2 and 4–7) has English-speaking employees and a cornucopia of maps, pamphlets, and newspapers in English. For border crossing information, *see* Crossing the Border *in* Tijuana, *above*. For

Most of the dancing in small bars and clubs on Coahuila is done by strippers. Women walking through this area of Tijuana may feel uncomfortable and should use caution at night.

information on tourist cards and visas, as well as the formalities involved in bringing a car into Mexico, *see* Chapter 1.

COMING AND GOING

BY BUS • The **Greyhound** bus station (tel. 619/357–1895 or 800/231–2222) is across the border from Mexicali in Calexico, directly in front of the pedestrian bridge. Hourly departures for San Diego (2 hrs, $17), Los Angeles (5 hrs, $27), and El Paso (14–18½ hrs, $88) keep this station open 5:30 AM–midnight. Luggage storage costs $4 for 24 hours or $2 for six hours. Mexicali's **Central Camionera** is in the Centro Cívico-Comercial on Independencia. Four companies operate from this station and share the same phone number (tel. 65/57–27–57). The counters to your right as you enter the station sell first-class tickets, those on the left sell second-class ones. **Élite** offers first-class service to many Baja towns and major cities on the mainland, with departures to destinations such as Guadalajara (32 hrs; $75 1st class, $65 2nd class) and Mazatlán (24 hrs; $65 1st class, $55 2nd class) every hour around the clock. Buses to Mexico City (42 hrs; $99 1st class, $80 2nd class) leave every two hours. **Autotransportes de Baja California (ABC)** has both first- and second-class service to points throughout Baja. Hourly buses leave for Tijuana (3 hrs; $12 1st class, $9 2nd class) and Ensenada (4 hrs; $12 1st class, $10 2nd class). Second-class buses depart for San Felipe (2½ hrs, $8) at 8 AM, noon, and 6 PM. First-class buses (2½ hrs, $10) leave at 4 PM and 8 PM. The station also has a 24-hour **Computel** office for long-distance calls; use a public phone to call collect. Reach the bus station from the center of Mexicali by catching the bus (40¢) that chugs down Altamirano, stopping a block west of the station. Otherwise, a cab to the station from the border or downtown costs $4.

BY CAR • Driving to Mexicali from Tijuana or Ensenada is relatively easy on Highway 2, although tolls along the road will run you about $3. **Budget** (in the Hotel Araiza, tel. 65/66–48–40; open daily 8–8) rents cars ($80 per day) that you can take all over Mexico with few restrictions. **Oasa** (López Mateos 850, tel. 65/52–82–15; open Mon.–Sat. 8–6, Sun. 9–2) sells auto parts and repairs cars.

BY TRAIN • The train station is at the south end of Ulises Irigoyen, north of the intersection with López Mateos. To get here, catch a bus marked FERROCARRIL (40¢) from Calle F at Madero, in front of the park. One first-class and one second-class train depart daily for Guadalajara, with connections to Mexico City. Both trains stop at all major cities on the way (the second-class train makes many more stops); and you can transfer at Los Mochis for the Copper Canyon train. The first-class train takes about 38 hours to reach Guadalajara and costs $53 for a comfortable reserved seat (make reservations 15 days to a month in advance). The second-class train to Guadalajara takes about two days and costs only $27. Second-class seats are not reserved, however, so arrive about four hours early. For more information, contact **Ferrocarril Sonora-Baja California** (tel. 65/57–23–86).

GETTING AROUND

Mexicali has two "downtowns," on opposite sides of town. The first, **La Frontera** (the border), a.k.a. *el mero centro* (the very center), is characterized by cheap hotels, taco stands, Chinese restaurants, and loads of street vendors. The **Centro Cívico-Comercial** (civic center) is home to government offices, the city hospital, the Calafia bullfighting arena, and the bus and train stations. Both areas are easily explored on foot, but to get from one to the other you'll need to take a city bus (40¢) down Boulevard López Mateos, the city's main thoroughfare. Buses to other parts of the city congregate near the border on the west side of Reforma, and on Altamirano near Madero. To reach the budget hotels in La Frontera from the bus terminal, cross the pedestrian bridge and wait directly on the other side for a bus marked CEN-TRO (40¢). Conveniently, their last stop is on Altamirano, near Hotel 16 de Septiembre and Hotel Altamirano (for both, *see below*). Taxis are not worth the expense ($5–$8) unless you can split the fare with a few friends or it's late at night. From the bus station, cab prices are preset, so don't bother bargaining.

WHERE TO SLEEP

The cheapest hotels are in the Frontera area and are accessible on foot from any of the local bus stops on Reforma or Altamirano. Most cheap hotels on Reforma are seedy and unsanitary; accommodations near the Centro Cívico-Comercial are more expensive, but they're also nicer. At **Hotel 16 de Septiembre** (Altamirano 353, tel. 65/52–60–70), near the Centro Cívico-Comercial, it's the bathrooms, rather than the rooms themselves, that make for a pleasant stay: The spacious tile showers are among the cleanest in Mexicali. Doubles run $7–$12 (cash only), some with private bath and air-conditioning. Carpeting and air-conditioning in each room make the **Hotel Plaza** (Madero 366, 1 block from border, tel. 65/52–97–59) reasonably comfortable. Basic doubles are $15, or $20 with TV and phone).

FOOD

The Frontera abounds with cheap places to eat, primarily taco stands and Chinese restaurants. At **Restaurant Buendía** (Altamirano 263, tel. 65/52–69–25), the Mexican-Chinese decor harmonizes with the Mexican-Chinese menu. Platefuls of chow mein, wontons, or enchiladas cost less than $4. Since 1945 **Cenduría Selecta** (Calle C 1510, tel. 656/2–40–47) has been attracting mobs of locals and tourists alike for its enchiladas, tacos, and carne asada burritos ($2). **Nevería Blanca Nieves** (Snow White's Ice Cream Shop; Reforma 503, tel. 65/52–94–85) has terrific salads, sandwiches ($2–$4), malts, and sundaes, as well as a great breakfast menu. All restaurants are cash only.

ENSENADA

Since the completion of the toll road between Tijuana and Ensenada in 1973, Ensenada has blossomed as one of Baja's most popular resort towns—increasingly with resort-style prices. Cruise ships call regularly at Ensenada's port, and passengers tired of shuffleboard head for the fine beaches nearby. Surfers catch waves 20 km (12 mi) north of the city at **Playa San Miguel,** while farther offshore sport fishers pursue yellowtail and marlin. By night, Ensenada offers a compact version of Tijuana-style nightlife, attracting crowds of hedonistic U.S. college students and Mexicans. But with a population of about 200,000, Ensenada is considerably smaller than Tijuana and its pace is less frenetic.

The missionaries who colonized much of Baja skipped Ensenada on their trek north because it lacked fresh water. The city's first major growth period came in the 1870s, after gold was discovered in Real de Castillo to the east. Following the discovery, Ensenada became the major supply center, seaport, and, for a while, even the capital of northern Baja. It also enjoyed a brief fling with the Hollywood jet set during Prohibition, serving as a playground for a tippling Southern California elite. With the repeal of Prohibition and the Mexican government's decision to make gambling illegal, tourism in Ensenada dried up. More recently, the loosening of restrictions on foreign ownership of beachside property has spurred a dramatic increase in the number of visitors here, foreign and native. Although ritzy hotels line the shore, the hills surrounding Ensenada are terraced with tar-paper shacks—home to the city's most recent migrants, who have come to look for work in northern Baja's booming construction industry.

BASICS

CASAS DE CAMBIO • American dollars are accepted (and expected) everywhere in Ensenada. **Banco Mexicano** and **Serfín** (both on Ruíz, at Calle 3; open weekdays 9–1:30) change cash and traveler's checks and give cash advances on Visa and MasterCard; Serfín has an ATM that accepts Plus and

Cirrus cards. **Cambio de Cheques** (López Mateos 1001-1, at Blancarte, tel. 617/8–14–59; open Sun.–Fri. 9–7, Sat. 9:30–3:30) changes cash and traveler's checks. They'll also allow you to make long-distance calls, including international credit card and collect calls, for a 50¢ fee.

EMERGENCIES • Dial 134 from any phone for the **police**; 136 for the **fire** department; or 132 for the **Cruz Roja** (ambulance).

LAUNDRY • **El Lavandero** has automatic washers ($1 per load) and dryers (25¢ for 10 min). If you prefer to leave the dirty work to someone else, same-day service is available ($1 extra per load). *Obregón 664, between Calles 6 and 7, tel. 617/8–27–37. Open Mon.–Sat. 7:30 AM–8 PM.*

MEDICAL AID • For an English-speaking doctor, contact **Dr. Antonio Orosco Soto** (Riveroll 679, between Calles 6 and 7, tel. 617/4–03–90), who has office hours daily 10–1 and 5–8. For 24-hour emergency service, call Dr. Orosco at home (tel. 617/6–42–29). Pick up prescriptions at **Farmacia Regia** (López Mateos 28, at Miramar, tel. 617/4–05–57; open Mon.–Sat. 8 AM–10 PM, Sun. 8 AM–9 PM).

PHONES AND MAIL • You can make collect calls from public phones along López Mateos or at the Cambio de Cheques (*see above*). The **post office**, near Hotel Riviera del Pacífico, will hold mail sent to you at the following address for up to 10 days: Lista de Correos, Administración 1, Avenida López Mateos, Ensenada, Baja California Norte, CP 22800, México. *López Mateos, at Floresta, tel. 617/6–10–88. Open weekdays 8–7, Sat. 9–1.*

SCHOOLS • The **Colegio de Idiomas de Ensenada** (Blvd. Rodríguez 377, tel. 617/6–01–09) offers six-week, intensive Spanish courses throughout the year. Classes are held weekdays and cost $125 per week, plus a one-time registration fee of $125. Family stays are also available ($20 per day, meals included).

VISITOR INFORMATION • The **tourist information booth** at the north end of the waterfront has a friendly, English-speaking staff and an ample supply of maps and pamphlets, but they don't know much about out-of-the-way places. *Costero, at Gastelum, tel. 617/8–24–11. Open weekdays 9–7, Sat. 10–4, Sun. 10–3.*

For a hair-raising, authentic Baja experience, take the carretera libre (free road) from Tijuana to Rosarito. Low-riders and produce trucks jockey for position on this potholed highway.

Baja's **Secretaría del Estado de Turismo,** farther south, has fewer pamphlets about local merchants but a more knowledgeable staff and better general information about Baja. *Centro de Gobierno, Costero 1477, at Las Rocas, tel. 617/2–30–22, ext. 3181 or 3182. Open weekdays 9–7, Sat. 10–3, Sun. 10–2.*

COMING AND GOING

Transportes Norte de Sonora (TNS) and **Autotransportes de Baja California (ABC)** are housed in Ensenada's bus terminal (Riveroll, at Calle 10). TNS (tel. 617/8–67–70) has first-class departures for Guadalajara (36 hrs, $60) at 3 PM, 8:30 PM, and midnight. Buses for Mexico City (48 hrs, $85 1st class, $72 2nd class) leave at 11:30 AM and 4:30 PM. ABC (tel. 617/8–66–80) has frequent first-class buses bound for San Quintín (3 hrs, $7), La Paz (19 hrs, $45), and towns in between. Buses depart 5:30 AM–8 PM for Mexicali (4 hrs; $12 1st class, $10 2nd class); at 8 AM and 6 PM for San Felipe (3½ hrs, $12); and hourly for Tijuana (1½ hrs, $5). The station has 24-hour luggage storage (50¢ for 5 hrs) and a caseta de larga distancia (open daily 7:30 AM–10 PM) for cash calls only. To reach the budget-hotel area from the bus station, turn right as you leave the station and walk eight blocks. It's a seedy part of town, so be careful walking alone at night. Colectivos (50¢) also run to the center of town until midnight. Taxis to the center are $3.

GETTING AROUND

Except for the beaches, which lie 10 km (6 mi) south of town and beyond, Ensenada is easy to cover on foot. The waterfront (Boulevard Costero) and the parallel tourist drag (López Mateos, a.k.a. Calle 1) serve as the town's focal points. The historic **Hotel Riviera del Pacífico** (*see* Worth Seeing, *below*), on López Mateos, serves as a good landmark. Avenida Juárez, about six blocks inland, is the main commercial street. To reach the **Estero** or **El Faro** beaches, flag down a yellow-and-white CHAPULTEPEC van from anywhere along the waterfront on Boulevard Costero; the vans stop within 3 km (2 mi) of the beach. You can also take a red-and-white CHAPULTEPEC bus from the depot on Calle 6, at Ruíz, or from Avenida Juárez. Get off at the ESTERO sign, and walk the 2–3 km (1–2 mi) to the beach. To reach **La Bufadora** (*see* Near Ensenada, *below*) take the yellow-and-white MANEADERO van ($2) all the way to Maneadero and change to a blue van ($1) for the remaining 26 km (16 mi). Vans and buses run daily 6 AM–10 PM. If you're in need of bike-related equipment, **Los Duran Bicicletas** (Riveroll 542, tel. 617/4–01–60) has parts and a knowledgeable staff.

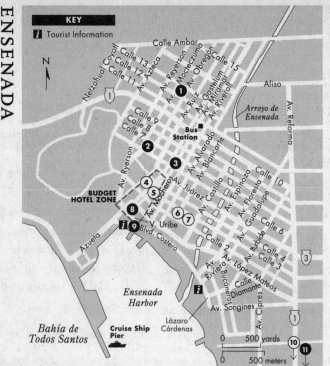

ENSENADA

KEY

ℹ️ Tourist Information

N

BUDGET HOTEL ZONE

Calle 13
Calle 12
Calle 11
Calle Ambar
Calle 15
Calle 9
Calle 8
Calle 7
Calle 10
Calle 6
Calle 2
Calle 4
Calle 3
Calle Diamante

Neizahual Coyotl
Av. Ryerson
Av. Reyerson
Av. Moctezuma
Av. Obregón
Av. Azteca
Av. Ruiz
Av. Gastelum
Av. Miramar
Av. Riveroll
Av. Alvarado
Av. Blancarte
Av. Macheros
Av. Juárez
Av. Castillo
Av. Espinoza
Av. Floresta
Av. Guadalupe
Av. Iturbide
Av. López Mateos
Av. Riviera
Av. Bucaneros
Av. Cipres
Av. Songines
Av. Reforma
V. Uribe
Blvd. Costero
Azueta

Bus Station

Aliso

Arroyo de Ensenada

Ensenada Harbor

Bahía de Todos Santos

Cruise Ship Pier

Lázaro Cárdenas

0   500 yards
0   500 meters

Sights ●
Beaches, **11**
Bodegas de Santo Tomás, **3**
La Diosa Tara, **1**
Fish Market, **9**
Museo de Historia/Hotel Riviera del Pacífico, **8**
Parque Revolución, **2**

Lodgings ○
Hotel Cinderella, **7**
Hotel El Pacífico, **4**
Joker Motel, **10**
Motel Gris, **6**
Motel Perla del Pacífico, **5**

WHERE TO SLEEP

The budget-hotel area is on Avenidas Miramar and Gastelum, between Calles 2 and 3. Miramar is a run-down street lined with bars, so if you arrive after dark, try Gastelum first. Hotels on these streets are usually clean but worn, and communal and private bathrooms are sometimes in need of a good scrubbing. Another good place to look for cheap lodging is the area around López Mateos. The best of the lot on Miramar is **Motel Perla del Pacífico** (Miramar 229, tel. 617/8–30–51). To compensate for the seedy location, they run a tight ship here, with no alcohol or visitors allowed. Rooms (and even communal baths) are clean and cost $8–$10, with private bath $12–$14 (cash only).

UNDER $10 • Hotel El Pacífico No. 1. El Pacífico is a popular stop for European cyclists on their way up or down the peninsula. The basic rooms cost $7 with bath, or $4.50 without. The private baths are surprisingly clean, and the communal ones are satisfactory, but the thin walls make for a potentially noisy evening. Ask and the owners may allow you to use the kitchen facilities. *Gastelum 235, between Calles 2 and 3, no phone. 30 rooms, 12 with bath. Luggage storage. Cash only.*

UNDER $15 • Hotel Cinderella. Run by a family, this quiet, tidy motel is gated to ensure no unwanted visitors. The small but clean double rooms with quirky bedspreads cost $12. *Castillo 198, at Calle 2, tel. 617/8–11–94. 8 rooms, all with bath. Luggage storage. Cash only.*

Joker Motel. It's hard to miss this eccentric, brightly colored hotel on Highway 1 south of town. All of the clean, spacious rooms have TVs and balconies with views of the sea. Doubles cost $14, with private bath $16. *Hwy. 1, Km 12.5, tel. 617/6–72–01. 40 rooms, 20 with bath.*

Motel Gris. Only two blocks southeast of López Mateos, this pleasant motel with friendly management attracts families and backpackers alike. Rooms with air-conditioning, TV, and big comfy beds cost $15 for one or two people. *Calle 2 No. 1180, between Castillo and Mar, tel. 617/8–26–13. 25 rooms, all with bath. Luggage storage. Cash only.*

CAMPING • Playa el Faro has a nice stretch of white sand for camping if you don't mind being 10 km (6 mi) from town. Facilities include toilets and showers. A site for a car with two people costs $7, motorcycles $2, and only 50¢ for people without a vehicle. La Bufadora (*see* Near Ensenada, *below*) is also a popular camping spot.

FOOD

Ensenada's specialty is fish tacos. You can find the best and cheapest at the many seafood stalls surrounding the **fish market** or in the pink **Plaza de Mariscos** (Costero, at Virgilio Uribe). Besides the mouth-watering tacos, piled high with cilantro, salsa, guacamole, onions, and tomatoes, you can also buy fresh seafood cocktails and *mariscos* (shellfish) prepared in a variety of ways. Cheap restaurants serving standard, nonfish Mexican dishes can be found between Calles 2 and 3 and between Miramar and Gastelum.

UNDER $5 • Mariscos de Bahía de Ensenada. Locals recommend Mariscos as the best place in Ensenada for fresh and inexpensive seafood, perfect for a long, sit-down meal. The tortilla-maker in the window attracts some tourists, but Mexicans usually outnumber foreigners. Anything that's not seafood is expensive, but shrimp, squid, and fresh fish cost $5 or less. *Riveroll 109, at López Mateos, tel. 617/8–10–15. Cash only.*

Pueblo Deli and Café. Locals and tourists come here to enjoy wine, beer, and California cuisine. It's a great place for breakfast, serving omelets ($4), French toast, and poached eggs. Vegetarians will be delighted by their salads. *Ruíz 96, between Calle 1 and Virgilio Uribe, tel. 617/8–80–55. Cash only.*

Restaurant-Bar Corralito. This 24-hour joint looks sketchy from the outside, and the interior is oddly decorated from floor to ceiling with old cigarette cartons. However, it draws large local crowds for terrific traditional Mexican chow. *Huevos rancheros* (ranch-style eggs; with spicy tomato sauce) served with lots of beans and tortillas costs $2.25. *López Mateos 627, tel. 617/8–23–70. Cash only.*

UNDER $10 • El Charro. El Charro serves excellent spit-roasted chicken, dished up with tortillas and condiments; half a chicken costs $8. The restaurant is built like a log cabin—complete with fireplace—and is situated at the heart of the tourist zone. A bottle of wine from the Bodegas de Santo Tomás (*see* Worth Seeing, *below*) is the perfect complement to your meal. *López Mateos 475, near Gastelum, tel. 617/8–38–81. No breakfast.*

The riches of northern Baja's waters are displayed at Ensenada's fish market, at the north end of Boulevard Costero. Visit in late afternoon to watch the pangas (fishing boats) arrive with the day's catch.

CAFES • Café Café. The hippest place in town is decorated with recycled furniture, paintings by local artists, and a rack of vintage clothing. Play a game of backgammon, drink coffee flavored with molasses ($1), or chat with Memo (the owner) and his friends about Zapatista politics. (¡*Que siga la lucha!*). *López Mateos, near Gastelum, tel. 617/8–35–44. Closed Tues. Cash only.*

WORTH SEEING

The remnants of Ensenada's "frontier" past are still visible in the northwest part of the city, especially along Avenida Reyerson. **Parque Revolución** (between Calles 6 and 7 and Obregón and Moctezuma) offers shady benches where you can escape the summer heat. **Bodegas de Santo Tomás** (Miramar 666, between Calles 6 and 7, tel. 617/8–25–09; open daily 9–4) is Baja's oldest commercial winery, founded by the Dominican fathers of the Santo Tomás mission. The grapes are grown 50 km (30 mi) south of the city, but wine production was moved to this large warehouse in the middle of Ensenada in 1934. Half-hour bilingual guided tours ($2), given daily at 11 AM, 1 PM, and 3 PM, end with wine tasting. The **Museo de Historia de Ensenada** (tel. 617/7–15–07; admission $1; open Tues.–Sun. 10–2 and 3–6), in the old **Hotel Riviera del Pacífico** on López Mateos, depicts Baja's history; afterward you can tour the gardens of the grand old resort hotel. Make the short climb up the hill overlooking Ensenada to find a statue of the serene Hindu goddess **La Diosa Tara**, a recent gift from the Nepalese government. Visiting her will bring you knowledge, compassion, and great views of Ensenada.

FESTIVALS

From May 15 to 19, the **Ensenada fair** marks the city's foundation with live musical performances, *baile folklórico* (folk dancing), and carnival rides. During the **Vendimia** (wine festival; August 2–11) local wineries exhibit their famed wines and the newly crowned Queen of the Harvest heads a raucous parade down Boulevard Costero.

OUTDOOR ACTIVITIES

The **El Faro** and **Estero** beaches, 10 km (6 mi) south of town, offer moderate waves for swimming. Rent a horse ($8–$10 per hr) on the beach and gallop along in the sand, or explore sand dunes in a four-wheel drive or ATV. You can rent ATVs ($20 per 3 hrs) at either El Faro or Estero. For directions to the beaches, *see* Getting Around, *above*.

WATER SPORTS • Ensenada is an angler's town. Most sportfishing outfitters are next to the fish market, just off Boulevard Costero, including **Gordo's Sport Fishing** (tel. 617/8–35–15), where they'll take you out to sea for $35 per day. If you prefer fish as swimming companions rather than entrées, try snorkeling at **El Faro** and **Estero** beaches, or off the **Banda Peninsula.** Here you can see surfperch, rockfish, barracuda, dolphins, and sharks (most of which do not eat people). Well-used masks, snorkels, and fins ($6 a day) can be rented from several beachfront *palapas* (thatched huts) in **Maneadero,** the area immediately south of Ensenada. Scuba equipment can be rented and scuba dives arranged in La Bufadora (*see* Near Ensenada, *below*).

The best surfing is north of Ensenada, but the rocky shore here is dangerous for beginners. Waves aren't as vicious near El Faro and Estero beaches; **Sam's Beach Toy Rentals,** at Estero, rents surfboards for $10 a day. They also rent boogie boards ($5 a day) and sea kayaks ($20 a day). Sam's is 1½ km (¾ mi) from Highway 1 at the Estero Beach turnoff; contact them through the Estero Beach Hotel (tel. 617/6–62–25).

AFTER DARK

Ensenada's nightlife centers around the intersection of López Mateos and Ruíz. Take your pick from a number of dark, neon-lit nightclubs that feature loud American music and crowds of college students from Southern California. The ever-popular **Papas and Beer** (López Mateos, at Ruíz, tel. 617/4–01–45) provides boogie and $2 beers nightly until 3 AM. At **Bar Andaluz** (inside the Hotel Riviera del Pacífico, tel. 617/7–17–30; closed Mon.), dance to Mexican music like salsa and cumbia with Ensenada's older, more cultured residents. **Hussong's Cantina** (Ruíz 113, at López Mateos, tel. 617/8–32–10) is a historic drinking establishment that has retained its character despite its popularity with tourists. A number of **billiard halls** line Calle 2 between Gastelum and Miramar. Afternoons are the best time to play; by night crowds (mostly local men) make it impossible. **Coyote Club** (Costero 1000, near Diamante; open weekdays until midnight, weekends until 3 AM) is the only gay bar in Ensenada.

NEAR ENSENADA

LA BUFADORA

Although the rugged cliffs south of Ensenada are spectacular in their own right, the main attraction here is the dramatic blowhole, La Bufadora, which sprays water and foam as high as 180 ft into the air. Local legend has it that the geyser's real source is a whale that ventured beneath the rocks as a calf and grew too big to escape. The blowhole is outside the town of **Punta Banda,** 45 minutes south of Ensenada, and is easy to reach via public transport (*see* Getting Around *in* Ensenada, *above*).

Dale's La Bufadora Dive (Calle 10 No. 320, just off the main road at La Bufadora, tel. 617/3–20–92; open weekdays 8–3, weekends 8–6) rents complete scuba equipment ($25) or snorkel gear ($15) and offers boat dives into the depths of La Bufadora ($50 for one or two people, $20 per additional person). Dives are daily at 9 AM and noon. Dale also rents out a cheery guest house ($10 per person per night) near his shop, which sleeps up to 15 people. Call for more information or reservations. **Rancho La Bufadora** (Calle 10 No. 305, right across from Dale's, tel. 617/8–17–72) has primitive campsites (no water or hook-ups) for $5 per night for a carload of two; each additional person is 50¢ extra. You can also camp at nearby **La Jolla Beach Camp** (Carretera La Bufadora, Km 12.5, tel. 617/3–20–05, fax 617/3–20–04), which charges $6 for two people and $1.50 for each additional person. The camp has showers and a minimart.

SAN FELIPE

Folks who love fishing, sailing, or off-roading congregate in San Felipe, on the northern coast of the Sea of Cortés. Although the extremely hot summers and desert surroundings prevented permanent settlement until the 1920s, in recent decades this small beach town has gained in popularity. With the completion of Highway 5 from Mexicali in 1951, fishermen came to San Felipe, soon to be followed by other sport lovers. Today sailors from all over Mexico and the United States show up in April and October to compete in Hobie Cat races. During **Carnaval** (Feb. 16–20) the town comes to life with parades, dances, and sporting events; over spring break (late March to early April), college students from the States turn the town into one big keg party. On June 1 **Día de la Marina Nacional** is celebrated with colorfully decorated boats, which parade through the water in front of the *malecón* (boardwalk). If you'd rather have the town to yourself, come in July and August, when temperatures averaging 37°C (100°F) drive most sane individuals away.

BASICS

CASAS DE CAMBIO • Prestaciones de Servicios Mitla (corner of Mar de Cortés and Chetumal, tel. 657/7–11–32; open daily 9–9) changes traveler's checks and cash. **Bancomer** (Mar de Cortés 165, tel. 657/7–10–51; open weekdays 8:30–2) has an ATM that accepts Visa.

MEDICAL AID • Dr. Ubaldo Espinoza Ángel (Mar de Cortés 238, tel. 657/7–11–43) speaks English and is available Monday–Saturday 5 PM–8 PM. For emergencies, call **Dr. Gerardo Olvera Duran** at his office (Mar de Cortés 238, tel. 657/7–11–43) or at his home (tel. 657/7–15–84). **Farmacia San Ángel Inn** (Chetumal, near Mar de Cortés, tel. 657/7–10–43) is open weekdays 9–9, weekends 9 AM–10 PM.

PHONES AND MAIL • The **post office** (Mar Blanco 187, tel. 657/7–13–30) is open weekdays 8–3 and Saturday 9–1; from Mar de Cortés, walk five blocks away from the beach along Chetumal and turn left at Mar Blanco. **Farmacia San Ángel Inn** (*see above*) charges $1 for collect and credit-card calls to the U.S. and Canada, and you can also make regular long-distance calls.

VISITOR INFORMATION • The staff here speaks some English and can tell you anything you want to know about San Felipe, but not much about the rest of Baja. *Mar de Cortés 300, at Manzanillo, tel. 657/7–11–55. Open weekdays 8–7, Sat. 9–3, Sun. 10–1.*

COMING AND GOING

The bus station is about a 10-minute walk from "downtown"—the strip along the water where you'll find all of the hotels, restaurants, and rental shops. **Autotransportes de Baja California (ABC)** buses leave San Felipe's terminal (Mar Caribe, between Manzanillo and the Pemex gas station, tel. 657/7–15–16) daily at 8 AM and 6 PM for Ensenada (3½ hrs, $12), and at 6 AM and 7:30 PM for Tijuana (6 hrs, $17). Buses leave for Mexicali five times daily (2½ hrs, $8). None venture onto the unpaved coastal roads south of San Felipe, however, so your best bet for exploring that area is to rent an ATV (*see* Outdoor Activities, *below*).

WHERE TO SLEEP

If you're lucky, you might find an empty room at **José's House** (Manzanillo 244, no phone), where clean, air-conditioned doubles cost $20 (including use of the kitchen and a big front porch), cash only. Look for the pink neon sign behind the tourist office. The popular **El Cortés** (Mar de Cortés, tel. 657/7–10–56) has modern, clean rooms (doubles $25), all with an ocean view, air-conditioning, and a TV. There's a bar and restaurant on site. The Cortés is south of the center of town, along the beach strip. Camping is your cheapest option in San Felipe, and there are plenty of RV trailerparks along Mar de Cortés. **Playa Laura RV** (Mar de Cortés 333, tel. 657/7–11–28) rents spaces for cars ($13) or pedestrian campers ($5); the managers will usually keep an eye on your bags. However, pitching a tent along the beach north of the trailer parks won't cost anything, and toilets (50¢) and showers ($1) are nearby.

FOOD

It's no surprise that the meal of choice in this fishing town is seafood. Fish and shrimp tacos, *ceviche* (diced fish marinated in lime juice), and clams are served from picnic tables along the malecón for 60¢– $5. At **Restaurant y Mariscos Puerto Padre** (Mar de Cortés 316, tel. 657/7–13–35) you can eat breakfast for $2; seafood entrées are $6. **Los Gemelos** (Mar de Cortés 136, near Chetumal, tel. 657/7–10–63) serves seafood and Mexican dishes ($4) and has heavenly air-conditioning. All are cash only.

OUTDOOR ACTIVITIES

The desert sands bordering San Felipe to the west and the dunes and dirt roads to the south are inviting landscapes for motorcyclists and ATV riders. Rent a vehicle at **Bahía ATV** (Malecón 122, no phone) for $11 an hour, or negotiate a full-day deal. Riding on the beach is illegal, so unless you're willing to risk the $100 fine, don't try it. The calm surf and strong winds of the Sea of Cortés are perfect for windsurfing; launch your sailboard at any beach south of **Punta Estrella**. Boards can be rented from **Charters Mar de Cortés** (El Dorado Travel Center, on Airport Rd., tel. 657/7–17–78 or 657/7–12–77) for $20 an hour. The wide beach in town is also good for catching rays, playing Frisbee, and swimming.

WATER SPORTS • Tommy Sport Fishing (Costero 176, no phone) organizes sportfishing tours—the catch often includes white sea bass, corvina, dorado, and yellowtail. Trips require four or five people and cost $25 per person.

Enchanted Island Excursions (tel. 657/7–14–31), just north of San Felipe, rents Hobie Cats ($10 per hr), Skippers (small boats; $20 per hr), and kayaks ($5 per hr), as well as a *panga* (fishing boat; $100 per day). Call and they'll come pick you up in San Felipe. They also offer several half- and full-day land tours ($15–$50) and rent a "Party House" ($100 per night) that sleeps up to 18 people.

SAN QUINTÍN AND LÁZARO CÁRDENAS

The twin towns of San Quintín and Lázaro Cárdenas parallel Highway 1 for several kilometers, their ugly cinderblock stores and restaurants doing nothing to attract tourists. Separated by a bridge and 3 km (2 mi) of highway, both towns lie humble and windblown, although Lázaro Cárdenas has more markets and restaurants to choose from. Sadly, this is the last place to stop and stretch your legs before enduring the long, long bus ride to southern Baja.

BASICS

In Lázaro Cárdenas, **Banco Internacional** (Ignacio L. Alcérraga, north side of park, tel. 616/5–21–01 or 616/5–21–02; open weekdays 8–5, Sat. 9–2:30) changes cash or traveler's checks and has an ATM that accepts most bank cards. At the south end of San Quintín, **Lavamática M.A.C.** (Hwy. 1, tel. 616/5–25–83; open Sun.–Thurs. 7 AM–8 PM and Fri. 7–4) has automatic washers and dryers ($1 each). North of the bus station in Lázaro Cárdenas, **Farmacia del Parque** (tel. 616/5–26–65) is open 24 hours and works with English-speaking **Dr. Ricardo Rojo Marín.** You can make long-distance calls to the States from the pharmacy's telephone for $1 per minute, or a five-minute collect call for 50¢. In Lázaro Cárdenas, the **post office** (Carretera Transpeninsular, no phone) is open weekdays 8–5, Saturday 9–noon. They'll hold mail sent to you at the following address for up to 10 days: Lista de Correos, Valle de San Quintín, Baja California Norte, CP 22930, México.

COMING AND GOING

First-class buses stop in San Quintín and at the **Autotransportes de Baja California (ABC)** bus station (Carretera Transpeninsular, tel. 616/5–30–50), at the southern end of Lázaro Cárdenas. From here, three buses a day head south toward La Paz (19 hrs, $41) at 1 PM, 5 PM, and 10 PM, stopping in Guerrero Negro (7 hrs, $14). Seven buses go north to Tijuana (5 hrs, $12) at 6 AM, 9 AM, 10 AM, noon, 3 PM, 5 PM, and 7 PM, and three buses destined for Mexicali (7 hrs, $20) leave at 7 AM, 1 PM, and 4 PM, stopping in Ensenada (3 hrs, $7). **Autotransportes Aragón,** a smaller station farther north, has more frequent buses to Ensenada and Tijuana. To travel between San Quintín and Lázaro Cárdenas, catch a blue-and-white or green-and-yellow microbus from anywhere along the highway. Microbuses run every 15 minutes, daily 6–6.

WHERE TO SLEEP AND EAT

Motel Romo (Hwy. 1, tel. 616/5–23–96) is close to the Lázaro Cárdenas bus station and has nice rooms with spotless baths for $12 for a double (cash only). You can camp for free on **Playa Santa María**—pitch your tent around Hotel La Pinta and use their bathrooms at no charge. **Palapa El Paraíso** (about 300 yds north of Pemex in San Quintín, no phone) dishes up huge steaming plates of the region's chocolate clams (named for the brown coloring on their shells) for $2. **El Gran Triunfo,** a white shack on the north side of Motel Romo, is open 24 hours. It serves gigantic bean burritos and tasty fish tacos.

BAJA CALIFORNIA SUR

Southern Baja is a land for escapists. Thrills here include camping, fishing, and swimming, exploring the miles of lonely beaches, and, during January through March, whale-watching. Southern Baja's main road, Highway 1, runs through a number of small towns that bear the imprint of the Spanish missionaries who founded them as outposts of "civilization": Today their crumbling adobe missions, built with Indian labor, still survive. Dirt roads crisscross the *Sierra* (the mountainous interior), connecting isolated hamlets, ranches, abandoned missions, and small fishing villages.

GUERRERO NEGRO

The only sign of civilization on the nine-hour drive between San Quintín (*see* Baja California Norte, *above*) and San Ignacio is the wind-chilled town of Guerrero Negro. The town straddles the dividing line between the states of northern and southern Baja; in town, a monumental metal statue of an eagle marks the exact middle of Baja California. Coyote roam the cacti-filled desert on one side of Guerrero Negro, while the other side is hemmed by white-sand dunes and the shallow San José estuary. It's a lonely place, with an economy driven primarily by the world's largest solar-evaporated salt mine. Unless you're fascinated by salt-production techniques, there's no reason to stop in this town outside of whale-watching season (January through March).

If you *are* here during the whale-watching season, you're in for a treat. Some 20,000 gray whales pass by during their annual migration from the Bering Sea to Baja, and many stop to birth their calves in the warm, calm waters of Scammon's Lagoon, 27 km (16½ mi) south of town. This lagoon, also known as **Laguna Ojo de Liebre** (Hare's Eye Lagoon), is within the bounds of **Parque Natural de Ballena Gris** (Gray Whale Natural Park), established to protect the whales from poachers. Bring binoculars to better spy the playful whales, who spout water and toss their 13-ft-wide flukes high in the air. Farther south, in **Laguna de San Ignacio** (*see* Near San Ignacio, *below*), you can hire a local fisherman to take you out in his boat for a close encounter with the giant sea mammals—whales sometimes swim so close to the boats that you can touch their barnacle-encrusted backs. The town's **Festival de Las Ballenas** (Festival of the Whales), held during the first two weekends of February, honors these giants with regional food, dances, and the selection of a local queen. Year-round you can view a 40-ft gray whale skeleton in the plaza outside the **Biblioteca Pública.**

No public transportation goes to the Laguna de San Ignacio. If you want to hitchhike, look around the western part of town in the morning for tourists who can give you a round-trip ride (you don't want to get stuck at the lagoon). You can also join an organized tour in town, although reservations are recommended, especially during January and February. **Cabañas Don Miguelito** (*see* Where to Sleep, *below*) runs day-long trips to the lagoon ($35 per person, including lunch) and to the Sierra de San Francisco mountains (*see* Near San Ignacio, *below*) to view ancient cave paintings ($60 per person). Tours operate April–June, October, and November. **Tours Mario's** (inside Restaurant Mario's, tel. 115/7–08–88, fax 115/7–07–88) also organizes whale-watching trips and two-day tours to the cave paintings ($35 per person), both only available during whale-watching season.

BASICS

You can change money at **Banamex** (Av. Baja California, tel. 115/7–05–55; open weekdays 8:30–1), which also has an ATM that accepts Plus, Cirrus, Visa, and MasterCard. In an emergency, call the 24-hour phone lines for **police** (tel. 115/7–16–15), **fire** (tel. 115/7–05–05), or **ambulance** (tel. 115/7–11–44). The **Clinica Hospital** (Zapata, tel. 115/7–04–33) is open 24 hours a day for urgent care. **Farmacia San Martín** (Zapata, tel. 115/7–11–11; open Mon.–Sat. 8 AM–10 PM, Sun. 9–4) fills prescriptions and offers telephone service, $1 for collect calls and $2 per minute for calls to the States. Guerro's **post office** (open weekdays 8–3) is on a sketchy, unnamed street—walk past the plaza and turn left at the Lion's Club. The office will hold mail for you for 10 days if sent to the following address: Lista de Correos, Guerrero Negro, Baja California Sur, CP 23940, México.

COMING AND GOING

Autotransportes de Baja California (ABC) and **Águila** both serve the **Terminal de Autobuses** (near Highway 1, on the motel strip, tel. 115/7–06–11). Six daily northbound buses pass through Guerrero Negro between 2:30 AM and 10 PM, stopping in San Quintín (7 hrs, $14), Ensenada (10 hrs, $21), and Tijuana (12 hrs, $25). Seven daily buses head south between 4 AM and 11 PM, stopping in San Ignacio (2 hrs, $6), Santa Rosalía (3 hrs, $13), Mulegé (4 hrs, $14), Loreto (6 hrs, $16), and La Paz (11 hrs, $28).

GETTING AROUND

Guerrero Negro is divided into two distinct halves: the old section around the square, and the new commercial and tourist strip on Zapata near the highway. A yellow minibus travels between the two every half hour, or it's a 20- to 30-minute walk. Taxis are also an option, as is jumping in the back of some kind soul's truck. Dirt roads lead from town to Scammon's Lagoon and Bahía de Tortugas, but unless you're with a tour, you'll need your own transportation to reach either.

WHERE TO SLEEP

Although the hotels near the bus station look cheap, only a few are within the budget traveler's reach. All fill up December–March, so call ahead for reservations. In the new part of town, reasonably priced options include **Hotel San Ignacio** (Zapata, tel. 115/7–02–70), doubles are $17; **Motel Las Ballenas** (behind El Morro, tel. 115/7–01–16), with tidy rooms cost $16 (double); and **Motel Brisa Salina** (Zapata, tel. 115/7–13–25), which charges $13 for doubles. All of the rooms at these hotels have air-conditioning and color TVs, but Motel Brisa Salina, with its well-kept courtyard, has the most charm of the

THE BOOJUM TREES OF BAJA

Mexico's boojum trees, shaped like upside-down carrots, seem like something out of a Dr. Seuss book. These odd trees only grow in a tiny section of the Baja California desert, near Highway 1, one hour south of Guerrero Negro. You can't miss them, since boojum trees can grow to be 90 ft tall and tower awkwardly over other desert flora such as datillos, elephant trees, and even giant cardon cacti.

The boojum's common name, "cirio," was given by Spanish missionaries who thought its hanging yellow flowers resembled the slender candles (cirios) used in churches.

three. On the right as you exit the bus station, look for **Malarrimo** (Zapata, tel. 115/7–02–50), which has 10 beautiful, quiet rooms with private baths and TVs for $25 (doubles). Malarrimo is run by the same management as the adjacent **Cabañas Don Miguelito,** an RV park that charges $10 per car space and $5 per tent space with two-person occupancy ($2 for each additional person).

FOOD

In Guerrero Negro you don't have to wander far from the bus terminal to eat well. **El Taco Feliz** (tel. 115/7–06–59), next door to the bus station, is praised by locals and has great Mexican dishes ($2.50–$15). If you're lucky, the friendly owner might even call up the local radio station and have them broadcast a *bienvenida* (welcome) for you. Around the first bend in Zapata there are a string of cheap eateries: **Café Alejandra** (just past the first Pemex station; cash only) sells egg dishes and burgers ($2). In the evenings, street vendors sell hot dogs smothered in beans and chile for $1.

NEAR GUERRERO NEGRO

THE LONELY COAST

About 35 km (21 mi) southeast of Guerrero Negro is the hot, dry Vizcaíno Desert. Although arid, this Biosphere Reserve is no barren wasteland: plants such as *tillandsia recurvata* (ball moss) and *datillo* (a.k.a. *yucca válida,* a plant that resembles the Joshua tree) thrive in the harsh environment and can grow to be several centuries old. The small farming community of **Ejido Vizcaíno** also thrives in the middle of the desert, using deep wells to grow crops such as tomatoes, onions, chiles, and grapes. At the peninsula's northern edge is a junk collector's dream come true: **Playa Malarrimo,** otherwise known as Scavenger's Beach. Here the shoreline lies perpendicular to the Pacific Ocean's currents, and the result is miles of washed-up, jumbled ocean debris. The southern side of the peninsula, from **Bahía de Tortugas** to **Punta Abreojos** (a prime surf spot) is an empty stretch of coastline. From January to mid-March you can see whales calving in **Laguna Ojo de Liebre,** and sea turtles laying eggs in the small **Bahía de Tortugas. Tours Mario's** (*see above*) arranges nature excursions to the area, and the people at **Casa de la Fauna** (Domingo Carballo y Ruíz Cortínez, tel. and fax 115/7–17–77; open weekdays 8–4) in Guerrero Negro have good maps if you'd like to explore on your own. To get to the Lonely Coast, take a bus toward San Ignacio and have the driver let you off at Ejido Vizcaíno. Ask around there for a guide; for a small fee, someone will undoubtedly show you around.

SAN IGNACIO

San Ignacio was built where an underground spring spilled out into the desert, creating an oasis filled with birds, insects, flowers, and fruit trees. Date palms, introduced by Jesuit missionaries, dominate the landscape. The tiny town is a good departure point for whale-watching at **Laguna de San Ignacio** or for exploring 300-year-old Rupestrian cave paintings in the **Sierra de San Francisco** and the **Sierra de Santa**

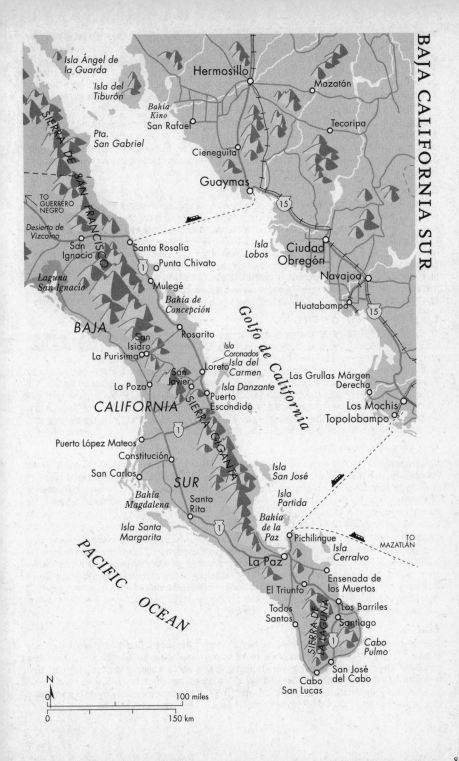

Isla Ángel de la Guarda

Isla del Tiburón

Hermosillo

Mazatán

Bahía Kino
San Rafael

Tecoripa

Pta. San Gabriel

SIERRA DE SAN FRANCISCO

Cieneguita

TO GUERRERO NEGRO

Desierto de Vizcaíno

Guaymas

15

San Ignacio

Santa Rosalía

Isla Lobos

Ciudad Obregón

1

Punta Chivato

Navajoa

Laguna San Ignacio

Mulegé

Bahía de Concepción

Huatabampo

15

BAJA

Rosarito

San Isidro

Isla Coronados

La Purisima

Loreto

Isla del Carmen

Golfo de California

La Poza

San Javier

Isla Danzante

Las Grullas Márgen Derecha

CALIFORNIA

Puerto Escondido

Los Mochis
Topolobampo

SIERRA GIGANTA

Puerto López Mateos

1

Constitución

Isla San José

San Carlos

SUR

Isla Partida

Bahía Magdalena

Santa Rita

Bahía de la Paz

1

Isla Santa Margarita

Pichilingue

TO MAZATLÁN

Isla Cerralvo

La Paz

PACIFIC OCEAN

Ensenada de los Muertos

El Triunfo

Todos Santos

Los Barriles

SIERRA DE LA LAGUNA

Santiago

Cabo Pulmo

1

San José del Cabo

N

Cabo San Lucas

0   100 miles

0   150 km

Marta. If you arrive from northern Baja, San Ignacio is the first town you'll encounter laid out in traditional Mexican fashion, with a zócalo at the center of everything. Life for San Ignacio's residents revolves around this tree-shaded square and the adjacent **Misión San Ignacio de Loyola.** Jesuits began constructing the mission's 4-ft-thick walls out of volcanic rock in 1716, but the structure wasn't completed until the Dominicans took over and finished the job in 1786. A particularly beautiful mass is held here Sunday at 11 AM. Next door, the free **Museo Local de San Ignacio** (open weekdays 9–4, Sat. 9–noon) has displays (in Spanish) about the region's cave paintings, including photographs and a small replica.

Many of the buildings around the square, shaded by Indian laurel trees, are more than a century old, their rough adobe walls layered with plaster and paint. Dates and grapes are harvested in the fall, and the town is justifiably proud of its locally made wine, goat cheese, and *cajeta* (a sweet made from goat's milk) for sale at the market on the zócalo. While usually sleepy, San Ignacio cuts loose during its annual five-day fiesta (end of July), with plenty of mariachi music and Tecate beer.

BASICS

You can get auto parts and 24-hour service at Autopartes Cadena (south side of highway, where the bus stops, no phone). The Centro de Salud (Independencia, at Valdina, no phone; open weekdays 8–2 and 4–6, Sat. 9–1) has an English-speaking **doctor.** Make **long-distance phone calls at Video Club Premiere** (on the plaza next to Jorge Fischer's store, tel. 115/4–03–97), where calls to the United States are $1.50 per minute (sorry, no collect or credit-card calls). The **post office** (open weekdays 8–3) is directly across the plaza from the video club. For information about the town and the surrounding area, ask Jorge Fischer at his grocery store-cum-**tourist information center** on the plaza (tel. 115/4–01–50; open daily 8–7). You can make reservations for his cave-painting and whale-watching tours (a good idea if you plan to be in the area Jan.–Mar.) by writing to him at: Domicilio Conocido, San Ignacio, Baja California Sur, CP 23930, México.

COMING AND GOING

The bus station consists of two shaded benches on the highway, 3 km (2 mi) outside town. The one next to the Pemex station is the stop for buses going north; cross the street for southbound buses. Seven buses go south to La Paz (6 hrs, $21) every day between 6 AM and 1 AM. Buses headed north to Tijuana (14 hrs, $19) and Ensenada (12 hrs, $17) pass through town five times a day. The staff at the store next to the Pemex station can tell you about changes in schedule, but you have to buy your ticket on the bus. The Pemex station is also an easy place to hitch a ride. The only way to ride from the bus stop into town is by taxi ($2), but the walk is pleasant, if sweaty. To return to the station, find one of the taxis that hover around the plaza day and night. If you're traveling by car, the road from Highway 1 to San Ignacio is easy, safe, and relatively well marked. The only thing you have to watch out for is tailgating, kamikaze bus drivers.

WHERE TO SLEEP

Running water can be sporadic at some San Ignacio hotels, so check the sink before you sign in. **Motel Posada** (Carranza, tel. 115/4–03–13) offers clean rooms ($20) with the most reliable water supply in town. To get here, follow the curving road that runs from the front of the mission. Family-run **Restaurant Chalita** (*see* Food, *below*) has two small, stuffy rooms ($11). Although there's a private entrance, the friendly owners encourage you to walk through their kitchen and backyard gardens. They also serve the best meals in town. Both are cash only.

CAMPING • San Ignacio has several fairly cheap campgrounds, although most have backbreakingly hard ground or are infested with insects. The best is **Las Candelarias,** a few hundred yards down the town's dirt road. Here you can camp for $2 in a well-maintained grove of date palms, but the bathrooms are simple outhouses without showers. The best swimming hole around is also here, which is free whether or not you're a guest. Right next door, **Trailer Park El Padrino** (1½ km/¾ mi south of Hwy. 1, near Hotel La Pinta, tel. 115/4–00–89) provides campgrounds ($7 per car) with toilets and showers, and their on-site restaurant serves cold beer and margaritas.

FOOD

There are only a few restaurants in town, the best of which is **Restaurant Chalita** (Hidalgo 9, west side of zócalo, tel. 115/4–00–82; cash only), where the elderly owners have turned their living room into a restaurant. The *comida corrida* (preprepared lunch special) costs $3, while the Mexican à la carte menu is less than $4. **Rene's Restaurant/Bar** (Hidalgo 39, no phone) has a thatched roof, a variety of breakfasts (including French toast), and simple dinners ($5–$7) of fish or shrimp. Stock up on camping supplies at Jorge Fischer's **CONASUP** grocery store (Hidalgo, on the plaza, tel. 115/4–01–90).

NEAR SAN IGNACIO

Gray whales stop in **Laguna de San Ignacio** between January and March during their annual migration from Alaska to Baja. The lagoon is two hours southwest of San Ignacio, 74 km (46 mi) along rough dirt roads, so you'll either need to drive a sturdy car or hitch and expect to be stranded for a while. Once there, hire a local fisherman to take you out in his boat (about $20). A little south of the lagoon is **Punta Abreojos,** a local surf spot with no amenities. To reach these places, follow Highway 1 south and watch for signs leading you to the dirt roads.

To reach the **cave paintings** in Sierra de San Francisco and Sierra de Santa Marta, you'll need to make a mule-back trek through Baja's high desert mountains. The trip is spectacular in its own right, and the caves are one of Baja's most incredible experiences. The now-faded, multicolored paintings depict giant men, fish, deer, hunting scenes, and religious rituals. When the missions in the area declined, many indigenous Baja Californians fled to the Sierra de San Francisco, where their descendants remain today, living off their gardens, goats, and, more recently, fees from guiding visitors to the caves. From San Ignacio you'll need to drive or hitch to reach the trailhead; once there, it's easy to find a guide. Admission to the caves, including a guide, is $10; mules to get you from cave to cave cost another $10 per day, and the trip to Sierra de San Francisco takes two to three days.

If you don't have your own transportation and don't want to hitch, talk to Oscar Fischer of San Ignacio's Motel Posada (see Where to Sleep, *above*), or his nephew, Jorge Fischer (see Basics, *above*). Both take up to six people on day-long trips to the caves for $120 (price includes guide and transportation by both car and mule). Jorge Fischer will drive you to Rancho San Francisco or Rancho Santa Marta, where you head out on mules to explore the caves. If you don't want to go back to San Ignacio immediately, you can camp at the caves, where local ranch hands cook dinner. Oscar also runs tours to the Laguna San Ignacio ($45 per person), a two-hour drive and two-hour boat ride. Jorge will do it for $20–$120 per person, depending on the number of people and type of boat. That said, the whale-watching is better and cheaper from Guerrero Negro (see above).

> *Santa Rosalía is home to Iglesia Santa Bárbara, a prefabricated iron church designed by Alexandre Gustave Eiffel (of Tower fame). It was imported from Europe by the mining company that founded the town.*

SANTA ROSALIA

Traveling south down Highway 1 from the U.S. border, Santa Rosalía is the first town you'll encounter on the Sea of Cortés. Founded by a French copper-mining company in the mid-1800s, Santa Rosalía looks unlike any other town in Mexico: As a company town, it was carefully laid out so that each rank of employees lived in a row of identical houses; the most important French mining officials were given houses in the hills high above town. All of the French-style buildings, with their long, sloping roofs, neatly fenced porches, and *mecedoras* (rocking chairs) were constructed with wood imported from Europe. Some locals have blond hair or East Indian features, testament to the varied ancestry of the town's original workers: native Californian, French, East Indian, and Chinese people.

When the mining company left in the early 1950s, Santa Rosalía's economy hit a slump and never recovered. Today, most residents make their living from the sea or by working in plaster mines on nearby Isla de San Marcos. Santa Rosalía is one of Baja's poorer towns, with an unkempt central square and houses in need of repainting. But although lodgings in this town may be a little sketchy, locals are kind to strangers—in two days you'll recognize everyone and everyone will recognize you. There are no good beaches in Santa Rosalía proper; explorers must go 3 km (2 mi) north of town to rocky **Playa Santa María** for surfing and clam-digging, or to the more isolated shoreline near the fishing village of **Punta Chivato.**

BASICS

Autopartes Plaza (Constitución, tel. 115/2–12–34; open daily 8 AM–9 PM) has a helpful, English-speaking staff and stocks almost any car part you could need. You can change cash and traveler's checks or get a cash advance on a Visa or MasterCard at **Bancomer** (tel. 115/2–02–65; open weekdays 8:30–2) or **Banamex** (tel. 115/2–09–84), both on Obregón, at Altamirano. There are new, working **Ladatel phones** on the plaza and around town. You can make collect calls by dialing 09 from the pay phone outside the ferry terminal (see below). The **post office** (Constitución, between Calle 2 and Altamirano, tel. 115/2–03–44; open weekdays 8–3, Sat. 8–noon) will hold mail sent to the following address for 10 days: Lista de Correos, Avenida Constitución, Santa Rosalía, Baja California Sur, CP 23920, México.

The **police** can be reached at 115/2–02–90 or 115/2–05–05; the **fire** department can be reached at 115/2–01–88, and the number for the **Cruz Roja** is 115/2–06–40. For less urgent medical attention, try **Farmacia Central** (Obregón, at Plaza, tel. 115/2–20–70, fax 115/2–22–70; open Mon.–Sat. 9 AM–10 PM, Sun. 9–1 and 7–10), where the English-speaking Dr. Eduardo Antonio Chang Tam can help with general medical problems. The pharmacy also has fax service and a caseta de larga distancia, but calls must be paid for in cash.

COMING AND GOING

BY BUS • Autobuses de Baja California (ABC) (tel. 115/2–01–50) buses run from the terminal south of town on Highway 1. The terminal is a quick taxi ride ($1.50) or 10-minute walk from downtown. Seven buses head south daily between 8 AM and 2 AM, stopping in Mulegé (1 hr, $3), Loreto (3 hrs, $7), and La Paz (8 hrs, $17.50). Five buses a day go north to Mexicali (16 hrs, $38), stopping in Guerrero Negro (3 hrs, $13) and Tijuana (14 hrs, $32). To reach the beach at Punta Chivato, hop on any southbound bus and ask the driver to let you off. You can also try to catch a ride at the Pemex station, on Highway 1 near the bus terminal.

BY FERRY • Sematur (tel. 115/2–00–13 or 115/2–00–14), offers biweekly ferry service from Santa Rosalía to Guaymas, in the state of Sonora (*see* Chapter 4). The ferry terminal is off Highway 1, a five-minute walk south from the center of town. Ferries to Guaymas (7 hrs; $15 regular class, $30 tourist class, which includes a four-person cabin) leave Wednesday and Sunday at 8 AM. To bring a car to the mainland, get a car permit from the **Delegación de Servicios Migratorios** offices, next to the ferry office (for more information on car permits, *see* Chapter 1). The office is open sporadically; the best time to catch them is around 3 PM on Tuesday and Friday, when the ferry arrives from Guaymas. Note that bringing a car is expensive: They charge by size, and even the smallest car costs $160.

WHERE TO SLEEP

The 110-year-old **Hotel Francés** (Jean Mitchel Cousteau, tel. 115/2–20–52) has a huge front porch with a view of the sea, an excellent place to sip a margarita while enjoying fresh seafood ($7–$10). The handsome rooms ($26) with showers and bathtubs are a worthwhile splurge; there's a hotel pool. **Hotel Minos** (Obregón, at Calle 10, tel. 115/2–10–60) charges $17 for rooms with air-conditioning and TVs. A cheaper option is the clean and centrally located **Hotel Olvera** (Plaza 14, tel. 115/2–00–57). Doubles are $11 ($13 with air-conditioning) and have TVs. Hotel Olvera accepts cash only. The closest place to camp is **RV Park San Lucas Cove,** on the beach 14 km (9 mi) south of Santa Rosalía, off Highway 1. They charge $6 a night per vehicle (cash only), and have 20 campsites with new flush toilets and hot showers.

FOOD

Santa Rosalía has a few decent restaurants, but the stands selling fresh fish tacos during the day and beef tacos or quesadillas at night are the way to eat well. Just be sure to get your snacks before everything closes at 10 PM. For a sit-down meal, **Steak House Don Ramón** (Constitución, at Plaza, no phone; closed Sun.) serves breakfasts ($2) of chimichangas or cheese omelets, and Mexican entrées for less than $4. The bakery **Panadería El Boleo** (Revolución, at Calle 4) was established to supply this French mining company town with authentic baguettes. If you're up before 8 AM, peek through the side doors and watch the bakers loading dough into wood-burning brick ovens. Both are cash only.

OUTDOOR ACTIVITIES

Other than poking around the rusty copperworks (officially closed to the public) near the harbor, there's not much to do here but read in the shade, sweat in the sun, or go fishing. For the latter, contact English-speaking Ángel Jesús Rodríguez (tel. 115/2–00–11), who works at the **Santa Rosalía Marina** (on the water where Americans anchor their yachts) Monday–Saturday 8–3. His friends take tourist groups on fishing trips ($20 per person, $100 minimum): a five- to six-hour trip in a boat that fits five people. Land-lubbers can take a walk up the hill to the Hotel Francés (*see* Where to Sleep, *above*) to admire the large houses in *La colonia francesa* (the French neighborhood).

MULEGE

The Santa Rosalía River courses through Mulegé, meandering through stands of date palms and creating a seaside desert oasis just 18 km (11 mi) north of the spectacular beaches of **Bahía de Concepción** (see Near Mulegé, *below*). The calm, warm waters here, in a wide spectrum of blues, contrast sharply with the surrounding semidesert landscape. Mulegé's own rocky beach lies at the mouth of the river, 2 km (1 mi) east of town along the main road; although the beach is not as white-sand spectacular as those farther south, it's a pleasant place to walk and decent for swimming. Best of all, camping here is free. Mulegé is also a popular departure point for trips to the Cochimi Indian **cave paintings** in the surrounding area (see Tours and Guides, *below*). A guide is required to visit the caves.

Although everything from T-shirt and curio shops to recently paved roads caters to the town's budding tourist industry, Mulegé hasn't completely lost its small-town charm, nor has it erased traces of its colonial past. One such relic is the **Misión Santa Rosalía de Mulegé,** built in 1766 and reconstructed in the early 1970s. The mission is on a hill overlooking town: Follow Calle Zaragoza south from the plaza, turn right after you pass under the bridge, then follow the road uphill. The free **Museo Mulegé** (open daily 9–1) is on a hill on the far north side of town. The building functioned as a prison from 1906 to 1975, and now houses artifacts from the original mission, old mining lamps from Santa Rosalía, and arrowheads unearthed in the area. To reach the museum, take Calle Principal to the dirt path at the base of the hill and start walking up.

BASICS

For auto parts and service, talk to the folks at **Refaccionaria Mulegé** (Gral. Martínez, at Zaragoza, tel. 115/3–00–41; open Mon.–Sat. 8–1 and 3–7). Mulegé doesn't have a bank, but **El Peso de Oro** (Moctezuma 7, no phone; open Mon.–Sat. 9–1 and 3–7) will change cash and traveler's checks. You can wash clothes at **Lavamática Claudia** (Moctezuma, tel. 115/3–00–57; open Mon.–Sat. 8–6). Free collect calls can be placed at the **Minisuper Padillo** (Zaragoza and Martínez, tel. 115/3–01–90; open Mon.–Sat. 8 AM–9 PM), which doubles as a pharmacy.

The cave paintings of Trinidad, San Borjitas, and Piedras Pintas depict traditional hunting and religious rituals and are said to be more than 14,000 years old.

TOURS AND GUIDES • The tourist office is run by Javier Aguiar, the owner of **Hotel and Restaurant Las Casitas** (Madero 50, tel. 115/3–00–19). He can provide you with information on kayaking tours, fishing expeditions, and trips to see the Cochimi Indian cave paintings in Trinidad, San Borjitas, and Piedras Pintas (a guide is required to visit the caves). Another guide, **Kerry Otterstrom,** has written a book on the area, *Mulegé–Baja California Sur: The Complete Tourism, Souvenir and Historical Guide of Mulegé,* available at **Mulegé Divers** (see Outdoor Activities, *below*). Kerry is considered the best guide in town; unfortunately, he has no phone number and is difficult to reach. You can try to hunt him down at the restaurant **El Candil** (corner of Zaragoza and Madero) daily between 4 and 6 PM. **Ramón Monroy** leads tours to the San Borjitas caves—look for him at his restaurant (Plaza Márquez de León, at Col. Benavides, tel. 115/3–02–23), distinguished by a 6-ft chicken painted on the door. The day-long tours cost $55 per person, but Ramón is willing to negotiate.

COMING AND GOING

Mulegé is small and easy to navigate. If you don't have a car, it's a 30-minute walk or a five-minute bus ride to Mulegé's beach. The better beaches of Bahía de Concepción are 18 km (11 mi) to the south (see Near Mulegé, *below*).

At the entrance to town is a shaded bench that functions as the bus station. You can buy tickets for the bus just behind the bench, at the restaurant that doubles as a bus terminal. Seven northbound buses pass through, with stops in Santa Rosalía (1 hr, $3) and Tijuana (15 hrs, $31). Eight buses per day go south to Loreto (2 hrs, $4) and La Paz (7 hrs, $15). You can ask at the terminal when the buses are expected to pass, but you should arrive a half hour early and be prepared to wait—schedules are rarely kept. Buy your tickets a day before traveling to guarantee yourself a seat.

WHERE TO SLEEP

You have several options, from dirt cheap to downright luxurious, in Mulegé. At **Casa de Huéspedes Manuelita's** (Moctezuma, tel. 115/3–01–75) the facilities are spartan, but the private baths are fairly clean, and you pay $7 for a double. **Hotel Suites Rosita** (Madero 2, no phone) is a deal if you're traveling with friends. The huge apartment-style rooms come complete with kitchenette, living room, and air-conditioning, and cost $17 for up to four people. Both of the above are cash only. **Hacienda** (Madero, tel. and fax 115/3–00–21) is the perfect place to treat yourself. The French-Canadian owner has carefully restored this historic hotel, which has a pool, bar, restaurant, and large ballroom with fireplace. Rooms ($25) are usually full, so reserve in advance.

CAMPING • Camping is free on Mulegé's beach 3 km (2 mi) east of town, but it's not as safe or as peaceful as the beaches farther south. **Orchard RV Park Resort** (south side of the river, tel. 115/3–03–00), a ½-km (¼-mi) walk from town, is the closest and most deluxe campground, with clean, white-tile bathrooms, a volleyball court, a bonfire pit, and shady fruit trees. One person in a tent costs $6, two people $7, and space for an RV costs $15. Farther up the road is **Villa María Isabel** (tel. 115/3–02–21), a smaller RV park with laundry service, a pool, and a bakery serving 60¢ chocolate chip cookies (bakery open Oct.–June). Tent camping costs $5 per person with use of all on-site facilities.

FOOD

The most inexpensive restaurants in Mulegé are near the bus stop on Highway 1: Join the crowds waiting for great guacamole at **Taquería Doney's** (righthand side of Moctezuma, 1 block west of the bus station; closed Wed.). Directly across from the bus station, **La Cabaña** (Moctezuma, no phone) serves an egg-and-tortilla breakfast for $2, as well as Mexican lunch and dinner plates for less than $4. On Friday from October to June, head for **Las Casitas** (Madero 50, tel. 115/3–00–19) for the "mariachi buffet" ($5), a huge Mexican dinner accompanied by live mariachi music. Mexican and seafood dishes of all kinds are served for $6–$10. On weekends the restaurant doubles as a disco that stays open until 2 AM. All restaurants are cash only.

OUTDOOR ACTIVITIES

Kayaking is popular on Mulegé's palm-fringed river. **Baja Tropicales** at Hotel Las Casitas (Madero 50, tel. 115/3–00–19) rents kayaks for $25–$35 per day. Roy and Becky Maehoff of **Mexico Adventures** (Palapa 17, in front of Ana's Restaurant on Playa Santispac, tel. 115/3–04–09) charge $25 per day for a kayak, $30 with drinks. They also rent snorkeling gear for $5 per day and arrange tours of Bahía de Concepción for $39, which includes a lunch of clams that you collect yourself. For fishing trips, the best in town is Mario Yee at **Captain's Sport Fishing** (fax 115/3–02–69), who has day-long expeditions for $150. The folks at Las Casitas (*see* Food, *above*) can help you get in touch with Mario.

The warm waters of Mulegé usually offer good visibility and teem with colorful aquatic life. The best diving spots are off the Santa Inez Islands and are accessible only by boat; Miguel and Claudia at **Mulegé Divers** (Gral. Martínez, tel. 115/3–00–59; open Mon.–Sat. 9–1 and 3–6) offer scuba-diving forays for $40–$50 per person, depending on how much equipment you rent. They do snorkeling trips for $25 ($30 with gear) and rent bikes at $10 for four hours ($2 per each additional hour).

NEAR MULEGE

BAHIA DE CONCEPCION

The most beautiful beaches in Baja lie along Highway 1, 32 km (20 mi) south of Mulegé. The highway runs along 40 km (24 mi) of curvy coastline, where hidden coves open onto white-sand beaches and electric-blue water—excellent for snorkeling, scuba diving, kayaking, swimming, and windsurfing. The first beach you'll hit heading south is **Playa Punta Arena** (20 km/12 mi south of Mulegé on Highway 1), popular among sailboarders. **Playa Santispac,** 24 km (15 mi) south of Mulegé, can turn into RV-camper hell overnight, but for the most part it's a mellow stretch of sand with good facilities. Local entrepreneurs provide tourists with palapas ($5 per night), showers ($1), and fairly inexpensive restaurants. Sign up with **Baja Tropicales** (next to Playa Posada Concepción, fax 115/3–01–90) for a $39 kayaking excursion, complete with a guide knowledgeable about the birds, fish, and shells of the area. They also rent snorkeling gear ($5). A few kilometers to the south, the beautiful beaches of **Playa Escondida, Playa Los Cocos, Bahía Los Burros,** and **El Coyote** remain unexploited, and have more modest facilities (i.e., pit toilets and scattered palapas). **Playa Requesón,** 14 km (8 mi) south of El Coyote, surrounds a bay so shallow that you can walk across the sand bar to a small island. To reach any of these places, catch a southbound bus from Mulegé and ask the driver to drop you off on the highway in front of your beach of choice. To return to Mulegé, simply flag down a northbound bus.

LORETO

Life in Loreto revolves around fishing and not much else. For many years, this town was only accessible to the wealthy or adventurous who flew in on private planes or arrived by yacht. Today it plays host to fishermen from all over, who cast for dolphinfish, marlin, and sailfish. The beaches in Loreto are small and grungy; a more popular diversion is the reefs around **Isla del Carmen, Isla Coronada,** and **Isla Danzante,** which offer good diving and snorkeling. However, both Mexican and gringo residents prize their privacy and don't exactly welcome newcomers with open arms. You'll probably want to make your stay here a short one.

If you do stop here, two sights in Loreto are worth your time. The **Misión de Nuestra Señora de Loreto,** built in the late 1600s in the shape of a Greek cross, was the first of Baja's missions and is still the town's social and religious center. Beautifully restored in the early 1970s, the chapel is impressive for its masonry, wood ceiling beams, and gilded altar bearing the figure of the **Virgen de Loreto**—famous throughout Baja for her miraculous powers. Every September 8, the statue is paraded down from her mountain shrine to Loreto, where a fiesta with music, dancing, eating, and drinking is held in her honor. Next to the church is the **Museo de las Misiones** (tel. 113/5–04–41; admission $1.50; open daily 9–4), which features relics from missions throughout Mexico.

BASICS

You can change money at **Bancomer** (Salvatierra, at Madero, tel. 113/5–03–15; open weekdays 8–2:30) and let the people at **Lavandería El Remojón** (Salvatierra 79, no phone; open Mon.–Sat. 8–8, Sun. 8–2) do your duds. For medical attention, look for the English-speaking Dr. Moreno at the 24-hour **Centro de Salud** (Salvatierra 71, near Hotel Salvatierra, tel. 113/5–00–39). Pick up prescriptions and supplies from **Farmacia de la California** (Salvatierra 66, tel. 113/5–03–41; open daily 8 AM–10 PM). Make long-distance phone calls at **Caseta Soledad** (Salvatierra, tel. 113/5–03–50; open Mon.–Sat. 8–1 and 3–9, Sun. 8–1), where collect and credit-card calls are $1.50. The **post office** (Deportiva, tel. 113/5–06–47) is open weekdays 8–3 and Saturday 9–1. The **tourist office** (Palacio del Gobierno, on Madero, tel. 113/5–04–11) is open weekdays 8–5.

Stingrays lurk in the shallow waters off Loreto's beaches; as you walk in the water shuffle your feet to avoid stepping on one. If you get stung, clean the wound thoroughly; the pain should ease in three to five hours.

COMING AND GOING

The bus station (tel. 113/5–07–67), served by **Autotransportes de Baja California (ABC)** and **Águila,** is at the beginning of Salvatierra and Paseo Tamará, a 10-minute walk east of the town center. Five buses a day travel south to La Paz (5 hrs, $12) between 8 AM and midnight. Northbound buses to Tijuana (18 hrs, $41) leave at 3 PM and 9 PM; two others bound for Santa Rosalía (3 hrs, $7) leave at 2 PM and 5 PM. Morning buses heading in either direction are often very crowded, but after a stop or two, there's more room.

WHERE TO SLEEP

Most hotels in Loreto are geared toward anglers who have a larger lodging allowance than the average budget traveler. Although **Motel Salvatierra** (Salvatierra 123, tel. 113/5–00–21) is not the cheapest hotel in town or the closest to the water, its rooms are clean and air-conditioned, and doubles ($15) have great bathrooms. It's only a 5- or 10-minute walk to the town plaza from here, and the bus station is almost next door. **Hotel San Martín** (Juárez 4, at Davis, no phone) caters to young travelers from all over the world in this less-than-backpacker-friendly town. Doubles with fans are $9, but the hotel sometimes closes during the off-season months of July and August. Both are cash only.

If you can forgo the facilities, camp for free on Loreto's beaches. Camping at **Loremar** (Zaragoza and Green, 1 km/½ mi south of town) or **El Moro RV Park** (closer to the center, on Rosendo Robles) is also cheap; Loremar is nicer, though, and offers camping for three people, toilets, and showers for $10.

FOOD

The cheapest restaurants in Loreto are on Hidalgo, at the fork in Salvatierra. Of these, **Restaurant Acapulco** takes the cake with its enormous comidas corridas ($2) and friendly clientele. Sit at a sunny table outside **Café Olé** (Madero, near zócalo, tel. 113/5–04–96), which serves oatmeal and fruit salad at breakfast, plus American favorites like burgers, fries, and banana splits, all less than $3. For seafood, follow the fisherfolk to **El Embarcadero** (Calle de la Playa, up from Hotel La Misión, tel. 113/5–01–65; closed Mon.). Steamed clams are $4, and a fish dinner is $5. Restaurants are cash only.

OUTDOOR ACTIVITIES

Prices for fishing trips vary, so shop around. **Alfredo's Sport Fishing** (Calle de la Playa, tel. 113/5–01–65) offers excursions costing a hefty $100 for two people (negotiable during the low season; boat and fishing licenses included), plus $8 per rod. Alfredo's also rents cars for $56 per day or 25¢ per kilometer. To rent a car for the trip to San Javier (*see* Near Loreto, *below*), they charge $57. **Diamond Eden**

Loreto (6½ km/4¼ mi south of town, tel. 113/3–03–77) rents equipment and arranges fishing ($120 for 2 people) and kayaking excursions.

Islas del Carmen, Coronado, and Danzante are the best places for scuba divers to see dorado, yellow-tail, sailfish, roosterfish, and even sea lions. Snorkeling is also popular in the shallow water surrounding Nopoló and Puerto Escondido. **Deportes Blazer** (Hidalgo 23, tel. 113/5–09–11; open Mon.–Sat. 9–1 and 3–7) rents scuba equipment for $27 and snorkeling gear for $8. You can also just rent tanks ($7). Guided underwater tours aren't offered, but the staff has good advice for those doing it on their own.

NEAR LORETO

SAN JAVIER

The one-street village of San Javier is in the mountains, 32 km (20 mi) southwest of Loreto. The main reason to make the one-hour trek from Loreto is to see the beautiful **Misión de San Javier,** a well-preserved mission built in Moorish style, with domes and exquisitely detailed stone carvings. Construction on the mission began in 1699, but was abandoned two years afterward due to Indian attacks. The mission was finally finished in 1759. The town and surrounding ranches are more modest than the mission—most people here grow their own food and herd goats. Their houses consist of large palapas with a small adobe building for cooking and storing belongings. Days in this mountain desert are hot and the sunlight is punishing, but evenings are serene and beautiful. If you're in the area December 1–3, don't miss the big **Fiesta de San Javier,** which resounds with music, dancing, drinking, and horse races. The road from Loreto to San Javier is rough, and while taxis do make the trip for a large sum ($50), it's best driven in a high-clearance car or jeep; from Loreto's center, head east into the mountains, following the road marked with an arrow off Highway 1. You can camp for free in San Javier near the dam, or rent a room from Doña Elena; ask around. Bring water purification tablets or a supply of drinking water—they don't sell bottled water here.

LA PAZ

Although beautiful desert beaches are only 15 minutes away by bus, La Paz is not a beach town. Rather, this capital of southern Baja is a sophisticated city with a university and a good museum. If you're coming from the backroads of Baja, the size of La Paz may come as a shock, but the city maintains an intimate and friendly atmosphere; in a matter of hours you'll be able to navigate La Paz's streets, stopping to greet people along the way. Sadly, many tourists bypass La Paz: Mainland-bound travelers are most likely to whiz through on their way to pick up the ferry to Mazatlán or Los Mochis, and a new airport outside Los Cabos has siphoned off tourists arriving by plane. Yet the ocean surrounding La Paz contains spectacular rocky reefs, a black coral forest, and an enormous variety of marine life. Those visitors who do stay here enjoy excellent scuba diving, snorkeling, and kayaking.

La Paz was founded by Hernán Cortés in 1535 during his search for pearls (pearl diving continued until the 1940s) and was later developed by Jesuit missionaries. The town's social life is split between the main plaza and the malecón, which is lined with restaurants and bars. On weekend evenings, after older residents have finished their promenade along the water, the malecón transforms into a hangout spot for local youth.

BASICS

AMERICAN EXPRESS

The travel agency **Turismo La Paz** provides AmEx services, including personal check–cashing for cardholders; they'll hold letters (not packages) for up to one month. *Esquerro 1679, La Paz, Baja California Sur, CP 23000, México, tel. 112/2–76–76 or 112/2–83–00. Behind Hotel Perla. Open weekdays 9–2 and 4–6, Sat. 9–2.*

CASAS DE CAMBIO

Banco Mexicano (Arreola, at Esquerro, tel. 112/2–31–55; open weekdays 8:30–1:30) has shorter lines than AmEx (across the street) and changes cash and traveler's checks. However, AmEx has a 24-hour ATM that accepts Visa, MasterCard, Cirrus, and Plus.

EMERGENCIES

You can dial 06 from any phone in La Paz to reach the **police, fire** department, or an **ambulance.**

MAIL

The post office is one block from the main plaza. They'll hold mail sent to you at the following address for up to 10 days: Lista de Correos, Centro La Paz, Baja California Sur, CP 23000, México. *Revolución, at Constitución, tel. 112/2–03–88. Open weekdays 8–7, Sat. 9–1.*

MEDICAL AID

For serious medical attention, the **Centro de Salud,** on the corner of Altamirano and 5 de Mayo, is open weekdays 8–8. The **Cruz Roja** (Domínguez, between Bravo and Ocampo, tel. 112/2–11–11) is open 24 hours. The **Farmacia Baja California** (Madero, on plaza, tel. 112/2–02–40) is open Monday–Saturday 7 AM–11 PM, Sunday 8 AM–10 PM.

PHONES

You can make collect calls from any pay phone by dialing 09. **Librería Contempo** (Arreola 25-A, at Obregón, tel. 112/2–78–75) has long-distance phones ($1.50 a minute to the U.S.) and is a good place for a private conversation. *Open weekdays 10–3:30 and 5–9:30, Sat. 10–9:30, Sun. 9–5.*

VISITOR INFORMATION

The staff at the **tourist office** is knowledgeable and speaks English, but be prepared to ask lots of questions, because they don't offer information voluntarily (they may also not be open when they're supposed to be). Pick up maps and southern Baja's free English paper, *Los Cabos News,* here. *Obregón, at 16 de Septiembre, tel. 112/2–59–39. Open weekdays 8–8.*

COMING AND GOING

BY BUS

Autotransportes de Baja California (ABC) and **Águila** buses stop at the **main bus station** (Jalisco, at Héroes de la Independencia, tel. 112/2–42–70), a 30-minute walk or a $2.50 taxi ride from downtown. Downtown city buses marked IMSS will also let you off three blocks from the terminal. To get downtown from the terminal, take any city bus and get off at the mercado municipal (Revolución, at Degollado). First-class buses for Tijuana (22 hrs, $47) and destinations en route depart La Paz four times daily. Eight buses depart daily for Cabo San Lucas and San José del Cabo ($7). The Pacific route through Todo Santos (1 hr, $3) takes 2½ hours to Los Cabos—an hour less than the route via Los Barriles (2 hrs, $4). Águila buses also depart from the more convenient **Terminal Malecón** (Obregón, near tourist office, tel. 112/2–78–98), with more frequent service to Cabo San Lucas at the same price. Eight buses depart daily for Los Cabos (via Todos Santos), and seven run via Los Barriles. The bus to the beaches and the ferry terminal in Pichilingue (10 per day, 20 min, $1) also leaves from Terminal Malecón. On weekends buses continue past Pichilingue as far as El Tecolote. The last bus back to La Paz departs Pichilingue at 6 PM.

BY FERRY

Sematur offers passenger and vehicle service from Pichilingue to Topolobampo (near Los Mochis) and Mazatlán, but buying tickets is a huge hassle if you don't plan ahead. Boats for Topolobampo depart Pichilingue Monday–Saturday at 11 AM, arriving at 7 PM that evening. On Tuesday, however, the ship carries "dangerous cargo," and women are forbidden on board! Seats cost $15. The boat to Mazatlán (18 hrs) leaves daily at 3 PM; a seat costs $20 and a berth in a four-person cabin costs $60. Ferry tickets can be purchased one day ahead of time from the **Sematur** office (5 de Mayo, at Guillermo Prieto, tel. 112/5–38–33; open weekdays 8–1 and 4–6, weekends 8–1), but it's easier to buy tickets in advance from **Agencia de Viajes Yurimar** (5 de Mayo, near Domínguez, tel. 112/2–86–00; open weekdays 9–7, Sat. 9–2). To reach the Sematur ferry station, go half an hour south of La Paz to Pichilingue (*see* By Bus, *above*). Arrive at the station an hour before departure.

If you want to take a vehicle to the mainland, you'll need to obtain a **car permit.** Contact the La Paz tourist office (*see* Visitor Information, *above*) for assistance, or go to the ferry terminal's *váscula* (weighing station; next to ferry station; open weekdays 8–1) in Pichilingue. Bring your passport, driver's license, and registration or ownership papers. Then, with permit in hand, go to the Sematur office (*see above*) to reserve a space on board. Price varies according to the size of the vehicle, but an average-size car costs about $100. Plan to arrive at the ferry terminal four hours prior to departure.

BY PLANE

From La Paz, **Aero California** (tel. 112/5–10–23) and **Aeroméxico** (tel. 112/2–00–91) serve Mazatlán ($83 one-way), Mexico City ($180 one-way), and Los Angeles ($230 round-trip). The airport is 8 km

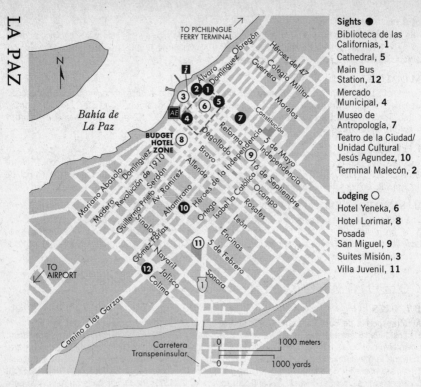

LA PAZ

TO PICHILINGUE
FERRY TERMINAL

*Bahía de
La Paz*

N

BUDGET
HOTEL
ZONE

TO
AIRPORT

Carretera
Transpeninsular

0   1000 meters

0   1000 yards

Sights ●
Biblioteca de las
Californias, **1**
Cathedral, **5**
Main Bus
Station, **12**
Mercado
Municipal, **4**
Museo de
Antropología, **7**
Teatro de la Ciudad/
Unidad Cultural
Jesús Agundez, **10**
Terminal Malecón, **2**

Lodging ○
Hotel Yeneka, **6**
Hotel Lorimar, **8**
Posada
San Miguel, **9**
Suites Misión, **3**
Villa Juvenil, **11**

(5 mi) north of town and taxis are the only transportation from town to the airport—a monopoly that is reflected in the price ($7).

GETTING AROUND

The downtown area doesn't follow the rest of the city's grid pattern, but most sights in La Paz are here, within easy walking distance of each other. Get your bearings from the cathedral and market (both on Revolución), which mark the limits of the downtown area. The malecón, called **Obregón,** runs along the water and is also a major reference point. To reach the main bus station, youth hostel, or theater and cultural center, catch a bus at the municipal market on Revolución at Degollado. The Pichilingue beach and Sematur ferry terminal are south of La Paz and are easily reached by bus (½ hr) from Terminal Malecón (*see* Coming and Going, *above*). From the ferry terminal, walk south for five minutes to Pichilingue beach. To reach any of the three beaches south of Pichilingue—**Puerto Balandra, Playa el Tecolote,** and **Playa el Coyote**—take the bus to Pichilingue, then hitch or catch a cab ($3). On the weekends, buses from Terminal Malecón run as far as Playa el Tecolote.

WHERE TO SLEEP

La Paz boasts a number of inexpensive lodgings with tons of character, especially in the downtown area. If you're traveling with several people, **Suites Misión** (Obregón 220, near Arreola, tel. 112/2–00–14) offers small, $25 suites that have a living room, kitchen, balcony with a sea view, and a bedroom with two double beds; reservations are necessary. The office is open 9–2 and 4–7:30; if it's closed, head next door to **Curios Mary** (tel. 112/2–08–15), the owner's jewelry and picture frame store. **Posada San Miguel** (16 de Septiembre, at Independencia, tel. 112/2–18–02) is a tiny, popular hotel with a pleasant inner courtyard. Doubles cost $11, but you must arrive by 1 PM to get a room. Camping in La Paz isn't worth it, considering the number of decent hotels in the city center for the same price. That said, campsites are abundant 2 km (1 mi) southwest of town and cost about $10 for two people with an automobile.

UNDER $25 • Hotel Lorimar. This hotel is a favorite among annual visitors to La Paz. It's on a small hill within walking distance of the malecón and has a communal patio with spectacular waterfront views. Each well-kept room ($22) has air-conditioning and a private tile bathroom. *Bravo 110, near Madero, tel. 112/5–38–22, fax 112/5–63–87. 20 rooms, all with bath. Restaurant.*

Hotel Yeneka. There are cheaper places around, but this is the funkiest hotel you'll find, with large, well-furnished rooms, a restaurant, and a resident pet monkey. The lobby resembles an artfully tended junkyard, complete with a rusty Model-A car. Doubles cost $20, and all have clean bathrooms. A bed in the new dormitory behind the hotel costs $12. *Madero 1520, between 16 de Septiembre and Independencia, tel. 112/5–46–88. 20 rooms, all with bath. Laundry ($2.50), luggage storage.*

HOSTELS

Villa Juvenil (CREA). In a sports complex outside the center of town, this hostel offers standard bunks ($4) in excessively air-conditioned single-sex dorms. The communal baths are well kept and there's a laundromat and grocery store nearby, but this place is rather inconvenient from downtown. Tell the staff if you'll be coming in after 11 PM so they can leave the gate open. Alcohol is not allowed. *5 de Febrero, at Carretera al Sur (Hwy. 1S), tel. 112/2–46–15. 70 beds. From bus station, walk down Jalisco and turn left on Camino a las Garzas. Or take bus marked CREA or 5 DE FEBRERO ($2). Reception open 7 AM–11 PM. Luggage storage. Cash only.*

FOOD

The nicest places to eat in La Paz overlook the water—though restaurants along the malecón are usually pricey. **El Camarón Feliz** (Obregón, at Bravo, tel. 112/2–90–11; no breakfast) is reasonably priced and right on the malecón, serving fish, crab, and *camarón* (shrimp) dishes ($5–$11). During happy hour (daily 6 PM–8 PM) drinks are two-for-one. Cheaper eats await downtown, especially at the daily **mercado municipal** (Revolución, at Degollado), where *loncherías* (snack bars) serve $3 comidas corridas. As you enter, the cooks yell out their offerings to draw your attention; visit **Conchería Colonial** (inside the market) for a seafood feast ($3).

UNDER $5 • Café Expresso. With patio tables overlooking the malecón, this is the place for hip locals to see and be seen. Scope out the crowd while munching on one of their deli-style sandwiches or sipping a cappuccino ($2). *Obregón, at 16 de Septiembre, tel. 112/3–43–73. No breakfast. Cash only.*

El Quinto Sol. La Paz's sole vegetarian restaurant/health food store sells granola, wheat germ, and vitamins. Mexican dishes are made with tofu or wheat gluten as a substitute for meat. For breakfast, have a bowl of yogurt, fresh fruit, and granola ($2.50). *Belisario Domínguez 12, at Independencia, tel. 112/2–16–92. 1 block from plaza. Closed Sun. Cash only.*

WORTH SEEING

La Paz is the place to stock up on high culture, especially if you've been trudging through the Baja backroads, where putting mainland-made salsa on a taco counts as a cultural activity. The modern **Teatro de la Cuidad** (Navarro, at Gómez Farías, tel. 112/5–00–04) presents folk dancing, music, and theater performances. Check the theater box office (open weekdays 10–1 and 4–8) when you arrive in town, because some excellent acts pass through La Paz and tickets are $10 or less. The theater is part of the **Unidad Cultural Jesús Agundez,** a complex that includes an art gallery and several monuments to heros of La Paz. **Biblioteca de las Californias** (across from the cathedral, in the old Municipal Palace, tel. 112/5–37–67) is a unique library with an extensive collection of material on Baja in both English and Spanish. They also have a free permanent exhibit of art depicting the missions of Baja and the colonial period. The library is open late May–September, daily 8–3; October–early May, daily 8–8. The small **Museo de Antropología** (5 de Mayo, at Altamirano; open weekdays 8–6, Sat. 9–2) provides information on the history and people of the peninsula and has an English-speaking docent to help you out. The museum has over 1,200 artifacts, as well as a botanical garden. A donation is requested, so leave a few pesos to be polite. If you're looking for something to do at night, head to **El Íntimo** (Esquerro 60; open Mon.–Sat. 7 PM–3 AM), one of La Paz's most popular bars. Besides offering live music every Monday, Friday, and Saturday night, they sell shots of Damiana ($1.50), a sweet liquor made from a native desert plant that's thought to be an aphrodisiac.

OUTDOOR ACTIVITIES

The beaches in La Paz are small and polluted, making swimming hazardous to your health. A better bet is to head to the beautiful, secluded beaches only minutes away from town. To the north are the gorgeous playas **Palmira, El Coromuel, Caimancito, Punta Colorada, Tesoro,** and **Pichilingue.** To reach them, take any bus bound for Pichilingue (*see* Coming and Going, *above*) and ask the driver to let you off at whichever beach you choose. Even better beaches, **Puerto Balandra, El Tecolote,** and **El Coyote,** lie beyond Pichilingue and can be reached by bus (weekends only), by cab ($10), or by thumb. El Tecolote is popular, with a restaurant, bar, and rest rooms. Puerto Balandra, a beautiful cove with white sandy beaches, shady palapas, and few gringos, was once a pirate's refuge.

The waters around La Paz also offer prime scuba diving. The most popular sites are around **Espíritu Santo** island, where clear waters provide excellent visibility almost year-round. For $96 per person, the English-speaking folks at **Viajes Palmira** (Obregón, between Rosales and Allende, tel. 112/2–40–30 or 112/5–72–78) offer a two-tank dive including equipment, guides, lunch, and a boat ride. Viajes Palmira also offers dive classes ($350 for a two-day course) and snorkeling trips to the island ($40). Full-day fishing trips including rods, licenses, a boat, and a guide are also available ($170 for two people), and whale-watching trips cost $80 per person in season (Jan.–Mar.). They also rent bicycles ($11 per day) and horses ($30 per day), and will take you on a sunset tour of the bay ($15, including champagne!). **Baja Diving Service** (Obregón 1665, near 16 de Septiembre, tel. 112/2–18–26, fax 112/2–86–44) offers an all-day scuba tour ($77), a one-tank night excursion ($45), and snorkeling ($40). They also rent kayaks ($50) and mountain bikes ($11 for 24 hrs), and sell fishing tackle and rods. If you're not keen on a package deal, rent scuba equipment here for $15. They also have four-day PADI certification courses for $400, equipment included. **Hotel Yeneka** (*see* Where to Sleep, *above*) offers guided kayaking tours ($42 per person per day) to the calm, reef-protected water about 30 minutes southwest of town.

LOS CABOS

In 1982 the Mexican government began a promotional blitz to propel Los Cabos into tourist consciousness. Its efforts were largely successful: Today San José del Cabo and Cabo San Lucas are Baja's primary tourist destinations. Unfortunately this popularity has turned Cabo San Lucas into a gringo Disneyland that's wall-to-wall luxury resorts and condominiums. San José del Cabo, on the other hand, has so far managed to avoid this fate and retains a certain modicum of charm and local identity. Several other towns in the Los Cabos area remain entirely off the beaten tourist path: Todos Santos is a lazy backwater, while Los Barriles and Buenavista are the secret playgrounds of surfers and windsurfers. The entire Los Cabos region offers kilometers of white beaches and warm, turquoise waters. But you'd better hurry—time is running out for the few gorgeous and isolated spots that remain.

SAN JOSE DEL CABO

Until recently, San José del Cabo dominated the tip of the Baja peninsula. Jesuits founded the town in the 1700s, taking advantage of an underground stream that surfaces nearby and creates a large natural estuary. The mission, zócalo, and other buildings erected during this period give San José del Cabo a sense of history; it still feels more like a real Mexican town than a tourist trap, despite all the slack-jaw gringos wandering about. The gazebo on the square is perfect for people-watching, while the 18th-century **Palacio Municipal** (Mijares, at Castro) is worth a peek for the cave-painting motifs in its courtyard. About 46 km (28 mi) northeast of San José del Cabo, **Cabo Pulmo** has the peninsula's only coral reef, and hundreds of brightly colored fish are visible in the clear water offshore.

BASICS

The best rates (and longest lines) for cashing traveler's checks are at **Bancomer** (Zaragoza, at Morelos, tel. 114/2–00–40; open weekdays 8:30–1:30). Rates at the exchange booth (tel. 114/2–00–40) farther up Zaragoza are not as good, but they're open Monday–Saturday 8 AM–9 PM and Sunday until 5. Almost all the restaurants, hotels, and shops in San José accept Visa, MasterCard, and AmEx, as well as traveler's checks. **Casitas y Casitas** (corner of Obregón and Hidalgo, tel. 114/2–24–64; open daily 8 AM–9 PM) has long-distance telephone service and charges $1 to make a collect call. Don't use the more upscale telephone office down the street near Zaragoza unless you want to pay twice as much for direct calls. The **post office** (Mijares, at Margarita Maza de Juárez, tel. 114/2–09–11; open weekdays 8–7, Sat. 9–1) will hold mail sent to you at the following address for up to 10 days: Lista de Correos, Blvd. Mijares, San José del Cabo, Baja California Sur, CP 23400, México.

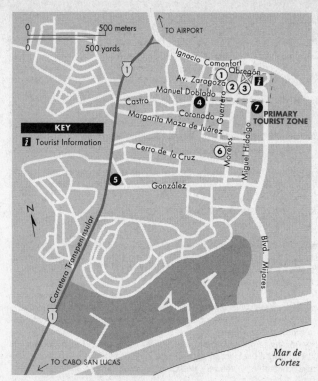

Sights ●
Bus Station, **5**
Mercado
Municipal, **4**
Palacio
Municipal, **7**

Lodging ○
Hotel Ceci, **2**
Hotel Colli, **3**
Hotel Consuelo, **6**
Hotel San José, **1**

KEY

i Tourist Information

TO AIRPORT

Ignacio Comonfort

Obregón

Av. Zaragoza

Manuel Doblado

Castro

Coronado

Margarita Maza de Juárez

Cerro de la Cruz

González

Guerrero

Miguel Hidalgo

Morelos

Blvd. Mijares

PRIMARY
TOURIST ZONE

*Mar de
Cortez*

Carretera Transpeninsular

TO CABO SAN LUCAS

500 meters
500 yards

The phone number for the **police** is 114/2–03–61 or 114/2–30–61; for the **Cruz Roja** (ambulance service), it's 114/2–03–16. **Lavandería VERA** (González, east of the bus station; open Mon.–Sat. 8–8) sells suds and has self-serve washers for $1.50; dryers are $2. Next to the zócalo, the **tourist office** (Zaragoza, at Mijares, tel. 114/2–04–46; open weekdays 9–3) carries mostly resort brochures and dispenses a tiny little town map. The staff's English isn't great, but they're eager to help.

COMING AND GOING

The bus station (tel. 114/2–11–00) is on González, near Highway 1, on the southwest edge of town. From here it's a 30-minute walk or $2 cab ride east down González and north up Mijares to the town center. Fourteen first-class buses leave daily for La Paz (2½–3½ hrs, $7), half traveling via Los Barriles (1 hr, $5) and the other half via Todos Santos (1½ hrs, $5.50). Ten first-class buses head to Cabo San Lucas (30 min, $1.50), and one leaves daily at 4 PM for Tijuana (26 hrs, $60); for more frequent departures to other destinations, transfer in La Paz. Another, more centrally located terminal is **Terminal Enlaces Terrestres** (Vicente Ibarra, at Doblado, no phone), about five blocks west of downtown. It has eight first-class buses daily to Cabo San Lucas (30 min, $1.50) that continue on to La Paz (2½ hrs, $7).

BY PLANE • The **Aeropuerto Internacional Los Cabos** is 11 km (7 mi) north of San José del Cabo. It's served by **Aero California** (tel. 114/3–08–48), **Mexicana** (tel. 114/3–04–12), **Alaska** (tel. 114/2–10–15), and **United** (tel. 114/2–28–81). **Yellow Taxi** colectivos shuttle people between the airport and San José del Cabo (15 min, $10) or Cabo San Lucas (30 min, $10–$15). They have a booth at the arrival gate and most of their yellow-and-black vans are air-conditioned. From town, any bus heading toward La Paz will drop you on the highway near the airport (15 min, $1), but you'll have to walk an easy 1½ km (¾ mi) from there.

WHERE TO SLEEP

If you've got camping gear, use it here—hotels are expensive and beautiful beach sites are plentiful along the coast. Otherwise, **Hotel Consuelo** (Morelos, above Cerro de la Cruz, tel. 114/2–06–43) is one of the cheapest places in town ($9 for a double), and it's a 10-minute walk from the center. Clean, well-ventilated **Hotel Ceci** (Zaragoza 22, near church, no phone) is smack dab in the center of the tourist zone; doubles are $9 with a fan, $10 with air-conditioning. **Hotel San José** (Obregón, at Guerrero, in

SURF'S UP IN ~~LOS CABOS~~

Los Cabos is rife with surfing spots that aren't on any official tourist maps, but surfers on pilgrimages from all over the world somehow still seem to find them. A few tips for newcomers: Nine Palms is for long-boarders, Punto Perfecto has Hawaii-size waves, and La Bocana is a freshwater estuary that has giant tubes, created when heavy rains open the river mouth. For consistently gut-wrenching waves, Playa Acapulguitos, Playa Monumentos, and Costa Azul are the beaches of choice for gringos and locals alike. Once you're in the vicinity, ask anybody with long hair and a tan to point you in the right direction.

front of Banco Serfín, tel. 114/2–24–64) has rooms with private bath ($10 doubles) and also offers laundry service and a long-distance caseta. All of the above are cash only. **Hotel Colli** (Hidalgo, near Zaragoza, tel. 114/2–07–25) offers quiet, secure doubles for $22, all with private bath. Rooms cost $4 more with air-conditioning, and prices rise during tourist season.

CAMPING • You can pitch your tent anywhere along the beach near town (though it's best to avoid the big hotels or the mosquito-ridden estuary), as long as you set up camp late, don't build a fire, and leave in the morning. A few kilometers down the road toward Cabo San Lucas you can set up at a more permanent surfer camp next to the **Costa Azul Hotel.** You can use the resort's outdoor showers on the beach to rinse off, but soaping up may get you some strange looks. Two trailer parks, **Brisas del Mar** and **Montanes de Palmillas,** outside town on the highway toward Cabo San Lucas, charge $15 for two people in a tent. They're expensive, but both have showers, flush toilets, a pool, laundry, and a restaurant.

FOOD

Food stalls at the daily **mercado municipal** (Castro, at Vicente Ibarra) serve seasonal fare and $2.50 comidas corridas—get here early, though, because food runs out by 4 PM. **El Café Fiesta** (Mijares 14, at Zaragoza, tel. 114/2–28–08) has endless refills on coffee and a patio from which to watch passersby. Their extensive vegetarian menu ($2–$4) ranges from lentil soup to tofu fajitas. **Café Rosy** (Zaragoza, at Green, no phone; closed weekends) is a more traditional Mexican restaurant with more traditional Mexican prices: Burrito and taco plates cost less than $3. Restaurants are cash only.

OUTDOOR ACTIVITIES

The water in front of most of San José's beach hotels conceals strong currents, and swimming can be dangerous; instead, both residents and tourists head to Hotel Palmilla's **Playa Palmilla,** 7 km (4½ mi) west of town. Rent surfboards ($15 a day), boogie boards ($8 a day), snorkel gear ($8 a day), fish tackle ($10 a day), and bicycles ($11 day) from **Killer Hook Surfshop** (Hidalgo, near Zaragoza, tel. 114/2–24–30; open Mon.–Sat. 9–8) The owner, Rafael, can fill you in on the best surf spots, as well as answer general questions about the surrounding beaches. For other choice local surf spots, *see box, above.* You can rent ATVs for $10 per hour ($40 for 9 hrs) at **Baja's Sports** (parking lot of Hotel Presidente, tel. 114/2–20–11; open daily 8–6).

AFTER DARK

For real disco action, head to Cabo San Lucas, a half-hour drive or $15 taxi ride away. Otherwise, **Bones** (Mijares, next to Hotel Presidente, tel. 114/2–02–11; closed Mon.) is a disco specializing in noisy explosions and fancy lightworks. Cover is $3 except Wednesday, when women get in free; drinks cost up to $5. **Iguana Bar & Grill** (Mijares 24, tel. 114/2–02–66) has live music on weekends. The crowd is a mix of locals and tourists.

CABO SAN LUCAS

Cabo San Lucas was originally a small fishing village where a few hardy or rich sportfishermen boated or flew in to battle with trophy-size marlin and sailfish. Over the past decade, however, spectacular growth has turned Cabo into a tourist nightmare. English is the lingua franca, U.S. dollars are expected, and precious water is used to grow lush grass in front of five-star hotels. The small town is congested, tacky, and expensive, although overdevelopment does mean all sorts of fancy water-sport equipment is available for rent. To discover Cabo as it existed before the landscape architects arrived (i.e., dirt roads and blowsy taco stands), stray a few blocks north of the tourist track.

BASICS

Money changers line Lázaro Cárdenas between Hidalgo and Matamoros, but U.S. dollars are preferred in most places, and credit cards and traveler's checks are widely accepted. Should you need pesos, **Bancomer** (Cárdenas, between Hidalgo and Guerrero, tel. 114/3–19–24) is open for money exchange weekdays 8:30–noon, and the **Serfín** branch (Cárdenas, at Morelos, tel. 114/3–01–91) in the Plaza Shopping Center has an ATM that accepts Visa, Plus, and Cirrus. The Cabo San Lucas **post office** (Lázaro Cárdenas, at 16 de Septiembre, tel. 114/3–00–48; open weekdays 9–6, Sat. 9–1) will hold mail sent to you at the following address for up to 10 days: Lista de Correos, Av. Lázaro Cárdenas, Cabo San Lucas, Baja California Sur, CP 23410, México. Public phones are common downtown, but you can place calls from most resort hotels in the area. For cash calls, the **Casa de Larga Distancia** (Lázaro Cárdenas, at San Lucas, tel. 114/3–00–80) is your best bet, but they charge a $1 connection fee if you call collect. There's no extra charge for local calls at the phones next to the elevators in **Hotel Plaza Las Glorias** (*see below*); just dial 0 first. You can make collect calls from pay phones by dialing 09 for the Mexican operator; don't use the blue phones that say DIAL 0 or you'll go bankrupt.

Forget the crowded, overpriced gringoville of Cabo San Lucas and get your rest and relaxation in La Paz, a big city with excellent beaches and the best selection of high culture on the peninsula.

For **police** call 114/3–00–57; for **Cruz Roja** (ambulance service) call 114/3–33–00. **Farmacia Rincón** (Blvd. Marina, in front of Plaza Las Glorias Hotel, tel. 114/3–07–95) is open 24 hours and has an English-speaking employee who can refer you to a doctor. **Libros** (Plaza Bonita, on Marina, tel. 114/3–31–71; open daily 9–9), has an adequate supply of best-sellers in English, as well as a selection of magazines and newspapers in both English and Spanish. The local **lavandería** (San Lucas, between 5 de Mayo and Constitución, tel. 114/3–20–25; open Mon.–Sat. 8–8) charges $2 for you to wash and dry your own clothes, or they will do it for you for $3.50. There are several booths around town that claim to be tourist information centers, but they generally can't offer more than a map and a smile. For thorough advice in English, visit the information desk at **Hotel Plaza Las Glorias** (Blvd. Marina, at center of town, tel. 114/3–12–20; information desk open daily 8–8).

COMING AND GOING

BY BUS • The **bus station** (Zaragoza, at 16 de Septiembre, tel. 114/3–04–00), two blocks north of downtown and 10 blocks from the hostel, is served by the **Autotransportes de Baja California (ABC)** and **Águila** bus lines. Frequent buses leave daily for La Paz (3 hrs, $7), San José del Cabo (30 min, $1.50), and Todos Santos (1 hr, $3). For other destinations, travel to La Paz and transfer.

BY PLANE • The Los Cabos airport is 48 km (30 mi) northeast of Cabo San Lucas and is shared with San José del Cabo; for more information, *see* Coming and Going *in* San José del Cabo, *above*. The cheapest way to reach the airport from Cabo San Lucas is on a bus (1 hr, $2) headed to La Paz via San José del Cabo, which will drop you off near the airport on Highway 1. If there are no taxis waiting to drive you the remaining 1½ km (¾ mi), the walk is easy. A taxi from Cabo to the airport (30 min) costs $10–$15.

WHERE TO SLEEP

In terms of lodging, Cabo San Lucas is the most expensive town in all of Baja California. At the **Hotel Mar de Cortés** (Lázaro Cárdenas 11, at Guerrero, tel. 114/3–00–32) rates for basic, well-maintained rooms start at $39 for one person, $44 for two. Perks include a tropical courtyard and inviting swimming pool. **Siesta Suites** (Zapata, tel. 114/3–27–73) has friendly management. All rooms have kitchenettes and TVs and cost $50 ($55 with air-conditioning). It's on a quiet side street about two blocks from the marina; reservations are essential in winter.

HOSTEL • **Las Villas Turismo Juvenil (CREA)** is the cheapest place to stay in Cabo San Lucas, drawing a mixed crowd of student and older travelers. It's in a quiet neighborhood about 10 blocks from the center of town (a $2 taxi ride). On the plus side, there is no curfew or check-in time, and a private room with bath costs $8–$10. Single-sex dorms are $5 per bed. Bring your own toilet paper. *Av. de la Juventud, 3 blocks east of Morelos, tel. 114/3–01–48. From downtown, follow Morelos 10 blocks. 2 dorms; 11 rooms, all with bath. Laundry. Reservations advised Nov.–Feb. Cash only.*

CAMPING • If you'd like to camp, head a few kilometers northeast from town to **Playa Migriño** or **Playa los Cerritos.** Both are gorgeous, secluded, free, and conveniently located on Highway 1 between Cabo San Lucas and San José del Cabo. For something more organized, **Club Cabo** (tel. 114/3–33–48) charges $6 for two people in a tent, $18 in an RV, and $40 for a cabana. **Vagabundos** (tel. 114/3–02–90) is visible from the highway and charges $18 for two people, regardless of whether you're in a 50-ft Winnebago or a four-ft-square tent. To reach any of these beach campsites, catch a bus bound for San José del Cabo ($1) and ask the driver to let you off.

FOOD

Surprisingly, Cabo San Lucas has several decently priced restaurants, on or north of Niños Héroes. Along Morelos (perpendicular to Lázaro Cárdenas) you'll find a number of authentic Mexican restaurants popular with locals: **Café Cabo** (Morelos, near Lázaro Cárdenas, no phone; cash only) has a cheery staff and serves big breakfasts ($3), plus sandwiches, hamburgers, and fajitas for less than $4. The omelets, salads, and sandwiches at **Mama's Royal Café** (corner of Hidalgo and Zapata, tel. 114/3–42–90; cash only) are all prepared with fresh, homemade ingredients and cost less than $6. For seafood, **Mariscos Mocambo** (Morelos, at 20 de Noviembre, tel. 114/3–21–22) is an undisputed favorite among locals. Seafood soup or crab in garlic sauce costs $6; grilled red snapper is sold by weight. At **Hippo's Fish 'N Chips** (Plaza de los Mariachis, on Blvd. Marina, no phone; cash only), a plate of crispy, English-style fish and chips is $5. For a fresh mango shake, add another $3.

SHOPPING

Two outdoor markets sell indigenous crafts to the hordes of cruise-ship passengers that arrive in Cabo daily. The market just past the marina on Boulevard Marina has the best prices on silver from Oaxaca and ceramics from Morelia. It's open daily 8–5. Another market, open daily 10–9, lies across from the Supermercado Plaza on Niños Héroes. It sells artesanía and crafts from all over Mexico. Small shops around the zócalo also offer real bargains.

OUTDOOR ACTIVITIES

Cabo San Lucas's warm, clear waters are ideal for water sports. You can rent everything from waterbikes and catamarans to Windsurfers and wave runners at **Plaza Las Glorias Beach Club** (at Hotel Plaza Las Glorias, Blvd. Marina, tel. 114/3–12–20; open daily 7–7). **Cabo Sports Center** (Madero, near Guerrero, tel. 114/3–42–72; open daily 9–9) rents snorkel gear ($10 per day), surfboards ($15–$20 per day), and boogie boards ($5 per day). The best swimming beach is **Playa El Medano,** but for snorkeling try **Playa Santa María** and **Los Barriles**—*tranquilo* (mellow) spots east of town. For the very daring, **Baja Bungee** sends people attached to a big rubber band off a 90-ft tower ($45 per jump); contact Alex Darquea at Siesta Suites (*see* Where to Sleep, *above*). You can get a $10 discount on your jump if you buy it with a $30 parasail ride at **The Activity Center** (near Las Palmas Restaurant, on Medano Beach, tel. 114/3–30–93), which serves as a ticket outlet for all of Cabo San Lucas's water sports and activities.

Los Arcos Beach and **Lover's Beach** are both south of town, at the tip of the rocky peninsula. Here the Pacific Ocean and the Sea of Cortés meet, the waves sculpting offshore rocks into weird formations. Many locals will try to lure you onto their boats for a trip to Lover's Beach, but the 30-minute hike is easy and offers spectacular views. Another option is to take a $7 ride in the **glass-bottom boat** that leaves periodically from behind Plaza Las Glorias Beach Club, daily 10 AM–6 PM.

SCUBA DIVING • If you're a certified diver, you won't want to miss Cabo—and if you aren't certified, this is a great place to learn. **Cabo Acuadeportes** (Cabo Water Sports Center; offices at Hotel Plaza Las Glorias, Hotel Pueblo Bonito, and Chileno Beach, tel. 114/3–01–17) arranges trips to dive sites at Pelican Rock, Los Arcos, and **Cabo Pulmo** (Baja's only coral reef). Dive trips cost $80, diving certification courses cost $400, and resort courses are $80 (all prices include equipment). **Dive Adventures** (Plaza Bonita, tel. 114/3–26–30) and **Cabo Diving Services** (Marina, across from Plaza Las Glorias, tel. 114/3–01–50) both have similar prices and trips; it's a matter of deciding where you'd like to dive and then calling to see who's going out there that day.

AFTER DARK

Cabo San Lucas is the center for nightlife in southern Baja. Every night the party-minded crowds drink $1 margaritas at **Río Grill** until 9 PM, then stagger off to the **Giggling Marlin** (tel. 114/3–06–06). The last stop is at **El Squid Roe** (tel. 114/3–06–55), where the sufficiently inebriated dance themselves silly to pop hits of the '80s; food and beer are served, but most people opt for tequila shots. All these bars are on Boulevard Marina (the main drag), which turns into Lázaro Cárdenas; none charge a cover. Just off the main drag lies the infamous **Cabo Wabo** (Guerrero, near Lázaro Cárdenas, tel. 114/3–11–88), owned by members of the '80s rock group Van Halen. Well-known, aging rock stars often play here on weekends, when the cover charge reaches a hard-to-justify $15.

NEAR LOS CABOS

TODOS SANTOS

Good (but sometimes dangerous) surf, free camping, and the absence of obtrusive hotels make Todos Santos the perfect place to escape from Cabo San Lucas's crowds. Founded by Jesuit missionaries in 1734, and subsequently abandoned due to resistance from the local Pericú people, Todos Santos was finally permanently settled by sugar-planting mestizos in the 19th century. When the sugarcane industry collapsed, the newly unemployed began growing chiles and raising beef cattle. Today Todos Santos remains a small town where life unfolds slowly around a shady zócalo. Despite the slow pace, adventurous visitors will find kayaking, sailing, and sailboarding easily accessible.

BASICS • There are no banks in Todos Santos, but **Baja Money Exchange** (1 block from the post office on Colegio Militar, no phone; open Mon.–Sat. 9–6) will hook you up with some pesos. The **post office** (Colegio Militar, near Marqués de León, no phone; open weekdays 8–1 and 3–5) is on the same block. **Farmacia Todos Santos** on Juárez is open daily 7 AM–10 PM, but you can knock at the door at any hour for emergency help. The **Centro de Salud** (Juárez, between Zaragoza and Degollado, tel. 114/5–00–95) is open 24 hours and Dr. Servín speaks English. Also on Juárez, **El Tecolote** English bookstore doubles as a gossip exchange for resident gringos. The staff will cheerfully tell you where the best beaches are, as well as trade used books (two for one) daily 9:30–5. Next door is **The Message Center** (tel. 114/5–00–03, fax 114/5–02–88; open Mon.–Sat. 8–5), where you can make direct international calls, call collect, use a calling card, receive phone messages, and send or receive faxes. This also serves as the town's travel agency.

COMING AND GOING • Buses depart from in front of **Pilar's O. G. Fish Tacos** (Colegio Militar, tel. 114/5–01–47) for Cabo San Lucas (1 hr, $3) every couple of hours 8 AM–9 PM; those continuing on to San José del Cabo leave four times daily (1½ hrs, $2.50). Frequent buses also leave for La Paz (1 hr, $2). You can store a few bags for free at Pilar's. From the bus stop, the zócalo is three blocks up the hill (toward La Paz) and one block west. Everything else of note lies in between.

WHERE TO SLEEP • Try the clean and affordable **Hotel Miramar** (Mutualismo, at Pedrajo, tel. 114/5–03–41). This tranquil retreat at the town's edge has parking, laundry service, and a swimming pool; double rooms cost $17. Clean, centrally located, and pool-blessed **Motel Guluarte** (corner of Juárez and Morelos, no phone) charges $15 for rooms with air-conditioning, $11 for those with a fan. Rooms upstairs have shared balconies equipped with rocking chairs. The sandy stretch of beach 2 km (1 mi) south of town is great for camping, but a dangerous place to swim. Buses headed for Cabo San Lucas will drop you off along the highway, but it's still a 2- to 3-km (1- to 2-mi) walk; although easy, hitching is not recommended for lone travelers.

FOOD • **Caffé Todos Santos** (corner of Centenario and Topete, no phone; closed Mon.) has all-you-can-eat blueberry or banana pancakes ($4), bagels and cream cheese, and real coffee for breakfast. Later in the day they serve sandwiches and salads. The food is good though the staff is brusque. **Restaurant Las Fuentes** (Delgado, at Colegio Militar, tel. 114/5–02–57) has patio tables. Typical Mexican fare costs less than $6. **Lonchería Karla** (Colegio Militar, opposite the park, tel. 114/5–02–93) has $2.50 plates of tacos, tamales, and other antojitos. All are cash only.

WORTH SEEING • Todos Santos's annual **art festival**, held around the third weekend in January, offers displays of local artists in the plaza and special exhibitions in all of the town's galleries. On October 12 the town celebrates its foundation with the **Día de la Virgen del Pilar.** Art exhibits, traditional food, and *baile folklórico* (folk dancing) are all part of the celebration. You can find out about other events that take place throughout the year through Professor Agundez at the **Casa de la Cultura** (Gral. Topete, no phone; open Mon.–Sat. 8–6), which also has a library and displays artifacts, paintings, and children's art. The **Misión de Nuestra Señora de Pilar,** built in 1733, is your typical mission; nevertheless, it offers a spectacular view of the Valle del Pilar and the ocean from its perch above town. One block west of the mission toward the water is the fabled **Hotel California,** of Eagles fame.

SONORA AND LOS MOCHIS

4

UPDATED BY KATE DEELY

Sonora has always resisted visitors. Long ago, the indigenous people of this region—the Yaqui, Seri, Guarijio, Mayo, and Papago—adapted to the region's sweltering deserts, but they were as fierce as the harsh soils they walked upon. European settlers in Sonora were thwarted by blistering summers and long battles with tribal residents. Although the indigenous people achieved a few successful rebellions, their traditional way of life was eventually destroyed by dammed rivers and barbed-wire fences. Agriculture became Sonora's buried treasure, rendering it the second-richest and second-largest state in Mexico. Today Sonora's proximity to Arizona attracts swarms of moneyed Tucson tourists, not to mention numerous *maquiladoras* (foreign-owned factories), where U.S. companies continue to benefit from the cheap cost of Mexican labor. It's no wonder Sonorans ask tourists in a cautious tone whether they are from "*el otro lado*" (the other side).

Travelers who favor cool breezes may wish to bypass Sonora during summer months, when the 37°C (100°F) heat can be almost unbearable. A few visitor-friendly areas exist, however. Nogales caters to day-tripping souvenir seekers, offering colorful markets full of woven blankets, wrought-iron furniture, and handmade crafts from all over the country. The barely sullied beaches of San Carlos, Bahía Kino, and Puerto Peñasco are the best spots to cool off in the Sea of Cortés, and the sleepy, colonial village of Alamos hearkens back to its mining-town days with narrow cobblestone streets and elegantly restored haciendas. Hermosillo, the bustling state capital, offers museums, parks, and a unique ecology center. Although it's not particularly pretty, you'll inevitably visit Los Mochis: The city is a transportation hub and essential stop if you plan to take a ferry to Baja or the train through the Copper Canyon (*see* Chapter 5).

NOGALES

The small, nondescript town of Nogales, Mexico, has grown to within inches of the border with Nogales, Arizona. Like Tijuana to the west, Nogales is famous for its shopping and attracts hordes of Arizonans bargaining for tacky knickknacks. This is the place to find that stuffed armadillo that's been eluding you elsewhere; blue glass from Guadalajara, silver from Zacatecas, and burnished pottery from Oaxaca also fill the stores, although you'll find these wares for lower prices farther south. The main shopping district lies close to the border, along the five blocks of alleyways that line Calle Ochoa between López Mateos

TO TUCSON ARIZONA

Nogales Nogales

Douglas

2 Coborca

Concepción

El Desemboque

Magdalena Cananea Agua Prieta

15

Puerto de
La Libertad

Santa Ana

El Dátil

Arizpe

Isla Ángel de
la Guarda

Nacozari
de García

Carbó

Bavispe

Isla del
Tiburón

15

Moctezuma

Kino Nuevo

Sonora Ures

Hermosillo

Papigochic

Bahía
Kino

San Rafael

KEY
|—|—| Rail Lines
- - - Ferry Lines

Cienaguita

Mt. Tetakawi Tecoripa

San Carlos 15

Guaymas

Yaqui

Santa Rosalía

Bahía
Guásimas

1

15

Pta.
Concepción

Isla
Lobos

Rosario

Rosarito

Ciudad
Obregón

Mavo

Golfo de California

Navojoa

Loreto

Huatabampo Alamos

Isla
Carmen

15

1

SIERRA DE LA GIGANTA

Río Fuerte

Las Grullas
Viejas

El Fuerte

Isla
San José

San Blas

Isla
Espíritu
Santo

Topolobampo Los
Mochis

Pichilingue

Guamúchil

N

La Paz

TO MAZATLÁN

0   50 miles

0   75 km

107

and Obregón. After a tough day of haggling, you can kick back with an overpriced margarita in one of the many bars overlooking Obregón. Nogales also boasts a decent bullfighting arena, which is especially lively during **Cinco de Mayo.** This festival, composed of bullfights, cockfights, horse races, and *artesanía* (handicrafts) exhibitions, celebrates Mexico's defeat of the French in the Battle of Puebla and lasts from the end of April until May 5.

Nogales serves as a major export depot for Sonora's rich agricultural produce but, like many of its border cousins, has also been affected by major economic changes over the past decade. Foreign (mostly U.S.) companies take advantage of cheap Mexican labor by setting up an increasing number of industrial parks and *maquiladoras* (foreign-owned factories, also called *maquilas*) in special duty-free zones outside the city (*see box titled* "Manufacturers of Misery," *in* Chapter 3). Though these factories employ the bulk of Nogales's residents, the town lacks the menacing criminal element found in other maquila-influenced border towns, such as Ciudad Juárez and Tijuana. The most negative impact of the maquilas in Nogales is environmental: The surrounding desert takes a great deal of toxic-waste abuse, resulting in a depressing lack of wildlife and flora.

BASICS

CASAS DE CAMBIO

Banks on the U.S. side don't change dollars into pesos, but you'll find a handful of currency-exchange offices that do on Grand Avenue, one block north of the border. South of the border, try **Casa de Cambio Gaby** (Morelos 18, near Ochoa, tel. 631/2–19–09; open weekdays 8–7, Sat. 8–noon). The ATM at **Bancomer** (López Mateos, 5 blocks south of border crossing, tel. 631/2–10–48) accepts Visa cards, and another Bancomer (corner of Ochoa and Obregón), about two blocks from the border, has an ATM that accepts Plus System cards. Unfortunately, ATMs in Nogales, Mexico, are often broken or out of cash, so you'll probably want to cross the pedestrian bridge back to the States and follow the lower ramp, which runs into Grand Avenue: One block down on the right-hand side, **Bank of America** (tel. 520/287–6553; open weekdays 9–6, Sat. 9–2) has a reliable ATM that accepts Plus cards.

CROSSING THE BORDER

Both the U.S. and Mexican customs offices at Nogales are open 24 hours a day. U.S. citizens and Canadians planning to stay in Mexico longer than 72 hours or traveling south of the border towns need tourist cards (*see* Chapter 1). To get one, present proof of citizenship at the **Mexican Government Border Office** (tel. 631/2–17–55; open 24 hrs), immediately to the right when you cross the border. Allow yourself extra time at border crossings because there can be backups due to staff shortages. If you've had a long, lascivious stay in Mexico, try to clean up (e.g., shave and get rid of the hangover) before going through customs or they may detain you for questioning, especially if you're under 21.

EMERGENCIES

Bilingual operators staff the emergency telephone service (tel. 91/525–001–23 or 91/525–001–51) 24 hours a day. Or call the **police** (tel. 631/6–15–64 or 631/2–17–67) or **fire** and **ambulance** services (tel. 631/4–07–69) directly.

MAIL

Your mail has a better chance of reaching its destination if you send it from the United States. The post office in Nogales, Arizona (300 N. Morley Ave., tel. 520/287–9246), six blocks from the border, is open weekdays 9–5. The *oficina de correos* (post office) on the Mexican side will hold mail sent to you at the following address for up to 10 days: Lista de Correos, Benito Juárez y Calle Campillo, Nogales, Sonora, CP 84000, México. *Benito Juárez, at Campillo, tel. 631/2–12–47. 2 blocks from the border crossing. Open weekdays 8–7, Sat. 8–noon.*

MEDICAL AID

Farmacia San Xavier (Campillo 73, 2 blocks from the border crossing, tel. 631/2–55–03) is open 24 hours daily and the staff speaks English. Several reputable, English-speaking doctors have offices on the first few blocks of Obregón. For general medical care contact **Dr. Roberto Belches Valenzuela** (tel. 631/2–37–21; appointment required), and for dental care contact **Dr. Rene Romo De Vivar** (Obregón 263, tel. 631/2–05–00).

PHONES

Working **Ladatel** pay phones can be found along major streets, and there is a *caseta de larga distancia* (long-distance telephone office) in the bus terminal. **Nabila** (tel. 631/2–01–42; open daily 8–6), a small bric-a-brac shop a few blocks down Obregón on the left-hand side, charges $1.50 to make a collect call and $1.50 per minute to dial direct.

VISITOR INFORMATION

The English-speaking **tourist office,** on the right as you cross the border, provides general information on accommodations and transportation and hands out a thumbnail-size city map. Fortunately, Nogales is easy to navigate. *López Mateos, at Internacional, tel. 631/2–06–66. Open daily 8–6.*

COMING AND GOING

Almost everything you could need or want to see is near the border-crossing area and easily accessible on foot. Local buses run to other parts of town from **López Mateos,** the main drag. Foot traffic fills Ochoa and Obregón. Taxis will charge you roughly $1 per km (½ mi), but be sure to negotiate a price before getting in.

BY BUS

The bus station in Nogales is 6 km (4 mi) from the center of town on Highway 15—you can get here on one of the local CENTRAL CAMIONERA buses (40¢) that runs along López Mateos. Three bus companies use the station: **Transportes Norte de Sonora** (tel. 631/3–17–00) and **Élite** (tel. 631/3–02–33) serve Baja as well as mainland Mexico, while **Transportes del Pacífico** (tel. 631/3–16–06) serves the western mainland. Four buses depart daily for Mexico City (1½ days; $94 1st class, $85 2nd class). Elite and Transportes Norte de Sonora each have

The Sonoran Yaqui fiercely resist outside domination. Mexican president Porfirio Díaz set the army against them in the 1890s, and Yaqui prisoners were sent to work building railroads in southern Mexico.

an evening departure for Mexicali (9 hrs; $26 1st class, $15 2nd class). Another option is to take any bus headed south to Santa Ana (2½ hours, $3.50 1st class, $3 2nd class) and transfer there to a Mexicali-bound bus. Buses also regularly leave Nogales for Tijuana (12 hrs; $34 1st class, $25 2nd class), Hermosillo (5 hrs; $10 1st class, $7.50 2nd class), Guaymas (7 hrs; $12 1st class, $11 2nd class), Los Mochis (12 hrs; $23 1st class, $11 2nd class), Mazatlán (17 hrs; $45 1st class, $35 2nd class), and Guadalajara (31 hrs; $73 1st class, $65 2nd class). The terminal has phones, luggage storage (50¢ per bag per hr), and a money-exchange booth.

On the Arizona side of the border, **Grey Line** (tel. 520/287–5628 in the U.S.; open daily 7 AM–9 PM) has frequent, direct service to Tucson (1½ hrs, $6.50) and other destinations throughout the States, and will let you stash your luggage in a locker ($1 per day). Collective taxi/vans go directly to the airport in Tucson from the Grey Line station for $11 per person. The station is to your left just off the ramp as you cross the border.

BY CAR

The state of Sonora has a smooth, four-lane highway and well-maintained toll roads. If you're driving less than 21 km (13 mi) across the border into Mexico, no special rules apply; bringing a car farther into Mexico is not complicated if you're properly prepared. U.S. rental cars are not permitted past the 21-km (13-mi) mark, but everyone else is allowed a permit for up to 6 months. An office at Kilometer 21 on Highway 15 at Aguazarca issues tourist cards and registers vehicles. Bring car registration papers (in your name), your driver's license, and your passport, plus a photocopy of each. After you sign a promissory note to bring your car back across the border, an identifying hologram sticker gets slapped on the car's windshield. The only catch is that you must leave Mexico by Highway 15 to stop by the same office on your way out of the country. A new program, called **Only Sonora** (tel. 800/4–SONORA in the U.S. or 800/6–25–55 in Mexico), also registers those traveling by car within the state. It's a good idea to purchase Mexican auto insurance ($8 per day) from the **Puerta de México Edificio Banderas** (government border office; tel. 800/446–8277; open Mon.–Sat. 7 AM–10 PM, Sun. 7–1), just over the border in Nogales.

BY TRAIN

The train station (tel. 631/3–02–05 or 631/3–10–91) is across from the bus station on Highway 15, 6 km (4 mi) outside town, and can be reached via any local bus marked CENTRAL CAMIONERA or FERROCAR-

RIL (40¢) or by taxi ($4 from the center). First-class trains depart daily at 4:30 PM for Benjamin Hill (2 hrs, $3), Hermosillo (5 hrs, $5), Sufragio (transfer point for the Copper Canyon; 11 hrs, $14), Mazatlán (19 hrs, $21), and Guadalajara (24 hrs, $23). For Mexico City, change trains in Guadalajara; for Mexicali, change in Benjamin Hill. Second-class service to these same destinations leaves daily at 7 AM, lacks air-conditioning, takes much longer, and costs about a third of the price of first class. Purchase tickets at the station and be sure to arrive at least 30 minutes prior to departure.

WHERE TO SLEEP AND EAT

If you're planning to travel farther into Mexico, you might be better off avoiding Nogales's overpriced hotels and taking an overnight bus straight out of town. **Hotel Yolanda** (Morelos, on a walkway just off Campillo, no phone) has decent rooms ($14 doubles) with private bathrooms and hot water, if you can tolerate the saggy beds and lack of ventilation. **Hotel Orizaba** (Juárez 29, near Campillo, no phone) provides similar conditions and prices ($12.50 doubles), except here you'll get your own fan instead of your own bathroom. The communal baths get nasty when the place is full, but they do have hot water. Across the street, **Hotel San Carlos** (Juárez 22, tel. 631/2–13–46) is pleasant, with air-conditioning, TVs, and clean bathrooms in each room, but you'll pay the price: Doubles cost $22. All hotels are cash only.

Restaurant Café Río Sonora (Ochoa, near Hidalgo, tel. 631/2–03–89; closed Mon.) serves the best and cheapest *comida corrida* (preprepared lunch special; $2). **Café Olga** (Juárez, at Campillo, tel. 631/2–16–41) is a popular breakfast spot, with hotcakes and eggs for just $3. **Elvira** (Obregón, tel. 631/2–47–73; no breakfast) serves typical Mexican fare, plus a free tequila shot with every meal. **La Fábula Pizza** (López Mateos, near Vásquez, tel. 631/2–20–48) serves up good Chicago-style pizza ($6 for a small) for lunch or dinner. You can also get your pizza *a domicilio* (delivered).

AFTER DARK

On weekends, Arizonans cross the border to whoop it up in Nogales. Tons of gringo bars line Avenida Obregón, all of which serve $2 beers, expensive cocktails, and American music. About 1 km (½ mi) from the border is **Mr. Don** (Obregón 1036, tel. 631/3–19–07; closed Mon.) a huge disco that plays everything from salsa to rap. On Friday there's no cover, and the $8 cover on Saturday includes an open bar. The popular **Epidaurus** (Privada Becerril and Corinto, just off Obregón, tel. 631/3–26–13; cover $9) attracts a bevy of locals and tourists with its mix of rap, techno, and traditional Mexican and rock favorites. Friday and Saturday the disco stays open until 3 AM. **Harlow's Discotheque** (Elías 21, no phone; closed Mon.–Wed.) offers all the latest in lasers, lights, and hip-hop music. Cover is $5.

NEAR NOGALES

PUERTO PENASCO

Founded as a fishing village in 1927, this quiet town sits on the northern coast of the Sea of Cortés. The town is ringed by the stifling **Desierto de Altar,** where the temperature often soars above 37°C (100°F) in summer. The best time of year to visit the area is late spring, when temperatures are milder and the cholla, saguaro, organ pipe, and barrel cacti are studded with red, yellow, and white blooms. Vacationing Arizonans in search of the sea congregate on the southern side of town, at **Miramar** and **Hermosa Bonita** beaches, armed with RVs, dune buggies, and Jet Skis. Besides hitting the beach, there is little to do or see here, except during festivals such as **Navy Day** (June 1), which Puerto Peñasco celebrates with mariachi music, boat parades, and beauty pageants. In mid-June there's an annual **fishing tournament,** during which you can eat enough seafood to just about grow fins yourself.

COMING AND GOING

To reach Puerto Peñasco from Nogales, take an **Élite** bus to Caborca (4 hrs, $10) and transfer there to a Puerto Peñasco–bound bus (2 hrs, $5). Trains also run from Puerto Peñasco to Mexicali (4 hrs, $8), Caborca (2 hrs, $5), Hermosillo (6 hrs, $8), and Ciudad Obregón (9 hrs, $8).

WHERE TO SLEEP AND EAT

Rich folk monopolize most of Puerto Peñasco's beachfront hotels, but **Motel Davis** (Emiliano Zapata 100, near Calle 13, tel. 638/3–43–14), only three blocks from the beach, offers well-maintained, air-conditioned singles and doubles for $10–$15 (cash only). If you're broke, try camping on peaceful **Playa Sandy** for $3. Pay at the booth at the entrance to the Cholla Bay private road. **Restaurant Los Arcos** (Eusebio Kino, at Tamaulipas, tel. 638/3–35–97) has breakfast specials for $2. You can also head for one of the many seafood stands near the end of Boulevard Kino, where fish tacos cost about 50¢. **La Cita Café** (Paseo Victor Estrella 72, tel. 638/3–22–70), in the old part of town, has been serving diner-style Mexican and American food since 1957. Breakfasts cost $3, a hamburger and milkshake $5. **Manny's Beach Club** (Playa Miramar, tel. 638/3–36–05) has a raging happy hour nightly 6–8 PM, when beers are $1 and Jimmy Buffett's "Margaritaville" is played over and over for the amusement of drunk gringos. They also have live music on weekends.

PARQUE NACIONAL EL PINACATE

On the road to Sonoita (Highway 8), 48 km (30 mi) north of Puerto Peñasco, lies Parque Nacional El Pinacate. The huge park—about 2,000 square km (1,240 square mi)—was declared a UN biosphere reserve in 1993, which put its 500 plant and animal species under protection. Because of its similarity to the moon's surface, the park's craters, sand dunes, and lava fields were used by NASA to train astronauts for moon walks. The most popular spots within the park, largely due to their accessibility to Highway 8, are Volcán Elegante and Volcán Colorado, but there are more than 600 other volcanic craters, as well as archaeological sites that date back almost 30,000 years. Because of high summer temperatures, visiting the park is recommended only between October and April. Going with a guide is strongly advised; the best is **Señor Munro** (tel. 638/3–32–09), Puerto Peñasco's town historian, who runs a photo studio in the commercial district. Day-long tours run about $50 per person, but you can get a group together and negotiate. The park is still largely undeveloped, so unless you're with a guide don't expect to find much more than vast expanses of parched, windblown earth—if you really want to go it alone, you'll need a truck or a car with four-wheel drive. You can camp in the park for free or at a neighboring *ejido* (farming community) for a few dollars: The latter is the safest option. When entering the park, you must register at the entrance booth off Highway 8.

> *Jesuit Father Eusebio Kino, who established a number of missions in northwestern Mexico in the late 17th century, reportedly drew a parallel between the Desierto de Altar and his vision of Hell.*

HERMOSILLO

Bustling and on the verge of modernization, the prosperous capital of Sonora boasts a state university and a population of almost a half million. Five-star hotels and American fast-food restaurants intermix with colonial plazas and narrow alleys, giving the city a unique, neither-here-nor-there feel. Like other large Mexican cities, Hermosillo is plagued by crime and poverty, though the university community imbues the city with a certain scholarly dignity. You probably won't spend much time here, but you could easily pass a day touring the city's sights and another day at the impressive **Centro Ecológico** (*see* Worth Seeing, *below*). Special events include **La Fiesta de la Vendimia** (The Grape Harvest Celebration) in mid-July, and Yaqui Indian dances, held during **Semana Santa** (Holy Week, the week preceding Easter).

BASICS

AMERICAN EXPRESS

The AmEx office in **Hermex Travel** sells traveler's checks, insurance, and plane tickets. Cardmembers may cash personal checks or receive mail (address to: Edif. Lupita, Hermosillo, Sonora, CP 83000, México). *Rosales, at Monterrey, tel. 62/13–44–15. Open weekdays 9–1 and 3–6, Sat. 9–noon.*

CASAS DE CAMBIO

A number of banks line Rosales, in the downtown area, and Eusebio Kino, in the northwest corner of town. **Bancomer** (Sonora, at Matamoros, tel. 62/12–13–62; open weekdays 9–1) changes traveler's checks and has a *caja permanente* (ATM) that accepts Visa cards. More ATMs can be found downtown, on Serdán between Juárez and Jesús García.

CONSULATES

United States. The consulate has an answering machine that is checked after hours. *Monterrey 141, behind Hotel Calinda, tel. 62/17–23–75. Open weekdays 8–4:30.*

EMERGENCIES

Dial 08 for emergencies, or call the **police** (tel. 62/13–40–46); **fire** department (tel. 62/12–01–97); or **ambulance** (tel. 62/4–07–69). The **Ángeles Verdes** (Green Angels; Calle Caridad 85, between Blvd. Kino and Lampazos, tel. 62/58–00–44 or 800/6–25–55) provide emergency car repair service.

LAUNDRY

Lavandería Automática de Hermosillo lets you wash and dry a load of your dirty duds for $3. *Corner of Sonora and Yáñez, tel. 62/7–55–01. Open Mon.–Sat. 8–8, Sun. 8–1.*

MAIL

The post office downtown will hold mail sent to you at the following address for 10 days: Lista de Correos, Blvd. Rosales, Hermosillo, Sonora, CP 83000, México. You can send or receive telegrams and faxes at the office next door. *Post office: Serdán, at Rosales, tel. 62/12–00–11. Open weekdays 8–7, Sat. 8–noon.*

MEDICAL AID

Farmacia Margarita (Morelia 93, at Guerrero, tel. 62/13–15–90) is open 24 hours. **Clínica del Noroeste** (Plaza Juárez, at L. D. Colosio and Juárez, tel. 62/12–18–90) provides 24-hour emergency service and has some English-speaking doctors. Nonemergencies are handled weekdays 8–8, Saturday 8–1.

PHONES

Pay phones are common on downtown streets, but finding one that works could take you all day. It's quicker to head to **Hotel Monte Carlo** (*see* Where to Sleep, *below*), which has working phones. Long-distance calls and faxes can be placed at **Farmacia Margarita**'s caseta (*see* Medical Aid, *above*; tel. 62/12–05–06), which charges $1.50 for a collect call and $2 per minute for direct calls to the United States. You can make no-surcharge collect calls at the bus station's caseta.

VISITOR INFORMATION

The **Secretaría al Fomento de Turismo** (Secretary of Tourism), in the Centro del Gobierno Edifico Estatal usually has someone on hand who speaks English, but anyone here will eagerly load you down with brochures and maps. *Blvd. Paseo Canal and Comonfort, 3rd floor, tel. 62/17–00–76. Open weekdays 8–4 and 5–9, Sat. 10–1.*

COMING AND GOING

With several hills around town to orient you, it's difficult to get lost in Hermosillo. The most prominent hill downtown is **Cerro de la Campana.** Highway 15 runs through Hermosillo and on to Nogales to the north. Boulevard Transversal transects the city northwest–southeast. Local buses are cheap (40¢ or less) and dependable, if not always fast. Taxis charge roughly $1 per km, but it may cost two or three times as much at night or from the bus station.

BY BUS

Three main bus companies serve Hermosillo's bus station (Blvd. Transversal 400): **Transportes Norte de Sonora** (tel. 62/13–24–16), **Transportes del Pacífico** (tel. 62/17–05–80), and **Élite** (tel. 62/13–40–50). To reach the station from downtown, take any bus marked CIRCUITO NORTE, PERIFERICO, or TRANSVER-SAL (40¢). Taxis charge $3.50 from the station to downtown, but you can pay less (about $3) if you walk away from the station and flag one down. Buses run north to Tijuana (14 hrs, $36), stopping in Nogales (5 hrs, $10) and Mexicali (10 hrs, $27); and south to Mexico City (31 hrs, $90), stopping in Guaymas (2 hrs, $4), Los Mochis (7 hrs, $15), Mazatlán (12 hrs, $31), and Guadalajara (26 hrs, $62). Luggage storage (30¢ per hour) and money exchange are available at the terminal.

BY TRAIN

The train station (tel. 62/15–35–77 or 62/10–34–57) is 3 km (2 mi) north of town, just off Highway 15. First-class trains leave for Mexicali (10 hrs, $17) and Nogales (5 hrs, $5) daily at 1 PM. Second-class service to these same destinations leaves at 5 PM, takes somewhat longer, and costs about one-third the price of first class. First-class trains for Guadalajara (24 hrs, $39) leave daily at 8 PM; second-class trains (minimum 27 hrs, $13) leave daily at noon. If you're bound for Mexico City, you'll need to change trains in Guadalajara. Buses marked EST. FERR. will take you from the market in central Hermosillo to the train station; a cab from the center costs $4.

WHERE TO SLEEP

The budget-lodging district (the area around Plaza Juárez) has improved somewhat since a government antiprostitution sweep closed many of the flophouses, but it's still unsafe for women traveling alone, and all travelers should avoid the area after dark. **Hotel Monte Carlo** (Juárez, at Sonora, on Plaza Juárez, tel. 62/12–08–53) is one safe option in the area—ignore the drunks hanging around outside, because inside you'll find clean, private bathrooms and good air-conditioning. Doubles cost $16. Quaint but affordable **Hotel Gandara** (Kino 1000, tel. 621/4–44–14) has doubles for $30. Its colonnaded gardens look like they've been transplanted from Spain. Both of the above are cash only. If you're travel-weary and looking to splurge, head to **Hotel San Andrés** (Oaxaca 14, near Plaza Juárez, tel. 62/17–30–99), which offers security and relative opulence. The big rooms have TVs, phones, and air-conditioning. The hotel also has a restaurant, bar, and shaded outdoor patio. Doubles cost $37.

FOOD

In Hermosillo you can go to dinner with $5 in your wallet and come back with a full belly and a pocket-ful of change. The downtown area is loaded with cheap taquerías and street vendors hawking everything from fruit to hot dogs. Those fresh fruits and vegetables are also sold at the daily **mercado municipal** (Matamoros, at Roberto Elías Calles). The baseball paraphernalia covering the walls of **Café Monte Carlo** (In Hotel Monte Carlo, Juárez, at Sonora, tel. 62/12–22–59, closed Sun.) adds ambience to this eclectic place. For breakfast, why not try a tongue omelet ($2) with pineapple juice? Chicken in green sauce, liver and onions, and other dinner items are less than $5. The wholesome fare at **Jung** (Niños Héroes 75, near Matamoros, tel. 62/13–28–82; closed Sun.) includes salads, sandwiches, and entrées ($2–$5) made with fresh fruits, vegetables, and whole-wheat breads.

WORTH SEEING

There's a certain charm to the decaying buildings and cramped alleyways of Hermosillo's historic dis-trict, near the budget-lodging area of Plaza Juárez. Even in the "newer" part of town, you can see traces of colonial history in the **Catedral de la Asunción** and the **Palacio de Gobierno,** on the central Plaza Zaragoza. The free **Museo de Sonora** (tel. 62/13–12–34; open Wed.–Sat. 10–5, Sun. 9–4), at the east-ern base of Cerro de la Campana, holds a fine collection of pre-Columbian artifacts. Nearby, the **Capilla del Carmen** occasionally holds a "mariachi mass"—a loud, colorful trumpet- and guitar-accompanied Sunday mass (10 AM). In **Parque Madero** (Jesús García, between P. Elías and Norwalk), jungle gyms, long slides, merry-go-rounds, and swings drive the local kiddies wild.

CENTRO ECOLOGICO DE SONORA

With more than 400 plant species and 240 animals, including wolves, hippos, and condors, this govern-ment reserve is concerned with education and preservation. In addition to the plant and animal exhibits, there is a library, a botanical garden, and a theater that shows documentaries on endangered species. The center also leads groups to a nearby observatory on Friday night (7:30–10:30) to observe the sky through a high-powered telescope; call 62/50–12–25 one week in advance for star-watching reserva-tions. *Carretera a Guaymas Km. 2.5, tel. 62/50–11–37, fax 62/50–12–36. From Plaza Juárez, take a LUIS ORSCI bus (15 min, 20¢) and ask the driver to let you off at centro ecológico; walk down the paved road about 10 min to the entrance. Admission: $1. Open June–Sept., Wed.–Sun. 8–6; Oct.–May until 5.*

AFTER DARK

At night, downtown Hermosillo (especially the area surrounding Plaza Juárez) is filled with men looking for trouble. Single women shouldn't even bother with the bar scene: the constant harassment it brings can be annoying or even dangerous. All travelers should avoid walking the streets at night—fortunately, buses and taxis are easy enough to find. For diehard club-crawlers, there's **Blocky'O Disco** (Rodríguez, at Juárez, tel. 62/15–18–88), a huge disco that plays Mexican and American rock and offers frequent drink specials. A little farther south, just off Rodríguez, you'll find **Nova Olimpia** (Frontera, at C. L. de Soria, tel. 62/17–30–13), where the music alternates nightly between cumbia, salsa, and disco. Both clubs charge a $5 cover for men and $3 for women. A few blocks farther south, **Marco 'n' Charlie's** (Blvd. Rodríguez 78, tel. 62/15–30–61; closed Sun.) is a popular, cover-free bar and grill for young, middle-class locals and the few gringos in town.

NEAR HERMOSILLO

BAHIA KINO

The two towns of Kino Viejo and Kino Nuevo share the Bahía Kino (Kino Bay) on the Sea of Cortés, and both are blessed with pristine beaches, warm, clear waters, and sizeable populations of manta rays and pelicans. Although both towns are easily reached from Hermosillo (about 120 km/75 mi away), they couldn't have less in common. The poor, sleepy fishing village of **Kino Viejo** was established in the 1700s by the Jesuit priest Eusebio Kino as a mission for Seri Indians; today it consists of a few stores, restaurants, and fishermen's houses strung along a dusty road. The charm of this town lies in its friendly atmosphere (sometimes a little too friendly for women traveling alone), cheap fresh seafood, and colorful sunsets. **Kino Nuevo,** about five minutes away from Kino Viejo by bus, is a haven for American retirees—their trim little houses blend into the desert landscape but seem out of place next to ramshackle shacks and coconut stands. The small, free **Museo de los Seris** (Mar de Cortés, at Calle Progresso; open daily 10–1 and 3–6) in Kino Nuevo gives out historical and cultural information on the indigenous Seris, who you may see selling the ironwood sculptures for which they are known. Local hustlers may try to persuade you to visit the **Isla del Tiburón** (Shark Island), home to the Seri Indians until they were forcibly resettled in the '50s. The island is now a fragile wildlife refuge for tortoises, rams, coyotes, and birds; please don't visit.

COMING AND GOING

Ten buses (1½ hrs, $5) run from Hermosillo to the Kinos daily 5:40 AM–5:30 PM. Buses depart from Hermosillo's old **Transportes Norte de Sonora** station (Sonora, between Revolución and González), rather than the main bus station. These buses pass through both Kinos every one or two hours, but walking and hitching between towns is also easy. To return to Hermosillo, catch the bus on the main road in either Kino between 6 AM and 5:30 PM.

WHERE TO SLEEP

Although you can do the Kinos in a day, you might regret missing the fiery sunset over the Sea of Cortés. Of the two Kinos, Kino Nuevo has the only hotels, the cheapest of which is **Hotel Saro** (midway down Kino Nuevo's main road, tel. 624/2–00–07), where clean doubles are $35. In the off-season, RV parks in both Kinos rent tent spaces for $5–$10, which includes use of their bathroom and shower facilities. In Kino Nuevo, try **Kino Bay RV Park** (tel. 624/2–02–16) at the end of the main road, or **Islandia Marina** (tel. 624/2–00–81), on the water near Puerto Peñasco and Guerrero. The latter has beach bungalows with kitchen facilities ($22 for four) right on the water. You can also string up a hammock or prop your tent under one of the many *palapas* (thatched huts) along the 18-km (11-mi) beach in Kino Nuevo for free. Camping here is generally safe, but you need to watch your stuff. Avoid camping on the beach in Kino Viejo; there's a lot of foot traffic here at night.

FOOD

Kino Viejo has a few good restaurants and a number of fish and taco stands. **Restaurant Dorita** (no phone), just opposite the police station/post office/Red Cross building on the main drag, serves good, cheap lunches (about $5) to fussing children and their exasperated parents. Also in Kino Viejo, **Restaurant Kino Bay** (Mar De Cortés, tel. 624/2–00–49) offers terrific ocean views. They serve fish tacos ($2) and other Mexican fare. In Kino Nuevo, you can wash down your shrimp cocktail ($4) with fresh lemonade while taking in the sea view at **La Palapa** (midway down the main road, tel. 624/2–02–10). All are cash only.

LA PINTADA

The archaeological site at La Pintada, 60 km (37 mi) south of Hermosillo off Highway 15, was once a refuge for Pima, Yaqui, and Seri Indians fleeing the Spanish. The site's main feature is **La Pintada cave**, in one of the canyons just off Highway 15. Inside the cave are vibrantly colored Rupestrian-era rock paintings dating to 9000 BC. These paintings depict deer, reptiles, and birds, as well as hunting rituals; the impressions of hands and feet around the paintings are thought to be the oldest such specimens on the continent. To reach La Pintada, catch a **TNS** (Transportes Norte de Sonora) bus from Hermosillo heading toward Guaymas (1 hr, $3) and ask the driver to let you off at La Pintada. From here, follow the dirt road 3 km (2 mi) to the site. La Pintada is open Monday–Saturday until dusk. Admission is free.

GUAYMAS

The port city of Guaymas is hot, humid, and smells like decaying fish. An extensive shrimp- and sardine-fishing fleet operates from these docks, and seafood processing is one of the main local industries—check out the town's **Monumento al Pescador,** an enormous statue of a fisherman grappling with a huge fish. All this fish makes Guaymas a memorable olfactory experience and little else, but if you're too broke to stay in San Carlos (see Near Guaymas, below), wandering along Guaymas's docks watching the fishing boats is one way to kill a few hours before or after frying your body on the nearby beaches. Another reason to visit is strictly practical: There is twice-weekly ferry service from Guaymas to Santa Rosalía on the Baja Peninsula.

BASICS

If your clothes are beginning to smell like fish too, **Guaymas Superlava** (García López 884, 1½ km (¾ mi) west of the bus station, tel. 622/2–54–00; open Mon.–Sat. 8–7:30) has automatic washers for $1.35 and dryers for $2.50. **Farmacia Benevides** (Serdán, at Calle 18, tel. 622/2–30–44) is a pharmacy open 24 hours. For more urgent medical attention, see **Dr. David Robles Rendón** (Serdán, at Calle 17, tel. 622/2–83–13 or 622/2–16–69), a general practitioner who doesn't speak English. His office hours are weekdays 9–1 and 4–8, Saturday 9–1.

You can change cash and traveler's checks for pesos at **Bancomer** (Serdán, at Calle 18; open weekdays 8:30 AM–12:30 PM) or head to the **Banamex** ATM (Serdán, at Calle 20), which accepts Plus and Cirrus cards. The public **phones** along the streets often don't work: Make local, long-distance, and international calls from the caseta at **Farmacia Eco San Alberto** (Calle 19, 1 block south of Serdán, tel. 622/4–20–44; open daily 8 AM–9 PM), which charges 20¢ to call collect. The **post office** (Av. 10, at Calle 20, tel. 622/2–07–57; open weekdays 8–7, Sat. 8–noon) has all the usual services and will hold mail sent to you at the following address for up to 10 days: Lista de Correos, Avenida 10, Guaymas, Sonora, CP 85400, México.

COMING AND GOING

In Guaymas, Highway 15 becomes García López. Avenida Serdán, which splits off from García López on the east side of town, is central to everything but the beaches and is served by rickety but well-marked local buses. Buses marked SAN CARLOS (60¢) make the 30-minute trip out to San Carlos from in front of the Comex building on Serdán, near Calle 16.

BY BUS

Here, buses are more convenient than trains as they run more frequently and the station is centrally located. Three bus lines, **Transportes Norte de Sonora** (tel. 622/2–12–71), **Transportes del Pacífico** (tel. 622/2–30–19), and **Élite** (tel. 622/2–12–71), operate from terminals across the street from one another on Rodríguez, near Calle 13, two blocks south of Serdán. Buses depart hourly, heading south to Mexico City (29 hrs; $75 1st class, $65 2nd class), with stops in Los Mochis (5 hrs; $10 1st class, $9 2nd class), Mazatlán (10 hrs; $32 1st class, $27 2nd class), and Guadalajara (24 hrs; $54 1st class, $44 2nd class); and north to Tijuana (17 hrs; $36 1st class, $31 2nd class), stopping in Hermosillo (2 hrs, $4), Nogales (7 hrs, $12), and Mexicali (15 hrs; $28 1st class, $24 2nd class). Transportes del Pacífico leaves frequently for Navojoa (3 hrs, $6), the transfer point for Alamos.

BY FERRY

The **Sematur** ferry terminal (tel. 622/2–23–24) is at the east end of town, just off Serdán. Ferries to Santa Rosalía, on the eastern Baja coast, run on Tuesday and Friday at 8 AM (7 hrs; $15 regular class, $30 tourist class, which includes a cabin). You can put a car on the ferry as well, but it's expensive—

they charge by size, and even the smallest car costs $160. You can buy tickets at the ferry terminal Monday and Thursday 8–3 or the morning of departure 6 AM–7:30 AM.

BY TRAIN

The train station (tel. 622/3–10–65) is 10 km (6 mi) south of Guaymas in a town called Empalme. To get here, take a red-and-white Transportes Norte de Sonora bus (50¢) marked EMPALME from any bus stop on Serdán or from the bus station; a taxi costs $5. If you're coming from the south, buses stop in Empalme on the way to Guaymas, but the bus stop is 1 km (½ mi) from the station. Northbound trains run to Mexicali (12 hrs, $18 1st class; 15 hrs, $11 2nd class), Nogales (6 hrs, $10 1st class; 8 hrs, $6 2nd class), and Hermosillo (1½ hrs, $4 1st class; 2 hrs, $2 2nd class). Southbound trains depart for Guadalajara, the transfer point for Mexico City (24 hrs, $35 1st class; 26 hrs, $20 2nd class).

WHERE TO SLEEP

There are plenty of clean, quiet, reasonably priced hotels on and near Serdán. **Casa de Huéspedes Lupita** (Calle 15 No. 125, tel. 622/2–84–09) is only a few blocks from Serdán and the bus terminals. Private-bath doubles cost $7–$9. Without bath the prices drop to $5–$7 and you might as well save your cash—the communal baths are pleasant, and the lukewarm water doesn't get any warmer in the pricier rooms. The same owner has recently opened **Casa de Huéspedes Marta** (Calle 13 and Av. 9, 3 blocks from Lupita, tel. 622/2–83–32), which offers private-bath doubles for $8, or $12 with air-conditioning. **Hotel Santa Rita** (Serdán, at Meza, tel. 622/4–14–64, fax 622/2–81–00), a short walk from the center of town, offers small doubles with TV and air-conditioning for $18. (A motel with the same name but higher prices lies less than a block away at Calle 9; don't let the taxi take you there.) All hotels are cash only.

FOOD

Serdán is lined with reasonably priced restaurants, bars, *loncherías* (snack bars), and taquerías serving fresh local seafood and typical Mexican dishes. Stock up on fresh fruit at the daily **mercado municipal,** housed in a long building one block south of Serdán, near the intersection with Yáñez. If you want to splurge, **Del Mar** (Calle 17, at Serdán, tel. 622/4–02–25) serves excellent fresh seafood dishes ($5–$8) like shrimp flambé and lobster burritos, and its cool, dark interior is a welcome respite from the summer heat. Del Mar's kitchen closes at midnight but the bar stays open until 2 AM. **Restaurant Las Cazuelas** (Av. 12, at Calle 15, tel. 622/2–65–96; no dinner Sun., closed Mon.; cash only) serves egg, rice, and bean breakfasts, as well as a tasty comida corrida ($3). **Restaurant Todos Comen** (Serdán, at Calle 15, tel. 622/2–11–00; cash only) has breakfast dishes for less than $3. At lunch or dinner, tuck into a huge Mexican combo plate ($3.50) with tacos, *flautas* (fried tacos), tostadas, and enchiladas. **Los Defines** (end of Sanchez Taboada, tel. 622/2–92–30; cash only) specializes in fresh fish ($5) and has postcard-perfect views of the harbor.

NEAR GUAYMAS

SAN CARLOS

The desert meets the azure waves of the Sea of Cortés at San Carlos, where Mt. Teta Kawi dominates the shoreline. An increasing number of diving enthusiasts from the United States call this town home, and when they're not underwater you'll find them putting on the golf courses and schmoozing at the nearby Club Med. If you have the cash, it's easy to participate in a number of water sports here, including sailing, kayaking, jet skiing, and fishing. San Carlos hosts an international fishing tournament in July and a multilevel sailing competition called **Cristóbal Colón** (Christopher Columbus) around October 12.

COMING AND GOING

Buses marked SAN CARLOS (30 min, 60¢) leave from Serdán in Guaymas every half hour, starting at 6 AM. The last bus returns to Guaymas from San Carlos at 9 PM. If you don't have a car, taxis provide the only means of transportation from San Carlos to the less-populated beaches. A taxi to **Frenchie's Cove** or **Lalo Cove** (both about 7 km/4½ mi from town) will cost $7; it's $8–$10 to **Catch 22** beach (a.k.a. **Playa Los Algodones**), 8 km (5 mi) away, and $7 to **Las Mangas,** 16 km (10 mi) away.

WHERE TO SLEEP

Hotels here are expensive, so unless you've got a tent, you may want to make San Carlos a day trip. **Hotel Fiesta** (at entrance to town, 1½ km (1 mi) down main road, tel. 622/6–02–29) and **Motel Crestón** (tel. 622/6–00–20) are the cheapest hotels, but both charge more than $30 for double rooms. Both have a pool and long-distance phone service, and Hotel Fiesta has a private beach and a restaurant. The more reasonably priced **Departamentos Ferrer** (1 block from the beach on Bajada del Comedor, tel. 622/6–04–67) has apartments ($25), equipped with air-conditioning and kitchenettes, which sleep up to four people. Make reservations at least two weeks in advance, as the place is full even during scorching summer months.

For $18 a night you can camp at **Teta Kawi Trailer Park** (behind Best Western, tel. 622/6–02–20, fax 622/6–02–48), just outside town on the road to Guaymas, or next door at **Totonaka Trailer Park** (tel. 622/6–04–81 or 622/6–03–23) and take advantage of the swimming pools and nearby laundry ($1.50). Both are cash only. Beach camping is legal, but keep an eye on your possessions. The best beaches for camping are **Playa San Francisco** (just before the entrance to town from Guaymas), **Lalo Cove,** and **Playa Los Algodones** (in front of Howard Johnson's).

FOOD

Food stands along the Carretera Turístico (the highway that runs through town) are the cheapest way to fill your belly. However, if you want to have a real sit-down meal, try **Rosaís Cantina** (tel. 622/6–10–00) on the main drag, which offers breakfast items, a salad bar, and entrées like pork chops, all less than $5. The **San Carlos Grill** (Plaza Comercial San Carlos No. 1, at turnoff to marina, tel. 622/6–06–09; no breakfast) specializes in "Lingo Gringo" (beef fillet; $5) and frosty margaritas. Both are cash only.

Club Med chose San Carlos for its sugary white-sand beaches and turquoise waters. A 60¢ bus ride from Guaymas will give you the same thing for a whole lot less.

OUTDOOR ACTIVITIES

Finding budget outdoor activities in San Carlos is, unfortunately, about as difficult as catching frostbite in Sonora. You can rent a bike ($10 for 5 hrs) at **El Mar Diving Center** (263 Creston, tel. 622/6–04–04), but make sure you carry plenty of water or you'll pass out from the heat. Another cheap option is to rent snorkel gear ($3 per day) at **Gary's** (near El Mar, on main road). Gary's also organizes fishing trips and has a 2½-hour snorkeling trip ($33) to the Aquarium Cove, one of the nearby attractions. If you have money to blow, you've come to the right place—everything from windsurfing equipment ($20 per hr) to Jet Skis ($55 per hr), to banana boat rides ($5.50 per hr) is available.

SCUBA DIVING • Divers and snorkelers are drawn to San Carlos for its accessibility and for its clear waters, which reach Jacuzzilike temperatures in the summer. **Gary's** (*see above*) has four-day certification courses for $414 that include five open-water dives and all equipment. His prices are competitive with those at **Cortés Explorations** (near the marina, tel. 622/6–08–08) and **El Mar Diving Center** (*see above*). If you're already certified, a two-tank dive to sites off nearby islands goes for $60 (add another $30 if you need equipment).

ALAMOS

This small city, 256 km (158 mi) southeast of Guaymas, is one of the oldest in northern Mexico. Once the land of the indigenous Guarijio people, Alamos was converted into a silver-mining town during the 18th century by European businessmen seeking their fortune. It may be difficult to reach, but once you get here, the narrow cobblestone streets, ranchers on horseback, and secluded haciendas with their elegant courtyards may charm you into staying longer than you had planned.

Entertainment in Alamos comes in the form of exploring the crumbling adobe buildings. The **Iglesia de la Purísima Concepción** has a towering three-tier bell tower and impressive Spanish colonial architecture, while the beautiful **Hotel Mansión de la Condesa Magdalena** (Obregón 2, tel. 642/8–02–21) is worth peeking into, even though you probably can't afford to stay—rooms run $60 and up. The **Plaza de las Armas** is a beautiful park that livens up with kids, couples, and people-watchers as soon as the sun dips below the horizon. At the north end of the plaza, the **Museo Costumbrista de Sonora** (admission 50¢; open Wed.–Sun. 9–1 and 3–6) merits a visit for its displays on Sonora's history. If you'd like an oral version of Alamos's history, **Pepe** at the Hotel Casa de los Tesoros (*see* Where to Sleep, *below*) gives a two-hour walking tour of the city ($7). Alamos is also famous for its *brincadores* (Mexican jumping beans; actually a kind of butterfly larva), which are found in the hills surrounding the city. September is the best time to catch the little guys, but they're usually hopping year-round.

BASICS

You can change cash or traveler's checks at the **Bancomer** (tel. 642/8–03–25; open weekdays 8:30–1) at the south end of Plaza de las Armas, but there are no ATMs anywhere in the city. The **post office** is next to the police station on Madero. There are no public phones on the streets, but **Polo's Restaurant** (tel. 642/8–00–01), at the far end of Zaragoza, has a small caseta that charges $1.50 for collect and credit-card calls. The **tourist office** (tel. 642/8–04–50), below Hotel Los Portales, is open weekdays 9–2 and 4–7, Saturday 9–2. You can rent **bicycles** ($1 an hr) on Plaza de las Armas next to Bancomer Monday–Saturday 8–1 and 3–6, but it's a bumpy ride along the cobblestone streets.

COMING AND GOING

Alamos is only accessible by car, or by local bus from the town of Navojoa. After the **Transportes del Pacífico** bus from Guaymas lets you off at the corner of Revolución and Guerrero in Navojoa, walk 10 minutes down Guerrero (toward the town center) to the small **Los Mayitos** terminal, at the corner of Rincón. Buses leave here for Alamos (1 hr, $1) every 40 minutes 6:30 AM–midnight. From Alamos, hourly buses (last bus 6:30 PM) make the return trip to Navojoa from the station on Morelos, at Plaza Alameda. If you're coming by car, head south on Highway 15 from Guaymas and look for the turnoff for Alamos in Navojoa.

WHERE TO SLEEP

The short walk to **Motel Somar** (Madero 110, tel. 642/8–01–95; doubles with fan $16, with air-conditioning $19) from the center of town is more than compensated for by the reasonably priced, comfortable rooms with fairly clean, private bathrooms. If you know you'll be staying here, ask the bus driver to drop you off when you see the MOTEL SOMAR sign on your left as you enter town. Next door, **Dolisa Motel** (Madero 72, tel. and fax 642/8–01–31) has doubles ($27) with TV, air-conditioning, and possibly a fridge (depending on the room). Both are cash only. The **Hotel Casa de los Tesoros** (Obregón 10, behind cathedral, tel. 642/8–00–10), a former convent, has been beautifully restored and offers air-conditioning, fireplaces, an inner courtyard with a pool, lots of elderly gringos in the winter months, and a restaurant serving Mexican and Puerto Rican food. Doubles cost $40 in summer months, $75 in winter.

CAMPING • The Dolisa Motel (*see* Where to Sleep, *above*) has a big dirt lot where you can pitch a tent ($5 for 2 people) or park an RV. The owner of Motel Somar will also let you camp in the back and charges whatever you can afford. There are a few RV parks where less than $10 will get you a two-person tent site with showers and a swimming pool; try **Trailer Park Acosta Ranch** (tel. 642/8–02–46), just over 1 km (½ mi) from town near the cemetery, or **Los Alamos Trailer Park** (tel. 642/8–03–32), at the entrance to town on the highway. RV parks are cash only.

FOOD

The vendors clustered around Plaza Alameda serve tacos and such for about $1. The **mercado municipal** (east end of the plaza) has inexpensive meats, cheeses, and locally grown fruits and vegetables, but you can eat almost as cheaply at some local restaurants. **Taquería Blanquita** (Antonio Rosales, next to the market) is packed with locals morning to night. Long, get-to-know-your-neighbor tables are generously stocked with chile and guacamole to dress the $2 comida corrida. **Antojitos Laura** (Rosales, just behind Plaza Alameda, no phone) serves to-die-for tostadas ($2) and guards their family recipe under lock and key. **Casa de Café** (Obregón 2, tel. 642/8–00–88), in the courtyard of an old mansion, serves cappuccinos, lattes, sticky buns, and scones that please locals and tourists alike. Restaurants are cash only.

LOS MOCHIS

The agricultural boomtown of Los Mochis, just over the Sonora–Sinaloa border on Highway 15, is surrounded by farmland. The city was founded in 1893 by Benjamin Johnston, a wealthy American who developed sugar production in this area. Another American, socialist Albert Owen, began the Chihuahua al Pacífico railroad line from Los Mochis and Chihuahua up into the Sierra Madre Occidental mountains. The rugged mountains forced Owen to abandon the project in 1893, but it was finally completed in 1961. Today most tourists passing through Los Mochis are only here to catch the famous train ride through Copper Canyon, or to board a Baja-bound ferry. Aside from this, Los Mochis and its environs boast few points of local interest—apart from the town's lively Sunday morning market, or the remains of Johnston's opulent estate and pleasant botanical garden.

BASICS

AMERICAN EXPRESS

The AmEx representative in **Viajes Araceli** changes traveler's checks and provides the usual cardholder services. The travel agency (open Mon.–Sat. 8:30–6:30, Sun. 10–1) also sells first-class plane, bus, and train tickets. *Álvaro Obregón 471-A Pte., Los Mochis, Sinaloa, CP 81200, México. Tel. 681/2–20–84 or 681/2–41–39. Open weekdays 8:30–1 and 3–6:30, Sat. 8:30–2.*

BOOKSTORES

Librería Los Mochis has a wide selection of literature in Spanish, as well as an occasional English newspaper. *Madero 402, at Leyva, tel. 681/5–72–42. Open daily 8 AM–10 PM.*

CASAS DE CAMBIO

A number of banks and several casas de cambio line Calle Leyva downtown. **Servicio de Cambio** (Leyva 271 Sur, near Juárez, tel. 681/2–56–66; open weekdays 8–7:30, Sat. 8–7) changes cash and traveler's checks. However, you can get much better rates at **Bancomer** (Leyva, at Juárez, tel. 681/5–80–01; open weekdays 8–1). You'll need to line up for the exchange window by noon. **Banamex** has three 24-hour ATMs in the downtown area; the most centrally located (Prieto and Hidalgo) accepts Visa, MasterCard, Cirrus, and Plus cards.

Bright-blue aguamalos (jellyfish) are abundant on the beaches of San Carlos. The jellyfish's sting is rarely fatal, though it is very painful; apply fresh lemon juice to the wound to stop the burning.

CAMPING SUPPLIES

Stock up on camping supplies for a trip to the Copper Canyon at **Equipos y Deportes** (Leyva, at Juárez; open daily 9–7).

EMERGENCIES

You can reach the **police, fire** department, or **ambulance** service by dialing 06 from any public phone.

LAUNDRY

The self-serve **Lavarama** is around the corner from the bus terminals. Automatic washers cost $2, dryers $2, soap 50¢, and they'll do it all for you for an additional 75¢ per load. *Juárez 225, tel. 681/2–81–20. Open daily 8–7.*

MAIL

The post office will hold mail sent to you at the following address for up to 10 days: Lista de Correos, Los Mochis, Sinaloa, CP 81281, México. *226 Ordóñez Pte., tel. 681/2–08–23. Open weekdays 8–6:30, Sat. 9–1.*

MEDICAL AID

Farmacia San Jorge (Flores and Independencia, tel. 681/5–74–74) is open 24 hours. For more urgent medical attention, the 24-hour **Centro Médico de Los Mochis** (Rosendo G. Castro, between Allende and Guillermo Prieto, tel. 681/2–74–26 or 681/2–01–98) has some English-speaking doctors, as well as a 24-hour pharmacy.

PHONES

There are brand-new **TelMex** pay phones all over downtown, from which you can make local or long-distance calls. At the quiet, air-conditioned **Fax Tel** (Leyva, between Hidalgo and Obregón, tel. and fax 681/8–10–20; open daily 8 AM–10 PM), you can make local or long-distance cash calls, free collect calls, and credit-card calls, or use the fax machine.

VISITOR INFORMATION

The small tourist office in the **Unidad Administrativa** building is cloaked by dark, reflective windows—but don't let that deter you. The English-speaking staff is happy to help. *Allende, at Cuauhtémoc, tel. 681/2–66–40. Open weekdays 8–3 and 5–8.*

COMING AND GOING

BY BUS

Unless you're heading straight to Chihuahua via the Copper Canyon, traveling by bus is the easiest way to leave Los Mochis. The **Élite** (tel. 681/2–17–57) and **Transportes Norte de Sonora** (tel. 681/8–49–67) terminal is on Juárez between Allende and Prieto. The **Transportes del Pacífico** (tel. 681/2–03–41) terminal is a few blocks north of downtown, on José María Morelos, between Leyva and Zaragoza. Both stations are open 24 hours, but neither offers luggage storage. The terminal on Juárez is the newest and busiest and offers first- and second-class service to Mazatlán (6 hrs; $40 1st class, $20 2nd class), Guadalajara (11 hrs; $75 1st class, $50 2nd class), Mexico City (24 hrs; $90 1st class, $40 2nd class), Nogales (12 hrs; $23 1st class, $11 2nd class), Mexicali (22 hrs; $40 1st class, $25 2nd class), Tijuana (24 hrs; $40 1st class, $25 2nd class), and Navojoa (3 hrs; $17 1st class, $15 2nd class).

BY FERRY

You can buy tickets for a **Sematur** ferry to La Paz (on the Baja Peninsula) at **Viajes Paotam** (Serapio Rendón 517 Pte., tel. 681/5–19–14) in Los Mochis Monday–Saturday 8–1 and 4–6, Sunday 10–noon. Be sure to buy tickets ($15) at least 24 hours in advance if you're determined to leave on a specific day. Tickets are also on sale at the ferry dock weekdays 8 AM–11 AM. Ferries leave from the dock in Topolobampo, 25 km (15 mi) west of Los Mochis, at 9 PM, and the trip takes about eight hours. Buses marked TOPOLOBAMPO (50¢) leave from the corner of Cuauhtémoc and Prieto every 15 minutes 6 AM–8 PM, stopping along Boulevard Rosendo G. Castro on the way out of town.

BY PLANE

The Los Mochis airport, 20 km (12 mi) south of town, is served primarily by **Aero California** (tel. 681/5–21–30 or 681/5–22–50, or 800/237–6225 in the U.S.) and **Aeroméxico** (tel. 681/5–25–70), which provide limited one-way service to major Mexican cities such as Guadalajara ($112) and Mazatlán ($100), and to U.S. destinations such as Tucson ($160). To get here, you'll need to take a taxi ($12).

BY TRAIN

The railroad station (tel. 681/2–93–85), on the outskirts of town 2 km (1 mi) southeast of downtown, is the southwestern terminus of the famous **Chihuahua al Pacífico** iron horse, which winds its way through the Copper Canyon region (*see* Chapter 5). If you only take one train ride in Mexico, this should be it. Two trains depart from Los Mochis: The first-class Vista departs daily at 6 AM, with stops in the Copper Canyon towns of Bahuichivo (6½ hrs; $13 1st class, $4 2nd class), Divisadero (7½ hrs; $15 1st class, $3 2nd class), and Creel (9½ hrs; $18.50 1st class, $3 2nd class), arriving in Chihuahua ($42 1st class, $9 2nd class) about 13 hours later. The second-class *Mixto* (also called *pollero* or *burro*) train departs Los Mochis on Tuesday, Thursday, and Saturday at 7 AM, and takes a whole lot longer than the first-class train to arrive at any given destination. Return trains depart from Chihuahua on Monday, Wednesday, and Friday. Buy tickets a day in advance if you can; travel agencies and most hotels sell tickets for the Vista train, but Mixto tickets are only available at the train station the morning of departure starting at 6 AM. During Semana Santa you'll have to fight everybody and their *abuelita* (grandmother) for tickets. To reach the station from town, look for taxis ($5) in front of Hotel Santa Rita on Leyva and Hidalgo; buses marked COL. FERR. go to the train station but don't operate in the early morning and are therefore useless to budget travelers, since this is precisely when the trains leave.

Travelers heading north to Mexicali ($21 1st class, $7 2nd class) or south to Guadalajara ($23 1st class, $7 2nd class) depart from the Sufragio station on the **Ferrocarril del Pacífico** line (tel. 681/4–01–28). To reach Sufragio, take a bus headed for El Fuerte from Calle Cuauhtémoc and Zaragoza (50 min, $2) and ask the driver to let you off at the Sufragio station.

GETTING AROUND

Los Mochis is easily navigated, and everything but the train station, airport, and ferry terminal is accessible on foot. The main streets Calles Allende, Guillermo Prieto, Zaragoza, and Leyva run parallel to one another, with hotels, drugstores, restaurants, and just about anything else you could need within Boulevard Castro and Avenida Madero. Budget lodging can be found close to Independencia on the west and Leyva on the north. City buses (20¢) are easily hailed all around town, and many originate at the **mercado,** on the corner of Guillermo Prieto and Cuauhtémoc.

WHERE TO SLEEP

Most budget accommodations in the downtown area need a good scrubbing but are fairly comfortable and conveniently located. **Hotel Fenix** (Angel Flores 365, tel. 681/2–26–23) offers doubles ($18) that are clean, carpeted, and air-conditioned, which is probably why it fills up fast. All rooms have TVs and phones. **Hotel del Valle** (Guillermo Prieto, at Independencia, tel. 681/2–01–05) is fairly modern, and its shabby but comfortable rooms have fans and bathrooms with occasional hot water. Doubles are $12–$15, depending on whether they have a TV and phone. The colonial-style **Hotel Montecarlo** (Ángel Flores 322 Sur, at Independencia, tel. 681/2–18–18) is tucked between a restaurant and a noisy bar in the downtown area, not far from the cathedral. All rooms (doubles $17) have air-conditioning, TV, phone, and clean bathrooms with hot water. Rooms on the second story have small balconies. All hotels are cash only.

FOOD

The downtown area teems with taco, fish, and fruit stands. The daily **mercado municipal** (Guillermo Prieto, at Cuauhtémoc Pte.) has raw edibles, a huge fish and meat market, and several decent *comedores* (sit-down food stands). **Restaurant Chic's** (Plaza Fiesta, at Rosales and Obregón, tel. 681/5–47–09), a few blocks west of downtown, seems characterless, but once the families start strolling in after mass it's a good place to people-watch. For less than $4, you can get the breakfast of tamales, chorizo, and beans, or the fresh fruit plate. **El Taquito** (Leyva, between Hidalgo and Independencia, tel. 681/2–81–19) looks like Denny's and tastes like Denny's, and just like Denny's it's open 24 hours. Mushroom omelets and French toast (both $3) are served for breakfast, and hamburgers and fries are on the menu for lunch. All of the above are cash only. **El Farallón** (Obregón, at Ángel Flores, tel. 681/2–14–28), specializing in fresh, spicy seafood, is a favorite of Los Mochis businessmen. Dishes such as calamari ($10) and *ceviche* (diced fish marinated in lime juice) come with tortillas and beans. **Jugos Chapala** (Independencia 366; cash only) pours fresh carrot, strawberry, papaya, and other juices for $1–$2.

WORTH SEEING

If you happen to be here on Sunday morning, be sure to visit the *tianguis* (open-air market), in the downtown shopping area (on Leyva, just across Rendon), where you can stock up on housewares, electronics, and trinkets. The city's locals flock here once church services are over, and the shops and stalls are packed with hagglers. Come early, though—everything closes down by 2 PM.

PARQUE ECOLOGICO DE SINALOA

This unassuming park occupies the grounds of sugar baron and town founder Benjamin Johnston's former estate, and is home to trees imported from around the world, including towering palms from Cuba and fuzzy cypress from Arizona. Near the entrance, a giant tree bears Indian carvings of an eagle, bear, snake, deer, and that ultimate animal, Mr. Johnston himself. *On Rosales, behind Woolworth shopping center, no phone. Open daily 8–7. Admission free.*

MUSEO REGIONAL DEL VALLE DEL FUERTE

Ensconced in a colonial-style house, this museum consists of a photography exposition and archaeological exhibits depicting the history and culture of the region. Traditional theater and *baile folklórico* (folk dancing) productions are also staged here throughout the year. Stop by for a calendar of events. *Obregón, just east of Rosales, no phone. Open daily 10–1 and 4–7. Admission 75¢.*

NEAR LOS MOCHIS

Buses headed for the towns of Topolobampo and El Fuerte depart Los Mochis from Cuauhtémoc, between Prieto and Zaragoza. Buses to Topolobampo (50 min, 50¢) leave daily about every half hour 7 AM–8 PM. If you're planning to take the ferry from Topolobampo to La Paz, don't get off at the first bus station in Topolobampo—the bus will continue on to the ferry dock. Buses to El Fuerte (1½ hrs, $2) depart a little less often, 7 AM–6 PM.

TOPOLOBAMPO

About 25 km (15 mi) west of Los Mochis is the town of Topolobampo, founded at the end of the 19th century by a bunch of Americans looking to set up a socialist utopia. This dream was quashed when the colonists began fighting amongst themselves, then Los Mochis sugar baron Benjamin Johnston managed to scoop up the water rights to the area and evict everybody. Today the harbor town is largely dependent on shrimping and industry. Sea lions frolic in the deep bay, and Isla El Farallón, just off the coast, is their breeding ground. You are most likely to come to Topolobampo only to get on or off the ferry, but if you do stay a day or two you can take advantage of the spectacular natural surroundings of this less-than-spectacular town. **El Yacht** (tel. 681/2–66–01), about ½ km (¼ mi) south of town on the highway, offers rooms (equipped with air-conditioning and TV) that fit five people for about $15. The hotel also has a private beach, a bar, and a restaurant built like a yacht, with a panoramic view of the bay and islands. El Yacht accepts cash only.

Although the harbor itself lacks swimming or sunning beaches, shell collectors will delight at scanning the shores. Boat rides to the five islands in the bay near Topolobampo can be arranged through Teodolfo Cital at the **Sociedad Cooperativa de Servicios Turísticos** (next to the customs building, on the water), which looks like a vacant, unfinished house. Teodolfo takes groups of eight people to the pristine **Playa Copas** ($30 a person), **Isla Santa María** ($45 a person), the duck sanctuary at **Isla Santuario** ($15 a person), or **Isla El Farallón,** where the sea lions play ($115 a person). He'll also take you on shorter fishing trips around the bay (45 min, $15). If you gather a group, you may be able to bargain for better prices. In September, *camarones* (shrimp) are practically spilling out of the ocean, and you can arrange a boat ride to watch the fishermen in action.

EL FUERTE

If your previous experiences of colonial architecture in northwestern Mexico have left you unimpressed, come to El Fuerte. Cobblestone streets, gracefully aging buildings, and newly remodeled haciendas with lush green gardens provide a scenic backdrop for this slow-pace town. El Fuerte was originally founded in 1564 as a gateway to the northern Indian territories of Sonora, Arizona, and California. It was not easily won land for the Spanish, however, and they spent the next 50 years fending off the fierce Tehueco, Sinaloa, and Zuaque Indians. In 1610 a fort was built here, and the following three centuries saw the area around El Fuerte grow into one of the most important commercial and agricultural centers in northwestern Mexico.

Today this small colonial city, 75 km (47 mi) east of Los Mochis, attracts fishermen bound for nearby **Lake Hidalgo** (11 km/6½ mi north), **Lake Domínguez** (19 km/11½ mi west), and the **Fuerte River** (a 10-minute walk west from the plaza), all known for their largemouth bass. If you didn't bring your fishing gear, you can swim in the lakes or the river, or simply enjoy the town's architecture. **La Iglesia del Sagrado Corazón de Jesús** (Church of the Sacred Heart of Jesus), built in 1854, the **Palacio Municipal,** and **La Casa de la Cultura** (admission free; open daily 10–7), surround the shaded **Plaza de Armas** at Degollado and Rosales. This plaza was voted one of the most beautiful in the state of Sinaloa by the state's residents, and has a graceful white gazebo surrounded by palm trees, rose bushes, and lush ferns. Perhaps the best reason to visit El Fuerte is to splurge on a room at **Hotel Posada Hidalgo** (Hidalgo 101, just off plaza, tel. 689/3–02–42, fax 681/2–00–46), a lovingly restored 19th-century hacienda with exotic gardens, outdoor patios, a swimming pool, and plenty of hammocks. The gracious staff is also more than willing to provide you with information on the city's attractions, whether or not you're a guest. Doubles cost $90. The adjoining **Disco Palace** (open Fri. and Sat. until 1 AM) attracts all the locals, who rock out to ranchero and mariachi music in their tightest Spandex. Stop by **Restaurant Supremo** (corner of Rosales and Constitución) for fresh bass ($5) or a ham-and-egg breakfast.

NORTH CENTRAL MEXICO AND THE COPPER CANYON

UPDATED BY JENNIFER BARTLETT

The north central states of Chihuahua and Durango are characterized by vast deserts, which encircle the magnificent Sierra Madre Occidental mountain range. Regal cacti and run-down *ranchitos* (small farms) freckle the landscape, and when farmers aren't working the tomato, chile, and corn fields, they can be heard wailing *ranchero* songs in the local bars. These farmers have been struggling with financial hardship for six years, thanks to a persistent drought, but the recent rains have brought some relief to withered crops and sickly livestock. Adversity is not uncommon to north central Mexico, though, and the people have a history of digging in their heels and fighting back: Two founding fathers of contemporary Mexico, Miguel Hidalgo and Pancho Villa, called this region home, and today north central Mexico remains at the forefront of popular dissent—Chihuahua being a long-standing bastion of support for the PAN (Mexico's leading opposition party; *see box, below*).

The highlights of this region begin to reveal themselves only after you pass the overpopulated, drug-infested border town of Ciudad Juárez. Indeed, the state of Chihuahua (which means "dry, sandy place" in the indigenous Tarahumara language) is famous for its natural beauty. Its Sierra Madre Occidental range comprises five large canyons sewn together by massive waterfalls, rivers, and hot springs. The most famous of these is **Las Barrancas del Cobre** (The Copper Canyon), which has been inhabited for centuries by the Tarahumara people. While many have been displaced due to the mining and lumber industries, 50,000 still uphold traditional customs on their original lands. The Chihuahua al Pacífico railway weaves 670 km (415 mi) through the canyon, conveniently stopping at popular jumping-off points for hiking and camping, such as Creel, Batopilas, and Bahuichivo. Many tourists are also attracted to the enigmatic pre-Columbian ruins of Paquimé and the lively, historic city of Chihuahua.

The dusty landscape around the town of Durango (the capital of the state of Durango) is what many people picture when they think of Mexico—probably because it has been used as the setting for a number of Hollywood westerns. The city itself is more a stopover point for travelers than anything else; however, once you get past the urban sprawl of the outskirts, you'll find a friendly colonial city perfect for a day or two of exploration.

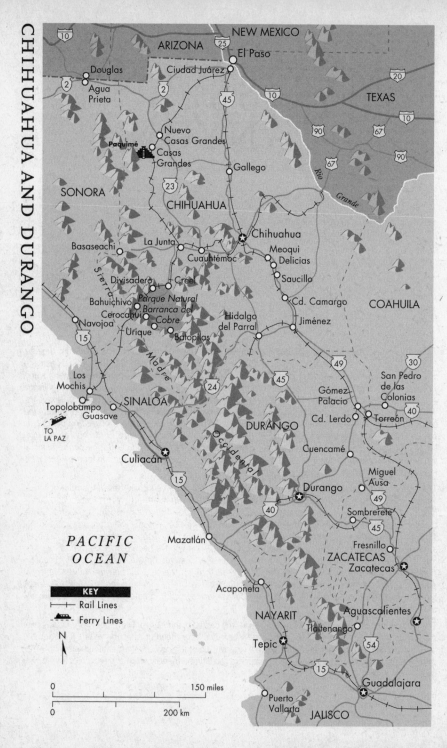

NEW MEXICO

ARIZONA

El Paso

Ciudad Juárez

Douglas

Agua
Prieta

TEXAS

Nuevo
Casas Grandes

Paquimé

Casas
Grandes

Gallego

SONORA

CHIHUAHUA

Chihuahua

Basaseachi

La Junta

Cuauhtémoc

Meoqui
Delicias

Saucillo

Divisadero

Creel

Cd. Camargo

COAHUILA

Bahuichivo

Parque Natural

Barranca del
Cobre

Cerocahui

Hidalgo
del Parral

Jiménez

Navojoa

Urique

Batopilas

San Pedro
de las
Colonias

Los
Mochis

Gómez
Palacio

Topolobampo

Guasave

SINALOA

Cd. Lerdo

Torreón

**TO
LA PAZ**

DURANGO

Cuencamé

Culiacán

Miguel
Ausa

Durango

Sombrerete

PACIFIC
OCEAN

Mazatlán

Fresnillo

ZACATECAS

Zacatecas

Acaponeta

Aguascalientes

KEY

Rail Lines

Ferry Lines

NAYARIT

Tlaltenango

Tepic

N

0   150 miles

0   200 km

Puerto
Vallarta

JALISCO

Guadalajara

CIUDAD JUAREZ

If you find yourself in Ciudad Juárez, leave fast. Only hang around if: (1) you're in the market for an inexpensive root canal; (2) you need a polyester wedding dress; or (3) you are wanted by the law on both sides of the border and need to hop jurisdictions easily. This sprawling city on the northern edge of Chihuahua state—just across the Rio Grande from El Paso, Texas—exhibits the worst of both Mexico and the United States. The passage of NAFTA (the North American Free Trade Agreement) in 1994 increased the number of *maquiladoras,* or *maquilas* (foreign-owned factories in duty-free zones) in and around Juárez, creating an unfavorable societal and environmental impact. The majority of Juárez's population is currently employed in the maquilas, and the cardboard settlements that have sprouted to house these people lack basic sanitation and are polluted by toxic waste.

Juárez, though a good example of emerging border culture, is an uninspiring tourist spot. However, if you're stuck here for a day, try to catch a bullfight at the **Plaza de Toros Monumental** (Paseo Triunfo de la República and López Mateos) or a rodeo at **López Mateos Charro** (Av. del Charro). Museum buffs can visit the free **Museo de Historia** in the **Antigua Aduana** building (16 de Septiembre, at Juárez, tel. 16/12–47–07; open Tues.–Sun. 10–6). The best time to catch a positive glimpse of the city is during festivals: The **Festival de la Raza,** celebrated during the first week of May, culminates in a **Cinco De Mayo** parade along Avenida Juárez. During the last two weeks of June, the **Feria Juárez** fills the city with dancing and theater, as well as arts-and-crafts displays.

"Throughout the ages the inhabitants of Chihuahua have always been warriors . . . because their environment has demanded of them more than their best efforts." –From a Mexican history book at the Paquimé Museum

BASICS

AMERICAN EXPRESS

The AmEx representatives at **Sun Travel,** in El Paso, Texas, can help with lost or stolen checks, insurance, and transportation arrangements. The office also sells traveler's checks, offers MoneyGram service, and holds mail for cardholders. The AmEx office in Juárez offers the same services. *3100 North Mesa, Suite B, El Paso, Texas 79902, U.S.A, tel. 915/532–8900, fax 915/533–6887. Open weekdays 8–5. In Juárez: Av. Lincoln 1320, Local (suite) 175, tel. 16/29–27–40. Open weekdays 9–6, Sat. 9-1.*

CASAS DE CAMBIO

Many money-exchange places line Avenida Juárez near the Stanton Street Bridge. **Cambios Juárez,** just yards from the bridge's entrance, is open daily 9–9, but most are only open until 5. After business hours, try **Banamex**'s 24-hour *cajas permanentes* (ATMs), on the corner of Avenidas Juárez and 16 de Septiembre.

CONSULATES

United States. *López Mateos Nte. 924, tel. 16/11–30–00, after hours in El Paso tel. 915/525–6066. Open weekdays 8–4:45.*

CROSSING THE BORDER

When entering Mexico, pick up a tourist card at the **Mexican Consulate** (E. San Antonio St., tel. 915/533–3644; open weekdays 9–1) in El Paso or at the immigration office (open 24 hours) near the Stanton Street Bridge in Ciudad Juárez. The bridge is eight blocks south of downtown El Paso on Santa Fe Street, and there's a 25¢ toll at the entrance and a 30¢ toll to return. If you travel farther than 32 km (19 mi) from the border or stay in Mexico more than 72 hours, you may be asked to show the card at checkpoints. For more information on tourist cards, *see* Chapter 1, or call the customs office at the border (tel. 16/16–08–25).

EMERGENCIES

You can dial 06 from any phone in Ciudad Juárez to reach the **police, fire** department, or an **ambulance.** Or dial 911 from any phone on the U.S. side of the border.

LAUNDRY

Lavandería Express (Hernán Baldez, just behind Mercado Juárez, no phone) will wash and dry your clothes for about $1 per kilo. Be prepared to wait two hours for the service.

MAIL

The slightly chaotic **post office** (downstairs level, Francisco Villa, Calle de la Peña just south of 16 de Septiembre) is open weekdays 9–7, Saturday 9–5, Sunday 9–noon. They'll hold mail for you for up to 10 days at the following address: Lista de Correos, Administración 1, Ciudad Juárez, Chihuahua, CP 32001, México.

MEDICAL AID

Unless you require emergency treatment, it's a good idea to hop over to El Paso for medical attention. In Ciudad Juaréz, **Hospital General** (Paseo Triunfo de la República 2401, tel. 16/13–15–71) offers emergency care but no English-speaking physicians. **Farmacia Iris** (16 de Septiembre, at Corona, tel. 16/14–89–90) is a pharmacy open Monday–Saturday 9 AM–10 PM.

PHONES

The **Ladatel** public phones in Ciudad Juárez are dependable for cash, credit- and calling-card calls, and even collect calls. For Mexican long distance, dial 01; to call El Paso, dial 001; for other international calls, dial 00 or your long-distance carrier's access number. Additionally, there are *casetas de larga distancia* (long-distance telephone offices) all along Avenida Juarez.

VISITOR INFORMATION

The tourist office inside the **El Paso–Juárez Trolley Co.** (1 Civic Center Plaza, El Paso, tel. 915/544–0061; open daily 8–5) provides information for travelers crossing into Mexico. Ciudad Juárez's new **tourist office** (Juárez 809, corner Acucenas, tel. 16/14–92–56; open weekdays noon–7, weekends 11–5) has a friendly staff that speaks excellent English.

VOLUNTEERING

The **Partido Verde Ecologista** campaigns to involve Mexico's youth in ecological projects such as water conservation and toxic-waste prevention. In Juárez, the group has an "eco-bus" that distributes literature and teaches poor communities about waste removal and clean water. Volunteers from both sides of the border are welcome. For more information write: Partido Verde Ecologista de México, Attn. Diego Cobo, Coordinador Nacional de la Juventud Ecologista, Callejón del Beso 235-C, FRACC Valle Verde, Ciudad Juárez, Chihuahua, México.

COMING AND GOING

BY BUS

The best way to reach Ciudad Juárez from El Paso is to catch a Greyhound bus (30 min, $5), which leaves every half hour from El Paso's Greyhound station (next to the convention center, tel. 800/231–2222 in the U.S.) and takes you right to Juárez's bus station (tel. 16/10–64–14). This monstrous terminal is way out of Juárez, at the junction of Highways 2 and 45. It's stocked with two long-distance telephone offices, a money-changing booth, a pharmacy, cafeterias, and 24-hour luggage storage (30¢ per hr). **Estrella Blanca** (tel. 16/29–22–29) provides hourly service to Chihuahua (4½ hrs, $14), Nuevo Casas Grandes (4 hrs, $9), Mazatlán (21 hrs, $49), Durango (14 hrs, $38), and Zacatecas (15 hrs, $47). Four buses also depart daily to Mexico City (26 hrs, $71). **Transportes Chihuahuenses** (tel. 16/29–22–29) serves the same routes, while **Omnibus** (tel. 16/10–64–45), **Turistar,** and **Futura** charge a few dollars more for *especial* first-class buses with air-conditioning, toilets, and movies. **Greyhound** bus tickets can be purchased at the Estrella Blanca counter for trips to Los Angeles ($35), Albuquerque ($20), and Denver ($40), as well as other U.S. destinations. To reach the bus station from downtown Juárez, take a bus marked CENTRAL CAMIONERA (20¢) and allow at least an hour. A taxi from Juárez will cost you about $7.

BY CAR

To cross the border with your car, present the registration (in your name), a current driver's license, and your passport, as well as photocopies of all three documents. If your documents are in order you'll be issued a car permit, usually valid for six months. You will be asked to provide a guarantee (like your credit-card number) that you'll bring the car back across the border once your permit expires; if you don't, you'll be charged a heavy fine. Those without a credit card will have to buy a bond of 1%–2% of the car's value from one of the bond sellers close to the border. Customs officials don't care if you buy Mexican insurance or not, but a policeman farther south (or the "other party" in case of an accident) might. Insurance is available from a number of companies near the border. All offer similar coverage— a basic liability/collision policy costs $10–$20 for 24 hours.

BY PLANE

The airport is far from the center of town, just off Highway 45. **Aeroméxico** (tel. 16/13–80–89, or 800/237–6639 in the U.S.) is the main carrier, with daily flights to Chihuahua ($105 one-way), Mexico City ($158 one-way), and Mazatlán ($164 one-way). A taxi from downtown to the terminal costs $10, but it's cheaper to grab a CENTRAL CAMIONERA bus (20¢), get off at the bus station, and take a taxi the rest of the way.

BY TRAIN

The train station (Juan Gabriel, tel. 16/12–31–88) is 12 long blocks down the tracks from the Stanton Street Bridge. Two trains leave Cuidad Juárez daily, heading south to Mexico City (12 hrs, $35 1st class; $20 2nd class), with stops in Chihuahua ($7 1st class, $3 2nd class), Zacatecas ($23 1st class, $13 2nd class), and Aguascalientes ($25 1st class, $14 2nd class). Tickets for the 10 PM first-class departure should be purchased in advance Monday–Saturday 9 AM–noon. They usually sell out, so plan ahead. The second-class train leaves at 7 AM, and tickets go on sale at 6 AM. If you're looking for a taxi from the station, it's better to walk a block or two toward downtown and hail one there, where prices are more reasonable.

GETTING AROUND

Juárez is spread out, and transport terminals are all far from each other. Fortunately, budget accommodations and restaurants are clustered along Avenida Juárez, between the Stanton Street Bridge and Avenida 16 de Septiembre. Unfortunately, finding local buses that travel to outlying points can be confusing because of the city's large number of one-way streets. Buses generally arrive and depart from Avenida Vicente Guerrero, one block south of Avenida 16 de Septiembre. Buses run until midnight and tickets (20¢) can be purchased from the driver. Taxis are plentiful, though not cheap—settle on a price before you get in, and don't hesitate to negotiate. Fares should run $1–$2 a kilometer (½ mi). If you want your own wheels, try **Hertz** (Paseo Triunfo de la República 2408-2, tel. 16/13–80–60), which rents cars for about $40 per day.

WHERE TO SLEEP

Most tourists stay in El Paso, so lodging options are limited in Juárez. The real cheapies are run-down and often charge by the hour, but there are several reasonable places on or near Avenida Juárez. That said, this area is not safe after dark, and if you happen to arrive in Juárez's bus terminal at night, call a taxi (tel. 16/12–00–17) rather than take a bus to downtown.

The small **Hotel Génova** (Moctezuma 569 Nte., off Colón and Lerdo, tel. 16/15–00–83) is off the beaten path—about six blocks from Avenida Juárez—but at least you won't be kept awake by noise from the downtown discos. The friendly staff will turn on the air-conditioning in your room at no extra charge, and patience will bring hot water to your shower. The $7 doubles come with bath. **Bombín Café Bary Hotel** (Colón, 1 block east of Juárez, tel. 16/14–23–20) is hot and dank, but the rooms ($14 doubles) are decent, and each has a private bathroom with hot water. On the east side of Juárez, **Hotel Morán** (Juárez 264 Nte., tel. 16/15–08–02) is a favorite with families. The small but comfortable rooms feature pink bedspreads and baths with cranky plumbing. Doubles are $18, with cable TV in every room. All are cash only.

FOOD

Restaurants and taco stands line Avenida Juárez, while the daily **mercado municipal** on Avenida 16 de Septiembre offers fresh fruit, vegetables, and cheeses. **Antojitos La Herradura** (2350 Hermanos Escobar and Belice, tel. 16/16–82–42) serves a *comida corrida* (preprepared lunch special; $5) that'll satisfy even the most ravenous traveler. For late-night cravings, the 24-hour **El Coyote Inválido** (Lerdo, at Paisaje Continental, tel. 16/14–25–71) is basic and economical. Its most popular dish is *pollo en mole* (chicken in chocolate-chile sauce; $3.50). Juárez's most tradition-steeped eatery, **Restaurant La Sevil-**

EL PARTIDO ACCIÓN NACIONAL

The PAN (Partido Acción Nacional) is the second most powerful party in Mexican politics. Its stronghold is in the northern, agricultural states of Sonora and Chihuahua, as well as in the state of Durango: In Casas Grandes, Chihuahua, a town consisting of one square block, the PAN office occupies half the block. You'll also see the PAN logo emblazoned on houses and stores throughout northern Mexico.

Considered to be ideologically right-of-center, the party was founded in 1939 in protest of reforms by the PRI (Partido Revolucionario Institucional), long the governing party in Mexico. Outlining welfare programs for the region's poor is one of the PAN's priorities, but the party mostly caters to middle- and working-class citizens, and it favors strong ties to the United States.

It appears that the PAN message is a popular one: In 1997 elections, the party gained control of the states of Colima, Nuevo León, and Querétaro. It now governs 7 of the 31 Mexican states, while the PRI is in charge of the rest.

Iana (Juárez, behind the old bullring, no phone), has been churning out the same dishes for 40 years. Try the pancakes for breakfast or the *picadillo con chile verde* (shredded beef with green chile sauce; $5) for lunch. All restaurants are cash only.

AFTER DARK

Every shuttered storefront on Avenida Juárez magically transforms into a disco or bar after dark, attracting teenagers from both sides of the border. Most places stay open until around 3 AM and charge a $3–$8 cover—arrive before 10 PM and you can often get in free. If you're a woman traveling alone, use caution, as Juárez's streets can be dangerous at night. Heavy-metal fans will like **Spanky's** (Juárez 887, tel. 16/14–70–35; closed Mon.–Wed.) where beer is served in *yardas* (yards). **Alive** (Juárez, ½ block from Stanton Street Bridge, tel. 16/12–50–63; closed Sun.–Wed.) is a popular dance spot where a $3 cover gives you access to the latest hip-hop played in a cavelike den. You'll find a more mellow scene at **Kentucky Club** (Juárez 629, tel. 16/14–99–90; open daily until midnight), a haven of Naugahyde couches, well-crafted mixed drinks, and decades-old sports memorabilia. You can also listen to strolling musicians at the **Plaza del Mariachi,** farther south on the east side of Avenida Juárez.

NUEVO CASAS GRANDES AND PAQUIME

Some 260 km (161 mi) southwest of Ciudad Juárez lie the twin towns of Nuevo Casas Grandes and Casas Grandes. Nuevo Casas Grandes is a two-horse town with the only hotels and most of the restaurants in the area—most visitors pass a night or two here on their way to either Ciudad Juárez or Chihuahua, visiting the **Paquimé ruins** (*see* Worth Seeing, *below*) in Casas Grandes as a day excursion. With wide, dusty streets and sauntering residents in full cowboy gear (including proudly displayed pistols), Nuevo Casas Grandes goes about its business, barely noticing the presence of a tourist or two. Believe it or not, Casas Grandes, just 8 km (5 mi) away, is even sleepier—the whole town occupies a single square block.

BASICS

Two casas de cambio, **Serfín** (open weekdays 9–1:30) and **Inverlat** (open weekdays 9–noon) have ATMs and change cash and traveler's checks. Both are across the street from each other on 5 de Mayo at Constitución. **Dr. Amaro Prieto Saldovar,** an English-speaking medical doctor, can be reached weekdays 12:30–3:30 at the **Farmacia de la Clínica** (5 de Mayo 404, tel. 169/4–07–70; open daily 9 AM–11 PM). The full-service **post office** (16 de Septiembre, 1 block east of Obregón, tel. 169/4–20–16; open weekdays 8–6, Sat. 8–1) is one block from **Geydi Teléfono Larga Distancia** (Obregón, near 5 de Mayo, tel. 169/4–12–71; open Mon.–Sat. 9 AM–10 PM), which has long-distance phones and fax machines.

COMING AND GOING

BY BUS

Nuevo Casas Grandes has two adjacent terminals: first-class **Omnibus** (tel. 169/4–05–02) and second-class **Estrella Blanca** (tel. 169/4–07–80), both on Obregón at 5 de Mayo, at the heart of downtown. Both send several buses daily to Ciudad Juárez (4 hrs, $9) and Chihuahua (5½ hrs, $11). Neither station offers luggage storage. To reach Casas Grandes and Paquimé from Nuevo Casas Grandes, hop a blue-and-gold bus marked CASAS GRANDES (30¢) on the corner of Constitución and 16 de Septiembre; after a 15-minute ride you'll be deposited at the *zócalo* (main plaza) in Casas Grandes. To reach Paquime from here, follow the PAQUIMÉ sign on Constitución; the 10-minute walk past the park will take you to the ruins. The last bus returns to Nuevo Casas Grandes at 8:30 PM.

WHERE TO SLEEP AND EAT

The few hotels in Nuevo Casas Grandes are rather expensive. Your best option is the comfortable and friendly **Hotel Juárez** (Obregón 110, next to Estrella Blanca, tel. 169/4–02–33), where clean doubles cost $8. The Hotel Juárez accepts cash only. **Motel Piñón** (Juárez 605, tel. 169/4–01–66) has a swimming pool and a private collection of ancient *ollas* (clay pots) from Paquimé. Doubles are $23. **Hotel Paquimé** (Juárez 401, tel. 169/4–13–20) has two categories of rooms to choose from: newly renovated (doubles $27) or nonrenovated (doubles $20). All include air-conditioning, TV, and phone. There is no lodging in Casas Grandes.

Restaurants and taco stands are plentiful in Nuevo Casas Grandes near the bus station or along Juárez. For a good sit-down meal, try **Denni's** (Juárez 412, at Urueta, tel. 169/4–10–75), which bears no relation to the U.S. chain. Big breakfast specials will set you back about $2. **Restaurante Constantino** (Juárez, across from Hotel Paquimé, tel. 169/4–10–05) makes great enchiladas ($3) and tacos and offers a full breakfast menu. The staff is friendly, the menu has English translations, and you can pay in American dollars! **Nevería Chuchy** (Constitución 202, tel. 169/4–07–09; closed Sun.) is a fun soda fountain with sandwiches, burgers ($1.50), and ice-cream cones—all the kids in town wind up here at some point during the day. In Casas Grandes, **El Pueblo** (off Juárez, tel. 169/2–41–22; no breakfast) draws residents from Nuevo Casas Grandes with great food, a full bar, and TVs showing American movies. House specialties include shrimp and steak ($6) and spicy chicken wings. For a shot of culture, try the *bebida nacional* (tequila). The bar **El Bandido** (Juárez and Del Prado, tel. 169/4–03–29) fills up on weekend nights with regulars in tight jeans and cowboy hats shakin' it to '80s hits. You might feel like you've stumbled into a Pace Picante commercial.

WORTH SEEING

If you're wandering around Casas Grandes, check out the free **Museo del Siglo XIX** (Independencia, ½ block from Pueblo Viejo; open Tues.–Sun. 10–5). This 19th-century stone house, now converted into a museum, features period paintings and furniture, as well as a room dedicated to the Mexican Revolution.

PAQUIME RUINS

Near the aspen-lined Casas Grandes River and sheltered by the burnt-sienna peaks of the Sierra Madre Occidental, Paquimé was inhabited by Pima, Concho, and Tolima peoples between AD 700 and AD 1500, and served as a center for trade with the Pueblo civilizations of the southwestern United States. Paquimé was a cosmopolitan settlement, whose residents raised fowl and manufactured jewelry; today, you can still see evidence of this worldliness, from the recently restored heat-shielding walls to the intricate indoor plumbing systems. Note the unique mixture of architectural styles: T-shape entrances (similar to those of Pueblo dwellings) coexist with Mesoamerican masonry techniques. The new high-tech museum on the site houses Paquimé artifacts and ceramics, displays a to-scale replica of the ruins, and offers descriptions in Spanish and English of the cultural, religious, and economic practices of the tribe. A small movie theater shows documentaries, and interactive touch-activated computers are scattered throughout the museum. Both the museum and the ruins are free and open Tuesday–Sunday 10–5.

CHIHUAHUA CITY

The city of Chihuahua, capital of Chihuahua state, lies on a high, hilly plain some 375 km (233 mi) south of Ciudad Juárez. Agriculture and lumber are the primary moneymakers here, so you won't get the feeling that you are a big, walking peso, as you may in its much poorer and more tourism-dependent neighbor to the north. Chihuahua has long played a leading role in Mexican history: Founded in 1709, it witnessed the execution of Independence leaders Padre Miguel Hidalgo and Ignacio Allende. In 1847 it fell to U.S. forces, and was occupied by Pancho Villa's army during the Mexican Revolution. The days of invading hordes are long over, however, and the primary reason that travelers visit today is to hop on the Copper Canyon train. There's no reason to leave quickly, however—a day or two can be spent contentedly exploring the city's cathedral and historical museums.

Touring the city allows you to get a good overview of Chihuahua state's diverse population. Most notable are the indigenous Tarahumara, whose multilayered, brightly colored clothing is akin to the style of dress in the Guatemalan highlands. Continued invasions by timber and mining interests have forced the Tarahumara deeper into the mountains, but desperate families travel into town for money and medical services. You may also see an occasional Mennonite in somber dress; these generally reclusive, German-speaking people live in the community of Cuauhtémoc, a short train ride from Chihuahua, and are best known for their famous Mennonite or Chihuahua cheese. A proliferation of Western-wear stores on Chihuahua's main streets, however, will confirm that the bulk of Chihuahua's residents favor cowboy hats and boots over any other garb.

BASICS

AMERICAN EXPRESS

The AmEx representative in the **Rojo y Casavantes** travel agency sells traveler's checks, holds cardholders' mail, replaces lost or stolen checks and AmEx cards, and offers MoneyGram service. However, the agency doesn't exchange traveler's checks or cash personal checks. *Guerrero 1207, Chihuahua, Chihuahua, CP 31000, México, tel. 14/15–58–58. Open weekdays 9–6, Sat. 9–noon.*

CASAS DE CAMBIO

Most banks change money weekdays 9:30–noon, and several on Avenida Independencia have ATMs. **Serfín**'s ATM (Independencia, at Juárez) accepts Visa, MasterCard, Cirrus, and Plus. **Bancomer** (Av. Libertad, facing the cathedral, tel. 14/10–35–35; open weekdays 8–5:30, Sat. 10–noon) changes traveler's checks and has 24-hour ATM machines. The best rates for cash (and the shortest lines) are at **Centro de Cambio Rachasa** (Independencia 401, at Victoria, tel. 14/15–14–14; open Mon.–Sat. 8–8.) They don't charge commission on traveler's checks, cash, or money orders, but their exchange rates are a few pesos lower than at the banks.

EMERGENCIES

You can dial 911 from any phone here for emergency assistance.

MAIL

The **post office** is in the Palacio Federal, just opposite the old Palacio del Gobierno. They offer all the usual services and will hold mail sent to you at the following address for up to 10 days: Lista de Correos, Administración 1, Chihuahua, Chihuahua, CP 31000, México. *Libertad, between Carranza and Guerrero, tel. 14/15–14–17. Open weekdays 8–5, Sat. 9–1.*

MEDICAL AID

Clínica del Parque (Calle de la Llave, at Calle 12a, tel. 14/15–74–11) offers 24-hour emergency service and has some English-speaking doctors, as well as a 24-hour pharmacy. For a dentist, go to **Central Médico Dental** (Niños Héroes 606, tel. 14/16–18–80; open Mon.–Sat. 9–1 and 4–8). About three blocks from the Palacio del Gobierno is the 24-hour **Farmacia Mendoza** (Aldama 1901, tel. 14/16–44–14).

PHONES

You'll find **Ladatel** public phones on the main square. Some take coins, while others take Ladatel phone cards, which can be purchased at the nearest kiosk or store that advertises Ladatel in the window. For cash calls, the Central Camionera (*see* Coming and Going, *below*) has a *caseta de larga distancia* (long-distance telephone office), but it doesn't allow collect or credit-card calls. The downtown **Servicio de Larga Distancia** (Independencia 808, near Morelos, tel. 14/10–24–00; open Mon.–Sat. 8–8) operates out of a pharmacy. Collect calls cost $1.50 for 15 minutes and calls to the U.S. are $1.80 per minute.

VISITOR INFORMATION

Topographical maps of the Copper Canyon are available though Chihuahua's **SECTUR** office (tel. 800/9–03–92 in Mexico). The **state tourism office** (Calle 11a, at Libertad, tel. 14/10–10–77; open Mon.–Sat. 9–7, Sun. 10–2) is in the Palacio de Gobierno. There's usually someone on duty who speaks English, and maps and brochures are plentiful.

COMING AND GOING

BY BUS

Chihuahua is a hub for bus transportation, and the companies serving its **Central Camionera** run routes all over Mexico. The modern terminal contains a phone office, 24-hour luggage storage (50¢ per hr), a video arcade, and a 24-hour cafeteria. Frequent first-class service is available to Creel (4½ hrs, $9), Ciudad Juárez (4½ hrs, $14), Mexico City (18 hrs, $49), Guadalajara (16 hrs, $40), Monterrey (12 hrs, $27), Zacatecas (15 hrs, $28), Aguascalientes (20 hrs, $32), and Nuevo Casas Grandes (5½ hrs, $11). To get here from downtown, take a city bus marked CENTRAL CAMIONERA (20¢) from the corner of Ocampo and Juárez. Buses marked E–179 CENTRO (20¢) run from the station to the center of town. If you arrive in town at night, your only choice is to take a taxi from the station to downtown: Don't let the driver charge you more than $5.

BY TRAIN

If you're on your way to Creel, the ride on the **Chihuahua al Pacífico** (Méndez, at Calle 24a, tel. 14/20–70–47), the famous Copper Canyon train, is much more scenic than traveling by bus. Trains run to Los Mochis (13 hrs; $42 1st class, $9 2nd class), stopping in Creel (5 hrs; $20 1st class, $4 2nd class), Divisadero (6½ hrs; $23 1st class, $5 2nd class), and Bahuichivo (8½ hrs; $26 1st class, $5.50 2nd class). The first-class *Vista* train leaves Chihuahua daily at 7 AM, passes through Creel around 12:30 PM, and arrives in Los Mochis at 9 PM. The second-class *Mixto* train runs Monday, Wednesday, and Friday, departing Chihuahua at 8 AM and arriving in Los Mochis anytime between midnight and 5 AM. The second-class train returns from Los Mochis on Tuesday, Thursday, and Saturday. As a rule, second-class trains always lollygag and arrive late, but all in all they aren't that bad: The windows open (they don't on first-class trains) and the crowd includes food vendors, musicians, and other colorful characters. To be certain of a first-class seat during Semana Santa (Holy Week, the week preceding Easter) and the first week in July (when Mexican schools get out), you have to shell out extra dough to buy your ticket in advance from **Mexico by Train** (tel. 800/321–1699 or fax 210/725–3659 in the U.S.). To reach the terminal, take a bus marked COL. ROSALIA or STA. ROSA (20¢) down Ocampo.

The station (tel. 14/13–00–93) for **El División del Norte** trains is at the north entrance to town, just off Avenida Tecnológico. From here you can catch first- and second-class trains to Ciudad Juárez and Mexico City. To get here, hop on a COLON (20¢) bus from downtown.

Sights ●

Catedral
Metropolitana
(Plaza de la
Constitución), **5**

Centro Cultural de
Chihuahua, **7**

Museo de la
Revolución
Mexicana, **10**

Palacio Federal, **1**

Palacio del
Gobierno, **2**

Plaza de Armas, **6**

Quinta Gameros, **8**

Lodgings ○

Hotel Carmen **4**

Hotel
Santa María, **9**

Posada Aida, **3**

KEY

AE American Express Office

i Tourist Information

GETTING AROUND

The downtown area, roughly 10 blocks by three, contains virtually all of the town's points of interest, including the **Plaza de la Constitución** (Chihuahua's zócalo) and the cathedral, as well as budget lodging and eateries. Odd-number streets lie north of **Independencia** (the core of the downtown area) and even-number streets are to the south. Buses for points all around the city leave from the corner of Ocampo and Juárez until about 8 PM. Tickets are 20¢ and can be bought from the driver. Taxis (usually consisting of a battered Subaru with a helpful driver) are relatively cheap, and, unless you've just stepped out of an expensive hotel, you can get practically anywhere for a few dollars.

WHERE TO SLEEP

Chihuahua's hotels are clustered southwest of the Plaza de la Constitución, and most are well maintained and clean. Those listed here are the best of the cheapies, and all have air-conditioning and hot water, though the latter is often limited in the evenings. **Hotel Carmen** (Juárez, at Calle 10a, tel. 14/15–70–96) is centrally located, clean, and comfortable, and each of its small rooms comes with a spotless bathroom. Doubles are $5.25, or $6.50 for a room with TV. Close to downtown, **Posada Aida** (Calle 10a No. 106, between Juárez and Doblado, tel. 14/15–38–30) is the best deal in Chihuahua: The sheets are fresh, the bathrooms clean, and the pleasant Spanish-style courtyard is a good place to unwind or play with the owner's dogs—they're Chihuahuas, of course. You'll pay $6.50 for a double with private bath. **Hotel Santa Maria** (1212 Aldama, tel. 14/10–35–37) has 27 rooms built around an inner courtyard. Double rooms are $7.50 and have TVs and tidy bathrooms. All hotels are cash only.

FOOD

Seafood stalls and hot dog stands crowd almost every corner in downtown Chihuahua, and fresh fruits, vegetables, meats, and cheeses are always available at the daily **mercado popular** (just north of Calle

4a, between Niños Héroes and Juárez). The excellent **Restaurant Los Olivos** (Calle de la Llave 202, between Calles 2a and 4a, tel. 14/10–01–61; no breakfast Sat., closed Sun.) serves organic fruits and vegetables, whole-wheat pancakes, vegetarian burgers, and egg dishes in a smoke-free environment with New Age music. A fruit plate smothered with yogurt, granola, and honey is $2.50. **El Taquito** (Venustiano Carranza 1818, 3 blocks south of the Palacio del Gobierno, tel. 14/10–21–44) serves up great tacos, burritos, *chiles rellenos* (stuffed chile peppers), and *enchiladas suizas* (tortillas stuffed with chicken or cheese, then baked in cream sauce). A meal with a bottle of sangria comes to about $6. Bright, cheerful **Ah Chiles** (Aldama, at Guerrero, tel. 16/37–09–77) attracts a crowd at any time of the day with its five-for-$2 taco specials and iced *refrescos* (soft drinks). All are cash only.

WORTH SEEING

In addition to the shaded plazas and cobblestone streets, there are plenty of cultural and historical sites to be explored here, and many are free. If you're interested in seeing where Padre Miguel Hidalgo joined the "choir invisible," walk over to the **Palacio del Gobierno** (Juárez, between Guerrero and Carranza). A plaque on the inner courtyard wall marks the spot where Hidalgo was executed by a firing squad. The Palacio also houses murals by Aarón Piña Mora, depicting historic events from the 16th century through the Mexican Revolution. The **Palacio Federal** across the street contains the tower in which Hidalgo was held prisoner before being executed. Although visitors can no longer climb the tower, the entrance has been turned into the **Calabozo de Hidalgo** (open Tues.–Sun. 9–7; admission 50¢), a small museum/cell containing Hidalgo's Bible, crucifix, and pistol. Efrén García Díaz, the museum's caretaker, will share relevant history. The **Centro Cultural de Chihuahua** (Ocampo, at Aldama, tel. 14/16–12–30; open daily 10–2 and 4–7) showcases art, theater, and dance throughout the year and posts listings of these events at its office, an old mansion three blocks from the cathedral (*see below*).

> *Ride the Chihuahua al Pacífico train while it's still cheap: The Mexican government has put the public railway up for sale, and once it's privatized, fares will probably be significantly higher.*

CATEDRAL METROPOLITANA DE CHIHUAHUA

This 19th-century baroque-style cathedral is dedicated to St. Francis of Assisi, and its exterior is adorned with statues of Francis and the 12 apostles. Inside, the **Museo de Arte Sacro** (tel. 14/10–32–38; open weekdays 10–1 and 3–6; admission 50¢) houses a collection of 18th-century religious art. *On Plaza de la Constitución, between Calle 2 and Independencia, at Libertad.*

MUSEO DE LA REVOLUCION MEXICANA

Quinta Luz, as the former home of legendary Francisco "Pancho" Villa is sometimes called, is Chihuahua's biggest attraction. One of his many wives, Luz Corral, gave personal tours of the building until her death in 1982, after which the house became a museum. The mansion was built by Pancho himself and is now dedicated to relating the history of the Mexican Revolution through photographs, treaties, maps, and artifacts—including weapons and the bullet-riddled 1922 Dodge Villa he was driving when he was assassinated. *Calle 10a No. 300, about 1½ km (¾ mi) from downtown, tel. 14/16–29–58. Take bus marked COL. DALES or OCAMPO south on Ocampo. Admission: 65¢. Open daily 9–1 and 3–7.*

QUINTA GAMEROS

This turn-of-the-century manor was built in French Nouveau style by one Manuel Gameros to impress his fiancée, who nevertheless turned her affection to another. It is now home to a museum displaying the mansion's original furniture, gilt-frame paintings, and ornate chandeliers, as well as the works of local artists and art students and several rotating exhibits. Odd touches include a reclining, headless nude on the upper reaches of the building's exterior, as well as a Little Red Riding Hood motif in the child's room, complete with a snarling wolf on the headboard of the bed. *Paseo Bolívar 401, at Calle 4a, tel. 14/16–66–84. Admission: 65¢. Open Tues.–Sun. 10–2 and 4–7.*

FESTIVALS

Chihuahuans like to consider themselves particularly spirited because of the historic role that their city has played in Mexican history. Three important annual festivals are worth attending: The **Feria de Santa Rita,** held during the last two weeks in May, is when Chihuahuans pay homage to their patron saint with

THE FOOTRUNNERS OF CHIHUAHUA

The name "Tarahumara" is a Spanish rendition of the Chihuahua region natives' original word for themselves: Rarámuri, or "footrunners." These people make their home in a 32,000-square-km (12,300-square-mi) stretch of the Sierra Madre Occidental, known as the Sierra Tarahumara.

For centuries, the people of this region have remained largely unaffected by modern civilization, despite numerous attempts by outsiders to enslave them as mine laborers or convert them to Christianity. Nonetheless, several aspects of Christianity have become part of their traditional religious rituals: The Virgin of Guadalupe festival (December 12) and Semana Santa (Holy Week, the week preceding Easter) are both celebrated with elaborate costumes and dancing, and the sun is honored as the symbol of God, or Onorúame, who is both the father and mother of the people.

Excessive logging and ongoing drought have destroyed the Tarahumara's farming lands, resulting in illness and malnutrition among the people and forcing many of them into Chihuahua city to beg. Others travel to the mountain towns of Creel and Divisadero to sell handicrafts to tourists. Those who remain deep in the canyons wage a constant struggle with the lumber industry—and with inconsiderate, overly curious tourists.

When traveling in the Copper Canyon, show respect for the land and its residents: Although entering the inhabited cliff-side caves and photographing the colorfully clothed women may seem appealing, ask for permission first, and comply if the request is denied.

food, music, and regional crafts at the fairgrounds on the Carretera al Aeropuerto. People call Santa Rita "The Governor's Fair," because it has evolved into a bureaucratic, expensive event that excludes the poor. Locals prefer the **Expoban** festival, a livestock competition and county fair held the second week of October at the Unión Banadera (just outside of town). On September 15, people come from all over the state to participate in **Mexican Independence Day** celebrations. There are fireworks displays at the Palacio del Gobierno and traditional *teatro del pueblo* (outdoor theater) put on by the Chihuahua Cultural Center.

AFTER DARK

Chihuahua is not a wild town, and movies are one of the more popular evening diversions. **Sala 2001** (Guerrero, at Escorza, tel. 14/16–50–00) and **Cinema Revolución** (J. Neri Santos 700, just west of Palacio Federal, tel. 14/17–52–22) both show Hollywood films ($1.50) with Spanish subtitles, plus the occasional Latin American or Spanish film. The disco **Robin Hood** (Ernesto Talavera, at Cuauthemoc; cover $3) is the only dance place around where gay couples are tolerated: Public displays of affection remain an exclusively heterosexual privilege in these parts. Although some hip-hop and rock dance music is played, most of what you'll hear is in the ranchero genre. **Alameda Corona** (Juárez, behind Club de los

Parados) is an outdoor bar with cheap beer and spirited mariachi music. Don't look for the signs, though—there aren't any. Just ask around for *la cervecería* (the brewery).

THE COPPER CANYON

With majestic 12,000-ft peaks and deep gorges plunging over 1 km (½ mi) into raging waters, the region known as *Las Barrancas del Cobre* (the Copper Canyon) humbles anyone in the presence of its beauty. In the late spring and early summer, the canyon's naked, dun-color rocks absorb the sun's intense heat, while the Apache pines and Chihuahua ash trees hold their breath until the arrival of giant gray thunderclouds in summer. By September, after the heavy rains, the canyons are thick with green layers of vegetation, which provide food for roaming deer, skunks, and salamanders.

A treasure for nature lovers, the five canyons and four main rivers in this area offer plenty of opportunities for hiking, mountain biking, and horseback riding. Guides are almost always recommended, not only because trails are rough and poorly marked, but because of the illegal marijuana fields in the area—these are guarded by men with shotguns and are extremely dangerous to stumble upon. The town of Creel, about halfway between Chihuahua and Los Mochis, is the most convenient takeoff point for camping and hiking trips, and has become a favorite among backpackers. The most popular times to visit are September and October, when the waterfalls are at their best, or during the weeklong festival of Semana Santa.

The Copper Canyon's second-class train has an unpredictable schedule and no reserved seating, but it provides the best opportunity to meet local campesinos (rural dwellers) and their poultry.

The Copper Canyon only became accessible to the public in 1961 with the completion of the Chihuahua al Pacífico railroad. It took nearly 100 years to complete and now boasts some 87 tunnels and 37 bridges. Long before the canyon was discovered by miners and tourists, however, the area was home to indigenous Tarahumara people (*see box, above*). The 50,000 Tarahumara that remain tenaciously maintain one of the most traditional indigenous cultures in North America. They continue to live in and around the canyons, farming and weaving pine-needle baskets, the majority of which are sold to tourists.

GETTING AROUND

BY BUS

Trains are the primary mode of transportation through the canyons, but you can shorten the train ride in either direction by taking an **Estrella Blanca** bus. Seven daily buses run between Creel and Chihuahua (4 hrs direct, 5 hrs indirect; $9 for both). If you attempt this, board at either Chihuahua or Creel, as boarding at intermediate points may leave you standing in the aisles for many leg-numbing hours due to lack of seats.

BY TRAIN

First-class **Vista** trains run daily between Chihuahua and Los Mochis in each direction. Second-class **Mixto** trains run from Los Mochis to Chihuahua on Monday, Wednesday, and Friday, and return from Chihuahua to Los Mochis on Tuesday, Thursday, and Saturday. Both stop in most small towns in between, including Cuauhtémoc, Creel, Divisadero, and Bahuichivo. The Vista is exponentially faster and more comfortable, with climate control, a snack bar, and bathrooms, but at $42 for the journey, it's almost four times the price of a second-class ride. The first-class train is popular in summer and during Semana Santa, so try to book ahead if you're traveling during these periods. Bring toilet paper and, for the mountainous areas, warm clothing; in first class you'll probably need a sweater even in the lowlands, as the train's air-conditioning is applied over-enthusiastically. Tickets for the Mixto are only available the morning of departure, so be prepared to fight tooth and nail for both tickets and seats during Semana Santa week and in the month of July.

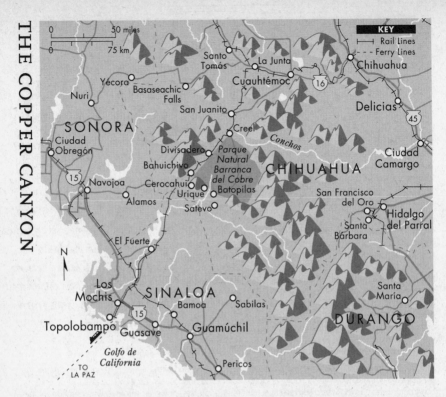

It is possible to make up to two 24-hour stops at stations other than your final destination. You need to ask for an *escala* (stopover)—a 15% surcharge added to the price of your ticket. The escala must be purchased in either Chihuahua or Los Mochis at the beginning of your trip, and it's only worthwhile during Semana Santa and the first week in July, when you are required to make reservations and plan all of your stops in advance. At less busy times of year, you can hop on and off the train at any station in the Copper Canyon without being charged extra. For specific information on prices and departures, *see* Coming and Going *in* Chihuahua, *above;* Creel, *below; and* Los Mochis *in* Chapter 4. Starting your trip in Los Mochis is recommended, especially since the Mixto leaving from Chihuahua will probably pass the Copper Canyon in the dark. If you're heading out of Chihuahua, the best views are on the right until you pass Creel and on your left from Creel to Los Mochis.

HIKING

Extreme temperatures, lack of resupply points, and a wide range of altitudes make hiking in the Copper Canyon a challenge. However, if you know where you're going and have the proper equipment, overnight trips are undoubtedly the best way to enjoy the canyons. You can pick up hiking supplies in Los Mochis (*see* Chapter 4) or Chihuahua: In Chihuahua, **Sears** (Libertad 104, tel. 14/16–52–72; open Mon.–Sat. 10–9, Sun. 11–7) is the most convenient place to purchase camping or hiking gear, and even tents and sleeping bags. Detailed topographical maps of the region are available through **SECTUR,** the state tourism office (tel. 14/16–21–06 in Chihuahua, or 800/90–03–02 throughout Mexico). Within the canyons, the best jumping-off points for hikes are Creel and Batopilas, and it's easy to find a guide in these places. Use your head though—holdups have been reported by tourists. Get someone moderately trustworthy (i.e., a hotel owner, rather than the guy hanging out on the corner) to refer you to a guide.

HITCHING

Hitchhiking is the only way to reach some points off the rail line. In rural areas it's fairly safe and common, but traveling in groups is always wisest. In any event, prepare for long periods of standing by the side of the road, especially on Sunday. Trucks may charge a few dollars, depending on the length of the journey; it's polite to ask.

CREEL

Set in a shallow valley high in the Sierra Madre, the growing town of Creel is a favorite stop on the Chihuahua al Pacífico line for travelers who want to explore the Barrancas without too much hassle. It's about halfway between Los Mochis and Chihuahua. The best way to enjoy the surrounding area, with its stunning green pine trees and jagged mountain peaks, is on bike, horse, or foot. Popular destinations include **Cusárare,** a waterfall 22 km (13 mi) away; **Rekohuata,** a group of hot springs 17 km (10 mi) south of Creel; Lake Arareco, 7 km (4 mi) south of Creel; and **San Ignacio,** 4 km (2 mi) south, past the town cemetery and a few Tarahumara caves. Even if you don't join a group tour from one of the hotels, it's a good idea to ask around about current trail conditions before setting off. The nearby attractions of **Batopilas** and **Basaseachic Falls** provide more opportunities for amusement, and are accessible by car: To get to either place, hitch a ride from *la carretera* (Creel's main road) or arrange a ride with one of the men waiting around the train station with trucks and vans.

BASICS

CASAS DE CAMBIO

Serfín (tel. 145/6–00–60; open weekdays 9–3), just east of the train tracks, changes money, does credit-card cash advances, and charges a "flexible" commission (no more than 2%) on traveler's checks. **Nuevo Horizonte Internacional** (no phone), across from Cafetería Gaby on the main road, has better rates and also does cash advances.

LAUNDRY

Lavandería Santa María (López Mateos 61, tel. 145/6–00–71; open weekdays 9–2 and 3–6, Sat. 9–2) belongs to the resortlike Pension Creel. They'll do your wash for you at less than $2 a load.

MEDICAL AID

There are a few English-speaking doctors at **La Clínica Santa Teresita** (Parroquia, behind Margarita's, tel. 145/6–01–05). The clinic offers dental service and 24-hour emergency care. **Farmacia Rodríguez** (López Mateos 43, tel. 145/6–00–52) is a pharmacy open Monday–Saturday 9–1 and 3–7.

PHONES AND MAIL

Papelería de Todo (López Mateos 30, tel. 145/6–01–22; open Mon.–Sat. 9–9, Sun. 9–6) charges 50¢ for collect calls. It also has a pay phone and a fax machine (fax 145/6–02–22). The **post office** (Enrique Creel 4, tel. 145/6–02–58; open weekdays 9–3) is in the Presidencia Municipal, south of the zócalo. They'll hold mail sent to you at the following address for up to 10 days: Lista de Correos, Presidencia Municipal, Creel, Chihuahua, CP 33200, México.

VISITOR INFORMATION

The **Complejo Turístico Arareco** (tel. 145/6–01–26; open Mon.–Sat. 9–5:30) on López Mateos has a decent map of the area and provides information on tours. The staff speaks some English, and arranges rowboat rentals for Lake Arareco ($3 per hr for up to 6 people) and rents bicycles ($2 per hr). Next to Serfín, **Artesanías Misión** (tel. 145/6–00–97; open Mon.–Sat. 9:30–1 and 3–6, Sun. 9:30–1) has English-language books and pamphlets on the Copper Canyon and the Tarahumara, as well as topographical maps.

COMING AND GOING

BY BUS

The **Estrella Blanca** terminal (tel. 145/6–00–73) is directly across the tracks from the train station. Buses depart Creel every 1½ hours between 7 AM and 5:30 PM for Chihuahua (4½ hrs, $9); the direct buses (daily at 7, 11:30, and 2:30) take an hour less at the same fare. Buy tickets for Batopilas at **Artesanías Raramuri** (tel. 145/6–02–79), across from Restaurant Lupita (*see* Food, *below*) on López Mateos. The Batopilas-bound bus (7 hrs, $8) departs at 7 AM on Tuesday, Thursday, and Saturday. On Monday, Wednesday, and Friday a van (5hrs, $9.50) departs at 10 AM.

BY TRAIN

The train tracks run along the west edge of town, and the station is very close to budget food and lodging choices. First-class trains depart daily: the train to Chihuahua (5 hrs, $20) leaves at 12:30 PM, and the one to Los Mochis (8½ hrs, $15) departs at 3:15 PM. The second-class train has a limited schedule: On Tuesday, Thursday, and Saturday it departs at 5:10 PM for Chihuahua ($4), and on Monday, Wednesday, and Friday it leaves at 2 PM for Los Mochis ($4). The first-class trains are rarely late; the second-class trains show up when they feel like it and take much longer to reach their final destinations, so be prepared to wait. You can buy both first- and second-class tickets on the train.

WHERE TO SLEEP

As soon as you step off the train you will be assailed by a passel of children beckoning you to **Margarita's** (Mateos 11, tel. 145/6–00–45). Make the kids happy and jump on the hotel's courtesy shuttle. Margarita's is a casual, family-run place that provides whatever type of accommodation you can afford, from a $3 bunk in a dorm room to a $13 double room with private bath (although the toilets are occasionally out of order). Breakfast and dinner are included in the price. A short distance away and under the same ownership, **Hotel Margarita Plaza Mexicana** (Chapultepec, near Mateos, tel. 145/6–02–45) offers rooms ($12–$28) with private baths; the rooms are more luxurious than at Margarita's and the atmosphere is more formal. When there's demand, the Margarita's staff leads guided tours ($7–$16 per person) to Cusárare and Basaseachic falls, Recohuata, La Bufa and Tarahumara caves, and Divisadero. They can also arrange horseback outings for about $4 an hour. Your other option, **Casa Valenzuela** (López Mateos 68, tel. 145/6–01–04) is usually semi-vacant, and the proprietor will accommodate your needs and budget. The communal bathroom is tiny and fairly clean, although sometimes without water, and the ceiling sags. The beds sag, too. Doubles are $11, and four of the eight rooms have private baths. Although **New Pensión Creel** (López Mateos 61, tel. 145/6–00–71, fax 145/6–02–00) is 1 km (½ mi) out of town, it's worth the trek for the clean and cozy two- to four-person rooms ($5.50 per person, including breakfast). This B&B has a spacious patio, kitchen, common area, and laundry, and tours of the canyon can be arranged with the staff for about $10 (half-day trip). To get here, walk south down López Mateos and turn left after Calle La Terminal. Look for the tin roof with PENSION CREEL in red letters. All hotels are cash only.

CAMPING

There is a campground next to Lake Arareco that costs $1.50 per person per night. The entrance is at the white house on the way to the lake. The only thing to prevent you from camping anywhere else for free is lack of a flat spot and the occasional scorpion.

FOOD

All of the following restaurants are on the main town road, Lópex Mateos, so stroll along and choose whatever strikes your fancy. **Mi Café** (López Mateos 21) has only one table and feels more like a home than a restaurant. Chicken tostadas and ceviche (diced fish marinated in lime juice) both cost $1. Another local favorite, **Restaurant Cabaña**, serves spit-roasted chicken, as well as wide variety of soups, tacos, burritos, and *antojitos* (appetizers), all priced less than $2. The specialty at **Restaurant Lupita** is *bistec ranchero* (steak cooked with tomatoes and onions; $3) served nightly until 10 PM. **Laylo's Lounge** (López Mateos 25, tel. 145/6–01–36) is a gringo-friendly bar with ESPN on color TVs. They pour beer and mixed drinks nightly until 1 AM. All of the above are cash only.

OUTDOOR ACTIVITIES

Creel is a convenient base from which to explore the natural beauty of the canyons and the rivers that tumble through them. You can rent mountain bikes or take off on hikes that last between one hour and several days. Just remember to take it easy while your body adjusts to the 7,668-ft altitude. Guided tours are available to almost any place in the area: Try Complejo Turístico Arareco (*see* Visitor Information, *above*), join a group from Margarita (*see* Where to Sleep, *above*), or arrange your own tour by asking around at the main plaza; many knowledgeable residents own trucks and will take you anywhere if the price is right.

Topographical maps of the region are available at Artesanías Misión (*see* Visitor Information, *above*) for $5, but they're little help if you don't know how to read them. A live guide is often a better idea—ask at Margarita. Creel is the base for long treks to Basaseachic Falls and Batopilas (*see* Near Creel, *below*), but those with less time or less ambition may prefer to meander over to the statue of Jesus in the hills, 15 minutes west of town, where you'll find a nice picnic spot. For an easy 1½-hour hike (this one along clearly marked trails), head to the nearby **Valle de las Monjas** (Valley of the Monks), so named for the rocks said to resemble a huddle of monks. Also close by is the **Valle de los Hongos** (Valley of the Mushrooms), where a few rock formations resemble overgrown toadstools (1-hr round-trip hike). While most of the Tarahumara caves in the area are abandoned, **Cueva Sebastián,** a few kilometers south of Creel at San Ignacio, is still inhabited and accessible by foot. The Tarahumara do not welcome visitors inside their homes, but there are tours available that have been given permission to enter the caves. To reach any of these places, ask directions from anyone in Creel.

NEAR CREEL

BASASEACHIC FALLS

A four-hour drive northwest from Creel are the magnificent Basaseachic Falls, which plunge more than 800 ft into a pool below. This area is most magnificent after the rainy season (July and August)—if it rains, that is. Tours can be arranged in Creel for groups of four or more (the ones from Margarita are $16 a person), or you can hitch from the town of **La Junta,** on the Pacífico rail line. If you do hitch, plan to stay overnight in the park—good, free camping spots abound. Hiking trails are a dime a dozen, and there's an excellent swimming hole at the waterfall's edge. There are no shops here, so bring your own supplies.

DIVISADERO

Only from Divisadero can you see the three canyons—Tararecua, Urique, and Cobre—merge, their seemingly endless peaks woven together by the meandering rivers below. Divisadero is on the Chihuahua al Pacífico line roughly one hour away from Creel; the train stops here for 15 minutes in the afternoon so tourists can snap pictures, buy handmade Tarahumara baskets, and peer over the canyon rim. If you want to stop and hike, you can catch a later train for a small

> *When the Batopilas mines were in full operation, they produced chunks of silver as big as basketballs—the profits of which were used, in part, to throw lavish high-society parties in the town's grand haciendas.*

surcharge. If you decide to spend the night, your best bet is either to hike away from town and camp (ask permission before pitching a tent on someone's land) or rent a room from a local family (up to $10 a night). Food and craft stands—selling cheap burritos and ridiculously high-price Tarahumara crafts—provide information on either option. Even if you're not one of the privileged guests enjoying the $100-per-night rooms at **Hotel Divisadero Barrancas** (tel. 145/6–00–99 or 14/15–65–75), you can rent one of their horses ($9 per person) or mountain bikes ($7 per person), or join a bus tour of the canyons ($7 per person). You can also hire a guide yourself for overnight trips down to the **Río Urique.** Less formidable is the 2-km (1-mi) hike from the north side of the hotel to an abandoned Tarahumara cliff dwelling.

BATOPILAS

About 140 km (87 mi) south of Creel, in the heart of the canyon region, is the tiny mining town of Batopilas. Beside the river of the same name, this rarely visited town is hard to reach, but provides great access to the canyons. The tiny town of **Satevo,** which has a spooky abandoned mission worth exploring, is an easy 4-km (2½-mi) hike south of Batopilas; about 6 km (4 mi) north is **La Bufa,** a forgotten gold mine. Both of these trails are marked, but a guide is recommended. A less adventurous trip allows you to explore the ruined mill (admission $1.50) across the riverbed from town. Beer drinkers beware: Batopilas has a *ley seca* (dry law).

COMING AND GOING

The cheapest bus to Batopilas departs Creel at 7 AM on Tuesday, Thursday, and Saturday (7 hrs, $8); a smaller and faster van (5 hrs, $9.50) departs Monday, Wednesday, and Friday at 10 AM. For more information, *see* Coming and Going *in* Creel, *above.* The return bus departs Batopilas at 5 AM (yes, AM) on Monday, Wednesday, and Friday. The trip takes six hours, arriving in Creel in time for the first-class Los Mochis train. The road out here has been called the best and worst in North America: The scenery is magnificent, but riding a rickety bus on a dirt road with no guardrail above 500-ft cliffs can be a little nerve-racking, especially on the switchbacks.

WHERE TO SLEEP AND EAT

To avoid Batopilas's steep prices, bring all necessary camping supplies with you, including food. You can swim and camp by the river, but it's not advised in the summer months, when the creepy-crawly insects are out in legion. Deforestation upstream has also increased the risk of flash floods, so exercise caution near the river. The best lodging is **Hotel Palmera** (tel. 145/6–06–33), about 1 km (½ mi) out of town along the river. The seven cool rooms ($8) with spotless bathrooms are a great place to nap after a feast at the adjacent restaurant. Gerardo, the hotel and restaurant manager, prepares *aguas frescas* (fresh-fruit drinks) from the hotel's mango trees and whips up salads ($2) made from the fresh vegetables in his garden; sometimes there's even *carne asada* (grilled meat) barbecued out on the patio. If the Palmera is full, choose one of the sweltering rooms ($5) at the **Hotel Batopilas** (across plaza from church). **Quinto Patio** (1 block from church, overlooking river) serves room-temperature sodas and typical Mexican chow for less than $2. Hotels are cash only.

BAHUICHIVO

Brick and mud houses and a few wandering chickens are about all you'll see along the winding dirt roads of this *muy tranquilo* (very mellow) small town. Bahuichivo hugs the railroad tracks 260 km (160 mi) north of Los Mochis and is the only departure point for exploring the nearby villages of Cerocahui and Urique. If you need to refuel before taking a bus or van out of here, head to **Restaurant Daniela,** just up the road from the train station. The friendly proprietor cooks up typical Mexican fare ($2) and rents out a few spacious, exceptionally clean upstairs rooms ($8.50). For medical help, see the reputable **Dr. Leyva**—his office is labeled FARMACIA ADRIANA and is near **Abarrotes Gabby,** a small grocery store. The few small markets here are poorly stocked, so buy the bulk of your supplies before arriving.

COMING AND GOING

Since Bahuichivo is a stop on the Chihuahua al Pacífico railway, it's the best place from which to set out for Cerocahui and Urique (*see below*). The first-class train from Chihuahua stops here at 3:30 PM, while the Los Mochis train gets in at about 12:15 PM. The second-class trains arrive whenever they feel like it. To reach Urique (2½ hrs, $4.75) from Bahuichivo, hop on the new bus or the white van, both marked TRANSPORTES CAÑON URIQUE, which meet the first-class trains. The vehicles occasionally wait for the second-class train, finally departing Bahuichivo at 6 PM. Both pass through Cerocahui (1 hr, $2) on their way to Urique. It's also possible to hitch between Cerocahui and Bahuichivo. Both **Hotel La Misión** and **Paraiso del Oso** in Cerocahui have gringo shuttles to and from the first-class trains, and they'll give you a ride for a minimal fee if they aren't already full of tour groups.

NEAR BAHUICHIVO

CEROCAHUI

Cerocahuis's twisting, no-name streets are nestled deep in one of the Sierra Madre's gorges, only 1½ km (¾ mi) above sea level. This isolated village offers perhaps the most spectacular stargazing in Mexico; when the electricity goes out after 11 PM, you're left standing amid oak and pine trees under a pantheon of stars. If you're fortunate enough to be here during Semana Santa, be sure to catch the *matachines* (Tarahumara dances) at the old **Jesuit mission.** Founded in 1680 and restored in 1940, the mission still operates a boarding school for Tarahumara children. Services are held in the school's *iglesia* (church) weekday nights at 7:30 (if the padre is in town) and Sunday at 8 AM and noon. On June 24, locals douse each other with water in homage to John the Baptist.

From July to August, water is also abundant in the nearby waterfalls (a 2-km/1-mi hike from town). You can also explore the abandoned **Sangre de Cristo** gold mines (3 km/2 mi from town). Each marked trail is short and can be maneuvered on horseback or foot—ask at **Hotel La Misión** (off the central plaza) for specific directions. You can also set out from Cerocahui on a two- to three-day trek/horseback ride to Batopilas (*see above*), but you'll need a guide. Information is available in limited English from the knowledgeable Eduardo Muños, at the small *artesanía* (handicraft) shop on the way out of town (toward the waterfall). He gladly leads hikes to anywhere (including Batopilas) for a negotiable price, and he (or someone at Hotel Misión) can also get you a horse to rent ($6 per hr).

WHERE TO SLEEP AND EAT • Double rooms with private baths and hot water are available at **El Raramuri** (tel. 145/6–05–99) for $10, cash only. It's the white house on the way out of town toward the waterfall. **Paraíso del Oso** (3 km/2 mi north of Cerocahui, tel. 142/1–33–72, or 915/598–6188 in the U. S.) offers everything from $9.50 bunk beds to $125 luxury suites, and the bilingual staff leads morning hikes into the canyons ($3.50). If you want to camp, they'll let you pick a spot behind the main lodge for $5. The restaurant in the El Raramuri hotel serves up decent local fare for around $2. The only other restaurant in town is diagonally across from the plaza; the menu changes daily, but meals are always less than $5.

URIQUE

Thirty-eight kilometers (24 mi) southeast of Cerocahui, the village of Urique features fantastic views of pointy canyon peaks rising above green hills. The gushing **Río Urique** meanders through it all, making Urique one of the most visually pleasing towns in the Copper Canyon. You can take day hikes along the river, or walk down the dirt road at the edge of town to explore **Chiflón,** an abandoned mine near the foot of a 3-ft-wide, 360-ft-long hanging footbridge. To reach Chiflón, follow Urique's main street north, then follow the GUADALUPE C sign to the banks of the river; it's about a 20-minute walk. This is a great spot for a swim, though during heavy rains the river is not safe for swimming. It's also a good idea to avoid Urique in early summer, as the river will be nearly dry and temperatures reach 37°C (100°F).

COMING AND GOING • A single bus or van (2½ hrs, $4.75) leaves daily at 8:30 AM from Urique's main road to meet the trains in Bauhichivo and returns to Urique sometime after 8 PM. If you're prone to carsickness, pray that the newer bus comes to meet the train instead of the elderly van—the road into Urique is a hair-raising one. A more expensive way to get here is to arrange a ride ($16 a person) through the Hotel La Misión in Cerocahui (*see above*); or try your luck at hitching.

Overlooking Cerocahui, Cerro de Gallego (Gallego Hill) was named at the end of the 19th century after Father Gallego, a padre from Urique who was found dead, wearing his priestly garb, in a nearby cave.

WHERE TO SLEEP AND EAT • Urique boasts three hotels, but your best bet is **Hotel Cañón Urique,** next to the huge ceiba tree on the main road. Rooms with private bath are about $5.50 per person (cash only), and those in the rear are the quietest. If you've brought camping equipment, ask for **Tom and Keith's house.** These friendly expatriates from the States have a great camping area under the mesquite trees by the river (just watch out for small, biting chiggers during the rainy season). A $2 donation is requested for use of the squat toilet and fresh water. The best food in town is at **Restaurant Plaza,** down the street from Hotel Cañón Urique. The owner is friendly and the patio out back is perfect for a late meal, when cool breezes come off the river. Ask for the $3 daily special.

DURANGO

Nestled in the Valle del Guadiana, the modern, industrialized city of Durango offers a hilly downtown area that retains some superb colonial architecture. If the dusty downtown landscape seems to strike a familiar chord, you're not crazy. The area has been used in a number of Hollywood productions, most of them westerns. The most recent movie filmed here was *Wagons East!,* a 1994 pioneer spoof starring Canadian comedian John Candy. The Durango tourist office, proud of the area's contributions to the film industry, often organizes weekend trips to two other nearby "western" towns used as film sets. Of these, **Villa del Oeste** (Village of the West) is the only one still used for moviemaking. Another set is known as **Chupaderos,** and although it has been forgotten by film, it has become a refuge for destitute Mexicans who have made their homes in the abandoned sets.

If you happen to pass through Durango in July, you can take part in the city's annual festivities. Durango wraps two weeks of **Feria Nacional** around two significant dates: July 8, the anniversary of Durango's 1563 founding by Francisco de Ibarra, and July 22, the day of the Virgen del Refugio. The festival has taken on national status, and people come from all around to bet on cockfights, bid on cows, and enjoy the music, food, and carnival rides.

BASICS

AMERICAN EXPRESS

AmEx services are provided by friendly, English-speaking representatives in the travel agency **Touris Viajes,** a few long blocks west of the Plaza de Armas. You can buy or change traveler's checks here and have lost or stolen traveler's checks or AmEx cards replaced. Cardholders can also have their mail held or cash a personal check. *20 de Noviembre 810 Ote., Durango, Durango, CP 34000, México, tel. 18/ 17–00–83, fax 18/17–01–43. From corner of Victoria and 20 de Noviembre, take the blue-and-white bus marked* TECNO. *Open weekdays 9–7, Sat. 10–5.*

CASAS DE CAMBIO

Serfín (20 de Noviembre 400 Ote., tel. 18/18–86–24; open weekdays 9–5) changes traveler's checks. There are several casas de cambio on 20 de Noviembre near the Soriana supermarket, just east of the Plaza de Armas. **Mundinero** (20 de Noviembre 806 Ote., no phone; open weekdays 9:30–2 and 4–6:30, Sat. 10–2), next door to the AmEx office, changes both cash and traveler's checks; unfortunately, the rates here are lousy.

EMERGENCIES

In the event of an emergency, contact the **police** (corner of Prolongación Felipe Pescador and Independencia, tel. 18/17–54–06). For an **ambulance,** call the Cruz Roja (corner of 5 de Febrero and Trabajo, tel. 18/17–34–44).

LAUNDRY

The friendly folks at **Lavandería Automática** will wash, dry, fold, and even deliver 3 kilos (6½ pounds) of your clothes for $3. *Lázaro Cárdenas 510a Sur, at Libertad, tel. 18/17–75–12. 7 blocks from Plaza de Armas. Open Mon.–Sat. 10–8, Sun. 10–2.*

MAIL

The full-service post office will hold mail sent to you at the following address for up to 10 days: Lista de Correos, Administración No. 1, 20 de Noviembre 500-B Ote., Durango, Durango, CP 34001, México. *20 de Noviembre, between Cuauhtémoc and Roncal, tel. 18/11–41–05. Open weekdays 8–7, Sat. 9–1.*

MEDICAL AID

Durango has two 24-hour emergency clinics: **Hospital San Jorge** (Libertad 249, tel. 18/17–22–10) and **Hospital de La Paz** (5 de Febrero 903, tel. 18/18–95–41). **Farmacia del Ahorro** (20 de Noviembre 100 Ote., no phone) is a 24-hour pharmacy.

PHONES

Several casetas de larga distancia line 5 de Febrero, and some **Ladatel** phones dot the Plaza de Armas. For cash calls, walk three blocks south of the plaza to the caseta at Bruno Martínez 206 Sur (tel. 18/13–30–01; open Mon.–Sat. 8 AM–9:30 PM, Sun. 8–3).

VISITOR INFORMATION

The staff of the state tourism office is multilingual, friendly, and helpful, but unfortunately has a limited supply of written information. *Hidalgo 408 Sur, tel. 18/11–21–39. West of plaza on 20 de Noviembre, left on Hidalgo. Open weekdays 8–3 and 6–8, weekends 10:30–2.*

COMING AND GOING

BY BUS

The **Central Camionera** is 4 km (2½ mi) east of the town center, but regular city buses and cheap taxis ($2 to the central plaza) make it accessible. The station is served by a number of national lines, including **Omnibús de México** (tel. 18/18–33–61), **Transportes del Norte** (tel. 18/18–30–61), **Estrella Blanca, Futura, and Transportes Chihuahuenses.** The latter three all share the same phone number: 18/18–37–21. First-class buses run daily to points all over Mexico, including Chihuahua city (9 hrs, $22), Ciudad Juárez (14 hrs, $38), Mazatlán (7 hrs, $10.50), Mexico City (12 hrs, $35.50), Monterrey (9 hrs, $24), and Saltillo (7½ hrs, $20). A small pharmacy, long-distance telephone service, and luggage storage (20¢ per hr) are available at the station.

BY TRAIN

Durango's train station (tel. 18/11–22–94) is right below the Cerro del Mercado, off Prolongación Felipe Pescador, about nine blocks north of the plaza. To get to most destinations (except Monterrey), you must change at another train station in some random town along the way and wait at least four–six hours for the next train. A first-class train to Mexico City (15 hrs, $18) departs at 6 AM. Another train departs for Ciudad Juárez (11 hrs, $19) at 7 AM, stopping in Chihuahua (8 hrs, $15) on the way. Other destinations include Monterrey (11 hrs, $7), Saltillo (9 hrs, $6.50), and Zacatecas (16 hrs, $5). The ticket office is open daily 5 AM–noon. To get here, catch a blue bus marked BRUNO MARTINEZ at 20 de Noviembre and Bruno Martínez, or walk 20 minutes south on Bruno Martínez from downtown.

GETTING AROUND

The main thoroughfare, **20 de Noviembre,** runs east–west. Victoria, Constitución, and Juárez are the main streets that intersect 20 de Noviembre in the heart of the downtown area. Parallel to 20 de Noviembre are Pino Suárez and 5 de Febrero on the south side, Negrete and Aquiles Serdán on the north side. The main square, called the **Plaza de Armas,** is off 20 de Noviembre, between Juárez and Constitución. Addresses contain cardinal directions—Nte. for north, Sur for south, Ote. for east, and Pte. for west—which indicate where they are in relation to the plaza. City buses (35¢) congregate near the plaza, and taxis charge 40¢ per kilometer.

The state of Durango is famous for its huge desert scorpions, but probably the only scorpion you'll encounter in town is a sticky, sweet caramel one, sold at candy shops and souvenir stands.

WHERE TO SLEEP

There are a few decent, central places, but budget hotels in Durango tend to be bottom-of-the-barrel. Around festival time (the first two weeks in July), either make reservations or expect to stay far from downtown, pay a lot, and get little. At **Hotel Gallo** (5 de Febrero 117, corner Progreso, tel. 18/11–52–90), rooms are sunny, spacious, and all have private baths. However, the low price (doubles $6) tends to attract a less than attractive crowd. **Hotel María del Pilar** (Pino Suárez 410 Pte., tel. 18/11–54–71) has rooms that are clean and relatively comfy, if a bit drab. The spotless bathrooms with copious hot water may help you forgive the peeling paint. Doubles cost $9.50. The **Hotel Posada Durán** (20 de Noviembre 506 Pte., at Juárez, tel. 18/11–24–12), next to the cathedral, is everyone's favorite. Large wooden doors, a bar, and a fountain-graced courtyard lead to impeccable rooms with hardwood floors, some with big glass doors that open onto balconies. The spotless bathrooms provide plenty of hot water. Doubles cost $12, and it's a good idea to make reservations. All hotels are cash only.

FOOD

There are almost no outstanding budget eateries downtown: A few small places serve *comidas corridas* (preprepared lunch specials) but not many distinguish themselves, unless you consider hot dogs a culinary novelty. The daily **mercado municipal** on 20 de Noviembre is a good place to get fresh fruits and vegetables; *fondas* (covered food stands) toward the back serve standard meals for about $1.50.

UNDER $5 • Café Opera. This chic little place serves excellent Italian cuisine, and the scent of garlic wafting from the doorway will instantly hypnotize your taste buds. Of the numerous pasta dishes, the *El mero barbero de Sevilla en Francia* (trout in a creamy almond sauce served with pasta) is highly recommended. For lighter fare, try the huge green salad ($2) doused in a garlic vinaigrette. *Negrete 1005, at Independencia, tel. 18/25–15–00. No breakfast. Closed Mon. Cash only.*

Sloan's. This small restaurant/bar hums with music and is always filled with young people (as well as a bizarre clutter of plane propellers, drum sets, and other kitschy junk). Delicious crepes and hamburgers cost around $2; a monster-size piña colada is $2.50. *Negrete 1003 Pte., just west of Hidalgo, tel. 18/12–21–99. Dinner only. Cash only.*

UNDER $10 • La Casa de la Monja. Despite the name (the nun's house), this colonial building has a rustic elegance. Sit beside the interior garden and fountain and enjoy the specialty *puntas de filete a la monja* (nun-style beef) or the *comida del día* (daily menu; $3). *Negrete 308 Pte., at Madero, tel. 18/11–71–62.*

WORTH SEEING

Most of Durango's interesting sights are within walking distance of the main **Plaza de Armas.** Durango's main church, the huge, baroque **Catedral Basílica Menor,** faces the plaza. It's actually the third religious structure to be built on this spot, started around 1691 and completed in 1770. The best of the outlying sights is the **Parque Guadiana** (on Carretera Durango–Mazatlán). Fourteen long blocks from the main plaza, this park is a favorite spot for sports-minded locals: Miles of dirt paths make it ideal for runners and bicyclists alike, and the huge public swimming pool ($1) is a great place to beat the afternoon heat. Just across the highway is the free **Zoológico Sahuatoba** (tel. 18/12–44–57; open Tues.–Sun. 10–6), where you can gawk at lions, panthers, hippos, and snakes. To get here, take a blue bus marked TIERRA Y LIBERTAD from the corner of Aquiles Serdán and Victoria.

MUSEO DE LAS CULTURAS POPULARES

This museum has a small but interesting display of artesanía from the Huichol, Tepehuano, and Tarahumara indigenous peoples. The friendly staff will walk you through the exhibit and explain everything to you (in Spanish), or you can wander on your own. You can purchase some of these crafts for a moderate price in the small gift shop, or try making your own in the museum's workshop (a mere $2.75 allots you all the supplies you need to create pottery, papier mâché masks, or paintings). *Juárez 302 Nte. and Gabino Barrera, no phone. 4 blocks north of Plaza de Armas. Open Tues.–Sun. 9–6.*

MUSEO REGIONAL DE DURANGO

Built in the second half of the 19th century by architect Stanislaus Slonecky, the Regional Museum of Durango was originally a private residence. Today the two-story building houses fossilized remains dating to the Paleozoic era. A mummified child (or extremely small adult) is also on display; its discovery in nearby El Mezquital has led some archaeologists to believe that a colony of pygmies once lived in Durango. The museum also houses paintings, textiles, and sculptures. *Victoria 100 Sur, between Aquiles Serdan and Negrete, tel. 18/12–56–05. 3 blocks from Plaza de Armas. Admission: 40¢. Open Tues.–Sat. 9–4, Sun. 4–8.*

PALACIO DE GOBIERNO

This impressive 18th-century baroque palace houses the offices of state officials, including that of Durango's governor. The reason to visit, however, is the impressive murals on the top floor, which depict the struggle for survival of Durango's indigenous population. On the ground floor you'll find an unfinished 1936 mural by painter Manuel Guerrero Lourdes. The state of Durango never got around to paying the master his salary, so he laid down his brush in protest midway through the project. *5 de Febrero, at Zaragoza. From Plaza de Armas, walk 4 blocks west. Admission free. Open weekdays 8–3 and 6–8.*

AFTER DARK

Nightlife isn't exactly hip-hoppin' in Durango, but things do liven up on weekends. Hang out with local youth at **Club 100** (Piñón Blanco 101, tel. 18/11–05–52; closed. Mon.–Wed.), on the highway to Mazatlán. Here, techno and rock music keep people dancing, and a "canta-bar" upstairs lets you try out your karaoke skills. To get here, catch a TIERRA Y LIBERTAD bus at Aquiles Serdán and Victoria; you'll have to get a taxi back into town when you're done. **Buchagas Pool and Snack Bar** (20 de Noviembre 310 Ote., tel. 18/12–40–64) is a respectable place to play eight ball (tables are $2 per hour).

NORTHEASTERN MEXICO

UPDATED BY PATRICIA ALISAU

The factories and processing plants that crowd Mexico's increasingly industrial northeastern states—Coahuila, Nuevo León, and Tamaulipas—contrast sharply with the *Dallas*-style ranches that occupy rolling acres just over the border in Texas. Since the North American Free Trade Agreement (NAFTA) went into effect in 1994, disillusioned job seekers from all over the country have flooded border towns like Nuevo Laredo, Matamoros, and Reynosa, looking for work in these *maquiladoras* (*see box titled* "Manufacturers of Misery," *in* Chapter 3).

Yet not every single town in northeastern Mexico is tied to the purse strings of foreign companies. Life, it seems, can still continue in the old, familiar ways—this despite the rising crime, falling wages, and growing hopelessness that inevitably arises with rapid modernization. In the border town of Reynosa, vendors from all over Mexico sell handmade crafts in open markets, while fresh red crab and baby shrimp are sold by the kilo in port towns like Tampico. In Saltillo, the slow-paced capital of Coahuila state and the original residence of revolutionary leader-turned-governor Venustiano Carranza, serape makers still produce the magnificently colored vests and blankets of their Tlaxcalan ancestors. Just 230 km (142 mi) south of the U.S. border is Mexico's third largest city, Monterrey, home to a number of excellent museums and one of Latin America's finest universities.

Although the northeastern landscape tends to be mostly dry and unbearably hot in the summer months, this does little to deter scores of U.S. day-trippers who cross the border in search of ethnic kitsch and cheap tequila shots. The coastal town of Tampico offers a verdant escape from this souvenir hell; its extensive stretches of beach provide refreshing relief from the city heat. If you're a serious nature lover, the Parque Nacional Cumbres de Monterrey, an hour from Monterrey, offers hiking, spelunking, and camping.

MATAMOROS

Matamoros is the easternmost border crossing between the United States and Mexico, linked with Brownsville, Texas, by a 330-ft bridge across the Río Bravo (or Rio Grande, as it's known in the States). It's in the state of Tamaulipas, 38 km (24 mi) west of the Gulf Coast. Half a million people call Matamoros home, and although most of the city's inhabitants are employed in maquiladoras, the recent devaluation

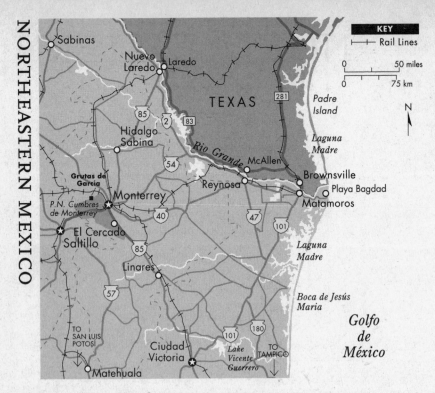

of the peso has left many jobless and desperate. On the streets, the ratio of men to women seems to be five to one, making it unpleasant for females to explore the city alone. This shouldn't be a major disappointment, however: There's not much reason you'd want to stick around here.

Still, if you're stranded in Matamoros, a few sights merit your perusal. Bullwhips, brightly colored serapes, ceramics, glass, and mounds of silver jewelry are sold at **Mercado Juárez** (Matamoros, at Calle 10) and at Matamoros's old market, **Pasaje Juárez** (Calle 8, across from Hotel Roma). Both are open Monday–Saturday 9–8, Sunday 9–2. The **Casamata** (Guatemala, at Santos Degollado, tel. 88/13–59–29; open Tues.–Sun. 9:30–5:30; admission free) was established in 1845 to defend the city against an anticipated U.S. invasion. It wasn't completed in time, however, and U.S. troops under Zachary Taylor were able to capture Matamoros easily in 1846. The fortress is now a museum housing photos and artifacts, mainly from the Mexican Revolution. The aging but regal **Teatro Reforma** (Calle 6, at Abasolo, tel. 88/12–51–20) hosts regional and local dance and drama, plus occasional art exhibits; check the Spanish monthly *Tu-Guía Matamoros,* available at the tourist office (*see below*). Nearby, **Calle Abasolo** is a pedestrian-only street that's great for people-watching. Matamoros explodes with dance, theater, and art during the huge **Festival Internacional de Otoño,** held the second week of October. During the last week of February, Matamoros's **Fiesta Mexicana** promotes U.S.–Mexican relations with parades and outdoor concerts.

BASICS

AMERICAN EXPRESS

American Express affiliate **Viajes Axial** offers extremely limited services. The office only replaces lost cards and holds members' mail. *Morelos 94–107, Centro, Matamoros, Tamaulipas, CP 87300, México, tel. 88/13–69–69. Open weekdays 8–6, Sat. 9–1.*

CASAS DE CAMBIO

Banamex (Calle 7, at Morelos, tel. 88/13–60–35; open weekdays 9–3) changes cash and traveler's checks. Its ATM accepts Plus, Cirrus, MasterCard, Visa, and American Express cards.

CONSULATES

United States. To avoid standing in the long line, show the guard your passport. *Calle 1 No. 2002, at Azaleas, tel. 88/12–44–02. Take the yellow* PRIMERA POPULAR/PUENTE *pesera (minibus) from the bus station. Open weekdays 8–5.*

CROSSING THE BORDER

If you're only staying in Matamoros a couple of days, simply show the scowling border guard your passport or any other photo ID. If you plan to travel more than 22 km (13 mi) into Mexico, get a tourist card (*see* Passports, Visas, & Tourist Cards *in* Chapter 1) at the crossing. Most of the yellow *maxitaxis* (buses) just over the bridge in Matamoros will take you to the downtown area.

EMERGENCIES

Contact the **police** at 88/17–22–05, the **fire** department at 88/12–00–03, and for **ambulance** service, the Cruz Roja at 88/12–00–44.

MEDICAL AID

Bótica Monterrey (Calle 6, at Nafarrete, tel. 88/17–09–48) is a 24-hour pharmacy. Emergency medical care is available at the 24-hour **Centro de Salud** (Calle 6, at Querétaro, tel. 88/17–49–30 or 88/17–19–16).

PHONES AND MAIL

It's cheaper and faster to send international mail from the United States than from Mexico. The Brownsville, Texas post office (1001 E. Elizabeth St., tel. 210/546–9462; open weekdays 9–5) is five blocks west of the international bridge. In Matamoros, the main **post office** will hold your mail at the following address for up to 10 days: Lista de Correos, Calle 6 No. 214, Matamoros, Tamaulipas, CP 87300, México. There's also a branch at the Matamoros bus depot, open daily 9–noon and 3–8. You can make collect and credit-card international calls from the **Ladatel** pay phones (not the overpriced orange ones) in Plaza Hidalgo, Plaza Allende, and the bus and train stations.

VISITOR INFORMATION

The Mexican government's **Turismo de Fronterino** office (Alvaro Obregon, at the international bridge, tel. 88/12–36–30; open weekdays 8–7) has an English-speaking staff and a few useful maps. One block east of the international bridge, the **Brownsville, Texas Chamber of Commerce** (Taylor and Elizabeth Sts., Brownsville, tel. 210/542–4341; open weekdays 9–5) has excellent street maps of Brownsville and Matamoros.

COMING AND GOING

For a city of its size, Matamoros is easily navigable. All north–south streets are numbered, and their cross streets form a neat grid. The city center is bordered by **Plaza Hidalgo** to the south and the **Mercado Juárez** to the north. The *puente internacional* (international bridge) connects Matamoros and Brownsville eight blocks north of downtown Matamoros. Walking is the easiest and fastest way to cross the border; the toll is 25¢ per pedestrian, $1.50 per vehicle. *Peseros* (minivans; 25¢) run every 10 minutes to the bridge, bus station, and American Consulate.

BY BUS

The **Central de Autobuses** (Calle 1, at Canales) is 25 blocks south of the international bridge. To get here, flag down a CENTRAL pesero at the international bridge or in Plaza Hidalgo. First-class **Autobuses del Oriente (ADO)** (tel. 88/12–01–81) serves Veracruz city twice daily (16 hrs, $38). **Omnibús de México** (tel. 88/13–76–93) sends several daily buses to Monterrey (5 hrs, $12), Reynosa (2 hrs, $3.50), and Nuevo Laredo (6 hrs, $12). **Transportes del Norte** (tel. 88/12–27–77) has one bus daily to Guadalajara (18 hrs, $39) and Zacatecas (12 hrs, $28) and four buses to Mexico City (15 hrs, $38). Inside the terminal you'll find a post office, plenty of Ladatel phones, a 24-hour cafeteria, and luggage lockers ($3 per day).

BY CAR

To cross the border with your car, present the registration (in your name), a current driver's license, your passport, and photocopies of all three documents. For more details on bringing a car into Mexico, *see* Chapter 1. Traveling to **Tampico** (501 km/310 mi, 7 hrs) is a long, dry drive on Highway 180 south. To reach **Monterrey** (338 km/210 mi, 4 hrs), head out on Highway 2 west toward Reynosa (104 km/64 mi, 1 hr); at Río Bravo, just before Reynosa, get on the smoothly paved toll road (tolls $4). This conveniently connects with Highway 40 southeast, which takes you directly into Monterrey (tolls $16). To reach **Mexico City** (990 km, 10 hrs), take Highway 180 south toward Tampico to Highway 70 west. This will hook up with Highway 105 south, which will take you to Highway 130 south at Pachuca (tolls $6).

BY PLANE

Aeroméxico (tel. 88/12–24–60) offers daily flights to Mexico City and other destinations. The airport is 17 km (10 mi) south of town, toward Ciudad Victoria. The frequent blue PEREÑO pesero from Plaza Allende (Independencia, at Calle 10) drops you off 800 ft from the gates. A taxi costs about $5.

WHERE TO SLEEP

Rooms in Matamoros are expensive by Mexican standards, but they're half the price of those in Brownsville. Budget hotels, virtually indistinguishable from one another, are clustered on and near Calle Abasolo. Keep in mind that Matamoros isn't the safest city in Mexico, and the cheaper hotels tend to attract a sketchy clientele. **Casa de Huéspedes Margarita** (Calle 4 No. 79, between Abasolo and Matamoros, tel. 88/13–72–78) has double ($10) rooms with air-conditioning, private bath, and plenty of hot water. The family that runs the place is always there, making it the safest budget option in town. At $9.50 for a double, the **Hotel Alameda** (Victoria 91, between Calles 10 and 11, tel. 88/16–77–90) won't break the bank. The immaculate rooms (all with private bath) are deliciously cool, and the snacks in the lobby rival those in any American movie theater. Parking is also available. Both of the above accept cash only. The **Gran Hotel Residencial** (Alvaro Obregón, at Amapolas, tel. 88/13–94–40) is considered the best in town and offers rooms ($45) with private bath, air-conditioning, TV, and parking; some rooms have garden views. There's a pool, bar, and restaurant on the premises.

FOOD

Head to the Mercado Juárez for tacos, *tortas* (sandwiches), and other cheap eats. Though run down, the **Café El Económico** (Calle 10 No. 1003, between González and Abasolo, tel. 88/12–14–58) is a mecca for starving travelers. A delicious meal consisting of a *guisado* (stew) of your choice, plus rice, beans, and tortillas, is only 75¢. Add another $1.50 for a helping of *gorditas* (fried tortillas filled with vegetables, beans, or meat). Local kids crowd around the orange Formica tables at **La Canasta** (Abasolo 706, between Calles 7 and 8, tel. 88/12–29–00), gobbling down the locally famous double burger with cheese ($1.75). The 75¢ burritos and 50¢ tacos are as cheap as they come. The air-conditioned **Las Dos Repúblicas** (Calle 9, at Matamoros, tel. 88/16–68–94) sells six *flautas* (fried tacos) or quesadillas for $4. Wash it all down with one of their 18-ounce margaritas. All of the above accept cash only.

AFTER DARK

Like other border towns, Matamoros attracts throngs of American tourists who cross the border for a night of unbridled indulgence. The frenzy reaches its peak during April and May, when U.S. colleges are on spring break. A popular place year-round is the restaurant/disco **Blanca White** (Álvaro Obregón 49, at Gardenias, tel. 88/12–18–59). The clientele, as the bilingual name suggests, is divided between Mexicans and Americans. A mellower crowd frequents the video-bar **La Tequila** (Álvaro Obregón 42, tel. 88/16–75–22), the best spot in town if you want to dance. There's no cover charge at either nightspot.

REYNOSA

Reynosa, across the border from McAllen, Texas, is a convenient starting point if you're bound for Mexico City, Monterrey, or El Bajío. It's also a typical border town with limited charm: With over 60 maquiladoras, it's one of Mexico's most industrial cities. That said, the city is not without its long-held traditions; agricultural goods are brought in weekly from as far as San Luis Potosí, Veracruz, and Sinaloa to be sold at Reynosa's spectacular open-air market, along with regional crops like okra, wheat, and corn. The **mercado municipal** (Colón, between Hidalgo and Morelos) stretches for two blocks, and on a typical day the smells of fruit, sweat, leather, and tamales waft through crowded streets. At night, tourists from Texas stop shopping and flock to downtown's upscale **Zona Rosa** neighborhood, for the raucous nightlife.

BASICS

AMERICAN EXPRESS

Erika Viajes, eight blocks north of the plaza, provides limited AmEx services: The staff won't cash personal checks, but they do replace lost traveler's checks and sell new ones. *Ávila Camacho 1325, at Ortíz Rubio, tel. 89/22–60–16. Open weekdays 9–6, Sat. 8:30–12:30.*

CASAS DE CAMBIO

You'll pass several casas de cambio on Zaragoza as you head downtown from the international border, most of which don't cash traveler's checks. However, **Banamex** (Juárez 650, at Guerrero, tel. 89/22–22–18; open weekdays 9–3) will cash them for you at good rates. It also has an ATM.

CROSSING THE BORDER

You can stay in Reynosa up to 72 hours without getting a tourist card, but if you plan to stay longer or venture more than 22 km (13 mi) into Mexico, you'll need to get one at the border crossing (*see* Passports, Visas, & Tourist Cards *in* Chapter 1). The border crossing over the Río Bravo costs 25¢ if you're walking and $1.50 to cross by car.

EMERGENCIES

In Reynosa, contact the **police** at 89/22–00–08, the **fire** department at 89/24–93–99, and for **ambulance** service, the Cruz Roja at 89/22–13–14.

MEDICAL AID

Farmacia López is a 24-hour pharmacy. *Aldama 101, at Hidalgo, tel. 89/22–84–84 or 89/22–96–67.*

PHONES AND MAIL

The only public phone within two blocks of Reynosa's bus station is at **7-Eleven**, across the street from the east side of the station. There's a cluster of **pay phones** in the main plaza, where you'll also find a **Computel** office (open daily 8 AM–10 PM). The main **post office** (corner of Díaz and Colón, near the train station; open weekdays 8–7, Sat. 9–1) will hold your mail at the following address for up to 10 days: Lista de Correos, Reynosa, Tamaulipas, CP 88620, México.

VISITOR INFORMATION

At the *puente internacional* (international bridge), you'll find the dusty **Delegación Estatal de Turismo** (tel. 89/22–11–89; open weekdays 8–8). The bilingual staff can only give you a few pamphlets and then send you on your way.

COMING AND GOING

A bridge over the Río Bravo links Reynosa with McAllen, Texas (which lies about 16 km/10 mi north of the border). Reynosa's small downtown area is laid out in a grid and can be crossed in less than 15 minutes. **Hidalgo** is the principal north–south axis, and **Morelos** the main east–west axis. Microbuses (25¢) run from the bridge to the plaza, the train station, and the bus depot at least every 15 minutes.

BY BUS

The **Central Camionera** (Colón 1001, tel. 89/22–84–08) is behind the Gigante supermarket, five blocks south and 10 blocks east of the main plaza. To get here, catch a C. CAMIONERA/OBRERO microbus (30¢) from the international bridge or the center of town. There have been a few thefts in and around the station, so use caution here, especially at night. Buses depart frequently for Matamoros (2 hrs, $3.50) and Río Bravo (½ hr, $1). Three first-class buses depart daily for Monterrey (3 hrs, $10). First-class **Omnibús de México** (tel. 89/22–33–07) sends buses west to Chihuahua (15 hrs, $31) and south to Mexico City (13 hrs, $34). **Transportes del Norte** (tel. 89/22–04–92) goes daily to Guadalajara (18 hrs, $34) and

Mexico City (15 hrs, $33). **ADO** (tel. 89/22–87–13) has first-class buses to Tampico (3 per day, 6½ hrs, $13), Tuxpán (3 per day, 10 hrs, $17), and Veracruz city (daily, 16 hrs, $36). The station and its *caseta de larga distancia* (long-distance telephone office) are open 24 hours; luggage storage is available 6 AM– 9 PM (25¢ per hr, $1 per day).

BY CAR

Travel to Monterrey (224 km/139 mi, 3 hrs) is easy sailing on Highway 40-D southwest (the toll is $16). Continue another hour past Monterrey on to Highway 40 to reach Saltillo. Travelers to Tampico (511 km/317 mi, 5 hrs) should take Highway 97 south to Highway 180 south.

WHERE TO SLEEP

Hotels in the Zona Rosa and around the central plaza cater to businesspeople and vacationers and are priced accordingly. Head toward the train station for the city's budget hotels; the cheapest rooms are found just north of the tracks. Frosty air-conditioning makes the immaculate little **Hotel Avenida** (Zaragoza 885 Ote., at Canales, tel. 89/22–05–92) a hard option to turn down; at $14 for a double, it's an affordable luxury. All rooms have TVs and open onto a plant-filled patio. The **Hotel Estación** (Hidalgo 305, tel. 89/22–73–02), just across the tracks from the train depot and a few blocks south of downtown, couldn't be more convenient. If you're tired enough, you won't even hear the roar of passing trains. Small rooms with air-conditioning cost $8—avoid the stuffy rooms with fans. Both hotels accept cash only. The $25 doubles at **San Carlos** (Hidalgo 970, on main square, tel. 89/22–12–80) are always full of Texans, who like the hotel's proximity to the market, restaurants, and nightlife. Rooms have air-conditioning, TV, and private bath.

FOOD

Cheap taco stands and carts selling *elote* (grilled corn on the cob) can be found on almost every street corner, and the piles of fresh fruit at the open market provide some of the cheapest snacks around. For sit-down restaurants, cruise the ***peatonal*** (pedestrian-only street) on Hidalgo from the main plaza to the train station. Elegant eateries abound on the main plaza.

The mirror-lined **Café París** (Hidalgo 815, tel. 89/22–55–35; cash only) is always full, so you may have to wait in the doorway until someone vacates one of the paisley-cushion booths. The delicious *comida corrida* (preprepared lunch special) is a steal at $1.75. Breakfast omelets are less than $2. **La Fogata** (Matamoros 750, tel. 89/22–47–72) is an elegant, air-conditioned restaurant/piano bar serving unusual dishes like *cabrito* (grilled baby goat; $7). Vegetarians won't find much here besides the *queso flameado* (cheese broiled in a smoky oven). There's live music nightly until midnight.

AFTER DARK

At night, Reynosa gets rowdy—and seedy. Fortunately, most of the serious drug trafficking, prostitution, and violence is relegated to the city's Zona Roja (red-light district), a good 10 blocks west of the city center. Better to stick to the **Zona Rosa,** a five-block section of streets bordering the international bridge, which fills nightly with party-minded students from both sides of the border. If you're pining for some country, ranchera, and norteña music, head to the cover-free **El Rodeo** (Allende 890, just south of the bridge, tel. 89/22–95–33), where the gaping mouth of an enormous plaster bull serves as the entrance. The large circular dance floor is suitable for any number of honky-tonk moves. **Fiesta Mexicana** (Ocampo 1140, at Allende, tel. 89/22–01–11) has a mellower atmosphere and an older crowd. The house band plays everything from *baladas* (ballads) to salsa, weekends until 3 AM. On "all you can drink" Fridays and Saturdays, the cover is $4.

NUEVO LAREDO

Of all the eastern border towns, Nuevo Laredo, just over the international bridge from Laredo, Texas, gets the largest onslaught of American souvenir-seekers. Shopping is the primary pursuit here, and you'll find a warren of stalls and shops along the seven-block stretch of **Avenida Guerrero** between the international bridge and the main plaza. Nuevo Laredo's shops stock a good selection of high-quality handicrafts imported from all over Mexico, available at only moderately inflated prices. Wander a few blocks off the main drag in any direction for better prices and smaller crowds. There's also a large **crafts market** on the east side of Guerrero, just north of the plaza.

Nuevo Laredo was founded after the Treaty of Guadalupe Hidalgo in 1848, which ended the Mexican-American War. The treaty established the Río Bravo (or Rio Grande) as the border between the two countries and forced Mexico to give up a substantial amount of territory. Many of Laredo's Mexican residents, suddenly finding themselves living in the United States, crossed the river and founded Nuevo Laredo on what had been the outskirts of town. Today, Nuevo Laredo's economy depends largely on gringos who head south for a few days of drunken revelry, returning home with hangovers and suitcases full of souvenirs. As is common in most border towns, Mexican men roam Nuevo Laredo's streets, hissing and calling to every lone woman in sight.

BASICS

AMERICAN EXPRESS

At AmEx agent **Lozano Viajes Internacionales** you can buy and replace AmEx traveler's checks, change traveler's checks, cash personal checks, and receive mail. *Paseo Reforma 3311, Col. Jardín, Nuevo Laredo, Tamaulipas, CP 88260, México, tel. 87/15–44–55. Open weekdays 9–5:30.*

CASAS DE CAMBIO

Change cash at one of several casas de cambio on Guerrero, just below the international bridge. To change traveler's checks, try **Lozano Viajes Internacionales** (*see above*) or **Divisas Terminal** (open Mon.–Sat. 6 AM–10 PM, Sun. 6 AM–8 PM) in the bus station. **Banamex** (Guerrero, between Canales and Madero, tel. 87/12–30–01) has an ATM that accepts Cirrus, Plus, Visa, and MasterCard.

Nuevo Laredo's vibrant commercialism takes the form of street vendors parading with yard-high stacks of straw hats, and of little kids hawking photos of the latest lucha libre (wrestling) heroes.

CONSULATES

United States. *Allende 3330, between Guanajuato and Nayarit, tel. 87/14–05–12. Open weekdays 8–12:30 and 1:30–5.*

CROSSING THE BORDER

Have your passport or other photo ID handy when crossing the border. If you plan on traveling farther south (22 km/13 mi or more) or will be staying in Mexico longer than 72 hours, cross the parking lot west of the international bridge and ask the immigration office for a tourist card (for more information, *see* Passports, Visas, & Tourist Cards *in* Chapter 1).

EMERGENCIES

Dial 06 from any phone in Nuevo Laredo to reach the **police, fire** department, or an **ambulance.**

MEDICAL AID

The **Cruz Roja** (Independencia 1619, at San Antonio, tel. 87/12–09–49) offers emergency and routine medical care. There are a number of well-stocked **Benavides** pharmacies throughout town; the one on Guerrero 702 (at Padre Mier, tel. 87/12–21–60) is open daily 8 AM–10 PM. **Farmacia Calderón** (Guerrero 704, tel. 87/12–55–63) is a 24-hour pharmacy.

PHONES AND MAIL

It's quickest and cheapest to drop foreign mail at the U.S. post office, about six blocks north of the border. Nuevo Laredo's main **post office** (corner of Reynosa and Dr. Mier, tel. 87/12–73–97; open weekdays 8–7, Sat. 9–12:30) is behind the Palacio Municipal. They'll hold your mail at the following address for up to 10 days: Lista de Correos, Nuevo Laredo, Tamaulipas, CP 88000, México. The building also has a telegram and fax service (both for sending only), open weekdays 9–7, weekends 9–noon. **Ladatel** pay phones can be found on Plaza Hidalgo, but it's cheaper to place international calls from the States; pay phones are across the international bridge, just past U.S. customs.

VISITOR INFORMATION

The **tourist office** (Puente Internacional No. 1, tel. 87/12–01–04; open daily 8–8) is housed in a large, dusty booth on the west sidewalk of the international bridge. They dispense tourist pamphlets and free maps of Nuevo Laredo.

COMING AND GOING

Nuevo Laredo is divided down the middle by Avenida Guerrero, which runs north–south from the **international bridge** to Avenida Reforma (which connects with the highway to Monterrey). The city's two main squares, **Plaza Juárez** and **Plaza Hidalgo**, are also on Guerrero, at the edges of the six-block area that makes up the central market. Buses marked PUENTE/CENTRAL and CAMIONERA/CARRETERA (50¢) run down Guerrero to the bus station; green-and-white COLONIAS 5 buses run from Plaza Hidalgo east to the train station.

BY BUS

The **Terminal Central Maclovio Herrera** (J. R. Romo 3800) is a 25-minute bus ride south of the bridge. Take a PUENTE/CENTRAL or CAMIONERA/CARRETERA bus (50¢) from the corner of Juárez and Victoria or from Galeano on the east side of the plaza. The 10-minute taxi ride costs $2. **Transportes Frontera** (tel. 87/14–09–88) runs buses every three hours to Mexico City (15 hrs; $46 1st class, $40 2nd class). Buses also leave hourly for Saltillo (4 hrs, $13 1st class; 5 hrs, $10 2nd class), San Luis Potosí (12 hrs, $29 1st class; 13 hrs, $25 2nd class), and Monterrey (3 hrs, $10 1st class; 3½ hrs, $8 2nd class). First-class **Omnibús de México** (tel. 87/14–06–17) serves nearby cities as well as Zacatecas (8 hrs, $27) and Guadalajara (14 hrs, $40). The caseta de larga distancia is open 24 hours a day, and the casa de cambio (open weekdays 6 AM–10 PM, Sun. 6 AM–8 PM) changes traveler's checks. Luggage storage is available Monday–Saturday 7 AM–10 PM, Sunday 7–5.

BY CAR

For those headed to Monterrey (224 km/139 mi, 2 hrs), Highway 85-D south is as quick and direct as they come (tolls $14). Travel to Mexico City (1,151 km/714 mi, 12 hrs) involves taking Highway 85-D south through Monterrey to Highway 57, which passes through San Luis Potosí and Queretaro. The grand total in tolls is around $23.

BY PLANE

Mexicana (tel. 87/12–22–11) flies to Guadalajara and Mexico City. The airport is 15 km (9 mi) south of town, and is not served by public transportation. A taxi costs about $3.

WHERE TO SLEEP

Hotels in Nuevo Laredo tend to be either outrageously expensive or dreadfully run-down; your best bet for something decent is in the area around Avenida Guerrero, between the bridge and central square. The streets stay lit until 9 or 10 PM, and Guerrero is almost always busy. Nevertheless, be careful of lurking thieves who target tourists.

Hidden among the casas de cambio near the bridge, **Los Dos Laredos** (Matamoros 108, at 15 de Junio, tel. 87/12–24–19) is fairly clean and friendly, with fluffy towels that make up for the wimpy water pressure. The throb of nearby discos can be heard late into the night, but you can't beat the $10 doubles. Check in before 6 PM on weekends as this place tends to fill up fast. Large, comfortable rooms with air-conditioning and color TVs are standard at the **Hotel La Finca** (Reynosa 811, tel. 87/12–88–83), where the hot water runs day and night. Doubles cost $18. But by far the cleanest, most reliable hotel in town is the **Hotel Romanos** (Dr. Mier 2402, tel. 87/12–23–91), where pearly white bedcovers and spotless bathrooms are complemented by blissfully cool air-conditioning and plenty of hot water. Doubles cost $15 and have color TVs. None of the above hotels accept credit cards.

FOOD

The dining scene here includes everything from cheap taco stands and fast-food joints to overpriced eateries catering exclusively to retired Texans. For moderately priced restaurants, explore the side streets south of the main plaza. After a long day of shopping (or a long night at the discos), visit mellow

Cafetería Modelo (Dr. Mier, at Ocampo, tel. 87/12–15–66) for huge all-day breakfasts ($2) like *huevos rancheros* (ranch-style eggs, with spicy tomato sauce, beans, and tortillas) or their special *plato mexicano* (two flautas, one burrito, one tamale, and beans). While mirrors and fluorescent lighting create a hospital-like atmosphere at **El Principal** (Guerrero 624, tel. 87/12–13–01), the meal-size *botanas* (appetizers) are a real bargain. Try the *queso panela de cabra* (goat cheese broiled in a smoky oven; $2) accompanied by a stack of piping-hot tortillas. The 24-hour **Restaurant Hotel Reforma** (Guerrero 806, between González and Canales, tel. 87/12–34–88) isn't much to look at, but it's always packed at lunchtime with hotel guests and local families. They come for the best comida corrida around—including salad, soup, dessert, and your choice of chicken or breaded beef, all for $4. All of the above accept cash only.

AFTER DARK

Nuevo Laredo's nighttime activities are every bit as frenzied as its daytime shopping. The most touristy and expensive discos are on the south end of Guerrero, but local crowds head one block south of 15 de Mayo to **Quintana Rock** (Victoria, at Matamoros, tel. 87/12–07–76), which plays everything from '70s hits to '90s disco, Thursday through Saturday until dawn. On Saturday, there's a $3 cover. The bars **Winery** (Matamoros 308, at Victoria, tel. 87/12–08–95) and **El Dorado** (Ocampo, at Belden, tel. 87/12–00–15) are popular with an older, more sophisticated crowd.

MONTERREY

In this metropolis of 3 million people, decadence and absolute poverty coexist side by side, a jarring reminder that Monterrey is the country's unchallenged industrial giant, as well as being the state capital for Nuevo León. In juxtaposition to the city's grand buildings and luxurious suburbs is the ring of squalid huts and smoke-belching factories known as the *cinturón de miseria* (belt of misery). Pollution is a serious problem here, and unless you confine yourself to Monterrey's sprawling but manageable center, it's likely you'll end up with a serious case of the urban-industrial blues.

After founding Monterrey in the late 1500s, the Spanish encouraged settlement in the region by granting vast tracts of land to a handful of families. The success of these sheep ranchers quickly created a wealthy elite, who, following the construction of a railroad in the 1880s, decided to invest in industry. The powerful Garza Sada family refined the art of mass-produced beer, and religiously reinvested the profits. They established glass factories and cardboard mills, and even manufactured their own beer barrels and delivery wagons. To ensure proper training for the future leaders of this vast industrial empire, the Garza Sadas founded the **Instituto Tecnológico de Monterrey,** now considered one of the best universities in Latin America.

Life in Monterrey, also known as "the Pittsburgh of Mexico," is hectic, and staying here can be quite expensive. Even so, those who take the time to wander the busy streets will encounter the region's best museums, good examples of colonial and modern civic architecture, and a spectacular central plaza that provides great views of the Sierra Madre, lush mountain peaks that encircle the southern edge of town. These pine-forest mountains are home to the **Parque Nacional Cumbres de Monterrey,** a national park known for several beautiful caves and waterfalls, as well as **La Silla** (The Saddle), a saddle-shape rock formation that you'll see on postcards everywhere.

BASICS

AMERICAN EXPRESS

The AmEx office appears disorganized, but the staff is patient and friendly. They cash personal checks, replace lost or stolen traveler's checks, and hold cardmembers' mail indefinitely at: San Pedro 215 Nte., Colonia de Valle, San Pedro Garza García, Nuevo León, CP 64220, México. *Pino Suárez 214, at Isaac Garza, tel. 8/318–33–85. Open weekdays 9–6, Sat. 9–noon. From Zona Rosa, take* RUTA *39 bus north on Pino Suárez; get off at Isaac Garza.*

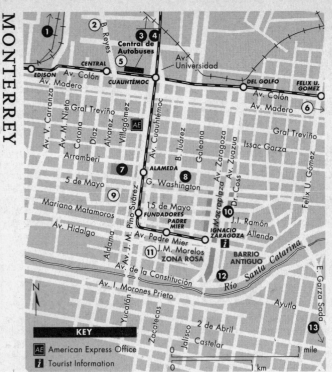

MONTERREY

Sights ●
Cervecería
Cuauhtémoc, **3**
Instituto
Tecnológico de
Monterrey, **13**
Mercado Juárez, **8**
Museo de Arte
Contemporáneo
(MARCO), **12**
Museo de Historia
Mexicana, **10**
Parque Alameda, **7**
Parque de los Niños
Héroes, **4**
Train Station, **1**

Lodging ○
Hotel Colonial, **11**
Hotel Estación, **2**
Hotel Posada de
Los Reyes, **9**
Hotel Victoria, **5**
Villa Deportiva
Juvenil, **6**

KEY
AE American Express Office
i Tourist Information

BOOKSTORES

The **American Bookstore** has a great selection of English books. *Garza Sada 2404-A, near Pemex station, tel. 8/387–08–38. Open weekdays 9–7, Sat. 10–7, Sun. 10–3.*

CASAS DE CAMBIO

Base Internacional (Pino Suárez 1217 Nte., tel. 8/372–86–22; weekdays 9–6, Sat. 9–1), just north of Colón and the Cuauhtémoc Metro stop, changes traveler's checks. **Banamex** (Pino Suárez 933 Nte.) also cashes traveler's checks for decent rates and has an ATM that accepts Cirrus, Plus, MasterCard, and Visa.

CONSULATES

Canada: *Edificio Kalos, Mariano Escobedo and Av. Constitución, Suite 108, tel. 8/344–32–00. Open weekdays 8–2.* **United States**: This office will replace birth certificates and lost passports, provide tax information and a notary public, and help in emergency situations. *Constitución 411 Pte., tel. 8/345–21–20. Open weekdays 8–2.*

EMERGENCIES

In an emergency, dial 06 or contact the **police** (Gonzalitos and Lincoln, tel. 8/370–00–48) or the **fire** department (tel. 8/342–00–53). For an **ambulance,** call the Cruz Roja (tel. 8/342–12–12).

LAUNDRY

At **Lavandería Automática,** you can get 4 kilos (9 pounds) of clothes washed for $3.50, or you can wash it yourself for 75¢ a load; drying costs 15¢ a minute. *Padre Mier 1102 Ote., at Antillón, tel. 8/42–11–88. Open weekdays 8–7, Sat. 8–5.*

MEDICAL AID

For medical attention, visit the 24-hour **Cruz Roja** clinic (Alfonso Reyes 2503, Col. del Prado, tel. 8/342–12–12), near the Plaza de Toros. Helpful pharmacies include **Benavides** (Morales 499, at Escobedo, tel.

8/345–91–91; open daily 7 AM–10 PM) and the 24-hour **Farmacia Medix** (Pino Suárez 510 Sur, in front of Hospital Zoria, tel. 8/342–90–02).

PHONES AND MAIL

The main **post office** is in the basement of the Palacio Federal building, at the north end of the Macroplaza. They'll hold your mail at the following address for up to 10 days: Lista de Correos, Administración 1, Monterrey, Nuevo León, CP 64000, México. *Washington, at Zaragoza, tel. 8/342–40–03. Open weekdays 8–7, Sat. 9–1.*

Phone calls from casetas are unjustifiably expensive here, so it's best to use one of the many **Latadel** phones scattered throughout the city. You can buy Latadel cards in 20- or 50-peso units at most supermarkets, drugstores, or 7-Elevens (look for the LATADEL sign in the store window).

VISITOR INFORMATION

Call the **tourist information line** (tel. 8/40–07–07) for up-to-the-minute information on current events as well as directions to major sights. **Infotour** (Padre Mier, at Dr. Coss, tel. 8/345–08–70, or 800/235–2438 in the U.S.; open Tues.–Sun. 10–5) stocks great brochures and maps and has a friendly English-speaking staff. Ask for a copy of "Enjoy Monterrey" to find out about museum exhibits, cultural events, and concerts.

COMING AND GOING

BY BUS

The huge **Central de Autobuses** (Colón, near Cuauhtémoc, tel. 8/375–32–38) is an impressive transport hub serving virtually the entire country. It's in the northwest section of Monterrey. Frequent first-class buses leave for Nuevo Laredo (3 hrs, $10), Reynosa (3½ hrs, $10), Matamoros (5 hrs, $12), Tampico (8 hrs, $20), Saltillo (1½ hrs, $2.50), and Mexico City (13 hrs, $36). Major first-class bus lines include **Omnibús de México** (tel. 8/374–07–16), which serves Chihuahua (12 hrs, $27) and Ciudad Juárez (18 hrs, $45), and **Transportes del Norte** (tel. 8/375–64–80), which, in conjunction with Greyhound, goes to San Antonio (7 hrs, $34), Dallas (12 hrs, $59), and Houston, Texas (10 hrs, $49). For other destinations, try **Transportes Zua Zua** (tel. 8/374–04–20) or **Tres Estrellas de Oro** (tel. 83/74–24–10). The terminal has a post office, 24-hour pharmacy, luggage lockers ($3 a day), Ladatel phones, and a medical center. Well-policed departure gates make this place perfectly safe.

The easiest way to get here is to take the Line 1 Metro to the Central stop. From downtown, catch the RUTA 39 bus, which runs from the Macroplaza north along Juárez to the bus station. From the bus station to downtown, catch the RUTA 45 bus at Bernardo Reyes and Colón or a RUTA 206 PERIFERICO bus on Suárez.

BY PLANE

The **Aeropuerto Internacional Mariano Escobedo** (tel. 8/345–44–32), equipped with luggage storage ($3 for 6 hrs) and a money-exchange booth, is 6 km (4 mi) northeast of downtown. The only way to get here is by taxi, which will cost about $8. **Aeroméxico** (tel. 8/343–55–60) and **Mexicana** (tel. 8/380–73–00) serve most domestic destinations.

BY TRAIN

Two daily trains pass through Monterrey's station (tel. 8/375–45–94). The first-class **El Regiomontano** leaves Monterrery at 7:50 PM and runs to Saltillo (2 hrs, $3) and Mexico City (14 hrs, $23 reserved seat, $47 sleeping berth). The **El Aguila Azteca** train offers second-class service (no sleeping berths) to Mexico City (20 hrs, $20), with stops in Saltillo (3 hrs, $3) and Querétaro (16 hrs, $15). Tickets are sold up to two days prior to departure at the station's TAQUILLA window (open daily 8–10 and 4–7.)

The train depot is six blocks northwest of the bus station and the Central Metro stop. To reach downtown, cross Venustiano Carranza in front of the train station, head east two blocks on Calzada Victoria to Bernardo Reyes, and take a RUTA 39 or RUTA 45 bus. To reach the bus station, get off at Colón; otherwise both buses will let you off at the Macroplaza. Your other option is to hoof it to the bus station and catch a bus there (*see above*).

GETTING AROUND

Monterrey is a sprawling monstrosity, and very few tourist sights are within walking distance of one another. Luckily, the extensive public transit system makes it easy to get around. If you're traveling by car, avoid rush hours (noon–2 and 4–7) and consider leaving your car at one of several moderately priced, downtown parking garages while you explore the city. Downtown, also called the **Zona Rosa,** the city's luxury hotel and shopping area, is bordered on the east by the **Macroplaza** and on the west by **Juárez.** The intersection of Juárez and Arramberi marks the official center of town, and addresses to the west of this intersection are followed by "Poniente" (Pte.); to the east by "Oriente" (Ote.); to the north by "Norte" (Nte.); and to the south by "Sur." Street numbers become larger the farther you move from the intersection.

BY BUS

Monterrey's loud, rickety, smoke-belching buses (20¢) go anywhere you need to be. The buses on each route are color coded, and the names of major stops are often painted across the windshield—sometimes they're even legible. There are a few fixed bus stops, marked by blue PARADA signs, but buses will stop anywhere; just wave madly at the driver. Most buses run until midnight, except the 24-hour RUTA 1 bus, which travels from Ciudad Universitario and Pino Suárez to the Technológico, then up Juárez to Universidad every 20 minutes. The tourist office (*see above*) offers all the bus information you may need to help make sense of the chaos.

BY METRO

Monterrey's Metro is a modern and efficient system that runs across the city both underground and along elevated tracks. Line 1 runs east–west from Exposición to the city's westernmost perimeter, and Line 2 runs roughly north–south from the Cuauhtémoc Brewery to the Macroplaza. Purchase tickets from station vending machines in units of one, two, four, or eight rides; each ride costs less than 30¢. The Metro runs daily 6 AM–midnight.

WHERE TO SLEEP

Monterrey's relative wealth, combined with a steady flow of business travelers, keeps hotel prices high. Most of the city's budget lodging is unfortunately clustered near the obnoxiously loud bus station.

UNDER $15 • Hotel Estación. The hotel's stern management keeps things clean and quiet and charges $13 for spartan double rooms with fans. Its location (close to the train station) and reasonable rates attract a mixed crowd, including some backpacking travelers. The bathrooms are small but decent, and the hot water flows readily. Rooms fill fast, so arrive early. *Victoria 1450, tel. 8/375–07–55. From the train station, cross Nieto and turn right. 25 rooms, all with bath. Luggage storage, parking. Cash only.*

Hotel Posada de Los Reyes. Conveniently located two blocks from Pino Suárez in the Zona Rosa, this hotel is admittedly a popular *hotel de paso,* so don't be surprised when well-groomed, smiling couples without suitcases pass through the doors. Despite all the activity, the cordial staff and guards create a secure and welcoming environment. Rooms are big enough to dance in, and vigorously air-conditioned. Doubles cost $14. *Aldama 446 Sur, between 5 de Mayo and 15 de Mayo, tel. 8/343–18–80. 23 rooms, all with bath. Cash only.*

UNDER $20 • Hotel Colonial. This basic hotel—the oldest in Monterrey–is ideally located in the Zona Rosa. The lobby is furnished in modest colonial style and features one of the last remaining manually operated elevators in the city. Recently remodeled rooms ($20) all have new color TVs, tile private baths, and carpeting. *Hidalgo Oriente 475, Escobedo, tel. 8/343–6791. 100 rooms, all with bath. Air-conditioning, luggage storage.*

Hotel Victoria. Although this hotel's proximity to the bus station is convenient and the manager tries to keep it decent for families, the exhaust-filled air has made for a slightly yellowed interior. Still, the rooms (doubles $16) are spacious and well-kept, and the water here is sizzling—just wait patiently for its grudging arrival. *Bernardo Reyes 1205 Nte., tel. 8/375–45–42. 1 block NW of the bus depot. 75 rooms, all with bath. Luggage storage. Cash only.*

HOSTELS

Villa Deportiva Juvenil. This enormous gymlike dormitory is situated above a school on the eastern side of the city, in the Parque Fundadora. It's easily accessible by Metro. Each of the seven single-sex dorms ($5 per bed) sleeps 20, and there's air-conditioning and a TV in every room. Best of all, the shared bathrooms are clean. There's also a grassy patio and a cafeteria serving meals for less than $2. A friendly crowd stays here, mainly Mexican high school and university students and recent graduates. *Madero 418 Ote., at Parque Fundidor, tel. 8/355–73–80. Take Metro Line 1 (direction: Exposición) to Y Griega; walk 1 block west on Colón, turn left on Preciliano Elizondo, and head south 1 block. 220 beds. Reception open daily until 7 PM; lockout midnight–6 AM. Luggage storage, parking, showers. Cash only.*

FOOD

Food stands in the major markets offer the best deal in town: a platter of grilled meats and rice-and-beans costs less than $2. Come early, as popular dishes usually run out by 2 or 3 PM. **El Pollo Loco** is a fast-food chain with several branches citywide; they serve generous chicken combination plates ($4). Monterrey's moderately priced, sit-down restaurants are concentrated in the Zona Rosa, especially around the Macroplaza.

UNDER $5 • La Casa del Maiz. Vegetarians, rejoice: Everything at this hip bohemian eatery can also be ordered meatless. Typical Mexican appetizers are large enough to eat as a meal, and the owners/chefs have added their unique touch to every dish: Try the *molletes,* thick bread rolls smothered with black beans, cheese, and *huitlacoche* (edible corn fungus), for $3. The walls are decorated with local art and the candlelit tables attract an artsy crowd at night. *Abasolo 870-B, between Diego de Montemayor and Dr. Cross, Barrio Antiguo, tel. 8/340–43–34. Closed Sun. Cash only.*

Los Girasoles. This is another meat-free haven in a city that seems to run on carne asada. The comida corrida ($3.25) features vegetable combinations like hot broccoli, spinach, and potato soup, or vegetarian "pescado" (grilled "fillet" of potato and shredded cheese). Dishes ordered a la carte are 90¢ each. Save room for dessert, usually fruit, yogurt, and granola. *Ocampo 961, at Cuauhtémoc, tel. 8/343–70–00. Closed Sun. Cash only.*

Las Monjitas. If you can stop giggling over the waitresses' nun outfits long enough to eat, you'll enjoy the tasty food at this taquería chain. Try the house specialty: sliced steak sautéed with peppers, onions, mushrooms, sausage, and bacon, served with a huge platter of tortillas for about $3.50. Live xylophone music accompanies the meal. *Morelos 240 Ote., at Galeana, tel. 8/342–85–37. Cash only.*

UNDER $10 • El Rey de Cabrito. Roast cabrito is a specialty dish in Monterrey, and this restaurant's name (King of Cabrito) might tip you off about what's on the menu here. No lie, it's probably the best roast kid you'll ever have. The owner keeps his own goat herds and has become so famous that he's constantly filling out-of-town orders. The cabrito, as well as beef steaks and ribs, costs about $8 a plate. *817 Constitutión Oriente, tel. 8/343–5560.*

WORTH SEEING

Monterrey offers a number of museums worth visiting, and many parks and plazas perfect for relaxing.

CENTRO CULTURAL ALFA

This five-story building complex resembles the "forbidden land" of *Planet of the Apes*; it was commissioned by an industrial megacompany to promote science and technology through interactive exhibits, art, and scientific experiments. Though it's designed for kids it's fun for folks of all ages. The impressive **Multiteatro** planetarium doubles as an Omnimax theater, presenting Spanish-dubbed films on everything from astronomy to history. Various galleries are packed with hands-on contraptions that will surprise your senses, test your perceptions, and tweak your reasoning. Science-themed modern art exhibits fill two whole floors, and the top floor features a collection of pre-Columbian and Mesoamerican artifacts. Also on the grounds are gardens, an aviary, a theater, and a playground with hands-on, gravity-defying equipment. *Gómez Morin 1100, Col. del Valle, tel. 8/356–56–96. At Parque Alameda (G. Washington, between Pino Suárez and Carranza) catch the free, navy-blue bus marked* DELFIN; *departures are Tues.–Sun., hourly 3 PM–8 PM. Admission: $3. Open Tues.–Sun. 3–9:30.*

CERVECERIA CUAUHTEMOC

The Cuauhtémoc Brewery—named for a famous Aztec ruler—is a powerhouse company that produces several brands of beer. The biggest draw here is its tree-lined **beer garden** (open Tues.–Fri. 9:30–5, weekends 10–6), which serves free samples of Cuauhtemoc suds. Free brewery tours are offered weekdays 9–1 and 3–6. On the grounds there's also a hodgepodge collection of museums, all open Tuesday–Saturday 11–8. The **Museo de Monterrey** (tel. 8/328–60–60) exhibits etchings, lithographs, and oil paintings. The **Salón de la Fama** (Hall of Fame) has a dizzying array of memorabilia from Mexico's baseball legends. The **Museo Deportivo** (Sports Museum) contains exhibits on Mexican boxing, bullfighting, and American college football. All museums are free. *Alfonso Reyes 2202, about 10 blocks north of the bus station, tel. 8/375–22–00. Take* RUTA *1 bus to Cuauhtémoc, at Anaya; cross the street and head south ½ block.*

MACROPLAZA

At the heart of Monterrey is one of the world's largest public squares, covering over 40 acres. The Macroplaza begins on Washington, runs past the **Palacio del Gobierno** (City Hall), and ends at the Santa Catarina riverbank. The southernmost boundary is marked by a beautiful Rufino Tamayo sculpture entitled *Homenaje al sol* (Homage to the Sun). The cascading fountains and blossoming trees in the square's gardens are a wonderful respite from the deafening roar of Monterrey's traffic. Stop in at Infotour (*see* Visitor Information, *above*) for a detailed brochure about this central plaza.

MUSEO DE ARTE CONTEMPORANEO (MARCO)

A huge black bird sculpture by artist Juan Soriano welcomes you into this architecturally daring (and air-conditioned) art center. The museum contains 11 exhibit halls with works by modern artists from around the world. A chic little café offers frequent poetry readings. *Zuazua, at Ocampo, next to the cathedral, tel. 8/342–48–20. Admission: $1.50; free Wed. and Sat. Open Tues. and Thurs.–Sat. 11–7, Wed. and Sun. 11–9.*

MUSEO DE HISTORIA MEXICANA

The newest addition to Monterrey's outstanding museum scene is situated just off the Macroplaza. Interactive exhibits on the second floor trace the history of Mexico—from the earth's creation up to the industrialization of Monterrey—with colorful, eye-jolting displays. The exhibit about the 1910 Mexican Revolution is one of the finest anywhere in the country. On the ground floor you'll find a pricey restaurant and gift shop, as well as special exhibits of works by famous Mexican artists, including Frida Kahlo and Pedro Coronel. *Dr. Coss 445 Sur (Paseo Santa Lucía), tel. 8/345–98–98. Admission: 75¢; free Tues. Open Tues.–Sat. 11–7, Sun. 11–8.*

EL OBISPADO

This tiny, hilltop baptistry is a superb sunset-watching spot. The baptistry, constructed in 1788, served as a fort in the Mexican-American War (1847) and during the French Intervention of the 1900s. Today it houses a number of interesting artifacts, including branding irons and serapes dating from the 17th century. *Far west end of Padre Mier, at Rafael Jóse Berger, tel. 8/346–04–04. From Macroplaza, take the* RUTA *15 pesero to Calle El Gollado; walk 15 min uphill. Admission: $1.50. Open Tues.–Sun. 10–4.*

PARQUE DE LOS NINOS HEROES

Meandering paths, lovely gardens, and a small man-made lake filled with rowboats—these are some of Parque de los Niños Heroes' delights. Several excellent museums also provide interesting stopping points within the park. Auto enthusiasts will be thoroughly impressed by the more than 20 cars on display at the **Museo del Automóvil.** At the **Museo de la Fauna,** a pantheon of stuffed wildlife inhabits the dimly lit rooms, including a 6-ft-tall polar bear and the head of an ivory-tusk elephant. In the **Museo de la Pinacoteca,** beautiful bronze and wood sculptures—including Fidias Elizondo's famous *La Ola* (The Wave)—are surrounded by paintings by artists from the state of Nuevo León. Admission to the park and museums is free, though you are encouraged to make a $1 donation for care of the park's animals. Make sure to get a map at the office to the north of the main entrance. *From Padre Mier, catch a* RUTA *17 bus and get off across from park entrance. To return to town, take* RUTA *18 bus to Juárez or Ocampo. Open Tues.–Sun. 10–6.*

AFTER DARK

The government recently revamped the **Barrio Antiguo,** a section of the Zona Rosa just southeast of the Macroplaza. On weekend nights the streets are closed to cars, and sidewalk cafés fill with throngs of artists, students, and tourists. Dozens of hip new bars and restaurants now line its cobblestone streets: Try **Bar 1900** (Hidalgo at Escobedo, in Barrio Antiguo), a swank, no-cover cantina with flamenco dancers on Thursday night.

Other clubs and bars are just west of the Zona Rosa. At **Pachanga** (Pino Suárez 849 Sur, tel. 8/340–45–23) you can do the cumbria Friday until 2 AM, no cover; on Saturday, women get in for $1 (men $2); and on Sunday everyone pays $2. For one of the best transvestite and cabaret shows around, head to **Antonio's Le Club** (Constitución 1471, at Carranza, no phone; closed Sun.), well worth the $8.50 cover charge. The show starts at 10:30, but if you get here early you can enjoy drinks at the zebra-stripe bar next door. To reach Antonio's, take a RUTA 126 or RUTA 130 bus to Carranza on Constitución, and walk one west block. To get back into town, hail a taxi ($2).

NEAR MONTERREY

LA CASCADA COLA DE CABALLO

An hour northwest of Monterrey, in the Sierra Madre mountains just off Highway 85, is the **Parque Nacional Cumbres de Monterrey**. One of the highlights of a trip here is a view of **La Cascada Cola de Caballo** (Horse Tail Falls), a dramatic waterfall that tumbles down from pine-forest heights. From the pool at the foot of the falls, you can then follow one of two short hiking paths that leads upstream. The waterfall is about 1 km (½ mi) from the park entrance, up a cobblestone road. You can rent horses ($3) at the ticket booth, or hop on a horse-drawn carriage ($2.50). *Admission: $1.50. Park open daily 9–6.*

COMING AND GOING

Horse Tail Falls lies 6 km (4 mi) up a winding road from the small town of **El Cercado**. From Monterrey's Central de Autobuses, **Autobuses Amarillos** buses run here every 15 minutes between 5 AM and 11 PM (45 min, $2). From the stop in El Cercado, walk two blocks to the town plaza and take a blue or orange pesero to the foot of the falls; the fare ($1 partway, $5 to the entrance) is higher on weekends. The last pesero heads back to the plaza at 7:15 PM; otherwise it's a long, mosquito-ridden walk back to town.

Carlos Saenz's painting "El Nacionalista," at Monterrey's Museo de la Pinacoteca, is of a gentleman whose eyes seem to follow you across the room. Leonardo da Vinci used the same technique for his Mona Lisa.

GRUTAS DE GARCIA

The awe-inspiring subterranean caverns of García have, sadly, been transformed into an overdone tourist attraction, the sort of place where stalagmites carry names such as Christmas Tree and the Hand of Death. But the impressive natural beauty of the caves overshadows the thick crowds and glittering signs. For $4 you can ride a tram to the cave entrance; it leaves every 10 minutes (daily 10–4) and fills up quickly. The more rugged alternative is to make the steep, 20-minute hike up the gorgeous mountain path from Villa de García. Bring water and a picnic lunch (if you don't feel like hauling food, there is a small restaurant here). A one-hour guided tour of the caves is included in the entrance fee ($3.25).

COMING AND GOING

The Grutas de García are just outside Villa de García. From Monterrey, catch one of the frequent MON-TERREY–VILLA DE GARCIA buses (1 hr, $1.25) from the corner of Colón and B. Reyes, opposite the Hotel Victoria (*see* Where to Sleep, *above*). Return buses leave Villa de García every 15 minutes.

SALTILLO

Set 5,300 ft up in the mountains, the capital of Coahuila state is a great place to take a deep breath and relax after the pollution and bustle of Monterrey. Saltillo's industrial complexes, including Chrysler and GM plants, are relegated to the suburbs, leaving the downtown plazas and parks clean and tranquil. The town is somewhat sleepy on the weekends, but during the week the streets overflow with foreigners and Mexicans from all walks of life.

Founded in 1575, Saltillo grew up around the grand **Plaza de Armas,** bordered by the elegant **Palacio del Gobierno** (government palace) and the **Catedral de Santiago.** The cathedral's elaborately carved stone facade—in Plateresque, baroque, and neoclassical styles—is considered one of the finest in Mexico. For a great view of the city, walk from the cathedral south along Hidalgo to the **Plaza de México.** If you're in town mid-July through early August, head to the fairgrounds to watch the entire town celebrate the **Feria Anual** (Annual Fair), with games, dancing, regional foods, carnival rides, crafts, and bloody *palenques* (cockfights). You'll always find colorful handicrafts and cheap, filling meals at the **Mercado Juárez,** Saltillo's vibrant marketplace.

BASICS

Change your cash and traveler's checks at **Serfín** (corner of Allende and Lerdo de Tejada, tel. 84/14–90–97; open weekdays 9:30–1). The bank also has a 24-hour ATM that accepts Cirrus, Plus, Master-Card, and Visa. **Operadora de Cambios** (Manuel Atuña 167, at Allende, tel. 8/14–12–96; open weekdays 9–1:30 and 3:30–6, Sat. 9–1) has better hours but worse rates. Dial 060 from any phone in Saltillo to reach the **police, fire** department, or an **ambulance.** You can phone home from the small cluster of **Ladatel** phones in Plaza Acuña, near the Mercado Juárez, or make international cash calls (no collect calls) from Café Victoria (*see* Food, *below*) for $1.50 per minute. The main **post office** (tel. 84/14–90–97; open weekdays 9–7, Sat. 9–1) will hold mail at the following address for up to 10 days: Lista de Correos, Victoria 453, Saltillo, Coahuila, CP 25001, México.

Don't expect much from Saltillo's **tourist office** (Periférico Echeverría 1560, 11th floor of Torre Saltillo building, tel. 84/15–17–14 or 91–800/8–24–20; open Mon.–Thurs. 9–3 and 5–8, Fri. 9–3); they can give you a decent free map, but that's about it. Also, the office is far from downtown; to get here, take the colectivo marked COMBI 9 (20 mins, 25¢) north from Aldama and Hidalgo, get off at Gigante Supermarket on Periférico Echeverría, and walk three blocks east.

COMING AND GOING

BY BUS

Saltillo's **Central de Autobuses** is about 2 km (1 mi) southwest of the centro. Most smaller second-class lines provide service to obscure destinations, but the major **Transportes Frontera** (tel. 84/17–00–76) has frequent service to Monterrey (1½ hrs, $2.50) and Mexico City (12 hrs, $28). Six first-class lines, among them **Omnibús de México** (tel. 84/17–03–15) and **Transportes del Norte** (tel. 84/17–09–02), offer frequent service to Guadalajara (10 hrs, $27), Ciudad Juárez (15 hrs, $40), and Matamoros (5 hrs, $16). **Greyhound** tickets for destinations in the United States and Canada (via Texas) are sold by **Auto-buses Americanos** (tel. 84/17–01–84). The bus station has a 24-hour long-distance and fax office and Ladatel phones that accept credit cards and coins. Luggage storage is available 6 AM–9 PM (20¢ per hr). To reach downtown, catch a bus marked CENTRO. To reach the station from downtown, catch the RUTA 9 bus on Aldama and Hidalgo. Local buses cost 25¢ per trip.

BY TRAIN

The **Estación de Ferrocarril** (tel. 84/12–88–79) is a large, impressive building a few blocks southwest of Parque Zaragoza on Emilio Carranza. To get here catch Bus 1B anywhere on Pérez Treviño, two blocks over from the plaza. To get back catch Bus 3 on Cristóbal Colón. Three trains a day connect Saltillo to eight other cities in the republic. The first-class **Regiomontano** heads south to San Luis Potosí (6 hrs; $7.50 1st class, $20 sleeper car) and Mexico City (12 hrs; $33 1st class, $42 sleeper car). The second-class **El Aguila Azteca** train heads south to Mexico City (17 hrs, $17) and north to Monterrey (2 hrs, $3). You may purchase train tickets in advance from any of the authorized travel agencies (open daily 9–5) just outside the station, or you can show up one hour before the train departs and pay the roving ticket collector on the train platform.

WHERE TO SLEEP AND EAT

Saltillo was overlooked when it came to supplying the budget travelers of the world with a comfortable place to spend the night. Those cheap hotels that do exist are in the city center, near Plaza Acuña. The **Hotel Bristol** (Aldama 405 Pte., tel. 84/10–43–37) is by far your best option, with mosquito-free rooms and clean private bathrooms. Doubles are $9. If you put your creature comforts first, try the downtown **Hotel Saade** (Aldama 397 Pte., tel. 84/12–91–20). Rooms have carpeting, TVs, phones, overhead fans, and private baths, and cost $18 for a double. Parking is available. Both accept cash only.

Saltillo doesn't offer fabulous cuisine, but you can grab a taco or slurp down some homemade soup at the *fondas* (covered food stands) in the **Mercado Juárez** in Plaza Acuña. Locals pack into **Taquería El Pastor** (Aldama 340 Pte., tel. 84/12–21–12) to wolf down $1 tacos filled with carne asada or *carne al pastor* (marinated pork). The house specialty at **Café Victoria** (Padre Flores 221, tel. 84/14–98–00) is the *palomas con aguacate* (flour tortillas filled with shredded beef and avocado; $2.50). They serve an excellent, filling, $2 comida corrida.

WORTH SEEING

Saltillo's winding streets may be colonial and quaint, but they're also confusing. Fortunately, most sights are within walking distance of the **Plaza de Armas** (Hidalgo, at Juárez), where the graceful **Catedral** shines in the strong Saltillo sun. Opposite the cathedral is the **Palacio del Gobierno,** a squat, rose-color building that houses government offices and beautiful murals illustrating the political history of Coahuila, painted by Salvador Almaraz y Tarazona.

Though many of Saltillo's artists have packed up and moved to Monterrey, a few galleries are still going strong. The free **Centro de Arte Contemporáneo** (behind cathedral, tel. 84/10–09–32; open weekdays 10–1 and 4–7, Sat. 10–1) houses everything from paintings to sculpture. The pleasantly cool **Instituto Coahuilense de Cultura** (Juárez, at Hidalgo, tel. 84/14–22–45; open Tues.–Sun. 9–7) exhibits sculpture, artesanía (handicrafts), painting, woodwork, and photography by artists from the state of Coahuila. The new **Museo de Aves de México** (Hidalgo, at Bolívar, no·phone; open Tues.–Sat. 10–6, Sun. 11–6; admission $2) is dedicated to the birdlife of Mexico, the only one of its kind in the country. It's housed in a restored 19th-century Jesuit school and has over 1,800 stuffed and mounted exhibits.

EL SERAPE DE SALTILLO

A small, rusting yellow sign swinging rhythmically in the afternoon breeze is the only marker for this fabulous serape store and factory. Everything from silver earrings and chocolate whisks to teacups and cured tree bark is for sale in the tiny store, but the real fun is watching nimble-fingered craftspeople make the colorful traditional serapes. *Hidalgo 305 Sur, no phone. Open Mon.–Sat. 9–1 and 3–7. Serape makers work weekdays only.*

AFTER DARK

Saltillo's streets are often empty by 11 PM. Local university students let off steam at **Sahara** (Blvd. Fundidores Km. 3.5, tel. 84/30–25–25; closed Sun.), a techno disco also frequented by tourists from nearby expensive hotels. The cover Thursday–Saturday is $4, but other nights are free. To get here, take the ZARAGOZA bus from Padre Treviño and Xicoténcatl. The $1 beers and eclectic music attract a more diverse crowd at **El Zaguán** (Ocampo 338, tel. 84/14–76–67), where candlelight is part of a heavy-handed colonial motif.

TAMPICO

Lush mango trees and endless white-sand beaches make Tampico one of the more enjoyable places to visit in northeastern Mexico. What originally served as a refuge for Huastecan tribes escaping the mosquito-ridden basin of the nearby Río Panuco is now a bustling port town of 600,000, with a large open market and a traffic-choked central plaza (**Plaza de la Libertad**). Although the humid, salty air has taken a toll on the city's older buildings, some well-preserved structures still line the **Plaza de Armas** and nearby sand-dusted streets. During the month-long **Feria de Abril** (April Fair), celebrating the anniversary of Tampico's founding, the plaza is home to live concerts, theater, and historical presentations. The **Museo de la Cultura Huasteca** (1 de Mayo, at Sor Juana Inés de la Cruz, inside Instituto Tecnológico de Cd. Madero, tel. 12/10–22–17; open weekdays 10–5; donations appreciated) displays artifacts and information relating to the indigenous Huasteca people. The nearby **Pirámide de las Flores,** a pyramid dating from the 12th century, receives a lot of hype for being the closest Huastecan ruin to Tampico, but it's rather unspectacular. If you're interested, take a bus marked BELLA-VISTA from the corner of 20 de Noviembre and Madero, two blocks southwest of the plaza, and tell the bus driver to let you off at the Pirámide.

BASICS

AMERICAN EXPRESS

The AmEx office is in **Viajes Pozos,** a travel agency about 10 minutes from downtown. The staff begrudgingly cashes personal checks, holds client mail, and sells and replaces traveler's checks.

Zapote 206, Colonia Águila, Tampico, Tamaulipas, CP 89220, México, tel. 12/13–72–00 or 12/17–14–76. From Plaza de Armas, take CHEDRAUE ECHAVERRIA *bus from in front of Tres Hermanos shoe store to Zapote, and walk ½ block toward Hidalgo. Open weekdays 9–2 and 4–6, Sat. 10–1.*

CASAS DE CAMBIO

Central Divisa (Benito Juárez 215 Sur, tel. 12/12–90–00; open weekdays 9–6, Sat. 9–1) changes both cash and traveler's checks at decent rates. **Bancrecer** (Díaz Mirón 407, at López de Lara) has an ATM that accepts Visa, MasterCard, Cirrus, and Plus cards.

EMERGENCIES

Dial 12/12–10–32 for the **police**; 12/12–12–22 for the **fire** department; or 12/12–13–33 for Cruz Roja, the **ambulance** service.

MEDICAL AID

Benavides is a large, well-equipped pharmacy right off the Plaza de Armas. *Olmos, at Carranza, tel. 12/19–25–25. Open Mon.–Sat. 8 AM–11 PM, Sun. 8 AM–10 PM.*

PHONES AND MAIL

The **post office** (3 blocks SE of Plaza de Armas, tel. 12/12–19–27) will hold mail sent to you at the following address for up to 10 days: Lista de Correos, Madero 309, Tampico, Tamaulipas, CP 89000, México. Clusters of **Ladatel** phones can be found on the Plaza de Armas. Purchase Ladatel cards at **Refresquería La Victoria** on the plaza.

VISITOR INFORMATION

The **tourist office** has a cheerful staff that will go out of their way to help you, but they seem to think "tourism" is limited to pricey group tours. Just pick up the free maps and be on your merry way. *20 de Noviembre 218, tel. 12/12–26–68 or 12/12–00–07, or 800/633–3441 in the U.S. From Plaza de Armas, walk north on Olmos, turn left on Obregón, left on 20 de Noviembre. Open weekdays 8–7, Sat. 9–2.*

COMING AND GOING

Downtown Tampico is easily explored on foot. It's centered around the **Plaza de Armas,** with the cathedral on the north side. **Carranza** runs along the plaza's northern border, with **Díaz Mirón** hugging its southern edge. Numerous *colectivos* (communal taxis; 25¢) and buses (25¢) marked PLAYA can be caught on the corner of Díaz Mirón and López de Lara heading toward the beach. Buses run 6 AM–midnight; colectivo service is 24 hours.

BY BUS

Tampico's **Central de Autobuses** has both first- and second-class terminals divided by a small verdant courtyard, making ticket-shopping a breeze. **ADO** (tel. 12/13–43–39) and **Transportes Futura/Transportes del Norte** (tel. 12/13–46–55) are major first-class carriers with service to Matamoros (6 hrs, $16) and Mexico City (9 hrs, $18.50). Second-class lines include **Transportes Frontera** and **Blancos,** which share a phone line (tel. 12/13–42–35). Destinations include Monterrey (8 hrs, $20), Reynosa (8 hrs, $12), and Mexico City (10 hrs, $18.50). Each terminal is equipped with Ladatel phones and casetas de larga distancia. To get downtown, catch a *micro* (minibus) marked CENTRAL CAMIONERA PERIMETRAL in front of the station; to reach the terminal, take the same micro from the corner of Madero and Colón.

BY CAR

Highway 80 runs through Tampico from Veracruz state. The highway continues north, where it connects to Highway 180, which leads to Matamoros and the Texas border. Highway 70 runs west from Tampico to San Luis Potosí. All three highways are toll-free and have four lanes. Car rental agencies in Tampico include **Budget** (tel. 12/28–05–56 or 12/27–18–80).

BY PLANE

The **Aeropuerto Francisco Javier Mina** (Universidad 700, tel. 12/28–21–95) is a small airport just northwest of town. **Mexicana** (tel. 12/28–21–95) and **Aerolitoral** (tel. 12/28–05–55) offer regular flights to Mexico City. To get downtown, catch an AVIACION POR BULEVAR micro to Carranza and walk four blocks to the Plaza de Armas.

BY TRAIN

Once a bustling doorway to the northeast, the **Estación de Ferrocarriles de Tampico** has been all but forgotten. Three lonely trains a day still lumber to San Luis Potosí (10 hrs, $6.50), Ciudad Victoria (4 hrs, $4), and Monterrey (10 hrs, $5). Tickets are sold daily 6–8 AM and 6–7 PM. *Aduana and Héroes de Nacozari, tel. 12/12–19–83.*

WHERE TO SLEEP

There are a few hotels with reasonable rates a few blocks from the Plaza de Armas, but the neighborhood tends to be unsafe and poorly lit late at night. Your best choice is the **Hotel Mundo** (Díaz Mirón 413, tel. 12/12–03–60), which offers spacious, clean, air-conditioned rooms with modern bathrooms, cable TVs, and telephones. Doubles cost $24.

Hotels along the beach tend to be pricey and a tad run-down. The bright red-and-white **Hotel Orinoco** (NW of beach entrance, off Casero, no phone) fills up fast, so arrive early in the day to stake your claim. Rooms are carpeted and cooled by noisy but relatively effective floor fans. Doubles cost $15, cash only. You can pitch a tent for free on **Playa Miramar**, about 5 km (3 mi) from downtown, and the fee to use the beach's showers and toilets is less than what you'd pay for a taco at one of the nearby hotels. For directions to the beach, *see* Outdoor Activities, *below.*

FOOD

It's possible to eat cheaply in Tampico, but only if you're not paranoid that eating at street stands will send you running for *el baño*. The food at the **mercado** on Juárez is cheap, cooked to order, and delicious: Try the *milanesa* (thinly sliced, breaded veal) with tortillas, beans, rice, salad, and a soft drink for $3. Most people flock to the downtown **Restaurant y Cafetería Emir** (Olmos 207, tel. 12/12–51–39) for the delicious *filete de sol* (fish fillet coated with egg and salted bread crumbs; $3). Factor in the beans, home fries, salad, and fresh bread that are included, and it's clear why almost no one finishes the dish. Just around the corner, the **Restaurante/Refresquería Élite** (Díaz Mirón 211 Ote., tel. 12/12–03–64) is also a good place for local fish dishes, as well as the $1.50 piping hot *sopa xochitl* (chicken soup flavored with tomato, avocado, onion, and cilantro). All of the above accept cash only.

OUTDOOR ACTIVITIES

Ten kilometers (6 mi) of white sand and blue-green waters make **Playa Miramar** a popular stretch of the Gulf of Mexico. The beach is divided into four sections; going from north to south you'll hit **Playa Darío, Playa Tampico, Playa Bañario,** and, finally, **Playa Escollera.** Beautiful views of the extensive shoreline can be had from the high-cliff entrance to Playa Escollera, at the southeast end of the city. Bring a picnic and hang out at the pleasantly cool, grassy spots just west of the cliff's edge. The best place for swimming and lounging is Playa Tampico. You'll have to bring your own towels, but showers are only 25¢ a pop at any of the hotels along the beach, and you can rent beach chairs for $3 at the palapas near the beach entrance. There are currently no businesses on the beachfront for the water-sport set, but the tourist office (*see* Basics, *above*) can arrange parasailing and boogie board rentals for you. To reach any of the beaches, catch a PLAYA micro or colectivo (both 25¢) from in front of Hotel Mundo on Díaz Mirón. Micros run about every five minutes during the day and every 20 minutes after 7:30 PM; the last bus from the beach leaves around 11 PM. Colectivos run later, but are extremely sporadic and should not be relied upon.

AFTER DARK

Eclipse (Universidad 2004, tel. 12/13–14–95) has dancing on Thursday night (cover $3); the rest of the week it's a video bar with a big-screen TV showing Mexican music videos. If you want to stay near the *centro,* try **El Globito** (north side of Plaza de Armas, no phone), a 24-hour juice bar/soda fountain with a jukebox that attracts a mixed-age crowd. The delicious smoothies and milk shakes ($1.50) are enormous, and the place stays lively late into the night.

EL BAJIO

UPDATED BY WENDY LUFT

Encompassing the states of Querétaro, Guanajuato, Michoacán, and San Luis Potosí, the Bajío is a spectacular mix of fertile valleys, dry hills sprinkled with strange cacti, town centers with tranquil plazas, and busy industrial zones. The term *bajío* (lowlands) is actually a misnomer—these fertile, mountain-ringed tablelands stand a good 5,500–7,000 ft above sea level. But it's more than altitude that distinguishes the Bajío from Mexico's crowded beach towns: In the Bajío's vibrant cities you'll find a rich colonial history and baroque architecture lacking in the coast's disco-studded resorts.

Rich in both agricultural and mineral resources, the Bajío has long been exploited for its abundant natural wealth. Archaeologists believe that even before the Spanish arrived, the region had nearly 750 active mines, which were probably worked by slave labor. The Spanish were lured here by silver lust, eventually finding incredibly lucrative veins throughout the region. During the 17th and 18th centuries, Guanajuato alone was responsible for 30%–40% of the world's silver production. In addition to mineral wealth, the Spanish also "discovered" the richness of the volcanic soil. Grand haciendas were established, producing a variety of Old World and New World crops, including corn, wheat, squash, grapes, and pears. Franciscan friars also colonized the region; by 1740, Father Junipero Serra, who later established the mission system along the California coast, had overseen the construction of five baroque churches in the remote highlands of Querétaro.

By the early 19th century, the newly wealthy conquerors had founded an exploitative economic system in the Bajío; untold numbers of indigenous laborers died building opulent churches and enormous mansions for those of Spanish descent. It is therefore not surprising that the battle for Mexican independence first arose in Querétaro and the small town of Dolores Hidalgo (in Guanajuato state), where leaders Ignacio Allende, Miguel Hidalgo, and Doña Josefa Ortiz de Domínguez began their revolutionary exploits. Towns throughout the Bajío are fiercely proud of these leaders' accomplishments, which earned the region the nickname "The Cradle of Independence."

Today, international agricultural and automotive companies have invaded the area, but thankfully the region is not an industrial wasteland—many colonial cities have been preserved as national treasures. As a result, the Bajío sustains a vibrant sense of history, made visible in its well-maintained baroque churches, narrow cobblestone streets, and excellent museums. Staunch traditionalism and progressive ideals coexist here in a strange harmony, resulting in a region rich in folklore and legends, as well as innovative cultural and artistic activity. Both Querétaro and Guanajuato boast thriving cultural centers, with active populations of artists, musicians, and students. The cities of Michoacán state have also pre-

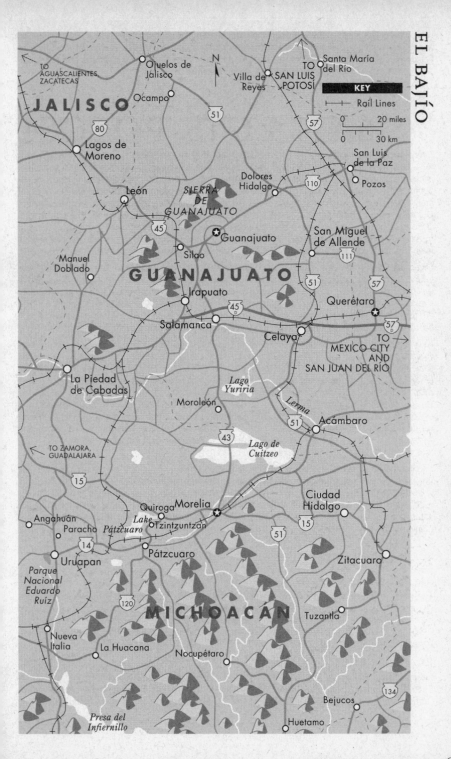

TO
AGUASCALIENTES,
ZACATECAS

Ojuelos de
Jalisco

N

TO
SAN LUIS
POTOSÍ

Santa María
del Río

Villa de
Reyes

KEY

Rail Lines

0   20 miles

0   30 km

Ocampo

JALISCO

80

51

57

San Luis
de la Paz

Lagos de
Moreno

Dolores
Hidalgo

110

Pozos

León

SIERRA
DE
GUANAJUATO

45

Guanajuato

San Miguel
de Allende

111

Manuel
Doblado

Silao

GUANAJUATO

51

57

Irapuato

45
D

Querétaro

57
D

Salamanca

Celaya

TO
MEXICO CITY
AND
SAN JUAN DEL RÍO

La Piedad
de Cabadas

Lago
Yuriria

Moroleón

Lerma

Acámbaro

51

TO ZAMORA,
GUADALAJARA

43

Lago de
Cuitzeo

15

Ciudad
Hidalgo

Quiroga Morelia

Lake
Pátzcuaro

Tzintzuntzan

15

Angahuán
Paracho

51

Parque
Nacional
Eduardo
Ruíz

14

Pátzcuaro

Uruapan

Zitacuaro

120

MICHOACÁN

Tuzantla

Nueva
Italia

La Huacana

Nocupétaro

134

Presa del
Infiernillo

Bejucos

Huetamo

served *artesanía* (handicraft) craftsmanship, stunning examples of which flourish in Pátzcuaro. San Miguel de Allende, well-known for its expatriate American population, is so laid-back that you may want to stay a few years. The more vigorous visitor can indulge in the natural parks, waterfalls, caves, and *balnearios* (swimming areas) of San Luis Potosí and Uruapan.

SAN LUIS POTOSI

At first glance, the capital of San Luis Potosí state might seem as sterile as a big town in the U.S. Midwest. Broom-wielding shopkeepers keep the sidewalks immaculate, and the town's skyscrapers and the occasional Burger King may remind you of Ohio rather than Mexico. But look beyond the recent development and you'll see numerous central plazas dotted with fine examples of baroque and neoclassical architecture—elegant reminders of the city's heyday as a colonial capital whose domain once encompassed most of northern Mexico, Texas, *and* Louisiana. Today the plazas, especially **Plaza de Armas,** serve as meeting places where well-dressed families stroll after mass, entertained by roving clowns and musicians. At the same time, protesters from opposition groups like El Barzón and the Zapatistas draw their own attention, while guards at the Palacio Municipal idly chat with one another.

Silver was discovered in the nearby hills of San Pedro in the 16th century, and "Minas del Potosí" was temporarily adopted as the city's name in the hope that the mines here would yield wealth equal to that found in Potosí, Bolivia. But the silver was soon depleted, and other minerals and a burgeoning dairy industry are now the basis of the city's economy. The mines in the San Pedro hills still function, but they are basically just tourist attractions. San Luis Potosí also generates its share of high culture, with abundant theatrical performances, concerts, and conferences—the majority of which are free.

As one of the oldest cities in central Mexico, San Luis Potosí maintains a rich tradition of religious festivals and fairs. In mid-January, pilgrims come to the shrine of **San Sebastián,** in the neighborhood of the same name, bearing artwork and offerings for the church. The city really fills up during **Semana Santa** (Holy Week, the week preceding Easter): On Good Friday the Passion of Christ is reenacted, followed by the Procession of Silence, in which men in hooded robes carry a model of Christ's body through the streets, mourning his death. In May, the 10-day **Festival de las Artes** features music, theater, and dance—much of it free to the public. In July contemporary dance troupes come to town for the **Festival de la Danza.** On August 25 the city celebrates its patron saint, **San Luis Rey,** with a parade and fiesta. The second half of August is also the time of the **Feria Nacional Potosina** (National Fair), celebrated with bullfights, cockfights, parades, and concerts.

Though there's plenty to see and do in San Luis, don't cheat yourself out of a visit to the beautiful, untouristed lands just beyond the city. **Santa María del Río,** a town specializing in the production of *rebozos* (silk shawls), is only a short day trip away, and campers or hikers can head to the caves and waterfalls of **Río Verde** and **Ciudad Valles.** The **Querétaro Missions** and the castle ruins of **Xilitla** are enthralling for anyone with the slightest interest in architecture. The ghost town of **Real de Catorce** also merits a visit—take the train for the full 19th-century effect.

BASICS

AMERICAN EXPRESS

The AmEx office in the **Agencia de Grandes Viajes** will deliver MoneyGrams, exchange traveler's checks, and replace lost checks for cardmembers and noncardmembers alike. The staff will also hold mail for you for up to 15 days at the following address: Carranza 1077, San Luis Potosí, San Luis Potosí, CP 78250, México. *10 blocks west of Plaza de Armas, tel. 48/17–60–04, fax 48/11–11–66. Open weekdays 9–7, Sat. 10–1.*

BOOKSTORES

Librería Cristal (Carranza 765, tel. 48/12–80–15) supplies a large and varied selection of books in Spanish. **Librería Española** (Othón 170, tel. 48/12–57–81) and **Librería Universitaria** (Álvaro Obregón 450, tel. 48/12–67–49) sometimes stock books in English. All are open Monday–Saturday 9–2 and 4–7.

CASAS DE CAMBIO

Banamex (Allende, at Obregón 355, tel. 48/12–16–56; open weekdays 9–noon) changes currency and cashes traveler's checks, and has a 24-hour ATM. Next to Café Pacífico (*see* Food, *below*), **Casa de Cambio** (Constitución 220, tel. 48/12–42–93) has good rates and long hours: Monday–Saturday 8:30 AM–9 PM, Sunday 9–5.

CONSULATES

United States. *Francisco de P. Moriel 103, Suite1, at V. Carranza, tel. 48/12–15–28. Open weekdays 8:30–1:30.*

EMERGENCIES

In an emergency, call the **police** at 48/12–10–36; for the **Cruz Roja** (ambulance service) dial 48/15–33–32.

LAUNDRY

Lavanderías Automáticas Superwash will clean 3 kilos (6½ pounds) of laundry for $1.75, or you can do the washing and drying yourself (75¢ per load). They offer same-day service if you drop your clothes off in the early morning. *Carranza 1093, tel. 48/13–93–22. 10 blocks west of Plaza de Armas. Open Mon.–Sat. 9–8, Sun. 9:30–2.*

MAIL

The full-service **post office** will hold mail sent to you at the following address for up to 10 days: Lista de Correos, Morelos 235, San Luis Potosí, San Luis Potosí, CP 78001, México. *Morelos 235, tel. 48/12–27–40. 2 blocks north and 1 block east of Plaza de Armas. Open weekdays 8–6, Sat. 9–1.*

MEDICAL AID

The **Beneficiencia Española** (Carranza 1090, tel. 48/13–40–48) and the **Cruz Roja** (Juárez 540, tel. 48/15–33–32) provide 24-hour medical service. **Farmacia La Perla** (Escobedo, at Los Bravo, tel. 48/12–59–22) is open 24 hours.

PHONES

Computel (Carranza 360, tel. 48/12–01–13; open Mon.–Sat. 7 AM–9 PM), three blocks west of Plaza de Armas, offers high-tech long-distance service with no charge for international collect calls; you can also make cash calls here. Several **Ladatel** phones are clustered along Obregón and Escobedo, near the Banamex.

SCHOOLS

The **Centro de Idiomas** (Zaragoza 410, tel. 48/12–49–55), associated with the Universidad Autónoma de San Luis Potosí, offers semester-long Spanish classes for about $60. For registration information contact: Lic. Angélica Chávez Calvillo, Centro de Idiomas, Universidad Autónoma de San Luis Potosí, Zaragoza 410, San Luis Potosí, San Luis Potosí, CP 78000, México.

VISITOR INFORMATION

The bilingual staff at the **Centro de Turismo** will earnestly try to answer questions and weigh you down with maps and brochures. They can also put you in touch with Daniel Acosta (tel. 48/16–58–11) who gives tours, in English, of the city's historical center ($3.50 per person). *Álvaro Obregón 520, tel. 48/12–99–06. ½ block west of Plaza de los Fundadores. Open weekdays 8–8, Sat. until 1.*

COMING AND GOING

BY BUS

The new **Central Camionera T.I.P.** (tel. 48/16–46–02) is just outside town, at Km. 2 on Highway 57 to Mexico City. **Flecha Amarilla** (tel. 48/16–98–12) provides frequent service to Mexico City (6 hrs, $17) and Guanajuato (4 hrs, $8). **Estrella Blanca** (tel. 48/18–29–63) serves Aguascalientes (3 hrs, $8) and Zacatecas (3 hrs, $6.25). **Omnibús de Oriente** (tel. 48/18–29–71) travels to Guadalajara (6 hrs, $15) and Ciudad Victoria (5 hrs, $13) every hour round-the-clock, as well as to intrastate destinations such as Río Verde (2 hrs, $5). **Omnibús de México** (tel. 48/16–81–72) sends three buses a day to Tampico (7 hrs, $16). Luggage storage is available at the station for about 25¢ an hour. There is also a *caseta de larga distancia* (long-distance telephone office) and a 24-hour pharmacy in the station. To get downtown from the terminal, catch the bus marked CENTRAL. From downtown, take any bus marked CENTRAL CAMIONERÓ from the Alameda. A taxi from the Alameda costs about $1.25.

BY CAR

To reach Zacatecas, take Highway 49 northwest for 186 km (115 mi). For Mexico City (453 km/270 mi), take Highway 57 south through Querétaro (200 km/124 mi) and continue to the capital. To reach Tampico (400 km/248 mi), take Highway 70 east through Ciudad Valles.

BY TRAIN

The **train station** (Othón, at 20 de Noviembre, tel. 48/12–36–41) is north of the Alameda. There are two trains daily to Mexico City: The first-class train (6 hrs, $10) departs at 3:45 AM, and the second-class train (9 hrs, $5) departs at 10:30 AM. Only second-class trains travel to Real de Catorce (3 hrs, $2.50) and Nuevo Laredo (15 hrs, $12), departing daily at 5:30 PM. Second-class trains depart for Monterrey (8 hrs, $12.50) at midnight. The ticket office is open daily 45 minutes prior to departure, but get in line at least 1½ hours before departure to buy a ticket. You can purchase tickets for the Monterrey train daily 10 AM–noon. From the station, buses run east to the Central Camionera and the youth hostel; ask the driver to drop you off at your destination.

GETTING AROUND

Central San Luis Potosí is laden with plazas; most attractions are within walking distance of the main plaza, **Plaza de Armas,** also known as **Jardín Hidalgo.** The city's grand **cathedral** is on this plaza, and its two bright-blue neon crosses form a shining nighttime reference point. Four main streets branch off from Plaza de Armas: Venustiano Carranza runs west–east, changing into Los Bravo as it crosses the north side of the plaza; Othón runs east–west and becomes Madero as it crosses the south side of the plaza; Hidalgo/Zaragoza borders the east side of the plaza; 5 de Mayo/Allende borders the west side. East of the plaza is the **Alameda,** a park surrounded by cheap restaurants, hotels, and the train station. City buses, which are rarely necessary in this small town, run 6 AM–11 PM and cost about 25¢.

WHERE TO SLEEP

The areas around Plaza de Armas and the Alameda offer reasonably priced rooms and convenience to tourist attractions.

UNDER $10 • Hotel Alameda. This is the cheapest place to stay without having to sacrifice too many comforts—rooms are small and dark but fairly clean, and the management is friendly enough. If you plan to use your bed for sleeping, the nonstop cumbia tunes from the bar next door may make it difficult. Doubles cost $5. *La Perla 3, tel. 48/18–65–58. Just off Othón, behind Pemex. 13 rooms, all with bath. Luggage storage. Cash only.*

Hotel Jardín Potosí. Sunny hallways welcome you to spacious rooms (doubles $10) with well-scrubbed bathrooms. Not all the rooms are as sunny as the courtyard, so ask to see a couple before you decide. The restaurant on the first floor is cheap and clean. *Los Bravo 530, tel. 48/12–31–52. From the Alameda, 1 block north on 20 de Noviembre and left on Los Bravo. 57 rooms, all with bath. Cash only.*

Hotel Progreso. A wood-panel foyer brimming with plants is the perfect prelude to clean, spacious rooms with wood floors, raised ceilings, and large spotless bathrooms. Basic doubles go for $10; rooms with TVs are a few dollars more. *Aldama 415, ½ block north of Plaza de San Francisco, tel. 48/12–03–66. 50 rooms, all with bath. Luggage storage. Cash only.*

UNDER $15 • Hotel Guadalajara. What this modern hotel lacks in personality it makes up for in creature comforts—such as clean rooms with private bath, telephone, and color TV. It's just a few steps from the railway station. Doubles cost $15. *Jiménez 253, tel. 48/12–46–12. One block north of Plaza de Armas. 33 rooms, all with bath. Luggage storage. Cash only.*

Hotel Plaza. Although this hotel is well past its prime, its central location and the balconies overlooking the plaza make it worthwhile. Large, carpeted rooms hint at the hotel's former glory, and the staff is extremely friendly and accommodating. In the lobby there are two TV viewing areas with lots of vinyl seating. Doubles cost $11. *Jardín Hidalgo 22, on Plaza de Armas, tel. 48/12–46–31. 27 rooms, 25 with bath. Luggage storage.*

HOSTELS

Villa Juvenil San Luis Potosí (CREA). This state-run hostel offers eight-bed, single-sex dorm rooms, attractively priced at $2.50 per bed. Also at your disposal are baseball and soccer fields and more than a dozen basketball courts. However, don't stay here unless you're looking for a quick place to rest before catching the next bus out—the neighborhood is sleazy and far from the center of town. There are no lockers. *Diagonal Sur, tel. 48/18–16–17. Just off the Juárez traffic circle, 7 blocks from the Plaza de Armas. 72 beds. Cash only.*

FOOD

San Luis Potosí boasts a number of regional specialties, including enchiladas *potosinas* (small, triangular enchiladas with cheese and red sauce) and *zahacuil* (Huastecan pork tamales). The food may be creative, but the ambience at most restaurants is not—the popular ones resemble diners, complete with vinyl booths and fake plants. Food stands on the plazas are few, but several hole-in-the-wall spots along Carranza and Othón offer cheap, standard Mexican fare. The daily **Mercado Hidalgo** (4 blocks north of Plaza de Armas, at Hildago) has vendors hawking fruits, vegetables, meats, fish, and poultry. **Panificadora La Noria** (Carranza 333, tel. 48/12–56–92) sells pastries and fresh breads beginning at 6:30 AM.

UNDER $5 • El Bocolito. This place benefits a cooperative for indigenous students, and its humble decor gives it a down-home feel. Unique specialties include *sarapes* (sautéed onions, peppers, ham, sausage, and cheese) and *bocolitos* (thick, tortilla-style bread stuffed with cheese, cilantro, and refried beans). *Guerrero 2, at Aldama, tel. 48/12–76–94. No breakfast Sun. Cash only.*

In the evenings, mariachi bands practice in San Luis Potosí's Jardín Escontría (on Los Bravo), turning the otherwise unattractive plaza into a romantic spot for an early evening stroll.

Café Pacífico. Within a two-block radius, you'll find three of these cheap and convenient San Luis "chain" diners. The one nearest the budget lodging area is open 24 hours. *Chilaquiles* (tortilla strips doused with salsa and sour cream) and enchiladas potosinas are popular menu items. Breakfasts cost $2.50–$3.50. *Constitución 200, at Los Bravo, tel. 48/12–54–14. 4 blocks east of Plaza de Armas. Cash only.*

Tropicana. Come to this semivegetarian restaurant for huge fresh fruit drinks (75¢–$1.50) with goofy names like "Tú y Yo" (You and I) and "Sensual," made with everything from strawberries and papaya to alfalfa sprouts and egg. The *comida corrida* (preprepared lunch special) runs $2. *Othón 355-B, tel. 48/12–81–69. On NE corner of Plaza del Carmen. No breakfast on Sun. Cash only.*

UNDER $10 • La Corriente. This restaurant pleases with stone- and tile-decorated walls and lots of greenery. A sampler of eight different dishes, including *chamorro pibil* (pork in sweet chocolate-chile sauce wrapped in banana leaf), costs only $6. *Antojitos* (appetizers) and cocktails are served after 7 PM. *Carranza 700, tel. 48/12–93–04. 6½ blocks west of Plaza de Armas. No dinner Sun. Cash only.*

WORTH SEEING

All of the sights below are within easy walking distance of the Plaza de Armas. Sunday is the best sightseeing day: Museums and churches are open, and the numerous plazas often have free daytime theater or early evening concerts. Pick up the monthly *Guiarte* from the tourist office (*see above*) for a schedule of events around town. Or check the billboard in front of **Fonart** (Plaza de San Francisco, tel. 48/12–75–21; closed Mon.), a government-run store with a good selection of crafts from all over Mexico. On **Mier y Terán,** opposite the south entrance to the Mercado Hidalgo (*see Food, above*), several shops sell regional crafts such as handwoven *rebozos* (silk shawls) from the village of Santa María del Río. The **Casa de la Cultura** (Carranza 1815, tel. 48/13–22–47; open Tues.–Fri. 10–2 and 4–6, Sat. 10–2 and 6–8, Sun. 10–2) and the **Centro de Difusión Cultural** (Universidad, at Negrete, tel. 48/16–05–25; open Tues.–Sat. 10–2 and 4–7, Sun. 10–2) both double as museums and cultural centers, showcasing local art and free films.

CHURCHES

San Luis Potosí is divided into seven *barrios* (neighborhoods), and the center of each one's social activities is its church. The most notable is the **Catedral** (Othón 105) in Plaza de Armas. Built in 1670, the cathedral's baroque facade features Italian marble statues of the 12 Apostles. The interior has been remodeled with neoclassical altars, although some baroque paintings still remain. Another major church is the **Templo de San Francisco** (Universidad 180), in the Plaza de San Francisco, which sports a pink-limestone baroque facade. It was built in 1686 to honor St. Francis of Assisi, and several paintings and stone carvings in the church depict scenes from his life. The unusual artwork inside the church—including a chandelier shaped like a boat and a toy truck in the hands of a statue of Sebastián de Apari-cio—symbolizes St. Francis's evangelical travels. Construction began in 1749 on the **Templo del Carmen** (Villerías 105), which sits in the Plaza del Carmen. This temple flaunts a *Churrigueresque* (ultra-baroque) facade and neoclassical structures in back. The interior contains an astonishing amount of gold leaf, most notably on the gold-covered altar of the Chapel of the Virgin. Mass times are posted in church entryways, but you can drop in anytime 8 AM–9 PM.

MUSEO NACIONAL DE LA MASCARA

This museum holds a collection of more than 1,000 ceremonial and decorative masks from all over Mexico. The written explanations in Spanish describe in detail the history and significance of the Mesoamerican masks and the festivals in which they are used. Not to be missed are the eerie exhibits of devil masks or the impressive *gigantes* (giants) of San Luis—eight huge puppets (about 10 ft tall) used in the festival of Corpus Christi. These represented royal couples from the four parts of the world known to Columbus—Asia, Africa, the Americas, and Europe. *Villerías 2, tel. 48/12–30–25. From Plaza de Armas, walk 2 blocks east on Othón, then right 2 blocks on Escobedo. Admission: 10¢. Open Tues.–Fri. 10–2 and 4–6, weekends 10–2.*

MUSEO REGIONAL POTOSINO

This museum, housed in a former Franciscan monastery, exhibits one of the largest collections of arti-facts from San Luis's Huasteca region, including a reproduction of a famous statue said to represent the young god Quetzalcoatl. The lower floor features an interesting series of early 20th-century photographs of the streets of San Luis, alongside current photographs of the same areas. Upstairs is the restored chamber of the Virgin de Aranzanzú, as well as a few 19th-century religious paintings. *Galeana 450, behind Templo de San Francisco, tel. 48/12–05–38. Admission free. Open Tues.–Fri. 10–1 and 3–6, Sat. 10–noon, Sun. 10–2.*

PALACIO DE GOBIERNO

The neoclassic, *cantera rosa* (pinkish stone) facade of this block-long edifice stands out as soon as you reach the Plaza de Armas. Construction was completed in 1825; in 1950 the building was restored to house the state government offices. Santa Ana and Benito Juárez are a few of the illustrious Mexican leaders who reigned from here. Upstairs, on your left, is the **Sala Juárez,** where you can't help but notice the wax figures of a kneeling "Princess Salm Salm" (Empress Carlota) and a mighty Juárez. As Juárez looks down at her, the princess begs for the life of her husband, Emperor Maximilian (Mexico's puppet ruler, installed by Napoléon III in 1864), who had been sentenced to death. The other rooms are filled with small photos of other Mexican presidents and furniture supposedly used by Juárez himself. *East side of Plaza de Armas. Admission free. Open weekdays 9–5.*

PARQUE TANGAMANGA

The Parque Tangamanga, a few kilometers southwest of Plaza de Armas, consists of more than 1,000 acres of lakes, trees, sports fields, and gardens—the best place to escape the smog and traffic of San Luis Potosí. Pedal carts ($1.50 per hour) are available for your exploring convenience. The free **Museo de Arte Popular,** inside the park, displays regional artesanía and a selection of pre-Columbian artifacts. There's also a **planetarium** and a huge open-air **Teatro de la Cuidad** (City Theater). To get here, catch the PERIMETRAL or RUTA 32 bus from Constitución near the Alameda; get off at Avenida Nacho, near the park's main entrance. To get back to town, walk four long blocks to Diagonal Sur and catch the bus heading back to the Alameda. *Tel. 48/13–11–86. Admission free for all attractions. Park open daily 6–6; museum and planetarium open Tues.–Sat. 10–1:45 and 4–5:45, Sun. 10–2:45.*

AFTER DARK

San Luis Potosí's nightlife is explosive Thursday through Saturday. One of the more popular bars in town is **Puff!** (Carranza 1145, tel. 48/13–65–53), where Lionel Ritchie, R&B, and rap tunes fill the air. Down-stairs, the disco (open Fri. and Sat. until 2 AM) plays Mexican and U.S. pop tunes. The cover is $8, but it's easily waived if you take advantage of the two-for-one specials offered 6 PM–midnight at the bar. The gay scene in San Luis is pretty lively, at least by Mexican standards. **Disco Sheik** (347 Prolongación a

Zacatecas, behind the gas station, tel. 48/12–64–57; open weekends 11 PM–dawn) is a popular, surprisingly modern disco/bar that hosts transvestite shows after midnight. **Chey's** (Mar Mediterraneo, behind Hotel Río) is a gay disco open on weekends. It's best reached by taxi, as it's quite a distance from the central plaza.

NEAR SAN LUIS POTOSI

SANTA MARIA DEL RIO

Perfect as a day trip, this sleepy, unassuming little town is famous for handcrafted cotton and silk rebozos. The shawls are made with a technique that originated in Asia, became part of Spanish tradition after the Moorish invasion, and arrived in Mexico with the conquistadores. You can see how the patterned shawls are woven (each one takes over a month to produce) at the **Escuela de Artesanía** (Jardín Hidalgo 5, tel. 485/3–05–68; open weekdays 9–7). A shawl made with synthetic fibers costs about $50, while a pure silk rebozo goes for $230 or more. To reach Santa María, take a Flecha Amarilla or Autobuses Potosínos bus from the Central Camionera; buses (2 hrs, $1.50) leave every 15 minutes 6 AM–11:45 PM.

REAL DE CATORCE

Perched among the high, desolate peaks of the northern *altiplano* (highlands), Real de Catorce is a dusty ghost town straight out of a B-grade western. Established in 1778 as a mining town, its glory days were in the 19th century. In the early 20th century, when the price of silver dropped, so did the population: from 144,000 to 2,700. Today, the town's residents number near 1,000, making exploration of the abandoned mines, baroque churches, and stone amphitheaters (once used for bull- and cockfights) a somewhat lonely experience—although the town's recent popularity with tourists has caused some souvenir shops to spring up. Huichol Indians from Nayarit and Jalisco visit Real de Catorce every autumn to harvest peyote in the nearby hills.

After trekking around town you can relax at one of the restaurants surrounding **Plaza Hidalgo.** An economic option for sleeping is the simple **Casa de Huespedes La Provincia** (Lanza Gorta, up from the Parroquia, no phone), where doubles go for $4 a night. In the nearby town of Matehuala, **El Real** (Morelos 20, tel. 488/2–25–94) is a classier option with rooms for $17. The only way to reach Real de Catorce is through the 2-km-long (1-mi-long) Ogarrio Tunnel. From San Luis, Estrella Blanca offers one direct bus per day to Real de Catorce (2½ hrs, $6) at 3:30 PM; alternately, catch one of the frequent buses bound for Matehuala (2 hrs, $4.50) and then transfer to a minibus for the rest of the journey.

RIO VERDE

Surrounded by acres of orange groves and fields of corn and chiles, the little town of Río Verde lives up to its name—even the *zócalo* (main plaza) is awash in green. In the lush countryside around town you'll find ample opportunities for swimming, camping, and hiking. The largest and most developed swimming area lies about 14 km (8½ mi) from town, off Highway 70, at **Laguna de la Media Luna.** This sparkling clear lake is popular with scuba divers and snorkelers for its varied aquatic plants and underwater fossilized trees. It was a pre-Columbian cultural center until it was abandoned for unknown reasons in the 12th century. You can camp here for $1. To rent snorkel or scuba gear, make arrangements at the restaurant/bar/disco/store **La Cabaña** (Carretera San Luis–Río Verde Km. 127.5, tel. 487/2–06–25).

Less developed, but just as popular with locals, are the double swimming holes, **Los Anteojitos** (Little Eyeglasses), 2 km (1 mi) south of town. You can usually camp nearby for free, but a caretaker may appear and charge you a dollar or two. A desertlike beauty surrounds the ponds of **El Charco Azul** and **Laguna El Coyote,** 18 km (11 mi) southeast of town. Both are very rustic, but camping is free and, according to locals, safe. Farther from town, spelunkers can explore the caves at **Las Grutas de Catedral** and **Las Grutas de Ángel,** where rock formations look vaguely like angels, altars, and pipe organs. The caves can be reached by a 3-km (2-mi) trail that leads out of the community of Los Alamitos; it's recommended that you hire a guide in the village for exploring the caves. Bring food, water, trekking clothes, and a sturdy flashlight.

Buses don't run on the backcountry dirt roads leading to Laguna de la Media Luna and other remote natural sights, but taxis will make the journey for $6–$10. Friendly *taxista* Salvador Hernández Castro is willing to drive just about anywhere; ask around for him at the Río Verde bus station, or call him at home (tel. 487/2–23–07). Maps of the area are available from the **Cámara Nacional de Comercio, Servicios,**

EMPEROR MAXIMILIAN OF MEXICO

French forces overran Mexico City in 1863, and shortly thereafter Napoléon III appointed Maximilian, an Austrian archduke, and his wife, Carlota, as the country's stand-in emperor and empress. Mexican president Benito Juárez was ousted, and the newly minted rulers moved into Chapultepec Castle (see Bosque de Chapultepec in Chapter 2), engendering immediate public resentment with their luxurious lifestyle.

Although Maximilian was never more than a puppet emperor to Napoléon III, he nevertheless had a well-developed sense of entitlement, and even after Napoléon withdrew French troops in 1866 and ordered Maximilian to abdicate, the emperor doggedly refused to give up his throne. Naturally, without France's support, Maximilian was quickly captured by Juárez's forces.

Maximilian was executed by firing squad on June 19, 1867, on a site in Querétaro now known as the Parque Cerro de las Campanas (Circuito Cerro de las Campanas, 2 blocks from Gómez Farías, tel. 42/15–20–75; open daily 6–6). The park harbors a chapel that was a gift from Austria and a small museum that chronicles the events leading up to the emperor's execution. Also here is a 66-ft-tall statue of the ousted President Benito Juárez, which marks the exact spot where Maximilian met his death.

To the bitter end an ardent aficionado of his adopted country, Emperor Maximilian's famous last words were "¡Viva México!" (Long live Mexico!).

y Turismo Río Verde (Jardín de San Antonio "F," Río Verde, tel. 487/2–08–02; open weekdays 9:30–2 and 4:30–7, Sat. 9:30–noon).

COMING AND GOING • Transportes Vencedor (tel. 48/18–29–41) sends buses hourly from San Luis Potosí to Río Verde (2 hrs, $5). The last bus back to San Luis Potosí leaves at 10:15 PM. From Río Verde, **Omnibús de Oriente** (tel. 487/2–01–12) and **Sistema** (tel. 487/2–12–88) make hourly runs to Ciudad Valles (2 hrs, $4).

WHERE TO SLEEP AND EAT • Hotel Plaza (Constitución "F," tel. 487/2–01–00) is right on Río Verde's main square, five blocks from the bus station. Doubles with bath cost $14, cash only. Food in Río Verde is hearty, if uninspired. Try the busy 24-hour **Restaurant Rivera** (Plaza Constitución "B," tel. 487/2–01–03), right on the zócalo, where you'll spend less than $4 on generous portions of tacos, enchiladas, and antojitos.

CIUDAD VALLES

The only reason to come to Ciudad Valles is to arrange excursions into the vast, untouristed countryside beyond the city limits—a region full of pristine rivers, waterfalls, and caves. The city itself has little to offer, unless you enjoy long blocks of cinderblock buildings and streets choked with speeding cars. The Valles **tourist office** (Carranza 53 Sur, tel. 138/2–01–44; open weekdays 9–1:30 and 4–7:30, Sat. 9–1) hands out free maps on the rare occasions when they're in stock. Groups of four or more can arrange excursions into the outlying tropical rain forest (see Outdoor Activities, below) with Ana Maria Musa or María del Carmen Castro at **Antani Viajes,** in the lobby of **Posada Don Antonio** (Blvd. México-Laredo 15, tel. 138/1–19–16). They speak some English and understand budget travel, so they won't push you into some expensive deal. The main bus line in Ciudad Valles is **Vencedor** (tel. 138/2–37–55); buses run hourly to Río Verde (2 hrs, $4), San Luis Potosí (5½ hrs, $10.50), and Tampico (2½ hrs, $6.50).

WHERE TO SLEEP AND EAT • Hotels here aren't particularly cheap, but **Hotel Boulevard** (Blvd. México-Laredo 19, tel. 138/2–01–28), on the main road, does have simple, clean rooms with fans for $7 (cash only). **Hotel Valles** (Blvd. México-Laredo 36 Nte., tel. 138/2–00–50) will let you camp on their extensive grounds for $6.50, which includes use of showers, bathrooms, and a glorious pool. A double here is $40. **Hotel San Fernando** (Blvd. México-Laredo 17 Nte., tel. 138/2–01–84) offers comfortable, air-conditioned rooms with TVs for $19 doubles; the hotel also sells maps of the region. The clean and airy **Restaurant Bonanza** (inside Hotel San Fernando) is open 24 hours and serves tasty enchiladas and pollo con mole (chicken in chocolate-chile sauce; $3.50). Lots of cheap food stands line Juárez, near Boulevard México-Laredo.

OUTDOOR ACTIVITIES • The dense tropical rain forest around Ciudad Valles is ripe for exploration but has little tourist infrastructure; to get you to where you want to go, be prepared to hike, haggle with taxistas, or hire the occasional guide. The following places can all be reached from Highway 70 and lie between Ciudad Valles and Río Verde: **Las Cascadas de Micos,** a series of cascades and swimming holes, lies 18 km (11 mi) north of Highway 70, just east of Valles. There's a no-frills campsite here that locals consider pretty safe. Bring plenty of drinking water and food. Farther east, midway to Río Verde, is **La Cascada Tamasopo,** where a confluence of mountain rivers and streams form several high falls that spill into swimmable pools. You'll pass the town of Tamasopo on the way, where you can stock up on food and water. Tamasopo also has campgrounds (with bathrooms). Just 2 km (1 mi) away are more pools at **El Trampolín,** which boasts a natural limestone bridge. **Vencedor** buses (tel. 138/2–32–81) leave the central station in Ciudad Valles seven times daily for Tamasopo (2 hrs, $2.50). Alternately, you can take one of the frequent Vencedor buses to Río Verde (1½ hrs, $2); get off at the Tamasopo crucero (intersection), and walk 8 km (5 mi) north to the falls. You can also hire a taxi from the crucero for $5.50.

A bit more remote is the **Cascada de Tamul,** a spectacular 36-ft-high waterfall. From Ciudad Valles, take a Vencedor bus headed for San Luis Potosí and ask the driver to drop you off at the crucero for Santa Anita on Highway 70; then hire a taxi or hitch south down the dirt road to the small town of Tanchachín. Here you can hire a guide (and his boat) to take you upriver to the falls. Ask for Don Catarino; he has the lowest prices. All in all, it'll take a good three hours to get here (the boat ride alone takes two hours).

If you're on your way to Xilitla (see below) from Ciudad Valles, consider stopping at **Sótano de las Golondrinas** (near the town of Aquismón, off Highway 85), a 1,240-ft vertical cave. It's home to hundreds of swallows, who swoosh out of the ground at sunrise and at dusk. Vencedor buses run regularly from Ciudad Valles to Aquismón (½ hr, $1.50); at Aquismón's main plaza you can arrange transport to the sótano (literally, basement). Don't pay more than $7 per person for the ride. The truck will let you off after about an hour in front of the 2-km (1-mi) trailhead to the sótano. Camping or staying here after dark is discouraged by locals.

XILITLA

Located on the slopes of the Sierra Gorda, Xilitla overlooks the deep green gorges cut by the Tahculín River. An Augustine church and convent were built here early in the Spanish Conquest (about 1557); their thick walls were designed to ward off Huastec attacks. About 3 km (2 mi) northwest from the main plaza, the ruins of a centuries-old mansion/castle lie moldering in the jungle. Built by Sir Edward James, the illegitimate son of King Edward VII of England, the house and gardens were designed to mimic the surrounding vegetation in a style that James claimed "integrated architecture with nature." Just outside the garden walls, you'll find **Las Pozas,** a series of waterfalls that plunges into several inviting pools. To reach the mansion you can take a taxi ($3), which leaves from the storefront of La Joyita, two blocks southwest of the plaza on Jardín Hidalgo. Or make the easy 30-minute walk: From the plaza, walk north on Melchón Ocampo, turn right where it dead-ends, and follow the rocky path all the way down (east) until you reach the freeway; from here, turn left, take the first dirt road to your left, and follow the LAS POZAS signs all the way to the mansion ruins and the falls (it's really not that difficult). Entrance to the ruins is $1.

For another adventure, experience the enormous saltpeter stalactites in the **Cueva de Salitre.** To get here, take a taxi ($2) from La Joyita or walk a leisurely 1 km (½ mi): Follow Melchón Ocampo north, turn right (east) on the second street, follow it to the highway, and take the fork to the left. The cave is behind a *taller* (auto-parts workshop); the entrance is through the first hut on the left after the Pemex station. There are no official guides nor an entrance fee at the cave. However, for a few pesos one of the worker's children will gladly guide you down the steep, rocky hill to where the cave is hidden.

COMING AND GOING • From Río Verde, one **Vencedor** bus (tel. 487/2–12–88) leaves at 6:45 PM for Xilitla (5 hrs, $6). In Ciudad Valles, **Vencedor** (tel. 138/2–32–81) buses run hourly to Xilitla (1½ hrs, $2.50).

QUERETARO MISSIONS

Nestled among the rugged hills of the Sierra Gorda is a series of five small missions, constructed in the mid–18th century under the saintly supervision of Father Junipero Serra. Each church has an elaborate facade carved in a baroque style, displaying both indigenous and Catholic iconography. Look for moons, stars, and the pagan mermaid—all symbols of the Virgin Mary. Elsewhere, life-size saints do battle with demons and dragons, surrounded by grapevines and blooming flowers. The largest of the five mission towns, **Jalpan,** has several hotels: The fancy **Mesón de Fray Junipero Serro** (Carretera Río Verde, tel. 429/6–01–64) charges $21 for a double. The more modest **Camino Viejo** (Carretera Río Verde, 330 ft north of bus terminal, tel. 429/6–01–85) charges $10.50 for a double. Jalpan also features the **Museo Histórico de la Sierra Gorda** (admission $1; open Mon.–Sat. 8–8), which employs drawings and dioramas to tell the story of the Sierra Gorda region and its inhabitants. The other four Querétaro missions— **Landa, Tancogol, Tilaco,** and **Concá**—are small, remote, and best visited as a day trip from Jalpan. Ask locals to point you to Concá's thermal springs, near the hotel Mesón de San Nícolas. Conveniently, Concá is a stopping point for buses between Jalpan and both Río Verde and Ciudad Valles.

COMING AND GOING • The fastest and most direct way to reach the Querétaro missions is by bus from Río Verde or Ciudad Valles. From Río Verde, **Vencedor** (tel. 487/2–12–88) runs hourly buses to Jalpan (2 hrs, $3.50) via Concá . From Ciudad Valles (3½ hrs, $4), **Vencedor** (tel. 138/2–32–81) buses also run hourly.

QUERETARO

Downtown Querétaro is a fine example of how past and present intermingle in Mexican cities: Centuries-old buildings house shops selling women's lingerie or household appliances, and fast-food joints do business in the shade of national monuments. Modern encroachments aside, the heart of Querétaro is a delightful stretch of tree-shaded cobblestone streets lined with colonial mansions, stately plazas, and well-kept gardens. And while this bustling, lively state capital now boasts a population of more than one million people, it's worlds away from the pollution and chaos of Mexico City: Women can walk alone at night on well-lit streets with a sense of security, and students from Querétaro's universities play chess in the cafés.

As the city's numerous historic landmarks indicate, some of the most important events in Mexican history took place in Querétaro. The signing of the 1917 constitution and the formation of the PRI (Institutional Revolutionary Party), Mexico's ruling party, both took place in Querétaro. The Treaty of Guadalupe Hidalgo, under which Mexico ceded Texas, New Mexico, and the California territories to the United States, was also signed here. Mexico's struggle for independence received a push from Querétaro resident Doña Josefa Ortiz de Domínguez, known as *La Corregidora* (wife of the Corregidor, or Spanish magistrate). She was later executed for her subversive activities; her heroism is commemorated in the **Plaza de la Corregidora** and **La Tumba de Doña Josefa.** Other historical landmarks include the **Convento de la Santa Cruz**—the site of Emperor Maximilian's imprisonment before his execution on the **Cerro de las Campanas** (Hill of the Church Bells), just north of town.

Queretaro explodes in music, dancing, and general revelry during its many annual festivals. A full-scale *pamplonada* (running of the bulls) occurs on July 26 as part of the **Fiesta de Santa Ana**—a celebration of one of the two patron saints of the city. A sip of the potent *ponche*—a delicious concoction made of cinnamon, water, sugarcane liquor, raisins, and *guayaba* (a type of tropical fruit), spiked with either red wine or rum—may make you think twice about joining the stampede. During the first two weeks of December, the city holds the **Exposición Ganadera,** a huge agricultural fair that includes more bullfighting and rodeos, along with carnival rides, music, and a lot of food. Mexican holidays such as Semana Santa, Day of the Dead, and Independence Day are also celebrated in Querétaro with style. The night before Easter Sunday, folks burn a model of Judas in effigy.

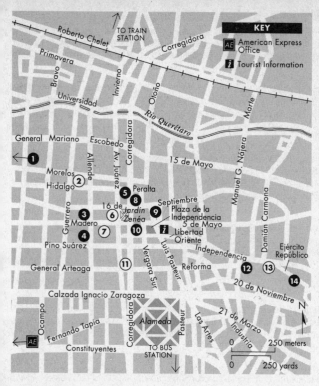

KEY

AE American Express Office

i Tourist Information

Sights ●

Convento de la Santa Cruz/Calzada de los Arcos, **14**

Cerro de las Campanas, **1**

Convento de la Santa Cruz, **12**

Museo de Arte de Querétaro, **4**

Museo Regional, **10**

Palacio del Gobierno Federal, **9**

Plaza de la Corregidora, **8**

Teatro de la República, **5**

Templo de Santa Clara, **3**

Lodging ○

Hotel Hidalgo, **7**

Hotel Plaza, **6**

Hotel San Francisco, **11**

Hotel Señorial, **2**

Villa Juvenil, **13**

BASICS

AMERICAN EXPRESS

Turismo Beverly is a travel agency that provides all American Express services, including emergency check cashing, traveler's check sales, and card replacement. Cardholders' mail will be held for up to 10 days if sent to the following address: Tecnológico Sur 1188–1, Local 1, Querétaro, Querétaro, CP 76030, México. *Tel. 42/16–12–60. From Alameda, take any bus west along Constituyentes to Tecnológico; walk south 1½ blocks. Open weekdays 9–2 and 4–6, Sat. 9–noon.*

BOOKSTORES

Unidad Cultural del Centro (16 de Septiembre 1, tel. 42/24–24–61; open Mon.–Sat. 9–8:30, Sun. noon–8) sells newspapers and tons of books (in Spanish) on Mexican history, literature, art, and film. **Fonart** (Angela Peralta 20, between Corregidora and Pasteur, tel. 42/12–26–48; open Mon.–Sat. 10–2 and 5–9), the government-sponsored artesenía store, sells books in English and the bimonthly magazine *Arte de Mexico,* which features photographs and essays on Mexican cinema, arts, and crafts.

CASAS DE CAMBIO

Bancomer (Juárez 15 Nte., tel. 42/12–06–77; open weekdays 8:30–3) cashes traveler's checks and exchanges currency. You can get cash advances on Visa or MasterCard from their 24-hour ATMs. **Casa de Cambio Acueducto** (Juarez Sur 58, tel. 42/14–31–89; open Mon.–Sat. 9–6) occasionally offers better rates.

EMERGENCIES

You can reach the **police** at 42/16–11–49. For **ambulance** service, call the Cruz Roja at 42/29–05–05.

LAUNDRY

Laundromats are scarce around the center of town, but **Lavandería Verónica** lies six short city blocks west of the zócalo. It'll cost $4 to clean 3 kilos (6½ pounds) of clothes. *Hidalgo 153, between Regules and Ignacio Pérez, tel. 42/16–61–68. Open weekdays 9–2:30 and 4:30–8, Sat. 9–3.*

MAIL

The **post office** will hold mail addressed to you for up to 10 days if sent to the following address: Lista de Correos, Administración 1, Allende Sur 19, Querétaro, Querétaro, CP 76001, México. *Tel. 42/12–01–12. From Jardín Zenéa, walk 2 blocks south on Juárez and turn right on Arteaga. Open weekdays 8–7, Sat. 9–1.*

MEDICAL AID

Grupo Médico Zaragoza (Zaragoza 39, tel. 42/16–76–38) is a large, centrally located medical center that provides most medical services 24 hours a day. Doctors Enriquez Espinosa, Hector Húgo Encorrada, and Antonio Solís all speak some English. **Farmacia Querétaro** (Constituyentes 17, at Ignacio de las Casas, tel. 42/12–44–23) is a pharmacy open 24 hours.

PHONES

Ladatel pay phones grace both the Jardín Zenéa and Plaza de la Independencia. Ladatel phone cards are sold in most kiosks or businesses displaying the LADATEL sign. The small kiosk, Libros y Revistas, on the corner of Juárez and Madero, always has an abundant supply of them and also functions as a **caseta de larga distancia** (tel. 42/12–79–55, fax 42/12–79–55; open daily 9–9). It costs $1.60 per minute for long-distance calls to the United States.

SCHOOLS

The **Universidad Autónoma de Querétaro** offers three-month summer and winter courses in all levels of Spanish. For more information, write to: Facultad de Lenguas y Letras, Centro Universitario, Cerro de las Campanas, Querétaro, Querétaro, CP 76000, México. *In Centro Universitario, Hidalgo, tel. 42/16–74–66. From Jardín Zenéa, take RUTA R bus to the university.*

VISITOR INFORMATION

The **Secretaría de Turismo** offers maps and detailed information about Querétaro. *Luis Pasteur 4, at 5 de Mayo, tel. 42/12–14–12. Open weekdays 9–2 and 5–8.*

COMING AND GOING

BY BUS

Querétaro recently opened a fancy bus station about 6 km (4 mi) south of the zócalo, composed of two separate buildings. Sala A sees mostly first-class bus lines, like **Omnibús de México** (tel. 42/29–03–29), which provides service to Aguascalientes (5 hrs, $6). Sala B deals with second-class bus lines such as **Estrella Blanca** (tel. 42/29–01–42), which goes to Zacatecas (5 hrs, $15), San Luis Potosí (3 hrs, $6.50), and Mexico City (3 hrs, $7); **Herradura de Plata** (tel. 42/29–02–45), which rumbles to San Miguel de Allende (1 hr, $2.50) every 40 minutes; and **Flecha Amarilla** (tel. 42/11–40–01), which sends five buses a day to Guanajuato (2½ hrs, $5). Each building has restaurants, phones, and luggage storage. Taxis wait at both salas; before embarking you need to buy a taxi ticket ($1.50 to the zócalo) from the kiosk near the exit. You can also take an *urbano* (local city bus) for about 50¢; walk to the end of Sala B and take the RUTA 8 minibus to the center. *Bernardo Quintano Sur, at Autopista México, tel. 42/29–00–61 or 42/29–00–62.*

BY CAR

Major highways connect Querétaro to the Pacific Coast, the Gulf Coast, and northern states, while the six-lane Highway 57 runs north to San Luis Potosí and southeast to Mexico City. Driving around within town is easier than in most Mexican cities, but since everything is within walking distance you don't really need a car. If you want a vehicle for day excursions beyond the city, try **Budget** (Constituyentes 73, tel. 42/13–44–98).

BY TRAIN

The small, second-class train station lies 1 km (½ mi) north of the historic center. Trains to Mexico City ($3.50) leave daily at 4 AM, 6 AM, and 5 PM. The train for Ciudad Juárez ($25) departs daily at 1 PM, and the train to Guadalajara ($5) leaves at 12:30 AM. No one in a responsible position is willing to hazard a guess as to how long these trips take, which may be an indication of the reliability of the service. To reach downtown, take the RUTA 8 minibus. *Héroe de Nacozar, at Invierno, tel. 42/12–17–03. Ticket sales daily 9–11 and noon–4.*

GETTING AROUND

Most sights, restaurants, and budget hotels are packed into the *centro histórico* (historic downtown area). At its center is **Jardín Zenéa,** also known as Jardín Obregón. The two main north–south drags near Jardín Zenéa are Juárez (on its west side) and Corregidora (on its east side). These two streets meet several blocks farther south at the **Alameda** (a park). On the north Jardín Zenéa is bordered by 16 de Septiembre and the south by Madero. Many of the city's cobblestone streets, called **andadores,** are closed to cars. On the few occasions that you may need a lift, white minibuses travel all over the city (destinations are painted on the front windshield) from 5 AM to 11 PM and cost about 30¢.

WHERE TO SLEEP

If you can afford to, it's wise to stay here in a moderately priced place rather than a bargain-basement hotel; most of Querétaro's budget lodging is near the noisy Jardín Zenéa. The more expensive hotels near the old bus station aren't much better, and the very cheapest hotels are only semiclean and attract a by-the-hour kind of clientele. During the Exposición Ganadera (first two weeks of December) hotels are completely booked; to play it safe, you may want to reserve a month or so in advance.

UNDER $15 • Hotel Hidalgo. Huge wooden doors open onto this hotel's sunny courtyard. Rooms have TVs and clean bathrooms, and some have balconies overlooking the cobblestone street. The friendly proprietors speak English, but they aren't around very often. Doubles cost $10. *Madero Pte. 11, tel. 42/12–00–81. 40 rooms, all with bath. Luggage storage. Cash only.*

Hotel Plaza. Rooms here are clean, bright, and come equipped with TVs and phones. It's right on the noisy central square, so ask for a room away from the street. Doubles run $13.50. *Juárez 23, tel. 42/12–11–38. 29 rooms, all with bath.*

Hotel San Francisco. On the bustling Avenida Corregidora, this dark and spartan hotel attracts mostly Mexican families and businesspersons. Rooms are clean (there's a lingering smell of disinfectant) and offer lots of hot water. Ask for a room away from the street if you're concerned about noise. Doubles with a "matrimonial bed" cost $8.50, and doubles with two beds are $9. *Corregidora 144 Sur, tel. 42/12–08–58. 58 rooms, all with bath. Luggage storage, TV. Reservations advised. Cash only.*

UNDER $25 • Hotel Señorial. Built in 1981, this sprawling four-story property has clean, modern rooms ($22) with telephones and TVs. Beds are covered with printed spreads that clash with the floral drapes. Rooms in front face a narrow, busy street, but traffic slows in the evening. There are purified water dispensers in the hallways. *Guerrero Norte 10–A, tel. 42/14–37–00. 45 rooms, all with bath.*

HOSTELS

Villa Juvenil (CREA). If you don't mind a 10-minute walk to the center of town, this is a good place to spend the night. It's clean and cheerful, and dorm beds cost $3 per person. The hostel's cafeteria even serves meals for less than $2. There's just one catch: The Villa locks its doors at 10 PM, just when nightlife gets rolling. It's enormously popular with high-school tour groups, so call ahead to be sure there's room. *Ejército Republicano, tel. 42/23–43–50. From Jardín Zenéa, south 1 block on Corregidora, then left on Independencia for 6 blocks; veer right at the fork to Ejército Republicano and continue to the crest of hill, right behind Convento de la Santa Cruz. 72 beds. Reception open daily 7 AM–10 PM. Luggage storage. No age limit. Cash only.*

FOOD

There are so many good, cheap things to eat in Querétaro that it's hard to know where to begin. By eating at food stands on the street, you can spend less than $7 on breakfast, lunch, *and* dinner (yes, all three combined). In the morning, vendors work the Jardín Zenéa and the streets surrounding the Alameda, selling 30¢ tamales and *atole* (a sweet, corn-based drink similar to hot chocolate). At lunchtime, stands sell 25¢ tacos or 75¢ fresh fruit cups doused with lime and chiles, and in the evening they sell freshly grilled corn on the cob (30¢). Also watch for Querétaro specialties like enchiladas *querétanas,* tortillas

A MIRACLE ON THE BATTLEFIELD

On July 25, 1531, a bare-hands battle between indigenous Otomí and Spanish conquistadors was fought where Querétaro's Convento de la Santa Cruz now stands.

According to legend, a miracle occurred in the heat of battle: The sun was eclipsed, the stars began to burn fiercely, and the apostle Santiago, patron saint of Spain, appeared in the sky astride a charging white horse, "deciding" the fight in favor of the Spanish.

The city of Santiago de Querétaro was founded on the site of the battlefield, with the white horse of the apostle gracing its coat of arms.

drenched in red chili sauce, fried in oil, then filled with cheese and onions and eaten like a taco. *Carnitas,* strips of slow-roasted pork served with tortillas and vinegar, are another favorite.

UNDER $3 • Café del Fondo. This popular café has a devoted bohemian following. The entryway displays posters for current concerts and art exhibitions, and artsy types lounge in the simple whitewashed rooms, dawdling for hours over *cafés exóticos* (cinnamon- or alcohol-spiked coffees). Cheap, filling breakfast and lunch specials are less than $2. *Pino Suárez 9, tel. 42/12–09–05. Cash only.*

La Mariposa. This popular café/ice-cream parlor has been around for more than 50 years, and its original peacock-blue decor is kept lovingly clean. Delicious milk shakes are $1.25 and sandwiches start at 50¢. Check out the tempting sweets at the back counter. *Peralta 7, tel. 42/12–11–66. 2 blocks north of Jardín Zenéa. Cash only.*

UNDER $5 • Comedor Vegetariano Natura. Though it looks like a 70s-style rec room with wood paneling and wall-size forest posters, the Comedor serves good vegetarian food. On the menu you'll find mushroom and cheese soy burgers, soy enchiladas, and healthful fruit and yogurt shakes. If you're suffering from a gastrointestinal disorder, the restaurant also sells natural remedies, including horsehair tea for dysentery. *Vergara 7, tel. 42/14–10–88. From Jardín Zenéa, 2 blocks east on 5 de Mayo, then right on Vergara. Closed Sun. Cash only.*

Restaurant Punto y Coma. University students flock here at midday for the *menú del día* (daily menu; $2–$4), which includes soup, tortillas, rice, an entrée, and dessert. Vegetarians will appreciate the terrific lentil soup. *16 de Septiembre 27, 1 block east of Jardín Zenéa, tel. 42/14–16–66. Cash only.*

UNDER $10 • Café Tulipe. Mexican and international students frequent this pleasant restaurant at night. Specialties here include *crema conde,* a soup made of black beans, cream, oregano, and *epazote* (an herb particular to Mexico); chicken in orange sauce; and fondue for two ($6). The prominently displayed dessert cart is sure to please your sweet tooth. *Calzada de los Arcos 3, tel. 42/13–63–91. Walk 1½ blocks west of the base of Ejército Republicano. Closed Mon. Cash only.*

WORTH SEEING

Though Querétaro is large and ever-expanding, most sights are in the compact centro histórico, within walking distance of the Jardín Zenéa. The tourist office (*see* Visitor Information, *above*) offers extensive and informative **walking tours** of the city, conducted in Spanish or (if you prearrange) English. The two-hour tours, held daily at 10:30 AM and 6 PM, start at the tourist office. They're a good way to get a sense of the city's history and cost just $1.50 (plus any museum entrance fees).

CONVENTO DE LA SANTA CRUZ

This functioning 16th-century convent is home to about 40 monks who serenely go about their business despite all the attention from tourists. Original furnishings and paintings are on display in several rooms, including the cell where Emperor Maximilian awaited his execution in 1867. In one of the convent's patios you'll find the famous **Árbol de las Espinas** (Thorn Tree), which has branches filled with cross-shape thorns; according to legend, the tree grows where a friar named Margil de Jesús buried his cane. The guides who lead 15-minute tours of the convent (in Spanish or English) ask for a small tip for their services. Just outside the convent is Querétaro's most important structure, the massive **Calzada de los Arcos,** an 18th-century aqueduct built of pink stone. Though the calzada no longer carries water, it is one of the largest aqueducts ever constructed in the Americas. *Tel. 42/12–02–35. From Jardín Zenéa, 1 block south on Corregidora, left on Independencia for 6 blocks. Donation requested. Open weekdays 9–2 and 4–6, Sat. 9–5, Sun. 9–4:30.*

MUSEO DE ARTE DE QUERETARO

This 18th-century building, once an Augustine monastery, was recently renovated and now houses a varied art collection. Most works date from the 16th, 17th, and 18th centuries, but several rooms on the ground floor are devoted to contemporary Mexican art and photography, including works by students from the University of Querétaro. *Allende 14, near Pino Suárez, tel. 42/12–23–57. Admission: $1.50; free on Tues. Open Tues.–Sun. 11–7.*

MUSEO REGIONAL

This regional museum is housed in an ornate building (formerly a Franciscan convent) that dates from the 16th century. The collection includes pre-Columbian artifacts from Querétaro state as well as items of historical import, including the coffin used to bring Emperor Maximilian's body to its final resting place and early copies of the first Mexican constitution. Films and other cultural events take place here after the museum has closed; check the entryway billboard for details. *Corregidora 3, SE corner of Jardín Zenéa, tel. 42/12–20–31. Admission: $2, free Sun. and Tues. Open Tues.–Sun. 10:30–4:30.*

PALACIO DEL GOBIERNO FEDERAL

Also called the Palacio Municipal or the Casa de la Corregidora, this enormous, neoclassical, 18th-century building was once the home of Querétaro's mayor-magistrate (El Corregidor) and his wife, Doña Josefa Ortiz de Domínguez (La Corregidora). The large room over the main entrance was where Doña Josefa was held under house arrest during the first rumblings of the War of Independence; it's now used as the governor's conference room and is not accessible to the public. As legend has it, Doña Josefa warned Juan de Aldama and Ignacio Allende that their plot to declare independence from Spain had been discovered. Allende rushed to tell Father Miguel Hidalgo, who then gave his famous call for liberty in the nearby town of Dolores Hidalgo; this speech, know as the "Grito de Dolores," became the spark that ignited public support for independence. Today, with its arched walkways and gracious courtyards, the palacio brightens the bureaucratic lives of municipal administrators whose offices are housed here. Tourists are allowed inside the building's courtyards and lobby. *5 de Mayo, at Pasteur, tel. 42/12–91–00. Open weekdays 9–9.*

TEATRO DE LA REPUBLICA

Some of the most important events in Mexican history took place at this imposing neoclassical building: In 1867 Emperor Maximilian received his death sentence here, and in 1917 statesmen gathered here to draft a new Mexican constitution. These days, it's the place to catch occasional plays and concerts. Ask at the box office to find out what's going on. *Angela Peralta 22, tel. 42/14–29–53. Open for viewing weekdays 10–2 and 5–8, Sat. 9–noon.*

TEMPLO DE SANTA CLARA

This 17th-century church sits in the tree-filled Jardín Madero. Exquisite baroque artwork and several gilded altarpieces grace the interior. Next to the church stands the **Fuente de Neptuno** (Neptune's Fountain), designed by renowned architect and Bajío native Eduardo Tresguerra. The fountain originally belonged to the monks of San Antonio, who sold it (along with part of their land) during hard times. *Madero, at Allende, tel. 42/12–17–77. Open Mon.–Sat. 10–1 and 5–7, Sun. 10–7.*

SHOPPING

The andadores in Querétaro's centro are chock-full of outdoor vendors hawking amusing trinketry, while shops lining Pasteur and Libertad are devoted to artesanía. Querétaro is also famed for its gemstones and opal jewelry; for quality merchandise at fair prices, visit **La Luna** (Pasteur 12–B, tel. 42/24–20–25) or **El Rubí** (Madero 3 Pte, tel. 42/12–09–84). At **Casa de las Artesanías** (Pasteur 16 Sur, tel. 42/14–12–35) you can pick up Talavera pottery made in Tlaxcala and Guanajuato, and locally made embroidered tablecloths and wood carvings. The huge **Feria de las Artesanías** (Juárez 49, tel. 42/14–11–98; open daily 9–9) is a good place to buy anything Mexican, from blankets to picture frames. Pick up a whimsical, hand-painted piggy bank ($1.50) for all those pennies you've saved budget traveling. The Feria also offers the best selection of inexpensive ceramic dishware and colorful glassware.

AFTER DARK

At night, Querétaro's historical center is taken over by a nocturnal animal, the lounge lizard. By 9:30 PM almost every café and restaurant around Plaza Corregidora echoes with the soulful crooning of a singer and his or her synthesizer accompaniment. Club-hoppers, on the other hand, favor the bars and discos lining Boulevard Bernardo Quintana, on the east side of town. For a quiet evening, head for Café Tulipe or Café del Fondo (*see* Food, *above*), both of which serve coffee and dessert until 10 PM. Querétaro is also the place to catch up on high culture, with plays, music, dance concerts, and art-film screenings taking place in various theaters around the city.

Quadros (5 de Mayo 16, tel. 42/12–04–45), housed in a former mansion three blocks from the Jardín Zenéa, doubles as an art gallery and performance space, with frequent jazz and folk concerts and occasional poetry readings. When it gets late, the crowd pushes away the tables and dances in the courtyard. **Freedom** (Constituyentes 119 Ote., tel. 42/23–32–12) and **Carlos 'N Charlie's** (Bernardo Quintana 160, tel. 42/13–90–36) both feature live rock and pop Thursday through Saturday.

CLUBS

The club scene here gets going just before midnight and continues until dawn. **Qiu** (Monte Sinai 103, tel. 42/13–04–21; closed Mon.–Wed.) is a glittering disco that plays mostly pop and charges a $6 cover. On weekends, the disco inside the Hotel Santa Maria, **La Iguana** (Universidad, no phone), attracts the largest gay crowd in town. You'll have to take a taxi to either one of these discos; the drivers know where they are and will charge you about $2–$3 to get you there from Jardín Zenéa. Salsa dancing is king at **Los Infiernos** (Bernardo Quintana 177, no phone; closed. Mon.–Tues.), where the atmosphere is laid-back enough to tolerate both amateurs and the John Travoltas–of–salsa. Cover is $3.

THEATERS AND CULTURAL CENTERS

Theaters in Querétaro offer performances to suit every type of artistic sensibility, and tickets are usually priced reasonably. The university-affiliated **Cómicos de la Legua** (Guillermo Prieto 7, tel. 42/12–49–11 or 42/12–51–82) specializes in classic European plays written in the 17th and 18th centuries. At the **Corral de Comedias** (Venustiano Carranza 39, tel. 42/12–01–65 or 42/12–07–65), nibble on bread and cheese and sip wine while seeing your favorite musicals, farces, and comedies performed in Spanish. The **Orquestra Filarmónica de Querétaro** (tel. 42/23–16–92) performs Friday night at 8 PM in the **Auditorio Josefa Ortiz de Domínguez** (Constituyentes, at Zimapán, tel. 42/13–02–88). Tickets can be bought at the auditorio the night of the show.

NEAR QUERÉTARO

SAN JUAN DEL RIO

Some 54 km (32½ mi) southeast of Querétaro is the town of San Juan del Río, a haven of wide sidewalks, shady central streets, and well-maintained colonial buildings. The 17th-century **Parroquia de Santo Domingo** (Zaragoza, at Juárez) church is worth a visit. Its most striking feature is the statue over the main altar—a Christ figure with African features. The **Museo de la Santa Veracruz** (2 de Abril, no phone; open weekdays 9:30–2 and 4–6, weekends 10:30–4) houses local pre-Columbian artifacts. On Avenida Juárez, a row of pleasant *portales* (porches) sell locally made, handwoven baskets and blankets. Querétaro state is famous for opals, and at **Lapidaria Guerrero** (Juárez Pte.4, tel. 427/2–14–81) these are cut and polished on site.

During the week of June 15, San Juan hosts an enormous festival in honor of its patron saint, San Juan Bautista. Bullfights, cockfights, bicycle races, and beauty contests ("Mister *y* Miss" San Juan) are held in conjunction with plays, concerts, and dance performances. Contact the friendly **tourist office** (Juárez 30, at Oriente, tel. 427/2–08–84) for details. **Hotel Layseca** (Juárez 9, tel. 427/20–01–10) offers large rooms ($17 doubles) around a gracious courtyard.

Clase Premier buses depart for San Juan del Río (40 min, $1.25) every 10 minutes from Sala A in Querétaro's Central de Autobuses; when you arrive at San Juan's bus terminal, just head out the front door and catch a bus marked CENTRO. The principal intersection in the downtown area is Juárez and Hidalgo. The last bus back to Querétaro leaves at 9:30 PM.

SAN JOAQUIN

About three hours northeast of Querétaro, in the high mountainous region called the Sierra Gorda, lies the tiny town of San Joaquín. Tourists stop here on their way to the nearby ruins of **Toluquilla** and **Ranas** (*see below*). Otherwise, this sleepy rural settlement is the type of place where the loudest noise is made by bickering backyard roosters and hens. The zócalo looks more like a wide sidewalk, but the many freshly painted houses have an air of prosperity. There's even a "luxury" hotel here: **Hotel Mesón de San Joaquín** (Guadalupe Victoria 4, tel. 429/2–53–19, ext. 118), a slightly upscale version of the basic cinderblock special (doubles $11). The manager, Mario Torres Camacho, is happy to answer questions about the town. The hotel's restaurant serves filling breakfasts ($2–$3) and a decent comida corrida ($3) of soup, *sopa seca* (rice or pasta; literally "dry soup"), a main dish, and dessert. The Mesón also has a bar that provides pretty much the only nighttime entertainment in town. You can camp for free at **Campo Alegro,** a small stretch of pine forest at the top of a nearby hill. According to locals, it's a safe place to pitch your tent. To reach the camp, walk up Guadalupe Victoria from either the Flecha Amarilla or Flecha Azul bus stop; once you reach the central church, follow the blue signs with pictures of pine trees on them.

If you're in Querétaro for Dia de Los Muertos or Christmas, you can enjoy holiday performances at Casa del Faldón, a 17th-century mansion at Primavera 43. Events are open to the public.

Both **Flecha Azul** and **Flecha Amarilla** send buses between Querétaro and San Joaquín (3 hrs, $2.50); the last Flecha Azul bus leaves San Joaquín at 3:30 PM. Flecha Amarilla's final bus leaves at 4:45 PM.

RUINS

**RANAS • ** These modest ruins, strategically located on a high slope, are thought to have served several simultaneous functions during their heyday in the 7th and 8th centuries: as ceremonial center, trading post, and defensive structure. The ceremonial center, made up of several pyramids, covers the top of a steep hill. On the flatlands below are a ball court and the remains of what may have been military structures. From ceramic shards found here, archaeologists believe that the original inhabitants had extensive contact with the larger cities of El Tajín (*see* Near Papantla de Olarte *in* Chapter 11) and Teotihuacán (*see* Near Mexico City *in* Chapter 2). The settlement was abandoned after the 11th century and taken over by the Chichimeca people sometime in the 16th century. Ranas won't overwhelm you with its architectural splendor (the buildings resemble huge party hats), but it will allow you to experience ruins as ruins, rather than as flashy, tourist-oriented reconstruction's of Mexico's indigenous past. To get here from San Joaquín, walk straight up Calle Insurgentes from the Flecha Amarilla bus stop and follow the signs at the top of the small hill; the ruins lie about 3 km (2 mi) from town. Guides are available onsite for tours; they are not paid, so a small donation is appreciated. *Admission: $1.25. Open daily 9–5.*

**TOLUQUILLA • ** Smaller and slightly more remote than Ranas, Toluquilla is similar in its history and architectural style. The ruins here include two ball courts that stretch along the crest of a mountain top, as well as walls and foundations that are thought to have been military fortifications. As at Ranas, the term "lowly workers" was taken literally here—those who cultivated the fields and worked in the mines probably lived below the city proper. Although the ruins themselves aren't much, the elevation—even higher than at Ranas—provides a glorious view of the Sierra Gorda's bluish peaks. To get here, your best bet is to take a *camioneta* (pickup truck) from San Joaquín's Flecha Amarilla station—just tell the driver you want to get off at Toluquilla. Walking will take a good 2½ hours, but if you so desire, walk back out of town along the main road, turn left at the blue sign with the picture of a pyramid on it, and follow the narrow highway. *Admission free. Open daily 10–4.*

SAN MIGUEL DE ALLENDE

The modest *pueblo* (town) of San Miguel de Allende, in Guanajuato state, draws artists, troubadours, and tourists like few other cities in Mexico—though it's difficult to explain why. Longtime residents will assure you (perhaps hoping you'll go away and chose Tijuana instead) that other Mexican towns are more picturesque, have better nightlife, or offer a wider range of cultural pursuits. And still, the foreigners keep arriving in droves. Many choose to stay on for a few weeks or months to study Spanish at one of the language schools; to paint, sculpt, or dance at the Bellas Artes; or simply to live their version of the low-rent good life.

San Miguel's popularity with foreigners supposedly started after WWII, when the GI Bill offered many Americans the financial means to travel abroad. Although all of Mexico was economically appealing, many were specifically drawn to San Miguel by the Instituto Allende, which offered Spanish language and Mexican culture classes. Today the gringo population of San Miguel is one of the largest in Mexico, a fact that causes some travelers to ignore this town in their quest for "authenticity." This is unfortunate, as not all the expatriates are boorish tourists, disrespectful of Mexican culture. Many play crucial roles in San Miguel society, helping to maintain the historical integrity of the town or performing social service work.

Natives of San Miguel don't let the gringo hordes get in the way of enjoying their *días de fiesta*. Some of the town's annual pageants and parades have been celebrated for decades or even centuries. The birth of the town's namesake, Ignacio Allende, is celebrated January 21 with a military parade. A procession featuring people in comical costumes takes place during the **Fiesta de San Antonio de Padua** (around June 12), which commemorates one of the town's patron saints. The first half of August brings San Miguel's **Festival de Música,** which features classical and jazz musicians from around the world. September 16 is the **Día de la Independencia,** celebrated with a marathon race and a reenactment of Father Miguel Hidalgo's famous freedom speech, the "Grito de Dolores." The third Saturday in September is **Sanmiguelada,** marked by a wild *corrida de toros* (running of the bulls). On the Friday closest to September 29th, a feast called "La Alborada" is held in honor of **San Miguel Arcángel,** the town's patron saint. The day is celebrated with a parade of *xóchiles* (huge decorations of flowers, plants, and corn) and *concheros* (shell dancers)—cultural remnants of San Miguel's indigenous past.

BASICS

AMERICAN EXPRESS

The AmEx representative, **Viajes Vertiz,** won't cash traveler's checks, but emergency check cashing is available. Mail for cardholders should be sent to: Hidalgo 1, AP 486, San Miguel de Allende, Guanajuato, CP 37700, México. *½ block north of Plaza Principal, tel. 415/2–18–56. Open weekdays 9–2 and 4–6:30, Sat. 10–2.*

BOOKSTORES

El Colibrí (Diez de Sollano 30, 1 block east of Plaza Principal, tel. 415/2–07–51; open Mon.–Sat. 10–2 and 4–7), in business for over 30 years, stocks an extensive selection of English-language paperbacks and magazines. **El Tecolote** (Jesus 11, inside Café de la Parroquia, no phone; open Mon.–Wed., Fri., and Sat. 10–5, Sun. 10–2) also carries books in English.

CASAS DE CAMBIO

Although the Plaza Principal is surrounded by several banks, **Casa de Cambio Deal** (Correo 15, tel. 415/2–29–32; open weekdays 9–6, Sat. 9–2) is your best bet because it doesn't charge a commission. **Banamex** (corner of Canal and Hidalgo) changes cash and traveler's checks and has an ATM.

CONSULATES

Canada: *Mesones 38–15, tel. 415/2–30–25. Open weekdays 11–2.* **United Sates**: *Macías 72, tel. 415/2–23–57, or 415/2–00–68 for emergencies. Open Mon. and Wed. 9–1 and 4–7, Tues. and Thurs. 4–7.*

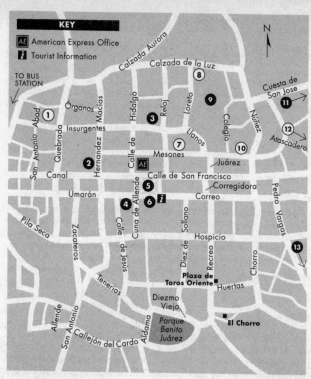

KEY

AE American Express Office

ℹ Tourist Information

TO BUS STATION

Calzada Aurora

Calzada de la Luz

Órganos

Insurgentes

San Antonio — Abad

Quebrada

Hernández

Canal

Hidalgo

Reloj

Calle de

Mesones

Loreto

Llanos

Colegio

Juárez

Umarán

Zacateros

Calle de Allende

Calle de Jesús

Cuna de Allende

Diezmo de Sollano

Hospicio

Recreo

Chorro

Pedro Vargas

Atascadero

Núñez

Cuesta de San José

Corregidora

Correo

Plaza de Toros Oriente

Huertas

Diezmo Viejo

Callejón del Cardo

Aldama

San Antonio

Allende

Tenerías

Parque Benito Juárez

El Chorro

Pila Seca

Canal

Sights ●

Bellas Artes, **2**

Biblioteca Pública, **3**

Jardín Botánico, **11**

Mercado Internacional Ramírez, **9**

El Mirador, **13**

Museo Histórico, **4**

Parroquia de San Miguel Arcángel, **6**

Plaza Principal (El Jardín), **5**

Lodging ○

Casa de Huéspedes, **7**

Hostal Internacional, **1**

Hotel La Huerta, **12**

Hotel Parador de San Sebastián, **10**

Quinta Loreto, **8**

EMERGENCIES

Contact the **police** at 415/2–00–22; for an **ambulance,** call 415/2–16–16.

LAUNDRY

Lava Mágico will clean a load of clothes for $3. If you drop off your clothes before noon, you'll get them back the same day. *Pila Seca 5, tel. 415/2–08–99. Open Mon.–Sat. 8–8.*

MAIL

The full-service **post office** will hold mail sent to you at the following address for up to 10 days: Lista de Correos, Correo 16, San Miguel de Allende, Guanajuato, CP 37701, México. *2 blocks east of Plaza Principal, tel. 415/2–00–89. Open weekdays 8–7, Sat. 9–1.*

MEDICAL AID

The English-speaking staff at the pharmacy **Botica Agundis** (Canal 26, tel. 415/2–11–98; open daily 10 AM–midnight) is particularly helpful. **Hospital de la Fé** (Libramiento a Dolores Hidalgo 43, tel. 415/2–22–33) provides 24-hour urgent medical treatment and can refer you to an English-speaking physician.

PHONES

The pay phones in San Miguel are in sad shape, but a couple of working **Ladatel** phones are clustered around the Plaza Principal. To place long-distance calls try the phones in the **Central de Autobuses** (*see* Coming and Going, *below*). In the center of town, **Caseta de Pepe** (Sollano 4, tel. 415/2–60–61, fax 415/2–62–55; open daily 8 AM–11 PM) charges about $1.50 per minute for direct calls to the U.S. and Canada. There's no charge to place an international collect call.

SCHOOLS

Although people from all over the world descend upon San Miguel for Spanish-language classes, they often end up speaking more English than Spanish. Study during the school year instead of the summer and you'll avoid the crowds of English speakers. Schools tend to offer courses in continuous four-week sessions, but most willingly offer private lessons as well. If you don't want to commit to an entire course, Spanish classes are also offered at the Hostal Internacional (see Where to Sleep, below). San Miguel is also the place to learn traditional jewelry making, pottery, and sculpture from local artisans, or to take lessons in traditional dance.

Academia Hispano Americano (Mesones 4, tel. 415/2–03–49, fax 415/2–23–33) offers Spanish and literature classes from beginning to advanced levels. Scholarships and homestays are also available. **Bellas Artes/Centro Cultural El Nigromante** (Macías 75, tel. and fax 415/2–02–89) is a fine arts school offering classes in dance, art, and music. For more information, contact Director Carmen Masip de Hawkins at: Macías 75, San Miguel de Allende, Guanajuato, CP 37700, México. **Centro Mexicano de Lengua y Cultura de San Miguel** (Orizaba 15, tel. and fax 415/2–07–63) offers individual and group instruction in Spanish, English, French, and Italian. Write to Josefina Hernandez at: Orizaba 15, Col. San Antonio, San Miguel de Allende, Guanajuato, CP 37755, México. **Instituto Allende** (Ancha de San Antonio 20, tel. 415/2–01–90, fax 415/2–45–38) is an internationally recognized fine arts school.

VISITOR INFORMATION

Pick up a copy of the local English-language newspaper, *Atención San Miguel* (50¢), for listings of events, religious services, and literary discussion groups. You can also visit the **tourist office** (south side of Plaza Principal, tel. 415/2–65–65; open weekdays 10–3 and 5–7, Sat. 10–5, Sun. 10–2); some of the staff members speak English, and they'll load you down with maps, brochures, and hotel listings.

COMING AND GOING

BY BUS

San Miguel de Allende's **Central de Autobuses** (tel. 415/2–50–43) lies about 10 minutes southwest from the center of town. The main bus lines here are **Flecha Amarilla** (tel. 415/2–00–84) and **Autotransportes Herradura de Plata** (tel. 415/2–07–25). Both lines provide frequent bus service to Mexico City (3½ hrs, $11), Querétaro (1 hr, $2.50), Guanajuato (1½ hrs, $3), Dolores Hidalgo (½ hr, $1.50), and San Luis Potosí (6 hrs, $6). The station offers long-distance telephone service (daily 7 AM–11 PM) and luggage storage (daily 7 AM–10 PM) for 50¢ per bag per eight hours. To reach downtown from the station, catch a local bus marked CENTRO.

BY CAR

To reach Mexico City (256 km/159 mi), head east on Highway 111 to Highway 57 south through Querétaro (69 km/45½ mi) and continue southwest on Highway 57-D. To Guadalajara (376 km/249 mi), take Highway 51 south to Highway 57-D east, then head east on Highway 110, and then farther east on Highway 90. To San Luis Potosí (160 km/100 mi), take Highway 57 north.

BY TRAIN

Trains depart San Miguel de Allende's **Calzada de la Estación** (tel. 415/2–00–07) daily at 1 PM for Mexico City (7 hrs; $8 1st class, $4.50 2nd class) and Querétaro ($2.50 1st class, $1 2nd class). Trains bound for Monterrey ($16 1st class, $9 2nd class) depart daily at 2:30 PM. Generally, trains are much slower and less reliable than buses. Tickets are sold daily noon–3. The bus marked CENTRO will take you from the train station to the center of town.

GETTING AROUND

San Miguel is a small town with picturesque, hilly cobblestone streets. Most attractions are easily explored on foot. The major streets change names around the central **Plaza Principal**: Canal runs east–west and becomes San Francisco as it crosses the north side of the plaza; Umarán runs east–west and becomes Correo as it crosses the south side of the plaza. The only buses you're likely to need are those that run up and down Canal to the bus and train stations; buses run from 7 AM to 10 PM and cost 30¢.

WHERE TO SLEEP

Hotels abound within walking distance of the Plaza Principal, with rooms ranging from reasonably priced to impossibly expensive. Prices listed here are for the low season; during high season (Oct.–Jan.) hotel prices soar by as much as 100%.

UNDER $10 • Hotel La Huerta. For inexpensive rooms ($10 doubles) in a quiet neighborhood, take a 10-minute walk from Plaza Principal. The basic rooms are clean and airy and open onto communal sitting rooms. *Cerrada de Becerra, tel. 415/2–08–81. From Plaza Principal, 1 block north on Reloj, right on Mesones 5 blocks, right on Atascadero, right on Cerrada de Becerra. 15 rooms, all with bath. Cash only.*

UNDER $15 • Casa de Huéspedes. The tiled, plant-filled courtyard is a charming enhancement to this tiny guest house. Rooms are large and well-lit, with balconies opening onto the street. The staff is amiable, and there's hot water 24 hours a day. Doubles run $13. *Mesones 27, tel. 415/2–13–78. 6 rooms, all with bath. Cash only.*

Hotel Parador de San Sebastián. This family-run establishment is more like a home than a hotel—and the owners have the most lovable dogs. Every room is clean and quaint with antique oak furnishings, and some boast small kitchens, complete with utensils. Doubles cost $14. *Mesones 7, tel. 415/2–07–07. 24 rooms, all with bath. Parking. Cash only.*

UNDER $30 • Quinta Loreto. Spacious, clean rooms with telephones and patios, a large garden, and free use of the pool and tennis court make the Quinta Loreto worth its price. Upstairs rooms have better views but aren't as breezy as those downstairs. Most guests here are foreign tourists. Doubles are $27, plus $5 for a TV. *Loreto 15, tel. 415/2–00–42. 38 rooms, all with bath.*

Chichimeca (a generic name for the nomadic bands who once inhabited northern Bajío) means "lineage of the dog." The Aztecs considered this term a compliment, and many dynasties proudly claimed it.

HOSTELS

Hostal Internacional. This hostel gives you an excellent deal for your money. Beds in the single-sex dorms cost $4–$5, breakfast included. Two private rooms are available for $8–$10. Rooms and bathrooms are cleaner than those in some hotels, and the friendly manager, Roberto, gets rave reviews from his guests. In return, guests are required to perform a 15-minute chore of their choosing. Introductory Spanish lessons ($1.50 per person) are held at the hostel weekdays 10 AM–noon. The crowd here is all ages, a mix of foreign and Mexican travelers. *Órganos 34, tel. 415/2–06–74. From Plaza Principal, 1 block west on Canal, right on Macías 3 blocks, and left on Órganos for 3 blocks. Curfew 11 PM, reception open daily 7 AM–11 PM. Kitchen, laundry, safe deposit boxes. No age limit. Cash only.*

FOOD

San Miguel caters to its large resident gringo population with a wide range of restaurants to suit all tastes and budgets. Restaurants downtown sell everything from Mexican staples to Italian and Lebanese cuisine. For *tortas* (sandwiches) and other local favorites, try the *comedores* (sit-down food stands) at the daily **Mercado Ignacio Ramírez** (Av. Colegio, tel. 415/2–28–44). Prices are very reasonable and the food stands are generally open until dusk. The baked goods at **Panadería La Espiga** (Insurgentes 119, tel. 415/2–15–80) are ideal for an inexpensive breakfast.

UNDER $3 • Las Palomas. Choose chicken mole, spicy pork, or *nopales* (grilled cactus) to fill your tacos, tostadas, or quesadillas. Whatever you choose, it's super cheap: Three tacos and a drink come to less than $2. The seating is arranged around the small kitchen so you can watch your food being prepared. *Correo 9, off of Diez de Sollano, no phone. Cash only.*

UNDER $5 • La Buena Vida. The menu at this patio restaurant features French, Italian, and Mexican specialties. There's also a juice and coffee bar. The well-balanced comida corrida, which includes soup, a main dish, fruit drink, and dessert, is a bargain at $4. *Hernández Macías 72, tel. 415/2–22–61. From Plaza Principal, walk 1 block on Canal to Hernández Macías then turn right and walk ½ block. Closed Sun. Cash only.*

El Ten-ten Pie. Tacos and burritos (some of them vegetarian) are served in a pleasant space filled with works by local artisans. The manager guarantees that meat for the 50¢ tacos is fresh and that vegetables are washed in purified water. You can also while away the hours here playing chess, dominos, or backgammon. *Cuna de Allende 21, tel. 415/2–71–89. No breakfast. Cash only.*

El Tomate. This small, clean eatery has a wonderful all-vegetarian menu; the *hamburgesa de espinaca* (spinach hamburger) is excellent. A huge sign hanging from the kitchen counter assures customers that all vegetables have been prepared hygienically. *Mesones 60, between Hidalgo and Macías, tel. 415/2–03–25. Closed Tues. Cash only.*

UNDER $10 • Mama Mía. The patio of this open-air restaurant is filled with huge trees and festooned with paper lanterns. On the menu you'll find Italian entrées like pizza and pasta ($3–$7). Live Andean or flamenco guitar music starts at 8 PM, making this a great place for drinks as well as food; it closes at 2 AM on Friday and Saturday. *Umarán 8, ½ block west of Plaza Principal, tel. 415/2–20–63.*

CAFES

Cafés in San Miguel de Allende are gringo hangouts where tourists and expats drink cappuccino. **El Buen Café** (Jesús 23, at Cuadrante, tel. 415/2–58–07; closed Sun.) pours excellent coffee drinks ($1). Sandwiches and crepes are less than $5. At **Café de la Parroquia** (Jesús 11, tel. 415/2–31–61) seating is available indoors or out. You can enjoy a scrumptious breakfast of hot cakes or French toast for $3; a huge cappuccino costs $1. These cafés accept cash only.

WORTH SEEING

Most sights are within a few blocks of the Plaza Principal. One that isn't is **El Mirador** (The Lookout), a popular place to view the sunset. It's up a steep hill and away from the center of town; ask a local to set you in the right direction. Strolling around the **Mercado Ignacio Ramírez** (*see* Shopping, *below*) is definitely a test in sensory overload: Squealing pigs and squawking chickens drown out blaring pop music.

BELLAS ARTES/CENTRO CULTURAL EL NIGROMANTE

This school of fine arts is housed in an 18th-century former convent. A peaceful central courtyard and fountain are surrounded by two floors of classrooms and studios. Murals by David Siqueiros (a contemporary of Diego Rivera) adorn the interior walls, and two small galleries on the first floor exhibit work by local artists. *Macías 75, tel. 415/2–02–89. 1½ blocks west of Plaza Principal. Admission free. Open Mon.–Sat. 9–8, Sun. 10–3.*

BIBLIOTECA PUBLICA

Besides having a great collection of books in both Spanish and English, San Miguel's public library acts as a center for the English-language community. Upcoming events are posted on the bulletin board in the library's foyer, and the town's English-language newspaper, *Atención San Miguel,* is sold at the front desk. On Tuesday and Thursday afternoons, people meet in the library's sun-filled courtyard from 5 to 7 for a free, informal English–Spanish exchange. Sunday at noon the library sponsors 1½-hour walking tours of notable local homes for about $15. *Insurgentes 25, tel. 415/2–02–93. Open weekdays 10–2 and 4–7, Sat. 10–2.*

MUSEO HISTORICO DE SAN MIGUEL DE ALLENDE

This grand mansion was the birthplace of Ignacio Allende, one of the key figures in Mexico's fight for independence. It's now a museum that exhibits Allende's clothing and personal effects, as well as pre-Columbian artifacts from Guanajuato state. Placards and posters will tell you more than you ever wanted to know about the history of San Miguel. *Cuna de Allende 1, tel. 415/2–24–99. SW corner of Plaza Principal. Admission free. Open Tues.–Sun. 10–4.*

PARROQUIA DE SAN MIGUEL ARCANGEL

This church is worth seeing, and indeed, it would be hard to miss. In the 18th century, the parish priest commissioned a stone carver, Cerefino Gutiérrez, to replace the original two-tower facade. Gutiérrez was an indigenous local with no formal training, and so he drew his plans in the sand every day with a stick. The resulting whimsical, pseudo-Gothic exterior contrasts sharply with the *mudéjar* (Moorish-influenced) interior. Parked outside the church on most days is San Miguel's answer to Good Humor, a horse-drawn cart where you can get mango, lemon, strawberry, and *cajeta* (sweet carmelized goat's milk) ice-cream cones for less than $1. *South side of Plaza Principal. Admission free. Open daily 7 AM–10 PM.*

SHOPPING

For centuries San Miguel's artisans have been praised for their fine crafts, ranging from woven straw baskets to metalwork. Popular souvenirs included woven-cotton and wool goods, folk art, silver jewelry, and housewares or decorative items made of brass and tin. The daily **Mercado Ignacio Ramírez,** behind

Plaza Cívica, is spread along six city blocks and sells just about everything. It's particularly active on Sunday, when country folk come to town to sell pigs, chickens, and succulent produce. **Lan Art** (Ancha de San Antonio, corner Orizaba, tel. 415/2–15–66) has excellent prices on hand-loomed bedspreads, rugs, and cushions. **Casa Maxwell** (Calle de Canal 14, tel. 415/2–02–47) is ideal for one-stop shoppers: This vast building offers folk art, ceramics, jewelry, furniture, glassware, metalware, modern clothing, and a lot more. **Veryka** (Zacateros 6A, tel. 415/2-21-14) deals primarily in Latin American folk art. They have a fine selection of *muertos* (skeleton figures used for Day of the Dead ceremonies) from Puebla.

AFTER DARK

San Miguel's bars and discos will not disappoint those looking for a party, and most stay open until about 6 AM. However, despite the town's large gay and lesbian population, conservative state laws prohibit "gay" bars from getting a license. **Laberinto's** (Ancha de San Antonio 7, tel. 415/2–03–62; closed Mon.) plays a mix of Latin and American dance music and is always crowded with locals on weekends. Cover charge is $5 (free on Thursday and Sunday). The discotheque **El Ring** (Hidalgo 25, 1 block from Plaza Principal; closed Mon.) is one of the most popular nightspots in town, complete with flashing laser lights and pulsating music. Cover is $6 (free to couples). **Mama Mia's** (*see* Food, *above*) has *three* bars (all no cover) with live classic rock, R&B, and reggae. There are two places in town where you can get your fill of American movies: **Villa Jacaranda Cine Bar** (Aldama 53, tel. 415/2–10–15) is a happening club that shows movies in English for about $6 (price includes one drink). **Cinema Gemelos** (Plaza Real de Conde, tel. 415/2–64–08) shows first-run Hollywood movies and has two-for-one nights on Tuesday and Wednesday.

Beat legend Neal Cassady, protagonist of Jack Kerouac's "On The Road," died in San Miguel in 1968 while walking on the railroad tracks.

OUTDOOR ACTIVITIES

One of the best-kept secrets of San Miguel is the **Jardín Botanico el Charco del Ingenio** (tel. 415/2–29–90; admission $1.50). This 116-acre park and garden is a popular picnic spot for locals, and it's adjacent to a canyon that offers hours of hiking and climbing opportunities. The newly replanted botanical garden features cacti, succulents, and various other regional flora. Elsewhere there's an old aqueduct and the ruins of a colonial mill. To reach the garden, catch a GIGANTE bus from the corner of Colegio and Mesones and get off at the Gigante shopping center. From here, walk west 20 minutes, following the (poorly marked) signs to the main entrance. Stay on the sidewalks on the way to the Jardín, rather than trekking through the hills at the end of Calzada de La Luz; several muggings have occurred in the hills. The park itself is fenced and guarded. *Park entrance is 4 km (2½ mi) from downtown, just behind Rancho Atascadero Hotel.*

Eight kilometers (5 mi) outside of San Miguel, on the road to Dolores Hidalgo, lies **La Gruta Balneario** (tel. 415/2–25–30 ext. 145), a longtime favorite local getaway. Basically, La Gruta Balneario is a series of three interconnected natural mineral pools, each a different temperature. The pools are outdoors and very clean; it costs $4 to soak your weary traveler's bones in them. The easiest way to get here is by taxi ($13), though you can take a bus from the Central de Autobuses toward Dolores or Atotnilco and ask the driver to let you off at the Balneario. (To return you'd have to stand in the road and flag down a San Miguel–bound bus.) The pools are open daily 8–5.

GUANAJUATO

If you visit only one city in the Bajío, let it be Mexico's colonial jewel, Guanajuato. Surrounded on all sides by green hills, the capital city of Guanajuato state charms travelers with its Churrigueresque churches, quiet parks, ornate theaters, colonial mansions, proud university, and flourishing arts tradition—all the legacies of a prosperous mining industry. Guanajuato was established as a World Heritage Site in 1988 and today it continues to be a vital, flourishing center for artists, dancers, musicians, and university students. The city's winding streets and subterranean roadways (built by miners in 1960) may make it easy to get lost, but you probably won't be in any hurry to leave.

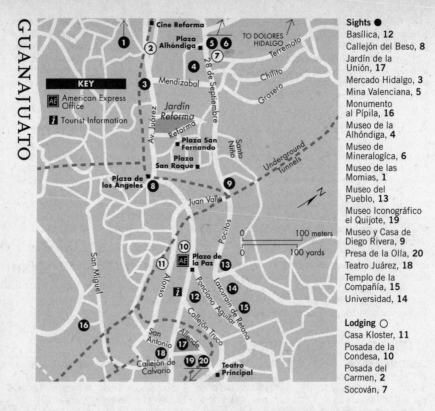

GUANAJUATO

KEY

AE American Express Office

i Tourist Information

Cine Reforma

Plaza Alhóndiga

TO DOLORES HIDALGO

Mendizabal

Jardín Reforma

Plaza San Fernando

Plaza San Roque

Plaza de los Angeles

Juan Valle

Plaza de la Paz

San Miguel

San Antonio

Callejón de Calvario

Callejón Truco

Allende

Teatro Principal

Terremoto

Chilito

Grasero

Av. Juárez

Reforma

Santo Niño

28 de Septiembre

Pocitos

Underground Tunnels

Alonso

Ponciano Aguilar

Lascurain de Retana

100 meters
100 yards

Sights ●
Basílica, 12
Callejón del Beso, 8
Jardín de la Unión, 17
Mercado Hidalgo, 3
Mina Valenciana, 5
Monumento al Pípila, 16
Museo de la Alhóndiga, 4
Museo de Mineralogíca, 6
Museo de las Momias, 1
Museo del Pueblo, 13
Museo Iconográfico el Quijote, 19
Museo y Casa de Diego Rivera, 9
Presa de la Olla, 20
Teatro Juárez, 18
Templo de la Compañía, 15
Universidad, 14

Lodging ○
Casa Kloster, 11
Posada de la Condesa, 10
Posada del Carmen, 2
Socován, 7

Besides Guanajuato city's significance as a major silver-mining town, it was also the scene of the first major military confrontation between rebel forces and royalist troops on September 28, 1810. Throughout the city you'll see monuments to Guanajuato's revolutionary heroes. The town of **Dolores Hidalgo,** where Father Miguel Hidalgo issued his famous freedom speech, is only an hour away, as is Pozos, an abandoned mining town ripe for exploration. Another of Guanajuato's claims to fame is as the birthplace of artist Diego Rivera; the house where he was born is now a museum. And finally, Guanajuato boasts one of the most bizarre and macabre museums in Mexico: the Museo de las Momias.

BASICS

AMERICAN EXPRESS

This office provides standard cardholder services and will cash AmEx traveler's checks. Send cardholder mail to: Viajes Georama, Plaza de la Paz 34, Guanajuato, Guanajuato, CP 36000, México. *Across from Plaza de la Paz, tel. 473/2–51–01 or 473/2–51–02. Open weekdays 9–2 and 5–7, Sat. 10–1.*

CASAS DE CAMBIO

Banamex (Plaza de los Ángeles, tel. 473/2–08–00; open weekdays 9–1:30) cashes traveler's checks and provides currency exchange. Its ATM accepts Visa, Cirrus, Plus, and MasterCard. **Centro Cambiario** (Plaza de la Compañía 2, in front of the post office, tel. 473/2–50–91; open weekdays 9–5, Sat. 9–1) has similar rates but better hours.

EMERGENCIES

Contact the **police** at 473/2–02–66; for **ambulance** service call Cruz Roja at 473/2–04–87.

LAUNDRY

Lavandería del Centro will wash, dry, and fold 3 kilos (6½ pounds) of laundry for $3. *Sopeña 26, near Museo Iconográfico del Quijote, tel. 473/2–06–80. From Jardín de la Unión, head west on Juárez. Open weekdays 9–8:15, Sat. 9–4.*

MAIL

The city's post office is near the University of Guanajuato. Mail sent to the following address will be held for you for up to 10 days: Lista de Correos, Guanajuato, Guanajuato, CP 36000, México. *Ayuntamiento 25, tel. 473/2–03–85. Open weekdays 8–7, Sat. 9–1.*

MEDICAL AID

Hospital Regional de Guanajuato (Carretera Guanajuato Cilao, tel. 473/3–15–73 or 473/3–15–76) provides 24-hour medical service and has a few English-speaking doctors. The tourist office (*see* Visitor Information, *below*) can tell you which of the city's pharmacies is currently on the 24-hour shift, or ask any pharmacist. **Farmacia El Fenix** (Juáez 104, tel. 473/2–61–40; open Mon.–Sat. 10–8) is a discount drugstore.

PHONES

Ladatel phones are sprinkled all along Juárez and on the northeast side of the Jardín de la Unión.

SCHOOLS

The **University of Guanajuato** (tel. 473/2–72–53) has an exchange program with several American universities, but you don't have to be a student to take Spanish-language and literature classes at its **Centro de Idiomas.** Programs run July–December and January–June. Four-week intensive Spanish-language summer sessions are also available: The registration fee is $110 and courses cost $550. Homestays with local families can be arranged. For registration information, contact: Lic. Patricia Begne, Centro de Idiomas, Universidad de Guanajuato, Lascurain de Retana 5, Guanajuato, Guanajuato, CP 36000, México.

In 1926, the Mexican government declared San Miguel de Allende a national monument, making it almost impossible to alter anything about the town. Thank the government if you trip over an uneven cobblestone.

The **Instituto Falcón** (tel. 473/2–36–94) is highly recommended by former attendees. All levels of Spanish language classes are offered, in addition to courses on Mexican culture and history. The registration fee is $50, while weekly tuition ($55–$110) depends on the number of sessions per day. Homestays are also available. For information, write to Jorge Barroso, Registrar, Instituto Falcón A.C., Callejón de la Mara 158, Guanajuato, Guanajuato, CP 36000, México.

VISITOR INFORMATION

The staff at the **tourist information office** (Plaza de la Paz 14, near Basílica, tel. 473/2–15–74, fax 473/2–42–51; open weekdays 8:30–7:30, weekends 10–2) is happy to answer questions and hand you a free city map.

COMING AND GOING

BY BUS

The **Central de Autobuses** (Carretera Guanajuato–Cilao Km. 8, tel. 473/3–13–33) is served by four bus lines: **Omnibús de México** (tel. 473/3–13–56), **Flecha Amarilla** (tel. 473/3–13–33), **Estrella Blanca** (tel. 473/3–13–44), and **Primera Plus** (tel. 473/3–13–33). Buses to Mexico City (4½ hrs, $12) leave seven times daily. Buses also leave frequently for León (1 hr, $1.75), San Miguel de Allende (1½ hrs, $3), Dolores Hidalgo (1½ hrs, $2), and San Luis Potosí (4 hrs, $8). From mid-morning to mid-afternoon, buses leave for Querétaro (2½ hrs, $5), Guadalajara (5 hrs, $10), and Morelia (4 hrs, $7). Luggage storage (50¢ per hr) is available 7 AM–9:30 PM. The bus station is 6 km (4 mi) west of the city; to get here from downtown, catch a bus marked CENTRAL on Juárez in front of Plaza de la Paz. To reach the center of town from the station, take a bus marked CENTRO.

BY CAR

To reach Mexico City (374 km/232 mi), take Highway 110 south to Highway 45-D east toward Querétaro (136 km/84 mi); just outside Querétaro, catch Highway 57-D straight to the capital. Tolls total $20. To Guadalajara (294 km/182 mi), take Highway 110 south and then Highway 90 west into the city.

EL CALLEJON DEL BESO

For a few coins, young men lingering around the "Alley of the Kiss" will tell you the following legend:

A young woman named Doña Carmen, the only child of a jealous father, fell in love with a man named Don Luis. When her father found out about the courtship he vowed to marry her off to an old, rich Spaniard. Her lovesick suitor Don Luis, noting the narrowness of the alleyway separating Doña Carmen's house from the one across the way, arranged to buy the neighboring house for a steep price. One starry night, when Doña Carmen went out onto her balcony, she was pleasantly surprised by the nearness of her lover. Swiftly her enraged father followed her and plunged a dagger into his daughter's heart. Don Luis was close enough to leave a kiss on his love's lifeless hand. Then, distraught with grief, he took his own life.

According to the legend, if you kiss your loved one on the third step leading up to the balcony where Don Luis died, you'll enjoy seven years of good luck.

To reach the alley from the Jardín de la Unión, walk west on Juárez to Plaza de los Ángeles, go up Callejón del Patrocinio, and take a left on Callejón del Beso.

GETTING AROUND

Whoever planned—or rather, didn't plan—Guanajuato was clearly asleep when the rest of Mexico's cities were being laid out using the simple grid system. At some point during your visit you will get lost. The most important street to remember is **Avenida Juárez,** the main thoroughfare. As you head east from Jardín Reforma, Juárez changes names twice, first turning into Obregón and then becoming Sopeña near the main plaza, **Jardín de la Unión.** Most directions in this chapter use the Jardín de la Unión as a reference point. City buses run 6 AM–10 PM and cost 30¢.

WHERE TO SLEEP

Most budget hotels are along Avenida Juárez, between the train station and the Cine Reforma. Conveniently, this area is also near many of the city's attractions and much of the action. As you continue east along Juárez toward the Jardín de la Unión, accommodations become more attractive and more expensive. If you're planning to arrive in mid-October, when the Cervantes Festival (*see* Festivals, *below*) is in full swing, you'll need to make reservations four to six months in advance. When hotels are full, the tourist office provides free information on families who will house travelers for low prices.

UNDER $10 • Casa Kloster. This wholesome hotel is your best option if you can live with a few house rules: Unwed couples must be discreet, and nighttime silence is strictly enforced. Run by the hospitable Pérez family, the Kloster features clean rooms, spotless communal bathrooms, and an interior courtyard filled with plants and chirping birds. It's extremely popular with backpackers, so be sure to call ahead. Rooms are $6.50 per person, with a 10% discount when more than two share a room. *Alonso 32, tel. 473/2–00–88. 17 rooms, 1 with bath. Cash only.*

Posada de la Condesa. This *posada* (inn) is cheaper than most of its neighbors. Rooms are cramped but clean, and all have private baths; there's hot water if you're patient. Doubles cost $9. *Plaza de la Paz 62, tel. 473/2–14–62. 22 rooms, all with bath. Cash only.*

UNDER $15 • Posada del Carmen. Run by a friendly, professional staff, this clean and cheerful place will even do your laundry ($4 for 3 kilos, or 6½ pounds). The cost is $12 for a double; prices go up during the Cervantes festival. *Juárez 111-A, tel. 473/2–93–30. 16 rooms, all with bath. Cash only.*

UNDER $20 • Socován. Don't be put off by Socován's gloomy, tunnel-like entrance: Open-air walkways, with views of surrounding mountains, lead to the guest quarters. Each room—simply furnished with bed, desk, and TV—has wood-beam ceilings and a modern bath. Off-season prices are $20 for doubles. *Alhóndiga 41-A, tel. 473/2–48–85. 37 rooms, all with bath.*

FOOD

Restaurants abound on Avenida Juárez and the surrounding side streets. A number of food stalls serve cheap Mexican fare at **Mercado Hidalgo** (Juárez, between Cine Reforma and Jardín Reforma), in the ornate former train station. The city has two great options for breakfast: **Panificadora Guanajuato** (Plaza de la Paz 53, tel. 473/2–18–69) sells scrumptious baked treats beginning daily at 7 AM. **café dadá** (Truco 19, tel. 473/2–50–95–4) serves heavenly 75¢ coffees made with fresh-roast coffee beans. They also do decent $2.50 hamburgers, good salads, and desserts. The above accept cash only.

> *In keeping with the illogical layout of the city, Guanajuato's main square, Jardín de la Unión, is actually a triangle and is therefore also known as the "wedge of cheese."*

UNDER $5 • Café Valadéz. Valadéz has been in business for more than 40 years but only recently swapped beer-soaked tables for an ersatz "tea shoppe" look. From the window seats you can see troubadours performing on the step of the Teatro Juárez, just across the street. *Molletes* (rolls slathered in refried beans and melted cheese) cost $2. *Jardín de la Unión 3, tel. 473/2–11–57. Cash only.*

El Café Galería. Vibrant artwork, multihued walls, and ceilings decorated with Mexican *artesanía* set the mood at Galería. Café fare includes hamburgers, yogurt with fruit and granola, and *tortilla española* (egg-and-potato omelet). *Sopeña 10, tel. 473/2–25–66. Cash only.*

Restaurant El Agora del Baratillo. This restaurant offers patio dining at wrought-iron tables covered with checkered tablecloths. The comida corrida ($5.50) is more expensive than any entrée on the menu, but it includes a glass of wine. Breakfast chilaquiles come with egg, fruit, yogurt, and coffee. *Jardín de la Unión 4, tel. 473/2–33–00. Near Hotel Posada San José. Cash only.*

UNDER $10 • Tasca de los Santos. At this candlelit restaurant near the basilica you'll be pampered by attentive waiters and enjoy delicious Spanish food. The pollo *al vino blanco* (in white wine; $5) and the tapas (Spanish appetizers) come recommended. *Plaza de la Paz 28, off Juárez, tel. 473/2–23–20. Cash only.*

WORTH SEEING

Most sights are near the centro and are easy to see in a few days' exploration on foot. Keep in mind that getting lost in Guanajuato is, strangely enough, one of the more enjoyable things to do here: You're sure to stumble across a charming side street, unusual curio shop, or stately colonial building. The maze of twisting *callejones* (alleyways) provides exciting opportunities to see less-touristed parts of the city.

BASILICA

The baroque facade of the 1693 **Basílica Colegiata de Nuestra Señora de Guanajuato** is painted a buttery yellow and resembles one of the pastries sold at the nearby Panificadora Guanajuato (*see* Food, *above*). The basilica's interior features sparkling crystal chandeliers and a bejeweled wooden statue of the Virgin, said to be the oldest existing Christian statue in Mexico. *Plaza de la Paz, near Juárez. Open daily 8–8.*

MINA VALENCIANA AND TEMPLO LA VALENCIANA

Founded in 1557, this prosperous mine once produced 20% of the world's silver as well as a fair share of other minerals. Although its yield isn't as generous today, it remains Mexico's top producer: Each of the 48 current miners dig up 7,257–18,143 kilograms (8–20 tons) of silver a day. The mine is open for visitors daily 8–7 and admission is 30¢. Local kids will proudly explain the architecture and history of the mine, in Spanish, for a $1.50 tip. On the way to the Mina Valenciana you'll pass the **Templo La Valenciana** (also called Templo de San Cayetano; open Tues.–Sun. 9–7). Legend has it that the Spanish mine owner who promised St. Cayetano that he would build a church in the saint's honor if the mine proved profitable. Another version claims that the church's construction was motivated by guilt over all the indigenous people who died working in the mine. Either way, the templo's Churrigueresque (ultra baroque) exterior is nothing compared to the five gold-plated altars inside. *From Plaza Alhóndiga, on 5 de Mayo, take a VALENCIANA bus. Buses leave every ½ hr.*

MUSEO DE LA ALHONDIGA DE GRANADITAS

This massive stone edifice started life as a granary in the 18th century and has since seen its share of history. During the first major battle of the War of Independence, supporters of Spanish rule hid here while waiting for Royalist forces to arrive. The strategy backfired when a miner known as *El Pípila,* on orders from Father Miguel Hidalgo, set the granary's door ablaze, allowing the rebel fighters to swarm in and massacre almost all of the loyalists. When several rebel leaders (including Allende and Hidalgo) were later captured and decapitated, their heads were hung from large hooks on the exterior walls (you can still see the hooks). Later, under Emperor Maximilian, the building became a jail. Today it's a museum that houses several excellent exhibits on Guanajuato's history. Contemporary art is displayed on the lower level, and huge, colorful murals by José Chávez Morado grace the stairwells. *28 de Septiembre 7, tel. 473/2–11–12. Admission: $1.75; free on Sun. Open Tues.–Sat. 10–1:30 and 4–5:30, Sun. 10–2:30. Free guided tours in Spanish Tues.–Fri. 10–2.*

MUSEO DE LAS MOMIAS

About a century ago, greedy bureaucrats dug up the city's graveyards, leaving at rest only those whose descendants had paid burial-plot fees. As it turned out, special properties of Guanajuato's soil have a preservative effect, and the recovered bodies remained in excellent condition. The cadavers, remnants of hair and skin intact, were judged fit for display in a local museum, which now has 108 mummified bodies in various states of undress. If you speak Spanish, the guided tour is fascinating. *Esplanada del Panteón, tel. 473/2–06–39. Take MOMIAS bus to the end of the line. Admission: $2; small donation requested for tour. Open daily 9–6.*

MUSEO DE MINERALOGIA

An exquisite array of over 20,000 different mineral specimens awaits you at this impressive museum. The collection of rare minerals, including some found only in Guanajuato, will bedazzle any rock lover. *Ex-Hacienda de San Matías, tel. 473/2–38–64. Catch PRESA–SAN JAVIER bus from corner of 5 de Mayo and 28 de Septiembre and get off at Escuela de Minas campus. Admission free. Open weekdays 9–3.*

MUSEO ICONOGRAFICO DEL QUIJOTE

This shrine to Cervantes features hundreds of scenes from *Don Quixote* as depicted by various artists, including Dalí and José Chávez Morada. *Manuel Doblado 1, tel. 473/2–67–21. From Jardín de la Unión, 1½ blocks up Sopeña. Admission free. Open Tues.–Sat. 10–6:30, Sun. 10–3.*

MUSEO Y CASA DE DIEGO RIVERA

Muralist Diego Rivera was born in this redbrick house in 1886 and lived here until he was six. Now beautifully restored and reopened as a museum, it displays some original furnishings, including the bed in which Rivera and his twin brother (who died in infancy) were born. The upper floors contain an excellent selection of Rivera's art, spanning various periods of his life. Films (most in Spanish) are shown for free Tuesday and Saturday. During the Cervantes Festival special performances (admission $7) take place on the patio. *Calle de los Pocitos 47, near Plaza de la Paz, tel. 473/2–11–97. Admission: $1. Open Tues.–Sat. 10–6:30, Sun. 10–2:30.*

TEATRO JUAREZ

The late 19th-century Juárez Theater is one of the most impressive buildings in Guanajuato. The neoclassical exterior features Doric columns, bronze lions, and giant statues of the muses. Inside, walls hung with red and gold velvet and the ornate furnishings reflect Moorish and French influences. The theater now serves as the principal venue of the annual Cervantes Festival. Year round, classical music concerts ($2–$7) take place Thursday evening at 8:30. *Jardín de la Unión, tel. 473/2–01–83. Open Tues.–Sun. 9–1:45 and 5–7:45, later hours during performances.*

UNIVERSIDAD DE GUANAJUATO

Founded as a Jesuit seminary in 1732, this institution became a state university in 1945. Notices advertising lectures, films, art exhibits, and concerts are posted on bulletin boards everywhere, and on the right side of the main entrance is a small, free gallery with temporary exhibits of contemporary art. *Lascurain de Retana 5, near Basílica, tel. 473/2–01–74. Closed weekends.*

Next to the University is the **Templo de la Compañía** (Lascurain de Retana; open daily 8 AM–6 PM), an elaborate baroque cathedral left over from the university's Jesuit days. On the opposite side of the university is the **Museo del Pueblo** (Calle de Los Pocitos 7, tel. 473/2–29–90; open Tues.–Sat. 9:30–7, Sun. 10–2:30; admission $1), which displays contemporary art on the first floor and has a small collection of colonial art upstairs.

FESTIVALS

One of the finest festivals in all of Mexico takes place annually in Guanajuato. During the **Festival Internacional Cervantino** (International Cervantes Festival; mid-October) the entire city becomes one sprawling stage, where artists, musicians, and dance troupes from around the world gather to honor Miguel de Cervantes, author of *Don Quixote.* Contact the tourist office (*see* Visitor Information, *above*) for more information, and make hotel reservations far in advance.

> *For a strange, sweet treat, try momias—hard, mummy-shape sugarcane candies that are sold at Guanajuato's Museo de las Momias and at many candy shops around town.*

SHOPPING

Mercado Hidalgo (Juárez, between Cine Reforma and Jardín Reforma) occupies a turn-of-the-century building with elaborate iron grillwork and glass windows. The second level is crowded with vendors of souvenirs and ceramics. About ½ block away, **El Cubilete** (Juarez 188, tel. 473/2–59–34) sells an interesting array of sweets, including momias. The **government-run handicrafts shop** (Plaza del Agora, behind Jardín de la Unión) displays pottery and other handicrafts made in this region. You can observe craftsmen at work making the exquisite *majolica* pottery designed by Guanajuato's most famous contemporary artisan, **Gorky González,** at his workshop (tel. 473/2–01–52) on Pacitas, near the Parque de las Embajadoras. Pieces range from $5 to $2,000.

AFTER DARK

Guanajuato is lively at night, when crowds fill the streets. On weekends at Jardín de la Unión, locals of all ages gather on the steps of the Teatro Juárez to see the student group *Las Estudiantinas* perform. The group dresses in troubadour garb and strums traditional instruments; the audience sings along at the top of their lungs and then follows the Estudiantinas as they make their way through the streets. Both the Teatro Juárez and the **Teatro Principal** (Hidalgo, near Allende, tel. 473/2–15–23) regularly screen international films, in English and Spanish. **El Rincón del Beso** (Alonso 21-A, tel. 473/2–59–12; closed Sun.) is a dimly lit, intimate bar that features live Latin folk music. Before, during, and after the show, the crowd is encouraged to sing along and even display their own musical or poetic talents. Music usually starts at 10, but show up earlier if you want to get a good seat.

BARS AND CLUBS

Café Truco 7 (Calle del Truco 7, tel. 473/2–83–74) is a mellow, comfortable joint with big wooden tables, excellent background music, and good cappuccino. Though the atmosphere is best at night, you can also grab breakfast or a light lunch here for less than $5. At **La Dama de las Camelias** (Sopeña 32, east of Jardín de la Unión, no phone; closed Sun.), the walls are fancifully decorated with turn-of-the-century costumes. Be sure to ask the bar's owner about the history of the colonial window in the corner—it's his pride and joy. **Guanajuato Grill** (Alonso 4, no phone) is a club playing thumping Mexican and American pop music. By night's end the crowd is usually dancing on the tables. From Jardín de la Unión, go south on San Antonio, then right on Alonso.

OUTDOOR ACTIVITIES

The hills surrounding Guanajuato offer several pleasant short hikes guaranteed to get your heart rate up in no time. The hills of **La Presa de la Olla** are a 30-minute walk from town, but the hike is half the fun. From Jardín de la Unión, walk left on Sopeña to Sostens Rocha, which curves left and passes the shady **Jardín Embajadores.** Then follow Paseo Madero south as it curves into Paseo de la Presa, an area lined by elegant colonial mansions. Follow Paseo de la Presa past the well-groomed **Parque Florencio Antillon** and the Presa de San Renovato until, at last, you hit Presa de la Olla. A couple of food stands and restaurants are at the top. Camping, however, is not advised, as *Chupacabras* (mythical goat-sucking creatures) are rumored to stalk the area. A much shorter but equally strenuous hike leads up San Miguel hill to the **Monumento al Pípila** (open daily 9–8), which honors the miner responsible for setting fire to the door of the Alhóndiga de Granaditas (*see* Worth Seeing, *above*). After conquering the steep, 10-minute climb up the steps you'll be rewarded with a stupendous view of the city. From Jardín de la Unión, walk left on Sopeña about 1½ blocks, and turn right on Callejón del Calvario; look for the SUBITA AL PIPILA sign.

NEAR GUANAJUATO

DOLORES HIDALGO

The town of Dolores Hidalgo's principal claim to fame is the site where Father Miguel Hidalgo y Costilla issued his stirring *grito* (call) for independence on September 16, 1810. The events that led up to the speech began when Spanish forces were tipped off to Ignacio Allende's plans to overthrow the government. Doña Josefa Ortiz de Domínguez, the Querétaro magistrate's wife and a sympathizer to Allende's cause, risked imprisonment to warn a fellow conspirator of Allende, who in turn gave word to Father Miguel Hidalgo. That night, Hidalgo gathered his parishioners together on the steps of the town's main church and gave his famous "Grito de Dolores," a speech that became the rallying cry of those struggling for freedom from Spanish rule. The "Grito" was sounded at the **Parroquia de Nuestra Señora de los Dolores** (on the Plaza Principal; open daily 7–2 and 4–8), which has a lovely Churrigueresque facade and a simple, serene interior. Hidalgo's former house, the **Casa de Don Miguel Hidalgo** (Morelos, near Hidalgo; admission $1.75) is now a museum exhibiting documents from the independence movement, including the order for Hidalgo's excommunication from the church. The **Museo de la Independencia** (Zacatecas 6; admission 75¢) displays paintings depicting the struggle for independence as well as some local crafts. Both museums are open Tuesday–Saturday 10–5:45 and are free on Tuesday. This town is also known for the quality of its ceramic ware and tiles; a few shops offer bargain prices. Dolores is best visited as a day trip from either San Miguel de Allende (40 km/25 mi away) or Guanajuato (50 km/31 mi away). Flecha Amarilla buses leave every 20 minutes from the Central de Autobuses in each city.

LEON

When you think León, think shoes. Think leather goods, such as purses, belts, and jackets, and then start thinking about shoes again. León is a huge, fast-pace, smoggy, industrial city. The most attractive part of this metropolis is the **Zona Peatonal,** where centuries-old buildings, like the **Palacio del Gobierno** and the **Parroquia del Sagrario,** sit side by side with modern high rises and, yes, dozens of shoe stores. In this city, rarely frequented by tourists, you may find yourself the object of some incredulous stares, but León is definitely the place to find fantastic bargains on leather goods. Flecha Amarilla buses leave from Guanajuato's and San Miguel's Central de Autobuses roughly every 10 minutes. The trip takes about 2½ hours ($1).

POZOS

Established as a mining camp in 1576, Pozos saw its population drop from 10,000 to 500 after the mines were abandoned in the 19th century. These days it's something of a ghost town, a lonely place with buildings overrun by cacti. The opportunity to explore these deserted structures, coupled with the clean crisp air, is the principal reason to visit. The **museum** on Ocampo, one block up from the **Plaza Principal,** is staffed by friendly folks who like to talk about Pozos's famed reproductions of pre-Columbian instruments; these include the *palo de lluvia* (rain stick), a snake-shape instrument filled with beads that makes a sound like rushing water when turned upside down. The sticks represent the feathered serpent god Quetzalcoatl.

In an attempt to promote Pozos's colonial history, Teresa Martínez and Juan José Arroyo (the unofficial resident historians) have opened two hotels: the luxurious **Hotel Casa Mexicana** (tel. 468/8–25–98 ext. 119), which charges a whopping $40 per person, and the **Hidalgo Bed and Breakfast** (Hidalgo 15, 2 blocks from Plaza Principal, tel. 468/8–25–98 ext. 116), which offers five spacious rooms and a communal bathroom for $12 per person, breakfast included. You can camp in town for about $1–$2. Talk to Teresa or Juan José to arrange camping, hiking, or horseback riding. To reach Pozos, take a Flecha Amarilla bus from either Guanajuato or San Miguel de Allende to San Luis de La Paz (1½ hrs, $4). From there, hop on a city bus, take a taxi, or make arrangements with Teresa or Juan José for the 10-minute ride into Pozos.

MORELIA

Morelia, the capital of Michoacán state, has not paved over its colonial past. There are still, in this expanding city of about 1 million, dozens of gracefully arched walkways, foliage-studded courtyards, and well-preserved lofty stone buildings that date to the days of the Spaniards. But this city with a rich past is one that chooses to live jubilantly in the present. On its streets, Morelia has its share of crowds, traffic, and street vendors. At the markets, longhaired youths wearing Metallica T-shirts mingle with *campesinos* (rural dwellers) from surrounding villages, creating an unmistakable contrast. Plaza-side cafés and a progressive arts scene lend Morelia a cultured air. You'll see relatively few foreign tourists here: While it's a popular vacation spot for Mexicans, the city remains largely unknown to the rest of the world.

Guanajuato's name comes from the Tarascan word "Quanas-huato," roughly meaning "place of many frogs."

Founded in 1541 by the Spanish, who named it Valladolid, the city became the provincial capital in 1580. The city's name was changed to Morelia in 1828, in honor of José María Morelos y Pavón, born here in 1765. Unlike earlier revolutionaries who were of the middle class, Morelos was a mestizo serf, and his heroic deeds garnered him unprecedented support from the Mexcian people. Although Morelos's personal fight for Mexico's independence ended with his death, others heeded his call and labored until his dream was materialized. Monuments, streets, and museums commemorate the city's independence-minded namesake. Special events include Morelos's birthday on September 30 and **Aniversario de Morelia** on May 18, both of which entail parades and fireworks. **Feria Regional de Morelia**, during the first two weeks in May, features bullfights and regional dances.

BASICS

AMERICAN EXPRESS
Gran Turismo Viajes provides all services for cardholders, including emergency check cashing. Cardholder mail should be sent to the following address: Carmelinas 323, Las Américas, Morelia, Michoacán, CP 58270, México). *1st floor of Bancomer building, across from Gigante shopping center, tel. 43/12–27–70. From downtown, take* RUTA ROJA *1 combi west. Open weekdays 9–2 and 4–6, Sat. 10–2.*

BOOKSTORES
Bazar Ocampo is a dusty bookstore with a decent collection of used English books. (Don't despair: Hidden somewhere between *The Sensual Woman* and *The Sensual Man* are a few intellectually stimulating paperbacks.) Pay $1 for paperbacks or exchange yours at a two-for-one rate. *Melchor Ocampo 242, no phone. From Plaza de Armas, 1 block north on Juárez, left on Melchor Ocampo. Open daily 9–8; sometimes closed 2–4 on weekends.*

CASAS DE CAMBIO
Banks that change traveler's checks and cash are plentiful near the cathedral. **Banamex** (Madero Ote. 63, tel. 43/12–27–70; open weekdays 9–5) changes cash and traveler's checks and has an ATM that accepts Cirrus and Plus cards. For similar rates and better hours, visit **Casa de Cambio Majapara** (Pino Suárez 166, at 20 de Noviembre, tel. 43/13–23–46; open weekdays 8:30–6:30, Sat. 8:30–4).

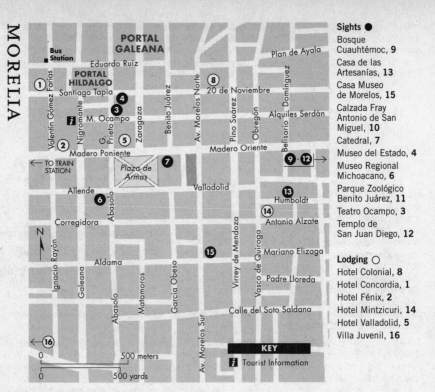

MORELIA

Sights ●

Bosque
Cuauhtémoc, **9**

Casa de las
Artesanías, **13**

Casa Museo
de Morelos, **15**

Calzada Fray
Antonio de San
Miguel, **10**

Catedral, **7**

Museo del Estado, **4**

Museo Regional
Michoacano, **6**

Parque Zoológico
Benito Juárez, **11**

Teatro Ocampo, **3**

Templo de
San Juan Diego, **12**

Lodging ○

Hotel Colonial, **8**

Hotel Concordia, **1**

Hotel Fénix, **2**

Hotel Mintzicuri, **14**

Hotel Valladolid, **5**

Villa Juvenil, **16**

KEY

🛈 Tourist Information

EMERGENCIES

Contact the **police** (Periférico Independencia 5000) at 43/16–32–60. For **ambulance** service, call the **Cruz Roja** (Ventura Puente 27) at 43/14–51–51.

MAIL

The full-service main post office will hold mail sent to you at the following address for up to 10 days: Lista de Correos, Morelia, Michoacán, CP 58001, México. *Madero Ote. 369, tel. 43/12–05–17. 3 blocks east of Plaza de Armas. Open weekdays 8–7, Sat. 9–1.*

MEDICAL AID

Hospital Memorial (Camelinas 2111, near the Social Security Clinic, tel. 15–10–47) offers 24-hour medical attention. **Farmacia Central** (tel. 43/13–67–94), at the west end of the bus station (*see* Coming and Going, *below*), is also open 24 hours.

PHONES

Make long-distance collect calls and send and receive faxes at either of **Computel**'s two central locations: one in the bus station (fax 43/13–92–81) and the other across the street from the cathedral (Portal Galeana 156, fax 43/13–62–56; open Mon.–Sat. 7 AM–10 PM). **Ladatel** phones are around the Plaza de Armas, and there are a few in working order at the post office (*see* Mail, *above*). Make collect calls at any phone by dialing 090 for the international operator.

SCHOOLS

At the **Departamento de Idiomas** of Universidad Michoacána de San Nicolás de Hidalgo, short-term Spanish language classes begin on the first day of every month. Fees are approximately $100 for one month. Semester-long courses in Purépecha (the indigenous regional language), Mexican literature, history, and philosophy are also offered. You don't have to be affiliated with the university to take advantage of their classes. For more details, contact Dr. Miguel García Silva at the Departamento de Idiomas,

UMSANH, Santiago Tapia 403, Col. Centro, Morelia, Michoacán, CP 58000, México, or call 43/16–71–01 between 8 AM and 2 PM.

VISITOR INFORMATION

Secretaría Estatal del Turismo is on the south side of Palacio Clavijero. Here you'll find a friendly staff ready to answer questions and dish out maps and information about upcoming cultural events. *Nigromante 79, tel. 43/12–80–81 or 800/4–50–23. Open weekdays 8–8, weekends 9–7.*

COMING AND GOING

BY BUS

Several bus lines pass through the busy **Central de Autobuses** (Eduardo Ruíz 526, 4 blocks NW of Plaza de Armas, tel. 43/12–56–64). **Flecha Amarilla** (tel. 43/13–55–89) takes the prize for most frequent departures and cheapest fares. Their buses travel to Guadalajara (5 hrs, $13), Mexico City (6 hrs, $13), and Uruapan (2 hrs, $5). **ETN** (tel. 43/13–41–37) has luxury buses with hourly service to Mexico City (4½ hrs, $16) as well as frequent departures for Guadalajara (3½ hrs, $18). The station itself is like a mini-city, offering long-distance telephone service, luggage storage (50¢ per 24 hrs), a post office, and a 24-hour pharmacy. To reach Plaza de Armas from the station, go left on Ruíz, then right (south) two blocks on Gómez Farías, and left on Madero. A taxi to downtown costs about $1.50.

For a mellow evening of people-watching and free local music, show up at Guanajuato's Jardín de la Unión on Thursday or Sunday evening around 7 PM.

BY CAR

Traveling to Mexico City via Super Carretera 15-D (304 km/188 mi, 3½ hrs), the tolls total $9–$11. It's well worth it: Road conditions are excellent and traffic is sparse. An alternative is the free Highway 15, which is rutted, heavily trafficked, and will add two hours of travel time. This is the "scenic route," though, and winds you through little villages and hills. To reach Guadalajara (367 km/228 mi, 4 hrs), take Highway 43 north for 27 km (16½ mi) and then head west on 15-D. West on Highway 14 will take you to Pátzcurao and Uruapan.

BY TRAIN

Morelia's train station lies 2 km (1 mi) west of town. The most comfortable way to get to or from the station is by taxi ($1.50), but the RUTA AZUL *pesero* (small bus) is also convenient. Trains depart daily at 10:30 PM for Mexico City (10 hrs; $5 first class, $2.50 second class). The train to Uruapan (4 hrs; $3 first class, $1.75 second class) leaves daily at 5:30 AM, with a second-class-only train at 5:30 PM. *Av. del Periodismo, tel. 43/16–39–12 or 43/16–39–65. Ticket office open daily 5 AM–6 AM and 10 PM–11 PM.*

GETTING AROUND

Most of Morelia's points of interest lie within a six-block radius of **Plaza de Armas** and the **Catedral.** Both are bordered on the north by the main avenue, **Madero,** called Madero Poniente to the west of the plaza and Madero Oriente to the east. Street names also change north and south of Madero and occasionally elsewhere without warning. Of the several nameplates posted on every street corner, the dark blue one usually corresponds to the name on your map.

BY BUS

You can catch 20¢ *combis* (VW vans) at the designated blue-and-white *parada* (bus stops)—or any street corner for that matter—by waving your hand at the driver. The colored strips on the VW bus are supposed to indicate its destination, though it's always wise to double-check with the driver.

BY CAR

Although downtown is usually thick with traffic, Morelia is fairly easy to navigate by car. As always, be alert for pedestrians and watch for narrow one-way streets that may (or may not) be marked by a black-and-white arrow. To rent a car, try **Budget Rent-A-Car** (Camelinas 2938, tel. 43/14–70–07).

WHERE TO SLEEP

If you've traveled to Morelia by bus and can't wait another minute to shower, you'll find a cluster of cheap hotels of dubious quality in front of the bus station. However, the better options are worth the four- to eight-block walk to Plaza de Armas. The tourist office provides a list of inexpensive hotels, but many of those are *hoteles de paso* (hotels that rent rooms by the hour). You're better off at any of the places listed below.

UNDER $10 • Hotel Colonial. Basic rooms with TVs are made more pleasant by their cleanliness, the friendly staff, and the immaculate central courtyard. Ask for a room away from the street; noisy cars and buses rumble by at all hours. Doubles cost $8.50. *20 de Noviembre 15, tel. 43/12–18–97. 25 rooms, all with bath. Luggage storage. Reservations advised. Cash only.*

Hotel Fénix. This hotel is popular with older Mexicans who leave their doors open to socialize. The rooms are not exactly loaded with amenities, but they're clean, cheap, and conveniently located a block from the Plaza de Armas. Street traffic can be annoying if your room is near the front. Rooms with private bath are $10 (double), and rooms without bath are $4. Hot water runs all day, and cheap breakfasts and lunches are served. *Madero Pte. 537, tel. 43/12–05–12. 30 rooms, 20 with bath. Cash only.*

UNDER $15 • Hotel Concordia. Rooms are spare and simply furnished, but the sheets are clean and the showers have hot water throughout the day. On weekends, Mexican families with young children frequent this spot and tend to rise (and wake others) early. Doubles cost $15. *Valentin Gomez Farias 328, tel. 43/12–30–53. 51 rooms, all with bath. Cash only.*

Hotel Mintzicuri. The two main attractions here are the hotel's sauna baths ($2) and the spectacular lobby murals. Rooms are smallish but clean and have TVs, phones, carpeting, and private baths. Doubles go for $12. This is the most luxury you'll get in Morelia for this price. *Vasco de Quiroga 227, tel. 43/12–05–90. 36 rooms, all with bath. Luggage storage, parking. Reservations advised.*

UNDER $20 • Hotel Valladolid. This hotel is immaculate, and most rooms have curtained balconies and handsome stone walls. It's surprisingly quiet despite its prime location on the Plaza de Armas, and the staff is so friendly you might not want to leave. Doubles cost $16 ($25 with TV). *Portal Hidalgo 245, tel. 43/12–46–63. 22 rooms, all with bath. Luggage storage.*

HOSTELS

Villa Juvenil. Serious budget travelers will like the Villa's low price ($3.75 per person), but you have to sleep in four-person, single-sex dorms, be in by 11 PM, and walk about 2 km (1 mi) or take the RUTA AMARILLA *combi* (VW van) to reach most of the attractions in town. The place is clean, the managers are young and hip, and there's a pool for guest use. Breakfast, lunch, and dinner each cost about $2. Sheets and towels are provided, and you get a 25% discount with a hostel card. *Chiapas 180, tel. 43/ 13–31–77. Inside Instituto Michoacáno de la Juventud y el Deporte; take Madero Pte. west to Cuautla, left 5 blocks to Oaxaca, right 4 blocks to Chiapas. 76 beds. Curfew 11 PM, reception open daily 7 AM– 11 PM. No age restrictions. Cash only.*

FOOD

Morelia teems with no-frills restaurants offering decent Mexican fare; most lie within a few blocks of Plaza de Armas. The farther you stray from the plaza, though, the cheaper the food: Stands on Gómez Farías, just outside the bus station, serve up the cheapest eats in town, with comidas corridas for just over $1. Several restaurants serve rich *sopa tarasca* (tomato and bean soup with tortillas, cheese, cream, and dried peppers), as well as other regional specialties. Sweet-toothed travelers should make a beeline for the **Mercado de Dulces** (Sweets Market), where you'll find *cocada* (coconut candy); the popular *morelianas* (condensed milk paste sandwiched between two *obleas,* or wafers); and *ate* (a chewy candy of guava, fig, or pear paste).

UNDER $5 • Cafédel Bosque. This 1960s-style restaurant looks tacky—it has floral carpeting and bright green booths—but the food is good. Morelia's university students favor Bosque's cheap sandwiches and burgers ($1.50), while specialties like pollo *moreliano* (with enchiladas, vegetables, and french fries) or *carne a la Mexicana* (beef grilled with onions, tomatoes, lemon juice, and served with salsa) cost a bit more. There's a small but pleasant terrace for outdoor dining. *Plaza Rebullones, at Acueducto, tel. 43/13-28-13. Cash only.*

Los Comensales. Here you can eat either indoors or outside, at an open-air courtyard filled with plants, flowers, and caged chirping birds. Specialties include pollo con mole and *paella* (Spanish-style, saffron-flavored rice with seafood, sausage, and chicken). The $3.50 comida corrida includes soup, pasta or rice, beans, an entrée, coffee or tea, and dessert. *Zaragoza 148, tel. 43/12–93–61. 2 blocks north of Plaza de Armas. Cash only.*

Restaurant Vegetariano Maná. Service is slow and indifferent, but the interior courtyard setting is bright and airy, and the price is right. Meatless comidas corridas cost $2, and an *energético* (fruit, yogurt, and granola) is 80¢. *Hidalgo 75, across from Casa Enrique, tel. 43/12–31–81. Cash only.*

UNDER $10 • El Rey Tacamba. This small restaurant near the cathedral serves only Michoacán specialties. The pollo moreliano ($5.25) comes with three enchiladas. Also good are *medallones en salsa chipotle* (beef fillet in chile sauce). *Portal Galeana 157, tel. 43/12–20–44. Cash only.*

CAFES

Hip young university students and families alike crowd **Café Catedral** (Portal Hidalgo 123, next to Hotel Casino, tel. 43/12–32–89) for its delicious $1.75 breakfasts. The café has a wide range of teas, like hibiscus and chamomile. On the second floor of the Teatro Ocampo, enormously popular **Café del Teatro** (Melchor Ocampo, at Prieto, no phone; open weekdays 8–3 and 5–10, Sat. 10–3 and 5–10, Sun. 5–10) is the best spot in town for a cup of coffee. Wood-beam ceilings and red velvet curtains will make you feel like you forgot your opera glasses. Grab a seat near the balcony overlooking the street and enjoy a cappuccino ($1) and dessert. Both cafés accept cash only.

Helados Torres, on Dolores Hidalgo's Plaza Principal, offers one-of-a-kind ice cream flavors like Corona beer, avocado, and even chicharrón (pork rind) for about 80¢ a cone.

WORTH SEEING

You don't have to look hard to find Morelia's downtown: Cars and pedestrians whiz through streets cluttered with racks of knockoff designer clothing, and buses loaded with passengers seem to stop at every corner. To catch up on what's happening in town, head to any newsstand for copies of the Spanish newspapers **La Voz** and **El Sol de Morelia**, both of which publish thorough listings of upcoming cultural events.

BOSQUE CUAUHTEMOC

Morelia's largest park, near an 18th-century aqueduct, provides a pleasant setting for a picnic. The park's free **Museo de Arte Contemporáneo** (Acueducto 18, tel. 43/12–54–04) exhibits contemporary art from all over Latin America, including works by Chilean painters and female graphic artists. *From Plaza de Armas, take any red combi (5 min, 20¢).*

CASA DE LAS ARTESANIAS

This former Francisan monastery houses a wide variety of handicrafts from all over Michoacán. The collection—from guitars to copper dishes—is varied and well-explained. Some pieces are available for purchase. The casa also provides workshops where you can watch artisans practicing their crafts. The adjacent **Museo de las Mascaras** contains more than 150 masks from throughout the state. *Ex-Convento de San Francisco, Humbolt and Fray Juan de San Miguel 129, tel. 43/12–12–48. Admission free. Open Mon.–Sat 10–3 and 5–8, Sun. 10–4:30.*

CASA MUSEO DE MORELOS

City namesake José María Morelos once owned this home then abandoned it to join the fight for independence. His life story is interesting, but unless you read Spanish you'll be restricted to simply admiring artifacts like Morelos's reading glasses. A collection of beautiful 19th-century carriages can be found in the courtyard. *Morelos Sur 323, tel. 43/13–26–51. Admission: $1.25, free Sun. Open daily 9–7.*

CATEDRAL

This 17th-century architectural marvel took more than 100 years to build. At more than 200 ft high, its bell towers are taller than those of any other church in Mexico. The cathedral's baroque exterior, however, gives way to a somewhat disappointing neoclassical interior, brightened only by warm rose- and gold-color ornamentation. Works of particular interest include a sculpture of Christ made from cane paste and a fantastic Churrigueresque (ultra-baroque) organ. *Open daily dawn–dusk.*

MUSEO DEL ESTADO

The Purépecha people once dominated almost all of Michoacán, as chronicled here via pre-Columbian artifacts. The Purépecha still populate the area, producing a wide range of handicrafts, some of which are on display. Other exhibits include artifacts from the independence movement and contemporary art. Especially worth a look is the section on Lake Pátzcuaro's fishing tradition. Explanations are in Spanish. *Prieto 176, tel. 43/13–06–29. Admission free. Open weekdays 9–2 and 4–8, weekends 9–2 and 4–7.*

MUSEO REGIONAL MICHOACANO

This museum traces the development of Michoacán from the beginning of the earth's creation to the present, bringing together a diverse collection of geological, archaeological, and artistic relics. The result is one of Morelia's more interesting museums. *Allende 305, near Abasalo, tel. 43/12–04–07. Admission free. Open Tues.–Sat. 9–2 and 4–6, Sun. 9–2:30.*

PARQUE ZOOLOGICO BENITO JUAREZ

Morelia's spacious zoo is one of the most enjoyable in Mexico, with picnic areas, a playground, a train, and a lake where you can rent boats. Eucalyptus-shaded trails wind past 89 animal species, most of which are being taunted by hordes of school kids. *Calzada Juárez, tel. 43/14–04–88. Take RUTA 1 combi and ask to be dropped off at the zoológico. Admission: 50¢. Open daily 10–5:30.*

CHEAP THRILLS

A pleasant way to spend the afternoon is to stroll to the aqueduct, a 15-minute walk down Madero Oriente from Plaza de Armas. Along the way you'll notice the famous **Tarascan Fountain**—a sculpture of robust bare-breasted women dutifully supporting huge baskets of fruit above their heads. The sculpture is a replica of the original, which mysteriously disappeared one night in 1940 and is rumored to currently reside somewhere in Spain. Continue your walk just beyond the aqueduct to **Calzada Fray Antonio de San Miguel,** a lovely tree-lined promenade. At the end of the Calzada, on Avenida Tata Vasco, you'll encounter one of the city's most beautiful churches, the **Templo de San Juan Diego.** In Morelia this is *the* place to get married, and ceremonies take place almost every Saturday. The walls inside the church are adorned with murals depicting the missionaries' arrival and the beginning of the Catholic conversion process. At the altar, San Juan Diego is faithfully kneeling, with his cloak of roses, in front of the Virgen de Guadalupe.

AFTER DARK

BARS AND DANCING

Morelia will not disappoint those who are seeking an evening of drinks and dancing. Most bars are open daily, but Thursday–Saturday nights are the liveliest. **Siglo XVIII** (García de León, at Turismo 20, tel. 43/24–07–47), a bar decorated in baroque style, is *the* hot spot in Morelia, so arrive before 10 PM to avoid waiting in line. There's a $10 cover Friday and Saturday, but women get in for half price. A popular disco, **Dali's** (Av. del Campestre 100, near Comercial Mexicana, tel. 43/15–55–14) has a good DJ, occasional live groups, and Salvador Dalí prints on the walls. Men pay $3 cover, but women get in free.

MUSIC AND THEATER

Morelia's Orquesta Sinfónica performs frequently in the **Teatro Ocampo** (corner of Melchor Ocampo and Prieto, tel. 43/12–37–34). The performance schedules change seasonally and prices average $6. They also feature *baile folklórico* (folk dancing) performances, as well as classic and contemporary dance. Contact the **Instituto Michoacáno de Cultura** (tel. 43/13–13–20 or 43/12–37–34) for more information.

At **La Casona del Teatro** (Aquiles Serdín 35, tel. 43/17–33–53), enjoy a cup of coffee, a glass of wine, or a light snack while watching a Spanish satire or comedy. Performances are Thursday–Saturday at 8:30 PM, Sunday at 7:30 PM. Admission is $3. The **Cantera Jardín** (Aldama 343, tel. 43/12–15–78) restaurant puts on dinner shows Thursday–Saturday at 9 PM. Programs and cover charges vary. For a night of chuckles (if you understand enough Spanish to get the jokes) check out **Corral de la Comedia** (Melchor Ocampo 239, tel. 43/12–13–74), which stages comedies Thursday–Saturday at 8:30 PM and Sunday at 7 PM. Cover is usually $3.50.

PATZCUARO

This cool, rainy city of 70,000 is the jewel of Michoacán state; bordered by a huge lake and green hills, it's a welcome sight for any traveler. Pátzcuaro's first inhabitants were the Purépecha, who justly named the area "Place of Stones." Much later, a string of Spaniards sojourned here, beginning with the unscrupulous Nuño de Guzmán. Guzmán, a member of Cortés's crew, created so much havoc in Pátzuaro that in 1536 Spain commissioned one Don Vasco de Quiroga to repair the damages. Don Vasco put a halt to the enslavement of the *indígenas* (indigenous people), chartered programs to educate them, and created industries that allowed the Purépecha to be self-sufficient; these deeds quickly earned him the endearing nickname *Tata* (Uncle) Vasco. Encouraged by Don Vasco, each village in Michoacán soon developed expertise in a specialized skill; the craftsmanship continues today and many fine goods can be found in the artesanía shops lining the streets of the city.

Despite its many charms this city has somehow avoided becoming another crowded tourist attraction, and few 20th-century intrusions mar its quaint colonial atmosphere. In keeping with an 18th-century mentality, most hotels enforce evening curfews and, with a few exceptions, the entire town goes to bed by 10 PM. You'll soon realize, though, that the reason you're in Pátzcuaro isn't for its nightlife, but for its convenience to the nearby lake region (about 3 km/2 mi from the town center). At **Lake Pátzcuaro** and the island of **Janitzio** (*see* Near Pátzcuaro, *below*), people of Purépechan descent still live.

Pátzcuaro's colonial charm is especially brilliant during festival time. If you find yourself here on **Día de los Muertos** (Day of the Dead; November 2), you'll see the town stay up past its bedtime for an all-night fiesta. Semana Santa is also a lively occasion, both in Pátzcuaro and in Tzintzuntzan (*see* Near Pátzcuaro, *below*). On Good Friday, locals reenact the Stations of the Cross, and on Holy Saturday they mourn Jesus' death with a candlelight procession. **Día de Nuestra Señora de la Salud** (Day of Our Lady of Health; December 8) honors the Virgin Mary with traditional Purépechan dances, including the *Baile de Los Viejitos* (dance of the old men).

BASICS

CASAS DE CAMBIO

Banamex (Portal Juárez 32, tel. 434/2–15–50; open weekdays 9–1) on Plaza Bocanegra changes cash and traveler's checks for good rates, which may explain the line. Half a block from the bank at Mendoza 16 is an ATM that accepts Cirrus, Plus, Visa, and MasterCard. **Casa de Cambio Multidivisas** (Padre Lloreda, at Buena Vista, tel. 434/2–33–83; open weekdays 9–6, Sat. 9–1) also changes cash and traveler's checks.

EMERGENCIES

Call the **police** at 434/2–00–04).

LAUNDRY

Lavandería Automática will wash, dry, and fold 3 kilos (6½ pounds) of your clothes for $2.50. Arrive early in the morning if you want same-day service. *Terán 16, tel. 434/2–39–39. 1½ blocks west of Plaza Quiroga. Open Mon.–Sat. 9–8.*

MAIL

The full-service post office will hold mail sent to you at the following address for up to 10 days: Lista de Correos, Administración de Correos, Pátzcuaro, Michoacán, CP 61600, México. *Álvaro Obregón 13, tel. 434/2–01–28. 1 block north of Plaza Bocanegra. Open weekdays 9–7, Sat. 9–1.*

MEDICAL AID

Clínica San Marco (Portal Hidalgo 80, tel. 434/2–19–98) provides 24–hour medical care. **Farmacia del Carmen** (corner of Romero and Navarrete, tel. 434/2–26–52) is a 24-hour pharmacy. Other pharmacies take turns handling the night shift; for current information check the billboard under Portal Hidalgo 1, on the west side of Plaza Quiroga.

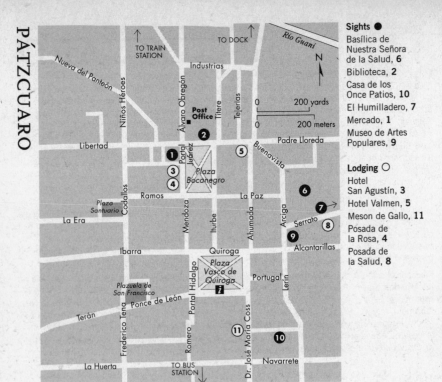

PÁTZCUARO

TO TRAIN STATION

TO DOCK

Río Guaní

N

Nueva del Panteón

Industrias

Niños Héroes

Álvaro Obregón

Post Office

Titere

Tejerias

0   200 yards

0   200 meters

Libertad

Padre Lloreda

①

Portal Juárez

②

⑤

Buenavista

③

Plaza Bocanegro

④

Ramos

Codallos

La Paz

⑥

Plaza Santuario

Mendoza

Iturbe

Ahumada

Arciga

⑦

La Era

Serrato

⑧

⑨

Ibarra

Quiroga

Alcantarillas

Portal Hidalgo

Plaza Vasco de Quiroga

Portugal

Lerín

Plazuela de San Francisco

Ponce de León

Frederico Tena

Romero

Dr. José María Coss

Terán

⑪

⑩

La Huerta

TO BUS STATION

Navarrete

Sights ●

Basílica de
Nuestra Señora
de la Salud, **6**

Biblioteca, **2**

Casa de los
Once Patios, **10**

El Humilladero, **7**

Mercado, **1**

Museo de Artes
Populares, **9**

Lodging ○

Hotel
San Agustín, **3**

Hotel Valmen, **5**

Meson de Gallo, **11**

Posada de
la Rosa, **4**

Posada de
la Salud, **8**

PHONES

Pátzcuaro's two main plazas, Bocanegra and Vasco de Quiroga, are surrounded by several casetas de larga distancia. **Hotel San Agustín** (*see* Where to Sleep, *below*) will let you place a collect call daily 8:30 AM–10 PM for a 75¢ fee. Your party can call back for the same price. Several **Ladatel** phones are in Plaza Vasco de Quiroga.

VISITOR INFORMATION

The staff at **Delegación Regional de Turismo** provides maps and attempts to answer questions. Ask to speak with Gerardo—he's a fountain of information. *Plaza Vasco de Quiroga 50–A, tel. 434/2–12–14. Open Mon.–Sat. 9–3 and 4–7, Sun. 9–3.*

COMING AND GOING

BY BUS

The **Central de Autobuses Pátzcuaro** (Libramiento Ignacio Zaragoza, tel. 434/2–16–18) is 1½ km (¾ mi) south of the town center. City buses (15¢) and vans (20¢) labeled CENTRO leave the station every five minutes or so, making stops at the town center and budget lodging area. **Autobuses del Occidente** (tel. 434/2–00–52) depart for Guadalajara (5 hrs, $11) daily at noon; Mexico City (5 hrs, $20) at 10:15 AM and 11:45 AM; and Morelia (1 hr, $2.25) every hour on the hour. **Autotransportes Galeana** (tel. 434/2–08–08) sends buses to Morelia (1 hr, $2.25) and Uruapan (1 hr, $2.25) approximately every 15 minutes. The station also has luggage storage (75¢ per bag per day), open 6 AM–10 PM and a caseta de larga distancia, open daily 7 AM–8:45 PM.

BY CAR

In town, traffic is minimal and street parking is relatively safe and abundant. The cautious car owner can pay $1.50 to park overnight at **Taurus**, a parking garage on Ahumada, a half block from Padre Floreda.

Leaving Pátzcuaro via Highway 14 takes you west to Morelia (56 km/35 mi) or east to Uruapan (62 km/38 mi). The four-lane road to Morelia is in excellent condition; to Uruapan it's much worse.

BY TRAIN

The **train station** (Paseo Lázaro Cárdenas, tel. 434/2–08–03) lies 3 km (2 mi) north of the town center, near the Janitzio boat docks. The train to Uruapan (2 hrs; $2 first class, $1 second class) leaves daily at 7 AM. The train to Mexico City (11 hrs; $1.25 first class, 45¢ 2nd class) leaves daily at 9:30 PM. First- and second-class service is available to Morelia (1½ hrs; $1.75 first class and 80¢ second class), leaving daily at 9:30 PM. The ticket office is open daily 7 AM–2 PM and 9 PM–10 PM. To reach the station from Plaza Bocanegro, take a bus or combi marked CENTRO-ESTACÍON LAGO (5 min, 20¢).

GETTING AROUND

You may have trouble finding street signs in Pátzcuaro—they're either high up on buildings or missing completely—but the central area is easily navigated. Minibuses (15¢) and vans (20¢) are convenient and frequent, and any local will point out where you can catch them. Most points of interest are within walking distance of the two main plazas: the small and busy **Plaza Bocanegra** (also called Plaza Chica), and **Plaza Vasco de Quiroga**, one block farther south. Streets change names at both plazas, and to add to the confusion, most businesses around Plaza Quiroga use *portal* (walkway) names instead of street names. Several blocks north of Plaza Bocanegra you'll find the train station, a few bars, the dock for boats to Janitzio, and a smattering of good seafood restaurants.

Every year during Carnaval (late February or early March), a group of Morelian musicians and dancers perform a bullfight reenactment called the "toritos de petate," with a fake bull and a man in drag.

WHERE TO SLEEP

Pátzcuaro's ritziest hotels line Plaza Vasco de Quiroga, while the slightly noisier Plaza Bocanegra offers many budget options. Many hotels in this quaint city impose a nightly curfew, usually around 10 PM.

UNDER $10 • Hotel San Agustín. Although this establishment lacks charm and can be a bit noisy, it wins praises for its tidy rooms and bathrooms, bright courtyard, ideal location, and low prices. Doubles cost $10. *Portal Juárez 27, on Plaza Bocanegra, tel. 434/2–04–42. 22 rooms, all with bath. No curfew. Cash only.*

Hotel Valmen. The main attraction at this modest hotel is its extremely friendly owner. Rooms are large and colorful (you have your choice of green or pink walls) and open onto a plant-filled courtyard. It's the best of the bargain hotels, but there's a 10 PM curfew. Doubles cost $9. *Padre Lloreda 34, at Ahumada, tel. 434/2–11–61. 16 rooms, all with bath. Luggage storage. Cash only.*

Posada de la Rosa. Only two doors down from Hotel San Agustín, this hotel is as quiet as it gets on Plaza Bocanegra. The clean rooms, some with amazingly mismatched bedcovers, suffice at $10 with private bath or $5.50 without. You'll need to bring your own toilet paper and towel. The curfew is 11 PM. *Portal Juárez 29, tel. 434/2–08–11. 12 rooms, 3 with bath. Cash only.*

UNDER $15 • Posada de la Salud. This cheerful establishment is priced a notch higher than the other budget hotels, but it's as sweet, quiet, and proper as the lady who runs it. Built in traditional Mexican style with a tile patio and a well-tended garden, it offers pleasant rooms with carved wooden furniture and large, clean bathrooms. Doubles cost $14. Curfew is 10 PM. *Serrato 9, tel. 434/2–00–58. 12 rooms, all with bath. Luggage storage. Cash only.*

UNDER $30 • Meson del Gallo. Located on a quiet side street near the Casa de los Once Patios (*see* Worth Seeing, *below*), this two-story hotel offers cozy, charmingly decorated modern rooms in a garden setting. All rooms have telephones. The patio is encircled by bougainvillea and fruit trees. Doubles cost $28, and suites (with small living room) are $30. *Dr. José María Coss 20, tel. 434/2–14–74. 20 rooms, all with bath. Luggage storage.*

FOOD

Pátzcuaro's restaurants serve many local specialties worth trying, including *pescado blanco* (whitefish); *charales* (tiny fish fried and served whole with lemon and chile); and *sopa tarasca* (bean soup garnished with cream, cheese, tortilla strips, chiles, and avocado). The best of the many fish restaurants are found near the lakefront. A huge open-air **market** operates daily on the west side of Plaza Bocanegra, with food stands open around the clock.

Travelers with a sweet tooth will want to stop by **Chocolate Joaquinita** (Enseñanza 38, tel. 434/2–45–14), where $3 buys a huge package of gritty but delicious homemade chocolate. The stands lining Plaza Vasco de Quiroga sell *helado de pasta,* a tasty, custardlike ice cream made from milk.

UNDER $3 • Hamburguesas y Tortas el Viejo Sam. If you're not a fan of seafood, you'll be happy to know there's a humble hamburger joint in town. Get 'em topped with cheese or ham for less than 75¢. Add french fries for 50¢. *Mendoza 15, no phone. ½ block south of Plaza Bocanegra. No breakfast. Cash only.*

UNDER $10 • Restaurante Hotel Posada La Basílica. The enormous windows here open onto an incredible view of Lake Pátzcuaro. Specialties include *caldo de pescado* (tomato-based fish consommé) and breaded trout ($4.50). Be prepared for a leisurely meal, as service is slow. *Arciga 6, tel. 434/2–11–08. From Plaza Bocanegra, east on Padre Lloreda, right on Buena Vista to Arciga. Closed Tues. Cash only.*

El Patio. The specialty at this low-key restaurant is a mouthwatering platter of pescado blanco (served with french fries, salsa, and vegetables; $7.50). At midday they serve a four-course comida corrida ($3.75). For a late-afternoon snack, opt for quesadillas with a side order of guacamole and a glass of locally made wine. *Plaza Vasco de Quiroga 19, tel. 434/2–04–84. Cash only.*

CAFES

Café de Flore. This charming Franco-Mexican enterprise serves delicious warm quiches (70¢) and tacos *al pastor* (filled with spicy roasted pork; 25¢ each). The friendly owner fusses over her French pastries—and gets great results. The café is especially popular with American and European tourists. *Portal Rayón 26, in front of the Basílica, tel. 434/2–19–46. Cash only.*

WORTH SEEING

Pátzcuaro's bustling *tianguis* (open-air market) is a good place to get a sense of the town. Here you'll find all kinds of fresh food, as well as vendors trafficking local handicrafts and cheap plastic toys. You can also get some good deals on handmade woolens, including sweaters, blankets, and serapes. The market stretches several blocks from the west side of Plaza Bocanegro. You can't miss it; there's always a giant crowd.

BASILICA DE NUESTRA SENORA DE LA SALUD

Two blocks east of Plaza Vasco de Quiroga is the Basílica de Nuestra Señora de la Salud, built atop a sacred Purépechan site by order of Don Vasco de Quiroga. (The Don is entombed near the basilica's entrance.) The most interesting artifact here is the **Virgen de la Salud** (Virgin of Health) made from cornhusk paste and orchid nectar. Walk behind the altar and you'll see a collection of *ex-votos,* or *milagros,* tiny silver charms that represent parts of the body and that are offered either in trust to become healed or in gratitude for a successful healing. The mass schedule is posted at the main entrance. *Open daily dawn–dusk.*

BIBLIOTECA GERTRUDIS BOCANEGRA

The public library is housed in the former Templo de San Agustín, which was founded in the 16th century. The present building dates from the 18th century. On the back wall is a phenomenal 1942 mural by Juan O'Gorman (one of Mexico's leading 20th-century muralists) illustrating the history of Mexico from pre-Columbian times to the Mexican revolution of 1910. *North side of Plaza Bocanegra. Open weekdays 9–2 and 4–6.*

LA CASA DE LOS ONCE PATIOS

Built in the 18th and 19th centuries by Dominican monks, this former convent was later broken up to make way for city streets, leaving only five of the original *once* (11) garden patios. Currently, it houses several craft shops. Come to watch the artisans in action and learn about their work. *Madrigal de las Altas Torres, 2 blocks from Plaza Quiroga. Open daily 10–2 and 4–8.*

EL HUMILLADERO

El Humilladero (The Place of Humiliation) is so named because it is where the Purépecha surrendered peacefully to the Spanish. Inside this Plateresque church is a stone cross with a 1553 carving of Christ. The church lies 3 km (2 mi) east of downtown on Calle Serato. Either make the 30-minute walk or catch a bus or van marked CRISTO from Plaza Bocanegra; they run 6 AM–9 PM and cost 50¢.

> *"Dying is nothing when you die for the Fatherland." –José María Morelos, 18th century Mexican revolutionary leader*

MUSEO DE ARTES POPULARES

This dilapidated edifice, which housed Colegio de San Nicolás in the 16th century, now functions as Pátzcuaro's crafts museum. On display are a variety of local wares, including ceramic dishes, intricately painted masks, and lacquered goods. In the back garden is a traditional Tarascan hut set on a 12th-century stone platform, the last remnant of the indigenous ceremonial center over which the basilica was erected. *Enseñanza, at Alcantarillas, tel. 434/2–10–29. 1 block east of Plaza Quiroga. Admission: $1.75, free Sun. Open Tues.–Sat. 9–7, Sun. 9–2:30.*

AFTER DARK

As you'd expect in a town where many hotels impose a 10 PM nightly curfew, Pátzcuaro is not famous for wild, dusk-til-dawn dance parties. If you're looking for a bar where you can relax and chat with other travelers, head to **El Campanario Video-Bar** (Portal Aldama 12, on Plaza Vasco de Quiroga, tel. 434/2–13–13). Take note: This relatively reputable establishment turns off the music videos at 10 PM to run an hour of tasteless American porn films.

NEAR PATZCUARO

JANITZIO

The indigenous Purépecha, who are practically the only inhabitants of the largest of Lake Pátzcuaro's five islands, call their isle *Xanichu.* The meaning of the name is disputed: Some claim it means "ear of corn," others argue it means "where it rains," and still others, "cornflower." During the rainy summer months there's no doubt which interpretation is most appropriate. The Purépecha are proud people who speak, write, and study in their native tongue. Many still fish the lake's waters as their forebears did, but their main source of income is from handicrafts sold to tourists. There are dozens of shops here to choose from.

Tecuena, Pacanda, and **Yunuen** are other islands on the lake, which also make worthwhile excursions. All are much less popular with tourists than Janitzio, lending them a completely different atmosphere. You can camp or sleep in a cabin on Pacanda by making advance reservations with **Instituto Nacional Indigena** (tel. 434/2–10–72). Cabins ($30 per night, double occupancy) are fully equipped with private bath, TV, hot water, and kitchenette. Transportation to the campsite is free.

COMING AND GOING

Boats run to and from Janitzio daily 8–5:30; the trip takes 20 minutes. Tickets can be purchased at the *taquilla* (ticket window) at Pátzcuaro's lakeside dock. Round-trip tickets cost $1.75 for Janitzio, $2 for the other islands. Boats leave whenever they're full, which might mean you'll have to wait. To reach the lakefront from downtown, go to the southwest corner of Plaza Bocanegro (Portal Juárez and Ramos) and catch a northbound bus or van marked LAGO. The last boats back to the mainland leave the islands around 5:30.

TZINTZUNTZAN

This tiny village, called "Place of Hummingbirds" in Purépechan, lies 18 km (11 mi) northeast of Pátzcuaro. Activities here include shopping, admiring the churches, or visiting the ruins, all of which you can accomplish in a single afternoon. In the center of town, next to the crafts market, is the 17th-century **Templo de San Francisco,** another of Vasco de Quiroga's legacies, with a newly redone, austere interior. The olive trees in the front courtyard, planted by Quiroga himself, still bear fruit. The **Templo de la Soledad** has its original facade and some elaborately clothed statues.

Roughly 1 km (½ mi) outside Tzintzuntzan are the crumbling remains of what used to be the Purépechan kingdom's religious and administrative capital, where Vasco de Quiroga based his evangelical mission. The huge ceremonial platform is topped with circular stone structures known as *yácatas,* which served as religious temples. There are no guides but a small museum offers information in Spanish about the Purépecha. To reach the ruins, walk back on the road to Pátzcuaro and turn left on a side road. You can't miss the ruins—they look like larger-than-life beehives. If in doubt, ask any villager for directions to the yácatas. *Museum admission: $1.50, free Sun. Open daily 10–5.*

COMING AND GOING

Autotransportes Galeana buses marked QUIROGA (½ hr, 75¢) leave Pátzcuaro's main bus terminal every 15 minutes, 6 AM–8:30 PM. Tell the driver to let you off at Tzintzuntzan's plaza. Return buses depart from the same plaza, with the last bus passing through around 8:30 PM.

URUAPAN

Situated near the center of Michoacán state, Uruapan is an unpleasant surprise for those expecting another picturesque town filled with well-preserved colonial architecture. With few exceptions, Uruapan—distinguished by blocks of dull modern buildings alongside older, unkempt colonial edifices—is difficult to appreciate. The city's only lure is its rich, natural surroundings and temperate climate: **Parque Nacional Eduardo Ruíz,** just blocks from the center of town, offers quiet retreat from city life. Other highlights include an excursion to the **Tzararacua** waterfall and a horseback ride to the inactive **Volcán Paricutín.**

Otomí and Chontal people took advantage of Uruapan's lush vegetation and free-flowing waters long before the Spanish arrived. When Father Juan de San Miguel showed up in 1531, he established a feudal *encomienda* system, reducing the indigenous peoples to serfs upon whose backs agrarian Uruapan grew and prospered. Today the town is known for its flower production; it's also the world's avocado capital, growing five different varieties of the divine fruit. Every November, the weeklong **Feria del Aguacate** (Avocado Fair) celebrates Urapan's fortunes. In fact, Uruapan finds some reason to break out the avocados and *charanda* (a local liquor) almost monthly. The biggest events include **Fiesta de San Pedro** (June 30), honoring the apostle Peter with a parade, band, indigenous dances, and lots of booze; **Fiesta de Santa María de Magdalena** (July 23), venerating the biblical saint with processions and dance performances reenacting battles between Moors and Christians; and **El Día de San Francisco** (October 4), commemorating Uruapan's patron saint with a dance by Purépechan women.

BASICS

CASAS DE CAMBIO

Banamex (Morelos, at Cupatitzio, tel. 452/3–92–90; open weekdays 9–5) changes traveler's checks and cash and has an ATM that accepts Cirrus and Plus cards. You can also change money and cash traveler's checks at **Divisas Tariacuri** (Portal Degollado 15, tel. 452/4–35–25; open weekdays 9–6, Sat. 9–2) on the east end of Jardín Morelos.

EMERGENCIES

To reach the **police** call 452/4–06–20. For **ambulance** service, call the Cruz Roja at 452/ 4–03–00.

LAUNDRY

Auto Servicio de Lavandería will wash, dry, and fold your laundry ($3 for 3 kilos, or 6½ pounds). They offer same-day service if you bring your clothes early in the morning. *Emiliano Carranza 47, at Jesús García, tel. 452/3–26–69. 6 blocks west of Jardín Morelos. Open Mon.–Sat. 9–2:30 and 4–8.*

MAIL

The full-service post office will hold mail sent to you at the following address for up to 10 days: Lista de Correos, Uruapan, Michoacán, CP 60001, México. *Reforma 13, tel. 452/3–56–30. From Jardín Morelos, walk 3 blocks south on Cupatitzio, left on Reforma. Open weekdays 8–7, Sat. 9–1.*

Handsome hand-carved wooden furniture is abundant in Michoacán state. The best time and place to buy is during the Tianguis Artesanal crafts festival, held in Pátzcuaro during the first week of November.

MEDICAL AID

Hospital Civil (La Quinta 6, tel. 452/4–80–40), in front of Parque Nacional, provides emergency service and a 24-hour pharmacy. The town's pharmacies rotate night hours on a monthly basis—ask any pharmacist to find out who's on duty.

PHONES

The caseta de larga distancia at **Restaurant Las Palmas** (Donato Guerra 2, tel. 452/3–34–41) charges a $1 connection fee for a collect call. **Ladatel** phones are a rare find, but there are some in working order south of the plaza, on the corner of Melchor Ocampo and Emiliano Carranza. Ladatel cards can be purchased at **Kodak Photo 30** (Portal Carrillo 14).

VISITOR INFORMATION

The **tourist office** provides maps and information on what to see and how to get there. *Ocampo 64, downstairs in Hotel Plaza, tel. 452/3–61–72. Open Mon.–Sat. 9–2 and 4–8, Sun. 10–2.*

COMING AND GOING

BY BUS

Several bus lines frequent the **Central de Autobuses de Uruapan.** One of the cheapest lines, **Flecha Amarilla** (tel. 452/4–39–82), sends buses to Guadalajara (2 per day; 6 hrs, $8.50), Mexico City (3 per day; 9 hrs, $16.50), Querétaro (3 per day; 6 hrs, $12), and San Luis Potosí (2 per day; 10 hrs, $17). The luxury line, **ETN** (tel. 452/3–86–08) takes passengers to Guadalajara (7 per day; 4½ hrs, $14), Mexico City (7 per day; 6 hrs, $25), and Morelia (2 per day; 2 hrs, $5). For short trips try **Ruta Paraíso** (tel. 452/4–33–50) or **Autotransportes Galeana** (tel. 452/4–33–50); both have service to Pátzcuaro every 15 minutes. To get downtown, take any bus marked CENTRO; on the return take a CENTRAL bus. A taxi to the center costs $1.50. *Carretera Pátzcuaro Km. 1, tel. 452/3–03–00. 3 km (2 mi) NE of Jardín Morelos. Caseta de larga distancia, luggage storage ($1.50 per day), pharmacy, post office, restaurant.*

BY CAR

The easiest way to reach Guadalajara from Uruapan is via the two-lane Highway 37 north to Super Carretera 15-D; just follow the signs. Tolls total $6 for the 159-km (99-mi), two-hour drive on 15-D. Traveling on the toll-free Highway 14 west will bring you first to Patzcuaro, then Morelia. Continue west to the 15-D west and you'll reach Mexico City.

BY TRAIN

The **train station** (Paseo Lázaro Cárdenas, at end of Av. Américas, tel. 452/4–09–81) lies 11 blocks south of the center of town. Buses marked CENTRO or 5A & PLAZA DE TOROS stop two blocks from the train station. A taxi directly to the station from downtown costs $1.50. Trains depart daily at 7:10 PM for Mexico City (12 hrs, $9 1st class), making stops at Pátzcuaro and Morelia. The ticket office is open daily 9–noon and 4–7.

GETTING AROUND

Although Uruapan is fairly large, as a tourist you're unlikely to stray far from three main areas: the bus station, **Jardín Morelos** (also known simply as "the plaza"), and the bars and clubs on Paseo Lázaro Cárdenas. Street names change as they cross the plaza, which makes navigating without a map confusing. To add to the chaos, streets immediately surrounding the Jardín often go by second portal names. The main street, bordering the plaza's southern side, is called **Emiliano Carranza** to the west and **Álvaro Obregón** to the east. Most buses (20¢) pass Jardín Morelos with routes or destinations written on their windshield. You'll have to take a taxi to sample the nightlife on Lázaro Cárdenas, since buses only run 6 AM–9 PM. Taxi fare is usually $1.50.

WHERE TO SLEEP

Most hotels immediately surrounding Jardín Morelos are way out of budget range. Fortunately, there are decent, inexpensive hotels within a short walk of the plaza. Tourism isn't big in Uruapan, so you shouldn't have trouble getting a room unless a festival is in full swing; in this case, reservations are advised. Camping is possible at Angahuan (*see* Near Uruapan, *below*).

UNDER $10 • Hotel del Parque. This place is popular with vacationing Mexican families. The basic, medium-size rooms are clean and airy, and you can watch TV in the lobby. While it's a seven-block walk to the city center, it's a stone's throw from Parque Nacional. Doubles cost $8.50. *Independencia 124, tel. 452/4–38–45. 14 rooms, all with bath. Parking. Cash only.*

Hotel Mi Solar. If spacious rooms, an indoor patio, and clean bathrooms with hot water do it for you, stay here. This establishment is popular with foreign travelers, making it a great place to exchange tales of life on the road. Doubles cost $8. *Juan Delgado 10, tel. 452/4–09–12. 2 blocks north of Jardín Morelos. 20 rooms, all with bath. Cash only.*

UNDER $20 • Hotel Regis. Tucked between busy storefronts, this hotel maintains a surprising degree of tranquility. Rooms ($20 doubles) feature tile or wood floors, and each has a decorative label on the door—from women's names to unidentifiable Tarascan nouns. A sunroof and comfortable hallway couches make this a bright and cheery place. *Portal Carrillo 12, near southern end of Jardín Morelos, tel. 452/3–58–44. 40 rooms, all with bath.*

FOOD

At the open-air **Mercado de Antojitos,** on the northeast side of Jardín Morelos, you'll have the opportunity to sample a variety of local dishes, including *churipos,* a hearty stew of chicken, pork, beef, veggies, and red chiles. Stands selling fruits, vegetables, tamales, fresh cheese, and grilled meats are open 24 hours and won't set you back more than $2.

UNDER $3 • Antojitos Yucatecos Cox-Hanal. You can eat your fill of Yucatecan cuisine here for less than $2. Try the *sopa de lima* (lime soup) or one of the many varieties of taquitos, and chase it down with a cold Montejo beer. *Emilio Carranza 37, no phone. 5 blocks west of Jardin Morelos. No breakfast. Closed Mon. Cash only.*

UNDER $5 • Boca del Río. This tiny joint overlooking Plaza La Ranita serves a *sopa de mariscos* (seafood soup) that is famous throughout the city. Another specialty is the ceviche (diced fish marinated in lime juice). *Juan Delgado 2, 1 block north of Jardín Morelos, tel. 452/3–02–03. Cash only.*

Comedor Vegetariano. Although not much to look at, this is the only vegetarian restaurant near the center that serves comidas corridas ($2). The tortas are delicious. *Corner of Morelos and Aldama, no phone. 2 blocks south and 1 block east of Jardín Morelos. Cash only.*

CAFES

Café La Lucha. Musicians often stop by to croon for a few pesos, making this homey café perfect for a leisurely afternoon. Tasty pies and pastries go well with La Lucha's café *de olla* (flavored with chocolate and cinnamon). *García Ortiz 20, tel. 452/4–03–75. ½ block north of Jardín Morelos. Cash only.*

Café Tradicional de Uruapan. The menu here features more than 20 teas and coffees, which you can customize with a scoop of ice cream or a shot of brandy. Light snacks include egg breakfasts ($2.50) and 50¢ tamales. *Carranza 5-B, no phone. ½ block west of Jardín Morelos. Cash only.*

WORTH SEEING

The best place to get a sense of Uruapan's hum and bustle is in **Jardín Morelos**. Though it's aesthetically uninspiring, the ice-cream vendors and frolicking children give the garden an air of liveliness. The open-air Mercado de Antojitos, at the plaza's northeast corner, offers bargains on everything from juice presses to jewelry. It's open daily dawn to dusk. For information on Uruapan's current diversions, including film and theater, contact **Casa de la Cultura** (García Ortiz 1, tel. 452/4–76–13).

DESTILADORA EL TARASCO

This distillery gives free tours in Spanish to those who want to know more about the local firewater, charanda. Here you can see the whole process, from the fermentation of sugarcane juice to its distilling and bottling. Naturally, tours end with free samples of charanda. Call beforehand to ensure that guides are available. *Carretera Terétan Km. 26, tel. 452/8–20–78. Catch a CALZONZIN pesero from the corner of Obregón and Miguel Silva. Open weekdays 9–2 and 4–7, Sat. 9–2.*

Pátzcuaro was the episcopal seat of Michoacán state until 1508, and its impressive colonial churches reflect the city's past ecclesiastical importance.

LA HUATAPERA

This large colonial structure, founded as a hospital by Father Juan de San Miguel, now functions as the **Museo Regional de Arte Popular**. You'll find artesanía from throughout the state displayed here. The patio out front is a popular gathering place for families and couples, who toss coins into the wishing well or chat on the moss-covered steps. On the museum's east is the **Templo de la Imaculada Concepción**; half a block to the west sits the **Templo de San Francisco**. Both have gorgeous cantera and Plateresque exteriors. *Museum tel. 452/4–34–34. North side of Jardín Morelos. Admission free. Museum open Tues.–Sun. 9:30–1:30 and 3:30–6. Churches open daily dawn–dusk.*

PARQUE NACIONAL EDUARDO RUIZ

This park is the best reason to visit Uruapan; you can lose yourself in the semitropical flora of Michoacán without stepping outside city limits. The west side of the park—where paved stone paths wind between streams, fountains, and waterfalls—offers the best scenery. English-speaking guides will happily tell you the legends behind the various fountains for $1.50. *Calzada La Quinta, at end of Independencia, 7 blocks west of Jardín Morelos. Admission: 20¢. Open daily 8–6.*

AFTER DARK

Paseo Lázaro Cárdenas and the nearby side streets are lined with bars that fill up on weekends. The crowd here is very young and party-minded, so join them at your own risk. **Euforia's** (Madrid 10, off Lázaro Cárdenas, tel. 452/4–12–86) is a video bar with all-you-can-drink Thursday nights ($7 for men, $1.50 for women). The disco **La Taberna** (Miguel Treviño, tel. 452/4–09–91) is in a 19th-century building that also houses a textile factory. Taberna plays a mix of American and Latin music and charges $3 cover for men, half price for women.

NEAR URUAPAN

PARACHO

The small indigenous town of Paracho is famous for its handcrafted guitars. Shops all over the state of Michoacán carry guitars, and all were made here. The town itself is of no particular interest—the "downtown" area basically consists of shops selling wooden crafts—but if you're a musician or are souvenir-shopping, Paracho merits a visit. Additionally, the town's weeklong **Feria Artesanal de la Guitarra** (late Aug.) attracts folkloric dance groups, *luthiers* (guitar makers), and the most talented guitarists from around Mexico. The tourist office in Uruapan (*see* Visitor Information, *above*) can provide more information about the festival. Buses to Paracho (45 min, $1.50) leave from Uruapan's Central de Autobuses approximately every half hour.

SAN JUAN PARANGARICUTIRO

The tiny village of **Angahuan**, off Highway 37 northwest of Uruapan, is nestled in the midst of green mountains. The town sees dozens of tourists daily during Semana Santa and the summer high season (June–August) but is far from being a tourist trap. Actually, it's just a clutch of wooden houses, a few dirt roads, and a handful of reserved residents. The reason to come here is to make hiking or horseback-riding arrangements at **Paradero Turístico de Angahuan** (opposite edge of town from the bus stop, tel. 452/5–03–83). The office rents cabins ($4 per person) and offers free camping facilities on site. It also rents horses ($4) for the trek to **San Juan Parangaricutiro,** a town buried by lava when Volcán Paricutín erupted in 1943. To hike the rugged 5-km (3-mi) trail, explore the ruins, and return before sunset, you'll need to start at dawn. Bring hiking essentials such as water, food, first-aid kit, and a buddy.

Once you arrive at San Juan Parangaricutiro, you'll have to clamber over twisted, moss-covered chunks of lava to see remnants of the buried town, including the top of a church. From your perch near the church you'll also be able to see Volcán Paricutín in the distance. You can also rent horses in Angahuan to make the longer journey to Paricutín itself; the six-hour round-trip trek should cost about $9 per person, guide included. From Uruapan's bus station, **Autotransportes Galeana** buses leave for Angahuan (1 hr, 50¢) every half hour. The last bus back to Uruapan leaves around 6 PM.

TZARARACUA

Ten kilometers (6 mi) south of Uruapan, on Highway 31, is the **Centro Turístico de Tzararacua**—the trailhead for a 2½-km (1½-mi) trek through a ravine to Tzararacua, a spectacular 142-ft waterfall and swimming hole surrounded by dense, tropical vegetation. You can rent horses ($3 round-trip) for the trip or set out down the long, rustic staircase on foot. This is the best day trip from Uruapan, though its popularity has resulted in a depressing amount of garbage strewn along the trail. **La Tzararacuita,** only 1 km (½ mi) away from the main waterfall, is smaller and cleaner. In addition to bringing food and water you'll need a guide if you plan to visit La Tzararacuita, since the trail is very poorly marked. To reach the trailhead, catch a TZARARACUA bus (50¢) from the south side of Jardín Morelos. Buses generally run every half hour, and the ride takes about 30 minutes. The last bus back leaves at 5:30 PM.

THE CENTRAL HIGHLANDS

UPDATED BY TRUDY BALCH

he states of Jalisco, Zacatecas, and Aguascalientes retain the flavors of their rich colonial history, with their winding cobblestone streets, classic *zócalos* (main plazas), and restored century-old mansions. The indigenous Huichol who live in the Central Highlands region, too, are concerned with preserving and maintaining the past—though old ways are quickly meshing with the new as local farmers and miners vie for service at the fax machine, and children watch MTV after a lesson in traditional dance. The people here have a strong sense of community and family, which even extends to travelers, especially international travelers, who seldom visit many parts of this fascinating territory. You'll find yourself welcomed here with honest, open hospitality.

The Central Highlands' historical significance and architectural splendor aren't its only attractions. Its cities tend to be rich in arts and culture, and as home to prestigious state universities many are also centers of intellectual discourse as well. Zacatecas city, like an oasis in a dry and nearly unpopulated terrain, is home to the works of 20th-century painter Francisco Goitia and the extensive international art collections of the Coronel brothers. Art assumes a more hands-on role in Aguascalientes city, a university town that's the perfect place to sample sculpture, painting, or *baile folklórico* (folk dancing); visitors are consistently greeted like long-lost relatives. Finally, Guadalajara, Mexico's second-largest city, is known as a bastion of traditional Mexican life: Here you'll have plenty of opportunities to enjoy mariachi music, dancing, and tequila.

ZACATECAS

Perched in hilly scrubland at an altitude of about 8,900 ft, the capital city of Zacatecas state is a charming maze of chaotic *adoquín* (paving stone) streets and alleyways, lined with beautiful colonial buildings and traversed by a Swiss-made *teleférico* (cable car). Much of its former wealth and glory is a product of nearby silver mines. The art museums here are fantastic, and the presence of a state university can make for lively weekend nights. Yet despite all these bonuses, relatively few foreign tourists visit the city.

OH, THAT MARIACHI MUSIC!

Around the world, mariachi music is probably the best known—and least respected—of Mexico's popular music. Mariachi music has been around since the 16th century, when Mexican bands started playing "son," a type of music originally from the Galicia region of northern Spain. At first, bands simply accompanied performers of popular dances such as the jarabe, but by the 19th century the musicians had gone solo. It wasn't until the modern age that blaring trumpets began to dominate the mariachi sound—commercial radio stations decided that raising the decibel level would make the music more popular.

Today, mariachi bands generally consist of two or more guitars, violins, the occasional harp, and, of course, trumpets. The typical tune thumps along at a rip-roaring pace, occasionally slowing down to draw tears from the listeners. Songs generally concern heartbreak, heavy drinking, and love for Mexico, and are punctuated by yelps and yodels from members of the band and the audience.

The musicians' mournful "ay-ay-ays" and their often-garish costumes lead many foreigners to regard the genre as tacky and trite. True, high-society Mexicans usually describe mariachi as "de pueblo" (lower-class), but most of them nevertheless know all the tunes by heart, and end up lustily singing along after a few shots of tequila. Sure enough, mariachi music sells, not only in the record stores, but also live, in places like Guadalajara's Plaza de los Mariachis or at El Parián in Tlaquepaque, where listeners will shell out up to $4 for a song.

Although indigenous people knew of the mineral riches of the area long before the conquistadors arrived, it was not until the Spanish forced the mining of local hills that the city of Zacatecas was founded. The first mining operations began in the mid-16th century, and by 1728 Zacatecan mines were producing one-fifth of the country's silver—a prosperity attested to by the extravagant old mansions that still line Zacatecas's streets. Silver mining tapered off during the fight for independence and declined even further during the Revolution, as political control of the area was hotly contested. Revered 19th-century statesman and politician Benito Juárez and his troops fought a decisive battle against local insurgents here in 1867, and Zacatecas was again the site of fighting in 1914, when Pancho Villa and his ragtag army routed 12,000 Huerta loyalists.

Despite the mining and fighting, Zacatecas remained a haven for intellectuals and artists, among them renowned 20th-century artists Francisco Goitia and Pedro Coronel, whose namesake museums are world famous. Other well-preserved Zacatecan cultural treasures include a stone aqueduct, colonial churches and haciendas, and one of the finest examples of colonial baroque architecture in all of Mexico, the **Catedral Basílica Menor.** Though currently home to a population of over 40,000, Zacatecas maintains a small-town attitude: Don't expect to do much here between 2 and 5 in the afternoon, when all the downtown businesses shut down for lunch. Straw hats and cowboy boots are almost mandatory gear for men of all ages, and solo women tend to disappear from the streets after 9 PM, while the student population takes over the cafés and plazas around the city.

BASICS

AMERICAN EXPRESS

Viajes Mazzocco, the AmEx representative, offers the usual services for cardholders, including emergency check-cashing and cardholder mail. *Enlace 115, Colonia Sierra de Alica, Zacatecas, Zacatecas, CP 98050, México, tel. 492/2–08–59. From cathedral, west on Hidalgo (which becomes Ortega), right on Enrique Estrada just before the aqueduct, left on Enlace after the Museo Goitia. Open weekdays 9–7, Sat. 9–2.*

CASAS DE CAMBIO

Banamex (Hidalgo 132, tel. 492/2–09–31; open weekdays 9–3) changes traveler's checks and currency and has an ATM that accepts MasterCard, Visa, Cirrus, and Plus cards. **San Luis Divisa** (Independencia 82, across from Jardín Independencia, tel. 492/4–33–24; open weekdays 9–6:30, Sat. 9–3) has better rates than the banks and also changes traveler's checks.

EMERGENCIES

In an emergency, dial the **police** at 492/2–01–80; for **ambulance** service call the Cruz Roja (tel. 492/2–30–05 or 492/2–33–23). Call the city's **toll-free tourist line** (tel. 91–800/9–03–92) for bilingual assistance with medical or legal problems.

LAUNDRY

Lavandería Indio Triste (Juan de Tolosa 826, no phone; open Mon.–Sat. 9–3 and 4–9), north of the zócalo, will dry and fold 1 kilo (2 pounds) of clothes for 75¢. Bring your load in before noon to get it back the same day. Just a few blocks northeast of Hotel Río Grande, **Lavandería Rosa Blanca** (López Mateos 129, tel. 492/2–97–80; open weekdays 8:30–7, Sat. 8:30–5) charges $1.35 to wash and dry 1 kilo (2 pounds) of clothes.

MEDICAL AID

The 24-hour **Clínica Hospital Santa Elena** (Guerrero 143, tel. 492/2–68–61) has English-speaking doctors on staff. For less urgent medical problems, visit the 24-hour **Farmacia ISSSTE-Zac** (Dr. Hierro 512, tel. 492/2–88–89). **Clínica Dental Zacatecas** (5 Señores 125, tel. 492/2–68–03; open weekdays 9:30–2 and 4–8, Sat. 10–2) offers free dental exams.

PHONES AND MAIL

The **post office** (Allende 111, tel. 492/2–01–96; open weekdays 8–7, Sat. 9–1) will hold mail sent to you at the following address for up to 10 days: Lista de Correos, Zacatecas, CP 98001, México. For collect calls, use the **Ladatel** phones near the cathedral. You can also make international calls from the *caseta de larga distancia* (long-distance telephone office; Callejón de Cuevas 103) in the *centro*. It's open weekdays 9–9, Saturday 9–2 and 4–8.

VISITOR INFORMATION

The **Módulo de Información de Turismo** (Hidalgo 93, no phone; open daily 10–2 and 4–8) has an English-speaking staff that doles out plenty of brochures, a great street map, and even computerized information. Ask for *Tips*, an English-language monthly calendar of cultural events and activities. For information by phone, contact their head office (tel. 492/4–05–52 or 492/4–03–93). There's also a small tourist office at the Central Camionera (*see* By Bus, *below*).

COMING AND GOING

BY BUS

The **Central Camionera** (Terrenos de la Isabélica 1) is on the western edge of town, and the RUTA 8 bus (20¢) runs from here to downtown and back from 6 AM until 10 PM. A taxi ride to the downtown area costs about $2. **Estrella Blanca** (tel. 492/2–06–84) first-class buses depart hourly for Aguascalientes (2 hrs, $5), Durango (4½ hrs, $11), Guadalajara (5½ hrs, $13.50), Mexico City (8 hrs, $24), and San Luis Potosí (3 hrs, $6.25). **Omnibus de México** (tel. 492/2–54–95) first-class buses travel to the above destinations, and a bus to Guanajuato (5½ hrs, $11) departs daily at 5:30 AM. The terminal offers luggage storage (50¢ per 3 hrs; open daily 7 AM–10 PM) and has a caseta de larga distancia.

BY CAR

Head north on Highway 54 to reach Monterrey (457 km/283 mi), south to reach Guadalajara (319 km/198 mi). To reach Mexico City (616 km/382 mi), take Highway 49 east through San Luis Potosí (191 km/118 mi) and continue south on Autopista 57, which passes Querétaro (203 km/126 mi) en route to Mexico City.

BY TRAIN

The **train station** (tel. 492/2–02–95) is just off González Ortega, south of downtown. Buses marked FERR stop near the terminal, but a taxi ride from downtown costs only $1.50. The daily northbound, first-class train to Chihuahua (17 hrs, $20) and Ciudad Juárez (22 hrs, $23) leaves at 9:50 AM. There are two daily southbound trains: The first-class train departs at 8:10 PM and the second-class train pulls out at 4:55 AM, making stops at Aguascalientes (3 hrs; $3 1st class, $1.75 2nd class) and Mexico City (15 hrs, $18 1st class only). Keep in mind that the second-class train is usually late and takes hours longer than the first-class one. Buy second-class tickets on the train; the ticket office for first-class tickets opens one hour prior to departure.

GETTING AROUND

It's easy to get lost in Zacatecas: The town is hilly, and there are many side streets, *callejones* (alleyways), and winding thoroughfares. Adding to the confusion, many main streets change names once or more. Fortunately, everything you could want to see is in or near downtown. From the north, the main thoroughfare, Juan de Tolosa, joins with Hidalgo and passes the **Catedral Basílica Menor**—the heart of the town and an easily visible landmark. As Juan de Tolosa continues south, it becomes González Ortega, which passes the **aqueduct**. Just to the east of and almost parallel to Juan de Tolosa is another busy street, Tacuba, lined with shops and restaurants. López Mateos, a street with many *talleres* (car-repair shops) and some budget hotels, passes through the southeast corner of Zacatecas, several blocks from the city's center. A good way to get a sense of the city's layout is to take a ride on its famous teleférico, which runs between hilltops on either side of the city; *see* Worth Seeing, *below*.

WHERE TO SLEEP

López Mateos, where many budget hotels are located, is an entertaining five-minute walk from downtown—speeding buses fill the streets and candy vendors crowd the narrow sidewalks. To reach López Mateos from the center, walk south on Tacuba (which becomes Aldama), and turn left on Ventura Salazar.

UNDER $15 • Hotel Gami. This fairly new, three-story hotel is a great place to meet other foreign travelers. The large rooms have new carpeting, TVs, and small, clean bathrooms. Doubles run $11. *López Mateos 309, tel. 492/2–80–05. 3 blocks east of the pedestrian bridge on López Mateos. 60 rooms, all with bath. Cash only.*

Hotel Río Grande. Rooms in this three-story hotel overlook either a central courtyard or the city. Medium-size rooms are bare but immaculate, with tile floors, comfortable beds, and 24-hour hot water. The place is popular with backpackers and vacationing Mexican families, all attracted by the great rates: Doubles run $9. *Calz. de la Paz 513, tel. 492/2–98–76. From the pedestrian bridge on López Mateos at Salazar, turn onto Calz. de la Paz; a HOTEL sign directs you up the hill. 64 rooms, all with bath. Cash only.*

UNDER $20 • La Condesa. A spacious, pastel-color entranceway and a smiling staff greet you, while large rooms with tile floors, clean bathrooms, and comfortable beds await upstairs. Some rooms have TVs and telephones. Many open to a communal patio, and though it may seem peaceful, the many Mexican families here can create quite a racket. The central location is a plus. Doubles cost $16. *Juárez 5, near Plaza Independencia, tel. 492/2–11–60. 61 rooms, all with bath. Laundry. Cash only.*

HOSTELS

The **Turismo Juvenil Villas** is nestled in a rural, almost woodsy, setting a few kilometers east of downtown. Soccer, basketball, and volleyball courts are available. Beds in the single-sex dorms cost a mere $3.50 per night. Lockout hours are 11 PM–7 AM, but you can make arrangements with the management if you plan to stay out later. The crowd here is mostly Mexican travelers in their 20s and 30s, though all ages are welcome. *Tel. 492/2–18–91 or 492/2–02–23. Take RUTA 8 bus from González Ortega or from Central Camionera; get off at Celaya (near railroad station and Pemex offices) and walk past the big orange-and-yellow building (you can't miss it); the hostel is next to Parque La Encantada. 70 beds. Reception open daily 7 AM–11 PM. Kitchen. Cash only.*

FOOD

Zacatecan restaurants cater to a wide variety of tastes, offering everything from Greek to Italian to Chinese cuisine. You also have a range of regional dessert specialties to sample, including *queso de tuna* (a hard, dark-brown candy made from prickly pears, available in July and August), *dulce de leche* (a milk candy that's so sweet it hurts your teeth), and *dulce de guayaba* (a candy made from guava fruit). Around Easter you can buy *capirotada* (bread pudding with raisins and cinnamon) and *melcocha* (multicolor sugar candy).

UNDER $5 • Restaurant Camino Real. This nondescript little eatery has all the right ingredients—it's clean, it's cheap, the food is great, and the service is efficient. Let the smiling owner bring you his specialty *carne becerra* (pork meat boiled, fried, and then sautéed in tomato, chile, and garlic sauce). Breakfasts go for $2. *López Mateos 420, ½ block south of pedestrian bridge, tel. 492/2-06-91. Cash only.*

Taquería y Rosticería La Única. La Única's clean, wood-panel dining area is behind a grill filled with roasting chickens and sizzling meats. A big plate of chicken, refried beans, salad, homemade potato chips, tortillas, and all the salsa and *rajas* (chile strips) you can eat is a steal at $2. Tacos ($1.50 for five) come in all flavors, from carne asada to *sesos* (brains) and *lengua* (tongue). *Aldama 243–245, tel. 492/2-57-75. From cathedral, SW on Hidalgo, left on Juárez to Aldama (also called Zamora). Cash only.*

UNDER $10 • La Cantera Musical. Local families and tourists come here for the good food, excellent taped mariachi music, and amusing mini-reproduction of the city's famous teleférico strung across the ceiling. The biggest seller is the *asado de Boda Jerezano* (pork with chiles, orange, and bay leaves, served with rice). The *platillo ranchero* ($5.50), a selection of appetizers such as quesadillas, *chicharrón* (pork rind), and guacamole, is perfect for two. *Tacuba T–2, tel. 492/2-88-28. Below Mercado González Ortega.*

El Dragón de Oro. The Golden Dragon serves Chinese food accompanied by jazz and country-and-western music. Standards like wonton soup, *sopa fu chuc* (a tofu and noodle soup), and *pollo almendrado* (almond chicken) are on the menu. Vegetarians will rejoice over the generous plate of chop suey, which could easily fill two. *Juárez, across from La Condesa Hotel, no phone. From the cathedral, SW on Hidalgo, left on Juárez to Plaza Independencia. No breakfast.*

WORTH SEEING

There's no way to see all of sprawling Zacatecas in a single day. Rather, allow yourself a full day for each area of town: the southwest (the aqueduct, Enrique Estrada park, and the Goitia museum); hilltop sights (the Mina el Edén, Cerro de la Bufa, and Teleférico); and the town center (the two Coronel museums, the cathedral, the Palacio del Gobierno, and the Museo Zacatecano). The free English-language weekly *Tips* has information on upcoming shows, concerts, and exhibits; it's available at the tourist office (*see* Visitor Information, *above*).

ACUEDUCTO DEL CUBO

This colonial aqueduct, with 39 high arches constructed of magnificent *cantera rosa* (pink quarry stone), is a strange and beautiful sight in the middle of the city. Just behind the aqueduct is the **Plaza de Toros,** Mexico's oldest bullring, which has been refashioned into the incredibly luxurious **Quinta Real Hotel** (tel. 492/2-91-04), where doubles are over $100 a night. The hotel bar is in the former bull pens, and a café occupies the spectator area. Across the street is **Parque Enrique Estrada** (not named in honor of the hunk from *CHiPs*), a gorgeous, lush park which has fountains, a waterfall, lots of strolling couples, and the Museo Francisco Goitia (*see below*). *From the cathedral, SW on Hidalgo (which becomes Ortega) for about 10 blocks.*

CATEDRAL BASILICA MENOR

The most imposing structure in Zacatecas is the **Catedral Basilica Menor** (corner Hidalgo and Aguascalientes, next to Plaza de Armas; open daily 8–2 and 4–8). It was built between 1612 and 1752, and the recently refurbished interior is as powerful in its neoclassical simplicity as the baroque exterior is in its dizzying complexity. Adjacent to the cathedral is the 1727 **Palacio de Gobierno** (Hidalgo 602; open weekdays 8–8), originally the mansion of a local silver baron. Inside you'll find a brilliant mural of Zacatecas's history painted in 1970 by the noted Zacatecan artist Antonio Pintor Rodríguez. Just down the street is the state-operated **Teatro Calderón** (Hidalgo 501, tel. 492/2-86-20). Built in the late 19th century, the theater flaunts beautiful stained-glass windows and is the venue for visiting national and international ballets, operas, and plays; check *Tips* for current schedules. Tickets run $2–$10, and the box office is open during performances only, daily 10–2 and 4–8.

CERRO DE LA BUFA

Atop the rugged Cerro de la Bufa—a hill thought by thirsty Spaniards to resemble a *bufa* (wineskin)—Pancho Villa defeated forces loyal to the dictator Victoriano Huerta in 1914. Beside being an important historic site, the mountain offers magnificent views of Zacatecas and the surrounding countryside. You can reach the top by a strenuous half-hour hike or take the Teleférico (*see below*), then explore the **Museo de la Toma de Zacatecas** (tel. 492/2–80–66; open Tues.–Sun. 10–4:30; admission $1), a museum with photographs, clothing, guns, and a cannon, all dating from Villa's victory. Adjacent to the museum is **La Capilla de la Virgen del Patrocinio,** an 18th-century chapel honoring the patroness of Zacatecas. Behind the chapel is a small mausoleum, the **Mausoleo a los Hombres Ilustres de Zacatecas.** Both the chapel and mausoleum are free and open daily 9–6. *SW on Hidalgo to Callejón Luis Moya, right on Calle de la Mantequilla, then left and up, up, and up, across the road to the path.*

EL MINA EDEN

The mine that supplied most of Zacatecas's silver from 1586 until 1964 is now a star tourist attraction with a macabre history. During peak production in the 1600s an average of eight slaves died each day in these dark, slippery tunnels. Conditions changed somewhat after independence and again with the Revolution, but mining continued (without electricity) until 1964, when incorrectly placed explosives caused the lower levels to flood. The mine's entrance is a vigorous 20-minute walk straight up Juárez, past the huge red IMSS hospital. From there you'll ride in a tiny mining train down into the underground tunnels (bring a sweater to combat the chill). The tour (45 min, $2) of the tunnels, though conducted in Spanish, is worthwhile. The mine is also now home to a disco (*see* After Dark, *below*). *Mina el Edén, tel. 492/2–30–02. From cathedral, SW on Hidalgo 4 blocks, right on Juárez (which becomes Torreón), and turn right after hospital. Open daily 11–6:30.*

MUSEO FRANCISCO GOITIA

This French-style mansion was built in 1948 for the governor of Zacatecas state, but now houses works by modern artists such as Pedro Coronel and his brother Rafael Coronel, plus an impressive collection of paintings by the 20th-century Zacatecan artist Francisco Goitia. Sadly, Goitia's most famous work, *Tata Jesucristo,* is in Mexico City, but an excellent reproduction is on display here. The museum's grounds overflow with well-tended flower beds and graceful fountains. *Enrique Estrada 102, tel. 492/2–02–11. From the cathedral, walk 6 blocks SW on Hidalgo, right on Miguel M. Ponce; the museum is just past the park. Admission: $1.50. Open Tues.–Sat. 10–1:30 and 5–7:30, Sun. 10–4:30.*

MUSEO PEDRO CORONEL

Zacatecas's favorite son, artist and sculptor Pedro Coronel, was also a collector with impeccable taste. This museum displays his own works together with some of his acquisitions: masterpieces by Goya, Miró, Cocteau, Kandinsky, Motherwell, Picasso, Chagall, and Dalí; ancient Greek pottery and statues; Indian, Chinese, Tibetan, and Japanese sculpture and artifacts; and a large collection of African and Latin American masks. Allow plenty of time to take it all in. *Plaza de Santo Domingo, at Fernando Villalpando, tel. 492/2–80–21. From the cathedral, walk 2 blocks west. Admission: $1.50. Open Mon.–Wed., Fri., and Sat. 10–2 and 4–7, Sun. 10–2 and 3–5.*

MUSEO RAFAEL CORONEL

One of the best museums in Mexico is known locally as **Museo de las Máscaras** (Museum of the Masks). It's formally named for Pedro Coronel's brother Rafael, who was also an artist, and is housed in an 18th-century former convent. The grounds are beautiful in their own right, while the collection of fanciful human and animal masks—some 3,700, used in regional festivals all over Mexico—is utterly astounding. *Off Vergel Nuevo, between Chaveño and Garcia Salinas, tel. 492/2–81–16. From the cathedral, NE on Hidalgo (which becomes Juan de Tolosa) and left at the fountain. Admission: $1.50. Open Mon., Tues., and Thurs.–Sat. 10–2 and 4–7, Sun. 10–5.*

MUSEO ZACATECANO

Time-worn colonial paintings and altarpieces contrast with vividly colored Huichol yarn tapestries, all displayed in the historic Antigua Casa de la Moneda, a 19th-century pink-stone building that once housed the Zacatecas mint. Also on display are photographs of the Huichol, a fiercely independent indigenous group (*see box, below*). *Dr. Hierro 301, tel. 492/2–65–80. From the cathedral, SW on Hidalgo to San Agustín; turn left and walk 1 block to Hierro. Admission: $1.35. Open Wed.–Mon. 10–5.*

TELEFERICO

This Swiss-made cable car offers unparalleled views of Zacatecas. It runs from Cerro de la Bufa (*see above*) on the east side of town to Cerro del Grillo (Cricket Hill) on the west. The ride is best combined with the Mina el Edén tour (*see above*), since at the end of the tour you have the option of taking an elevator to the top of Cerro del Grillo. Otherwise, you'll have to climb a steep flight of stairs next to the mine entrance, or make the even steeper trek up Cerro de la Bufa. The 10-minute ride costs $1.50 each way. *Cable car operates Tues.–Sun. 10–6:30, weather permitting. To reach Cerro del Grillo station from town center, NE on Villalpando (which becomes Genaro Codina) and west on Callejón de García Rojas.*

AFTER DARK

Zacatecas is best on weekend nights, when a half dozen discos roar to life with the latest dance mixes. **El Elefante Blanco** (The White Elephant; Paseo Díaz Ordaz 2, tel. 492/2–71–04; closed Sun.–Wed.), near the Cerro del Grillo teleférico station, offers great views of the Zacatecas skyline. **La Marcha** (Dr. Hierro 409, tel. 492/2–03–89; closed Sun.–Tues.) is popular with a young and wealthy local crowd. **El Malacate** (tel. 492/2–30–02 or 2–37–27; closed Mon.–Wed.), also known as La Mina, is deep in the Mina El Edén (*see* Worth Seeing, *above*). It's a gimmicky, touristy place where drinks cost $2. Cover at all three discos is $5. One low-key, high-culture option in this college town of bars and clubs is the video center at the **Biblioteca Mauricio Magdaleno,** across from Plaza Independencia. It has nightly screenings of Mexican films and dubbed or subtitled foreign films.

AGUASCALIENTES

A large and expanding industrial city, Aguascalientes, capital of the state of the same name, may disappoint those expecting the charming historical details of other highland destinations. This city is a tangle of pastel-color modern buildings and neon signs, with the occasional colonial building scattered here and there. But although Augascalientes rates low on the aesthetic scale, and the *aguas calientes* (thermal waters) that originally attracted colonists to the region have all been paved over, the city has a proud, continuing tradition as a fine arts stronghold.

The main reason to come to Aguascalientes is to visit the museums displaying works by famous Mexican artists Saturnino Herrán, Jesús Contreras, and Enrique Díaz de León. The city is also home to a state university, which means you'll find plenty of young, sociable students, most of whom are extremely friendly and curious about foreign visitors. In fact, Aguascalientes is so devoid of tourists that people bend over backwards to lend a hand—a welcome reception for the world-weary traveler. One of the best times to visit is during the **Feria de San Marcos,** a monthlong festival starting the second week in April. It attracts thousands of people, including Mexican and international artists, musicians, actors, dancers, and poets. The grandiose parades, cockfights, bullfights, concerts, and partying in the streets reach a crescendo on St. Mark's day (April 25). However, the celebration continues for another one to three weeks.

BASICS

AMERICAN EXPRESS

All cardmember services are provided here, and they'll hold cardmember mail sent to: Avenida Independencia 2351, Centro Comercial Galerías, Local 5556, Aguascalientes, Aguascalientes, CP 20130, México. *Tel. 49/12–43–36. From 5 de Mayo, take Bus 5 or 6 to the shopping center; the AmEx office is next to Walmart. Open weekdays 9–6, Sat. 9–1.*

CASAS DE CAMBIO

Banamex (Plaza de la Patria, at 5 de Mayo, tel. 49/16–65–70; open weekdays 9–5) changes currency and has an ATM that accepts Visa, MasterCard, Cirrus, and Plus cards. **Mónitron** (Juan de Montoro 120, tel. 49/15–79–79; open weekdays 9–5, Sat. 9:30–1) has longer hours but poorer rates.

EMERGENCIES

In an emergency, call the **police** at 49/14–30–43 or 49/14–20–50. For **ambulance** service, call the Cruz Roja (tel. 49/15–20–55 or 16–42–00).

LAUNDRY

For $1, **Lavamatic** will wash a kilo of your clothes or let you wash 3 kilos (6½ pounds) yourself. *Juan de Montoro 418–B, 4 blocks east of Plaza de la Patria, tel. 49/16–41–81. Open Mon.–Sat. 9–8.*

MEDICAL AID

The 24-hour **Hospital Hidalgo** (Galeana Sur 465, south of Plaza de la Patria, tel. 49/15–31–42) has some English-speaking doctors. For less urgent medical problems, visit the 24-hour **Farmacia Sánchez** (Madero 213, east of Plaza de la Patria, tel. 49/15–66–10).

PHONES AND MAIL

Ladatel phones, along with coin-operated phones, are in Plaza de la Patria. The **post office** (Hospitalidad 108, tel. 49/15–21–18; open weekdays 8–6, Sat. 9–5) will hold mail for you for up to 10 days if sent to the following address: Lista de Correos, Aguascalientes, Aguascalientes, CP 20000, México. *From Plaza de la Patria, walk 1 block east on Madero, 1 block north on Morelos, and right on Hospitalidad.*

SCHOOLS

Dance schools, music schools, and even museums around the city offer short courses in various subjects. Both the **Casa de la Cultura** (*see* Worth Seeing, *below*) and **Centro Cultural Los Arquitos** (Alameda, at Héroe de Nacozari, tel. 49/16–92–42) offer dance, ceramics, music composition, and poetry summer classes ($6–$16 per month).

VISITOR INFORMATION

The **Dirección General de Turismo** doesn't offer much, except a city map and friendly conversation. Some of the staff speaks English. *First floor (planta baja) of Palacio de Gobierno, Plaza de la Patria, tel. 49/16–03–47 or 49/15–11–55. Open weekdays 8:30–3 and 5–7, Sat. 10–1.*

COMING AND GOING

BY BUS

The 24-hour **Central Camionera** is on the southern edge of town, just off Avenida de la Convención. Numerous bus lines rumble through here, including **Omnibus de México** (tel. 49/78–27–70) and Estrella Blanca's first-class line, **Futura** (tel. 49/78–20–54). Both zip to Guadalajara (3 hrs, $13), Mexico City (6½ hrs, $20), and Zacatecas (2 hrs, $5), among other destinations. The bus station has a high-tech, long-distance telephone office as well as luggage storage (50¢ per hr). A taxi into town costs $1.50; local bus lines 3, 4, 9, 12, and 13 all head to the city center and cost 25¢.

BY CAR

To reach Cuidad Juárez (1,360 km/845 mi), take Highway 45 north past Zacatecas. To go to Mexico City (500 km/300 mi), take Highway 45 south, then transfer to the 45-D at Celaya (tolls on this road total $10). Highway 45-D is a scenic route that winds through several colorful towns, such as León and Querétaro. To reach Guadalajara (260 km/145 mi), drive east on Highway 70 and continue south on Highway 54.

BY TRAIN

The train station (tel. 49/15–28–38) lies on the eastern edge of town, some 5 km (3 mi) from downtown. First-class trains depart daily at 7 PM for Ciudad Juárez (24 hrs, $25), with stops at Zacatecas and Chihuahua, and at 10:55 PM for Mexico City (11 hrs, $12), with a stop in Querétaro.

GETTING AROUND

Perhaps as a nod to abstract art and *cubísmo* (cubism), the haphazard streets at Aguascalientes's center form triangles and trapezoids rather than actual "blocks." To add to the confusion, streets change names as they cross the main square, the **Plaza de la Patria.** For example, south of the plaza, Juárez becomes Colón while 5 de Mayo becomes José María Chávez. East of the plaza, Carranza becomes Madero. One street that doesn't change names is López Mateos, a major thoroughfare two blocks south of the plaza. Most of the city's attractions are within walking distance of the Plaza de la Patria. Bars and nightclubs are concentrated on López Mateos.

WHERE TO SLEEP

Downtown is the place to be if you're a budget traveler: Though the hotels listed below may lack in sophistication, they compensate by putting you right in the middle of things. Make reservations well in advance if you plan to arrive during the Feria de San Marcos (in April).

UNDER $10 • Hotel Rosales. At this funny little hotel, an endless succession of halls leads to hidden inner courtyards, dizzying tile patterns adorn the floor, and spiral staircases lead to rooms at odd levels. The woman who manages the place, despite her sweetness, seems to have been affected by the strange surroundings. Basic doubles are $8. *Victoria 104, tel. 49/15–21–65. ½ block north of Plaza de la Patria. 50 rooms, all with bath. Cash only.*

UNDER$15 • Hotel Imperial. Wrought-iron staircases, an inner courtyard, and large, clean rooms are what you'll find here. All rooms have phones, and some have TVs and small balconies. Doubles cost $12, with picturesque view $16. Groups of 10 or more get one room free. *5 de Mayo 106, north side of plaza, tel. 49/15–16–50. 66 rooms, all with bath. Laundry, luggage storage. Cash only.*

Hotel Señorial. Rooms here have less character than those at Hotel Rosales, but they're also in better repair and far quieter. The management is extremely helpful and speaks some English. Doubles ($11.50) have phones and TVs. *Colón 104, tel. 49/15–16–30. SE corner of Plaza de la Patria. 32 rooms, all with bath. Cash only.*

HOSTELS

Villa Juvenil Aguascalientes. This is the cheapest place to sleep in town. Dorm beds ($4) are eight to each small, single-sex room. The communal bathrooms are spacious and clean, the staff is pleasant, and if you ask nicely, they may even let you use the pool (normally open only to Villa Juvenil members). *Av. de la Convención, at Jaime Nuno, tel. 492/70–06–78 or 492/70–08–63; ask for "albergue." From downtown on López Mateos, take Bus 12, 23, or 24. From Central Camionera, take Bus 20. Reception open daily 7 AM–11 PM; curfew 11 PM. 64 beds. Cash only.*

The Spanish dubbed Aguascalientes ciudad perforada (perforated city) because of the many catacombs and tunnels that indigenous peoples had built beneath it prior to the conquest.

FOOD

If you want to meet some of Aguascalientes's hungry students, head to **Jugos Acapulco** (Allende 106, 1 block north of Plaza de la Patria, tel. 49/18–15–20; cash only). A big favorite here is the hamburger with fries, for $1.25. They also serve delicious, all-natural *cerveza de raíz* (root beer).

UNDER $2 • Lonchería Max. This little taquería satisfies the late-night munchies of students, bar-hoppers, and Mexican families 'til 1 AM or so. Max himself reads minds and will usually have another taco (30¢) or sandwich (75¢) prepared for you just when you want one. Crowds are thickest on week-ends. *López Mateos, between 16 de Septiembre and Enrique Díz de León, no phone. Cash only.*

UNDER $5 • Restaurant Mitla. The classiest budget restaurant in Aguascalientes has service with a smile, in dress whites and ties, no less. Specialties include *tampiqueña tradicional* (beef in salsa, served with tortillas), *mollete* (soft roll topped with beans and cheese), and several filling breakfasts ($3–$4). *Madero 220, tel. 49/16–36–79. East of Plaza de la Patria. cash only.*

Restaurant Vegetariano "Devanand." Despite the name, this is not just a vegetarian restaurant—it's vegan! The all-you-can eat buffet ($3.50) features dishes like brown rice, carrot and raisin patties, and tofu stew. Breakfast features soy yogurt, granola, honey, fresh juice, and a tofu dish. The outdoor patio is graced with a fountain and a statue of Swami Guru Devanand. *Emiliano Zapata 201, at Libertad, tel. 49/18–27–21. 5 blocks east of Plaza da la Patria. Cash only.*

WORTH SEEING

The **Plaza de la Patria** is the heart of downtown and the site of political demonstrations and musical con-certs. Shade trees and plenty of fountains make it a lovely place to pass an afternoon. Look for **Exedra,** a monument to King Carlos IV built in 1807 and later capped with the eagle-and-serpent symbol of revolu-tionary Mexico. The plaza's **Palacio de Gobierno** (open Mon.–Sat. 7 AM–9 PM, Sun. 7–1) is a fantastic example of colonial architecture, built with sandstone and *tezontle* stones that give it a deep-red hue. Inside, 111 arches open onto two inner courtyards. The Palacio's real highlight, however, is the massive, colorful, and forceful murals by Chilean painter Osvaldo Barra, detailing the history of Aguascalientes. Barra, whose mentor was none other than Diego Rivera, worked on these murals in 1961–62, 1989, and 1991. Three blocks west of the plaza is verdant **Jardín San Marcos,** favored by picnicking families dur-ing the day and courting couples in the evening. Adjacent to the Jardín is the huge **Plaza San Marcos,** which hosts craft stands, performers, and arcade games every year during the Feria de San Marcos.

BASILICA DE NUESTRA SENORA DE LA ASUNCION

This beloved cathedral has had a few face-lifts since its construction in 1575. The most recent work involved its two towers: The north one (the one with the clock) wasn't completed until 1946, which accounts for the difference in color. The neoclassic cantera rosa facade opens to a white interior lavished with gold and marble trim. The cathedral's *pinacoteca* (painting room) displays oil paintings by 18th-century artist Miguel de Cabrera, including one of the 12 Apostles. The pinacoteca is opened only by request, and never during mass. *East end of Plaza de la Patria. Mass held every 1½ hrs daily 6–2 and 4–9.*

CASA DE LA CULTURA

The Casa, just behind the cathedral, is the artistic and social headquarters of Aguascalientes. Built in 1625 as a hacienda for a prominent Spanish family, the building has since been used as a monastery, seminary, and correctional school. Today it hosts art exhibits, films, and recitals, as well as classes in dance, music, theater, pottery, and language. Something exciting is always happening here, so be sure to ask about upcoming events. *Carranza 101, tel. 49/15–00–97. West of Plaza de la Patria, just past Galeana. Admission free. Open weekdays 9–2 and 5–8, weekends 10–8.*

MUSEO DE AGUASCALIENTES

Self-taught architect J. Refugio Reyes Rivas undertook the construction of this bright orange building at the turn of the 20th century, creating an edifice in the neoclassical style (with a few random details from his other favorite styles thrown in for good measure). Works by the famous local artist Saturnino Herrán are paired with appropriate quotes from Ramón López Velarde, a famous local poet and friend of the painter. Other rooms showcase changing exhibits by contemporary artists. *Zaragoza 505, tel. 49/15–90–43. From Plaza de la Patria, walk 3 blocks east on Madero, left on Zaragoza. Admission: 75¢; free Sun. Open Tues.–Sun. 11–6.*

Across the street from the Museo de Aguascalientes is the **Templo de San Antonio,** a bizarre structure with some neoclassical elements and a tall, domed bell tower. The interior is a riot of colorful murals depicting events in the life of Saint Anthony, the patron saint of lost causes.

MUSEO DE ARTE CONTEMPORANEO

This small but exquisite museum concentrates on local and national artists of the abstract, surreal, and *arte fantástico* (which blends common elements of everyday life into fantasy) movements. Exhibits rotate every two months and include winning pieces from the city's annual art contest honoring San Marcos. *Juan de Montoro 222, tel. 49/18–69–01. 1½ blocks east of Plaza de la Patria. Admission: 75¢; free Sun. Open Tues.–Sun. 10–6.*

MUSEO DE JOSE GUADALUPE POSADA

This small museum is dedicated to the artist and journalist whose political cartoons and prints helped stir dissent against dictator Porfirio Díaz during the Revolution. The museum occasionally offers printing and painting classes. *North side of Jardín del Encino, tel. 49/15–45–56. From Plaza de la Patria, walk S on José María Chávez, left on Pimentel. Admission: 75¢. Open Tues.–Sun. 10–6.*

Next door is the **Parroquia del Encino,** a baroque church with a black statue of Christ, as well as huge 19th-century oil paintings depicting the Stations of the Cross. *Open daily 6–1 and 4–9. Mass schedule posted at entryway.*

AFTER DARK

Aguascalientes's hip bars and nightclubs are a $2 taxi ride from the center. Both **The Station** (Carretera al Campestre 129, tel. 49/12–09–91) and **IOZ** (Miguel de la Madrid, no phone) are crowded Friday and Saturday with beautiful people dancing to techno and pop. There's no cover and beers are $2. **El Cabús** (Salida a Zacatecas, at Luis Donaldo Colosio, tel. 49/73–00–06; closed Mon.–Wed.), in the Hotel Las Trojes, dominates the dance-music scene, with crowds of up to 400. Cover is $4, though women usually get in free before 10 PM.

A quieter scene prevails at **Café Parroquia** (Hidalgo, just before López Velarde, no phone), where bohemians spend hours conversing over cappuccinos ($1) and cigarettes. **La Querencia** (Alarcón 105, between Zapata and Allende, tel. 49/18–06–57; closed Sun. and Mon.) is a bar with a café atmosphere. Its hip, artsy crowd loves the live music on Friday and Saturday. **Teatro de Aguascalientes** (Av. Aguascalientes, at Chávez, tel. 49/78–55–56 or 49/78–54–14) and **Teatro Morelos** (Plaza de la Republica,

GUADALAJARA

Despite urban sprawl, streets choked with smoke-belching buses, and a burgeoning population of almost 6 million, Guadalajara somehow retains a traditional feel that is usually only present in smaller Mexican towns. The city's devotion to its rich heritage isn't so surprising when you consider that it's the birthplace of three things typically Mexican: the woeful love songs of mariachi bands, the flirtatious *jarabe tapatío* (known to gringos as the Mexican hat dance), and heart-pumping *charreadas* (rodeos). City officials know that tourists love these things and have taken steps to preserve and promote all three traditions, as well as other cultures and practices of the "typical" (some would say "stereotypical") Mexican.

Elements of tradition are also evident in Guadalajara's politics. The city has long been characterized as politically conservative, particularly because of the strong influence the PAN (Partido de Acción Nacional) has gained here in the last few decades (*see box titled* "El Partido Acción Nacional," *in* Chapter 5). But the PAN's and, consequently, Guadalajara's conservative bent is an understandable response to the city's problems. This is a city where impoverished children can be seen sleeping on the sidewalks, and—as in Mexico City—the gray haze of air pollution only seems to worsen as Guadalajara swallows surrounding suburbs. Big-money drug smugglers are rumored to call the city home, and despite the best efforts of elected officials to combat drug trafficking and increase police patrols, Guadalajara is no doubt still on the DEA's top 10 list.

If you're at Aguascalietes's Plaza de la Patria at 6 PM, you'll witness the Ceremonía de la Bandera (flag ceremony), when prancing soldiers march the Mexican flag into the Palacio de Gobierno for the night.

These big problems rarely touch the average traveler, however, and if you never leave the downtown area, it is easy to believe that you are in one of Mexico's finest cities. A simple stroll around the *centro histórico* (historic center) will open your eyes to the beauty of clean, clearly marked cobblestone streets and *pasajes peatonales* (pedestrian walkways), surrounded by immaculately preserved colonial buildings. Plentiful taxis, a well-organized bus station, and enormous mercados make Guadalajara easily accessible and aesthetically pleasing. The large number of students at the public Universidad de Guadalajara ensures a wide array of cultural offerings, and the gay population here is energetic and active, though not as "out" as many would like to be. The presence of both groups lends Guadalajara a constant hum of activity, from lively *peñas* (clubs featuring Latin American folk music) to transvestite shows.

Guadalajara's suburbs and neighboring towns offer further adventure and excitement for travelers. In the towns of Tlaquepaque and Tonalá, you'll find fine local handicrafts for sale, while Zapopan's basilica draws religious pilgrims from around the country. The nearby Lake Chapala, Mexico's largest lake, is a favorite getaway for tapatíos and retired Americans. In the nearby town of Tequila, you can tour distilleries and even taste free samples of Mexico's national drink.

BASICS

AMERICAN EXPRESS

Services provided by this AmEx office include: traveler's check exchange, personal-check cashing, and cardholder mail. *Vallarta 2440, Guadalajara, Jalisco, CP 44100, México, tel. 3/615–89–10. From downtown on Juárez, take PAR VIAL or Bus 500 W to Plaza los Arcos. Open weekdays 9–2:30 and 4–6, Sat. 9–1.*

BOOKSTORES

Both **Librería México** (Plaza del Sol, tel. 3/121–01–14) and **Sandi's** (Tepeyac 718, tel. 3/121–08–63; closed Sun.) stock popular magazines and some paperbacks in English. **El Libro Antiguo** (Pino Suárez 86, no phone; closed Sun.), 1½ blocks north of downtown's Plaza de la Liberación, deals in new and used books, for sale or trade, in Spanish and in English (though most of the English-language paperbacks have titles like *Impatient Virgin* and *Lovers and Libertines*).

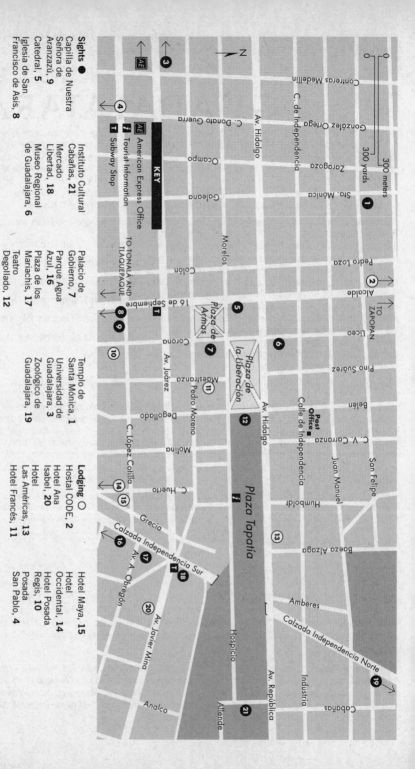

GAUDALAJARA

Sights ●

Capilla de Nuestra
Señora de
Aranzazú, **9**
Catedral, **5**
Iglesia de San
Francisco de Asis, **8**

Instituto Cultural
Cabañas, **21**
Mercado
Libertad, **18**
Museo Regional
de Guadalajara, **6**

Palacio de
Gobierno, **7**
Parque Agua
Azul, **16**
Plaza de los
Mariachis, **17**
Teatro
Degollado, **12**

Templo de
Santa Mónica, **1**
Universidad de
Guadalajara, **3**
Zoológico de
Guadalajara, **19**

Lodging ○

Hostal CODE, **2**
Hotel Ana
Isabel, **20**
Hotel
Las Américas, **13**
Hotel Francés, **11**

Hotel Maya, **15**
Hotel
Occidental, **14**
Hotel Posada
Regis, **10**
Posada
San Pablo, **4**

KEY

AE American Express Office
ℹ️ Tourist Information
T Subway Stop

222

CASAS DE CAMBIO

Banamex (Juárez 237, at Corona, tel. 3/679–32–52; open weekdays 9–3) changes traveler's checks and currency and has an ATM that accepts Cirrus and Plus cards. Banamex also gives cash advances on MasterCard or Visa. For longer hours, try any of the casas de cambio cluttering López Cotilla between Corona and Maestranza; **Multidivisas Delta** (López Cotilla 224, tel. 3/613–16–37; open weekdays 9–5, Sat. 9–3) has good rates.

CONSULATES

For countries not listed below, call the **Consular Association** (tel. 3/616–06–29). **Canada**: *Hotel Fiesta Americana, Aurelio Aceves 225, Local 31, tel. 3/615–62–15. Near Glorieta Minerva. Open weekdays 8:30–5.* **United Kingdom**: *Eulogio Parra 2539, at Montreal, tel. 3/616–06–29. Open weekdays 9–3 and 5–8.* **United States**: *Progreso 175, 1 block E of Chapultepec, tel. 3/825–27–00 or 3/825–29–98. Open weekdays 8–4:30; American Citizen Services office open weekdays 8–11:30 for walk-in appointments.*

DISCOUNT TRAVEL AGENCIES

University faculty and students frequent **Agencia de Viajes Universidad de Guadalajara** (Juárez 976, basement level, at Enrique Diz de León, tel. 3/825–85–52), so its staff knows all about cheap travel. From downtown, take the PAR VIAL or Bus 500 west on Juárez. **Mapamundi** (Hidalgo 2009, between Victoriano Salado Alvarez and Tomás V. Gómez, tel. 3/616–37–97) has a friendly, English-speaking staff who can help with international travel plans. From downtown, take the PAR VIAL or Bus 500 west to Avenida Vallarta; get off between Francisco de Quevedo and Duque de Rivas and walk two blocks north to Hidalgo.

> *Guadalajara, a city of 6 million, has a surprising small-town feel. Introduce one tapatío (as they call themselves) to another and they'll rapidly find that they have a friend or associate in common.*

EMERGENCIES

For the **police** call 3/617–60–60; for the **fire** department call 3/619–52–41 or 3/623–08–33; for **ambulance** service call Cruz Roja (tel. 3/613–15–50, 3/614–56–00, or 3/614–27–07).

LAUNDRY

At **Lavandería Lavarami** (Río Juárez 1520-A, ¾ mi SE of Parque Agua Azul, tel. 3/657–16–83; open Mon.–Sat. 9–8, Sun. 10–2) you can get 3½ kilos (9 pounds) of your clothes washed, dried, and folded for $3.75. They'll also pick up and deliver laundry with a minimum charge of $11. Doing your own clothes costs $3 per load. **Quickwash** (López Cotilla 1234, tel. 3/826–51–85; open Mon.–Sat. 8:30–8, Sun. 9–3), four blocks west of Agencia de Viajes Universidad (*see* Discount Travel Agencies, *above*), will wash, dry and fold up to 4 kilos of clothes for $4.50. Self-service costs $2–$3 per load.

MAIL

The full-service post office will hold mail sent to you at the following address for up to 10 days: Lista de Correos, Administración de Correo 1, Guadalajara, Jalisco, CP 44100, México. *Independencia, at Carranza, tel. 3/614–74–25. One block north of Plaza Tapatía. Open weekdays 8–6, Sat. 9–1.*

MEDICAL AID

Both **Hospital del Carmen** (Tarascos 3435, near the Plaza México shopping mall, tel. 3/813–00–42) and **Hospital Regional ISSSTE** (at the northern end of Av. de las Américas, near Avila Camacho, tel. 3/633–03–18 or 3/633–00–44) are open 24 hours. Carmen Hospital has English-speaking doctors on staff, while the Regional Hospital is closer to downtown. **Farmacia Guadalajara** (Javier Mina 221, 2 blocks east of Mercado Libertad, tel. 3/617–85–55) has 24-hour service.

PHONES

You can make collect or phone-card calls at any working **Ladatel** phone in Plaza Tapatía or Plaza de la Liberación. You can also make direct-dial calls at **Caseta Telefónica** (Morelos 417, at Colón, tel. 3/614–76–84; open Mon.–Sat. 9–8:30), but rates are higher than with a Ladatel card.

SCHOOLS

The **University of Guadalajara** offers five-week, intensive Spanish language courses, as well as classes on Mexican culture, literature, and history. Contact its **Centro de Estudios Para Extranjeros** (open weekdays 9:30–5) for more information, or write to: Lic. Jocelyne Gacel, CEPE, Apdo. Postal 2130, Guadalajara, Jalisco, CP 44100, México. *Tomás V. Gómez 125, at México, tel. 3/616–39–82.*

The **Departamento Escolar** at the **Instituto Cultural Cabañas** (*see* Worth Seeing, *below*) offers classes in Nahuatl (the Aztec language) and Maya. You can also study Latin American literature, art, theater, folklórico dance, and music. Classes are typically offered fall and spring semesters, though a few take place during the summer. For information write to: Dirreción Escolar de la Secretaría de la Cultura, Instituto Cultural Cabañas, Cabañas 8, Plaza Tapatía, Guadalajara, Jalisco, CP 44100, México. *East end of Plaza Tapatía, tel. 3/617–43–22 or 3/617–44–40. Open weekdays 9–8.*

VISITOR INFORMATION

The helpful, English-speaking staff at the **Secretaría de Turismo de Jalisco** office in Plaza Tapatía gives out detailed maps of the city as well as information about upcoming cultural events. Several small tourist information booths scattered around Plaza de Armas, Plaza de la Liberación, and Plaza Tapatía also offer some assistance to travelers. *Morelos 102, tel. 3/658–22–22 or 91–800/3–63–22. Open weekdays 9–8, weekends 9–1.*

COMING AND GOING

BY BUS

The **Central Camionera Nueva,** the main bus station, is on the Carretera Libre a Zapotlanejo (Free Highway to Zapotlanejo) between Tlaquepaque and Tonalá, about half an hour southeast of downtown. This station handles service to destinations over 100 km (60 mi) away. The huge, horseshoe-shape structure is divided into seven terminals, each with its own bus lines, restaurants, luggage storage area (the Terminal 1 storage is open 24 hours), and Ladatel phones. The cheapest way to reach downtown is via Bus 275 (20¢), which runs the length of Avenida 16 de Septiembre. Taxis to downtown cost $3, but you must purchase your ticket from a booth in the terminal.

Hundreds of buses depart daily from the Central Camionera Nueva. The problem lies in deciding which line to take in a station that stretches for almost 1 km (½ mi). You can purchase tickets for a number of first-class lines from many local travel agencies at no additional charge, sparing you the hassle of hunting for the line's *taquilla* (ticket counter) inside the terminals. If you're not one to plan ahead, try second-class **Flecha Amarilla** (Terminal 1, tel. 3/600–05–26) for the cheapest fares and slowest buses. Destinations include Morelia (12 per day; 6 hrs, $13) and Mexico City (24 per day; 9 hrs, $26). **Autobuses del Occidente** (Terminal 2, tel. 3/600–00–55) runs regular first- and second-class buses to Morelia (3–5 hrs, $13). First-class **Rojo de los Altos** (Terminal 2, tel. 3/679–04–55) buses go to Ciudad Juárez (24 hrs, $45) and Zacatecas (5½ hrs, $13.50). **ETN** (Terminal 2, tel. 3/600–04–72) is a reliable but pricey deluxe first-class line with frequent departures to Aguascalientes (3 hrs, $13.50), Manzanillo (4½ hrs, $21), and Mexico City (8 hrs, $36).

Destinations within 100 km (60 mi) of Guadalajara are served by the old bus station, **Antigua Central Camionera** (R. Michel, between Los Angeles and 5 de Febrero). **Autotransportes Guadalajara Chapala** (tel. 3/619–56–75) buses depart every 30 minutes from 5:20 AM to 9 PM for towns around Lake Chapala ($1.75). **Rojo de los Altos** (tel. 3/619–23–09) buses leave for Tequila ($2) every 15 minutes, 6 AM–9:15 PM. To reach the station from downtown, take Bus 110 (20¢) south on 16 de Septiembre.

BY CAR

To reach Mexico City (511 km/317 mi), take Highway 15-D southeast and be ready to fork over $40 in tolls. You could also take the free Highway 15, but road conditions are less safe, and you'll be driving an extra 129 km (80 mi). For Puerto Vallarta (366 km/250 mi), take Highway 15-D west and pay $15 in tolls.

BY PLANE

Guadalajara's **airport** (tel. 3/688–52–48 or 3/688–51–27) lies 30 km (18 mi) from downtown off the Carretera a Chapala, (Hwy 44). It's served by **Aero California** (tel. 3/826–19–62), **Aeroméxico** (tel. 3/669–02–02), **American** (tel. 3/616–40–90), **Continental** (tel. 3/647–44–46), **Delta** (tel. 3/630–35–30), and **Mexicana** (tel. 3/112–01–01).

The cheapest ride from the airport to the center of town is aboard a **Transportaciones Terrestres** (tel. 3/812–42–78) bus (40 min, 70¢). Buses leave from the front of the airport every hour on the hour, 5 AM–9 PM. Buses to the airport leave from Enrique Díaz de León 954, corner of España. Taxis between the airport and downtown cost $9.50; buy your ticket from the taxi office (tel. 3/688–58–90) outside the airport. Reservations at least 24 hours in advance are recommended for taxi travel to the airport.

BY TRAIN

The **train station** lies two blocks southwest of Parque Agua Azul. The train to Mexico City leaves daily at 9 PM and takes 12 hours. Sleepers with two beds are available Friday–Sunday and cost $32, but seats are a steal at $13 first class, $8.50 second class. The first-class train to Mexicali (38 hrs, $53) leaves daily at 9:30 AM, with a stop in Mazatlán (10 hrs, $14.75). Much cheaper and slower is the second-class train to Mexicali (nearly 3 days, $30), which leaves daily at noon. All train tickets should be purchased prior to the day of departure to ensure availability. The station has a long-distance telephone office and a few shops selling snacks. *South of downtown, tel. 3/650–08–26 or 3/650–10–82. Tickets for Mexicali-bound train sold weekdays 9–1, Sat. 9 AM–11 PM, and Sun. 8:30–9:30 AM; tickets for Mexico City train sold daily 9 AM–8 PM. Take Bus 62 S on Calz. Independencia or Bus 54 S on 16 de Septiembre.*

GETTING AROUND

Although Guadalajara is the second largest city in Mexico, it's easy to get around if you stick to the area of downtown known as the centro histórico; conveniently, this is where most of the sights are. At the heart of the centro are three adjoining plazas: sprawling **Plaza Tapatía**, the much smaller **Plaza de la Liberación,** and the smallest, **Plaza de Armas.** The plazas are roughly bordered by Hidalgo/República to the north, Morelos/Hospicio to the south, Alcalde/Avenida 16 de Septiembre to the west, and Calzada Independencia (not to be confused with Calle Independencia, a smaller street) to the east. Streets switch names as they cross over the two main streets, **Hidalgo/República** and **Calzada Independencia.** A few blocks south of the plazas is another main street, **Juárez,** which leads west into the university district (where it changes names to Vallarta). Traveling west on Juárez you'll cross several major north–south streets, including Federalismo, Chapultepec, and Avenida de las Américas. At the far western edge of town, Juárez intersects the **Glorieta Minerva** (a traffic circle). Traveling east of the centro, Juárez changes names to **Javier Mina** as it crosses Calzada Independencia. To make sense of it all, pick up a detailed street map from any tourist booth (*see* Visitor Information, *above*).

BY BUS

Hundreds of buses and minibuses ply the Guadalajara streets daily 6 AM–10 PM. Each costs 20¢ per ride. For destinations along Calzada Independencia Sur, such as Parque Agua Azul and the train station, hop on Bus 62 or 60. Bus 258 runs south on Calzada Independencia Sur to the Plaza del Sol shopping mall and to López Mateos, where many bars and clubs are located. The PAR VIAL, a trolley that runs west on Juárez/Vallarta to Glorieta Minerva, and returns east to the centro historico via Hidalgo, passes the American Express office and the university. Blue **Tur III** buses (70¢) offer air-conditioned comfort: The 707 runs west on Juárez/Vallarta, while the 706 goes south on 16 de Septiembre to Tlaquepaque and Tonalá. The tourist office (see Visitor Information, *above*) can map out bus routes for you if needed.

BY CAR

Traffic in Guadalajara can get fairly ugly, especially during rush hours. It's safest to keep your car in a hotel parking lot overnight, rather than on the street—though street parking is available. The parking garage **Mulbar** (Corona, next to Hotel Posada Regis, tel. 3/614–89–40) costs $3 a day. Rental-car companies are clustered near 16 de Septiembre and Niños Héroes and include **Budget** (Niños Héroes 934, tel. 3/688–52–16) and **Dollar** (Federalismo Sur 540-A, tel. 3/826–79–59). Several rental agencies also have offices at the airport.

BY SUBWAY

The *tren ligero* (light-rail train) is the fastest way to travel long distances in Guadalajara. It runs both above and below ground, traveling north–south along the length of Federalismo, as well as east–west along Juárez/Javier Mina. Light green T signs indicate subway stations; the downtown stations are at Juárez near Federalismo, Juárez near 16 de Septiembre, and Javier Mina at Calzada Independencia. *Fichas* (tokens; 20¢), which you'll need to board, can be purchased from machines within the stations; use exact change or the machines will eat your money. Trains run daily 6 AM–10:30 PM.

BY TAXI

Taxis are the only way to get around Guadalajara late at night. Fortunately, they're easy to find on the streets. Cabs also line up in front of expensive hotels, but these charge higher rates than those you hail yourself. A ride from the center of town to the bar and club area around Plaza del Sol should cost about $4. As the night wears on, taxis raise their rates by $1 or more.

WHERE TO SLEEP

The drawback to nearly all budget hotels in Guadalajara is the noise from street traffic, but you can often avoid it by requesting a room facing away from the street or on a high floor. On the plus side, this is a city where most hotel proprietors will go out of their way to make guests feel comfortable. Choose a hotel downtown and you'll be near centro historico sights as well as all the bus lines to take you elsewhere—the safest choices are within a five-block radius of Plaza Tapatía. Neighborhoods southeast and northeast of the plaza also have plenty of cheap accommodations, but you should use extra caution and take cabs at night. If all the hotels below are booked, the **Hotel Maya** (López Cotilla 39 between Huerto and Grecia, tel. 3/614–54–54) is a decent alternative, with clean doubles for $13.50. All rooms have baths, and some have telephones and TVs.

UNDER $15 • Hotel Las Américas. This hotel, conveniently located across from Plaza Tapatía, provides bright, clean, carpeted rooms with TVs and phones. The area is fairly safe, but traffic makes it noisy; request a room on the top floor or facing away from the street. Singles and doubles cost $9.50–$11 (high-end rooms have fans and color TVs). *Hidalgo 76, tel. 3/613–96–22. 3 blocks east of Teatro Degollado. 49 rooms, all with bath. Luggage storage. Cash only.*

Hotel Occidental. The Occidental is clean and its staff is young and outgoing; you won't have trouble making friends here, especially if you're female. It's situated on a grungy side street, but the brightly painted halls and rooms are sure to cheer you up once you're inside (if the smell of disinfectant doesn't knock you out first). The *matrimonial* (double) beds were made with a very slim couple in mind. One-bed doubles run $6.75, two-bed doubles $10, plus $1.75 if you want a TV in your room. *Villa Gómez 17, between Molina and Huerto, tel. 3/613–84–06. 3 blocks south of Plaza Tapatía. 51 rooms, all with bath. Cash only.*

Posada San Pablo. This immaculate hotel offers the most for your money: a sunny courtyard, a reading room stocked with books in English, a kitchen (kitchen privileges cost $1.50 per day), and a back patio with a barbecue. The owner, Lilly, and her family take great pride in making guests feel at home. Basic doubles cost $9 ($10.50 with bath). *Madero 429, between Ocampo and Donato Guerra, tel. 3/614–28–11. 10 rooms, 3 with bath. Laundry. Reservations advised. Cash only.*

UNDER $20 • Hotel Posada Regis. This establishment offers small, carpeted rooms and an atmosphere of faded elegance. Carmen and Lolita, the proprietors, will do all they can to ensure your stay is a pleasant one. Doubles ($16) all have telephones, and prices go down if you stay a week or longer. *Corona 171, at López Cotilla, tel. 3/613–30–26. 18 rooms, all with bath. Laundry, luggage storage. Cash only.*

UNDER $35 • Hotel Francés. The Hotel Francés is surprisingly affordable for a place so elegant. Built in 1610 as Guadalajara's first hotel and trading post, it has huge rooms ($30) with TVs, phones, wood floors, ceiling fans, and sparkling bathrooms. On Friday, mariachi bands entertain guests all night long; other evenings feature live jazz groups. The young, peppy staff will do anything to please you. *Maestranza 35, tel. 3/613–11–90 or 3/613–09–17. Behind Palacio del Gobierno. 67 rooms, all with bath. Luggage storage.*

HOSTELS

CODE. This youth hostel, affiliated with a sports complex, has four 20-bed dorm rooms ($3.50 per person). The communal bathrooms and showers are clean, well-maintained, and even have toilet paper. The one drawback is the 11 PM curfew. *Prolongación Alcalde 1360, just north of Glorieta La Normal, tel. 853–00–11 ext. 130. From downtown, Bus 231 on Alcalde; get off ½ block past the traffic circle. 80 beds. Check-in daily 8–2 and 3–9. Luggage storage (bring your own padlock). Closed Christmas and Easter. Cash only.*

FOOD

Though restaurants serving international cuisine like Italian and Chinese abound in Guadalajara, foreigners and Mexicans alike come here for that "authentic Mexican experience." So dig into those tamales *con mucho gusto,* and consider sampling regional specialties like *tortas ahogadas* (literally "drowned sandwiches," generously bathed in a spicy tomato-base sauce) and *jericalla* (a rich, sweet custard). You'll find both at lunch counters around town and at stands in Mercado Libertad (*see* Worth Seeing, *below*).

DOWNTOWN

The city center doesn't cater to people searching for a fine dining experience, but you'll find lots of cheap fast food here, particularly tortas. On Moreno (1 block north of Juárez), tons of small shops offer afternoon specials, such as five tacos or three tostadas for $1. Mercado Libertad teems with food stalls selling the cheapest meals in town, but one jocose resident ominously called those meals *platillos de cólera* (plates of cholera), so watch out. For an inexpensive breakfast, try the 80¢ baked goodies at **Croissants Alfredo** (Morelos 229, across from Plaza de la Liberación, no phone).

UNDER $2 • Gorditas Estilo Durango. University students short on cash come here for *gorditas* (thick corn tortillas stuffed with sausage, cheese, or shredded beef; $1 apiece). The menú del día features soup, refried beans, an entrée, and a drink. *Moreno 552, at Enrique Díaz de León, tel. 3/825–81–19. Closed Sun. Cash only.*

Taco Cabana. This economical eatery is always packed with families. Mexican music blares from the jukebox and the two-for-one beer specials add to the lively environment. Breakfasts run less than $2, or choose from a variety of 40¢ tacos. *Pedro Moreno 248, at Maestranza, tel. 3/613–11–90 ext. 19. Cash only.*

UNDER $5 • La Chata. In business for over half a century, this cheerful restaurant serves excellent traditional Mexican food at decent prices. *Sopes* (fried tortillas topped with beans, salsa, and meat or cheese) are $2, but the house special is the *platillo jalisciense* (one-quarter of a chicken, french fries, a sope, one enchilada, and one flauta; $4.50). *Corona 126, tel. 3/613–05–88. 2 blocks south of Plaza Tapatía. Cash only.*

> *For the tourist's-eye view of Guadalajara, take a ride on one of the numerous calandrias (horse-drawn carriages) that crowd the centro histórico. A 45-minute scenic tour costs $13.50.*

Krishna Prasadam. The East Indian music and pictures of Hindu deities might give the impression that you've been magically transported out of Mexico. The delicious *comida corrida* (prepeprared lunch special; $2.75), which includes soup, tofu and peppers in tomato sauce, breaded vegetables, a hearty salad, whole-wheat tortillas, fruit, and a yogurt drink, captures flavors of the Far East. *Madero 694, between Federalismo and Penitenciaria, tel. 3/826–18–22. Closed Sun. Cash only.*

Restaurant Panamericano. Though the place is a bit worse for the wear, Panamericano's hearty chicken *mole* (chocolate-chile sauce) more than makes up for the lack of ambience. *Chilaquiles* (eggs and tortilla strips doused with salsa and sour cream) are the best breakfast in town for less than $1.50. *Plaza de los Mariachis 47, tel. 3/617–61–00. Cash only.*

Restaurant Sandy's. Despite its generic name, this restaurant delivers an out-of-the-ordinary menu plus a pleasant terrace with views of the shady Plaza de la Rotonda. Choices include a burger with mushrooms ($3.50) or an overflowing platter of vegetables and shrimp. *Independencia, at Alcalde, upstairs, tel. 3/614–42–36. Cash only.*

AVENIDA CHAPULTEPEC/AVENIDA AMERICAS

The peaceful, residential area between Avenidas Chapultepec and Américas is full of upscale restaurants, though there are still plenty of options for budget travelers. From downtown, catch a westbound PAR VIAL bus.

UNDER $5 • Ecocafé. Full breakfasts at this 100% vegetarian restaurant cost $2. The comida corrida includes salad bar, soup, entrée, and fresh fruit drink for $3. Also on the menu are sandwiches, soyburgers, naturally grown coffees, pastries, yogurt, and juices. An adjacent shop sells natural foods and soaps. *José Guadalupe Zuno 1961, near Chapultepec, tel. 3/825–87–26. 2 blocks south of Av. de la Paz. Cash only.*

Los Itacates. This Mexican power-lunch place specializes in traditional dishes such as *coachal* (shredded chicken and pork with corn) and *pollo itacates* (one-quarter of a chicken with cheese enchiladas, potatoes, and rice). The breakfast buffet is $3. *Chapultepec Nte. 110, tel. 3/825–11–06. 4 blocks north of Vallarta. Cash only.*

PLAZA DEL SOL

Plaza del Sol is a massive open-air shopping mall popular with the nouveaux riches of Guadalajara. Its neon lights and pulsing rock music may soon have you longing for the gritty taco stands of downtown. On the plus side, the food here is excellent, if a bit expensive. From downtown, catch Bus 258 south on Calzada Independencia Sur.

WANT TO BUY AN $80 CHICKEN?

If you're interested in learning more about Mexican culture—and the Mexican psyche—drop by Veterinaria Gallero (Calz. Independencia Sur 500, tel. 3/658-18-40; open weekdays 9:30-2 and 4-7, Sat. 9:30-2), a store in Guadalajara that specializes in fighting cocks.

These aren't your ordinary, run-of-the-mill chickens. There are about 60-70 different breeds of fighting cocks, which fight with various types of weapons attached to their feet—from the inch-long "arma de filo" (blade) to the shorter "navaja corta" (razor). The starting price for one of the specially bred and trained birds is a whopping $80.

For the past few years, cockfights have only been permitted during public festivals in Mexico. The friendly staff at Veterinaria Gallero will happily answer your questions about cockfighting and tell you where to view one.

Normally, wagers for cockfights are about $10-$20, though they can climb as high as $20,000. Losses like this can be a double disaster, for not only are you suddenly destitute, but your favored cock is a heap of dead feathers.

UNDER $5 • Los Arcos. The specialty at this low-key restaurant is *barbacoa* (barbecued lamb; $5), a Mexican favorite. Another house special, *misiote,* is made with lamb, chicken or pork wrapped in maguey leaves and cooked with pine nuts, almonds, and raisins. *López Mateos Sur 1850, next to Hotel Posada Guadalajara, no phone. Cash only.*

CAFES

Cafés line Chapultepec, and many offer live music in the afternoons and evenings. Elsewhere in the city, **Café La Paloma** (López Cotilla 1855, 1 block west of Av. de las Américas, tel. 3/630-01-95; cash only) offers live music and occasional poetry readings. There are always a few bohemian types scattered among the Guadalajaran youth, all smoking and looking cool. La Paloma's specialty is *Saltapérico* (Kahlua, Rompope, vodka, pineapple juice, and a shot of espresso; $2.50).

WORTH SEEING

Most of Guadalajara's sights are on or around the Plaza Tapatía, in the centro histórico. However, to visit Tlaquepaque, Tonalá, and Zapopan—you'll need to board a city bus.

CENTRO HISTORICO

CATEDRAL • Completed in 1618 after 57 years of work, Guadalajara's religious centerpiece has since undergone numerous modifications, resulting in an eclectic combination of baroque, Renaissance, Moorish, and neo-Gothic styles. Its twin yellow spires were added in 1854 after an earthquake destroyed the original towers. Inside the cathedral is a fine collection of religious art reflecting Guadalajara's colonial-era wealth and importance: The altar and statue dedicated to Our Lady of the Rose, carved from a single piece of balsa, were gifts from King Carlos V of the Holy Roman empire in the 16th century. King Ferdinand VII of Spain presented the 10 silver-and-gilt altars in gratitude for aid during the 19th-century Napoléonic Wars. North of the entrance are remains of St. Innocence that were brought here from catacombs in Rome. The cathedral's mass service is especially beautiful and solemn—if you choose to attend, do so with respect. *Hidalgo, at Alcalde. Open daily 8–7. Mass schedule posted at entryway.*

CHURCHES • The baroque **Iglesia de San Francisco de Asis** is one of Guadalajara's first churches. Columns with vinelike ornamentation line the entryway. To the right of the main altar are statues of Santo Niño de Atocha and Santo Niño de la Misericordia; both saints are sacred to Mexican children and are showered with toys by those who visit them. *16 de Septiembre, at Prisciliano Sánchez. Mass schedule posted at entryway.*

The **Capilla de Nuestra Señora de Aranzazú** is the only surviving chapel of the six that once surrounded the Iglesia de San Francisco. Its three richly detailed, brightly painted, gold-embellished wooden *Churrigueresque* (ultra-baroque) altarpieces are considered among the finest in the world. In such a small church, their size and presence seem almost overpowering. *16 de Septiembre, at Prisciliano Sánchez.*

The **Templo de Santa Mónica** was built in 1773 for the Augustinian nuns who lived next door. With its ornate gold interior, the church is an excellent example of baroque architecture. In the northwest corner of the building is a statue of St. Christopher with mestizo features. Mass is held every hour daily 7:30 AM–9:30 PM. *Santa Mónica, at San Felipe.*

INSTITUTO CULTURAL CABANAS • Built between 1805 and 1810, this building served as an orphanage until 1979, when it was transformed into the city's cultural center. An important example of neoclassical architecture, the building is home to 23 magical courtyards, several art galleries, a small theater, and a snack bar. In the late 1930s, José Clemente Orozco painted a series of murals on the ceiling and walls of the building's main chapel, including what is considered his finest work, *The Man of Fire.* Also displayed here are some of Orozco's lithographs and paintings. Excellent tours are given in both Spanish and English (guides work on a volunteer basis and should be tipped $1.50). *Hospicio 8, tel. 3/617–43–22 or 3/617–44–40. Admission: $1.50; free Sun. Open Tues.–Sat. 10:15–6, Sun. 10:15–3.*

MERCADO LIBERTAD (SAN JUAN DE DIOS) • This sprawling market, heavily promoted by the local tourism department, is just a larger version of those found all over Mexico. Though people have been buying and selling on this location for more than 400 years, the existing structure was built in the 1950s—and looks it. That said, even the pickiest shopper or cultural anthropologist will find heaven in its three stories of jam-packed stalls, selling everything from *artesanía* (handicrafts) such as leather *huaraches* (sandals) and Mexican blankets, to *fayuca,* inexpensive electronics sold without warranties, instructions, or even packaging. *Javier Mina, at Calz. Independencia Sur. Open daily 10 AM–8 PM.*

MUSEO REGIONAL DE GUADALAJARA • The museum's displays of pre-Columbian artifacts are impressive, and the exhibit tracing Jalisco's history is interesting (if you read Spanish). There's a collection of colonial paintings, the most impressive of which is the newly restored *Alegoría del Paraíso de las Monjas Carmelitas.* In this 17th-century painting, a crucified Jesus' spurting blood turns into a field of flowers, plants, and trees, while a group of Carmelite nuns looks on approvingly. *Liceo 60, tel. 3/614–99–57. Admission: $2; free Sun. and holidays. Open weekdays 9–6:45, Sun. 9–3.*

PALACIO DE GOBIERNO • The governor of New Galicia had this stately Churrigueresque mansion built in 1643. It was here that independence fighter Miguel Hidalgo decreed the abolition of slavery in 1810, and where the country's first indigenous head of state, Benito Juárez, was almost assassinated by his enemies in 1858—before Don Guillermo Prieto stopped the would-be killers with the now-famous phrase, "*Los valientes no asesinan*" (The brave do not kill). All of these revolutionaries have been immortalized in bronze in the **Sala Jalisco,** which doubles as a gallery for portraits of Jalisco's past governors. However, the main attraction here is definitely Orozco's dramatic *Social Struggle,* a huge painting of a white-haired Hidalgo leaping away from the chaos of war, fascism, communism, and ecclesiastical oppression. It hangs in the stairwell to the right of the Sala Jalisco. *Corona, between Morelos and Pedro Moreno. Admission free. Open daily 9–8:45.*

Across the street from the Palacio de Gobierno is the **Plaza de Armas.** At its center is a wrought-iron kiosk decorated with half-naked women—a gift from France in 1910. Today the dark-green structure is surrounded by small children who feed flocks of pigeons, while others beg for money. Political protestors occasionally congregate in the plaza as well. Free concerts take place Tuesday, Thursday, and Sunday at 6:30 PM.

TEATRO DEGOLLADO • One of Guadalajara's most cherished possessions is this neoclassical opera house, modeled after Milan's La Scala and opened in 1866. Above the stately Corinthian columns flanking the theater's entrance is a relief depicting Apollo and the nine Muses. The interior was painstakingly restored in 1988, and worth a look even if you don't plan to attend a performance. The university's renowned **Ballet Folklórico** performs here Sunday at 10 AM; tickets are $2–$11. Year-round there are also performances by the Filarmónica de Jalisco, other visiting orchestras, dance groups, singers, theater groups, and, of course, the opera. Operas take place in September and October, and tickets are

$2.75–$33.50. *Belén, at Hidalgo, tel. 3/614–47–73. Box office open daily 10–1 and 4–7. Theater open to the public weekdays 10:30–11 and 12:30–1.*

UNIVERSIDAD DE GUADALAJARA • The University of Guadalajara's administrative offices are housed in a beautiful turn-of-the-century building. Two famous Orozco murals are on view in the auditorium, one on the dome and another behind the stage. Also here is **Museo de las Artes de la Universidad de Guadalajara** (open Tues.–Sat. 10–8, Sun. 10–6; admission 70¢, free Sun.) a top-flight contemporary art museum. Across Avenida Juárez is the university's main building (a large cement structure); take the elevator to the top floor for views of southeastern Guadalajara. Or, take the elevator to the basement to watch movies at **Cine Foro** (*see* After Dark, *below*). One block south of the university is the pseudo-gothic **Templo Expiatorio** (Madero, at Escorza), so dark and imposing that you almost expect to hear Gregorian chants drifting from the choir. *Juárez, at Enrique Díaz de León. Take the* PAR VIAL *west on Juárez and ask to be let off at the university.*

ZOOLOGICO DE GUADALAJARA • With 32 hectares (79 acres) to cover and more than 1,500 animal species to gawk at, you'll need plenty of energy and a full afternoon to see the whole zoo. Luckily, a 70¢ train travels the circumference of the park, stopping midway at the Barranca de Huentitán, where you can see part of the canyon that borders the city. *Paseo del Zoológico 600, tel. 3/674–10–34 or 3/674–44–88. Take Bus 60 or 60-A N on Calz. Independencia to zoo entrance. Admission: $1.85. Open Tues.–Sun. 10–6.*

SOUTH OF THE CENTRO HISTORICO

Guadalajara's premier urban getaway is the **Parque Agua Azul.** Nine hectares of eucalyptus, pine, and jacaranda forest surround shady paths, benches, and idyllic lawns. There's also a small orchid greenhouse and a huge aviary inhabited by parrots, peacocks, and other exotic birds. *Calz. Independencia Sur, south of Niños Héroes, tel. 3/619–03–28. Bus 62 S on Calz. Independencia to Niños Héroes. Admission: 50¢. Open Tues.–Sun. 10–6.*

At the northern end of the park is the **Casa de Artesanías de Jalisco,** a government-run crafts store organized like a museum, with craft samples from many regions of Mexico. Prices here tend to be high, making it a good place to check out quality items before buying from street vendors. *González Gallo, at Calz. Independencia Sur, tel. 3/619–46–64. Open weekdays 10–6, Sat. 10–5, Sun. 10–3.*

The **Teatro Experimental de Jalisco,** next to the park's main entrance, performs everything from Shakespeare to Mexican avant-garde. Check the bulletin board near the park entrance, take a look at "Tentaciones" (*see* After Dark, *below*), or call 3/619–37–70 for more information.

Across Calzada Independencia Sur from the park, the **Museo de Arqueología del Occidente** is small, well-organized, and packed with pottery made by the indigenous peoples of western Mexico. The museum shop sells display items at high prices. *Calz. Independencia Sur, at Av. del Campesino, no phone. Admission: 20¢. Open Tues.–Sun. 10–2 and 4–7.*

TLAQUEPAQUE

Guadalajara's elite founded Tlaquepaque as a country retreat, but automobiles and housing developments slowly encroached on this rustic hamlet. The town's spacious manors remained in disrepair until the 1960s, when artists converted many of the buildings into studios. Today, central Tlaquepaque has a lively and colorful pedestrian zone lined with gallery after gallery of high-priced handmade crafts and rustic furniture. Vendors on the street often offer a better deal and sometimes even a better selection.

The main street in Tlaquepaque is pedestrians-only **Independencia. Artmex la Rosa de Cristal** (Independencia 232, tel. 3/639–71–80) sells hand-blown glass; visit the artists' studios (Contreras Medellí 173; open weekdays 8–1, Sat. 8–noon) to witness the ancient craft of glassblowing for yourself. The free **Museo Regional de la Cerámica** (Independencia 237, tel. 3/635–54–04; open Tues.–Sat. 10–6, Sun. 10–3), housed in an old country estate, exhibits the work of expert potters and operates a small gift shop. Independencia ends at the lively **El Parián plaza** (Independencia, at Madero). Named after the Chinese section of Manila, the plaza is a great place to grab a beer and refuse the advances of wandering portrait artists and mariachi bands. Several bars are on the outskirts of the plaza, while the gazebo in the center is often given over to local musicians. For maps, festival information, and other tidbits, head to the **tourist office** (Donato Guerra 160, inside the Centro Cultural el Refugio, tel. 3/659–02–38; open daily 9–7). *From downtown, take Bus 275 or 706 S on 16 de Septiembre; after traveling ½ hr down Revolución, look for brick arches followed by a traffic circle; get off and walk NW to Independencia.*

Restaurants here are expensive, so if you want a sit-down meal, go where it's worth the extra pesos. **Fonda la Medina** (Independencia 195, tel. 3/657–94–67) serves savory Mexican specialties on a beau-

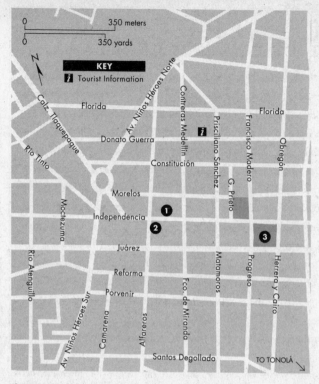

TLAQUEPAQUE

Artmex la Rosa
de Cristal, **1**
Museo Regional
de la Cerámica, **2**
El Parián Plaza, **3**

Map labels:
0 — 350 meters
0 — 350 yards

KEY
i Tourist Information

Calz. Tlaquepaque
Florida
Av. Niños Héroes Norte
Contreras Medellín
Prisciliano Sánchez
Francisco Madero
Florida
Obregón
Donato Guerra
Río Tinto
Constitución
G. Prieto
Morelos
Independencia
Mochtezuma
Juárez
Río Atengullo
Reforma
Matamoros
Progreso
Herrera y Cairo
Porvenir
Av. Niños Héroes Sur
Camarena
Alfareros
Fco. de Miranda
Santos Degollado
TO TONOLÁ

tiful outdoor patio with trickling fountain. Soups and salads run $2, main dishes cost $5. At **Birriería El Sope** (Donato Guerra 142, tel. 3/659–23–33; closed Fri. during Lent), meat lovers can sample a $3 plate of *birria* (roasted goat or pork stew).

TONALA

This smaller, humbler version of Tlaquepaque is also a famous crafts center. In fact, many of the ceramics and other crafts sold in Tlaquepaque are made in Tonala, so prices here tend to be cheaper. A small **tourist information booth,** on the Plaza Principal, has a friendly staff that hands out maps and brochures. Plaza Principal hosts a *tianguis* (open-air market) Thursday and Sunday 8–4. The free **Museo Nacional de la Cerámica** (Constitución 110, tel. 3/683–04–94; open Tues.–Fri. 10–2 and 3–4:30, Sat. 10–3, Sun. 10–2) displays a range of Mexican pottery old and new, and has a workshop and small store. The **Santuario del Sagrado Corazón** (Madero, corner Juárez) has a brightly painted interior and large paintings of the 14 stations of the cross. Behind the altar is a striking representation of Jesus Christ rising from a cloud-shrouded earth. **Lienzo Charro González Valle,** on Avenida Tonaltecas, stages a full-blown *charreada* (rodeo), complete with lasso tricks and wild-horse taming on Saturday at 4 PM. Tickets are $2; for more information, call or visit the main tourist office (Av. de las Tonaltecas 140 Sur, tel. 3/683–17–40; open weekdays 9–3, Sat. 9–1). *From downtown, take Bus 275 or 706 S on 16 de Septiembre, past Tlaquepaque.*

ZAPOPAN

The suburb of Zapopan lies 7 km (4½ mi) northwest of downtown Guadalajara. It boasts the magnificent **Basílica de Zapopan,** an 18th-century structure with an ornate baroque facade and a tile dome. The basilica is home to the **Virgen de Zapopan,** a 10-inch figurine regarded as one of Mexico's most powerful miracle workers. Veneration of the virgin culminates in a pilgrimage every October 12, when more than 1 million faithful tapatíos honor the figurine's return to the basilica after her annual tour of every parish church in Jalisco state. The small **Museo Huichol,** at the east end of the basilica, is run by Franciscan monks who proselytize among the Huichol people (*see box, below*). The museum exhibits colorful clothing, beadwork, and unique, elaborate renditions of Huichol myths "painted" entirely with yarn.

THE STRUGGLE
OF THE HUICHOL

Most Huichol Indians live in northern Jalisco, southern Nayarit, and Zacatecas, in a remote 592,800-acre reservation established in 1953. The Huichol remain a proud people with age-old traditions, though recently their independent ways have resulted in an ugly conflict with neighboring landowners: The ownership and territorial boundaries of many acres that the Huichol had rented out to farmers and cattle breeders are currently in dispute. There have been allegations of human rights violations perpetrated by Nayarit police as well as by the current "tenants." The Mexican government's Human Rights Commission (CEDH) has been investigating the alleged violations since 1993 and has granted limited financial and political support to the Huichol in the interim. A recent constitutional amendment affirms the CEDH's measures, by recognizing the autonomy of the Huichol and other indigenous communities within Mexico. Yet even with these advances, ownership of land continues to be a heated issue in the region. In late 1996, proposals to set up a 3,600-square-km (1,400-square-mi) nature preserve on Huichol land has drawn protests from Huichol leaders.

Most items are for sale, and proceeds benefit the Huichol people. Zapopan's **visitor information** center is in the Casa de Cultura (Vicente Guerrero 233, tel. 3/633–24–12 or 3/636–6727; open weekdays 9–8). *To reach Zapopan, take Bus 275 N on 16 de Septiembre.*

CHEAP THRILLS

Guadalajara offers plenty of fun excursions and diversions that are cheap or free. Follow Calzada Independencia Norte to the northeastern edge of Guadalajara to find the 2,000-ft-deep canyon **Barranca de Oblatos.** On weekends, the canyon park fills with families who come to enjoy its spectacular views and varied vegetation. Take Bus 60 north on Calzada Independencia Norte to the last stop. The park is open daily 7–7 and admission is 20¢. The **Cola de Caballo** (Horsetail) waterfall plummets over a cliff into the depths of the canyon. Though you can't swim in the falls, it makes a lovely spot for a picnic. To reach the waterfall, take Bus 275 or 54 on 16 de Septiembre to Glorieta La Normal; transfer to the Ixcatán bus to Parque Dr. Atl (20–30 min total). The waterfall park is open Tuesday–Sunday 10–6, and admission is 75¢.

You can spend the whole day browsing the rows of stands in **El Baratillo,** Mexico's second-largest outdoor market. The market (open Sun. 7–4) is a huge maze that covers some 30–40 city blocks, primarily around Calle Esteban Loera, several blocks east of Mercado Libertad. Just when you think you've seen it all—shoelaces, cassettes, vegetables, new and used clothes, heavy machinery, live pigs and goats—something else pops up. *Take PAR VIAL bus east on Hidalgo until you see the market.*

If you haven't worn out your dancing shoes yet, head out to the tiny town of **Santa María Tequepexpan,** where a *tardeada* (afternoon dance) is held at the bullfighting arena after Sunday sporting events. This is cowboy culture in all its glory, with men in Marlboro-man gear swinging their partners to lively ranchera music. Admission is $1, and the fun lasts from about 5 to 10 PM. Before starting off, check with the Guaudalajara tourist office to make sure a dance and bullfight will take place during your visit. *Take tren ligero south to Periférico Sur station; ask someone to point you toward Santa María Tequepexpan (a 10-min walk).*

FESTIVALS

Lake Chapala (*see* Near Guadalajara, *below*) is the place to be for **Carnaval** (late February or early March). The **Fiestas de Tlaquepaque** (mid-June to early July), celebrate the artesanía of Tlaquepaque with music, dancing, cockfights, and loads of food and drink. The **Fiesta de Santiago Apostol** (July 25) is an all-day fair that takes place in Tonalá, culminating in the *Danza de los Tastoanes,* an indigenous dance reenacting the Spanish conquest. The **Fiestas de Octubre** (October) is Guadalajara's monthlong commercial and cultural fair. On October 12 Guadalajara also celebrates the **Día de la Virgen de Zapopan** (*see* Worth Seeing, *above*), when 1 million pilgrims walk the 7 km (4½ mi) between Guadalajara's cathedral and Zapopan's basilica.

AFTER DARK

Guadalajara once rivaled Mexico City as a place where you could dance until dawn, but local ordinances now require that the sidewalks be rolled up at 2 AM. That said, plenty of discos and bars have special contracts with the city government to keep things hopping after hours. Keep in mind that buses stop at around 10 PM, making taxis ($4–$6) your only late-night option back to the budget lodging area. The daily paper *Siglo 21* lists entertainment options around the city, including movies, theaters, galleries, music, and dance. Its Friday "Tentaciones" section has the most expansive coverage. The Sunday edition of *El Informador* also provides a listing of upcoming events, as does the English-language weekly the *Guadalajara Colony Reporter.*

Bars and discos are clustered around Chapultepec and Vallarta, though you'll need money, connections, and/or fancy clothes to get past the bouncers. Many gay and lesbian clubs are on or near Obregón and Calles 50–60, in an eastern portion of the city rarely frequented by tourists; the best way to reach them from downtown is by cab. For an evening of mariachi music (*see box, above*), head for El Parián in the suburb of Tlaquepaque (*see* Worth Seeing, *above*). A tableside serenade costs about $4. Strolling musicians also work the **Plaza de los Mariachis** in downtown Guadalajara, next to the Iglesia San Juan de Dios and Mercado Libertad, but the area is more safely visited by day rather than by night.

The three main plazas of the centro histórico, **Plaza de Armas, Plaza de la Liberación,** and **Plaza Tapatía,** fill with frolicking people of all ages during the evenings, especially on weekends. Caricaturists and marimba players call out to passersby, while mimes, puppeteers, and musicians enthrall the crowds. In the bandstand of Plaza de Armas, the Guadalajara Municipal band gives free concerts Tuesday at 6:30 PM, while the Jalisco State band plays Thursday and Sunday at 6:30 PM.

BARS

Babel. Guadalajara's number-one alternative hangout is a long, dim bar with a dance floor on the back patio. Patrons average at least five visible piercings. Expect a $2 cover if there's live rock, usually weekends. *Vallarta 1480, at Chapultepec, tel. 3/615–63–61. Open weekends until 3 AM. Closed Sun.*

Black Beards. This bar is a Guadalajara institution, featuring occasional live rock with no cover and an older crowd. *Justo Sierra 2194, corner Américas, tel. 3/615–38–79. Open weekends until 3 AM. Closed Mon. and Tues.*

La Cripta. The dimly lit corridors of "the Crypt" are the haunts of Guadalajara's wealthiest alternative crowd. A 2-liter pitcher of beer costs $5. On weekends, there's a $1.50 cover for live, loud rock. *Tepeyac 4038, at Niño Obrero, tel. 3/647–62–07.*

La Maestranza. This rustic tavern doubles as a *museo taurino* (bullfighting museum). The padded leather tables and chairs are cozy perches for the young, party-minded crowd. There are free *botanas* (snacks) to go with the tequila and beer on tap. *Maestranza 579, between López Cotilla and Madero, tel. 3/613–58–78.*

CINEMAS

Dozens of theaters around the city show recent, undubbed American and international films. You'll find current listings in the daily paper *Siglo 21.* **Cine Foro** (Juárez, at Enrique Díaz de León, tel. 3/825–88–88), in the basement of the Universidad de Guadalajara administration building; **Cine Cinematógrafo** (Vallarta 1102, several blocks west of Cine Foro; tel. 3/825–05–14); and **Cine Teatro Cabañas** (tel. 3/617–43–22 or 3/617–44–40), at the Instituto Cultural Cabañas (*see* Worth Seeing, *above*), are all good venues for quality movies. Tickets average $2.75. **Videosala** (Libertad 1690, corner Venezuela, tel. 3/825–66–53), also near the university administration building, shows Mexican and international art films ($2) on weekdays. Its monthly program guide is available on site, or at the information booth in the university administration building.

DANCING

Guadalajara has its share of big, flashy, expensive discos, which attract a well-heeled twenty-something crowd. If you're among the "chosen" few (literally—bouncers here can be tough), the latest dance beats await you inside. Cavernous **Lado B** (Vallarta 2451, corner Francisco de Quevedo, tel. 3/615–71–76) plays the usual rock, pop, and techno, but without a dance floor (you shake it next to your chair). The bi-level **La Marcha** (Vallarta 2648, corner Arcos, tel. 3/615–89–99) is a baroque-style disco, while **La Mákina** (Vallarta 1920, near Chapultepec, tel. 3/615–23–25) is done up in an industrial motif. The Greek-theme **Persepolis** (Vallarta 2503, tel. 3/615–75–46) tries for the over-25 crowd and offers an airier *ambiente,* complete with waterfall and outdoor patio. Covers at any of these run $11–$14 for men, less than $4 for women, and usually includes an open bar.

Of the *salones* (dance halls) that host live *bandas* playing traditional Mexican music, **Salón Corona** (López Mateos 2380, tel. 3/647–08–82) is one of the best. Women get in free Monday–Thursday (men pay $3). Also renowned is **Copacabana** (López Mateos, tel. 3/631–45–96; closed Mon.), which plays live salsa and merengue for a $4 cover. **Casino Veracruz** (Manzano 486, at Av. del Campesino, tel. 3/613–44–22; closed Mon.) has tropical and salsa music, $2 cover.

GAY BARS AND CLUBS

During weeknights, the place to be is **Máscaras** (Maestranzas 238, at Prisciliano Sánchez, tel. 3/614–81–03). At this no-cover bar, masks adorn lavender-color walls while contemporary Mexican and American pop blares from the jukebox. Dance clubs heat up Wednesday through Sunday: **Mónica's** (Obregón 1713, near Calle 64, no phone) is mostly for gay men; **La Malinche** (Obregón 1230, near Calle 48, tel. 3/643–65–62) attracts gays and non-gays, and features lots of Latin music; and **El Taller** (Calle 66, No. 30, near Gigantes, tel. 643–98–32) plays techno for an all-gay crowd. **S.O.S.** (Av. de la Paz 1413, at Enrique Díaz de León, tel. 3/826–41–79) is a hot club for both gays and lesbians (Wednesday night for men, Thursday for women, everyone welcome on other nights). All of the above charge a $2.75–$3.50 cover, and Mónica's, La Malinche, and S.O.S. feature transvestite shows. **Angels** (Av. de la Paz 2030, ½ block west of Chapultepec, tel. 3/615–25–25) is an upscale place attracting gay men, lesbians, and non-gays. It's cover-free and also houses a restaurant.

LIVE MUSIC

Many of the city's bars (*see above*) frequently host live music, usually American-inspired rock. **Peña Cuicacalli** (corner Niños Héroes 1988 and Chapultepec, at Glorieta Niños Héroes, tel. 3/825–46–90) is the granddaddy of Guadalajara's *casas de canto* (literally, "houses of song"). The peña attracts an enthusiastic mixed-age audience, for music ranging from folk to salsa to nueva canción and rock. Music starts around 8:30 PM, and the cover runs $2–$8. **La Peñita** (Vallarta 1110, tel. 3/825–58–53; closed Mon.) is a friendly restaurant with live music similar to Cuicacalli's. Sundays are free; other nights you pay $2–$8 to hear jazz, Afro-Antillean, blues, and Latin American music. The music starts at 9 PM (6 PM on Sunday). An attractive newcomer on the same music scene is **El Solar** (Av. de la Paz 1840, tel. 3/825–31–68) in a restored turn-of-the-century house.

NEAR GUADALAJARA

LAKE CHAPALA

Mexico's largest lake, bordered by lush, almost tropical mountains, is a pleasant place to spend the weekend. Although the lake itself is plagued by severe ecological problems—the water from the Río Lerma is severely polluted, and huge pipelines pump water daily toward Guadalajara—this does little to diminish the beauty of the natural surroundings. The town of Chapala is a popular retirement community for Mexicans, Canadians, and Americans, and during the week you may hear more English than Spanish in the town's restaurants. On weekends, families from Guadalajara dominate the boardwalk, and the air is full of the cries of vendors hawking ice cream and fried fish. Get away from it all by taking a boat to **Isla de los Alacranes** (Scorpion Island). It costs $13.50 for the boat ride (15 min each way) plus 30 minutes on the island, or $16 for the ride and an hour on the island. Boats for hire line up by the pier at the southern end of Madero, just past the intersection of Paseo Ramón Corona.

COMING AND GOING

Buses leave from Guadalajara's old bus station (*see* Coming and Going *in* Guadalajara, *above*) every half hour 5:30 AM–9 PM (45 min, $1.75). Return buses depart from the bus station on Madero in Chapala; the last bus is at 8:15 PM.

WHERE TO SLEEP AND EAT

The cheapest place to stay in Chapala is the **Casa de Huéspedes Las Palmitas** (Juárez 531, behind the market, tel. 376/5–30–70). Basic rooms in this converted old house cost $10.75 doubles, cash only. The **Villa Montecarlo** (Hidalgo 296, 1 km/½ mi west of Madero, tel. 376/5–22–16 or 376/5–21–20) is a sprawling hilltop establishment with simple rooms and two thermal water pools. Doubles cost $30. A number of fairly decent restaurants hug the lakeshore, and they're not too outrageously priced; try **La Playita** (Acapulquito Local 4, tel. 376/5–41–40) for big plates of fish and shrimp *al ajo* (with garlic; $5.75). The English-speaking staff at Chapala's **tourist office** (Aquiles Serdán 26, tel. 376/5–31–41; open weekdays 9–7, weekends 9–1) eagerly doles out information.

TEQUILA

The town of Tequila—as you may have already guessed—is the home of Mexico's national drink. Most locals work the fields of agave, or are employed in one of the town's 10 tequila distilleries that ship the firewater to more than 90 countries around the world. Well-known brands like Cuervo and Sauza produce their stuff here. **José Cuervo** (Blvd. José Cuervo, 3 blocks from the bus station, tel. 374/2–00–11) gives tours Monday–Saturday 10–1, ending with free samples. Groups of six or more should make an appointment. The **Herradura** distillery, about 14 km (8 mi) closer to Guadalajara in the town of Amatitán, is widely regarded as makers of Mexico's best tequila. Tours (Mon.–Thurs. and Sat. 10–1) are free but you need an appointment; call the Herradura office (tel. 374/5–00–11 or 374/5–01–99) and ask to speak to Salvador Huerta. For help finding other tequila factories, stop by the **tourist information booth** (outside the town hall, tel. 374/2–00–12 or 374/2–00–13) on Tequila's main plaza.

On Chapala's boardwalk, vendors hawk sodas, candy, and nuts that are perfect for snacking. Grab a bag of pistachios, take a seat on a nearby bench, and watch the passersby.

COMING AND GOING

Buses (1½ hrs, $2) leave from the old bus station (*see* Coming and Going *in* Guadalajara, *above*) every 20 minutes, daily 6 AM–9:15 PM. The return schedule is similar.

THE PACIFIC COAST

UPDATED BY WENDY LUFT

ourneying along the Pacific Coast, you'll constantly encounter one thing: the ocean. Aquamarine swells provide a scenic backdrop to beachside *palapas* (thatched-roof huts) and palm trees; rolling waves offer a playground for boogie boarders, Jet Skiers, and surfers; and the salty waters offer up a smorgasbord of fresh seafood that is sliced, diced, and spiced into tasty regional dishes. Many cities regularly celebrate the ocean as their source of livelihood: San Blas blesses the sea in a joyous festival, Manzanillo holds world-renown sailfish tournaments, and Mexcaltitán kicks off the opening of its shrimping season with fireworks and a fiesta. With all this going for it, it's not surprising that the Pacific Coast has been a haven for beach-seeking tourists since the 1950s, when the region was targeted by the Mexican department of tourism as a means of luring foreign currency to boost the flagging economy.

If you're looking for action, you've come to the right place. Cities such as Ixtapa/Zihuatanejo, Puerto Vallarta, and Acapulco are guaranteed to keep you entertained day and night with their myriad water sports centers and flashy discos. Conversely, though tourists and their freely spent pesos keep the coast's fishermen and hotel owners in business, the influx of foreigners has resulted in a pervasive "Americanization" throughout the region. For the most part, traditional dress and customs are relegated to the countryside, and restaurants that actually serve *Mexican* food have only recently gained favor in the Perrier-and-pizza world of beach resort towns. But don't despair. Much of the Pacific Coast remains relatively underdeveloped, and beach towns such as Barra de Navidad, Pie de la Cuesta, and San Blas still offer peace and quiet in traditional Mexican fashion.

Those who think the Pacific Coast is all sun and surf will be surprised by the states of Sinaloa, Nayarit, Jalisco, Colima, and Guerrero: Farmland, volcanoes, and mountains take over once you're out of sight of the Pacific Ocean. The towering Sierra Madre Occidental and Sierra Madre Sur mountain ranges attract hikers. Inland towns such as Tepic and Santiago Ixcuintla are home to the *indígenas* (indigenous people), the Huichols and Coras. Their world is far removed from the resort towns, but they still depend on profits from the tourist industry for their cultural and financial survival. Whatever you do on the Pacific Coast, whether you choose to visit mountain villages, hit the powerful surf, maneuver through a tropical jungle, or hike an active volcano, do it in the tourist off-season (June–Sept.), when the hotels empty out and the prices drop significantly.

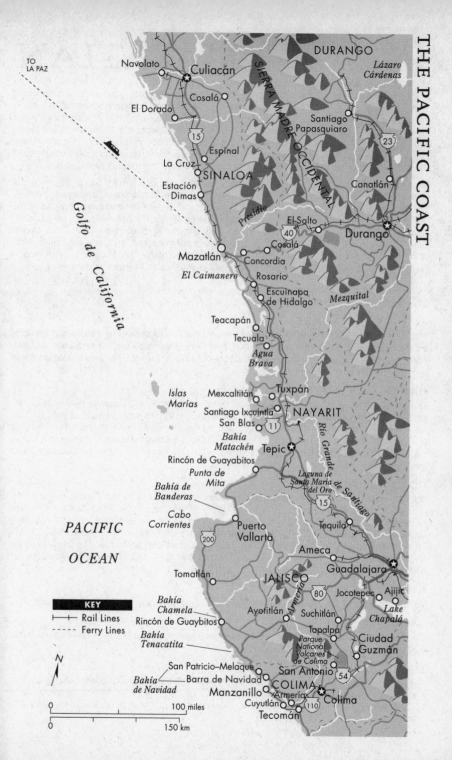

TO LA PAZ

Navolato
Culiacán
DURANGO
Lázaro Cárdenas
Cosalá
El Dorado
Santiago Papasquiaro
Espinal
SIERRA MADRE OCCIDENTAL
15
La Cruz
SINALOA
Canatlán
23
Estación Dimas
Presidio
El Salto
Durango
40
Cosalá
Mazatlán
Concordia
El Caimanero
Rosario
Escuinapa de Hidalgo
Mezquital
Teacapán
Tecuala
Agua Brava
Golfo de California
Islas Marías
Mexcaltitán
Tuxpán
Santiago Ixcuintla
NAYARIT
San Blas
11
Bahía Matachén
Tepic
Río Grande de Santiago
Rincón de Guayabitos
Punta de Mita
Laguna de Santa María del Oro
Bahía de Banderas
15
Cabo Corrientes
Puerto Vallarta
Tequila
PACIFIC
200
Ameca
Guadalajara
OCEAN
Tomatlán
JALISCO
80
Jocotepec
Ajijic
Bahía Chamela
Ayotitlán
Suchitlán
Lake Chapalá
Rincón de Guaybitos
Tapalpa
Bahía Tenacatita
Parque Nacional Volcanes de Colima
Ciudad Guzmán
San Patricio–Melaque
Barra de Navidad
San Antonio
54
Bahía de Navidad
COLIMA
Manzanillo
Armería
Colima
Cuyutlán
110
Tecomán

KEY
+ Rail Lines
- - - Ferry Lines

N

0   100 miles
0   150 km

MAZATLAN

Mazatlán, with a population of 400,000, offers a glimpse of the Pacific Coast's dual identities. While the new **Zona Dorada** (Golden Zone) is packed with luxury time-share condos, glitzy resorts, and more than 1 million tourists a year, **Mazatlán Viejo** (Old Mazatlán) rolls along as a flourishing seaport, shrimp-packing city, and sport-fishing haven. Combine the two and Mazatlán has something for the merrymaker and the mellow alike: Party-minded travelers can hit the beaches and discos with a vengeance, and resort-weary souls can drink in the folk dance, art, and colorful colonial-style buildings of Mazatlán Viejo. Mazatlán, it seems, has always catered to visitors, from the pre–Spanish conquest pirates who rested at their "Island of Mazatlán," to gold-driven miners in search of riches, to today's diverse tourists.

Mazatlán's party atmosphere really kicks in during **Carnaval,** the city's biggest fiesta, celebrated just before Lent (usually February). Thousands of tourists, both domestic and foreign, descend on the town for six days and nights to enjoy music, dancing, fireworks, and parades. **Semana Santa** (Holy Week, the week before Easter) is a smaller festival that draws reveling Mexicans with its religious reenactments, parades, and music. The changing seasons also bring different kinds of visitors to Mazatlán. During summer, the resort town becomes the humid playground of American students and Mexican tourists. When the mercury drops from the scorching 90s to the comfortable 70s, Mazatlán's winter season begins, and older visitors from the United States and Canada flock to the expensive hotels.

BASICS

AMERICAN EXPRESS

This office delivers MoneyGrams and changes traveler's checks at a decent rate. In addition, cardholders can cash personal checks and have mail held. *Av. Camarón Sábalo, Plaza Balboa, Local 4, Mazatlán, Sinaloa, CP 82110, México, tel. 69/13–06–00. 1 block north of Dairy Queen. Open weekdays 9–6, Sat. 9–noon.*

CASAS DE CAMBIO

The Zona Dorada teems with *casas de cambio* (money-changing offices). **Banamex** (Flores, at Juárez, tel. 69/82–77–33; open weekdays 8:30–noon) exchanges cash and traveler's checks at the best rates in town. They charge no commission and also have ATMs that accept Cirrus and Plus cards. Places to change money are scarcer downtown; try the **Casa de Cambio Camiga** (Belisario Domínguez 2, at Flores, tel. 69/85–00–03; open Mon.–Sat. 9–1:30 and 3:30–7) in Plaza Concordia. The rates here aren't great, but there's no commission on traveler's checks.

CONSULATES

Mazatlán doesn't have an actual **United States** consulate, but you can contact the U.S. consular representative, Geri Nelson (Loaiza 202, in Zona Dorada, tel. and fax 69/16–58–89). Geri's office, open weekdays 9:30–1:30, is in the Hotel Playa Mazatlán complex. Or in an emergency call the U.S. consulate in Hermosillo (tel. 62/17–23–75). **Canada's** representative, Fernanda B. Romero (tel. 69/13–73–20, fax 69/14–65–55), is in the same complex, across the street from Geri's office. Her office hours are weekdays 9–1. Citizens from other countries should contact the tourist office at Olas Altas 1300 for information on consulates in Mexico City.

EMERGENCIES

You can dial 06 from any phone in Mazatlán to reach the **police, fire** department, or an **ambulance.**

LAUNDRY

The 24-hour **Lavandería Romy** will wash, dry, and fold a load of clothing ($2) in as little as three hours. *120 Hidalgo, near 5 de Mayo, tel. 69/82–80–42.*

MAIL

The post office will hold mail sent to you at the following address for up to 10 days: Lista de Correos, Administración Postal No. 1, Centro, Benito Juárez y 21 de Marzo, Mazatlán, Sinaloa, CP 82001, México. You can send or receive telegrams at the office next door. *Juárez, at 21 de Marzo, tel. 69/81–21–21. Open weekdays 8–7, Sat. 8–1.*

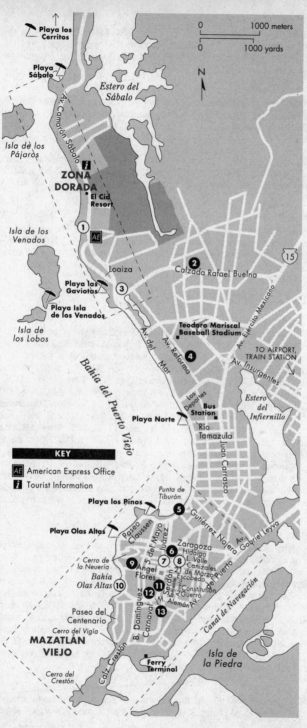

Playa los
Cerritos

Playa
Sábalo

Estero del
Sábalo

Sights ●

Acurario
Mazatlán, **4**

Mercado Central, **6**

Monumento al
Pescador, **5**

Museo
Arqueológico, **9**

Plaza de Toros, **2**

Plaza Machado, **12**

Plaza Revolución
and Basílica, **11**

Teatro Ángel
Peralta, **13**

Lodging ○

Casa de Huéspedes
El Castillo, **8**

Hotel Belmar, **10**

Hotel
Bugambilias, **1**

Hotel del Centro, **7**

Hotel San Diego, **3**

N

Isla de los
Pájaros

ZONA
DORADA

El Cid
Resort

Av. Camarón Sábalo

AE

15

Loaiza

Calzada Rafael Buelna

Isla de los
Venados

Playa las
Gaviotas

Playa Isla
de los Venados

Isla de
los Lobos

Teodoro Mariscal
Baseball Stadium

Av. del Mar

Av. Reforma

Av. Ejército Mexicano

Av. Insurgentes

TO AIRPORT,
TRAIN STATION

Bahía del Puerto Viejo

Los
Deportes

Bus
Station

Estero
del
Infiernillo

Playa Norte

Río
Tamazula

Juan Carrasco

KEY

AE American Express Office

i Tourist Information

Punta de
Tiburón

Playa los Pinos

Gutiérrez Nájera

Playa Olas Altas

Paseo
Claussen

5 de Mayo

Juárez

Zaragoza
Hidalgo
V. Valle
Canizales
de Marzo
Escobedo
Constitution
Guerro

Av. Gabriel Leyva

Cerro de
la Neuería

Ángel
Flores

Serdán
Aquiles
Serdán
Leandro
Valdez

Av. del Puerto

Bahía
Olas Altas

Constitution
M. Alemán Av.

Canal de Navegación

Paseo del
Centenario

B. Domínguez

Carnaval

Calz. Crestón

Cerro del Vigía

**MAZATLÁN
VIEJO**

Cerro del
Crestón

Ferry
Terminal

Isla de
la Piedra

0 — 1000 meters
0 — 1000 yards

MEDICAL AID

Miguel Ángel Guzmán Elizondo (Nelson 1808, tel. 69/81–25–87, or 69/81–51–17 after clinic hours) is a locally respected, English-speaking doctor. He sees patients weekdays 10–2 and 5–8, Saturday 10–1; consultations cost $12–$20. The 24-hour **Farmacia Cruz Verde** (Gutiérrez Najera 901, at Obregón, tel. 69/81–22–25) handles minor problems and prescriptions.

PHONES

You'll find pay phones on almost every other block throughout the Zona Dorada and Mazatlán Viejo. To place cash calls, make free collect calls, or send faxes, visit **Computel** (corner Rodolfo T. Loaiza and Camaróon Sábalo, tel. 69/16–02–67; open 24 hrs).

SCHOOLS

The **Centro de Idiomas** in Mazatlán Viejo offers Spanish instruction at all levels, with small class sizes. Twenty hours of instruction per week costs $140, plus a $105 registration fee. Homestays are available for $130–$150 per person per week. *Belisario Domínguez 1908, Mazatlán, Sinaloa, México, CP 82000, tel. 69/82–20–53, fax 69/85–56–06.*

VISITOR INFORMATION

The huge federal **tourist office** has a helpful staff, some of whom speak English. You'll be sure to leave with an armful of pamphlets and maps. *Camarón Sábalo, at Tiburón, tel. 69/16–51–60, fax 69/16–51–66. 4th floor of Banrural building, across from Holiday Inn. Open weekdays 8:30–2 and 5–7:30 (open Sat. 9–1 for phone calls only).*

COMING AND GOING

BY BUS

The immense **Central Camionera** (Carretera Internacional Km. 1203, at Chachalacas, tel 69/82–02–87) is divided into two sections: One is devoted to long-distance first-class buses, and the other to second-class buses. First-class buses are speedy, clean, and air-conditioned, while second-class buses are cheap, roomy, and slow. **Transportes Pacífico** (tel. 69/82–05–77) offers first-class service to Mexico City (16 hrs, $45), Guadalajara (7 hrs, $21), and Tijuana (26 hrs, $64). **Élite** (tel. 69/81–36–80) sends a daily first-class bus to Acapulco (25 hrs, $60), with stops in Puerto Vallarta (8 hrs, $18) and Manzanillo (12 hrs, $30); buses to Tepic (4½ hrs, $12) leave every hour. Second-class **Transportes Norte de Sonora** (tel. 69/81–38–46) buses stop in Mazatlán hourly on their way to Guadalajara (9 hrs, $17.50), Mexico City (19 hrs, $39), Tijuana (29 hrs, $56), and Nogales (17 hrs, $35). **Estrella Blanca** (tel. 69/81–53–81) runs second-class buses six times a day to Durango (7 hrs, $10.50); from there, you can transfer to a Monterrey-bound bus (17 hrs, $45). Luggage storage is available at the station ($1 per 4 hrs), and there's a **Computel** phone office (tel. and fax 69/85–39–31) where you can make cash calls. To get downtown or to the market from the bus station, catch any bus marked INSURGENTES on Avenida Ejército Mexicano; or walk to the *malecón* (boardwalk) and take a southbound CAMARON SABALO bus. The northbound CAMARON SABALO bus will take you to the Zona Dorada. A taxi to the Zona Dorada costs about $2.

BY FERRY

Sematur makes the 18-hour ferry crossing to La Paz on the Baja peninsula at 3 PM, every day except Thursday and Saturday. An uncomfortable reclining seat costs $20, and a berth in a four-person cabin is $60. A two-person cabin with private bathroom is $80 per person. Vehicles can be ferried as well, but price varies according to size; the average-size car costs about $100. Purchase or reserve ferry tickets in the office at the ferry landing on Playa Sur (Prolongación Carnaval, tel. 69/81–70–21; open weekdays 8–3:30, Saturday 9–1). The travel agency **Turismo Coral** (5 de Mayo 1705, tel. 69/81–32–90; open weekdays 8–2 and 3–7, Sat. 8–2), in Mazatlán Viejo, sells ferry tickets at no additional charge. Make reservations several days in advance (even earlier during Easter holidays), and arrive at least an hour before the boat departs. To reach the ferry terminal, take the PLAYA SUR bus from the market. The terminal has luggage storage ($1.50 per day). The boat has a high-price restaurant and snack bar; consider stocking up on edibles and drinking water before you board.

BY PLANE

Mazatlán's airport (tel. 69/82–23–99) is a 40-minute drive from town. Taxis make the trip for around $15, and *pulmonías* (golf cart–like vehicles) charge $10. Cheaper still are *combis* (VW vans), which operate as *colectivos* (communal taxis). They charge roughly $4 and travel between the airport and Mazatlán's major hotels. Carriers that serve Mazatlán from the United States include **Aeroméxico** (Camarón Sábalo 310, tel. 69/14–11–11), **Alaska Airlines** (in airport, tel. 69/85–27–30), and **Mexicana** (Paseo Claussen 101-B, tel. 69/82–77–22). Domestic carriers include **Aero California** (tel. 69/13–20–42) and **Aviación del Noroeste** (tel. 69/14–38–33), both with offices in the El Cid Hotel on Camarón Sábalo. Numerous booths inside the airport terminal provide free information on hotels and transportation. There are a few international phones but no luggage storage area.

BY TRAIN

Mazatlán lies on the Pacific rail line, one of the most efficient routes in Mexico. The train station (tel. 69/84–67–10) is northeast of Mazatlán Viejo, on Avenida Ferrocarril in the Colonia Esperanza. To get here, take a taxi ($2) or hail one of the buses labeled ESPERANZA from Olas Altas. The first-class northbound train leaves daily at 8:15 PM, making stops at Culiacán (4 hrs, $5), Nogales (19 hrs, $21), and Mexicali (26 hrs, $30). The second-class northbound train leaves at 2 PM; fares are approximately half the first-class prices, and travel times are much, much longer. Southbound trains stop in Tepic (5 hrs, $6 1st class; 6 hrs, $3.50 2nd class) en route to Guadalajara (10 hrs, $14.75 1st class; 12 hrs, $6 2nd class). Departure time is 2 PM daily for first class, and 5 AM for second class. First-class trains fill up quickly, so reserve seats the morning of departure. The ticket office is open daily 9–1 and 3–5.

GETTING AROUND

Mazatlán has two primary neighborhoods: Mazatlán Viejo, at the southern end of the city, and the Zona Dorada (Golden Zone) to the north. Mazatlán Viejo is the civic and commercial center and includes the city's malecón. This walkable area centers around **Plaza Revolución,** the city's zócalo (main plaza). It includes the **Basílica de la Inmaculada Concepción,** Mazatlán's main church, on Avenida Benito Juárez. **Olas Altas,** a relatively quiet strip of beach, lies along the waterfront in Mazatlán Viejo, about seven blocks east of the basilica. Avenida del Mar connects Old and New Mazatlán, running north along Playa Norte to Valentino's disco, where its name changes to Camarón Sábalo. The Zona Dorada, with its resort hotels, crowded beaches, and time-share condos, begins here.

The open attitude of the Pacific Coast's beach towns draws many vacationing gays and lesbians. Acapulco is the traditional gay mecca, though Puerto Vallarta and San Blas are gaining popularity.

The Zona is so spread out that walking between restaurants and sights here can be time-consuming. Fortunately, buses run from the central market to just about anywhere in town; purchase the 20¢ ticket on board. Bus stops are rare, but you can flag a bus at any streetcorner by waving your hands. The SABALO-BASILICA bus travels from the downtown market to the Zona Dorada and runs 5 AM–10 PM. Otherwise, pulmonías tear around the streets of Mazatlán and are your cheapest option. Arrange the fare (and say your prayers) before boarding. If you're feeling adventurous, rent a scooter ($5.50 per hour or $18 per day, helmet included) at one of the rental shacks on the south end of the Zona Dorada.

WHERE TO SLEEP

For a resort town, Mazatlán has a surprising number of decent, cheap hotels. In Mazatlán Viejo you'll find budget digs behind the Monumento al Pescador and in the area east of the basilica; there are even a few pockets of sanity within the glitzy Zona Dorada. Prices listed below are for the low season—if you're in town around Carnaval, Semana Santa, or the Christmas and New Year holidays, expect to pay quite a bit more. The information booths inside the airport (*see above*) do make reservations for budget hotels, and the service is free. If you're only in town for a night, the best of the hotels near the bus station is the **Hotel Emperador** (Río Panuco, tel. 69/82–67–24), where each room has a color TV. Doubles cost $8; air-conditioning is $3 extra.

MAZATLAN VIEJO

UNDER $10 • Casa de Huéspedes El Castillo. The spacious, country-kitsch rooms here boast rocking chairs, fans, soft mattresses, and quirky dressers. The year-round price is a mere $6 for two. The nine rooms share just two (surprisingly well-kept) bathrooms. *Teniente José Azueta 1612 Nte., between Canizales and 21 de Marzo, tel. 69/81–58–97. 9 rooms, none with bath. Luggage storage. Cash only.*

UNDER $15 • Hotel Belmar. With the beach out front and a gigantic pool in the back, you'll feel like you've discovered budget paradise. Elegant rooms come with either fan and ocean view ($13 doubles) or air-conditioning and no view ($19 doubles). All rooms have balconies and TVs. Prices triple during Easter week and Carnaval. *Olas Altas 166 Sur, tel. 69/85–11–11. 100 rooms, all with bath. Luggage storage. Reservations advised.*

Hotel del Centro. The aging rooms here are small and slightly run-down, though blessedly air-conditioned. Each floor has a small lobby with potted plants and rocking chairs. Doubles cost $13, plus $1.50 for a TV. Prices are the same year-round. *Canizales 705 Pte., ½ block from Basílica, tel. 69/81–26–73. 19 rooms, all with bath. Luggage storage. Cash only.*

ZONA DORADA

UNDER $15 • Hotel Bugambilias. Tucked away in the heart of Zona Dorada is this charming hotel. Clean, good-size rooms with bath are $14 a double. Ten apartments with kitchenettes run $20 for two people ($7 for each additional person). The top level has a sun-tanning area and great ocean views. *Camarón Sábalo, at Costa Azul, tel. 69/14–00–29. Luggage storage.*

UNDER $25 • Hotel San Diego. Many of the Zona Dorada's discos are conveniently located across the street from the San Diego. Medium-size rooms flaunt newly tiled floors, ornate bedspreads, TVs, and large bathrooms; each floor has a deck with ocean views. Fan-cooled rooms with one bed cost $11. Air-conditioned rooms are $15 for one bed, $25 for two beds. Prices rise about $3 during Easter week. *Rafael Buelna, at Av. del Mar, tel. 69/83–57–03. 63 rooms, all with bath. Luggage storage.*

CAMPING

The Zona Dorada has a few trailer parks that charge $10–$14 per night for a tent space. The best is **Mar Rosa** (Camarón Sábalo 702, near Holiday Inn, tel. and fax 69/13–61–87), with showers, 24-hour security, and a waterfront location. They charge $12 for a two-person tent, plus $3 for each additional person. Of the public beaches, only **Isla de la Piedra** (*see* Outdoor Activites, *below*) permits camping. There are no facilities.

FOOD

A surprising number of inexpensive eateries are scattered throughout this wealthy town—of course, there are plenty of expensive restaurants, too. The daily **mercado municipal** (city market; Avenidas Serdán at Melchor Ocampo) has stalls selling fresh produce and cheap tacos. Likewise, dozens of palapas on Playa Norte sell cheap seafood; a whole fried fish costs $2. Mazatlán is known for its *mariscos* (shellfish) and *camarones* (shrimp), so look for specialty dishes like *caldo de* (soup of) camarones and camarones *rellenos* (stuffed with bacon and cheese).

MAZATLAN VIEJO

UNDER $5 • Cenaduría Conchita. This small, red-and-white restaurant is a local favorite for hearty traditional Mexican food. The $2 *comida corrida* (preprepared lunch special) includes steak or chicken, fresh fruit, soup, beans, a fruit drink, and dessert. *Canazales 603, at Nelson, no phone. Closed Sun. Cash only.*

Panamá Restaurant y Pastelería. The largest branch of this popular bakery/restaurant chain is in Mazatlán Viejo. For breakfast, try the *huevos divorciados* (literally, "divorced eggs"), one with green sauce, the other with red, separated by a dollop of beans. Later in the day, savor anything from chef salad to beef tenderloin fajitas ($4). *Juárez, at Valle, tel. 69/85–18–53. Cash only.*

Royal Dutch. Originally an in-home bakery, this place is now also a café with intimate courtyard dining, nightly live music (6–10), and an expansive menu of soups and sandwiches. A breakfast of two eggs, hash browns, and toast costs $2. Breads and desserts are made on the premises. *Juárez 1307, at Constitución, tel. 69/81–20–07. Closed Sun. Cash only.*

UNDER $10 • Karnes en Su Jugo. A family-run café on the malecón, this establishment specializes in *carnes en su jugo* (literally, "beef in its juice"), a traditional Mexican stew with chopped beef, onions, beans, and bacon. For $5 it's a satisfying meal, especially when eaten with a basket of homemade tortillas. *Av. del Mar 550, tel. 69/82–13–22. Cash only.*

ZONA DORADA

UNDER $5 • Jungle Juice Restaurant and Bar. The name says it all: This Zona Dorada joint has a terrific selection of fresh juice drinks ($1.50). Menu items include shrimp-stuffed avocado; fresh fruit salad with yogurt; soyburger with fries; and a $2 egg, potato, and toast breakfast. The bar is popular with locals and foreigners alike. *Calle de Las Garzas 101, between Laguna and Camarón Sábalo, tel. 69/13–33–15. Cash only.*

Mucho Taco. This bright-blue sidewalk stand in the heart of the Zona Dorada serves fresh and tasty tacos with a variety of fillings. It's open 24 hours, to the delight of revelers in search of a late-night nosh. *Camarón Sábalo, no phone. Cash only.*

UNDER $10 • Restaurant Bar La Costa Marinera. The seafood entrées can be expensive, but the ocean views, live mariachi music, and gourmet cuisine make for an enchanting experience. For $10, try the Chef's Special: fish soup, grilled shrimp, and flan. *Camarón Sábalo, between Hotels Ocean Palace and Luna Palace, tel. 69/14–19–28. No breakfast.*

WORTH SEEING

The best way to see Mazatlán Viejo, with its mix of crumbling old colonial mansions and tidy newer homes, is on foot. At its center is the **Plaza Revolución,** from which the blue-and-gold spires of the adjacent basilica rise above the downtown buildings. A few blocks away, **Plaza Machado** (Constitución and Carnaval) is surrounded by elegant colonial-style buildings that have been turned into cafés and restaurants with outdoor seating. Follow Avenida del Mar north toward the Zona Dorada and you'll pass the unusual **Monumento al Pescador** (Fisherman's Monument): an enormous statue of a voluptuous nude woman reclining on an anchor, her hand extended toward a fisherman, also naked, hauling in his nets.

ACUARIO MAZATLAN

Halfway between the Zona Dorada and Mazatlán Viejo is this aquarium/zoo, offering an aviary swarming with chirping birds and tanks full of tropical fish, turtles, and crocodiles. Visitors can observe fish in a feeding frenzy four times daily, followed by a sea lion show and a film about sharks (although the film is in Spanish, Anglophones won't have a hard time understanding what the sharks are doing to the smaller fish). *Av. de los Deportes 111, 2 blocks off Av. del Mar, tel. 69/81–78–17. Admission: $3. Open daily 9:30–6:30.*

MUSEO ARQUEOLOGICO

This large museum is one of Mazatlán's few nods to pre-Columbian Mexico. It features a fascinating permanent display of local artifacts, including war objects, burial ornaments, and pictures of women with cranial and dental deformation (a beauty custom still practiced in some parts of Mexico). Intriguing temporary exhibits display works by international painters, sculptors, and ceramicists. The museum houses the **Casa de la Cultura** (literally, House of Culture), which hosts lectures and occasional concerts. *Sixto Osuna 76, 1 block east of the beach, no phone. Admission: $1. Open Tues.–Sun. 10–1 and 4–7.*

PLAZA DE TOROS

Bullfights are held here most Sundays between December and April. You can buy tickets in advance at Valentino's disco (*see* After Dark, *below*) and some of the city's large hotels, as well as at the bullring the day of the fight. The cheapest seats are about $19. Fights start at 4 PM. *Rafael Buelna, near Zona Dorada, tel. 69/84–16–66.*

TEATRO ANGELA PERALTA

This striking neoclassical opera house was built in 1860 following Italian style but with Mexican flair. It was declared a historic monument in 1990 and, after a two-year restoration, now hosts the music and dance performances of Mazatlán's flourishing arts community. The interior is spectacularly ornate, enhanced by stellar acoustics and excellent climate control. The season schedule is posted at the box office, to the right of the entrance. Tickets are $3.50–$6. All performances are in Spanish. *Constitución, at Carnaval, tel. 69/82–44–47. Box office open daily 8:30–2 and 4–7.*

CHEAP THRILLS

On Sunday, locals of all ages gather in front of the cathedral near the Palacio Municipal to hear *bandas* (bands). The tourist office and the Casa de la Cultura (*see* Museo Arqueológico, *above*) offers calendars of these and other cultural events. If you're looking for some moderate exercise, take one of the following three strolls: The walk to the **Cerro de la Nevería** (Icebox Hill), in Mazatlán Viejo, off the malecón along Paseo Claussen, takes you past beautiful homes and various lookout points. Just south of Olas Altas, about halfway down the peninsula, is **Cerro de la Vigía** (Lookout Hill). It was originally used by the Spanish to keep watch for pirates—hence the rusty cannon here today. It's a steep climb up the Paseo del Centenario to the top of the hill, but there are vista points along the way where you can catch your breath. Farther down

THE BULLFIGHT: ART OR SPORT?

Is bullfighting a bloodthirsty sport in which an innocent animal is brutally murdered, or is it a fair match between an artist dressed in his "suit of light" and a thoroughbred bull bred especially for this purpose?

Mexicans consider "la corrida de los toros" an elegant art rather than a simple sport, but you can decide for yourself at a number of bullfighting arenas along the Pacific Coast. The dramatic man-and-beast competition was imported to Mexico centuries ago by the Spaniards, and to this day the three-act event continues to draw large, cheering crowds to arenas all over the country.

A day of bullfighting begins with a gala parade, followed by the corrida (bullfight), which consists of three matadors and six bulls; each matador has 16 minutes to triumph over his opponent the bull. The quick death of a bull brings thunderous applause and scores of tossed roses; a slow struggle results in a loud chorus of boos.

Audience members who choose to root for the bull will also win an unpopular response.

the peninsula from Olas Altas is the **Cerro del Crestón** (Cockscomb Hill), which offers the most stunning views. It's a 30-minute hike to the *faro* (lighthouse) at the top, where you can marvel at the sea and the city.

OUTDOOR ACTIVITIES

Each of Matzatlán's half-dozen beaches offers a unique scene and a whole new crowd. **Playa Sábalo** and **Playa Las Gaviotas** are worked by strolling vendors who rent boogie boards and Jet Skis, or offer five-minute parasail rides. Local favorite **Playa Norte** is cluttered with palapa restaurants selling seafood. **Olas Altas,** farther south in Mazatlán Viejo, has dangerous surf but offers the best sunset-watching. If you're looking to escape the crowds altogether, head for the quieter beaches north of the Zona Dorada, such as **Playa Bruja** and **Playa Cerritos.** To reach these, take a CERRITOS bus from the Zona Dorada and hop off when you see the signs.

You can rent almost any kind of water sport equipment in Mazatlán. Vendors on the beach near Valentino's disco rent surf- and boogie boards for $5 an hour. At the **Aqua Sports Center** (tel. 69/13–33–33), next to El Cid Hotel, you can rent a Hobie Cat ($25 per hr), boogie board ($4 per hr), or snorkeling gear ($8 for 6 hrs). They also offer parasail rides ($20) and arrange scuba-diving excursions to the reefs at **Isla de los Venados** (15 min away by boat). The one-tank dive ($50) for certified divers includes equipment and transportation. Uncertified divers can participate if they first take a $10 resort course. A trip to the island to simply snorkel and lounge in the sun costs $9, snorkeling equipment and round-trip transportation included. Another popular activity in Mazatlán is sportfishing, for mahimahi, red snapper, saltfish, and marlin. More than a dozen sportfishing fleets operate from the docks south of the lighthouse. A full day of fishing costs $60–$75 per person on a party boat or around $300 for a private charter (prices include boat, guide, and bait and tackle). Charter companies to contact include **Bill Heimpel's Star Fleet** (tel. 69/82–26–65), **Flota Faro** (tel. 69/81–28–24), and **De Oro** (tel. 69/82–31–30).

Sports abound at **Isla de la Piedra,** an island with palm-fringe, white-sand beaches dotted with shady palapas. Here you'll find volleyball nets, boogie boards ($2 an hr), horseback riding ($6 an hr), and banana boat rides ($3 for 10 min). You can camp wherever you please, though facilities are nonexistent. To reach the island, take a boat (10 min, 50¢) from the dock at the corner of Avenida Playa Sur and Calle Barranza, just past the ferry terminal. Boats depart frequently, daily 6–6.

SHOPPING

The daily **Mercado Central,** between Calles Juárez and Serdán, is a sprawling expanse of open-air stalls selling produce, meat, fish, and handicrafts at the lowest prices in town. It takes some searching to find quality handicrafts, but that's part of the fun. In the Zona Dorada, particularly along Avenida Camarón Sábalo and Avenida Rodolfo T. Loaiza, you can buy everything from piñatas to designer clothing. Leather shops are clustered along the southern end of the Zona Dorada. The **Mazatlán Arts and Crafts Center** (Av. Rodolfo T. Loaiza 417, tel. 69/13–50–22) is the best place in town for browsing. It's filled with shops, boutiques, and you can see craftsmen making *huaraches* (leather sandals), painting plates, and sculpting figures from coconuts. **La Carreta** (Playa Mazatlán, tel. 69/13–83–20) has the finest selection of high-quality Mexican folk art in town. **Sea Shell City** (Av. Rodolfo T. Loaiza 407, tel. 69/13–13–01) has two floors packed with shells that have been glued, strung, and molded into every imaginable shape, from lamps to necklaces. Check out the enormous fountain upstairs, covered with thousands of shells.

AFTER DARK

Most of Mazatlán's nightclubs are in the Zona Dorada. Frequented by rowdy twentysomething gringos and done-up Mexican tourists, they offer a certain kind of fun. **Señor Frog's** (Av. del Mar, tel. 69/82–19–25) is a popular restaurant that morphs into a multiroom disco after 11 PM. There's no cover but be prepared to wait in line to get in. **Valentino's** (Punta del Malecón, tel. 69/84–16–16) has a disco overlooking the sea and a *canta bar* (karaoke room) that gets everybody laughing. Cover is $2.50, which includes free drinks from 9 PM to 4 AM. **Bora Bora** (tel. 69/84–16–66), next door, is a gringo-ized outdoor disco that plays more rap and less techno than the clubs listed above. The bar **Café Pacífico** (Constitución 501, tel. 69/81–39–72) attracts an older, more sedate crowd, while gay nightlife centers around **Pepe El Toro** (Av. de las Garzas 18, tel. 69/14–41–76).

NEAR MAZATLAN

CONCORDIA

In the foothills east of Mazatlán, Concordia makes for a pleasant day trip from Mazatlán. This small *pueblo* (town) was founded in 1565 and is known for its beautiful wooden furniture and brown clay pottery, which can be found in shops along the highway. Church-goers, cooing couples, and rambunctious kids gather at the zócalo, which is the heart of this mining village. The 18th-century **Iglesia de San Sebastián,** which stands on the zócalo, is considered the only truly baroque church in the state of Sinaloa. The **Hotel Rancho Viejo** (El Vado Carretera Mazatlán–Durango, tel. 69/68–02–90) has basic double rooms ($10). Second-class buses to Concordia (1 hr, $1.25) leave from Mazatlán's main bus station every 15 minutes, daily 6 AM–8 PM. The last bus back to Mazatlán leaves at 7 PM.

COSALA

This former mining town is high in the mountains, surrounded by lush, unspoiled forest. It's worth the three-hour bus ride if you enjoy camping and swimming; you'll probably want to spend at least two or three days, since transportation to the region is sparse. Within the town you can visit the free **Museo de Minería e Historia** (open Tues.–Fri. 9–7, weekends 10–3) on the main plaza. It displays locally mined rocks and minerals and some fossilized bones. The modern, air-conditioned **Hotel Ray Cuatro Hermanos** (on the plaza, tel. 696/5–03–03) offers rooms for $10.

The best attractions, though, are outside of town; you can arrange transportation through the English-speaking guide/taxi service **Palacio Municipal** (next to the museum, tel. 696/5–03–40). Just 15 minutes away is the **Balneario de Vado Hondo,** where you can swim in a cool pond surrounded by three waterfalls. It's 3 km (2 mi) from the highway leading into town; any Mazatlán- or Culiacán-bound bus can get you to the crossroads. You can also visit the unchartered **Gruta México,** a dark cave with pre-Columbian hieroglyphics. Bring your own flashlight, and consider hiring a guide in town. To reach the cave, catch the 1 PM bus to Canzal (15 min, $1) and walk two hours to the cave. The same bus goes to the **Presa del Comedero** (1 hr, $3), a large, murky lake ideal for fishing. Local fishermen will take you out on their boats for a small fee. You can camp near the falls or the lake, but be sure to buy all your food and drinking water beforehand.

COMING AND GOING

The bus to Cosalá (3 hrs, $5.50) leaves the main bus station in Mazatlán daily at 10 AM, returning at 1 PM. You can also take any Culiacán-bound bus to Espinal (1½ hrs, $3.50), where Cosalá-bound buses pass by every hour or so. Buses headed for Espinal from Cosalá (1½ hrs, $3.50) leave at 5:45, 7, and 10 AM and 2 and 3:30 PM.

SAN BLAS

On the Nayarit coast between Mazatlán and Puerto Vallarta lies a run-down town of less than 10,000. Though this looks like a place you'd want to skip, its proximity to pristine tropical forest makes San Blas the perfect stop for the adventure traveler or the amateur naturalist. Hit the trail, swat away the relentlessly biting *jejene* insects, and you'll enjoy iridescent waterfalls, swollen river canals, and outrageous tangles of colorful vegetation. Egrets, ibises, and woodpeckers are among the 300 different bird species native to this region, and even if you don't see them, you will certainly hear their calls.

San Blas is sometimes called the *puerto olvidado* (forgotten port), referring both to the dearth of tourism and lack of government funds. One plausible reason for San Blas's unpopularity is the vicious biting insects that plague it during the rainy season (mid-June through October). The written records of Spanish explorers remark on the number of mosquitoes and jejenes, and describe in detail how the local people took cover at dusk. But San Blas wasn't always a sleepy tropical backwater. In its heyday from the 1500s to the 1800s it was an important Pacific port with a peak population of more than 30,000. Mazatlán and Manzanillo later eclipsed San Blas, leaving only a few stone ruins as testaments to the town's former glory. To visit one of the ruins, make the 15-minute hike from town to **Nuestra Señora del Rosario,** a fort built in 1769 and now garrisoned only by sun-loving iguanas. After San Blas's decline as a port town, the hill was used by pirates to hide the riches they seized. To get here, follow the main road out of town; before the bridge, veer right past the restaurants and follow the stone road up the hill on your right.

BASICS

CASAS DE CAMBIO

Banamex (Juárez 26, off the zócalo, tel. 328/5–00–30; open weekdays 8:30 AM–11 AM) changes cash and traveler's checks, but lines are often long and the bank sometimes charges unwarranted commissions or runs out of cash altogether. Fortunately, its ATM accepts Cirrus and Plus cards. Across the street is the **Agencia de Cambio** (Juárez 21, no phone; open Mon.–Sat. 8–2 and 4–8).

EMERGENCIES

The **police station** (corner Sinaloa and Canalizo, tel. 328/5–00–28) is open 24 hours and handles all emergencies.

MAIL

The full-service **post office** (Sonora, at Echevarría, 1 block NE of the bus station, tel. 328/5–02–95; open weekdays 8–1 and 3–5, Sat. 8–noon) will hold mail sent to you at the following address for up to 10 days: Lista de Correos, San Blas, Nayarit, CP 63740, México.

MEDICAL AID

The **Centro de Salud** (Teniente Azueta, at Campeche, tel. 328/5–02–32) is six blocks west of the zócalo. **Farmacia Botica Mexicana** (Juárez 7, at Batallón, tel. 328/5–01–22; open daily 8:30–1:30 and 5–9) has an English-speaking owner and plenty of mosquito repellent.

PHONES

There is a public **Ladatel** phone in the Palacio Municipal, on the zócalo. From the zócalo's *caseta de larga distancia* (long-distance telephone office; Juárez 3, tel. and fax 328/5–06–11; open daily 8 AM–10 PM) you can place cash calls or pay 75¢ for a five-minute long-distance collect or credit-card call.

VISITOR INFORMATION

Federico at **Posada Portola** (*see* Where to Sleep, *below*) is friendly and very knowledgeable about the area. The staff at **Delegación de Turismo Municipal** (Juárez 60, tel. 328/5–00–21), across from McDonald's restaurant, offers up-to-date information and hands out brochures and maps. Hours are theoretically daily 9–noon and 8–9, but may vary.

COMING AND GOING

The **bus station** (tel. 328/5–00–43) is on the corner of Sinaloa and Canalizo, just off the zócalo. One bus leaves daily at 9 AM for Guadalajara (5 hrs, $11.50), and four buses depart daily for Santiago Ixcuintla (1½ hrs, $2.75) and Las Varas (1½ hrs, $3.50). Buses to Santa Cruz (30 min, 80¢) leave on the hour 6 AM–5 PM; they also leave from the corner of Sinaloa and Canalizo at 8:20 AM, 10:30 AM, 12:30 PM, and 2:30 PM. The buses to Santa Cruz stop at several tiny beach towns en route. Buses to Puerto Vallarta (3½ hrs, $6) depart daily at 7 AM and 10 AM. Buses to Tepic (1½ hrs, $2.50) leave almost hourly between 6 AM and 7 PM. Daily at 5 PM, a bus chugs to Mazatlán (5 hrs, $2.75).

WHERE TO SLEEP

If you arrive in San Blas by bus, you will likely be greeted by hotel owners trying to get your business for the night. Be sure to check out the competition before agreeing to anything. Wherever you stay, if you're here between June and October, inspect the windows, screens, and doors for any possible insect-size entryways—or prepared for a fun-filled evening swatting mosquitos. Hotel prices vary depending on the season; the prices listed below apply during summer and fall, but expect to pay a few dollars more in winter and during Semana Santa. San Blas is one town where you don't want to go with the cheapest possible hotel—those charging $15 or less a night are too awful to even mention.

San Blas is the place to ponder the chemical interaction between suntan lotion and insect repellent: "Will they neutralize each other, leaving me unprotected, or will I simply burst into flames?"

UNDER $20 • Posada Portola. Each of the spacious bungalows here is graced with kitchen, living/dining room, and a separate, good-size bedroom. The gregarious owner, Federico, will cheerfully rent you a bike or car, wash a load of laundry (35¢ per piece), or even make your plane reservations. Double-occupancy bungalows cost $18–$20 per night, plus $4.50 for each additional person. *Paredes 118, just past Yucatán, tel. and fax 328/5–03–86. From the church, 1 block west, then a few blocks north. 8 bungalows, all with bath. Luggage storage.*

UNDER $25 • Hotel Bucanero. This place, right across from the tourist office, is an all-in-one hotel and entertainment center. You can take a dip in the swimming pool, admire the owner's stuffed crocodile, or shoot a game of pool. Doubles cost $25. *Juárez 75, tel. 328/5–01–01. 2 blocks west of zócalo. 30 rooms, all with bath. Luggage storage. Cash only.*

Posada del Rey. A block and a half from the beach, near where the fishing boats come in, you'll find this sleepy hotel. Though the third floor has a bar that stays open 'til the wee hours, the atmosphere is so lethargic you're still guaranteed to get a good night's rest. Rooms cost $24 with ceiling fan or $27 with air-conditioning. *Campeche 10, tel. 328/5–01–23. 14 rooms, all with bath.*

CAMPING

If you intend to camp in San Blas be sure to have good screens and plenty of repellent. The summer months bring torrential rains and tides so high that beach camping is out of the question. In winter, however, the palapa restaurants on the beach will often let you use their facilities. They charge up to $4 for the privilege. Try **Restaurante de Federico y Lucia** on Playa Borrego; the owners will keep an eye on you, and even let you borrow one of their three hammocks for the night. **Trailer Park Coco Loco** (Teniente Azueta, down Batallón, tel. 328/5–00–55) is conveniently close to the beach. Facilities include decent bathrooms with hot water and an overpriced bar. RV spaces are $9; tents cost about $7.50. There are 100 sites.

FOOD

San Blas is a fishing town, so the seafood is fresh and inexpensive: A lunch of fried fish at a beach restaurant runs $4. San Blas is also proud of its *pan de plátano* (banana bread). The sweet-smelling

loaves ($1.50) are sold at **Tumba de Yaco** (Batallón 219, tel. 328/5–04–62; cash only) by a local group
of surfers who call themselves Team Banana. If you're in the mood to whip up your own meal, swing by
the daily market on the corner of Batallón and Sinaloa.

Huichol paintings and stuffed crocodiles decorate the snazzy **Restaurante y Bar Cocodrilo** (Juárez, at
Canalizo, on the zócalo, tel. 328/5–06–10). Specialties include filet mignon ($4) and spaghetti with Ital-
ian sauce, but they also serve tacos and enchiladas. **McDonald's** (Juárez 36, ½ block west of the zócalo,
tel. 328/5–01–27), not related to the American fast-food chain, does delicious *huevos rancheros*
(ranch-style eggs, with spicy tomato sauce, tortillas, and beans; $1.75). Their dinner special ($3) is
enormous: grilled chicken with enchiladas, french fries, beans, chips, salad, and tortillas. With its elegant atmosphere, **La Hacienda** (Juárez 41, tel. 321/5–07–72; no breakfast, closed Tues.) is the talk of
the town. The food is delicious, particularly the house special, *pescado gaviota* (fillet of sea bass stuffed
with shrimp and served with cheese sauce; $5). All of the above accept cash only.

OUTDOOR ACTIVITIES

San Blas offers plenty of outdoor diversions, including a fascinating boat ride through surrounding jungle (*see* La Tovara, *below*). You can rent bikes at **Posada Portola** (*see* Where to Sleep, *above*) for $5 a
day, even if you're not a paying guest. You can also ask here for Toño Palma, who will take you out on a
boat to watch whales or to fish for tuna and red snapper. His prices vary and are negotiable. Contact
Lucio at the tourist office (*see* Basics, *above*) to join a four-hour nature hike ($10) past waterfalls,
streams, and canyons. Lucio also offers jeep tours ($10) to a nearby coffee plantation, where you can
learn about coffee harvesting and purchase the freshly roasted beans. Both tours leave at 8 AM and must
be reserved a day in advance.

If you're simply looking to stroll along a sandy beach, head for **Playa Borrego**; San Blas's main beach is
1 km (½ mi) from the town center. Just off the coast, **Isla del Rey** (Island of the King) sports a lighthouse
and an empty beach and is the place to go if you're suddenly seized by a severe case of misanthropy. To
get here, take a boat (40 min, 50¢) from the dock next to the customs house anytime from dawn till dusk.
Additional beaches lie to the south of San Blas, along the **Bahía Matanchén** (*see* Near San Blas, *below*).

LA TOVARA

San Blas's famous jungle boats cruise down the Río San Cristóbal to the freshwater spring La Tovara. As you glide through thick mangrove swamps, keep your eyes open for crocodiles, exotic birds, turtles, and the fake huts used in the film *Cabeza de Vaca* (Cow's Head). Boats embark on the cruise (3 hrs; $17.50, 4-person maximum) from the bridge just outside of San Blas. For a shorter, cheaper tour ($15, 4-person maximum), take the SANTA CRUZ bus to Matanchén (10 min, $1) and hire a boat at the embarcadero where the bus drops you off. Boats run until sundown, with no set schedule; if you catch a boat before 8 AM you'll have some time to swim in the freshwater spring before most tourists arrive.

AFTER DARK

Summer months in San Blas are sleepy, but December to May this little town is pretty lively. Keep an eye open for signs announcing shows by Los Bucaneros, a talented local band that plays salsa, merengue, and other tropical tunes. At **Disco La Fancy** (Yucatán, at Canalizo, no phone) you can shake it until 3 AM for a $2 cover. The smaller and less modern **Disco La Fitte,** a block down from McDonald's (*see* Food, *above*) is open until 2 AM and charges a $1.50 cover for a pool-playing, kick-up-your-heels kind of night. Both discos play a mixture of rock, techno, salsa, merengue, and romantic music. **Restaurant y Bar Cocodrilo** (*see* Food, *above*) sports a large bar with dim lights and *rock en español*. The gay scene in San Blas is large and close-knit; **La Hacienda** (Juárez 41, tel. 328/5–07–72; open Wed.–Mon. until midnight) is a restaurant and bar popular with gay men. On the second and fourth Saturday of the month, **Mike's Bar** (above McDonald's) hosts a transvestite show. Mike himself sings for couples of all persuasions Thursday–Sunday.

Heavy winter rains sometimes raise the water level around Mexcaltitán by as much as 10 ft. In the worst flooding, helicopters must fly in food and purified drinking water for its 1,900 inhabitants.

NEAR SAN BLAS

BAHIA MATANCHEN

Several splendid beaches lie along the **Bahía Matanchén,** just south of San Blas. The first and best is **Playa Las Islitas,** which is famous among surfers for the 1-km-long (½-mi-long) wave that occasionally appears in summer or fall—depending on some fortuitous conjunction of equinoctial and lunar forces. You can rent surfboards ($2 per hour) or boogie boards ($1.50 per hour) from Juán at Tumba de Yaco (*see* Food, *above*), in San Blas. Juán also gives surf lessons for all levels ($4.50 per hour).

Farther south along the bay, the beaches are rockier. They're also less infested with mosquitoes. **Playa los Cocos,** a beautiful beach with lots of coconut trees, is adjacent to the oyster-harvesting town of **Aticama.** You can snack on oysters in town and camp at the trailer park on the beach—it isn't attractive, but it does offer cheap, secure tent camping for about $5. Buses run from San Blas (corner Sinaloa and Paredes) along the bay to Playa Las Islitas (10 min, 25¢), Aticama (20 min, 55¢), and Playa Los Cocos (25 min, 65¢) at 5:20 AM, 8:20 AM, 10:30 AM, 12:30 PM, and 2:30 PM. Buses also leave on the hour from San Blas's main bus station, daily 6 AM–5 PM. The last returning bus passes through Playa Los Cocos at 4:35 PM.

SANTIAGO IXCUINTLA

This midsize city is surrounded by ranchlands, 40 km (24 mi) northeast of San Blas. Its main attraction is the **Centro Cultural Huichol** (*see box, above*), 10 blocks east of the plaza on Calle Zaragoza. It's also the departure point for boats to Mexcaltitán (*see below*). Cheap hotels surround Santiago's plaza and the central market; at **Hotel Santiago** (Ocampo y Arteaga, tel. 323/5–06–37) most of the rooms have TVs. Rooms cost $8–$9, plus $3.50 if you'd like air-conditioning. Second-class **Transportes Norte de Sonora** (tel. 323/5–04–17) buses run from Santiago's **bus station** (Primera Correjidora, north side of pueblo) to Tepic (every 30 mins; 1 hr, $3.25), San Blas (2 times daily; 1½ hrs, $2.75), and Mazatlán (4 times daily; 4 hrs, $8). Half a block away, **Transportes del Pacífico** (tel. 323/5–12–12) sends buses to the dock for Mexcaltitán (five times daily; 1 hr, $1.25).

MEXCALTITÁN

The village of Mexcaltitán, believed to be the mythical first city of the Aztecs, sits on an island in the middle of a saltwater lagoon. The town's name means "the place of the temple of the moon" in Nahuatl, and legend describes how an eagle with a serpent in its beak landed here, marking it as a suitable building spot for the Aztec kingdom. The arrival of the Spaniards, however, scared the eagle back into flight. Its next landing spot was Tenochtitlán (present-day Mexico City), which ultimately became the Aztec capital. You can see the ancient carved-stone figure of the eagle and serpent and learn about Mesoamerican culture at the modern **Museo del Origen** (tel. 323/2–02–11; open Tues.–Sun. 10–2 and 3–5), on Mexcaltitán's main plaza. The museum houses indigenous art, maps, and costumes that tell the story of ancient Aztec culture, aided by TV monitors and recorded music. For a tour of the lagoon, find José or Edy at the Embarcadero Tuxpán on the east edge of the island. They'll charge you $4.50 per boat (it fits up to four), and you'll see lots of birds and fish during the relaxing ride. On June 29, the villagers (plus a few thousand visitors) celebrate the opening of the shrimping season and honor the patron saints of the city, Pedro and Pablo. The annual fiesta features all-night dancing, lively bands, and lots of home-cooked seafood.

You can reach Mexcaltitán by taking a bus from Santiago Ixcuintla (*see above*) to Embarcadero Batango, and then jumping on a boat (15 min, 50¢) to the village. Boats depart after the buses arrive; the last boat returns to the mainland at 6 PM. If you miss the boat, **Hotel La Ruta Azteca** (Venecia 5, south of the plaza, tel. 323/2–02–11 ext. 128) offers air-conditioned rooms ($10). Fresh shrimp and shellfish are on the menu at **La Alberca** (tel. 323/2–02–11 ext. 134), on the west edge of the island, and **Restaurante Lomochina.** The latter is on a small island that is a free, three-minute boat ride from Mexcaltitán. Both restaurants fill up with locals, tourists, and mariachi musicians in the late afternoon. A local favorite is the Aztec dish *taxtihuilli* (shrimp in a cornmeal sauce with herbs and spices; $4).

TEPIC

The capital of the agricultural state of Nayarit, Tepic is not a city to linger in if you're craving a hammock, an ice-cold coconut drink, and a wide expanse of sandy white beach. However, the city's bus station is a hub for transportation throughout western Mexico, so your travels between Puerto Vallarta and San Blas or Los Mochis might make Tepic a like-it-or-not part of your itinerary. For local people, Tepic is a center of commerce: The indigenous Huichol and Aztec come down from the hills to buy supplies, and nearby ranchers and tobacco farmers, their faces darkened and wrinkled from labor in the sun, can be found chatting on street corners or making purchases in shops that sell leather goods, tools, ammunition, and chemical fertilizers.

If you're going to be in the city for more than a few hours, head for the free **Museo Regional de Antropología e Historia** (México 91, at Zapata, tel. 32/12–19–00; open weekdays 9–7, Sat. 9–3), near the zócalo, where you'll find a fine collection of pre-Columbian clay figurines. Two blocks northeast is the small, free **Museo Casa de los Cuatro Pueblos** (Hidalgo 60 Ote., tel. 32/12–17–05; open weekdays 9–2 and 4–7, Sat. 10–2). Also known as the Museo de Artes Populares, the museum hosts a five-room collection of Cora and Huichol clothing, wood- and leather work, and sculpture. The **Ex-Convento de la Cruz de Zacate** (México, at Calzada del Ejército) was built to guard a grass cross that, legend has it, miraculously appeared nearby in 1540. The building now houses a ballet academy, an art store, and a progressive theater group. To escape Tepic's noise and general drabness, take a stroll through **Paseo La Loma** (Insurgentes, at Colegio Militar), a large park with pine and eucalyptus trees and a miniature train—hop aboard for a ride reminiscent of "The Little Engine That Could."

BASICS

Banamex (Av. México, at Zapata, tel. 32/12–02–42; open weekdays 8–2) has an ATM that accepts Cirrus and Plus cards and changes traveler's checks. **Agencia de Cambio Serna** (México 139 Nte., at Zapata, tel. 32/16–55–30; open Mon.–Sat. 8–8) sometimes gives slightly better rates. The full-service **main post office** (Durango 36 Nte., tel. 32/12–01–30) is open weekdays 8–7, Saturday 8–noon. The best place to make long-distance phone calls is the bus station, where you can place collect or credit-card calls (75¢ each) daily 7 AM–9 PM. For basic first aid try **Farmacia Benavides** (Hidalgo 6, at México, tel.

32/12–08–33; open daily 7 AM–midnight), near the zócalo. For ambulance service contact **Cruz Roja** (tel. 32/13–11–60). The **tourist office** (México 178-A Nte., tel. 32/12–19–05; open Mon. to Sat. 9–8), one block south of the cathedral, provides maps of town and of the entire Nayarit state, as well as handfuls of tourist brochures, most of which are in Spanish. The knowledgeable staff speaks some English.

COMING AND GOING

Central Tepic is walkable, with casas de cambio, restaurants, hotels, and most of Tepic's points of interest lying along **Avenida México** (the main commercial street), between Avenida Insurgentes and Avenida Victoria. Near Avenida Insurgentes is the Palacio Municipal and the Plaza de los Constituyentes; the basilica lies closer to Avenida Victoria. The main street crossing Avenida México is Avenida Insurgentes. Buses (15¢) traverse all these main thoroughfares.

BY BUS

Tepic's bus terminal is on Avenida Insurgentes, about six blocks east of Avenida México. **Transportes del Pacífico** (tel. 32/13–23–20) sends frequent second-class buses to Mazatlán (4½ hrs, $12), Guadalajara (4 hrs, $10), Los Mochis (12 hrs, $30), Mexicali (30 hrs, $68), and Tijuana (32 hrs, $70). Service to Puerto Vallarta (3½ hrs, $7) leaves on the half hour 3 AM–8 PM; if you ask the driver, he will let you off at Rincón de Guayabitos or any other beach en route. Buses to San Blas (1½ hrs, $2.50) leave on the hour; those to Santiago Ixcuintla (1½ hrs, $2.75) leave every 45 minutes. **Omnibús de México** (tel. 32/13–13–23), with first-class service only, has hourly buses to Guadalajara (3½ hrs, $11), evening service to Mexico City (11 hrs, $35), and one daily bus at 6 PM to Cuidad Juárez (28 hrs, $65). Luggage storage is available at the station ($1 per 7 hrs). To get downtown from the station, take a ESTACION FRESNOS bus.

The gray buildings of downtown Tepic stand in marked contrast to the colorful Huichol embroidery and yarn paintings sold in the town's many daily outdoor markets.

BY TRAIN

To reach the **train station** (tel. 32/13–48–61) from downtown, hop on a ESTACION FRESNOS bus, which passes the train station on its way to the bus station. Trains travel north from Tepic to Mexicali (32 hrs, $45 1st class; 38 hrs, $25 2nd class), with stops in Culiacán (8 hrs, $13 1st class; 10 hrs, $8 2nd class), Sufragio (10 hrs, $16.50 1st class; 12 hrs, $10.25 2nd class), and Nogales (23 hrs, $43 1st class; 28 hrs, $19.50 2nd class). The northbound train leaves daily at 1:50 PM (1st class) and 5:15 PM (2nd class). The southbound train leaves at noon (2nd class) and 2 PM (1st class), traveling as far as Guadalajara (5 hrs, $7 1st class; 6 hrs, $4 2nd class). Departure times may vary from season to season—call ahead to check. Tickets go on sale an hour before departure.

WHERE TO SLEEP

Tepic has a few inexpensive hotels near the bus station. These are convenient for weary travelers but a 10-minute bus ride from downtown. Turn left out of the bus station, make another immediate left, and walk one block to **Hotel Nayar** (Martínez 430, tel. 32/13–23–22). The bathrooms are clean and have hot water, and it's not a bad choice considering the price: Doubles are $6.50. **Hotel Sarita** (Bravo 112 Pte., tel. 32/12–13–33) is close to the basilica and has colonial-style furniture and clean, fan-cooled rooms. Rooms with one bed cost $7, $9.50 with two beds. **Hotel Altamirano** (Mina 19 Pte., tel. 32/12–71–31), just off the zócalo and behind the Palacio Municipal, has quiet doubles for $10. All hotels are cash only. There is no campground in town, so those with a tent should head for the Laguna de Santa María del Oro (*see* Near Tepic, *below*).

FOOD

Food is generally cheaper in Tepic than in the seaside resorts, and better than you might expect: The fresh seafood here comes straight from San Blas. Grill joints can be found along Avenida Insurgentes below the park, and super-cheap grub is also sold near the bus station on Avenida Victoria, close to México. If you're in the mood for fruit and snacks, you'll find a daily **market** on the corner of Puebla and Zaragoza.

For delicious vegetarian food, try **Girasol** (tel. 32/13–42–93), in Paseo La Loma park. Soyburgers and *pozole* (hominy soup, served with fresh onions, ground chile, and oregano) are each $1.75. The owner's brother runs **Restaurant Vegetariano Quetzalcoatl** (León 224 Nte., at Lerdo, tel. 32/12–22–84; closed Sun.), north of downtown. At **Restaurant Altamirano** (México 109 Sur, near Palacio Municipal, tel. 321/12–71–31; no lunch), the high ceilings, stone walls, and sounds of frying tortillas create an "authentic" atmosphere. *Lengua en salsa* (beef tongue in salsa) or *pollo en mole* (chicken in chocolate-chile sauce) cost $3. **Café Juventus** (Zacatecas 120 Nte., between Hidalgo and Zapata, tel. 32/16–41–72) serves coffee and beers ($1), and is popular with students from the city's university. All of the above are cash only.

PUERTO VALLARTA

Puerto Vallarta is famous for its wide beaches, charming cobblestone streets, and the whitewashed, red-roof buildings stacked on its steep hillsides. Unfortunately, many of the latter are condos and time-shares. Like most of the Pacific Coast's resort towns, Puerto Vallarta has a gringo-ized hotel zone—the *Zona Hotelera*—which is completely separate from the "Mexican" part of town. The downtown area acts as a kind of common ground, full of pleasant cafés and good restaurants. Puerto Vallarta's biggest draw, however, is its ideal location, nestled between lush tropical hills and the rugged coastline of the Bahía de Banderas.

Puerto Vallarta's transformation from sleepy farming and fishing village to popular tourist destination was the result of a few fascinating twists of fate. In the early 1950s, Mexicana Airline "discovered," developed, and promoted the resort town to combat rival Aeroméxico's monopoly on flights to Acapulco. In 1964, Puerto Vallarta was the setting for John Huston's *The Night of the Iguana,* and in the 1980s, it was a frequent port of call for *The Love Boat.* Word of the city's charms soon spread far and wide, and Puerto Vallarta grew up into a big, bustling, multimillion dollar resort. You may not care for all of its fancy resort hotels, but you might want to overlook them. The rustic beauty of old Vallarta, the green waves of the Pacific, the crooning of strolling mariachis who wander palm-fringe beaches all make a visit here worthwhile.

If you don't mind higher hotel prices, Puerto Vallarta is best visited during the fiesta-filled winter season. The **Christmas** festivities begin in November: On November 22, the **Fiesta de Santa Cecilia** honors the patron saint of musicians with a parade beginning at 5 AM. In the evening everyone heads to the malecón for mass; the fiesta beer starts to flow soon afterward. December 1–12 sees daily parades honoring the Virgin Mary with mariachis and *baile folklórico* (folk dancing). The town is beautifully decorated December 15–24, and daily dancing and piñata parties liven things up. During the entire month of May, residents of Puerto Vallarta honor their city with the **May festival** that includes parades, bullfights, regattas, games and cultural events, street fairs, dancing, and fireworks.

BASICS

AMERICAN EXPRESS

The office sells traveler's checks and changes them at a good rate. Cardholders can cash personal checks and have their mail held here. *Morelos 660, at Abasolo, Col. Centro Puerto Vallarta, Jalisco, CP 48300, México, tel. 322/3–29–55. Open weekdays 9–6, Sat. 9–1.*

CASAS DE CAMBIO

Puerto Vallarta has many casas de cambio, usually in tiny storefront booths. All of them change cash and traveler's checks at average rates. **Cambio de Moneda** (Libertad 349, tel. 322/2–09–13; open Mon.–Sat. 9–9, Sun.10–9) is near the mercado. Across the street, the bank **Bital** (Miramar, at Libertad, tel. 322/2–02–27; open Mon.–Sat. 8–7) has an ATM that accepts Plus, Cirrus, Visa, and MasterCard.

CONSULATES

Both the **Canadian Consulate** (tel. 322/2–53–98; open weekdays 9–5) and the **U.S. Consulate** (tel. 322/2–00–69; open weekdays 10–2) are at Zaragoza 160 in the Vallarta Plaza building.

EMERGENCIES

In an emergency contact the **police** at 322/2–01–23. For **ambulance** service, call the Cruz Roja 322/2–15–33.

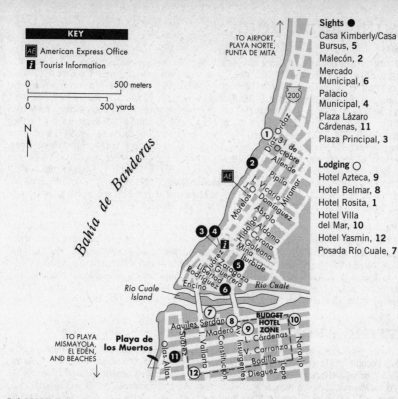

KEY

AE American Express Office

i Tourist Information

0 — 500 meters

0 — 500 yards

N

Bahía de Banderas

TO AIRPORT,
PLAYA NORTE,
PUNTA DE MITA

200

31 de
Octobre
Ordaz
Allende
Pipila
I. Vicario
J.O. Domínguez
Morelos
Miramar
Absolo
Hidalgo Aldama
Corona
Galeana
Mina
Iturbide
Juárez
Zaragoza
Libertad Guerrero
Rodríguez
Encino

Río Cuale
Island

Río Cuale

TO PLAYA
MISMAYOLA,
EL EDÉN,
AND BEACHES

Playa de
los Muertos

Aquiles Serdán
Suárez
I. Madero
Av. Insurgentes
A. Vallarta
L. Cárdenas
V. Carranza
Constitución
Badillo
Dieguez
Naranjo
Tepe
Olas Altas

BUDGET
HOTEL
ZONE

Sights ●

Casa Kimberly/Casa Bursus, **5**

Malecón, **2**

Mercado Municipal, **6**

Palacio Municipal, **4**

Plaza Lázaro Cárdenas, **11**

Plaza Principal, **3**

Lodging ○

Hotel Azteca, **9**

Hotel Belmar, **8**

Hotel Rosita, **1**

Hotel Villa del Mar, **10**

Hotel Yasmin, **12**

Posada Río Cuale, **7**

LAUNDRY

Lavandería Acuamatic will wash, dry, and fold 3 kilos (6½ pounds) of clothes for $2.25. *Constitución 279, south of Río Cuale, tel. 322/1–64–90. Other location: Madero 289, north of Río Cuale. Open daily 9–2 and 4–8.*

MAIL

The **post office** is a half block from the malecón, at Juárez. They offer the usual services and will hold mail sent to you at the following address for up to 10 days: Lista de Correos, Morelos 444, Puerto Vallarta, Jalisco, CP 48301, México. *Tel. 322/2–18–88. Open weekdays 8–7, Sat. 9–1.*

MEDICAL AID

The **CMQ** clinic (Badillo 365, ½ block east of Insurgentes, tel. 322/3–19–19) provides 24-hour emergency medical care. English-speaking doctors are available daily 5 PM–8 PM, and appointment prices start at $20. Next door, **Farmacia CMQ** (tel. 322/2–29–41) is also open 24 hours.

PHONES

You'll find **pay phones** on the Plaza Principal and the malecón. Both the **Transportes del Pacífico** (Insurgentes 282, tel. 322/2–10–15) and **Élite** (Carranza 322, tel. 322/3–27–70) bus stations have casetas de larga distancia, open 7 AM–10 PM. The charge for a collect call is $2 at either location.

VISITOR INFORMATION

The **Delegación Regional de Turismo** (Blvd. Fco. Medina Ascencio 1712, across from the Sheraton, tel. 322/3–08–44, fax 322/2–02–43; open weekdays 9–7, Sat. 9–1) is the central office for the state of Jalisco and has all the brochures, maps, and information you'd ever need. Closer to town is the branch office in the Palacio Municipal (tel. 322/2–02–42; open weekdays 9–5). Both offices have friendly, English-speaking staffs.

COMING AND GOING

BY BUS

Puerto Vallarta does not have a central bus station. Instead, bus lines each operate out of individual buildings, all of which are south of the Río Cuale, on or near Avenida Insurgentes. The **Élite** (Badillo 11, at Insurgentes, tel. 322/3–11–17) bus to Hermosillo (24 hrs, $61) departs at 3 PM, with stops in Tepic (3 hrs, $8) and Mazatlán (8 hrs, $18). Buses leave for Manzanillo (5 hrs, $11) at 7 AM and 1 PM; the 1 PM bus continues on to Acapulco (18 hrs, $41). Four first-class buses depart every evening for Mexico City (14 hrs, $36), and an even more plush bus leaves at 8:30 PM ($49). **Transportes del Pacífico** (Insurgentes 282, tel. 322/2–10–15) sends first-class buses to Guadalajara (6 hrs, $17) every hour between 7 AM and 1 AM. Buses to Tepic (3½ hrs, $7) leave every half hour from 4:15 AM to 8 PM. **Transportes Norte de Sonora** (Carranza 322, between Insurgentes and Constitución, tel. 322/2–66–66) has second-class service to San Blas (3½ hrs, $6) and Mazatlán (8 hrs, $16.25). Luggage storage is available at the Norte de Sonora depot. **Transportes Cihuatlán** (Madero 296, at Constitución, tel. 332/2–34–36) has first-class service at 11:30 AM and 4:30 PM to Manzanillo (5 hrs, $11) and to intermediate points such as Bahía Chamela (3½ hrs, $4.50) and Barra de Navidad (4 hrs, $9).

BY PLANE

Puerto Vallarta's international airport is 6 km (4 mi) north of town, near the major resorts. **Aeroméxico** (Plaza Genovesa, tel. 322/4–27–77) and **Mexicana** (Centro Comercial Villas Vallarta, in the Zona Hotelera, tel. 322/4–89–00) have daily flights to Guadalajara ($68 one-way) and Mexico City ($100 one-way) as well as select U.S. cities. **Alaska, American, Continental,** and **Delta** also serve Puerto Vallarta. From downtown, city buses (25¢) marked AEROPUERTO, IXTAPA, or JUNTA will drop you off on the highway, a hop, skip, and jump from the terminals. You can also take an airport taxi to or from the town center for $6.50.

GETTING AROUND

Puerto Vallarta is divided into three parts. The northern section, **Zona Hotelera,** is a long stretch of hotels, shopping centers, and overpriced restaurants. The pedestrian-friendly downtown is known as **Viejo Vallarta** (Old Vallarta) and extends along the banks of the Río Cuale. The southern section is dominated by **Playa de los Muertos,** the most popular beach within city limits. The **malecón** begins at Díaz Ordaz in the Zona Hotelera and runs south past the **Plaza Principal** (also called the Plaza de Armas) in Viejo Vallarta.

To reach the Zona Hotelera from downtown, hop a HOTELES, AEROPUERTO, or MARINAS VALLARTA bus (25¢) on Insurgentes or Juárez. Buses return along Morelos and, south of the Río Cuale, along Insurgentes. Buses run 5 AM–11 PM. You can also take one of the many taxis roaming Vallarta; the city's aggressive drivers will probably flag *you* down for a ride. **Moto Gallo** (Badillo 324, tel. 322/2–16–72; open daily 9–7) rents Honda scooters ($7 per hr, $35 per day) but you'd have to be a very experienced or foolhardy rider to brave Puerto Vallarta's congested streets.

WHERE TO SLEEP

Almost all budget hotels lie just south of the Río Cuale. Most are along Madero, close to the bus stations and less than 10 blocks from the beach. Remember that hotel prices jump as much as 30% between November and April. There are no campgrounds in Puerto Vallarta, and camping is not permitted on beaches within city limits. The exception is during Semana Santa, when temporary campgrounds are set up to accommodate the crowds.

UNDER $10 • Hotel Azteca. A discount rate for families means this cheap hotel fills with crying children and working locals. On the plus side, there's an airy courtyard and the owners are particularly friendly. Doubles cost $8, with kitchenette $11. Prices hold year-round. *Madero 473, tel. 322/2–27–50. 47 rooms, all with bath. Luggage storage. Cash only.*

Hotel Villa del Mar. This spacious hotel, decorated with posters of James Dean and Brooke Shields, is a steal during summer, when clean rooms with balconies and fancy beds cost $10 for a double. For $15 you can have an apartment-style, double-occupancy room with kitchenette. *Madero 440, 3 blocks east of Insurgentes, tel. 322/2–07–85. 49 rooms, all with bath. Luggage storage.*

UNDER $20 • Hotel Belmar. The nicest of the budget hotels, the Belmar has tile floors, framed artwork on the walls, cheerful striped bedcovers, and sparkling bathrooms. Some rooms have balconies overlooking the street, and others open onto the inner courtyard. Rooms cost $16 for a double (rates go up $4 during high season). Ask for a room with TV—it's the same price. *Insurgentes 161, at Serdán, tel. 322/2–05–72. 29 rooms, all with bath.*

Hotel Yasmin. A lush courtyard, clean rooms, and a fine location—one block from Playa de los Muertos—makes this place worth the extra cash. It's in Viejo Vallarta, upstairs from the Café de Olla (*see* Food, *below*). In summer, doubles cost $15, but prices are hiked during winter. *Badillo 168, tel. 322/2–00–87. 27 rooms, all with bath. Luggage storage. Cash only.*

UNDER $30 • Hotel Rosita. You'll pay a bit more here for convenience to the beach and malecón. In low season, doubles cost $26. The suites ($30) have high ceilings, brick walls, air-conditioning, a tile bathroom, and a comfortable king-size bed. *Díaz Ordaz 901, at north end of malecón, tel. 322/3–20–00, fax 332/3–21–51. 112 rooms, all with bath. Luggage storage, pool.*

Posada Río Cuale. This small, friendly inn on the south side of Río Cuale has an excellent gourmet restaurant onsite (aptly named Le Gourmet) and a pleasantly landscaped pool area. The beds are big and comfortable, and the hotel itself is refreshingly quiet. Doubles are $25 (high season $45) and have air-conditioning. *Auiles Serdán 242, tel. 322/2–04–50. 21 rooms, all with bath.*

FOOD

Puerto Vallarta tempts taco-weary travelers with a wide range of restaurants, including many French and Italian ones. Only a few of these are budget-priced. At the city's daily **market,** just north of the Río Cuale, you can get a good comida corrida for $3.

UNDER $5 • Café de Olla. This place swarms with gringos, but service is surprisingly efficient. Delicious *chiles rellenos* (stuffed chile peppers; $4) come with rice, beans, tortillas, and tons of cheese. The eponymous *café de olla* (coffee flavored with chocolate and cinnamon) goes well with breakfast ($2). *Badillo 168, between Olas Altas and Pino Suárez, tel. 322/3–16–26. Closed Tues. Cash only.*

Cenaduría el Campanario. This family-run restaurant is typically packed with locals and savvy tourists enjoying excellent Mexican fare, including 60¢ tamales and a hearty *pozole* (hominy soup) made with chicken or pork and served with chopped lettuce, onion, oregano, radishes, chilis, and sardines. *Hidalgo 339, at Independencia, tel. 322/3–15–09. Closed Sun. Cash only.*

UNDER $10 • Archie's Wok. Founded by Archie Alpenia (who was formerly a private chef to director John Huston), Archie's dishes up the best Asian food in town. Specialties include Hoisin ribs ($6.50) and Thai coconut fish ($7.50). *Rodríguez 130, tel. 322/2–04–11. Near pier at Playa de los Muertos. Closed Sun.*

La Dolce Vita. The oven-baked pizzas ($6) and freshly made pastas here are nothing like the pale imitations served in most of Mexico's "Italian" restaurants. A zesty cheese pizza easily feeds two hungry people. *Díaz Ordaz 674, north end of malecón. tel. 322/2–38–52. No breakfast; dinner only on Sun.*

Andale. A Playa los Muertos hangout that's a great spot for an afternoon beer with locals, Andale also serves superb dinners like fettucini with scallops ($5), and an unusual chicken dish with white wine, pineapple juice, and jalapeño peppers ($6.50). *Paseo de Velasco 425, tel. 322/2–10–54.*

CAFES

Jugos y Café Malibu (Morelos, at Guerrero, tel. 322/2–29–44) is the place to go for fresh-squeezed juice ($1) or an authentic espresso. Euro-style **Café San Cristóbal** (Corona 172, between Juárez and Morelos, tel. 322/3–25–51; closed Sun.) supplies its fresh-roasted beans to restaurants around the city. A platter with cheese, bread, and fruit costs $1.50. Come to **A Page in the Sun** (Olas Altas 399, 1 block from Playa de los Muertos, no phone; closed Sun.) to sip a café latte ($1), buy used books in English, or get a tarot card reading ($7). All of the above accept cash only.

WORTH SEEING

Although the beaches are the main attraction in Puerto Vallarta, a pair of downtown sights are worth a look. **Casa Kimberly** (Zaragoza 445, behind the Guadalupe church, tel. 332/2–13–36) is connected by a bridge to **Casa Bursus.** The first *casa* (house) was a gift from Richard Burton to Elizabeth Taylor in the '60s; the second was named by Burton and his second wife, Susy, using the combination of their two names. Tours of the opulently furnished casas are given daily 9–6.

In recent years, art galleries have sprouted up around town. **Galería Pacífico** (Insurgentes 109, tel. 322/2–19–82), in Viejo Vallarta, shows leading local and international artists and is recognized as the best in town. **Galería Uno** (Morelos 561, tel. 322/2–09–08) has long been a center for the local artists' community and features various Latin American artists. **Galería Javier Niño** (Plaza Marina C-4, tel. 322/2–08–00) features psychedelic, Huichol-inspired paintings done in a singular style known as "Vallarta Art." Pick up information about the city's cultural events from the owners of **Gallería Vallarta** (Juárez 263, tel. 322/2–02–90), where you'll find indigenous art and bronze sculptures.

OUTDOOR ACTIVITIES

Most of the things to do in Puerto Vallarta involve splashing around the waters of the Bahía de Banderas. That said, there are a few enjoyable ways to pass the time on land. **Bike Mex** (Guerrero 361, 1 block north of the market, tel. 322/3–16–80; open Mon.–Sat. 8:30–2 and 4–8) organizes beginner- through advanced-level mountain-biking trips, which range from four-hour excursions ($30) to three-day adventure tours ($360). Prices include food, bikes, and equipment. **Horseback riding** along Río Cuale is another option. Rent horses ($7 per hr) near Olas Altas, at the end of Carranza, daily 9–6.

BEACHES

On sunny days, **Playa de los Muertos** is packed with tourists and vendors. It's also a popular place to watch the sunset. The gloomy name (literally, "Beach of the Dead") stuck after a battle with the Spanish took place here. Parasailing costs $30, banana boat rides $6, inner tubes 50¢, and boogie boards $3 per hour. Snorkel gear ($10 for 24 hrs) or guided snorkel ($22) or dive trips ($49) are available through **Chico's Dive Shop** (Díaz Ordaz 772-5, tel. 322/2–18–95). They also offer longer dive excursions for certified divers, as well as a $200 certification course.

The underwater **Parque Nacional Los Arcos** protects a set of large rocks that have been sculpted by wave erosion to form arches and caves. Chico's and other dive shops will take you scuba diving in these protected waters filled with tropical fish, sea turtles, and moray eels. Night diving (recommended for experienced certified divers only) reveals rarely seen neon fish and slumbering sea turtles. You can see many of the same tropical fish by snorkeling at **Playa Mismaloya.** Take a RUTA 2 combi (20 min, 25¢) from Plaza Lázaro Cárdenas (corner of Vallarta and Badillo) and get off at the Arcos Hotel. Walk down to the rocky beach, and swim out yourself. Playa Mismaloya is also a good sunning and swimming beach. Detour inland 2 km (1 mi) on the dirt road from Playa Mismaloya and you'll find the restaurant **Chino's Paradise,** where *Caveman,* starring former Beatle Ringo Starr, was filmed. Five kilometers (3 mi) farther is **El Edén,** a restaurant near where *Predator* was filmed. Keep walking uphill to reach Puerto Vallarta's largest waterfall, where you can swim, slide down rocks, or play Tarzan on one of several rope swings. To visit the falls on horseback ($20 round-trip) contact Victor at **Rancho Manolo** (tel. 322/8–00–18).

The beaches of **Las Animas, Quimixto,** and **Yelapa** are on the southern side of the Bahía de Banderas, past Playa Mismaloya, and are best reached by boat. Las Animas has a white-sand beach and choice waters for parasailing and waterskiing. The 200-family beach community of Quimixto recently installed its first "road"—a cobblestone walkway leading to a large waterfall 15 minutes inland. Yelapa is the most upscale of the three, with a small colony of expatriates leading the good life in pricey cabañas. The cheapest way to get here is by water shuttle (45 min, $11 round-trip), which leaves daily at 11 AM from the pier at Playa de los Muertos and returns at 4 PM. Boat cruises to the beaches, with meals and snorkeling equipment included, start at $25 per person.

AFTER DARK

There are a million discos in Puerto Vallarta, most of which extort an outrageous cover or charge scandalous prices for drinks. Americanized bars and dance spots are clustered on the north end of the malecón. Chic clubs also abound on Juaréz and Vallarta, and the Zona Hotelera is more expensive still.

To avoid the dance scene altogether, walk over the bridge from Insurgentes to **Le Bistro** (Río Cuale island 16-A, tel. 322/2–02–83; closed Sun.), one of the sleekest restaurant/bars in town. Sit at the black-and-white bar or in the dinner lounge and listen while a DJ spins your favorite jazz tunes.

DISCOS

Of Puerto Vallarta's classier discos, the only one in Viejo Vallarta is **Cactus** (Vallarta 399, tel. 322/2–60–37), a self-proclaimed "Disco Club and New Age Bar." Cover is $13 for men, $5 for women. Wednesday and Sunday nights the cover price includes an open bar. Other discos are at the resorts, a 15–20 minute, $2–$5 taxi ride north of town. **Christine's** (tel. 322/4–69–90), in the Hotel Krystal, plays rock, salsa, and techno; cover is $6. **Collage** (Marina Vallarta, tel. 322/1–05–05) is the best disco in town, playing techno and rock music until 5 AM nightly. The $8 cover gives you access to pool tables and video games. If you prefer live salsa and *música tropical* and want to mingle with some more down-to-earth Mexicans, head to **Le Carrusel** (in front of Seguro Social building, tel. 322/3–28–09).

GAY/LESBIAN BARS AND DISCOS

The downtown **Zótano** (Morelos 101, no phone) means "basement" in Spanish and has an appropriately underground feel, attracting a mixed straight and gay clientele. **Los Balcones Bar** (Juárez 182, 1 block south of Plaza Principal, tel. 322/2–46–71) is a popular gay tourist hangout, with tables that overlook the street. The large **Club Paco Paco** (Vallarta 266, between Carranza and Ardenas, tel. 322/2–18–99) attracts a mixed local/tourist lesbian and gay crowd to its downstairs dance floor and upstairs pool table and video games. The newest gay disco in town, **Studio 33** (Juárez 728, at Vicario, tel. 322/3–11–65), features the area's best strip and drag shows Friday–Sunday at 1 AM.

NEAR PUERTO VALLARTA

PUNTA DE MITA

The Punta de Mita, north of Puerto Vallarta on the Bahía de Banderas, offers beaches ideal for surfing and swimming. For decades this was a pristine area unspoiled by development, but sadly that era has come to an end; construction of a Four Seasons luxury hotel on Punta de Mita should be completed in 1998. The landscape here is drier and more desertlike than you'll find along most of the Pacific coastline, and the views of the bay and mountains are fantastic. The beach is often crowded, especially around the restaurants and the main beach, **Playa El Anclote,** but a short walk along the coast in either direction brings you to solitary stretches of sand. Next to the pier, English-speaking Chuy at **Sol y Arena** (no phone) makes boat trips (half an hour each way) to **Isla Marietas,** home to many seabirds; if you want to camp on the island, arrange a pickup time with the boat captain. Round-trip transport for up to five people is $44. Chuy also makes boat trips to other "hidden beaches" ($22 per hour for up to five people) and will rent you surfboards ($14 a day) and snorkel gear ($4 for 3 hrs). If you've got your own surfboard, head straight to Punta de Mita, a 15-minute walk from Playa El Anclote. For beautiful, isolated beaches, get off the bus to or from Punta de Mita at **Playa Destiladores, Cruz de Huanacaxtle,** or **Arena Blanca.** If you want to spend the night, you can camp anywhere along Playa El Anclote, or head uphill to the **Hotel Punta de Mita** (Hidalgo 5, no phone), where a beautifully furnished room five minutes from the beach is $15. Head back down to the beach to **Restaurante Rocío** for BBQ fish ($7) and lobster ($10). They'll even whip up a vegetarian dish, and all meals include a free drink of your choice.

COMING AND GOING

Transportes Medina (Brasil 264, at Guatemala, tel. 322/2–47–32) in Puerto Vallarta has service to Punta de Mita (1 hr, $1.50) every 10 minutes from 6:10 AM–9 PM. To reach the bus terminal from downtown, take any CENTRO bus (15 min, 25¢), which will let you off two blocks south of the station. When thinking about bus schedules, keep in mind that because they're in different time zones, 2 PM in Punta de Mita is 3 PM in Puerto Vallarta.

RINCON DE GUAYABITOS

Located 70 km (43 mi) northwest of Puerto Vallarta, this beach town offers similar tourist services but without the sky-high prices. The area around Guayabitos is virgin forest, and colorful tropical flowers and lush foliage line the town streets. The golden beach, in the sheltered cove of Jaltemba, has calm, clean waters perfect for banana boat rides ($3 per person) and jet skiing ($25 an hr). You can also go sportfishing ($16 per hr) and take glass-bottom boat tours to the nearby island; walk to the southern end of the beach for rentals and information on all of these activities. If you're up for a little sunning, walk past the boat docks and around the rocks to the small, quiet **Playa Los Ayala.** For surfing, hop in a taxi ($1) and head 10 minutes south to **Playa Lo de Marcos.**

Each year during the first few days of November, Rincón de Guayabitos hosts a **Fly-In,** in which more than 100 airplanes put on air shows for an audience representing more than 300 countries. For further information, contact the town's **tourist office** (next to the church, tel. 327/4–06–93).

COMING AND GOING

From Puerto Vallarta, hop on one of **Transportes del Pacífico**'s Tepic-bound buses and get off at the crossroads for Guayabitos (1½ hrs, $3.50). To return to Puerto Vallarta, take a combi from Avenida Sol Nuevo to La Peñita de Jaltemba (10 min, 25¢), where there's a Pacífico bus terminal.

WHERE TO SLEEP AND EAT

Guayabitos is the choice vacation spot for many Mexican families, and its bungalows are filled to capacity during Christmas, Easter, and the month of July. Between November and March, an onslaught of travelers from Canada and the United States visit, causing prices to rise. The fact that accommodations are mostly six-person bungalows with kitchenettes means lodging can be especially pricey for solo travelers. **Bungalows Zapotlanijo** (Sol Nuevo 18, tel. 327/4–00–02) is slightly run down but cheap: A bungalow for up to four people costs $12.50 ($18.50 in the high season). For beautiful, modern bungalows right on the beach, **Bungalows El Paraíso** (Tabachines 5, tel. 327/4–02–99) has prices ranging from $32 for two people to $47 for six. Camping is allowed along the beach. Both accept cash only. The **Restaurante Toñita II** (in Hotel Costa Alegre, tel. 327/4–02–42) is on the beach and serves delicious shrimp ($3) and a special Mexican plate ($4.50) that comes with a chile relleno, tacos, enchiladas, rice, beans, and the meat of your choice. Guayabito's lush vegetation means you'll also find vendors on the streets and at the beach selling mangoes and fresh pineapple juice.

BAHÍA DE NAVIDAD

If simple living and sandy beaches entice you, look no farther than the Bahía de Navidad (Christmas Bay). There are two towns, **San Patricio-Melaque** and **Barra de Navidad,** on this tranquil bay in the southernmost part of Jalisco state. In 1989, the government gave the whole string of beaches from the bay north to Puerto Vallarta the name *Costalegre* (Happy Coast), designating the area as a tourist zone. Many who vacationed at these towns 10 years ago lament that tourism has ruined the beaches' natural beauty, but locals heartily welcome the business. The sandy shores are still clean, the prices still reasonable, and the pace still decidedly laid back.

The town of San Patricio-Melaque is most popular with vacationers from Guadalajara, many of whom own beach homes that sit idle most of the year. Tourists from the States and Canada alight here during winter months, but in general, Melaque has fewer wealthy gringo tourists than Barra de Navidad does, making it more accessible to the budget traveler. Melaque also feels more like a Mexican town, particularly in the evening, when people gather in the main square under the neon glow of the church cross. As in Barra de Navidad, the best and only pastime here is sunning on the golden sand and cooling off in the rolling waves. San Patricio-Melaque's patron saint is, of course, **San Patricio**, and the merrymaking in his honor begins on March 10, ending on his feast day, March 17. During this time, there is a weeklong party, which includes a solemn mass and blessing of the fishing-boat fleet, as well as folk dancing and a cake-eating contest.

Six kilometers (4 mi) down the beach from Melaque, Barra de Navidad boasts cool, brisk breezes that make for choppy afternoon waves. Most action happens at the hotels and restaurants along the small peninsula that stretches toward Isla de Navidad; Avenida Veracruz, where locals and tourists mingle, is a pleasant place for a stroll at any time of day. The unfinished **Iglesia de Cristo** is off the town square, leaving Barra de Navidad somewhat centerless. In the church, note that Christ's hands are by his side instead of attached to the cross: Local myth describes how Christ's hands fell from the cross to push the water away and save the town during the 1973 hurricane. Barra de Navidad's annual **Fiesta de San Antonio de Padua** (June 5–13) honors the town's patron saint. Don't count on sleeping a wink during the unremitting fireworks and resonating tuba tunes.

BASICS

BOOKSTORES

Beer Bob's Book Exchange. Bob has a fascinating collection of best-sellers and novels available for sale or trade. *Mazatlán 61, in Barra de Navidad, no phone. Open weekdays 1–4.*

CASAS DE CAMBIO

There's a casa de cambio in the **Centro Commercial Melaque** (Gómez Farías 27-A, behind Farmacia Nueva, tel. and fax 335/5–53–43). The casa will exchange traveler's checks and cash at no commission. In Barra de Navidad, you can change money at the nameless **casa de cambio** (Veracruz 212-C, tel. 335/5–61–77) on the main strip. Both places are open Monday–Saturday 9–2 and 4–7, Sunday 9–2.

EMERGENCIES

The number for the **police** in Melaque is 335/5–50–80; in Barra, call the police at 335/5–53–99.

LAUNDRY

In Barra, **Lavandería Jardín** (Jalisco 70, tel. 335/5–61–35; open weekdays 9–2 and 4–7, Sat. 9–noon) charges $2 for 3 kilos (6½ pounds) of laundry.

MAIL

Postal service for both Barra and Melaque is conducted through Melaque's post office. They'll hold mail sent to you at the following address for up to 10 days: Lista de Correos, Melaque, Jalisco, CP 48980, México. *Clemente Orozco 13, at Gómez Farías, tel. 335/5–52–30. Open weekdays 8–3, Sat. 8–noon.*

MEDICAL AID

If you need a doctor while you're in the Bahía, Melaque's **Centro de Salud** (tel. 335/5–62–20) is at the corner of Corona and Gómez Farías. For minor problems, stop by the **Farmacia Melaque** (López Mateos, ½ block east of the square, no phone; open daily 8 AM–10 PM). In Barra, **Farmacia Rubio** (Veracruz 332, by the bus station, tel. 335/5–54–12) is open daily 9–2 and 4–9.

PHONES

Pay phones line Gómez Farías in Melaque and Avenida Veracruz in Barra. You can make cash calls and use the fax machine in Melaque at the Centro Comercial Melaque, in the casa de cambio listed above. In Barra, **TelMex** (Jalisco 16, tel. and fax 335/5–52–37; open daily 9 AM–10 PM) has long-distance service.

VISITOR INFORMATION

Barra is home to the sole tourist office in the Bahía. The staff is extremely helpful but does not speak English. The brochures, laden with lovely pictures, lack substance, but the maps are accurate. *Calle Jalisco, tel. 335/5–51–00. Open weekdays 9–8.*

COMING AND GOING

The bus station in Melaque (tel. 335/5–50–03) is on the corner of Gómez Farías and Carranza, and comes equipped with a restaurant. From here, **Transportes Cihuatlán** (tel. 335/5–50–03), also known as Autocamiones del Pacífico, sends second-class buses to Guadalajara (6½ hrs, $10.50) and Puerto Vallarta (4 hrs, $9). Though second-class buses are fine, it's worth laying out an extra couple of bucks to take a faster *plus* bus, with videos and chilling air-conditioning; *plus* buses leave five times daily to Guadalajara and Puerto Vallarta, stopping in Barra de Navidad at Avenida Veracruz, between Avenidas Pilipinas and 21 de Noviembre. There's no formal bus station in Barra, but the **Flecha Amarilla** (Gómez Farías 34, tel. 335/5–61–10) office sends buses hourly to Manzanillo (1½ hrs; $3 1st class, $2.25 2nd class).

GETTING AROUND

Barra de Navidad is more like one big neighborhood than a town. **Avenida Veracruz,** two blocks east of the beach, is the main commercial street. The farther south you go, the more restaurants and hotels you'll find clustered near the malecón, which runs along a strip of land dividing the lagoon from the sea. Green-and-white minibuses (10 min, 25¢) constantly shuttle between Barra and Melaque. In Barra, flag down buses on Veracruz.

Melaque has a longer row of hotels and restaurants ringing the northern part of the crescent bay. The budget hotel zone is conveniently located in the few blocks between the bus station and the beach, near Avenida Carranza. Many services and restaurants, as well as the daily mercado, are also near the bus station. Flag down minibuses to Barra on Juárez.

WHERE TO SLEEP

Hotels raise their prices December–April, particularly around the Christmas and Easter holidays. Of the hotels listed below, Posada Pacífico and Hotel Delfín are in Barra de Navidad, while Bungalows Villa Mar and Posada Pablo de Tarso are in Melaque. If all of these are full, try Melaque's **Hotel Hidalgo** (Hidalgo 7, tel. 335/5–50–45), a quiet, well-maintained hotel facing the beach. Doubles run $7.50, cash only.

UNDER $15 • Posada Pacífico. Veteran travelers consider this the best budget hotel in town. Each room is different, reflecting the owner's intent to treat every guest like a member of the family. His son, Ernesto, is into ecology, and if you ask, he'll show you pictures of what Barra de Navidad looked like 10 years ago. Doubles cost $11, and bungalows with kitchenettes cost $12.50–$19. Prices jump $2–$5 in high season. *Mazatlán 136, at Michoacán, Barra de Navidad, tel. 335/5–53–59. 1 block from both beach and bus station. 24 rooms, all with bath. Laundry, luggage storage. Cash only.*

UNDER $20 • Bungalows Villa Mar. The English-speaking owner here is very accommodating. Bungalows have kitchen and bathroom and sleep up to eight people; during high season the rate is $20 for two people, plus $5 for each additional person. Low season prices are a few dollars less. *Hidalgo 1, a few paces from Gómez Farías, Melaque, tel. 335/5–50–05. 5 units, all with bath. Laundry ($3), luggage storage. Cash only.*

Posada Pablo de Tarso. The elegant rooms in this two-story hotel surround an alluring garden and swimming pool. Air-conditioned rooms with wooden furniture, velvetlike bedspreads, and TVs cost $20 for two people. Bungalows with kitchenette, fan, and TV cost $26 for up to three people. *Gómez Farías 408, between Guzmán and Orozco, Melaque, tel. 335/5–51–17. 27 rooms, all with bath. Cash only.*

UNDER $25 • Hotel Delfín. Here you'll get immaculate rooms and efficient service. Large rooms open onto a shared balcony, and guests (many of them German) have access to a pool, makeshift fitness room, and free breakfast buffet. Doubles are $25, with a 20% discount in the low season. Reservations are advised in winter. *Morelos 23, tel. 335/5–50–68. 22 rooms, all with bath. Luggage storage.*

CAMPING

Camping on the beach in either town is discouraged by hotel owners. Rather, the tourist office recommends camping on the undeveloped section of beach between Barra and Melaque. In Melaque, the **Trailer Park La Playa** (Gómez Farías 250, 1 block from the bus station, tel. 335/5–50–65) is a well-maintained parking lot/campground that's crowded with RVs in winter. Tent spaces cost $8.

FOOD

The daily **market** in Melaque on López Mateos, near the zócalo, is a good place to stock up on cheap, fresh produce. Melaque's beach, sprinkled with palapas that serve seafood at moderate prices, is another option. In Barra, Avenida Veracruz is lined with inexpensive food stalls and restaurants. Only some of these amiable restaurants are open during the day, but those that are serve full breakfasts for about $2. The more expensive seafood restaurants on the south end of the bay are prime spots for watching the setting sun.

UNDER $5 • César and Charly. This Melaque seafood restaurant has a patio that spills out onto the beach. It's not as good as Los Pelícanos (*see below*), but you can get a delicious meal of grilled fish ($4) without having to walk as far. *Gómez Farías 27-A, Melaque, tel. 335/5–56–99. Past Centro Comercial Melaque toward water. Cash only.*

Los Pelícanos. The best of Melaque's palapas is run with motherly care by Italian-born, ex–New Yorker Philomena "Phil" García. Her ham and eggs would make Dr. Seuss green with envy, and rumor has it that Robert Redford occasionally flies in for breaded octopus ($4). You may have to wait for one of the whimsical booths, and don't leave without trying one of the icy margaritas ($3). *5th palapa from end of beach, Melaque. Cash only.*

Restaurante Velero's. Overlooking the lagoon in Barra de Navidad, this restaurant enjoys cool breezes all day long. The restaurant has funky tablecloths and chairs and sweeping views of the bay. Both the ceviche (diced fish marinated in lime juice; $4) and shrimp salad are delicious. *Veracruz 64, Barra de Navidad, no phone. No breakfast. Cash only.*

UNDER $10 • Restaurant y Café Crepes Ámbar. Run by a French-Mexican couple, this romantic Barra de Navidad restaurant serves savory French wine and a large variety of delicious seafood, vegetarian, and sweet crepes ($2–$6). Flamenco music plays throughout the night. *Veracruz 101-A, Barra de Navidad, no phone. No breakfast. Cash only.*

OUTDOOR ACTIVITIES

The main diversions here—apart from bayside margarita-sipping—are swimming, surfing, splashing, or surveying the sunset. Barra's beaches have rougher waves than Melaque's, and Melaque offers better views of the rocky peninsula, local lagoon, and distant mountains. For surfing, trek 1 km (½ mi) around the bend past Melaque to the pristine beach on the other side of the crescent bay. The **Isla de Navidad**, also called "Colimilla," is actually a peninsula accessible only by boat. Arrange a ride (15 min, $5) to Isla de Navidad (and its first-rate beachfront restaurants) with someone from Barra's **tourist-boat cooperative** (Veracruz 40, no phone).

A popular activity in the Bahía is fishing: The Barra tourist-boat cooperative charges $16 per hour for up to eight people, equipment included, to troll the coastal waters for marlin, tuna, and sailfish. There is no minimum number of hours for a trip.

AFTER DARK

The Bahía is known for its slow pace and tranquility. Even on weekends, the main social activity after 10:30 PM consists of local men drinking in front of liquor stores. There are two nightclubs: **Disco La Tanga** (Gómez Farías, at Av. La Primavera, tel. 335/5–50–01; closed Mon.–Wed.) in Melaque plays lively disco and techno and charges $3 cover. In Barra, **El Galeón** (Morelos 24, in Hotel Sands, tel. 335/5–50–18) plays salsa, merengue, and disco for a $1.50 cover. **Bar Terraza Jardín** (Jalisco 71, tel. 335/5–65–31) is a karaoke bar that really gets going after 9 PM.

If you're loco for coconuts, try an atole de coco, a sweet drink made with coconut water and corn syrup. It's sold at stalls on Avenida Veracruz in Barra de Navidad.

NEAR BAHIA DE NAVIDAD

BAHIA CHAMELA

South of Puerto Vallarta, Highway 200 swings inland and doesn't meet the coast again for 150 km (93 mi), until it touches Bahía Chamela. This bay is isolation with a capital "I"—one long stretch of unsullied beaches developed only in patches, such as the self-contained Lu Bay Village and Club Med's Playa Blanca resort. You'll find an older RV crowd from the States here in winter, while Mexican holidays (August, December, and Easter) herald the arrival of families from Guadalajara. During the rest of the year, you can expect relative seclusion (along with fewer open hotels and restaurants) in this dry, breezy, coastal area. Thatched-hut restaurants and campgrounds are the primary services along most of the bay.

At the far northern end of Bahía Chamela is the rocky **Punta Perula,** from which you can take a short boat trip to **Isla La Pajerera,** a small island that is home to many migrating birds. It's a designated ecological sanctuary. Fishermen at Punta Perula give rides to and from the island ($5 round-trip). South of Punta Perula lies a sweeping crescent of sand that includes the beaches **Playa Fortuna** and **Playa Chamela,** as well as the nesting areas of myriad exotic seabirds. At the south end of the bay, camping opportunities abound, and there's a small store where you can pick up supplies. **Villas Polinesia Camping Club** (Carretera 200 Km. 72, tel. 328/5–52–47) is 5 km (3 mi) outside of the small town of Chamela. Polynesian-style two-story huts with bathrooms cost $31 for two people, $35 for three or four. Since the only restaurant is a 15-minute walk back to the highway from the villas, the accommodating staff will cook for you if given advance notice (winter only).

COMING AND GOING

To reach Bahía Chamela, take one of the hourly second-class buses traveling from Barra de Navidad (1½ hrs, $2.50) or Melaque (1 hr, $2.50) toward Puerto Vallarta; they'll drop you off at the crossroads leading to Chamela. For the 4-km (2½-mi) trek inland to the beach, you can try to snag a taxi from the highway, but you'll probably have better luck either hitchhiking or, if you can handle it, walking an hour in the sweltering heat.

MANZANILLO

The city of Manzanillo, with a population of just 110,000, is built along the twin, crescent-shape Manzanillo and Santiago bays. Altogether, it's home to 20 beaches and the busiest Pacific seaport in Mexico. The city was named Manzanillo because export of locally grown *manzanilla* (chamomile, an herb used for tea) significantly increased with the start of the region's shipping industry. Today, the port's industrial clutter forms a menacing skyline, and spilled oil and debris have spoiled the beaches in Manzanillo proper. However, in spite of the bays' pollution, fish in the area flourish. Manzanillo claims to be the *pez vela* (sailfish) capital of the world, and marlin and red snapper are regularly reeled in as well.

Don't be scared away by Manzanillo's urban sprawl. The city has much to offer the budget traveler, and there are several outlying beaches where you won't have to scrape tar off your feet after a swim. In town, you'll find quaint neighborhoods, white-stucco buildings, cobblestone streets, fountains, and giant sculptures—reflecting Manzanillo's Mediterranean, Moorish, and Spanish influences. Foreigners receive a genuinely hospitable welcome here, and if you stay away from the resorts, you'll only see a handful of foreign tourists. On the other hand, Mexican tourists abound, especially wealthy Guadalajarans; expect prices to rise everywhere during Christmas and Easter.

BASICS

AMERICAN EXPRESS

The city's AmEx representative is the travel agency **Bahías Gemelas,** in the Salahua neighborhood. Cardholders may cash personal checks and receive mail. MoneyGrams are available. *Blvd. Costero Miguel de la Madrid 1556, Manzanillo, Colima, CP 28200, México, tel. 333/3–10–00. Near IMSS building. Open weekdays 9–2 and 4–7, Sat. 9–2.*

CASAS DE CAMBIO

Banamex (México 136, in Manzanillo, tel. 333/2–01–15; open weekdays 9–2:30) changes money and has ATMs that accept Plus, Cirrus, MasterCard, and Visa. There's another Banamex in the Commercial Mexicana building on Boulevard Costero, in the Salahua neighborhood. **Farmacia Americana** (*see* Medical Aid, *below*) also changes money.

EMERGENCIES

You may dial 06 from any phone in Manzanilla for emergency assistance. The number for **police** is 333/2–10–04. For **ambulance** service contact the Cruz Roja (tel. 333/2–59–83).

LAUNDRY

Lavandería Casablanca charges $1.25 per piece or $4 for 9 kilos (20 pounds) of laundry. *Across from bus station, tel. 333/2–16–54. Open Mon.–Sat. 10–2 and 4–7.*

MAIL

The post office in downtown Manzanillo will hold mail sent to you at the following address for up to 10 days: Lista de Correos, Manzanillo, Colima, CP 28200, México. *Juárez, at 5 de Mayo, tel. 333/2–14–61. Open weekdays 8–7, Sat. 8–1.*

MEDICAL AID

Hospital Civil (Calle Hospital, Col. San Pedrito, tel. 333/2–19–03), off the Carretera a Santiago as you leave downtown Manzanillo, charges on a sliding scale. **Hospital Naval** (tel. 333/3–27–40), on the naval base in Colonia Las Brisas, has better facilities but is more expensive. **Farmacia Americana** (México 224, tel. 333/2–37–55) is open daily 9 AM–10 PM.

PHONES

Computel (Morelos 144, ½ block from Jardín Obregón; open daily 7 AM–10 PM) offers phone and fax services. Calls to the States cost $1 for two minutes, but on Sunday there's a 33% discount.

VISITOR INFORMATION

The **tourist office** has lots of brochures on Manzanillo but lacks information on nearby towns. The staff is friendly and speaks some English. Tourist information is also available at many hotels and the local

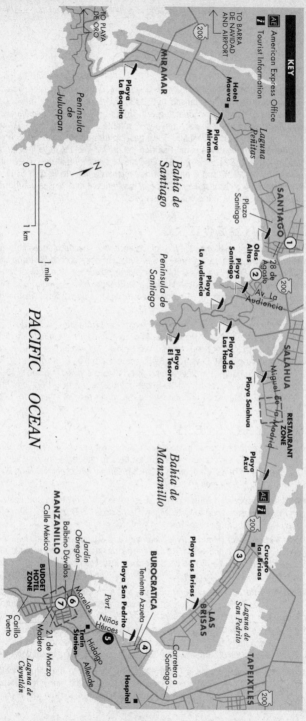

MANZANILLO

KEY

AE American Express Office

i Tourist Information

Sights ●
Museo de
Arqueología, **5**

Lodging ○
Hotel Brilla Mar, **2**
Hotel Colonial, **7**
Hotel María
Cristina, **1**
Hotel Miramar, **6**

Hotel Parador
Marbella, **3**
Hotel San Pedrito, **4**

TO BARRA
DE NAVIDAD
AND AIRPORT

200

MIRAMAR

Playa
La Boquita

Hotel
Maeva ■

Playa
Miramar

Laguna
Peritita

Península
de
Juluapan

TO PLAYA
DE ORO

N

0   1 km
0   1 mile

Bahía de
Santiago

PACIFIC OCEAN

Plaza
Santiago

SANTIAGO ①

28 de
Agosto
② Olas
Altas

Playa
Santiago

Av. La
Audiencia

Playa
La Audiencia

Península de
Santiago

Playa
El Tesoro

Playa de
Las Hadas

Playa Salahua

SALAHUA

Miguel de la Madrid

RESTAURANT
ZONE

Playa
Azul

AE i

200

Bahía de
Manzanillo

③

Playa Las Brisas

Crucero
las Brisas ■

LAS
BRISAS

Laguna
de San Pedro

Laguna de
San Pedrito

Carretera a
Santiago

TAPEIXTLES

200

BUROCRATICA

Teniente Azueta

Playa San Pedrito

④

Port

Jardín
Obregón

Balbino Dávalos
Calle México

MANZANILLO

BUDGET
HOTEL
ZONE

⑦

Carillo
Puerto

Morelos

Madero

21 de Marzo

Hidalgo

Allende

⑥

Niños
Héroes

⑤ Train
Station

Hospital ■

Laguna de
Cuyutlán

263

AmEx agent (*see above*). *Blvd. Costero Miguel de la Madrid Km. 9.5, tel. 333/3–22–77. Open weekdays 9–3 and 6–8.*

COMING AND GOING

BY BUS

The **Central Camionera** is east of town, best reached from the city center by taxi (5–10 min, $1.50–$2). **Autotransportes del Sur de Jalisco** (tel. 333/2–10–03) buses (30 min, 50¢) run to Armería and Tecomán every 15 minutes, connecting with buses to El Paraíso, Cuyutlán, and Boca de Pascuales. Buses to Colima (1½ hrs, $1) depart every 30 minutes. **Élite** (tel. 333/2–01–35) buses leave for Acapulco (11 hrs, $26) at 12:30 PM and 5 PM, passing through Zihuatanejo (6 hrs, $18) en route. **Transportes Cihuatlán/Autocamiones del Pacífico** (tel. 333/2–02–15) have first- and second-class buses to Guadalajara (4¼ hrs; $21 1st class, $11 2nd class) every 90 minutes. They run hourly buses to Barra de Navidad (1½ hr, $3), and a midnight bus to Puerto Vallarta (5 hrs, $11). To reach Colonias San Pedrito, Las Brisas, or Santiago, catch one of the frequent local buses that depart from the back of the station. Luggage storage at the bus station costs $1 per 24 hours.

GETTING AROUND

Manzanillo is an unusual town by Mexican standards. There's Manzanillo proper, which is the city's downtown, and then there are a string of self-sufficient neighborhoods strung along the two bays, Bahía de Santiago and Bahía de Manzanillo. Traveling northwest from downtown, you'll encounter **San Pedrito, Brisas, Azul, Salahua, Las Hadas,** and **El Tesoro** on Bahía de Manzanillo. **La Audiencia, Santiago, Olas Altas, Miramar,** and **La Boquita** are on Bahía de Santiago. Each neighborhood has its own corresponding beach.

Downtown, Manzanillo's zócalo is better known as the **Jardín Obregón.** On its north side it's bordered by Avenida Morelos and the waterfront. **Calle México,** the main commercial street, extends south from the Jardín and leads to budget hotels and banks. Buses (20¢–45¢) marked SANTIAGO and LAS HADAS depart for various points along the bays from the bus stop half a block east of the Jardín on Morelos, and from Manzanillo's Central Camionera (*see* Coming and Going, *above*). The ride is 15–45 minutes, depending on your neighborhood/beach of choice. Buses operate daily 7 AM–11 PM; after hours you can depend on taxis. It's about $4.50 to taxi from Santiago to the center of town.

WHERE TO SLEEP

Cheap hotels are concentrated in downtown Manzanillo, near the pleasant Jardín Obregón. They're a short bus or taxi ride away from the good beaches. To stay right on the waterfront you should be prepared to spend a bit more, particularly in the Santiago neighborhood and on La Punta peninsula. Hotel prices jump during Christmas and Easter.

Camping is only allowed during the high season (around Christmas and Easter), when the free trailer park on **Playa Miramar** (next to Hotel Maeva, tel. 333/5–05–95) opens. Latrines and showers are available free of charge during the season.

UNDER $15 • Hotel Miramar. The Miramar's odd staircases lead to huge, tile balconies, and doors straight out of *Alice in Wonderland*. Rooms on the top floor catch cool breezes. Doubles cost $12; all are equipped with fans and hot water. It's downtown, just steps from the zócalo. *Juárez 122, ½ block from Jardín, tel. 333/2–10–08. 38 rooms, all with bath. Luggage storage. Cash only.*

Hotel San Pedrito. Although staying near the port in a dumpy part of the city might not seem appealing, this hotel does offer pool, tennis courts, picnic area, and proximity to San Pedrito beach. Doubles cost $11. *Teniente Azueta 3, San Pedrito, tel. 333/2–05–35. Laundry (25¢ per piece), luggage storage.*

UNDER $20 • Hotel Colonial. This downtown Manzanillo hotel is reminiscent of an 18th-century mansion. Large, clean rooms ($18.50) are equipped with air-conditioning and TVs. *Bocanegra 28, at México, tel. 333/2–10–80. 36 rooms, all with bath. Laundry, luggage storage, restaurant.*

Hotel María Cristina. The María Cristina is ideally located in the affluent neighborhood of Santiago. Rooms cost $20 with fan, $30 with air-conditioning. There's a funny, fish-shape pool in the back, and you're not too far from the beach. *28 de Agosto 36, between Morelos and Hidalgo, Santiago, tel. 333/3–09–66. 21 rooms, all with bath.*

UNDER $35 • Parador Marbella. This hotel is reasonably priced considering its prime location right on Las Brisas beach. The pleasantly decorated rooms ($35) all have private bath, air-conditioning, and TV. Rooms that face the ocean have tiny, palm-shaded balconies. *Carretera Santiago-Manzanillo, Las Brisas, tel. 333/3–08–61. 94 rooms, all with bath.*

FOOD

Manzanillo's restaurants accommodate all budgets. Downtown, the food stalls at the daily **market** (Cuauhtémoc, at Madero) are the cheapest places to eat. Food is freshest at lunchtime. Budget restaurants are also downtown around the Jardín Obregón. In Santiago, look for restaurants around the Jardín Santiago. In Salahua, you'll find a cluster of restaurants near the American Express office (*see* Basics, *above*). With the exception of Ramada Tanilo's, all of the restaurants listed below are in downtown Manzanillo.

UNDER $4 • Chantilly. Of all the restaurants surrounding downtown's Jardín Obregón, this is the most popular. The food ($2–$4) at this cafeteria-style spot is traditional Mexican (tacos, enchiladas, and quesadillas) and service is brisk. *Madero 60, at Juárez, tel. 333/2–01–94. Closed Sat. Cash only.*

Plaza La Perlita. On a sunny day, opt for one of the wrought-iron outdoor tables at this seafood restaurant. A regular shrimp cocktail costs $2, a huge one $3. A fish fillet, cooked to your liking, is $4. Evenings at 9 PM live musicians show up to play romantic tunes for starry-eyed couples. *Niños Héroes, across from train station, tel. 333/2–27–70. No breakfast. Cash only.*

Manzanillo is known for its annual sailfishing tournaments in February and November. Tournament participants set a world record in 1957, catching more than 300 sailfish within three days.

Restaurant Roca del Mar. This bargain joint, decorated with indigenous art and overlooking a garden, serves a filling comida corrida ($3) of soup, rice, an entrée, and tortillas. For vegetarians, there are meatless soups and quesadillas. *21 de Marzo 204, tel. 333/2–03–02. Cash only.*

UNDER $10 • Ramada Tanilo's. Mexican tourists flock to this waterfront restaurant on Playa La Boquita. You'll dine to live mariachi music mixed with the gentle sound of lapping waves. House specials include shrimp in garlic sauce and *almejas vivas* (live clams; $4); locals claim the latter dish is an aphrodisiac. The most convenient way to get here is by taxi. *Playa La Boquita, no phone. Take SANTIAGO bus to Playa Miramar and walk 15 min north on the beach, or ask the bus driver to drop you off at La Boquita and taxi ($1) the rest of the way. Cash only.*

WORTH SEEING

Besides the friendly people and miles of beachfront, Manzanillo's main attraction is the outstanding **Museo de Arqueología,** run by the University of Colima. The museum houses a collection of some 18,000 artifacts (about 5,000 are displayed at a time) from all over Mesoamerica, including important pieces discovered around Manzanillo. The two *tumbas de tiro* (tunnel-shape, multichamber tombs), found in the archaeological site of Las Golondrinas and reconstructed here, are especially fascinating. *San Pedrito traffic circle, tel. 333/2–22–56. From downtown, take any westbound bus marked SALAHUA or SANTIAGO. Admission free. Open Mon.–Sat. 10–2 and 5–8, Sun. 10–1.*

OUTDOOR ACTIVITIES

Manzanillo's biggest attractions are its beaches, with waters much cooler and a bit murkier than its southern neighbors. Note that beaches immediately around the port in Manzanillo are dirty and unsafe for swimming. The best beach closest to downtown Manzanillo is **Playa Las Brisas,** a 20-minute bus ride from downtown. On the peninsula separating Bahía de Santiago from Bahía de Manzanillo is the peaceful **Playa La Audiencia,** surrounded by green hills. This beach is dominated by the luxurious Las Hadas resort (the setting for the Bo Derek flesh fantasy *10*). **Agua Mundo** (tel. 333/4–20–00 ext. 759), inside the Las Hadas resort, rents windsurf boards ($30 per hr), kayaks ($15 per hr), and snorkeling equipment ($12 per 6 hrs). They also offer sunset tours at 5 PM daily; the two-hour cruise costs $15 and includes two drinks. To get here, take a bus to the Las Brisas *crucero* (crossroads) and transfer to a LAS HADAS or AUDIENCIA bus.

Boca de Pascuales is famous for its huge, aggressive waves, making it a year-round hot spot for "surfos"—kamikaze surfers who ride the waves for hours and who stretch out their surfing safaris by living on a few dollars a day.

Indeed, the only people who will want to visit Boca de Pascuales are surfers, fans of surfers, or those looking for an inexpensive, isolated beach upon which to do absolutely nothing but watch surfers (as a spectator sport, surfing can be a thrill; there's nothing like watching a puny human battle an 18-ft wave).

The Manzanillo tourist office doesn't provide information on conditions here, so snag a surfer and beg him or her to advise you, or try calling one of the town's two phone numbers (332/9–13–32 or 332/4–21–56). You can camp anywhere along the beach in Boca de Pascuales, and a few hotels offer basic rooms.

To reach Boca de Pascuales, take a bus to Tecomán (1 hr, $1.50) from Manzanillo. The depot for transfer buses (20 min, 50¢) is one block to the right as you leave Tecomán's main bus terminal.

For surfing and boogie boarding, head for the appropriately named **Olas Altas** (high waves) beach, near Santiago. All the way at the end of the strip of beaches, about 35 minutes by bus from downtown Manzanillo, is **Playa La Boquita,** a sheltered beach popular with local families and tourists staying at nearby resorts. Here you can rent boogie boards ($1 per hr) and horses ($5 per hr), take a banana boat ride ($5 for 10 min), and enjoy wonderful seafood right on the beach (*see* Food, *above*).

AFTER DARK

Manzanillo's nightlife centers around one neighborhood, Salahua, which can be reached by taking a MIRA-MAR or SANTIAGO bus. The largest disco, **Vog** (Blvd. Costero, tel. 333/3–18–75), is open nightly during the high season but only Friday and Saturday during the off-season. Cover is $4 for women, $8 for men. There's no cover at the adjacent **Bar de Félix,** where the atmosphere is a little more mellow. **El Navegante** (Blvd. Costero Km. 6.5, no phone) is decorated like a ship, with mermaid statues and colorful murals. The bar gets people dancing on the tables, even on Sunday night, and stays open until the last person leaves.

NEAR MANZANILLO

South of Manzanillo is a stretch of coast dotted with golden beaches even prettier than the ones surrounding town. Hotels exist in the area, but beach camping is free and encouraged. To reach Cuyutlán or El Paraíso from Manzanillo, first catch a TECOMAN bus to **Armería** (40 min, $1.25), which leaves every half hour from the Manzanilla bus station. Buses leave Armería for Cuyutlán and El Paraíso (½ hr, 50¢) every 40 minutes 6 AM–8 PM from the mercado, three blocks behind and to the right of the Manzanillo–Armería bus stop.

CUYUTLAN

Arriving in Cuyutlán through lush banana plantations and towering palms, you'll feel like you've discovered a tropical paradise. Beware, however: The crashing waves and powerful ocean currents here can turn a dip in the sea into a serious struggle. The most developed of the three beach resorts outside Manzanillo, Cuyutlán fills up with Mexican vacationers during August, Christmas, and Easter. The rest of the year it's like a ghost town: The rainbow-hue umbrellas fold up, and the beach takes on a lonely, run-down air.

Cuyutlán is best known as the home of the *ola verde* (green wave). No one agrees on what ola verde is, but they certainly talk about it a lot: Some swear it was a tidal wave that wiped out the entire town of Cuyutlán in 1942, while a tourist brochure claims that the ola verde happens every April and May, when the sun shines on the waves at a certain angle, making them look green. Still others believe it's just a local name for the phosphorescent algae that glows sparkly green in the water. The other attraction in Cuyutlán is the modest **Museo Bodega del Sal** (open daily 8–6:30; donation requested). The museum's displays show how locals strain salt from the nearby lagoon and crush it into crystals by hand for domestic use. To get here, follow the green signs ½ block from the zócalo.

WHERE TO SLEEP AND EAT

Cuyutlán has a good selection of affordable beachfront hotels, though prices double in the high season. Located at the northern end of the boardwalk, **Hotel Tlaquepaque** (Veracruz 30, tel. 332/6–40–11) has plain rooms ($6 per person) cooled by sea breezes. Ask for a discount if you plan to stay a while. **Hotel Morelos** (Hidalgo 185, 2 blocks from the zócalo, tel. 332/6–40–13) has 37 rooms ($7.50 each) with private baths, fans, and three meals included. Both hotels accept cash only. Next door, the **Hotel Fénix** (Hidalgo 201, tel. 332/6–40–82) serves seafood and has a happy hour with two-for-one drinks. You can pitch a tent for free on Cuyutlán's sandy beaches, except during Christmas and Easter week, when it's $3 a night. Stay near the hotels for safety reasons. The helpful staff at **Junta Municipal** (Hidalgo 144, tel. 332/6–40–14) has tourist brochures and is open 24 hours daily.

EL PARAISO

Smaller and less-developed than Cuyutlán, El Paraíso has one short road, Avenida de la Juventud, that runs the length of the town, passing oceanfront hotels and restaurants. The surf here isn't too strong, making it a better place to take a dip than neighboring Boca de Pascuales (*see box, above*) and Cuyutlán. The town is wondrously small, and the beaches are more often than not yours and yours alone.

WHERE TO SLEEP AND EAT

Camping here is a breeze: No permit is required: Just set up your tent on the beach and head to **Hotel Paraíso** (tel. 332/8–10–09) for 25¢ showers. The Paraíso has the nicest rooms ($16.50) in town, and also has a restaurant and pool. Pick a restaurant, any restaurant, in El Paraíso—they all serve fresh fish for around $3.

COLIMA

Colima, the easygoing capital of the state with the same name, is a gleaming city of well-maintained colonial buildings and safe, tidy streets. Although the towering volcanic peaks that surround Colima are also impressive, a visit here is really about Mexican history and culture. Colima was the third city founded by the exploring Spaniards, but its true history reaches much, much farther back: Archaeologists have discovered tombs filled with ceramic figurines that indicate humans inhabited the area as early as 1500 BC. Many of the unearthed animal figurines are now on display in Colima's museums, while others were whisked away to museums in Mexico City. In addition to numerous museums, Colima offers a lively arts scene filled with poetry readings and performance art. Signs for these events are posted all around town, at the tourist office, and at the **Casa de la Cultura** (*see* Worth Seeing, *below*). Colima also boasts a thriving literary scene that revolves around the University of Colima, which puts out 10 local newspapers and is constantly publishing new books of poetry and prose. Despite the potential for highbrow snobbery, Colima's friendly, politically progressive residents will make Mexican and international travelers alike feel welcome.

BASICS

BOOKSTORES

Galería Universitaria (Torres Quintero 62, tel. 331/2–44–00; open daily 9–3 and 4:30–9), just off the Jardín Principal, carries books in Spanish about Mexican art and culture. **Las Palmeras** (Portal Medellín 16, tel. 331/2–38–60; open daily 8 AM–11 PM) is a magazine- and newsstand next to Hotel Ceballos on the Jardín Principal. It's stocked with American publications like *Time, Newsweek,* and *National Geographic,* as well as many Mexican magazines.

CASAS DE CAMBIO

Several banks on Madero have ATMs, but most accept only Visa and MasterCard. The ATM at **Bital** (Madero 183, near Jardín Nuñez, tel. 331/2–36–24; open Mon.–Sat. 8–7) accepts Plus and Cirrus cards, and the bank changes cash and traveler's checks. **Casa de Cambio Majaparas** (Morelos 200, at Juárez, tel. 331/4–89–98; open weekdays 9–2 and 4:30–7, Sat. 9–2) offers better rates for cash, but not for traveler's checks, which they change into U.S. dollars only.

EMERGENCIES

Dail the **police** at 331/2–18–01; call the **fire** department at 331/2–58–58.

MAIL

The full-service **post office,** on the northeast corner of Parque Núñez, will hold mail sent to you at the following address for up to 10 days: Lista de Correos, Col. Centro, Colima, Colima, CP 28001, México. *Madero, at Núñez, tel. 331/2–00–33. Open weekdays 8–7, Sat. 8–noon.*

MEDICAL AID

The 24-hour **Hospital Civil** (San Fernando, at Ignacio Sandoval, tel. 331/2–02–27) provides medical care. For minor problems, try the 24-hour **Farmacia Sangre de Cristo** (Medina 83, tel. 331/2–20–30).

PHONES

There are public phones on all four corners of the Jardín Principal. You can place cash calls at **Farmacia Colima** (Madero 1, at Constitución, tel. 331/2–00–31; open Mon.–Sat. 8:30 AM–9 PM, Sun. 9–2), also on the Jardín. They charge 50¢ to make a collect call.

VISITOR INFORMATION

For official information about Colima, city or state, talk to the immensely helpful staff at the air-conditioned **tourist office.** *Portal Hidalgo 20, west side of Jardín Principal, tel. 331/2–83–60. Open weekdays 9–3 and 5–9, weekends 10–1.*

COMING AND GOING

BY BUS

The **Central de Autobuses de Colima** (tel. 331/4–10–60) is at the northeastern edge of town. Catch any 4 CENTRO bus or take a taxi (about $1) to reach downtown. The major bus lines are **Estrella Blanca** (tel. 331/2–84–99) and **Omnibús de México** (tel. 331/4–71–90). Both offer first-class service to Guadalajara (3 hrs, $9) and Manzanillo (1½ hrs, $3.50) every two hours 4 AM–11 PM. Buses to Mexico City (12 hrs, $29) leave four times a day. **ETN** (tel. 331/2–59–99) runs deluxe, air-conditioned buses with reclining seats to Mexico City (10 hrs, $41), Guadalajara (2½ hrs, $13), Morelia (6 hrs, $7.50) and Manzanillo (1½ hrs, $5). Like the rest of Colima, the station is extremely clean. Cheap eateries, pharmacies, and luggage storage (25¢ per hour per bag) are on the premises.

The **Central de Autobuses Sub-Urbana** (Carretera Colima–Coquimatlán, tel. 331/4–47–50) sends second-class buses to towns within the state of Colima. Buses bound for Armería (50 min, $1), Manzanillo (1½ hrs, $1.50), and Tecomán (45 min, $1) depart every 15 minutes 4 AM–10:30 PM. To reach Zihuatanejo, first take a bus to Tecomán (1 hr, $1) and transfer to Zihuatanejo (3 hrs, $11). Buses for nearby villages such as Suchitlán (50¢) and San Antonio/Laguna La María ($1) leave frequently during the day. The bus station is a 20-minute walk southwest on Cuautéhmoc from the Jardín Principal. RUTA 2 combis (10 min, 20¢) leave frequently from Morelos between Medellín and Ocampo, dropping you right at the station. A taxi ride to the station from downtown costs $1.

BY CAR

Colima is on the toll road connecting Guadalajara to Manzanillo. To get from town to the Volcanes de Colima (*see Near Colima, below*), take Highway 16 north for 7 km (4½ mi), then cut northeast for 11 km (6½ mi) to San Antonio and then another 2 km (1 mi) northeast to Laguna La María.

GETTING AROUND

You can orient yourself on a clear day by looking for the volcanoes just outside of Colima—they're to the north. Otherwise, the parks along Avenida Madero are landmarks that make downtown Colima easy to navigate. The **Jardín Libertad** (also known as the zócalo or the Jardín Principal) is at the corner of Avenidas Madero and Reforma. This is the center of town, where families and couples gather in the evening. Four blocks east of here is the massive **Parque Núñez**. The **Universidad de Colima** is 10 minutes northwest of town on Boulevard Camino Real. From Parque Núñez, RUTA 1 combis run frequently to the university. Most of Colima's modern fleet of microbuses (25¢ per ride) stop at the corner of Reforma and Díaz; on Medellín along the Jardín Quintero; or on Avenida Rey Colimán, near the southwest corner of Parque Núñez. A taxi ride anywhere in the city shouldn't cost more than $2–$3.

WHERE TO SLEEP

Colima doesn't boast a huge selection of hotels, but the dearth of tourists here means finding a room is still fairly easy. Budget hotels are clustered near the center of town and are popular with Mexican businessmen.

UNDER $10 • Casa de Huéspedes Familiar. Slightly worn but clean rooms sit above the house and garden of the friendly manager, Señora Saucedo. Doubles cost $6.50. *Morelos 265, near the Pemex station, tel. 331/2–34–67. 10 rooms, 8 with bath. Luggage storage. Cash only.*

> *Long ago at La Campana, people were once sacrificed for their blood, which was thought to replenish the lava of the volcano god and the red fire of the sun god.*

Hotel Núñez. Rooms in this converted colonial house surround a courtyard shaded by a huge old mango tree. The rooms are small and plain, but the communal baths are spic and span. Rooms are $4, or $8 with private bath. You can't find a better place for the price and many travelers know this: Arrive early, especially if you want a room with a TV ($1.50 extra). *Juárez 88, on Jardín Núñez, tel. 331/2–70–30. 32 rooms, 16 with bath. Luggage storage. Cash only.*

Hotel San Lorenzo. Though it's just a few blocks from the zócalo, this hotel sits in a quiet *barrio* (neighborhood) often overlooked by budget travelers. Spacious rooms have fans, large closets, and homey floral bedspreads. There's also a pleasant communal sitting area. Rooms cost $8 for two people. *Cuauhtémoc 149, at Independencia, tel. 31/2–20–00. 3 blocks west of the zócalo. 17 rooms, all with bath. Cash only.*

FOOD

Colima prides itself on its *antojitos* (appetizers), such as enchiladas with sweet sauce, ceviche, and *pozole blanco* (hominy soup made with chicken or pork). Restaurants are scattered throughout the city, but there are dozens of cheap ones near the Jardín Principal.

UNDER $5 • Ah Qué Nanishe. The name means "Oh, how delicious!" in Zapotec, and the Oaxacan specialties at this downtown eatery usually evoke that kind of response. For a true culinary adventure, try chicken tamales with mole (chocolate-chile sauce) or *huitlacoche* (edible corn fungus, considered a delicacy in Mexico). Sweet tamales are 50¢. *5 de Mayo 267, 4 blocks west of Jardín Principal, tel. 331/4–21–97. No breakfast. Cash only.*

Livornos Pizza. At this pizzeria and pub, $3 buys you a small vegetarian or meat pizza plus a drink. Strike up a conversation with the congenial manager about Colima's upcoming cultural events, or catch a CNN newscast on the satellite TV. *Constitución 10, near the cathedral, tel. 331/4–50–30. No breakfast. Cash only.*

Restaurante Samadhi. The walls here are decorated with indigenous paintings and ceramics, and tables overlook the sunny, palm-filled courtyard. Samadhi makes a unique version of sangría, with blended pineapple, celery, radish, and orange juices; it's surprisingly good. It also offers some meatless dishes for vegetarians. The buffet breakfast ($3) is a smorgasbord of yogurt, fruit, eggs, crepes, juice, and coffee. *Medina 125, 3 blocks north of Parque Núñez, tel. 331/3–24–98. No dinner Thurs. Cash only.*

EXCUSE ME, IS THAT REAL LAVA?

In case a volcanic eruption occurs while you are visiting Colima, here are a few tips:

(1) Remain calm.

(2) Click your heels together three times and chant, "There's no place like Colima."

(3) Sacrifice your annoying travel companion to appease the angry volcano god.

Then maybe, just maybe, the Volcán de Fuego will return to its fitful slumber for another few years.

Mexican and American geologists continue to predict that this impressive and constantly active volcano will soon explode into plumes of fiery lava. They say that such an eruption would not only destroy the stands of pines and evergreens in the fertile valley below, but also threaten many of the state of Colima's inland and coastal towns with burning rocks, sulfuric vapors, ash, mudslides, and earthquakes.

Sounds awful, doesn't it? Yet for Colimans, fear of the Volcán de Fuego—which has already erupted five times during this century—is simply a way of life.

WORTH SEEING

The **Jardín Principal** has been the heart of Colima since the city's founding and is a good place to begin your explorations. On the south side of the Jardín is the free **Museo Regional de Historia de Colima** (Morelos 1, at Reforma, tel. 331/2–92–28), where you'll find a few exhibits of pre-Columbian pottery and local crafts, as well as an occasional university art exposition. On the east side of the Jardín is the 19th-century, neoclassical **Santa Iglesia Cathedral** (Reforma 21, tel. 331/2–02–00), with a plain white exterior that gives way to a lavish interior. Next door is the beautiful **Palacio de Gobierno** (tel. 331/2–04–31), built at the turn of the century. Its mural portraying the history of Mexico was painted by Coliman artist Jorge Chávez Carrillo in honor of Independence leader Padre Miguel Hidalgo.

Cultural events are hosted at the Museo Regional, the Casa de la Cultura (*see below*), and at the highly respected **Universidad de Colima,** home to the Museo de Culturas Populares (*see below*) and the well-stocked bookstore **Galería Universitaria** (*see Basics, above*). It also has a huge sports facility, the **Polideportivo,** which has swimming pools and soccer fields that are free and open to the public. To reach the university, take a RUTA 1 bus (15 min, 25¢) from Jardín Núñez. The Polideportivo is the huge building on your left, about five minutes outside of downtown.

LA CAMPANA RUINS

Opened to the public in 1996, these ruins date all the way back to 1500 BC, and were used by the Capacha tribe until AD 700–900. When the Spaniards arrived in the 16th century, Franciscan monks built churches around some of the ruins, but the majority of the ancient structures were abandoned—and therefore survived the centuries relatively intact. The 50-hectare (124-acre) site is still under excavation, and new sites will be opened to the public as archaeologists complete their work. Currently you can observe magnificent tombs, an administrative-religious center, a vast drainage system, and some living quarters. Look carefully at the stone foundations and you'll see carved hieroglyphics and engraved maps. *Av. Tecnológico, at Villa de Alvarez, tel. 331/3-49-45. From Jardín Núñez, take RUTA 1 combi (15 min, 25¢). Admission: $1. Open Tues.-Sun. 9-6.*

CASA DE LA CULTURA

The Casa de la Cultura (Galván Norte, at Ejército Nacional, tel. 331/3-06-08) houses a permanent collection of works by Coliman artists, as well as visiting exhibitions. The gallery is open Tuesday–Sunday 8 AM–8:30 PM, and admission is free. The Casa also shows foreign and national art films (75¢); check the postings on the theater door for current films and showtimes. The Casa's playhouse showcases local theatrical productions weekends at 8 PM, and tickets are a reasonable $1.50. **Café Dalí,** within the Casa, is a good place to stop in for a drink and to listen to live music (nightly 9–11).

MUSEO DE ARTES POPULARES MARIA TERESA POMAR

Next door to the Casa de la Cultura, this excellent museum is dedicated exclusively to pre-Hispanic ceramic ware from the Colima area. On display are a collection of ceramic figurines. Many are of dogs, which the early people of the area held as sacred animals (and also favored as a source of food). *Galván Nte., at Ejército Nacional, tel. 331/2-31-55. From Jardín Núñez, take RUTA 1 combi to the university. Admission free. Open Tues.-Sat. 10-2 and 5-8, Sun. 10-1.*

MUSEO UNIVERSITARIO DE CULTURAS POPULARES

This university crafts museum is not particularly impressive, but it has a wonderful gift shop. Outside the museum, under a giant banyan tree, an artisan makes reproductions of pre-Columbian ceramics (typically he's there Monday–Saturday 9–3). Go to Room 30 in the museum building to find out about cultural events at the university. *Gallardo, at 27 de Septiembre, tel. 331/2-68-69. Admission free. Open Tues.-Sat. 9-2 and 4-7.*

AFTER DARK

To experience Colima's version of a *peña* (musical gathering) head for **Café Colima** (Jardín Corregidora, tel. 331/2-80-93). Spectators sing along with local musicians during the performances (Sun. 9 PM–midnight). The seats are under an awning in the Jardín Corregidora, and fancy food, beer, wine, and a variety of coffees are all for sale. To get here, take a RUTA 9 bus from Medellín, at Jardín Quintero.

You'll run into plenty of friendly students from the University of Colima at the city's bars, restaurants, and clubs. Both **Atrium** (Felipe Sevilla del Río 574, tel. 331/3-04-77) and the nearby **Grillos** (in front of Plaza Country, tel. 331/4-88-44) start serving food and alcohol around 5 PM but don't really get going until 8 PM. For dancing, try the disco **Cheer's** (Zaragoza 521, tel. 331/4-47-00; closed Sun.-Wed.), where cover is $3 and all domestic drinks cost $1.50. If you're in the mood to wax prosaic en español about Aristotelian theory, Colima's club of philosophers, the Mesa de Despelleje, meets nightly at 9 PM in **Los Naranjos Restaurant** (Gabino Barreda 34, tel. 331/2-00-29) A taxi from the zócalo to any of these nightspots should cost about 75¢.

NEAR COLIMA

VOLCANES DE COLIMA

Just north of Colima in the Parque Nacional Nevado de Colima are two volcanoes known as the Volcanes de Colima (one is actually in the state of Jalisco, but nobody seems to mind). The taller one, at 14,220 ft, is the **Volcán de Fuego** (Fire Volcano). As it has recently been rumbling ominously, belching smoke, and, in 1994, spewing lava, it's completely off-limits to visitors.

However, 9 km (5½ mi) away lies the extinct 12,790-ft **Volcán Nevado de Colima**—a hiker's paradise. Also called the Volcán de Nieve (Snow Volcano), it offers stunning views from its snowy peak. Allow three days for the entire round-trip trek, and pack food, drinking water, a first-aid kit, and other hiking gear, as well as layers of clothing to keep you warm at night and cool during the day. About two-thirds of the way up the volcano is a no-frills hostel called **La Joya,** where you can stay for free in a cabaña with a fireplace (and little else). From La Joya it's a three- or four-hour hike up to the volcano's summit. To reach Volcán Nevado from Colima, take a Guadalajara-bound bus from the Central de Autobuses de Colima, get off in Ciudad Guzmán (40 min, $4), and transfer to a bus to the town of Fresnito, at the base of the volcano. From here, you'll need to hitch a ride, or find someone willing to drive you to La Joya (it's about 37 km/23 mi) for a fee. Either option shouldn't be too difficult, as townspeople are accustomed to plenty of hikers making the trip.

The small town of **San Antonio** lies at the base of the Parque Nacional Nevado de Colima, and is an ideal place for viewing the volcanoes without having to expend much energy or time. Reach the town by hopping a bus from the Sub-Urbana bus station in Colima.

LAGUNA LA MARIA

Laguna La María is a vacation retreat poised on the edge of the Parque Nacional Nevado de Colima. Its verdant, isolated lakeshore is not easy to reach from Colima. Once you're here the lake offers great camping, swimming, and fishing—although frequent afternoon rains may force day-trippers to take refuge under the *casitas* (covered picnic tables). Pay 25¢ at the park entrance for day use or $1.50 to camp anywhere along the shore. Public bathrooms (without showers) are accessible to campers, but the lack of restaurants means you'll be packing in your food. You can also stay at **Cabaña La María** (right by the lake), which has clean cabins ($20–$25) with small kitchens and bathrooms. It's wise to make reservations; contact the Avitesa travel agency (tel. 331/2–69–70) in Colima. From the Central de Auto-buses Sub-Urbana in Colima, SAN ANTONIO buses leave for Laguna La María at 7 AM, 1:20 PM, 2:30 PM, and 5 PM. From the bus stop it's a 15-minute walk to the lake. Buses return at 9 AM, 3 PM, and 3:50 PM.

IXTAPA
ZIHUATANEJO

If you must choose only one resort on the Pacific Coast to visit, let it be Ixtapa/Zihuatanejo. A four-hour drive up the coast from Acapulco, this resort area—comprised of two towns side-by-side—is less expensive and less frenetic than its big brother to the south. The two towns, **Zihuatanejo** and **Ixtapa,** are only 6 km (4 mi) apart and have a combined population of just 20,000. Each has a distinct personality: Zihuatanejo is a sleepy fishing village, and Ixtapa is a sizzling tourist-oriented resort. Both share a common natural setting of green, sparsely settled hills and beautiful white-sand beaches.

Zihuatanejo has maintained the feeling of a typical Mexican town despite its active fishing industry and a mellow beachside tourist zone. It has a bustling mercado and side streets that close to vehicles in the evening. It makes a good base for budget travelers, who'll get to experience Mexican culture firsthand before zipping off to Ixtapa's prettier but busier beaches 15 minutes away. Zihuatanejo also has local craft shops, inexpensive seafood restaurants, and affordable hotels and guest homes right on the water-front. Near town, **Playas La Ropa** and **Las Gatas** on Zihuatanejo Bay are two of the most serene beaches in the area, attracting scuba divers and snorkelers alike.

In contrast, Ixtapa is one long strip of hot pavement, perfectly manicured lawn, and chunky modern buildings. Just 20 years ago, this area was nothing but acre after rolling acre of coconut and banana plantations, but all that changed once Ixtapa was targeted for development by the federal tourism department, Fonatur. Today you'll find plenty of luxury hotels, expensive boutiques, and air-conditioned, American-style restaurants, but you'll also get some of the prettiest beaches on the coast, free of the fishing boats (and their debris) that plague Zihuatanejo. There's also a thriving night scene, dominated primarily by foreigners. With these two cities you get the best of both worlds—dip into Ixtapa's liveliness and clear waters, then beat a retreat to peaceful and affordable Zihuatanejo.

BASICS

AMERICAN EXPRESS

Cardholders can receive mail and cash personal checks at this office, which caters to upper-class travelers. *Area Comercial, Blvd. Ixtapa, Ixtapa/Zihuatanejo, Guerrero, CP 40880, México, tel. 755/3–08–53. In the Hotel Krystal shopping arcade. Open Mon.–Sat. 9–6, Sun. 9–2.*

CASAS DE CAMBIO

Banks seem to be on every street corner in Zihuatanejo. **Banamex** (Cuauhtémoc 4, near Nicolás Bravo, tel. 755/4–21–96; weekdays 9–3) changes traveler's checks and has an ATM. In Ixtapa, **Bital** (Blvd.

Ixtapa, tel. 755/3–06–41; open Mon.–Sat. 8–7) changes traveler's checks and cash. Keep your eye on posted rates around town, as casas de cambio often offer better exchange rates than the banks. **Central de Cambio** (Galeana 6, tel. 755/4–28–00; open daily 8 AM–9 PM) in Zihuatanejo is worth a try.

EMERGENCIES

For the **police,** call 755/4–20–40. For the **fire** department call 755/4–75–51. For **ambulance** service, contact the Cruz Roja at 755/4–20–09.

LAUNDRY

Lavandería Super Clean, in central Zihuatanejo, charges $1 per kilo (2 pounds), with a 3-kilo (6½-pound) minimum. *González 11, at Galeana, tel. 755/4–23–47. Open Mon.–Sat. 8–8.*

MAIL

Zihuatanejo's **post office** (tel. 755/4–21–92; open weekdays 8–7, Sat. 9–1) is hard to find. Walk up Guerrero away from the water, turn right onto Morelos, turn right again onto a dirt road two blocks past the Pollo Feliz restaurant, and look for the white TELECOM building in front of you. The office will hold mail sent to you at the following address for up to 10 days: Lista de Correos, Domicilio Centro SCT, Zihuatanejo, Guerrero, CP 40881, México. You can also just drop your letters at any *buzón* (mailbox) in town. There is no post office in Ixtapa.

MEDICAL AID

In Zihuatanejo, the **Centro de Salud** (Hospital General; Paseo de la Boquita, at Calle Palma, tel. 755/4–20–88) charges $1.50–$4 for a consultation. There are no 24-hour pharmacies in town, but **Farmacia del Centro** (Cuauhtémoc 20, at Nicolás Bravo, tel. 755/4–20–77) is open daily 7 AM–9 PM.

PHONES

There are two pay phones in front of Zihuatanejo's Palacio Municipal on Álvarez. At the **Central de Cambio Juiball** (Galeana 6, tel. 755/4–28–00; open daily 8 AM–9 PM) you can make long-distance cash calls but not collect calls.

VISITOR INFORMATION

Don't be misled by the booths you'll see around town advertising tourist information—these are really fronts for time-share operations. The real **tourist office** (Álvarez, near Cuauhtémoc, tel. 755/4–22–07 ext. 120; open weekdays 9–3 and 6–8, Sat. 9–2) is next door to Zihuatanejo's Palacio Municipal.

COMING AND GOING

BY BUS

Zihuatanejo's new bus station is on the highway leading out of town. To reach downtown Zihuatanejo from here, take any bus or combi marked ZIHUATANEJO or CENTRO (10 min, 25¢). You'll be let off on either Juárez or Morelos, both just a few blocks from most of the town's budget hotels. To return to the station, head to the corner of Juárez and Ejido and board a combi marked CORREO. Ixtapa doesn't have a bus station of its own; to get here, you have to take a local bus (15 min, 30¢) from the intersection of Morelos and Juárez in Zihuatanejo.

Estrella Blanca (tel. 755/4–34–77) is the main bus line that operates out of the Zihuatanejo station. Direct buses to Acapulco (4 hrs, $6) depart hourly, daily 6–6. The bus to Huatulco (13 hrs, $16) leaves at 7:45 PM and stops in Puerto Escondido along the way. Buses depart at 10 AM and noon for Mazatlán (20 hrs, $34), stopping in Manzanillo (9 hrs, $12) and Puerto Vallarta (12 hrs, $21). Buses to Mexico City (10 hrs, $22) leave four times daily. The above are all first-class buses. You can travel second class to Acapulco and Mexico City, but the extremely long travel time and lack of air-conditioning makes it an unpleasant experience.

BY PLANE

The international airport (tel. 755/4–22–37 or 755/4–26–34) is 11 km (6½ mi) east of Zihuatanejo on the Carretera Costera (Hwy. 200). **Aeroméxico** (tel. 755/4–20–18), **Mexicana** (tel. 755/4–22–08), and a few U.S. carriers serve the airport. A one-way flight to Mexico City averages about $100. Taxis take care of all transportation between the airport and Zihuatanejo (15–20 min, $6) or Ixtapa (25 min, $7.50).

TOURISM 101: RESORT TOWNS

In the 1960s, the Mexican government decided that tourism was a solution to the country's economic woes. It would bring an influx of foreign currency, which would help repay foreign debt. A department of tourism, Fonatur, was formed, and after careful consideration, five sites were chosen to become megaresorts: Acapulco, Cancún, Ixtapa, Los Cabos, and Bahías de Huatulco. These billion-dollar babies have enjoyed varying success: Cancún, a paradise carved from the Yucatecan landscape, reigns supreme, while Huatulco is still growing.

True to plan, increased tourism has brought a flood of foreign dollars—but exactly how much money remains in the country? Construction money stays, since Mexican law requires local labor on resort projects. Fees for water and electricity remain, as does money spent by tourists in Mexican-owned businesses. However, Hyatt and Sheraton chains—among many other prominent foreign-owned businesses—are cropping up all along the Mexican coast, and their profits certainly go elsewhere.

Indeed, more than half the profits from tourism in developing countries like Mexico are funneled back to the so-called First World. To add to the dilemma, funds left in the country often fuel short-term growth at the expense of long-term health and safety. It's said that Fonatur, backed by private investment dollars, has been responsible for hacking down coconut and banana plantations in Ixtapa, as well as destroying entire indigenous neighborhoods to construct gringo playgrounds.

GETTING AROUND

Zihuatanejo is easily explored on foot, with budget hotels, restaurants, shops, and the beach all near the town's center. This area is marked by Álvarez and the beach to the south, Juárez to the east, 5 de Mayo to the west, and Morelos to the north. Ixtapa has one main thoroughfare, the Paseo de Ixtapa, which is essentially a 3-km (2-mi) strip of hotels and shopping arcades. To reach Ixtapa from Zihuatanejo (15 min, 15¢), catch one of the blue-and-white buses from the corner of Morelos and Juárez. You can catch a bus back to Zihuatanejo anywhere along Ixtapa's Paseo de Ixtapa. Buses run daily 6 AM–10 PM.

WHERE TO SLEEP

Downtown Zihuatanejo is packed with inexpensive hotels, many of which are near the waterfront. Staying in Ixtapa is pretty much out of the question for budget travelers—the cheapest hotel there will charge you $70 for a room. The prices listed below apply in Zihuatanejo's low season. Expect to pay a bit more from mid-November through April.

Beach camping is only allowed at **Playa La Ropa,** south of Playa La Madera in Zihuatanejo. Alternately, you can pitch a tent at the hostel (*see below*) and use their bathrooms and showers for $2.50 a night.

UNDER $10 • Casa Elvira. The Elvira's sweet, elderly proprietress has added homey touches to each room, like flowered curtains, mirrors, and a calendar. The rooms are clean, but the bathrooms seem neglected. That said, you can't beat the price: $10 for a double, plus $1.50 during high season. *Álvarez 52, near 5 de Mayo, tel. 755/4–20–61. 6 rooms, 4 with bath. Luggage storage. Cash only.*

Hotel Casa Aurora. The narrow entryway to this hotel is hidden between souvenir shops and grocery stores. Inside you'll find a plant-filled, tile courtyard. Second-floor rooms have large, shady decks with comfortable lounge chairs, and all rooms have handsome flagstone floors. Rooms are $9 year-round, plus $5 for air-conditioning. Discounts are possible for longer stays. *Nicolás Bravo 27, near Juárez, tel. 755/4–30–46. 15 rooms, all with bath. Cash only.*

UNDER $15 • Hotel Rosimar. This breezy, clean hotel has sitting areas on every floor, each with a view of the street. Rooms have modern tile bathrooms, floral comforters, and their very own TVs. Doubles cost $15. *Ejido 12, between Galeana and Guerrero, tel. 755/4–21–39. 16 rooms, all with bath. Laundry, luggage storage. Cash only.*

UNDER $25 • Hotel Raúl Tres Marías. This hotel overlooks Zihuatanejo Bay and is worth the money. Each floor has a communal deck with tables, chairs, and terrific views. Rooms ($25) with cement floors are ample, clean, and air-conditioned. Expect a 15% increase in rates during the high season. Don't get this place confused with the hotel by the same name at La Noria 4—that one may be cheaper, but it doesn't have hot water. *Álvarez 52, tel. and fax 755/4–67–06. 1 block from the beach. 17 rooms, all with bath. Luggage storage.*

According to local legend, an ancient Tarascan king built a barrier of rocks at Playa Las Gatas to ensure calm waters for his maidens. Today it's a popular snorkeling spot near Zihuatanejo.

UNDER $35 • Irma. This colonial-style beauty was one of Zihuatanejo's original hotels. It sits on a bluff overlooking Madera Beach, which is accessible by stairway. Almost all of the recently remodeled rooms (doubles $35) have air-conditioning, and all have TV, telephone, a small balcony, and two double or one king-size bed with handpainted headboards. *Playa la Madera, tel. 755/4–21–05. South of town. 73 rooms, all with bath. Restaurant, bar, 2 pools, laundry, luggage storage.*

HOSTEL

Villa Juvenil. This friendly, crowded place is just outside town, less than 1½ km (¾ mi) from the waterfront, and unfortunately borders the foul-smelling marina. Facilities are rudimentary but clean, and it's a good place to meet other travelers. A bed in one of the single-sex dorms costs $4. Breakfast costs about $2, and lunch and dinner are each $2.50. Be careful if you're going out at night—the front door is locked at 11 PM, after which you have to enter through a side door. *Paseo de las Salinas, tel. 755/4–46–62. West on Morelos until it becomes Paseo de las Salinas, left at the fork. 64 beds. Reception open 7 AM–10:30 PM. Luggage storage. Cash only.*

FOOD

The restaurants in Ixtapa tend to be fussy and overpriced, but a few small restaurants serving *comida típica* (typical Mexican food) can be found by walking inland from the resort strip. In contrast, Zihuatanejo has a good selection of low-key seafood eateries, many of which are right on the beach. For a quick breakfast treat, try **Panadería Francesa** (González 15, tel. 755/4–27–42). The warehouse-size bakery offers a wide selection of *pan dulce* (sweet rolls) and breads. All of the restaurants listed below are in Zihuatanejo.

UNDER $5 • La Sirena Gorda. Seafood tacos are the specialty at this waterfront restaurant: two tasty smoked-fish tacos cost $3; octopus tacos are $4. The name means "the fat mermaid," and ceramic mermaids and other knickknacks adorn the tables and the busy bar. *Paseo del Pescador 20-A, near the pier, tel. 755/4–26–87. Closed Wed. Cash only.*

Tamales Atoles Any. This fun and lively place specializes in tamales ($2–$3) of all varieties, including sweet ones. They also have soups, *queso fundido* (melted cheese), and vegetarian selections. *Ejido, at Guerrero, tel. 755/4–73–73. Cash only.*

UNDER $10 • Mamacita's El Chiringuito. This funky restaurant/bar is decorated with guitars, ponchos, and skinny tinsel skeletons. They make the best guacamole around, and a house specialty, Chiringuito shrimp ($6.50), is delicious. The bar offers an international selection of wines. *Corner of Alvarez and 5 de Mayo, no phone. No breakfast.*

Restaurant Bar Tata's. At this lively beachfront restaurant, super-hip waiters bop to the beat of Top 40 pumping from the loudspeakers. Specialties include *filete a la tampiqueña* (steak served with enchiladas, beans, and rice; $6.50) and breaded red snapper with rice and tortillas. Drinks are two-for-one during happy hour (5 PM–7 PM). *Paseo del Pescador, at Guerrero, tel. 755/4–20–10. No breakfast.*

WORTH SEEING

The **Museo Arqueológico de la Costa Grande** uses maps, figurines, paintings, and photographs to trace human settlement in America, specifically in the Costa Grande region (an area that includes present-day Acapulco). The museum also displays ceramic objects and primitive carvings from this region's original settlers, the Zaputecas. *Plaza Olof Palme, on the beach in Zihuatanejo, tel. 755/4–75–52. Admission: 60¢. Open Tues.–Sun. 10–6.*

OUTDOOR ACTIVITIES

The beaches at Las Gatas and Isla Ixtapa are highly regarded scuba-diving spots, and shops along the waterfront in Zihuatanejo, Playa Las Gatas, and Isla Ixtapa rent equipment to certified divers. The NAUI-certified **Zihuatanejo Scuba Center** (Cuauhtémoc 3, near Álvarez, tel. 755/4–21–47) has an English-speaking staff. For $70, beginners get pool lessons and one dive, while certified divers get an all-day trip. Deep-sea fishing is also popular here; the **Cooperativa de Pescadores** (Paseo del Pescador, at 5 de Mayo, tel. 755/4–20–56) charters boats for $130–$260 per day.

ZIHUATANEJO

Playa La Madera, a pretty stretch of sand with inviting water, is a 10-minute walk from the town center. To get here, follow Álvarez east for 1 km (½ mi) until you reach a set of stairs leading over a canal; cross over and continue following the water. When you hear surf, cut to the right, past one of the big hotels. **Playa La Ropa** has clean, calm waters perfect for swimming or waterskiing. The best way to get here is by taxi ($1–$2). If you choose to walk (25 mins), follow the route to Playa La Madera; keep to the right on the main road (the Paseo Costera), always heading up. As the road descends and the ocean comes into view, cut through the nearest hotel, or follow the road until it winds to the beach. You can also get here by walking 15 minutes north from Playa Las Gatas (*see below*).

The last beach off the Paseo Costera is the protected **Playa Las Gatas,** with calm water that hides a rocky bottom—use caution when wading. Las Gatas is, however, perfect for snorkeling, as flippers will protect your feet. Colloquially named for the sharks that used to frequent the waters, Las Gatas now only attracts marlin, yellowfin sailfish, parrotfish, needlefish, and other colorful sea creatures. To get here from Playa La Ropa, walk south along the beach for 15 minutes; or take a pleasant 10-minute boat ride ($2 per person round-trip) from the *muelle* (pier) in Zihuatanejo. Boats run daily 8:30–5.

IXTAPA

The resort hotels on **Playa Ixtapa** all rent water-sports equipment, charging fairly uniform prices. Choose between boogie boards ($4 per hr), banana boats ($2.50 for a 20-min ride), parasailing ($20 for an 8-min flight), waterskiing or wave runners (both are $20 per 30 mins), and snorkeling ($20 for 4 hrs). Try **Hotel Fontán** (Playa Ixtapa, tel. 755/4–20–56) for friendly, courteous service. **Playa del Palmar** is a long, sandy stretch bordering the Ixtapa hotels, ideal for swimming, snorkeling, and boogie boarding. To the northwest are several more pristine beaches, including **Playa Quieta, Playa Linda,** and Ixtapa's **Club Med** (near Playa Linda, tel. 755/2–00–44), where equipment and instruction for innumerable sports, as well as a gargantuan buffet lunch, is yours for $20. To reach Playa del Palmar from Zihuatanejo, take a minibus to Ixtapa from the intersection of Morelos and Juárez. Get off at any of the towering hotels and cut through to the beach. **Isla Ixtapa,** off the shore of Playa Quieta, has three good swimming, sunbathing, and snorkeling beaches. There are a few restaurants on the island, but no place to stay. The best thing about Isla Ixtapa is the hour-long boat trip from the pier in Zihuatanejo ($5 per person round-trip). Boats leave at 11:30 AM and return at 4 PM. Daily 8–5 they also leave every 15 minutes from Playa Quieta ($2 per person round-trip).

AFTER DARK

Evenings in Ixtapa/Zihuatanejo may not be as hedonistic as those in Acapulco, but don't get ready for bed yet. Most of the action is where the tourist dollars are: Ixtapa. The ubiquitous Mexican chain **Carlos**

'n' Charlie's (Paseo del Palmar, at the northwest end of the hotel strip, tel. 753/3–00–85) draws locals and tourists, who shake it until 3 AM. Cover is $5 for men, $2.50 for women. Also open until 3 AM, **Señor Frog's** (Centro Comercial La Puerta, tel. 755/3–06–72) is the place to go if you want to have a few icy tropical drinks and end the night dancing on the tables with strangers. Next to the Hotel Kristal in Ixtapa is **Christine's** (tel. 755/3–03–33; open daily 10:30–3), which caters to a rich and sophisticated crowd of Mexicans vacationing from Mexico City. Cover is $6 (free on Mon., ladies free on Wed.). Over in Zihuatanejo, the only nightclub/disco is the tourist-free **Roca Rock** (5 de Mayo, at Nicolás Bravo, tel. 755/4–33–24; closed Sun.–Wed.), which pulls in the city's gays and lesbians and features a nightly drag show. Near the main bus station, the small **Bar Bohemio** is popular with locals and sometimes hosts live guitar music. The happy hour at **Restaurant Bar Tata's** (see Food, above) is also popular. For a more sedate evening, catch a movie at Zihuatanejo's **Cinema Paraíso** (Cuauhtémoc, near Nicolás Bravo, tel. 755/4–23–18), which shows American movies with Spanish subtitles on an enormous screen.

NEAR IXTAPA/ZIHUATANEJO

BARRA DE POTOSI

If even mellow Zihuatanejo is too touristed for you, make a midweek trip to the slow-pace seaside village of Barra de Potosí, a 30-minute bus ride southeast of Zihuatanejo. During the week, there's absolutely nothing to do in Barra de Potosí but to relax, swim, enjoy fine weather and food, or chat with locals. If you can rouse yourself from your hammock, the rugged *morros* (cliffs) offer a number of hiking trails with breathtaking views of the Pacific. Note that the restful atmosphere of Barra de Potosí is shattered on weekends, when its beaches fill with teenagers lugging boomboxes and volleyballs. Each Sunday night, a *norteño* (country-and-western) band strolls around town strumming traditional tunes.

Sunday night around 9 PM, the basketball court at the center of town in Zihuatanejo fills up with locals who've come to watch their friends and family perform traditional dances and music.

Another reason to visit Barra is for the seafood. Here, red snapper with rice and tortillas will set you back only $3. **Palapa Bacanona** (two palapas from the end of the beach) serves $1 quesadillas and cold *refrescos* (soft drinks). Visitors are welcome to take a siesta or spend the night free of charge in the hammocks slung beneath the restaurant's eaves. The bright-pink **Hotel Barra de Potosí** (tel. 755/4–82–90) offers charming rooms overlooking a pool, restaurant, and, of course, the beach. Basic rooms are $12, studios with a kitchenette and small living room cost $25.

COMING AND GOING

To reach Barra from Zihuatanejo, catch a VW combi or one of the white minibuses that runs along Juárez, first verifying that the driver is stopping at the town of Los Achotes (30 min, 25¢). These minibuses run daily 9–8. From Los Achotes, *camionetas* (small flatbed trucks) run to Barra de Potosí every half hour, daily 9–5. The trip through the tropical countryside takes about 10 minutes.

ACAPULCO

Acapulco's air hangs thick with grime; the smell of freshly grilled fish intermingles with the stench of open sewers; and the ocean is a murky shade of brown. Once the crowning star of the Pacific Coast, this tourist town isn't aging so gracefully. However, in the luxury-hotel zone, which has existed in all its tacky brilliance for 40 years, tourists still cruise the strip—shopping, supping, and spending. Acapulco Viejo, at the other end of the bay, is a popular area for budget travelers, especially Mexicans and Europeans. The area around Playa Caleta is a crush of handicraft vendors, but for most visitors, Acapulco's main draw isn't the beach, it's the discos, which are expensive, flashy, loud, crowded, and rock all night. If that's your idea of fun, this is your heaven. But if you've arrived here expecting something different, and now wish to escape this "Mexico City with a beach" (as one Mexican woman put it), head to the quieter town of Pie de la Cuesta, 45 minutes from the center of town.

Sights ●

Mercado
Municipal, **5**

Parque Acuático
Cici, **1**

Parque Papagayo, **4**

Plaza de Toros
Caletilla, **10**

La Quebrada, **9**

Zócalo, **6**

Lodging ○

Casa Mama
Helene, **7**

Hotel Lupita, **2**

Hotel Misión, **8**

Hotel Playa
Suave, **3**

0 ——— 880 yards
0 ——— 800 meters

KEY

AE American Express Office

ℹ Tourist Information

Cortines

Ruiz

Av.

Av. Cuauhtémoc

ZONA
DORADA

Av. W. Massieu

AE

Playa
Hornitos

Av. Durango

J. S. Elcano

Av. Constituyentes

Niños Héroes
18 de Marzo
Av. Cuauhtémoc

Costera Miguel Alemán

ℹ Playa
Hornos

Av. Ejido

Prol. D. H. de Mendoza

La Cuesta

Av. Cuauhtémoc

Av. 5 de Mayo

Calz.
Pie de la

Av. V. Guerrero

Morelos

*Bahía de
Acapulco*

**ACAPULCO
VIEJO**

Juárez

Av. J. L. Mateos

Malecón

1te.
Azueta

TO AIRPORT
AND PUERTO
MÁRQUÉZ →

La Quebrada

**BUDGET
HOTEL
ZONE**

Cost. M. Alemán

← TO
PIE DE
LA CUESTA

Av. Pozo
del Rey

*Península de
las Playas*

Gran Vía Tropical

A C A P U L C O

Av. López Mateos

Playa
Caleta

Playa
Caletilla

Playa
Roqueta

*Isla la
Roqueta*

PACIFIC OCEAN

If you're in town in May, check out the **Festival de Acapulco,** an affordable music celebration that features singers and bands from around the world. Also in May is the **Festival de Gastronomía,** a huge food fair that encompasses the **Feria de Paella** held in the Hotel Acapulco Plaza. Call the hotel (tel. 74/85–90–50) for more information on the paella festival.

BASICS

AMERICAN EXPRESS

The main AmEx office is in the heart of the luxury-hotel strip. It handles MoneyGrams, replaces lost or stolen AmEx cards and checks, and changes traveler's checks at rates comparable to those at the banks in Acapulco Viejo. Cardholders can cash personal checks or receive mail here as well. *789 La Gran Plaza, Acapulco, Guerrero, CP 39670, México, tel. 74/69–11–00. Open weekdays 9–2 and 4–7, Sat. 9–2.*

CASAS DE CAMBIO

Dozens of casas de cambio line the luxury-hotel strip. In Acapulco Viejo, **Banamex** (Costera Miguel Alemán 211, near the zócalo, tel. 74/83–70–20; open weekdays 9–3) changes money and has an ATM that accepts Plus and Cirrus cards. **Consultoria International** (Costera Miguel Alemán 48-3, Centro Comerical La Piluda, tel. 74/84–31–08; open daily 9–9) also changes money.

CONSULATES

In the Club del Sol Hotel (Costera Miguel Alemán, tel. 74/85–72–07), you'll find the **United States** consulate (tel. 74/85–72–07), open weekdays 10–2, and the **Canadian** consulate (tel. 74/85–66–21), open weekdays 9–1. The **United Kingdom** consulate is at Las Brisas Hotel (Carretera Escénica, tel. 74/84–66–05) and is open weekdays 1–8.

Acapulco has a high crime rate. After dark, stay off the beaches and out of sparsely populated areas. Women in particular should take common-sense precautions such as traveling in a group rather than alone.

EMERGENCIES

Call 74/85–06–50 for the **police** and 74/84–41–22 for the **fire** department. For **ambulance** service contact the Cruz Roja (tel. 74/84–41–00).

LAUNDRY

At **Lavandería Coral,** you'll pay 75¢ per kilo (2 pounds) to get your clothes washed, dried, and folded. Same-day service is available if you drop off your clothing before noon. *Juárez 12, 1 block west of zócalo, tel. 74/80–07–35. Open daily 9–2 and 4–7.*

MAIL

The main **post office** is on the Costera, a few blocks east of the zócalo. The office will hold mail for you for up to 10 days if sent to the following address: Lista de Correos, Costera Miguel Alemán 215, Acapulco, Guerrero, CP 39301, México. *Tel. 74/82–20–83. Open weekdays 8–7, Sat. 8–1.*

MEDICAL AID

For an English-speaking doctor, call the 24-hour **Servicio Médico Especialista** (in Hotel Club del Sol, opposite Plaza Bahía, tel. 74/85–80–66). One of the service's doctors, Dr. Luís Roberto García Ruíz, charges $30 for a consultation and makes hotel calls anywhere in Acapulco for an additional $15. In an emergency, go to the **Cruz Roja** (tel. 74/85–41–00) on Ruíz Cortínez. To reach either from the zócalo, follow Constituyentes north until it becomes Ruíz Cortínez—the hospital and clinic are on the 600 block. The 24-hour **Farmacia Emy** (Costera Miguel Alemán 176-C, tel. 74/84–53–33) can assist with minor medical complaints.

PHONES

There are pay phones on the zócalo, and calls can be placed from the convenient **Caseta Telefonica** (Costera Miguel Alemán 215, tel. and fax 74/82–87–19; open Mon.–Sat. 8–8) near the post office. It costs $2.50 a minute to call the United States, and collect calls cost $1.50.

VISITOR INFORMATION

Acapulco's streets are patrolled by **tourist police** dressed in white—they answer questions, give directions, and come to the rescue if you have a problem. The main **tourist office** (Costera Miguel Alemán 187, a few blocks west of the Ritz, tel. 74/86–91–67; open weekdays 9–2 and 4–7) has an extremely helpful staff that will send you away with an armful of reading material, much of it in English. The **tourist assistance bureau** (Costera Miguel Alemán 4455, tel. 74/84–44–16; open daily 8 AM–midnight), in the luxury hotel area, is equally helpful.

COMING AND GOING

BY BUS

The **Central de Autobuses Líneas Unidas del Sur** (Ejido, between Calles 6 and 7, tel. 74/86–80–29), commonly called Estrella Blanca, is in Colonia La Fábrica and can be reached from the zócalo on any bus marked EJIDO or CENTRAL. Buses labeled CALETA or CENTRO make the trip in the opposite direction. The Estrella Blanca bus company has its own taxi company (tel. 74/82–90–59), which will take you to the zócalo for $2. They also make pickups anywhere in the city between 7 AM and 10 PM; call for reservations. A number of companies serve the bus station, but **Estrella Blanca** (tel. 74/69–20–30) has both first-class and *futura* (deluxe) service to most destinations. With futura buses, you get reclining seats, air-conditioning, beverage and snack service, an onboard toilet, and video movies. First-class buses to Mexico City (7 hrs, $14) leave every hour between 6 AM and 2 AM, stopping in Cuernavaca (5 hrs, $11.50). First-class buses to Taxo (4 hrs, $10), stop in Chilpancingo (2 hrs, $4.50) and Taxco (4 hrs, $9). Direct futura buses to Mexico City (5 hrs, $18) leave on the same schedule. First-class direct buses also run to Zihuatanejo (4 hrs, $6) and Huatulco (9 hrs, $13), with a stop in Puerto Escondido (7 hrs, $10). You can catch buses from a number of other companies to far-flung destinations like Guadalajara, Monterrey, and Tampico. The station offers luggage storage (25¢ per hour).

BY PLANE

Acapulco's airport is 30 km (18 mi) east of the city on Highway 200. There's no public transportation to the airport, and taxis cost $7–$10. A cheaper alternative is **Shuttle Aeropuerto Acapulco** (tel. 74/66–99–88); the shuttle costs $4 per person and operates daily 7 AM–10 PM. If you call 24 hours in advance, they'll pick you up at your hotel. **Continental** (tel. 74/66–90–46) has international flights only. For domestic flights, try **Aeroméxico** (Costera Miguel Alemán 286, tel. 74/85–16–00).

GETTING AROUND

Acapulco can be divided roughly into three sections: the city itself, known as Acapulco Viejo (Old Acapulco); the Zona Dorada, a.k.a. the strip, where all the fancy hotels are; and the Zona de Amantes, a rarefied district containing the ritziest hotels and flashiest clubs. Most of the budget hotels in Acapulco are in Acapulco Viejo, around the zócalo—which is also called **Plaza Álvarez**. The zócalo is easy to locate as it's home to the city's cathedral. Bordering the zócalo to the south is the Costera Miguel Alemán, an 8-km (5-mi) bayside thoroughfare that passes through each section of the city. As you move east along the Costera, away from the zócalo, you'll encounter the **Parque Papagayo,** several beaches, the **Fuente Diana** traffic circle, and finally the Zona Dorada. The Zona Dorada stretches from the tunnel on the Costera to the naval base, and includes **Parque Acuático CiCi.** The walk from the zócalo to CiCi takes just over an hour.

Buses are by far the cheapest way to get around Acapulco, with fares averaging 12¢ for regular buses and 25¢ for the air-conditioned **Acatur** buses. Buses marked LA BASE and HORNOS run in both directions along the Costera 6 AM–10 PM. Taxis are more expensive, particularly the cleaner, larger cars. Stick to the white VW bugs for the cheapest rates. Since taxis are unmetered, don't be afraid to haggle—remember that if the first *taxista* (cabbie) won't lower his price, another will be along in 30 seconds.

WHERE TO SLEEP

The ritzy Zona Dorada hotels have prices that appeal to lottery winners, international debutantes, and Texas oilmen. But budget travelers should not despair: It's easy to find budget lodging off the strip, and competition keeps prices low. The best budget lodgings are clustered around the zócalo and in the Caleta area in Acapulco Viejo. These areas are generally safe, but use caution (and consider taking a taxi) at night. There are also a handful of budget options several blocks past the Fuerte de San Diego, within binocular-view of the ritzy part of town. Note that many hotels in Acapulco charge by the person, rather than by room or by bed. Wherever you stay, expect prices to jump substantially in the high season (December–April).

NEAR THE ZOCALO

UNDER $10 • Hotel Misión. This place has the most charm of any budget hotel in Acapulco. The atrium is filled with philodendrons, mango trees, and wicker rocking chairs, and the rooms are decorated with assorted artwork and classy wood furniture. Powerful fans keep the rooms cool, and each has a dimly lit bathroom. Rates are $9 per person. *Felipe Valle 12, 3 blocks west of the zócalo, tel. 74/82–36–43. 27 rooms. Luggage storage. Cash only.*

UNDER $15 • Casa Mama Helene. This slightly worn hotel is Mama Helene's house—as evidenced by the Ping-Pong table, bookshelves, aquarium, plants, and Mama Helene sitting around with her friends. Doubles are $15 ($20 high season). *Juárez 12, 3 blocks west of the zócalo, tel. 74/82–23–96. 30 rooms, all with bath. Luggage storage. Cash only.*

NEAR THE STRIP

UNDER $10 • Hotel Lupita. Statues of cherubs and mermaids surround the hotel's entrance and small pool. Narrow hallways open to spacious rooms ($7–$10 per person). The hotel is across from Parque Papagayo and a block from the beach. *Gómez Espinoza, right off the Costera, tel. 74/85–94–12. 16 rooms, all with bath. Cash only.*

UNDER $15 • Hotel Playa Suave. This is a reasonable place to stay if you want to be as close to the beach as possible. The 30 rooms are dark but clean, and each has a bathroom. A breezy but noisy hallway leads to a restaurant, a swimming pool, and parking. Rooms cost $15, plus $4 for air-conditioning. *Costera Miguel Alemán 253, just west of Hotel do Brasil, tel. 74/85–12–56. Luggage storage. Cash only.*

CAMPING

During high season, camping is allowed on the police-patrolled beach at Puerto Marqués (*see* Outdoor Activities, *below*). Otherwise, the city's high crime rate makes camping a foolhardy choice. The **Playa Suave Trailer Park** (Costera Miguel Alemán 276, tel. 74/85–14–64) lies between Acapulco Viejo and the strip, a block away from the beach. For $7.50, one or two persons can comfortably and safely pitch a tent here and have access to private bathrooms, showers, and drinking water.

FOOD

Cheap restaurants abound in Acapulco Viejo, just west of the zócalo. Here you'll find literally hundreds of small, clean establishments frequented by locals; the best selection is along Juárez. Alternately, you can explore the *fondas* (covered food stands) in the city's daily market; try **Fonda Christie** or **Fonda Doña Lupe.** A meal at either costs about $2. To reach the market, take a HOSPITAL bus heading inland from the zócalo. There are three warehouse-size **grocery stores** on the Costera, between Acapulco Viejo and the strip. They sell yogurt, fresh fruit, deli meats, and freshly baked bread.

NEAR THE ZOCALO

Restaurante Ricardos (Juárez 9, tel. 74/82–11–40), near the zócalo, is a local favorite serving traditional Mexican food. A meal of soup, beans, an entrée, and dessert costs $2. The open-air **Cafetería Astoria** (Plaza Álvarez, tel. 74/82–29–44) is tucked away in a secluded corner of the zócalo. They serve Mexican and American dishes like club sandwiches, enchiladas, and *chilaquiles rojos* (tortilla strips and chicken in red sauce; $1.75). You can also while away the hours here with a cappuccino ($1) and some *pan dulce* (dessert pastries). **Café La Parroquia** (Costerma Miguel Aleman, on the west side of zócalo, tel. 74/82–47–28) is a combination sidewalk café and restaurant that serves a mishmash of German, Mexican, and American fare. Sausage and sauerkraut costs $4.50 and breakfast runs $1.50–$3. **Tepoznieves** is the best place in town for ice cream (30¢ per scoop). They serve the usual chocolate, vanilla, and strawberry, plus exotic flavors like coconut, mango, and rose petal. There are two branches: One is next to Café La Parroquia on the zócalo and the other is in front of the city Convention Center. All of the above are cash only.

El Amigo Miguel (Juárez 31, at José Azueta, tel. 74/83–69–81) serves the town's freshest seafood and offers a second-floor balcony with views of Acapulco Bay. The restaurant has two branches on the same street; the nicer one is farther off the beach. You'll find everything from fish soup to lobster ($9) on the menu. A fillet of sole with vegetables, rice, and warm bread costs $2.50. **La Casa de Tere** (Alonso Martín 1721, two blocks from Costera Miguel Alemán, tel. 74/85–77–35; cash only) is a spotlessly clean, open-air establishment hidden away in a downtown commercial district. They serve an outstanding *sopa de tortilla* (spicy soup with tortilla strips, avocado, and cheese; $1.25), and their comida corrida, which includes soup, an entrée, and dessert, is a bargain at $3.50.

ON THE STRIP

Don't come to the strip expecting to find a budget meal. Your best option is **El Zorrito** (Costera Miguel Alemán, just east of the Ritz, tel. 74/85–37–35), where the food is good and reasonably priced. They serve hamburgers, onion rings, and fried chicken ($4), as well as the hearty *filete a la tampiqueña* (steak served with a chicken taco, chicken enchilada, guacamole, and beans; $6.25). Large crowds of young people flock here in the afternoon. The 24-hour **100% Natural** (Costera Miguel Alemán 200, just west of Parque Papagayo, tel. 74/85–39–82) is a natural-foods restaurant, with several other locations around Acapulco. The green salads, steamed vegetable dishes ($3–$4), and soyburgers are fresh and skillfully prepared. (Warning: The branch on the zócalo is an imitation and not worth your time). The above are cash only.

WORTH SEEING

Most points of interest are along Acapulco's main thoroughfare, the Costera Miguel Alemán. The **Casa de la Cultura** (Costera Miguel Alemán 4834, 1 block east of Cici, tel. 74/84–38–14; open weekdays 9–2 and 5–8, Sat. 9–2) displays pre-Colombian art and houses a small theater. At the daily **mercado municipal** (near Cuauhtémoc and Mendoza) you'll find all kinds of food and crafts, including painted ceramic statues, shell earrings, and Guatemalan vests and backpacks. To reach the market, take a HOS-PITAL bus heading inland from the zócalo. On Sunday head to the zócalo or Parque Papagayo. Local bands play at both locations around sunset.

PARQUE ACUATICO CICI

Acapulco's ultimate amusement park draws crowds of waterlogged tourists of every age. The gigantic park on Costera Miguel Alemán features dolphin shows, water rides on a man-made lake, steep and slippery water slides with names like "Kamikaze," and even access to the beach. *Tel. 74/84–19–70. From Acapulco Viejo, take a LA BASE or HORNOS bus; the park is on right, just past the convention center. Admission: $5. Open daily 10–6.*

PARQUE PAPAGAYO

This sprawling beachside amusement park—complete with a roller rink, tobaggans, an aviary, and two artificial lakes—is primarily a hangout for local youth and, on weekends, families. Admission is free, but the rides cost up to $1.25 each. *Costera Miguel Alemán, at Manuel Morin, tel. 74/85–96–23. Open daily 10–8.*

PLAZA DE TOROS CALETILLA

Bullfights take place here almost every Sunday between Christmas and Easter. Fights start at 5:30 PM and the cheapest tickets, available at the bullring, are $12.50. It's just a few minutes' walk northwest of Playa Caletilla (*see* Outdoor Activities, *below*). *Av. Circunvalacán, Fracc. las Playas, tel. 74/82–11–81.*

LA QUEBRADA

A 10-minute walk northwest of the zócalo, these beautiful cliffs offer breathtaking views of the ocean and surrounding landscape. Acapulco's famous divers, the **Clavadistas** (tel. 74/83–14–00), risk their lives daily on La Quebrada, plummeting 200 ft into the rock-filled waters below. To add to the excitement, some divers fling themselves off the cliffs while clenching flaming torches. Divers accept/expect small gratuities, and there's a $1.25 admission fee to enter the viewing area. Dives take place daily at 1, 7:30, 8:30, 9:30, and 10:30 PM. **La Perla** restaurant (Plazuela La Quebrada, tel. 74/83–11–05) also offers a spectacular view of the diving action. The $10.50 cover charge includes two drinks and the view. To reach the cliffs, walk straight up La Quebrada, the street that begins directly behind the cathedral on the zócalo.

OUTDOOR ACTIVITIES

The beaches lining Acapulco Bay may look beautiful, but the bay is quite polluted with sewage and debris. Beaches near Acapulco Viejo are a bit cleaner: Try **Playa Caleta** or **Playa Caletilla,** both of which offer boogie board rentals and banana boat rides. Before the strip was built these two beaches were Acapulco's hot spots, but they now cater more to Mexican tourists than to foreigners. Across the bay from the beaches lies **Isla Roqueta,** which is accessible from either beach by boat. The island has calm waters and a lighthouse with spectacular views, and the boat ride (10 min, $3 round-trip) is pleasant. Buy a ticket on the wharf from the offices marked ISLA ROQUETA (tel. 74/83–12–15), or on the beach from a roaming ticket seller. To reach the wharf, board a bus marked CALETA heading west along Costera.

The cleanest beaches in Acapulco lie on the **Bahía de Puerto Marqués,** east of the city near the air-port freeway. Here the water is clean enough for snorkeling, waterskiing, and swimming. **Playa de Puerto Marqués** is the most developed of the bay's beaches, and usually fills up with Mexican tourists on weekends. From Costera 5 de Mayo, take the bus marked PUERTO MARQUES (30 min, 15¢). **Princess Beach,** named for the hotel that dominates its skyline, lies beyond Playa de Puerto Marqués. The waves are big here, and swimmers should be very careful. Buses don't run to Princess beach so catch a cab ($1).

All kinds of water sports are popular on Acapulco's beaches—though you might want to choose one that requires the least amount of contact between you and the water. **Divers de Mexico/Fishing Factory** (Costera Miguel Alemán 100, a few blocks west of the zócalo, tel. 74/82–13–98) charges $55 per person for seven hours of marlin-, sailfish-, and tuna-fishing. All equipment and an English-speaking captain are included.

AFTER DARK

Acapulco's disco scene is legendary. Mirrored walls, strobe lights, laser beams, and pounding music are in excess here, and things only slow down slightly during the low season (December through April). Covers average $13–$23 year-round, and in many clubs you'll pay $5 for a drink. Women get the best bargain here, as many discos offer cover-free "ladies' nights." Otherwise, watch for clubs advertising a *barra libre* (free bar). This means there's a hefty cover charge, but all drinks are included in the price. If you want to go all out, you can pay a bit more to dance the night away on one of the ships that cruise Acapulco Bay. **Bonanza Cruise** (Costera Miguel Alemán, a few blocks southwest of the zócalo, tel. 74/82–49–47) has a dinner cruise (7:30 PM; $38) that features an open bar and show. Their sunset cruise (4:30 PM; $10) features an open bar with domestic drinks, a disco, and live music. If you're looking to escape the club scene altogether you can play pool at **Los Amigos** (in front of Hotel Condesa) or **La Plaza de Mariachi** (Costera Miguel Alemán, at Mendoza). A handful of new, sparkling movie theaters line the Costera in the Zona Dorada, including **Cinepolis** (Costera Miguel Alemán, at Massieu, tel. 74/86–43–56) in La Gran Plaza. Whatever you do, use caution when walking city streets at night, or take a cab; Acapulco has a high crime rate.

A mellow mix of salsa and rock plays at Acapulco's discos until around midnight, when the dance floor officially opens. From then on, it's strictly the thumping beats of house and techno.

On the strip, dozens of bars vie for the attention of gringos. Two of the most popular are the chains **Carlos 'n' Charlie's** (Costera Miguel Alemán 112, tel. 74/84–00–39) and the **Hard Rock Café** (Costera Miguel Alemán 37, tel. 74/84–66–80). Get to Charlie's early unless you'd like to wait in line. The Hard Rock frequently offers live music. For live tropical and salsa music, try **Nina's** (Costera Miguel Alemán 2909, tel. 74/84–24–00) and **Salon Q** (Costera Miguel Alemán 23, tel. 74/81–01–14). Both places open nightly at 10 PM and charge $12 cover (open bar included).

DISCOS

After a visit to **Andromeda** (Costera Miguel Alemán, corner Fragata Yucatán, tel. 74/84–88–15) you'll agree that Acapulco is the disco capital of the world. The exterior looks like a castle, the interior's decorated like a submarine/aquarium, and it features fabulous sound, light, and video effects. The place is always crowded with wealthy young locals and *chilangos* (Mexico City residents), who can afford the hefty $25 cover (open bar included). The **Palladium** (Carretera Escénica Las Brisas, tel. 74/81–03–00) is part of an international chain with locations in San Francisco, New York, and Los Angeles—which might explain why decorations include ghetto graffiti on the walls. It's packed throughout the week, despite the $20 cover for men, $15 for women (free for women Tuesday and Thursday before 12:30 AM). Down the hill from Palladium is **Extravaganza** (tel. 74/84–71–64), which features an open bar on Monday and Wednesday. Covers range from zip to $20, depending on your gender and day of the week. All of the above discos are open nightly until 6 AM, and enforce a hip dress code (no swimsuits and flip-flops, please).

But wait, there's more: Popular with the 18–30 crowd, **Baby O** (Costera Miguel Alemán, near Nelson, tel. 74/84–74–74) is packed almost every night of the week during high season. The jungle decor seems to bring out the real party animals—don't say you haven't been warned. There's no cover for women, but men pay $7 weeknights, $15 weekends (open bar included). Doors open at 10:30 PM. At **B&B** (Gran Vía Tropical 5, tel. 74/83–04–41), you'll hear American music from the '60s and '70s on the first floor and romantic Mexican pop on the second. Cover is $5 and drinks are $2–$3. This club is a distance from the zócalo, so take a cab. **Disco Beach** (Costera Miguel Alemán, tel. 74/84–70–64) is an open-air disco with ocean views—its the most famous of Acapulco's many legendary pick-up spots. Expect lots of young muscle men and among the opposite sex, plenty of bleached blondes. The drinks are always $1 at **Disco Beach Terraza** (tel. 74/84–82–30), upstairs from Disco Beach.

GAY/LESBIAN BARS AND DISCOS

The gay bars in Acapulco are as wild and crazy as all the other clubs. Most are clustered near Condensa Plaza, across from the Fiesta America Condensa. **Disco Demás** (Privada Piedra Picuda, tel. 74/84–13–70) is the best dance club, but it doesn't heat up until about 1 AM. **Relax** (Lomas del Mar 4, tel. 74/84–04–21) is smaller and charges a $4 cover. **Open House Bar** (Plaza Condesa, tel. 74/84–72–85) has a tiny, no-cover disco; it's most crowded in the early evening, and then everyone goes to Relax or Disco Demás. **Bar La Malinche** (Privada Piedra Picuda, tel. 74/81–11–47) also has a small no-cover disco, but most come here to converse at the bar. All of the above feature strippers at midnight, and Demas and Relax have drag shows.

NEAR ACAPULCO

PIE DE LA CUESTA

The sandy beach of Pie de la Cuesta is only 15 km (9 mi) northwest of Acapulco. The beach itself has incredibly forceful currents and riptide; two or three swimmers, usually foreigners, drown each year. However, on the other side of the road is **Laguna de Coyuca**—a lake of *agua dulce* (sweet, fresh water). Locals and tourists take advantage of Coyuca's calm waters for swimming, waterskiing, and lazing around. **Tres Marías** (Fuerza Aerea Mexicana 375, tel. 74/60–00–11) offers waterskiing ($30 per hr). **Club de Ski Chuy** (Fuerza Aerea Mexicana 67, tel. 74/60–11–04) offers leisurely boat tours (4½ hrs, $5) departing daily at 11 AM. Boat tours journey to the lake's *barra* (sandbar), a beautiful swimming area, passing mangrove swamps and the **Isla de los Pájaros,** a bird sanctuary inhabited by pelicans, flamingos, and storks. To reach Pie de la Cuesta from Acapulco, catch an eastbound PIE DE LA CUESTA bus (½ hr, 15¢) on Costera, across the street from the main post office.

WHERE TO SLEEP

Pie de la Cuesta's beach is not safe for camping, and women especially should use caution at night around the beach and the laguna. The **Acapulco Trailer Park** (Fuerza Aerea Mexicana 381, tel. 74/60–00–10) is right on the beach and charges $8 for one or two people. Bring your own tent, and the park will provide water, bathrooms, showers, and security. The hotel **Villa Nirvana** (Playa Pie de la Cuesta 302, tel. 74/60–16–31), just steps away from the ocean, offers clean, airy rooms ($20) with fans and terraces. Discounts are available for stays of three or more nights during the low season, and owners Rosanna and Stan are friendly, helpful, and speak English. **Bungalows María Cristina** (Fuerza Aerea Mexicana 351, tel. 74/60–02–62) offers homey bungalows on the beach, across the street from the tranquil lagoon. Year-round rates are $20 for one or two people, or $42 for a four-person bungalow with kitchenette. Additional persons are $4 each.

FOOD

Restaurants in Pie de la Cuesta are famous for their fresh seafood. The main strip, Fuerza Aerea Mexicana, is lined with small hotels, most of which sport their own beachfront restaurant. During low season, **El Zanate** (Fuerza Aerea Mexicana 693, tel. 74/60–17–09) has a $1.50 comida corrida. In the high season they have a wide selection of fresh fish and "whatever else the gringos want." **Tres Marías** (*see above*) is popular with locals for its cordial service. There are two locations: a remodeled, more popular branch by the lagoon and another across the street on the beach. The specialty is the fried fish fillet ($6.50), but tacos are three for $2.25. These restaurants accept cash only.

CENTRAL CITIES

UPDATED BY PATRICIA ALISAU

Although American culture has saturated Mexico's border towns and beach communities, the central region—consisting of the states of Tlaxcala, Puebla, Morelos, and part of Guerrero—has managed to remain true to traditional Mexican culture. Despite the U.S. chain stores and restaurants that have gradually moved in and set up camp here, this is still a world of mariachis, artesanía (handicrafts), and Mexican-owned businesses.

As you travel throughout this region, you'll notice that the struggle to resist outside influences isn't just a recent phenomenon. Almost all of the area's early civilizations—the Toltec, Mixtec, Zapotec, Tlahuic, and Xilanca tribes—were strongly affected by the Maya and Aztec, either through trade or warfare. The Spaniards arrived and eventually won religious and cultural dominance, building their colonial churches on or near indigenous pyramids. But Spanish settlement was not met with passivity here: One of the most dramatic battles ever fought against the Spanish, the War of Independence, took place in the town of Cuautla. In 1862, French invaders were driven out of the region during a decisive battle at Pueble, commemorated annually on Cinco de Mayo; and Emiliano Zapata issued his 1910 call for land reform from the town of Ayala. Throughout the region look for imposing stone fortresses and bullet-riddled palaces that stand as reminders of the turbulent War of Independence and the Revolution of 1910.

The central cities' pre-Columbian and colonial past are what draw Mexican tourists here. There are numerous museums, ruins, and gardens to explore, and the entire town of **Taxco** (including its delicious dozens of silversmiths' shops) was declared a national monument in 1928. To truly experience central Mexico, however, make time to sample the curative waters in Tlaxcala, feast on Puebla's renowned version of mole (chocolate-chile sauce), learn to speak Nahuatl from the Tlahuican healers in Tepoztlán, or attend mass in Taxco's Iglesia de Santa Prisca.

TLAXCALA

Tlaxcala, meaning "the land of corn" in Nahuatl, is a tiny state, only 2½ times the size of Mexico City. It's also one of the poorest Mexican states: Most of its inhabitants rely on their *milpas* (small plots of land on which corn is grown) for subsistence. Tlaxcala city, the state's capital, lies just two hours east of chaotic

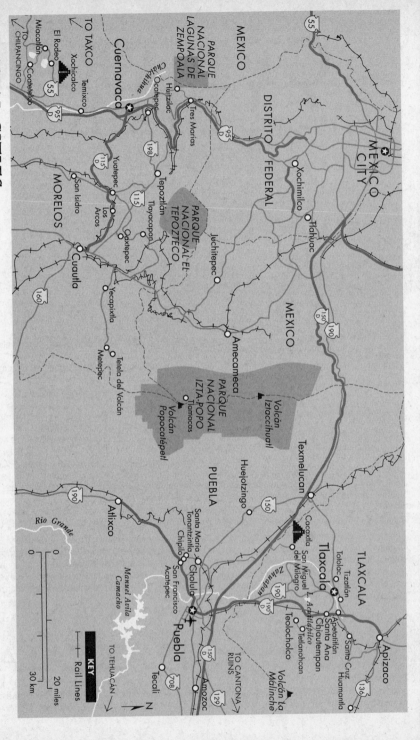

CENTRAL CITIES

MEXICO

DISTRITO FEDERAL

MEXICO CITY

PARQUE NACIONAL LAGUNAS DE ZEMPOALA

TO TAXCO

Cuernavaca

Miacatlán
El Rodeo
Xochicalco
Temixco
TO CHILPANCINGO
Coatetelco
55
95 D

Huitzilac
Ocotepec
Tres Marias
Chalchihua

198
115 D
Yautepec
San Isidro
Los Arcos
Tepoztlán
Tlayacapan
Oaxtepec
115

PARQUE NACIONAL EL TEPOZTECO

MORELOS

Cuautla

Yecapixtla
Melepec
Tetela del Volcán

160

Xochimilco
Tlahuac

55

95 D

190

150 D

MEXICO

Amecameca

PARQUE NACIONAL IZTA-POPO

Volcán Iztaccíhuatl

Tlamacas
Volcán Popocatépetl

Texmelucan

Huejotzingo

150

PUEBLA

190

Atlixco

Río Grande

Santa María Tonantzintla
Chipilo
San Francisco Acatepec
Cholula

Manuel Ávila Camacho

Puebla

Tecali

708

Cacaxtla
San Miguel del Milagro
Tizatlán
Tololac

Zahuapan

190

190 D

150 D

Amozoc

129

TO TEHUACÁN

Santa Ana
Chiautempan
Apetatitlán
Tlaxcala
TLAXCALA
Santa Cruz
Huamantla
Tetlanohcan
Teolocholco
Volcán la Malinche
TO CANTONA RUINS

Apizaco

136

KEY
Rail Lines

N

0   20 miles
0   30 km

Mexico City, but with a population of only 8,000 it could hardly be called urban. Perhaps because of the town's small size, its friendly residents won't hesitate to introduce themselves to foreign visitors. Tlaxcalans remain proud of both their indigenous heritage and the fact that their town was the first Catholic diocese in Mexico.

The delicate arches surrounding the *zócalo* (main plaza) and the terraces overlooking the streets are just two traits that characterize Tlaxcala city as inviting and tranquil. The close proximity of many worthwhile historic and geologic attractions makes it a good place to base yourself for a day or three of leisurely sightseeing: Explore the **Cacaxtla** archaeological ruins, hike the **Volcán La Malintzi,** and dip into curative waters supposedly brought to the New World by the Virgin Mary.

BASICS

CASAS DE CAMBIO

Change currency or traveler's checks at **Banamex** (Plaza Xicohténcatl 8, just east of Independencia, tel. 246/2–25–36; open weekdays 9–3). The bank's 24-hour ATMs accept Plus, Cirrus, Visa, and MasterCard. You can also change cash and traveler's checks at the **Casa de Cambio** (Independencia 3, at Morelos, tel. 246/2–90–85; open weekdays 9–4).

EMERGENCIES

In an emergency, dial the **police** at 246/2–07–35; for **ambulance** service contact the Cruz Roja (tel. 246/2–09–20).

LAUNDRY

Lavandería San Felipe charges $1 per kilo (2 pounds) of laundry. *Guridi y Alcocer 30, between Juárez and Lira y Ortega, no phone. Open weekdays 8–7, Sat. 8:30–2.*

MAIL

The full-service post office on the zócalo will hold mail sent to you at the following address for up to 10 days: Lista de Correos, Tlaxcala, Tlaxcala, CP 90000, México. *Plaza de la Constitución 20, at Morelos, tel. 246/2–00–04. Open weekdays 8–8.*

MEDICAL AID

Central Médico (Guridi y Alcocer 40-A, between Juárez and Lira y Ortega, tel. 246/2–58–51) provides 24-hour medical services and has an English-speaking doctor on staff. For less serious medical problems, visit the 24-hour **Farmacia Mora** (Guerrero 10, at Independencia, no phone).

PHONES

To make a collect call, use one of the many pay phones around town. **Ladatel** phones on the main plaza allow long-distance calls, but first you'll have to buy a card at the **telephone office** (Guridi y Alcocer 7; open weekdays 8–4) or at **Gómez-Esparza Papelería y Fotografía** (Julian Carrillo, at Lira y Ortega, tel. 246/2–34–57; open Mon.–Sat. 9–8). For cash calls and faxes, try the *caseta de larga distancia* (long-distance telephone office; Independencia 10, on the west side of Plaza Xicohténcatl, fax 246/2–10–49; open Mon.–Sat. 9–8:30).

VISITOR INFORMATION

The information desk at the **Secretary of Tourism** is staffed by eager young people who hand out numerous flyers. They can arrange for guided tours of the nearby attractions when given a week's notice. *Juárez, at Lardizábal, tel. 246/2–00–27. Open weekdays 9–7, weekends 10–6.*

COMING AND GOING

BY BUS

The **Central Camionera** (tel. 246/2–03–62) is eight blocks west of the zócalo. From here, **ATAH** (tel. 246/2–02–17) runs buses to Mexico City (2 hrs, $4.50) every 15 minutes 4:30 AM–11:30 PM. **Flecha Azul** (tel. 246/2–33–92) sends second-class buses to Puebla (45 min, 1) every eight minutes 5:30 AM–9 PM. To reach the zócalo from the bus station, take any CENTRO or SANTA ANA *colectivo* (communal taxi; 25¢). Those marked CENTRAL head to the bus station from the corner of Lira y Ortega and Lardizábal.

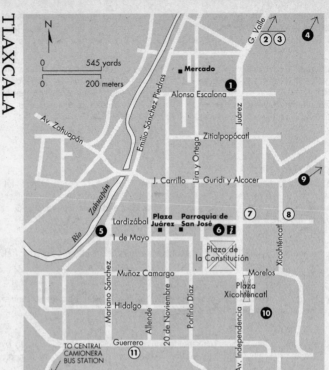

TLAXCALA

N

0 — 545 yards
0 — 200 meters

Mercado

Alonso Escalona ①

Av. Zahuapán

Emilio Sánchez Piedras

Zitlalpopócatl

Juárez

Lira y Ortega

J. Carrillo   Guridi y Alcocer ⑨

Río Zahuapán

⑤ Lardizábal **Plaza Juárez** **Parroquia de San José** ⑦ ⑧
1 de Mayo ■ ⑥ 🛈

Plaza de la Constitución

Mariano Sánchez

Muñoz Camargo Morelos

Hidalgo Plaza Xicohténcatl

Xicohténcatl

Allende

20 de Noviembre

Porfirio Díaz

Av. Independencia

⑩

Guerrero
TO CENTRAL CAMIONERA BUS STATION ⑪

G. Valle ②③ ④

Sights ●
Basílica de Ocotlán, 9
Ex-Convento de San Francisco, 10
Jardín Botánico, 4
Museo de Artes y Tradiciones de Tlaxcala, 5
Palacio de Gobierno, 6
Palacio de la Cultura, 1

Lodging ○
Albergue de La Loma, 11
Hotel Jeroc's, 2
Hotel Mansión de Xicohtencatl, 7
Hotel Plaza-Tlaxcala, 3
Posada Mary, 8

BY CAR

From Tlaxcala, it's an easy two-hour (120-km/74-mi) drive to Mexico City on Highway 190-D. Three toll stops, totaling a whopping $11, keep this highway in good shape. The *libremento* (free highway), via Santa Ana, takes you on a smooth ride to Puebla (1 hr) with no toll fees.

GETTING AROUND

Tlaxcala is a walkable city. The zócalo at its center is named **Plaza de la Constitución.** The main street is called Independencia on the south side of the zócalo. As Independencia runs north, it becomes Juárez, then Guillermo Valle, and finally Boulevard Revolución. Most everything of interest lies near or along Independencia/Juárez in the downtown area.

Colectivos (communal taxis) travel up and down the main street, to the Central Camionera, and to neighboring towns. These can also be called *rutas* or *combis,* although usually only VW vans (and VW van look-alikes) are called combis. Northbound colectivos leave from the stop on Independencia at Plaza Xicohténcatl; those heading south, west, and to the Central Camionera depart from the northwest corner of the intersection of Lira y Ortega and Lardizábal. Colectivos cost 25¢ per trip and stop running at about 10 PM. Taxi stands are situated on the south side of the zócalo and at Parroquia de San José. Most taxi fares within Tlaxcala should cost less than $2, while a ride to nearby Santa Ana averages $4. Unless you have heavy luggage, though, a taxi isn't necessary in such a small town.

WHERE TO SLEEP

Tlaxcala's visitors are few and far between, and the town's hotels reflect that fact. With no business to speak of, many hotel owners tend to doze off in front of the TV and forget that they have a place to run. Reservations are only required during fairs and festivals (*see* Festivals, *below*), as well as during the first week of July, when summer sessions start at the university. If the places listed below are full, your only alternative is a luxury hotel. The most affordable of these is **Hotel Jeroc's** (Revolución 4, tel. 246/2–15–77), which charges $44 for a double. For this you get a restaurant, bar, dance club (*see* After Dark, *below*), pool, and tennis courts.

UNDER $10 • Hotel Mansión de Xicohténcatl. Not exactly the mansion it claims to be, this place is right at the heart of town. Rooms are clean but drab, and a few have small balconies. If you're a woman traveling alone, you might get some unwanted attention, otherwise the hot showers and great location make it worth your while. Doubles cost $8.50. *Juárez 15, tel. 246/2–19–00. 1 block north of the zócalo. 18 rooms, all with bath. Cash only.*

Posada Mary. This establishment, at the center of town, is cheap—double rooms with private bath cost $5.50. You also get access to a casual restaurant and a young, friendly manager at your service. The rooms are small and unspectacular, however, with no amenities. *Xicohténcatl 19, at Lardizábal, no phone. 10 rooms, all with bath. Laundry, luggage storage. Cash only.*

UNDER $20 • Albergue de La Loma. Come here if you want to pamper yourself—the clean rooms are large and airy and equipped with phones, TVs, carpeting, and a panoramic view of Tlaxcala. The hotel is perched atop a hill overlooking Tlaxcala, about four blocks from the *centro* (downtown). Doubles cost $19. *Guerrero 58, at Allende, tel. 246/2–04–24. 24 rooms, all with bath. Restaurant, bar, luggage storage.*

Hotel Plaza-Tlaxcala. Next door to Hotel Jeroc's (*see above*) sits this popular but quiet hotel, complete with sprawling garden. The remodeled rooms have white-and-blue decor and color TVs with cable. It's pretty far from the center of town, but rooms are a bargain at $12 for a double. *Revolución 6, tel. 246/2–78–52. From the bus station or centro, take a SANTA ANA combi; you'll see Hotel Jeroc's sign on left. 12 rooms, all with bath. Restaurant, luggage storage. Cash only.*

FOOD

Most of Tlaxcala's restaurants are clustered around the zócalo and Plaza Xicohténcatl. International restaurants are gaining popularity with the locals, but you'll still find plenty of eateries serving regional specialties like *pollo tocotlán* (chicken with maguey cactus salsa, wrapped in paper and then cooked). The taco stands off 20 de Noviembre, near Plaza Juárez, stay open late and serve the cheapest food in town. Drinks are room temperature, the salsa is hot enough to make your ears smoke, and you'll probably have to eat standing up, but tacos are 20¢ each. Also look for *rosticerías* (restaurants specializing in roasted chicken), where a whole chicken with a side of tortillas, beans, *rajas* (chile strips), and salsa costs about $2. Several rosticerías are near the daily **market** (Alonso Escalona, between Emilio Sánchez Piedras and Lira y Ortega).

UNDER $5 • La Fonda del Convento. You'll find this popular restaurant on the cobblestone path that runs between the Ex-Convento and Plaza Xicohténcatl. The *carne fonda del convento* (flank steak served with rice, fries, beans, guacamole, and an enchilada) costs $3.50; the *comida corrida* (preprepared lunch special) costs $5. *Calzada de San Francisco 1, tel. 246/2–07–65. Closed Sun. Cash only.*

Los Portales. Among the multitudes of restaurants crowding the zócalo, choose this one for its excellent $2 breakfast: enchiladas or ham and eggs, served with fresh-squeezed orange juice, a melon slice, coffee, and all the bread and jam you can eat. At other times of day they serve steaks, hamburgers, and the regional specialty *pollo en pipián* (chicken in chile and pumpkinseed sauce). There's al fresco dining on the porch, and salsa and merengue music fill the air on Friday and Saturday nights. *Independencia 8, on the west side of the zócalo, tel. 246/2–54–19. Cash only.*

El Quinto Sol. Vegans will rejoice at the presence of soy milk on the breakfast menu, though it's served hot and tastes suspiciously like *atole* (a sweet, corn-based drink). Add bread, fruit, yogurt, and granola, and you have breakfast for $1. The lunch menu varies, offering creative dishes such as soy "steak." *Juárez 15, at Lardizábal, tel. 246/2–49–28. Next to Hotel Mansión de Xicohténcatl. Closed Sun. Cash only.*

UNDER $10 • El Mesón Taurino. As you'd expect from a restaurant adjacent to the town's Plaza de Toros, this spot has an authentic bullfighting theme. If you're an animal lover, you might try dining in the patio room or outdoors in the garden, as the dining room is hung with the mounted heads of bulls who lost the fight. Though it's open all day, it's best known for dinner; the menu includes pasta dishes ($3–$4), filet mignon, and *filete Cacaxtla* ($6; steak topped with *huitlacoche* (edible corn fungus) and chile strips). *Independencia 12, at Guerrero, tel. 246/2–43–66. No breakfast on weekends.*

WORTH SEEING

Tlaxcala's main points of interest all lie within walking distance of the zócalo and can be seen in a day or two. **Plaza de la Constitución** is quieter than most Mexican zócalos; goods are only sold here during weekend markets and annual festivals. Along the western side of the plaza sits **Casa de Piedra**, a colonial-era house with a distinctive stone facade. Legend has it that the doctor who lived here allowed his poor patients to pay with a chiseled stone in lieu of cash. In this manner he went about building his house, stone by stone. Dominating the adjacent **Plaza Xicohténcatl** is a monument to the *cacique* (chieftain) of that name, who was hanged by the Spaniards for refusing to slaughter Aztec people during the assault on Tenochtitlán. From the plaza, follow the **Paseo de la Amistad** (Friendship Walkway), where courting couples, kids on bikes, and elderly folks alike enjoy the sunshine.

BASILICA DE OCOTLAN

This hillside temple is one of Mexico's national treasures, as it's considered the region's best example of the ornate Churrigueresque (ultra-baroque) style. The basilica's gleaming white-plaster facade is carved with intricate figures and flanked by two 109-ft towers. These are symbolically tiled in red and sky blue: Red and white are the colors of the flag of the ancient kingdom Tlaxcallan, and blue symbolizes the Virgin, in whose honor the shrine was built in 1640. According to church history, the Virgin once appeared here to a pious *indígena* (indigenous person) who was praying for the end to a severe epidemic raging through his village. In answer to his prayers, the Virgin caused curative waters to flow from the hillside.

The most dazzling room of the basilica is the **Chamber of the Virgin**. It took indigenous sculptor Francisco Miguel Tlayoltehuamintzin and Spaniard metalworker Miguel Jose de Santa Maria 25 years to complete, and every single inch glimmers with gold plating. Unfortunately, this room has recently been declared off-limits to tourists, who were apparently too interested in obtaining free souvenirs. If you can wrangle permission to view it, you won't be disappointed. Inside the basilica on the main altar you can see the wooden statue of **Our Lady of Ocotlán** that, according to legend, was carved from the trunk of a tree by unknown hands and later survived a devastating fire unscathed. Opposite the basilica's entrance is a small alley leading to a carefully preserved papier mâché miniature of the building. A sign here reads "Así se apareció la Virgen de Ocotlán" (Thus appeared the Virgin of Ocotlán).

To sample the curative waters that the Virgin brought to the hillside, walk 10 minutes down the steep cobblestone road to **Capilla del Pocito de Agua Milagrosa,** a tiny, round chapel housing a well filled with sweet, fresh water. The chapel walls are brightly decorated with a series of murals designed by Desiderio Hernández Xochitiotzin (*see* Palacio de Gobierno, *below*) that depict biblical themes related to water. Although a plaque by the well quotes the Virgin as saying that the tiniest drop of this water will bring perfect health, locals and tourists alike take it away by the bucketfuls. Bring an empty water bottle or buy one of the brightly colored jugs for sale along the way. *From the zócalo, walk north on Juárez, right at Guridi y Alcocer, left at Calzada de los Misterios, then uphill 2 km (1 mi). Or take* OCOTLAN *combi from the bus station and get off at the basilica. Admission free. Open daily dawn–dusk.*

EX-CONVENTO DE SAN FRANCISCO

More than just a religious site, this former monastery was witness to some key moments in the republic's history. One of the oldest parts of the structure, the **Capilla Abierta** (Open Chapel), is thought to be the earliest 16th-century construction of its type in Mexico. Upstairs and across the courtyard is the **Catedral de Nuestra Señora de la Asunción** and a beautiful view of Tlaxcala city. Built in 1526 after Tlaxcala was declared the first diocese in "New Spain," the cathedral is known for its gold-studded cedar ceiling, carved in the geometric mosarabe style. Here the four caciques of Tlaxcala were converted at the baptismal font, with Cortés and Alvarado acting as godfathers. The small **Museo Regional de Tlaxcala** (admission $1; open daily 10–5), next to the convent, specializes in Tlaxcalan archaeology and 18th-century paintings. *From the zócalo, walk 1 block south past Plaza Xicohténcatl and turn left at Calzada de Capilla Abierta. Mass is held daily at 6 PM.*

JARDIN BOTANICO TIZATLAN

This conservation garden sprouts flora characteristic of the *altiplano* (highland) region. Plants are labeled with both scientific and common names, and some have descriptions of their medicinal and practical uses. The Jardín is a good place for picnics or trysts, so bring a lunch or a lover. Tours (in Spanish only) are available weekdays; call 246/2–39–96 for reservations. Also in the garden, the **Sala Miguel Lira** theater (tel. 246/2–46–85) shows international art films ($1.25) Tuesday–Sunday. *From the zócalo, take* SANTA ANA *combi to Camino Real (just before the aqueduct); follow the path to the left about 100 yds. Admission free. Open daily 9–5.*

MUSEO DE ARTES Y TRADICIONES DE TLAXCALA

A visit to this living history museum is surprisingly entertaining. In the first room, filled with paintings and ancient artifacts, Spanish-language videotapes explain the early history of Tlaxcala. Outside is an original stone steam bath used by the Otomí for bathing and healing. Two chatty Otomí women will take a break from their weaving to guide you (in Spanish) through the replica of a typical rural house. There's also an area upstairs dedicated to the process of spinning and dying wool yarn used in weaving. Ask permission before taking photographs. *Emilio Sánchez Piedras 1, at 1 de Mayo, tel. 246/2–23–37. Admission: $1.25. Open Tues.–Sun. 10–6.*

PALACIO DE GOBIERNO

Now the state headquarters, this palace was built around 1550 to house traveling Spanish viceroys. The interior walls are covered with spectacular, colorful murals painted by local artist Desiderio Hernández Xochitiotzin, who had close ties to Diego Rivera. The murals depict symbolic and prophetic figures; the stairwell, for example, illustrates the heavens overrun by fantastic creatures, as gods plunge headfirst to the earth. Other murals proudly depict the Tlaxcalan alliance with Cortés, a marked contrast to other parts of Mexico where the Spaniards are shown as the oppressors. You can wander around the building for as long as you like, so long as you steer clear of the government offices. Spanish-speaking guides from the tourist office provide better information about the murals than the explanations painted on the walls. *North side of zócalo, tel. 246/2–00–06. Admission free. Open daily 8–8.*

PALACIO DE LA CULTURA

This sprawling building, surrounded by an immaculate garden, houses Tlaxcala's cultural center. The first floor contains a **Sala de Cultura** with temporary exhibits by Tlaxcalan and national artists. Check the bulletin board at the entrance for upcoming musical events. *Juárez, at Alonso Escalona, tel. 246/2–27–29. Admission free. Open Mon.–Sat. 9–8.*

Several of Tlaxcala's mariachi bands have shops on Camargo between Díaz and Allende, and welcome visitors. They practice here in the afternoon before suiting up to serenade the lunch and dinner crowds.

FESTIVALS

Carnaval. The best festival in Tlaxcala is Carnaval, celebrated the week prior to Ash Wednesday. The event is characterized by bullfights and street parades in which people dance around wearing masks and costumes. Each village uses a specific color or design for its masks. *Late Feb.*

Celebración de las Cuatrocientas Familias. In 1591 a group of 400 Christianized Tlaxcalan families left Tlaxcala under orders from King Philip II of Spain and Pope Gregory XIV to go forth and colonize the north of "New Spain." The Celebration of the 400 Families, an impressive reenactment of their departure, takes place at the ruins of the **Convento de Nuestra Señora de las Nieves** in the town of Totolac (½ km/¼ mi from Tlaxcala, on the road to San Martín Texmelucan). The highlight is a candlelight procession. *July 6.*

Fiesta de la Asunción. This two-week festival in Huamantla (*see* Near Tlaxcala, *below*) celebrates the Assumption and the Virgin of Charity. A figure of the Virgin is paraded through the streets, which are carpeted with flowers arranged in symbolic designs. The procession ends when the sun rises, and a Pamplona-style running of the bulls begins. *Aug. 15.*

Fería del Pan. In the town of Totolac (½ km/¼ mi from Tlaxcala, on the road to San Martín Texmelucan) is a typical Tlaxcalan festival with dancing and fireworks. The bread baked for the festival, Pan de Fiesta, is famous throughout Tlaxcala state, and can be purchased year-round in the pueblitos of San Juan de Dolac and San Juan de Huactzinco. The fruit-filled breads are only sold in private homes; look for posted signs. *Oct. 8–13.*

The **Tlaxcala Fair** features bullfights, *charreadas* (rodeos), cockfights, indigenous dances, carnival rides, and exhibitions of local handicrafts. The fair lasts two weeks. *Late Oct.–early Nov.*

AFTER DARK

Though the cafés on the zócalo are crowded in the evenings, Tlaxcalans generally retire early. During festivals and in July and August, students from Mexico City descend on Tlaxcala, causing things to pick up a bit. As for the rest of the year, if you go out after 10 PM, you've missed whatever action there was. You can always catch a movie: Both **Cinema Tlaxcala** (tel. 246/2–19–62), on the south side of the zócalo, and **Cinemas 1 y 2** (G. Valle 113, tel. 246/2–35–44), 6½ blocks north of the centro, show fairly recent Hollywood films with Spanish subtitles, as well as Mexican films. Shows cost $1.50.

The best bar in town is **La Valentina** (1 de Mayo 9, between Allende and Sánchez, no phone; closed Sun.). A DJ mixes rock music, except Thursday when there's *música protesta* (protest music), which despite its name is slow and romantic. On weekends, live bands play alternative rock in English and Spanish. **Bar Tendido 7** (Plaza de la Constitución 19, at Porfirio Díaz, tel. 246/2–86–87) offers live music, Thursday–Saturday. **Royal Adler's** (Revolución 4, tel. 246/2–15–77; closed Sun.–Tues.), in Hotel Jeroc's, is the most decent and popular disco at present. The attire is dressy, cover is $1.50, and drinks run $2.

NEAR TLAXCALA

CACAXTLA

Cacaxtla (place where the water dies in the earth), 19 km (12 mi) southwest of Tlaxcala city, consists of a group of pyramids covering a space the size of four football fields, each with an amazing view of the endless cornfields from their respective summits—a sure sign of the strategic importance of these citadels in pre-Columbian times. In 1975 a series of vivid polychrome murals was discovered here—one of the most important Mesoamerican archaeological finds in the past 50 years. Today you can still see these astonishingly well-preserved works, which are unique in their realistic style and detail. The current theory holds that the murals were painted by the Olmeca-Xicalanca, a group of warrior merchants who arrived in the Tlaxcala Valley around 2,000 BC. The Olmeca-Xicalanca either were descendants of the Maya or had plenty of contact with the Maya, which explains why their murals contain elements more commonly found in southern Mexico. The murals date back to AD 600 and consist of five colors—white, red, yellow, blue, and black—produced from nopal cactus juice mixed with ground yellow ochre, ground charcoal, and red hematite. The figures adorned with blue body paint represent sacrificial victims, and the five-pointed stars are symbols of the planet Venus. The murals appear to have been deliberately preserved by the Indians: Archaeologists have discovered a layer of fine sand protecting the murals and a heavier filler added before each new part of the buildings was constructed. The most modern, 20th-century protective covering is an ugly, towering metal dome that you'll see from the entrance.

The first set of murals, painted on columns flanking the entrance to a small room, depicts barefoot blue dancers. Archaeologists refer to this room as the **Star Chamber,** because the dancers are surrounded by five-pointed stars. It may have been here that captives were prepared for sacrifice. The next mural to the right represents water, fertility, and trade. Note that the ears of corn are actually human faces. The **Red Temple** is identifiable by the bands of red paint that run along the bottom of the walls, like a sea of blood. Unfortunately, the general public is not allowed inside the Red Temple: Murals depicting prisoners are painted on the floor of the temple and are too fragile to be walked upon.

The **battle mural** for which Cacaxtla is most renowned is found just beyond the Red Temple. This mural depicts the aftermath of a real-life battle; the 48 victors wear jaguar pelts, and the vanquished wear bird headdresses. A final set of murals is in **Building A,** to the right of the battle mural. The murals here line up with the two small pyramids on the east and west sides of the structure. The date on the **north mural** (denoted by the eye of a reptile in indigenous glyphs) corresponds with the supposed incarnation of the wind god Enecatl. On the border of these murals are pictures of various sea creatures, reflections of the Olmec-Xicalanca origins on the Gulf of Mexico.

In January of 1993 excavation began at **Xochitecal** (known as Pyramid of the Flowers) on the hill opposite Cacaxtla. The 2-km (1-mi) climb through the fields from Cacaxtla is a hot and sweaty one, but definitely worth it. The site consists of three civic-religious temples that you may enter. Human remains and close to 5,000 clay female figures have been discovered here. You'll also find three monolithic fonts and four anthropomorphic monuments of engraved basalt stone. A small onsite museum displays many of the small, clay figurines that have been unearthed. *Admission for both sites: $2. Open Tues.–Sun. 10–5. Cacaxtla murals open for viewing Tues.–Sun. 10–1. Spanish-speaking guides available onsite for tours (1 hr, $5.50 per group) of Cacaxtla.*

If you make the trek out to Cacaxtla, you might as well visit the town of **San Miguel del Milagro,** on a cobblestone pathway just before the entrance to the pyramids. The archangel Michael supposedly appeared here in 1630, asking Diego Lázaro de San Francisco, a local Indian boy, to tell the townspeople of a curative well. When he did not follow the order, the boy was struck with illness, only to be cured with the waters that the angel brought him. As in Ocotlán (*see* Basílica de Ocotlán *in* Worth Seeing, *above*) a fountain of healing water bubbled forth, and to this day the **Santuario de San Miguel** is a destination for pilgrims. You can take some of the water from the **Pocito de Santa Agua** (Well of Holy Water), in the courtyard outside the church, during one of its sporadic distributions. The church itself is filled with 17th- and 18th-century paintings depicting angels, biblical stories, and the tale of St. Michael's curative water. At the lacquered **Chinese Pulpit** and **Cuarto de Exvotos,** to the right of the church, you'll find offerings—photographs, pairs of crutches, and handwritten notes—that healed pilgrims have left in gratitude.

COMING AND GOING

From Tlaxcala, take a TEXOLOC bus from the Central Camionera, and ask to be let off at the calzada (30 min, 70¢). You'll be dropped off at a crossroads where combis wait to take people to San Miguel and Cacaxtla (5 min). You'll then be dropped at the entrance to the ruins. If you're arriving from Puebla, catch a SAN MARTIN bus (1 hr, 90¢) from the CAPU terminal; you'll also be dropped off at the crossroads.

The Olmeca-Xicalanca, like the Maya, believed that the first human beings were made of tender ears of corn.

HUAMANTLA

The town of Huamantla, 45 km (28 mi) west of Tlaxcala city, was founded in 1534 and provides enough well-preserved colonial sights for a full day's explorations. For those interested in seeing bullfights, these take place in town June–August and are well publicized. The baroque **Convento de San Luis Obispo** is across the street from the free **Museo Taurino** (Allende Nte. 203, no phone; open Wed.–Sun. 9–2), which features bullfighting posters, costumes, swords, and photographs. The nearby **Museo Nacional del Títere** (National Museum of the Puppets; admission $1.50; open Tues.–Sun. 10–2 and 5–8) showcases various puppets and marionettes. To reach Huamantla, take an ATAH bus (1 hr, $1) from the Central Camionera in Tlaxcala.

PARQUE NACIONAL LA MALINTZI

The Parque Nacional La Malintzi is at an average altitude of 14,800 ft, the highest region in Tlaxcala. The park is best known for the beautiful La Malintzi volcano that slumbers peacefully within its boundaries. Guides for the three-hour trek to the summit of La Malintzi aren't necessary, but they're sometimes available on weekends and charge $5–$7 per person. Hiking within the forest here is also great, except during the rainy season (July–September), when the trails become slick and treacherous.

The Parque Nacional lies 43 km (26½ mi) southeast of Tlaxcala city and can be reached by bus in 1½ hours. From the Central Camionera or the daily market in Tlaxcala, take a bus to Huamantla; from there catch another bus to **Centro Vacacional La Malintzi** (tel. 246/2–40–98), a government-run resort. You can camp here for $3 per person, or rent one of the six-person cabins for $33 a night. There's a restaurant here, but it's pricey, so stock up in Tlaxcala with food and water for the hike.

SANTA CRUZ

If you've seen enough churches and museums, take a break at **Centro Vacacional La Trinidad,** 15 km (9 mi) northwest of Tlaxcala city in the town of Santa Cruz. The La Trinidad resort lies on the banks of the Río Tequixquiatl, and you can swim in the cool water, go boating, and, on the weekends, ride horses. Rooms in the adjoining **Hotel Balneario** (tel. 246/1–03–33) are $35 for a six-person cabin, or you can camp ($3 per person) on the hotel grounds with your own tent and equipment. Toilets, showers, and a water cistern are available in the tree-shaded camping area. Colectivos (70¢) run from the Central Camionera in Tlaxcala to directly in front of Hotel Balneario.

PUEBLA

Puebla, like its neighbor Mexico City 125 km (78 mi) to the south, is overwhelmingly urban. Music stores blast the latest Mexican hits onto crowded sidewalks; taxis and buses weave crazily down narrow cobblestone streets; and traffic cops stand at impossibly congested intersections, calmly licking ice-cream cones. Although your first instinct may be to run and hide, this cosmopolitan state capital will seem less chaotic once you get to know some of its 2 million friendly residents and the easy rhythms that dictate their daily lives. It's a prosperous town, with textiles, Talavera ceramics, and a Volkswagen plant bolstering the local economy.

Vibrant Puebla city is like a living museum, and as you walk through its streets you'll discover a stunning blend of Spanish and indigenous architecture, trimmed in exquisite Talavera tile. Puebla is also the original home of the famous mole, and almost anything you eat here, whether prepared on a makeshift streetcorner brazier or in a fancy restaurant, is wonderful. In fact, this is the only Mexican city where a kitchen, **La Cocina de Santa Rosa,** is considered a valid tourist attraction.

BASICS

AMERICAN EXPRESS

The AmEx office in the Plaza Dorada shopping center is a five-minute bus ride from downtown. The staff will exchange, replace, and sell traveler's checks, and deliver MoneyGrams. Cardholders can also cash personal checks, replace lost cards, and have their mail held at the following address: Plaza Dorada 2, Local 21–22, Puebla, Puebla CP 72530, México. *Tel. 22/37–55–58. From 13 Ote. and 2 Sur, take PLAZA DORADA bus. Open weekdays 9–6, Sat. 9–1.*

BOOKSTORES

Librerías de Cristal has an enormous selection of Spanish books, magazines, videos, and compact discs, and a smaller selection of English books. *Reforma 511, between 5 Nte. and 7 Nte., tel. 22/42–44–20. Open Mon.–Sat. 9:30–8:30.*

CASAS DE CAMBIO

Exchange traveler's checks at **Bancomer** (3 Pte. 116, tel. 22/32–00–22; open weekdays 8:30–2:30). Many of the banks along Reforma offer 24-hour ATMs that accept Plus and Cirrus system cards, but those at **Banamex** (Reforma 135, tel. 91–800/9–03–83) are the most reliable. **Casa de Cambio Puebla** (5 de Mayo, tel. 22/37–74–73; open Mon.–Sat. 9–1:30 and 4:30–6) is four blocks from the Plaza Dorada shopping center.

EMERGENCIES

Dial 06 from any public phone in Puebla for **police, fire,** or **ambulance** service.

LAUNDRY

Lavandería Roly charges $3 to wash and dry 3 kilos (6½ pounds) of laundry and $1 for self-service. *7 Nte. 404, at 4 Pte., tel. 22/32–93–07. Open Mon.–Sat. 8 AM–9 PM, Sun. 8–2.*

MAIL

The main post office is two blocks south of the zócalo. Mail will be held for up to 10 days if sent to you at: Lista de Correos, 5 Oriente y 16 de Septiembre, Sur C, Puebla, Puebla, CP 72000, México. *Tel. 22/42–64–48. Open weekdays 8–8, Sat. 9–1. Other location: 2 Ote. 411, between 6 Nte. and 4 Nte. To send mail to this branch, write "Adm. 1" before "Sur C."*

MEDICAL AID

Hospital Universitario (13 Sur, at 25 Pte., tel. 22/43–12–77) provides 24-hour emergency service and some of its staff speaks English. For 24-hour pharmacy service and free delivery to your hotel, try **Drogería Medina** (4 Pte. 107, tel. 22/32–37–89, fax 22/42–09–52).

PHONES

Puebla probably has the highest percentage of functioning **pay phones** of any city in Mexico. Casetas de larga distancia are also pretty abundant: Just look for the blue sign with a picture of a telephone and the word LADA. **Printaform** (2 Sur 104, tel. 22/46–68–14; open weekdays 9–2 and 4–8, Sat. 10–2) is right on the zócalo and lets you make cash calls. **Helados Holanda** (16 de Septiembre 303, tel. 22/42–61–55; open daily 9–9) has long-distance service and a fax machine, but you can't make collect calls.

VISITOR INFORMATION

There are two tourist offices in Puebla. The **Oficina de Información Turística** (5 Ote. 3, tel. 22/46–12–85; open daily 9–8:30) is the state office, staffed by a helpful crew that provides good maps of the city and the state. If you want a guided tour, the person to ask for is **George Estrada,** who speaks English. With 30 years of experience and a great sense of humor, he leads tours to the town of Cholula ($19 per person) and the ruins at Cantona ($38 per person); for both *see* Near Puebla, *below.* Prices include transportation; tours require a minimum of three persons. The nearby **municipal tourist office** (Portal Hidalgo 14, tel. 22/46–10–93; open weekdays 9–8) can also give you tons of information.

COMING AND GOING

BY BUS

Puebla's main bus terminal, **CAPU** (Blvd. Nte. 4222, tel. 22/30–19–03), is served by a number of bus lines. **Autobuses Unidos (AU)** (tel. 22/49–74–05) runs frequent buses to Mexico City (2 hrs, $4) and Veracruz city (5 hrs, $9.50), and sends three daily buses to Oaxaca city (8 hrs, $10) at 8:30 AM, 7:30 PM, and 11:30 PM. **Estrella Blanca** (tel. 22/49–75–61) serves Acapulco (7 hrs, $23) every two hours until 11:30 PM. **Cristóbal Colón** (tel. 22/49–73–27) buses depart for Salina Cruz (10 hrs, $24) twice daily. Besides serving many of the

La Malintzi volcano, in a national park 43 km (26½ mi) southeast of Tlaxcala city, was named after the woman who was the translator and mistress of Hernán Cortés.

destinations listed above, **Autobuses del Oriente (ADO)** (tel. 22/49–70–42) also sends buses daily at 9 PM to Mérida (21 hrs, $41) and at 11:45 AM to Cancún (24 hrs, $48). Several local companies, such as **Flecha Azul,** cruise to Tlaxcala (45 min, $1). The terminal has luggage storage (25¢ per hour; open daily 7 AM–10:30 PM), a tourist information booth, a police station, and a bank (open daily 9 AM–noon) that changes money. Several cafeterias, a pharmacy, and nearby shops ensure that you'll be occupied as you wait for your bus.

Unfortunately, the CAPU bus terminal is nowhere near downtown Puebla. To get here you have to take either a combi or a cab. Authorized taxis (prepay the fare at the booth inside the terminal) charge $3 to the zócalo, where most of the budget hotels are. The RUTA 48 combi (20 min, 30¢) will get you closest to the zócalo—about five blocks away.

BY CAR

The new Oaxaca–Veracruz highway makes traveling by car fast (3½ hours to either destination) and easy, but not cheap: Tolls to Oaxaca total $13, and to Veracruz a whopping $23. To reach Mexico City, take the Puebla–Mexico freeway and pay $8 for two hours of easy driving.

BY PLANE

Puebla doesn't have its own airport, but the **Puebla–Mexico City airport bus service** shuttles between Puebla's CAPU bus terminal (*see* By Bus, *above*) and the Mexico City International Airport. The nonstop service is hourly, daily 5:30 AM–10 PM; tickets for the 2½-hour ride cost $6.50. If you arrive in the Mexico City airport and need a ride to Puebla, look for the bus service's ticket counter in the baggage claims area.

GETTING AROUND

Puebla's streets might seem confusing at first, but they can be mastered with the help of the free maps provided by the tourist office (*see* Visitor Information, *above*). Streets are organized by number, in relation to the zócalo, and according to cardinal directions: *norte* (north; nte.), *sur* (south), *oriente* (east; ote.), and *poniente* (west; pte.). Two exceptions to the rule are **5 de Mayo,** which becomes **16 de Septiembre** south of the zócalo, and **Avenida Reforma,** which becomes **Avenida Ávila Camacho** after passing the zócalo going east–west.

The *calles* east of the zócalo are even-numbered, and those west of the zócalo are odd-numbered. All of these are labeled "sur" and "norte." The *avenidas* north of the zócalo are even-numbered, while odd-

HOLY MOLE, THE SECRET SAUCE

According to local legend, Puebla's famous mole sauce was invented centuries ago by the Aztec as a topping for human flesh. A more plausible explanation involves a nun, Sor Andrea de la Asunción, who lived in Puebla's Santa Rosa convent during the 18th century. Apparently, Sor Andrea wanted to create for the Archbishop of Puebla a special dish blending Spanish and Mexican cuisines. So she began with four types of chiles—mulato, ancho, pasilla, and chipotle—and then added almonds as a symbol of Spain. Raisins, plantains, and chocolate sweetened the mix; sesame seeds and peanuts thickened the sauce; and cloves, cinnamon, and anise enhanced the flavoring.

numbered ones are south of it. All avenidas are labeled "oriente" and "poniente." Puebla's streets are surprisingly safe for a city its size, and even solo women can walk around alone hassle-free. Areas to avoid at night, however, are 6 Poniente between 7 Norte and 11 Norte, and the area northwest of 20 Poniente and 3 Sur.

BY BUS

Puebla's extensive system of colectivos (25¢) run daily 6 AM–11 PM. However, in an effort to control noise and protect historic buildings from air pollution, colectivos and combis don't travel the streets nearest the zócalo. The closest they come is 11 Poniente, about five blocks away.

BY CAR

Driving within Puebla can be a harrying experience. The cobblestone roads are one-way in downtown and are crowded with honking cars, hordes of pedestrians, and policemen with obnoxiously loud whistles. Parking can be hard to find on the street, but parking lots are an easy option. Car rental offices in the city include **Budget** (Juárez 2927-8, tel. 22/30–39–76) and **National** (Juárez 2318-M, tel. 22/48–50–48). Both rent sedans for about $40 per day to those who are at least 23 years of age and in possession of a driver's license, credit card, and passport.

WHERE TO SLEEP

All of the hotels described below are within a few blocks of the zócalo, in the colonial **Centro Histórico** (historical center) of the city. The only hotel anywhere near the CAPU bus station is the quiet and modern **Hotel Terminal de Puebla** (Carmen Serdán 5101, tel. 22/32–79–80) where rooms cost $16.50 for two. Solo travelers may not want to look for lodging west of Calle 7 Norte. The numerous brothels here make for a seedy atmosphere, and even a brief walk in the area can be uncomfortable.

UNDER $5 • Hotel Venecia. Established in 1897, Hotel Venecia isn't much to look at, but it's clean, and the clientele consists of friendly Mexican families. None of the rooms have private baths, but there's hot water all the time. Doubles cost $4, plus $1.50 for a TV. *4 Pte. 716, tel. 22/32–24–69. 2 blocks north and 3 blocks west of the zócalo. 36 rooms, none with bath. Cash only.*

UNDER $15 • Hotel Santander. Entering this hotel's huge enclosed courtyard surrounded by opulent terraces will make you feel as if you arrived in a mansion. The very clean and quaint rooms come with endless hot water, TVs, and if you're willing to pay, phones and private bathrooms. Doubles run $10–$15, depending on the amenities. The hotel fills up with Mexican and foreign travelers, so it's a good idea to reserve ahead of time if you want a cheaper room. *5 Pte. 111, tel. 22/46–31–75. 1 block west of the cathedral. 33 rooms, 13 with bath. Restaurant, luggage storage. Cash only.*

UNDER $30 • Hotel Colonial. This charming place—a former 16th-century convent—is a favorite of American and European students taking courses at the university across the street. Fittingly, the entire place is done up in colonial style, with antiques, dark-wood paneling, and a 95-year-old hand-cranked elevator. Rooms are spacious, tiled, clean, and fairly quiet, and all are equipped with phones and TVs. There's also a library, money exchange, and a fifth-floor terrace with great views of Puebla. On Sunday, the pedestrian-only street out front comes alive with local artists displaying their works for sale. Doubles cost $27, triples $30. *4 Sur 105, tel. 22/46–46–12. 1 block east of the zócalo. 70 rooms, all with bath. Restaurant, laundry ($2.50), luggage storage. Reservations advised.*

Hotel Imperial. From the busy pool table and restaurant on the first floor to the remodeled split-level rooms complete with TVs, phones, and filtered tap water, you'll feel like you've died and gone to traveler's heaven. There are also safes for your valuables and a complimentary breakfast (daily 7:30–10:30 AM). The owner, Juan José Bretón Avalos (*el Licenciado*), is one of the most helpful guides in all Puebla. Rooms cost $23 for a double. *4 Ote. 212, between 2 Nte. and 4 Nte., tel. 22/42–49–81. 65 rooms, all with bath. Laundry, parking, luggage storage.*

FOOD

Puebla's nuns had a special gift for culinary creation, and are credited with inventing the Mexican favorites *mole poblano* (*see box, above*) and *chiles en nogada* (chiles stuffed with beef and covered in a walnut sauce and pomegranate seeds). For a particularly filling and original lunch, try the 50¢ *tacos árabes* (Arabian tacos; seasoned beef and a yogurty sauce, rolled in pita bread) at **Taquería La Oriental** (Portal Juárez 107, no phone) on the west side of the zócalo. Oddly enough, these tacos can be found only in Puebla. You can pick out the little shops where they're sold by the rotisserie stands out front. Sugar addicts will want to stroll down **Calle de los Dulces** (Street of Sweets; 6 Ote., between 5 de Mayo and 4 Nte.), past numerous shops selling Puebla's

Puebla is the site of the famous battle of May 5, 1862, when 2,000 Mexicans defeated 6,000 French troops. The annual Cinco de Mayo holiday, celebrated all over Mexico, recognizes this important victory.

famous fruit candies. Specialties include *camote* (candied yam) and a meringue concoction called *beso del ángel* (angel's kiss). **Super Churrería** (2 Sur, at 5 Ote., tel. 22/35–01–15) serves chocolate-dipped ($1) and traditional *churros* (15¢). The twisted, sugary pastries dipped into melted chocolate will send you floating away into ecstasy. The above places accept cash only.

UNDER $5 • San Francisco el Alto Mercado (Garibaldi). What used to be a market has now been turned into this enclosed setting for about 15 *fondas* (covered food stands). In this lively place you'll find traditional poblano food, such as a plate of chicken mole, rice, beans, and chiles en nogada (in season July–Sept.). On weekend nights mariachis play for the working-class crowd, and the market ends up resembling a rowdy bar. *14 Ote., at 14 Nte., no phone. 5 blocks north and 6 blocks east of the zócalo. Open 24 hrs. Cash only.*

Super Soya. This fun joint is a haven for die-hard vegetarians, health nuts, and ice cream fanatics. The yogurt/ice cream bar in the building's front offers creative, nutritious concoctions in waffle cones that smell better than they taste. In back you'll find a health food store and restaurant serving mouthwatering *platos del día* for just $2. *5 de Mayo 506, tel. 22/46–22–39. 3 blocks north of the zócalo. No breakfast Sun. Cash only.*

UNDER $10 • Fonda de Santa Clara. Typical comida poblana is served in this famous restaurant, decorated with *papel picado* (traditional Mexican cut-paper decorations) and *lupe muñecas* (papier-mâché dolls). Although it caters to tourists and the food isn't cheap, you'd be hard pressed to find their seasonal specials anywhere else. The menu features *gusanos de maguey con salsa borracha* (maguey worms in chile sauce; $10) in April and May, and *chapulines* (fried grasshoppers; $6) during October and November, as well as more conventional dishes, like mole poblano and chiles en nogado. The *café de olla* (coffee flavored with cinnamon and brown sugar; $1) is delicious. *3 Pte. 307, tel. 22/42–26–59. 2 blocks west of zócalo. No breakfast. Other location: 3 Pte. 920 (no breakfast; closed Sun.).*

Restaurant Hotel Colonial. This glass-dome restaurant is packed at lunch. The clientele includes regulars who come for the food, and exchange students who come to socialize. The menú del día (served daily 1:30–5 PM; $4) is certainly filling: It includes soup, rice with fried plantains, a vegetable dish, an entrée with black beans on the side, dessert, and coffee. *4 Sur 105, tel. 22/46–46–12. 1 block east of the zócalo. Cash only.*

Villa del Mar. The food's so good, people actually line up to lunch at this terrace seafood restaurant. Try the cocktail ($5) made of shrimp, octopus, or oyster, seasoned with cilantro, onion, avocado, chili, and

THE CHINESE
WOMAN OF PUEBLA

Mirrah, the China Poblana (Chinese Woman of Puebla), became a beloved resident of the city in the 17th century. Legend claims that she was a Mongol princess, captured by Acapulco pirates when she was a girl, and then sold as a slave to the viceroy of Mexico. A Pueblan merchant and his wife adopted the young woman and raised her as their daughter.

Once she was settled in her new home, Mirrah adapted her native Chinese style of dress to that of her new country, using the green, red, and white of the Mexican flag. The costumes that she sewed were so beautiful and unusual that local women began to imitate her, and Mirrah kindly taught them to sew in the Chinese style. A modern version of her dress, elaborately embroidered and sequined, is worn by Pueblan dancers performing the jarabe tapatío (hat dance).

Mirrah died at 80 years of age in 1668 and is buried in the Iglesia de la Compañía de Jesús, one block east of the zócalo.

sugar. Another excellent choice is the shrimp brochette with onion, bacon, and tomatoes. *Juárez 1920, in Zona Esmeralda, tel. 22/42–31–04. Take* RUTA *7 combi from 11 Ote. and 16 de Septiembre. Or walk 8 blocks west from the zócalo, then 3 blocks south to Juárez. No breakfast. Cash only.*

CAFES

Café del Artista. This cozy café/bar is in the Plazuela del Torno, an artsy hilltop neighborhood. At night, it fills with soft candlelight and the pleasing strains of live guitar music (daily from 7 PM). A cappuccino costs $1.25. *8 Nte. 410, at 6 Ote., tel. 22/42–15–27. Closed Sun. Cash only.*

Teorema. This dimly lit café/bookstore has the feel of a literary salon, with professors and international students engaged in earnest conversations about art and politics. Live music begins nightly at 9:30, varying from blues to rock to traditional guitar. The menu includes beer, wine, desserts, and coffees; try the *Ira bien* (coffee with five liqueurs and cream; $2.50). *Reforma, at 7 Nte., tel. 22/42–10–14. Cash only.*

WORTH SEEING

Almost all of Puebla's museums are free on Tuesday and closed on Monday, with the exception of the **Museo Amparo,** which is free Monday and open daily. **La China Poblana** (6 Nte. 1, no phone) is equal parts restaurant and tourist attraction; everywhere you look there is *papel picado* (decorative paper cutouts) and other assorted kitsch, plus a life-size mannequin dressed in a flashy China Poblana costume (*see box, below*). The food isn't exceptional, but it is reasonably priced (entrées cost $2.75–$3.50).

One of the nicer areas in town for a leisurely stroll is the fashionable **Plaza de los Sapos,** where shops sell typical Pueblan wares, restaurants beckon with their rich aromas, and fountains provide the soothing sounds of running water.

AFRICAN SAFARI

This zoo, founded in 1972 on the outskirts of Puebla, is considered by many to be the best in the country. The animals here roam around freely, while you, the visitor, snap photos from the safety of a bus or private car. More than 3,000 animals representing 250 African species live here, including lions, giraffes, and zebras. African Safari buses ($1.75) leave every hour 10–4 from Puebla's CAPU (*see* By Bus *in* Coming and Going, *above*). *Tel. 22/35–86–07. Admission: $5. Open daily 10–5.*

CASA DE ALFENIQUE

Known as the wedding-cake house, this 17th-century mansion is now a state museum. Exhibits on the second floor focus on Puebla's history and archaeology. On the third floor is a re-creation of a colonial-era residence and a small chapel. Also here is the original dress of the legendary China Poblana (*see box, below*). *4 Ote. 416, tel. 22/41–42–96. 2 blocks north and 1 block east of the zócalo. Museum admission: $1.25. Open Tues.–Sun. 10–5.*

CASA DE LA CULTURA

This grand, two-story building was once the residence of Juan de Palafox y Mendoza, the Archbishop of Puebla, and later served as a convent and then a civic building. It now houses the Casa de la Cultura (literally, House of Culture), complete with concert and lecture hall, movie theater (*see* Cinemas and Theaters, *below*), playhouse, and art galleries. Sharing the second floor is the luxurious **Biblioteca Palafoxiana,** a library that dates back to 1646. Monks used to study on the uncomfortable-looking pull-out benches along the walls. Next door to the library is the newly opened **Sala del Tesoro Bibliográfico,** with rotating displays of antique books. The oldest book in the collection is a 1493 history of the world from the beginning of time to the date of publication. Miguel Ramírez Meya, the head librarian, is hard of hearing and very protective of the library and books, but he's more than willing to lecture you on anything to do with the library and possesses a wealth of library lore. Both libraries are nonlending. *5 Ote. 5, tel. 22/46–19–66. Across from the cathedral. Casa de la Cultura admission free. Library admission: $1.25. Open Tues.–Sun. 10–5.*

CATEDRAL DE LA CONCEPCION INMACULADA

Construction on the cathedral began in 1575, and it's clear why it took 90 years to complete: This is one of the largest cathedrals in Mexico, with 14 chapels and the highest bell towers in the country. According to local legend, one of the towers' bells, too heavy to be lifted by mere men, was installed by angels. The massive, gray-blue stone building is an example of the *mudéjar* (Moorish-influenced) style and boasts marble floors and a beautiful altar carved from gray onyx, as well as 300-year-old paintings and an 18th-century pipe organ. The altar at the center also functions as a crypt: The bishops of Puebla are buried here, and every November 2 (Day of the Dead) the crypt is opened to the public. The bell tower on the north side of the church has a stairway (admission 70¢; open daily 11–2) with beautiful views of Puebla at the top. *On the zócalo. Cathedral open daily 7–12:30 and 4–8.*

CONVENTO SECRETO DE SANTA MONICA

The convent first opened in 1688 as a spiritual refuge for women whose husbands were away on transatlantic business trips, later became a home for "fallen" women, and was finally dedicated as an Augustinian convent for women who chose to give their lives to the church, as well as for young girls whose wealthy parents chose an ecclesiastical life for them. In the 1850s, the Reform Laws of Benito Juarez required that all religious buildings be abandoned and turned over to the government. Nevertheless, the convent continued to function until 1934, requiring the nuns to completely withdraw from the outside world (sympathizers slipped them food through secret compartments). Today, Spanish-speaking guides show visitors the peepholes through which the nuns watched mass performed in the church next door, and tour the underground crypt where nuns were buried. In a gruesome display you'll see the preserved 130-year-old heart of the convent's founder. Religious art fills the twisting hallways. The velvet paintings from the 1850s are startling; as you move from one side of the painting to the other, the faces and feet of the subjects seem to change position. *18 Pte., near 5 de Mayo, tel. 22/32–01–78. 9 blocks north of the zócalo. Admission: $1.25. Open Tues.–Sun. 10–5.*

Around the corner is **Señor de las Maravillas,** a much-visited statue of Christ that is believed by poblanos to perform miracles. The figure is said to be made from corn paste, but it looks remarkably similar to plaster. According to legend, the statue was fashioned by a fugitive carpenter hiding out in the convent. He and the Mother Superior both dreamed of the Señor on the same night, after which she ordered him to create this figure or be turned over to the police.

EX-CONVENTO DE SANTA ROSA

The centerpiece of this remodeled convent is a huge, tile colonial kitchen—the supposed birthplace of mole poblano. Most of the building is now devoted to the **Museo de Artesanías,** featuring folk art from Puebla state's seven regions. From 1697 to 1861, the building was a convent, after which it became a private psychiatric hospital. After serving a lengthy stint as an apartment building, it was remodeled and opened as a museum in 1972. Free tours are offered in Spanish only. *14 Pte. 301, tel. 22/46–45–26. 1 block west and 6 blocks north of the zócalo. Admission: 70¢. Open Tues.–Sun. 10–5.*

FUERTES DE LORETO Y GUADALUPE

A popular destination for both poblanos and tourists, these two forts are the main attraction of a hilltop park complex. **Fuerte de Loreto** is dedicated to the Battle of Puebla (May 5, 1862), and the original cannons used to defeat the French army now guard the grave of victorious General Zaragoza. Other aspects of the battle are exhibited in the **Museo de Historia** within the fort, but don't make a special trip just to see the museum. Across the plaza is the **Fuerte de Guadalupe,** which is not as well preserved. The complex features a cluster of museums: the **Museo de Antropología Regional,** exhibiting artifacts from the early Puebla Valley cultures; the **Museo de Historia Natural,** with realistic wildlife scenes; and the excellent **planetario** (planetarium), featuring shows for stargazers hourly noon–6 PM. Admission prices are separate for each museum ($1.25 each) but it's all free on Sunday. *Take FUERTES combi from 8 Nte., at 10 Ote, or RUTA 72 combi from anywhere on 5 de Mayo after 8 Pte., and get off at Monumento Zaragoza; museums are to the east. Open Tues.–Sun. 10–4:30.*

IGLESIA DE SAN FRANCISCO

Built in the 18th century, this church houses the preserved body of Franciscan Friar Sebastián de Aparicio, who is credited with convincing the Indians to stop carrying heavy loads on their backs and let oxen do the work instead. His skeleton is covered with a monk's robe, there's a mask covering his face (reportedly because so many people have picked pieces from it), and his decomposed toes peek out from beneath his robe. It's not a sight for queasy stomachs. Above the friar's body hangs Hernán Cortés's personal statue of the Virgin Mary, the famous *Conquistadora.* Her bloodstained gown is enough to make you shudder. *8 Nte., at 5 de Mayo. 3 blocks east and 5 blocks north of zócalo. Admission free. Open daily 9–7:30.*

IGLESIA DE SANTO DOMINGO

This church dates from 1659 and acquired its fame because of the **Capilla del Rosario** (Chapel of the Rosary), a baroque chapel with a surfeit of gold leaf and glitter that took 40 years to build. Locals refer to it as the eighth wonder of the world, and it is quite a sight to behold. Notice the tiny dog with a firebrand in its mouth at the feet of St. Domingo; it's an image that came to the saint in a dream and represents the light of God. Free and interesting eight-minute tours are offered in Spanish 9:30–12:30 and 4–6. Three doors north of the church lies the free **Museo Bello Zetina** (tel. 22/32–47–20; open Tues.–Sun. 10–5), the preserved home of the wealthy José Luis Bello family. The ornate home displays paintings and ceramics from around the world and includes a living room decorated in the French style during the reign of Napoléon III. *5 de Mayo 407, 1 block north of the zócalo. Church open daily 7 AM–8 PM.*

MUSEO AMPARO

The airy, terra-cotta-color colonial building used to function as a hospital. Now it serves as a huge museum specializing in both *virreinal* (viceregal) and Mesoamerican art, with beautiful examples of Mayan, Olmec, and other artifacts on display. Interactive computer displays inform visitors about selected pieces in the museum. Signs in English and Spanish guide you through the exhibits or you can listen to a recorded audio tour (70¢ plus $1 deposit). Guides are available for tours in Spanish for $7 per hour (there's a free tour Sunday at noon). *2 Sur 708, at 9 Ote., tel. 22/46–46–46. 2½ blocks south of the zócalo. Admission: $1.25; free Mon. Open daily 10–6.*

MUSEO DE LA REVOLUCION

Known as **Casa de los Hermanos Serdán,** this former house of Aquiles Serdán and his sister Carmen now honors these two heroes and their band of revolutionaries who perished here in 1910. The group was killed after 14 hours of gunfight with the police and 500 federal army soldiers who were sent to arrest them on conspiracy charges. Though the building's facade is intact, it bears the violent marks of the fight. In the parlor, pierced mirrors still hang on bullet-riddled walls, and broadsheets calling for revolution, published by the Serdán family, are on display. The assassination of Aquiles Serdán and his followers is believed by many to be the event that launched the Revolution of 1910. *6 Ote. 206, tel. 22/42–10–76. 3 blocks north of the zócalo. Admission: 1.25; free Tues. Open Tues.–Sun. 10–4:30.*

FESTIVALS

Every year on Mardi Gras (six weeks before Easter), the residents of the nearby town of Huejotzingo reenact the kidnapping of a *corregidor's* (magistrate) daughter as part of the story of the Mexican triumph against the French. The costumes and masks of **Carnaval de Huejotzingo** are elaborate, and the festival is noisy and sometimes dangerous—the tradition of shooting colored gunpowder at celebrants often results in injuries. Buses to Huejotzingo (1 hr, $1) depart from the CAPU bus terminal; the last bus back to Puebla leaves the village at 9 PM. The **Feria Regional de Puebla** (April 23–May 20) celebrates the diversity of Puebla, combining agricultural and livestock expositions, industrial and mechanical productions, cultural and sporting events, and the best of *cocina poblana* (Pueblan cooking) and artesanía. On May 5, known as **Cinco de Mayo,** the city commemorates the 1862 Battle of Puebla, in which the Mexican army defeated French invaders. The city center is transformed for a day as fireworks, a military parade, sporting events, and traditional music take over. During the monthlong **Festival de San Agustín** (Aug.), Pueblans celebrate with music, dancing, and fireworks. On August 28 (St. Augustine's feast day) it is customary to prepare chiles en nogada (*see* Food, *above*). The **Fiesta de San Francisco de Asis–Cuetzalán** (Oct. 4) is two weeks of indigenous dances, a *tianguis* (open-air market), and general merrymaking in the tiny town of Cuetzalán (*see* Near Puebla, *below*). Dancers wear traditional white robes and *tocas de lana* (large, turbanlike hats almost 1½ ft tall).

SHOPPING

The *majólica* techniques developed in Talavera de la Reina, Spain, are today used for making tiles and other ceramic ware in Puebla. You can learn about the process at **Uriarte** (4 Pte. 911, tel. 22/32–15–98), a factory and shop devoted exclusively to beautiful Talavera ceramics. Free tours in English and Spanish take place daily 9–6. If the workers aren't too busy,

> *The tiny town of Amozoc was originally an ancient Nahuatl settlement on a low mountain range. Its name means "where there is no mud" in Nahuatl, and today it is famous for its intricate silver work.*

they may even let you try your hand at the potter's wheel. You'll find more Talavera pieces, including dishes and vases, at **El Parián** (6 Nte., between 4 Ote. and 2 Ote.), a market that's been around since 1796. Nowadays the more artistic pieces are mixed in with a lot of cheap stuff, but it's a fun place to poke around and haggle. Across the street is the **Barrio del Artista** (8 Nte., at 6 Ote.), where painters and sculptors open their studios to visitors. On 5 Oriente and 6 Norte you'll find an upscale antique market known as **Mercado de Los Sapos,** popular with students and wealthy locals. Fakes have been known to circulate in this market of late, so know your antiques or suffer the consequences.

If you're interested in intricate silver work visit **Amozoc,** 16 km (9½ mi) east of Puebla. This town is famous for *charrería* (silver rodeo gear). Basically, that means lots of shiny souvenir spurs and horse bridles. Amozoc's Sunday mercado is a gastronomic extravaganza, known for its fresh fish, avocados, and *pulque* (an alcoholic beverage made from the fermented juice of the maguey cactus). Second-class AMOZOC buses ($1) leave from the corner of 14 Oriente and 18 Norte in Puebla. Ask to be let off near the zócalo; the town is very small, so you'll have no trouble finding your way around. The last bus to Puebla leaves at 6 PM from Amozoc's main plaza.

Tecali, under an hour's drive from Puebla, is where you'll find the workshops of numerous onyx craftsmen, as well as shops selling their work. **Casatellez,** near the town center, is a store specializing in the local artesanía. From Puebla's CAPU, catch an Autobuses Unidos bus to Tepeaca and transfer there to Tecali; or take a 90¢ combi from the corner of 10 Poniente and 13 Norte in Puebla.

Those interested in Catholic paraphernalia will find plenty in Puebla's stores, including incense, rosaries, and electric "candles" with lights that flicker (for those opposed to the shameless consumption of wax). At **Librería Mariana** (Calles 2 Sur and 3 Ote., across from zócalo) you can buy prayer cards (20¢ each) identifying all those saints you've seen in churches around the city.

AFTER DARK

Pueblans tend to hit the sack around 10:30 on weeknights, but on weekends everyone is out for some sort of adventure, usually involving tequila. In any case, the scene here is amiable; strike up a conversation and you'll be sure to make some new friends.

BARS

Just a five-minute walk southeast of the zócalo, **Plaza de los Sapos** is surrounded by popular bars and restaurants. At Western style **La Bóveda** (6 Sur 503-C, tel. 22/46–55–90), sawdust covers the floor, while the songs of a bohemian, lyrical guitarist fill the air. Next door, **D'Pasadita** is decorated with antique clocks and other unique memorabilia. Speakers blast Mexican and U.S. rock, which seems to please the gregarious crowd. **Los Alambiques** (6 Sur 504, tel. 22/46–35–65) sports a lively gay scene on weekends, while an older gay crowd heads to **El Ceroso** (6 Sur 506-F, tel. 22/32–42–89). The 80-year-old tavern **La Pasita** (3 Sur 504, at 5 Pte.) might be the only bar in the world that serves *La Pasita* (a liqueur made from raisins). Shots of this and other regional liqueurs cost $1 each.

DANCE CLUBS

At **News** (Atlixco 3102, tel. 22/31–13–30; closed Sun.–Wed.), young locals and tourists dance to techno and pop under a constellation of tiny lights. A slightly older crowd lines up for **Freedom** (Circuito Interior 2907, tel. 22/37–74–07; closed Mon.), with rock music and occasional live bands. For the greatest variety, head to the **Zona Esmeralda** district, also called **La Juárez**, on Juárez west of 18 Sur. Most places here charge a $2 cover. This district is far from the center of town, so take a taxi ($1.50).

CINEMAS AND THEATERS

New releases from the United States, either dubbed in Spanish or with Spanish subtitles, are shown at **EcoCinema** (4 Ote. 210, tel. 22/32–19–55). At the Casa de la Cultura (*see* Worth Seeing, *above*), **Cinemática Luis Buñuel** shows $1.25 international and cultural films Wednesday–Sunday at 5 PM and 7:30 PM and free weekend matinees. Both **Teatro Espacio 1900** (2 Ote. 412, tel. 22/46–17–30) and **Teatro Hermanos Soler** (Hotel Camino Real, tel. 22/46–98–15) produce live theater on the weekends. Tickets cost about $4, and events are posted at their respective addresses.

NEAR PUEBLA

There are enough ancient ruins, indigenous villages, and historical points of interest in the region surrounding Puebla to keep you occupied with sightseeing for more than a week, should you wish. Cantona is a new and exciting archaeological site, reachable only by private car or a tour from Puebla. Other attractions are accessible by bus or combi.

CANTONA

Cantona is one of the most recent and spectacular archaeological finds in Mexico, opened to visitors in 1995. The outstanding feature here is the 24 ball courts, which is more than are found at any other known ruin in the country. From afar, Cantona looks like a massive military fortress; up close, it's all nononsense, drab, and solid. Though there's none of the beautiful ornamentation found at other Mexican ruins, it has a striking presence nonetheless. In all, archaeologists have mapped 500 raised cobblestone streets, alleys, and lanes crisscrossing a 13-square-km (5-square-mi) area—which makes this larger than Teotihuacán (*see* Near Mexico City *in* Chapter 2), Cantona's likely archenemy during its heyday in the 7th through 9th centuries AD.

The Cantona ruins are divided into three sections and, so far, only the southern area is open to the public. The highest point, the **Acropolis,** was where civil and religious headquarters stood, as well as palaces of the ruling elite. Be prepared for plenty of hiking—much of it uphill—when you visit the site, and wear sturdy walking shoes or boots. Cantona is 125 km (77½ mi) northeast of Puebla city: Take Highway 129 to Highway 125 to Oriental, then turn onto the dirt road leading to the site. In the rainy season, you can only navigate the access road with a four-wheel drive. There is no public transportation to Cantona, so your only other option for visiting is by guided tour; George Estrada at Puebla's Oficina de Información Turística (*see* Visitor Information *in* Puebla, *above*) leads tours for $38 per person (3-person minimum), transportation included. *Admission: $1.25. Open Tues.–Sun. 9–5.*

CHOLULA

Only 20 minutes east of Puebla by bus, the town of Cholula is gringo friendly, with signs and menus in English, and shops and restaurants that accept credit cards. Best of all, the 65,000 Cholulan residents are extremely helpful and much less harried than their Pueblan neighbors. The women of this town are much more open to conversation than they are in many other places, an aspect of life here that will put female travelers at ease. The town's centro is small and quiet, and much of it caters to the multitude of tourists passing through to see the **Great Pyramid** (*see* Worth Seeing, *below*). Cholula is also home to respected Universidad de las Américas.

Before the Spanish Conquest, Cholula reportedly had hundreds of temples and rivaled Teotihuacán as a cultural and ceremonial center. The *mercado-santuario* (market-sanctuary) system was developed here in AD 1200, whereby satellite cities of Cholula exchanged cultural ideas and began trading with the Gulf region and Oaxaca. When Cortés arrived, colonialism and Catholicism were strictly enforced, and according to local legend, conquering Spaniards built a church for each day of the year atop the ruins of Cholulan temples. Although the number is exaggerated, there are approximately 70 churches in Cholula and the surrounding areas today.

COMING AND GOING

In Puebla, catch a PUEBLA/CHOLULA combi (30¢) from the bus stop on the corner of 11 Norte and 14 Poniente, or take an Estrella de Oro or Estrella Roja bus from CAPU (*see* Coming and Going *in* Puebla, *above*). Buses run about every 10 minutes and cost 50¢. The bus stop in Cholula is at the corner of 5 de Mayo and 5 Poniente; to reach the zócalo from here, walk south on 5 de Mayo for three blocks. To reach Cholula by car, take the Puebla–Cholula highway ($2.50 toll).

Pueblans like to joke that their neighbors, the Cholulans, strike the perfect balance between faith and sin by living in a town with an equal number of bars and churches.

WHERE TO SLEEP

Cholula doesn't offer many affordable hotels. The oldest hotel in Cholula, tiny **Hotel Reforma** (4 Sur 101, tel. 22/47–01–49) is run by a friendly, talkative señora. Doubles with bath cost $7–$10. The 70-room **Hotel Las Américas** (14 Ote. 6, tel. 22/47–22–75) charges $10 for a double, with private bath. It's close to the nightclub zone, but a 10-minute hike from the zócalo and most bus stops. Both hotels accept cash only.

Campsites are available at the invitingly named **Trailer Park Las Américas** (30 Ote. 602, tel. 22/47–01–34), a five-minute bus ride west of Cholula. Pitching a two-person tent costs $5. Hot showers and swimming facilities are available, but it's not the most scenic spot.

FOOD

Several restaurants serving Italian food are clustered on the zócalo: **Los Jarrones** (tel. 22/47–02–92) serves good pizzas, huge burgers, and salads, all priced less than $3. **Güero's** (Hidalgo 101, tel. 22/47–21–88), on the road to the pyramid, is the most popular joint in town. Locals love the nachos, pizza, and *comida típica* (traditional Mexican food) priced $4 for a meal. Two traditional restaurants near the pyramid, **La Lunita** (Morelos, at 6 Nte., tel. 22/47–00–11) and **La Pirámide** (Morelos 416, tel. 22/47–02–54) are popular with locals and serve chicken with mole or *pipián* (chile and pumpkinseed sauce), and *filete milanesa* (breaded steak) for $3. All of the above accept cash only.

WORTH SEEING

CHIPILO • A five-minute bus ride past the villages of Santa María Tonantzintla and San Francisco Acatepec (*see below*) is a town with a startling population of blond, blue-eyed north Italian immigrants. Chipilo was founded in 1882 when dictator Porfirio Díaz imported a group of white, Catholic Venetians in an attempt to "save the nation." The inhabitants adamantly proclaim themselves *mexicanos* who just happen to uphold Italian traditions and speak Italian. The town's excellent sausage, cheese, and dairy products—which make their markets and Italian restaurants famous throughout the region—are an excellent reason to visit. **El Correo Español** (tel. 22/83–05–29), on the road to Chipilo, serves excellent Spanish and Italian food for less than $10. **Centro Artesanal** (tel. 22/83–07–82; open daily 10–7), also on the main road, sells beautiful arts, crafts, and hand-carved wood furniture. To reach Chipilo from Cholula, take a CHIPILO bus (15 min, 30¢) from 5 de Mayo and 6 Poniente and tell the driver where you're headed. From the bus you'll see a lone sign for the town across from the Central Artesanal.

GREAT PYRAMID • Cholula's Great Pyramid actually consists of seven different structures built one on top of the other by seven successive cultures. The final pyramid has a base measuring 14,800 square ft and would have been the largest in the world if it had not been finished. Construction started under the Cholulteca, a mix of people from several regions of Mexico, but ended around AD 650 when they were attacked and conquered by warriors from nearby Cacaxtla. Later arrivals, the Toltec, made further additions and dedicated the Great Pyramid to the god Quetzalcóatl. Centuries after them the Aztec, who also worshipped Quetzalcóatl, moved in and used the pyramid as a ceremonial center. The $2 admission (free Sunday) entitles visitors to explore nearly 6 km (4 mi) of underground tunnels built by archaeologists during the Great Pyramid's excavation. Guides, available at the tunnel entrance, charge $4.50 per person ($5 for the English version) for a one-hour tour of the site. *Open daily 10–5.*

A museum across the road from the pyramid explains what you'll see in the tunnels. Also outside the Great Pyramid compound is a smaller, nicely restored pyramid built by the Toltecs and dating to AD 1300. If you're not totally exhausted, hike up the hill just past the site's exit to the small **Iglesia Nuestra Señora de los Remedios,** built in 1666 on top of a precolonial temple. Adjacent to the Iglesia is the **capilla** (chapel) where people leave offerings to the Virgin Mary, such as charms, long braids of hair, baby clothes, and letters. To reach the Great Pyramid from Cholula's zócalo, walk east (away from the volcanoes) along Morelos for three blocks.

SANTA MARIA TONANTZINTLA/SAN FRANCISCO ACATEPEC • Separated by a five-minute bus ride, these villages, 3 km (2 mi) south of Cholula, are home to a pair of unique colonial churches. The **Iglesia de Santa María Tonantzintla** took almost 300 years to build and is the only church in the republic designed and built exclusively by Indians. The interior is a curious mix of baroque and indigenous aesthetics—an explosion of bright colors and gilt. On the plaster ceiling, look for images of indigenous gods such as Quetzalcóatl (god of the sun) and Tlaloc (god of rain). Also, note that the angels and cherubs have Indian features (as does the Jesus on the cross to the left of the altar) and that the statue of the Virgin is framed in neon. The graves of children taken by an early death are marked by the stones in the path leading up to the church.

The village of Acatepec boasts the 16th-century **Iglesia de San Francisco Acatepec,** decorated on the outside with blue, yellow, and green Talavera tiles. Inside, the recently remodeled interior (the original was destroyed by fire in 1939) rivals that of Santa María Tonantzintla's church in amount of gilt per square inch. Both churches are open to visitors daily 10–6. Red-and-white CHIPILO buses leave from the corner of 5 de Mayo and 6 Poniente in Cholula; ask the driver to let you off at either church. Buses run frequently, so it's easy to hop on another to reach the second church.

ZOCALO • Down the hill, seven blocks east of the Great Pyramid, is Cholula's zócalo, which supposedly has the longest *portal* (porch) in Latin America. Along the portal are several shops, boutiques, and restaurants. Try to visit the zócalo on Sunday (market day), or a saint's day celebration (considering the number of churches in the area, each celebrating at least 10 feast days annually, stumbling across one shouldn't be difficult). Facing the zócalo is the mustard-yellow **Convento Franciscano,** resembling a medieval castle. It was built in 1549 on the site of a temple dedicated to Quetzalcoatl; Cortés's troops and their Tlaxcaltecan allies massacred thousands of Cholulans here. The **Capilla Real** (Royal Chapel) inside the convent is unique in that it has 49 domes, inspired by the Great Mosque of Córdoba, Spain.

AFTER DARK

With the Universidad de las Américas on the east side of town, Cholula is enough of a happening place that even Pueblans come here for a change of scene. **Keops** (14 Ote., at 5 de Mayo) is a bright purple building that houses the area's only gay disco. The place to go Thursday–Saturday nights is **Wilo** (tel. 22/47–21–06), with no cover charge and $1 beers. The place is jammed by 11, presided over by a friendly owner best known as *el chofo* (the chauffeur).

CUETZALAN

Although this town is four hours north of Puebla, it's worth visiting, as the indigenous population has preserved many of its traditional customs. The best day to visit is Sunday (market day) when the Totonac and Nahua peoples come down from the *cerro* (hill)—the men dressed in striking *huipiles* (embroidered tunics), and the women in elaborate, towering headdresses. Most people are here to attend a Catholic mass given in Totonac, the local language. On October 4, the feast day of St. Francis is celebrated (*see* Festivals *in* Puebla, *above*). The place to stay is **Hotel Posada Viky** (Guadalupe Victoria 16, tel. 233/1–02–72), which charges $7 per person. There is a **tourist office** (Miguel Hidalgo, tel. 233/1–00–04) in Cuetzalán, although the office in Puebla (*see* Visitor Information *in* Puebla, *above*) provides information as well. From Puebla's CAPU terminal, **VIA** buses depart daily 6:20 AM–7:15 PM for Cuetzalán ($1).

CUERNAVACA

Cuernavaca lies in the shadow of the great Popocatépetl volcano, on the rich agricultural plateau of Morelos state. Despite problems of poverty, pollution, and population growth (the city will soon have 2 million residents), Morelos's prosperous state capital continues to attract a steady stream of visitors. Travelers come from all over the world to study in the city's numerous language schools, visit historical sites, or simply laze in its plazas amidst flowering trees and fountains. Mexicans make up the largest tourist group and many wealthy and famous *chilangos* (residents of Mexico City), attracted by Cuernavaca's mild year-round climate, buy second homes in Cuernavaca. However, these are only the most recent groups to shape Cuernavaca's character. At the ancient ruins of nearby Xochicalco, bas-relief sculptures suggest that this once-powerful religious center was influenced by the Maya, who dwelled south of Morelos. In the 1300s, the indigenous Tlahuican struggled against the Aztec, who attempted to enforce their supremacy by building new structures around existing Tlahuican pyramids. Ruins of these imposing structures can still be found in Cuernavaca and neighboring Tepoztlán. However, it wasn't until Cortés's brutal devastation of most native cities two centuries later that Tlahuican rule crumbled.

Despite this history of foreign domination, *cuernavaquenses* (Cuernavaca residents) aren't easily pushed around. The state of Morelos, where revolutionary leader Emiliano Zapata began his movement for agrarian reform, was a whirl of activity during the Mexican Revolution in the early 1900s. Today, however, people here take things slow and easy, often pausing to practice English with willing foreigners.

BASICS

AMERICAN EXPRESS

The AmEx office is in the **Marin travel agency,** in the Las Plazas shopping center. Exchange traveler's checks, cash personal checks, or have your mail held at the following address: Edificio Las Plazas, Local 13, Gutemberg 101, Col. Centro, Cuernavaca, Morelos, CP 62000, México. *Across from the zócalo, tel. 73/14–22–66. AmEx service available weekdays 9–2 and 4–6, Sat. 10–1.*

BOOKSTORES

A unique **bookstore** with a small selection of English books is in Jardín Borda (*see* Worth Seeing, *below*). For a wide selection of Spanish books, visit the **Libería Cristal** (Gutemberg 3, Edificio de las Plazas, Local 38, tel. 73/12–70–00; open Mon.–Sat. 10–9). They also sell tapes, videos, posters, and greeting cards.

CASAS DE CAMBIO

You'll find several casas de cambio along Dwight Morrow, near the budget lodging area. Among the most reputable are **Gesta** (Lerdo de Tejada 2, tel. 73/18–22–87) and **Master Dollar** (Dwight Morrow 7-B, tel. 73/12–93–71), both open weekdays 9–6, Saturday 9–2. **Banamex** (Matamoros 6, at Arteaga, tel. 73/18–17–35; open weekdays 9–5) changes money and has ATMs that accept Plus, Cirrus, Visa, and MasterCard.

EMERGENCIES

Dial 06 from any telephone in Cuernavaca for **police, fire,** or **ambulance** service.

LAUNDRY

Only two blocks from the budget hotel area, **Tintorería y Lavandería Morelos** charges $3 to clean 3½ kilos (7½ pounds) of laundry. They offer same-day service if you hand over your clothes before 10 AM. The staff is friendly and helpful and can also answer general tourist questions about Cuernavaca. *Matamoros 406, tel. 73/10–05–10. Open Mon.–Sat. 9–8.*

MAIL

The **post office** will hold your mail at the following address for up to 10 days: Lista de Correos, Administración 1, Cuernavaca, Morelos, CP 62001, México. Faxes, telexes, and telegrams can be sent and received at the **telecommunications office** (tel. 73/14–31–81, fax 73/18–00–77) in the same building. *SW corner of Plaza de Armas, tel. 73/12–43–79. Open weekdays 8–7, Sat. until 1.*

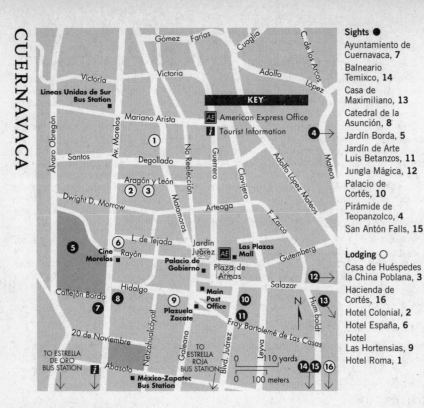

CUERNAVACA

Sights ●

Ayuntamiento de
Cuernavaca, **7**

Balneario
Temixco, **14**

Casa de
Maximiliano, **13**

Catedral de la
Asunción, **8**

Jardín Borda, **5**

Jardín de Arte
Luis Betanzos, **11**

Jungla Mágica, **12**

Palacio de
Cortés, **10**

Pirámide de
Teopanzolco, **4**

San Antón Falls, **15**

Lodging ○

Casa de Huéspedes
la China Poblana, **3**

Hacienda de
Cortés, **16**

Hotel Colonial, **2**

Hotel España, **6**

Hotel
Las Hortensias, **9**

Hotel Roma, **1**

MEDICAL AID

Some of the staff at **Hospital Civil** (Domingo Diez, at Guadalajara, tel. 73/11–22–09) speaks English. Next door is the 24-hour **Farmacia Cuernavaca** (Dr. Gómez Azcarte 200, Col. Lomas de la Selva, tel. 73/11–41–11, fax 73/17–47–59).

PHONES

Cuernavaca's zócalo is graced with several **Ladatel** phones; dial **09** to make an overseas collect call. **Caseta Morelos** (Pasaje Galeana 4, tel. 73/18–30–31; open daily 8 AM–9 PM), in a minimall across from Plaza de Armas, charges $1.50 per minute for cash calls to the United States, and 25¢ per minute for collect calls.

SCHOOLS

Cuernavaca is home to dozens of schools offering intensive language and cultural classes, including **Encuentros** (Encuentros Comunicación y Cultura, AP 2-71, CP 62158, Cuernavaca, Morelos, México; tel. 73/14–07–78) and the **Spanish Language Institute,** which is run by **Language Link** (Box 3006, Peoria, IL, tel. 800/552–2051, fax 309/692–2926).

Classes at **Cuauhnáhuac Escuela Cuernavaca** are limited to eight students per Spanish class. Registration is $70, and weeklong classes cost $180 ($600 per month). For more information write to: AP 5-26, Cuernavaca, Morelos, CP 62051, México. *Morelos Sur 123, Col. Chipitlán, tel. 73/12–36–73 or 73/18–92–75. U.S. contact: Marcia Snell, tel. 800/245–9335 ext. 154.*

Another highly respected school in Cuernavaca is the **Center of Bilingual Multicultural Studies** (tel. 73/17–06–94, fax 73/17–05–33). Placement is into one of four levels, and grammar classes never comprise more than five students. Cost of instruction runs $170–$230 per week. For more information write to: San Jerónimo 304, Col. Tlaltenango, AP 1520, Cuernavaca, Morelos, CP 62000, México.

VISITOR INFORMATION

Although English-speaking, friendly, and eager to help, the staff at the **state tourist office** is coping with severe budget cuts. Spanish information on language schools and various sights will be photocopied for you, but the free map is less than useful—significant streets are covered by advertising logos. Better maps can be purchased at most *papelerías* (stationery stores) for $5. For tourist information in English, your best bet is to chat with Joel or Alex at **Tintorería y Lavandería Morelos** (*see* Laundry, *above*). At least one of them is usually around, and they are authorities on day trips and nightspots. *Morelos Sur 802, tel. 73/14–38–72. Take RUTA 4 combi down Galeana to Himno Nacional, then walk 1 block west. Open Mon.–Sat. 8 AM–9 PM.*

VOLUNTEERING

Desarrollo Integral de la Familia (DIF) provides health care, education, and counseling to communities in Morelos. If you plan to be in the area for two weeks or longer and are interested in volunteering, contact Alejandro Vera Jiménez. *Chapultepec 25, tel. 73/15–51–68. Take a RUTA 11 combi from corner of Las Casas and Leyva.*

COMING AND GOING

During April, Cuervavaca hosts a two-week Feria de la Primavera (Spring Festival), established by horticulturists in 1865 to promote the local flower industry.

BY BUS

Those traveling by bus will find themselves at one of Cuernavaca's four bus stations. The largest is **Lineas Unidas de Sur** (Morelos 503, at Arista), two blocks from the budget lodging area. It houses the **Estrella Blanca/Flecha Roja** lines (tel. 73/12–81–90), which send hourly buses to Mexico City (1 hr, $3). First-class *directo* (direct) buses to Acapulco (5 hrs, $11.50) leave every two hours; air-conditioning and a TV bump the price up to $14.50. Directo buses to Taxco (2 hrs; $4 deluxe, $3 1st class) depart every three hours until 10:30 PM. Hourly *ordinario* (indirect) buses to Acapulco (7 hrs, $8.50) stop in Chilpancingo (3 hrs, $5). The station offers luggage storage (75¢ for 5 hrs, 20¢ each additional hr).

A 10-minute walk from the zócalo, the dark and dingy **Estrella Roja** station (Galeana 401, at Cuauhtémotzin, tel. 73/18–59–34) serves Cuautla (1 hr, $2) every 30 minutes 6:15 AM–10:15 PM; transfer in Cuautla for Oaxaca city. Buses to Puebla (3½ hrs, $4) leave every hour 5 AM–7 PM. The budget hotels are seven blocks from the station—take any CENTRO combi down Morelos to Aragón y Léon.

The remaining two bus stations are less significant. You'll probably only visit **México-Zacatepec Autos Pullman de Morelos** (Abasolo 12, at Netzahualcóyotl, tel. 73/14–36–50) to reach Xochicalco (*see* Near Cuernavaca, *below*); buses to Coatlán or Miocatlán will drop you off at the Xochicalco crossroads. On the outskirts of the city center, **Estrella de Oro** (Morelos Sur 900, tel. 73/12–30–55) is a *de paso* station, which means buses only stop here en route to somewhere else, and departure times are not dependable.

BY CAR

The new Mexico–Acapulco highway passes through Cuernavaca and is in excellent condition. Tolls total $5.50 to Mexico City and $48 to Acapulco. To reach Puebla, drive on the Cuernavaca–Cuatla highway until you see the sign for Cuatla–Puebla.

BY PLANE

Cuernevaca doesn't have its own airport, but Mexico City's International Airport is just an hour's drive away. **Aerotransporte Terrestre** (tel. 73/18–91–87) buses make the trip ($6) hourly, Monday–Saturday 5 AM–midnight. If you're arriving in Mexico City and need transportation to Cuernavaca, look for the ticket kiosk in the main concourse beneath the giant Á.

GETTING AROUND

Exploring Cuernavaca is not difficult; the budget hotel zone, major sights, and main bus stations are all within walking distance of one another. The zócalo, at the center of town, is actually composed of two plazas: **Jardín Juárez** and **Plaza de Armas**. The main streets in Cuernavaca are Morelos, with northbound traffic only, and on either side of Morelos, Obregón, and Matamoros/Galeana, both of which allow only southbound traffic. Colectivos and combis are the major means of daytime travel within Cuernavaca besides walking. Drivers cram in as many passengers as possible, and the 25¢ fare will get you almost anywhere in town. The name of the final destination is painted with whitewash on the front window, but routes vary, so double-check before boarding. You'll have to travel by taxi if you plan to sample Cuernavaca's nightlife, as colectivos stop running after 10 PM. Negotiate your fare before you get in—taxis don't have meters. Generally the fare within the centro is $1.50, plus an additional $1.25 for travel to outlying neighborhoods. Late at night, fares shoot up to as much as $5. A reliable cab service is **Radio Taxi Ejecutivo** (tel. 73/22–12–02).

WHERE TO SLEEP

Cuernavaca's budget lodging area lies along and around Aragón y León, a few blocks south of the Lineas Unidas de Sur bus station and north of the zócalo. The city's hotels tend to fill up on Fridays and weekends, so be sure to make reservations. If the places below are booked, try the beautiful **Hotel Las Hortensias** (Hidalgo 22, tel. 73/18–52–65), which has a pleasant courtyard and lumpy beds. A double here is $17. The hotel accepts cash only.

UNDER $10 • Casa de Huéspedes la China Poblana. Tucked behind the restaurant of the same name, this hotel is clean and spacious, though unattractive. Rooms ($7 doubles) all have tidy private baths. *Aragón y León 110, tel. 73/12–37–12. 17 rooms, all with bath. Luggage storage. Reservations advised. Cash only.*

Hotel Roma. The sunny courtyard with palm trees is more inviting than the hotel's clean, basic rooms with tiny bathrooms. Still, you can't beat the prices: Doubles cost $9, and quads are only $15. *Matamoros 17, tel. 73/18–87–78. 1 block east of Flech Roja station. 40 rooms, all with bath. Cash only.*

UNDER $20 • Hotel Colonial. This hotel is at the center of the budget lodging area, but it's a step above the competition. The large, clean rooms have high ceilings, and some boast wrought-iron terraces. Others don't even have windows, so ask to see a few before paying. The young staff is friendly and helpful, and silence is observed beginning at 10 PM. Doubles cost $13–$16. *Aragón y León 104, tel. 73/18–64–14. 14 rooms, all with bath. Luggage storage. Cash only.*

Hotel España. This hotel lives up to its name, with Spanish-style arches, patterned tiles, and palm trees. The first floor contains a Spanish restaurant, a reception area, and a small lounge. Clean rooms ($20 doubles) occupy the second and third floors and surround a courtyard with potted flowers. Although all rooms have TVs, the furniture is worn, some rooms reek of cigarette smoke, and the noise level can be bothersome in rooms that face the street. *Morelos 200, at Rayón, tel. 73/18–67–44. 24 rooms, all with bath. Reservations advised. Cash only.*

UNDER $55 • Hacienda de Cortés. This old hacienda dates to the 16th century and indeed once belonged to Hernán Cortés. It's in the nearby town of Atlacomulco, a $2 cab ride from downtown Cuernavaca. Rooms lack TVs but are beautifully decorated with traditional old Mexican furnishings. (For TV addicts, there's a television room off the lobby.) Outside, lovely gardens, patios, and a pool beckon. Doubles cost $54. *Plaza Kennedy 90, Atlacomulco, tel. 73/15–88–44. Take RUTA 8 combi from corner of Morelos and Ortega. 22 rooms, all with bath. Restaurant, bar, luggage storage. Reservations advised.*

FOOD

Small, cheap restaurants abound in the budget lodging area and on the streets surrounding the zócalo. Most serve a mix of *antojitos* (appetizers) and tourist grub such as burgers and fries. On your culinary tour of town, look for the following Morelos specialties: *tamales de frijole* (bean tamales) from Axochiapan; *tamales de bagre* (catfish tamales) from Miacatlán; mole *verde,* also called mole *pipián* (the same recipe as Puebla's famous mole poblano but with green salsa instead of red), from Laguna de Coatetelco; *cecina de yecapixtla,* a dry, salty beef; and *tacos acorazados,* tortillas filled with rice, beans, or whatever your heart desires.

In addition to the eateries listed below, try **Los Arcos** (Jardín de los Héroes 4, tel. 73/12–44–86), a popular patio restaurant with a sparkling fountain, shady trees, and a generous $3 comida corrida. **La Universal** (Guerrero 2, tel. 73/18–67–32) serves stingier portions of traditional food to a crowd of gringos, but the $2 daiquiris may prompt you to forget its faults. These two restaurants accept cash only. The daily **Mercado Principal** (central market; off Guerrero, north of the zócalo) also offers cheap eats, but this market has a reputation for being particularly unhygienic.

UNDER $5 • Gin Gen Comida China. If you're looking for a break from tacos and *tortas* (sandwiches), this sharp, red-and-white restaurant won't disappoint. Mexican/American fare fills the breakfast menu and Chinese food is served afternoon and evening. The restaurant is run by a husband and wife team; she is the chef and he is the artist whose paintings grace the walls. Both are well-versed in many languages and create an entertaining environment. *Rayón, at Alarcón, tel. 73/18–60–46. Cash only.*

Naturiza. For generous portions of creative vegetarian cooking, come here. The menu changes daily, featuring seasonal delights like creamed carrot soup and cauliflower dumplings. Comidas corridas run $2.50, and the à la carte breakfasts, like granola and yogurt or omeletes, are even cheaper. You can buy vitamins at a small counter in the back of the restaurant. *Alvaro Obregón 327-1, between Victoria and Ricardo Linares, tel. 73/12–46–26. Closed Sun. Cash only.*

Restaurant El Salto. In the village of San Antón, this off-the-beaten-track eatery fills daily with savvy *cuernavaquenses*. The menu includes fish, chicken, and game dishes, served in pottery made in the village. The most expensive entrée is pigeon for two ($4); other specialties include garlic soup, cactus tamales, and a bowl-size rum-and-tequila "Convento" ($2.50). *Bajada del Salto 31, San Antón, tel. 73/ 18–12–19. Take RUTA 4 combi from Artega, at Morelos. Cash only.*

UNDER $10 • Los Pasteles de Vienes. Continental cuisine and European-style pastries are served here, while lace curtains and jazz music float on the breeze. Its location, around the corner from the Teatro Ocampo (*see* After Dark, *below*), makes it a great spot to grab a cappuccino after the show. Recommended dishes include the veal cutlet in wine and mushroom sauce ($8), asparagus and ham in béarnaise sauce, and spinach crepes. *Lerdo de Tejada 302, at I. Comonfort, tel. 73/14–34–04. Cash only.*

La Strada. Rub shoulders with expats as you savor Italian food on a candelit colonial patio. You can't go wrong with the fish dishes, pastas, or pizzas. On weekends, the chef whips up specials-of-the-day that include main dishes for $7.50–$9. Friday evening there's a guitarist. *Salazar 3, tel. 73/18–60–85. Around the corner from Palacio de Cortés. No breakfast. Closed Mon. Reservations advised for dinner.*

For a glimpse at daily life in Cuernavaca, visit Mercado Principal López Mateos. Here, women hawk mounds of chiles, and eloquent herbolarios (herb vendors) will guarantee a cure for whatever ails you.

WORTH SEEING

The zócalo is the heart of Cuernavaca; it's made up of the **Plaza de Armas,** where you can unwind beside the fountain, and the more lively **Jardín Juárez,** the oldest park in the city. There are enough attractions near the zócalo to fill an entire day of sightseeing. Other points of interest, particularly Casa de Maximiliano, the Jungla Mágica, San Antón Falls, and Pirámide de Teopanzolco, are in outlying *colonias* (neighborhoods), for which you'll need to take combis. Most museums and historical sites are closed on Monday.

AYUNTAMIENTO DE CUERNAVACA

Also known as the Palacio Municipal, the Ayuntamiento displays murals by 17th-century Spanish muralist Salvador Tarazona. These depict Cuernavaca's history and scenes from the Tlahuican civilization. *Morelos 199, at Callejón Borda. Admission free. Open weekdays 8–8.*

BALNEARIO TEMIXCO

This aquatic park offers 15 swimming pools, 10 wading pools, multiple water slides, sports fields, gardens, and a full bar. Originally a 16th-century sugar plantation, it was used as a fort in the Mexican Revolution and as a prisoner-of-war camp during World War II. From downtown, it's an 8-km (5-mi) 30-minute bus ride; ask the driver to let you off at the gate. *Emiliano Zapata 11, Col. Temixco, tel. 73/25–03–55. Take TEMIXCO combi from Galeana. Admission: $4.50. Open daily 9–6.*

CASA DE MAXIMILIANO

This old adobe house was bought by Emperor Maximilian in the 1860s, and is known as the Casa del Olvido (House of Forgetfulness). One reason given for this name is that the French-appointed emperor came here to escape political and domestic troubles. Another is that he "forgot" to build a room for his wife, Carlota—but made sure to include a small cottage in the garden for his lover, La India Bonita. Today the Casa is home to the **Museo de Medicina Tradicional,** which features exhibits about the me-

THE FOLK MEDICINE OF MORELOS

Morelos is infused with a rich history of herbal-medicine practice that dates back to the Aztec. At that time, traditional healers categorized illnesses by four possible causes: infliction by the gods, a person's own negative energy, the casting of an evil spell, or a loss of destiny. The traditional healers of today use two categories: natural (such as parasites or rheumatism) and supernatural (such as the evil eye or ghostly spirits), further subdivided into "hot" ailments (fever, nervousness, shock) and "cold" ailments (sterility, bronchitis).

When the Spaniards arrived in the 16th century, they adopted elements of Mexican herbology to enrich their less-sophisticated European medicines. Two centuries later, the birth of botany initiated the empirical study of medicine, but in Morelos herbal medicine was still viewed with respect. Even today, modern medicines are expensive or simply unavailable in rural Mexican communities— and local people continue to have a strong faith in the healing properties of herbology. Herbs are harvested in the state of Morelos's 300 rural communities; curanderos (natural healers) flock to the mercados on weekends to offer advice and sell their concoctions; and several stores in Cuernavaca still sell natural antidotes for every ailment imaginable, from hangnails to herpes.

To study the history of herbology and purchase healing plants, visit Casa de Maximiliano (see above) and the weekend mercado in Tepoztlán (see Near Cuernavaca, below). You'll find many ancient healers at either place.

dicinal and religious uses of Mexican plants and herbs since pre-Columbian times (*see box, above*). Many of the plants described in the museum can be found in the adjoining botanical garden and some are also available for purchase. *Matamoros 14, Col. Acapantzinga, tel. 73/12–59–55. Take RUTA 6 combi from Degollado, between Guerrero and Clavijero. Admission free. Open daily 9–5.*

CATEDRAL DE LA ASUNCION

From the early 16th to late 19th century, this cathedral complex also housed a convent and three *capillas* (chapels) within its high walls. The **Capilla Abierta de San José** was designed with only a partial roof so the unbaptized indigenous people, used to worshipping outside, would feel more at home—and would therefore be more likely to convert. The **Capilla de la Asunción Gloriosa de la Virgen María** was started in 1529 by Hernán Cortés and completed in 1552. Inside, newly uncovered remnants of early 17th-century frescoes, supposedly painted by a Japanese immigrant, depict the crucifixion of Christian missionaries in Japan. Near the entrance gate to the cathedral grounds, the **Templo de la Tercera Orden de San Francisco** took 13 years to build due to the elaborate gilded ornamentation. The newest structure is the **Capilla de Carmen,** which dates from the late 19th century and has beautiful *retablos* (altarpieces). Sunday at 11 AM and 8 PM, you can witness a "mariachi mass." *Hidalgo 17, at Morelos, tel. 73/12–12–90. 3 blocks west of the zócalo. Admission free. Open Mon.–Sat. 9–2 and 4–8, Sun. 9–8.*

JARDIN BORDA

The mansion, landscaped grounds, and botanical gardens of the Jardin were built in the 18th century by Manuel de la Borda as a gift for his father, José de la Borda, Taxco's silver millionaire. The gardens were patterned after those in Andalucía, Spain. In 1865 the Jardín Borda became a symbol of imperial Mexico when the estate was turned into a summer retreat for Emperor Maximilian and his wife, Carlota. Today, more than 100 varieties of fruit trees and ornamental shrubs, all original plantings, continue to flourish here. The six refurbished front rooms of the mansion now house the **Centro de Arte Jardín Borda,** where you can view the work of local and international artists. The **bookstore** (open Tues.–Sun. 11–3 and 6–10), sells classical music on CD, rare Frida Kahlo postcards, and books (some in English) on topics ranging from Picasso's works to Mexican cooking. **Cine Morelos** (*see* Cinemas and Theaters, *below*) hosts international and cultural films here Friday at 7:30 PM. *Morelos 103, at Hidalgo, tel. 73/12–92–37. Admission: 70¢, free Wed. Open Tues.–Sun. 10–5:30.*

JUNGLA MAGICA

It's not Disneyland, but it is an amusement park. This Mexican wonderland boasts water slides, a haunted house, a small aquatic park, a natural lake, an aviary, a chilling serpentarium, and a planetarium. *Chapultepec 27, tel. 73/15–34–11. From corner of Las Casas and Leyva, take* RUTA *11 combi and ask the driver to let you off at Jungla Mágica; walk 1 block downhill on Chapultepec. Admission: $3.50; rides and attractions an additional 10¢–60¢. Open Tues.–Sun. 9:30–6.*

PALACIO DE CORTES

Built for Hernán Cortés by Tlahuican laborers, this imposing building has been a potent symbol of power throughout Cuernavaca's history. At first it followed a simple plan, but as Cortés gained wealth, influence, titles, and a wife, the palace grew. It later passed into the hands of the Spanish crown and, during the War of Independence, was used as a prison for revolutionaries José María Morelos, Ignacio López Rayón, and Nicolás Bravo. During the Revolution of 1910, the palace was abandoned and later became the office of the municipal government. These days the palace houses the **Museo Cuauhnáhuac,** which displays some of Diego Rivera's finest murals dramatizing the history and horrors of the conquest, colonialism, and the Revolution. To the right of the palace is the **Jardín de Arte Luis Betanzos,** where indigenous artists sell everything from brightly painted wooden toys to beautiful handworked silver. *Juárez, at Hidalgo. Admission to Palacio and Museo: $2; free on Sun. Open Tues.–Sun. 10–5.*

> *The scrolled ironwork on the bandstand in the center of Cuernavaca's Jardín Juárez was designed by Gustave Eiffel, of Paris Eiffel Tower fame.*

PIRAMIDE DE TEOPANZOLCO

This small, Tlahuican ceremonial center predates the Aztec presence in Cuernavaca, as its name (Place of the Old Temple) suggests. When the Aztec conquered the Tlahuican, they began building a new temple around the old one to prove their superiority. They, in turn, were interrupted by the Spanish conquest. The temple's unfinished remains were rediscovered in 1910, and today you can hike up the stairs of the 30-ft central pyramid. *From the east side of Mercado Principal, take* RUTA *19 combi for 15 min. Admission: 75¢. Open daily 10–4:30.*

SAN ANTON FALLS

Although this 132-ft waterfall cascades into a dirty brown pool, the sidewalks that wind around and under the falls make a trip here worth your while. Also fun is strolling through the barrio of San Antón, where vendors sell Virgin Mary figurines and terra-cotta pots of colorful flowers. While here, stop for a meal at **Restaurant El Salto** (*see* Food, *above*), a half block from the waterfall. *Bajada del Salto, Barrio de San Antón. From Arteaga and Morelos, take* RUTA *4 combi, then walk downhill on Av. del Salto for 3 blocks; a sign on your right leads to the falls. Admission: 70¢. Open weekdays 10–6, weekends 8–6.*

AFTER DARK

On weekends, crowds vacationing from Mexico City add to Cuernavaca's mix of fun-loving locals, university students, and travelers. You can listen to live music on Thursday and Sunday in **Jardín Juárez,** and just about every weekend at **Jardín Borda** (*see* Worth Seeing, *above*). For your own private concert, hire one of the mariachi bands that loiter on the northeast corner of **Plaza de Armas.** The **Catedral de la Asunción** occasionally sponsors choral performances.

BARS

The cafés on the zócalo are among the most pleasant places to enjoy a beer. **Harry's Bar** (Gutemberg 5, tel. 73/12–76–39), where yuppie chilangos and cuernavaquenses hang out, is the first place any resident will send you. During the week, international students and locals flock here for loud music and videotaped sports games. On weekends Harry's becomes a pickup joint. The bar labeled "second best" by locals is **Sapo-Sabio** (Madero 503, Col. Mira, tel. 73/18–48–83; closed Sun.–Tues.), 15 minutes out of town in the Francisco Madero area. It, too, plays U.S. and Mexican rock music.

CINEMAS AND THEATERS

Teatro Ocampo (tel. 73/18–63–85), on the Jardín Juárez, is home to Cuernavaca's talented repertory company. Posters around town display upcoming events; tickets cost about $4. **Cine Morelos** (Morelos, at Rayón, tel. 73/18–84–18) screens a variety of international films (with Spanish subtitles) and regularly hosts national and international music and dance performances. Events are posted at a booth on the corner of Morelos and Rayón. **Cinematográfica Las Plazas** (Gutemberg 101, tel. 73/14–07–93), in Las Plazas shopping center, shows mostly Hollywood films with Spanish subtitles.

DANCING

Cuernavaca offers a number of flashy clubs with high cover charges. Two happening discos are **Baby Rock** (Nueva Italia 11-N, tel. 73/13–90–97), a classy Mexican chain that's a favorite among international language students, and **Barba-Zul** (Prado 10, Col. San Jerónimo, tel. 73/13–19–76), north of the centro. **Zumbale** (Chapultepec, tel. 73/22–53–43; closed Sun.–Wed.) plays salsa and merengue music to a mostly local crowd, and RUTA 17 and RUTA 20 buses from Degollado pass right by it. Cover at all three is $7 for men, free for women. **Shadé** (López Mateos, east side of Mercado Principal) is a large gay disco where DJs spin a variety of music until 5 AM Wednesday–Saturday. Catch a cab ($1) from the zócalo.

NEAR CUERNAVACA

TEPOZTLAN

The small town of Tepoztlán lies north of Cuernavaca, in a valley surrounded by lumpy mountains that have been shaped by wind and water. The Nahuatl Indians are the largest indigenous group here, and they'll happily discuss their unique customs and rich heritage with foreigners. Show up at the town's weekend mercado and you'll find everyone from curanderos to Nahuatl authors eager to bend your ear.

To learn more about the fascinating history and mysticism of this town and its people, begin with a hike to the towering **Pirámide Tepozteco.** The walls surrounding the pyramid are covered with bas relief murals representing the 20 symbols of the days, the gods of the cardinal points, and various mythological and historical figures. The pyramid was named in honor of Tepoztécatl, the Nahuatl god of *pulque* (an alcoholic beverage made from the fermented juice of the maguey cactus). According to legend, the gods Mayahuel and Patécatl discovered how to ferment maguey into pulque. Tepoztécatl, one of their 400 children, went on to learn the curative and stimulative properties of pulque. The path leading to the Tlahuican ruins begins at the end of Avenida Tepozteco, a 15-minute walk past Tepoztlán's small town plaza. From there, it's a steep, hourlong climb up the cerro where the pyramid lies. A small stand at the top sells water and soft drinks for about 75¢ each. On Sunday everyone and his *abuela* (grandmother) is out here making the climb. *Admission: $2, free Sun. Open daily 10–4:30.*

Although the Tlahuican, related to the Nahuatl, were continually attacked by the Aztec, they were never truly conquered until Cortés arrived in 1521. At that time, Christianity was strictly imposed, and it's rumored that a Dominican friar tore down the Tepoztécatl statue that used to reside inside the pyramid, sending its fragments to the nearby town of Oaxtepec to serve as the cement for a new convent. The **Ex-Convento de la Natividad de la Virgen María** was thusly constructed, with imposing walls more than 6 ft thick. The convent is known for its syncretic *tequitqui* style, in which Christian and indigenous symbols mingle in faded frescoes. Notice the subtle image of Quetzalcoatl, god of the sun, painted into the intricate black-and-white border design running high along the antechamber walls. Take a peek in the **Iglesia de la Asunción** next door and in the **Museo Arqueológico Colección Carlos Pellicer,** which exhibits precolonial artifacts and photos of various archaeological sites. *Next to the mercado, 1 block east of Av. Tepozteco. Museum entrance on Calle de la Conchita, a small road behind the church, tel. 739/18–51–01. Museum admission: $1.25 Open Tues.–Sun. 10–6.*

COMING AND GOING

Tepoztlán-bound buses (1 hr, 75¢) leave every half hour until 9 PM from Mercado Principal in Cuernavaca. To reach town from Tepoztlán's bus station (a 10-minute walk), follow the highway downhill; it will become Avenida Tepozteco, which leads straight to the pyramid. The last bus back to Cuernavaca leaves at 8:30 PM.

WHERE TO SLEEP

Tepoztlán fills up fast on weekends and holidays, particularly since budget lodging is scarce here. Reservations are advised during those periods. If you're willing to pay $35 ($40 with meals) for a double, try **Casa Iccemanyan** (Calle del Olvido 26, tel. 739/5–08–99). The hotel has a beautiful swimming pool and a patio restaurant. Much cheaper is **Las Cabañas** (Cinco de Mayo 54, no phone), a tiny, family-run hostel on the edge of town. It has five small, clean rooms ($10) with communal bath. Both of the above hotels accept cash only. The **Posada de Tepozteca** (Paraiso 3, tel. 739/5–00–10) has modern rooms ($39 for a double) plus a restaurant, bar, two pools, a garden, and a tennis court.

If you're looking to camp, head for **Campamento Meztitla** (Rte. 2, tel. 739/5–00–68) on the Tepoztlán–Yautepec highway. You'll need to take a taxi (15 min, $3.50) from town to get here. Camping costs $4 per person per night, or $10 to rent a six-person tent. Toilets, showers, and drinking water are provided. The staff will also fill you in on the exciting hiking opportunities offered by nearby Parque Nacional el Tepozteco. The boundary of this large park is just north of town.

FOOD

There are several good restaurants along Avenida Tepozteco. Try the chicken mole ($5) at local favorite **Los Colorines** (Tepozteco 13, tel. 739/5–01–98). For Mexican and Hindu cuisine, stop by the **Restaurante Vegetariano Govinda** at the **Proyecto Milenio** (Tepozteco 19, tel. 739/5–17–15). The "om" burgers are delicious. The Proyecto also houses the adjoining **Café la Arábica,** where you can sip coffee and peruse the book collection. You can also use the Proyecto's long-distance phone and fax services. All of the above are cash only.

On September 8th and 9th, Tepoztláns honor Tepoztécatl, the Nahuatl god of pulque. In a time-honored attempt to erase "pagan" practices, the local convent holds its own festival at the same time.

XOCHICALCO

Located 38 km (24 mi) southeast of Cuernavaca, the ancient city of Xochicalco (Place of the House of the Flowers) sits atop terraced hills overlooking a valley and a town of the same name. These partially excavated ruins are the most fascinating in Morelos state, displaying elements of both Olmec and Mayan architecture. The Toltec, Mixtec, and/or Zapotec may also have inhabited this site at various points in time. Some believe that Xochicalco was a ceremonial center where scholars met to calibrate their calendars. In any case, when the Spaniards arrived in the early 16th century, it's believed that the people of the valley came from miles around to protect the ancient city by burying it under rocks and earth. The pre-Columbian ruins of both Xochicalco and Teopanzolco (see Worth Seeing in Cuernavaca, above) weren't rediscovered until the Mexican Revolution. During a battle in the early 1900s, Emiliano Zapata and his troops noticed that bullets ricocheted off the hill they were holding; they later discovered that the bullets had been bouncing off grass-covered stone walls.

Opened in April 1996, the **Museo de Sitio de Xochicalco,** about 300 yds from the ruins, showcases a huge collection of archaeological pieces excavated here over the years. The museum's six rooms contain intricate hieroglyphics and statues of the gods; Room 2 has a perfectly preserved statue of *Señor de Rojo* (sun god). The museum guides possess an extensive knowledge of the site and its history, so feel free to ask questions.

The center of Xochicalco is the **Plaza Ceremonial** (Plaza 1), at the city's highest base elevation. Only priests were allowed here, in what is believed to be the main ceremonial enclosure, while people of the valley congregated to trade goods in a bazaar far below. The intricately carved **Pirámide de la Serpiente Emplumada** (Pyramid of the Feathered Serpent) depicts the alignment of the calendars of several Indian tribes. These are presided over by the god Quetzalcoatl, shown as a headdressed serpent with two mouths, two tongues, and a fan of feathers for a tail. His left hand discards an erroneous date (represented by a hieroglyph) while his right hand pulls up a correct one. The correct date has been identified as 13 Monkey, of the 260-day Mesoamerican calendar. You can climb the steep staircase of the **Temple of the Stelae,** also on the Plaza Ceremonial, to get a commanding view of the surrounding hills and the valley below.

Down the hill in the **main plaza** (Plaza 2) is the **Two Glyph Stelae Square,** arranged to chart the sun's path through the day. Below this is a ball court—one of many found in ruins throughout Mexico. It is believed that the game played here involved two teams of five men each, with competitors attempting to get a small, hard ball through the circular stone hoops on either end of the court.

The underground **observatory,** one of 32 interconnected tunnels below the pyramids, was used to trace the sun's path throughout the year: At noon on the summer solstice (usually June 21), the sun's rays would completely illuminate the chamber's interior. This event held great religious significance, as for one moment each year the celestial, the terrestrial, and the subterranean worlds were united.

The small snack bar at the ruins offers nothing substantial, so bring along a picnic lunch. The guards are strict about the "no camping" rule here, so take care not to miss the last bus of the day. *Admission: $2; free Sun. Ruins open Tues.–Sun. 10–5. Observatory open daily 10–4.*

COMING AND GOING

Autotransportes Chapultepec is the only bus line that runs from the bus station in Cuernavaca all the way to the Xochicalco site. Their CUENTEPEC–ALPUYECA buses (50¢) leave from Cuernavaca's Mercado Principal every hour 5:30 AM–8 PM. Fewer buses take you back, however, passing the ruins at approximately 1, 3, 6, and 7 PM. If you have a car, take Highway 95 (Mexico–Acapulco) until you see a fork in the road. Bear to your right and you'll see the ruins gleaming in the sunlight at the top of the hill. If you reach Alpuyeca or El Rodeo Lake, you've chosen the wrong road.

CUAUTLA

Hotter, drier, and less built-up than Cuernavaca, Cuautla is the second-largest city in Morelos state and a stopover with only limited appeal. Located about 12 km (7½ mi) southeast of Cuernavaca, its dusty provinciality belies the fact that this is a favorite vacation spot for many middle-class Mexicans drawn here by the town's famed mineral baths. The tradition of a wealthy elite soaking in sulphur water reportedly dates back to Moctezuma (Montezuma), who apparently enjoyed the restorative powers of these springs. The city was built into a prosperous colonial spa by the Spanish in the 17th century, but today the palm-lined streets roar with traffic, and the natural hot springs are now more like unkempt public pools than therapeutic spas.

The town's few remaining historical attractions are clustered in the town center and are a source of local pride. Cuautla was a revolutionary stronghold during the War of Independence and the Mexican Revolution, and both rebel leader Emiliano Zapata and revolutionary priest José María Morelos are honored here. In 1812 Morelos and his 3,000 men held the city for 72 days against an attacking Royalist force of 20,000. It was only when starvation set in that they surrendered. The Battle of Cuautla is commemorated by an impressive statue of Morelos, who is posed waving a machete over the Plaza Galeana.

Across from this statue is the church that served as Morelos's headquarters, the **Iglesia de San Diego,** and the adjacent **Convento de San Diego.** This graceful convent was later converted into a railway station and today houses the town's **Casa de la Cultura.** The convent also contains Cuautla's helpful **tourist office** (Galeana, tel. 735/2–52–21; open weekdays 8–6, Sat. 8–5, Sun. 8–3) and the tiny, free **Museo José María Morelos** (open Tues.–Sun. 10–5), featuring historical items from the wars of Spanish conquest.

It's a five-minute walk south on Galeana from the convent to the zócalo. On its northeast corner is the **Palacio Municipal** (tel. 735/2–65–11); on the west side is the **Iglesia de Santo Domingo** (tel. 735/2–00–06), which served as a hospital during the War of Independence and was defended by four cannons, one on each corner. At the southeast corner of the zócalo sits **Casa de Morelos** (Callejón del Castigo 3, tel. 735/2–83–31), Morelos's home while defending Cuautla. This small building, with peeling paint and a white doorway, now houses the free **Museo de la Independencia** (open Tues.–Sun. 10–5).

A 15-minute walk south of the zócalo on Guerrero brings you to **Jardín Revolución del Sur** where Emiliano Zapata is buried. Zapata was assassinated at Chinameca, 31 km (19 mi) away, and his image assumed renewed political meaning with the armed uprising of the Zapatista Army in Chiapas. Facing the Jardín is **Iglesia Señor del Pueblo,** named in Zapata's honor.

COMING AND GOING

Although it's the second largest city in Morelos, Cuautla is fairly easy to explore on foot—but be prepared for frequent street-name changes and a paucity of street signs. The city is shaped roughly like an L, with the centro at the crook and the Alameda a few blocks north of the zócalo, on Galeana. Most colectivos run on Zavala/Reforma and Alvaro Obregón, and cost about 15¢.

There are two neighboring first-class bus stations in Cuautla. **Cristóbal Colón** (2 de Mayo 97, at Reforma, tel. 735/2–31–68) is four blocks from the zócalo. It serves Mexico City (every 15 mins; 1½ hrs, $3.50) and Oaxaca city (3 per day; 7 hrs, $10). **Estrella Roja** (Costeño, at Vásquez, tel. 735/2–05–49) serves Cuernavaca (every 15 min; 1 hr, $2), Mexico City (every 20 min; 2 hrs, $3.25), and Puebla (1 per day; 3 hrs, $2.50). To get from either station to the zócalo, walk three–four blocks west. From the Estrella Roja station in Cuernavaca, buses to Cuautla leave every 15 minutes between 6 AM and 10 PM.

WHERE TO SLEEP

Cuautla's hotels aren't the cheapest in the region, but prices aren't ridiculous. **Hotel Central** (Fin del Rul 21, off Plaza Galeana, no phone) has very basic rooms grouped around a grassy courtyard. Some of the bathrooms here are very small and dark, so ask to see a few rooms (doubles $11) before paying. The **Villa Juvenil Cuautla** (Unidad Deportiva Morelos, tel. 735/2–02–18), a hostel, is the best deal in town. The parklike grounds are well groomed, and it's only $3.50 for a dorm bed and use of the sparkling-clean communal bathrooms. The hostel is 10 minutes from the Cristóbal Colón bus station: Walk west on 2 de Mayo, right on Niños Héroes, over the bridge, and enter the parking lot to your right. If you get lost, just keep asking where the Villa Juvenil is; everyone in town knows. There is no age limit at the youth hostel. All of the above accept cash only.

FOOD

There's no lack of cheap dining establishments in Cuautla. On the northeast side of the zócalo, the cafe-teria **Colón** (tel. 735/2–23–17) sells cheap comida corrida and offers a good view of the square. Also try **Mario** (Ramierez Ferrara 10, tel. 735/2–08–16), which serves traditional Mexican food; **Cafetería y Jugos Alameda** (Galeana 40, tel. 735/2–24–52), where you can slurp milk shakes and juices; or the popular burger joint **Las Tortugas** (Plaza Fuerte de Galeana 84, tel. 735/2–35–08). For a more formal dinner, try the restaurant in **Hotel Colonial** (José Perdiz 18, tel. 735/2–21–64), known for its $7 *cabrito colonial* (specially cooked goat meat). All of the above accept cash only.

OUTDOOR ACTIVITIES

Splashing around in one of Cuautla's many *balnearios* (spa and swimming areas) isn't all it's cracked up to be; the mineral baths are often like municipal swimming pools. Beware: pools are jammed with schoolkids July–September, December, and the week before Easter. **Oaxtepec** (Carretera México–La Pera–Oaxtepec, tel. 735/6–01–01), is possibly the best of the resorts, with 25 pools, a cable car, and water slides. Catch a blue OAXTEPEC combi (½ hr) from three blocks north of Cuautla's zócalo and have $6 ready for admission. **Las Estacas** (Carretera México–La Pera–Ticumán, tel. 734/2–14–44), about 24 km (13 mi) outside town, features a spring-fed river that floats guests through a patch of jungle. The resort also has a restaurant and camping facilities; admission is about $4. **Aguas Hediondas** (tel. 735/2–00–44) is a sulphur spring whose name means "stinking waters." If you can stand the rotten-egg stench, the water circulating in the pools is fresh and rumored to possess curative properties. Here you can rent a private, covered "family" pool ($5 per hour) that accommodates up to 10 people. General admission is $2. To reach the sulphur springs, catch the AGUAS HEDIONDAS combi either across from Plaza Galeana or just past the Niños Héroes bridge, in front of Unidad Deportiva.

TAXCO

Taxco is a medieval-looking city with twisting, cobblestone streets, red-tile colonial houses, dozens of sil-versmiths' shops, and busload upon busload of tourists, most of them bent on bringing half the town's silver supply home in their carry-on luggage. The town, so picturesque it hardly seems real, was built into a narrow cleft in the Sierra Madre mountains. As the city grows, it creeps higher into the mountains, and now many streets sport steep grades and sharp right-angle turns. It's what makes this town of just 150,000 unique, compared to sprawling Puebla and Cuernavaca.

Overlooking Taxco's peaceful zócalo is the **Iglesia de Santa Prisca.** This incredibly ornate, pink-stone church is a testament to the silver industry that sustains this town. Cortés's men set up the first silver mine in the Americas here in 1531, but it was only briefly profitable, and the aqueducts at the city's western entrance are the only structures remaining from that period. Following a 200-year lull, however, a more lucrative silver vein was found—this time by one lucky José de la Borda. According to local leg-end, the Frenchman accidentally discovered this vein when his horse stumbled on a rocky pathway. The

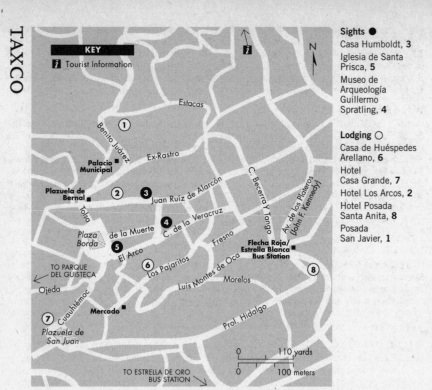

TAXCO

KEY

i Tourist Information

Sights ●
Casa Humboldt, **3**
Iglesia de Santa Prisca, **5**
Museo de Arqueología Guillermo Spratling, **4**

Lodging ○
Casa de Huéspedes Arellano, **6**
Hotel Casa Grande, **7**
Hotel Los Arcos, **2**
Hotel Posada Santa Anita, **8**
Posada San Javier, **1**

church, often simply called "La Prisca," was Borda's ostentatious gift to the city, and is the source of the local aphorism: "If God gives to Borda, Borda gives to God." The Borda family built a few of the mansions that surround the zócalo, but the restaurants and shops that now fill these buildings indirectly owe their existence in part to yet another foreigner, U.S. college professor William Spratling. Spratling settled here in the 1930s, and his innovations in handwrought silver design inspired the tourist industry that thrives here today.

BASICS

CASAS DE CAMBIO

Taxco's silver shops usually accept U.S. dollars, or you can change money at the banks along Cuauhté-moc. **Banco Confia** (Plaza Borda 2, tel. 762/2–01–92) exchanges currency weekdays 9–1. **Monedas Continentales** (Plazuela de San Juan 5, tel. 762/2–12–42; open weekdays 9–3 and 5–7, Sat. 9–2), also changes traveler's checks and dollars. **Banamex** (Plazuela del Convento 2, down Juárez from zócalo) has a 24-hour ATM that accepts Plus, Cirrus, Visa, and MasterCard.

EMERGENCIES

In an emergency, contact the **police** at 762/2–06–66; for **ambulance** service call the Cruz Roja at 762/2–32–32.

LAUNDRY

The 24-hour **Lavandería la Cascada** (Delicias 4, tel. 762/2–17–21) is in Bora Bora Pizza, half a block west of the zócalo. The minimum load is 4 kilos (9 pounds) for $3.

MAIL

The post office is next to the Estrella de Oro bus station. They'll hold your mail for up to 10 days at the following address: Lista de Correos, Taxco, Guerrero, CP 40200, México. *Av. de Los Plateros 124, no phone. Open weekdays 8–7, Sat. 9–1.*

MEDICAL AID

There are many pharmacies near the zócalo and Plazuela de San Juan. A particularly well-stocked one is **Farmacia Guadalupana** (Hidalgo 8, tel. 762/2–03–95; open daily 8:30 AM–10 PM). For more urgent medical attention, the **Clínica de Especialidades** (Av. de Los Plateros, near Hotel Posada de la Misión, tel. 762/2–11–11) offers 24-hour emergency care.

PHONES

There are working pay phones on the zócalo and all over Taxco, where you can place collect or credit-card calls. A more expensive option ($3–$5 for collect calls) is to make your call from **Farmacia de Cristo,** down the street from Plazuela de San Juan. *Hidalgo 18, tel. 762/2–11–19. Open daily 8 AM–9 PM.*

VISITOR INFORMATION

Taxco's tourist office is run by a helpful, English-speaking staff. Although it's a 10-minute walk or combi ride from the zócalo, have your questions answered here rather than by the dubious self-appointed guides who stand on the highway. *Av. de Los Plateros 1, tel. 762/2–22–74. From Plaza Borda, take a combi marked ZOCALO to the gas station. Open weekdays 9–2 and 4–7, Sat. 9–1.*

COMING AND GOING

BY BUS

Taxco has two bus stations. The **Estrella Blanca/Flecha Roja** station, a few blocks downhill from Plaza Borda, offers first-class and deluxe service (deluxe has air-conditioning). Buses serve Mexico City (3 hrs; $7 deluxe, $4.50 1st class) and Cuernavaca (2 hrs; $4 deluxe, $3 1st class); Acapulco (4 hrs, $13 deluxe, $9 1st class). *Av. de Los Plateros 104, tel. 762/2–01–31.*

Many Taxco shops make milagros, tiny silver or tin pieces representing the human eyes, arms, heart, or legs. These are pinned to the skirts of saints in churches as an appeal for healing an illness or deformity.

The **Estrella de Oro** bus line also has first-class and deluxe service to Mexico City, Acapulco, and Cuernavaca, with rates comparable to Flecha Roja's. Combis marked LOS ARCOS run between the two bus stations, while ZOCALO combis make the loop between the stations and the zócalo. You can also walk uphill 10–15 minutes, keeping the spires of Santa Prisca church in sight. A taxi to the zócalo will cost 75¢. *Av. de Los Plateros 126, tel. 762/2–06–48.*

BY CAR

The new Highway 95 runs through Taxco, leading to various destinations. Driving south takes you to Chilpancingo (2 hrs, toll free) and to Acapulco (4 hrs, $32 toll). Drive north to reach Cuernavaca (1 hr, $7 toll) and Mexico City (3 hrs, $19 toll).

GETTING AROUND

Taxco is fairly accessible by foot, and most sights and budget hotels are clustered around the town's zócalo, **Plaza Borda.** As you move away from the zócalo, the twisted, steep streets become increasingly difficult to navigate. When you need a rest, hop on one of the many 15¢ combis roaming the area—that is, if you haven't already been run over by one. Combis labeled LOS ARCOS travel the length of Avenida de Los Plateros (formerly Avenida John F. Kennedy), which traverses the lower part of the city from north to south. Plaza Borda is uphill from Avenida de Los Plateros, easily identifiable by the pink spires on the **Iglesia de Santa Prisca.** The main west–east road is Benito Juárez, which most people still call by its old name, Las Grutas. Taxco's other main square is **Plazuela de San Juan,** 1½ blocks southwest of Plaza Borda, up Cuauhtémoc.

WHERE TO SLEEP

Taxco is a popular tourist destination, and its hotel owners are aware of this. Rooms here are not cheap. The less-expensive hotels surround Plaza Borda and the Flecha Roja bus depot; you won't find any real bargains, but you'll find some compensation in the picturesque setting and great views. Reservations are a good idea on holidays and weekends, especially Semana Santa (Holy Week, the week preceding Easter) and during July, August, and December. There are no camping facilities in Taxco.

UNDER $10 • Casa de Huéspedes Arellano. Only the most determined budget travelers will be able to find this well-hidden hotel, although every Taxco resident knows where it is—just keep asking and you'll get there. Although the administration can be brusque, and the decor and standard of cleanliness leave a bit to be desired, it's the cheapest hotel in town and relatively quiet. Doubles cost $9.50, with private bath $12.50. *Pajaritos 31, tel. 762/2–02–15. Down alley to right of the cathedral, right through the market, then 3 levels down. 13 rooms, 5 with bath. Laundry, luggage storage. Cash only.*

UNDER $15 • Hotel Casa Grande. Probably the best deal for the price, this large, old, stone building is clean and well kept. Rooms vary from plain with small, grungy bathrooms, to nicely decorated with elaborately tiled bathrooms and terrace views of the town. Beware: Some beds are flea-ridden and the noise from the street video arcade next door can get annoying. All rooms are the same price (doubles $13) so ask to see several. *Plazuela de San Juan 7, tel. and fax 762/2–11–08. 12 rooms, all with bath. Luggage storage. Cash only.*

Hotel Posada Santa Anita. The good news about this hotel is that it's near the bus stations and is clean and nicely furnished. The bad news is that it's a 10-minute uphill hike any time you want to go to the zócalo. Rooms can be small, but those in the back are quiet and have a charming view of Taxco. Doubles cost $15. *Av. de Los Plateros 106, tel. 762/2–07–52. 29 rooms, 23 with bath. Luggage storage. Cash only.*

UNDER $20 • Hotel Los Arcos. This hotel was originally a gift for a viceroy of "New Spain," as Mexico was known during the Colonial era. Some rooms have lofts, with beds overlooking the sitting area, and all open onto a cool patio of brick, stone, and tile. The hotel is quiet and gorgeous and the clientele mostly consists of middle-age travelers. Doubles are $17. *Juan Ruíz de Alarcón 12, tel. 762/2–18–36. 24 rooms, all with bath. Luggage storage. Reservations advised. Cash only.*

Posada San Javier. This quiet inn features courtyards, bougainvillea, and a large pool. The spacious, clean rooms are $20 for a double. Ángel Cervantes, the receptionist, is friendly, garrulous, and eager to offer information about Taxco shopping and day trips. *Estacas 1, tel. 762/2–31–77. 18 rooms, all with bath. Luggage storage. Reservations advised. Cash only.*

FOOD

If you're not careful, Taxco's tourist-friendly restaurants will empty your wallet without filling your stomach. Cheap meals can be had in the taquerías near the Flecha Roja bus depot and in restaurants on the side streets surrounding the zócalo. Purchase inexpensive fresh fruits and vegetables as well as baked bread from one of the many *panaderías* (bakeries) in the daily **mercado** (*see* Shopping, *below*), down the alley to the right of the cathedral. The specialty of the region is cooked iguana; locals say it's an aphrodisiac, and that it tastes just like chicken. Find out for yourself at **Casa Borda** (Plazuela de Bernal 1, ½ block from the zócalo, no phone; cash only) where $4 buys a plate of fried iguana and rice.

UNDER $3 • Jugos y Tortas Restaurante Cruz. Whitewashed walls adorned with folk art add charm to this family-run restaurant, a favorite with locals looking for a quick lunch. Tacos are 75¢, the $1 tortas are some of the best in town, and a burger, fries, and soda go for $2. *El Arco 11, tel. 762/2–70–79. 2 blocks from the zócalo. Cash only.*

UNDER $5 • La Concha Nostra. The Hotel Casa Grande's second-story bar/restaurant overlooks Plazuela de San Juan and draws both locals and travelers for its Italian and Mexican cuisine (not to mention the MTV and cable sports broadcasts). The calzone with ham, olives, and mushrooms is mouthwatering. Traditional breakfasts of juice, coffee, fruit, and eggs cost $2. *Plazuela de San Juan 7, tel. 762/2–11–08. Cash only.*

Restaurant Sante Fé. Ask anyone in Taxco where they spend their precious pesos when taking the family to dinner, and they'll point you toward this colorful restaurant, around the corner from Plazuela de San Juan. The comida corrida features an entrée such as *chile relleno* (stuffed chile pepper) or chicken in garlic sauce, with soup, beans, rice, tortillas, and dessert, all for $3.50. Sandwiches and enchiladas are less than $2.50. *Hidalgo 2, tel. 762/2–11–70. 1 block east of Plazuela de San Juan. Cash only.*

UNDER $10 • Pizza Pazza. The delicious aroma of pizza and garlic bread wafts across the zócalo from this pleasant place. The view is terrific and so is the pizza. A large cheese pie for two–three people is only $5, with everything $10. Other specialties include spaghetti, *queso fundido* (cheese fondue), and *pozole* (hominy soup). *Calle del Arco 1, next to the cathedral, tel. 762/2–55–00. No breakfast.*

WORTH SEEING

Taxco itself is its own major tourist attraction, which is why the Mexican government declared the city a national monument in 1928. If you're athletic, simply wandering along Taxco's many cramped alleys and stairways makes for a strenuous but pleasant urban hike. The **Plaza Borda,** where local families gossip and mingle among the wrought-iron benches and well-kept walkways, is a pleasant place to pass an evening. It's also where you'll find the town's stunning **Iglesia de Santa Prisca** (*see* Taxco, *above*).

CASA HUMBOLDT

This 18th-century mansion is named after Alexander von Humboldt, a German explorer who visited Taxco in 1803 and later traveled throughout South America, making maps and conducting scientific surveys. The interior was recently reconstructed and is adorned with 16th-century artifacts found during renovations of the Ex-Convento and the La Prisa church. *Juan Ruíz de Alarcón 6, tel. 762/2–55–01. Admission: $2. Open Mon.–Sat. 10–5.*

MONTE TAXCO RESORT

A 10-minute ride on a *teleférico* (tram) takes you from the north side of Taxco to the luxurious resort of Monte Taxco, with its swimming pools, gardens, golf course, and spa. It costs $4 to use the pool and $3 to take a 20-minute horseback ride around the grounds. The views from the resort's bar are spectacular. Trams run every five minutes, daily 8 AM–7 PM, and cost $2.50 round-trip. Alternately, the trip costs $2 one-way by taxi. *Tel. 762/2–13–00. From the zócalo, take ARCOS/ZOCALO combi and ask to be let off at the teleférico; walk up the hill on the south side of the street.*

The 18th-century Iglesia de Santa Prisca on Taxco's zócalo is considered one of the finest examples of baroque architecture in Mexico.

MUSEO DE ARQUEOLOGIA GUILLERMO SPRATLING

A short walk from the Iglesia de Santa Prisca, this museum was formerly the house of American professor William Spratling. It now consists of three galleries: two dedicated to pre-Columbian artwork and artifacts, the third to rotating exhibits of contemporary art. The museum is fairly small, and its collection isn't extraordinary. *Delgado 1, tel. 762/2–16–60. Admission: $2, free Sun. Open Tues.–Sun. 10–3.*

FESTIVALS

Taxco celebrates all the usual Mexican holidays as well as two unique events. The weeklong **Feria Nacional de La Plata** (Silver Fair), held in December, features the crowning of a Silver Queen and several silver exhibitions. **El Día del Jumil** (Day of the Jumil Bug), held the first weekend in November, honors an insect supposedly found only in Cerro de Huizteco, a town near Taxco. Traditional healers use the bugs for medicine, while others crush them to make a tasty salsa. During the festival, families and groups of friends camp on the cerro near town and sing and drink in between bug-hunting expeditions. All this merrymaking is destroying what was once virgin forest; nevertheless, the entire town of Taxco moves to the hill for the night. The cerro is 6 km (4 mi) away, a short ride by taxi or combi.

SHOPPING

Prices in Taxco's endless procession of silver shops are uniformly high—the shopkeepers have figured out that many foreigners are rich and gullible. **Los Castillos** (Plaza Bernal 10, tel. 762/2–06–52) displays some of the most beautiful and ornate silver work in town. However, if you're looking to actually buy, stick to the vendors and small, crowded shops below street level for better prices. To reach these stores, head down Cuauhtémoc from Plaza Borda and turn down the small alley at Banco Mexicano Somex. Also try the stores in the **El Pueblito** complex, down Hidalgo from Plazuela de San Juan and across from the park. Another place featuring jewelry is **Rancho Guillermo Spratling,** just outside town on Highway 95. Take a cab or combi. Most shopkeepers have two price tiers: *Mayoreo* is the wholesale price given to those who buy at least $100 worth of silver, and *menudeo* is the price per gram for people buying less. Authentic silver is priced by weight and intricacy of workmanship.

Taxco's daily **mercado,** extending from the cathedral to **Avenida de Los Plateros,** is another good place to purchase less-expensive silver, as well as just about anything else. Haggling is common, though two-thirds of the initial price is usually about the best you'll do. The market really heats up on weekends when merchants from nearby towns come to hawk their wares.

AFTER DARK

Most nights the zócalo is the hottest spot around—the place where Taxco youth flirt and local families gather for nightly gossip. Buy yourself a bag of popcorn from one of the street vendors and settle onto a park bench to watch the nighttime spectacle unfold. If you're lucky, you may see a small parade of ado-lescents dressed as if for a wedding: This is a party for a girl's quinceañera, celebrating her 15th birth-day and the passage into womanhood.

The town's few drinking-and-dancing establishments close fairly early, even on weekends. Your best bet is the bars and restaurants next to the zócalo. **Restaurant/Bar Paco** (Plaza Borda 12, tel. 762/2–00–64) serves $1 beers and has the best views of the city. **Bar Berta** (Plaza Borda 9, tel. 762/2–01–72), a charming little place where the signature cocktail of Mexico, the margarita, was supposedly invented by the now-deceased owner, Berta. You won't find margaritas on the drink list, but you will find something called a "Berta" (tequila, club soda and lime juice). For dancing, try **Windows,** the disco at the **Monte Taxco Resort** (*see* Worth Seeing, *above*). It's especially lively during summer. Cover runs $4.

VERACRUZ

UPDATED BY PATRICIA ALISAU

The state of Veracruz is a narrow, verdant crescent of land on the southeastern coast of Mexico, warmed and watered by the tropical breezes that drift off the Gulf of Mexico. Much of Veracruz's uniqueness derives from the diversity of its population; the prolonged interaction of African, Spanish, and indigenous peoples has produced a rich array of cultural traditions, including especially vibrant festivals celebrated all over the state.

Ever since that fateful Good Friday in 1519, when Hernán Cortés dropped anchor along this lush green coast, Veracruz has been a popular gateway to Mexico for the rest of the world. But even before the Spanish arrived, Veracruz was the site of several powerful civilizations. The most ancient of all Mesoamerican groups—the enigmatic Olmec—ruled the coast as early as 1200 BC; the monumental carved basalt heads they left behind provide mute testimony to their former power and glory. Originators of the calendrical system adopted by the Maya, the Olmec are considered to be the "mother culture" of Mesoamerica. Little is known about the city-states that followed after the Olmec, but the ruins at El Tajín, near Papantla de Olarte, indicate that a highly complex culture—perhaps the early Totonac people— governed the northern area of the state between AD 600 and 900. When the Aztec came along and conquered this region, they left the area and its people ripe for rebellion: At Zempoala, the Totonac became the first allies of Cortés's conquering army. Soon after the Spanish came into power, they brought in boatloads of African slaves to fulfill their labor needs; by 1640, nearly 150,000 people of African descent were living in the region.

Today, Veracruz state is relatively wealthy due to cattle, coffee, and a thriving oil industry. The region is still largely undiscovered by foreign tourists, which keeps the prices low and makes Veracruz attractive to Mexican vacationers seeking delicious seafood and Caribbean music. Along the coast, the serene beaches of Tuxpán are the perfect place to relax, while the many marimba bands in Veracruz city will keep you dancing all night long. The hilly, tobacco-growing region of Los Tuxtlas lures visitors with its many lakes and waterfalls. Jalapa, the state capital, boasts a progressive university population, colorful markets, and many lively *peñas* (musical gatherings).

VERACRUZ CITY

The city of Veracruz is a raucous, sweaty port town. With its Caribbean flavor, lively music, and multiracial population, the city holds a special place in the hearts of many Mexican tourists, who come to admire the welcoming, ready-to-celebrate attitude of the *jarochos,* as the city's residents are known. The exuberance of the city's more than 1 million inhabitants never falters, even when heavy flooding or strong *nortes* (winds) sweep the unsuspecting streets. Multicultural influences are most evident in Veracruz city's famous cuisine and music; an African slave created the popular seafood dish known as *pescado a la veracruzana,* and Cuban immigrants brought over the slow, sensual rhythms of *danzón* (a tropical dance). In the white-tile main square, salsa music, the African xylophone music known as *marimba,* and birds chattering as loudly as monkeys in the palm trees overhead all compete for your attention. Jarochos and tourists sit in outdoor cafés, soaking up the scenery and savoring the strong coffee and potent cigars that are hallmarks of the region.

As one of the principal ports serving landlocked Mexico City, Veracruz city has been a bitterly contested prize in many of the country's conflicts. An array of forts and walls, originally built as protection against pirates, have seen plenty of action in the ensuing centuries. Pirates sacked the city a number of times, most viciously in 1683, when a Frenchman known as Lorenzillo held the town hostage for three days and carried off enormous quantities of booty. The French invaded again in 1838, and the United States seized the town twice, first in 1847 and again in 1914. The most dramatic of the fortifications—the castle at San Juan de Ulúa—is one of the city's most popular tourist attractions.

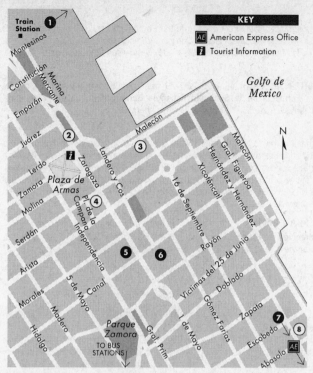

KEY

AE American Express Office

i Tourist Information

Sights ●
Acuario, **7**
Fuerte de San Juan de Ulúa, **1**
Instituto Veracruzano de la Cultura, **6**
Museo de la Ciudad, **5**

Lodging ○
Gran Hotel Balneario Royalty, **8**
Hotel Amparo, **4**
Hotel Hawaii, **3**
Hotel Sevilla, **2**

Golfo de Mexico

BASICS

AMERICAN EXPRESS

The travel agency **Viajes Olymar** serves as the AmEx representative in Veracruz. The agency provides the usual services for cardholders, including personal check cashing and cardholder mail. It also delivers MoneyGrams, sells traveler's checks, and exchanges currency. *Ávila Camacho 2221, Veracruz, Veracruz CP 91700, México, tel. 29/31–34–06. South of downtown. Open weekdays 9–1:30 and 4–6, Sat. 9–noon.*

CASAS DE CAMBIO

Exchange rates are uniform around town. **Bancomer** (Juárez, at Independencia, tel. 29/32–74–34) changes money weekdays 9–1, and you'll have to arrive early to make it through the lines. For longer hours, try **Casa de Cambio Puebla** (Juárez 112, tel. 29/31–24–50; open weekdays 9–5), or use the 24-hour ATM at **Banamex** (Independencia 1027, near Juárez, tel. 29/32–47–00).

CONSULATES

United States. *Víctimas del 25 del Julio 384, between Gómez Farías and 16 de Septiembre, tel. 29/31–58–21. Open weekdays 9–1.*

EMERGENCIES

In an emergency, dial **06** from any telephone in Veracruz city. Call the **police** at 29/38–05–67 or 29/38–06–93; for an **ambulance,** dial 29/37–55–00 or 29/37–54–1. **Oficinas Para la Seguridad del Turista** (tel. 91/800–90–392) operates a 24-hour, toll-free, bilingual hotline to provide legal and medical help for tourists in Veracruz.

LAUNDRY

The bad news at **Lavandería Automática del Parque** is that there are no self-service machines; the good news is that it's relatively cheap to have the staff do the job for you, at 50¢ per kilo (2 pounds). *Collado 23, between Juan de Dios and Begrete, tel. 29/31–06–75. Open weekdays 8–2 and 4–8, Sat. 8–3.*

MAIL

The central **post office,** a magnificent building dating from the Porfirio Díaz era, will hold mail sent to you at the following address for up to 10 days: Lista de Correos, Administración No. 1, Veracruz, Veracruz CP 91700, México. *María Mercante 210, tel. 29/32–20–38. Open weekdays 8–8, Sat. 9–1.*

MEDICAL AID

Benavides (Independencia 1291, at Serdán, tel. 29/31–89–29; open daily 8 AM–10 PM) is a big, convenient drugstore downtown. **Farmacia de la Sociedad Española Beneficencia** (16 de Septiembre, between Escobedo and Abasolo, tel. 29/32–05–59) is a 24-hour pharmacy.

PHONES

Latadel phone cards are the only way to go if you don't want to have the irritation of shoving coins into the phone every minute. Buy phone cards at kiosks displaying the LATADEL sign out front. The *zócalo* (main plaza) is sprinkled with Ladatel phones, or try the ones inside Gran Café la Parroquia (*see* Food, *below*), which is quiet and air-conditioned. To make an international collect call from any of these phones, dial **09.** Caseta Lissy (5 de Mayo 1085, between Lerdo and Juárez, tel. 29/34–99–96; open daily 8 AM–9 PM) charges $3 per minute for long-distance calls.

VISITOR INFORMATION

The bilingual staff at the **Direccion de Turismo Municipal** has few helpful pamphlets but a lot of enthusiasm. *Palacio Municipal, on the zócalo, tel. 29/32–19–99. Open Mon–Sat. 9–9, Sun. 10–1.*

COMING AND GOING

BY BUS

The main bus terminal (Díaz Mirón 1698, tel. 29/37–57–44) is 4 km (2½ mi) south of the zócalo. The main bus company is **Autobuses del Oriente** (ADO; tel. 29/37–57–22), which serves Jalapa (2 hrs, $3) every 15–30 minutes between 5:30 AM and 11 PM; Mexico City (9 hrs, $14); and Reynosa (16 hrs; $36). First-class buses run to both San Andrés Tuxtla (2½ hrs, $4.75) and Santiago Tuxtla (2 hrs, $4.50) every 15–30 minutes 7 AM–midnight daily; buses head for Catemaco (3 hrs, $5) every few hours 9:30–5:30. For those headed farther south, **Cristóbal Colón** (tel. 29/07–57–22) runs to Oaxaca city (6 hrs, $18) daily at 11 PM, and to Tuxtla Gutiérrez (11 hrs, $25) daily at 6 PM. **Cuenca** (tel. 29/35–54–05) also has service to Oaxaca city (9 hrs, $10) daily at 7 AM and 8 PM. The station offers luggage storage ($2.50 per day), public phones, and a *caseta de larga distancia* (long distance telephone office).

Autobuses Unidos (AU; tel. 29/37–23–76) and **Transportes Los Tuxtlas** (tel. 29/37–28–78) operate from the second-class bus station on the same block and offer frequent service to Jalapa (3½ hrs, $2) and San Andrés Tuxtla (3 hrs, $3.75). Any city bus marked DIAZ MIRON on Avenidas Zaragoza or 5 de Mayo near the zócalo will stop by both the first- and second-class terminals. A taxi from the zócalo to the terminal should cost no more than $2.

BY CAR

Highway 140, a modern, well-maintained freeway runs northwest to Jalapa. Highway 180 runs along the Gulf coast from Nuevo Laredo to Mérida, while Highway 150 heads southwest to Córdoba. You can rent a car at **Avis** (Collado 241, tel. 29/32–98–34), **National** (Díaz Mirón 1036, tel. 29/31–17–56), or **Budget** (Díaz Mirón 1123, tel. 29/31–21–39), all of which also have booths at the airport.

BY PLANE

The airport lies 15 km (9 mi) southwest of Veracruz city. **Mexicana** (tel. 29/32–22–42) has three direct flights a day to Mexico City ($110–$144 one way). Subsidiary airlines offer service to Cancún, Cozumel, Merida, Tuxtla Gutierrez, and other major Mexican cities. A taxi to the airport costs $8–$9.50. A cheaper alternative is the minivan ($6) that runs between the office of **Transportación Terrestre Aeropuerto** (Hidalgo 826, between Canal and Morales, tel. 29/32–32–50) and the airport.

BY TRAIN

The train station (tel. 29/32–32–72) is a romantic 19th-century building about five long blocks from the zócalo. The **Jarocho** train departs nightly at 10 PM for Mexico City (10 hrs). Classes of service include: first-class *especial* (seats in air-conditioned cars; $10.50), sleeper car ($25), and second class ($7). A second-class-only train departs daily at 8:20 AM for Mexico City (12 hrs, $7). Trains also depart daily for Jalapa (5 hrs, $2) at 7:30 AM, and for Orizaba (5 hrs, $2.50) at 8 AM. Tickets for all trains are sold at the *taquilla* (ticket booth) Monday–Saturday 6–11 and 2–9. If you're traveling first class during peak tourist season (July, August, and holidays), buy your tickets in advance—they're available up to a month before the departure date. To reach the station, follow María Mercante until it ends, then turn right.

GETTING AROUND

Downtown Veracruz centers around two plazas: the **Plaza de Armas,** also known as the zócalo, and the larger **Parque Zamora.** The two are connected by Avenida Independencia, the city's busy shopping street. While this downtown area is compact and walkable, you'll need to take buses (25¢) to the outlying beaches and some tourist sights. Most of the useful buses run along Molina and Zamora, just behind the cathedral. The *malecón* (boardwalk) parallels the seashore and is called Molina in the downtown area, becoming Boulevard Manuel Ávila Camacho (referred to by everyone as *el bulevard*) as it heads south. This winding street hugs the southern coast of Veracruz, passing Playa de Hornos and Playa Mocambo before arriving in Boca del Río. Fortunately, most other streets adhere to a grid system.

WHERE TO SLEEP

More than 60 hotels are scattered throughout this small city, so finding a place to stay is relatively easy. Because Veracruz city is a popular vacation spot for Mexicans, prices tend to be higher during holidays like Semana Santa (Holy Week, the week preceding Easter) and Carnaval (February/March), as well as the months of July and August. Lodging in the older, noisier section of downtown may be cheap, but the quality is low and the area is unsafe at night.

The Huastec of the Veracruz coast were regarded as the greatest runners in the Aztec empire. They delivered fresh fish to the Aztec capital of Tenochtitlán (near modern Mexico City), a 377-km (234-mi) dash.

NEAR THE ZOCALO

Hotels near the zócalo tend to be less expensive than those near the beach, although luxuries like air-conditioning will bump up the price in either location. The hotels listed below are in the middle of the action, but the all-night noise might make you wish you'd taken a room in a less busy area.

UNDER $15 • Hotel Amparo. Big rooms, friendly staff, and plenty of hot water make this hotel one of the best deals in town. Rooms on the main courtyard tend to be cleaner and cooler than interior rooms. The lobby TV is *always* on, and the same old crowd of *cuates* (buddies) are slouched on the uncomfortable chairs in front of it day in and day out. Doubles are only $9.50. *Serdán 482, between Zaragoza and Independencia, tel. 29/32–27–38. 64 rooms, all with bath. Luggage storage. Cash only.*

Hotel Sevilla. This small hotel is right off the zócalo. Everything here is light blue—the walls, the tiles, and the sheets. Rooms tend to be noisy, especially those that open onto Zaragoza, but all have ceiling fans, TVs, and clean bathrooms with plenty of hot water. Doubles are $13. *Morelos 359, between Lerdo and Juárez, tel. 29/32–42–46. 30 rooms, all with bath. Cash only.*

UNDER $40 • Hotel Hawaii. This little jewel of a hotel overlooks the malecón. It offers comfort, class, and eager-to-please personnel. Each impeccable guest room (doubles $38) comes with a pair of queen-size beds, air-conditioning, phone, cable TV, purified water, and a neat little bathroom. Guests can have all the free coffee they want from the hotel's coffee shop. *Insurgentes Veracruzanos 458, tel. 29/31–04–27. 32 rooms, all with bath. Coffee shop, room service, laundry, parking, luggage storage.*

NEAR THE BEACH

If you're a light sleeper you may want to keep distance between yourself and the boardwalk, as the social scene here, although more mellow than in the city itself, often continues until 10 PM.

UNDER $15 • Gran Hotel Balneario Royalty. Known to locals as "El Royalty," this gigantic building is one of the largest budget hotels in the city. Many of the pastel-color rooms have breezy balconies with nice views of the bay, and all have phones and TVs. Rooms with ceiling fans cost $15 double; add an extra $5–$7 for air-conditioning. *Abasolo 34, at Ávila Camacho, tel. 29/32–39–88. 270 rooms, all with bath. Restaurant, luggage storage.*

FOOD

Veracruz offers a mind-boggling array of culinary choices, from tempura to lasagna; watch for Afro-mestizo specialties like *tortillas de plátano* (banana tortillas), *tamales de calabaza con camarones* (pumpkin and shrimp tamales), and *huachinango a la veracruzana* (red snapper cooked with tomatoes, onions, and olives). Seafood is also a star attraction here, and the **municipal fish market,** one block south of the zócalo, has scores of stands where vendors cook all kinds of seafood dishes until late into the night. The stretch of Serdán between Zaragoza and Madero also offers plenty of inexpensive restaurants. For fresh vegetables, fruits, nuts, and cheeses, visit the daily **outdoor market** on Guerrero between Juan Soto and Serdán. Fresh bread and pastries at **Panadería País** (corner Molina and 5 de Mayo, tel. 29/32–12–13) make for a cheap and tasty breakfast. For a real treat, try one of the *nieves* (sherbets) at **Nevería Jimenez** (Zamora, at Landero y Cos); among the tastiest of the tropical flavors are mamey, guanábana, and cacahuate.

UNDER $5 • A Donde Tu Quieres. This pastel-hue, air-conditioned eatery offers pleasant respite from the city's heat and humidity. Relax with a cold glass of *sangría* (red wine sweetened with fruit), while *música criolla* (daily 3–midnight) fills the air. The $2 *comida corrida* (preprepared lunch special) features a fresh meat or seafood dish. *5 de Mayo 1039, tel. 29/34–91–61. Cash only.*

Gran Café La Parroquia. Veracruz's busiest and most venerable café is best known for its sandwiches, crepes, egg dishes, and coffee. When you want some *café con leche* (coffee with milk), tap your glass with your spoon and a waiter armed with pitchers of hot milk and coffee will scurry over. Hearty specialties include *tortilla parroquia* (chile-and-onion omelet cooked in chicken broth; $2) and *frijoles con plátanos fritos* (black beans with fried plantains). The enormous sidewalk café **Gran Café del Portal** (Independencia 105, across from the cathedral, tel. 29/31–27–59), housed in a former monastery, is run by relatives of La Parroquia's owners, and has a similar menu, as well as similar prices and atmosphere. *Gómez Farías 34, on the malecón, tel. 29/82–25–84 or 29/32–25–84. Cash only.*

Tortas Koy Koy. On delightful Parque Zamora you'll find this unpretentious little shop. Besides burgers and fries, tacos, and tamales, it serves excellent *tortas* (sandwiches) made with fresh roasted chicken, pork, or beef, served with beans, cheese, tomato, avocado, and a side of pickled vegetables. *Manuel Doblado s/n, tel. 329/1–50–49. Cash only.*

UNDER $15 • Pardiño's. The chef at this modest restaurant makes guest appearances at European food fairs. Specialties include skillfully prepared grilled sea bass, crabs *salpicón* (chopped finely with cilantro, onion, and lime), and of course the favorite local dish, huachinango a la veracruzano. Also delicious are the simple, fresh appetizers, like shrimp cocktail with generous chunks of avocado. *Landero y Coss 146, at malecón, tel. 29/32–28–76. Other location: Zamora 40, in Boca del Río, tel. 29/86–01–35.*

WORTH SEEING

Most tourist attractions are near the zócalo and are easily accessible by foot or are served by convenient public transportation. The malecón is a whirl of activity, with men selling boat rides, kids driving tiny toy cars, and scores of tacky souvenir shops. If you plan on visiting at night (a popular weekend activity among courting young jarochos), watch out for the street brawls that break out all too frequently. Parque Zamora is a more mellow spot, with a decorative old trolley car at its center.

ACUARIO

The aquarium, a short bus ride from downtown in a shopping plaza on Playa de Hornos, draws flocks of locals on weekends. The main attraction is an enormous round tank with 3,000 different marine species native to the Gulf of Mexico, including nurse sharks, manta rays, barracudas, and sea turtles. Scary shark movies are shown near the exit, and if that doesn't give you second thoughts about a dip in the sea, take a look at the very large shark outline drawn on the far wall—it's the actual size of one caught off the coast not so long ago. *Plaza Acuario, tel. 29/32–79–84. Take the* VILLA DEL MAR *or* BOCA DEL RIO *bus from the corner of Molina and Zaragoza to VIPs plaza on Ávila Camacho. Admission: $2. Open daily 10–7.*

FUERTE DE SAN JUAN DE ULUA

Built on the ruins of a Totonac temple, and now a miniature city in itself, the island fort of San Juan de Úlua is a maze of moats, ramparts, and drawbridges in the middle of Veracruz's busy port. Connected to the mainland by a causeway, this "island" was witness to some of the most momentous events in Mexican history: Cortés landed here in 1519, touching off the chain of events that would lead to Spanish colonization. In 1535, fortification of the island began (using ground coral and oyster shells to build walls) to ward off pirate attack. A few centuries later, the fort served as a prison, housing revolutionary and president-to-be Benito Juárez, among other notables. A museum on the premises displays old photos, 16th-century Spanish suits of armor, and a cannon. *Tel. 29/38–51–51. From the zócalo, take* SAN JUAN DE ULUA *bus. Admission: $2; free Sun. and holidays. Open daily 9–4:30.*

INSTITUTO VERACRUZANO DE LA CULTURA

The bright blue Veracruz Cultural Institute building was a hospital until atrocious conditions caused health authorities to close it down in 1975. The massive 18th-century structure, with its long, arched hallways and green, tree-filled garden, now hosts cultural events and rotating art exhibits. Ask for a schedule of events at the reception desk. *Canal, at Zaragoza, tel. 29/31–66–45. Admission free. Open Sun.–Tues. 9–3 and 6–9.*

MUSEO DE LA CIUDAD

The city museum is a good place to orient yourself. The region's history is narrated via artifacts and displays, and scale models of the city give you a sense of the lay of the land. Also exhibited are copies of pre-Columbian statues and contemporary indigenous art. *Zaragoza 397, near Morales, tel. 29/31–84–10. Admission free. Open Tues.–Sun. 9–4.*

FESTIVALS

Carnaval. Since 1925, jarochos have been celebrating the eight days prior to Lent with Los Bacanales (Bachanalia), a hedonistic tribute to Bacchus, Greek god of wine. Festivities typically start out with the burning of an effigy, a doll named Mal Humor (bad humor): In 1996, Mal Humor was called "Devaluación," for the devaluation of the peso, and in 1997 it was "Chupacabras," for a mythical goat-sucking creature thought to be killing local livestock. People come from all over the region to dance in the streets and gorge themselves on food and drink. The party ends when the Carnaval King and Queen, dressed in black, burn another effigy, "Juan Carnaval." *March and April.*

Veracruz city has been one of Mexico's most important ports since the day Hernando Cortés and his 600 men landed in 1519— mainly because it's a gateway to landlocked Mexico City.

Las Ramas and **EL Viejo.** Navidad in Veracruz is far from puritanical, with festivities starting up 10 days before Christmas. For the first big event, families go door to door, holding branches decorated with lanterns and singing *las ramas*—clever and funny improvised songs designed to make the neighbor open the door, listen, and offer treats for outstanding performances. Rama competitions take place in the zócalo December 20–25, when contestants vie for cash prizes. Midnight on December 31st sees the burning of an effigy named El Viejo (the old man), who symbolizes the old year. El Viejo is carried to his fiery end in the zócalo, while songs are sung in his honor. *December.*

AFTER DARK

The Plaza de Armas comes alive Tuesday and Friday nights after 8 PM, when it hosts open-air dances. There's live marimba music and the crowds come dressed in their finest. Sunday night the dancing takes place in Parque Zamora. When you've had enough of the zócalo gaiety, try one of the traditional bars just south of Plaza de Armas, such as **El Rincon de la Trove,** on the pedestrian-only side street Lagunilla. The bar serves seafood, and drink prices are lower than what you'll find on the square. The clientele is mainly young couples.

Discos and video bars are plentiful along the malecón, especially as you move south toward the beaches of Villa del Mar. Buses marked BOCA DEL RIO make the journey here from Ávila Camacho until about 10:30 PM, but you'll have to catch a cab ($2) to get back. **Ocean** (Ruíz Cortínez 8, at Ávila Camacho, tel. 29/37–63–27) is a flashy, modern discotheque, while **Blue Ocean** (Ávila Camacho 9, tel. 29/22–03–66) is a video bar with a light show. Both play a wide variety of music, draw a young, local crowd, and are open Thursday–Saturday nights. Ocean charges a cover ($8) on Saturday only; Blue Ocean charges $4 at the door Thursday–Saturday and has a small dance floor and some pool tables.

Teatro de la Reforma (5 de Mayo, at Rayón, near Parque Zamora, tel. 29/31–79–99) showcases dance and music performances two to three times a week. Buy tickets ($5–$20) or inquire about the schedule at the theater's box office.

OUTDOOR ACTIVITIES

Boat tours (30 min, $2) of the Veracruz bay leave from the malecón daily 7–7 whenever they're full. The ride includes a talk (in Spanish) on Veracruz history. Longer trips to nearby **Isla Verde** (Green Island),

Isla de en Medio (Middle Island), Isla de los Sacrificios (Island of Sacrifices), and Isla de Pájaros (Island of Birds) leave daily from the small dock near the Instituto Oceanográfico, on Ávila Camacho, and from the beach next to the Plaza Acuario. All four islands are blessed with clean and quiet beaches. However, in an effort to preserve the islands and mitigate damage caused by tourists, the Mexican coast guard randomly rotates the availability of each island; the *lancha* (motorboat) guides will tell you which ones are currently accessible. Cost is usually $5–$7 per person, but bargaining is acceptable; the old men near the Instituto tend to give better deals. Before you decide to spend the larger part of the day sunning on the islands, make sure your guide doesn't charge by the hour.

Landlubbers can rent bicycles ($1 per hr or $5 per day) and motor scooters ($23 per day) at **Bicicentros Lezama** (Juan de Dios Peza 180, near Parque Zamora, tel. 29/31–04–32; open daily 9–8).

BEACHES

Veracruz's mainland beaches are much less inviting than you might expect: Although some locals aren't deterred from swimming, the shoreline is dirty, and the water is fairly polluted. The beaches of Isla Verde, Isla de en Medio, and Isla los Sacrificios (*see above*) are cleaner, but you're still swimming in the same water. For lazing in the sand, the **Playa Cancunito** on the Isla de Pájaros is the best choice. **Villa del Mar** is the beach closest to downtown, 2 km (1 mi) south along the malecón but is also the most crowded. Locals frequent the beaches behind the Torremar Resort, 6 km (4 mi) south of Villa del Mar, known as **Playas Curazau**. The long, uninterrupted stretches of white sand are good for soaking in the sun, and they're cleaner and less built up than at **Playa Mocambo**, 2 km (1 mi) farther south.

Better beaches lie farther from town. About 4 km (2½ mi) south of Playa Mocambo is **Boca del Río,** a small fishing community at the mouth of the Río Jamapa, which is quickly getting swallowed up by the urban sprawl of greater Veracruz. Though Boca's beach gets dirtier as you move closer to the center of town, it's uncrowded, and the water is relatively unpolluted. Don't expect a charming little seaside village, though: Boca is basically a suburb by the sea. Its beaches can be reached via any of the BOCA DEL RIO buses that run along the malecón, leaving from Calle Serdán, a block east of the zócalo. Playa Curazau and Playa Mocambo are en route.

If you want to find water conducive to good snorkeling and scuba diving, head 20 km (12 mi) south of Veracruz city to the village of **Antón Lizardo.** Off its coast lie tiny islands, low-lying coral reefs, and two 19th-century shipwrecks, the *Valientes* and the *Ana Elena.* You can rent snorkel gear ($3 per hr) or scuba equipment ($18 per hr) at the local branch of **Tridente** (Pino Suárez, at Av. de la Playa, tel. 29/34–08–44), which also arranges boat rides to the islands. Three-hour boat trips are $10 per person (six-person minimum), and it's a good idea to call ahead and reserve at least a day in advance. **Autobuses Unidos** serves the town frequently from the main bus terminal in Veracruz city (20 min, $2). The last bus back to Veracruz leaves the station at Antón Lizardo around 8:30 PM.

NEAR VERACRUZ CITY

TLACOTALPAN

The town of Tlacotalpan looks much the same as it did 100 years ago, when one-time resident President Porfirio Díaz attempted to remake its dock area into an important trade center for Veracruz. The Revolution came, Porfirio went, and Tlacotalpan didn't modernize—a stroke of luck if you're an architecture buff or a weary traveler. This sleepy, riverside village's pristine colonial architecture and Popsicle-color houses truly soothe the senses. Laze away the day on a riverboat ride or in the quiet zócalo, listening to the plaintive songs of the old-timers strumming their guitars.

Touring Tlacotalpan takes no time at all. The **Museo Salvador Ferrando** (Alegre 6, in Plaza Hidalgo, no phone; open weekdays 10–5; admission $1) features Tlacotalpan furniture and crafts from the past century. A 15-minute walk to the western edge of town takes you to the **cemetery,** with marble mausoleums and Italian angels that have unfortunately suffered some looting. The zócalo features the Moorish architecture of the **Iglesia de la Candelaria,** home to the Virgin of Candelaria for 200 years. During the **Festival de la Candelaria** (February 2) the Virgin is bedecked with hundreds of shimmering candles and sailed down the river with a full regatta. Two days prior to the event, the town warms up with masquerades and a running of the bulls à la Pamplona.

BASICS

Inverlat (Carranza, below Hotel Doña Lala) changes money weekdays 9–1:30. It has a 24-hour ATM that accepts MasterCard only. The **Oficina de Correos** (Pablo Díaz 3, off Plaza Zaragoza; open weekdays 8–3) offers the usual postal services. For telephone and fax services, visit **Servicios Multiples** (Alegre, at Iglesias, tel. 288/42–0–21; open daily 8 AM–10 PM), where a long-distance call costs about $2.25 per minute. You can pick up a small pamphlet and map of the city at **Museo Salvador Ferrando** (*see above*) for $2.

COMING AND GOING

Tlacotalpan is centered around two main squares, the Plaza Zaragoza and Hidalgo park (which lie right next to each other). Within one or two blocks of the squares lies the river, most of the restaurants, and just about all of the sights. The **ADO** and **Cuenca** terminal (Beltrán 43, 1 block west of Plaza Zaragoza, tel. 288/4–21–25) has bus service hourly 6:15 AM–10:15 PM to Veracruz city and 7:35 AM–8:35 PM to San Andres Tuxtla. For motorists, Highway 180 connects Tlacotalpan to Veracruz city.

WHERE TO SLEEP AND EAT

The **Hotel Doña Lala** (Carranza 11, tel. 288/4–25–80) has dark wooden staircases and hallways that lend it a 19th-century atmosphere. The yellow rooms are clean and bright, though a bit bare. Rooms for two people cost $19 ($21.50 with air-conditioning). Just two storefronts down is the **Hotel Reforma** (Carranza 2, tel. 288/4–20–22). Rooms here are clean, but smaller and more modest than the big, airy lobby would have you think. Doubles run $13 ($18 with air-conditioning). Hotel Reforma accepts cash only. You can camp for free at the far north side of the river, known as **Cancha del Bosque**; just go into the Palacio Municipal, on the zócalo, to ask for permission. **Doña Leo** (Gutiérrez Zamora 1, at Carranza, tel. 288/4–24–58) dishes up big, economic breakfasts (less than $1.50) and a generous comida corrida. Just a block away from Plaza Zaragoza, a string of fresh seafood restaurants line the riverside, serving local specialties like *robalo al ajillo* (a type of freshwater fish cooked with garlic) and *mojarra* (freshwater bass cooked with lime and chiles, oranges, or garlic).

> *Veracruz's port-city swagger has earned its inhabitants the nickname jarochos (rude ones).*

ZEMPOALA RUINS

Thick sugarcane fields surround the ruins of Zempoala, while the irregular peaks of the Sierra Madre Oriental rise dramatically in the distance. Located one hour north of Veracruz city, just outside the small town of **José Cardel,** Zempoala's pyramids are not particularly exciting architecturally, but they do have a distinguished history. This sizeable Totonac town of 30,000 was the first settlement to rebel against Moctezuma's empire: Resentful over the excessive tributes they had to pay to the Aztec, the Totonac allied themselves with Cortés's army. Meanwhile, Cortés's first scouts reported that the city was made of silver, so brightly did its white-stucco pyramids gleam in the moonlight. Time has now worn away the plaster, revealing surprisingly uniform, rounded riverbed stones beneath.

The **Templo Mayor** lies directly in front of you as you enter the site. Its steep staircase ascends 13 levels to the faint remains of a three-room shrine on top. To the right of the Templo Mayor sits a smaller pyramid, **Las Chimeneas** (The Chimneys), named after the remains of four round towers in front of it. Cortés may have lodged at the top of this temple; before this, the chimneys were probably used for storage. Behind Las Chimeneas, out in the cane fields, lies another small structure, called **Las Caritas** (Little Faces) for the many pottery heads that once decorated its walls. Today you'll only find graffiti scratched into traces of the original paint. The **Gran Pirámide** (also known as the Temple of the Sun) and the **Temple of the Moon** are at the western edge of the site, next to a stand of jacaranda trees.

All of Zempoala's ruins lie close together, so a walk around the site shouldn't take more than 20 minutes. At the entrance you'll find friendly guards happy to discuss the region (in Spanish) or sell you colorful, informative pamphlets (some in English) for 50¢. **Adolfo Velasco** is a student who works as an English-speaking guide Friday and Saturday from September through June, and every day in July and August. He requests a small donation for his work. The site is open daily 9–6, and admission is $1.25.

COMING AND GOING

To reach Zempoala from Veracruz city, take a **TRV** bus (tel. 29/37–57–32) from the second-class bus station to José Cardel (45 min, $1). Buses leave every 10 minutes between 8 AM and 7 PM. In José Cardel, turn left out of the **bus station** (tel. 296/2–01–69) and walk one block to the corner of Zapata and Avenida Cardel, on the zócalo. From here, white *micros* (minibuses) marked ZEMPOALA and *colec-*

tivos (collective taxis) can take you to the ruins (15 min, 50¢) 6 AM–8 PM. The last bus returns to Veracruz city from José Cardel at 10:30 PM. To reach Zempoala from Jalapa, catch a TRV bus from the central bus station in Jalapa (1½ hrs, $2).

WHERE TO SLEEP

If you want to stay overnight in José Cardel, **Hotel Garelli** (Flores Magnón, at Juárez, tel. 296/2–05–69) is basic and clean. Its jovial owner charges $4 per person. If you're dying for air-conditioning, try the frilly pink rooms at **Hotel Cardel** (Zapata, at Martínez, tel. 296/2–00–14); doubles here are $17. Both hotels accept cash only. You can camp at the ruins for free if you first obtain permission from the head caretaker, Feliciano Concha Bas, who can be found around the entrance daily 9–6.

LOS TUXTLAS

The small volcanic mountain range of Sierra de Los Tuxtlas meets the sea 140 km (87 mi) south of Veracruz city. The area, simply known as Los Tuxtlas, has lakes, waterfalls, rivers, mineral springs, and beaches, making it a popular stopover for travelers heading east from Mexico City to the Yucatán. The region's three principal towns—Santiago Tuxtla, San Andrés Tuxtla, and Catemaco—are tucked away in mountains about 650 ft above sea level, lending them a heavenly coolness even in summer.

The Los Tuxtlas region was once a center of Olmec culture, and Olmec artifacts and small ruins abound, especially around Santiago Tuxtla. Today, the economic life of Los Tuxtlas depends on cattle ranching, cigar manufacture, and tourism. Though much of Los Tuxtlas architecture is of the 1960s school (i.e., lots of unadorned cement), all three towns are laid out in the colonial style, around a main plaza and a church, and retain a certain charm. Residents of the towns, particularly Santiago and San Andrés, are warm and friendly, and still treat foreign travelers with an air of novelty. The largest of the three towns is San Andrés, which is also the local transport hub and a good base from which to explore the entire region. From Santiago, you can visit the ruins at Tres Zapotes; the town also has an informative museum where you can learn about the region's indigenous heritage. Lake Catemaco is popular among Mexicans as a summer and Christmas resort; it's also the place to go for a *consulta* (consultation) with a brujo or curandero, should you have any questions that require spiritual clarification or supernatural intervention.

BASICS

CASAS DE CAMBIO

The only places in the Tuxtlas to change money are in San Andrés: **Bancomer** (Madero 20, tel. 294/2–00–41) changes currency and traveler's checks weekdays 9–1. **Banamex** (Madero 4, tel. 294/2–13–50; open weekdays 9–1:30) only changes traveler's checks, but it has a 24-hour ATM that accepts Plus, Cirrus, MasterCard, and Visa.

EMERGENCIES

The **Cruz Roja** (González Boca Negra 242, tel. 294/2–05–00) in San Andrés provides emergency medical care for all three towns. In an emergency, contact the **police** in San Andrés at 294/2–02–34, in Santiago at 294/7–00–92, and in Catemaco at 294/3–00–55.

MEDICAL AID

Farmacia Garysa (Madero 3, tel. 294/2–44–34) in San Andrés is open 24 hours, and you can get just about any prescription drug or remedy there.

PHONES AND MAIL

The largest **post office** (tel. 294/2–01–89; open weekdays 8–8, Sat. 9–1) in the region is in San Andrés, on the corner of 20 de Noviembre and La Frauga, one block downhill from the main square. Mail will be held for you for up to 10 days at the following address: Lista de Correos, San Andrés Tuxtla, Veracruz, CP 95701, México. There are a few small **phone offices** in all three towns—just look for the blue-and-white signs marked LARGA DISTANCIA. One of the most convenient is in San Andrés at **Casetea "Pipisoles"** (Madero 6-B, tel. 294/2–25–88; open daily 8 AM–9 PM), just past the Banamex.

COMING AND GOING

The transport hub for Los Tuxtlas is San Andrés's **ADO** terminal (Juárez 762, tel. 294/2–08–71), a short six blocks from the zócalo. Buses for Veracruz city (2½ hrs, $4.75) leave hourly between 5 AM and 8 PM. Several luxury overnight buses, with air-conditioning, free movies, and soft drinks depart for Mexico City (9 hrs, $20) around midnight, and there are also frequent departures for Villahermosa (5 hrs, $10) and Jalapa (8 hrs, $8).

Second-class buses based in San Andrés link the three towns of Los Tuxtlas; from San Andrés to either Catemaco or Santiago it's a 15-minute ride (50¢). Santiago-bound buses leave the **Terminal de los Rojos** station (Juárez, 1 block past ADO on Hwy. 180) in San Andrés every 10 minutes. You don't have to go to the station to board the bus for Catemaco—just wait on Highway 180 around the corner from the ADO terminal for one of Rojos's CATEMACO buses, which pass every 10–15 minutes. In Catemaco, the second-class company operates a small station two blocks from the main square. In Santiago, the bus stop is at the corner of Morelos and Ayuntamiento, three blocks from the plaza. All three towns are connected by Highway 180 (known locally as the Carretera de Golfo), which is narrow but well-paved. Heading southeast, it hits Santiago de las Tuxtlas, then San Andrés, and on to Catemaco.

SAN ANDRES TUXTLA

To find out what it was like to be imprisoned at San Juan de Ulúa fort in the 19th century, squat in the small subterranean cell known as el purgatorio (purgatory). Maintain this position for two or three years.

San Andrés Tuxtla is the largest and most modern town in Los Tuxtlas, with approximately 80,000 inhabitants. A graceful, red-dome cathedral presides over the central plaza, which is surrounded by relaxed, open-air cafés. Bordering the plaza, the main street running east–west is **Madero**; the main streets running north–south are **Juárez** and **Rascón.** In the summer evenings, you'll find the zócalo filled with groups of kids walking around in the warm rain, eating homemade *paletas,* which are Mexican desserts like flan or *arroz con leche* (rice pudding) frozen on a stick. The pleasant atmosphere, cool temperatures, and convenient location make this an ideal stopover for travelers feeling abused by too many hours on the bus. To sample traditional curative teas and medicinal herbs, visit **Farmacia Homeopática La Esperanza** (Juárez 264, at Hidalgo, tel. 294/2–08–79), two blocks from the zócalo on the way to the ADO station. The **Fábrica de Puros Santa Clara** (5 de Febrero 10, tel. 294/2–12–00) is a huge cigar factory where you can see experts making fine cigars (as much as $92 for a box of 24). If you buy a box, they'll print your name or slogan on each cigar at no extra charge.

WHERE TO SLEEP

On a quiet side street near the cathedral lies the spotless **Hotel Catedral** (Pino Suárez 3, tel. 294/2–02–37). A night here costs $4 for one person, $6 for two; most rooms have large comfortable beds, and all have clean bathrooms with decent plumbing. The hotel accepts cash only. At **Hotel San Andrés** (Madero 6, tel. 294/2–06–04), all 31 rooms ($13 doubles, $3 extra for air-conditioning) are graced with Diego Rivera prints and private balconies. **Hotel de Los Pérez** (Rascón 2, tel. 294/2–07–77) is your best bet at the high end. All rooms ($20 doubles) come with phones, TVs, blissfully quiet air-conditioners, and spotless bathrooms. The hotel also has a decent restaurant.

FOOD

San Andrés is not renowned for its restaurants. If you want quality seafood or regional specialties, make the short trip to Catemaco. Otherwise, the cafés near the zócalo on Madero serve cappuccino and fixed-price breakfasts. In the afternoons, the restaurant at **Hotel del Parque,** right on the zócalo, serves a filling comida corrida for $3. The small, outdoor **Caperucita Roja** (Juárez 108, tel. 294/2–05–11) whips up sandwiches and tacos at rock-bottom prices. Or escape to **Restaurante Tortacos** (tel. 294/2–31–00), in the cool, quiet La Fuente shopping center (corner of Juárez and Argudín); the *pollo con mole poblano* (chicken in chocolate-chile sauce) and mojarra costs $2. This is also the place to satisfy late-night cravings—it's open nightly until 3 AM. **El Fénix** (Constitución 125) is a big supermarket where you can stock up on picnic supplies. All of the above are cash only.

OUTDOOR ACTIVITIES

In the wet, tropical hills of Los Tuxtlas, opportunities abound for day trips to local swimming holes, rivers, and beaches. Just 3 km (2 mi) outside San Andrés, the **Laguna Encantada** (Enchanted Lagoon) fills a small volcanic crater; the lake gets its name from its strange propensity to rise in the dry season and fall during the rains. Some taxis will brave the rutted road to the lake for $5. More easily reached and more impressive is **Salto de Eyipantla**, 20 km (12 mi) from town on Highway 180. A roaring, 132-ft-wide waterfall crashes 165 ft into shallow, churning pools. It's a popular picnic spot with the locals. The falls are served by greenish micros marked SALTO that run every 5–10 minutes from the zócalo in San Andrés. Micros cost about 50¢, and it's a 20-minute ride to the falls.

CATEMACO

On the western shore of Lake Catemaco, 12 km (7 mi) southwest of San Andrés on Highway 180, the town of Catemaco is now almost entirely devoted to tourism, but has lost little of its eccentric character. Inhabited by approximately 40,000 people of Spanish, African, and indigenous descent, Catemaco is dotted with *consultorios* (consulting rooms), where brujos ply their trade. If you'd like to sample their services, ask a townsperson for a recommendation—most residents have snuck off for a *limpia* (spiritual cleansing) once or twice themselves.

In stark contrast to their beautiful surroundings, the muddy foothills of Catemaco are home to rows of makeshift houses and shacks. The town's center of activity is its lakeside walkway, or malecón, just two blocks downhill from the bus station and the zócalo. The malecón contains what little nightlife Las Tuxtlas has to offer, namely the discotheque **Luna 90**, and the bar **El Pescado Loco**. It also bustles with seafood vendors, souvenir stands, inexpensive eateries, and men hawking boat rides—all set against the gorgeous backdrop of lake and mountain. Look closely and you might see *changos* (monkeys), parakeets, and white herons along the shore. Take a tour in a lancha to **Isla de los Changos** (Monkey Island) for a peek at a troop of whimsical-looking baboons with bright red behinds. The baboons were brought from Thailand by the University of Veracruz for research purposes and now supplement their vegetarian diet with fish (yes, you can actually see them diving for lunch). University researchers ask that you do not feed the monkeys or attempt to interfere with their natural behavior. On the way to visit the monkeys, you'll pass by **Isla de Garzas,** a nesting spot for herons, and **El Tegal,** a grotto where the Virgin allegedly made a local appearance. It's now a shrine lit with countless votive candles. The lancha tours also include stops at a couple of other beaches and a swimming hole, a ride past floating aquatic flowers, and a visit to Nanciyaga (*see* Outdoor Activities, *below*). You can get off and walk around at most places, except for Isla de los Changos and Isla de Garzas. Lancha tours costs $21 for one to six people.

The town's other attractions include the gaudy church on the zócalo dedicated to Catemaco's patron saint, the Virgen del Carmen, who appeared in 1714 to Juan Catemaxca—a local fisherman for whom the town is named. Every year on May 30, locals descend upon the malecón, where lanchas await to take them out to the **Monumento a Juan Catemaxca** for ceremonial offerings of fish, flowers, and fruit. If you're in town on the first Friday in March, don't miss the conference of brujos who gather on the misty hillside of **Cerro Mono Blanco** (Hill of the White Monkey), overlooking Lake Catemaco, to conjure up the spirits.

WHERE TO SLEEP

Hotel Los Arcos (Madero 7, at Mantilla, tel. 294/3–00–03) provides comfortable rooms equipped with phones, TVs, private bathrooms, and balconies overlooking the lake. There's even a small pool in the courtyard. Doubles cost $20, with air-conditioning $23. At **Posada Koniapan** (Revolución, at malecón, tel. 294/3–00–63), air-conditioned rooms on the ground floor cost $19, while upstairs rooms with ceiling fans cost $16. All rooms have balconies facing the lake. The Koniapan sits at a quiet end of the malecón, and a good-size pool beckons from the grassy front yard. Both places accept cash only.

FOOD

The malecón is lined with small restaurants overlooking the lake. Most serve seafood, including mojarra that's usually priced about $2 a plate. **Las 7 Brujas** (tel. 294/3–01–57; cash only) is a two-story bamboo hut with a great view of the lake, not to mention delicious *robalo al ajillo* (freshwater fish cooked with garlic; $4). **La Ceiba** (tel. 294/3–00–51; cash only) is the most economical of the sit-down eateries on the malécon and serves an outstanding *ceviche de jaiba* (crab marinated in lime juice; $3). Those who want to try the regional specialty *ceviche de tegogolos* had better be adventurous in two ways: (1) not mind eating *tegogolo* (a type of snail that lives in the lake), and (2) be able to withstand its reputed aphrodisiac qualities. There's always the **mercado** (market) just off the malecón, where *comedores* (sit-down food stands) sell hearty meals for less than $2, and a cocktail of shrimp, oysters, or octopus won't cost more than $2.50.

OUTDOOR ACTIVITIES

For mud and mineral water baths, sweatlodge rituals, and guided tours of the rain forest, head to the self-proclaimed ecotourist paradise of **Nanciyaga** (tel. 294/3–01–99; open daily 8:30–7). It's a simple, locally managed resort on the edge of Lake Catemaco. For the $1.25 admission fee you'll be treated to a guided tour of the forest plus an introduction to the history and rituals of the *temascal* (sweat lodge). A session in the temascal runs $9.50 (reservations required) and a mud facial costs $6. You can rent cabañas here for $10–$32 per night, which entitles you to a free mud and mineral water bath. Nanciyaga can be reached by bus (15 min, 50¢) from the zócalo in Catemaco, or by lancha from Catemaco's malecón (10 min, $4–$6). If you're driving, take the Coyame highway southwest from San Andrés to Nanciyaga. About a 15-minute drive past Nanciyaga is **Río Cuetzalapan,** a cold-water mountain stream popular for swimming and fishing.

NEAR CATEMACO

The Gulf Coast beaches, 1½ bumpy hours by bus out of Catemaco, are one of Los Tuxtlas's great secrets. Though they don't offer the white, sugary sand of Cancún, their desolation and lack of commercial development lends them a certain special appeal. Indeed, foreign tourists rarely venture this far

Veracruz city is the birthplace of the song "La Bamba," and of Yuri, Mexico's answer to American pop chanteuse Madonna.

down the coast, unless they're staying at one of the few isolated hotels scattered among the region's tiny fishing villages. Buses marked SONTECOMOPAN leave Catemaco at the corner of Revolución and the malecón every 20 minutes ($1.50). The 25-minute ride down narrow Highway 180 takes you through some beautiful ranching country before stopping at **Sontecomopan,** a small town on the shore of a quiet lagoon. Near the lagoon lies **Poza Enano,** a freshwater swimming hole frequented by locals. They say the reflections in the water make you look like an *enano* (dwarf). From Sontecomopan, lanchas ($3) will take you to the small, pleasant beach called **La Barra.** If you're still on a quest for the perfect stretch of sand, pickups ($1) from Sontecomopan run down the dirt road toward other Gulf Coast beaches. About 10 km (6 mi) along this road is the stop for **Playa Jicacal** and **Playa Escondida,** two of the most attractive beaches in the region. When you get off the bus, follow the marked trail downhill for about 1 km (½ mi) to the sandy expanse of Playa Jicacal. Playa Escondida lies on the other side of the promontory at the far end of the beach (use care when swimming here, as locals claim the area is frequented by sharks). Pickups leave Playas Jicacal and Escondida for the return trip to Catemaco as late as 8 PM, but you'd be crazy to try hiking back up the hill after nightfall. On top of the promontory, the basic **Hotel Playa Escondida** (no phone; cash only), with double rooms for $10, is your best overnight option. You're allowed to camp, but the beach is narrow, and locals warn that it's unsafe.

The farthest beach, at a spot along the sand most resembling a town, is **Montepío,** the end of the line for the SONTECOMOPAN bus; the last bus to return to Sontecomopan leaves at 7 PM. If you want to spend the majority of your day on the beaches rather than on a bus, stay overnight. Camping isn't safe here so try the **Hotel San José** (tel. 294/2–10–10), which charges $10 for a double, cash only. You can usually find someone around town who will rent a horse ($2 per hour) if you feel like gallivanting about.

SANTIAGO TUXTLA

With its winding streets, red-tile roofs, and small daily market, Santiago Tuxtla, northwest from San Andrés on Highway 180, has managed to retain more of its colonial character than Tuxtla's other two towns. Most visitors come to see the nearby ruins of **Tres Zapotes,** an ancient Olmec settlement. A huge carved-stone Olmec head dominates the town's zócalo, and the **Museo Tuxteco** (no phone; open Mon.–Sat. 9–6, Sun. 9–3; admission $1.50), also on the plaza, displays a collection of Olmec and early Huastec pieces, including clay sculptures, obsidian blades, and a skull showing evidence of ritual deformation. The museum's director, Dr. Fernando Bustamante, is an expert on local indigenous cultures and more than willing to answer (in Spanish) any question you may have. He is usually at the museum weekday mornings.

LOVE LOST? LET A BRUJA HELP

Do you want to gain the undying love of someone who has spurned you? If so, bring his/her photo and between $70 and $140 to a Los Tuxtlas "bruja" (witch), who will perform a "trabajo" (spell-casting) for you.

A cheaper option ($5–$30) is to purify your own soul with a "limpia," which cleanses your aura of the negativity that causes blockages in luck and love. In the typical cleansing, you will be placed in front of an altar that sparkles with Catholic icons and is often bedecked with strings of Christmas lights. The special objects used in the ritual have a European-pagan tradition: The egg is a symbol of new life and fertility, while the basil plant is believed to be so powerful that smelling too much of it will cause a scorpion to grow in your brain. Both objects are doused with "sacred" water and brushed all over your body while Catholic incantations are intoned a mile a minute by the bruja. The ritual culminates with the bruja blowing the water onto you and then pouring it over your head—a baptism of sorts.

Does it work? Who knows, but many claim to experience a lingering feeling of euphoria and cleanliness . . . at least until the sacred water (Avon perfume) wears off.

Call Nanciyaga (see Outdoor Activities, below) to make an appointment for your limpia ($5). In Catemaco, José Luis Martínez Miros (tel. 294/3–07–91) is reputed to be a genuine curandero, but his limpia fees tend to be on the steep side ($14–$28). He also performs trabajos but at higher prices.

The Tres Zapotes ruins lie 21 km (13 mi) west of town. Though once an important Olmec ceremonial center occupied as early as AD 100, the ruins are now fairly unspectacular. Little remains of the original site, except for **La Camila,** a burial mound that rises above the cornfields outside town. This large mound (almost 50 ft tall) is locally regarded as an important nexus of spiritualism and cosmic energy. But unless you wish to exercise a lively imagination, skip the strenuous walk through the overgrown ruins and head for the **museum** in the village of Tres Zapotes. From the entrance to the ruins, hang a left on the dirt road and walk for 1 km (½ mi) until you come to a large grassy field, where you'll find the outdoor museum. Here you'll see **Stela C,** a slab of bas-relief carving, with the date 7.16.6.16.18 (the 3rd of September 32 BC) inscribed upon it in the bar-and-dot calendrical system. This stela is one of the earliest examples of the "Long Count" calendar, suggesting that the Olmec were the originators of a system the Maya would later adopt and perfect.

COMING AND GOING

The only way to make the bumpy, 25-minute trip from Santiago Tuxtla to the Tres Zapotes ruins is by colectivo (50¢) or by taxi ($5.75). Both leave from **Los Pozitos** bar (just over the bridge from Hidalgo) in Santiago Tuxtla. You may have to wait over an hour to leave in a colectivo, as they only depart when they're full.

WHERE TO SLEEP

Casa de Huéspedes Morelos (Obregón 15, at Morelos, tel. 294/7–04–74) is the cleanest of Santiago's few budget lodging options and feels like what it is: someone's cramped but comfortable home. There's no air-conditioning, but each room has a fan, and the owner doesn't mind if you use her washboard and clothesline. Rooms cost $10 for a double, cash only.

FOOD

The area near the bus terminal houses several inexpensive *fondas* (covered food stands), and near the zócalo there's a daily market that sells fruit and bread. At **Parrilla la Ribera** (Castellanos Quinto 43, tel. 294/7–06–73) the chicken tacos are a steal ($1 for five), and the owner, Señor Gutiérrez, is super friendly. To get here, walk down Morelos to Victoria and turn left after you cross the bridge. **Restaurant Los Faisanes** (5 de Mayo, at Comonfort, tel. 294/7–02–00) is spotless and attractive. It serves decent seafood like *robalo al ajillo* (freshwater fish cooked with garlic; $4); satisfying breakfasts cost $2. Both places are cash only.

JALAPA

There's an air of mystery in the Tuxtlas; townspeople whisper about local brujos (witches) and curanderos (healers) who read tarot cards, prescribe herbal remedies, and cast spells.

Home to 800,000 *xalapeños* (as the city's residents are called), Jalapa is perched on the side of a mountain, between the coastal lowlands of Veracruz and the highlands of the central plateau. Just over 5,000 ft above sea level, the city has a pleasant climate that will come as a surprise to travelers arriving from Veracruz city, which swelters on the coast some 100 km (60 mi) to the southeast. The cool temperatures also bring rains and winds, and townsfolk joke that you can sometimes experience all four seasons in one day. This is the capital of the state of Veracruz and a university town, also called "The Athens of Veracruz" for its thriving arts scene. The presence of the Universidad Autonoma de Veracruz makes for a heady cosmopolitan mixture: You are as likely to meet long-haired intellectuals sipping espressos in cafés as you are to see wizened *campesinos* (rural dwellers) bringing their livestock and produce to market. The city's arts community runs the gamut from smaller experimental dance and theater troupes to a symphony orchestra and a state theater that attracts big-name performers. Jalapa also boasts the finest anthropology museum outside Mexico City.

BASICS

AMERICAN EXPRESS

The travel agency **Viajes Xalapa** functions as the local AmEx representative and provides all AmEx services, including exchanging traveler's checks and holding cardholders' mail. *Carillo Puerto 24, Jalapa, Veracruz, CP 91000, México, tel. 28/17–87–44. 3 blocks east of Parque Juárez. Open weekdays 9–1:30 and 4–7, Sat. 9–1.*

CASAS DE CAMBIO

Five blocks west of Parque Juárez, **Casa de Cambio Jalapa** (Zamora 36, tel. 28/18–68–60; open weekdays 9–2 and 4–6) offers excellent rates on currency. You can also change money on weekday mornings at several banks near Parque Juárez. **Bancomer** (Lázaro Cárdenas, at Ferrocarril, tel. 28/14–43–22; open weekdays 8:30–2) only changes traveler's checks. **Banamex** (Xalapeños Ilustres 3, tel. 28/15–64–01) has similar rates; changes both cash and traveler's checks; and has an ATM that accepts Cirrus, Plus, Visa, and MasterCard.

EMERGENCIES

In an emergency, dial **06** from any telephone in Jalapa. For the **police,** call 28/17–22–80, and for **ambulance** service contact the Cruz Roja (tel. 28/17–34–31).

LAUNDRY

Easy Launder has "easy" prices: For 50¢ a kilo (2 pounds), someone will wash, dry, and fold your clothes and return them to you the same day. *201-C Ávila Camacho, at Mártires 28 Agosto, no phone. 7 long city blocks east of Parque Juárez. Open Mon.–Sat. 9–8.*

MAIL

The full-service **post office** (Diego Lenyo, at Zamora, tel. 28/11–03–40; open weekdays 8–8, Sat. 9–1) is seven blocks west of Parque Juárez. The post office will hold mail sent to you at the following address for up to 10 days: Lista de Correos, Administración No. 1, Jalapa, Veracruz, CP 91000, México. Next door, the **Centro de Servicios Integrados de Telecommunicaciones** (Zamora 70, tel. 28/17–71–60; open weekdays 8–6, Sat. 9–noon) offers fax, telegram, and telex services.

MEDICAL AID

You'll find many pharmacies on Calle Enríquez. The 24-hour pharmacy in **Super Tiendas Ramón** (Revolución 171, at Sagayo, tel. 28/18–09–35) has a staff that speaks English.

PHONES

You can make a long-distance collect call by dialing 09 from any of the **Ladatel** phones clustered in front of the Palacio del Gobierno (Enríquez, at Revolución). Alternately, the long-distance service inside the **Restaurant Mariscos** (Zaragoza 70, tel. 28/17–84–36; open daily 7 AM–11 PM) charges $1.50 per minute for international calls.

SCHOOLS

The **Escuela Para Estudiantes Extranjeros,** of the Universidad Veracruzana, offers six-week summer and four-month semester programs for foreign students. The department can also tailor courses to your needs and arrange homestays. Contact Maestra Berta Cecilia Murrieta Cervantes (who speaks English) by phone for more information or write to: Escuela Para Estudiantes Extranjeros, AP 440, Jalapa, Veracruz, CP 91000, México. *Juárez 55, 2nd floor, between Lucío and Revolución, tel. 28/17–86–87, fax 28/17–64–13.*

VISITOR INFORMATION

The restaurant **La Sopa** (*see* Food, *below*) hands out a trilingual brochure (Spanish, English, French) with detailed information about and a map of Jalapa. The friendly staff at the **tourist office** is not terribly well informed, and if you don't ask for the green *folleto* with a map of Jalapa, you'll just get an unreadable map and useless pamphlets. *Av. de las Américas, 1st floor of Torre Ánimas building, tel. 28/12–72–84. From Parque Juárez, walk west on Hidalgo, ½ block past Baderas, then take a pesero marked CENTRO TORRE ANIMAS or SEC. Open weekdays 9–3 and 6–9, Sat. 9–1.*

COMING AND GOING

BY BUS

Jalapa's attractive, modern **Central de Autobuses de Xalapa** (20 de Noviembre Ote. 571, tel. 28/18–92–29), commonly known as CAXA, lies 2 km (1 mi) east of the city center. It's served by the first-class **Autobuses del Oriente (ADO)** line (tel. 28/18–98–55 or 28/18–92–40), as well as the second-class **Autobuses Unidos** (AU; tel. 28/18–70–77). ADO has frequent departures to Veracruz city (2 hrs, $3), Mexico City (5 hrs, $10.50), Catemaco (4½ hrs, $8.50), Papantla (4 hrs, $8), and Puebla (3 hrs, $6). AU has equally frequent service and slightly lower prices. The terminal has a 24-hour pharmacy, a long-distance phone office, and 24-hour luggage storage (25¢ per hr). To reach the center of town from the station, walk down the wide stone stairs to the local bus stop and catch any bus marked CENTRO. To reach the terminal from downtown, catch a bus marked CAXA going east from Enríquez, between Clavijero and Revolución.

BY TRAIN

The small **Estación Nueva Miguel Alemán** (tel. 28/15–17–64) is in the northern section of Jalapa. Two painfully slow second-class trains creep to Mexico City (7½ hrs, $3.50) and Veracruz city (5 hrs, $2) daily. A cab from here to downtown should cost less than $2.

GETTING AROUND

Jalapa's hilly, winding cobblestone streets can test the stamina of even the fittest traveler, but there are plenty of beautiful parks where you can stop and catch your breath. And keep a city map handy, as many major streets change names once or more. **Parque Juárez** is the city's emotional, if not geographic, heart. Enríquez runs along the northern edge of the park; as it heads east past the purple Banamex building it becomes Zamora, and as it heads west past the **Teatro del Estado** (state theater) it becomes Ávila Camacho. Allende flanks the southern edge of the park, Zaragoza radiates from its east side, and Revolución branches from its northeast corner.

The most important city bus routes originate in front of the **3 Hermanos** shoe store on Enríquez, two blocks east of Parque Juárez. Buses (25¢) and colectivos (30¢) run 5 AM–11 PM. Taxis, which roam all main streets, are also relatively cheap and extremely convenient. They don't have meters—just get in, name your destination, and don't pay more than $1.

WHERE TO SLEEP

Because Jalapa functions as the seat of state government, a university town, and the only big city in a poor but heavily settled rural area, it offers plenty of lodging choices. You'll find several clean, comfortable, and surprisingly cheap hotels right in the center of town.

UNDER $10 • Hotel Plaza. Rooms at the Plaza are tidy and fan-cooled, and the bathrooms have hot water, soap, and clean towels. Some rooms are a bit gloomy, but all of them are spacious. The hotel is on busy Enríquez, and rooms facing the street are more airy—and more noisy—than their interior counterparts. Doubles cost $7. The reception desk is at the top of a flight of stairs at the end of a long, yellow-tile hallway next to Enrico's restaurant. *Enríquez 4, tel. 28/17–33–10. 36 rooms, all with bath. Luggage storage. Cash only.*

The precolonial name for San Andrés was Zacoalcos, meaning "locked-up place." Some say it referred to the surrounding rugged hills and narrow valleys, which made it difficult to find a way into the town.

Hotel Principal. This immaculate hotel is a short walk from Parque Juárez. The rooms (doubles $9–$10) are big and comfortable, with phones, TVs, and ceilings high enough to accommodate any visiting giraffes—just get an interior room or the traffic will set your teeth rattling. The tidy bathrooms are, oddly enough, configured to allow you to use the toilet and sink while showering. *Zaragoza 28, tel. 28/17–64–00. 3½ blocks east of Parque Juárez. 40 rooms, all with bath. Laundry, luggage storage. Cash only.*

UNDER $20 • Hotel Posada del Virrey. A Spanish coat of arms is engraved into every available window at the Virrey. Tastefully decorated and immaculate rooms offer TVs, phones, and modern bathrooms, and some rooms even have small, wrought-iron balconies. Doubles cost $19. *Dr. Lucío 142, tel. 28/18–61–00. 40 rooms, all with bath. Restaurant, laundry, luggage storage, safe-deposit boxes.*

Las Margaritas. This charming, sunny hotel has brightly colored daisies painted on all the chairs and doors, and bowls of flowers are scattered around the lobby. Big picture windows offer great views of Jalapa. Rooms are spacious and equipped with phones and TVs; doubles cost $15, and triples $22. *Benito Quijano 10, ½ block from the bus station, tel. 28/12–43–25. 29 rooms, all with bath. Coffee shop, luggage storage. Cash only.*

CAMPING

Camping is permissible 40 minutes outside Jalapa, on the shores of the **Río Pescados.** The area is safe, and you can stock up on food supplies at stores in the nearby town of Jalcomulco. If you're driving, take the Las Trancas exit from Jalapa towards Veracruz city, which turns into the Coatepec/Huatusco highway. This will bring you to the town of Jalcomulco, where you'll find river access. Or catch a southbound JALCOMULCO bus ($3) from 7 de Noviembre, between Úrsulo Galván and Allende; buses leave every 20–40 minutes.

FOOD

If you eat all your meals at the markets on Altamirano, you'll spend less than $5 for breakfast, lunch, and dinner combined. You might even develop a taste for *hormigas chichantanas* (dried ants), a local delicacy. Down the hill from the markets, along Lucío, you'll find health-food stores, bakeries, and the superstore **Chedraui Centro** (Lucío 28, tel. 28/18–71–77), which has an extensive grocery section. **Callejón Diamante,** a narrow, cobblestone alleyway off Enríquez, is where you'll find a handful of bright, cheery restaurants serving flavorful meals to crowds of hungry university students. You'll know you've found the Callejón when you spot the white-and-red, second-story restaurant La Fonda (*see below*).

UNDER $3 • La Sopa. Modest little La Sopa is a favorite of all kinds of xalapeños—from blue-collar workers to students to local politicians. They're here for the bargain comida corrida that includes garbanzo-bean soup, chicken with rice, fresh tortillas, vanilla pudding, and an *agua fresca* (fresh-fruit drink). The place is usually packed, but once you get a table the service is prompt and polite. La Sopa has live music Thursday–Saturday after 9 PM. *Antonio M. de Rivera (a.k.a. Callejón Diamante) 3-A, tel. 28/17–80–69. Comida corrida served daily 1–5 PM. Closed Sun. Cash only.*

UNDER $5 • El Macondo. This tidy, blue-wall restaurant attracts students from the nearby university, who come for the unusual gourmet menu. House specialties include vegetarian pizza, *espaguetti al ajo* (garlic pasta), and *choriqueso macondo* (goat cheese, sausage, and chiles served with tortillas). *Morelos 13, at Alonso Guido, tel. 28/18–52–15. Closed Sun. Cash only.*

La Fonda. At this cozy, popular eatery you can watch as the cooks make fresh tortillas or prepare regional delicacies served in big, clay pots. *Hongos de la casa* (wild mushrooms cooked with garlic and purple chiles; $2.50), *camote con piña* (yam and pineapple pudding), and *tepache* (fermented pineapple juice) are all local favorites. *Callejón Diamante 1, tel. 28/18–45–20. Closed Sun. Cash only.*

Restaurant Parroquia. This bustling restaurant is *the* place for breakfast in Jalapa, and the tables are always filled with white-hair professor types, slouching school kids, and university students. Anxious patrons tap their glasses with spoons to call for another *lechero* (coffee and steamed milk) to go with that basket of sweetbreads. Breakfast or lunch will only set you back $3. *Zaragoza 18, 2 blocks east of Parque Juárez, tel. 28/17–44–36. Cash only.*

WORTH SEEING

Let the terraced gardens of the central **Parque Juárez** be your starting point for exploring Jalapa. The park offers gorgeous views of Mexico's highest peak, the 18,400-ft Pico de Orizaba, originally known as Citlaltépetl, a favorite with mountain climbers. Next to the park is the massive **Palacio del Gobierno** (Enríquez, at Revolución; open weekdays 6 AM–9 PM), where you may find machine gun–toting guards protecting the government offices from either university professors seeking a 100% salary hike or the indigenous campesinos demanding improvements in education and medical aid. Directly across the street, the imposing **catedral,** crowded with dozens of life-size saint statues, opens its doors daily 8–1 and 4–8. A short bus ride away is the Museo de Antropologia de Jalapa (*see below*), the finest anthropology museum outside Mexico City.

CENTRO DEL ARTE

This small, free cultural center hosts exhibitions of everything from photography and sculpture to finger painting. A billboard on the wall by the entryway provides the scoop on current cultural events. *Xalapeños Ilustres, at Insurgentes, no phone. From Parque Juárez, walk east on Enrique until it forks; Xalapeños Ilustres will be the street to your left. Open Mon.–Sat. 11–8, Sun. 11–6.*

JARDIN BOTANICO FRANCISCO JAVIER CLAVIJERO

These well-kept botanical gardens about 2 km (1 mi) outside town display more than 1,500 varieties of flora gathered from throughout the state of Veracruz. A small arboretum houses species of palm trees, and a large pond showcases a vast array of aquatic plants. Hilly stone walkways and narrow stairways lead into the woods, where most plants sport placards that bear their Spanish and scientific names and explain any useful properties the plants possess. Buses marked COATEPEC BRIONES will bring you here from the stop in front of the **Teatro del Estado** (corner of Ignacio de la Llave and Ávila Camacho) for 25¢. *Carretera Antigua a Coatepec Km. 2.5, no phone. Admission free. Open Tues.–Sun. 10–5.*

LA ZONA DE LOS LAGOS / CASA DE ARTESIANAS

One of the most beautiful and popular recreation spots in Jalapa is a series of lakes nestled in a narrow, wooded canyon. In the morning it's crowded with joggers, and occasional cultural events take place in its huge amphitheater. Four-person paddleboats ($2 per hr) are available on weekends. Jalapa's state-run handicrafts center, the **Casa de Artesanias** (Paseo de los Lagos, tel. 28/17–08–04; open weekdays 9–8, Sat. 10–1) is housed in a beautifully renovated colonial mansion that sits on a hill overlooking the lakes. Inside the center is a studio with rotating art and craft exhibits and a shop selling a limited supply of locally produced crafts and clothing. Fruit wines ($3 a bottle) are also sold. *From Parque Juárez, straight down the hill on Herrera, right on Domínguez, left on Dique. Park admission free. Open daily dawn until dusk.*

MUSEO DE ANTROPOLOGIA DE JALAPA

With more than 29,000 pieces on display, Jalapa's esteemed anthropology museum is second only to Mexico City's. The building's long central corridor opens out onto extensive gardens and displays stunning artifacts from the Olmec, Totonac, and Huastec, the primary indigenous cultures of Veracruz. Highlights include massive stone Olmec heads, lively, grinning Remojadas figurines, graceful jade masks, and a burial mound complete with bones, ritually deformed skulls, and ceremonial statuettes. There is also an exhibit on the clothing and customs of contemporary Totonac and Huastec cultures. Guided tours by English-speaking students are available weekdays, but you must call in advance for an appointment. *Av. Jalapa, tel. 28/15–07–08. Take ALVARIO PANTEON or MERCADO TESORARIA bus from corner of Revolución and Abasolo. Admission: $2. Open Tues–Sun. 9–5.*

PARQUE ECOLOGICO MACUILTEPEC

This park was once a pre-Columbian town called Mzcuilxochitlan (Place of the Flower God). More recently, the Veracruz state government declared the spot an ecological reserve because of its historical richness and to protect the lush subalpine forest that covers the mountainside. A paved trail winding up the mountainside offers great views of Jalapa, and it's a favorite with joggers and strolling couples. You can picnic at the *parillas* (barbecue pits), or ascend to the mountaintop, where famous historical figures from Veracruz's history are buried inside a pink, art nouveau pyramid. The park itself is on an inactive volcano; at the entrance you can gaze into the extinct crater, now a soccer field. *Miguel Alemán, no phone. Take MIGUEL ALEMAN bus from in front of Palacio Municipal. Admission free. Open daily 10–5.*

AFTER DARK

Jalapa is home to the jalapeño pepper. With almost every bite of this city's fiery hot, spicy food, you'll be reminded of where you are.

Jalapa sleeps Sunday through Wednesday, but Thursday through Saturday you'll find lots of sizzling venues showcasing live music. Check the city newspaper *El Diario de Jalapa,* available at newsstands, for details on events around Jalapa. **La Sopa** (*see* Food, *above*) is a popular student hangout, mostly due to the free salsa and danzón offered Thursday–Saturday nights from 9 to 11 PM. Two doors away, the popular salsa club **El Callejón** (Callejón Diamante 7, tel. 28/18–77–46) draws an enthusiastic crowd with live shows 10 PM–2 AM. More laid-back is the live samba and jazz at the restaurant/bar **La Casona del Beaterio** (Zaragoza 20, tel. 28/18–21–19); there's no cover, and you can linger over coffee and dessert as long as you like. **Juanote** (Xalapeños Ilustres 22, tel. 28/12–48–50) is a funky restaurant with artwork scattered across its colorful walls. Juanote features local live music and theater and dance performances Monday–Saturday from 10 PM to 2 AM. Cover is more expensive on weekends, but usually runs 75¢–$1.50. On the other side of Parque Juárez, about four blocks along Ávila Camacho, you'll find **B42** (Ávila Camacho 42, tel. 28/12–08–93), a video bar and rock club packed with well-dressed students and young professionals. Local groups play here Friday and Saturday 11 PM–2 AM, and cover is $3. The upscale **La 7a Estación** (20 de Noviembre, near CAXA) is the biggest, fanciest disco in Jalapa. It features pop music, and is free before 10 PM; after that, cover costs $5.

Agora (SW corner of Parque Juárez, downstairs, tel. 28/18–57–30) is a cultural center that shows classic and avant-garde films. Stop by after 6 PM to see what's planned; it's open daily 9–9, and admission is free. While you're here, you can also inquire about performance schedules for the **Orquestra Sinfónica de Jalapa,** which performs in the **Teatro del Estado** and often gives free concerts during its off-season (early June to mid-August).

NEAR JALAPA

COATEPEC

Just 8 km (5 mi) southwest by highway from Jalapa, the one-time colonial city of Coatepec is now a center for coffee and orchid cultivation. The town is bereft of any kind of "café society," and most of the quality coffee beans get exported—though you can find some packaged for sale in Coatepec stores. Blooming orchids are on display at the **Invernadero María Cristina** (Miguel Rebolledo 4, tel. 28/16–03–79; open Mon.–Sat. 8–6), near the main square. **Licores Finos Bautista Gálvez** (Hernández y Hernández 5, no phone) sells fruit wines and also serves free samples. At the 32-acre ecotourism wonderland **Agualegre** (Río La Marina, 5 blocks NW of plaza, no phone), you can enjoy four swimming pools, a water slide, a restaurant, and many trails for horseback riding or hiking, then camp in the jade-green hills.

The ritual of the "voladores" (fliers) was originally performed on the spring equinox as a tribute to the Totonac gods of the sun and rain. Dressed in bright red trousers, black boots, and tasseled red caps, voladores dive backward off a small platform at the top of an 82-ft pole; tied at the ankle, they swing upside down in the air, each one twisting 13 full rotations to mark the months of the lunar calendar. The four fliers circle the pole 52 times, once for each year of the cycle of the Totonac calendar. A fifth man, the "caporal" (prayer-giver), sits atop the pole and keeps rhythm with flute and drum. Modern voladores fly for the crowds every Saturday and Sunday afternoon in Papantla de Olarte next to the cathedral and at the ruins of El Tajín.

Admission is $2, plus $3 for a campsite; an hour of horseback riding through the reserve costs $6. Guided trips to sites as far off as Xico (*see below*) can be arranged with advance notice.

COMING AND GOING

To reach Coatepec from Jalapa, first catch a bus marked TERMINAL (10 min, 15¢) from the stop in front of the **3 Hermanos** shoe store on Enríquez; it'll drop you at a string of bus stands near the rusty, white TERMINAL EXCELSIOR sign. From here, blue buses marked COATEPEC (15 min, 30¢) leave every 5–10 minutes. The last bus back to Jalapa departs at approximately 9 PM.

XICO

About 19 km (11½ mi) southwest from Jalapa, Xico (pronounced He-koe) is a tiny town at the base of the steep Perote foothills. The area is filled with coffee plantations and is also one of the few places left on earth where donkeys are the major mode of transportation. Influenced by the heavy Spanish presence in the 16th century (Cortés passed through Xico on his way to the Aztec capital of Tenochtitlán), this very traditional town holds bullfights and *pamplonadas* (running of the bulls) each year as part of the **Feria de Santa María Magdalena** (July 22). However, Xico's year-round selling point is the roaring, 132-ft **Cascada de Texolo,** a strenuous 3-km (2-mi) walk from town. A cobblestone path leads through banana plantations to the falls, which are not easy to find. From the entrance to town on the main street (at the sign marked ENTRADA), walk uphill. Where the path forks, bear left and follow the CASCADA TEXOLO sign down the unpaved road. At the next fork, take the high road. You can swim in the small pool at the bottom of the waterfall, and a restaurant near the waterfall serves a $2 comida corrida; the owner moonlights as a taxi driver and will take you back to Xico ($3) if you're too tired to walk.

Be sure to leave Xico for Jalapa before nightfall, as there are no hotels here. The food is great, though, and almost all the restaurants near the plaza serve excellent dishes with a famous local variation of mole sauce. Another local specialty is *verde,* a liqueur made with herbs.

COMING AND GOING

To reach Xico from Jalapa (40 min, $1), first catch a bus marked TERMINAL from the stop in front of the **3 Hermanos** shoe store on Enríquez; it'll drop you at a string of bus stands, near the rusty, white TERMINAL EXCELSIOR sign. From here, blue buses marked XICO leave every 5–10 minutes. The last bus back to Jalapa departs at approximately 9 PM.

PAPANTLA DE OLARTE

Papantla de Olarte sits amid tropical hills, 250 km (420 mi) northwest of Veracruz city. The town's character is distinctive, largely due to its mix of Spanish and indigenous residents. The **Festival of Corpus Christi,** held nine weeks after Easter, celebrates both the Spanish-Catholic sacrament of the Eucharist and ancient Totonac harvest rituals. A focal point of the festivities is the ornate **cathedral,** which is festooned with enormous wreaths of flowers, vanilla leaves, and ears of corn. Traditional Totonac dances are performed outside. On weekends year-round, you can watch a Totonac ritual in which four *voladores* (fliers) plummet from an 82-ft pole set up next to the cathedral (*see box, above*). Otherwise, this is a sleepy town where Totonac men in flowing white pants lead their donkeys through crowded streets, and where daily activity is centered around a traditional, tile zócalo shaded with palm trees. Papantla's main draw, however, is its proximity to the extensive ruins of **El Tajín** (*see* Near Papantla, *below*). You'll find a small number of Mexican and foreign tourists using Papantla de Olarte as a base for exploring the ruins, but the town is far from the beaten tourist track.

BASICS

CASAS DE CAMBIO

Papantla lacks a casa de cambio, but the **Banamex** (Enríquez 102, tel. 784/2–01–89; open weekdays 9–1:30), two blocks east of the zócalo, changes both cash and traveler's checks. It also has a 24-hour ATM that accepts Cirrus, Plus, Visa, and MasterCard.

EMERGENCIES

In an emergency, dial the **police** at 784/2–01–93; for **ambulance** service contact the Cruz Roja (tel. 784/2–01–26).

MAIL

The **post office** is down the hill from the zócalo; walk one block south on 20 de Noviembre, turn left on Serdán, right on Azueta, and then look for the CONSULTORIO MEDICO sign; the post office is in the same building. Mail will be held for you for up to 10 days if sent to the following address: *Lista de Correos, Azueta 198 Altos, Papantla, Veracruz, CP 93400, México Tel. 784/2–00–73. Open weekdays 9–4, Sat. 9–1.*

MEDICAL AID

Farmacia Médico is the biggest pharmacy in Papantla, and it's right on the zócalo. The staff doesn't speak English but is good at charades. *Gutiérrez Zamora 3, tel. 784/2–19–41. Open daily 7:30 AM– 10 PM.*

PHONES

The three **Ladatel** (phone card) phones in town are down the hill in the **Teléfonos de México** caseta (5 de Mayo 201, tel. 784/2–05–35), which only offers long-distance services. **Farmacia Médico** (*see above*) also has a caseta de larga distancia, but it only places collect calls.

VISITOR INFORMATION

The **tourist office** has an attentive staff that hands out free maps and loads of good advice. Margarita Pérez is especially helpful, speaks some English, and will gladly make arrangements for you to visit a nearby vanilla plantation. *Palacio Municipal, in zócalo, tel. 784/2–01–77. Open weekdays 9–3 and 6–9, Sat. 9–1.*

COMING AND GOING

Situated just off the modern Highway 180, Papantla can be easily covered on foot. The zócalo, or **Parque Telléz,** is bordered by the cathedral to the south and Calle Enríquez to the north. The first-class **Autobuses del Oriente (ADO)** station (Juárez 207, tel. 784/2–02–18) is a five-minute walk downhill from the zócalo. Eight buses leave daily for Jalapa (4 hrs, $8), and five leave for both Veracruz city (4 hrs, $8) and Mexico City (5½ hrs, $9.50). The second-class **Transportes Papantla** station (20 de Noviembre, tel. 784/2–00–15)

THE TOTONAC'S DANGEROUS GAME

To the Totonac of the ancient city of El Tajín, "playing ball" meant more than just sport. Although the original purpose of the Totonac's ball game may have been solely athletic, the game's outcome soon came to be considered a divination of the gods.

Totonac ball was played between two teams of three players each, in H-shaped courts that had been blessed by priests of the city's temple. At El Tajín there are 16 such ball courts. The object was to pass the ball through an "aro"—a ringlike fixture carved from stone, which was attached to the side of the court's wall—using only the waist, hips, or forearms.

The winners of each game were believed to be spiritually superior to the losers. Because of this, some modern researchers are now inclined to believe that the captain of the winning team, not the losing team, was ritually sacrificed at the end of the game; sacrifice to the gods was the highest honor a Totonac individual could receive and was akin to becoming a demigod oneself. Numerous bas-reliefs at El Tajín depict the postgame sacrifice, with the death god looking on.

lies two blocks downhill from the zócalo behind the 15-10-15 superstore; buses serve the surrounding villages and a few major cities in Veracruz, such as Jalapa (6½ hrs, $7), Veracruz city (6½ hrs, $6.50), and Zempoala (3½ hrs, $5). Buses to Poza Rica (20 min, $1) run every five minutes between 4 AM and 11 PM. Once in Poza Rica, you can transfer to an ADO bus for a direct ride to farther destinations.

WHERE TO SLEEP

Hotels in Papantla are either cheap and lousy or expensive and passable, but almost all are within a block or two of the zócalo. If you have cash to burn, the **Hotel Premier** (Enríquez 103, tel. 784/2–00–80) sports large rooms ($24 doubles) with modern bathrooms and tiny balconies overlooking the square. Despite the lack of aesthetics at **Hotel Pulido** (Enrique 205, tel. 784/2–00–38), rooms are inexpensive: $8.50 doubles, cash only. Test the ceiling fans in a few rooms before you bed down; some are rickety and look like they're about to do a cartwheel off the ceiling. **Hotel Tajín** (Núñez y Domínguez 104, 1½ blocks west of the cathedral, tel. 784/2–01–21) offers lovely views of the city plus the convenience of laundry service and an upscale in-house restaurant. The clean rooms (with TVs, phones, and large bathrooms) are worth the price: Doubles run $23 ($29 with air-conditioning).

CAMPING

At **Pipos** (Lorenzo Collado, tel. 784/2–39–32) campsites ($2) include use of a swimming pool. You can camp for free about 10 minutes away from the El Tajín ruins, on the **Río Molino.** According to locals, it's safe, and the restaurant **El Mirador** (near the bridge) will satisfy your hunger pangs. Catch a 25¢ Transportes Papantla bus (see Coming and Going, above) marked EL CHOTE, and get off at El Chote; cross the street, and take a 50¢ SAN ANDRES or MARTINEZ DE LA TORRE bus and get off before you arrive at the bridge. Both buses run every 20 minutes until 7 PM. From El Tajín, walk to the highway, then catch any bus going southeast; ask the driver to let you off at Río Molino.

FOOD

Papantla doesn't offer many fancy culinary options, but you'll be hard-pressed to spend more than $5 on a meal here. Your cheapest option is to choose from the fondas in the daily market (between Azueta and 20 de Noviembre). The restaurant at **Hotel Tajín** (*see* Where to Sleep, *above*) is one of the better places in town, serving generous breakfasts and $2–$3 comidas corridas. **Restaurante Plaza Pardo** (Enríquez 105, south side of the zócalo, tel. 784/2–00–59) doubles as a gift shop with tacky souvenirs but specializes in delicious chicken tacos ($2) and sweet aguas de fruta ($1). **Restaurant Enríquez** (Reforma 100, no phone) on the northeast corner of the zócalo, serves tasty seafood dishes ($3) and bite-size tacos (20¢). All accept cash only.

NEAR PAPANTLA DE OLARTE

EL TAJÍN

Just 15 minutes outside Papantla is El Tajín, the ruins of an extensive city that dates to AD 100. Although the central buildings have all been identified, excavated, and restored, many more structures remain hidden under thick jungle growth. Archaeologists speculate that the entire city covered about 58 hectares (146 acres), and that smaller, related outposts could be spread over several thousand acres.

The arts department at the Universidad Autonoma de Veracruz puts on performances running the gamut from modern dance to Shakespeare. These take place on campus and in the august Teatro del Estado (state theater).

Little is known about the people who built El Tajín. Early theories attributed the complex to either the Totonac or Huastec, the two most important cultures of the Veracruz area. Today, local Totonac people claim it as part of their heritage—"Tajín" is a Totonac word meaning "thunder"—although archaeologists remain unconvinced. Various clues reveal that whoever built El Tajín also had important ties to other Mesoamerican cultures. Archaeological motifs that adorn the pyramids here, such as the repeated scroll pattern (symbolizing sea shells) and the step-and-fret design (symbolizing lightning), also show up at Teotihuacán (*see* Near Mexico City *in* Chapter 2) and Xochicalco (*see* Near Cuernavaca *in* Chapter 10).

Guided tours of the site are not available, but the blue-shirted guards who pace the complex know a great deal about the site and are willing to share their knowledge with visitors. Start exploring at the unremarkable **Plaza del Arroyo,** near the entrance to the ruins; this is likely to have been the city's commercial center. Pass by the four large pyramids of the plaza to reach El Tajín's ceremonial heart. Here, a squat statue of Mictlantecuhtli (a god of death) guards the central stairway to a steep, soot-color pyramid (Structure 5). This pyramid adjoins the central **ball court** (shaped like a wide H), which is famous for the series of bas-relief carvings that adorn its walls (*see box, above*). At the northern corners of the court are two panels depicting pre- and post-game rituals. In each panel look for the eerie death god, depicted floating out of a jar.

Behind Structure 5 stands the ornate **Pyramid of the Niches.** Also known as the *edificio calandario* (calendar building), it has seven levels punctuated by 365 square cubby holes—one for each day of the solar year. Now bleached white, this pyramid, like all buildings at El Tajín, was once painted in vivid reds and blues—surely that must have been an impressive contrast to the surrounding green hills. Past the steep rise to the north lies **El Tajín Chico,** which is thought to have been where administrative buildings once stood and where the elite had their private residences. The most important structure here is the **Building of the Columns.** Three of the columns, carved with complex narrative scenes, are now housed in the onsite museum (near the entrance). Several carved human figures on the columns, such as 13 Rabbit, bear names taken from the 260-day Mayan ceremonial calendar, but the nature of the relationship between El Tajín and the Mayan empire remains unknown.

The El Tajín ruins are open Tuesday–Sunday 9–6 and admission is $2.50, except on Sunday, when it's free. Don't worry about finding food—the entrance is lined with fondas that sell cheap eats and tacky souvenirs, and there's even a big cafeteria-style restaurant onsite. El Tajín is a good place to see the voladores (*see box, above*); their pole is right outside the entrance. Performances take place on weekends, beginning at noon and continuing hourly; they also perform during the week if enough people show up. Donations are the only wages the fliers receive.

COMING AND GOING

The EL TAJÍN/CHOTE buses ($1 round-trip) that run along 16 de Septiembre in Papantla will take you to the ruins; catch them at the bus stop behind the cathedral. The last bus back from El Tajín to Papantla leaves at 5:45 PM.

TUXPAN

Tuxpán is a peaceful riverside town of approximately 140,000 residents that lies an hour and a half north of Papantla. The city's main attraction is **Playa Tuxpán,** also known as **Playa Norte** among locals—rather than being a single beach it's a 42-km (26-mi) stretch of beaches along the Gulf Coast. White sandy beaches, an emerald-green river, and a mellow atmosphere makes Tuxpán a prime destination for any-one seeking solitude—though the area is still relatively unknown to foreigners. The surf isn't huge here, but there's enough action to warrant shelling out $2 to rent a surfboard for the day. You'll find them for hire at the seafood and beer stands in the pine grove next to the beach.

Tuxpán itself is a pleasant town, composed of winding streets lined with two-story buildings. Juárez, the main road, runs parallel to the Tuxpán River and is home to numerous diners, hotels, and shops. The **Parque Reforma** is the center of social activity in town and is scattered with cafés, fruit stands, and more than 100 open-air tables. On the western edge of the Parque is the **Museo Arqueológico** (tel. 783/4–61–80; admission $1; open weekdays 9–7, Sat. 9–2), a small museum displaying Huastecan pottery, crafts, and several ancient burial mounds. Lanchas shuttle passengers across the river to the **Casa de Fidel Castro** (Obregón, no phone), where Cuba's Fidel Castro lived for a time in 1956 while planning the overthrow of dictator Fulgencio Batista. Tuxpán was chosen by Castro as a base camp because it offered a direct pas-sage to Cuba through the Gulf. The casa is now a free museum, open daily 9–5. The interior is bare save some black-and-white photos of Fidel together with former Mexican president Lázaro Cárdenas.

BASICS

CASAS DE CAMBIO

Bancomer (Juárez, at Escuela Médico Militar, tel. 783/4–00–09; open weekdays 9–1:30) changes cash and traveler's checks. **Banamex** (Juárez, at Corregidora, tel. 783/4–08–40) has a 24-hour ATM that takes Cirrus, Plus, Visa, and MasterCard.

EMERGENCIES

In an emergency, contact the **police** at 783/4–02–52; for **ambulance** service contact the Cruz Roja (tel. 783/4–01–58).

MEDICAL AID

The 24-hour **Farmacia Benavides** (15 Juárez, tel. 783/4–51–93) is a gleaming modern pharmacy with amply stocked shelves.

PHONES AND MAIL

The full-service **post office** (Mina 16, between Ocampo and Colón, tel. 783/4–00–88; open weekdays 8–7, Sat. 8–1) will hold mail for you for up to 10 days at the following address: Lista de Correos, Admin-istración 1, Tuxpán, Veracruz, CP 92801, México. You can make both long-distance and local calls at the ADO station (*see* Coming and Going, *below*).

VISITOR INFORMATION

The small **tourist office** is in the red municipal building across the street from the cathedral. The friendly staff only speaks Spanish, and maps are in chronic short supply. *Juárez 23, tel. 783/4–01–77. Open daily 10–3 and 5–7.*

COMING AND GOING

Highway 180 runs through Tuxpán, making it a snap to get here from Tampico to the north or Veracruz city to the south. Central Tuxpán is small and easily explored on foot; Juárez, the main street, runs parallel to the Tuxpán River, one block inland. Boat rides across the river cost mere pennies. Frequent PLAYA buses run east along Reforma, the street that borders the river's edge. The easiest place to flag down buses in the centro is along the river dock, at the corner of Rodríguez and Reforma.

Tuxpán doesn't have a central first-class bus terminal; instead, each line has its own depot. Bus tickets are a prized commodity during such holidays as Semana Santa and Christmas, as well as during the months of July and August. To avoid getting stuck here during high season, it's best to buy your ticket at least two days prior to your intended departure. The **Autobuses del Oriente (ADO)** station (Rodríguez 1, tel. 783/4–01–02), five minutes east of Parque Reforma on Juárez, is the most convenient, with nine buses a day to Mexico City (6 hrs, $10.50) and seven buses a day to Papantla (1½ hrs, $2.25). If you can't get a ticket at the ADO terminal, try **Omnibús de México** (Independencia 50, tel. 783/4–11–47), which has a depot 1 km (½ mi) farther down the river, near the bridge. Their service schedule is similar to ADO's. Take a bus marked PLAYA going east along the riverside, on Reforma, and get off at Reforma and Independencia, where the terminal is located. Second-class buses operate from the outdoor **Terminal ABC** (tel. 783/4–20–40) on Cuauhtémoc. Buses travel to Tampico (4½ hrs, $6.50), Nuevo Laredo (15 hrs, $27.50), Monterrey (12 hrs, $20.50), and Reynosa (10 hrs, $17).

WHERE TO SLEEP

Tuxpán's hotels tend to be expensive, but you'll find a few moderately priced establishments near the center. If you have the funds, opt for **Hotel Florida** (Juárez 23, tel. 783/4–02–22), where all rooms have TVs, air-conditioning, and phones. Doubles cost $23. **Hotel El Huasteco** (Morelos 41, tel. 783/4–18–59) lies just a block east of Parque Juárez, and its 40 rooms tend to fill up fast. The rooms are basic but clean and air-conditioned. Laundry and luggage storage is available. One-bed doubles cost $9, two-bed doubles $11, and the hotel accepts cash only. At the **Hotel Posada San Ignacio** (Melchor Ocampo 29, 1 block north of the zócalo, tel. 783/4–29–05), potted plants fill the small central courtyard. Rooms in this attractive hotel ($10 for two beds, cash only) are spotless and all have fans. Sparkling-clean tile bathrooms have plenty of hot water. If the places mentioned above are full, try the bare but passable **Hotel del Parque** (Humboldt 11, on the zócalo, tel. 783/4–08–12), where doubles cost $9, cash only.

Local legend has it that a bishop used to perform exorcisms on the red fish that swam through Agua Bendita and Cajón de Pextla, two small arroyos (canyons) in Xico.

CAMPING

Although it's free and legal to pitch a tent on **Playa Tuxpán,** in recent years it has become increasingly less safe. It's also possible to camp on **Isla Lobos** (*see* Outdoor Activities, *below*), but you must first obtain a permit from the Coast Guard office (tel. 783/4–03–43), about 3 km (2 mi) from the Tuxpán's centro, on the road to Playa Tuxpán. Permits can take up to four days to process, so plan ahead. The **Unidad Deportiva** (Colonia Jardines, tel. 783/4–42–09) is not as close to the beach, but it is extremely secure, has a pool, and campsites are free. From the center of town, take the UV (Universidad Veracruzana) bus, which heads west along the river, and get off at the Coca-Cola factory.

FOOD

You'll find most restaurants congregated on Juárez, near the center of town. There are also several good, cheap taco stands up the street from the ADO depot. The menu at **Antonio's** (Juárez 25, at Garizurieta, tel. 783/4–16–02) runs the gamut from prohibitively expensive to budget-friendly. The *desayuno americano* (American breakfast; $3.50) includes eggs, toast, jam, juice, and tea. A plate of chicken enchiladas costs $4. There's also a full bar here, and Friday and Saturday nights feature live music beginning at 9 PM. Hungry locals pour into **Cafetería el Mante** (Pipila 8, at Juárez, tel. 783/4–57–36; cash only), especially for breakfast. The most popular dish is *bocoles rellenos* (fried dough filled with egg, meat, or cheese; 50¢).

FESTIVALS

Recent efforts to bolster tourism in Tuxpán include instigation of the **Carnaval de la Primavera** (last week of April). It's no competition for the Carnaval of Veracruz city; extracted from the pre-Lent significance that Carnaval usually holds, Tuxpán's festival is simply a rowdy way to celebrate spring with dancing, drinking, and music.

The **Día del Niño Perdido** (December 17) commemorates the day young Jesus "got lost." At 8 PM, the electricity in Tuxpán is shut off, and the whole city is illuminated by thousands of votive candles in an effort to light Jesus' way back home. The event lasts several hours, with groups of children walking through the street, calling out to the lost Christ. Tuxpán is the only city in the world that celebrates this unique holiday.

OUTDOOR ACTIVITIES

Playa Tuxpán is the most accessible beach in the area, about 7 km (4½ mi) east of downtown Tuxpán. The beachfront here is lined with cheap *palapa* (thatched-hut) restaurants selling everything from crab burritos to ice-cold coconuts. Palapas closest to the bus stop charge the most; farther down the beach you can chow on dishes like *ensalada de camarones* (shrimp salad) for only $3. For picnic supplies, visit the fresh fruit stands on the river dock (Reforma, at Rodríguez), where the lanchas are. The **Dauzan** bakery (Juárez 15, tel. 783/4–37–77) sells hot fresh rolls and pastries. In **Tamiaula,** a small village just north of Tuxpán, you can hire a fishing boat for the 45-minute journey to the prime scuba diving sites around **Isla Lobos** (Island of Wolves). In the shallow water offshore there are a few shipwrecks and colorful reefs that are home to a large variety of sea life, including pufferfish, parrotfish, damselfish, and barracuda. Certified divers can rent scuba gear from **Aquasport** (just before Playa Tuxpán, tel. 783/7–02–59), at the rate of $32 per person for four hours. It's best to round up a group, since the lancha ride costs $160 for 1–10 people.

To reach Playa Tuxpán, pick up a PLAYA bus near the dock where the lanchas leave to cross the river (near Rodríguez and Reforma). The last bus back to town leaves the beach at about 8:30 PM. Buses to Tamiaula (30 min, $1) leave from the Terminal ABC (*see* Coming and Going, *above*).

OAXACA

UPDATED BY JANE ONSTOTT

O axaca comes closer to the Mexico of tourists' imaginations than any other state in the country. Here customs dating back 10,000 years are alive and well, not just relegated to museums. Artisans, farmers, fishermen, and oral historians still practice their traditional arts throughout the state. And indigenous peoples such as the Zapotec, Mixtec, Huave, and Triqui—isolated from 20th-century adaptations by the Sierra Madre mountains—continue in lifestyles more or less unchanged for centuries. More than 16 distinct Indian languages are spoken in Oaxaca, and cultures within this mountainous southern state vary as greatly as the landscape, which encompasses sunset-color canyons, cacti-carpeted deserts, tropical jungles, scrubby coastland, and thriving towns.

Unfavorable economic conditions, particularly in the Mixteca region and the Isthmus of Tehuantepec, have for years made Oaxacans into a *pueblo peregrino* (nomadic people). In search of work at a decent wage, hundreds of thousands of *campesinos* (rural dwellers) have abandoned their families and migrated to Northern Mexico, Baja California del Norte, and the United States, where they can earn as much in one hour as they can in a day in Oaxaca. Aside from the presence of beggars in Oaxaca city and other urban centers, however, these economic hardships remain invisible to many travelers to the state, and the Oaxacans are determinedly cheerful.

At the confluence of three river valleys sits the state's capital, Oaxaca city. Pre-Columbian sites such as Monte Albán and Mitla are easily accessible from here, as are many small towns filled with artisans and craftspeople. Farther from the city, the landscape changes drastically: To the south, the Sierra Madre mountains drop sharply to the sea, forming a long stretch of Pacific Coast beaches frequented by everyone from backpacking hippies to vacationing Mexican families. Puerto Escondido is *the* surfer mecca, while Puerto Ángel, a cliffside fishing village, is a peaceful place to snorkel and enjoy some stunning views. Although the Isthmus of Tehuantepec is often viewed as a dull, dusty gateway to Chiapas and Tabasco, this is partly because the region reacts to the modern world by clinging to its old traditions and customs. You may not be wowed by exquisite scenery in the isthmus, but the friendly people and the intricacies of Zapotec culture will make your stay, however brief, a pleasant one.

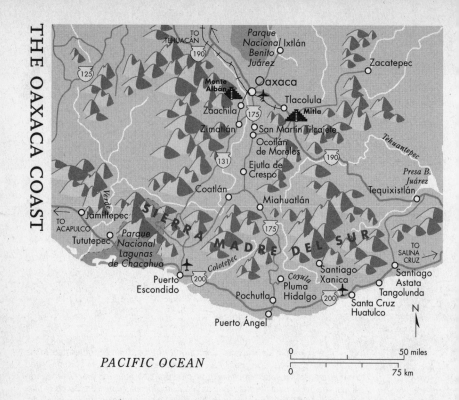

Parque
Nacional Ixtlán
Benito
Juárez

TO
TEHUACÁN

190

125

Zacatepec

Monte
Albán

Oaxaca

Tlacolula

Mitla

Zaachila

175

Zimatlán

San Martín Tilcajete

Ocotlán
de Morelos

131

Ejutla de
Crespó

190

Tehuantepec

Presa B.
Juárez

Tequixistlán

Coatlán

Miahuatlán

175

SIERRA

MADRE   DEL   SUR

TO
SALINA
CRUZ

Verde

TO
ACAPULCO

Jamiltepec

Tututepec

Parque
Nacional
Lagunas
de Chacahua

Colotepec

Coyula

Santiago
Xanica

Santiago
Astata

Tangolunda

Puerto
Escondido

200

Pluma
Hidalgo

200

Santa Cruz
Huatulco

Pochutla

Puerto Ángel

N

PACIFIC OCEAN

0   50 miles

0   75 km

OAXACA CITY

Oaxaca city, more formally known as Oaxaca de Juárez, is a bustling metropolis, a melange of the many indigenous cultures who call this state home. The city's *zócalo* (main plaza) is a microcosm of the area's diversity: Women from the Triquis' mountaintop weaving villages sit alongside colorfully garbed Tehuanas from the isthmus. To further sample the region's cultural richness, rent a bike from Pedro Martínez (*see* Getting Around, *below*) and head to the *pueblos* (towns) surrounding the capital; Oaxaca city is a logical base for this type of exploration. Not surprisingly, scores of budget travelers journey to the city, and plenty of cheap food and lodging choices provide comfort after sightseeing excursions to the ruins of Monte Albán or the village of Arrazola. When you're tired of bumpy bike or bus rides, the numerous cathedrals and museums sprinkled throughout town provide a few days of relaxed strolling and sightseeing.

BASICS

AMERICAN EXPRESS

The AmEx office, inside the travel agency **Viajes Micsa** (NE corner of zócalo), exchanges all traveler's checks at no commission. They also replace lost checks, deliver MoneyGrams, cash personal checks, hold mail, and replace AmEx cards. *Valdivieso 2, Oaxaca, Oaxaca CP 68000, México, tel. 951/6–27–00, fax 951/6–74–75. Open weekdays 9–2 and 4–6, Sat. 9–1.*

CASAS DE CAMBIO

Although the banks around the zócalo give slightly better rates for dollars and traveler's checks, casas de cambio have longer hours and much shorter lines. If you must pinch pesos by changing at the bank, arrive as early as possible to avoid a lengthy wait. The banks **Banamex** (Hidalgo 821, 1 block east of

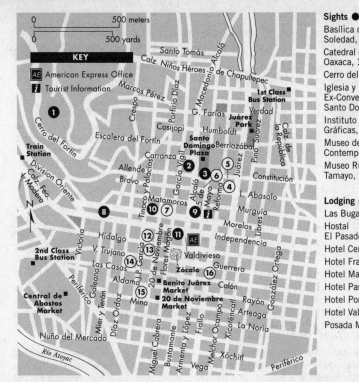

Sights ●

Basílica de la
Soledad, **8**

Catedral de
Oaxaca, **11**

Cerro del Fortín, **1**

Iglesia y
Ex-Convento de
Santo Domingo, **3**

Instituto de Artes
Gráficas, **2**

Museo de Arte
Contemporáneo, **9**

Museo Rufino
Tamayo, **10**

Lodging ○

Las Bugambilias, **4**

Hostal
El Pasador, **16**

Hotel Central, **14**

Hotel Francia, **13**

Hotel Maela, **5**

Hotel Pasaje, **15**

Hotel Pombo, **7**

Hotel Vallarta, **12**

Posada Margarita, **6**

zócalo, tel. 951/6–59–00; open weekdays 9–1)˙and **Bancomer** (García Vigil 202, tel. 951/6–76–43; open weekdays 9–1:30) both change traveler's checks, and Bancomer has an ATM that accepts Plus, Cirrus, MasterCard, and Visa cards. Several casas de cambio are on the streets around the zócalo; they're generally open Monday–Saturday 8–8, Sunday 9–3.

CONSULATES

Australia/Canada: *Dr. Liceaga 119, Oaxaca, Oaxaca CP 68000, México, tel. 951/3–37–77, fax 951/5–21–47. Open weekdays 11–2.* **United Kingdom**: *Alcalá, at Allende, Plaza Santo Domingo, Oaxaca, Oaxaca CP 68000, México, tel. 951/6–72–80 or 951/3–08–65. Open weekdays 9–3 and 6–8.* **United States**: *Alcalá 201, Int. 204, Oaxaca, Oaxaca CP 68000, México, tel. 951/4–30–54. Open weekdays 10–5.*

EMERGENCIES

For all emergencies, dial 06 from any phone in Oaxaca city; no coins are necessary. For the **fire** department, call 951/6–22–31. The **Green angels** (tel. 951/6–38–10) will help with road emergencies, free of charge. For **legal** aid, call 91–800/9–03–92. The **tourist police** who patrol the downtown area are friendly and can help with questions and concerns.

INTERNET SERVICES

You can send and receive e-mail ($1.30 per message) and surf the net ($8 per hour) at **Makedonia** (Trujano 122, tel. 951/4–07–62; open daily 8 AM–10:30 PM.

LAUNDRY

Superlavandería Hidalgo (J. P. García 200, at Hidalgo, tel. 951/4–11–81; open Mon.–Sat. 9–6) charges $2.75 for up to 3½ kilos (7½ pounds) of laundry. **La Espuma** (Yagul 405, tel. 951/4–41–82) offers same-day pickup and delivery service for 75¢ a kilo (2 pounds), but you must contact them before 10 AM.

MAIL

The **post office** (just off zócalo, facing the cathedral, tel. 951/6–26–61; open weekdays 8–7, Sat. 9–1) will hold mail sent to you at the following address for up to 10 days: Lista de Correos, Administración 1, Oaxaca, Oaxaca CP 68001, México. However, you can only pick up mail weekdays 8–2. Next door, **Telecomunicaciones de México** (corner Independencia and 20 de Noviembre, tel. 951/6–49–02; open weekdays 8–6, Sat. 9–4) provides telegram, money order, and fax service.

MEDICAL AID

The **Cruz Roja** (Armenta y López 700, tel. 951/6–44–55) offers free, 24-hour medical service and emergency care. The **Sanatorio del Carmen** (Abasolo 215, tel. 951/6–26–12) is open 24 hours; English-speaking doctors are only available during the day. If you need a dentist or medical specialist, the tourist office (*see* Visitor Information, *below*) can refer you to someone who speaks English. The 24-hour **Farmacias del Ahorro** (Calzada Niños Héroes 1102, tel. 951/5–50–00), next to the first-class bus station, offers delivery service.

PHONES

Oaxaca's pay phones do not accept credit cards and international calling cards, but you can use them at **Teleplus** telephone offices. These offer competitive prices on faxing and international calls, with discounts weekdays after 7 PM, all day Saturday, and Sunday until 5 PM. *Alacalá 1000, tel. and fax 951/6–65–10. Open daily 7 AM–10 PM. Other downtown locations: 20 de Noviembre 820, tel. and fax 951/4–60–79; Hidalgo 820, tel. and fax 951/4–11–98.*

SCHOOLS

Oaxaca has a number of reputable language schools, most of which will arrange homestays for attendees. The **Instituto Cultural de Oaxaca**, based in a gracious 19th-century home, charges $100 per week for its limited-enrollment classes. Tuition covers cultural workshops, a daily conversation hour, and seven hours a day of intensive language instruction. *Juárez 909, tel. 951/5–34–04. Mailing address: A. P. 340, Oaxaca, Oaxaca CP 68000, México.*

The **Centro de Idiomas** at the Universidad de Benito Juárez offers intensive Spanish programs to small groups in a more institutional setting. Classes cost $80 per week or $200 per month. You'll also have the opportunity to meet local students eager to practice their English. *Burgoa, between Armenta y López and Bustamente, tel. 951/4–00–49. Mailing address: Centro de Idiomas, UABJO, A. P. 523, Oaxaca, Oaxaca CP 68000, México.*

VISITOR INFORMATION

Stop by the **Oficina de Turismo** (5 de Mayo 200, at Morelos, tel. 951/6–48–28; open daily 9–8), where the bilingual staff is more than happy to assist you. Pick up a free copy of the English-language *Oaxaca Times* or *Oaxaca* for details on local events and festivals. The bilingual *Guía Cultural* (75¢), which lists free and inexpensive films, art exhibits, and music and theater performances, is available here or at magazine stands on the zócalo. **Sedetur** (Independencia, at García Vigil, tel. 951/4–77–33; open daily 9–8) provides free maps and bus schedules.

COMING AND GOING

BY BUS

Oaxaca's crowded and noisy first-class bus terminal (Calzada Niños Héroes 1036) is 11 long blocks north of the zócalo—a 20-minute walk or a $1.25 taxi ride from downtown. The service **Cristóbal Colón** (tel. 951/5–12–14) runs frequent buses to Mexico City (6 hrs, $17) and San Cristóbal (2 per day; 12 hrs, $14). **Autobuses del Oriente (ADO)** (tel. 951/5–17–03) has frequent service to Puebla (8 hrs, $12.50), Veracruz city (6 hrs, $18), and Salina Cruz (5 hrs, $8).

The **second-class station** (corner Trujano and Periférico, tel. 951/4–57–00 or 951/6–22–70) is south of the railroad tracks and across from the Central de Abastos market. The bus companies based here serve nearby towns, as well as major cities like Tapachula (10 hrs, $16) and Mexico City (6 hrs, $15). **Estrella del Valle** and **Autobuses Unidos (AU)** both run to Puerto Escondido (7½ hrs, $9.50), Santa Cruz Huatulco (6½ hrs, $8), and Pochutla (7 hrs, $8.50).

BY PLANE

The **Aeropuerto Nacional de Oaxaca-Zozocatlán** (tel. 951/1–54–22) is 8 km (5 mi) south of town. At least two daily flights go to Mexico City (1½ hr, $90 one-way). Tickets can be purchased at the airport or from agencies downtown; try **Cid de León** (Morelos 602, tel. 951/4–18–93). **Transportes Terrestres Aeropuerto** (Alameda de León s/n, in front of cathedral, tel. 951/6–27–77) will shuttle you between the airport and your hotel (although they try to get backpackers to walk to their offices, they will pick you up at your hotel if asked). Cost is $1.30 one-way. The office is open Monday–Saturday 9–2 and 5–8.

BY TRAIN

Every night at 7 PM, **El Oaxaqueño** trains depart from the **train station** (Madero and Periférico, tel. 951/6–26–76 or 951/6–48–44) and chug to Mexico City ($13.50 1st class, $7.75 2nd class) via Tehuacán and Puebla. The ride takes a grueling 15–24 hours, depending on weather, mechanical failures, and the whims of the conductor. The Oaxaca station is a 15-minute walk from the center of town—for safety's sake, take a taxi at night. Tickets must be bought on the day of departure; purchase a second-class ticket only if you are really broke or love farm animals. The ticket office is open daily 6:30–11 and 3:30–7.

GETTING AROUND

At the heart of walker-friendly Oaxaca is the **zócalo,** bordered by the mammoth cathedral and the **Parque Alameda de León.** North of the zócalo is the posh part of town, where you will generally find (or avoid) pricier hotels and restaurants. The **Periférico** circles the city center. Southwest of the zócalo, at Las Casas and the Periférico, you'll find the **second-class bus station,** the huge **Central de Abastos** market, and the Zona Roja (red-light district). The hill that overlooks Oaxaca, **Cerro del Fortín** (Fort Hill), is a 20-minute walk northwest from the zócalo. Keep in mind that most streets change names as they cross Avenida Independencia going north–south and Bustamante/Alcalá going east–west.

Oaxacans are politically active, and demonstrations in front of government buildings and around the centro (downtown) are common—whether they be for indigenous rights or better pay for schoolteachers.

Buses are plentiful in Oaxaca, though you won't need them to get around the downtown area. Taxis are best for getting to and from the bus and train stations after dark, when the southwest section of town gets a bit dicey. Standard taxi fare within downtown is $1–$2.50 per trip, but agree on a price before getting in—taxis are unmetered. **Martínez Mountain Bikes** (J. P. García 509, tel. 951/4–31–44; open Mon.–Sat. 9–2 and 4–8) rents good-quality bikes ($10 per day). Knowledgeable owner Pedro provides maps and excellent advice for routes of varying difficulty.

WHERE TO SLEEP

There are two main budget-hotel areas in Oaxaca: one north and one south of the zócalo. Hotels on the quiet, residential north side often cost a few pesos more. The south side, near the markets and second-class bus station, caters to working-class Mexicans and shoestring travelers. The tourist office provides lists of local families with rooms to let; the rates ($5–$15 per night) often include laundry service and meals. If you're desperate for a room, the tourist office is open late and will call around, free of charge, until they find you a place to sleep.

Relatively new to Oaxaca (and, indeed, all of Mexico) is the *recámara con desayuno* (bed-and-break-fast). At **Las Bugambilias,** double rooms ($15 per person) all have private baths and the price includes a filling breakfast. Owner Mariana Arroyo skillfully administers Aztec *temascals* (vapor baths) and massages, for a bargain $25 per blissful hour. *Reforma 402, between Abasalo and Constitución, tel. and fax 951/6–11–65. 8 rooms, all with bath. Restaurant, luggage storage. Reservations advised. Cash only.*

SOUTH OF THE ZOCALO

UNDER $15 • Hotel Pasaje. A courtyard with potted plants, festive tiling, and a gregarious green parrot make the Pasaje a favorite among budget travelers. The clean, comfortable rooms have desks and private baths with hot showers. Ask to try out the beds in your room first—some have uncomfortable mattresses. Doubles are $10.50. *Mina 302, between J. P. García and 20 de Noviembre, tel. 951/6–42–13. ½ block west of 20 de Noviembre market. 18 rooms, all with bath. Luggage storage. Reservations advised. Cash only.*

ON THE MENU IN OAXACA CITY

Modern Oaxacan food is based on local ingredients and traditional recipes, elements of which predate the Spaniards' arrival. Oaxaca's markets are the best places to sample any of the following delectable regional specialties without paying tourist prices.

CHAPULINES: *fried grasshoppers prepared with tangy chile and lime sauce. They go down a bit easier if you remove the legs first. According to local mythology, one taste will charm you into never leaving Oaxaca.*

JICUATOTE: *jiggly, sweet, white gelatinous dessert made with milk, cloves, cinnamon, and cornmeal. It's served in tubs or cut into cubes and is usually colored red on top.*

TEJATE: *beverage made from the flowers and roasted seeds of the cacao tree, plus corn, coconut milk, sugar, water, and spices. The result, a white paste suspended in brown liquid, is served in a huge bowl—it may look deadly, but is actually nutritious and tasty.*

TLAYUDAS: *huge, flat tortillas spread with refried beans and topped with Oaxacan string cheese, cilantro, fresh vegetables, and guacamole.*

Hotel Vallarta. The clean, freshly painted rooms here are antiseptic and plain, but blessed with amenities: private bathrooms, purified water, towels, soap, and desks. For an extra $1.50, they'll throw in a TV. Doubles with one bed cost $11; with two beds it's $12.50. *Díaz Ordaz 309, between Trujano and Las Casas, tel. 951/6–49–67. 3 blocks SW of zócalo. 30 rooms, all with bath. Luggage storage. Cash only.*

NORTH OF THE ZOCALO

UNDER $10 • Hotel Pombo. The Pombo has recently joined the 20th century, switching to gas-powered water heaters instead of wood-burning ones. The rooms are nothing to shout about, but the management is friendly, and the location, just northwest of the zócalo, couldn't be better. *Morelos 601, tel. 951/6–26–73. 2 blocks NW of zócalo. 32 rooms, all with bath. Cash only.*

Posada Margarita. This inexpensive hotel is on a quiet street just across from Labastida park, a half block from the tourist corridor. Rooms have closets and firm beds; those on the second story are quietest. The hotel's refrigerator is stocked with soft drinks and beer, and its small courtyard is just the place to relax and enjoy a few. Doubles are $10. *Labastida 115, tel. 951/6–28–02. 4 blocks NE of zócalo. 18 rooms, all with bath. Parking. Cash only.*

UNDER $20 • Hotel Francia. The Francia is where writer D. H. Lawrence stayed during his 1925 visit to Oaxaca. Mexico's colonial past is recalled in the dramatic rooms of the old hotel, with high ceilings and tile floors. Doubles cost $16. *20 de Noviembre 212, between Hidalgo and Trujano, tel. 951/6–48–11. 1 block west of zócalo. 45 rooms, all with bath. Luggage storage. Reservations advised.*

Hotel Maela. This new hotel has clean, bright doubles ($14) with tasteful furnishings. It's on a quiet, residential street near El Llano, an urban park where local kids kick soccer balls and grownups jog around the perimeter. *Constitució 206, tel. 951/64–65–18. 6 blocks NE of zócalo. 11 rooms, all with bath. Luggage storage, parking. Reservations advised. Cash only.*

HOSTELS

Hostal El Pasador. This is the cheapest place to sleep in town, which means you'll be shacking up with other bargain-hunting globe-trotters in the single-sex dorms ($4.50 per person) and rooftop cabañas. The management plans to open a vegetarian restaurant on the premises. *Fiallo 305, tel. 951/4–13–51. 2 blocks east and ½ block south of zócalo. Reception open daily 6 AM–11 PM. Kitchen, laundry, luggage storage ($1.25 per item per day). Cash only.*

FOOD

Spicy Oaxacan cuisine is famous throughout Mexico. If you have an adventuresome attitude, the *comedores* (sit-down food stands) at the **Central de Abastos** and the **20 de Noviembre markets** offer a great selection of local specialties that won't break the bank. Go in the early afternoon, while the cooking pots are still full and fresh, and look for a clean, tidy kitchen. Restaurants south of the zócalo are generally cheap and cater to a local crowd, while those on the zócalo itself are expensive and tourist-oriented.

SOUTH OF THE ZOCALO

UNDER $5 • Café Alex. At this popular restaurant, diners share the back patio with cages full of chattering parrots and parakeets. The menu features Oaxacan cooking, and the *comida corrida* (preprepared lunch special) is an exceptional deal: portions are large, and they usually offer a vegetarian entrée. A breakfast of juice, fruit salad, and granola costs less than $2. *Díaz Ordaz 218, at Trujano, tel. 951/4–07–15. No dinner Sun. Cash only.*

Cafetería Tayu. This local favorite is just across the street from the bustling 20 de Noviembre market. The simple comida corrida ($2) includes a meat entrée, soup, rice or spaghetti, *agua fresca* (fresh fruit drink), and a dessert. Be prepared to share your table with savvy Oaxacans. *20 de Noviembre 416, tel. 951/6–53–63. Closed Sun. Cash only.*

NORTH OF THE ZOCALO

UNDER $5 • Antojitos de los Olmos. Although the owner has recently relocated after years on the tourist corridor, she still serves the town's best *atole* (a sweet, corn-based drink, similar to hot chocolate) to crowds of loyal customers. The *antojitos* (appetizers; $1 apiece) are also delicious—tamales, tacos, and quesadillas are cooked before your eyes. *Morelos 403, tel. 951/6–44–10. Mon.–Sat. evenings only; closed Sun. Cash only.*

Cafetería Morgan. The curmudgeonly owner notwithstanding, this tiny place draws plenty of locals and travelers alike. Mexican or international breakfasts ($3) include a cup of their authentic Italian cappuccino; pastas are the highlight of the evening meal. *Morelos 601-B, no phone. Closed Sun. Cash only.*

El Mesón. The all-you-can-eat, buffet-style breakfasts and lunches ($2.50) at this low-key spot are a great way to sample the region's famed dishes. Choose from *mole oaxqueño* (Oaxacan mole, a sauce made with chocolate and chiles), *pozole* (hominy soup served with fresh onions, ground chile, and oregano), dozens of types of tacos, and much more. *Hidalgo 805, at Valdivieso, tel. 951/6–27–29. Cash only.*

Flor de Loto. Come here for a tantalizing array of vegetarian and regional specialties, in addition to excellent soups and breads. It's a cool, fresh space filled with original art. The comida corrida ($3) includes soup, salad, main dish (veg or nonveg), dessert, and fruit drink. *Morelos 509, tel. 951/4–39–44. Cash only.*

Nutritortas Gigantes. This hole-in-the-wall shop serves a variety of *tortas* (sandwiches) priced at just over a dollar—they even do a sandwich stuffed with *chapulines* (*see box, above*). Other options include tostadas, quesadillas, and fruit cocktail. *Nicolás Bravo 216, tel. 951/6–64–69. 4 blocks NW of zócalo. Cash only.*

Pozole. The best *pozole* (hominy soup) south of Mexico City is served here, just across from the cathedral. The chicken-based soup ($1.50) comes in three varieties: Michoacán (red broth, radishes, and chiles), Guerrero (green broth, pork rind, and avocado), and Jalisco (clear broth). *Independencia, at Alameda de León, no phone. Just west of zócalo. Dinner only. Cash only.*

Quickly. Quickly is probably how you'll attack the *chilaquiles* (tortilla strips doused with salsa and sour cream). Also worthwhile is the dubiously named but tasty *gringa* hamburger ($2), loaded with ham, bacon, and tomato. The *tlayudas* (*see box, above*) are popular with locals. *Alcalá 100-B, ½ block north of zócalo, tel. 951/4–70–76. No breakfast weekends. Cash only.*

Restaurant Morelos. The friendly owners of this regional-food restaurant serve up a filling comida co-rrida ($2), with cream or broth soup, black beans, rice, main course, dessert, and fruit drink. There are also à la carte and breakfast offerings. *Morelos 1003, 2 blocks NE of zócalo, tel. 951/6–05–58. Closed Sun. Cash only.*

CAFES

El Gecko (5 de Mayo 412, at Plaza Fray Gonzalo Lucero, tel. 915/4–80–24; closed Sun.) has an open-air patio that's drenched in flowering purple vines in season; the coffee is fine and the ambiance pleasant, although the help can be a bit surly. On a hot day, you'll love their iced cappuccino. **Coffee Beans** (5 de Mayo 400, no phone) is just a few doors down from El Gecko, and sells coffees from around Mexico and Latin America—whole bean, ground, or by the cup as cappuccino or espresso. Both cafés serve snacks and desserts, cash only.

WORTH SEEING

Oaxaca boasts a wealth of Roman Catholic churches, convents, and monasteries dating from the colonial period, only a few of which are mentioned below. Some have been converted into government offices and museums, but many remain active places of worship. It's possible to see most of Oaxaca's important sights in a day or two; check the maps in *Oaxaca* or *Oaxaca Times* for suggested walking tours.

BASILICA DE LA SOLEDAD

This 17th-century baroque church contains a black velvet–draped figure of Nuestra Virgen de la Soledad (Our Lady of Solitude), to which believers ascribe healing powers. On December 18, the **Danza de la Pluma** (Feather Dance), a dramatization of the Conquest, is performed here as part of the festival in her honor. Behind the church is the **Museo Religioso de la Soledad** (tel. 951/6–75–66; open daily 9–2; admission 35¢), which displays a kitschy collection of trinkets dedicated to the Virgin. The church is particularly breathtaking at sunset, when it reflects a golden glow. *Independencia 107, at Galeana, no phone.*

CATEDRAL DE OAXACA

Construction of the cathedral began in 1544 but was interrupted by earthquakes, leaving this magnificent structure unfinished for another 200 years. The beautifully carved baroque facade depicts the assumption of the Virgin Mary, and inside is a glorious bronze altar imported from Italy. The cathedral also houses the Señor del Rayo, a giant gold-and-silver crucifix that, legend has it, miraculously survived a fire that started with a bolt of lightning. *Independencia 700, on the zócalo, tel. 951/6–44–01.*

CENTRO FOTOGRAFICO ALVAREZ BRAVO

This new museum houses permanent and rotating exhibits of contemporary Mexican and international photography, as well as a Braille library. Free art films are shown Friday–Sunday, usually at 6 PM; check the *Guía Cultural* for details. *Murguía 302, tel. 951/4–19–33. Admission free. Open Wed.–Mon. 9:30–6.*

CERRO DEL FORTIN

Fort Hill dominates the city and has been a site of festivals and celebrations since pre-Columbian times. A long flight of stairs leads up the Cerro from Avenida Crespo, about 2 km (1 mi) northwest of the zócalo. Crowning the Cerro is an open-air auditorium used during **La Guelaguetza** (*see* Festivals, *below*), as well as a planetarium and observatory. *El mirador* (the lookout point) has amazing views of the city. It's also the site of a huge bronze statue of Oaxacan native Benito Juárez, the first indigenous president of the Mexican republic. His famous phrase, "*El respecto al derecho ajeno es la paz*" (Respect for the rights of others is peace) is engraved on the statue's base. *From zócalo, walk 7 blocks north along Díaz Ordaz, then climb stairs.*

IGLESIA Y EX-CONVENTO DE SANTO DOMINGO

Santo Domingo, built in the 16th century, is one of Oaxaca's most ornate houses of worship. The rose-color exterior is striking, but it pales in comparison to what lies inside: The entryway's ceiling is decorated with an amazing mural of church benefactors, and busts of saints and martyrs loom in every corner and archway. The adjacent monastery, built in 1619, now houses the **Museo Regional de Oaxaca.** Exquisite Mixtec artifacts from the tombs of Monte Albán are displayed here, including skulls encrusted with jade and turquoise, gold earrings and ornaments, and elaborately carved jaguar bones. The church and museum complex is currently undergoing renovation and expansion, with plans to open a botanical garden and café in 1998. *Constitución at 5 de mayo, 5 blocks NE of zócalo, tel. 951/6–29–91. Museum admission: $2; free Sun. Open Tues.–Fri. 10–6, weekends 10–5.*

INSTITUTO DE ARTES GRAFICAS

This often overlooked but splendid library, art gallery, and café complex features a collection of books (in Spanish, English, German, and French) on art, architecture, photography, and more. The gallery has rotating shows of graphic art. You can relax over a book (your own, not from the collection!) in the breezy café at the building's rear. *Alcalá 507, across from Santo Domingo, tel. 951/6–69–80. Donation suggested. Open Wed.–Mon. 10:30–8.*

MUSEO DE ARTE CONTEMPORANEO DE OAXACA (MACO)

This excellent museum is dedicated to contemporary Oaxacan artists but occasionally features big-name European exhibits as well. Free art films are shown Friday–Sunday, usually at 6 PM. There is a café at the museum's back patio. *Alcalá 202, tel. 951/4–71–10. Admission: $1.30. Open Wed.–Mon. 10:30–8.*

MUSEO DE ARTE PREHISPANICO "RUFINO TAMAYO"

Pre-Columbian artifacts from all over Mexico are displayed in this beautifully restored colonial mansion. The collection, which belonged to Rufino Tamayo, one of Mexico's premier 20th-century artists, is arranged chronologically to give an idea of the artistic developments that preceded the Conquest. *Morelos 503, tel. 951/6–47–50. Admission: $1.50. Open Mon. and Wed.–Sat. 10–2 and 4–7, Sun. 10–3.*

CHEAP THRILLS

Oaxaca is one of the best cities in the country in which to sample traditional arts and culture, and many events and exhibits are free. Consult the *Guía Cultural* (*see* Visitor Information, *above*) for a comprehensive monthly listing of activities throughout the city. The **Casa de la Cultura Oaxaqueña** (González Ortega 403, tel. 951/6–24–83) hosts free films, dance, theater, art, and musical events. Stop by weekdays 9–9 or Saturday 9–2 to find out what's going on. **Art galleries** throughout the city host openings that are free to the public; look for notices posted around downtown. You'll get an inside look at local painters' works—and if you're lucky, some free *mezcal* (distilled spirit made from the blue maguey cactus) and tacos, too. Head to the **zócalo** for all kinds of free music. There's usually a concert on Sunday at noon, and night and day, itinerant mariachi bands roam the zócalo serenading anyone who'll buy a song. The Oaxaca state band gives free marimba concerts in the zócalo's gazebo on Monday, Wednesday, Friday, and Saturday at 7 PM. Tuesday and Thursday nights feature salsa and mariachi numbers. From the gazebo, make a small detour to the **Palacio del Gobierno** (south side of zócalo) to inspect Arturo García Bustos's beautiful murals depicting Oaxaca's pre-Columbian and revolutionary history; admission is free. The **Biblioteca Circulante de Oaxaca** (Alcalá 200, no phone) has an extensive selection of books in English and more than 50 different magazines—everything from *The New Yorker* to *Rolling Stone*.

> *"La Guelaguetza" can be figuratively translated as "The Zapotec Contribution." This is a festival of community ties, and is celebrated by expatriate Oaxacans living as far away as Los Angeles and San Diego.*

FESTIVALS

The most famous and stunning Oaxacan festival is **La Guelaguetza,** which is celebrated annually the first two Mondays following the Fiesta de la Virgen del Carmen (*see below*). The festivities, which take place atop the Cerro del Fortín (*see* Worth Seeing, *above*), summon thousands of Oaxacans (and tourists) to the capital to exchange gifts and perform folk dances representative of their regions. The preceding week is filled with music, parades, and cultural events. The best tickets cost upward of $35 and are sold at tourist agencies throughout the city; a better idea is to pack a pair of binoculars and arrive early (8 AM) on the day of the performances to secure a free seat in the upper seating levels. You can also catch less-touristed versions of the festivities in nearby villages; enquire at the tourist office for more information.

A bizarre display of Oaxacan craftsmanship and creativity can be seen on the **Noche de los Rábanos** (Night of the Radishes), on December 23. Everything from the NASA moon landing to the resurrection of Christ is re-created using only carved radishes, toothpicks, and moss. Equally impressive dioramas are constructed using corn husks and tiny dried marigolds. The following evening, Christmas Eve, features an impressive collection of floats, bands, and giant dancing dolls that are paraded around the zócalo in a traditional parade.

Other Oaxacan festivities include **La Virgen del Carmen** on July 16, when the Virgin's likeness is paraded around the Templo del Carmen Alto on García Vigil; the **Bendición de los Animales** on August 31, when family pets and farm animals are brought to church to be blessed and draped in garlands of flowers; **El Señor del Rayo** during the third week of October, when firework displays dominate the landscape; **La Virgen de la Soledad** on December 8–18, culminating in processions to the Basílica de la Soledad and in the Danza de la Pluma (*see* Worth Seeing, *above*).

SHOPPING

Oaxacan artisans are famous for the quality and inventiveness of their work—everything from unglazed and glazed pottery to colorful cotton hammocks, handloomed rugs made with natural or synthetic dyes, leather goods, cutlery, wooden and ceramic masks, brightly painted wooden figurines, handloomed textiles, and much more! If you only want to browse, explore the expensive boutiques along the Andador Turístico and the shops north of the zócalo. The **MARO** women artisans' collective (5 de Mayo 204, tel. 951/6–06–70; open daily 9–8) stocks an excellent selection of reasonably priced regional crafts and textiles, include serapes (woolen ponchos), shawls, embroidered shirts and dresses, and handloomed table and bed linens. Government-run **ARIPO** (García Vigil 809, tel. 951/4–40–30) sells a wide selection of Oaxacan treasures, while **FONART** (M. Bravo 116 at García Vigil, tel. 951/6–57–64) has a great selection of utilitarian and decorative pottery, glassware, lacquerware, and papier mâché from elsewhere in the republic. Both charge fair prices.

The **Central de Abastos** market, across from the second-class bus station, is a labyrinth of stalls selling leather bags, shoes, hammocks, exotic fruits, witchcraft, gory pieces of meat—in all, there are miles of merchandise. On Saturday, the traditional market day, you'll find a larger-than-usual display of regional crafts: Black-and-green ceramics, gold filigree jewelry, *alebrijes* (brightly painted wooden animals), rebozos (shawls), engraved knives, and *huipiles* (intricately embroidered tunics). The smaller **Benito Juárez** market, bordered by Flores Magón and Las Casas lies just one block southwest of the zócalo and is ringed by *artesanía* (handicrafts) vendors. The **20 de Noviembre** market, on Aldama south of the Benito Juárez market, contains mostly produce stalls and cheap *comedores* (sit-down food stands).

AFTER DARK

The heart of Oaxaca's nightlife is the zócalo. Families stroll the main square until about 11 PM, when the younger set heads to the discos to shake it until the wee hours. Bars surrounding the zócalo offer live music nightly, ranging from marimba to nuevo flamenco to Andean flute music. For the price of a coffee or drink you can enjoy these patio concerts.

BARS

If you're not content simply having a beer on the zócalo, the saloon-style **La Casa del Mezcal** (Flores Magón 209, no phone) dispenses *mezcal*, tequila's sister drink, in many different flavors and concentrations. The house closes its swinging wooden doors at 11 PM. **Café/Bar Hipótesis** (Morelos 511, tel. 951/4–74–08; closed Sun) is an intimate, late-night spot that offers sangria ($2), an eclectic selection of shelved literature, and live piano and guitar duets Thursday–Saturday at 9:30 PM. Gay bars in Oaxaca are very discreet; **502** (Porfirio Diaz 502, no phone) is identified only by the street number on the outside wall.

CINEMA

A half-dozen movie theaters show subtitled or dubbed American movies; check *Oaxaca* or the *Oaxaca Times* for listings. Right off the zócalo is **Plaza Alameda** (Independencia 508, at 20 de Noviembre, tel. 951/6–11–99; admission $2). Both the **Centro Fotográfico Alvarez Bravo** and the **Museo de Arte Contemporaneo** offer free screenings of foreign films with English subtitles; for both, *see* Worth Seeing, *above*.

DANCING

The friendly club **Candela** (Ignacio Allende 211, tel. 951/4–12–54; closed Sun.) heats up with live salsa and Caribbean rhythms. A shot of mezcal is less than $2, and gay couples, rhythmically impaired gringos, and single women will feel at ease jumping about on the dance floor. Depending on the band, the cover charge runs $2–$5. Another good salsa venue is **Los Tres Patios** (Cosijopi 208, between Porfirio Díaz and García Vigil, no phone; closed Sun.), where you can dance under the covered patio. Cover is usually about $2. If you prefer technopop, flashing lights, and clouds of smoke, go to **Universo** (Porfirio

Díaz 219, tel. 951/6–42–36; closed Sun.–Wed.). Cover is $3, and it's as packed with young people as it is with attitude.

LIVE MUSIC

El Sol y La Luna (M. Bravo 209, tel. 951/4–81–05) is a mellow and romantic place, candlelit and decorated with antiques. Live music fills the back room Friday and Saturday after 9 PM, while the bar is open Monday–Saturday. There's also an international menu with delicious crepes ($3). Cover is $3.

NEAR OAXACA CITY

Within 50 km (31 mi) of Oaxaca city are a number of important pre-Columbian ruins, most notably Monte Albán and Mitla. Nearby are indigenous communities that maintain distinct languages, customs, and histories, as well as ties to the sacred ruins. The Oaxaca valleys are also dotted with small towns whose inhabitants have lived for generations largely from a particular craft, such as pottery, carving, or weaving; these artisans have earned a national and, in some cases, international reputation. A visit to the indigenous communities on their market days, combined with a trip to the ruins, is an unobtrusive way to gain an appreciation of the culture of this region. As in all of Mexico, admission to the ruins described below is free on Sunday and holidays. Bring a flashlight for exploration of the ruins' tombs.

MONTE ALBAN

High on an artificially leveled plateau overlooking Oaxaca city lie the ruins of Monte Albán, the great ceremonial center of the Valles de Oaxaca. The Zapotecs began building Monte Albán as early as 500 BC, and at the height of its power the center had a population of over 40,000—more than any European city of that time. The evidence that Zapotec, Mixtec, Olmec, and Aztec civilizations all lived here has baffled archaeologists in their attempts to piece together Monte Albán's history, but they now believe the site was appropriated by the Mixtecs after it was abandoned by the Zapotecs in the 8th century. The Mixtecs in turn abandoned the site 500 years prior to the arrival of the Spaniards, who on discovery named the ruins Monte Albán. Archaeologists today disagree about the origin of the Spanish name: it may mean "white mountain" or be a corruption of the Spanish surname Montalván.

The site covers an area of more than 40 square km (14 square mi), but the most impressive structures are in the **Gran Plaza.** At each end of the plaza are ceremonial platforms aligned along a north–south axis. The acoustics here are such that sound carries clearly from one platform to the other. Start your exploration of the ruins at the monument to Dr. Alfonso Caso, the Mexican archaeologist who began excavations in 1930. Moving clockwise, you'll first encounter the **Juego de Pelota** (ball court). Its capital I shape and sloping side walls are distinctive to the region. In contrast to the contests played in the ball courts of the Yucatán, those in Monte Albán are not believed to have ended in sacrifice.

Next is a structure known as **Edificio P,** where a tunnel runs from the inner stairway in one corner to the central altar. Zapotec priests may have used the tunnel to appear, as if magically, during ceremonies. Next door is **El Palacio,** apparently the residence of a high-status Zapotec. The central patio is circled by nine chambers, some with sleeping ledges. Beneath the structure are subterranean passageways not open to the public. Looming above the plaza is **Plataforma Sur** (South Platform), where bas-relief figures with closed eyes are believed to represent vassals who paid tribute to Monte Albán. There is evidence of five distinct epochs of construction in this edifice.

Edificio L, more commonly known as the **Edificio de los Danzantes** (Building of the Dancers), is one of the oldest buildings at the site and is covered with carvings of human figures. Originally the figures were thought to represent swimmers, acrobats, or dancers; the current theory is that the bas-relief figures represent enemies who were either tortured or mutilated to prevent procreation, and possibly sacrificed as well. In **Mound IV,** the next building over, archaeologists constructed a tunnel that lets you view an enormous *talud* (altar) of large stones. Some are carved with dancing figures, indicating that later inhabitants may have stripped older buildings and recycled the stones.

The massive **Plataforma Norte** (North Platform) completes the circle. A path behind the platform leads to the entrances of a number of tombs: **Tomb 104** contains some of the site's best-preserved carvings and murals, which are said to depict the day the deceased passed away and scenes from their most notable lifetime achievements. Others suggest that the paintings could be written formulas soliciting the benevolence of the gods.

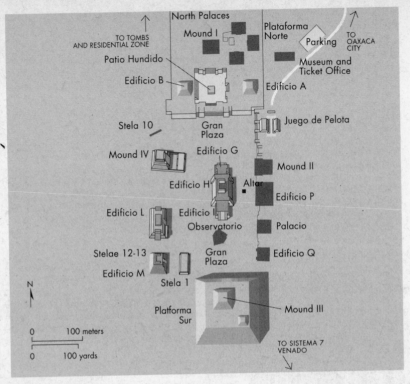

The **Observatorio** and **Edificios I, H,** and **G** are in the middle of the plaza. The arrowhead-shape struc-ture close to Plataforma Sur is the observatory, otherwise known as **Edificio J.** Its dancing figures appear upside down or placed on an incline, suggesting that they may have been recycled from older buildings. The depictions of captives, however, were probably designed for this building.

Tombs 7, 72, and 105, currently not on display, were not built by the Zapotecs, who originally inhab-ited Monte Albán, but by the Mixtecs, who used the city as a necropolis. Tomb 7, behind the visitor's center to the left, divulged some of the richest art finds in the world, now on display in the Museo Regional de Oaxaca (*see* Worth Seeing, *above*).

COMING AND GOING
Buses from **Hotel Mesón del Ángel** (Mina 518, tel. 951/6–53–27 or 951/4–31–52) in Oaxaca city run to Monte Albán (20 min, $1.50 round trip). There are half-hourly departures 8:30 AM–3:30 PM; the last bus returns at 5:30 PM. The fare allows only two hours at the site, which is barely enough time, but you can come back on a later bus for an 80¢ surcharge—negotiate with your driver. If you'd rather go the cheap route, catch a bus to Colonia Monte Albán (the town) from the second-class bus station in Oa-xaca city for 30¢. From the colonia, the 30-minute walk to the ruins is beautiful but painfully steep. The ruins are open daily 8–5, and admission is $2 (free Sunday and holidays).

MITLA AND THE EASTERN VALLEY
While most visitors head in this direction just to see the ruins of Mitla, along the way there are a number of smaller archaeological sites and a scattering of villages that produce handmade crafts. If you're plan-ning to visit several towns, consider staying in one of the newly built **YU'U** (House of the Tourist) cabañas set up in Teotitlán del Valle, Tlacolula, or Santa Ana del Valle. They offer comfortable dorm-style cabins (most with kitchens) and super-clean bathrooms for less than $5 per person. Get details and make reservations at the tourist office in Oaxaca city.

Mitla-bound buses (1 hr, 50¢) leave Oaxaca city's second-class bus station every 15 minutes and drop you off less than a mile from the ruins. In Oaxaca city, you can also catch the Mitla-bound buses on Calzada de Niños Héroes, east of Calzada de la República, although there may be standing room only. Return buses pass by the drop-off point on the main highway until 8 PM.

THE ROAD TO MITLA

All buses for Mitla (*see above*) pass the places listed below—just let the driver know where you'd like to get off, and sit close to the front so he doesn't forget about you. The highway is well marked, and everything is easily accessible from the road. The first stop out of Oaxaca city on your way east is the 2,000-year-old **Tule tree** in the tiny town of Santa María del Tule. It's supposedly the largest *ahuehuete* (cypress tree) in the world. Farther on, you'll come to the crossroads for the partially unearthed Zapotec ruins of **Dainzú**. From the main road, walk about 20 minutes to the site. The main attraction at Dainzú is its many carved bas-reliefs, some depicting ball players in full costume; the ruins are open daily 8–5, and admission is $1.

After Dainzú, you can hop off the bus at the crossroads for the village of **Teotitlán del Valle**. Teotitlán's inhabitants specialize in woven *tapetes* (rugs), some still colored with dyes handmade from dried insects or native plants. Further down the road to Mitla is the **Chagoya Mezcal Factory** (open daily 9–5), where free tours teach visitors the traditional methods used to make this potent drink. Next the bus passes the crossroads for the town of **Tlacolula**, known for its lively Sunday market—quite possibly the best in the area.

Oaxacan civic groups are currently battling a plan by the national government to make Monte Albán more attractive to tourists by adding a monorail from Oaxaca city, an aerial tram, and a huge parking lot.

More spectacular than Dainzú are the ruins at **Yagul**, about halfway between Tlacolula and Mitla. Yagul is believed to have been a residential area for Zapotec priests and aristocrats. It features a grand **Palacio de 6 Patios** (Palace of 6 Patios) and a restored **Juego de Pelota**. A scramble up the path to the right of the entrance will give you a panoramic view of the ruins as well as of the valley below. Yagul is open daily 9–5; admission is $1.

MITLA

The name Mitla (Mictlán) is Nahuatl for "place of the dead" or "place of rest." Mitla's Zapotec name is *Lyobaa*. Here, 44 km (27 mi) southeast of Oaxaca city, the Zapotecs established a massive burial ground in 100 BC. The Mixtecs conquered the site in 1250 and it remains important to indigenous families to this day. According to popular myths, the Aztec god Quetzalcoatl (a plumed serpent, part snake and part bird) came here in search of bones that would aid in the formation of man.

Of the five groups of square structures at Mitla, only two have been fully excavated and restored. The **Conjunto de Columnas** (Group of Columns) was part of an official's private home. Inside the north structure is a room covered from stone floor to wooden ceiling with three distinct patterns of *greca* (mosaic) unique to Mitla, composed of thousands of pieces of well-cut stone set in clay to form geometric patterns. These particular grecas represent air, earth, and water and at one time were coated with stucco and painted red. Some believe that this room was a library and that the patterned greca hold coded knowledge. Also in this group you'll see what is popularly referred to as the **Columna de la Vida** (Column of Life). According to legend, you can tell how many years you've got left by embracing the column and calculating the space left between your outstretched hands. Presumably, the longer your arms, the sooner you can expect to die. The site is directly in front of the Iglesia San Pablo, about a mile uphill from where the second-class bus lets you off. The ruins are open daily 8–5 and admission is $1.25.

Downhill from the ruins, near the center of Mitla village, the free **Frissell Museum** (open Sun.–Fri. 9–5) exhibits beautiful pottery recovered from Mitla and nearby sites. The adjacent restaurant, **La Sorpresa**, serves delicious, wholesome meals.

SOUTH OF OAXACA CITY

In the valley to the south of Oaxaca city you can meet the personalities behind the colorful pottery, embroidered blouses, and carved wooden creatures that fill the city's markets and shops. All the villages listed below are 20 minutes to one hour away via second-class bus from Oaxaca city. Arrazola lies just off the road to Zaachila; these two towns make an enjoyable day trip when combined with San Martín Tilcajete and Ocotlán. Friday is market day in Ocotlán.

ARRAZOLA

Five kilometers (3 mi) off the main road between Oaxaca city and Zaachila is the small village of Arrazola, internationally famous for its wood carvers, who create fantastic animals called *alebrijes* out of copal wood (copal is also valued for its resin, which is used to make incense). These small, wooden coyotes, lizards, and mythological figures fetch anywhere from a few dollars to a few hundred dollars—the most expensive are those bearing the name of Don Manuel Jiménez, one of the town's best-known artisans and the originator of the brightly colored pieces. To get here, take a bus bound for Zaachila, get off at the Arrazola crossroads (remind the driver or he's bound to forget the stop), and walk or wait patiently for a *colectivo* (communal taxi) to take you the 3 km (2 mi) into Arrazola. Direct colectivos to Arrazola (50¢) depart Oaxaca city infrequently from the corner of the Periférico and Prolongación de Victoria, just east of the Mercado de Abastos and south of Galeana street. The trip takes about 40 minutes.

ZAACHILA

Eighteen kilometers (11 mi) south of Oaxaca city, Zaachila was once the Zapotec capital, then a Mixteca city. It's also the site of ruins that were never looted, thanks to the townspeople's devotion to their ancestors' graves. When archaeologists discovered the tombs in Zaachila, residents insisted on being involved in the excavations. There are two tombs here: One tomb is empty, its artifacts having been removed to museums. The other tomb has tiny grecas similar to those found in Mitla (*see above*) and a mural depicting two figures. One figure, wearing a long alligator mask, represents the god of death. The other carries a bag of copal resin and is thought to represent a priest. The ruins are open daily 8–5, and admission is $1. Hourly buses to the ruins and the town of Zaachila (30 min, 50¢) depart from the second-class bus station in Oaxaca city.

SAN MARTIN TILCAJETE

In this tiny town, you'll be invited into private homes to see fantastically painted toy animals, the sale of which supports entire families. It's well worth the half-hour bus ride and 20-minute walk. Buying here—rather than in the markets of Oaxaca city—means you can be sure the money goes straight to the artist. To reach this hospitable town, ask the driver of any bus headed to Ejutla to drop you off at the road leading to San Martín, and walk or hitch the rest of the way (it's a 15–20 minute walk). Catch buses at the second-class bus station in Oaxaca city.

OCOTLAN

This wonderful little town is home to the famous Aguilar sisters: Guillermina, Josefina, Irene, and Concepción, all of whom are skilled pottery painters in their 50s. You can visit their homes and workshops on Continuación de Morelos, near the entrance to town. The best day to come is Friday, when Ocotlán holds its small market. It takes about an hour on the Ejutla bus to reach Ocotlán ($1); catch buses at the second-class bus station in Oaxaca city.

THE OAXACA COAST

The Sierra Madre del Sur mountain range hugs the Oaxacan coastline for almost 400 km (250 mi). Much of this region is undeveloped, and most visitors do their frolicking at three main tourist destinations: Puerto Ángel, Puerto Escondido, and the Bahías de Huatulco. Within the last decade, the latter two spots experienced soaring popularity and a flurry of construction, but the devaluation of the peso has brought much of the commercialization to a halt. Nonetheless, developers still like to predict that Huatulco will eclipse Cancún as the premier resort destination in Mexico by the year 2000.

Sporting opportunities abound here. In Puerto Escondido, surfers from around the world congregate to ride the Mexican Pipeline at Playa Zicatela. Snorkelers head out to the calmer waters at nearby Puerto Angelito and Carrizalillo, or to Estacahuite near Puerto Ángel. Scuba enthusiasts make their way to Roca Blanca off the shores of Cacoletepec. Many travelers, however, come here simply to kick back and enjoy the sunshine and ocean breezes. Zipolite beach, near Puerto Ángel, is famous as a hippie hangout, while the town of Santa Cruz Huatulco is the Mexican government's latest target for development as a high-class resort area. It's still a camper's paradise—but that won't last long.

PUERTO ESCONDIDO

Puerto Escondido is much less flashy and pretentious than most of Mexico's coastal hot spots, and it's one of the few resort towns left that doesn't serve as a port of call for cruise ships. Still, Puerto Escondido's two beaches do draw the tourists hordes: Zicatela beach is the site of surfing contests in August and November; and Playa Principal is a favorite of vacationing Mexican families. High seasons for tourism are Christmas, Semana Santa, and the months of July and August. If you decide to visit during any of these peak times, make reservations well in advance and prepare yourself for the *pachanga* (party). Standing in marked contrast to this unabashed tourism is the "other" Escondido, which lies north of the resort areas, on the other side of the Carretera Costera (Highway 200). This is where the locals live and where you'll find the post and telegraph offices, the bus stations, and a more typical Mexican town atmosphere with cheap food, busy streets, and friendly people.

BASICS

CASAS DE CAMBIO

The most conveniently located casa de cambio is on Pérez Gasga, across from Farmacia Cortés; it's open weekdays 9–2 and 5–8. **Banamex** (Pérez Gasga 314, tel. 958/2–03–52; open weekdays 9–1:30) changes currency and traveler's checks and has a 24-hour ATM.

LAUNDRY

Lavamática del Centro (Pérez Gasga 405A, tel. 2–03–19; open daily 8–8) charges $1 per kilo (2 pounds). **Lavandería Automática** (Pérez Gasga s/n, no phone), next to the Banamex office, has similar prices and hours. **Silvia's Place** (Calle del Morro s/n, next to the Swill Shop, no phone; open Mon.–Sat. 7–3) charges one peso per item.

Many towns in southern Mexico, such as Mitla, Ocotlan, and Tlacolula, have Nahuatl names. Some once belonged to the Aztec empire, and others were named by Aztec guides who traveled with the conquistadors.

MEDICAL AID

Emergency medical care is available at **Comisión Nacional de Emergencia** (Tlacochahuaya, at Fracc. Bacocho), the free **Cruz Roja** (Marina Nacional, at Pérez Gazga, tel. 958/2–01–46), or at the **Centro de Salud** (Pérez Gasga 409, tel. 958/2–60–16), where the English-speaking Dr. Luis Flores is on staff. All three clinics are open 24 hours.

PHONES AND MAIL

You can make collect and cash calls at the **caseta de larga distancia** (long-distance telephone office) on Pérez Gasga by the Andador Unión, a stairway connecting Pérez Gasga to the Carretera Costera. There are also public phones that accept credit cards in front of the pharmacy at the west end of Pérez Gasga. The **post office** (Calle 7 Nte., at Oaxaca, tel. 958/2–09–59) is a long, uphill walk on the inland side of the highway. They'll hold mail sent to you at the following address for up to 10 days: Oficina de Correos, Puerto Escondido, Oaxaca, 71980, México. You can send or receive telegrams, money orders, and faxes at the **telegraph office** (tel. 958/2–09–57) next door. Both the post and telegraph offices are open weekdays 9–7, Saturday 9–noon.

VISITOR INFORMATION

The main **tourist office** (Calle 5 Pte., at the Carretera Costera, tel. 958/2–01–75; open weekdays 9–2 and 5–8, Sat. 9–1) is at least a half-hour walk west from town, but they do provide maps and some hotel and touring information. There's also a minuscule **tourist-information booth** on Pérez Gasga, across from the Hotel Roca Mar. It's manned by Gina, who provides friendly, intelligent, useful information on hotels, guided tours, and street directions daily until 1 PM, and occasional evenings between 5 and 7:30 PM.

COMING AND GOING

Puerto Escondido is split in two by the **Carretera Costera** (Coastal Highway; Highway 200). Uphill to the north is the untouristed part of town, where locals live. The street that snakes south down the hill from the highway and then east along the coast is Pérez Gasga, popularly known as the **Andador Turístico** (tourist walkway). The Andador runs parallel to the main beach, **Playa Principal,** and is where many of the town's hotels and restaurants are located. **Zicatela,** the town's famous surfing beach, lies just southeast of town.

BY BUS

All of the town's bus terminals are north of the Carretera Costera, a 15-minute walk (or $1.50 taxi ride) from hotels on the Andador Turistico. **Estrella del Valle-Oaxaca Pacífico** (Hidalgo at Av. 3ra Oriente, tel. 958/2–00–50 or 958/2–09–53) has first-class service to Oaxaca city (3 per day; 7½ hrs, $9.50), Acapulco (4 per day; 7 hrs, $10), Salina Cruz (5 hrs, $7), and Pochutla (hourly; 90 min, $1.50). You can also flag down buses for Pochutla along the highway—there's one every 15–20 minutes. **Cristobal Colón** (Primera Norte 207, tel. 958/2–10–73) sends first-class buses to San Cristóbal (2 per day; 12 hrs, $19); book your seats in advance.

BY PLANE

The airport (Km 3 on the Carretera Costera, tel. 958/2–04–92 or 958/2–04–91) is served by several airlines: **Mexicana** (tel. 958/2–04–14 or 958/2–00–98) flies daily to Mexico City (1 hr, $100), while **Aeromorelos** (tel. 958/2–06–53) and **Aerovega** (Peréz Gasga, at Marina Nacional, tel. 958/2–01–51) fly small planes to Oaxaca city (30 min, $45). **Transportes Aeropuerto y Turístico** (tel. 958/2–09–45) handles transportation to and from town (10 min, $2) in VW vans; look for their signs at the airport. You can also make arrangements with your hotel to be picked up by a **Transportes Terrestres** (tel. 958/2–01–15) van; cost is $1.25.

WHERE TO SLEEP

During Christmas, New Year, Semana Santa, and surfing championships, as well as the entire months of July and August, prices for accommodations are often double the prices listed below. Make reservations well in advance for these peak periods. During the low season look for ROOM FOR RENT/RENTAN CUARTOS signs; these are often cheaper than the hotels and give you the added benefit of meeting a friendly Mexican family.

ANDADOR TURISTICO

UNDER $10 • Cabañas Aldea Marinero. Not to be confused with the nearby Bungalows Marinero, this small cluster of hammocks and huts lies on a sandy lane just off Playa Marinero. The brick-floor cabañas ($4 per person) have cots, electric lights and outlets, and mosquito netting. The communal bathrooms are semi-clean. *Playa Marinero, no phone. 14 cabañas, none with bath. Restaurant, bar. Cash only.*

Hotel Mayflower. This hotel boasts spotless rooms, all equipped with ceiling fans, private baths, hot water, and balconies with ocean views. Doubles are $13. Dorm-style accommodations ($5.50 per person) with kitchen access are the best value in town. The rooftop bar draws a diverse crowd during happy hour (daily 5–10 PM). *Andador Libertad, just uphill from Pérez Gasga, tel. 958/2–03–67, fax 958/2–04–22. 12 rooms, all with bath. Bar, laundry, luggage storage, safe-deposit boxes. Reservations advised. Cash only.*

UNDER $20 • Hotel Casablanca. This two-story hotel offers large, adequately furnished rooms ($18.50) with ceiling fans. Bathrooms are clean and have plenty of hot water. Outside, there's a small, shaded pool surrounded by a grassy area with umbrella tables and lounge chairs. The hotel restaurant overlooks the pool. *Pérez Gasca 905, tel. 958/2–01–68. 21 rooms, all with bath. Restaurant, bar. Cash only.*

ZICATELA

UNDER $20 • Bungalows/Cabañas Acuario. The cabañas here are simply furnished, but some of the larger ones have full kitchens. A two-person cabaña is $16.50, a two-person bungalow (basically, a cabaña with a kitchen) about $24. The friendly, laid-back management can provide information on sightseeing, surfing, and scuba lessons. They also operate a pharmacy and a phone/fax office in front of the hotel. *Calle del Morro, tel. 958/2–03–57 or 958/2–10–27. 26 cabañas and bungalows, all with bath. Restaurant, pool. Cash only.*

Rockaway Surfer Village. A wall encloses this well-kept, beachfront village of cabañas. It's an idyllic place where guests drink beer on the porch of the surf shop or splash in the clean, freshwater pool. Cabañas with portable floor-model fans, mosquito netting, and private bathrooms run $13 for one person or $20 for two. *Just west of Bruno's, tel. 958/2–06–68. 12 cabañas, all with bath. Restaurant, bar. Reservations advised. Cash only.*

CAMPING

Camping is illegal on Puerto Escondido's beaches, except at designated campgrounds: **Cabañas el Eden** (Calle del Morro s/n, no phone) is behind Bruno's Restaurant on Zicatela beach. It offers six camp-sites for tent or van (as well as six plain, tiny rooms with fans) for $2. At **Neptuno** (Pérez Gasga, tel. 958/2–03–27) tent sites cost $1.50, and next door at **Las Palmas,** car camping costs $8 for two people. Both of these are on the beach.

FOOD

Seafood is king in Puerto Escondido, and you can sample dishes made from fresh lobster, fish, shrimp, squid, and cuttlefish. A smattering of cafés, comedores, and *paleterías* (Popsicle shops) along Pérez Gasga make for good snacking. Locals shop for produce at the daily **Mercado Benito Juárez,** near the post office.

UNDER $5 • Bruno's. This Zicatela beach joint fills with expat surfers who are into healthy food, mellow music, and leisurely service. There's a happening bar and a rotating menu featuring Thai, Japanese, and Indian food. *South end of Playa Zicatela, no phone. Closed Mon. Cash only.*

Carmen's Bakery. You'll find this bakery on a sandy lane off Playa Marinero. Hungry beachcombers come to feed on ter-rific breakfasts (free refills on coffee), delicious sandwiches ($1.50), and freshly baked breads. The same owner runs **Cafecito,** a popular surfer's hangout at Zicatela beach. *Entrada Playa Marinero s/n, across from Hotel Flor de María, tel. 958/2–08–60. Cash only.*

If you want a glimpse of what life in Puerto Escondido was like before all the fishermen became tour operators, visit the fish market on the west end of Playa Principal. Fish are sold daily from 6 AM.

La Gota de Vida. The specialty here is homemade vegetarian food, including fresh tempeh and tofu; the veggie tamales ($1.50) and mushroom pâté are both excellent. There's also a juice bar. Rumor has it the owner is looking to relocate—ask around town for information. There's a second La Gota on Zicatela Beach at Calle del Morro. *West end of Pérez Gasga, no phone. Cash only.*

La Pergola Mexicana. An extensive selection of cheap, fresh seafood dishes ($2), as well as traditional comidas corridas and breakfasts, keep this place packed with savvy locals and tourists alike. *Pérez Gasga, near casa de cambio, tel. 958/2–12–36. Cash only.*

La Posada del Tiburón. For a no-worry, no-hurry beachfront meal, check out this clean, friendly place serving a pleasing selection of seafood and Mexican dishes. From your table you'll be able to watch the fishing boats coming and going. The fruit salad ($2) is divine. *Playa Marinera, tel. 958/2–07–86. Cash only.*

OUTDOOR ACTIVITIES

The beaches around Puerto Escondido offer a variety of sporting opportunities. If you want to snorkel (best at Puerto Angelito and Carrizalillo), boogieboard (best at Playa Principal and Carrizalillo), or surf (best at Zicatela), you'll save money by renting equipment in town for the entire day, rather than paying an hourly rate at the beach. For surfing equipment, lessons, and advice, visit **Bungalows/Cabañas Acuario** (*see* Where to Sleep, *above*). They also rent scuba gear. **Mango Club** (Pérez Gasga 605-E, tel. 958/2–04–06; open daily 9–8) rents snorkel gear ($5 per day), motorcycles ($32 per day), and bicycles ($15 per day) with a deposit or a credit card.

Green Iguana Tours (Calle del Morro s/n; no phone), behind Cafecito Restaurant on Zicatela Beach, runs three-hour river trips on the nearby Colotepec River. A truck takes you to the river, where you climb aboard rubber inner tubes and float tranquilly downriver. The trip costs $10, with a two-person minimum.

PLAYA PRINCIPAL

The main beach parallels the Andador Turístico and is a favorite spot for strolling, sunning, sailing ($10 per hr), and horseback riding ($6.50 per hr). You can hire a *lancha* (motorboat; $10 per hr) to go to

Puerto Angelito, Carrizalillo, or out to sea to frolic with local sea turtles. The eastern section of Playa Principal, called **Playa Marinero,** is separated from the rest by a lagoon. It's ideal for swimming, exploring tidepools, and learning to surf.

ZICATELA

The town's famous surfing spot lies east of Playa Marinero. Along with Hawaii's North Shore and Australia's Barrier Reef, Zicatela is considered one of the top surfing beaches in the world; waves here roll in with impressive force. **Las Olas** (Calle del Morro s/n, no phone) rents boogieboards and surfboards (each $6.50 per day), plus an $80 deposit, which is refunded at the end of the day if the equipment is undamaged. If you do venture into the water, use caution: The swift current can be deadly. If you're not a surfer, you can rent horses or four-wheelers from vendors who set up tents on the sand.

PUERTO ANGELITO

It's about a 20-minute walk or a $2 taxi ride to this small inlet and the neighboring beach of **Manzanillo.** The calm water attracts families with young children, and it's a great area for swimming and snorkeling. Sure enough, young boys rent the necessary snorkel gear for about $2.50 an hour. To get here, walk west along Pérez Gasga until it curves uphill toward the highway. From there, follow Camino a Puerto Angelito, to a set of cement stairs leading down to the beach.

CARRIZALILLO

Relatively free of the families that crowd Puerto Angelito, this U-shape cove with tricky ocean currents draws snorkelers and strong swimmers. You can make the dusty, hourlong trek by walking west along the Carretera Costera toward Bacocho; the sign pointing to Carrizalillo is visible from the carretera. Or take a motor-boat ride from Puerto Angelito or Playa Principal (*see above*) and have them return to pick you up later. **Bacocho,** the most westerly beach, is safest for swimming.

AFTER DARK

During major holidays, surfing championships, and summer months, the Andador Turístico is itself the party, with locals checking out the tourists, surfers mingling with sightseers, and everybody out having a good time. The Andador is also lined with dozens of bars and clubs, which are absolutely dead in the low season but become jam-packed when everyone's in town. At the east end of the Andador, **Bananas** (Pérez Gasga, tel. 958/2–00–05) offers canned pop music and games like Ping-Pong and Foosball. **Barfly** (Pérez Gasga, no phone) has an extensive drink list and a rickety roof deck with views of the Andador. Downstairs, surfers down beer after beer while watching reruns of old surfing championships. **Babalu** (Pérez Gasga, no phone) plays live Latin rhythms nightly starting at 10:30 PM. **Montezuma's Revenge** (Pérez Gasga 613, tel. 958/2–19–17) also offers live music most evenings. **El Tubo** is an out-of-the-way bar that rocks nightly until 3 AM in high season. It's down a flight of stairs on the beach side of Pérez Gasga; look for the sign with a surfer riding a wave.

NEAR PUERTO ESCONDIDO

Going with a guide will save you time, money, and hassles: Ana Márquez, a native Mixteca, has an office in the **Hotel Rincón del Pacífico** (Pérez Gasga s/n, tel. 958/2–00–56 or 958/2–20–01).

ZAPOTALITO AND
PARQUE NACIONAL LAGUNAS DE CHACAHUA

About 74 km (46 mi) west of Puerto Escondido is a tropical park encompassing the **Chacahua** lagoon, deserted beaches, and much wildlife. The town of **Zapotalito,** many of whose inhabitants are descended from African slaves, is near the entrance of the park. Your options for passing the day here are numerous: You can enjoy the pristine beaches, lunching on banana tortillas and grilled fish sold by kids at **Playa Chacahua,** or visit the *crocodrilario* (alligator hatchery) in Chacahua village. The hatchery workers will show you small bathtubs full of tiny, squirming alligators, their eyes still shut but their jaws already snapping. It takes about an hour to cross the lagoon to the village of Chacahua in a hired boat. Closer to Zapotalito (about a 45-minute boat ride down the river) is **Playa Cerro Hermoso,** a windswept beach at the mouth of the lagoon. Here you can hunt for rare black orchids or play in the gentle surf.

Tours ($25) by Ana Márquez (*see above*) are a good way to see the park and Zapotalito, as they include transportation to, from, and within the park. If you prefer to hire a guide in Zapotalito, catch an early Acapulco-bound bus (1 hr, $1) and ask to get off at the road leading to the park. It's about a 10-km

(6-mi) hike or hitch to Zapotalito. Park admission is free, but boat rentals run about $60. To make it worth your while, go with a group and allow a full day for the excursion.

PUERTO ANGEL

Puerto Ángel, 11 km (6½ mi) off the main highway, is touted by tourism officials as an unspoiled beach paradise. In fact, the tranquil fishing village *has* managed to stave off much of the development and commercialization that has slowly crept up on Puerto Escondido. And now that Santa Cruz Huatulco is receiving all of the developers' attention, it looks as though the Navy will remain the most influential force in town for some time to come. A rustic atmosphere prevails in Puerto Ángel: You can join the locals for a swim in the bay off the main beach, or arrange for a day of snorkeling or sightseeing by boat from one of the coves on either side of town.

Puerto Ángel's bay has become more polluted in recent years, but local families still splash around in gentle waves off **Playa Panteón.** The beach is in a sheltered cove just west of town, reached by walking along the Andador just west of the town's *muelle* (dock). You can rent snorkel equipment ($8 per day) here, or take a boat trip—ask around for Sr. Byron, who leads excursions by bicycle or boat. A 20-minute walk east of town will take you to **Estacahuite,** where you can rent snorkel gear on the beach and explore the offshore coral reef. Beyond Estacahuite, the next beach is **La Mina,** a pristine, palm-shaded paradise.

Chacahua is the Mixtec word for river shrimp; these are the tiny critters you'll see kids selling by the bagful on the streets of Puerto Escondido.

BASICS

There are no banks or casas de cambios in Puerto Ángel, and hotels in town change currency only. However, **Gundi and Tomás** (*see* Where to Sleep, *below*) will change your traveler's checks at a lousy rate. There aren't any pay phones in town; **Ferretería Velasco** (in front of the naval base, tel. 958/4–30–10; open Mon.–Sat. 9–9) charges $1 to make an international collect call, while **Hotel Soraya,** at the entrance to town, has a phone for local and long-distance calls. The **post and telegraph offices** (open weekdays 9–3) lie along the main road, near the entrance to town. For medical care, both the **Centro de Salud** (no phone; take stairway up to Rincón Sabroso—it's past the church) and the naval base's emergency center at Playa Principal are open 24 hours. There is currently no **visitor information** center in Puerto Ángel. Another option if you need to change money, send a letter, or make a long-distance call, is to hop on a bus to the nearby town of Pochutla (30 min, 50¢).

COMING AND GOING

There's no direct bus service to Puerto Ángel, so you'll need to take a bus to the town of **Pochutla** and catch a colectivo, bus, or cab from there. The bus to and from Pochutla (30 min, 50¢) runs every half hour, 6 AM–8 PM. Frequent colectivos run the same route for about 50¢; a taxi shouldn't cost you more than $3.

GETTING AROUND

Puerto Ángel is a tiny town, but finding places can be somewhat complicated since very few have numbered street addresses. The highway from Pochutla turns into Avenida Principal at the entrance to town, and later becomes Boulevard Virgilio Uribe. The bus will drop you off or pick you up at *el árbol* (the tree) on the main street just before the naval base. Farther on, the road crosses a dry creek bed and then forks just after the supermarket—the high road leads to Zipolite, the low road to Playa Panteón.

WHERE TO SLEEP

Most of Puerto Ángel's hotels are perched atop rocky hillsides, and reaching them often requires climbing a healthy number of stairs. The rewards for your efforts include unobstructed ocean breezes, in-house restaurants serving well-prepared local cuisine, and great views of the cove. One of the best of these hotels is **Hotel Alex** (tel. 958/4–30–03), where double rooms with fans, mosquito nets, and private bath go for $11 (one bed) or $13.50 (two beds). To reach the hotel, follow the main road across the bridge and continue uphill. At **La Buena Vista** (tel. and fax 958/4–31–04), comfortable, fan-cooled double rooms cost $22.50. La Buena Vista is on the same hill just past Alex's; it's on the left. **Casa de Huéspedes El Capi** (Playa Panteón, tel. 958/4–30–02) is a bargain beachside option, with clean but cramped rooms costing $11 for a double. **Pensión Anahí** (Pedro Sainz s/n, just past Playa Panteón, no phone) is a favorite of locals: it's small, clean, and friendly and has a small restaurant. Double rooms cost $5. All hotels are cash only.

UNDER $10 • Gundi y Tomás. This homey hilltop guesthouse provides several options for shoestring travelers: You can sleep in a double ($10) or a hammock ($3). Rooms are basic, with communal bath and no hot water. *Up the stairs just west of el árbol, no phone.16 rooms, none with bath. Café, laundry, luggage storage. Cash only.*

UNDER $15 • Pensión Puesto del Sol. This red-roof guest house is nestled amid a profusion of hibiscus flowers and lemon and pomegranate trees. The lobby/library has a profusion of plants and tempting hammocks. All of the.simple, clean rooms have mosquito screens and fans; the spotless bathrooms, both private and communal, have cold water only. Harold, the German proprietor, will share his maps and bus schedules (and perhaps a beer) in the open-air lounge. The cheapest doubles are $11, $13 with bath. Recently renovated rooms cost $17, and two new rooms with private terraces are a good deal at $20. *Tel. 958/4–30–96. From el árbol, follow road toward Zipolite; it's up the hill just beyond supermarket. 14 rooms, 8 with bath. Breakfast, laundry, luggage storage. Cash only.*

Posada Cañón de Vata. This hotel is set in a tranquil canyon just behind Playa Panteón. Rooms run $15–30 for a double, depending on whether or not you want a private bath and/or a stunning view. The bilingual owners are friendly and freely give advice on all of Puerto Ángel's offering. When it's not raining, outdoor yoga classes ($7 each) are conducted by resident swamis. The posada also offers holistic massages, and their patio restaurant features vegetarian fare. *Playa Panteón, tel. and fax 958/4–30–48. 20 rooms, 17 with bath. Restaurant, luggage storage. Closed May and June. Cash only.*

FOOD

Avoid the *palapa* (thatched hut) restaurants selling overpriced seafood along Playa Principal—the best cooking is served in the hotels listed above. You needn't be a guest to partake of their cuisine, although reservations are required of nonguests for lunch at Cañón de Vata. Gundi y Tomás offers healthy breakfasts for less than $2, including granola with yogurt and fruit, fruit smoothies, and homemade whole-wheat bread. La Buena Vista serves delicious, authentic Oaxacan cooking, such as mouthwatering veggie tamales ($3.50), *chiles rellenos* (stuffed chile peppers), and Kahlúa flan.

UNDER $5 • Restaurante Beto. This patio-style restaurant is wrapped in heavy jungle foliage. It's just the place to sip a beer or enjoy Oaxacan dishes like *atún al mojo de ajo* (tuna in garlic; $2). *Tel. 958/4–30–11. Follow main road past naval base and turn right at fork; it's just past Puesto del Sol. No breakfast. Cash only.*

NEAR PUERTO ANGEL

CHACALAPA

This quiet town, nestled in a green valley, is just 12 km (7 mi) from Pochutla. Here you'll find Tom Bachmaier, an artist who etches Oaxacan landscapes on small bamboo beads. Even if you're not interested in buying, stop by his meticulous home to admire his beautiful work and garden. Across the path is **Alberca El Paraíso** (closed Tues. and Wed.), a swimming pool filled with turquoise mineral water from a nearby natural spring. Octavio Ramos, who owns the pool and surrounding ranch, will happily guide you through the forest, identifying all sorts of strange-looking, edible tropical fruits. There's a $1 charge to use the pool for a day; if you're drawn in by the warmth of the Ramos family, you can enjoy free use of the pool and stay in one of the four cabañas ($7.50) with hot water, private baths, and ceiling fans. On Thursday and Friday, Octavio organizes daylong excursions ($10.50) that include use of the pool and nature trails, lunch, and round-trip transportation from Puerto Ángel. Make reservations at Pensión Puesto del Sol (*see* Where to Sleep, *above*). To visit these two households on your own, catch a northbound microbus (25¢) in Pochutla, across from the Freedom Language School. Ask for the *callejón* (alley) that leads to "La Alberca" and walk about 2 km (1 mi).

ZIPOLITE

A sweaty 30-minute walk west from Puerto Ángel brings you to Zipolite (Beach of the Dead). It's like entering a lost world of the 1960s and '70s: You'll hear lots of Led Zepplin and Bob Marley music and see lots of spaced-out, scruffy hippy gringos. Most people come to experience the scene (or to see how long they can stretch their skinny budget), but the recent influx of wealthier, better groomed daytrippers from Puertos Ángel and Escondido have given Zipolite a more touristy feel than before. Nudity is common on the western end of Zipolite beach, and the southern section, known as **Playa del Amor,** has a pretty active gay scene. Be *extremely* cautious about swimming here: The name Beach of the Dead refers not, as some seem to think, to the Grateful Dead, but to the many lost to its swift currents each year.

COMING AND GOING • Buses (30 min, 50¢) run to Zipolite from Puerto Ángel and Pochutla approximately every half hour 6 AM–8 PM. If coming from Puerto Escondido, you can avoid a stop in Pochutla by getting off the bus at the crossroads for San Antonio on the Carretera Costera. From there, catch a direct bus to Manzunte or Zipolite (20 min, 25¢). Taxis between Pochutla and Zipolite cost about $2.50, but most Zipolite taxi drivers retire for the evening around 9 PM.

WHERE TO SLEEP AND EAT • A hammock in a communal palapa on the beach fetches $1.50, and if you want a little privacy you'll pay $5. Fans, mosquito netting, and lockable security boxes also cost more. Flush toilets are rare, and while showers and *regaderas* (cold-water showers) are abundant, in some places there's no water 10 AM–6 PM. Ask before you pay. Also keep in mind that theft is common, so consider leaving the bulk of your stuff in Puerto Ángel.

Some people never stray from the sand, but the *posadas* (inns) up in the hills are worth the extra effort. One of the coolest is **Shambala,** also known as Gloria's, on the hillside at the western end of the beach. Sprawling over most of the cliff, the posada has meditation altars, a café, and a patio restaurant serving mostly vegetarian food. Spectacular views of a secluded bay are an extra bonus. Your lodging options range from a beach cabaña ($7.50) to a hammock hook ($1) and no one is turned away for lack of space. Luggage storage and a safe-deposit box are provided, and drug use is not allowed. **Lo Cósmico,** just east of Shambala, offers clean, cool palapas slung with two hammocks for $6.50. Open-air terraces with hammocks are slightly cheaper.

> *West of the town of Mazunte is Punta Cometa, a cactus-ridden set of cliffs with a fantastic view of the coast. Ask anyone in Mazunte to point out the path.*

Zipolite has no daily market, but the cheapest and best eats can be found right in your hotel. You can get a California-style granola breakfast in Shambala's restaurant, or try their tasty chicken mole ($2.50) or vegetarian turnovers. For pizza, try **Gemini's** on the eastern end of the beach or **El 3 de Diciembre** (in front of La Puesta disco on main road), which serves an exquisite slice of cheesy pie ($1). A battalion of palapas catering to hungry travelers loom on the beach, serving seafood and tortilla dishes at exorbitant prices.

MAZUNTE AND PUNTA COMETA

Just outside of Zipolite, you'll notice a cluster of dilapidated, rusty buildings on the far end of the beach—these were once centers for processing 2,000 sea turtles daily for their meat and shells. The packing plants are now closed, and just past them in Mazunte is a center for the turtles' protection. The **Centro Mexicano de la Tortuga** (tel. 958/4–30–55 or 951/4–30–63) offers educational tours in Spanish and English Tuesday–Sunday 9–4. You can watch eight of the 10 species of sea turtles that inhabit Mexico's coastal waters swim in huge tanks and aquariums. Baby turtles are only kept on display a short time, after which they're released or used in conservation research. The $1.25 entrance fee goes toward conservation and education projects. The center is always looking for volunteers to help protect the sea turtle's coastal habitat, especially during June and July, when turtles come ashore to lay their eggs. Write to: A.P. No. 16, Puerto Ángel, Oaxaca, CP 70902 México, or fax 958/4–30–63 for more details. Buses make the journey to Mazunte from Zipolite (10 min, 25¢), Puerto Ángel (20 min, 40¢), and Pochutla (45 min, 75¢). You can stay in Mazunte with local families or in beachside cabañas ($3).

BAHIAS DE HUATULCO

The area often referred to simply as Huatulco consists of nine bays spread out over (12 mi) of coast. At the heart of it all is **Santa Cruz Huatulco,** which as late as 1986 was a small fishing village of simple adobe huts on a pristine bay. That was before the Mexican government chose it as the site of a luxury tourist development meant to duplicate Cancún's success in attracting foreign sunseekers and their money. However, due to the government's policy of "responsible ecodevelopment," the outlying bays and the forests that ring them remain relatively unspoiled.

Huatulco's bays, from west (closest to Puerto Ángel) to east, are: San Agustín, Chachacual, Cacaluta, Maguey, Órgano, Santa Cruz, Chahué, Tangolunda, and Conejos. Santa Cruz and Tangolunda are the most developed, while Órgano, which can usually only be reached by boat or footpath, is the most pristine. The rapidly growing town of **La Crucecita** (five minutes inland from Santa Cruz by bus) is where most of the people who work in Santa Cruz's boutiques and hotels live, shop, and eat, and is the budget traveler's base for the area.

BASICS

You'll find banks and tourist offices in Santa Cruz Huatulco: **Bancomer** (Blvd. Santa Cruz, at Pochulta, tel. 958/7–00–03; weekdays 9 AM–1:30 PM) has an ATM and changes traveler's checks. The **Banamex** (tel. 958/7–03–22) bank next door offers the same services and similar hours. You can find maps and helpful English speakers at the **Asociación de Hoteles y Moteles** (Blvd. Santa Cruz, at Monte Albán, tel. 958/7–08–48; open weekdays 9–6, Sat. 10–1); **SEDETUR** (in the same building at Asociación de Hoteles, tel. 958/7–15–41); at the **kiosk** (open daily 9–2 and 4–7) just east of Santa Cruz's main plaza; and at the **Tourist Information Center** (Benito Juárez, across from Hotel Fa-sol, tel. 958/1–03–88) in the town of Tangolunda.

The post office, telephones, and medical services are all in La Crucecita: The **post and telegraph offices** (south of the Plaza Principal, on Chahué) offers fax service. Ladatel **public phones** are on the south side of La Crucecita's Plaza Principal. For medical aid contact **IMSS** (Blvd. Chahué s/n, next door to Telmex, tel. 958/7–02–64) or the **Cruz Roja** (Carrizal, at Bahías de Huatulco, tel. 958/7–11–88).

COMING AND GOING

For long-distance bus service you'll need to go to the town of La Crucecita. Direct **Cristóbal Colón** (corner Ocotillo and Gardenia, La Crucecita, tel. 958/7–02–61) buses head to Oaxaca city (2 per day; 7 hrs, $12) and reservations are recommended. Buses also go to Pochutla (every 15 minutes; 1 hr, $1), Salina Cruz (5 per day; 3 hrs, $4), Juchitán (4 hrs, $5.50), San Cristóbal de las Casas (11 hours, $16), and Mexico City's Tasqueña terminal (1 per day; 13 hrs, $27.50). **Estrella Blanca** (Gardenia, at Paloma Real, tel. 958/7–01–03) buses depart from the terminal behind the Corona beer deposit for Mexico City (1 per day; 13 hrs, $27) and Acapulco (5 per day; 8 hrs, $13). There are daily flights to Oaxaca city and Mexico City from the **Santa María de Huatulco airport** (tel. 958/1–90–04 or 1–90–05), about 12 km (7 mi) west of La Crucecita, just north of the Carretera Costera. **Transporte Terrestre** runs colectivos to and from the airport ($4), or you can arrange a taxi ride (tel. 958/7–08–88) for less than $10.

GETTING AROUND

Huatulco's bays are extremely spread out, and though they're now accessible by paved roads, it's still a bit of a haul to get from one to the other. The three central bays—Tangolunda, Chahué, and Santa Cruz—are serviced by blue *urbanos* (city buses; 20¢). They run daily from 6 AM to 11 PM, but there are about half as many on the weekends as on the weekdays. Taxis between La Crucecita, Santa Cruz, and Tangolunda shouldn't cost more than $1.50 per trip.

Colectivos ($2) leave early in the morning along the Santa Cruz–Chahué road and from the crossroads for Santa María Huatulco to take workers out to Conejos, Maguey, and Cacaluta. To reach Santa Cruz from La Crucecita, catch one of the frequent buses (50¢) that run past the Plaza Principal and along the main road. To reach Órgano, walk over the hill on the east end of Maguey; it should take about half an hour. To reach San Agustín and Chachacual, catch any bus toward Pochutla and get off at the crossroads for Santa María Huatulco. From here it's a $3.50 taxi ride or $1 colectivo (if you're lucky enough to get one) to the bay of your choice. Another option for all the bays is to show up at the Santa Cruz marina bright and early and arrange a ride with someone boating out to one of the beaches to work. If you find someone willing, expect to pay between $2 and $7.

WHERE TO SLEEP

Bahía de Huatulco's budget hotels are all inland, in the town of La Crucecita. **Posada Primavera** (Palo Verde, between Bugambilias and Gardenia, tel. 958/7–11–67) has clean and relatively inexpensive rooms ($17) with fan and private bath. At **Posada Michelle** (corner Gardenia and Palma Real, tel. 958/7–05–35) simple doubles with cable TV and private bath are $17 with fan, or $26 with air-conditioning. The **Hotel Las Palmas** (Guamuchil 206, tel. 958/7–00–60) charges $22 for a room with TV, hot water, and air-conditioning. It's just a block from La Crucecita's main plaza, and has a restaurant and bar. All hotels are cash only, and Las Palmas does not accept reservations during holidays and the summer high season.

Trailer Park Los Mangos (right-hand side of road, between La Crucecita and Santa Cruz, no phone) provides the cheapest official campsites near Bahía Chahué. Tent sites are $2.50 per person, with access to communal bathrooms and showers. Camping is not permitted on the developed beaches (Santa Cruz and Tangolunda) but is tolerated on Chahué.

FOOD

Bargain tacos, tortas, and comidas corridas abound in La Crucecita. Both **La Crucecita** (Bugambilias 501 and Chacahua, tel. 958/7–09–06) and **Restaurante Tropicana** (Guanacastle and Gardenias, tel. 958/7–06–61) serve good breakfasts and $2 comidas corridas. Both are cash only. In Santa Cruz, the 24-hour comedores on Monte Albán at Andador Coyula serve $2 comidas corridas to local workers. Expect to pay $5–$15 for lunch or dinner in a tourist-oriented restaurant. These are around the plaza in La Crucecita and in the hotels in Tangolunda and Santa Cruz bays. There are quite a few pleasant thatch-roof restaurants on the beach at Santa Cruz Bay—the most famous of which is **Doña Celia's.** The seafood entrées are pricey but good, and the beachfront location is worth the extra bucks.

OUTDOOR ACTIVITIES

Budget travelers aren't what the Mexican government had in mind when they built up Huatulco, but you can still have some fun without draining your pockets. Most people come here simply to lie on exquisitely groomed or exceptionally empty beaches. The most accessible, but least attractive beaches are **La Entrega** (near Santa Cruz) and **Chahué,** and no one seems to mind if you spend a day on the fine sands in front of the pricey resorts at Tangolunda. Snorkeling is best at Cacaluta and Chachacual, and you can rent snorkeling gear ($5 per day) at most places around town and on the beaches. There are on- and off-road bike paths to several of the bays, and you can rent mountain bikes ($20 per day) from **Jeep Safaris** (Benito Juárez, in the small commercial plaza across from the Sheraton Hotel, tel. 958/1–03–23) or **Rent-a-Bike** (in the Oasis Restaurant, Flamboyant esq. Bugambilias, La Crucecita, tel. 958/7–06–69) for guided or unguided tours. Telephone first to make sure there are bikes in stock.

In the plazas and marketplaces of isthmus towns, you'll hear and see Zapotec merchants hawking geta tzuki (small, dense loaves of bread) and geta bingi (tortillas stuffed with shrimp).

The best way to see Huatulco without breaking the bank is to hop aboard a daylong bay cruise ($20 per person). Tour boats typically visit two or three pristine, outlying beaches, with stops to swim and eat lunch (bring money for snacks or pack your own). Book tours through **Servicios Turíticos del Sur** (Hotel Sheraton, Tangolunda Bay, tel. 958/1–00–55, ext. 784) or **Sociedad Cooperativa Tangolunda** (tel. 958/7–00–81). The latter is the boat-owners' cooperative at the marina on Santa Cruz Bay.

THE ISTHMUS OF TEHUANTEPEC

Stretching 215 km (133 mi) from the Caribbean to the Pacific, the isthmus encompasses parts of both Oaxaca and Tabasco states. Most tourists do not consider it a destination in itself, but a stop along the gringo trail between Oaxaca and Chiapas, a place to switch buses or fill up the gas tank. True, in comparison to the Oaxacan coast or the Chiapan highlands, the isthmus may seem dusty, hot, and provincial. If, however, you're interested in meeting friendly locals, you'll find the region rather hospitable. The large Zapotec population here has resisted being "Mexicanized," and works hard to maintain a unique culture, with distinctive local costumes, festivals, foods, and even Zapotec poetry.

The three main cities on the isthmus are Salina Cruz, Tehuantepec, and Juchitán. Despite the fact that they are all within 32 km (20 mi) of one another, they have developed in very different ways. Salina Cruz has the most modern conveniences, Tehuantepec is the sleepiest, and Juchitán, recognized as the cultural center of the isthmus, is where the Zapotec influence is most prominent.

SALINA CRUZ

Salina Cruz is an industrial port city with a friendly populace. It's a convenient base from which to explore the rest of the isthmus, as well as a good stopover point between the Oaxaca coast and Chiapas—but that's about it. If you need a day at the beach, catch the VENTOSA bus (20 min, 20¢), which runs every half hour from the corner of 5 de Mayo and Acapulco (SE corner of zócalo) to **Bahía La Ven-**

tosa, a clean, windswept stretch of coast 10 km (6 mi) south of town. From where the bus drops you off, head northwest (left) toward the sandy strip of beach. On the rocky eastern end of the bay, at the edge of a rugged cliff, stands a lighthouse once used for navigation by the Spanish explorer Cortés. Back in town, there's not much to do except chat with oil workers.

BASICS

Bancomer (NW corner of plaza, at Camacho, no phone; open weekdays 8:30–noon) has an ATM and exchanges currency. For medical aid, both **IMSS** (on the Carretera Transístmica, 1½ km from the center of town, tel. 971/4–15–72) and the **Centro de Salud** (corner Camacho and Frontera, near post office) are open 24 hours. For the best rates on international and domestic calls and fax service, head to **SONEX** (corner Camacho and Mazatlán, tel. 971/4–56–21, fax 971/4–57–10; open daily 8 AM–11:30 PM). The **post office** (Camacho 44 at Frontera, no phone) is open weekdays 8–7, Saturday 9–2.

COMING AND GOING

Cristóbal Colón (5 de Mayo 412, tel. 971/4–02–59), two blocks from the plaza, sends buses to Tapachula (3 per day; 9 hrs, $13), Tuxtla Gutiérrez (2 per day; 6 hrs, $9), and San Cristóbal (1 per day; 8 hrs, $10) in Chiapas, as well as Huatulco (2½ hrs, $4.50) and Puerto Escondido (5 hrs, $7) on the Oaxaca coast. There are several buses daily to Oaxaca city (5 hrs, $8) and two evening buses to Mexico City (12 hrs, $32.50). Frequent micros and second-class buses also depart daily from the railroad tracks for Puerto Escondido and Santa Cruz. Frequent local buses to Tehuantepec (30 min, 50¢) and Juchitán (1 hr, $1) leave from the same location.

WHERE TO SLEEP

Hotels in Salina Cruz cater to Mexican businessmen and tend to be expensive. **Hotel Fuentes** (Camacho 114, tel. 971/4–34–03) has clean rooms with color TVs and fans ($8) or air-conditioning ($12). A few doors down, **Hotel Posada del Jardín** (Camacho 108, tel. 971/4–01–62) offers secure doubles ($9) with industrial-strength fans. You'll pay $2 more for rooms with TVs. All hotels are cash only.

FOOD

You'll find taco stands and women selling dried fish and seafood around the market on 5 de Mayo (NE corner of zócalo). **La Pasadita** (Camacho 603-A, tel. 971/4–28–48) serves the best shrimp cocktail ($2.50) in Salina Cruz. **Café Istmeño** (east side of plaza, tel. 971/4–17–40) serves great coffee and desserts, and the tiny shop next door sells tasty tortas ($1). **Jugos Hawaii** has two locations, both on Camacho north of the plaza, and each offers a wide selection of fresh fruit drinks and Mexican snacks. All are cash only.

TEHUANTEPEC

Tehuantepec, Nahuatl for "Jaguar Hill," is the most inviting of the main isthmus towns. It's a sleepy place that has seen little modern development. The main tourist attraction is its free **Casa de la Cultura** (Callejón Rey Cosijopi, near Guerrero, tel. 971/5–01–14; open weekdays 10–2 and 4–6, Sat. 10–1:30), a renovated 16th-century convent that houses an anthropology museum and a gallery with exhibits of photography and contemporary art. Director Julín Contreras provides tourist information, usually 11 AM–noon. Other staff members can answer questions about local festivals and events. The Casa de la Cultura welcomes volunteers interested in helping curate cultural exhibitions and restore their building. Minimum commitment is one month. For more information, contact Julín Contreras at the Ex-Convento Dominico, Tehuantepec, Oaxaca, 70760, México, fax 971/5–08–35.

Just 12 km (7 mi) outside town is **Guiengola**, a former Zapotec fortress that was the locus of battles between the Zapotecs and Aztecs. The breezy mountain site offers good views of the surrounding area, although the isthmus landscape isn't overly impressive. For a guide you can hire one of the boy scouts who congregate at the Palacio Municipal on Saturday morning.

Locals often gather in the neighborhoods surrounding Tehuantepec for festivals, or *velas* (vigils), honoring patron saints. At the Jasmine Vigil, held during the third week of May, festivities include displays of typically rich and ostentatious Tehuana dress, lots of marimba music, and, best of all, women pelting the local men with fruit to assert their superiority as matriarchs.

BASICS

Bancomer and Serfin, near the zócalo, have ATMs and change money weekdays 9–noon. Both the **Centro de Salud** (Guerrero, 3 blocks NE of plaza) and the **Cruz Roja** (corner of Roberto E. Salazar and Soto, near Carretera Transístmica) offer emergency care. **El Paraíso** (5 de Mayo 1, tel. 971/5–02–12; open daily 8 am–10 pm) provides long-distance and collect-call service. The **post office** (corner Hidalgo and 22 de Marzo) is open weekdays 8–6, Saturday 9–1.

COMING AND GOING

Long-distance buses operate out of the terminal at the north side of town, on the Carretera Transístmica (Transisthmus Highway). From here, **Cristóbal Colón** (tel. 971/5–01–08) serves Oaxaca city (8 per day; 5 hrs, $8), Tuxtla Gutiérrez (4 per day; 5 hrs, $6), and San Cristóbal (8 hrs, $11.50). Buses traveling through Tehuantepec from Oaxaca city may be full and reservations are not accepted. To get a seat for the ride to San Cristóbal, make a reservation for travel to Tuxtla Gutiérrez, then catch one of many buses from there to San Cristóbal. **Istmeños** buses to Juchitán (30 min, 50¢) and Salina Cruz (30 min, 50¢) depart every half hour from the highway, two blocks east of the plaza. During daylight hours, local buses (15¢) depart for the main bus terminal from the northwest corner of the plaza.

WHERE TO SLEEP

The regal **Hotel Donaji** (Juárez 10, tel. 971/5–00–64, fax 971/5–04–48), two blocks southeast of the plaza, is built around a simple but peaceful courtyard. A double with private bath costs $11, with air-conditioning $16.50. One block south and west of the plaza is **Hotel Oasis** (Ocampo 8, tel. 971/5–00–08). Doubles with hard beds, lumpy foam pillows, and ceiling fans are $11.50, with air-conditioning $15. The **Casa de Huéspedes Istmo** (Hidalgo 31, tel. 971/5–00–19) is a great value: Ample rooms with ceiling fans, desks, and firm beds cost less than $5 per person. Rooms overlook a large cement courtyard enlivened with a few potted mango trees. All hotels are cash only.

There are no taxis in Tehuantepec, only motocarros (open-air, three-wheel ATVs). A hair-raising, thrill-a-minute ride to anywhere in town costs a mere 15¢.

FOOD

On the west side of the main plaza is Tehuantepec's covered market; several fine comedores are clustered on the top floor. **El Portón** (Juana C. Romero 54, 1 block south of zócalo; no dinner Sun.) sells fresh, simple Oaxacan food. Big servings of enchiladas, chiles rellenos, or pozole cost $1.25 apiece. Two blocks southwest of the plaza is **Café Colonial** (Juana C. Romero 66, tel. 971/5–01–15), where a filling comida corrida with fish and fresh fruit costs $2.25. These places are cash only.

JUCHITAN

The town of Juchitán buzzes with Zapotec culture, but is seldom visited by gringos. The people here are warm and friendly, though the town itself, 26 km (16 mi) from Tehuantepec, is hot and dusty, and the most colorful part of the landscape is the sturdy Tehuana women in their flowered skirts and mismatched embroidered blouses. The **Mercado 5 de Septiembre** (Gómez, east of zócalo) is the place to observe Juchitán's matriarchal society, with boisterous women hawking the goods that give them economic power. It's also a good place to stock up on fresh, cheap produce, or purchase a hammock. The free **Casa de la Cultura** (corner Belsario Dominguez and 5 de Septiembre, tel. 971/1–13–51; open weekdays 9–2 and 4–7, Sat. 9–1) is a regional arts center housed in the 16th-century **Iglesia San Vicente Ferrer**. The contemporary collection includes works by 20th-century Oaxacan artist Rufino Tamayo. Visit in the early afternoon, when Juchitán children attend catechism and sing church hymns. About 10 km (6 mi) outside of town you'll find an estuary called **Mar Muerto** (Dead Sea), ideal for fishing and boating; for a few dollars you can arrange to ride with one of the local fishermen. To get to the Mar Muerto, take a green bus labeled 7A SECC (35¢) from Calle 2 de Abril, behind the market in Juchitán. Ask the driver to let you off at the junction to the beach; from there you can hitch or catch another local bus. A taxi from town costs $6.50. Don't confuse this Mar Muerto with the one farther away from town.

Like Tehuantepec, Juchitán likes to go crazy with dance, food, and libations, all in the name of this or that patron saint. Most of the 26 local festivals happen between April and September, the largest one being the **Vela de San Vincente Ferre.** The festival occurs in May and features bullfights, parades, and women pelting helpless men with fruit—a distinguishing characteristic of festivals throughout the isthmus. For information on how to participate (or how to avoid getting fruit pulp in your hair), talk to the folk at the Casa de la Cultura (*see above*).

BASICS

Banamex (5 de Septiembre, at Gómez, tel. 971/1–17–12; open weekdays 10–noon) exchanges currency only, while **Bancomer** (16 de Septiembre, between Gómez and Hidalgo) has an ATM machine. For medical attention, go to the 24-hour **IMSS** (eastern end of Gómez, at 2 de Noviembre). The **Centro de Salud** (Libertad, near Gómez) offers emergency medical service daily 8–3. **Ladatel** phones are all along 16 de Septiembre; fax and long-distance phone service is available in the bus terminal. The **post office** (corner 16 de Septiembre and Gómez, no phone) is open weekdays 8–6.

COMING AND GOING

The main bus terminal (16 de Septiembre, 10 blocks north of zócalo, tel. 971/1–20–22) is open 24 hours and houses **Cristóbal Colón, ADO, Sur,** and **AU** buses, as well as the local **Istmeño** company. Many long-distance buses stop here on their way from larger cities and arrive in the wee hours—which means you may have trouble finding an empty seat during holidays and summer months. For connections to San Cristóbal de las Casas, consider taking a bus to Tuxtla Gutiérrez and then transferring.

Cristóbal Colón offers first-class service to Tapachula (6 hrs, $10), Tuxtla Gutiérrez (5 hrs, $11.50), Oaxaca city (5 hrs, $8), and San Cristóbal (8 hrs, $13). Second-class Sur buses travel to Pochutla (5 hrs, $7), and Huatulco (3½ hrs, $5). Istmeños buses depart from outside the main terminal, near the highway, every half hour for Tehuantepec (30 min, 50¢) and Salina Cruz (1 hr, $1).

WHERE TO SLEEP

Hotel Juchitán (16 de Septiembre 51, tel. 971/1–10–65) is close to the bus station. Its clean doubles cost $6.50, with air-conditioning $9. The **Hotel Malla** (tel. 971/1–27–30 or 971/1–19–27) is actually *above* the bus station; doubles are $8.75. **Casa de Huéspedes Echazarreta** (Juárez 23, south side of plaza, tel. 971/1–12–05) offers secure doubles ($6.50) just off the plaza. All hotels listed above have fans and private baths. The new **Hotel López Lena Palace** (16 de Septiembre 70, tel. and fax 971/1–13–88) is equipped with restaurant, bar, and parking. Its clean, bright rooms have cable TV, air-conditioning, and telephones; doubles are $20. All hotels are cash only.

FOOD

Juchitán is regionally famous for its seafood. The popular **Mariscos Sylvia Juchitán** (2 de Abril, between Aldama and Hidalgo, tel. 971/1–22–35) serves an enormous *vuelve a la vida* ("back to life" seafood cocktail; $4), crammed with chunks of octopus, shrimp, conch, oysters, avocado, onion, and cilantro. **Restaurant Casa Grande** (Juárez 12, south of zócalo, tel. 971/1–34–60) has linen tablecloths and a cool courtyard; their *aguacate relleno de camarones* (avocado stuffed with shrimp; $2) is a delicious and filling treat. Both places accept cash only.

CHIAPAS AND TABASCO

UPDATED BY PATRICIA ALISAU

The states of Chiapas and Tabasco occupy a narrow strip of land bordered by the Gulf of Mexico, the Pacific Ocean, and Guatemala. Mountains, swampy lowland, volcanoes, cloud forests, and thick jungle characterize this region, which was at the heart of the great Olmec and Classic Mayan empires, and which was hotly contested by many Mesoamerican civilizations. Despite the shared history of these two states, however, the present-day contrast between them couldn't be more striking. The oil boom of the 1970s gave Tabasco many air-conditioned buildings, massive cement expressways, and modern, flashy hotels—an urban setting in which indigenous people are a rare sight. In contrast, the larger and more mountainous state of Chiapas retains its colonial, and even precolonial, traditions and structures; Spanish is a *second* language for much of its indigenous population. However, although Chiapas provides Mexico with abundant agricultural goods and enough electricity to light up Mexico City, it remains one of the poorest states in the country.

It was partially in response to this type of regional inequity that, in January 1994, the Zapatista National Liberation Army (EZLN) invaded the historic Chiapan city of San Cristóbal de las Casas and effectively thrust some of Chiapas's chronic problems into the political limelight. Although the many middle-class mestizos (people of mixed ancestry) who lost businesses during the uprising remain unsympathetic to the cause, most *indígenas* (indigenous people) extend their thanks to the Zapatistas. Since peace talks began in 1995, Chiapas has received much more governmental attention and an influx of social services. However, army repression has been on the rise, and local people continue to lack any sort of real control over government policies. While the *diálogos* (dialogues) drag on, the state remains relatively safe for travel. The press's coverage of the situation has actually attracted more visitors, many of whom come to express solidarity with the Zapatistas and to view firsthand the reality behind the conflict. Prepare for a passive but continuous military presence; check with the **U.S. State Department** (tel. 202/647–5225 for 24-hour recorded information) in Washington, DC on current conditions before wandering around outlying areas; and make sure your documents are handy and in order at all times.

The natural wonders of Chiapas have received less fanfare than its politics but are impressive to even the most worldly of travelers. The state contains a large tract of endangered rain forest and is home to vital indigenous cultures unlike any others in the country. The hilly terrain near San Cristóbal is the living fabric of Maya culture, with a multitude of indigenous groups speaking several Maya dialects. San Cristóbal itself, just two hours from the hot and humid state capital of Tuxtla Gutiérrez, offers a cool climate, pine forests, and some of the country's best-preserved colonial architecture. The residual effects

Bahía de Campeche

Ciudad del
Carmen

Laguna de
Términos

Frontera

Paraíso

Comalcalco

CAMPECHE

186

TO
VERACRUZ

Villahermosa

180

TABASCO

Río Grijalva

Río San Pedro

Catazajá

Tacotalpa

186

199

Palenque

Tenosique

Teapa

187

Palenque

195

Agua Azul

Misol-Ha

Río Usumacinta

Pantelho

199

Toniná

Najá

Sumidero
Canyon

San Andrés
Larrainzar
San Juan
Chamula

Ocosingo

Chenalho

Tenejapa

Oxchuc

Yaxchilán

TO
JUCHITÁN

Tuxtla
Gutiérrez

Zinacantán

Río Lacantún

TO
BONAMPAK
RUINS

Lacanjá

Bonampak

Chiapa de
Corzo

San Cristóbal
de las Casas

SELVA
LACANDONA

TO ARRIAGA
& TONALA

CHIAPAS

190

Amatenango
del Valle

Río Lacanjá

Las Rosas

Comitán

SIERRA

Tzimol

La Trinitaria

Chinkultic

Parque Nacional
Lagos de
Montebello

TO SALINA
CRUZ

MADRE

Presa de la
Angostura

190

**Tenam
Puente**

200

DE

CHIAPAS

Ciudad
Cuauhtémoc

La Mesilla

Motozintla

GUATEMALA

Escuintla

Acapetahua

Huixtla

Volcán
Tacaná

KEY

Rail Lines

Las
Palmas

Unión
Juárez

N

Golfo de
Tehuantepec

Tapachula

Talismán

0   20 miles

Puerto
Madero

0   30 km

Ciudad
Hidalgo

of the Zapatista occupation still linger here: On every other corner you'll find indígenas hawking Subco-mandantes Marcos and Tacho dolls.

The coffee- and cacao-growing region of southern coastal Chiapas is almost never visited by the pack-age-tour crowd. The town of Tapachula has a strong Chinese and German presence and is a gateway to Guatemala. From here you can hit a few undeveloped beaches or head for the beautiful mountain town of Unión Juárez, perched below Volcán Tacaná amid foothills dotted with coffee plantations. Farther inland are Comitán and the Parque Nacional Lagos de Montebello, home to more blue-green lakes than one person could ever swim in; surrounding the park are several Maya archaeological sites worth your exploration.

The eastern region of Chiapas is mostly rain forest, though more and more acreage is being lost to cat-tle ranching. Here you'll find the famous ruins of Palenque and Toniná, along with rivers and waterfalls where you can escape from the heat. In the southeast section of Chiapas, the Lacandón rain forest hides the remote ruins of Yaxchilán and Bonampak. This ever-shrinking paradise is home to the Lacandón Indians, whose culture and religious rites are considered by many to be more closely related to the ancient Maya than those of any other living group. Conversion to Evangelical Protestantism and co-opta-tion by well-meaning social service groups are just two of the struggles the Lacandón continue to face since contact with Western society.

Tabasco also has dense jungles, dotted with midsize Mayan ruins and intriguing caves. However, most of this state's natural treasures are rarely explored by foreigners. Even the state's beaches are hidden paradises where you can feast on seafood and tropical fruit concoctions for far less money than at resort towns farther north. By no means is Tabasco an untouched Eden: While the oil boom brought new busi-nesses to and built new cultural institutions in the state capital, Villahermosa, stretches of the Gulf coast-line were contaminated by oil spills. The majority of Tabascans now enjoy a relatively high standard of living, though at a cost to the environment that could be quite high. Residents counter by pointing proudly to the fact that oil money paid for the draining of the basin containing La Venta, the largest Olmec archaeological find in Mesoamerica.

TUXTLA GUTIERREZ

Tuxtla Gutiérrez isn't exactly easy on the eyes: As Graham Greene declared in 1939, "The ugly new cap-ital is like an unnecessary postscript to Chiapas, which should be all wild mountain and old churches and swallowed ruins . . ." This busy administrative and university city with its long, well-lit commercial strip evokes images of Las Vegas, Nevada. Unless you're desperate for a hot shower, want a dose of unadulterated mestizo culture, or are stuck waiting for a connection to Oaxaca city, San Cristóbal, or the Yucatán, it's unlikely you'll want to spend more than a day or two here. However, in the midst of all the cement structures and super-expressways, you'll find pleasant surprises such as a great zoo, botanical gardens, and cultural museums. A short trip outside the city takes you to the colonial town of Chiapa de Corzo, the departure point for boat rides through the spectacular Sumidero Canyon.

Tuxtla became the capital of Chiapas in 1892 after a bloody battle in the old capital of San Cristóbal de las Casas. Tensions arose because of Tuxtla's support of dictator Porfirio Diaz's land policy, which favored a few ladinos (Spanish descended) families over the indigenous *campesinos* (rural dwellers). To this day, Chiapas's fertile land is concentrated in the hands of a tiny, powerful fraction of the population.

BASICS

AMERICAN EXPRESS

The AmEx representative in Tuxtla is **Agencia de Viajes Marabusco.** Cardholders can cash personal checks, receive cash advances on AmEx cards, or have their mail held. Anyone can change money, receive a MoneyGram, or have lost traveler's checks replaced. Mailing address: Pl. Bonampak, Local 14, Sedetur, Tuxtla Gutiérrez, Chiapas, CP 29030, México. *Av. Central, tel. 961/2–69–98 or 961/2–84–49. From Plaza Principal, take AV. CENTRAL colectivo west on Av. Central. Open weekdays 9–2 and 4–7, Sat. 9–2.*

CASAS DE CAMBIO

Bancomer (Av. Central, at 2a Pte. Nte., tel. 961/2–82–51) and **Banamex** (1a Sur Pte. 141, tel. 961/2–87–44) both change traveler's checks weekdays 10–noon. You'll have to wait longer than you would at one of the casas de cambio but you'll get slightly better rates. Bancomer also changes currency and offers cash advances on credit cards. If you're low on money after hours or on weekends, **Cafetería Bonampak** (Blvd. Belisario Domínguez 180, tel. 961/3–20–50 ext. 127; open daily 7 AM–midnight) will change cash or traveler's checks or give you a cash advance on your credit card.

EMERGENCIES

In an emergency, call the **police** at 961/2–16–76. For **ambulance** service contact the Cruz Roja (tel. 961/2–00–96).

LAUNDRY

Lavandería La Burbuja will wash and dry 3 kilos (6½ pounds) of clothes for $4. *1a Nte. Pte., at 3a Pte. Nte., tel. 961/1–05–95. Open weekdays 8–8, Sat. 8–2.*

MAIL

The **post office** (NE corner of Parque Central, tel. 961/2–04–16) will hold mail sent to you at the following address for up to 10 days: Lista de Correos, Tuxtla Gutiérrez, Chiapas, CP 29002, México. Next door, the **telegram office** (tel. 961/2–02–81) sends packages and faxes. Both are open weekdays 8–7, Saturday 9–1.

MEDICAL AID

The **Centro de Salud** (9a Sur Ote., at 2a Ote. Sur, tel. 961/2–03–15; open Mon.–Sat. 7:30–noon) is open for walk-in appointments. Free, 24-hour medical attention is available at the **Cruz Roja** (5a Nte. Pte. 1480, tel. 961/2–00–96). For less urgent medical assistance get help at the 24-hour **Farmacia del Ahorro** (Av. Central, at Calle Central, tel. 961/2–26–54).

PHONES

Blue **Ladatel** phones can be found in front of the movie theaters near the plaza and on every other corner downtown. Cash calls can be made from *casetas de larga distancia* (long-distance telephone offices), as can collect calls, which generally cost $1–$2 per call. There's a convenient caseta on 2a Norte Oriente, outside Hotel Plaza Chiapas (*see* Where to Sleep, *below*), that's open daily 9–8. Several others are on 2a Oriente Norte, just east of the plaza.

VISITOR INFORMATION

The state-run **tourist office** is staffed by helpful young people fresh out of college who speak decent English. While you're here, ask for a copy of *La Cartelera,* a free monthly publication that lists cultural events taking place in Tuxtla and other Chiapan cities. Photocopied brochures with maps and practical information about other towns in Chiapas are also available. *Blvd. Belisario Domínguez 950, next to Hotel Bonampak, tel. 961/2–55–09 or 91–800/2–80–35. From Plaza Principal, take AV. CENTRAL colectivo west on Av. Central. Open weekdays 9–3 and 6–9.*

COMING AND GOING

BY BUS

The first-class **ADO/Cristóbal Colón** station (2a Nte. Pte. 268, tel. 961/2–16–39) is two blocks west of the plaza's northwest corner. Buses to San Cristóbal (2 hrs, $2.25) leave frequently 5 AM–9 PM. Every day after 1 PM, several regular first-class buses and two plush, toilet-equipped "Maya de Oro" buses leave for Mexico City (12 hrs; $31.50 regular, $35 Maya de Oro), stopping in Puebla (10 hrs, $27) and Córdoba (9 hrs, $21). The red *juguería* (juice bar) across from the station will hold luggage all day (until midnight) for 40¢. Lock your bags and don't leave any money or valuables in them.

Transportes Tuxtla Gutiérrez (3a Sur Ote. 712, tel. 961/2–02–30), near the San Roque market, offers both first- and second-class service to Ocosingo (3½ hrs, $3.25), Palenque (6 hrs, $6), Tapachula (8 hrs, $8.25), San Cristóbal (2 per day; 2 hrs, $1.75), and Villahermosa (8½ hrs, $6). Inquire at the window about service to other destinations in Chiapas. **Tuxtla-Chiapa** buses leave from the corner of 3a Oriente Sur and 3a Sur Oriente for Chiapa de Corzo (30 min, 40¢) every 5–10 minutes, daily 6 AM–8 PM.

BY PLANE

The **Aeropuerto Francisco Sarabia** (Carretera Panamericana, 10 km west of Tuxtla, tel. 961/5–10–11) is commonly known as "Terán." **Aerocaribe** (tel. 961/2–00–20) serves Mérida, Cancún, Villahermosa, and Oaxaca city; a one-way flight to Mexico City costs about $100 during peak tourist seasons. **AVIACSA** (tel. 961/2–80–81) flies to Merida, Oaxaca city, Tapachula, Monterrey, and Mexico City. **Mexicana** (tel. 961/1–14–90) soars thrice daily to Mexico City (1 hr, $100). Taxis ($2.75) are the best means of transport to Terán from downtown, and your only option when going in the opposite direction.

GETTING AROUND

Although Tuxtla is a large, sprawling city, it's fairly easy to navigate. Two main thoroughfares, the north–south **Calle Central** and the east–west **Avenida Central,** a.k.a. **Boulevard Ángel Albino Corzo,** intersect at the main plaza and divide the city into quadrants. All the other streets are named and numbered according to their position relative to the main plaza, called the **Plaza Principal.** Avenidas are labeled with a number, then "Sur" (south) or "Norte" (north; nte.), followed by either "Oriente" (east; ote.) or "Poniente" (west; pte.), for example, 2a Sur Oriente. Calles are labeled in the opposite manner, for example, 2a Oriente Sur.

BY BUS

Colectivos (communal taxis; 30¢) run throughout the city 6 AM–9 PM. Destinations are plainly marked on the front windshields, and stops are indicated on the street by blue signs. Unlike those in many Mexican cities, the colectivos here only pick up passengers at marked stops. **Microbuses** (50¢) are bigger and run to Tuxtla's outlying sights, such as the zoo and botanical gardens. They can be hailed on most main streets and their destinations are also clearly marked. To reach the American Express office, the state tourist office, Hotel Bonampak, and the discos from the centro you'll need to take an AV. CENTRAL colectivo down Avenida Central until it turns into Boulevard Belisario Domínguez on the western outskirts of town.

In the morning and early afternoon, look for people sitting around Tuxtla's plaza supping from hollowed gourds. They're enjoying their daily pozol, a traditional porridgelike drink made with cornmeal.

BY CAR

Budget (Blvd. Domínguez 2510, tel. 961/5–13–82), **Dollar** (5a Nte. Pte. 2260, tel. 961/2–89–32), and **Hertz** (Blvd. Domínguez 180, tel. 961/1–39–50) are the best budget rental agencies in town. The going day rate for a sedan is $36, which includes insurance, 200 free km (100 mi), and a full tank of gas. The rate almost doubles for those under age 25.

BY TAXI

Taxis run 24 hours and are necessary if you want to return from one of the discos late at night. The most you should pay within city limits is $1.50; agree on the price before getting in.

WHERE TO SLEEP

Most hotels in Tuxtla are modern and bland but relatively clean, and cheap rooms are easy to come by. Rather than ambience, look for a working fan and clean sheets.

UNDER $10 • Hotel Casablanca. The Casablanca features a pleasant courtyard filled with plants, and all its rooms have ceiling fans. The clean bathrooms are stocked with towels, soap, and toilet paper. Doubles are $10. Hot water pours from the showers 24 hours a day. *2a Nte. Ote. 251, 1 block NE of plaza, tel. 961/1–03–05. 52 rooms, all with bath. Luggage storage. Cash only.*

Hotel La Catedral. A maze of stairways and corridors leads to sparkling clean and quiet rooms. All have ceiling fans, TVs with local channels, and private bathrooms with hot showers. Doubles are $10, triples $13. *1a Nte. Ote. 367, at 3a Ote. Nte., tel. 961/3–08–24. 30 rooms, all with bath. Cash only.*

Hotel Plaza Chiapas. Clean rooms come complete with fans and cheery pink bathrooms with hot water and towels. Those seeking air-conditioning should head to the cheap eatery downstairs. Doubles are $8, triples $10.75. *2a Nte. Ote. 299, at 2a Ote. Nte., tel. 961/3–83–65. 2 blocks NE of zócalo. 34 rooms, all with bath. Restaurant. Cash only.*

Hotel San Antonio. The 20 exceptionally clean rooms—all with fans and private bathrooms—are often full, but it's worth a try. Doubles cost $6.75, triples $8. *2a Sur Ote. 540, tel. 961/2–27–13. Around eastern corner from 2nd-class bus station. Reservations advised. Cash only.*

HOSTELS

INDEJECH Villa Juvenil/Chiapas. This clean hostel is in a youth sports center, and provides single-sex dorm-style accommodations ($2.25 per person) complete with clean sheets, pillowcases, and towels. Meals ($1.25) are available at the cafeteria whenever there are enough people staying. It's an excellent deal, even with the cold showers and 11 PM curfew. *Ángel Albino Corzo 1800, at 18a Ote., tel. 961/3–34–05. 70 beds. From downtown, take a colectivo east along Av. Central for about 10 min. Reception open daily 8 AM–9 PM. Cash only.*

FOOD

Because people from all over the state come here on business, Tuxtla offers a chance to sample cuisine from almost anywhere in Chiapas. Most restaurants serve traditional favorites, including tamales, crumbly Chiapan cheese, and spicy tacos laden with chiles. This prosperous city also has plenty of health-food stores catering to its large middle class, and most restaurants offer a selection of vegetarian dishes. Cheap *tortas* (sandwiches), tacos, and *jugos* (fruit juices) are easy to come by near the bus stations, and the centro swarms with snazzy eateries and patio cafés; look for the striped umbrellas just off the plaza.

UNDER $5 • Las Pichanchas. The menu here includes tamales *chiapanecos* (with meat, chocolate-chile sauce, olives, and raisins wrapped in banana leaves) and *milanesas de ternera* (breaded cuts of veal). Live marimba music (2:30–5:30 PM and 8:30–11:30 PM) adds to the festive atmosphere, and *baile folklórico* (folk dancing) performances take place in the evening at 9. *Av. Central 837, tel. 961/2–53–51. Cash only.*

Restaurante Imperial. This centrally located restaurant serves tasty and inexpensive local fare such as *entomatadas de pollo* (chicken in tomato sauce). The ample *menu del día* (daily menu; $3) includes soup, a meat entrée, tortillas, a drink, and dessert. *Calle Central, at 2a Nte. Ote., no phone. Cash only.*

Restaurante Vegetariano Nah-Yaxal. Vegetarians are in for a treat here. Tasty tortas made with soy beef on whole wheat, or *chilaquiles* (tortilla strips doused with salsa and sour cream) are both $2, and the mammoth Energética Nah-Yaxal (fruit salad smothered in yogurt and granola) is $2.50. Cookbooks for sale include *The Power of Respiration* and *Sprouts: The Most Perfect and Complete Natural Food. 6a Pte. Nte. 124, tel. 961/3–33–16. Closed Sun. Cash only.*

Trattoria San Marco. Of all the eateries near the plaza, this place wins the prize for variety. Specialties include spaghetti bolognesa and crepes ($3–$4). Come and enjoy a cappuccino or beer alongside executives, teenagers, and a cadre of chess players. *Behind cathedral, tel. 961/2–69–74. Cash only.*

WORTH SEEING

Tuxtla's main attractions lie in three distinct areas: **Parque Madero,** in the northeast; **Parque Zoológico,** to the southeast; and the city center, which contains **Parque Central,** the sprawling **Plaza Cívica,** and the **cathedral,** which houses one of the world's first musical clocks. You'll need to use public transportation to reach the zoo from the center, but the other two areas can be easily reached on foot. The city's daily **mercado,** just two blocks south of the *zócalo* (main plaza), is a dimly lit maze where sellers hawk giant papayas, wheels of local cheeses, crispy *chicharrón* (pork rind), and costume jewelry.

PARQUE MADERO

At the intersection of 5a Norte Oriente and 5a Oriente Norte, six blocks northeast of the plaza, the Parque Madero complex brings together a variety of indoor and outdoor wonders, all within easy walking distance of each other. The park's central landmark is the **Teatro Emilio Rabasa,** which hosts frequent free cultural events. Two tree-lined walkways extend from the theater: The western path, lined with bronze busts of famous Mexican leaders, winds its way to the museums and botanical garden; the eastern path cuts through a children's park. Immediately outside Parque Madero is **Teatro Bonampak,** an open-air theater for cultural events. Consult *La Cartelera* (*see* Visitor Information, *above*) for a list of special performances at both theaters.

MUSEO REGIONAL DE CHIAPAS • This sleek, air-conditioned museum provides a look at Chiapas's past and present. Permanent exhibits of Mayan artifacts trace the growth of early indigenous civilization. Look for oddly shaped ancient skulls: Cosmetic cranial deformation was performed on noble Maya children. Across the courtyard and upstairs is an exhibition on the Spanish invasion: Contrasting with huge colonial paintings of the Virgin Mary and numerous Spanish artifacts are historical narratives and images of the enslavement and displacement of indigenous peoples. Exhibits are in Spanish only. *Admission free. Open Tues.–Sun. 9–4.*

JARDIN BOTANICO • Run by the Chiapan Botanical Institute, this botanical garden displays native trees, flowers, and medicinal plants, providing a sense of the scope of preservation efforts being undertaken across the state. The winding paths that crisscross the garden are filled with amorous teenagers strolling through canopies of bamboo, mango trees, and twisting vines. There's also a hothouse building with orchid species from around Chiapas state. *Admission free. Orchid house open Tues.–Sun. 10–1; garden open Tues.–Sun. 8–6.*

PARQUE ZOOLOGICO

This zoo, one of the best in Latin America, features a selection of the spectacular and diverse flora and fauna of Chiapas. Concrete paths climb through lush tropical canopies ringing with the songs of birds and insects. More than 100 species of native Chiapan creatures, many of them endangered, wander here in an approximation of their natural surroundings. There's an environmental education center, an aviary, and even an insect zoo filled with giant roaches and huge, hairy spiders. The zoo affords rare glimpses of tapirs, black panthers, *guacamayas* (macaws), and the spectacularly plumed quetzal bird. *SE of town, off Libramiento Sur. Take a CERRO HUECO or ZOOLOGICO bus, which leave every ½ hr from 1a Ote. Sur, between 6a and 7a Sur Ote. Donations encouraged. Open Tues.–Sun. 9–5.*

The Chiapan rain forest is home to 40% of all plant species unique to Mexico, yet it's rapidly disappearing as a result of the government's eagerness to sell the highly marketable wood.

AFTER DARK

In addition to the movie theaters near the plaza, you'll find a wide variety of nightlife options in Tuxtla. The music of street performers—which can be anything from a marimba ensemble or romantic balladeer to a military band—is common in the Parque Central, especially on Sunday. For authentic and free marimba, stroll to the appropriately named **Parque de la Marimba** (Av. Central, 7 blocks west of Parque Central) weekdays 7 PM–10 PM, rain or shine. *La Cartelera* (*see* Visitor Information, *above*) provides the rundown on more folkloric cultural events. The nameless **café** beneath Hotel Serano (Av. Central 230) serves great coffee to crowds of convivial codgers.

BARS

The clientele at Tuxtla's bars and cafés tends to change as the evening wears on. Early in the evening, the college crowd congregates to find out where the real action will be taking place later that night. Next, middle-age regulars come around to listen to live bands and/or watch *fútbol* (soccer) on TV. Check out **Bar El Nucu** (Hotel María Eugenia, Av. Central 507) for throaty Mexican ballads Thursday–Saturday. **La Cascada** (Hotel Camino Real, Blvd. Belisario Domínguez 1195) is an outdoor bar constructed around a series of pools. There's romantic live music nightly. It attracts a well-heeled older crowd who sip $3 cocktails. You'll need to take a cab ($1) to get here from downtown.

DANCING

Tuxtla's discos tend to host events like bikini and "best legs" contests. The cover is generally about $2–$4 (less for women), and Friday and Saturday tend to be the liveliest. Some boogeying options include **Freeday** (Blvd. Los Laureles, at Blvd. Belisario Domínguez) and **Colors** (Hotel Arecas, Blvd. Belisario Domínguez Km. 1080, tel. 961/5–11–29). Colors charges a $4.25 cover on weekends that includes all you can drink. The best way to reach these clubs from the centro is by taxi ($1).

CHIAPA'S LOVELY LACQUERWARE

Chiapa's master artisans are famous throughout Mexico for the art of lacquerware. Their beautiful lacquered objects are created by a centuries-old, labor-intensive process: First a dried gourd is rubbed with fat, then with a natural colorant (such as charcoal or earth), and finally the gourd is buffed to a smooth finish. This process is repeated at least four times before the gourd is ready to be intricately hand-painted.

The most common type of lacquerware is the "jícara" (bowl), used to serve food and drink such as "pozol" (a corn-based gruel). The Popol Vuh (an ancient Maya codex) described the importance of the jícara in its creation myth: "The sky is no more than a immense blue jícara, the beloved firmament in the form of a cosmic bowl."

The impressive and free Museo de la Laca (Lacquerware Museum; open Tues.– Sat. 9–2 and 4–6, Sun. 9–1), in Chiapa de Corzo, behind the cathedral on the top floor of the 16th-century Ex-Convento de Santo Domingo, has an extensive collection of lacquered bowls from all over the state.

NEAR TUXTLA GUTIERREZ

CHIAPA DE CORZO

After the hustle and bustle of Tuxtla Gutiérrez, you might not guess that a mellow riverside town awaits you only 15 km (9 mi) to the east. But Chiapa de Corzo is the type of place where the loudest sounds you'll hear are crowing roosters and the clang of church bells. The town was once an important pre-Columbian center because of its strategic location on the Río Grijalva, and today you'll find the ruins of a **pre-Classic Mayan site** on private property just outside of town, behind the Nestlé factory. To reach the ruins, follow the signs from the center and ask the owner's permission to enter the site during daylight hours. Chiapa de Corzo's other attractions are clustered around the large **main plaza,** with its colonial clock tower and 16th-century fountain representing Queen Isabella's crown (the latter in the Moorish-influenced *mudéjar* architectural style). The **Palacio Municipal**—just off the zócalo in the arched **Plaza de Ángel Albino Corzo**—has murals depicting scenes from local and national history, including portrayals of the Chiapa Indians, who threw themselves into the Sumidero Canyon to escape enslavement by the Spanish.

Nearly every Tuxtlan you meet will ask if you've taken the boat ride through the **Cañón del Sumidero** from Chiapa de Corzo. The locals' opinion of the place is exalted but justified: Gliding between the 1-km-high (½-mi-high) canyon walls is an experience not to be missed. The best way to enjoy the Cañón del Sumidero is to take the two-hour cruise along the Río Grijalva. The canyon is full of birds, crocodiles, and iguana, and your pilot will be more than eager to maneuver into caves and close to shore to point them out. In July and August, heavy rains create four waterfalls, the largest of which is the **Árbol de Navidad,** a conical plume of water that cascades down the green canyon wall in the shape of a giant Christmas tree. If you opt not to take the boat ride through the canyon, you can take a taxi from Tuxtla or Chiapa to any of four *miradores* (lookouts), which afford a bird's-eye view of Sumidero.

Those who would rather be in the water should head to **Cascada El Chorreadero,** a waterfall and swimming hole 7 km (4½ mi) east of Chiapa on the road to San Cristóbal. The site is most beautiful in the rainy season (June–September), when the waterfall is strongest. Go on a weekday if you want some solitude. To reach the falls, take any bus from Chiapa or Tuxtla toward San Cristóbal or pay $1.50 for a taxi. Return buses run along the highway all night long, though it's wisest to leave by sunset.

COMING AND GOING

Direct microbuses to Chiapa de Corzo (30 min, 40¢) leave from the corner of 3a Oriente Sur and 3a Sur Oriente in Tuxtla every 5–10 minutes, 6 AM–8 PM. Chiapa's bus station is one block east of the zócalo on 21 de Octubre, but you can always jump on a bus as it passes the Parque Central. Several daily buses also depart for San Cristóbal (1 hr, $1) from here. To reach the zócalo from the station, follow the signs for the post office. Taxis between Tuxtla and Chiapa are also readily available and cost about $3.

Boat tours of the Sumidero Canyon originate from Chiapa's *embarcadero* (dock) and from the town of Cahuaré (about five minutes before Chiapa when approaching from Tuxtla). To reach Chiapa's embarcadero from the zócalo, head past the cathedral and down the hill on Calle 5 de Febrero for two blocks. Boats charge $4 per person (minimum 12 persons) for the two-hour tour. Trips run daily, from 7 AM until around 4 PM. Come in the morning if you're alone and want to get in on a group deal.

WHERE TO SLEEP AND EAT

Chiapa is an easy day trip from Tuxtla and even from San Cristóbal, so few visitors stay the night. **Hotel Los Ángeles** (Julián Grajales 2, southern end of zócalo, tel. 961/6–00–48) is the only budget lodging in town. The slightly grimy but spacious rooms cost $10.75 for doubles, all with fans. The hotel accepts cash only. During December, Semana Santa (Holy Week, the week preceding Easter), July, and August, reservations are advisable.

The fountain in Chiapa's plaza is connected to an underground spring of sweet, pure water that helped townspeople to survive the epidemics that swept through much of Mexico in colonial times.

Central Chiapa has a number of food stands and small eateries. For a little extra money and a lot more ambience, head down the hill to one of the restaurants at the embarcadero and try the local fare. You'll also get a view of the river and perhaps some live marimba music. **El Ausente** (embarcadero, no phone), a local favorite, serves a whopping plate of prawns fried in garlic ($5) with tortillas and condiments. **Jardines de Chiapa** (Francisco I. Madero 395, 1 block from zócalo toward pier, tel. 961/6–01–98) serves tasty and unusual local specialties unavailable elsewhere, including *sopa fiestero* ($1.50) a soup with shredded chicken, avocado, hard-boiled eggs, tomatoes, onions, cheese, and noodles, and *chiplín con bolita* (balls of corn paste, tomato sauce, and cheese cooked with a local tarragonlike herb). Dinners run $5–$10. Don't confuse this restaurant with another one of the same name on the zócalo. On a corner just outside the Museo de la Laca (*see box, above*), a local family sells some of the best pozol (corn gruel) in Chiapas: Try both the *blanco* (which is eaten with chile and salt) and the sweet *cacao* (chocolate). On weekdays pozol is only served before noon—don't sleep in and miss out!

FESTIVALS

Every January, Chiapa de Corzo plays host to the lively **Fiesta de Enero.** The festival is kicked off on January 9 with a series of dances, including **La Chuntá,** in which local men dress up as women. On January 15, street dancers perform the **Parachico,** wearing wooden masks and mimicking Spanish conquistadores. The **Combate Naval,** a re-creation of a famous naval battle, takes place on January 21 on the river and is followed by a day or two of festivities.

SAN CRISTOBAL DE LAS CASAS

The capital of Chiapas until the 1890s, San Cristóbal still maintains an unmistakably colonial feel. Crisp mornings see Chiapan highlanders in traditional dress flood the city's markets, main plazas, and church steps to sell homegrown produce and woven clothing. European backpackers heading to and from Guatemala are a common sight on the streets, and the city has recently been receiving an even larger

ZAPATISTAS:
A CRY FOR ACTION

On January 1, 1994, San Cristóbal de las Casas made headline news around the world when the Zapatista National Liberation Army (EZLN) swiftly captured the town's zócalo as a stage for demanding national agrarian reform.

The occupying Zapatistas (the group's name honors Mexican revolutionary hero Emiliano Zapata) consisted largely of indigenous peoples, the Tzeltal and Tzotzil, led by the charismatic Subcommandante Marcos. Their stated objective was to focus international attention on their demands for democratic reform, land redistribution, and improved education and health care for the region's desperately poor indigenous population. Though the occupation left the municipal palace in shambles, it succeeded in calling attention to the ruling elite's moral commitment to the poor and exploited.

Contrary to reports in the international press, most of the initial armed conflicts took place around Ocosingo and the Lacandón jungle, not in San Cristóbal itself. But even as the EZLN continues to occupy an area deep inside the Lacandón jungle, their actions have great impact on Chiapas' second-largest city. On April 10, 1996, more than 5,000 indígena farmers gathered at San Cristóbal's zócalo as part of a statewide protest.

San Cristóbal also remains a base for foreign volunteers of nongovernmental organizations, who are helping to bring stability and comfort to the region's residents during seemingly fruitless, possibly endless rounds of peace talks.

international crowd that is eager to show solidarity with the Zapatistas. The large expatriate population means San Cristóbal is well equipped to cater to visitors; you'll even find good coffee and a variety of healthy food. Here you can meet other travelers, find out which outlying areas are currently safe to visit, and discuss border-crossing strategies.

BASICS

BOOKSTORES
La Pared (Hidalgo 2, tel. 967/8–63–67) buys, sells, trades, and rents more than a thousand guidebooks, fiction, and nonfiction titles in several languages. They're open daily 10–2 and 4–8, Sunday 9–1 during tourist high seasons; hours are shorter in the off-season. They also provide the best fax and phone services in town. **Chilam Balam** (open daily 9–8) has two locations in town: Insurgentes 18, at Madero; and Guadalupe Real 20, at Utrilla. It's one of the best bookstores in southern Mexico, with the latest English-language works on Mexican archaeology, anthropology, history, and travel, plus a fine selection of maps.

CASAS DE CAMBIO
Bancomer, Banamex, and **Serfín,** all clustered around the zócalo, exchange currency weekdays 9–11 AM. Banamex offers advances on both Visa and MasterCard but won't change traveler's checks. For

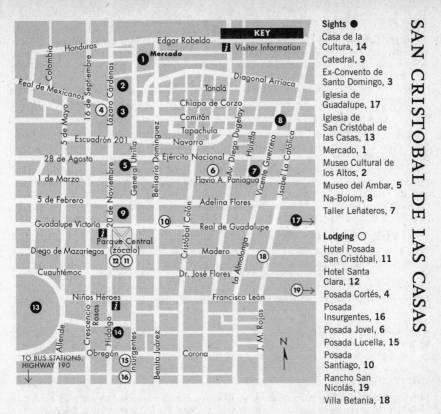

KEY

i Visitor Information

Sights ●

Casa de la
Cultura, **14**

Catedral, **9**

Ex-Convento de
Santo Domingo, **3**

Iglesia de
Guadalupe, **17**

Iglesia de
San Cristóbal de
las Casas, **13**

Mercado, **1**

Museo Cultural de
los Altos, **2**

Museo del Ambar, **5**

Na-Bolom, **8**

Taller Leñateros, **7**

Lodging ○

Hotel Posada
San Cristóbal, **11**

Hotel Santa
Clara, **12**

Posada Cortés, **4**

Posada
Insurgentes, **16**

Posada Jovel, **6**

Posada Lucella, **15**

Posada
Santiago, **10**

Rancho San
Nicolás, **19**

Villa Betania, **18**

after-hours or weekend currency exchange, go to **Agencia de Cambio Lacantún** (Real de Guadalupe 12-A, tel. 967/8–25–87; open Mon.–Sat. 9–2 and 4–8, Sun. 9–noon), half a block from the zócalo.

EMERGENCIES

There are several different **police** units scattered around town; call 967/8–05–54 in an emergency. For **ambulance** service call the Cruz Roja (tel. 967/8–07–72).

LAUNDRY

Lavorama (Guadalupe Victoria 20-A, tel. 967/8–35–99; open Mon.–Sat. 9–7, Sun. 9–2) washes and irons your clothes in a couple of hours for $1 per kilo (2 pounds).

MAIL

The **post office** will hold mail sent to you at the following address for up to 10 days: Lista de Correos, San Cristóbal de las Casas, Chiapas, CP 29200, México. *Cuauhtémoc 13, at Crescencio Rosas, tel. 967/ 8–07–65. Open weekdays 8–7, Sat. 9–1.*

MEDICAL AID

The **Hospital Regional** (Insurgentes, at Santa Lucía, tel. 967/8–07–70) offers 24-hour emergency care. **Cruz Roja** (Prolongación Ignacio Allende 57, tel. 967/8–07–72) does the same, and it's free. **Farmacia Regina** (Diego de Mazariegos, at Crescencio Rosas, tel. 967/8–02–41) is open 24 hours; after 10 PM, knock on the metal door for service.

PHONES

To use the **Ladatel** public phones in front of the Palacio Municipal, buy your Ladatel Plus cards at the telephone office (corner of Niños Héroes and Miguel Hidalgo) before 1:30 PM weekdays, or at **Agencia de Cambio Lacantún** (*see above*). **El Puente** (*see* Schools, *below*) claims they will beat anyone's rate for long-distance and collect calls. They're open Monday–Saturday 7 AM–10:30 PM.

SCHOOLS

The **Centro Bilingüe**, in the **El Puente** cultural center, offers Spanish classes year-round for about $140 per week, including 15 hours of one-on-one instruction per week and room and board with a local family. Their cultural center hosts craft workshops, videos, and live music on a regular basis. A comfortable café, travel agency, and art gallery complete the package. Preregistration from the states is subject to higher tuition and a nonrefundable $75 registration fee. *Real de Guadalupe 55, tel. and fax 967/8–22–50. Mailing address: Real de Guadalupe 55, San Cristóbal de las Casas, Chiapas, CP 29230, México.*

TOURS AND GUIDES

Privately run tours to nearby ruins and the surrounding indigenous communities are cheaper than those arranged by travel agencies. Talk to Moisés at **Casa Margarita** (Real de Guadalupe 34, tel. 967/8–09–57) for information about trips to Toniná, the Sumidero Canyon, Palenque, Agua Azul, and the Lacandón jungle. Prices may seem steep to budget travelers ($130 per person for a minimum of four people to see the Lacandón jungle, Yaxchilán, and Bonampak; around $20 per person for day trips to Palenque and other sites), but keep in mind that the cost includes a bilingual guide, transportation, and several meals. For a guided visit to nearby villages, meet Mercedes Hernández Gómez (*see* Near San Cristóbal, *below*) on the zócalo at 9 AM.

VISITOR INFORMATION

The staff at the **state tourist office** (Hidalgo 3, next to La Pared, tel. 967/8–65–70; open Mon.–Sat. 9–8, Sun. 9–2) can answer questions about the entire state of Chiapas and has lots of information on citywide cultural and sporting events, plus good city maps. The **municipal tourist office** (tel. 967/8–06–65; open Mon.–Sat. 9–8, Sun. 9–2), at the zócalo, on the ground floor of the Palacio Municipal, has a staff that speaks English and French. They provide free maps and their bulletin board is a good source of local information.

VOLUNTEERING

Na-Bolom (*see* Worth Seeing, *below*) accepts volunteers willing to donate a minimum of three months to photo archival, reforestation, and cultural preservation projects. Room and board are provided for full-time volunteers. *Mailing address: Volunteer Program, Vicente Guerrero 33, San Cristóbal de las Casas, Chiapas, CP 29220, México.*

Global Exchange offers several volunteer opportunities in and around San Cristóbal, including working in civilian peace camps, attending seven-day human rights delegations, and working in San Cristóbal's international peace center. Volunteers should be fluent in Spanish, knowledgeable about the current political situation, and able to support themselves in Mexico. *Write to: Global Exchange, Attn. Ted Lewis, 2017 Mission St. Suite 303, San Francisco, CA 94110. In the U.S., tel. 415/255–7296, fax 415/255–7498.*

COMING AND GOING

BY BUS

From the first-class **Cristóbal Colón** bus terminal (Insurgentes, about 8 blocks south of zócalo, tel. 967/8–02–91), buses depart daily for Mexico City (4 per day; 21 hrs, $32). The line's luxury "Maya de Oro" bus ($35) departs at 4:30 PM. Buses also leave daily for Oaxaca city (4 per day; 12 hrs, $14); Ocosingo (4 per day; 3 hrs, $3); Palenque (7½ hrs, $6), with two buses at 9 AM and frequent buses in the evening; Tapachula (4 per day; 9 hrs, $10); Tuxtla Gutiérrez (2 hrs, $2.25) and Comitán (1½ hrs, $2), hourly 6:30 AM–10 PM; Mérida (14 hrs, $20) at 5:30 PM and 7:30 PM; and Cancún (21 hrs, $35) at 4:35 PM. It's wise to book ahead since buses fill up quickly.

At the second-class **Transportes Tuxtla Gutiérrez** (Allende, ½ block up from Carretera Internacional, tel. 967/8–48–69) bus terminal, 10 buses per day serve Palenque (8 hrs, $6), with a stop in Ocosingo (3½ hrs, $3). There's hourly service to Tuxtla Gutiérrez (2 hrs, $2.75) and Comitán (2 hrs, $1) during the day.

GETTING AROUND

Most sights are within easy walking distance of the center, and the outlying attractions are only a 20- or 30-minute walk away. The hub of the town is the zócalo, otherwise called the **Parque Central,** which is bordered on the north by the cathedral. Although they're clearly labeled, remember that all streets change names as they cross the zócalo.

BY BIKE

Los Pinguinos (5 de Mayo 10-B, tel. 967/8–02–02; open daily 9–2 and 3:30–6:30) rents bikes for $2 an hour or $10 a day; guided tours of the surrounding area are $9 for a half day, $18 for a full day.

BY BUS

Crowded colectivos and cramped combis run until about 10 PM, charging 20¢ per ride. Major routes are north–south along Insurgentes/Utrilla (from the Carretera Internacional to the market), and east–west along Real de Guadalupe/Guadalupe Victoria. To get a ride, flag down one of the always attentive drivers at any point on the road and pay him directly. To get off, shout "¡Se baja!" (Someone's getting off!).

BY TAXI

Taxis await passengers in front of the cathedral on the north side of the zócalo. Rates within the city and to and from the bus stations are standardized; without baggage the cost is $1, with baggage $1.50. Rates to surrounding sites and villages are negotiable.

WHERE TO SLEEP

Loads of budget hotels—many with colonial flourishes—have sprung up here in the last two decades. Competition keeps prices low and cleanliness standards high. Several good *posadas* (inns) are along Insurgentes, just north of the Cristóbal Colón terminal. Especially noteworthy are **Posada Insurgentes** (Insurgentes 73, no phone) and **Posada Lucella** (Insurgentes 55, tel. 967/8–09–56), with cheap ($4–$5 per person), warm rooms. Both accept cash only. No matter where you stay, make sure the hot water is in working order; the morning air in San Cristóbal can be chilly. Look on bulletin boards at the tourist office and in bookstores for rooms for rent in people's homes: Clean and hospitable digs can be had for $2–$5 per person during busy tourist seasons, when hotels fill up quickly.

The **Baños Mercedarios** (1 de Marzo 55, tel. 967/8–10–06; open Mon.–Sat. 6 AM–7 PM, Sun. 6 AM–2 PM) can make for a relaxing treat if you're stuck at a hotel without hot water. Choose between a private steam or dry-heat sauna followed by a shower. The whole ritual comes to less than $3. Soap, towels, razors, and refreshments cost about 50¢ each.

UNDER $10 • Posada Cortes. This snug little inn opened in 1995 and remains the best-kept secret in town. Spacious rooms each have comfortable beds and tile floors, and two overlook charming Plazuela Mexicanos. It's in a tranquil residential neighborhood, two blocks from the mercado and four blocks from the Parque Central. You may not want to stay here during the two-week religious festival staged in the plazuela in August. Doubles cost $9. *Plazuela Mexicanos, near 16 de Septiembre, tel. 967/8–74–86. 10 rooms, all with bath. Luggage storage. Cash only.*

Posada Jovel. Ideally located a few blocks from the hustle and bustle of the center, this posada's third-floor doubles with private bath ($8) offer cool views and plenty of hot water. Avoid the tiny, cell-like second-floor singles with communal baths ($4.75). The friendly family serves a good breakfast and rents horses for touring. *Flavio A. Paniagua 28, between Cristóbal Colón and Dugelay, tel. 967/8–17–34. 19 rooms, 9 with bath. Laundry, luggage storage. Cash only.*

Posada Santiago. Santiago's small rooms are dark but comfortable. Clean doubles ($9.50) have private baths with hot water. The rooftop terrace and cheery café are good places to socialize with other travelers. *Real de Guadalupe 32, tel. 967/8–00–24. 9 rooms, all with bath. Luggage storage. Cash only.*

Villa Betania. This hotel offers a homey refuge on the sleepy east side of town. Spacious doubles ($8) are spotless and have private baths with hot water. The Salazar family encourages you to use their kitchen and rooftop terrace, or you can watch TV with them in the living room. *Madero 87, tel. 967/8–44–67. 4½ long blocks east of zócalo. 7 rooms, all with bath. Kitchen, laundry, luggage storage. Reservations advised. Cash only.*

UNDER $20 • Hotel Posada San Cristóbal. The huge rooms in this grand old building have high ceilings, white walls, dark plank floors, antique furniture, and tall, heavy French doors that block all light and sound. Newly remodeled bathrooms and balconies off every room are a plus. Doubles are $19. *Insurgentes 2, 2 blocks south of zócalo, tel. 967/8–38–42. 10 rooms, all with bath. Luggage storage. Cash only.*

UNDER $30 • Hotel Santa Clara. If you want to see how wealthy folk lived in colonial days, book a room at this 16th-century mansion. The hotel, once home to conquistador Diego de Mazariegos, has beam ceilings, antique furnishings, hardwood floors, and a distinct air of past grandeur. The best rooms are the ones with balconies overlooking the zócalo. Folk dancers occasionally entertain in the hotel bar, and a cage of brilliantly colored guacamaya birds amuse guests with their squabbling. Doubles cost $29. *Insurgentes 1, tel. 967/8–08–71 or 967/8–11–40. 40 rooms, all with bath. Restaurant, bar, coffee shop, pool, travel services.*

Na-Bolom. Each of the cozy but rustic rooms at this cultural center (*see* Worth Seeing, *below*) is decorated with crafts, photographs, and books from and about a specific indigenous community. Guests staying at Na-Bolom get a free tour of the house, access to the library, and plenty of helpful advice about the area. Doubles are $27. *Vicente Guerrero 33, tel. 967/8–14–18. 14 rooms, all with bath. Restaurant, luggage storage.*

CAMPING

Rancho San Nicolás Camping and Trailer Park (tel. 967/8–00–57), less than 2 km (1 mi) east of town, is ideally situated at the end of Francisco León. Facilities include kitchens, electricity, and hot water for showers. Camping for two people costs $4; a cabin for two is about $8, cash only. To get here, catch a RANCHO SAN NICOLAS combi (20¢) on Francisco León.

FOOD

San Cristóbal's large expatriate presence has had a decisive influence on its culinary offerings. In addition to Chiapan fare, many restaurants and cafés serve yogurt, whole-wheat bread, green salads, and pizzas; some eateries even offer separate vegetarian menus. The Sunday brunch at **Na-Bolom** (*see* Worth Seeing, *below*) is a must. The spread includes dishes made with organic vegetables and salads straight from the garden, as well as meat entrées, drinks, and dessert.

For more typically Chiapan fare, locals flock to **Los Merenderos** (Insurgentes, near Iglesia de San Francisco), a group of cheap food stands that stay open until the wee hours. On Saturday, look for red lamps hanging outside homes: They signal that freshly made tamales (20¢) and *atole* (a sweet, corn-based drink, similar to hot chocolate) await within.

UNDER $5 • Casa de Pan. This bakery/restaurant/expat hangout is run by friendly baker extraordinaire Kippy Nigh, formerly of Colorado. Fresh bread, the best bagels in Mexico, organic salads, and veggie empanadas with curry ($2) are served on the quiet patio. Popular breakfast plates ($2.50) include fresh fruit, tea, and bread. There's live music weekend nights. *Navarro 10, at Domínguez, tel. 967/8–04–68. Closed Mon. Cash only.*

Comedor Familiar Normita II. Sit down in Norma's recently refurbished kitchen and enjoy the tasty enchiladas in red sauce ($2) or *pozole* (hominy soup served with fresh onions, ground chile, and oregano; $2). A fireplace helps take the bite out of the cold mountain air. *Benito Juárez 6, at José Flores, no phone. Closed Sun. Cash only.*

La Galeria. This Italian eatery is San Cristóbal's oldest social center as well as a Thursday-night dance club. It's housed in an attractive colonial building. On the menu you'll find 11 different pizzas, Neopolitan dishes like lasagna with eggplant, and Mexican dishes like pozole. Art exhibits, a billiards table, and occasional screenings of American movies make it more than just another restaurant. *Hidalgo 3, tel. 967/8–15–47. Cash only.*

La Langosta. Let La Langosta (The Lobster) satisfy your cravings for authentic colonial cuisine. There's lobster on the menu, of course, as well as intriguing specialties like *chalupas coletas* (deep-fried tortillas smothered in sliced pork, refried beans, chopped vegetables, cheese, and salsa; $3); tamales stuffed with either pork or chicken, chopped prunes, almonds, spicy chocolate sauce, and bits of chile; and *tascalate*, a cold drink made with corn meal, sugar and anise. *Madero 9, tel. 967/8–22–38. Cash only.*

Madre Tierra. "Mother Earth" serves up homemade yogurt, whole-wheat bread, and big bowls of vegetable soup ($1.75). The best deal is the *platos del día* ($3.25), with your choice of chicken or vegetarian entrée. The patio makes for a good place to enjoy a casual beer when it's not raining. And the restaurant's bakery makes brownies, cookies, muffins, and tarts that are widely regarded as the best in town. *Insurgentes 19, 3 blocks south of zócalo, tel. 967/8–42–97. Cash only.*

UNDER $10 • El Fogón de Jovel. This touristy place caters to noisy European tour groups. It serves traditional Chiapan fare in an open-air colonial patio setting. The *parrilla coleto* (Chiapan mixed grill; $6) pairs the best of local meats with a salad; plenty of vegetarian selections, and a tamale sampler ($2.50) round out the menu. A full bar of regional moonshine cocktails ($1) is backed by live marimba daily. *16 de Septiembre 11, tel. 967/8–25–57.*

CAFES

Espresso, cappuccino, tea, and pastries are always at hand in San Cristóbal. **Café Bar Los Amorosos** (Dr. José Felipe Flores 12-A, at Blvd. Domínguez, tel. 967/8–49–28), in the Jaime Sabines cultural center, is the preferred haunt of local intellectuals and artists. The patio out back is an ideal spot to sample the bevy of coffee drinks (50¢–$1) and philosophize. Locals spend hours playing chess and reading newspapers at **Cafetería San Cristóbal** (Cuauhtémoc 2, at Insurgentes, no phone; closed Sun.). Coffee and espresso are 50¢; the excellent desserts are $1. The spacious, sunlit parlor above the popular café/art gallery/handicrafts shop **La Galería** (Hidalgo 3, south of zócalo, tel. 967/8–15–47) lures locals and foreigners alike with their excellent pies and cakes (less than $2) and live music weekends after 8:30 PM. The **Casa de las Imágenes** (Blvd. Domínguez 11, no phone) is a multipurpose space housing a café, art gallery, bookstore, and occasional foreign films. All of the above are cash only.

WORTH SEEING

San Cristóbal is an amalgamation of many neighborhoods, each with its own church and patron saint, but the center of town is the **Parque Central,** or zócalo. The **Hotel Santa Clara,** on the south side of the zócalo, was supposedly the house of conquistador Diego de Mazariegos and is adorned with stone sirens and the royal lions of Castille, Spain. On the north side of the zócalo is the **Catedral.** It was first constructed in 1528 as a run-of-the-mill church, but 10 years later the pontiff declared it a cathedral, and paintings, altars, and an ornate facade were added. San Cristóbal's daily **market** (8 blocks north of zócalo on Utrilla) is a huge conglomeration of stalls selling vegetables, tropical fruits, medicinal herbs, poultry, and cassettes blaring reproduced regional music and American pop. Most produce comes from the small plots of land farmed by local Tzotzil and Tzeltal people. The **Casa de Cultura** (Hidalgo, across from Iglesia del Carmen, no phone) sponsors a diverse range of cultural events, including concerts, films, and lectures.

Sunday Spanish Mass at San Cristóbal's cathedral (held 6 AM, noon, and 7 PM) is given by Bishop Samuel Ruíz when he's not busy mediating peace talks between the Mexican government and the EZLN.

For a good view of the city, walk seven blocks east of the zócalo on Real de Guadalupe and continue up the stairs to the yellow-and-white **Iglesia de Guadalupe.** You can see even farther from the **Iglesia de San Cristóbal de las Casas,** at the opposite end of the city, west of Allende. A 15-minute climb to the top leads you to the vista point and a quirky cross made from discarded license plates.

CENTRO DE ESTUDIOS CIENTIFICOS NA-BOLOM

This cultural center, museum, library, garden, home, and guest house is devoted to the study and preservation of the culture and rain forest environment of the Lacandón Indians. The center was established by the late Frans and Gertrude Blom, a Danish/Swiss couple who dedicated much of their lives to the study of and advocacy for the Lacandón people. The house has a comfortable library (open Mon.–Thurs. 8–3, Fri. 8–11:30 AM) housing more than 5,000 books on Chiapan culture, as well as travel guides, the Bloms' writings, and other books on Mexico. Frans's collection of religious art is on display in the chapel; an exhibit of Lacandón artifacts fills the museum; and Gertrude's black-and-white photos of Chiapan Indians decorate the halls of the house. The bookstore sells volumes of Gertrude's photography as well as Frans's map of the Lacandón jungle, supposedly the best available.

Hour-long tours ($2) take place twice a day and are followed by a film. Rooms (*see* Where to Sleep, *above*) and meals ($3.50–$5) are some of the best in town. Make reservations in the morning for meals, and reserve far in advance for rooms. *Vicente Guerrero 33, at Comitán, tel. and fax 967/8–14–18. Tours given Tues.–Sun. at 11:30 and 4:30 (in Spanish) and at 11:45 and 4:45 (in English).*

MUSEO CULTURAL DE LOS ALTOS DE CHIAPAS

At this small museum focusing on local history and culture, all posted explanations are in Spanish, but you'll glean some information even if you can't read the signs. The upstairs exhibits focus on the *encomienda* system, by which the conquistadores were awarded the right to exact tribute from certain groups of Indians, and on the quantities of booty the Spanish sent back to Europe. Textiles from surrounding indigenous communities are displayed downstairs. *Next to Ex-Convento de Santo Domingo. Admission free. Open Tues.–Sun. 9–6.*

A ONE-MAN, WALKING MUSEUM

A longtime resident of Chiapas, Señor Sergio Castro has dedicated his life to preserving indigenous cultures, working closely with the Tzotzil community of Chamula. At his home he keeps a one-of-a-kind collection of indigenous textiles. He is also one of the best resources in the area for Chiapan history and current events—in French, English, Italian, and Spanish. Señor Castro entertains small groups at his house (Guadalupe Victoria 47, tel. 967/8-42-89) nightly after 6 PM; call for an appointment. Donations are encouraged.

MUSEO DEL AMBAR DE LOS ALTOS DE CHIAPAS

Amber, which is the petrified sap of ancient trees, is displayed and sold at this tiny museum. It comes from the Simojovel Valley and Totolapa, the only two areas in Mexico where amber is still mined. After excavation, the dark-yellow amber is carefully polished then set in earrings, necklaces, and other ornaments and sold at a moderate price—especially when you consider that bugs trapped in this amber have been carbon-dated to the Jurassic period. Be sure to check out the display of ants, beetles, butterflies, and mosquitoes trapped in the resin, as well as the carvings in amber of Mayan figures. *Utrilla 10, 2 blocks north of zócalo, tel. 967/8-35-07. Admission free. Open Sun.–Fri. 10–8.*

TALLER LENATEROS

This award-winning press has been producing handmade stationery, books, and silk screens—all made of 100% natural and recycled materials—for some 20 years. The facility is open to the public for free tours (in English and Spanish) that guide visitors through the paper-making process. Their publication, *La Jícara*, is an excellent literary review featuring major Mexican writers and Maya poets, and it's printed with silk-screen and original block prints. *Flavio A. Paniagua 54, tel. 967/8-51-74. Donations encouraged. Open Mon.–Sat. 9–5.*

FESTIVALS

With its many neighborhoods each beholden to a particular patron saint, San Cristóbal seems to throw a celebration almost every week. Chiapans really cut loose during the annual **Fería de la Primavera y la Paz,** which takes place the week after Easter Sunday. Bull- and cockfights, folkloric dance, parades, and choral music all take place in the carnival-like atmosphere of the fairgrounds south of town. Most events are free. On November 22, the **Fiesta de Santa Cecilia**, honoring the patron saint of musicians, is held. Other festivals include the **Fiesta de San Cristóbal** (July 25) and the **Fiesta de la Virgen de Guadalupe** (Dec. 12–14). Check with the state tourist office (*see* Visitor Information, *above*) for a comprehensive list of events, prices, and locations.

SHOPPING

Once upon a time, San Cristóbal was divided into sectors, each dedicated to a particular trade or skill. Those in the sector of La Merced, for example, were known for their candle work, and would sell or trade candles to the merchants in the central sector, who were skilled in making sweets and *embutidos* (jam-filled candies). The tradition still continues: The sector of San Antonio is well-known for its fireworks, La Cerrería for its carpentry, and San Ramón for its baked goods. Shops crowd **Real de Guadalupe** and **Utrilla,** selling quality woven and leather goods and amber jewelry. You can also buy Guatemalan goods in many of these shops—but they cost a lot more than they would across the border. The finest weaving is to be found in the cooperatives Sna Jolobil and J'pas Joloviletik (*see below*) and the government-run Casa de Las Artesanías de Chiapas (*see below*). Don't buy amber off the street—it could easily be plastic or glass.

CASA DE LAS ARTESANIAS DE CHIAPAS

This store/museum is run by a government program meant to encourage handicraft production while improving the quality of life in indigenous villages. The handicrafts for sale are quality controlled, and the excellent ethnographic museum is free. *Hidalgo, at Niños Héroes, tel. 967/8–11–80. Open Mon.–Sat. 9–2 and 5–8.*

SNA JOLOBIL AND J'PAS JOLOVILETIK

Housed in the 16th-century **Ex-Convento de Santo Domingo,** Sna Jolobil (Calz. Lazaro Cardenas 42, tel. 967/8–26–46) functions as an outlet store for a weaver's cooperative made up of about 800 Tzotzil and Tzeltal women. The cooperative's aim is to preserve Mayan techniques of weaving on the back-strap loom, and to ensure that the artisans receive a fair price for their work. Local *huipiles* (embroidered tunics), wool vests, brocade shirts, and ribboned hats are displayed and sold here, though at prices quite dear. Depending on the tourist flow, the store is open Monday–Saturday 9–2 and 4–7, Sunday 9–2. **J'pas Joloviletik** (Utrilla 43, tel. 967/8–28–48; open Mon.–Sat. 9–1 and 4–7, Sun. 9–1) just across the street is another weaver's cooperative store.

AFTER DARK

San Cristóbal holds tightly to Mexican colonial traditions: In the evenings, especially on Sunday, everyone congregates on the zócalo, strolling with cotton candy or popcorn purchased from the numerous stands. Many restaurants feature live music around dinnertime (starting around 8 PM), usually without a cover charge. The few spots that stay open past midnight cater strictly to tourists. For the best salsa and *nueva canción* (Latin American folk music), try **La Galería** or **Casa de Pan** (*see* Food, *above*), where the music starts around 9 PM. **Las Velas Bar** (Madero 14, no phone) has live music (salsa, rock, and reggae) starting at around 11 PM; crowds drink $1 beers until 3 AM. Cultural center **El Puente** (*see* Schools, *above*), run by California expatriate Bill English, shows free, smart international films Tuesday–Saturday at 8 PM.

> *Shamans in the Chiapan highlands use a variety of materials to heal the sick: Eggs and white chickens remove impurities, while Coke or Pepsi causes burping, a sign that evil spirits are leaving the body.*

OUTDOOR ACTIVITIES

Trails for hiking and mountain biking abound in the mountains surrounding San Cristóbal (for information on bike rentals and tours, *see* Getting Around, *above*). You can also take horseback-riding excursions to Chamula or **Las Grutas de San Cristóbal,** a set of dank, stalactite- and stalagmite-filled caves about 11 km (6 mi) southeast of town. The caves are open daily 9–4, admission is 40¢, and you need to bring a flashlight. (You can also reach the caves on any Comitán-bound bus.) Two-hour horseback trips from **Hotel Real del Valle** (Real de Guadalupe 14, tel. 967/8–06–80) cost $25–$30 per person. Many individuals post flyers in budget hotels about horse rentals, which are usually considerably cheaper than private tours.

The **Huitepec Ecological Reserve,** just 3 km (2 mi) out of town, is alive with hundreds of birds, bright flowers, and 600 species of plants. There's a 4-km (2½-mi) loop trail that affords a quiet, 1½-hour hike up through the cloud forest on the side of the Muktevitz volcano. The reserve is run by **Pronatura** (Juarez 9, tel. 967/8–50–00), a San Cristóbal–based conservation group that buys land and establishes parks to preserve wildlife for educational purposes and to promote sustainable farming alternatives. To reach the reserve, take a colectivo bound for Chamula or Zinacantán from the market and ask to be let off at Huitepec; or hire a taxi ($2) from town. Sign up in advance for group tours (donations encouraged) at the Pronatura office. Admission to the park is free, and it's open Tuesday–Sunday 9–5.

NEAR SAN CRISTOBAL

Several indigenous communities, each 30 minutes to two hours from San Cristóbal, make easy and enjoyable day trips. The best day to go is Sunday, when Tzotzil and Tzeltal people from the surrounding highlands congregate in the markets to sell livestock, fruits, vegetables, and textiles. Wonderful tours to Chamula and Zinacantán are led by Mercedes Hernández Gómez, who grew up in Zinacantán and

FATHER, SUN, AND HOLY GHOST

While pre-Hispanic religions are still practiced in various forms throughout Mexico, the beliefs of many modern indigenous people combine the symbols and deities of their ancestors with both the Catholicism carried across the Atlantic by the Spaniards and by the Protestantism of more recent missionaries. For example, the conventional exteriors of Catholic churches in the Indian pueblos of Chiapas often give way to pine-strewn, candlelit interiors redolent of the fumes of copal, an incense sacred to the Maya. In religious texts and paintings, the sun god of the Maya pantheon has been recast in the figure of Saint John the Baptist—who has taken on many of his attributes—and Jesus Christ is worshipped as his younger brother.

Even before the Spanish arrived in Mexico, however, the groundwork was laid for a union of Christian and native religions. The symbol of the cross, for example, was a potent one for ancient Mexico; it is said that just before he disappeared from the Earth, the feathered serpent god Quetzalcoatl planted a giant wooden cross on the beach in Veracruz that resisted all efforts to pull it down. The cross also symbolized the ceiba tree that held up the Mesoamerican world, and, indeed, life itself: The stone covering the sarcophagus of Lord Pakal, 7th-century ruler of Palenque, depicts his descent into the underworld with a giant cross (representing life) emerging from his body.

Today, pine branches (another symbol of life) are tied to crosses overlooking Chiapan highland towns, a testament to the blending of Mesoamerican and European beliefs.

speaks English. Look for Mercedes's umbrella daily (except major holidays) around the kiosk in San Cristóbal's zócalo. The tour ($8) includes transportation and is well worth the price.

All villages listed below are accessible by infrequent bus service or VW colectivo, with the exception of Zinacantán and Chamula, which are served frequently. If you do choose to go on your own, dress conservatively, leave your camera at home, and stick to the main public areas—injudicious wandering will not be appreciated.

SAN JUAN CHAMULA

Chamula's wood-and-mud houses and the surrounding cornfields are spread across a small valley. Residents are recognizable by their dark blue shawls, embroidered blouses, and ribboned braids for women; and shirts, wool serapes, and leather belts for men. The religion of the Chamula people is unique in that it's a hybrid of Mayan rituals and Catholicism: In their church you'll see patron "saints" not found in the Bible, and the cross they've erected is not the Catholic cross, but a broader Mayan style than you'll find in archaeological stelae around the region. Also atypical of a Catholic church, the floor is carpeted with pine needles and devoid of pews. Shamans heal sick villagers here and conduct other ceremonies. Ever since Evangelical Protestant missionaries arrived in 1968, outsiders have been treated with detached suspicion. Heed posted warnings against photography when you enter the church (admission 70¢) and keep your distance from worshippers.

The best time to visit Chamula is during the Sunday morning market, when thousands descend from their parishes to the ceremonial center to shop, socialize, visit shamans, and take care of business. One of the most impressive Chiapan festivals is San Juan Chamula's **Carnaval,** one week before Ash Wednesday, when Chamulans dance atop fire to purify their souls. Colectivos to Chamula (20 min, 70¢) leave from the San Cristóbal market.

ZINACANTAN

The people of Zinacantán wear elaborate, bright pink tunics (for the men) and beautifully embroidered ponchos or colorful shawls with red borders (for the women). This quiet town's main industry is the cultivation and sale of chrysanthemums and gladiolas. Sunday morning brings a small market (come early for the freshest flowers) and religious services; if you're lucky you may also catch the town's elders, wearing ceremonial white shorts with high-backed Mayan sandals, as they exit the church playing handmade guitars, harps, and drums. The free **Ik'al Ojov museum** (Isabel la Católica, at 5 de Febrero; open daily 9–6) presents a collection of local clothing, historical photography, and musical instruments. To reach Zinacantán, take a VW colectivo (30 min, 70¢) from the San Cristóbal market. There is also a footpath between Zinacantán and Chamula, but it has been the site of several assaults and should be avoided.

In Chamula, you'll notice mirrors behind the saints in the church and tiny mirrors sewn onto women's blouses. Chamulans believe that a mirror's reflection helps to ward off evil.

SAN ANDRES LARRAINZAR

The Tzotzil village of San Andrés is about half an hour north of Chamula by bus. The people here are friendly, and the Sunday market is interesting for the brocade shirts sold here. San Andrés continues to make international headlines as the host town for peace negotiations between the Zapatistas and the Mexican government. Be sure to make the 15-minute trek from the center of town to the **Iglesia de Guadalupe,** which offers a stunning view of the surrounding highlands. The town's major festivals include the Fiesta de Santiago Apóstol (July 24–26), the Fiesta de la Virgen de Guadalupe de Santa Lucía (December 12–13), and the Fiesta de San Andrés (November 30), featuring drunken dancing, music, and loads of pyrotechnics. Buses to San Andrés (45 min, $1) leave from San Cristóbal's market. There are no hotels, so leave early to catch a colectivo from the church back to San Cristóbal.

CHENALHO

The less-touristed town of Chenalhó lies about an hour's bus ride north of San Cristóbal through tiny settlements and dramatic mountain scenery. On Sunday, a market takes place in front of the Iglesia de San Pedro, in the center of town. The major festival (June 27–30) here honors San Pedro and features a terrific procession of horses, children, women, and men in their traditional garb, chanting in Tzeltal as they carry a statue of their patron saint into the incense-fogged church. Buses (70¢) depart from San Cristóbal's market. If you don't plan to stay over, plan a morning visit, since colectivos become scarce in late afternoon.

AMATENANGO DEL VALLE

This Tzeltal town, about 39 km (22 mi) south of San Cristóbal on the road to Comitán, is known for its pottery—done entirely by women working by hand, without the aid of a pottery wheel. People work out of their houses and are likely to invite you in to look at their wares if you show an interest. The major festivals here are celebrations of patron saints: San Francisco is honored April 28–30, San Pedro Mártir on October 4, and Santa Lucía on December 13. Any Comitán-bound bus (40 min, 70¢) will get you here.

PALENQUE

The ruined Classic Maya city of Palenque is truly magical. As you watch the morning mist rise over the temples and listen to the unmistakable calls of the howler monkeys reverberate through the jungle, it's hard not to be awestruck. The nearby, modern-day town of Palenque isn't half as impressive, but it remains surprisingly friendly despite recent rapid growth. The Zapatista uprising shut down a number of businesses in the mid-1990s, but tourism has returned at unprecedented levels—which means you'll have to share the ruins with the busloads of package tourists who descend daily on Palenque's archaeological sites. Start your day early and plan a leisurely exploration of the ruins and rain forests: The exotic jungle vistas from atop Palenque's temples are not to be missed.

BASICS

CASAS DE CAMBIO

Queue up early and expect to wait up to an hour to exchange traveler's checks and receive Visa card advances at either **Bancomer** (Juárez 96, tel. 934/5–03–21) or **Banamex** (Juárez 62, tel. 934/5–04–90), both a few blocks west of the Parque Central. Both are open weekdays 10–noon and have ATMs. **Viajes Yax-ha** (Juárez, at Aldama; open daily 8 AM–9 PM), along with most other travel agencies, changes cash and traveler's checks at lousy rates.

LAUNDRY

If you drop off your clothes early in the morning, **Lavandería Mundo Maya** will wash and dry a 3-kilo (6½-pound) load ($2) by the end of the day. *Jiménez 2, 1 block south of Parque Central, no phone. Open Mon.–Sat. 7–7.*

MEDICAL AID

The **Centro de Salud** (Prolongación Juárez, no phone; open weekdays 7 AM–8 PM), at the west end of town, charges $2 for a general consultation. Next door, the **Hospital Regional** (tel. 934/5–07–33) has expensive 24-hour emergency service. **Farmacia Lastra** (Juárez, at Allende, no phone) is also open 24 hours.

PHONES AND MAIL

The blue Ladatel **phones** around the Parque Central are plagued by vandalism, but if they're in working order, they're your best bet (dial 09 for an international collect call). The 24-hour **caseta de larga distancia** (long-distance telephone office; Juárez, next to Hotel Misol-Ha, tel. 934/5–04–24) offers the best phone and fax service in town. The **post office** (open weekdays 8–1 and 3–6, Sat. 8–1) in the Casa de Cultura on the south side of Parque Central has the usual services and will hold mail sent to you at the following address for up to 10 days: Lista de Correos, Palenque, Chiapas, CP 29960, México.

TOURS AND GUIDES

A number of travel agencies offer charter flights and other package deals to Bonampak, Yaxchilán, Tikal, and the Lacandón jungle. Two-day trips to Yaxchilán and Bonampak, including transportation, meals, lodging, and guides, cost $80 per person. Day trips to Yaxchilán (by van and boat) and Bonampak (by van and two-hour hike) cost $65 and $55 per person, respectively. Most trips require a minimum of four people. Other options include jungle tours, horseback riding, and fishing trips. Most agencies are clustered around Avenida Juárez, between Allende and Abasolo, and coordinate with each other in rounding up groups. Travelers who have taken the trips advise that you establish a big group and then haggle like mad.

STS (Jiménez 6, in Hotel Palenque, tel. 934/5–13–54) is run by young, enterprising students who are eager to please (which means they'll often undercut the competition). Pick up a flyer from Francoise or Fernando for a free map of town and additional discounts on their already low prices. Other reputable agencies include **Viajes Misol-Ha** (Juárez 48, tel. 934/5–04–88), **Viajes Toniná** (Juárez 105, tel. 934/5–02–09), and **Viajes Yax-Ha** (Juárez 123, tel. 934/5–07–67).

VISITOR INFORMATION

There are two state-run tourist offices in town: The smaller office (Juárez, at Abasolo, in Mercado de Artesanías; open weekdays 8 AM–9 PM, Sat. 8–7) has an English-speaking staff, but tends to be short on maps. The main office (Jiménez, at 5 de Mayo, tel. 934/5–03–56; open weekdays 9–3 and 6–9), on the southeast end of the park, has a friendly but somewhat disorganized staff. They hand out travel agencies' business cards and distribute maps of the city.

COMING AND GOING

BY BUS

All bus stations are downhill and within walking distance of the Parque Central on Avenida Juárez. First-class, air-conditioned **ADO/Cristóbal Colón** buses (5 de Mayo, at Juárez, tel. 934/5–13–44) serve Mex-

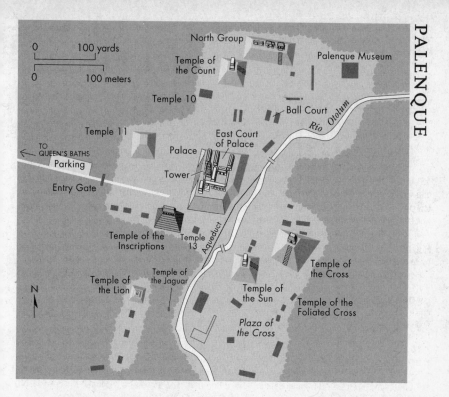

North Group
Palenque Museum
Temple of the Count
Temple 10
Ball Court
Río Otolum
Temple 11
East Court of Palace
TO QUEEN'S BATHS
Parking
Palace
Tower
Entry Gate
Temple of the Inscriptions
Temple 13
Aqueduct
Temple of the Cross
Temple of the Lion
Temple of the Jaguar
Temple of the Sun
Temple of the Foliated Cross
Plaza of the Cross
N

0   100 yards
0   100 meters

ico City (1 per day; 14 hrs, $35) and Villahermosa (10 per day; 1½ hrs, $5). The Mérida-bound bus (3 per day; 9 hrs, $17) stops in Campeche (6 hrs, $13). There are also buses for San Cristóbal (5 per day; 7½ hrs, $6) and Tuxtla Gutiérrez (4 per day; 7½ hrs, $7), stopping in Ocosingo (2 hrs, $3) on the way.

Second-class **Transportes Tuxtla Gutiérrez** (Júarez, at 20 de Noviembre, tel. 934/5–12–33) has six daily buses that leave from the end of Avenida Juárez and run to Tuxtla Gutiérrez (6 hrs, $6) and San Cristóbal (8 hrs, $6), stopping in Ocosingo (2½ hrs, $3.50). The station has daylong luggage storage with purchase of a ticket. If you want to try your luck at getting to the Lacandón jungle without paying exorbitant package prices, check with **Autotransportes Río Chancala** (5 de Mayo 120, opposite Hotel Kashlan, no phone; open daily 6 AM–8 PM) about their early departures for Lacanjá and Bonampak (5 hrs, $6).

BY PLANE

The Palenque **airport** opened in 1996 and is served by two Mexican air carriers, **Aviacsa** and **Aerocaribe** (tel. 934/5–06–18). Both offer service to Mérida, Tuxtla Gutiérrez, Cancún, Chetumal, and Oaxaca city in Mexico, as well as Flores, Guatemala, and Belize City, Belize. Taxis will take you the 16 km (10 mi) into town.

GETTING AROUND

Palenque is easily explored on foot. Most hotels, restaurants, and bus stations are within blocks of its **Parque Central** or along the main street, **Avenida Juárez.** In typical Chiapan fashion, *calles* run north–south and *avenidas* run east–west. Taxis congregate on the east side of the park and charge $1.50 for a ride to the train station or to the Mayabell campground (*see below*), and a bit more for a trip to the airport. Taxis are not necessary for a trip to the ruins or Agua Azul, which are both served by frequent bus service.

Microbuses and colectivos are run by **Transportes Palenque** (20 de Noviembre, at Allende, 3 blocks east and 2 blocks south of park) and **Transportes Chambalu** (Allende, at Juárez, 3 blocks east and 1 block north of park). Both offer service to the ruins (30¢) every 10 minutes, daily 6–6. Package plans to Misol-Ha and Agua Azul leave at 9 AM, 10 AM, and noon, spending 30 minutes at Misol-Ha and three to four hours at Agua Azul. The whole deal lasts about six hours and costs $8, which is a bargain since it includes admission. It costs almost $6 to reach these places on your own, and you can't count on front-porch delivery to the sites on local buses.

WHERE TO SLEEP

You can find fairly cheap dives as well as the purest air-conditioned luxury in Palenque, although most places fall in the middle- to upper-price range. If you want to sleep surrounded by jungle, camp out at Mayabell (*see below*) or rent a hammock in Agua Azul (*see* Near Palenque, *below*). In town, various posadas—offering simple fan-equipped rooms with toilet paper, clean towels, and luggage storage—are the cheapest accommodations. At **Posada Santo Domingo** (20 de Noviembre, at Allende, tel. 934/5–01–46), doubles cost $8, cash only. One final consideration is the time of year you're in town: Prices jump by about 15% in July, August, November, and December. Prices listed below are for the off-peak season.

UNDER $10 • Hotel Misol-Ha. Straightforward lodging in the heart of the city, Misol-Ha is refreshingly quiet and clean. Doubles are $10. All have fans, hot water, and access to sunny communal balconies. *Juárez 14, tel. 934/5–00–92. 28 rooms, all with bath. Luggage storage. Cash only.*

Hotel Posada San Juan. On a dirt road well off the tourist track, San Juan feels like it's in a cooler climate than the rest of Palenque. The pleasant, fan-cooled doubles ($10) are a real deal. *Off Allende, near corner of Emilo Rabasa, tel. 934/5–06–16. From park, walk down Juárez to Allende, turn left and walk 4 blocks. 18 rooms, all with bath. Luggage storage. Cash only.*

UNDER $15 • Hotel Lacroix. This unique place has been an institution since 1956, when archaeologists arrived to begin excavating the ruins. Painted on the lobby walls are replicas of letters written by colleagues of the late French archaeologist Señor Lacroix, who owned Palenque. The few rooms with fans and cold-water baths tend to fill quickly. Doubles cost $13. *Hidalgo 10, tel. 934/5–00–14. ½ block east of NE corner of park. 8 rooms, all with bath. Luggage storage. Cash only.*

UNDER $40 • Tulija. If the heat and mosquitoes have gotten to you, opt for this cheerful, air-conditioned oasis. Smallish rooms have color satellite TVs and phones, and some face a pleasant garden. Doubles cost $39. It's a 10-minute walk or $1 taxi ride from downtown and the first-class bus station. *Carretera Ruinas Km. 27.5, tel. 934/5–01–65. 48 rooms, all with bath. Restaurant, bar, pool.*

HOSTELS

Youth Hostel Posada Canek. Because it's the cheapest in town, and the best place to meet fellow travelers, beds ($4 per person) in the comfortable coed rooms fill up fast. Private doubles with clean shared baths are $9. Come in around the 10 AM checkout to be sure of securing a bed. *20 de Noviembre 43, across from Posada Charito, tel. 934/5–01–50. 8 rooms, all with bath; 10 dorm beds. Laundry, luggage storage. Cash only.*

CAMPING

Mayabell (tel. 934/5–05–97 for reservations) is known worldwide as a hip home-away-from-home for wandering minstrels, craftspeople, and shaman wanna-bes. Pitching a tent runs $3 per person, stringing your own hammock costs about $2 per night, and renting a hammock is another $3 (plus a $13.50 deposit). Cabañas for two with private bath are $15 (plus a $13.50 deposit). Payments are accepted in cash only. Communal bathrooms lack hot water but are usually clean, and there's a full-service restaurant on the premises. The campground is on the road to the ruins, several kilometers out of town. Take a colectivo (35¢) headed for the ruins for about 10 minutes and tell the driver to let you off at Mayabell.

FOOD

Most restaurants along Avenida Juárez and around the park cater to tourists, many of whom are Mexican nationals. For a simple, cheap meal, try the snack stands on the uphill side of the square, where you can purchase tortas, *licuados* (fruit smoothies), and corn on the cob all for less than $1. The daily **mercado** (4 blocks south of zócalo) is a good place to stock up on bread, cheese, and fruit to snack on while visiting the ruins. For cheap beer (50¢) and tacos (35¢), head to local favorite **Chan-Bahlum** (Hidalgo, 2 blocks from park; cash only).

UNDER $5 • Restaurante El Rodeo. The Rodeo serves a decent, ample *comida corrida* (preprepared lunch special; $3). Their eponymous burger comes with ham, cheese, bacon, and all the trimmings.

Upstairs from El Rodeo, **El Patio's** terrace is perfect for sipping coffee or beer. The management also changes traveler's checks at the bank rate and is a good source of information on the surrounding area. *Juárez 10, tel. 934/5–02–03. Cash only.*

Restaurante Maya. Popular with Mexicans and international travelers alike, this restaurant/bar has served quality local food since 1958. However, its popularity means you may wait an eternity for service. The best deals are the sandwiches ($1.50–$2.50) and breakfast specials ($3). Breakfasts include fruit, bread and jam, eggs, black beans, a stack of tortillas, and coffee. The pleasant atmosphere and view of the Parque Central may move you to linger over an after-dinner cappuccino ($1.20). *Independencia, at Hidalgo, tel. 934/5–00–42. Cash only.*

Restaurante Mero-Lec. Live romantic music and starlight seating are extra perks here, but the real attraction is the good food at terrific prices. A shrimp cocktail or a hearty order of tacos is just $2.50. After dinner you can have a drink or play a game of Ping-Pong. *No phone. From traffic circle on highway to ruins, walk along dirt path (follow neon signs) to Centro Turístico la Cañada; it's on your right. Dinner only. Live music Wed.–Sat. 9:30 PM–midnight. Cash only.*

Restaurante Yunyuén. This restaurant in Hotel Vaca Vieja serves generous *antojitos* (appetizers) for $1.50 and light meals of yogurt and fruit for just $2. The entertaining bilingual menu advertises tantalizing "sparro gas" (asparagus). *5 de Mayo, at Chiapas, tel. 934/5–03–77. 3 blocks east of park. Cash only.*

WORTH SEEING

In June, 1997 an Australian archaeologist and his crew were attacked by indigenous people when they tried to remove an ancient Maya altar from El Cayo, a set of ruins 80 mi southeast of Palenque.

Palenque's ruins retain more of a lost-in-the-jungle feel than any of Mexico's other easily accessible sites. No one should miss scaling these ancient ruins for the view of the surrounding vegetation: It's hard to imagine that what you see is only a fraction of the ancient city, while the rest lies buried under dense foliage. The city—probably founded in the 3rd century and abandoned for unknown reasons in the 9th—was at the height of its glory in the 7th century under a ruler named Pakal. He is represented in numerous bas-reliefs and is most remembered for his tomb, one of the most important archaeological finds of this century.

You should allow about a day to see everything here. Guidebooks to the ruins are not sold on the premises, but you can buy a pamphlet with a map and description of each major structure. The English version is $1.50, the Spanish 50¢. For more in-depth explanations, join a private tour ($15–$20 per group); these can be arranged at the entrance to the ruins or in advance through a local travel agency. The ruins are open daily 9–5, and the entrance fee is $2.25, free on Sunday. Colectivos shuttle frequently between the town and the ruins (*see* Getting Around, *above*).

PALENQUE MUSEUM

This museum features bits and pieces from the site's digs as well as a general overview of the religious, social, and political structures of the Maya. Most notable are the stone slabs covered with hieroglyphics and the carved stone sculptures of Maya faces. Also on the premises is a government handicrafts shop with remarkable weavings from all over Chiapas. It's a good idea to hit the museum before getting bedraggled and sweaty at the ruins. To get here, catch a colectivo (30¢) along the main road in town. *1 km (½ mi) before ruins on main highway. Admission: $2. Open Tues.–Sun. 9–4:15.*

TEMPLE OF THE INSCRIPTIONS

This structure wins the building-you're-most-likely-to-see-on-a-postcard contest. If you're not afraid of heights, the spectacular view from the top of the 86-ft pyramid provides a sense of the vast lands once under Palenque's domain. It's also the vantage point from which to see the surrounding buildings' roof combs—vertical extensions that are characteristic of southern Maya architecture. The climb is less steep and taxing if you ascend from the back side.

From the top of the pyramid you can descend to Pakal's tomb, a chamber 5 ft below ground. The six-toed Chan-Bahlum, Pakal's son, buried his father here in AD 683 and then had the entire 125-ft space above the tomb filled with debris. Mexican archaeologist Alberto Ruíz uncovered the tomb in 1952 after spending four years plowing through the rubble, finally thwarting Chan-Bahlum's efforts to deter grave robbers and nosy academics. Ruíz found Pakal's body wrapped in red cloth and decorated with jade jewelry, a stunning jade death mask, and other items to ensure his comfort in the next world. These are now exhibited at the Museo Nacional de Antropología in Mexico City (*see* Chapter 2). At the site you can see the tomb's 5-ton lid, intricately carved with a likeness of Pakal as a young man descending through the gateway to the afterworld. The enormous crypt is comparable to the huge tombs found in Egypt. The tomb is open daily 10:30–4.

TEMPLE 13

In 1994, a royal tomb was discovered in the depths of the small and unassuming Temple 13, adjacent to the Temple of the Inscriptions. It was discovered after a visiting French psychic felt peculiar vibrations around the temple, indicating, she told archaeologists, the presence of a tomb. They dug and found what probably are the remains of Pakal's mother or grandmother. The tomb is currently being studied and will open to the public in the near future.

PALACE

Next to the Temple of the Inscriptions, in the center of the site, is a cluster of buildings that includes steam baths, latrines, dwellings supposedly inhabited by priests, and rooms for religious ceremonies. From the center tower you can see walls covered with stucco friezes and masks in relief, many depicting Pakal and his dynasty.

PLAZA OF THE CROSS

Across the river, to the east of the Temple of the Inscriptions, a wide plaza holds four pyramids constructed by Chan-Bahlum. The **Temple of the Cross** holds an image of a cross, representing the ceiba tree; the **Temple of the Foliated Cross,** which looks like a gingerbread house with giant keyholes for windows, has a stone slab whose hieroglyphs recount the Maya's struggles for survival in the jungle. The **Temple of the Sun** has a depiction of a shield, the symbol of the sun god. **Temple 14** has an underworld scene done in stucco relief that an inscription notes was completed 260 days after Pakal's death. Modern Maya culture is certainly far removed from the Classic period, but symbols such as the cross and shield retain their significance. In contemporary indigenous villages, for example, crosses decorated with pine branches still mark sacred places of worship.

TEMPLE OF THE JAGUAR

This tiny temple is just off a short trail to the south of the Temple of the Inscriptions—follow the dirt path into the jungle alongside the Otolum River. The temple features a slippery stairwell leading to an exposed chamber. The trail continues on to smaller ruins amid dense jungle, ending 8 km (5 mi) uphill at a friendly village.

QUEEN'S BATHS

Pakal's wife reportedly dipped her queenly body into the various small waterfalls and pools that dot a 3-km (2-mi) trail leading to the ruins from the museum. Swimming is not permitted, but the guard will let you cool your feet in the pools. *From Palenque Museum, walk across street to path leading through dense vegetation; the Queen's Baths begin about 330 ft along path.*

NEAR PALENQUE

MISOL-HA AND AGUA AZUL

Rivers snake through the Chiapan rain forest, forming crashing waterfalls and deep swimming holes. **Misol-Ha** and **Agua Azul** are two such places, and are popular tourist stops for Mexican families, especially during high seasons. Eighteen kilometers (10 mi) down Route 199 from Palenque, the single towering cascade at Misol-Ha thunders into a deep, cold, green pool. Here you can swim, sun on the rocks, or poke around behind the falls, where a cave leads to a subterranean pool, more falls, and lots of bats.

Forty-six kilometers (27 mi) farther south toward Ocosingo is Agua Azul, which, during the rainy months (July–Sept.) isn't quite the vibrant blue depicted in postcard photos. Nevertheless, it's still a treat to float down the river or play on the rope swing. To get away from the clutter of families, snack shacks, and souvenir vendors, follow the trail leading upstream from the main swimming area for about 2 km (1 mi). Once there, you'll find pools that alternate with waterfalls in a steplike pattern. You can climb from one level to the next in the water, but watch for areas of slippery rocks (clearly marked with skulls and crossbones and multilingual warnings).

COMING AND GOING

Microbuses from **Transportes Chambalu** and **Transportes Palenque** (*see* Getting Around *in* Palenque, *above*) run directly to both Misol-Ha and Agua Azul from Palenque, and the journey takes about two hours one way. If you prefer to go at your own pace, all buses bound for Ocosingo or Yajalón from Palenque pass the *cruceros* (crossroads) for Misol-Ha and Agua Azul. The Misol-Ha crossroads is about 3 km (2 mi) from the falls, and the ride will cost you 70¢. The 1½-hour ride to the crossroads for Agua Azul costs $1.25, and the bus lets you off about 5 km (3 mi) from the river. The downhill walk is on a narrow, hot, paved road; watch out for microbuses swerving around corners. When you enter Agua Azul, you may be asked to pay an entrance fee of 70¢ ($3 if you come by car), depending on how attentive the guards are. To return to Palenque, hook up with a colectivo for around $3.

WHERE TO SLEEP AND EAT

At the base of the Misol-Ha waterfall are several family-style cabañas with all the modern amenities—refrigerators, stoves, ovens, and cooking utensils. The simple double-occupancy cabañas ($16 in low season, $20 high season) have private baths with hot water, mosquito screens, and color TVs. Pitching a tent costs $16 year-round. There is a full-service restaurant at the site.

Locals at Agua Azul hang cardboard signs outside their houses advertising spots to camp or hang a hammock for a small fee. You can hang your own hammock upriver at Agua Azul for $2–$3, or rent one for an additional $2–$3 from the locals; tent spots are also $2–$3. There is a group of *comedores* (food stands) at the uppermost falls, and they all serve three cheap meals daily.

Palenque's rulers often intermarried, and birth defects were seen as marks of divinity. Pakal, who was clubfooted, may have married both his mother and a sister. His son, Chan-Bahlum, had 12 toes and 11 fingers.

OCOSINGO AND TONINA RUINS

Located 20 km (12 mi) south of Palenque, Ocosingo is an unassuming town. It was here, in January 1994, that the Zapatista rebels confronted the Mexican army in one of the bloodiest battles of the uprising. Peasants suspected of rebel activity were executed by the army in Ocosingo's central plaza—images of the victims made newspaper front pages worldwide. These events have contributed to an attitude of wariness and suspicion in Ocosingo, but the little-known ruins of **Toniná,** just over 10 km (6 mi) away, are still worth a visit. A Maya city that reached its height in AD 500–1000, Toniná's ruins are tough to reach without a car, but well worth the effort. Experts say the site housed a prison for warriors captured in the many battles Toniná waged against its neighboring city-states. Passageways wind through Toniná's imposing seven-tier pyramid and descend into tombs complete with stone sarcophagi and still-discernible depictions of jaguars, skeletons, and the god of the underworld clutching the heads of decapitated prisoners. A small, on-site museum displays a fair selection of Toniná statuary; many of these pieces were also decapitated, supposedly by the invading forces of a rival city. The site and museum are open daily 9–4; the caretaker will show you around by request. Admission to the pyramid and museum is $1.50, free on Sunday.

COMING AND GOING

Frequent buses connect Ocosingo with San Cristóbal and Palenque. The **Cristóbal Colón** station (Carretera Ocosingo–Palenque Km. 2, tel. 967/3–04–31) is a 20-minute walk from the zócalo along 1a Avenida Oriente Norte. From here, first-class buses depart for Palenque (2 hrs, $3) and Tuxtla Gutiérrez (5 hrs, $4). **Transportes Tuxtla Gutiérrez,** in the second-class bus station 3½ blocks up the hill on 1a Avenida Norte Poniente, has the most reliable service to Tuxtla (3½ hrs, $3.25), San Cristóbal (3½ hrs, $3), and Palenque (2½ hrs, $3.50).

There is no public transportation to Toniná, so unless you have a car or want to take a tour from Palenque or San Cristóbal, you'll need to go to the Ocosingo market around 9 AM and ask around until you get on a truck that passes the road leading to the ruins ($1 is a reasonable fee). Your best bet is finding someone headed to Guadalupe, a town just past the ruins, but make it clear you want to go to Toniná. Don't be fooled by the road signs for Toniná—the first, which is about 2 km (1 mi) from Ocosingo, is a good three-hour walk from the site. With luck, you'll be let off at the last crossroads, a 20-minute walk from the ruins. Be sure to head out early to hitch a ride for the return trip, as traffic is light and you may be in for a 3½-hour walk back to town. If it's late, you might be able to cajole a ride home from the people who work at the site and museum. You'll be expected to pay $1 for the ride.

THE LACANDÓN
TRUE PEOPLE

With the arrival of the Spanish in Chiapas, many diverse Maya groups fled deep into the Lacandón jungle; the Spaniards chose not to follow them into such unfamiliar and inhospitable territory. These Maya banded together and called themselves Hachack-Winick (the True People). They lived peacefully in the rain forest—in complete isolation from the rest of the world—until they were contacted by anthropologists during this century.

Today the continued existence of the Lacandón people is in jeopardy. Only 350 remain, and they are under great pressure to assimilate. Phillip Bayer, a Baptist missionary, spent 12 years trying to convert the people of Najá with meager results. When he heard the last two elders of Lacanjá had died, he rushed in and successfully converted virtually all of southern Lacandón to Christianity in just a couple of years.

In Najá however, the elder Chan K'in Viejo has bestowed upon his many sons the task of preserving Lacandón social and cultural traditions. To the many who have turned away from their culture, Chan K'in warned that to "cut the umbilical cord connected to one's traditions" means to "be denied the key to the heavens." Sadly, this great patriarch died in 1997 (he was well over 100 years old), and some predict that traditional Lacandón culture will now fall apart.

Indeed, the children that Chan K'in Viejo fathered with his three wives (the youngest of which is said to have been conceived when Chan K'in was 102) are estimated to comprise 35% of the population of Najá.

WHERE TO SLEEP AND EAT

Ocosingo's few hotels are nothing to write home about, but worth considering—this would be a long, exhausting day trip from either San Cristóbal or Palenque. For rooms with a cabaña-in-the-jungle feel, head to **Hotel Agua Azul** (1a Ote. Sur 127, tel. 967/3–03–02). The cheap, clean rooms here come with private baths and hot water; doubles cost $6.25. Fans in every room of **Hotel Bodas de Plata** (1a Sur, at 1a Pte., just south of Palacio Municipal, tel. 967/3–00–16) cool things off during the midday heat, while the piping hot water warms you on chilly Ocosingo mornings. Doubles are $13. **Hotel Central** (Central 5, tel. 967/3–00–24) provides small, comfortable rooms furnished with tiny black-and-white TVs, fans, and bathrooms with plenty of hot water. From the restaurant downstairs you can view the happenings on the zócalo. Doubles cost $11.50. All of the above accept cash only.

Another option is the new **Rancho Esmeralda** (no phone, fax 967/3–07–11), run by a couple of expat Americans. The rustic, five-cabin lodge is set on a macadamia nut farm and is just a 10-minute walk from the ruins. Cabins ($24–$35) lack electricity and indoor plumbing, but there's a common bathhouse and several outhouses. Meals (breakfast $2–$4, lunch $4, dinner $5) are served family-style and include vegetarian dishes; just about everything you'll eat has been grown on the farm. Activities include horseback-riding, birding, hiking, volleyball, badminton, and lawn bowling. From Ocosingo, it's a $5 taxi ride; turn off at the sign along the dirt road 1 km (½ mi) before Toniná.

Ocosingo's morning **market** (downhill on 2a Avenida Sur Oriente, on the left just before the dusty lot) is the place to stock up on fruit, bread, fresh tortillas, and locally made cheese. Good, cheap tacos (30¢) are prepared in front of you at **El Buen Taquito** (tel. 967/3–02–51), on Avenida Central near the zócalo. Fill up on quesadillas made with local cheese (3 for $1) at **La Michoacana** (Central Ote. 3, on zócalo, tel. 967/3–02–51), or order *sincronizadas* (tortilla sandwiches; 70¢) with cheese, ham, onions, chiles, and avocados. The patio at **Restaurante La Montura** (below Hotel Central, tel. 967/3–05–50) is a great place to enjoy a platter of spicy chicken chilaquiles ($3), or *plátanos fritos* (fried plantains) with cream.

THE LACANDON RAIN FOREST

The Lacandón rain forest is not as pristine as its remote location might suggest. Humans have encroached everywhere, stripping it of its precious wood and razing the land for cattle ranches and farms. A road built through the heart of the forest—connecting Palenque with Najá—will soon be linked with a road to Ocosingo, ostensibly to bring package tours to unspoiled lagoon areas such as **Metzaboc** and **Miramar**. In reality, these projects afford the military better access to what is the last Zapatista stronghold. The forest is still home, however, to the Lacandón Indians—considered to be the living indigenous group most similar to their Maya ancestors—and contains the two important Maya archaeological sites of Bonampak and Yaxchilán. Most of the southern Lacandón live in Lacanjá, and until very recently, most of them worshipped at Yaxchilán (the northerners worshipped at Palenque). These days northerners worship at Yaxchilán, while most of the southerners have converted to Christianity. Though some Lacandón only speak a dialect of Maya, many of those living in Lacanjá now speak Spanish. Lacandón crafts, including bows, arrows, and seed jewelry, are for sale in the region's towns.

Health workers at Chiapan archaeological sites routinely carry injections to counteract bites by the nahauyaca, a striped, fanged snake whose poison can be fatal to victims left untreated longer than 15 minutes.

NAJA AND LACANJA

Most Lacandón people now live in or around these two main towns, and a number of them are quite rich, having sold their land rights to lumber companies. Neither Najá nor Lacanjá offers hotel lodging, but local families will often let visitors sling hammocks in their homes. It is advised to bring a letter of introduction from Na-Bolom (*see* Volunteering *in* San Cristóbal, *above*), and to come with a purpose other than a vague interest in experiencing Lacandón life. In the past, exposure to outsiders has brought some tragic results to the Lacandón people, resulting in justifiable skepticism and suspicion on their part. Be respectful and bring your own provisions plus food gifts such as sugar and salt. Check with Na-Bolom for more information about events coordinated through the new **casas de cultura** in Najá and Lacanjá.

The most reliable road into the Lacandón jungle runs straight to Lacanjá, a four- to six-hour trip from Palenque. Najá is closer, but on a poorer road, and takes about seven hours to reach from Palenque, or six hours from Ocosingo (*see* Ocosingo and Toniná Ruins, *above*). Driving on your own is not advised due to the current political situation in the region. Buses depart daily for Najá from Ocosingo at 9 AM. From Palenque, **Transportes Chamcala** buses go to Lacanjá via the San Javier military installation, daily at 10 AM and 2 PM. You should bring a tent or hammock, and locals will tell you where you can spend the night. Before venturing off into the jungle, it's a good idea to pick up a map, available in bookshops and at Na-Bolom. You might also check travel agencies in San Cristóbal and Palenque for organized tours to the region.

BONAMPAK

In the grand scheme of things, this small ceremonial center played only a minor role during the late Classic Maya period. What's notable about Bonampak, built between AD 400 and 700, are the colorful frescoes in three excavated rooms, complete with altars that seem to depict an epic. Room 1 supposedly illustrates preparation for a war; Room 2, scenes from the battle (Yaxchilán under the reign of Governor Chaan Muan is the supposed foe); and Room 3, the various bloodletting rituals associated with victory, plus the passing of Bonampak site to a young heir. The first white explorers to the region were on a 1946 National Fruit Company expedition looking to build a road through the rain forest. They stumbled upon this tiny palace, its murals preserved in vivid color by a thin coating of limestone. Excavations took place soon after (National Fruit footed much of the bill), and several partially destroyed buildings and a plaza were uncovered. The colors in rooms 2 and 3 are rather faded, and some claim that seeing the reproductions in Mexico City's anthropology museum will save you a lot of time and unnecessary effort. Don't believe it: Seeing the remnants of a great civilization in its original context, plus the adventure of getting to the site, is worth the trip. Just don't expect comic-strip clarity on the walls. The site is open daily 9–5. Admission is $2, free on Sunday.

COMING AND GOING • Transportation to the ruins is most easily set up through a travel agency (*see* Tours and Guides *in* Palenque, *above*); guided tours usually last two to three days. You can also get here by bus. From Palenque, make the six-hour trip on one of the frequent **Transportes Lagos de Montebello** buses to Lacanjá; from Lacanjá, walk the 13 km (7 mi) to the ruins. Bring all you need to be self-sufficient for a few days, plus gifts of food or cigarettes for the caretakers.

YAXCHILAN

The Yaxchilán ruins lie on the shores of the Usumacinta River, 32 km (19 mi) northeast of Bonampak, at the Guatemalan border. This ceremonial center, built between AD 500 and 800, was considerably more important than Bonampak and is still considered sacred by the present-day descendants of the Maya. For several years, the Lacandón people were prevented from worshipping at Yaxchilán because it was feared they would damage the temple. Today access has been restored, and inhabitants of the northern Lacandón once again perform their ceremonies here.

The site was ingeniously constructed around the twisting Usumacinta River, and therefore remains accessible only by boat. The highlight is the series of high temples, many with stelae and glyphs. Carvings depict the two most important rulers: Jaguar Escudo (Shield Jaguar), in power during the 7th century, and Jaguar Pájaro (Bird Jaguar), who ruled a century later. You'll probably have to fork out a tidy sum for a visit here, so try to see everything you can—don't miss the series of temples dedicated to Jaguar Pájaro, set high on a hill, deeper in the jungle behind the eastern structure. Excavations are ongoing here and promise to reveal many more Mayan secrets.

There's a large *palapa* (thatched hut) for sleeping in Yaxchilán, but no facilities; bring a hammock and a mosquito net. You can bathe and fish in the river, and have your catch or any other food prepared (for a small fee) by the woman who cooks for the guards. You'll pay a $2 fee to enter the ruins (free on Sunday). Spanish-language guided tours are free and mandatory.

COMING AND GOING • Transportation is usually arranged by travel agencies. The trip typically involves a four-hour bus ride to the border town of Frontera Echeverría (called Corozal on the Guatemalan side) and a one-hour boat ride to Yaxchilán, where you can see the ruins and camp before heading on to Bonampak (*see above*). STS (*see* Tours and Guides *in* Palenque, *above*) does the two-day trip for $80 a person. You can also try to arrange boat transportation with a local resident in Lacanjá for about $20, or from Frontera Echeverría for $50 each way (up to eight people).

COMITAN AND LAGOS DE MONTEBELLO

Though usually only used as a stopover for those traveling to and from Guatemala, the town of Comitán has a pleasantly cool climate, some unusual little museums, and a pretty zócalo planted with ceiba trees and bougainvillea vines. The real draw to this area, however, is the Parque Nacional Lagos de Montebello, with over 2,000 acres of pine-forested hills dotted with lakes in brilliant shades of blue, green, and gray.

Comitán was originally a Tzeltal-speaking Maya community called Balún-Canán, meaning "Place of the Nine Stars," and it remains a primary Tzeltal trading post. Its current name is derived from the name given by the Aztec: Comitlán, which translates from Nahuatl as "Place of the Potters." You can see remnants of Maya civilization dating back as far as AD 900 at the Chinkultic and Tenam Puente ruins (*see* Near Comitán, *below*) and in town at an archaeology museum in the Casa de Cultura (*see* Worth Seeing, *below*).

BASICS

CASAS DE CAMBIO

Bancomer (1a Av. Sur Ote. 10, SE corner of zócalo, tel. 963/2–02–10; open weekdays 9:30–11:30 AM) exchanges cash and traveler's checks and gives advances on Visa cards. It also has a 24-hour ATM.

CONSULATES

The **Guatemalan Consulate** (Calle 1a Sur Pte. 26, at 2a Av. Pte. Sur, tel. 963/2–26–69; open weekdays 8–4:30) may open up shop for you on Saturday if you pay an "overtime surcharge." For specific information on visas and border crossings, *see box, below.*

CROSSING THE BORDER

The border crossing at **Ciudad Cuauhtémoc** doesn't quite live up to its billing as a city, but it's reported to be less dicey than those further south, near Tapachula. In any case, it affords good scenery and frequent transportation from La Mesilla, Guatemala, to the heart of the Guatemalan *altiplano* (highlands). The border is open daily 8 AM–6 PM. For general border information, *see box, below.*

If you're coming from Guatemala, pickup trucks (50¢) and taxis ($1) bridge the 3-km (2-mi) gap between La Mesilla, Guatemala, and Ciudad Cuauhtémoc, Mexico. From Cuauhtémoc, sporadic buses make the trip to Comitán (1½ hrs, $2.25) from the Cristóbal Colón terminal across from the immigration office. If you reach the border too late, don't despair; there is a very civil hotel next door to the bus terminal and a restaurant across the street. For information on how to reach the border from Comitán, *see* Coming and Going, *below.*

Since 1981, the area around Comitán has become home for thousands of indígenas who fled Guatemala's Ixcán jungle during that country's brutal Scorched Earth counterinsurgency campaign. Many remain.

LAUNDRY

Lavandería Takana (Calle 1 Sur Pte., at 2a Av. Pte. Sur, next to Guatemalan Consulate; open Mon.–Sat. 9–2 and 4–8) washes and dries your clothes for $1 a kilo (2 pounds). If you can't get next-day service there, try **Lavandería Chulul** (2a Av. Pte. Sur, around corner from Restaurant Alis), which has identical hours.

MAIL

The **post office** provides the usual services and will hold mail sent to you at the following address for up to 10 days: Lista de Correos, Comitán, Chiapas, CP 30000, México. *Central Belisario Domínguez Sur 45, tel. 963/2–04–27. Open weekdays 8–7, Sat. 9–1.*

MEDICAL AID

The **Centro de Salud** (Calle 7 Sur Ote. 3, tel. 963/2–36–49 or 963/2–01–64; open weekdays 8 AM–3 PM) is well prepared to treat cholera or *turista*. At the **Cruz Roja** (Calle 5a Nte. Pte., tel. 963/2–18–89), doctors are on call 24 hours and speak some English.

PHONES

There are **Ladatel** phones on the zócalo, at the southeast corner and along the west side. **Caseta Maguis** charges a 20¢-per-minute commission on international collect calls, and a $1.25 fee if the party doesn't accept your call. *Calle 2 Sur Pte. 6, at Av. Central Belisario Domínguez, tel. 963/2–29–55, fax 963/2–43–52. Open Mon.–Sat. 8 AM–9 PM, Sun. 9–2 and 5–8.*

VISITOR INFORMATION

The tourist office in the Palacio Municipal on the zócalo is stocked with an excellent selection of brochures, as well as good maps of the city and region. The staff is well versed in local history, geography, and transportation options, but doesn't speak English. *Tel. 963/2–40–47. Open Mon.–Sat. 9–3 and 6–9, Sun. 9–2.*

COMING AND GOING

The first- and second-class bus terminals are on the highway—called Boulevard Belisario Domínguez or Carretera Internacional—west of the center. Cross the highway and catch a frequent CENTRO colectivo (20¢) to the plaza or take a taxi ($1). To get back to the terminals, hop on a CARRETERA INTERNACIONAL colectivo, which leaves from the east side of the zócalo daily 6 AM–9 PM.

The first-class **Cristóbal Colón** station (Blvd. Belisario Domínguez Sur 43, tel. 963/2–09–80) is on the highway about 12 blocks southwest of the center. Frequent buses to Tuxtla Gutiérrez (3½ hrs, $4.25), with stops in San Cristóbal (1½ hrs, $2), leave daily 6:30 AM–7 PM. Buses leave for the Guatemalan border town of Ciudad Cuauhtémoc (7 per day; 1½ hrs, $2.25) 8 AM–11:30 PM and continue to Villahermosa (8½ hrs, $10) at 6:30 PM. Two buses leave daily at noon and 2 PM, making the 22-hour haul to Mexico City; it's $32 for regular first-class and $37.50 for deluxe buses with extra-comfortable reclining seats, TV, and beverage service.

Second-class **Transportes Tuxtla Gutiérrez** and **La Angostura** (tel. 963/2–10–44 for both) buses leave from the station at Boulevard Belisario Domínguez Sur 27. The buses serve Tuxtla Gutiérrez (4 hrs, $3) and San Cristóbal (2 hrs, $1) 5 AM–7:30 PM. Buses for Ciudad Cuauhtémoc (2 hrs, $1.75), on the Guatemalan border, leave daily. Buses to Tzimol (30 min, 50¢) and La Mesilla (45 min, 70¢) leave about every half hour, daily 8–5, as do colectivo pickup trucks. To reach the station from the zócalo, head six blocks west on Calle Central Benito Juárez Poniente, turn left, and go 1½ blocks down the highway.

GETTING AROUND

Comitán is easy to navigate once you master its grid system. **Calle Central Benito Juárez** runs east–west, while **Avenida Central Belisario Domínguez** ("el boulevard") runs north–south. The two divide the city into quadrants. All *calles* run east–west, all *avenidas* north–south. The Palacio Municipal (with its clock facade) sits on the north side of the zócalo, and the Santo Domingo Church on the east side. The number in each street name indicates how far it is from either Avenida Central Belisario Domínguez or Calle Central Benito Juárez. For example, Calle 2 Sur Poniente runs east–west two blocks south of Calle Benito Juárez in the southwestern quadrant of the city. As the street crosses Avenida Central Belisario Domínguez into the southeastern quadrant of the city, it's called Calle 2 Sur Oriente.

WHERE TO SLEEP

Many of Comitán's budget hotels are near the center of town. The climate here is cooler than in most other areas of Chiapas, so when it comes to choosing a room, hot water should be more of a consideration than fans or air-conditioning. If there's no room at the places listed below, first try **Posada Las Flores** (1a Av. Pte. Nte. 17, tel. 963/2–33–24) then **Posada San Miguel** (1a Av. Pte. Nte. 19, tel. 963/2–11–26) next door. Both have clean double rooms for about $3 per person, cash only. If you'd like to camp, head to Lagos de Montebello (*see* Near Comitán, *below*).

UNDER $10 • Hospedaje Montebello. An amiable young couple runs this rather noisy but clean and traveler-friendly place, which is usually full by evening. The hot water is erratic in the private bathrooms, but the communal showers are reliable. Doubles are $6, with private bath $8. Calle 1 Nte. Pte. 10, at 1a Av. Pte. Nte., tel. 963/2–35–72. 14 rooms, 8 with bath. Luggage storage. Reservations advised. Cash only.

Posada Continental. Squeaky clean singles with communal bathrooms (stocked with soap, towels, and toilet paper) go for $3. Doubles without bath are $5, and a double or single room with bath goes for $5–$8. 1a Av. Pte. Sur 12, tel. 963/2–37–52. 13 rooms, 8 with bath. Luggage storage. Cash only.

UNDER $25 • Hotel Internacional. Just one block south of the center, this spacious hotel with perfumed, spotless rooms and plentiful hot water is an affordable luxury for two or more. Doubles are $21. Jovial Mexican businessmen tend to be the primary clientele here. Central Belisario Domínguez Sur 16, tel. 963/2–01–10. 28 rooms, all with bath. Restaurant, luggage storage.

FOOD

The affordable restaurants lining Comitán's zócalo serve international dishes and regional specialties, plus delicious coffee made from locally grown beans. Try **Restaurant Nevelandia** (west side of zócalo, tel. 963/2–00–95; cash only) for cheap tacos and quesadillas, or breakfast specials ($3.50) of eggs, tortillas, beans, fruit, and coffee. The daily **market**, in a huge, tan building one block east of the zócalo, is the place to find fruit, vegetables, and Ocosingo cheese.

UNDER $5 • Café Gloria. You can find both regional and nonregional treats in this family-owned restaurant, including locally grown coffee and tasty *sopes* (fried tortillas topped with beans, salsa, and meat or cheese) at three for $2. Other dishes are similarly priced, and all come with four kinds of homemade salsa. Little boys sometimes serve as waiters here, and they'll introduce each dish to you as if it's a person. *Av. Central Belisario Domínguez Nte. 22, tel. 963/2–16–22. Dinner only. Cash only.*

UNDER $10 • Restaurant Alis. Local immigration officials and their families come here for excellent typical Comitecan food. Their *platón chiapaneco* (plate of Chiapan meats; $6) includes *butifarras* (beef sausage) and *cecina* (dry, salted beef), and is enough for two–three people. Their five-course lunch specials are a tasty bargain for less than $5. *Central Benito Juárez Pte. 21, tel. 963/2–12–62. Cash only.*

WORTH SEEING

Comitán has some fine examples of colonial architecture and several well-curated museums. The 16th-century **Iglesia de Santo Domingo** on the zócalo displays elements of the Moorish-influenced mudéjar style. Just off the northeast corner of the zócalo stands the **Iglesia del Calvario,** whose columns and gables probably got their Islamic influences via Andalucía, Spain.

CASA DE CULTURA

The casa encompasses an archaeological museum, a multimedia performance space, an extensive library, and a café. The **archaeological museum** displays Mayan artifacts from the sites near Comitán. Especially notable is the display of bones and ornately decorated pottery found in the caves of Cam-Cum and Los Andasolos. *Calle 1 Sur Ote., no phone. Next to Santo Domingo, east side of zócalo. Museum behind Casa de Cultura. Admission free. Open Tues.–Sun. 10–5.*

MUSEO DE ARTE HERMILA DOMINGUEZ

This museum, two blocks south of the center, features modern works by Mexican artists, including famous Oaxacan muralist Rufino Tamayo. Many of the pieces deal with mystical themes, depicting mestizo and indigenous people and their connections to the earth, sky, and water. *Av. Central Belisario Domínguez Sur 53, no phone. Admission: 60¢. Open weekdays 10–1:45 and 4–6:45, Sat. 10–1:45.*

MUSEO DR. BELISARIO DOMINGUEZ

Dr. Domínguez was a statesman and proponent of preventive medicine who represented Chiapas in the Senate under President Francisco Madero, just after the Mexican Revolution. After Madero was assassinated by U.S.-backed General Victoriano Huerta in 1913, Dr. Domínguez publicly denounced Huerta as a brutal tyrant. Predictably, Domínguez was then murdered. Once his home, this extensive, well-organized museum displays the doctor's pharmaceuticals, menacing-looking medical instruments, photographs, letters, and other personal belongings. *Av. Central Belisario Domínguez Sur 35, tel. 963/2–13–00. Admission: 25¢. Open Tues.–Sat. 10–6:45, Sun. 9–12:45.*

FESTIVALS

Comitán has many festivals, some barrio-specific and others citywide. The **Festival de San Caralampio** (Feb. 8–22), featuring floats, flowers, music, and processions, is one of the biggest religious events of the year. Caralampio was a pious Christian who was burned to death by nonbelievers in his native Greece. Years later, a rancher named Raymundo Solís, inspired by a book about Caralampio, commissioned a statue of him for his ranch. At the time, a cholera epidemic was devastating Comitán, and when no one on Don Solís's ranch was affected, townspeople attributed this to the protection of Caralampio. Other festivals include **Semana Santa** (Holy Week, the week preceding Easter) and the **Feria de Agosto** (early Aug.), a 10-day festival of Comitecan agriculture, theater, and cuisine in honor of Santo Domingo.

AFTER DARK

The Zapatista uprising in 1994 brought an end to free musical performances on street corners and in the zócalo, but there are still plenty of venues to hear live music at no charge. **Helen's Enrique** (Av. Central Belisario Domínguez Sur 19, across from zócalo, tel. 963/2–17–30) is a prime hangout serving delicious cappuccinos. Nightly after 8 PM there's live Mexican pop. The bar in **Restaurant Nevelandia** (*see* Food, *above*) has an equally mellow scene, with nightly live *ranchera* and *banda* music. **El Rincón de la Guitarra** (Calle 1 Sur Ote. 13, no phone) offers live music of the Mamita-come-home-with-me-tonight ilk, nightly after 7 PM. It also offers some dangerous drinks ($2.50 apiece), like the Muppet (tequila with Squirt) or the Cucaracha (tequila, anise, and Kahlúa).

NEAR COMITAN

Many come to Comitán simply to enjoy the surrounding lake country, but there are also some quiet towns and Mayan ruins to visit nearby. Gringos rarely visit the area so prepare for plenty of attention. The town of **Tzimol,** set in a green valley 8 km (5 mi) southwest of Comitán, is where sugar has been cultivated with the same farming methods for hundreds of years. The town is known for its *panela* (hardened cakes of sugarcane used in Chiapan pastries). A 15-minute bus ride past Tzimol brings you to **La Mesilla,** from which a 5-km (3-mi) path leads to great swimming at an isolated waterfall called **El Chiflón.** Any La Mesilla local can direct you to the path once you get to town. **Transportes La Angostura** buses serve both towns (*see* Coming and Going, *above*). You'll want to catch the last bus back at 4:30 PM.

Twenty-five minutes by bus northwest of Comitán is the attractive little town of **Villa Las Rosas.** To get here from Comitán, take a direct **Transportes Cuxtepeque** (Blvd. Belisario Domínguez 12, at Calle 1 Nte. Pte., tel. 963/2–17–28) microbus (they leave every half hour) to the center of Las Rosas. If you decide to go to the freshwater spring **Manantial el Vertedor,** just outside of town, take another micro (60¢) from the center of Las Rosas to the Manantial bridge (first ask the driver if he's going to "el puente al manantial"). From the bridge it's a 1-km (½-mi) hike down a dirt road; follow the muddy path behind the dam and you can take a cool dip in the clear pool. In May and June, locals erect tiny shrines (dedicated to the rain god) by the pool's edge.

Eight kilometers (5 mi) south of Comitán is the Maya-Toltec site of **Tenam Puente.** Some feel that once the site is fully unearthed, it may prove to encompass an area larger than that of Palenque, and so far archaeologists and INAH workers have dug up several good-size pyramids, three ball courts, and a tomb with a mummy. The site is open to visitors daily 8–5; admission is $2, free on Sunday. To get here, catch any bus or colectivo marked LAGOS (35¢) and get off at the signs for Tenam Puente. To get back, walk to the highway and take any bus headed back to town (last bus passes around 6 PM). Licenciada María Trinidad Pulido, who is in charge of the archaeological museum at the Casa de Cultura (*see* Worth Seeing, *above*), is very knowledgeable about the site and can answer all your queries.

LAGOS DE MONTEBELLO

Set among pine trees, blackberry bushes, and maples, the 60-or-so blue, gray, and green lakes of the **Parque Nacional Lagos de Montebello** afford spectacular hiking and swimming opportunities. The most popular lakes are those closest to the road, such as lakes Esmeralda, Ensueño, Agua Tinta, La Encantada, and Bosque Azul. A 45-minute walk on the unpaved road from the park gates leads to **Lago Montebello,** the larger **Laguna Tziscao,** and a dozen tiny lakes. A bus continues north past this junction and parks at Lago Bosque Azul. Two dirt paths lead into the forest from here; the one to the left takes you to a riverside picnic spot called **El Paso del Soldado,** while the other takes you to **San José El Arco,** a natural limestone arch and series of *grutas* (caves). Bring a flashlight to explore the caves (as well as a few small offerings to leave for the gruta gods). Little boys will offer to guide you; their services are well worth a $1.25 donation.

At Bosque Azul, older boys will offer to take you to more isolated lakes on foot or horseback. Be sure to agree on a price before setting out ($2 an hour is acceptable) and wear a watch, since most guides aren't too concerned about getting you back in time for the last bus. The lakes **Peinita** and **Bartolo,** surrounded by white cliffs that offer spectacular views of the surrounding farmland and mountains, are best reached accompanied by a guide. You can pick up a useful map of the lakes at the tourist office in Comitán (*see* Visitor Information, *above*).

Just beyond park boundaries are the Mayan ruins of **Chinkultic** (terraced well). This site has a number of stelae, a ball court, and pyramids from which you can admire the surrounding lakes. You can also swim in the deep *cenote* (spring-fed water hole) from which Chinkultic takes its name. The ruins are a half-hour hike from the main road that leads to the lakes, and buses between Comitán and the park pass the turnoff; ask the driver to let you off at Chinkultic. The ruins are open daily 8:30–4; admission is $2, free on Sunday.

COMING AND GOING

Colectivos and combis from **Transportes Comitán-Montebello** (2a Av. Pte. Sur 17, between 2a and 3a Calles Sur Pte., tel. 963/2–08–75) terminate at Lago Bosque Azul; they leave every half hour, 5:45 AM–4:45 PM. The trip takes about an hour and costs $1.25. The last bus back to Comitán leaves Bosque Azul around 4 PM.

WHERE TO SLEEP AND EAT

You can easily stay in Comitán and make day trips to the lakes. If you want to stay overnight, bring warm gear as nights here are chilly. The restaurant at Lago Bosque Azul offers simple cabañas ($3), and Doña Maria at **Posada Las Orquideas,** at the turnoff for the ruins, offers basic cabins ($3 per person) and cheap meals. Out here, however, camping is the way to go. It's free, and officially permitted at Bosque Azul and La Encantada, which are outfitted with palapas, fire pits, and restrooms. The village of Tziscao on the south end of the park has lodging ($5 per person) as well as camping sites ($2). Bring your own food.

TAPACHULA

The southernmost city of any size in Mexico, Tapachula lies at the center of the Soconusco mountain region, which extends from the Chiapan mountains to the coast and down into southwestern Guatemala. Significant numbers of European and Asian immigrants—many fleeing World War II and the Communist Revolution in China—were attracted to the area by its coffee- and cacao-driven prosperity, and modern-day Tapachula is still home to a diverse population. Guatemalans come here to shop, do business, find work on the plantations, or escape political persecution, while budget travelers are attracted by the city's amenities and proximity to the border. All this activity has rendered Tapachula a bustling, cosmopolitan town that's even blessed with budget hotels and good cappuccino.

Tapachula, which means "Place of Sour Prickly Pears" in Nahuatl, was originally designated a tribute-paying region of the Aztec empire. Payment was in colored feathers, jade, jaguar pelts, and cacao.

The Izapa archaeological zone, where easy hikes through cacao fields lead you to infrequently visited ruins, lies close to the city. A bit farther away, at the foot of the Tacaná volcano, the cool mountain town of Unión Juárez offers limitless camping, hiking, and swimming.

BASICS

CASAS DE CAMBIO

BITAL (2a Av. Nte., at Calle 1 Pte., tel. 962/5–05–01; open weekdays 10–noon) changes traveler's checks and cash. **Serfin** (Calle 1 Pte., at 4a Av. Nte.) doesn't change money, but has a 24-hour ATM. The **Casa de Cambio** (4a Av. Nte., at Calle 3 Pte., tel. 962/6–51–22; open Mon.–Sat. 7:30–7:30, Sun. 7–1) is the only place in town to exchange Central American currencies, but it does so at poor rates.

CONSULATES

Get a visa ($5) for travel into Guatemala at the **Guatemalan Consulate.** Bring along a photocopy of your passport for faster service. *Calle 2 Ote. 33, at 7a Av. Sur, tel. 962/6–12–52. Open weekdays 8–4.*

CROSSING THE BORDER

Two border crossings lie within easy reach of Tapachula and both are open 24 hours a day, 365 days a year, to accommodate the constant flow of migrant workers. The **Talismán/El Carmen** crossing, 15 km (9 mi) north of Tapachula, is the most convenient for travelers, with frequent onward buses for Quetzaltenango and Guatemala City close at hand. **Ciudad Hidalgo/Tecún Umán** lies farther out of the way—some 40 km (24 mi) south of Tapachula—and sees little tourist traffic. For more general border advice, *see box, below.*

Frequent VW colectivos ply the routes to the Talismán border, leaving every few minutes from outside Tapachula's Unión y Progreso terminal (Calle 5 Pte., between Avs. 12 and 14 Nte.). The 45-minute trip costs 50¢. **Paulino Navarro** buses service Ciudad Hidalgo (45 min, $1) every 15 minutes. Taxis from Tapachula cost $1.50 to Talismán and $3 to Hidalgo.

LAUNDRY

Lava Ropa will wash and dry 3 kilos (6½ pounds) of clothing for $2. *Av. Central Nte. 33, between Central Ote. and Calle 1 Ote., tel. 962/6–35–25. Open Mon.–Sat. 8–8.*

MAIL

The **post office** is a seven-block trek from the centro. They offer all the usual services and will hold mail sent to you at the following address for up to 10 days: Lista de Correos, Tapachula, Chiapas, CP 30700, México. *Calle 1 Ote. 32, at 7a Av. Nte., tel. 962/6–39–22. Open weekdays 8–7, Sat. 9–1.*

MEDICAL AID

Like the name says, **Farmacia 24 Horas** (8a Av. Nte. 25, at Calle 7 Pte., tel. 962/6–24–80) is open round the clock. In a medical emergency, call the **Cruz Roja** (tel. 962/6–19–49).

PHONES

There are two blue **Ladatel** phones on the southwest corner of the zócalo and a few more a block south of the zócalo on Calle 1 Poniente, at 6a Avenida Norte. To make an international collect call dial 09 for an operator.

VISITOR INFORMATION

Housed in the Casa de Cultura, the **SEDETUR** office has two wonderful employees, Magui and Amelinda, who are very proud of their region. They can help you plan treks into the countryside or provide information on crossing into Guatemala. *Between Palacio and Museo, west side of zócalo, tel. 962/5–54–09. Open weekdays 9–3 and 6–9.*

COMING AND GOING

BY BUS

The first-class bus terminal (Calle 17 Ote., at 3a Av. Nte., tel. 962/6–28–81) is about 12 long blocks north of the center. To get here, either take a taxi (75¢) or a CRISTOBAL COLON or LOMA DE SAYULA combi (20¢) up Avenida Central Norte. **Cristóbal Colón** and **UNO** offer first-class direct service to San Cristóbal (6 per day; 9 hrs, $10) and Oaxaca city (2 per day; 14 hrs, $22). Four buses a day go to Salina Cruz (9 hrs, $13) and Mexico City (24 hrs, $36); the evening luxury service is worth the extra bucks.

If your next destination is San Cristóbal (10 hrs, $7) or Comitán (6 hrs, $4), second-class **Transportes Sur** (Calle 9a Pte. 63, between 12a and 14a Avs. Nte.) offers the most frequent service, with about 10 departures per day to each city. **Autobuses General Paulino Navarro** (Calle 7 Pte., at Av. Central Nte., tel. 962/6–31–02), four blocks northeast of the zócalo, offers two second-class buses a day to Tuxtla Gutiérrez (7 hrs, $9) and frequent service to nearby towns and border crossings. **Unión y Progreso** (Calle 5 Pte., between 12a and 14a Avs. Nte., tel. 962/6–33–79) collectivos serve Talismán and Unión Juárez infrequently 5:30 AM–8 PM for 50¢. Frequent colectivos (75¢) also depart for Ciudad Hidalgo and Talismán from the bus stations and along 10a Avenida Norte, near the market.

BY PLANE

Aeroméxico (tel. 962/6–20–50), **AVIACSA** (tel. 962/6–31–47), and **Taesa** (tel. 962/6–37–32) take off from the airport (Carretera 225 Km. 22, tel. 962/6–22–91) for Mexico City. Fares cost $90–$120 one way. All planes depart daily at 7:30 AM, with an additional Taesa flight weekdays at 5 PM. Call or stop by the airport bus office (2 Av. Sur 40, tel. 962/5–12–87) in advance to make arrangements for a colectivo pickup at your doorstep ($4). Private taxis from the airport charge $8.

GETTING AROUND

The city's main sights and many budget hotels are clustered around the zócalo, at the intersections of Calles 3 and 5 Poniente and 4a and 6a Avenidas Norte. Most of the city is easily walkable, but colectivos (20¢), which run daily 5 AM–10 PM, and taxis ($1) crowd the streets and can move you around town cheaply. Two long boulevards, the north–south Avenida Central Norte/Sur and the east–west Calle Central Oriente/Poniente, divide the city into quadrants. Even-numbered calles are south of Avenida Central Poniente/Oriente, and odd-numbered calles are north of it. Even-numbered avenidas are west of Calle Central Norte/Sur, and odd-numbered avenidas are east of it.

WHERE TO SLEEP

Many better-than-average budget hotels are concentrated around the city center.

UNDER $10 • Hospedaje Colonial. Although it looks like another hole-in-the-wall from the street, this downtown hotel is overflowing with character—and potted plants. According to the owners, "hanging herbs keep the bats away," and the beautiful gardens keep the guests happy. The front door is perpetually locked, and if you come in past 11:30 PM you'll earn the owners' extreme displeasure. Rooms are $6 per person. *4a Av. Nte. 31, tel. 962/6–20–52. 10 rooms, all with bath. Luggage storage. Cash only.*

Hospedaje Las Américas. This hotel is just steps away from the mercado and the second-class bus stations. The quiet, clean rooms open onto a tree-filled central courtyard, making them a terrific deal at $10 a double. *10a Av. Nte. 47, tel. 962/6–27–57. 20 rooms, all with bath. Luggage storage. Cash only.*

Hotel Cervantino. Four blocks from the center, this is an exceptionally clean hotel, and all rooms have fans and tables. The management is friendly and extremely helpful. Doubles cost $8. Add a few dollars more if you'd like a TV in your room. *1a Av. Ote. 6, tel. 962/6–16–58. 21 rooms, all with bath. Luggage storage.*

UNDER $15 • Hotel Puebla. You pay a premium for excellent location at this four-story hotel right next to the Palacio Municipal. Spacious rooms have fans, hot water, and access to communal balconies overlooking the Parque Central. Doubles are $12. *Calle 3 Pte. 40, behind Palacio Municipal, tel. 962/6–14–36. 40 rooms, all with bath. Luggage storage. Cash only.*

FOOD

Tapachula has a number of 24-hour restaurants, most of them clustered around the zócalo. **La Flor de Michoacán** (6a Av. Nte., at Calle 7 Pte., no phone) is filled with Guatemalan workers watching TV and slowly sipping 70¢ licuados and nibbling 20¢ tacos into the wee hours. **La Parrilla** (8a Av. Nte. 20, west of zócalo, tel. 962/6–51–98), open daily until midnight, offers cheap sandwiches and breakfasts, as well as beef fillet ($6) with baked potato. Both are cash only.

UNDER $3 • El Mestizo. Savory one-dollar Chinese entrées beckon from the window of this cross-cultural comedor. Pozole ($2) and pancakes ($1) are served up lickety-split. *Calle 7 Pte. 32-A, between 8 and 10 Avs. Nte., no phone. Cash only.*

UNDER $5 • Restaurant Longyin. You won't find any fortune cookies, but the chop suey ($4) and chow mein ($3) are served in heaping portions, with extra MSG, in a commodious open-air setting. The restaurant offers a unique opportunity to spice your Chinese food with salsa picante. *2a Av. Nte. 36, tel. 962/6–24–67. Cash only.*

WORTH SEEING

The labyrinthine **Mercado Sebastián Escobar** (behind the cathedral) is a two-block indoor/outdoor market where tropical fruits, vegetables, live birds, and every trinket you can imagine are sold. The indoor part is open in the morning only, and the fruit selection is best before midday. Also worth a visit is the **Museo Regional del Soconusco,** inside the art deco **Palacio Municipal** (just west of zócalo, tel. 962/6–35–43). The museum displays bits of stelae and other artifacts from nearby ruins, as well as photos of excavation sites. Admission is $1.25 (free Sunday) and it's open Tuesday–Sunday 10–5. Next door is the **Casa de Cultura** (admission free; open daily 9–9). Upstairs, regional displays of arts and crafts appear from time to time. Marimba, classical, and ambient music is often featured in the **Parque Central**'s gazebo at 6 PM. Check with the Casa de Cultura for a schedule of free events. The **Banana Safari** and **Chula Zoo** complex (Libramiento Sur Km. 1, no phone; open daily 9–5) offers a glimpse of wild animals on a former banana plantation. Admission is $1.25. To get here, take a taxi ($2) from the center.

If you're in town the first two weeks of March, you'll witness the **Feria Internacional,** Tapachula's big yearly bash in celebration of the agricultural, artistic, and commercial richness of the area. Another big event is the **Feria de San Agustín,** which celebrates the town's patron saint with songs, libations, and dance August 20–28.

NEAR TAPACHULA

The seldom-visited **Izapa** archaeological zone is only 15 minutes from Tapachula on the road to Talismán. The ruins are said to provide a link between Olmec and early Mayan cultures. Closest to Tapachula are groups A and B, about 20 minutes down a jungle path marked by a sign at the highway. Group A is in a sad state of neglect. Continue farther along the path and through the cacao fields to Group B, where you'll find a huge pyramid and some better-preserved stelae. The largest and most impressive ruins (Group F) are visible from the highway and are less than a kilometer farther along the path, on the left-hand side.

TIPS FOR TRAVEL TO GUATEMALA

To facilitate onward passage into Guatemala, arrive at the border checkpoint early in the day and have your passport and Mexican tourist card handy. You should also have small denominations of both American dollars and Guatemalan quetzals on hand to help wend your way through the excessive border town bureaucracy. Though you should rebuff shifty moneychangers and their poor rates, realize this may be your last opportunity to get rid of unwanted pesos.

Guatemalan tourist cards cost $5, regardless of your nationality; if you're planning a lengthy visit, be insistent that you receive the 90-day tourist card, rather than a 30-day one (which you'll have to jump through hoops to renew). Check with the consulates in Comitán and Tapachula (see above) for the latest requirements.

Border crossings in Chiapas are at Ciudad Cuauhtémoc, Talismán, and Hidalgo—for details on hours and transportation for each, see Basics in Comitán and Tapachula, above.

This fully restored ceremonial center—complete with pyramids, a ball court, altars, and stelae—enjoyed its heyday around 300–200 BC. To reach the sites, take one of the frequent Talismán-bound colectivos from either of Tapachula's second-class stations and ask the driver to let you off at Izapa. Buses (60¢) run 5:30 AM–8 PM. The sites are open daily 8–5; admission is $2, free on Sunday.

UNION JUAREZ

If you're going to be in the area for any length of time, do not fail to visit Unión Juárez, 30 km (18 mi) northeast of Tapachula. This coffee-growing town clings to the base of the dormant **Volcán Tacaná** (13,500 ft). The town offers good food and lodging, plus proximity to great swimming and hiking. Its steep cobblestone roads wind through coffee plantations and cool, lushly forested valleys crisscrossed by rivers. Close to town, the **Cascadas de Muxbal** (Muxbal Waterfalls) have a deep pool for swimming and are situated in a narrow canyon hung with gargantuan ferns. There are also pools for bathing on the nearby **Río Mala.** If you're up for a short hike, two sublime vantage points each lie about an hour's trek out of town: **Pico de Loro** (Parrot's Beak) is a rock outcropping that affords a beautiful view of Guatemala and the ocean. **La Ventana** (The Window), the other vista point, is on a hill overlooking a forested valley. Ask for directions and maps at the Palacio Municipal on the zócalo during business hours. If you're looking for something more challenging, the climb to the top of Tacaná is a daylong enterprise. You'll have to spend the night on the summit in some simple huts (free of charge); bring a warm bedroll. Ask Don Humberto Ríos at **Restaurante La Montaña** or Roberto Moody at **Posada Aljoad** (*see* Where to Sleep and Eat, *below*) about guide service and accommodations for a climb up the volcano. Whatever you choose to do, head out early in the morning, since the fog and rain arrive like clockwork every afternoon.

COMING AND GOING

Direct buses between Tapachula and Unión Juárez are hard to come by. The simplest way to get here is to catch a minibus or combi from 12a Avenida Norte in Tapachula to the town of Cacahuatán (40 min, 70¢), where you can squeeze into one of the always-crowded VW buses that frequently make the trip to Unión Juárez (1 hr, $1).

WHERE TO SLEEP AND EAT

Pay $14 a night for a double room or $25 for a private chalet at the A-frame **Hotel Colonial Campestre** (Hidalgo 1) and enjoy hot water, TVs, phones, and even a disco. Your other option is to join nature enthusiasts and groups of young hikers at the **Hotel Posada Aljoad** (Mariano Escobedo, right off zócalo), where doubles cost $10 and the hot water is temperamental. Neither hotel has a private phone line, but you can call the community phone line (tel. 962/2–02–25) for lodging information in Spanish. **La Montaña** and **Restaurante Carmelita,** both on Avenida Juárez in the zócalo, serve three tasty meals daily at shoestring prices. Don't leave without trying La Montaña's *plátanos fritos* (fried plantains; $1.50).

VILLAHERMOSA

Villahermosa, as the capital of Tabasco state, is largely the product of the region's rich oil reserves, which in the '70s brought prosperity and expansion to the city. Huge luxury hotels, active cultural centers and museums, and the massive Tabasco 2000 complex—with its decadent, postmodern architecture—are among the additions. The capital of Tabasco was originally established farther north under the name of Santa Maria de la Victoria, but was relocated after British, French, and Dutch pirates repeatedly looted the area for cacao and *palo de tinta* (a tree used for making dyes) during the 16th and 17th centuries. The city was moved south, away from the river connecting it to the pirates' sea route, and was renamed San Juan Bautista. In the late 1700s, King Felipe II of Spain gave it its final name: Villahermosa. The region came back into prominence in the world market in the early 1900s, when exports of bananas and cacao began to flourish.

Festivals are an important part of local life: **La Feria del Desarrollo** (Development Fair), held during late April and early May, celebrates the diversity of culture in the state of Tabasco, with all 17 municipalities showcasing their typical dances, arts, and music. There's also a parade of decorated boats down the Río Grijalva, with fireworks and general revelry. The main action takes place in Parque de la Choca, past the Tabasco 2000 building. In February, **Carnaval** is especially big here, with music, dance contests, and processions. Ash Wednesday is marked by citywide water-balloon fights.

At its worst, Villahermosa is an excessive jumble of streamlined '70s-style cement buildings, expressways reminiscent of Los Angeles, and garish superstores filled with imported furniture, housewares, and clothing. At its best, Villahermosa is an oasis of culture, with museums, a beautiful archaeological park, and an excellent ecological reserve. Many affordable hotels serve as a base for exploring the rest of the state, where nontouristed beaches and quiet towns await. At any rate, be prepared for a brief bit of culture shock, especially if you've been tramping around the rural, remote Chiapan highlands.

BASICS

AMERICAN EXPRESS

The air-conditioned **Turismo Nieves** travel agency also runs a full-service American Express desk that will hold mail, replace lost cards, and cash personal checks for cardholders, as well as deliver Money-Grams and exchange or replace traveler's checks for all travelers. Mailing address: American Express, Turismo Nieves, Sarlat Incidencia 202, Villahermosa, Tabasco, CP 86000, México. *Sarlat Incidencia 202, at Fidencia, tel. 93/14–18–88. From Zona Luz, walk 1 block north on Carranza past Parque Juárez and turn left. Open weekdays 9–6, Sat. 9–noon.*

BOOKSTORES

If you read Spanish, **Librería Bookworm de Cultura** (27 de Febrero 603, Plazuela la Aguila, tel. 93/12–24–24) has a large selection of novels and books on Tabasco's natural and cultural heritage. **Librería El Alba** (Madero 616, tel. 93/12–22–24) also has Spanish novels, textbooks, and crafts. Both are open Monday–Saturday 8–8.

CASAS DE CAMBIO

At last count, there were nine banks squeezed in among the shops and budget hotels of the Zona Luz area. All the major banks—**Banamex, Bancomer,** and **BITAL**—have ATMs and will change U.S. dollars and traveler's checks weekdays 10–5.

For longer hours, head to **Blahberl** (27 de Febrero 1537, tel. 93/13–34–19; open weekdays 8:30–6:30, Sat. 8:30–4). They change Canadian dollars as well as currency from most major European countries. For a commission, you can also cash personal checks written in U.S. dollars. To get here, take a cathedral-bound bus down 27 de Febrero and ask to be let off at *el reloj con tres caras* (the clock with three faces).

EMERGENCIES

For emergencies, dial **06** from any telephone in Villahermosa. The **police** can be reached at 93/15–39–14 or 93/15–43–45.

LAUNDRY

Acua Lavandería (Reforma 502, tel. 93/14–37–65; open Mon.–Sat. 8–8), just outside of the Zona Luz near the river, will wash 1 kilo (2 pounds) of clothes for about $1. Same-day service is 50¢ more. **La Burbuja** (Bastor Zozaya 621, at Joaquín Camelo, no phone; open weekdays 8–8, Sat. 8–4) offers reliable next-day service at $1 per kilo.

MAIL

Villahermosa's most convenient post office for travelers is in the Zona Luz. They'll hold mail sent to you at the following address for up to 10 days: Lista de Correos, Villahermosa, Tabasco, CP 86001, México. *Sáenz 131, tel. 93/12–10–40. Open weekdays 8–7, Sat. 9–noon.*

MEDICAL AID

For 24-hour emergency medical service go to **Cruz Roja** (Cesar Saudino, Col. Primera de Mayo, tel. 93/15–55–55). Pharmacies abound in the Zona Luz, but all close by 9 PM. **Farmacia Mariana** (27 de Febrero 626, tel. 93/14–23–66), a few blocks up from the Zona Luz, is open 24 hours.

PHONES

You can't walk 10 paces in the Zona Luz without running into a **Ladatel** phone. From these you can make international calls using a Ladatel Plus card, sold at most *papelerías* (stationery stores) in the area. To make an international collect call dial 09 for operator assistance. If you want to make a cash call, head for the caseta in **Café Barra** (Lerdo de Tejada 608; open Mon.–Sat. 7–1 and 3:30–10). It charges a small fee for unaccepted collect calls. There is also a 24-hour caseta across from the ADO station (*see* Coming and Going, *below*).

VISITOR INFORMATION

The **Tabasco Tourism Institute** offers the free magazine *Mundo Maya*, a blurry map of the city, and information on cultural events. The topsy-turvy office is ensconced within an unmarked stone building. To get here, take the TABASCO 2000 or PALACIO MUNICIPAL bus from either the *malecón* (boardwalk) or Parque Juárez. *Paseo Tabasco 1504, Tabasco 2000 Complex, tel. 93/16–36–33. Open weekdays 9–3 and 6–9.*

COMING AND GOING

BY BUS

The first-class bus station (Francisco Javier Mina 297, at Lino Merino) is big and efficient, with a computerized reservation system. **ADO** (tel. 93/12–76–92), **Cristóbal Colón** (tel. 93/14–22–40), and **UNO** (tel. 93/14–20–54) all provide frequent service to the following destinations: Chetumal (9 hrs, $15), Mérida (9 hrs, $19), Mexico City (16 hrs, $30), Oaxaca city (16 hrs, $22), Palenque (1½ hrs, $5), Tapachula (16 hrs, $22), Teapa (1½ hrs, $1.50), and Tuxtla Gutiérrez (6½ hrs, $9). Be sure to buy your ticket in advance, as lines are always long and seats sell out. The station houses a couple of overpriced places to eat, as well as 24-hour luggage storage ($1–$2 per day). To reach the city center, walk 12 long blocks southeast or take a bus marked PARQUE JUAREZ. Buses marked CENTRO will take you to the Palacio Municipal; those marked CENTRAL will take you to the Central Camionera (*see below*). A collective taxi from the station to the center costs 65¢.

The huge **Central Camionera** (Ruíz Cortínez 501, east of intersection with Javier Mina, tel. 93/12–47–03) is the city's second-class bus station. Buses range from clean and plush to fleabags on wheels, and serve a dizzying array of destinations more frequently and cheaply than the first-class buses. Ticket-sellers from a zillion different bus companies will get you to Mexico City ($20), Puebla ($16), Jalapa ($14), Veracruz city ($9), Palenque ($2), and Teapa ($1). To arrive here from the Zona Luz, take any bus marked CENTRAL along the malecón.

Buses to the coast and Comalcalco leave from the **Transportes Somellera** terminal (Ruíz Cortínez, at Llergo, tel. 93/14–41–18). There is service to Comalcalco (1½ hrs, $1.50) every half hour and to Paraíso (2 hrs, $2) every hour. The easiest way to get here is to take a bus to the Central Camionera, cross the bridge over the highway, and walk three long blocks down Ruíz Cortínez toward the Hotel Maya Tabasco. A block or so past the hotel you'll see the station on your left.

BY PLANE

The airport (tel. 93/12–18–30) is served by **Aeroméxico** (tel. 93/12–15–28), **AVIACSA** (tel. 93/14–47–70), **Mexicana** (tel. 93/12–11–64), and **Aerolitoral** (tel. 93/12–15–28). There are daily flights to Acapulco, Cancún, Havana, Los Angeles, Mazatlán, and Mérida, as well as several daily flights to México City ($56–$88 one-way). No public transportation serves the airport. Taxis charge $8 for private service or $5 for collective service into town, a 30-minute trip. Luggage storage ($3 per day) is available at the airport.

GETTING AROUND

Sprawling Villahermosa can be difficult to navigate (even with the blurry map given out at the tourist office) but a few prominent landmarks, abundant city buses, and cheap taxis help somewhat. The center of town is bordered by three avenues, along which lie many of the major points of interest. The main highway is **Ruíz Cortínez,** a huge expressway with swift and deadly traffic. The Central Camionera, the Transportes Somellera terminal, and the largest food market are all here. Cortínez turns south at the **Parque Museo La Venta**—you'll see the rectangular *mirador* (viewing tower) jutting out where it intersects with **Paseo Tabasco,** another main avenue. This street runs from the **Tabasco 2000 complex** in the west—with its huge, black mushroom of a water tower—to the **malecón,** which runs along the bank of the Río Grijalva, in the east. CICOM (*see* Worth Seeing, *below*) is south of the center on **Carlos Pellicer,** which is the name the malecón takes on just past the roundabout where it hits Paseo Tabasco.

The bus system in sprawling Villahermosa can be confusing— so confusing, in fact, that you'll probably see more than one local anxiously asking the bus driver for reassurance about the route.

Taking all of the above into consideration, the streets that will be most important to you are: Francisco Javier Mina, which heads north to Cortínez and the bus stations along the highway; Méndez, which runs from Llergo to the malecón and crosses Javier Mina; and Madero, which runs eight long blocks from Cortínez to the malecón, parallel to Javier Mina. Follow the one-way flow of traffic north on Madero and you'll pass the **Parque Benito Juárez,** at the northeast corner of the **Zona Luz.** The Zona Luz (or Zona Remodelada) is a recently remodeled pedestrian-only area bordered by Madero on the east, Zaragoza on the north, Castillo to the west, and 27 de Febrero to the south. This is where you'll find the best budget lodging and restaurants.

BY BUS

Destinations are usually marked on bus windshields, but routes are often very roundabout. To reach the tourist office or La Venta, take either the TABASCO 2000 or PALACIO MUNICIPAL bus from Madero, one block north of Parque Juárez. From the same stop, you can catch buses for CICOM (*see* Worth Seeing, *below*). For buses to the second-class bus station or market, take either the CENTRAL or MERCADO bus from the malecón to the highway. Bus fare is 20¢.

BY TAXI

Taxis can be hard to come by in the city, especially private cabs. Most taxi drivers pack their Nissans with passengers colectivo-style; rides are cheap within the city (60¢–$1), but are a rip-off to the airport and Yumká, neither of which are served by public transit. In front of the first-class bus station and on Madero near Reforma, wait in line at a taxi stand and someone will find you the right car once you announce your destination. Taxis (30 min, $5–$8) are unfortunately the only way to the airport. Call 93/15–83–33 for a pickup.

WHERE TO SLEEP

Villahermosa has a number of large hotels with standard rooms and competitive prices. Since many hotels have permanent residents, you may have to check a few before you find space, but most places will store your luggage for you while you look. The best time to search is noon–1, the usual checkout time. Fans or air-conditioning are more important here, and easier to come by, than hot water. Budget hotels are clustered in the Zona Luz, on Madero and along side streets such as Lerdo de Tejada. The quietest hotels overlook pedestrian walkways. **Hotel Tabasco** (Lerdo de Tejada 317, tel. 93/12–00–77) is the cheapest hotel in town that still maintains reasonable standards of cleanliness. Doubles cost $6.75, cash only.

UNDER $10 • Hotel Madero. The conscientious proprietor has seen to it that this is one of the cleanest, most comfortable budget hotels in the city. The rooms are decorated in various tranquil shades of blue, the bathrooms have hot water, and the staff is more than eager to help you find your way around town. Doubles are $9. *Madero 301, tel. 93/12–05–16. 28 rooms, all with bath. Luggage storage. Cash only.*

Hotel Oriente. This modest, fairly clean (although somewhat dark) hotel, on a busy section of Madero, is a decent value. Request the "penthouse" rooms (Nos. 43 and 44), with cross-ventilation from three sets of windows. Doubles are $10. Luxuries like air-conditioning and a TV cost a few dollars more. *Madero 425, tel. 93/12–11–01. 22 rooms, all with bath. Luggage storage. Cash only.*

Hotel Palma de Mallorca. The majesty of this hotel is fading fast, but rooms are all large and airy. Rooms with fans cost $9 a double. The hot water in the shower eventually arrives if you wait patiently. *Madero 510, tel. 93/12–01–45. 36 rooms, all with bath. Luggage storage. Cash only.*

Hotel San Miguel. This is one of the more popular budget places and is consistently full. The clean, basic rooms all have phones, TVs, and private baths. Doubles are $7. For a few dollars more you'll get air-conditioning. *Lerdo de Tejada 315, tel. 93/12–15–00. 45 rooms, all with bath. Luggage storage. Reservations advised. Cash only.*

Hotel Santa Lucia. This centrally located hotel provides well-furnished, clean doubles ($9) with hot water and real bathtubs. Some rooms are darker than others, but all go quickly. Make sure your fan works before settling in. *Madero, between Lerdo de Tejada and Reforma, no phone. Next to Hotel Don Carlos. 30 rooms, all with bath. Cash only.*

UNDER $25 • Hotel Don Carlos. This recently remodeled downtown hotel has long been popular for its friendly atmosphere and good service. Rooms all have cable TVs, phones, and air-conditioning; the suites have mini-bars. Doubles are $22. *Madero 422, tel. 93/12–24–99. 80 rooms and 14 suites, all with bath. Restaurant, bar, lounge, parking.*

UNDER $45 • Hotel Cencali. The Cencali is a classy colonial-style inn inside the parklike new hotel zone with lakes and lush greenery. Cheerful rooms have views of either the lakes or the lagoon; some also have balconies overlooking groves of coconut palms and almond trees. Air-conditioned rooms cost $44 for a double. The easiest way to get here is by taxi ($2.50) from the stand at the first-class bus station. *Juárez and Paseo Tabasco, tel. 93/15–19–99. 119 rooms, all with bath. Restaurant, bar, pool, parking.*

FOOD

Variety is not a problem in Villahermosa; frozen yogurt shops, bakeries, and supermarkets fill the Zona Luz. The large, enclosed **Mercado Pino Suárez** (Bastar Zozaya, 2 blocks west of Río Grijalva) is open mornings and has a good selection of fruit and bread, plus a dozen or so cheap taco stands. You can also cool off with a *paleta* (popsicle) or a ladle of liquid heaven from the many *agua fresca* (fresh-fruit drink) stands featuring icy vats of tamarind, lime, pineapple, horchata, and other thirst quenchers. **Mini-Leo** (Juárez 504) is a citywide chain serving burgers, fries, tacos, quesadillas, and the like. **Las 2 Naciones** (Juárez 533, tel. 93/12–12–22; closed Sun.) has tempting pastries perfect for a quick, cheap breakfast.

UNDER $5 • Aquarius. You'll find vegetarian sandwiches, soups, and yogurt, as well as medicinal teas and vitamins at Aquarius's two locations. A filling sandwich with beans, cheese, avocado, and alfalfa sprouts costs $1.25. Serious health-food nuts can detoxify their systems with a beet, carrot, and celery juice concoction called *vampiro*, which leaves the mouth bright red. Wheat breads are also sold here by the loaf. *Zaragoza 513, in Zona Luz, tel. 93/12–05–79. Closed Sat. Other location: Javier Mina 309, 2 blocks from ADO bus station, tel. 93/14–25–37. Cash only.*

La Noria. A welcome addition to the Villahermosa eating scene, this Lebanese enclave serves homemade hummus (chickpea spread; 50¢) and tabbouleh (salad made with cracked wheat, mint, and tomato), as well as an authentic barrage of breads and brochettes. Owner Señora Amalin Yabor Elías has been trying to wean locals away from greasy foods for five years, and the trend is finally starting to catch on. *6a Av. Méndez 1008, tel. 93/14–16–59. From first-class bus station, walk 2 blocks south on Mina, right on Méndez. Closed Sun. Cash only.*

El Torito Valenzuela. The specialty here is tender, meaty tacos (35¢–65¢ each), made with pork, beef, or even brains, then loaded with cilantro and onion and served on fresh, handmade tortillas. The *queso fundido* (cheese fondue), quesadillas, and hearty breakfast specials are also excellent. Their comida corrida ($3) is more than one person should ever eat in one sitting: soup, tortillas, entrée, french fries, beans, rice, fried plantains, a drink, and dessert. *27 de Febrero, at Madero, tel. 93/14–18–89. Cash only.*

UNDER $10 • Birbiri's. Locals swear by the seafood at this out-of-the-way, teal-and-pink restaurant. After your shrimp in garlic, sip a drink from the full bar and enjoy the singer who performs nightly. *Madero 1032, tel. 93/12–32–41. Closed Sun. Cash only.*

WORTH SEEING

Villahermosa is rich with places to stroll: along the malecón, through Benito Juárez Park, above the river at the end of Aldama, and around the Zona Luz. Sunday is family day, which means bigger crowds everywhere in the city.

MUSEUMS

Most of Villahermosa's museums offer free guided tours in Spanish. The museums in the Zona Luz are cheap (or free), only a short walk from the budget lodgings, and hold worthwhile evening events. All museums are closed Monday and free on Sunday.

PARQUE-MUSEO LA VENTA • Villa's most touted attraction, this sprawling park displays all the major finds from the La Venta archaeological site, on the border with Veracruz state. The site was threatened by oil drilling in the late '50s, but saved by arts patron and poet extraordinaire Carlos Pellicer Cámara. The junglelike park has dirt paths that wind past 30 or so Olmec artifacts, like giant carved heads, mosaics, and stelae. Provided there's a group of four or more, free guided tours in Spanish leave every half hour from the entrance; tours in English can be arranged with guides at the entrance for around $5. Buy your tickets before 4 PM and bring bug repellent for the 30- to 40-minute walk through the steamy jungle. *Ruíz Cortínez, tel. 93/15–22–28. From Parque Juárez, take a TABASCO 2000 bus, get off at corner of Paseo Tabasco and Ruíz Cortínez, and walk NE along lakeshore to entrance. Admission: $2. Open daily 9–5.*

MUSEO REGIONAL DE ANTROPOLOGIA CARLOS PELLICER CAMARA • This museum in the CICOM cultural center (*see below*) emphasizes the Olmec's influence on the cultures that succeeded them, particularly the Maya to the south and the Huasteca to the north. There are a few well-worn Olmec heads, altars, and stelae, as well as a number of pieces from as far away as Nayarit, Chihuahua, and the Yucatán. *CICOM, Carlos Pellicer 511, tel. 93/12–95–21. Catch any CICOM bus along Madero. Admission: 60¢. Open daily 9–8.*

MUSEUMS IN THE ZONA LUZ • Near the budget lodgings are three museums, each worth at least a quick look. The small, free **Casa-Museo Carlos Pellicer** (Sáenz 203, tel. 93/12–01–57) has miscellanea that once belonged to this famous Tabascan poet, who funded the excavation of La Venta and helped save its treasures from destruction. Most interesting is the plaster cast of his face (taken at his death). The free **Museo de Cultura Popular** (Zaragoza 810, tel. 93/12–11–17) has mannequins dressed in local costumes, as well as a collection of Tabasco's famous carved gourds. In the back is a "typical" hut and a small pond with a few live *pejelargartos* (alligator gars), a kind of large, toothy, freshwater fish popular in regional dishes. The largest of these museums is the **Museo de Historia de Tabasco** (Juárez, at 27 de Febrero, no phone), with displays chronicling the history of Tabasco from pre-Hispanic times through the modern industrial age. It houses mostly posters and illustrations, but there are also a few old books, colonial uniforms, and even an antique X-ray machine that once belonged to a Villahermosan doctor. The interior is covered with many beautiful tiles, hence its nickname *La Casa de los Azulejos* (House of Tiles). Admission is 65¢. All three museums are open Tuesday–Sunday 10–4.

CULTURAL CENTERS

Villahermosa's numerous free cultural centers are a testimony to the fact that Tabasco's oil revenues were put to good use. Galleries, music, and dance performances are all available at the places below free (or almost free) of charge.

CENTRO CULTURAL DE LA UNIVERSIDAD AUTONOMA DE TABASCO • Just steps away from the Zona Luz, this cultural center sponsors a wide variety of events and has two galleries showcasing local artists. There are free films (in English or with English subtitles) Wednesday night, and "cultural Thursday" features music, dance, or performing arts. *27 de Febrero 640, tel. 93/12–45–57. Open weekdays 8 AM–9 PM.*

CENTRO CULTURAL DE VILLAHERMOSA • Across from the Zona Luz, this air-conditioned center has wonderful art exhibits from all over Mexico, plus foreign films, concerts, a shop dedicated to Tabasco's crafts, and a good café. All performances and exhibits are free. *Madero, at Zaragoza, tel. 93/14–55–52. Open Mon.–Sat. 10–9.*

CICOM • The Center for the Investigation of Olmec and Maya Cultures (CICOM) lies along the malecón, just west of the Río Grijalva. Of main interest is the Museo Regional de Antropología Carlos Pellicer Cámara (*see above*). Near the museum is the **Teatro Esperanza Iris,** a modern, plush, red-curtained center for national and regional events. Major events, such as performances by the National Ballet, tend to be jam-packed and cost $3–$7. The frequent lesser-known attractions—such as local dance and folk music performances—are often free and usually only half full.

CICOM also houses the mammoth **public library** (open Mon.–Sat. 9–8, Sun. 9–6), where you'll find an impressive collection of books in Spanish and English (look on the shelves upstairs and to the right for English titles). On Sunday, free movies (in English or with English subtitles) are shown three times a day in the auditorium to the left of the main library entrance. On weekdays, videos are shown at 7 PM. There's also a good bookstore here. *Carlos Pellicer, south of Paseo Tabasco. From Parque Juárez, take a CICOM bus. Open Tues.–Sun. 10–4.*

ART GALLERIES

Calle Sáenz in the Zona Luz features two small art galleries. Located in an old house, the **Galería Tabasco** (Sáenz 122, tel. 93/121–43–66; open Tues.–Sat. 3–8) features exhibits by local artists. Styles range from your basic still-life oil paintings to surreal dreamscapes. Just up the street is **Galería El Jaguar Despertado** (Sáenz 117, tel. 93/14–12–44; open Tues.–Sat. 4–10 PM), a combination café, art gallery, and bookshop. Admission to both galleries is free.

YUMKA CENTRO DE INTERPRETACION Y CONVIVENCIA CON LA NATURALEZA

Yumká, the Mayan name for a magical dwarf who looks after the jungles, is a 617-hectare (250-acre) ecological park featuring a tropical rain forest, savanna, and lagoon, each with its corresponding flora and fauna. Yumká's brochures highlight the imported African animals that draw Tabascans into the park, but the main focus is actually the Tabascan rain forest and lagoon ecosystems. The two-hour guided tour—led by professional biologists—takes you through the rain forest by foot, across the savanna by open-air tram, and over the lagoon by raft. Dr. Luis Palazuelos, who oversees the operation, can provide further details for those interested. *No phone. From Restaurant Turístico La Venta (outside of Parque La Venta on hwy), take a YUMKA bus ($1) or a taxi ($4.50). Admission: $2. Open daily 9–5.*

AFTER DARK

For a modern and apparently cosmopolitan city, most of Villahermosa goes to bed surprisingly early. Around dinnertime (6:30–8 PM) is the prime time to be out and about, as this is when street bands and dancers entertain crowds at the city's plazas. **Café Casino** (Juárez 531, at Zaragos) and **Café Barra** (Lerdo de Tejada 608), both open Monday–Saturday 9–9, offer cappuccino, espresso, and lively crowds. By 10 PM, however, the Zona Luz is a virtual ghost town. You've one good option if you're in the mood for dancing, and that's **Tequila Rock** (tel. 93/16–44–00), a modern, neon-lit extension of the Holiday Inn in Tabasco 2000. The young and trendy spend their weekend evenings here. Frequent events at Villahermosa's cultural centers (*see* Worth Seeing, *above*) are another way to entertain yourself during the evenings.

BARS

For a variety of live Latin music, head to the bar in **Hotel Don Carlos** (Madero 518, tel. 93/12–24–99), just across from the Zona Luz. Bands start about 9:30 PM and keep swingin' until 1:30 in the morning. There's no cover, no minimum, and drink prices aren't too outrageous: $2 for a beer, $2.75 for a margarita. **Baccarat "Ladies Bar"** (Sánchez Marmol 410, across from Parque Juárez, tel. 93/14–17–50) is a small, upstairs place with soft lights, wood paneling, and velvet seats. Live, mellow jazz plays weekend nights, 8–11. Contrary to the name, most of the clientele seems to be single and male, but the atmosphere is relatively relaxing.

NEAR VILLAHERMOSA

COMALCALCO

One of the easternmost Maya sites, Comalcalco is best known for the fired brick with which all of its lasting edifices were constructed—it's the only known site in the Maya empire where these kinds of bricks were used. Because the jungle in these parts had no rock, the Chontal Maya who lived here used a mixture of clay, sand, and ground conch shell to form thin reddish bricks that were fired and used for 282 buildings covering an area of 10 square km (4 square mi). The city was built in the 7th century, and its sloping roofs (suitable for repelling heavy rains) and stucco figures show evidence of the influence of Palenque (*see above*).

Comalcalco has two major groups of buildings and many unexcavated grassy mounds. **Temple I,** the main pyramid, is on the large plaza. A flight of red-painted steps leads you up to the **Great Acropolis** and **Temples IV–VII.** Temple VI features a huge stucco mask representing the sun god. From the hill of the acropolis, you can enjoy a view of the thick jungle canopy punctuated by cacao plantations. Since the temples at the site lack description, visit the **museum** first for a chronological breakdown of the site. The ticket window closes at 4 PM. Don't forget the insect repellent. *Admission to site and museum: $2, free Sun. Open daily 10–4:30.*

COMING AND GOING

Buses to Comalcalco leave every half hour from **Transportes Somellera** in Villahermosa (*see* Coming and Going, *above*). The last buses back to Villahermosa leave Comalcalco's main bus station, known as **La Central/Comalcalco** (Méndez 411, tel. 931/4–00–27), around 6 PM. From the Comalcalco station you can take a microbus (25¢) directly to the ruins or to the highway drop-off point for the ruins, a 1-km (½-mi) walk away. Comalcalco has modest hotel and food offerings, but it's easier to make this a day trip from Villahermosa. Tabasco's coast is only 21 km (12 mi) from the Comalcalco ruins; you can catch a bus (35¢) marked PARAISO at the intersection of the highway with the road from the ruins.

THE TABASCAN COAST

Although once pristine, Tabasco's coastline suffered a sort of black death during the '70s oil boom. Currently the effects aren't readily apparent in the beaches listed below. Rather, the most visible uncleanliness now stems from humans too lazy to pick up their trash. Few foreign travelers travel to the Tabasco coast, while Mexicans only hit these beaches on weekends and Semana Santa. Lodging choices on the beaches tend to be no more than a scattering of palapas with hammock hooks; however, most are within day-trip distance of towns with hotels and restaurants, such as Villahermosa, Comalcalco, and Paraíso.

The beaches with the most facilities (showers, lockers, shaded restaurants, and palapas) are **Limón** and **El Bellote,** both within a short bus ride of the medium-size city of **Paraíso.** Both have long stretches of white sand and pleasant shallow water with small wavelets. Palm tree–lined **Limón** has family-size cabañas that go for $18 (rates double in April), lots of palapas, and a few restaurants offering grilled chicken. A better place to eat is in El Bellote at **Restaurante/Bar Viña del Mar,** which offers a never-ending list of tasty Atlantic-coast seafood dishes for less than $6 apiece. Sometimes a local Mexican jazz ensemble will play during dinner. Nearby, the staff at **La Posta** gives out information on boat rentals to beach spots along the Laguna Mecoacán ($6 for a boat ride) and places to hang your hammock ($3 a night). Limón has endless rows of coconut trees, giving you a better chance to hang your hammock for free.

Colectivos leave for the beaches fairly frequently from Paraíso's bus station. Second-class **Transportes La Somellera** buses run between Paraíso and Villahermosa (1½ hrs, $2), and microbuses leave from Comalcalco (15 min, 20¢), or take a taxi for $3 from Comalcalco.

TEAPA

Tabasco is not all oil fields and bug-filled wetlands. The air feels remarkably clean and fresh in the city of Teapa, just one-hour's drive through banana fields south of Villahermosa. The town's pretty **zócalo,** shaded by enormous trees, houses a community library at one end. The Río Teapa runs right through town, offering lazy swimming (the best spot is just off the main street near the zócalo). Otherwise spend your time taking excursions out of town for a cooling swim, a healthful sulfur bath, or some subterranean exploration.

The Puyacatengo river in **Tacotalpa,** a short bus ride away on the road between Teapa and Villahermosa, has rapids and is a popular place with locals. Camping is safe here if you're not alone; there are no real facilities though, so bring everything you'll need to be self-sufficient for a few days. A 6-km (4-mi) bus ride toward the town of Pichucalco and a $2 entrance fee will buy you pleasant camping and almost unlimited hedonism at **El Azufre Spa,** where the noxious sulfur springs are known for their healing properties. Once you've paid the entrance fee, you're free to store your stuff in the administration office, enjoying use of the pools, palapas, and picnic tables.

If you prefer something a bit more strenuous, you can roam around inside the **Grutas de Coconá,** a set of spectacular caves out in the country. A bus marked MULTIGRUTAS leaves for the caves every half hour or so from Teapa's zócalo. To walk here, go down Méndez to the Pemex station and turn right onto Carlos Madrazo—a green sign alerts you—and follow the road about 2 km (1 mi) until it turns to countryside; you'll find the grutas shortly thereafter. Once here, pay the 50¢ fee and enter the caves, where you'll hear only the squeaking of tiny bats and the dripping of water. The caves may not be lighted, so bring a flashlight and see if you can make out the figures of King Kong and his family, a giant peanut, a cow's tongue, a headless chicken, and, of course, Jesus Christ in the rocks. Be careful about going solo or late in the afternoon, as robberies have been known to occur. The caves are open daily 10–4.

COMING AND GOING

Autotransportes Villahermosa Teapa (Méndez 218, tel. 932/2–00–07) has hourly buses to Villahermosa ($2 1st class, $1 2nd class) between 5 AM and 8 PM. The station can be hard to find—look for a small square with a giant tree in the middle, and lots of maroon taxis parked outside; it's about five blocks from the zócalo, where the island in the middle of the main road begins. Arrive early, as buses fill quickly and folks line up for tickets long before they go on sale (15 minutes before departure).

GETTING AROUND

Teapa has one main street that passes the zócalo. It begins as 21 de Marzo, changes to Carlos Ramos at the Pemex station, and changes again to Gregorio Méndez as it approaches the zócalo. Many of the city's side streets are pedestrian walkways, and the town is definitely manageable on foot. Buses and colectivos to the grutas and other attractions leave from the zócalo and from the lime-green clock on the outskirts of town.

WHERE TO SLEEP AND EAT

The **Hotel Azufre** (for directions see El Azufre Spa, above) rents huge rooms ($14) that sleep one to four persons, all with fans and private bathrooms. Price includes admission to the spa. **Casa de Huéspedes Miye** (Méndez 211, 2 blocks from zócalo, tel. 932/2–04–20) has small rooms and plant-strewn hallways. Singles with communal baths are $4, doubles $5; rooms with private baths for one or two are $10. There's no hot water, but you probably won't need it. Pastel rooms, a cheery patio, and a lobby filled with porcelain animals make the **Hotel Jardín** (Plaza Independencia 123, tel. 932/2–00–27) unique. The airy rooms with bath (cold water) are $7.50 for doubles. All of the above accept cash only.

Restaurants in Teapa tend to be either expensive or of the greasy-food variety. It's best to stick to the 50¢ sandwiches from any of the many hole-in-the-wall joints like **Café y Antojitos Queta** (across from Casa de Huéspedes Miye), rather than endanger your digestive system exploring more ambitious fare. Another safe option is the **market** right across from the lime-green clock, open early morning to late afternoon.

THE YUCATAN PENINSULA

UPDATED BY PATRICIA ALISAU AND DAN MILLINGTON

At the heart of the ancient Maya city of Chichén Itzá stands El Castillo, a soaring 89-ft pyramid honoring the god Kukulcán. Every year at the spring and autumn equinoxes, the sun casts a shadow on the temple that makes it appear as if the serpent god is slithering down the pyramid to the city's sacred well. In a way, this monument of astrological precision embodies everything that attracts visitors to the Yucatán: the ingenuity of the ancient Maya, whose ruined cities dot the peninsula, and an attraction to the sun that manifests itself today in the form of pale gringos tanning themselves on the beaches of Cozumel, Cancún, Playa del Carmen, and Isla Mujeres.

Encompassing the states of Yucatán, Campeche, and Quintana Roo, as well as the nation of Belize and part of Guatemala, the Yucatán Peninsula covers 113,000 square km (70,000 sq mi). Much of the peninsula is vast, scrubby desert covering porous limestone ("one living rock," as an early Spanish priest put it). Portions of the peninsula are dotted with *cenotes* (spring-fed water holes), clumps of jungle, and telltale mounds hiding unexcavated ruins. The peninsula's eastern coastline has everything you could ask for—clear Caribbean waters, unbroken stretches of beach, stunning coral reefs, and tropical temperatures. Although much of this land is being sold to Mexican and foreign resort developers (causing nearby families to rely more heavily on the tourist trade for their survival), so far only Cancún has been transformed into a truly obscene tourist complex. Isla Mujeres, Playa del Carmen, and Tulum, though tourist-oriented, remain mellow vacation destinations with prices that appeal to the budget traveler.

Many visitors to the Yucatán are attracted by the Maya ruins—ancient cities dating back as far as 2000 BC. Although hundreds of Maya sites dot the Yucatán, only a handful have been excavated. Tulum and Chichén Itzá are the best known, although Uxmal, near Mérida, and Cobá, within easy reach of Caribbean beaches, are also important sites. If you're prepared to forgo the most famous Maya ruins in favor of less spectacular or unexcavated ones, you can wander through entire ruins with only iguanas and monkeys for company.

Often overlooked in the sprint for the beaches and ruins, though, are the Yucatán's colonial-era towns. Huge baroque churches, old mansions, and winding cobblestone streets give these towns a distinctly European look, albeit one patined by tropical heat and humidity. The peninsula was one of the first areas of the New World to be settled by the Spanish, and the legacy of the colonists lives on in towns such as Mérida and Campeche. In other areas of the Yucatán, the Maya people and the culture are very much

Golfo de México

Po

Santa
Clara
Telchac
Puerto
Chabihau
D

Progreso
Yucalpetén
Chicxulub
Puerto
Telchac

Chelem
Motul
Te

Sisal
261
Tixkokoh
Izan

Punta Baz
Dzibilchaltún

Parque Natural
Río Celestún
Hunucmá
Mérida
Kanasín
Hoctún

Umán
180

Celestún
Acanceh
Holca

Punta Nimún
281

Maxcanú
Telchaquilo

Calcehtok
Mayapán
YUC

Oxkintok
Muna

Xpukil

Santa
Elena
Ticul

Santa
Cruz
Uxmal
184
Oxkutzcab

Kabah
Loltún
Tekax

Sayil
Chacmultún

Bolonchén
de Rejón
Labná
Tzucacab

Xlapak

Grutas
Xtacumbilxunaan

Tenabó

Tinúm

Campeche

Punta
Seybaplaya
180
Hopelchén

Vicente
Guerrero

Edzná

Dzibalchén
Chunchintok

La Joya
Hochob

Champotón

CAMPECHE

Río Champotón

Sabancuy

Francisco
Escárcega
186

Xpujil
Río

186
Becan
186

Río Bec

261

Q

e Natural
an Felipe

Parque Natural
Río Lagartos

Santa
Teresa

Sinaí

Cabo
Catoche

Isla
Contoy

San
Felipe

Río
Lagartos

Holbox

Isla Holbox

El
Cuyo

Chiquilá

Punta Sam

Isla
Mujeres

m
avo

Yucatán

Cancún

Puerto
Juárez

Sucilá

Tizimín

Kantunilkin

Tunkas

X-Can

Puerto Morelos

n
Pisté

Chichén
Itzá

Valladolid

Chemax

Punta
Bete

ankanché

Dzitnup

Playa del Carmen

San Miguel

cabá

Cobá

Xcaret

Paamul

TÁN

Akumal
Chemuyil

Palancar
Reef

Cozumel

Xel-Ha

Xcacel

Punta Sur

Tihosuco

Parque
Natural de
Quintana Roo

Tulum

Boca Paila

Santa Rosa

Punta Allen

Sian Ka'an
Biosphere
Reserve

Punta Pájaros

Polyuc

Felipe Carrillo
Puerto

Tupak

INTANA ROO

Punta Herrero

Limónes

Caribbean Sea

Punta El Placer

Laguna de
Bacalar

Puerto Bravo
Punta Río Indio

scondito

Bacalar

El Cocal

Majahual

Nicolás
Bravo

Cenote
Azul

Ucum

Bahía de
Chetumal

Chetumal

Bahía de
Corozal

Palmar

unlich

Xcalak

BELIZE

N

Cayo
Centro

0   30 miles

0   40 km

alive. Indeed, traveling here from elsewhere in Mexico is like entering another country: Most of the population is *mestizo* (people of mixed ancestry), and a fair amount are pure Maya, identifiable by their broad faces, dark skin, and short stature. Maya, not Spanish, is the predominant language in many country towns and villages.

Christianity for many *yucatecos* (Yucatecans) is a mix of Catholicism and traditional animism, a belief that the sun, the earth, the plants, the animals, and the rain are all gods. This melding of the ancient and the new is the result of a particularly bloody and cruel period of colonization. Since Hernán Cortés landed on the shores of the Yucatán in 1519, the Maya have battled for their land and their freedom. The Spanish burned religious texts, including astronomical works, and destroyed stone idols. Disease and forced labor decimated the Maya, but the Spanish never really succeeded in breaking their resistance. In the 1840s, after losing much of their lands, the Maya recaptured a good portion of the peninsula during the War of the Castes, but they failed to follow through and take the principal city, Mérida. The inevitable retaliation of the *hacendados* (landowners) resulted in the extermination of nearly half the Maya population. Not until 1935, when the Chan Santa Cruz people signed an accord with the government, did the fighting cease.

Here, as in much of Mexico, poverty is always present, aggravated by the peninsula's thin, parched topsoil. Increasingly, Yucatecans are turning away from agriculture to more lucrative jobs; after oil, tourism is the second-largest industry here. As is the case with most tourist-driven economies however, the Yucatán's fragile environment has suffered unfortunate side effects. The destruction of delicate coral reefs to make room for new cruise ship piers has many residents and visitors questioning the relative costs and benefits of opening up paradise to so many people.

CANCUN

If you're a newcomer, Cancún's warm, aquamarine waters and sugar-sand beaches will instantly enchant you. You'll think, "This is *it*. How could it be better than this?" Then you'll start listening to more experienced Yucatán travelers and you'll wise up. You'll realize that there's no soul behind Cancún's flashy exterior. That you don't have to max out your credit cards to experience hedonism. That it's not necessary to always share your fun with 18-year-olds dancing enthusiastically on tables. And with this coming of age you'll toss the easily accessible but culturally limited Cancún aside for less-touristed spots such as Playa del Carmen and Isla Mujeres; places that leave you with the same satisfied feeling, but where you can wake up in the morning with wallet and dignity intact.

BASICS

AMERICAN EXPRESS
The office makes travel arrangements, replaces lost cards and checks, cashes personal and traveler's checks, changes cash, and holds customers' mail for up to 30 days. Mailing address: Avenida Tulum 208, Cancún, Quintana Roo, CP 77500, México. *Av. Tulum 208, between Calles Agua and Viento, tel. 988/4–54–41. Open weekdays 9–6, Sat. 9–1.*

CASAS DE CAMBIO
Cancún's many casas de cambio are open until 9 or 10 PM. Rates at banks are better, but the lines are long. **Banamex** (Av. Tulum 19, tel. 988/4–54–11) and **Banco del Sureste** (Sunyaxchen 64, at Yaxchilán, tel. 988/4–51–61) change money weekdays 9–1:30. Both banks have an ATM that accepts Plus and Cirrus cards, and you can also get cash advances with a Visa or MasterCard.

CONSULATES
Canada. *Plaza Caracol 2, Paseo Kukulcán, 3rd floor, tel. 988/3–33–60. Open weekdays 9–5.*

United States. If you're unlucky enough to lose your passport or if you're involved in an accident or robbery, the U.S. consulate can help. *Plaza Caracol 2, Paseo Kukulcán, 3rd floor, tel. 988/3–22–86. Open weekdays 9–1.*

EMERGENCIES
In an emergency, dial **06** from any telephone in Cancún. The **police station** (tel. 988/4–19–13) is downtown, next to the banks on Avenida Tulum. For 24-hour **ambulance** service, contact the Cruz Roja (Labná 2, at Yaxchilán, tel. 988/4–16–16).

LAUNDRY

Lavandería Lavamorena does up to 3 kilos (6½ pounds) of your laundry for $2. *Grosella 105, at Xel-ha, Supermanzana 25, tel. 988/7–30–29. In front of post office. Open Mon.–Sat. 8 AM–9 PM.*

MEDICAL AID

The **Hospital Americano** (Viento 15, at Av. Tulum, tel. 988/4–61–33) is open 24 hours. **Farmacia París** (Yaxchilán 32, in Edificio Marruecos, tel. 988/4–30–05) is also open 24 hours. The tourist information booklet *Cancún Tips* provides a list of English-speaking doctors.

PHONES AND MAIL

You can place collect calls from **Computel** (Av. Tulum, near bus terminal, tel. and fax 998/7–42–24; open daily 7 AM–10 PM); the service charge for five minutes is $1. The **post office** (Sunyaxchen, Supermanzana 28, tel. 988/4–14–18; open weekdays 8–7, Sat. 9–noon) will hold mail sent to you at the following address for up to 15 days: Administración 1, Lista de Correos, Cancún, Quintana Roo, CP 77501, México.

VISITOR INFORMATION

The **Secretaría Estatal de Turismo** (Av. Tulum, next door to Palacio Municipal, tel. 988/4–80–73; open daily 9–9) has a knowledgeable, English-speaking staff ready to shower you with brochures. The magenta building is marked by a FUNDACIÓN LOLITA DE LA VEGA sign. Your best printed resource is the ubiquitous **Cancún Tips.** The publication's frank and helpful staff (Av. Tulum 29, near bus station, tel. 988/4–10–37 or 988/4–32–38), on duty weekdays 8–7, is a valuable source for the most up-to-date discounts offered by local sport and tour companies.

Kukulcán is the Maya name for Quetzalcoatl, the feathered serpent god of the Toltec and Aztec pantheons. Depictions of Kukulcán are plentiful at the ruins of Chichén Itzá.

COMING AND GOING

BY BUS

The bus station is downtown, on Uxmal near Avenida Tulum. Two major bus companies, the first-class **Autotransportes del Oriente** (ADO; tel. 988/4–55–42 or 988/4–48–04) and the second-class **Autotransportes del Sur** (ATS; tel. 988/4–48–04), serve most points in Quintana Roo and the Yucatán, as well as other major cities in Mexico. Buses leave frequently for Mérida (4 hrs, $8.50 1st class), Valladolid (3 hrs, $3 2nd class), Chichén Itzá (3 hrs, $6 1st class; 4 hrs, $4 2nd class), and Chetumal (6 hrs, $8 2nd class), stopping at smaller towns en route. Buses for Playa del Carmen ($2) and Puerto Morelos ($1) depart every 15 minutes from the southeast side of the station. The bus stop for Puerto Juárez, where you can catch a ferry to Isla Mujeres, is on the east side of Avenida Tulum near the Monumento a la Historia. The budget hotels are within walking distance of the station; you can store luggage at the station (75¢ per hour) while you look. To reach the Zona Hotelera from the station, cross Avenida Tulum and catch a HOTELES bus.

BY CAR

The drive from Cancún south to Tulum is a pleasant one: There are no tolls, and Highway 307 is well maintained. The road to the ruins near Valladolid and Mérida, however, is another story. Many an unsuspecting driver has paid through the nose after taking the *carretera de cuota* (toll road) to Mérida, which costs $24 ($12 at the Nuevo X-Can toll stop and $12 at the Pisté stop). The toll is charged in both directions. Highway 180, which is a *carretera libre* (free road), follows the same route as the toll road but passes through small towns. Sure, it's a little slower and bumpier, but the savings and scenery are worth it. To avoid the toll road, take the highway out of Cancún and keep going straight—a CUOTA sign on your right will try to lure you in, but don't bite.

RENTAL CARS • You can rent cars at the airport, in hotels, and all along Avenida Tulum; try **Avis** (in the airport, tel. 988/3–08–03). VW Bugs typically cost $35 a day, but look around for discounts and check for coupons in *Cancún Tips*.

BY PLANE

Cancún's airport is the largest and busiest on the peninsula and is a frequent destination for many U.S. airlines. Domestic airlines include **Aeroméxico** (Coba 80, tel. 988/4–35–71 or 988/6–00–59) and **Mex-**

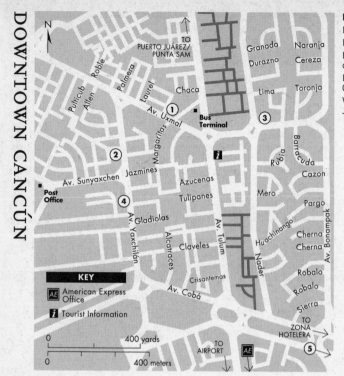

DOWNTOWN CANCÚN

N
↑

TO
PUERTO JUÁREZ/
PUNTA SAM

Roble
Palmera
Pulticub
Allen
Laurel
Av. Uxmal
Margaritas
Chaca

Granada
Durazno
Naranja
Cereza

Lima
Toronja

Bus
Terminal
①

②
Jazmines
Av. Sunyaxchen

Post
Office

Azucenas
Tulipanes

Rubia
Barracuda
Cazon

Mero

Pargo

③

ℹ

④
Av. Gladiolas
Av. Yaxchilán
Alcatraces
Claveles
Av. Tulum

Crisantemas
Av. Cobá

Huachinango
Cherna
Cherna
Av. Bonampak
Nader

Robalo
Robalo
Sierra

TO
ZONA
HOTELERA →

Lodging ○
Hotel Alux, **1**
Hotel Canto, **2**
Hotel El Rey
del Caribe, **3**
Hotel Villa Rossana
Cancún, **4**
Villa Deportiva
Juvenil Cancún, **5**

KEY
AE American Express
Office
ℹ Tourist Information

0 ———— 400 yards
0 ———— 400 meters

TO
AIRPORT

AE

⑤ →

icana (tel. 988/6–01–20). The casas de cambio at the airport, humorously named $EXCHANGE, have awful rates; you're better off changing your money downtown.

AIRPORT TRANSIT • Unfortunately, no public bus system serves the airport. A taxi into Cancún costs about $18 and a *colectivo* (communal taxi) costs $7; you'll see the station wagons lined up outside as you leave the terminal. No colectivos return to the airport from downtown Cancún, so you must take a taxi.

GETTING AROUND

Cancún is divided into two sections: the **Zona Hotelera** (Hotel Zone), where you'll find all of the monstrous resorts, and the **centro** (downtown). The centro is on the mainland, while the Zona Hotelera is built along an elbow-shape sand bar. The centro is divided into dozens of numbered zones—some only one block long—called *supermanzanas,* and addresses are often designated as "S. M." followed by a number. **Avenida Tulum** is the main street at Cancún's center, and it's lined with restaurants and shopping centers selling expensive Mexican crafts. Only one street, **Paseo Kukulcán,** runs through the Zona Hotelera. Buses marked HOTELES, CENTRO, and HOTELES/DOWNTOWN run west from the centro down Avenida Tulum, then through the Zona Hotelera, returning along the same route. These city buses (50¢) run every few minutes 5 AM–2 AM.

BY TAXI

Taxis are as expensive as you'd expect in a resort town. Fare within downtown should be around $1.50—or an outrageous $6 to the Zona Hotelera, and about $18 to the airport.

WHERE TO SLEEP

If you're traveling on a budget in Cancún, your hotel room will be downtown, away from the water. If you want to stay near the beach, your only reasonably priced option is the youth hostel (*see below*). Camping is not permitted on Cancún's beaches.

Keep in mind that during the high seasons (Nov.–Apr., July, and August) room prices rise by $10 or more, and vacancies are nonexistent. During these periods you should make reservations two weeks to one month in advance. The prices listed below are for the low season.

UNDER $20 • Hotel Alux. This thoroughly sanitized place has air-conditioning and hot showers. Doubles are $17. *Uxmal 21, tel. 988/4–05–56. ½ block north of bus station. 32 rooms, all with bath. Laundry, luggage storage. Cash only.*

Hotel Canto. This hotel offers air-conditioned rooms with large, clean bathrooms and purified water. If you get lonely, hang out in the lobby and watch cartoons with the kids. Doubles are $17. *Yaxchilán 22, at Sunyaxchen, tel. 988/4–12–67. 23 rooms, all with bath. Luggage storage. Cash only.*

Hotel Villa Rossana Cancún. This centrally located hotel is cheap, and you're bound to meet other budget travelers. The singles are huge, and some rooms have decks that look out above the city. Doubles cost $20 with ceiling fans, $30 with air-conditioning—but the ceiling fans should keep you sufficiently cool during most of the year. *Yaxchilán 68, just north of Sunyaxchen, tel. 988/4–19–43. 10 rooms, all with bath. Luggage storage. Cash only.*

UNDER $30 • Hotel El Rey del Caribe. If atmosphere is more important than proximity to the beach, this is the place: It's set in a junglelike garden with tropical plants, a pool, and a Jacuzzi. Rooms are spacious and comfortable, with kitchens and clean bathrooms. Doubles cost $30, plus $5 for each additional person. *Uxmal, at Náder, tel. 988/4–20–28. 23 rooms, all with bath. Luggage storage. Reservations advised.*

The story of how Cancún became a tourist mecca is a local favorite: Looking for a new location for a money-making resort, the Mexican government asked a computer to come up with a site.

HOSTELS

Villa Deportiva Juvenil Cancún. This large hostel is the cheapest place in town and the only budget lodging on the beach. Ping-Pong tables, a volleyball net, and a swimming pool are some of its appealing qualities. The single-sex dorm rooms are all equipped with bunks and lockers—and some even have views of the sea. The hostel attracts the most travelers in the winter months (December–March): If you stay here during the rest of the year, you just might have your own room. The place stays fairly clean, though bathrooms lack toilet paper and hot water; during the rainy season, ants and mice tend to seek refuge here. Beds cost $4 (plus $4 deposit for sheets and towels). The Villa also lets travelers camp on its grassy lawns and use the facilities for $2 per person. *Paseo Kukulcan Km. 3.2, tel. 988/3–13–37. 480 beds. Luggage storage. Meal service during high season. Cash only.*

FOOD

Food isn't cheap in Cancún, but if you're willing to stick to typical Mexican fare, it's affordable. In the Zona Hotelera, the budget pickings are extremely slim—guests at the youth hostel might want to stock up at **Deliquor,** a 24-hour minimarket 660 ft east of the hostel. Downtown, look for cheap eateries on Avenidas Uxmal and Cobá and nearby streets. **Comercial Mexicana** (Av. Tulum, at Uxmal; cash only) serves prepreared food by weight, from spaghetti ($2 per pound) to black beans and rice ($1 a pound). **Mercado 28** (Av. Xel-Ha, across from post office), a faux-colonial shopping mall, has an array of *loncherías* (snack bars) serving cheap, homemade meals and *antojitos* (appetizers). The morning **mercado,** held daily behind the post office, is a good place to purchase fresh fruit.

UNDER $3 • Rincón Yucateco. Low prices and a pleasant outdoor patio make this low-key restaurant a great place to fill up on soup ($1.75) or *parmuchas* (crisp, bean-filled tortillas topped with sliced chicken). *Uxmal 24, next to Hotel Alux, no phone. Cash only.*

UNDER $5 • Lalos & Denise. This restaurant makes a strained attempt to integrate Mexican and Canadian culture, but who comes to Cancún for culture? A plate with three red enchiladas, three chicken tacos, or three meat burritos costs $4, and they'll even throw in a free beer or Coke. *Av. Tulum 26, north of Palacio Municipal, tel. 988/4–54–45. Cash only.*

Restaurant Tlaquepaque. Candy-color tablecloths and high-back bamboo chairs give the Tlaquepaque the air of an oversize dollhouse. The owner is charming and a true connoisseur of Mexican cuisine—his ceviche (diced fish marinated in lime juice) is delicious. Four tacos cost $3.25. *Yaxchilán 59, no phone. Next to Hotel Villa Rossana. Cash only.*

UNDER $15 • La Parrilla. La Parrilla's dining room is a labyrinth of colorful tables, and it's popular with tourists and locals alike. You'll find yuppie tourists sharing the *parrillada mexicana* ($13), a two-person feast of grilled beef, pork, chicken, and vegetables, served with tortillas, salad, beans, and rice. Vegetarians will delight in the *nopalitos* (cactus- and onion-filled tacos topped with cheese and salsa; $2.25). The bar stays open until 4 AM. *Yaxchilán 51, tel. 988/7–61–41. No breakfast.*

OUTDOOR ACTIVITIES

Water sports in Cancún are fun but overpriced, and you probably won't see any Mexicans doing them. Street vendors and hotels offer fairly consistent prices for **parasail rides** ($35 for 15 min) and **waverunners** ($40 for 30 min). If you plan on **windsurfing** (about $15 per hour), be aware that the current can get pretty strong beyond the shoreline. Lifeguards keep a good watch, but you might want to get their attention before heading out just to be sure. Windsurfing rentals and lessons can be arranged at **Aqua World** (Paseo Kukulcán Km. 15, tel. 988/5–22–88).

BEACHES

Beaches in Cancún face either the Caribbean Sea or the calmer Bahía de Mujeres, but the ones on the Caribbean side are constantly being eroded by passing hurricanes. Posted warning flags indicate current water conditions: Green or blue means calm waters, yellow means caution, and red or black signifies danger. Note that though many of the best beaches are bordered by wall-to-wall luxury hotels, all of Cancún's beaches are open to the public. If you're discreet, you can make use of hotel facilities such as hammocks, lounges, swimming pools, bars (the kind that charge $3.50 for a Coke), and showers.

The best beaches on the Caribbean are **Playa Chac Mool** and those in front of the **Hyatt Cancún** and **Sheraton** hotels, all of which are near **Punta Cancún,** the northeast point of the Zona Hotelera. Calm **Playa Linda,** near the youth hostel, is just 10 minutes from town by bus, and **Playa Tortugas,** another mile farther along Paseo Kukulcán, boasts some of Cancún's clearest water. If you're bent on avoiding the crowds, head to **Playa Ballenas** (Kukulcán Km. 14, just north of Cancún Palace Hotel), where rocky outcroppings and bigger waves make for slightly hazardous swimming but beautiful views. There are even a set of **nude beaches,** near Club Med, at the southern end of the Zona Hotelera. Buses don't make it all the way out here, so you'll need to take a taxi. To reach the beaches along the Zona Hotelera, hop one of the HOTELES buses (50¢) and tell the driver where you're going.

DEEP SEA FISHING

Cancún is known as one of the best game-fishing spots in the world, with year-round barracuda, red snapper, bluefin, grouper, and mackerel. **Aqua Tours** (Kukulcán Km. 6.25, tel. 988/3–04–00) arranges four- to six-hour tours ranging in price from $70 to $99. Beer, bait, and gear are all supplied.

SNORKELING

Despite the incredible clarity of the water, snorkeling off the beaches around Cancún is not as rewarding or affordable as at some other Caribbean resorts; it's usually cheaper to snorkel from Isla Mujeres (*see below*). Many marinas in town offer tours to **Los Chitales** (2 km/1 mi north of Cancún) or **Punta Nizuc,** a tropical underwater grove just south of Cancún. Snorkeling tours usually run $40 for 3½ hours (including lunch and beer), or you can rent your own gear (about $25 a day) and head to Punta Nizuc by bus—take the HOTELES bus to Westin Regina resort, 2 km (1 mi) from the best snorkeling spots.

AFTER DARK

The great advantage Cancún has over other Caribbean coastal towns is its exuberant night scene, but its bars and discos are generally what you'd expect: they offer stiff, fruity drinks of every type imaginable, and are bedecked with pseudo-Maya motifs and flashing lights. Discos in Cancún are known for their discriminatory policies: Several places in the Zona Hotelera prohibit Mexicans from entering. The places listed below do not follow this policy.

If you are in downtown Cancún on a Friday night, head to the park behind Calle Tulipanes. At around 8 PM, a special show called **Noche Caribeña** (Caribbean Night) features songs, dances, poetry readings, and a raffle. On Sunday evening at 7:30, cultural events such as a *baile de jarana,* a typical Yucatecan dance, are held in the **Parque Las Palapas,** between Avenidas Yaxchilán and Tulum. Both events are for locals, giving you a chance to escape the tourist crowd.

BARS

The majority of bars in Cancún feature "shows"—usually female strip acts. If this doesn't appeal to you, ask at the door whether there are any shows planned. One lively bar without a striptease is **No Way, José** (Cobá 89, at Nader, tel. 988/4–22–80), which offers televised sporting events and nightly karaoke. For $7 you'll get unlimited drinks and a nasty hangover; otherwise, beers bought à la carte cost about $1.25. A diverse crowd parties at **Karamba** (Av. Tulum 9, tel. 988/4–00–37), a gay bar with $1.50 beers and a small dance floor, as well as occasional events like "The Queens Transvestite Show."

DANCING

There are plenty of places to dance away the night in Cancún providing that you're willing to pay the price: Cover charges are a high $8, but many set aside one day a week (usually Monday) for free admission. Check *Cancún Tips* for special club offers. **La Boom** (Paseo Kukulcán Km. 3.5, near Villa Deportiva Juvenil, tel. 988/3–11–52) boasts a smoky multilevel dance floor with artificial stars and extravagant light displays. It's always crowded. In the same building, **Tequila Rock** encourages patrons to dance on the bar after they've downed a few $4 margaritas. The city's salsa club, **Batachá** (Hotel Miramar, Zona Hotelera, tel. 988/3–17–55) starts up at around 11 PM, when happy couples fill the bamboo-bedecked dance floor and breezy patio.

NEAR CANCUN

PUERTO MORELOS

South of Cancún is the tranquil fishing town of Puerto Morelos, a welcome change from the resort frenzy to the north. It's a fairly upscale place, benefiting from the crowds of gringos who make this a day trip from Cancún in rented 4x4s. There isn't much to do in town—locals affectionately call it *Muerto* (Dead) Morelos. Nor are the nearby beaches so exceptional; if you want to relax on the sand, travel a couple of kilometers south to more secluded, attractive shores. The real draw to Morelos lies in the sea just off-shore, in the form of a coral reef where you can snorkel or dive. **Sub Aqua Explorers** (SW corner of zócalo, tel. 987/1–00–78), run by Mexican brothers Shedor and Hitamar Muñoz, rents snorkel equipment ($6 per day), offers diving trips ($55 for 2 tanks, $40 for 1 tank, or $100 for a cavern dive), and fishing trips ($80 for 2 hrs). If you're staying overnight, consider **Posada Amor** (Javier Rojo Gómez, tel. 987/1–00–33), a quirky little hotel just south of the *zócalo* (main plaza) that offers doubles with communal bath ($22) or with private bath ($32). For $20 you can stay in a rustic *palapa* (thatched hut) complete with mosquito netting and feel like you're part of the Swiss Family Robinson. The posada accepts cash only. **Restaurant Las Palmeras** (Av. Rafael Melgar; closed Sun.) serves typical seafood dishes for about $6–$7.

COMING AND GOING

ATS buses (30 min, $1) run daily from Cancún's bus station to Puerto Morelos every 20 minutes 8–8:30 en route to Playa del Carmen. Be sure to let the driver know that you wish to disembark in Puerto Morelos. Seven daily buses return to Cancún, with the last bus returning around 5 PM. Return tickets ($1) are sold at *el crucero*: the junction of Highway 307 and the road leading east into town. A man sitting on a bench at the junction will sell you a ticket. If you're continuing on to Playa del Carmen, buy your ticket at the *caseta* (booth) on the opposite (west) side of the highway.

ISLA MUJERES

At first sight, Isla Mujeres, just 10 km (6 mi) east of Cancún, is just your stereotypical resort: A handful of expensive restaurants and soulless hotels jostle for space with souvenir shops selling piles of conch shells and machine-made Maya figurines. But Isla Mujeres has retained a sweet and simple essence that attracts budget travelers from all over the world. They come for the quiet and peaceful white beaches, as well as for the snorkeling and diving opportunities. Still, the main reason to come to the island is to loaf, relax, lounge, laze, idle, nap, snooze, or simply do nothing at all. Virtually the only time the town rouses itself is during the **Regata del Sol al Sol,** celebrated annually in late April. The fiesta

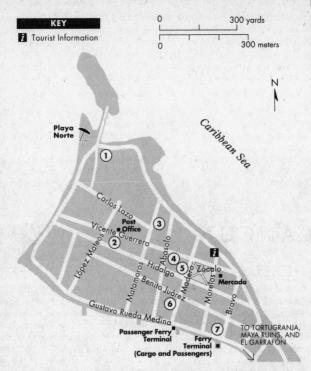

KEY

i Tourist Information

0 ——————— 300 yards

0 ——————— 300 meters

N

Playa Norte

Caribbean Sea

Carlos Lazo

Post Office

Vicente Guerrero

López Mateos

Abasolo

Hidalgo

Matamoros

Benito Juárez

Madero

Morelos

Bravo

Zócalo

Mercado

Gustavo Rueda Medina

Passenger Ferry Terminal

Ferry Terminal
(Cargo and Passengers)

TO TORTUGRANJA, MAYA RUINS, AND EL GARRAFÓN

Lodging ○

Hotel Caribe Maya, **5**

Hotel Carmelina, **4**

Hotel Casa Maya, **1**

Hotel Gomar, **7**

Hotel Osorio, **6**

Hotel Xul-Ha, **2**

Poc-Na, **3**

celebrates the end of a boat race begun in St. Petersburg, Florida, and the arrival of the contestants is greeted here with parades, parties, and fireworks. At its conclusion there's a basketball game between Mexican and American teams—the Mexican team always wins.

How the island got its alluring name ("Island of the Women") is open to debate. According to one fanciful story, pirates stashed their women here while they were out at sea plundering Spanish galleons groaning with gold. A more plausible explanation is that the island is named for the many Maya female figurines found here by Francisco Hernández de Córdoba, the commander of a Spanish expedition, who "discovered" the island in 1517. The subsequent history of the island is a common one in the Caribbean: It was indeed a hideaway for pirates that later became a fishing village. During the late 1960s and '70s the island was a haven for hammock-toting hippies, but the neo-hippies of the 1990s prefer Zipolite beach on the Oaxacan coast (*see* Near Puetro Ángel *in* Chapter 12).

BASICS

CASAS DE CAMBIO

Banco del Atlántico, on your right as you come off the ferry from Puerto Juárez, offers good exchange rates. *Rueda Medina 3, between Morelos and Bravo, tel. 987/7–00–05. Money exchange counter open weekdays 9–4:30.*

LAUNDRY

Tim Phó does up to 4 kilos (9 pounds) of laundry for $2.50, often in less than two hours. *Juárez, at Abasolo, tel. 987/7–05–29. 2 blocks from zócalo. Open Mon.–Sat. 7 AM–9 PM, Sun. 8–2.*

MEDICAL AID

The **Centro de Salud** (Guerrero 5, tel. 987/7–00–17) offers 24-hour emergency service. **Dr. Antonio Salas** (Hidalgo, next to Farmacia Lily, tel. 987/7–04–77) speaks English and makes house calls round the clock. **Farmacia Lily** (Madero, at Hidalgo, tel. 987/7–01–64) is open Monday–Saturday 9–9:30, Sunday 9–3:30.

PHONES AND MAIL

The **post office** will hold mail sent to you at the following address for up to 10 days: Lista de Correos, Isla Mujeres, Quintana Roo, CP 77400, México. *Guerrero, at Mateos, tel. 987/7–00–85. Open weekdays 8–7, Sat. 9–1.*

There is a long-distance **telephone office** in Hotel María José (Rueda Medina 9-B, at Madero, near ferry terminal; open daily 9–9). You can also find coin- and card-operated phones scattered about the town. Buy phone cards at **Yamili Crafts & Shirts** (Hidalgo 4, tel. 987/7–05–20; open Mon.–Sat. 9–9, Sun. 9–3). You can place or receive a fax at **Telecomm** (Guerrero, next to post office, fax 987/7–01–13; open weekdays 9–3).

VISITOR INFORMATION

The **tourist office** (tel. 987/7–03–16; open weekdays 9–2 and 7–9) is in Plaza Isla Mujeres at the north end of the main shopping street, Avenida Morelos. Make sure to pick up a copy of *Islander,* a free monthly publication with good maps of the island and general tourist information. For a free map and some friendly advice, you can also try the **tourist information booth** at the Puerto Juárez ferry dock, in downtown Isla Mujeres.

COMING AND GOING

You can reach Isla Mujeres from either Puerto Juárez or Punta Sam, both north of Cancún. From Puerto Juárez, older ferries chug to Isla (40 min, 75¢), as well as quicker, air-conditioned ferries (15 min, $2). Both types of ferries run daily 7–7:30. Puerto Juárez is 15 minutes from Cancún by bus (50¢)—catch one marked PUERTO JUAREZ from any of the bus stops on Avenida Tulum. A taxi will cost about $3.

Although it's farther from Isla Mujeres than Puerto Juárez, Punta Sam is the best departure point if you're bringing a car over to the island. Ferries (45 min, $1) leave every two to three hours. The cost of transporting a car starts at about $8, depending on the car's size. To reach Punta Sam from Cancún, drive north up Avenida Tulum, turn right (east) on Avenida Portillo, and follow the signs to Punta Sam.

GETTING AROUND

The island of Isla Mujeres is only about 8 km (5 mi) long and less than a kilometer wide, and most travelers stay in the town at the northern tip of the island. The majority of shops and restaurants are on the west side of town, and the zócalo is at the town's southernmost end, at Morelos and Benito Juárez.

BY BUS

The only bus on the island (35¢) runs down the main street at the ferry docks, passing the designated bus stops just north of the taxi stands every half hour. From here the bus heads south to Playa Lancheros, then turns around and makes its way through the residential areas on the island's edge before heading back into town.

BY MOPED AND BIKE

Consider renting a bicycle or moped to see the "other" Isla Mujeres, consisting of locals' houses and unspoiled coastal vistas. Several places around town rent mopeds for about $8 per hour, $25 per day (gas included); you'll usually need to leave a deposit or your ID. You can rent bicycles for only $3.50 per day at **Micha's Motorent** (Abasolo 13). **Sport Bike** (Juárez and Morelos, just below zócalo, tel. 987/2–00–36; open daily 8–5) rents bikes with locks ($4.50 for a 24-hour period).

BY TAXI

Because the island is small, taxis are a pleasant and affordable way to get around. For regulated rates, try the taxi stand near the two ferry docks. A taxi from town to the Tortugranja (*see* Worth Seeing, *below*) costs $2.50.

WHERE TO SLEEP

Most hotels on Isla Mujeres are in town. Prices double during high season (Nov.–Apr., July, and Aug.). The prices listed below reflect the low-season range.

Camping is not allowed on Isla Mujeres and police do patrol the beaches. The one exception is at Poc-Na (*see* Hostels, *below*), which will let you camp on their stretch of beach for the regular $2.50 room fee.

UNDER $15 • Hotel Caribe Maya. This hotel near the main ferry terminal is comfortable, clean, and bugless, and the water gets so hot you can actually steam your clothes in it. The $10.50 fan-only rooms (doubles) stay pretty cool, but air-conditioned rooms are available for $14. They also rent mopeds ($20 per day) and offer trips to Isla Contoy (*see* Near Isla Mujeres, *below*) for $22.50. There's a 6% usage fee on credit cards. *Madero 9, tel. 987/1–04–23. From Rueda Medina, head east on Madero about 2 blocks. 25 rooms, all with bath. Luggage storage. Reservations advised Dec.–Apr.*

Hotel Carmelina. You may see the occasional *cucaracha* (cockroach), but rooms here are large and sunny, with fans and clean bathrooms. Ask for a top-floor room; they're bright, cheery, and overlook the rest of town. Doubles cost $14, plus an additional $2.50 for air-conditioning. They also rent bicycles ($3.50 per day). *Guerrero 4, tel. 987/7–00–06. From ferry, walk up Morelos and left on Guerrero. 18 rooms, all with bath. Laundry, luggage storage. Cash only.*

Hotel Osorio. You'll spot Osorio by its bright red-and-green balconies overlooking the street. Beds are small, and the place is not exactly picturesque, but rooms are about as cheap as they get—$10.50 for a double. The hotel also offers daily trips to Isla Contoy for $25. *Madero 10, at Juárez, tel. 987/7–02–56. 40 rooms, all with bath. Luggage storage. Reservations advised Dec. and Jan. Cash only.*

Hotel Xul-Ha. If you can see past the ruinous appearance of this hotel's unoccupied portion, you'll appreciate the value of the available rooms. Bathrooms are pleasantly grunge-free, and large shower stalls with piping hot water provide a welcome end to a long day at the beach. Doubles cost $10.50. *Hidalgo 23, tel. 987/7–00–75. From Rueda Medina, east on López Mateos 1 block, then left on Hidalgo. 11 rooms, all with bath. Luggage storage.*

UNDER $25 • Hotel Casa Maya. Romantics will love the breezy beachside palapas and inviting patio hammocks of this small hotel. Common areas include a bright, cozy living room, kitchen facilities, and a shaded terrace. Doubles with a spotless shared bath (you share with one other room) cost $25. A double with private bath goes for $35. Reservations are recommended during the high season. *Calle Zazil-Ha, tel. 987/7–00–45. At Playa Norte, near abandoned Zazil-Ha Hotel. 10 rooms, 7 with bath. Luggage storage.*

Hotel Gomar. If cleanliness and convenience are your top priorities, stay here. Located directly across the street from the Puerto Juárez ferry, this hotel allows you to drop your bags and take a siesta immediately upon arrival. Doubles ($18; high season $45) come with steamy hot water, cooling fans, and ocean views from the common balcony. *Medina 150, tel. 987/7–05–41. 16 rooms, all with bath. Luggage storage. Reservations advised Dec.–Apr.*

HOSTELS

Poc-Na. Budget travelers and adventure seekers from all over the world converge here for good company and comfortable hammocks. Hang out on the rooftop or play your guitar under the large palapa that doubles as a dining room and living area. The single-sex dorm rooms ($5 per person) have bunks and hammock hooks, and you can use towels, sheets, and pillows for a $7 deposit. The hostel's restaurant serves pizza and huge pasta dishes that two people can share for $3. The food is, as one visitor put it, "brilliant." *Matamoros, tel. 987/7–00–90. From main ferry docks, north on Rueda Medina, east 4½ blocks on Matamoros toward east coast beach. Meal service, laundry, luggage storage. Cash only.*

FOOD

Inexpensive *loncherías* (snack bars) are scattered throughout town, including four on Avenida Guerrero between Matamoros and Mateos. Small sandwiches or a plate of tacos cost under $2, while main dishes, such as fish, cost about $3. Especially good is the tiny, nameless lonchería on Guerrero between Matamoros and Abasolo. The daily **market** on Guerrero at Mateos is a good place to stock up on fruit or snacks. **Panadería La Reina** (Madero, at Juárez, no phone) sells fresh pastries and great banana bread.

UNDER $5 • Cafecito. Sitting at a table decorated with seashells, you understandably may think that you've fallen into a tourist trap. Once you tuck into the Belgian waffles (smothered with whipped cream and strawberries) or sample the crepes (with ice cream, chocolate sauce, and bananas) you probably won't care. Breakfast lovers take note: A variety of egg dishes cost under $2. *Matamoros 42, at Juárez, tel. 987/7–04–38. Closed daily noon–6 PM. No dinner Sun. Cash only.*

Chen Huaye. The name of the place means "always here," which describes where you might be after you discover *chaya,* a green drink made from a tropical plant resembling spinach (Popeye never had it so good). There are Silvio Rodríguez tapes in the stereo and pink flamingos on the wall. The chicken *tor-*

tas (sandwiches), at $1.25 a pop, make the wallet as happy as the soul. *Bravo 6, no phone. Near zócalo, between Juárez and Hidalgo, behind basketball courts. Closed Tues. Cash only.*

El Nopalito. Start your day in a spiritual way at this small café hidden within a crafts store. Festively painted wood tables seem in harmony with the New Age flute music. The French toast is buried under a blizzard of powdered sugar and comes with honey and fresh marmalade. *Corner Guerrero and Matamoros, tel. 988/7–05–55. Breakfast only. Closed Sun. Cash only.*

The Red Eye Cafe. A bright red-and-white awning marks this open-air café where expat couple Gus and Inga serve hearty American breakfast dishes that have a German flair. Egg dishes are accompanied by fresh, authentic German sausage made by an expat German in Cancún. *Hidalgo, between Matamoros and Madero, no phone. No dinner. Closed Tues. Cash only.*

Restaurant Portales. This small place has whitewashed walls, an outdoor grill, and live music. Take advantage of the all-you-can-eat lunch buffet (daily 12:30–3:30; $5) and then stick around for a swim in their pool. *Juárez 32, between Mateos and Matamoros, tel. 987/7–05–06. Lunch only. Cash only.*

WORTH SEEING

MAYA RUINS

The island's Maya ruins are just that—ruins—and there's little for the casual visitor to see. A small sandstone building at the southern tip of the island was once a temple to Ixchel, the Maya goddess of fertility. Female figurines, believed to be votive offerings, were found here by Hernández de Córdoba and provide the most plausible explanation of the island's name. Despite the temple's disrepair, the striking effect of the waves breaking on the steep cliffs below is spectacular. Ask the lighthouse keeper if you can climb to the top floor for the beautiful view; if you're lucky, he may also have some ice-cold Cokes for sale. You should tip the keeper about $1 if you do climb the lighthouse stairs. *From town, follow road as far south as possible and walk up dirt path. Or, take bus to Playa Lancheros and walk 2 km (1 mi).*

TORTUGRANJA

Among many ardent save-the-sea-turtle enterprises dotting the Quintana Roo coastline, this is probably the most elaborate. The Tortugranja turtle farm is government funded and features a small informational museum as well as multilingual guides who give detailed information on the life cycle and mating habits of the turtles. The best time to come is near the end of the egg-laying season (May–October), when newly hatched baby turtles can be found darting around the central building's shallow, raised tanks. It gets hot here, so bring water. Some snorkeling tours include a stop at the Tortugranja. *Tel. 987/7–05–95. Take the (only) bus, get dropped off at Mondaca, and walk north 20 min. Admission: $1.50. Open daily 9–5.*

OUTDOOR ACTIVITIES

BEACHES

Northwest of town is **Playa Norte,** a wide, white-sand beach. It's the traditional topless beach, but until the Europeans arrive in July and August, mammary toasting is not all that common. A plethora of water sports are available at Playa Norte, including snorkeling, sailing, and water skiing; for details on rentals, *see* Snorkeling, *below.* You can use the bathrooms and showers on the beach near Hidalgo for $1.

The three modest beaches on the west coast of the island—**Playa Paraíso, Playa Lancheros,** and **Playa Indios**—don't have the fine white sand you'd expect from a Caribbean island. The shallow sea is rocky and full of seaweed, making it a less than ideal place to swim and snorkel. Still, Playa Paraíso sees its share of visitors, as it's a popular harbor for tourist boats from Cancún. The beach has quite a few restaurants, a number of small stands selling souvenirs, and clean bathrooms. Someone may ask you to pay an entrance fee, but the beaches are government-owned and the fee is a scam. From town, take a bus, bicycle, or moped south down the main road about 4 km (2½ mi).

SCUBA DIVING

Isla Mujeres offers some exciting and unusual diving trips. Aside from the obvious attraction of the coral reefs, divers have a chance to explore the **Sleeping Shark Caves** (*see box, below*). Diving trips to the coral reefs around the island (such as the Chitales, Banderas, and Manchones reefs) cost $20–$65,

SHHH... DON'T WAKE THE SHARKS

The underwater caverns off Isla Mujeres attract a dangerous species of shark—though nobody knows exactly why. Stranger still, once the sharks enter the caves they enter a state of relaxed nonaggression seen nowhere else. Naturalists have two explanations, both involving the composition of the water inside the caves (it contains more oxygen, more carbon dioxide, and less salt). According to the first theory, the decreased salinity of the water inside the caves causes the parasites that plague sharks to loosen their grip, which allows the remora fish (the sharks' personal vacuum cleaner) to eat the parasites more easily. Perhaps the sharks relax in order to facilitate the cleaning, or maybe their deep state of relaxation is a side effect of having been scrubbed clean.

Another theory is that the caves' combination of fresh- and saltwater may produce a euphoric feeling in the sharks, similar to the effect scuba divers experience on extremely deep dives (most divers call the feeling "getting narc'd"). Whatever the sharks experience while "sleeping" in the caves, they pay a heavy price for it: A swimming shark breathes automatically and without effort (water is forced through the gills as the shark swims), but a stationary shark must laboriously pump water to continue breathing. If you dive in the caves of the sleeping sharks, be cautious: Many of the sharks are reef sharks, a species normally responsible for the largest number of attacks on humans. Dive with a reliable guide and be on your best diving behavior.

depending on how many tanks you use, how much gear you need to rent, and where you go. Trips to the Sleeping Shark Caves are usually about $15 more than other dives, and there's no refund if you don't see a shark. If you're not certified, you must take the $80, three-hour introductory course and then you'll be able to dive with an instructor. However, you'll have to retake the course every time you dive with a different company or in a different location. If you're really serious about getting into diving, consider taking a **PADI certification course.** The course usually lasts 4–5 days, costs around $350, and includes four tanks worth of diving: two in shallower waters and two deep-water dives. Once you have a certificate, you can dive anywhere you want at cheaper rates. Carlos Gutiérrez at **Mexico Divers** (Rueda Medina, near ferry dock, tel. 987/7–02–74) is a good person to talk to if you're considering taking the plunge. His prices for dives by certified divers are also reasonable. **Bahía Dive Shop** (Rueda Medina, near ferry dock, tel. 987/7–05–00) offers trips to all of the locations listed above.

SNORKELING
The island is fringed by coral reefs, and in many places you can just wade in and start snorkeling. Remember that coral is a living organism—walking on or just touching the coral will kill it, thus ruining the reef for both the fish that live there and for the tourists who follow after you to see it. **Marina Amigos del Mar** (Playa Norte, near Hidalgo, tel. 987/7–03–92) rents almost every type of water equipment, including snorkeling equipment ($5 per day), aqua cycles ($8.50 per hr), sailboats ($7.50 per hr), Windsurfers ($7.50 per hr), and kayaks ($5 per hr). If you want to snorkel close to town, the best spot is on the northern corner of the island, across from the bridge connecting the town to a small peninsula with a luxury hotel.

A few years ago the **Parque Nacional El Garrafón,** at the southern tip of the island, was a paradise for snorkelers. There's still a lot to see here, but as a result of 1988's Hurricane Gilbert much of the coral has died, and many of the fish have found new homes. What remains are hundreds of day-trippers from Cancún, floating on the surface of the water like fat, white fish. The tourist-oriented park includes a diving center, shops, a restaurant and snack bar, bathrooms, showers, and tiny lockers ($1.50). The dive shop rents snorkels, masks, and fins for about $4. You can easily bike to El Garrafón, or take the bus to Playa Lancheros and walk the rest of the way. *Admission: $1.75. Open daily 9–4.*

You can also take a 1½- to 3-hour snorkeling trip to the huge coral reef of **Manchones.** Here, brightly colored fish will surround you, and you may even see some barracuda. What you won't see are the bevy of floating tourists fresh off the boat from Cancún. Another option is **El Farrito Reef,** which is supposed to be the best snorkeling experience off Isla Mujeres. All agencies in town, as well as the one at El Garrafón, offer almost identical snorkeling trips ($20 per person) to Manchones and El Farrito Reef. Both trips usually include a visit to a couple of small coral reefs, and all trips should include use of snorkeling gear. Poc-Na (*see* Where to Sleep, *above*) offers a particularly good trip at prices sometimes below average. If you want to rent snorkeling gear and hit the beach by yourself, La Isleña, (*see* Isla Contoy, *below*), rents the snorkel, mask, and fins for $4 per day.

AFTER DARK

Buho's Bar allows you to enjoy your margaritas in a swing or even a hammock (although the latter can get pretty messy) while watching the sunset during the two-for-one happy hour (5:30 PM–sunset). A sand-dusted crowd of younger Mexicans goes to **Las Palapas** (Hidalgo, at Playa Cocos) for merengue and disco dancing right on the beach. There's no cover and drinks are two-for-one from 9 PM until midnight. **Cuba Ron** (Guerrero, at Morelos) serves a mean *mojito* (rum with mint, lime, and soda water; $2) and features live music on weekends. The **zócalo** is also a fun place to hang out at night, with music, games, and stands selling sticky, sweet fried plantains. Check the postings at Poc-Na (*see* Where to Sleep, *above*) to find out about other goings-on around town.

NEAR ISLA MUJERES

ISLA CONTOY

Isla Contoy, 45 minutes north of Isla Mujeres by boat, is a bird sanctuary where you can see brown pelicans, cormorants, frigate birds, herons, and flamingos in their lush natural habitat. Snorkeling is also a popular pastime here, although visibility off the thin strip of white-sand beach depends on the weather—if it's windy and the waves are rough, don't expect to see much. You can only visit Isla Contoy on an organized tour, but luckily most travel agencies and several hotels in town offer day trips to the island. Poc-Na (*see* Where to Sleep, *above*) arranges daylong sailboat trips to the island for $18 per person ($20 per person for fewer than 10 people), including snorkeling and fishing equipment as well as food and drink. **La Isleña** (Morelos, at Juárez, tel. 987/7–05–78) arranges four-hour tours ($30 per person) that include food, drink, and snorkeling equipment. They usually require a six-person minimum, but you may be able to talk them down to four. Tours consist of a boat ride, a stop on the beach to snorkel and eat lunch, and a spot of bird-watching on the island.

PLAYA DEL CARMEN

Like Cancún, Playa del Carmen is a tourist-oriented beach town. Also like Cancún, the town has experienced explosive growth in recent times, growing from a few thousand to over 30,000 inhabitants in the last five years. Unlike Cancún, Playa maintains a charming, small-town feel. Musicians fill the almost magical *malecón* (boardwalk) and surrounding streets, providing harmony for the breaking waves and the sounds of people conversing in dozens of different languages. After a day in Playa, you'll begin to recognize people on the street. After a week here, you'll feel like you're at home. And if Playa's mellow sand-and-sea atmosphere begins to bore you, convenient day trips to Maya ruins and isolated cenotes are plentiful.

Depending on when you go, you'll find two different types of visitors. The Playa del Carmen of July, August, and December through April is a destination for vacationing Mexicans as well as foreign package tourists who spill over from Cancún and Cozumel. The beaches are packed, gasoline from the boats pollutes the water in the harbor, and hotel prices skyrocket. The rest of the year, Playa is relatively peaceful, with a group of hip, young travelers taking advantage of empty hotels offering great deals.

BASICS

CASAS DE CAMBIO

The **money exchange center** (corner of 5a Av. and Juárez) offers lousy rates, but it's open daily 8 AM–10 PM. **Banco del Atlántico** (corner 10a Av. and Juárez, 1 block from bus station, tel. 987/3–03–62) changes cash and traveler's checks weekdays 8–noon. **Bancomer** (corner 25a Av. and Juárez, 4 blocks from 5a Av., tel. 987/3–04–08) has an ATM machine which takes Visa, Cirrus, and Plus cards.

LAUNDRY

Maya Laundry washes clothes for $1 per kilo (2 pounds) and underwear and socks for 15¢ a pair. *Calle 2, at 5a Av., tel. 987/3–02–61. Open Mon.–Sat. 8–8.*

MEDICAL AID

There's a **24-hour medical clinic** (tel. 987/3–03–14) on Avenida Juárez, three blocks inland from 5a Avenida. **Farmacia La Salud** (corner of Juárez and 30a Av., tel. 987/3–10–50) is open daily 8 AM–midnight to serve your late-night antacid needs.

PHONES AND MAIL

The full-service **post office** (Juárez, between 15a and 20a Avs., no phone; open weekdays 8–7, Sat. 9–1) will hold mail sent to you at the following address for up to 10 days: Lista de Correos, Playa del Carmen, Quintana Roo, CP 77710, México. Public, card-operated **phones** are near the post office on Juárez and across from the bus station on 5a Avenida and Juárez. The **Computel** long-distance phone office (Juárez, ½ block NW of bus station, tel. 987/3–04–69) is open daily 7 AM–10 PM.

VISITOR INFORMATION

Playa's **information booth** supplies free maps and copies of *Destination,* the free monthly tourist magazine, which has useful tips, phone numbers, a map, and snippets of Quintana Roo history. They also sell Latadel cards. *Juárez, at 5a Av., no phone. Between bus station and zócalo. Open daily 7 AM–11 PM.*

COMING AND GOING

The malecón, also known as **5a Avenida,** is the social center of town. Playa del Carmen's main street is **Avenida Juárez,** also known as Avenida Principal, and runs perpendicular to the beach. All other avenues run parallel to the beach and are numbered in multiples of five. Calles are numbered in multiples of two and run perpendicular to the beach.

BY BUS

ADO and **ATS,** both with first- and second-class service, operate out of the town's **bus depot** (corner 5a Av. and Juárez, tel. 987/3–01–09) which is conveniently located one block from the beach. Second-class buses depart hourly 6 AM–8 PM for Tulum ($1.50), stopping in Xcaret (50¢), Akumal ($1), and Xel-Ha ($1.25), as well as other coastal destinations. Five buses travel daily to Chetumal (4 hrs, $8.25 1st class; 5 hrs, $6.50 2nd class), Mérida (4 hrs, $11 1st class; 7 hrs, $8.25 2nd class), and three buses travel daily to Cancún (1 hr; $2 1st class, $1.50 2nd class). There's also direct service to Cancún and to Tulum (1 hr; $1.75 1st class, $1.50 2nd class) every two hours. The four other bus lines that operate out of this terminal have similar schedules and prices.

WHERE TO SLEEP

As Playa del Carmen becomes increasingly popular with tourists, even its budget hotels have been quick to raise their prices. In July, August, and December–April, rates tend to run as much as $5–$15 higher than those listed here. Most budget hotels are on 5a Avenida close to the beach or on Juárez near the bus station.

Camping on the beach is not allowed in Playa del Carmen. However, you can pitch your tent ($4) in the yard of La Ruina (*see below*) and have full access to their facilities.

UNDER $10 • La Ruina. More like an international hippie commune than a hotel, this spot on the beach is the cheapest and by far the most colorful place to stay in Playa. Hang your hammock in a communal open-air palapa ($5 per person) and stash your stuff in a locker (locker and hammock rental $1 each), or rent a double-occupancy cabaña ($12, plus $4 for each extra person). You can also pitch a tent in the grass for $4. The shared bathrooms are passable, and the women's shower farthest west usually has hot water (which means it has devotees of both sexes). *Calle 2, on beach, tel. 987/4–11–23. From bus station, 1 block left on 5a Av. and first right. 21 huts, 32 palapa spaces. Luggage storage. Cash only.*

UNDER $15 • Hotel Playa del Carmen. The walls and floors here gleam with fresh paint, and dark-wood dressers and doorways have a nice, cooling effect. It's $15 for a double only three blocks from the beach. *Juárez, at 10a Av., tel. 987/3–02–94. 1½ blocks from bus station. 17 rooms, all with bath. Laundry, luggage storage. Cash only.*

Posada Mayeli. Rooms here aren't anything spectacular, but it's a great place to be—the owners are so friendly you'll soon feel like one of the family. Plus, you're just seconds away from the heart of Playa, its malecón. Bare, fan-equipped doubles cost $15. *Calle 2a Nte., at 5a Av., no phone. Behind Pez Vela restaurant. 6 rooms, all with bath. Luggage storage. Cash only.*

UNDER $25 • Copa Cabañas. Even if you don't like Barry Manilow's song *Copacabana,* you'll love this place with its large garden and colorful lights. Double ($25) cabañas come complete with attractive tile-work, an outdoor patio and hammock, and sometimes even an ocean view. A Jacuzzi in the courtyard clinches the deal. *5a Av., at Calle 10, tel. 987/3–02–18. 10 cabañas, all with bath. Luggage storage. Cash only.*

Posada Marinelly. Lonely travelers appreciate the incredibly friendly family that owns this place. The large rooms are bare, but the floors sparkle and the fan somehow manages to keep things pretty cool. The owners are happy to help you with the temperamental plumbing. Doubles cost $19. *Juárez, at 10a Av., tel. 987/3–01–40. Next to Hotel Playa del Carmen. 10 rooms, all with bath. Cash only.*

HOSTELS

Villa Deportiva Juvenil Playa del Carmen. This hostel is out in the boonies, about a kilometer (½ mi) from civilization and (more importantly) far from the beach. The pink sex-segregated dorm rooms (18 persons per room) are bare and basic; your $4 buys you a bunk and a locker (bring your own lock). The bathrooms are clean but lack toilet paper, hot water, and shower walls. A $4 deposit is required. *Calle 8, at 30a Av., no phone. From bus station, walk up Juárez 5 blocks, right on Av. 30a and continue NE 4 blocks to Muscle Beach Gym; hostel is just beyond gym, down a short dirt road running NW. 198 beds. Luggage storage. Cash only.*

FOOD

An array of restaurants and loncherías makes it easy to eat cheaply in Playa del Carmen. Supermarkets and stores line 5a Avenida, but you'll find better deals on Juárez. **El Super del Ahorro** (Juárez, at 30a Av., tel. 987/3–03–06) offers the best selection of foods at reasonable prices. Across the street, **Frutería Marsan** sells fresh fruits and vegetables. **Panificadora del Carmen** (Juárez, at 10a Av.) starts selling delicious pastries daily at 6 AM. Most restaurants are also on 5a Avenida, and a few cheap taco stands dot the intersection of Juárez with 10a Avenida.

UNDER $3 • La Cabaña del Lobo. Join the locals for *huevos rancheros* (ranch-style eggs, with spicy tomato sauce, beans, and tortillas; $1.50) or a ham and cheese sandwich ($1) in this clean, cool restaurant. *Juárez, between 5a and 10a Avs., no phone. Cash only.*

UNDER $5 • Media Luna. To find this hidden little vegetarian spot, look for a rusting sign with a white *media luna* (half moon) on a black background. The menu features delicious creations like crepes stuffed with banana, mango, granola, and fresh sweet cream; cheese sandwiches made with juicy tomatoes and whole-wheat bread; and *café frío* (iced coffee with milk, cream, vanilla, cinnamon, and sugar; $1.25). *5a Av., 4½ blocks from Juárez, no phone. Closed Sun. Cash only.*

Pez Vela. This lively restaurant serves elaborate fish and meat dishes accompanied by all the chips and salsa you can handle. Try the Veracruz-style squid, in a fresh tomato sauce flavored with onions, olives, and capers, or the ceviche ($3). Save your beer money for another place though: One measly Corona costs $1.75. *5a Av., at Calle 2, tel. 987/3–09–99. Cash only.*

Sabor. A mellow, newspaper-reading crowd comes to this bakery/café to nibble tasty pastries and cookies or to indulge in a vast array of exotic fruit drinks—including a blend of banana, pineapple, and chocolate. Tofu enthusiasts shouldn't leave here without trying the odd-looking soy tacos ($2). *5a Av., next to Pez Vela, no phone. Cash only.*

UNDER $10 • Mascaras. In Spanish, the name means "masks," and indeed masks from all over the world decorate the walls at this Italian bistro. The menu features fancy *nuevo*-Italian foods like calamari in garlic and oil and pizzas topped with smoked salmon. *Av. Juarez, next to La Ruina Hotel, tel. 987/3–10–53.*

La Parilla. The Parilla is the tourist's social center of Playa del Carmen, and a boisterous crowd holds sway in its open-air terrace. The menu features true gringo food, like chicken fajitas. Strolling mariachis show up nightly. *5a Av., at Calle 8, no phone.*

OUTDOOR ACTIVITIES

Playa del Carmen is a beach town—and beach is just about all it offers. If you don't like sand and swimming, keep on going. The beaches here are spectacular long stretches of white sand (perfect for barefoot walks or lounging with a book) and the surf is free of seaweed. The best section of beach in town is near La Ruina (*see* Where to Sleep, *above*), though during peak season (June–Nov.) litter and the lack of trees turn some people off. Walking south along the beach a couple of kilometers brings you to a narrow, deserted stretch backed by thick vegetation. More than 1 km (½ mi) north of Playa del Carmen is a series of protected lagoons with few visitors beyond the occasional local fisherman.

When you tire of sunning and swimming, it's possible to organize snorkeling, diving, and fishing on charter boats but these trips may break the bank: A small-boat fishing excursion can cost up to $150 for six people. Jaime at **Price Tours** (5a Av., ½ block from Juárez, tel. 987/3–09–25) can arrange big- and small-boat fishing. For snorkeling, try **Seafari Adventures Dive Shop** (5a Av., at Juárez, tel. 987/3–09–01; open daily 8–1 and 5–10); a trip runs $30 per person, including lunch and drinks. Scuba-diving tours go to a number of reefs lying just offshore: **Playacar Divers** (in front of Plaza Marina Playacar, south of ferry dock, tel. 987/3–04–49) and **Tank-Ha Dive Center** (5a Av., between Calles 8 and 10, tel. 987/3–03–02), next to Hotel Maya Bric, offer comparable prices and a professional dive staff. A two-tank dive is $55, and a snorkeling trip to the shallower reefs is $25 per person, with a minimum of two people. Snorkel equipment rental costs $5 per day; to snorkel off the beach, head around the point north of the Blue Parrot Inn to a small coral reef.

AFTER DARK

Almost every hour is happy hour at the **Blue Parrot** (6 blocks north of Juárez, on the beach), where couples sip banana daiquiris ($2.50) and a live rock band plays nightly 8–11 PM. Pick your bar-side swing and take advantage of two-for-one drink specials (offered noon–3, 6–8 PM, and 11 PM–3 AM). After the Blue Parrot, move on to **Caribe Swing** (Calle 4, on the beach), where a local reggae band keeps the dance floor packed until 4 or 5 AM. **Café Sofia** (Calle 2, between 5a Av. and the beach) screens videotapes of recent U.S. movies daily at 3, 5:30, and 8 PM. The movies are free but you are expected to order a beer or snack.

NEAR PLAYA DEL CARMEN

THE COASTAL ROAD

Highway 307, the road running between Playa del Carmen and Tulum, passes some of the most spectacular beaches in the Caribbean, as well as a variety of lagoons that support a vast array of fish and wildlife. The PLAYA DEL CARMEN–TULUM bus runs hourly 6 AM–8 PM (*see* Coming and Going *in* Playa del Carmen, *above*) and will stop at or near any of the places listed below, with the exception of Punta Bete, which is north of Playa del Carmen. From Tulum, you can take a bus running north along the highway every half hour until 9 PM. Either way, be sure to tell the driver where you want to get off.

PUNTA BETE

Punta Bete, especially the southern end of it, is isolated and idyllic, with kilometers of pristine white sand, coconut palms, and gentle waves curling in from the sea. The only thing missing is garlanded dancers singing "Bali Hai." If you can't arrange that, try the snorkeling, which is excellent just 65–215 ft offshore. Schools of fantastically colored fish, octopus, and stingrays are within wading distance; slap on those fins on the southern end of the beach, as the northern part of Punta Bete is more rocky. Overnight visitors can hang their hammocks in a palapa for about $3 at either **Palapas Los Pinos** or **Palapas Playa Xcalacoco.** For an extra $3, you can rent a hammock. At Xcalacoco, you have the additional options either to pitch your own tent ($4 per person) or rent a cabaña ($15–$23, depending on size). Clean showers and a restaurant are footsteps away. Both Palapas Los Pinos and Xcalacoco rent snorkeling gear (about $6 a day) and offer snorkeling and fishing expeditions (about $20 per person per day). Both places accept cash only.

COMING AND GOING • If you've got the energy, the 1½-hour, 12-km (7½-mi) walk from Playa del Carmen north to Punta Bete takes you along a gorgeous stretch of beach. Start early in the morning before the sun gets too high. Otherwise, take an ADO or ATS bus (75¢) heading toward Cancún, tell the bus driver to let you off at Punta Bete, and walk 30 minutes down the bug-ridden, paved road. To get back to Playa del Carmen, wave down the same bus heading the opposite direction.

Playa del Carmen isn't known for its archaeological sites, but locals take pride in the ruins of Xaman-Ha, in the woods behind the Continental Plaza Hotel.

XCARET

No more than 10 km (6 mi) south of Playa del Carmen (40 km north of Tulum) lies Xcaret (ISH-carey), where Maya women used to come for purifying bathing rituals before canoeing to Cozumel. Although the site is still surrounded by lagoons, cenotes, and voluptuous jungle brush, it's about as authentically Maya as Disneyland. The main attraction is a 1,750-ft underground river, which would make for beautiful snorkeling if it weren't already packed to capacity with tourists. You can rent snorkeling equipment for $6; lockers are 30¢. Snacks and drinks at the park's eateries are similarly overpriced. The biggest drawback is the entrance fee, an astounding $30 Monday–Saturday. "Bargain" Sunday will still cost you $25. The fee goes toward the park's upkeep and the preservation of endangered animal species and also allows you access to the light show, music, and dancing of "Xcaret at Night," which starts at 6 PM. *Open daily 8:30 AM–10 PM.*

COMING AND GOING • Your best bet is to get here early and make a day of it. Take a bus (50¢) from anywhere along the highway—it passes about every half hour—and ask to be dropped off at Xcaret. From there, walk 20 minutes to the park's entrance, or wait for the free tourist tram.

PAAMUL

About 10 km (6 mi) south of Xcaret is Paamul, the famous nesting site of an endangered species of giant turtle that can weigh more than 200 pounds. During June and July, the female turtles emerge from the ocean at night to lay as many as 200 eggs each. They may like Paamul's beach, but you probably won't—it doesn't have the white sandy expanses found in tourist brochures. Ah, just as well let the turtles have this beach. Snorkeling over the reef, about 1,200 ft offshore, is excellent, and **Scuba Mex** (next to Restaurant Arrecifes, tel. 987/4–17–29) rents snorkeling equipment for $6 a day. For $25 per person they'll take you out to the reef in a boat for three hours and give you a few drinks. Otherwise, just slip on your fins and swim on out.

COMING AND GOING • Take any Tulum-bound bus and ask to be dropped off at Paamul; it's a five-minute walk down the road to the beach. To return, flag down the bus on the opposite side of the highway. Note that buses pass here most frequently during the early part of the day. Around 4 or 5 in the afternoon you may have to resort to a taxi or hitchhiking.

YAL-KU LAGOON

Yal-Ku has everything that nearby Xel-Ha has, without the commercial gloss, tourist crowds, or high price. But don't count on this paradise lasting forever, because Xel-Ha's owner has plans to develop Yal-Ku lagoon into a similar tourist park. Come in the morning to beat the crowds; you'll have access to interesting underwater cavern formations, where schools of small, yellow-nose barracuda gather. The parrotfish here munch coral so loudly that you can actually hear them chew. *Take a PLAYA DEL CARMEN–*

TULUM bus and ask to be dropped off at Hotel Club Akumal Caribe. From inside hotel's gates, walk north 3 km (2 mi) and follow signs to lagoon. Admission free. Open daily 8–4:30.

XCACEL

About 14 km (9 mi) south of Yal-Ku, Xcacel (pronounced ISH-ka-sel) provides an excellent refuge from the string of pricey tourist stops along the highway. The beach is free of rocks and seaweed, and there are usually just a handful of RVs and campers here. There's also a small, privately funded turtle farm (where you can look as long as you don't touch). The impressive Xcacel cenote, dark with salt- and freshwater animal life, lies at the beach's southern end and is reached by a swampy jungle path rife with scurrying hermit crabs. Just south of the cenote is a giant coconut grove where some of the area's only remaining *palmeras reales* (royal palms). To arrange diving and snorkeling trips in the nearby breathtaking underwater caves and cenotes, visit Buddy in the camper just west of the turtle farm, or call Tony and Nancy Derosa of **Aquatic Tech** (tel. 987/5–90–20) in nearby Akumal. *Take a PLAYA DEL CARMEN–TULUM bus and ask to be dropped off at Xcacel. Admission to beach $1.50; $2 extra to camp overnight.*

XEL-HA LAGOON

Xel-Ha ("clear water" in Maya) is a national park that is home to parrotfish, angelfish, manta rays, and giant barracudas, as well as the tourists who love them. Underwater caverns filled with coral (and, in one case, a Mayan altar) make for interesting snorkeling. Though tourists and their various ointments have polluted the lagoon—resulting in the current prohibition of sunscreen lotions—the place remains maddeningly popular. If you're determined, come early in the morning, before the rush starts, and explore the entire lagoon; don't be afraid to stray from where the tourists are swimming. Admission is a whopping $10, and on the northeast side of the lake, you can rent snorkeling equipment ($6), lockers ($1 plus a $2 deposit), and towels ($1). There are an assortment of snack bars selling overpriced food and drink. *40 km (25 mi) south of Playa del Carmen, 15 km (9 mi) north of Tulum, no phone. Take a PLAYA DEL CARMEN–TULUM bus and ask to be dropped off at Xel-Ha.*

COZUMEL

If you want to dive, come to Cozumel—it's as simple as that. Noted oceanographer Jacques Cousteau raved about the coral reefs that ring this island, 19 km (12 mi) offshore from Playa del Carmen. While Cozumel is not the paradise it once was (tourism has killed a lot of the coral), it's still the best site on the Yucatán Peninsula. Most famous of all the reefs is the sheer **Palancar Reef,** where underwater visibility can often extend more than 200 ft. Divers can experience a range of underwater excitement at dozens of other reefs as well, including plunging walls, caves, and even a phony airplane wreck left behind by a Mexican film crew on location in 1977. Just keep in mind that most visitors to Cozumel are prepared to drop a bundle on diving, so it's not exactly a budget paradise. Though you'll find reasonably priced restaurants, dive resorts charging upward of $100 a day tend to be the norm for accommodations.

During Maya times, Cozumel was a sacred island covered with temples and shrines dedicated to Ixchel, the goddess of fertility. Maya women from all over what is now Central America and southern Mexico were expected to make the pilgrimage here at least once in their lifetime to pray and leave offerings. Unfortunately, many temples were ransacked by Cortés in 1519, and the U.S. military destroyed others while constructing an airstrip during World War II. What does remain are vast tracts of thick jungle covering the entire northeast half of the island, as well as much of its interior. Even if you're only on Cozumel a couple of days, it's worth renting a scooter or bike to explore the teeming jungles and swamplands.

BASICS

AMERICAN EXPRESS

The AmEx representative here is **Fiesta Cozumel.** The office cashes and issues traveler's checks but doesn't give cash advances. *Calle 11 Sur 598, between Pedro Joaquín and 25a Av. Sur, tel. 987/2–07–25. Follow Rafael Melgar south to Calle 11, take a left, and walk 6½ blocks. Open weekdays 8–1 and 4–8.*

CASAS DE CAMBIO

Most banks and casas de cambio are in downtown San Miguel, the one and only town on the island. You can change cash or traveler's checks at **Banco del Atlántico** (Calle 1 Sur 11, southern corner of zócalo,

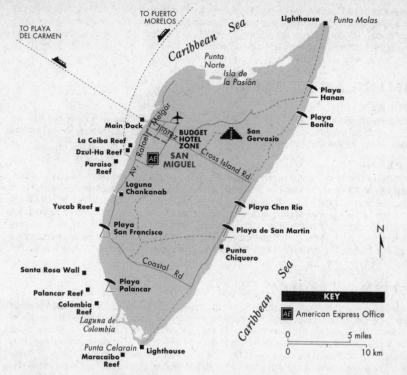

TO PLAYA
DEL CARMEN

TO PUERTO
MORELOS

Caribbean Sea

Lighthouse Punta Molas

Punta
Norte

Isla de
la Pasión

Playa
Hanan

Playa
Bonita

Main Dock

La Ceiba Reef

Dzul-Ha Reef

Paraiso
Reef

BUDGET
HOTEL
ZONE

San
Gervasio

AE
SAN
MIGUEL

Av. Rafael Melgar

Juárez

Cross Island Rd.

Laguna
Chankanab

Yucab Reef

Playa Chen Río

Playa
San Francisco

Playa de San Martin

Punta
Chiquero

Santa Rosa Wall

Coastal Rd.

Playa
Palancar

Palancar Reef

Colombia
Reef

Laguna de
Colombia

Caribbean Sea

N

Punta Celarain Lighthouse
Maracaibo
Reef

KEY

AE American Express Office

0   5 miles
0   10 km

tel. 987/2–01–42; open weekdays 9–2, Sat. 10–1), or use its ATM that accepts MasterCard, Cirrus, and Visa. **Cambio de Moneda** (5a Av. Sur, between Calle 1 Sur and Rosado Salas, tel. 987/2–21–97 or 987/2–21–65; open daily 8 AM–9 PM), one block from the waterfront, has good exchange rates. However, American dollars are gladly accepted all over the island.

EMERGENCIES

In an emergency, contact the **police** (Rafael Melgar, at Calle 13 Sur, tel. 987/2–00–92). For **ambulance** service dial 987/2–06–39.

LAUNDRY

Margarita Laundromat charges $2.50 per load to wash, 50¢ per 10 minutes of drying, and sells detergent. *20a Av. Sur, at Calle 3 Sur, tel. 987/2–28–65. Open Mon.–Sat. 7 AM–9 PM, Sun. 9–5.*

MEDICAL AID

For 24-hour medical assistance, call or visit **Dr. Gustavo Ambriz** (Calle 5 Sur 21-B, 4 blocks south of ferry dock, tel. 987/2–16–71 or 987/2–14–30). He specializes in travel medicine and diving-related problems and has a decompression tank. **Farmacia Dori** (Rosado Salas, at 15a Av. Sur, tel. 987/2–05–59) is open daily 7 AM–midnight.

PHONES AND MAIL

The full-service **post office** (Rafael Melgar, at Calle 7 Sur, tel. 987/2–01–06; open weekdays 9–6, Sat. 9–noon) will hold mail sent to you at the following address for up to 10 days: Lista de Correos, Cozumel, Quintana Roo, CP 77600, México. At **Computel** (Calle 1 Sur 165, between 5a and 10a Avs., tel. 987/2–41–54, fax 987/2–40–87; open daily 7 AM–10 PM) you can make local and long-distance calls. Farmacia Dori (*see above*) sells Ladatel phone cards.

VISITOR INFORMATION

The Blue Guide is a free, pocket-size publication with important phone numbers and a small map of the city. Pick one up at any hotel or at the ferry dock. Cozumel's **Oficina Estatal de Turismo** is difficult to find and often closed, but they do have some interesting information on island flora and fauna and can supply you with free maps of the island as well as a self-guided tour of the San Gervasio ruins (*see* Worth Seeing, *below*). *Edificio Plaza del Sol, tel. and fax 987/2–09–72. From tall clock on east side of zócalo, head east behind farmacia toward Centro de Convenciones, then head north and look for tower on the left. Office is on west side of upper-level balcony. Open weekdays 8:30–3.*

COMING AND GOING

BY FERRY

The **Cruzeros Maritimo** (tel. 987/2–15–08) ferry departs from Playa del Carmen for Cozumel (45 min; $3.25 one-way, $7 round-trip) every two–three hours daily 5:15 AM–8:45 PM. The ferry leaves from the pier just in front of Plaza Marina Playacar in Playa.

BY PLANE

Cozumel has a small international **airport** (tel. 987/2–06–47), with flights to and from the States on **Continental** (tel. 987/2–08–47). Fares vary dramatically, but a reasonable low-season round-trip fare from Houston to Cozumel is about $420. **Mexicana** (tel. 987/2–29–45) and **Aero Cozumel** (tel. 987/2–34–56) offer service to cities all over Mexico, including Cancún, Mérida, and Mexico City. **Aero Banana** (tel. 987/2–50–40) flies to nearby Isla Mujeres and Cancún. To reach town from the airport, walk two minutes out of the terminal to the *glorieta* (traffic circle) with the large statue of a sparrow and then catch a taxi (10 min, $3.50). The CIRCUMNAVEGACION bus will take you from the airport to the ferry terminal at the heart of town for a mere 25¢.

GETTING AROUND

Cozumel is the largest of Mexico's islands, 53 km (33 mi) long and 14 km (9 mi) wide. **San Miguel de Cozumel,** on the western coast, is the one and only town on the island. Inland you'll find residential areas, and stretching along the coast south of San Miguel are dozens of expensive, exclusive diving resorts. It's easy to get around San Miguel on foot, since the streets are laid out in a grid and run either parallel or perpendicular to the coast. Apart from the main avenues, all streets have numerical designations. The avenue running along the malecón is **Rafael Melgar**; parallel avenues are numbered in multiples of five (5a Avenida is followed by 10a Avenida and 15a Avenida). **Avenida Benito Juárez,** the main avenue, begins at the ferry dock and divides the town into two halves: north and south. Streets and avenues north of Juárez receive the appellation Norte; those to the south, Sur. To further confuse the situation, streets north of Juárez have even numbers, and those to the south have odd numbers. The main **plaza** is directly adjacent to the ferry dock, between 5a Avenida and the malecón at Avenida Juárez. The rest of the island is circled by a single road along the perimeter, making it easy to explore, and several other roads and trails cut across the island through the low-lying jungle.

BY BUS

There are three bus routes in Cozumel, connecting downtown to the *colonias* (residential areas). The CIRCUMNAVEGACION bus (25¢) is most useful for visitors; it runs up Calle 11 from Rafael Melgar and turns north on 65 Avenida; after passing through the eastern colonias, it returns to town via Boulevard Aeropuerto. The bus runs every 20 minutes until about 7:30 PM.

BY SCOOTER

The most popular way to explore the island is by scooter. The going rate is $20–$25 for 24 hours, but bargaining is not out of the question. **Rentadora Leo** (5a Av. 199, at Rosado Salas, tel. 987/2–43–81) charges $20 for same-day returns. Don't neglect to wear a helmet, or you'll be fined $25.

BY TAXI

Taxi rates are regulated by the government, so you have the right to report any excessive charges to the local **Sitio de Taxis** (Calle 2 Nte., between 5a and 10a Avs., tel. 987/2–00–41), and you may even get your money back. Within town, you shouldn't be charged more than $2; if you're going as far as Laguna Chankanab, you'll have to pay about $6. Taxi rates rise slightly after midnight. If you take a taxi from the ferry dock, ask to see the driver's *tarjeta de tarifas* (rate card) to make sure you're getting a fair price.

WHERE TO SLEEP

After Cancún, Cozumel is the most expensive place on the peninsula. Hotels and resorts along the beach tend to cater to scuba divers with money to burn, and they charge a pretty penny for all that pampering. Budget travelers can choose between staying in the hotels in San Miguel, most of which are within a few blocks of the central plaza, and camping (*see below*) on one of the outlying beaches.

UNDER $15 • Hotel Posada Edém. This is the cheapest downtown hotel, and it's conveniently located next to a taxi stand, bakery, and the main plaza. You may find a few skittering bugs in the somewhat gloomy rooms, but overall this place is clean and well-kept. The owner is happy to have guests join him in the lobby to watch Mexican soap operas. Double rooms are $11, with air-conditioning $24. *Calle 2 Nte. 12, between 5a and 10a Avs. Nte., tel. 987/2–11–66. 14 rooms, all with bath. Luggage storage.*

UNDER $25 • Hotel Kary. Spacious rooms, free *agua purificada* (purified water), and a refreshing courtyard pool will make you forget you're a budget traveler. Doubles with or without air-conditioning are $22. If you're a party of three, beware: Apparently your right to a third towel is not guaranteed, and you may have to tackle the maid to get one. *25a Av. Sur, at Rosado Salas, tel. 987/2–20–11. From ferry dock, 2 blocks south (right) and 5 blocks east. 17 rooms and 2 suites, all with bath. Luggage storage. Cash only.*

Hotel Pepita. Located on a somewhat run-down street, this lovely hotel is a welcome surprise, with complimentary coffee provided in the photo-filled lobby. Rooms are small but sunny and surprisingly quiet, with refrigerators, air-conditioning, and colorful bedspreads. Doubles are $25. *15a Av. Sur, at Calle 1 Sur, 3 blocks from main pier, tel. 987/2–00–98. 30 rooms, all with bath. Cash only.*

UNDER $30 • Hotel Cozumel Inn. The sunny balconies of this three-tier hotel look out onto a plant-filled inner patio with a small pool. Tiny but tidy bedrooms come equipped with shoebox-size bathrooms, and the patio rooms are perfectly positioned for the occasional afternoon breeze. Doubles are $26, plus an extra $5 for air-conditioning. *Calle 4 Nte. 3, at Rafael Melgar, tel. 987/2–03–14. 30 rooms, all with bath. Luggage storage. Cash only.*

Hotel Marycarmen. Rooms here have wood furniture, air-conditioning, and great bathrooms, plus plush bedding with satin ruffles. The small atrium is ideal for sunbathing, and the location is central. Doubles cost $27. *5a Av. Sur 4, between Calle 1 Sur and Rosado Salas, tel. 987/2–05–81. From ferry dock, 1 block inland and 1½ blocks right. 27 rooms, all with bath. Luggage storage.*

Posada del Zorro. Down-and-out scuba-diving junkies flock here. The walls are patched with blistering paint and the bathrooms are rust-tinted and bare, but at least there aren't any noticeable nonhuman life forms scurrying around. Large rooms with two double beds are only $30 for one or two people, plus $5 for each additional person. *Juárez, at 30a Av., 6 blocks east of ferry dock, tel. 987/2–07–90. 6 rooms, all with bath. Luggage storage. Cash only.*

CAMPING

You can camp for free at **Playa del Sol** or **Playa Casita,** both a short walk south of town, or try the secluded beaches on the southern and eastern portions of the island. None of Cozumel's beaches are patrolled, and there have been several incidents of theft recently; use caution and do not leave your belongings unattended. If you plan to camp on Cozumel's beaches during the sea turtle's egg-laying season (May–Oct.), you'll need to get permission from the **Zona Federal** (Edificio Plaza del Sol, second floor, near Visitor Information Office, tel. 987/2–09–66). During any other time of year, permission isn't necessary.

FOOD

Surprisingly, Cozumel has plenty of reasonable dining options. The daily **mercado** (Rosado Salas, at 25a Av.) sells fresh fruits and vegetables. Several *loncherías* (snack bars) in the market offer breakfast deals and main dishes for less than $2. **Panaderia La Cozumeleña** (Calle 3, at 10a Av., tel. 987/2–01–89) bakes the world's greatest pastry, a cross between a *churro* (a long, spiral, sugared doughnut) and a cream puff. Three cost about $1.

UNDER $5 • La Casa del Waffle. A couple of windsurfers named Raul and Jeannie got together and formed this waffle joint to finance their aquatic habit. Delicacies include excellent pancakes, waffles Benedict, and the waffle supreme ($4), a waffle freighted with fruit, syrup, and whipped cream. Bathing suit–clad tourists stop here for a bite to eat and end up staying for the bottomless cup of coffee. *Juárez,*

ENDANGERED
YUCATAN REEFS

The Yucatán offers some of the most stunning coral reefs in the world. Once a reef has been damaged, it repairs itself very slowly, growing at a rate of just 1 cm every 10 years. To preserve the reefs for future visitors, observe a few rules: Don't touch the coral while snorkeling, as even a brief encounter will kill it. Be careful where you drop anchor when mooring a boat; a 30-pound weight can do a lot of damage. And although coral is often made into colorful souvenirs and jewelry, you'll do the reefs a favor if you don't buy such trinkets.

between 20a and 25 a Avs., no phone. Closed daily 1–6 PM. Other location: Ground floor of Vista del Mar Hotel, Av. Melgar, 4 blocks south of ferry dock, tel. 987/2–05–45. No dinner Sun. Cash only.

Casa Denis. At this open-air eatery, breathe in the fresh air while you admire the adjacent Virgin Mary altar. The book-size menu offers choices such as avocado soup, fresh fish kabobs, and *enchiladas suizas* (enchiladas with cheese sauce). Beers are less than $1.50 apiece. *Calle 1 Sur, between 5a and 10a Avs., ½ block east of zócalo, tel. 987/2–00–67. Closed Sun. Cash only.*

Restaurant Toñita. The *comida típica* (traditional Mexican food) served here is cheap, and the menu changes daily. A meal of soup, a meat dish, vegetables, rice, and tortillas will run you about $3. Strategically placed fans keep the place somewhat cool. *Rosado Salas, between 10a and 15a Avs., 2½ blocks east of zócalo, tel. 987/2–04–01. Closed Sun. Cash only.*

UNDER $10 • Los Moros del Morito. This restaurant is a hidden treasure, worth the extra effort a visit requires. The setting is festive and the portions are decadent, which are two reasons why this place is so popular with locals and expat residents of Cozumel. Seafood and typical Mexican fare includes everything from fish shish kabobs ($7) to enchiladas with rich mole (chocolate-chile sauce). *35a Av. Sur, between Calle 3 and Morelos, tel. 987/2–28–67. From malecón, walk inland 8 blocks on Rosada Salas, right on 35a Av. Sur. Closed Tues. Cash only.*

CAFES

Café Caribe. For travelers in a serious Nescafé rut, Café Caribe is a blessing: It's a European-style coffeehouse that plays jazz and classical music, and serves excellent iced cappuccino ($2). The pastry selection is decent, and the owner runs a paperback exchange. *10a Av. Sur, between Rosado Salas and Calle 3 Sur, tel. 987/2–36–21. Cash only.*

WORTH SEEING

The wild and rocky eastern coast of Cozumel is well worth exploring: It remains undeveloped despite the paved road that runs along its shoreline. You can swim in some places, especially **Punta Chiquero, Chen Río,** and the beach at **Punta Morena Hotel.** At other points, however, the strong undertow makes a leisurely dip dangerous. You can get a great view of the island from the top of the lighthouse on **Punta Celarain** (southern tip of island, at end of 4-km/2½-mi dirt road), which looks out over the pounding surf.

SAN GERVASIO RUINS

The restored ruins of San Gervasio are situated in 10 acres of jungle at the center of the island. The site is said to have been used as a ceremonial center throughout several Maya periods, and the remains of fertility shrines, residential units, and mural paintings are still visible today. Information for a self-guided tour is available at the **Oficina Estatal de Turismo** (*see* Visitor Information, *above*). To get here, take the cross-island road until you see the sign for San Gervasio, then turn right on the dirt road (which may be washed out during the rainy season) and head northeast to the ruins. **Turismo Aviomar** (5a Av., between Calles 2 and 4 Nte., tel. 987/2–04–77 or 987/2–05–88) offers a two-hour tour of the ruins for $35. Tours leave weekdays at 9 and 11 AM, but call ahead to check availability. You can also take a taxi to the ruins, but it'll cost $30 round-trip. San Gervasio is open daily 8–5, and admission is $3.50.

MUSEO DE LA ISLA DE COZUMEL

This handsome museum is a necessary stop for anyone wanting to learn more about the island's spectacular array of unique terrestrial and underwater plants and animals. Clearly drawn, color-coded maps with English subtitles explain the island's geographic history and the development of the island's ecological riches. In addition to life-size nature scenes and an entire room dedicated to the origins and nature of coral, the museum also has a gallery delineating the history of the Maya, complete with replicas of important ruins and artifacts found on the island. The doorman is also a great source of information—if business is slow, he'll walk through the museum with you. *Rafael Melgar, between Calles 4 and 6 Nte., tel. 987/2–14–34. Admission: $2, free Sun. Open daily 9–5.*

OUTDOOR ACTIVITIES

Prime snorkeling and diving spots can be found all around the island, though equipment rental and transport to the reefs is not cheap. Most trips, however, are well worth the pesos: The wide variety of marine life combined with the astonishing visibility of Cozumel's clear Caribbean waters makes this one of the most outstanding adventures in Mexico.

SNORKELING

Snorkeling is a cheap and easy way for nondivers to explore Cozumel's sea life. Particularly good is the snorkeling off the beach on the western coast, especially in the area between Hotel Sol Caribe and Playa Maya. Equipment rental costs about $6 at any of the dive shops in town; a boat trip to snorkel the shallow reefs is about $20. Try **Bel Mar Aquatics** (Hotel La Ceiba, 1 km/½ mi south of ferry dock on Rafael Melgar, tel. 987/2–16–65), **Blue Bubble Divers** (corner 5a Av. Sur and Calle 3 Sur, tel. 987/2–18–65, www.qssolutions.com/bluebubble), or **Diving Adventures** (Calle 5 Sur, at Rafael Melgar, tel. 987/2–30–09, or 888/338–0388 from the U.S.).

On Sunday night, local bands gather in Cozumel's main plaza to play everything from mambo and salsa to jarana, a fast-pace Yucatecan dance that requires the tiptoeing performer to sidestep an invisible bull.

LA CEIBA REEF • La Ceiba Reef, in front of La Ceiba Hotel, is a good place to snorkel or dive. A 400-ft trail has been marked out on the reef, starting at a fake airplane wreck (it was sunk during the filming of a movie) and continuing past several interesting coral formations. *4 km (2½ mi) south of San Miguel; a taxi costs $3. Admission free.*

DZUL-HA • Dzul-Ha Reef boasts two important features: free admission and few tourists. About 2 km (1 mi) south of La Ceiba Reef (*see above*), Dzul-Ha doesn't plant airplane wrecks or religious icons to amuse snorkelers. What you will see are beautiful angel fish, amazing coral formations, and even starfish on the ocean floor. You can rent equipment for $6 at the Blue Bubble dive shop branch on the beach beside the reef, or just bring your own. *6 km (4 mi) south of town, across from Hotel Club de Sol; a taxi costs $4.*

LAGUNA CHANKANAB • This national park 9 km (5½ mi) south of San Miguel is the most popular snorkeling spot in Cozumel. At the center of the park is a lagoon separated from the beach, fed by an underwater cave; a large botanical garden with replicas of Maya dwellings surrounds the lagoon. Swimming is no longer allowed in the lagoon (paddling tourists were slowly killing it), but snorkeling in the clear waters of the adjacent bay is spectacular, as is diving at the offshore reef. Once underwater, you can see interesting coral heads, a myriad of tropical fish, and a large statue of Christ, sunk for the entertainment of divers. The drawback here is that it's quite crowded: Head elsewhere if you want a solitary snorkel. Four dive shops on the premises rent snorkeling and diving equipment. A taxi to Chankanab costs about $7. *Admission: $5. Open daily 9–5:30.*

SCUBA DIVING

Diving is the raison d'être of tourism in Cozumel. Dozens of dive shops offer all levels of instruction, as well as a wide range of boat trips; anybody, from beginner to expert, can find a suitable dive. Beginners hone their skills on the shallow **Yucab Reef,** close to shore and just south of Laguna Chankanab. Expert divers will want to head for the more challenging (and thrilling) reefs, such as **Maracaibo, Santa Rosa Wall,** and **Colombia.** You must be a PADI- or NAUI-certified diver to rent diving gear and take diving trips; at the more reputable agencies, the staff will also test your diving ability before letting you attempt advanced dives. The good agencies may be more expensive, but you're paying for expert dive masters and well-maintained (or new) equipment. **Aqua Safari** (Rafael Melgar 429, between Calles 5 and 7 Sur, tel. 987/2–01–01), **Cozumel Equalizers** (Rosado Salas 72, at 5a Av. Sur, tel. 987/2–35–11), and **Dive Paradise** (Rafael Melgar 601, tel. 987/2–10–07) are among the most reputable dive shops. Four-day certification courses cost about $315. Two-tank boat dives cost about $50 (usually with a six-diver minimum), and night dives are $30.

PALANCAR REEF • The most famous of Cozumel's reefs, Palancar lies about 1½ km (¾ mi) from Playa Palancar on the island's southwestern shore. The reef stretches intermittently for about 5 km (3 mi) and offers divers a range of underwater experiences. The best-known formation is the **Horseshoe,** a collection of coral heads that form a horseshoe curve right at the drop-off. The visibility—some 200 ft in places—is extraordinary.

PARAISO REEF • Just north of the Stouffer Presidente Hotel, near San Miguel, this reef lies 40–73 ft deep and has excellent star- and brain coral formations. The northern part of Paraíso may be affected by the new pier construction (*see box, below*). The southern part is farther offshore but merits taking a boat to see the extensive marine life there. **Diving Adventures** (Calle 5 Sur, at Melgar, tel. 987/2–30–09) offers daily dive trips to Paraíso for $35.

AFTER DARK

Although Cozumel boasts the usual gringo-packed bars, chain operations like Carlos 'n Charlie's and Hard Rock Café are not your only options for a memorable night. **Joe's Reggae Bar** (10a Av. Sur, at Rosado Salas, tel. 987/2–32–75) is free of high-school students celebrating graduation. No cover charge, bottomless popcorn baskets, live music, $1.75 beers, and quirky Fiji-meets-Rome decor make it a delightful place to kick back for the evening. Around the corner, **Raga** (Rosado Salas, between 10a and 15a Avs., no phone) presents live pop music Monday–Wednesday 9:30 PM–midnight and Thursday–Saturday 10:30 PM–1 AM.

TULUM

The ancient Maya city of Tulum is set against a breathtaking backdrop of talcum-powder beaches, rocky cliffs, and clear Caribbean waters. Many tourists come here on organized day trips from Cancún, and they linger only long enough to take a few pictures, buy some souvenirs, and then scurry back to their air-conditioned hotel rooms. However, the pristine beaches south of the ruins attract a different sort of crowd—mostly friendly young Europeans—who come here to sell handmade jewelry and tie-dyed shirts, or just to hang around soaking up the sun's rays.

Tulum was built and rebuilt in various stages, beginning sometime between AD 700 and 1300 with the Putún-Maya people. This tribe was also associated with Mayapán, one of the most powerful Maya city-states in the region. Originally named *Zama* (Maya for "dawn"), Tulum was intended as an observatory and ceremonial center. Burial platforms surround the leftover buildings and the tiny, windowed observatory hovers above the old city. Juan de Grijalva, who sighted the city in 1518 when his Spanish expedition sailed past the coast, compared Tulum, with its red, white, and blue buildings, with Seville. The city was still occupied by the Maya at the time of the Spanish conquest: One of the images in the Temple of the Paintings depicts Chaac riding a horse, an animal introduced by the Spanish.

COMING AND GOING

The ancient city of Tulum is 63 km (39 mi) south of Playa del Carmen and 127 km (79 mi) south of Cancún. The first-class **Premier** bus station (tel. 987/2–33–66) is downtown, across from the Maya Hotel. It serves Mérida and Valladolid. Second-class buses can be caught at the terminal opposite the first-class station; from Tulum there's frequent second-class service to Playa del Carmen (2 per hr; 45 min, $1.50), Cancún (2 per hr; 1½ hrs, $3), Chetumal (5 per day via Bacalone; 3½ hrs, $6.50), Cobá (4 per day; 45 min, $1), and Valladolid (1 per day; 2½ hrs, $4). One lone bus heads to Mérida (5 hrs, $8) at 1:30 PM. Hitchhiking along the main highway is common and relatively easy.

GETTING AROUND

The *crucero* (turnoff) for the Tulum ruins and budget lodging is about 4 km (2½ mi) north of the modern town of Tulum. To reach the ruins, ask the driver to let you off at the crucero, then walk east down

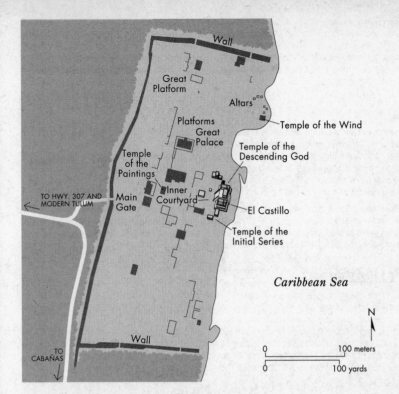

Caribbean Sea

N

| 0 | | 100 meters |
| 0 | | 100 yards |

the paved road for five minutes, toward the coast. There's also a $1 trolley bus running from the parking lot just south of the crucero to the entrance to the ruins. As you enter the ruins, another paved road heads south along the coast to the cabañas and beaches. It's a five-minute taxi ride ($1.50) from the ruins and campgrounds to the modern town of Tulum, which is equipped with one budget hotel, a handful of restaurants and fruit stands, and a few other basic services.

WHERE TO SLEEP

The cabañas that lie along the beach south of the ruins are your cheapest (and most primitive) lodging option. You'll need to arrive no later than 9 PM to register with the cabaña managers before they return to town. **Hotel Maya** (Av. Tulum 32, across from bus terminal, tel. 987/1–20–34) has doubles for $13. Rooms are clean and, unlike the cabañas, have electricity, but the only good reason to stay here is to catch the 6 AM bus to Cobá. The hotel accepts cash only.

UNDER $15 • Cabañas Don Armando. The owner is pleased to announce that there are "no hippies" at Don Armando. The well-constructed cabañas are comfortable, with beds on cement platforms, hammock hooks, sand floors, and windows. The bathrooms are clean and locked (you get a key). Light sleepers beware: A nearby disco plays loud, obnoxious music every night until about 2 AM. Cabañas cost $10 with one bed and one hammock, $12 with two beds, and $14 for a beachfront hut with one bed and one hammock. Camping costs $4 per person. *1 km (½ mi) south of ruins, tel. 987/5–05–96. 24 cabañas. Restaurant, laundry, luggage storage. Cash only.*

Cabañas El Mirador. This place is quiet and rarely crowded, though its two cabañas with beds ($11 each) go quickly. Cabañas with hammocks are $7.50 for two people, and hammock rental is $2. The showers are communal, though single-sex. The friendly owners serve up a hearty plate of spaghetti at Restaurant El Mirador (*see below*), which overlooks the cabañas. *On the beach, 1 km (½ mi) from ruins, no phone. 20 cabañas. Restaurant, laundry, luggage storage. Cash only.*

Cabañas Los Gatos. After one night's rest in these palm-shaded cabañas, you may decide to stay indefinitely. A 20-minute walk south of the other cabañas, Los Gatos sits atop a rocky promontory that overlooks the vigorous surf. Cozy cabañas have small double beds swinging from sturdy knotted ropes, mosquito-net canopies, wood furniture, and elegant candleholders. Cabañas with one bed cost $12. Those with two beds (for 3 or 4 people) cost $20. *Follow road 2 km (1 mi) south past ruins. Or walk south along beach about 20 min. Cash only.*

FOOD

The restaurants outside the ruins and at the crucero are nothing spectacular, and in fact are also ridiculously expensive. Skip them in favor of one of the downtown eateries, or take your meals at one of the cabaña sites. **Don Armando** (*see* Where to Sleep, *above*) offers main dishes such as fish, chicken, eggs, and beans for under $5 and beer for less than $1. The food is particularly good but pricey at **Restaurant El Mirador** (*see* Cabañas El Mirador, *above*): a pile of hot cakes costs $2, while chicken fajitas or a big plate of spaghetti with shrimp costs around $5.

In town, **Restaurant Maya** (in Hotel Maya, across from bus terminal) serves a filling meal of chicken tacos, rice, and vegetables for $3.25. The 24-hour **Restaurant Ambrosia** (next to bus terminal) serves tasty *salbutes* (fried tortillas topped with chicken, lettuce, onion, and tomato) and generously cheesed quesadillas for $3.50 apiece. All of the above are cash only.

WORTH SEEING

Tulum wasn't constructed as a fortress of defense, but the structure's thick walls and watchtowers proved useful in times of war. The city's most prestigious inhabitants (priests, astrologers, and carpenters) were shielded from contact with peasant farmers by a 23-ft-thick wall. The city's castle and the nobles' homes surrounding it are evidence of three different building phases, each using the previous structure as a base from which to erect the building's next level. There are some reliefs carved into the stucco walls of the buildings, but frescoes were the most prevalent form of decoration in Tulum. *Admission: $5.50, free on Sun. Parking: $2. Open daily 8–5.*

TEMPLE OF THE PAINTINGS

This small yet well-preserved structure consists of two temples, one inside the other. Large stucco masks, probably representing the god Kukulcán, stare from the corners of the outer facade. The mask on the southern corner, with one eye open and one shut, symbolizes the duality of the Maya belief system, which held that evil and darkness (the closed eye) are as much a part of nature as goodness and light (the open eye).

Inside the temple, the murals are divided into three sections, symbolizing the three realms of the universe: the underworld, the mortal world, and the heavens. Archaeologists point to the depiction of Chaac riding a horselike animal as an indication that the murals were completed or reworked after the Spanish arrived. Unfortunately, the images are difficult to see from the entrance, and visitors are not allowed inside the temple.

EL CASTILLO

The most impressive structure at Tulum, El Castillo is not a castle as its name would suggest, but a small, two-chamber temple built atop a tall pyramid that stands on the edge of a steep cliff. The stairway that leads to the temple has recently been closed to visitors, but you can still scramble up to the base of the pyramid and then gaze at the sea down below.

TEMPLE OF THE DESCENDING GOD

Immediately north of El Castillo, this temple is a small, elevated structure that received its name from the beautiful relief carved above the doorway. The stucco carving depicts a deity diving headfirst from the sky. Some archaeologists believe that the figure is a honeybee (look closely and you'll see that it has wings and a strange pointed tail, and carries what seems to be a flower), a creature of central significance in Yucatecan Maya religion, medicine, and commerce.

TEMPLE OF THE WIND

This small structure north of the Temple of the Descending God was acoustically designed to whistle when winds blew through at a velocity of 160 km (99 mi) per hour or greater. The storm warning whistle can be heard 34 km (21 mi) away.

OUTDOOR ACTIVITIES

The many cenotes scattered throughout the Tulum/Cobá area are worth a look, if not a swim. One of the most beautiful is the **Gran Cenote,** first discovered when Hurricane Gilbert (1988) caved in its porous limestone roof, exposing the cenote's cavernous interior. To reach the Gran Cenote, take a taxi ($2.50) about 4 km (2½ mi) west on the road opposite the crucero. The family that lives on the land surrounding the cenote usually charges a small entrance fee ($2.50).

NEAR TULUM

COBA

This site, covering more than 70 square km (43 square mi), has been largely ignored by archaeologists and the Mexican government. Dense jungle envelops much of it, which will give you that "Indiana Jones" feeling that you've stumbled onto something unknown and exotic. Distances between the structures are all 1–2 km (½–1½ mi), so wear comfortable walking shoes, carry plenty of drinking water, and douse yourself in insect repellent. The jungle that surrounds the ruins is no less an attraction, and plenty of paths wend their ways through the undergrowth. Snorkeling or swimming in the many lakes is not recommended, as the lakes are home to several families of crocodiles.

Cobá is one of the oldest known settlements on the peninsula. It was built around several shallow lakes and marshes during 400 BC but didn't develop into a full-scale city until roughly AD 500. The city's inhabitants mysteriously abandoned it 600 years before the arrival of the Spanish, and the ruins weren't discovered again until the late 19th century. The remains of more than 30 roads, once paved with smoothed stones, indicate that Cobá was a large commercial center. The two huge pyramids that archaeologists have unearthed here bear some resemblance to the structures at Tikal, Guatemala, suggesting commercial or kinship ties with the wealthy Maya of the Petén jungle. More than 6,500 structures at Cobá have been identified but have yet to be excavated.

Start your exploration at the group of temples closest to the main entrance, known as **Grupo Cobá.** The first of these temples is the enormous pyramid called the **Iglesia**; at 85 ft high it's the second-largest on the peninsula. The vigorous climb to the top rewards you with a fantastic view of two lakes, the jungle surrounding the ruins, and Nohoch Mul (which is in fact the largest pyramid on the peninsula). In front of the Iglesia is a small shrine where local Maya occasionally leave offerings to the gods; please do not remove anything from the shrine.

Continue past Grupo Cobá and follow **Lake Macanxoc**'s eastern edge; after about 1,000 ft you'll pick up the trail to **Grupo Macanxoc** and the **Stelae Group.** More than 30 deteriorating but intricately carved stelae have been found at Cobá, depicting imperious rulers standing on the backs of captives, subjects, and slaves. After the Stelae Group, walk back up the way you came and bear right after the path to reach **Las Pinturas** (The Paintings). Here the Maya covered their buildings with stucco and then adorned the stucco with paintings. Unfortunately, the pyramidal temple bears only scant remnants of frescoes on its walls. At the foot of the pyramid lie 13 square stone wells, thought to be altars or sites for offerings to the gods.

Finally, retrace your steps from Las Pinturas to the main trail and then follow the signs to **Nohoch Mul,** the Yucatán's tallest Maya structure. It's well worth the trek to see this pyramid, which soars 135 ft from the jungle floor. The climb is not for the unfit, but the view from the top is superb. Chances are you'll have the summit to yourself, a rarity in this region. The temple on top of the pyramid is thought to have been constructed long after the pyramid itself was finished, and it's said that the temple was used as a pen for jaguars at one point. The bones of birds and small animals were found inside. Note the carvings of diving gods on the front wall of the temple. *Admission: $5.50, free on Sun. Open daily 8–5.*

COMING AND GOING

Four daily buses make the trip to Cobá from Tulum (45 min, $1), with the last bus leaving at 6 PM. The last bus back to Tulum leaves at 4:30 PM. If you miss the last Cobá–Tulum bus, take a taxi to the main highway (10 km/6 mi, about $2.50) and flag down a Valladolid–Tulum bus.

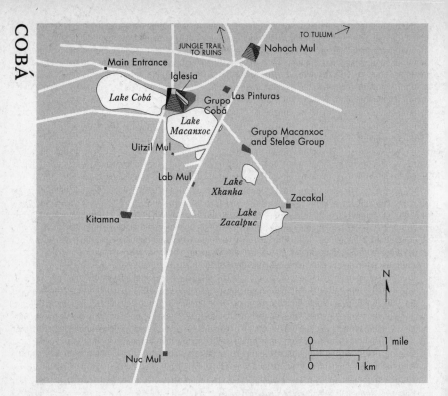

SIAN KA'AN BIOSPHERE RESERVE

This expanse of quiet bays, deserted beaches, mangrove swamps, and jungle is populated with birds, crocodiles, jaguars, and boars. Look carefully and you may spy the blossoms of rare orchids as well. Within the reserve, **Isla Pájaros** is home to more than 300 species of migratory and nonmigratory birds, including flamingos, herons, and egrets. Also of interest are the narrow canals that ribbon the reserve; these are believed to have been built by the ancient Maya.

For budget travelers, Sian Ka'an is only affordable as a day trip: Cabañas at the northern entrance of the reserve start at about $60, and lodging in the fly-fishing resort of **Boca Paila** is even steeper. Camping is not permitted within the reserve. Restaurants are few and far between, and those that exist are expensive. During the tourist season (December–April, July, and August), taxis depart sporadically for Sian Ka'an from the intersection about 3 km (2 mi) south of the Tulum ruins (just past Cabañas Los Gatos), or you can try calling **Victor Barrera,** a local cab driver (tel. 987/1–21–18) to arrange for a pick up. Drivers should fill up at the gas station in Tulum before making the trip out. Cancún-based **Amigos de Sian Ka'an** (tel. 988/4–95–83) runs tours to the reserve ($40 per person); the six-hour tour leaves daily at 9 AM from Cabañas Ana y José in Tulum and includes a three-hour boat ride, a bilingual guide, refreshments, and snacks. For more information on the reserve itself, contact Alfredo Arreyano at the **SEMARANAP** office (tel. 988/3–05–63) in Cancún.

CHETUMAL

Travelers come to Chetumal, at the southern tip of Quintana Roo, for one reason: to use the city as a springboard for trips to Belize and Guatemala. Here you'll find the **Museo de la Cultura Maya,** which offers an excellent overview of Maya history and culture. It's the best museum of its kind in Mexico. The **mercado nuevo,** 10 blocks north of the city center, is a bustling and chaotic daily market that attracts fruit and vegetable vendors—on foot, bike, or truck—from all over the state. On the city's outskirts are beautiful lagoons that make for worthwhile day trips.

BASICS

CASAS DE CAMBIO
Bancomer (tel. 983/2–53–00) and **Banamex** (tel. 983/2–11–22), both on Juárez at Obregón, change money weekdays 9–2 and have ATMs that accept MasterCard, Visa, and Cirrus cards. If you need Belizean dollars, try one of the casas de cambio on Héroes, such as **Centro Cambiario** (Héroes 67, at Zaragoza, tel. 983/2–38–38). However, you should wait to change the bulk of your money in Belize, where you'll get a better rate.

CROSSING THE BORDER
TO BELIZE • American and British Commonwealth citizens do not need visas to enter Belize, but they do need passports. For additional information, contact the **Belizean Consulate** (Obregón and Juárez, next to Bancomer, tel. 983/2–01–00; open weekdays 9–2 and 5–8, Sat. 9:30–2). For information on reaching the Mexico–Belize border, *see* Coming and Going, *below.*

TO GUATEMALA • For information on visas and tourist cards, *see box titled* "Tips for Travel to Guatemala," *in* Chapter 13. You can also contact the **Guatemalan Consulate** (Chapultepec 354, at Cecilio Chi, tel. 983/2–30–45; open weekdays 9–5).

A stela is a large stone, vaguely rectangular, with smooth sides covered by inscriptions. The Maya carved dates, astronomical happenings, and special events into the stelae, perhaps as a historical record.

MEDICAL AID
There are a number of clinics near the budget hotel area. The **Centro de Salud** (Juárez 147, at Aguilar, tel. 983/2–00–95) is open weekdays 8–2:30. The **Cruz Roja** (tel. 983/2–05–71) provides 24-hour emergency medical service. For minor medical needs, visit **Farmacia Canto** (Héroes, at Gandhi, tel. 983/2–04–83; open Mon.–Sat. 7 AM–11 PM, Sun. 7–5).

PHONES AND MAIL
The full-service **post office** (Plutarco Elías, at 5 de Mayo, 2 blocks east of Héroes, tel. 983/2–25–78; open weekdays 8–7, Sat. 9–1) will hold mail sent to you at the following address for up to 10 days: Lista de Correos, Chetumal, Quintana Roo, CP 77000, México. The **Ladatel** phone cards used here are sometimes be different from those used in Playa del Carmen and Cancún. If your card doesn't work, purchase a new one at **Super Las Arcadas** (*see* Food, *below*).

VISITOR INFORMATION
The **tourist booth** (Héroes, at Águilar, in front of mercado viejo, tel. 983/2–36–63; open Mon.–Sat. 8:30–1:30 and 6–9) dispenses information and free maps. The **Dirección de Turismo** (Palacio Municipal, on Bahía, 1 block west of Héroes, tel. 983/2–08–55; open weekdays 9–2:30 and 4–7) has a helpful English-speaking staff.

COMING AND GOING

BY BUS
Chetumal's **Central de Autobuses** (Insurgentes, at Belice, about 15 blocks north of downtown, tel. 983/2–98–77) is a $1 taxi ride from downtown. Frequent first- and second-class buses leave for Cancún (5½ hrs, $9.50 1st class; 6 hrs, $8 2nd class) and Playa del Carmen (4 hrs, $8.25 1st class; 5 hrs, $6.50 2nd class). Buses head to Tulum (3½ hrs, $6.50) every two hours 12:30–6:30 PM. The first-class bus to Campeche leaves at noon (6 hrs, $12), and second-class buses leave at 4:30 AM and 3:30 PM. Four first-class buses head to Mérida (8 hrs, $10 1st class; 9 hrs, $8.50 2nd class). One bus makes the trip to Palenque (8 hrs, $14.50) at 10:15 PM , and three buses a day leave for Mexico City (23 hrs, $40). The 24-hour station has a Computel office (open daily 7 AM–10 PM), a restaurant, and luggage storage (20¢ per hr).

A SHORT HISTORY OF THE MAYA

The Maya first settled in the lowlands of Guatemala, Mexico, and Belize and then moved north onto the Yucatán Peninsula. Hence, the height of the Classic period in the north occurred as the southern centers were being abandoned. The following divisions are commonly used by archaeologists who study the Maya.

PRE-CLASSIC PERIOD (1500 BC–AD 300): At this time, farming replaced the nomadic lifestyle. Monumental buildings with corbeled arches and roof combs appeared, as did the first hieroglyphics and a calendar system.

CLASSIC PERIOD (AD 300–900): During this period, the Maya developed a unique art, language, science, and architecture. Temples and pyramids built with precise relation to one another illustrate the close tie between religion and aesthetics. Buildings were placed on superstructures atop stepped platforms and were often decorated with bas-reliefs and ornate frescoes. The population's growing dependence on agriculture inspired the creation of the highly accurate Maya calendar, which is based on planting cycles. Economy and trade flourished, and the Maya began to observe class distinctions; the wealthiest lived extremely lavish lifestyles around great ceremonial centers. Toward the end of this period, more palaces were constructed on top of or in place of temples, evidence of the growth of secular authority and centralized political rule. Examples of Classical period architecture are found at Uxmal and Sayil.

POST-CLASSIC PERIOD (900–1520): This period of decline is marked by increased military activity and the growth of conquest states. The Toltecs of central Mexico invaded the Yucatán, and this ultimately led to an increasingly warlike society, more elaborate temples and palaces, and a greater number of human sacrifices. At the same time, the quality of craftsmanship fell; for example, carved-stone building facades were replaced at this time by carved stucco. Mayapán is an example of post-Classic architecture.

Servicio San Juan provides daily direct service from Chetumal's main bus terminal to Flores, Guatemala at 2:30 PM ($28). **Batty's** buses run to Belize (4½ hrs, $4.50) every half hour 11:30 AM–7:30 PM from the mercado nuevo (Segundo Circuito, at Calzada Veracruz, 10 blocks north of downtown). Pay the Batty's bus fare in Belizean dollars—you'll get a better exchange rate.

To reach Bacalar, Cenote Azul, or Laguna Milagros (*see* Near Chetumal, *below*), take one of the small buses that leave from the station at Hidalgo and Francisco Primo de Verdad. Buses for Xcalak ($5) leave at 7 AM from the corner of Avenida 16 de Septiembre and Gandhi. To reach Calderitas, take a *combi* (a VW van that operates as a collective taxi) from the station on Belice, between Colón and Gandhi.

BY PLANE

The small airport (2 km/1 mi outside of Chetumal) only handles flights to destinations in Mexico, Guatemala, and Belize. Carriers serving the airport include **Aeroméxico** (tel. 983/2–83–06) and **Aerocaribe** (tel. 983/2–66–75). A one-way ticket from Chetumal to Guatemala City should cost about $90. Be forewarned that Aerocaribe only flies to and from Guatemala City three days a week. To reach downtown, either take a taxi ($2.50) or walk east on Revolución (the main street north of the airport), which becomes Águilar.

GETTING AROUND

It's easy to get around Chetumal on foot, and almost everything you need is in the downtown area. The most important street running north–south is **Avenida Héroes,** where the **mercado viejo** (old market), budget lodging, and tourist information booth are all located. The bus station is about 15 blocks north of the center; the **mercado nuevo** (new market), where buses depart for Belize, is five blocks south of the bus station. Taxis are cheap and abundant: Within the downtown area, you shouldn't pay more than 50¢; north of Insurgentes, you'll have to pay 75¢.

WHERE TO SLEEP

The best place to seek budget lodging is in the blocks surrounding the plaza at the intersection of Héroes and Águilar; you'll find the hotels squeezed between cheap loncherías and bookstores.

Would you like to know your Maya birthdate? At Chetumal's Museo de la Cultura Maya you'll find cogged wheels that match dates on the Roman calendar to dates on the 18-month Maya calendar.

UNDER $15 • Hotel Real Azteca. Shiny wooden carvings of Maya gods and modern-looking hieroglyphics decorate this unabashedly tourist-friendly hotel. A circular stairway winds up to air-conditioned rooms equipped with TVs and black-and-white checkered bathrooms reeking of air freshener. Bring your own agua purificada, as they charge 50¢ a glass here. Doubles are $13. *Belice 186, between Águilar and Gandhi, tel. 983/2–06–66. 30 rooms, all with bath. Luggage storage. Cash only.*

Hotel Ucum. The dark-wood furniture in the freshly painted rooms create a homey atmosphere here. Beds are small and rickety, but adequate, and bathrooms have piping-hot water. Doubles are $7.50, with air-conditioning $12.50. *Gandhi 167, between Héroes and 16 de Septiembre, tel. 983/2–07–11. 58 rooms, all with bath. Restaurant, luggage storage. Cash only.*

UNDER $20 • Principe. This hotel is in a quiet residential neighborhood eight blocks from the center of town. Ask to see a few rooms first, as some have missing toilet seats or backed-up drains; all rooms have air-conditioning and satellite TV. The hotel has a swimming pool and a friendly, helpful staff. Doubles cost $18.50. A taxi from the center of town costs 50¢. *Héroes 326, tel. 983/2–47–99. 52 rooms, all with bath. Restaurant, bar, luggage storage. Cash only.*

UNDER $40 • Los Cocos. This downtown luxury hotel has a huge garden and pool, as well as spacious, modern rooms with color TV, phone, air-conditioning, and bathroom toiletries. Doubles cost $36.50. *Héroes 138, at Chapultepec, tel. 983/2–05–44. 60 rooms, all with bath. Restaurant, bar, coffee shop, parking, safety-deposit boxes.*

HOSTELS

Albergue Juvenil CND. CND is clean, well staffed, and one of the best-run hostels on the peninsula. Four-person, wood-shuttered rooms have fans and lockers; beds are $4 and HI cardholders get a 10% discount. The 11 PM curfew is negotiable with the friendly manager. You can pitch your tent on the hostel's lawn for $1 per person. There are no age restrictions. *Naval, at Veracruz, tel. 983/2–34–65. 1 block north of Obregón and 5 blocks east of Héroes. 66 beds. Restaurant, luggage storage. Cash only.*

FOOD

In Chetumal you'll find Yucatecan food—sometimes with a Belizean influence—including lime soup and *tikinchic* (fried fish seasoned with sour orange). If you're trying to save money, pick up fresh fruit at **Frutería La Merced** (Héroes, at Cristóbal Colón). There's a convenient bakery, **Pan La Terminal,** at Héroes and Colón.

UNDER $5 • Restaurant/Super Las Arcades. Open-air seating and clean wood tables make this a preferred spot among tourists, but 24-hour service and consistently good food also win it a regular crowd of locals. Large appetites can be sated with the *cubana* ($1.75), a bulging sandwich stuffed with ham, beef, cheese, and breaded chicken, slathered in salsa, and accompanied by potato chips. For light eaters, there's yogurt and granola. An elaborate selection of egg, bean, and rice dishes averages $2–$3. *Héroes 74, at Zaragosa, no phone. Cash only.*

El Vaticano. On a corner across from the old market, this seafood joint is a nice place to sit outside and sip a beer. They serve large plates of fresh fish for much less than in Cancún or Playa del Carmen, and excellent dishes with fried, grilled, or marinated conch in lemon and garlic are $3.75. *Belice, at Gandhi, no phone. No dinner Sun. Cash only.*

UNDER $10 • Sergio's. What started out as a tiny pizza parlor has grown into a bustling two-story restaurant. Not only do they serve the best pizza in town (try the smoked oyster or "super seafood special" pizzas), they also grill rib-eye, T-bone, and sirloin steaks for around $7. *Obregón 182, at 5 de Mayo, tel. 983/2–23–55. Cash only.*

WORTH SEEING

Museo de la Cultura Maya. If you plan to check out any of the peninsula's ruins, or if you've already done so and are looking for a refresher on Maya history and culture, this outstanding museum is worth a visit. Inside you'll find interactive computers that offer a variety of information on Maya history as well as facts about regional plants and animals. You can also view glass-encased replicas of the peninsula's ancient temples and hieroglyph-covered stelae. Virtual realists will get a kick out of the subterranean models of Uxmal and Tulum, which you can peer down at through brightly lit glass floor panels. A central gallery exhibits contemporary photography, sculpture, and paintings. *Héroes, at Colón, just north of mercado viejo, tel. 983/2–38–68. Admission to permanent exhibit: $3; admission to central gallery free. Open Tues.–Sun. 9–7.*

NEAR CHETUMAL

Calderitas, a beach town 8 km (5 mi) north of Chetumal, is the closest place to take a dip in the ocean. To get here, take one of the minibuses (10 min, 25¢) that run every half hour from the bus stop in back of the mercado viejo (Belice, between Colón and Gandhi). Diving enthusiasts should head for **Banco Chinchorra,** a 42-km (26 mi) coral reef littered with shipwrecks, about two hours offshore from **Xcalak** beach. Two buses leave daily for Xcalak (5 hrs, $4) at 6 AM and 3:30 PM from the bus terminal. If you need snorkeling and diving gear, you can rent it right on the beach or at **Costa de Cocos,** 1 km (½ mi) before the bus stop in Xcalak. Chetumal's major water attractions, however, are inland: Laguna Milagros, Cenote Azul, and Laguna de Bacalar (*see below*) are all easily reached by combi ($1) from the corner of Hidalgo and Primo de Verdad in Chetumal. The last buses head back to Chetumal around 7 PM.

CENOTE AZUL

If you have time to visit only one place near Chetumal, it should be Cenote Azul, 30 km (19 mi) north of Chetumal. This, the largest cenote in the world, measures 292 ft deep and 722 ft across. Its name derives from the intensity of its blue waters, home to an array of beautiful fish. Diving is dangerous here due to strong underwater currents and poor visibility, but careful floaters can see plenty from the water's surface (bring your own gear—there aren't any shops here). The cenote is especially popular on weekends. From Chetumal, take any minibus toward Laguna de Bacalar and ask the driver to let you off at Cenote Azul. To get back, stand on the roadside and flag down a passing bus or minibus.

LAGUNA DE BACALAR

About 40 km (25 mi) north of Chetumal, this is a favorite destination for day-tripping locals. Also known as *Laguna de Siete Colores* (Lagoon of Seven Colors), the lagoon changes color according to the time of day and the depth of the water; its warm, shimmering waters are safe for swimming and attract families on holidays and weekends. An hour-long boat ride around the lagoon and down the adjoining Río Depiratas costs about $30 for up to eight people, and a three-hour boat trip to Chetumal Bay costs $100 for up to 10 people. For more information concerning either trip, ask any of the staff at the **Club de Vela** sailing club or talk to the bartender at **Restaurant Ejidal.** The restaurant serves fish fillet and shrimp dishes ($4–$5) prepared to your taste, and several other nearby restaurants offer comparable prices. Camping at Ejidal costs $2, including use of the toilet and shower facilities, but you'll have to move out at daybreak, since the restaurant/bar is open all day. To reach Ejidal, walk away from the central square toward the water, turn left on the road that runs along the water, and continue about 2,625 ft. While in Bacalar, take a look at the perfectly preserved **Fuerte San Felipe Bacalar,** just east of the park. The fort has an impressive view of the area, and the main room serves as the town museum. The fort is open Tuesday–Sunday 10–6; admission $1.25.

LAGUNA MILAGROS

The area surrounding Laguna Milagros is unspectacular, but the lagoon's warm waters are inviting and peaceful. This also a safe place to pitch a tent free of charge: From the main road, walk straight about 330 ft to the water, and on your left you'll see the patio and lawn of an abandoned restaurant just waiting for your hammock or tent. If you didn't bring food, you can choose between four restaurants at the lake, including **El Campesino** and **Las Brisas del Caribe.** The 12-km (7-mi) trip here by minibus takes 15 minutes, and the lake is about 360 ft from the main road. Catch a bus back to Chetumal at one of the stops on the road.

CAMPECHE

Campeche, one of the few walled cities in the Americas, charms its visitors with lofty churches, Moorish arches, and cannon-laden forts, all within its crumbling walls. It was through Campeche that Mexican gold and silver were shipped to Spain during the 16th and 17th centuries, making it the target of raids by Dutch and English pirates. A brutal pirate attack in 1663 resulted in the massacre of almost the entire population of Campeche, spurring the construction of its sturdy forts. Today, Campeche is all business, serving as a meeting place for executives from Mexico's oil industry and bustling with the daily transport of goods from nearby towns to be sold in the main market. Still, Campeche's colonial sights, along with its refusal to succumb to blatant tourism, makes the city a pleasant place to spend a day or two.

BASICS

AMERICAN EXPRESS

Anyone can replace lost traveler's checks at the AmEx office run by the **Viajes Programados** travel agency. However, the office does not change money or cash personal checks. Cardholders can pick up mail sent to: Prolongación Calle 59, Edificio Belmar, Apartado Postal 82, Campeche, Campeche, CP 24000, México. *Behind Ramada Inn, tel. 981/1–10–10. Open weekdays 9–2 and 5–7, Sat. 9–1:30.*

CASAS DE CAMBIO

Bancomer (16 de Septiembre 120, tel. 981/6–66–22) changes money weekdays 9–2. On weekends, your only option is the **Ramada Inn** (Ruíz Cortínez 51, tel. 981/6–22–33), where you can exchange money daily 5 PM–10:30 PM. The ATMs at **Bancomer** and **Banamex** (corner of Calles 10 and 53, tel. 981/6–06–29) accept Visa, MasterCard, Cirrus, and Plus.

EMERGENCIES

In an emergency, dial **06** from any telephone in Campeche. The **police** station (Resurgimiento, ½ block west of Hotel Alhambra, tel. 981/6–23–29) is open 24 hours.

MEDICAL AID

The **IMSS** (López Mateos, at Baluartes, tel. 981/6–09–20 or 981/6–42–33) offers 24-hour, walk-in emergency service. For minor medical needs, try **Farmacia Canto** (Calle 10, at Calle 55, tel. 981/6–52–48; open Mon.–Sat. 8–2 and 5–9, Sun. 9–1).

PHONES AND MAIL

There are very few coin-operated phones in Campeche; try the main bus terminal on Gobernadores or the public library (Calle 12, between Calles 61 and 63). Buy **Latadel** cards at **Tel Mex** (Calle 10, between Calles 61 and 63; open weekdays 8–1:30). **Computel** (Calle 8 No. 255, fax 981/1–01–29;

open daily 7 AM–10 PM) lets you place international collect calls. The **Oficina de Correos** (16 de Septiembre, at Calle 53, 2 blocks east of Parque Principal, tel. 981/6–21–34, fax 981/6–52–10; open weekdays 8–8, Sat. 9–1) is the joint post/telephone office; it offers fax, telex, and mail services. They'll hold mail sent to you at the following address for up to 10 days: Lista de Correos, Oficina Urbana 1, Campeche, Campeche, CP 24000, México.

VISITOR INFORMATION

For information about the city's churches, museums, and upcoming public events, ask the ticket man at the **Puerta de Tierra** (*see* Worth Seeing, *below*). The friendly and enthusiastic staff at the **state tourist office** (Calle 12, between Calles 53 and 55, tel. 981/6–67–67 or 981/6–55–93; open weekdays 9–3 and 6–8) gives out information on Campeche and nearby ruins.

COMING AND GOING

BY BUS

The main bus terminal is on Gobernadores, about a kilometer (½ mi) north from Parque Principal and just outside the city walls. The terminal is actually composed of two adjoining stations, offering first- and second-class service respectively. **Autobuses del Oriente** (ADO; tel. 981/6–28–02), the principal first-class carrier, runs daily trips to Mérida (2½ hrs, $5), Mexico City (18 hrs, $38), and Veracruz city (14 hrs, $25). You can store luggage here for 50¢ per day, and the station is open 24 hours. The dusty and dilapidated second-class bus depot (tel. 981/6–23–32), adjacent to the ADO depot, is only open until 7 PM; from here you can catch frequent buses to Hopelchén (1½ hrs, $1.50), Bolonchén (2 hrs, $2.25), and Dzibalchén (2 hrs, $2.25). Five daily buses also leave for Iturbide (3 hrs, $2.50), Uxmal (2½ hrs, $3), Santa Elena (3 hrs, $3.25), and Mérida (4 hrs, $4.50). To reach town from the ADO terminal, turn left onto Gobernadores; the first fort you reach marks the beginning of the old town. Otherwise, catch a bus (35¢) across the street and ask to be left near the Parque Principal.

BY CAR

If you can afford it, having a car will make exploring the region much easier. **Maya Rent-a-Car** (Ruíz Cortínez, at Calle 59, tel. 981/6–22–33, fax 981/1–16–18; open Mon.–Sat. 9–2 and 5–8), in the Ramada Inn, rents Volkswagen bugs for $44 a day, including insurance and unlimited mileage. You'll need to show your passport and license. The agency also provides maps and information on road conditions. The roads leading to the outlying ruins and caves are well maintained; there's the occasional dirt road, but your average VW bug can take you just about anywhere you want to go.

GETTING AROUND

Virtually everything of interest lies inside the walls of the *villa vieja* (old city) and is easily accessible on foot. Even-numbered streets run parallel to the waterfront, and odd-numbered streets run perpendicular. At the center of town, the zócalo is bordered by Calles 8, 10, 53, and 55. The malecón that runs along the water is named **Avenida Ruíz Cortínez**. It is the location of Campeche's more expensive hotels, such as the Ramada Inn. The market and the bus terminal are on the southeast side of Campeche on Avenida Circuito Baluartes Este and Avenida Gobernadores, respectively. Local buses (35¢) run daily 5 AM–11 PM, stopping at the mercado and in front of the **Palacio de Gobierno** (malecón, at Calle 61).

WHERE TO SLEEP

Hotels in Campeche tend to host more businesspeople than tourists. If you arrive at the bus station in the wee hours, you're better off paying the cab fare (about $1.75) to any of the following hotels (all in the old city) rather than staying in one of the noisy, overpriced dives near the station.

UNDER $10 • Hotel Colonial. This beautiful, chandelier-adorned hotel, a former colonial, has a shady rooftop patio and a pleasant, palm-fringed inner courtyard. The sparkling-clean rooms (doubles $10) have ceiling fans *and* air-conditioning, good mattresses, window screens, and phones. They get snatched up pretty quickly, especially during July and August. Reservations are accepted until 7 PM. *Calle 14 No. 122, between Calles 55 and 57, tel. 981/6–22–22. 30 rooms, all with bath. Luggage storage. Cash only.*

UNDER $15 • Hotel El Regis. This new hotel is in an old colonial home, just two blocks from the plaza. A wrought-iron staircase leads from a pleasant atrium up to the balconied rooms with high ceilings. Each has a black and white Art Deco tile floor and a bathroom with shower. Some rooms also have air-conditioning and TV. The front door closes at 11 PM, but a friendly night watchman opens up for late arrivals. *Calle 12 No. 148, between Calles 55 and 57, tel. 981/5–31–75. 7 rooms, all with bath. Luggage storage. Reservations advised. Cash only.*

Hotel Lopez. Cheerful pink, yellow, and white walls and an open, airy ambience make this little two-story hotel a pleasant place to stay. Rooms include colonial-style desks and armoires, luggage stands, and easy chairs. The hotel's restaurant serves its version of Continental fare. Double rooms cost $12, with air-conditioning $19. *Calle 12 No. 189, between Calles 61 and 63, tel. 981/6–33–44. 39 rooms, all with bath. Restaurant, luggage storage. Cash only.*

Posada San Angel. Although the lobby is sunny and filled with plants, the dark rooms are somewhat disappointing. Brightly colored fish paintings do add a note of gaiety, and the bathroom does come complete with shower curtain, toilet seat, *and* lid; if you've just been camping in the jungle, you'll probably be in seventh heaven. Doubles cost $13 (plus $2.50 if you'd like air-conditioning). *Calle 10 No. 307, across from Catedral de la Concepción, tel. 981/6–77–18. 14 rooms, all with bath. Luggage storage. Cash only.*

FOOD

Campeche's seafood dishes have a well-deserved reputation throughout Mexico. Local specialties include *pan de cazón* (finely shredded baby shark layered with tortillas, beans, fresh tomato purée, and avocado) and *camarón chiquito* (a type of tiny shrimp). Many of the city's better restaurants, as well as a handful of small sandwich shops, line Calle 8 across from the Parque Principal. If you're pinching pennies, go to the huge, frenzied daily **market** on Gobernadores just outside the city wall. Here you can buy luscious regional fruits such as *pitaya* (a pink fruit that tastes like pineapple) and mamey, as well as *panuchos* (Yucatecan tacos; tortillas stuffed with beans, then fried and topped with chicken, lettuce, onion, and tomato), tacos, and tamales for less than 25¢ apiece.

Yucatecans claim Campecheans do everything backward, citing examples like the speed bump on the road from Campeche to Mérida: First you hit the bump, then a sign warns about it.

UNDER $5 • La Perla. Whirring fans and the constant buzz of the TV keep locals at their tables after a filling meal of shrimp or conch with rice. Also good is the fish filet stuffed with shrimp and shellfish ($2.75). Beer and tequila run about 50¢ each. *Calle 10, between Calles 57 and 59, in same building as Lonchería Colón, tel. 981/6–40–92. Cash only.*

Restaurant La Parroquia. Despite the warehouselike atmosphere, La Parroquia is an excellent place to eat, featuring a huge menu, low prices, slow but friendly service, and many daily specials. It's also a wonderful place to people-watch. A plate of rice and fried plantains or a fluffy pile of pancakes with hot honey and syrup costs 75¢ each. Also worth a try are the generously stuffed *torta de camarones* (French bread crammed with chunky shrimp salad) and *jamaica*, a sweet juice made from the iced pulp of boiled hibiscus. *Calle 5 No. 8, 1 block west of Parque Principal, tel. 981/6–80–86. Open 24 hrs. Cash only.*

Restaurante Portales. Campechean couples and families come here evenings to enjoy snacks like a *torta claveteado* (ham sandwich flavored with honey) and the best *horchata* (rice drink flavored with cinnamon) in town. Orange-and-white checkered tablecloths and a cobblestone courtyard give the place a festive air, and a nearby vendor serves up coconut ice cream (40¢) for dessert. *Calle 10 No. 86, at Plaza San Francisco, tel. 981/1–14–91. From Parque Principal, walk 8 blocks NE on Calle 10. Or take a taxi ($1) to Plaza San Francisco. Cash only.*

UNDER $10 • Marganzo. For occasional live music and truly fabulous regional dishes served by suave waiters in festive costumes, head for Marganzo. Seafood specialties are pricey, but the delicious shrimp or crab salads are under $4. Their pan de cazón, the regional specialty, is outstanding. *Calle 8 No. 268, between Calles 57 and 59, tel. 981/1–38–99.*

WORTH SEEING

A walk through Campeche is like taking a short course on the military and commercial history of the Spanish colonies. Forts that protected the city from marauding pirates still stand, as do centuries-old churches and graceful merchant's homes. The city's recently restored museums are stocked with newly found artifacts from the nearby ruins of Edzná and Calaknul. Most of the interesting colonial buildings in Campeche are within the old city, and all are easily accessible on foot.

A **city tour** by trolley car leaves from the north side of the zócalo daily at 9:30 AM, 6 PM and 8 PM. The one-hour, bilingual tour costs $1, and tickets can be purchased aboard the trolley. It takes in the historic center, malecón, and fortresses.

CIRCUITO DE BALUARTES

Five years after much of the city was wiped out by pirates in 1663, the first stones of a new defense system were laid. The fortifications were to consist of a 10-ft-thick wall running around the city, protected by seven *baluartes* (watchtowers). Even ships had to pass through the four gates that controlled access to the city. The construction took more than 35 years but effectively ended Campeche's role as the Yucatán's 98-pound weakling. Today, it's possible to follow the Circuito de Baluartes around to the various watchtowers, many of which are now government buildings.

Aside from admiring the forts and watchtowers themselves, visitors can enjoy the museums, exhibits, and even gardens found inside many of them. Of particular interest is the **Baluarte de Santiago,** in the northern corner of the city, which was demolished at the end of the last century and reconstructed in the 1950s. Today it houses a beautiful **Jardín Botánico,** where you can admire a wide variety of regional flora, such as tiny orchids from the Campechean jungle. *Calle 8, at Calle 49, tel. 981/6–68–29. Admission free. Open daily 9–2 and 5–8.*

Another relic of the old city wall is the **Baluarte de San Carlos** (Calle 8, at Calle 65), on Campeche's east side. Completed in 1676, the baluarte is now the site of the **Museo de la Ciudad** (admission free; open Tues.–Sat. 8–8, Sun. 8–2), which hosts a collection of photos, maps, and models illustrating Campeche's history. The real attraction, however, is the fort itself: Standing in the turrets, you can imagine yourself fending off menacing pirates. Farther along Calle 8 stands the **Baluarte de la Soledad,** now the three-room **Dr. Roman Pina Chan Museum of Stelae** (Calle 8, between Calles 55 and 57, tel. 981/6–91–11; admission: 50¢; open Tues.–Sat. 8–8, Sun. 8–1). It showcases some 20 Maya stelae, mostly from the ruins of Cayal, Acannuíl, and Xcalumkin.

The most impressive of the city's forts is the **Fuerte de San Miguel.** Located at the city's highest point, San Miguel is surrounded by a moat, and a rooftop ringed with cannons offers impressive views of Campeche's shoreline ports. The San Miguel fort now hosts the new **Museo de Cultura Maya** (Museum of Maya Culture; admission: 50¢, free Sun.; open Tues.–Sat. 8–8, Sun. 8–1), a consolidation of Campeche's most important precolonial artifacts. Funerary offerings, which are among the majority, include five exquisite jade masks from tombs at Calakmul; small human figures from the island of Jaina; jade ear disks; and beautifully crafted ceramic urns and *petates* (grinding stones). *Take the LERMA bus from in front of the market for about 10 min.*

The **Fuerte de San Jose,** at the opposite side of the city from Fuerte San Miguel, houses a new **Museo de Armas y Barcos** (Museum of Arms and Ships) dedicated to the town's colonial period. Old swords, armor, guns, cannon, and models of captured pirate ships are all on display. *Take BELLA VISTA/SAN JOSE DEL ALTO bus from the market for about 10 min. Fort admission: 50¢, free Sun. Open Tues.–Sat. 8–8, Sun. 8–1.*

CHURCHES

The beautiful **Catedral de la Concepción** (on the zócalo, between Calles 8 and 10) dates from the 18th century. Inside, note the illustrations of the Stations of the Cross, each placed under a fan so that worshippers can keep cool while they reflect on Christ's burden. As you approach the altar, look for the small but brilliant stained-glass windows under the cupola at the front of the church. Other beautiful churches in the old city include the **Iglesia de San Francisquito** (Calle 12, between Calles 59 and 61), which dates from the 18th century, and the **Iglesia de Jesús El Nazareno** (Calle 55, at Calle 12), which features dramatic, elaborate icons in flashy altars. Farther away from Campeche's center is **Iglesia San Francisco** (Plaza San Francisco, at Calle 10, 8 blocks NE of zócalo), reportedly the setting for the first mass ever held in Latin America. Campeche's churches are open weekdays 9–noon, Saturday 5–7 PM, and all day Sunday.

AFTER DARK

On weekends the malecón is the place to be—it's perfectly safe to cruise the well-lit walk until around midnight, which is when most Campecheans retire for the evening. Lovers can take advantage of the free *música romántica* in the Parque Principal on Sunday night, usually starting around 8 PM. The light show at **Puerta de Tierra** (Gobernadores, toward old city from main bus station) rehashes Campeche's history of pirate invasions in Spanish, French, and English. The two-hour spectacle is performed by local musicians and dancers at 8:30 PM on Friday year-round and costs $2. Ask at the tourist office (*see above*) for more information.

BARS AND DISCOS

Commonly acknowledged as the hippest disco in town, **Atlantis** (Ruíz Cortínez 51, in Ramada Inn, tel. 981/6–22–33) is decorated like a ship, with netting, railings, portholes, and a fish video screen. Promotions vary by night, whether it be two-for-one drinks or free margaritas for women. Usually only men get slapped with the $4–$5 cover. Atlantis is open Thursday through Saturday until 5 AM. For a more diverse crowd of locals, try **Dragon** disco (Resurgimiento 87, in front of Hotel Alhambra on the malecón, tel. 981/6–42–89), which is open Friday and Saturday nights year-round and Thursday in December, July, and August. Friday night features salsa and merengue music until 4 AM. Saturday, the club is host to a mix of Latin and American music until 5 AM. Cover hovers around $4 (sometimes free). **Mazehual** (Gobernadores 551, across from Pemex station, tel. 981/1–11–74), a vast, palapalike beer hall, features a variety of music, including live funked-out '50s tunes sung by satin-bedecked soloists striding around in 10-inch heels. There's no cover and beers are only $1, but the place shuts down for the night at 10:30 PM.

NEAR CAMPECHE

EDZNA

A mere 60 km (37 mi) southeast of Campeche city lies Edzná, the most famous set of ruins in the state. Evidence suggests that this large site may have been settled as early as 600 BC, and the city certainly thrived during the late Classic period, from AD 600 to 900. The beauty here lies in the overall building scheme rather than in the ornamentation of individual structures. Later styles of architecture (as seen at Uxmal, for example) may be more elaborate, but according to some they signal the decline of the Maya civilization. Edzná's Classic style is characterized by superb stelae; many of these are still onsite, although they have been moved to a roped-in, palapa-covered gallery outside the ruins, where guards can keep an eye on them.

Edzná's main attraction is the **Temple of Five Stories,** an example of early Puuc architecture situated on the Plaza Central. Climb the stairway of the **Gran Acrópolis** (the structure on your left as you enter the ruins) and of the 102-ft temple itself to reach the 23-ft roof comb on its top story. The roof comb was once decorated with a mask of Chaac (the rain god) which seemed to change expression as the sun rose and fell. The mask is believed to be the origin of the name Edzná, meaning "House of the Facial Expressions." Edzná can also be translated as "House of Echoes," probably referring to the amazing acoustics among the principal buildings—standing in the doorway at the top of the pyramid, you can hear the voice of someone at the far end of the Gran Acrópolis. Several other excellently restored buildings cluster around the Gran Acrópolis, including the **House of the Moon,** the **Temazcal** (sweat house), and three additional structures. On the first three days of May, the sun reaches its zenith over Edzná, illuminating various stelae on the Acrópolis. In ancient times this probably marked a sacred ceremony for the sun god, Itzámna. Vicious mosquitoes breed in the swamps and stagnant water holes surrounding Edzná, so bring repellent. *Admission: $2, free Sun. Open daily 8–5.*

COMING AND GOING

In Campeche, **Servicios Turísticos Picazh** (Calle 16 No. 348, between Calles 57 and 59, tel. 981/6–44–26) has organized tours to Edzná departing from the Puerta de Tierra (Calle 59, at Gobernadores) at 9 AM and 2 PM. They can also pick you up at your hotel. The cost is $9 per person for a minimum of two people; an extra $3.50 per person pays your admission and gets you a guided tour of the site. A less reliable option is to take a PICH bus (1 hr, $1.50) from **Terminal Joaquín Pacheco** (Alameda, at Salvador, SW of market) in Campeche and ask the driver to let you off at the Edzná ruins. From there you'll only have to walk about 1,000 ft to the site. The bus schedule is never guaranteed: One bus leaves daily around 6:30 AM and another at around 10:30 AM, but other departure times vary. Be sure to ask the driver what time you should wait at the entrance to the ruins for a return bus to Campeche; a bus usually passes by Edzná at around 2 PM. If you're in a car, take Highway 180 toward Mérida, then change to Highway 188, following signs to Edzná.

THE MENNONITES OF HOPELCHEN

Hopelchén is home to a community of tall, blue-eyed people who look as if they've just stepped out of Little House on the Prairie. Their typical garb of overalls and straw hats for men and cotton dresses and head scarves for women perpetuates the illusion of being in the frontier-era American Midwest. The Mennonites are actually descendants of 16th-century Swiss Anabaptists and continue to speak a German dialect even while living in the depths of the Yucatán. They left Zacatecas in search of land to pursue their agricultural interests (cheese is their main product), winding up in Holpechén in 1985. Their creed includes separation from the outside world, conformity to scripture, and an aversion to modern technology. Orthodox "horse-and-buggy" Mennonites shun all contact with the modern world, but the Mennonite sect in Hopelchén is less strict. Around here you'll often see Mennonite men accepting car rides and conversing in Spanish with the locals; the women rarely communicate with anyone except other Mennonites.

CHENES RUINS/X'TACUMBILXUNAAN

Any comprehensive tour of the peninsula's Maya archaeology should include the Chenes ruins. The remote ruins at **Hochob** are rarely visited, in part because reaching them is tough, even if you have a car. Those who persevere will see one of the purest styles of Chenes architecture, which is characterized by elaborate decoration. A set of *grutas* (caves) is more accessible than the ruins: **Grutas X'tacumbilxunaan** (pronounced shta-koom-bil-sho-*non*) lie just off Highway 261. **Servicios Turísticos Picazh** (Calle 16 No. 348, Campeche, tel. 981/6–44–26) arranges pricey trips to the caves, but with a little fortitude you can get there on your own. The easily accessible ruins of **Dzibilnocac,** only a kilometer outside of Iturbide, are the best bet for those short on time.

VISITOR INFORMATION

José William Chan (tel. 982/2–01–06) is *the* source for information on the Chenes Ruins. He can also tell you just about everything you need to know about Maya culture or other sights in the area. He rents bikes ($3.25 per day); guide services cost $8–$10, depending on the number of people and your financial means. If you want to visit the ruins by car, José can usually rent you one for about $13 (for your own use) or $20 (for him to accompany you). If you brought your own car, you can just pick him up along the way. José lives about 900 yards from the plaza, in Dzibalchén, on the road heading out of town toward Iturbide. Follow his signs reading TOURIST INFORMATION, or ask anyone in town where Maestro William lives.

COMING AND GOING

It's virtually impossible to make the bus journey to any of the Chenes ruins and return to Campeche in one day. It's best to stay the night in **Hopelchén,** 53 km (33 mi) east of Campeche, en route to Mérida, and leave early in the morning for the ruins. Starting at 8 AM, six buses leave Campeche daily for Hopelchén (1½ hrs, $1.50). The **ATS** station in Hopelchén is across from the park, two doors down from the hotel, marked by a disconcerting BURGER CHEN sign. From Hopelchén, six direct buses run daily 8–8 to Dzibalchén (45 min, 75¢), which serves as the crossroads for Hochob and El Tabasqueño. Buses leaving Hopelchén at 9:30 AM, 2:30 PM, and 5:15 PM also stop at Dzibalchén before continuing on to Iturbide (1 hr, $1). The last bus back to Holpechén leaves Iturbide at 3:30 PM; the final bus from Dzibalchén leaves at 5:30 PM. Five buses depart Hopelchén for Mérida daily 7:30 AM–6:30 PM (2½ hrs, $3). Campeche-bound buses also leave frequently.

WHERE TO SLEEP AND EAT

The only hotel in the area is **Los Arcos** (Calle 20, at Calle 23, tel. 982/2–01–23) in Hopelchén, which offers huge, sunny rooms and clean bathrooms with hot water, priced at $6.50 doubles. The hotel accepts cash only. In Holpechén, several open-air loncherías line the avenue between the church and Los Arcos, where you can eat like a king: two fat tamales and a Coke cost less than $1. The restaurant at Hotel Los Arcos serves chicken (Kentucky-style) and fries ($1.50) along with cold beers. **Casa Alpuche** (tel. 982/2–00–07), the minisupermarket across from the park, supplies a reasonable selection of foods and is open daily 7:30–2 and 5:30–9.

WORTH SEEING

DZIBILNOCAC • Among the scattered dirt mounds hidden in the thick vegetation here are two buildings which, until a few years ago, were unrecognizable. Recently, however, the western pyramid has been excavated and reconstructed and now stands in almost perfect condition. Masks of the rain god Chaac cover the uppermost temple, and the curled pattern of his nose is repeated in relief on all sides. A neighboring structure, as yet unrestored, houses the remains of beautiful red-and-green frescoes. Admission to the ruins is free, and the site is open daily 8–5. To reach Dzibilnocac (pronounced Tsee-bil-no-KAK), walk 1 km (½ mi) west of Iturbide on the dirt road leading out of town. Don't be intimidated if you encounter a large bull chained near the entrance to the ruins: As long as he's tethered he's as harmless as an iguana.

Annually on the first three days of May (the beginning of the Maya planting season) anthropologist Elvira del Carmen Tello stages a traditional ancient Maya ceremony at Edzná.

HOCHOB • Reaching this site deep within the rain forest is not easy, but Hochob's appeal lies in its splendid isolation. There is little here to suggest that you aren't the first to discover this long-lost civilization, a sensation that is heightened if you camp overnight. Only the central plaza has been excavated, but countless other buildings lie unexplored under the thick vegetation. The main building is the **Temple of Chaac,** a rectangular building 132 ft long and 23 ft high. Look carefully at the facade to see a giant image of the rain god: The motifs on the lintel above the entrance to the temple are his eyes, and the open door represents his mouth. Admission is free; the site is open Tuesday–Thursday and weekends 8–3.

Getting to Hochob is difficult, even if you have your own car. There is no public transportation, so your only option is to drive, bike, or walk the 13 km (8 mi) from Dzibalchén. Take the road toward Campeche north for 1 km (½ mi), then turn left onto a dirt road leading to the tiny village of Chencoh. The 8 km (5 mi) to Chencoh are clay, sand, and rock—not ideal for traversing on a bike. The trek is even worse if it's raining—bicycles (and cars) will slowly grind to a stop after 25 pounds of pottery has attached itself to the tires. Hitching is nearly impossible unless you're naturally a very lucky person.

GRUTAS X'TACUMBILXUNAAN • Two kilometers (1 mile) from the town of Bolonchén and 34 km (21 mi) north of Hopelchén are the Grutas X'tacumbilxunaan (Caves of the Hidden Girl). The name comes from a local legend that the Maya once lost a young girl here when they were searching for water. The colorful caves are unbelievable, especially if you see them before heading on to the Loltún Caves in the Puuc Region, which spoil you for anything else. The main caves are lighted, but bring a flashlight in case the electricity fails, and plan to spend about an hour exploring their nooks and crannies. Below the main caverns (and accessible only to those with climbing equipment, lanterns, and a sense of adventure) are seven underground wells, each of a different color. The surreal two-day excursion to the seven wells is rarely attempted; should you wish to try it you'll need to negotiate the trip price with a guide who has the necessary equipment. Guides can be found around the caves during open hours. You may also camp for free at the site, but be prepared to share your flesh with thirsty mosquitoes. An attendant charges $1.25 to visit the site (open daily 8–5) and will offer his services as a guide in Spanish; it's customary to tip him few dollars if he acts as your guide.

X'tacumbilxunaan lies on Highway 261 between Hopelchén and Bolonchén. Take the Mérida-bound bus from Hopelchén (30 min, 75¢) and ask the driver to drop you at the *grutas* (caves). The turnoff point for the caves is well marked, and the entrance is close to the road. On the way back, catch the same bus traveling in the opposite direction—the last one passes the caves at about 7:30 PM.

CHAAC, GOD OF RAIN AND RIVER

To the Maya, water was sacred, and Chaac—the god of rain, rivers, cenotes, lakes, and oceans—was their most revered god. Look for his visage (identified by a long, curling nose) on ruins throughout the peninsula, especially in areas such as Chenes and Puuc, which were (and continue to be) drier than other regions. Ch'a Chak, a dusk-to-dawn ceremony with both Catholic prayers and Maya offerings and divination, is still performed by the Maya to appeal to Chaac for rain.

THE PUUC REGION

The Puuc Hills, a low-lying mountain range covering about 156 square km (97 square mi), contain six major archaeological sites with some of the most distinctive Maya architecture on the peninsula. You'll want to dedicate at least three days to the region: one to see the main site at Uxmal; another for the surrounding Maya ruins of Kabah, Sayil, Labná, and Xlapac; and a third to explore the spectacular caves at Loltún.

Puuc architecture is considered the most perfectly proportioned of all Maya building styles. The lower facades of Puuc buildings are typically smooth and plain, contrasting with elaborate upper facades decorated with intricate mosaics. Among the most common motifs used in the mosaics are X-shape lattices, geometric designs, serpents, and masks. It is a highly complex architectural style that draws on the simple idea of the *choza,* or one-room thatched hut, common in the region (stylized representations of the choza appear on the greatest works, such as the archway at Labná). Later Puuc architecture is almost ridiculously top-heavy with decoration—mosaics bursting with serpents and masks—and reflects a Toltec influence.

BASICS

VISITOR INFORMATION

If you want to buy a guidebook to the Puuc Hills (a good idea since there are no guides at the smaller sites), purchase it before you leave Mérida or Campeche. One thorough, reasonably priced guide is Jeff Karl Kowalski's *Guide to Uxmal and the Puuc Region* (Dante, 1990). The book ($5) can be purchased at any Dante bookstore in Mérida (*see Basics in Mérida, below*). Otherwise, Uxmal has a large tourist center, which runs half-hour documentaries on the archaeological, cultural, and environmental riches of the Yucatán. A small museum in Uxmal also displays a few archaeological remains with descriptions printed in Spanish. Apart from small tourist shops selling crafts and soft drinks, smaller sites have no amenities, not even toilets.

WHEN TO GO

The best time to visit the Puuc Region is between February and May. In these months, there are few tourists, little rain, and pleasant temperatures.

COMING AND GOING

The Puuc route snakes its way from Campeche to Mérida, and many travelers take in the sights on their way between the two towns. The main attractions, Uxmal and Kabah, are about 25 km (15½ mi) apart along Highway 261. To reach Uxmal from Campeche, take one of the **buses** (5 per day, 2½ hrs, $3) that leave from the second-class station at Gobernadores. From Mérida's main second-class station (Calle 70, between Calles 69 and 71), six second-class buses make the 1½-hour trip ($1.50) to Uxmal daily;

or take the daily direct bus ($6 round-trip) that leaves Mérida at 8 AM and returns from Uxmal at 2 PM. To return to Mérida or continue on to Kabah from Uxmal, flag down a bus along Highway 261—north to Mérida or south to Kabah. The problem is getting them to stop: Some of the bus drivers consider passengers an unnecessary nuisance and won't stop even if you wave your arms madly. If you're coming by car from Mérida, take Avenida Internacional south to Umán and then hop on Highway 261—the journey to Uxmal is about 97 km (60 mi).

All of the other sites in the Puuc region—Labná, Xlapak, Sayil, and the Loltún Caves—lie along the 48-km (30-mi) back road that runs from Highway 261 to the town of Oxkutzcab and Highway 184. If you have the money, rent a car in Campeche or Mérida and you'll be able to spend as much time as you want at each site. Exploring the lesser-known Puuc ruins by bus can be frustrating. The **Ruta Puuc ATS** bus ($4.50) leaves Mérida's second-class station daily at 8 AM and stops for 25 minutes at each site, giving you just enough time to scan the plaques, climb a few rubbled steps, and poke your nose into a crevice or two. You get an added hour and a half at Uxmal before returning to Mérida between 4 or 5 PM. The bus stops at the plaza in the town of Santa Elena both coming and going.

WHERE TO SLEEP

Many people visit the Puuc region as a day trip from Mérida, since lodging options here are severely limited. But if you want to explore the area in depth, it doesn't make sense to keep commuting back and forth; staying in the small towns of **Santa Elena, Ticul,** or **Oxkutzcab** (see below) is a more convenient option. You can also camp for $4 a night at Loltún (see Oxkutzcab and the Loltún Caves, below) as long as you don't mind sleeping next to a gaping black hole in the ground.

For more comfortable camping, check out the **Sacbé Campgrounds,** about 1½ km (¾ mi) outside of Santa Elena; the town is 15 km (9 mi) west of Ticul along Highway 261, halfway between Uxmal (to the north) and four other major archaeological sites (to the south). The campground is clean and pleasant, and you can sling a hammock or pitch a tent for $2. They have three bungalows ($8) with fans and mosquito nets. The cheerful owners speak English and French, know the local bus schedules, and offer insider information about free activities, shortcuts to sites, and local wildlife. They also cook a reasonably priced breakfast or dinner for guests. *Just south of road to Santa Elena. From Mérida or Campeche, take any bus that travels down Hwy. 261 and ask driver to let you off at "campo de beisball/Km 127." From Ticul, take a colectivo truck to Santa Elena and walk north 1½ km (¾ mi) on hwy. Cash only.*

TICUL

The small town of Ticul, 86 km (53 mi) south of Mérida, is a convenient base from which to explore the Puuc region. The town itself has little to offer, other than an old-fashioned shoe manufacturing center: Piles of high heels can be seen poking out of plastic milk crates strapped to the bicycles of local shoe-makers on their way to the **market** (Calle 23, between Calles 28 and 30). At the market, prices for unadorned shoes run about $5–$10, depending on size. Hand-embroidered shoes cost $75 and up. **Camita España** hand-makes shoes and is hired out on special occasions by women around town. You can visit her at her home (Calle 32, between Calles 25 and 27, Colonia San Román) or you can drop by her store, **La Camita** (corner of Calles 28 and 23, near the market). To see the cobblers in action, pay a visit to **Abigail y Aurora** (Calle 30, between Calles 17 and 19, tel. 997/2–04–45), where an extensive two-level factory supplies everything from patent-leather party shoes to fat-buckled leather sandals.

BASICS

Banco Atlántico (Calle 23, tel. 997/2–02–48), diagonally across from the plaza, changes money weekdays 9–1:30. Medical aid is available at the 24-hour **Centro de Salud** (Calle 27, between Calles 30 and 32, tel. 997/2–00–86).

COMING AND GOING

Combis leave Mérida for Ticul ($1.75) from the Parque San Juan whenever they are full. Buses also make the 80-minute trip from the second-class bus station in Mérida every hour 6 AM–7 PM for about the same price. To reach Ticul from Campeche or Hopelchén, you'll have to take a Mérida-bound bus along Highway 261 and change at Santa Elena (2 hrs, $3), where combis await incoming buses to take passengers on to Ticul 5:30 AM–6 PM.

To reach Uxmal and Kabah from Ticul, take a combi (20 min, 50¢) to Santa Elena from the plaza or from the combi station (Calle 30 No. 214, at Calle 25); from Santa Elena catch the Campeche-bound bus to

Kabah (50¢) or the Mérida-bound bus to Uxmal ($1). To reach Loltún, your best bet is to take a combi (20 min, 50¢) to Oxkutzcab. They idle near the plaza in Ticul at Calle 25, between Calles 26 and 28.

WHERE TO SLEEP AND EAT

The little old man who runs **Hotel San Miguel** (Calle 28 No. 213, between Calles 21 and 23, tel. 997/2–03–82) speaks Maya, but his Spanish is rough. The clean doubles ($5) have hot water and fans. The woman who works at **Hotel Sierra Sosa** (Calle 26 No. 199, between Calles 21 and 23, tel. 997/2–00–08) in the afternoons speaks excellent English. The simple rooms have comfortable beds, fans, and hot water, but street noise can be annoying in the front rooms, so request a room in the back. Doubles are $8 ($12 with air-conditioning). They have laundry facilities and will hold your luggage. Both hotels accept cash only.

Unlike the at Puuc sites, Ticul has plenty of cheap eateries. Head to the daily market (Calle 23, between Calles 28 and 30) for fruit or food from one of the many *fondas* (covered food stands). **Lonchería Mary** (Calle 23, between Calles 26 and 28, no phone) serves 50¢ licuados and 10¢ tamales. **Restaurant Los Almendros** (Calle 23, between Calles 26 and 28, tel. 997/2–00–21), a branch of the famous Mérida restaurant, has excellent Yucatecan dishes ($3–$4) and accepts credit cards. **Cafetería y Pizzería La Góndola** (corner of Calles 23 and 26, tel. 997/2–01–12) serves spaghetti and pizzas ($3–$4), and they'll even deliver a pizza to your hotel room.

UXMAL AND THE PUUC ROUTE

Although the well-tended lawns crawling with plaid-clad tourists provide an unfortunate reality check at Uxmal (pronounced oosh-MAHL), you'll soon lose yourself in the beauty and scale of the buildings. The *Chilam Balam,* a chronicle of the Maya of this region, says that Uxmal was founded in the mid-6th century. Uxmal means "built three times," but the structures were apparently reconstructed at least five times. No one knows exactly who used these buildings, but one theory suggests that the Xiú (pronounced SHEE-oo), a people from the central Mexican plain, occupied Uxmal briefly in the 10th century. Some evidence of this remains in inscriptions, but their paucity suggests that the Xiú's stay was relatively short. Whatever the case, the city was abandoned soon afterward.

The satellite Puuc towns of Kabah, Sayil, and Labná are not as large or as historically impressive as Uxmal, but their remote setting in the Puuc Hills adds to their appeal. Many of the temples and pyramids remain hidden by the low vegetation, and tropical birds flit among the ruins. If you're making a thorough tour of the Puuc ruins, it's worth your while to check these sites out, but if you're pressed for time head directly to Uxmal.

UXMAL

The archaeological ruins are open daily 8–5. Admission is $4, free on Sunday. Maya history and culture is the focus of the nightly light-and-sound shows (Spanish $3.25, 7 PM; English $5, 9 PM).

The magnificent **Pyramid of the Magician** is the first thing you'll see when you enter the archaeological site. The first stage of the pyramid's construction dates to the 6th century, and five temples were added during the next 300 years. The pyramid has an unusual oval base and stands 129 ft tall; to reach the fifth temple, you'll have to climb 150 narrow steps at a 60° angle. Then climb down the west side to the temple just below it, which has an entrance framed by the mouth of a huge mask of Chaac. Most impressive is the careful stone-by-stone construction and the way the shape of the pyramid seems to change when viewed from different angles.

Behind the pyramid is the Nun's Quadrangle, an imposing complex of four long, narrow buildings around a central courtyard. The complex received its name from the Spanish, who thought the layout and the 74 small rooms inside resembled a European convent. Its real purpose remains unclear: Red handprints covering one wall have led to speculation that the building was associated with Itzamná, the god of sun and sky. However, images of Chaac, the rain god with the distinctive hooked nose, are also prevalent. Many walls are decorated with geometric patterns and animal carvings, including images of a two-headed serpent representing Itzamná, the Maya god of sun and sky. Facing the Nun's Quadrangle is a four-building complex called the **Cemetery Group.** Now badly decayed, the structures were once decorated with carved skulls and bones.

Head southwest from the Nun's Quadrangle to reach the **juego de pelota** (ball court). The badly deteriorated complex used to have stone bleachers from which spectators watched the competitors knock balls through stone rings using only their hips, elbows, and knees. Close to the ball court is the **House**

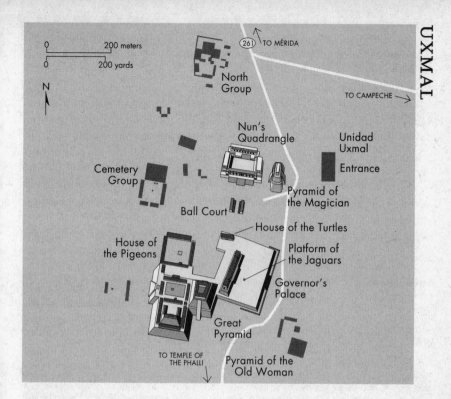

0 200 meters
0 200 yards

N

TO MÉRIDA

261

TO CAMPECHE →

North Group

Nun's Quadrangle

Unidad Uxmal

Entrance

Cemetery Group

Pyramid of the Magician

Ball Court

House of the Turtles

House of the Pigeons

Platform of the Jaguars

Governor's Palace

Great Pyramid

Pyramid of the Old Woman

TO TEMPLE OF THE PHALLI

of the Turtles, a simple, typically Puuc structure. The upper half of the building, which consists of a series of rooms, is most interesting: A series of columns supports a cornice sculpted with small turtles (use your imagination here, as they look more like muffins). The Maya believed that turtles would appeal to Chaac on behalf of drought-stricken humans.

Set on a large raised platform, the **Governor's Palace** is one of the finest examples of pre-Columbian architecture in Mesoamerica. Its 351-ft length is divided by three corbeled arches, creating narrow passageways or sanctuaries. The friezes along the uppermost section of the palace are as intricate as any in Maya architecture, with carvings of geometric patterns overlaid with plumed serpents and Chaac masks. These mosaics supposedly required more than 20,000 individually cut stones.

Southeast of the Governor's Palace is a badly deteriorated pyramid with a rectangular base and the remains of a temple on its top. Now covered by vegetation, the whole complex is known as the **Pyramid of the Old Woman,** referring to a Maya legend that claims the Pyramid of the Magician was built by an old witch and her dwarf son, who was hatched from an egg. Continuing south from the Pyramid of the Old Woman, you'll reach the small **Temple of the Phalli.** Suspended from the cornices, the phalli were used to channel rain into storage containers. Most phalli have been destroyed or stolen, but you can see one lone phallus in the museum at the tourist center.

Southwest of the Governor's Palace are the remains of the **Great Pyramid.** The structure is in poor condition and cannot compare with the Pyramid of the Magician, but the view from the 108-ft mound is rewarding and the climb up the reconstructed stairway is relatively easy. Inside the temple at the top is a shrine to Chaac. Small bowls are carved into parts of the mask, presumably to hold water or small offerings. Behind the Great Pyramid is the **House of the Pigeons,** a long building topped by eight triangular belfries perforated with what appear to be pigeonholes, hence the name of the building. No one has a clue as to what the place was actually used for. About ½ km (¼ mi) south from the House of the Pigeons is a small building half-covered by dirt and vegetation. The geometric carvings on its facade look like a centipede, giving the building the name Chimez (Maya for centipede).

SOME HELPFUL PHRASES IN MAYA

B'ish a ka' ba?	What is your name?
Im ka' ba. . .	My name is. . .
Baax a kajal?	Where are you from?
In kajale'. . .	I live in. . .
Bis a wool?	How are you?
Jach kimac in wool	I'm content.
Takin jahnal	I'm hungry.
Takin ukik a sis bah	I want something cold to drink.

WHERE TO SLEEP • Of the Puuc sites, only Uxmal has accommodations, most of which are expensive hotels. If you insist on staying in the area, head for **Rancho Uxmal,** a hotel 6 km (4 mi) north of the ruins. Doubles here are $22. You can pitch a tent or hang a hammock in the cement-floor palapas (and still have use of bathrooms, hot showers, and an enticing swimming pool) for $2 per person, plus $1.75 per hammock rental. *Hwy 261, no phone. From Uxmal, flag down a Mérida-bound bus and ask to be let off at Rancho Uxmal. 20 rooms, all with bath. Restaurant, laundry, luggage storage. Cash only.*

KABAH

About 25 km (15½ mi) south of Uxmal, Kabah is among the most impressive sites in the Puuc region and dates from AD 850–900. Highway 261 splits Kabah in two: The most interesting structures uncovered so far lie on the eastern side of the road, while the ruins on the western side remain partly hidden beneath dense vegetation. You should devote at least an hour to seeing the main sights here, if possible.

The **Codz Pop** is the principal structure at Kabah. The west side of the structure has a fantastic facade decorated with nearly 300 masks of Chaac, to whom the building was dedicated. The name Codz Pop means "coiled mat," possibly a reference to the distinctive Chaac noses, which curl like rolled-up mats. The noses may have been used as supports for lanterns, in which case the wall would have been brilliantly lit and visible for miles. Some archaeologists have suggested that the building had a legal or military function. Behind the Codz Pop are two structures built in the plainer, more traditional Puuc style: **El Palacio,** a palace that featured over 30 chambers, half of which still remain; and the **Temple of the Columns,** with well-preserved columns at the back of the building.

On the west side of the road are several more magnificent structures, still largely unexcavated. Over hundreds of years, the roots of jungle vines and trees have transformed the **Great Pyramid,** once the most important temple in Kabah, into a mound of rubble. Traces of a stairway appear on its southern side. Nearby, the **Arch of Triumph** marks the end of a *sacbé,* a raised road leading from Kabah to Uxmal; the link to Uxmal demonstrates that Kabah was a politically important center. Southwest of the arch is the newly excavated **Templo de las Manos Rojas** (Temple of the Red Hands), which features in its first chamber some red hand imprints similar to those seen in Uxmal. The handprints have been interpreted as either the signatures of the ancient architects or the marks of Itzamná, the Maya god of the sun. *Admission: $1.25, free Sun. Open daily 8–5.*

SAYIL

Meaning "the place of the ants" in Maya, Sayil, 10 km (6 mi) south of Kabah, is best known for its magnificent **palace.** Built in AD 730, the palace is 213 ft long, with more than 50 rooms on three levels. The second level is decorated with columns similar to those found in Greek temples. The sculpted frieze above these columns features masks of Chaac, as well as images of the Descending God, an upside-down figure diving from the sky to the earth in order to grant the wishes of the Maya. Also visible is the Blue Lizard, a snakelike figure. South of the palace is the badly decayed **El Mirador,** which features a rooster-comb roof and a **juego de pelota.** Don't leave Sayil without getting a good look at the city from a distance—the best view is from the hill across the road from the entrance. *Admission: $1.25, free Sun. Open daily 8–5.*

LABNA

Probably the oldest of the Puuc cities, Labná (4 km/2½ mi from Xlapak) is thought to have been built during the early Classic period (about AD 500). Labná means "the old house" in Maya, but it probably received this name after the city was abandoned. Only a few structures have been uncovered at Labná, but they are exquisite. The best-preserved structure is the corbeled **arch,** whose stones stand without the aid of any mortar; once part of a larger building, the arch now stands alone, except for two surviving rooms that are richly decorated with geometric patterns, mosaics, and small columns. The **palace,** probably built some time in the 9th century, is the other major structure at Labná. The largest complex in the Puuc Hills, it sits on a huge platform more than 449 ft long. Despite its size, the palace isn't nearly as inspiring as the palace at Sayil. However, the decorations on its facade are noteworthy. Another impressive structure at Labná is **El Mirador,** a pyramid with a temple on top. The pyramid is little more than rubble today, but the temple has survived. *Admission: $1.25, free Sun. Open daily 8–5.*

OXKUTZCAB AND THE LOLTÚN CAVES

Sixteen kilometers (10 mi) southeast of Ticul, the small town of Oxkutzcab (pronounced osh-kootz-KAAB) is seldom explored by tourists. Most foreigners who do come here promptly board a bus or taxi to the nearby caves at Loltún. Ticul works better as a base town for the Puuc Route, but if you decide to spend the night in Oxkutzcab, try **Hospedaje Trujeque** (Calle 48 No. 102-A, between Calles 51 and 53, tel. 997/5–05–68), which has pleasant rooms with private bathrooms and hot water costing $7.50 a double. The huge daily **market** (Calle 51, between Calles 48 and 50) draws produce sellers and buyers from throughout the region.

You'd be crazy to hike or bike around Hochob during the rainy season (June–August): gallons of water pour from the sky, and rattlesnakes come out of their burrows to avoid drowning.

The Grutas de Loltún are the largest and most spectacular caves on the peninsula and definitely deserve your time. About 19 km (12 mi) east of Labná and 10 km (6 mi) west of Oxkutzcab, Loltún consists of a maze of underground caverns filled with enormous stalagmites and stalactites. Archaeologists have had a field day here, unearthing evidence about the Maya and their ancestors, who inhabited these caves for more than two millennia. Religious ceremonies were held in the **Catedral,** a vast chamber crowded with stalagmites and stalactites. Some formations in the center of the chamber resemble an altar. In another cavern you can see the soot from cooking fires and the remains of *metates* (stones used for grinding corn). The caves also contain several carvings of figures and some hieroglyphs, a few of which date back to 2000 BC, as well as a handful of black-ink paintings. Over thousands of years, dripping water has carved the cave's rocks into bizarre shapes, and tour guides find no end of amusing resemblances, including the Virgin of Guadalupe, a dolphin's head, a camel, a jaguar, and an eagle. Especially interesting are two semihollow rock formations extending from the ceiling to the floor. If you tap them the right way, they produce musical tones (though according to local legend, only virgins can coax the rocks into producing their sweet tones).

You cannot enter the caves without a guide. Guided tours leave every 1½ hours, daily 9:30–3; if you arrive after 3, you'll be forced to wait until the following day. Guides expect a tip for their troubles—a dollar or two each is appropriate. The floor of the dark caves is slippery and uneven, so bring a sturdy pair of shoes. *Admission: $3, free Sun.*

COMING AND GOING

Combis leave from the Parque San Juan in Mérida (Calle 62, between Calles 69 and 67) for Oxkutzcab whenever they're full; ADO buses leave from Mérida's bus terminal (Calle 71, between Calles 68 and 70) about every three hours, 9 AM–8:30 PM. Both combis and buses take 1½ hours and cost $3. From anywhere besides Mérida, you'll have to go to Ticul first and catch a combi (20 min, 50¢) from Calle 25 (between Calles 26 and 28) to Oxkutzcab. The last bus leaves Ticul at 7 PM. To reach Loltún from Oxkutzcab, you'll have to wait until one of the trucks carrying workers to the fields (and stray foreigners to the tourist attractions) fills up—wait in front of the market. The trip costs only 50¢ and takes about 20 minutes. If you don't want to wait around, you can hire one of the many taxis or combis to take you to the grutas for about $4.

THE SNAKE CHARMERS OF TICUL

Don Toribio Na'a Tzul, a 72-year-old snake expert, and his equally knowledgeable wife, Juana María Yam, live on Calle 31 No. 181, at Calle 24, in Ticul. The Maya couple has been curing snake bites and making medicines from snake venom and meat for decades. They prescribe powdered rattlesnake meat as a cure for people in the beginning stages of cancer, and rattlesnake oil to alleviate the symptoms of rheumatism. For a mere 10 pesos you can even buy a powdered snake potion that will make your love pursue you endlessly for the rest of his or her life—just put a little snake powder in that person's taco, wait eight days, then repeat the dose. Warning: The effects of the potion are supposedly irreversible! Don Toribio and Juana María speak only limited Spanish, but if you bring a Maya-speaking interpreter, you can hear hundreds of stories about the Yucatán's various species of snakes, including the boa roja, a snake that cries like a baby, and the chicotera, which laughs like a woman.

Of course, if you are unfortunate enough to be bitten by a snake, you should seek medical attention immediately. In the meantime, Don Toribio suggests eating a whole lime (peel and all) to calm yourself. Try to slow the circulation from the bitten area to the rest of your body by squeezing the area above the bite, and remain motionless to prevent the venom from traveling farther in your bloodstream. It's good to eat something, as food will help to absorb the venom.

There are three ways to return from Loltún: Wait (and hope) for the truck to come back; wait for a combi outside the entrance of the main parking lot; or hitch. Hitching is pretty easy (especially if you've made friends during the cave tour) and isn't dangerous during the day. From Oxkutzcab, combis leave for Ticul from Calle 52 (between Calles 51 and 53) or from the northwest corner of the park (the last leaves at 7 PM). Buses leave for Mérida from Oxkutzcab every half hour until 9 PM.

MERIDA

Mérida is the largest and most elegant city on the Yucatán Peninsula, perfect for a romantic Yucatecan vacation; after only a short stay here you'll come to love Mérida's sophisticated beauty. From aging, tranquil neighborhoods to frenzied commercial districts, each sector of the city has a distinct ambience: The Paseo de Montejo is a broad street harboring restored mansions, sidewalk cafés, and ritzy hotels. In the Parque Central, tourists and locals mingle near the cathedral and the Palacio de Gobierno, which are both monuments to the 500-year struggle between European and Maya culture. In fact the city itself is built on the site of the Maya settlement of T'hó, whose temples and columns reminded the Spanish of the Roman ruins at Mérida, Spain. The colonists forced the Maya to dismantle their temples and used the masonry to create new buildings, churches, and mansions. Like its buildings, Mérida's residents are the result of a merger of indigenous and European cultures: Their traditions, their cooking, and their language blend Maya and Spanish aesthetics.

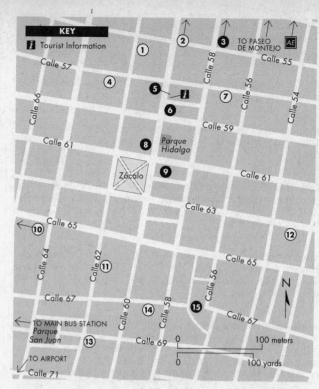

KEY

i Tourist Information

Calle 57

Calle 58

Calle 55

TO PASEO
DE MONTEJO

Calle 56

Calle 66

Calle 54

Calle 59

Calle 61

Parque
Hidalgo

Zócalo

Calle 61

Calle 63

Calle 65

Calle 64

Calle 62

Calle 56

Calle 65

Calle 67

Calle 60

Calle 58

Calle 67

TO MAIN BUS STATION
Parque
San Juan

Calle 69

100 meters

TO AIRPORT

Calle 71

100 yards

N

Sights ●
Catedral, **9**
Iglesia de la
Tercera Orden, **6**
Mercado
Municipal, **15**
Museo Regional
de Antropología, **3**
Palacio de
Gobierno, **8**
Teatro Peón
Contreras, **5**

Lodging ○
Casa San Juan, **13**
Hotel América, **14**
Hotel Casa
Bowen, **10**
Hotel Dolores
Alba, **12**
Hotel Galería
Trinidad, **2**
Hotel Montejo, **4**
Hotel Mucuy, **7**
Hotel Trinidad, **1**
La Paz, **11**

Mérida is a wonderful place to laze around for a few days and also a good base from which to explore the Gulf Coast and the ruins of the Puuc Hills. If you only have one day to spend in Mérida, try to make it a Sunday, when the central streets are closed off and the whole city turns out for festivities like Yucatecan folk dancing and an especially grand market. The best time to visit is generally during the dry season, November–April.

BASICS

AMERICAN EXPRESS

AmEx sells traveler's checks and offers emergency check cashing as well as lost-card and lost-check services. They hold clients' mail for up to a month. *Paseo de Montejo 494, Mérida, Yucatán, CP 97000, México, tel. 99/24–43–26. Between Calles 43 and 45. Open weekdays 9–2 and 4–5, Sat. 9–noon.*

AUTO PARTS/SERVICE

The **Ángeles Verdes** (Green Angels), a government-funded road service agency with a small office in Mérida, answers questions about service, tolls, and other car-related matters. *Calle 14 No. 102, between Calles 73 and 75, tel. 99/83–11–84. Open daily 8–8.*

CASAS DE CAMBIO

Most banks are on Calle 65, between Calles 60 and 62, and change money weekdays 9–12:30. Casas de cambio have poorer rates but longer hours: **Profesionales en Cambio** (Calle 61 No. 500, between. Calles 60 and 62, tel. 99/24–06–31) is open daily 8 AM–9 PM. The **Banamex** ATM at the corner of Calles 56 and 59 accepts Visa, MasterCard, Cirrus, and Plus cards.

CONSULATES

For information about Belize, visit the **United Kingdom/Belize Vice-Consulate**: *Calle 53 No. 498, between Calles 56 and 58, tel. 99/28–61–52. Open weekdays 9–1 and 4–5.* **United States**: *Paseo de Montejo 453, at Colón, tel. 99/25–50–11. Open weekdays 7:30–4.*

EMERGENCIES

In an emergency, dial **06** from any telephone in Mérida. The **police** station (tel. 99/25–25–55) is on Calle 72, between Calles 39 and 41.

LAUNDRY

La Lavamática La Fé charges $2 to wash and dry 3 kilos (6½ pounds) of clothing. *Calle 61 No. 518, between Calles 62 and 64, tel. 99/24–45–31. Open weekdays 8–7, Sat. 8–4.*

MAIL

The **post office** will hold mail sent to you at the following address for up to 10 days: Lista de Correos, Administración Urbana 1, Mérida, Yucatán, CP 97000, México. *Calle 65, at Calle 56, tel. 99/28–54–04. Open weekdays 7–7, Sat. 9–1.*

MEDICAL AID

Farmacia Noemi Virginia (Calle 67 No. 550-D, between Calles 66 and 68, tel. 99/24–52–90) is open 24 hours. For medical attention, visit the 24-hour **Clínica Yucatán** (Calle 66 No. 528, at Calle 65, tel. 99/24–93–91). The **Cruz Roja** (Calle 68, between Calles 65 and 67, tel. 99/28–53–91, or 99/24–98–13 for emergencies) offers 24-hour ambulance service.

PHONES

You can find **Ladatel** telephones on the zócalo, at the Palacio Municipal, and in parks around the city. Dial **09** for international collect calls. You can only call direct from *casetas* (booths); the **Caseta de Larga Distancia** (long-distance telephone office; Calle 60, at Calle 61, tel. and fax 99/24–19–07) charges $2.75 per minute for calls to the United States.

SCHOOLS

The **Academia de Cultura e Idiomas** offers beginning through advanced Spanish courses, including classes geared toward scientists, businesspeople, and anthropologists. Four-week programs entail four hours of class per day and cost $300 for the first two weeks, $110 for each additional week. The school arranges affordable homestays for students. *Calle 13 No. 23, tel. and fax 99/44–31–48. Take SAN ANTO-NIO bus from corner of Calles 56 and 59. Mailing address: Apartado 78-4, Mérida, Yucatán, CP 97100, México.*

TOURS AND GUIDES

Shop around for tours to the Maya ruins near Mérida, as prices for day trips fluctuate widely from agent to agent. Guided trips to Uxmal and Chichén Itzá should cost about $30. Reliable travel agencies include **Ceiba Tours** (Colón 498, at Calle 60, tel. 99/20–44–77; open weekdays 8–7, Sat. 8–2) and **Eco-Turismo Yucatán** (Calle 3 No. 235, between Calles 32 and 34, tel. 99/20–27–72).

VISITOR INFORMATION

The **tourist information center** at Teatro Peón Contreras has a knowledgeable staff that speaks English fairly well. They also have copies of *Yucatán Today,* a free magazine with general information and some maps. Information booths at the airport and the bus station stock similar material. *Calle 60, between Calles 57 and 59, tel. 99/24–92–90. Open daily 8–8.*

COMING AND GOING

BY BUS

Mérida is home to several bus terminals, the biggest and most confusing of which is **Unión de Camioneros del Yucatán** (Calle 70, between Calles 69 and 71). From here, **ADO** (tel. 99/24–83–91) has first-class service to Cancún (4 hrs, $8.50) and Villahermosa (9 hrs, $19), as well as frequent first-class service to Campeche (2½ hrs, $5). Other destinations include Chetumal (4 per day; 8 hrs, $10), Palenque (2 per day; 9 hrs, $17), and San Cristóbal de las Casas (1 per day; 14 hrs, $20). **ATS** (Calle 69, between Calles 68 and 70, tel. 99/23–22–87) sends second-class buses every three hours 6 AM–7 PM to Uxmal (1½ hrs, $2), Hopelchén (3 hrs, $3.25), and Maxcanú (1 hr, 75¢).

Buses to smaller, nearby towns leave from various points around the city. Buses to Dzibilchaltún (hourly; 1 hr, 60¢) or Umán (every ½ hr; 45 min, 50¢) leave from the corner of **Parque San Juan** (Calle 64, between Calles 69 and 71). To reach Hunucmá (1 hr, $1), Sisal (1½ hrs, $1.25), or Celestún (2 hrs, $1.75), go to the station on **Calle 71** (between Calles 64 and 66, around corner from Parque San Juan).

Frequent buses to Mayapán (1½ hrs, $1.25), and Dzilam de Bravo (2 hrs, $1.75) leave from the station at **Calle 50** (between Calles 65 and 67). Buses for Progreso (1 hr, $1) leave every 20 minutes 6 AM–9 PM from the station on **Calle 62** (between Calles 65 and 67).

BY CAR

Avoid the expensive toll road, unless you care to pay $6 to Valladolid, plus another $10 to Cancún (tolls are 40% lower from January through June). To drive the free road instead, veer to the right at Kilometer 67 of Highway 180 as you leave Mérida. The *carretera de cuota* (toll road) and the *carretera libre* (free road) go through the same places, but you can't get off the toll road (which, admittedly, is much faster) until Valladolid. If you're going the other direction, you're in luck—there are no tolls between Campeche and Mérida.

BY PLANE

Mérida's airport is 7 km (4 mi) west of the city's central square. **Aeroméxico** (Paseo Montejo 460, tel. 99/27–90–00) flies to Cancún ($60 one-way) and Mexico City ($162 one-way). **Aerocaribe** (Paseo Montejo 500-B, at Calle 47, tel. 99/28–67–90) flies to Oaxaca city ($135 one-way) and Villahermosa ($79 one-way) It's fairly easy and cheap to get to town: Just take Autobus 79 (AVIACION) to the corner of Calles 67 and 60 downtown. The half-hour trip costs about 25¢. A combi to your hotel costs $5 for up to four people.

In Ticul you are likely to hear Maya spoken as often as Spanish. One important discrepancy between the two languages is that in Spanish, malo means bad, while in Maya, malo means good.

GETTING AROUND

Despite its size, Mérida is easy to explore, with most of the interesting buildings and budget hotels clustered near the zócalo. Streets are numbered, not named, with odd-numbered streets running east–west and even-numbered streets running north–south. The **zócalo** is bordered by Calles 60, 61, 62, and 63.

BY BUS

You won't need to use the bus to see the sights in Mérida's center, but if you want to go beyond the area immediately surrounding the zócalo, bus travel is a cheap option. City buses (25¢) run daily 5 AM to midnight; some buses stop earlier, so be sure to ask the driver. Buses leave from Calle 59 between Calles 56 and 58, and from Calle 56 between Calles 59 and 67, near the market. Destinations are marked on the windshields.

BY CAR

Most rental agencies are on Calle 60, between Calles 55 and 59. At about $25 a day (including insurance and unlimited mileage) the cheapest place is **México Rent-a-Car** (Calle 60 No. 495, between Calles 57 and 59, tel. 99/27–49–16; open Mon.–Sat. 8–1 and 5–8, Sun. 8–1). Despite the too-good-to-be-true price, their VW bugs seem to be in good condition. However, their other cars seem less reliable. **National InterRent** (Calle 60, between Calles 55 and 57, tel. 99/23–24–93; open daily 7 AM–10 PM) charges about $30 a day (including insurance and unlimited mileage); to rent a car here you must be age 21 or older and possess a credit card.

BY TAXI

Regular taxis are very expensive, so look for combis (50¢). Tell the driver where you want to go before you get in, and he'll tell you if it's on his way. Combis leave from the zócalo, the market area, and Parque San Juan at Calles 67 and 62. If you need a ride to the airport, call a radio taxi (tel. 99/23–49–62 or 99/23–13–17) for pickup. These are cheaper than the *sitios,* the taxis that park at taxi stands.

WHERE TO SLEEP

Mérida's best budget hotels are conveniently located near the zócalo—many of these are converted old mansions or town houses. The majority of the budget hotels near bus station are unpleasant and to be avoided.

UNDER $10 • Hotel Casa Bowen. The wood and wicker furniture, wrought-iron railings, and open-air lending library in the lobby will make you look forward to coming "home" each night. Big windows let light into the rooms, and ceiling fans or air-conditioning keep things cool. Doubles cost $10. Suites ($12) have their own kitchens, equipped with stove and fridge. *Calle 66 No. 521-B, between Calles 65 and 67, tel. 99/28–61–09. 25 rooms, all with bath. Laundry, luggage storage. Cash only.*

Hotel Montejo. A gorgeous courtyard decorated with colonial-style arches are what you'd expect in a hotel of this caliber in Mérida. Elegant doubles cost $10. Air-conditioned rooms are a mere $1.25 more. *Calle 57 No. 507, between Calles 62 and 64, tel. 99/28–03–99. 22 rooms, all with bath. Restaurant, luggage storage. Cash only.*

UNDER $15 • Hotel América. The simple rooms here have private bathrooms (most with hot water), but the beds are a bit uncomfortable. A couple of blocks from the zócalo, the hotel is popular with families, less so with foreign travelers. Doubles cost $11. *Calle 67 No. 500, between Calles 58 and 60, tel. 99/28–58–79. 43 rooms, all with bath (30 with hot water). Meal service, luggage storage. Cash only.*

Hotel Galería Trinidad. This funky hotel is decorated with everything from weatherbeaten sculptures to avant-garde Mexican paintings to inflatable Mickey Mouse dolls. After admiring the lobby and hallways, though, you'll probably be disappointed by the relatively bland rooms. The swimming pool is refreshing but is sometimes neglected (it tends to flood when it rains). Rooms start at $9 for doubles with a shared bath. Air-conditioning is an extra $2.50. *Calle 51, at Calle 60, tel. 99/23–24–63. 30 rooms, 27 with bath. Luggage storage. Cash only.*

Hotel Mucuy. The Mucuy's owners will make you feel like part of the family and are eager to share information about the city and nearby ruins. The immaculate rooms have good window screens, overhead fans, and views of the hotel's garden (a pleasant place for postcard-writing). There's a book exchange and communal refrigerator in the lobby, and someone's always around to keep things secure. Doubles cost $11.25. *Calle 57 No. 481, between Calles 56 and 58, tel. 99/28–51–93, fax. 99/23–78–01. 22 rooms, all with bath. Luggage storage. Cash only.*

Hotel Trinidad. Oddly carved wood columns, tons of plants, and a hodgepodge of paintings give this place a homey, atticlike feel. The communal bathrooms aren't luxurious, but they're kept relatively clean. Guests can enjoy coffee and toast with eggs or cereal (not included with lodging) on the hotel's central patio. Doubles with private bath start at $11.25. *Calle 62, between Calles 55 and 57, tel. 99/23–20–33. 20 rooms, 10 with bath. Laundry ($1 per piece), luggage storage. Cash only.*

UNDER $20 • Hotel Dolores Alba. When you emerge from your cozy room with a clean bath, lively paintings, and red-tile floor, pull up a chaise lounge and daydream by the pool. Rocking chairs fill the common areas, along with a guitar and chess set. Doubles cost $20. Air-conditioning is an extra $3. *Calle 63 No. 464, between Calles 52 and 54, tel. 99/28–56–50. 50 rooms, all with bath. Breakfast room, pool, laundry, luggage storage. Cash only.*

UNDER $25 • Casa San Juan. You won't mind paying extra for the pampering you'll receive that this new bed-and-breakfast in a mellow, old colonial mansion. The original beam ceilings, tile roof, sunny patio, sitting rooms, and 18th-century fountain have been beautifully restored. Personable Cuban owner Pablo D'Costa really knows how to please his guests: Breakfast with eggs, juice, fruit, sweet rolls, and coffee is served in a cozy dining room or on a terrace. Guest bathrooms have big, fluffy towels and complimentary soaps and shampoos. Doubles with air-conditioning and private bath cost $25. *Calle 62 No. 545-A, between Calles 69 and 71, 3 blocks south of zócalo, tel. 99/23–68–23, fax. 99/86–29–37. 6 rooms, all with bath.*

FOOD

Eating is one of the highlights of a trip to Mérida: Yucatecan food is delicious, and nowhere is it better prepared than here. Naturally, the larger, sit-down restaurants are expensive, but many small loncherías and street stands around town sell antojitos, tortas, and panuchos and salbutes—all for under $1. The second floor of the **mercado municipal** (Calles 65 and 67, between Calles 54 and 56) has more than 20 simple loncherías offering full lunches for under $3; on the north side of the market are dozens of stands selling amazingly fresh ceviches and full-size shrimp and conch cocktail cups for $2–$3. The municipal market is also a wonderful place to buy fresh fruits and vegetables brought daily from the villages.

UNDER $5 • Amaro. Lilting music and flickering candles make this shaded courtyard restaurant—in a converted mansion—almost embarrassingly romantic. Vegetarian delights include delicious grilled green peppers stuffed with savory tofu, onion, and cheese. *Calle 59 No. 507, between Calles 60 and 62, tel. 99/28–24–51. Cash only.*

Café y Restaurante El Louvre. This is Mérida's answer to the American coffee shop. Stout waiters with little black bow ties and white shirts patrol the restaurant and yell orders to the cook, who stands behind a glass counter hacking at a pot roast. The hot lime soup ($1) with chicken and fried tortilla is delicious. Huge daily specials are only $2.25. *Calle 61, at Calle 62, on the zócalo, tel. 99/24–50–73. Open 24 hrs. Cash only.*

Restaurante Nicte-Há. Raucous groups of men wearing *guayaberas* (hand-embroidered cotton shirts) flock here to enjoy delicious Yucatecan specialties at amazingly cheap prices. The *combinación yucateca* is a must—for only $3.75 you get a panucho, papadzule, pollo pibil, tamale, and a Yucatecan sausage. Vegetarians can feast on rice and banana soup or *frijoles kabax* (savory whole-bean soup; 75¢). *Calle 61, between Calles 60 and 62, tel. 99/23–07–84. Cash only.*

UNDER $10 • Portico del Peregrino. Dining is either inside, in an immaculate old colonial home with its original doors and windows, or outside, on a leafy green patio where candles light the tables at night. The menu features Mexican and international cuisine, such as eggplant with layers of chicken and cheese, and seafood casserole cooked in wine. *Calle 57 No. 501, between Calles 60 and 62, tel. 99/28–61–63.*

Restaurant Express. The food at this European-style café is quite good and servings are abundant, but plan to spend $4–$5 for typical Yucatecan dishes. The specialty is pollo pibil, or try the *chilaquiles* (tortilla strips doused with salsa and sour cream). Save room for special desserts such as *pasta de guayaba* ($1), a square of luscious guava paste wrapped in a cool blanket of creamy cheese. *Calle 60, at Calle 59, tel. 99/28–16–91. Cash only.*

Southeast of Sayil's ancient city center stands a lone stela representing the importance of fertility to Maya culture. The carved male figure appears, at first glance, to have three legs—this is not the case.

WORTH SEEING

Since Mérida was founded, wealthy residents have invested an enormous amount of money and pride in their city, and the government continues to dole out funds to keep the city's colonial heritage in good shape. Museums, galleries, and stores are stocked with antiques and artwork from ancient, colonial, and contemporary times, and every week new listings of dance, theater, and music performances appear. For information on upcoming events, pick up the free weekly magazine *Yucatán Today* at the tourist office or check the local newspaper, *Por Esto* (25¢).

The sites listed below are only part of what makes Mérida interesting. Take the time to walk the blocks surrounding the zócalo and you will find old mansions, churches, and theaters. Some restoration efforts are better than others, but even if you walk into a run-down hotel, you're likely to see beautiful stained glass, original hardwood furniture, oil paintings dating back one or two hundred years, columns, marble and ceramic tiles, and beautiful courtyards.

CHURCHES

The splendid twin-spire **cathedral** (Calle 60, at Calle 61; open daily 7–noon and 5–8) stands austerely at the front of the zócalo. It looks more like a fort than anything else and is a subtle reminder of how difficult the Spanish found it to convert the Maya to Christianity. Built in 1561 entirely of stone (much of which came from razed Maya buildings), the cathedral was indeed designed for defense—gunnery slits, not windows, stare out onto the square. The interior is rather bleak, having been ransacked during the Mexican Revolution and never restored. However, the pillagers did not touch **El Cristo de las Ampollas,** which translates as "Christ of the Blisters." Legend has it that a local peasant once claimed he saw a tree burning all night, but that the tree was not consumed by the flames. A statue of Christ was carved from the tree and placed in a church in a nearby town. Later, the church burned down, but the statue survived, albeit covered in blisters.

The **Iglesia de la Tercera Orden** (Church of the Third Order), across from Parque Hidalgo at Calles 60 and 59, was built by Jesuit monks in the 17th century. The stones of the facade come from the great pyramid of T'hó; if you look carefully, especially on the Calle 59 side, you can still distinguish Maya designs on them. *Open daily 7–11 and 5–8.*

MERCADO MUNICIPAL

Mérida's gargantuan municipal market, occupying the area between Calles 65 and 67 and Calles 54 and 56, is considered by many travelers to be the best on the peninsula. If you're hunting for a hammock, hold out for the fine ones sold here (*see* Shopping, *below*). You'll also find a huge selection of embroidered shirts and dresses, ceramics, silver, and some crazy-looking, wood-eating insects called *maquech,* which have jewels and gold chains glued to their hard, shell-like backs. There's even a saint-repair shop, **La Reina de Tepeyac** (bottom floor of market, across the aisle from Edmundo Pinzon Lara Artesanías y Ropa Típica), in case your traveling icon has been damaged. *Market open daily 6–5.*

MUSEO REGIONAL DE ANTROPOLOGIA

This museum, about a kilometer (½ mi) from the zócalo, is worth visiting despite the $2 admission and lack of air-conditioning. Exhibits consist mainly of Maya artifacts, including figurines of the Maya messenger between the gods and man, Chac Mool, and artifacts retrieved from the sacred cenotes at Dzibilchaltún and Chichén Itzá. There are also reconstructions of burial chambers. *Paseo de Montejo, at Calle 43. Admission: $2, free Sun. Open Tues.–Sat. 8–8, Sun. 8–2. From zócalo, take northbound* PASEO DE MONTEJO *bus or walk 9 blocks.*

PALACIO DE GOBIERNO

Built in 1892 on the northern side of the zócalo, the Governor's Palace is a beautiful example of neoclassical architecture, with Doric columns topped by arches. Inside, on the second floor, murals by Fernando Castro Pacheco, a Yucatecan painter, depict the tumultuous history of the Yucatán, including the Caste War (*see box, below*), in which the Maya fought against Mexicans of European descent. *Calle 61, between Calles 60 and 62. Admission free. Open daily 8 AM–9:30 PM.*

TEATRO PEON CONTRERAS

In front of the Iglesia de la Tercera Orden (Church of the Third Order) stands this theater, yet another city landmark. The current building dates from 1877 but has undergone several transformations, the most drastic in 1905, when Italian artists gave it a neoclassical design. The theater hosts classical music recitals and ballets on Tuesday at 9 PM; check *Por Esto* for current shows. For ballet, plays, and concerts, same-night seats go on sale at 9 AM. Ballet tickets vary in price, sometimes starting as low as $3. *Calle 60, at Calle 57. Ticket box office open Mon.–Sat. 9–9, Sun. 9–1:30.*

SHOPPING

Mérida is the best place on the Yucatán Peninsula to buy a hammock, but the experience can be like looking for a used car. Salesmen are aggressive and will tell you anything, so visit at least two shops and don't be afraid to bargain. Street vendors near the zócalo and the bus station offer the best bargains, but it's wiser to cruise the shops along Calle 58 near the market (between Calles 63 and 69) to see what's out there. The best places to go are **El Hamaguero** (Calle 58, between Calles 69 and 71, tel. 99/23–21–17), which makes and sells their own hammocks, and **Artesanías Uxmal** (Calle 58, between Calles 63 and 65, tel. 99/23–36–33). In both of these places, be ready to bargain and have some prices in mind before walking in.

Hammocks come in several sizes—single, double, matrimonial, large matrimonial, and family. Judge the size for yourself by hefting the hammocks and comparing how much each weighs, rather than trusting the salesman's claims. The larger hammocks are probably your best bet, since they allow you to sleep diagonally, which is better for your back. Prices vary, but the smallest ones should be no more than $8 for the cotton-nylon type, $11 for nylon only. Matrimonial hammocks cost about $15 for cotton-nylon, $20 for nylon. Cotton and nylon-cotton hammocks are the most comfortable, however pure nylon hammocks last longer, and the colors don't fade. Whether you buy a cotton or a nylon hammock, the end-strings should be nylon for greater strength. Also, several long, straight strings should run along each side of the hammock for stability. Ask the salesman to hang the hammock for you, and see how closely it's woven; the closer the weave, the better the hammock.

AFTER DARK

The bar and disco scene in Mérida isn't terribly exciting. Locals are usually content just strolling around the zócalo, though things do liven up a bit on the weekends, when the city goes all out, staging huge cultural events and folkloric shows that are often free. For more information on upcoming events, visit the tourist information center (*see above*) or the **Oficina de la Cultura del Ayuntamiento** (Calle 62 between Calles 61 and 63, tel. 99/24–69–00), inside the Palacio Municipal.

BARS

Music by Gloria Gaynor and Madonna characterize **Kabukis** (Calle 84, between Calles 61 and 65, across from zoo; open Thurs.–Sat. until 3 AM), which is frequented by a predominantly gay crowd. A mellow bar during the early evening, Kabukis turns into a sizzling disco after 10 PM, and transvestites strut their stuff nightly at 12:30 AM. Cover is $2.75 Thursday and $5.25 Friday and Saturday; two drinks are always included in the charge. Waiters in giant sombreros carry drinks (beers $1.50, piña coladas, $2) to patrons at intimate wrought-iron patio tables at **Panchos** (Calle 59 No. 509, between Calles 60 and 62, tel. 99/23–09–42; open daily until 2 AM). The lack of cover and the lively bands that take the stage keep it a favorite among locals. **Pancho Villa's** (Calle 60, between Calles 55 and 57, tel. 99/24–22–89) is popular with locals and tourists who don't want to travel to the popular discos. Pancho Villas is open nightly until 3 or 4 AM and serves $1.25 beers and $1.50 margaritas. The music is mostly Latin rock and pop music, but the dance floor is rarely packed.

DANCING

The dance scene downtown is nonexistent. The really slick discos, popular among the upper-class youth, line Prolongación Montejo. A taxi from Mérida costs about $4. Serious dancers should go to **Kália** (Calle 22 No. 282, between Calles 37 and 39, tel. 99/44–42–35; open Wed.–Sat. until 3 AM), where an 18- to 40-year-old crowd works up a healthy sweat on a multiplatformed stage lit by a huge video screen. The cover charge is $4.75 for men, $3.50 for women. Downtown, a somewhat older crowd dances to salsa at **Estelares** (Calle 60 No. 484, between Calles 55 and 57, tel. 99/28–28–58; open Thurs.–Sat. until 3 AM). Cover is $1.50.

NEAR MERIDA

Yucatán state is home to many impressive ruins and breathtaking caves, many just a short bus ride from Mérida. However, in your rush to visit the blockbuster attractions, don't overlook the numerous *pueblos* (villages) scattered around the region; these provide a window on the real Yucatán, the Yucatán of today. Most of the region's towns flaunt quaint colonial churches, the largest and most elaborate of which can be seem at **Umán**, 18 km (11 mi) southwest of Mérida, and **Hunucmá**, 29 km (18 mi) west of Mérida. For details on how to reach these two towns, *see* Coming and Going, *above*.

You haven't really experienced the Yucatán until you've sampled one of the region's staple dishes: Poc chuc (grilled pork marinated in orange juice) and pollo pibil (marinated chicken baked in banana leaves) are among the favorite regional meat dishes. A non-meat favorite is papadzule (hard-boiled eggs wrapped in a tortilla with pumpkin sauce).

CALCEHTOK AND OXKINTOK

The spectacular caves at Calcehtok (Maya for "Bleeding of the Deer's Throat") are unknown to all but the most ambitious travelers because they aren't easily accessible without a car. Although they are only 70 km (43 mi) southwest of Mérida and about 15 km (9.3 mi) from Maxcanú, you'll have to wait an eternity for transport to the village of Calcehtok and then hike 3 km (2 mi) on a dirt road to get to the caves. But the rewards are great: After the first immense chamber, where sunlight illuminates tropical plants and singing, swooping birds, it's pure silence, except for the sound of water dripping from stalactites and the occasional chirping of a bat or two. Don't continue exploring unless you're an expert or have enlisted the help of a guide: **Roger Cuy** and his sons have been leading tours of the caves for three generations, and Roger's grandfather actually discovered them. You'll find the Cuys in the adobe house marked by a CAVE TOURS sign, adjacent to the bus stop in Calchetok village. A complete tour lasts up to six hours, but you can ask to return at any point during the tour (2–3 hours may be plenty to get a good feeling for what's here). Roger doesn't charge a set fee, but $5 an hour is about right, a bit more if you have a large group. Ropes and ladders, sticky mud, buzzing bees, and lots of bat guano are involved in a cave trip—it's not for the weak of heart or the less than agile. A flashlight of your own is also helpful.

COMING AND GOING

Getting to Calcehtok and Oxkintok by public transport is tiring and time-consuming. From the main bus station in Mérida, take a Maxcanú-bound bus; they make the one-hour trip every hour or so. The detour for Calcehtok is a few hundred yards before Maxcanú—just tell the driver you want to get off at the *grutas* (caves). From here, either hitchhike or catch a minitruck taxi to the village. From Calcehtok, it's 5 km (3 mi) to Oxkintok and 3 km (2 mi) to the caves. You may be able to arrange transport in the village; otherwise you'll have to walk or hitch. If you're visiting the caves, pick up Roger in the village. If you're driving from Mérida, take Highway 180 toward Campeche and turn off at the detour for Calcehtok.

CASTE WARS: MAYA REBELLION

When Mexico achieved independence from Spain in 1821, the Maya did not celebrate the event. The new government neither returned their lost land nor became more tolerant of their religion. In 1847, a Maya rebellion began in Valladolid. Within a year, the Maya had conquered all of the Yucatán except Mérida and Campeche. Just as the Maya prepared for a final, decisive assault, the winged ant (symbolic of coming rains) made an early appearance. The Maya took the insects' arrival as an omen, packed up their weapons, and returned to the fields to plant the sacred corn, without which they could not survive.

Help for the Spanish settlers then arrived with a vengeance from Mexico City, Cuba, and the United States. The Maya were mercilessly slaughtered, their population plummeting from 500,000 to 300,000. Survivors fled to the jungles of Quintana Roo and held out against the Mexican government until 1974, when the region officially accepted statehood with Mexico.

WHERE TO SLEEP AND EAT

In between the village of Calcehtok and the turnoff to the Oxkihtok ruins you'll find paradise; that is, **Paraíso Oxkihtok Cabañas y Restaurantes.** The clean cabins ($8) here have printed curtains and private baths. At the restaurant, order some beers (60¢) or Cokes and you'll get all the salbutes and *empanadas* (fried tortillas filled with mashed potatoes) you can eat. Paraíso accepts cash only. For reservations call the village's communal telephone line (tel. 992/8–21–87).

MAYAPAN

A day trip to Mayapán, about 52 km (32 mi) southeast of Mérida, is a must for every amateur archaeologist. The ruins, dismissed by many as cheap imitations of Chichén Itzá, are nevertheless impressive. Even more astounding is the fact that so few tourists come this way. Mayapán was built during the post-Classic period and inhabited by the Cocam, a tribe of Mexican origin. The Cocam, along with the Xiú of Uxmal and the Itzá of Chichén Itzá, formed a powerful alliance that lasted from about AD 1000 to 1200, when Mayapán broke off and established its hegemony over the already weakened Maya empire. The city's dominance lasted only a couple of centuries, however—a coup d'état by a noble family ousted the rulers, leading to the city's demise some time before 1450.

The buildings of Mayapán have not fared as well as those of Chichén Itzá. The most interesting building is the **Great Pyramid,** similar to El Castillo at Chichén but without the temple chamber at the summit. The **Temple of Chaac,** next to the pyramid, is a long, low building decorated with carved masks of the rain god. This is also an excellent place to check out colorful birds like the *chachalaca,* which can be heard calling from its perch in the surrounding flora. The site's rock-rimmed cenote sustains a bonanza of floral life, including banana trees and a dark-leaf avocado tree. *Admission: $1.25, free Sun. Open daily 8–5.*

COMING AND GOING

From the station at Calles 50 and 67 in Mérida, hourly buses (1½ hrs, $1.25 round-trip) travel down Road 18 to Telchaquillo and the Mayapán turnoff. Ask the driver to drop you off at "*las ruinas.*" Buses from Mayapán back to Mérida are pretty frequent until 5:30 PM; after that it's a long wait for the last return bus at 8 PM. There are no hotels anywhere in the area.

DZIBILCHALTUN

Dzibilchaltún (pronounced tsee-bil-chal-*toon*) is one of the most visited archaeological sites in the region, perhaps because of its proximity to Mérida. As popular as it is, Dzibilchaltún will not impress most visitors. Most of its archaeological riches lie underground, and the two remaining buildings cannot compare with the grandeur of Uxmal and the Puuc Hills, or even of Mayapán. Still, Dzibilchaltún's location, within a natural park just 20 km (12 mi) north of Mérida, makes it an accessible half-day trip. The site was first inhabited in about 2000 BC, reaching its apogee during the Classic period, from AD 600 to 900, when it became a major ceremonial and residential center. In the late 1500s it was turned into an open chapel and, about 200 years later, a cattle ranch. Remains of all three epochs litter the city "center." At the southern end of a well-maintained 65-ft-wide sacbé is the **Temple of the Seven Dolls,** noteworthy for its structural elegance. The temple received its name from the seven clay dolls unearthed from its floor.

Near the ruins is the **Cenote Xlacah,** a natural, freshwater pool that was once (judging from the bones found inside) used by the residents of Dzibilchaltún for religious ceremonies and sacrifices. The large and excellent **museum** at the entrance to the ruins displays pottery samples found in the cenote, as well as the original seven dolls from the temple. Outside the museum is a garden with dozens of intricately carved stelae and some sculpted figures of the *jugadores de pelota* (ball players), with their heavily ornamented sumo wrestler–like belts. *Admission to ruins and museum: $3, free Sun. Open daily 8–8.*

Mérida's Banamex on Calle 63 has a facade that depicts Francisco de Montejo (who destroyed the Maya city of T'hó to create Mérida) and his Spanish soldiers standing on the heads of the vanquished Maya.

COMING AND GOING

Buses to Dzibilchaltún (45 min, 50¢) leave Mérida from the station at Parque San Juan every hour. Otherwise, you can catch a bus or combi heading north along Highway 261 to Progreso. These drop you at the turnoff to the ruins, which lie about 6 km (4 mi) down a side road. To return to Mérida or Progreso, flag down a passing bus or combi at the end of the driveway to the ruins (a five-minute walk); they run every one–two hours, cost 80¢, and the last one leaves for Mérida at 7 PM. Otherwise, flag down a bus to either Mérida or Progreso from the highway.

THE GULF COAST

If you're in Mérida and you'd like to spend a day or two at the beach, try the Gulf Coast. Beaches here have a look all their own, quite different from the azure perfection of the Caribbean coast. The coast road between Progreso and Dzilam de Bravo passes by savannas and *aguadas* (shallow ponds), grassy dunes, palm tree groves, and the dark blue sea. Birds fly in patterns overhead or float in the waters, seemingly oblivious to the magnificent summer storms that occasionally pass through. The modern beach houses you'll see here belong to wealthy residents of Mérida, who use them only on weekends and summer vacations. During the rest of the year, you'll share the miles of white beaches with just a handful of fishermen. Note that in most of these villages accommodations are limited or nonexistent.

PROGRESO

Progreso is a growing tourist resort, catering mainly to residents of Mérida who make the 32-km (20-mi) pilgrimage to its beaches during the weekends and latter half of summer. During the winter months, a large contingent of Canadian visitors arrive, trading their miserable snowy winter for some sun and fun. Yet Progreso maintains a small-town atmosphere, and most locals live their lives independent of all these tourists. Its beaches are nice enough, although the town itself is charmless, with cold cement architecture.

COMING AND GOING • In Mérida, Progreso-bound buses (1 hr, 60¢) leave every 20 minutes between 6 AM and 9 PM from the station on Calle 62 between Calles 65 and 67. Buses back to Mérida leave the Progreso bus station (Calle 29, between Calles 80 and 82) every 15 minutes between 5:30 AM and 9:30 PM; combis (60¢) leave for Mérida every 10 minutes until 9:30 PM from Calle 31, between

Calles 78 and 80. Buses for Dzilman de Bravo ($1.50) leave Progreso (Calle 82, between Calles 29 and 31) at 7 AM and 2 PM.

WHERE TO SLEEP • During the low season, you should have no problem getting a room in one of Progreso's several hotels. Each of the large, sandy rooms ($18) at **Playa Linda** (Av. Malecón, at Calle 76, tel. 993/5–05–23) has two double beds and hammock hooks, as well as a kitchenette with a table, chairs, and a burner; rooms on the second floor have balconies. **Hotel Progreso** (Calle 78, at Calle 29, tel. 993/5–00–39) offers immaculate rooms and some of the nicest bathrooms in the Yucatán. It's five short blocks from the beach, but the added comfort is worth the walk. Doubles are $9.25, plus $5–$6 for air-conditioning and TV. Both hotels accept cash only.

FOOD • Progreso is a port town surrounded by fishing villages, so it's no surprise that seafood is a staple at the town's restaurants. Head for the **market** (corner of Calles 27 and 80; open daily 6–6) to buy fresh fruits and vegetables or to eat in one of the many fondas or loncherías. For fresh bread and drinks, try the supermarkets and bakeries on Calle 27. **Sol y Mar** (Av. Malecón, at Calle 80, tel. 993/5–29–79; cash only) is a great place to enjoy a beer (80¢) while crunching on free nachos and *botanas* (seafood chip dips). Shrimp dishes, prepared in various styles, are $4–$5.

CELESTUN

On the tip of a narrow strip of land that separates the estuaries of Río Esperanza from the Gulf of Mexico, Celestún is one of the most-visited places around Mérida, and with good reason. Set in the middle of the **Parque Natural Río Celestún,** the town offers pretty beaches and large colonies of exotic birds. Star billing goes to the park's pink flamingos, thousands of which gather in the waters of the estuary. To see the flamingos up close, you'll need to rent a boat (approaching on foot is illegal, and could net you a large fine). Tours leaving from the beach are ridiculously expensive, so your best bet is to walk about 1½ km (¾ mi) southeast from the zócalo, where you can hire a boat at the dock under the bridge that spans the river. The boat tour generally includes visits to the flamingos' hangout, an *ojo de agua* (freshwater spring), and the Isla de los Pájaros (Bird Island). The boat guides often clap their hands and make a lot of ruckus to scare the flamingos—if you'd prefer to leave the poor birds in peace, let the guide know. Tours ($23–$38 for up to six people) last one–two hours.

The beaches at Celestún are speckled with glittering white shells, and the warm, clear waters make for pleasant swimming. If you can arrange to stay here for the night, be sure not to miss the magnificent sunset over Celestún's calm, misty waters. Buses for Celestún leave Mérida almost every hour from the bus station (Calle 71, between Calles 64 and 66) and cost about $1.75. From Celestún, first-class buses return to Mérida about every two hours, the last one leaving Celestún at 8:30 PM.

WHERE TO SLEEP AND EAT • The few budget accommodations on the beach fill up during July and August and on weekends. **Hotel María del Carmen** (Calle 12, at Calle 15, tel. 993/6–20–51) offers clean new rooms (doubles $19), all with nice ocean views and some with great sundecks. **Hotel San Julio** (Calle 12 No. 93-A, no phone), also on the beach, has comparable rooms at $10–$12 a double. Both hotels accept cash only. Camping is free along the beach, but stay within the town limits or you might get some unwanted attention from locals. Free camping on the beach in front of Hotel María del Carmen is allowed. There are plenty of restaurants on the main street between the zócalo and the beach, and on the beach itself. Most serve only seafood, but **Restaurant La Playita** (Calle 12, between Calles 7 and 9, no phone) always has one nonseafood dish for about $2. Fish fillets are about $3.25 and shrimp dishes run $4–$5.

DZILAM DE BRAVO

Seventy-five kilometers (46½ mi) northeast of Mérida is Dzilám de Bravo, a bird-watcher's paradise. (Unfortunately, sand flies make the beach a sunbather's nightmare.) You can get a fisherman to take you out to see the birds for a few dollars. If you're feeling rich or are traveling with a fairly large group, consider a day trip to the **Bocas de Dzilám,** a group of freshwater springs flowing from the sea floor about 40 km (25 mi) away; the region around the springs is an avian extravaganza, with colonies of pelicans, albatross, and seagulls. The one-day excursion, including stops at various beaches and islets, costs $60–$70 for up to six people. To arrange a trip, ask around for Javier "Chacate" Nadal (Calle 11, 2 blocks east of park, tel. 991/82–20–50 ext. 164). Dzilám's sole decent hotel is **Hotel y Restaurant Los Flamencos** (Calle 11 No. 120, between Calles 22 and 24, no phone), which offers clean, basic rooms, some with great sea views. Rooms cost only $7.50, but unfortunately the bathrooms are tiny and lack hot water. The other option is to stay at **Cabañas Totolandia,** on the beach 2 km (1 mi) west of town. A cabaña with private bath costs $8.30 (up to four people). Both places accept cash only. **Restaurante El Pescador** (Calle 11, across from the park, no phone) serves seafood specials like fried fish with salad and tostadas ($2.25) and breaded shrimp ($4.50).

COMING AND GOING • From Mérida, take one of the nine daily buses (2 hrs, $1.40) from the Auto-buses del Noroeste station (Calle 50, between Calles 65 and 67). To return to Mérida, catch the bus out-side the store at the southern end of the park—the last bus leaves around 5 PM). Two buses also depart from Progreso (2 hrs, $1.25) at 7 AM and 2 PM, traveling along the coastal road to Dzilám. From the park, you can catch a COSTERA bus back to Progreso and Telchac at 9 AM and 4 PM.

IZAMAL

Tourism boosters often point to Izamal, 70 km (43 mi) east of Mérida, as the quintessential colonial city of the Yucatán. The well-kept buildings around the main plaza do indeed recall the peninsula's colonial past, but actually most weren't constructed until the 19th century. There isn't any reason real to spend time in Izamal, but a stop does break up the long bus trip between Mérida and Valladolid or Cancún. While you're here, visit the **Convento de San Antonio de Padua,** a magnificent example of colonial architecture. Built in 1533 by Franciscan monks, the monastery is the largest of its kind in the Yucatán. The bright-yellow complex is built on top of ancient Maya ruins and contains a church, a chapel, a sac-risty, and a grassy atrium surrounded by arched galleries. *Admission free. Open daily 6 AM–8 PM. Mass held daily at 6:30 AM and 7:30 PM.*

Two blocks north of the main plaza are what remains of the **Pyramid of Kinich Kakmo,** whose summit is the highest point for miles around. The large pyramid and four other scarcely discernible structures are all that remain of the ancient Maya city of Itzamal, founded in AD 500 and named after the Maya sun god Itzamná. The site has deteriorated but remains interesting both for its proximity to the colonial city and the fact that it is of pure Maya design, free of Toltec or Aztec influence. *From main plaza, follow Calle 28 north past the park to where it runs into Calle 27. Admission free. Open daily 8–5.*

COMING AND GOING

Buses for Izamal (15 per day, 2 hrs, $1.70) leave Mérida from the station on Calle 50 (between Calles 65 and 67). You can also catch a bus here from Valladolid (2 per day, 2 hrs, $2.50). The best way to see Izamal is en route from one city to another, since you can see everything in an hour or two and be on the next bus out of town. To do so, take an early bus to Izamal and ask permission to store your luggage at the station (or ask any local policeman if he will store your luggage at the police station). To reach Chichén Itzá from Izamal, take a bus from in front of Restaurant Wayné Né (Calle 33, at Calle 30) to Kan-tunil (45 min, $1.25). Buses for Kantunil leave about every two hours, with the last bus leaving at 5 PM. Wait in Kantunil for the next bus to Valladolid, and tell the driver to let you off in Chichén Itzá (45 min, $1). Restaurants and loncherías are plentiful around the zócalo, and there's a daily market in front of the monastery complex.

CHICHEN ITZA

Chichén Itzá is probably the most complex and interesting archaeological site on the peninsula, and the second most crowded after Tulum. Located only 120 km (74 mi) east of Mérida and 157 km (97 mi) southwest of Cancún, Chichén can be explored on a day trip from either town. A better idea, though, is to stay in the nearby village of Pisté, or even in Valladolid, and save yourself the two- or three-hour morn-ing bus ride to the ruins. Another advantage of staying nearby is that you can avoid the crowds. Around midday the tour buses arrive in force, and the mass of humanity completely changes the feel of the place. Better to arrive early in the morning, when relatively few people are around and the sun's heat isn't as intense.

Chichén Itzá is Maya for "mouth of the wells of Itzá," a reference to the area's cenotes, around which the Maya first settled. Humans built this site into a major metropolis around AD 520, centuries before Maya tribes emigrated from northern Guatemala. The new occupants modified many of the existing buildings, creating an eclectic architecture. For this reason, visiting Chichén is like being at several sites at one time, and trying to make sense of everything can be exhausting. Those who have been to Uxmal (and other Puuc and Chenes ruins) will notice similarities between the buildings there and the ones clustered around the observatory here—both include choza motifs, Chaac masks, and elaborate lat-ticework on the upper facades. Additional features at Chichén Itzá, such as columns and carvings of serpents, jaguars, and eagles, are typical of a later Toltec-Maya style. The buildings surrounding **El**

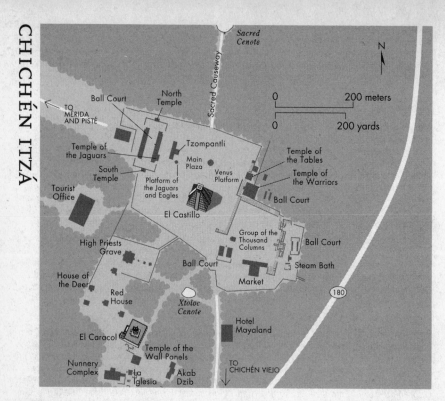

Castillo, as well as the great pyramid of Kukulcán itself, were constructed from scratch by the Toltec-Maya and reflect the growing influence of war and the military. Look here for exquisite stone carvings glorifying human sacrifice, and for images of the messenger god Chac Mool, whose semirecumbent figure waits everywhere, ready to receive offerings from the high priests.

COMING AND GOING

First- and second-class buses leave Mérida (2½ hrs, $3.25), Cancún (3 hrs, $6), and Valladolid (40 min, $1.25) on the hour for Chichén Itzá; there are also three daily buses from Playa del Carmen (5½ hrs, $7.50). Hourly second-class service returning to Valladolid and Cancún ends at 8 PM, to Mérida at 9 PM. Most buses stop at the ruins, the bus station (about 770 yards from the zócalo) in the nearby village of Pisté, and in downtown Pisté. If you have luggage in the bus's storage compartment, you'll have to get off at the bus station. Most restaurants, hotels, and handicraft stores line **Calle 15,** the road leading from Pisté's zócalo to the ruins. You can walk between the two easily (it's only 2½ km/1½ mi), or take a taxi for about $1.

WHERE TO SLEEP

Accommodations near Chichén Itzá are geared toward wealthy tourists; budget travelers will do much better in the small village of Pisté, a few kilometers to the west. Pisté is a characterless town, but it's cheap. During the fall and spring equinoxes (Sept. 20, 21 and Mar. 20, 21), be prepared to settle for any amount of square footage you can get; even the fleabag hotels are packed, and sleeping next to a stranger on the floor of a private kitchen is not a rarity. The cheapest option in town is at the **Posada No-velo** annex of the Stardust Hotel (Calle 15, next to the bus station, tel. 985/1–01–22). The annex has nine clean double rooms ($12.50), all with private bath and plenty of hot water. You also have access to a swimming pool. The posada accepts cash only.

UNDER $20 • Posada Olalde. Located down a side street from Pisté's main strip, this family-owned hotel offers quiet, cozy rooms with wood furniture and a little bit of charm. The bathrooms are immaculate and have hot water. Doubles cost $19. *Calle 6 No. 49, no phone. From bus station, walk toward town, left at El Carrousel restaurant, continue down dirt road 500 ft. 6 rooms, all with bath. Kitchen, laundry sink, luggage storage. Cash only.*

UNDER $25 • Hotel Dolores Alba. This family-run hotel is a longtime favorite of foreign travelers. Rooms are clean and simple and have access to a small swimming pool surrounded by hammocks. There's free transportation to the ruins, and breakfast and dinner are served family-style in the dining room for under $7. Doubles are $22.50, plus an additional $2.50 for air-conditioning. *Carretera Pisté–Cancún, 1½ mi south of Chichén, tel. 99/28–56–50 for reservations. Ask any bus driver along this route to stop at Dolores Alba. Dining room, pool, luggage storage.*

FOOD

Eating in Pisté is affordable as long as you avoid overtly tourist-oriented restaurants. For drinks, snacks, and fresh bread, head to the small convenience stores along Calle 15, just east of Pisté's zócalo. The **market,** open each morning, is just east of downtown Pisté. In front of the plaza are three loncherías, where you can get tortas, salbutes, or panuchos for less than 75¢ each.

UNDER $3 • Restaurant Sayil. This tiny restaurant is almost like being invited into someone's cozy kitchen. Flowered tablecloths cover three long tables watched over by a small ceramic Virgin Mary. The menu is limited, but they'll usually make a vegetarian dish to order. Main dishes such as poc chuc, pollo pibil, and beef filete cost $2; for the same price you get a giant plate of rice, beans, and tortillas. *Calle 15 No. 57, west of bus station, no phone. Cash only.*

UNDER $5 • Restaurant El Parador Maya. This small, family-owned restaurant cooks up delicious daily specials, though neighbors often just drop by for a few *cervezas* (beers). It's a good place for breakfast, with a delicious vegetable-filled huevos rancheros. At other times of day you can fill up on regional dishes like poc chuc, pollo pibil, and salbutes. El Parador is open only when there are customers; if the door is closed and you're here between the hours of 7 AM and 11 PM, just knock. *Calle 15, 2 blocks east of zócalo, no phone. Cash only.*

Restaurant Los Pájaros. This restaurant has a festive thatch roof that's popular with tiny emerald-green geckos—they like to hide inside it during rainstorms. The menu ranges from sandwiches ($1.25) and vegetable soup to delicious poc chuc. Beers are $1. *Calle 15, 2 doors west and across street from El Carrousel, no phone. Cash only.*

WORTH SEEING

Give yourself a day to explore Chichén Itzá, or two days if you prefer to move at a leisurely pace. The ruins can be divided into three groups according to location: **North Group** (El Castillo and surrounding ruins), **South Group,** and **Chichén Viejo.** If you want to visit the less-frequented ruins that lie deep in Chichén Viejo, you'll need to make special arrangements with a tour guide. The park caretakers will also occasionally take visitors out to Chichén Viejo for a small fee; caretakers are identifiable by shirts or caps bearing the letters INAH. For the main set of ruins, **guided tours** (2 hrs, $26 for up to six people) are available in Spanish, French, German, or English. Make sure your guide is certified; Eddy Garrido and Victor Olalde are two reliable guides who speak Spanish, English, and French. A **sound and light show** takes place nightly at El Castillo. It's an entertaining overview of the ancient city's history and the fall of the Maya empire. The show in Spanish at 7 PM costs $3.50; the English version at 9 PM costs $4.75. Chichén has bathrooms, as well as an expensive refreshment stand serving cold drinks and snacks. This is a large site, so bring plenty of drinking water. *Admission: $4, free Sun. Parking: $3.50. Open daily 8–5.*

NORTH GROUP

The first building you see when you enter Chichén is the awe-inspiring **El Castillo.** Ninety-one steps up is a temple to Kukulcán, the feathered serpent deity. By the base of one balustrade is the carved head of a giant serpent; at the spring and fall equinoxes, the afternoon light hitting the balustrade forms a shadow that resembles the slithering form of Kukulcán descending the pyramid toward the Sacred Cenote. This kind of symbolism abounds in El Castillo: for example, the four stairways face the cardinal directions and the number of steps totals 365, the number of days in the year. Fifty-two panels on the sides stand for the 52 years in the sacred Maya calendar and the 18 terraces symbolize the 18 months in the Maya year.

The **Temple of the Jaguars** stands northwest of El Castillo. The columns that support the temple's lower enclosure are thought to depict the Maya cosmogony, or creation of the world and all of its beings: Plants, fish, fowl, serpents, and men spring from the head of a god. Inside the enclosure, a detailed mural of a village scene depicts soldiers and townspeople.

The **Ball Court,** just west of the Temple of the Jaguars, is similar to others found at ancient centers in Mexico—but this one is bigger and more elaborate. The long, rectangular stadium features two stone circles embedded high in the walls, into which players tried to shoot a large, rubbery ball using only their hips, elbows, and knees. On either side of the ball court are two small temples decorated with images of warriors and of the god Kukulcán. From the north temple you can clearly hear the voice of anyone in the south temple—the sound travels amazingly well along the walls of the court.

Tzompantli means "place of the skulls" in Toltec, and this T-shape platform is indeed decorated with the carved images of hundreds of human skulls. Tribes from the west used to display the fleshless skulls of defeated captains stacked one on top of the other on stakes, and some think that the Maya-Toltecs used this platform for similar purposes.

Immediately southeast of the Tzompantli is **The Platform of Jaguars and Eagles,** a small rectangular structure with a staircase on each side. Supposedly both the eagles and jaguars carved here represent the kings of certain city-states. Scroll-like designs coming out of their mouths suggest that they may be discussing the plight of the sacrificial victims whose hearts they clutch.

Many sacrifices took place at the **Sacred Cenote,** a well about 1 km (½ mi) from the main ceremonial area. The cenote was considered to be the dwelling place of Chaac, the rain god. It was once believed that young virgins were hurled into these waters when the city was in dire need of rainfall, but scuba-diving archaeologists have since discovered skeletons belonging to individuals of all ages. The slippery walls were impossible to climb, and most sacrificial victims could not swim well enough to survive until noon, when the survivors were supposedly fished out to relate the stories of what they had learned from the spirits in the water. Thousands of gold and jade artifacts, highly precious to the Maya, have also been dredged from the murky depths of the cenote. First explored by Edward Thompson in 1903, the Sacred Cenote was excavated twice during the ensuing six decades, both times resulting in the salvaging of precious jewelry and artifacts. During the second set of dives, a special chemical was used to make the water clearer, enabling divers to recover more than twice what had been previously found. In the process the chemical also killed off most of the cenote's marine life.

Carved soldiers adorn the rectangular columns fronting the **Temple of the Warriors.** The upper facade of the temple features gruesome masks of Chaac, as well as a sculpted eagle with a fierce serpent head projecting outward from the stone surface. A closer look reveals the head of a human being emerging from the serpent's mouth. Just southwest of the temple, you'll notice the **Group of a Thousand Columns,** a large plaza surrounded by intricately carved columns that probably once supported arches and a roof. Nobody knows the plaza's original purpose.

There is no evidence to suggest that the **Market,** just south of the Group of a Thousand Columns, was actually used for selling, but some have speculated that the columns supported a palapa-style roof under which vendors sold their merchandise. In Chichén's **steam bath,** right next to the market, you can still see the stone benches on which bathers gathered. A tiny doorway leads to a room containing two benches and a hearth where stones were heated, then sprinkled with water to produce steam. Steam baths were popular for ritual purification all over pre-Columbian Mesoamerica.

SOUTH GROUP

Following the road southwest of El Castillo you'll reach the **High Priest's Grave,** with its succession of underground chambers. As is typical with Maya sites, most of which are randomly named, no priest was found buried here. Most likely, Edward Thompson (the first explorer of the area) said this was a "High Priest's Grave" so he could get funding to continue his excavations. Farther along the road past the High Priest's Grave is the small **House of the Deer,** a Puuc-Chenes style building from the late Classic period. The house owes its name to the mural of a deer that once decorated a wall. Next door is a similar building known as the **Red House,** named after the remnants of red paint found inside. The building is pure Puuc-Chenes style, and hieroglyphs on its frieze date to AD 870.

El Caracol, also called The Observatory, is the second most famous building in Chichén Itzá, after El Castillo. During the life span of this city it was enlarged and renovated several times, making it a strange amalgamation of shapes and styles. Astronomers probably used this building to observe the motion of the sun and stars in order to plan festivals, ceremonies, planting cycles, and other important events. A spiral staircase (hence the name *caracol,* which is Spanish for "snail" or a "conch") leads to a small observation chamber. The chamber's slitted windows are oriented toward key astronomical points. Southeast of the Caracol is **Akab-Dzib,** a 9th-century building. Akab-Dzib means "obscure writing" in Maya, and if you look at the lintel of the southern doorway you'll notice a carving of a priest sitting on a throne surrounded by hieroglyphics.

La Iglesia stands behind the less interesting **Temple of the Wall Panels,** just southeast of El Caracol. It is a beautiful example of Puuc architecture, adorned with masks of Chaac and other geometrical motifs. In between the masks are animal gods—a bee, snail, turtle, and armadillo—which represent the four Bacabes, the beings that hold up the heavens. Next door to La Iglesia is the **Nunnery Complex,** a strange cluster of buildings named by Spaniards who thought it resembled a European convent (in actuality, it was probably a palace). Chenes designs adorn the east building, whose doorway is the gaping mouth of Chaac. The form of the central building, with its classic corbeled arches, seems to have suffered a bit from several additions.

CHICHEN VIEJO

Two kilometers (1 mi) down a path from the Nunnery Complex is group of poorly preserved ruins known as the **date group.** Here, two Atlantes (godlike figures who supposedly balance the weight of the world above their large heads) stand atop a black block carved with Maya dates and hieroglyphs dating back to AD 879. If you're tired of dodging video cameras and potbellied tourists in order to get a glimpse of the ruins, try heading down the path to a barely excavated group of ruins about a kilometer (½ mi) from Chichén's more popular sites. Among the rubble lies what is thought to be a ceremonial center. The **House of the Phalli** displaying early Maya triangular arches and the only examples of Toltec-influenced columns, was supposedly the place where virgins came to "know" a man's body. Indeed, numerous phallic reliefs jut out from the temple's walls. About 20 minutes farther into the jungle is another group of ruins, most badly decayed, with the exception of the **Temple of the Three Lintels,** a beautiful Puuc-Chenes building similar to structures at Uxmal. The three-room building was supposedly used by healers, who brought the ailing here to be cured. Unless you're a real bushwhacker, it is *not* recommended that you go any further than the date group on your own. Instead, strike up a deal with an official guide. Groups of four or five may end up paying $10–$15 each for the excursion. Try to go in the morning, as the afternoon often brings rain, animals, and *lots* of mosquitos.

NEAR CHICHEN ITZA

BALANKANCHE CAVES

A mere 6 km (4 mi) from Chichén Itzá are the immense Balankanché caves, thought to have been used as a Maya ceremonial center in the 10th and 11th centuries. In 1959 a local tour guide stumbled upon the stalactite-filled caves and discovered a number of ceramic and carved artifacts inside. The images engraved on some of the artifacts are thought to represent Tlaloc, the Toltec god of rain. Although the cave's length and size are impressive, and the bulbous, petrified stalactites are fascinating to observe at eye level, a visit to the caves is only recommended if you're not heading on to the more impressive caves of Loltún (*see* Oxkutzcab and the Loltún Caves, *above*). The Balankanché caves are open daily 9–4; tours accompanied by audio cassettes, which tell an indiscernible story in Spanish, English, and French, supposedly leave every hour but are canceled unless at least two participants show up. Don't worry if you can't understand the tape—the small museum at the entrance to the caves is much more informative. To reach Balankanché, take any second-class bus between Chichén Itzá and Valladolid, and ask the driver to drop you "*en las grutas.*" From the road it's a few hundred yards to the caves. On the way back, flag down a bus on the road. Admission, including the mandatory audio tour, is $6, free on Sunday. A separate $2.50 admission is required for the sound-and-light show held in the caves daily at 11 AM and 3 PM (English), 9 AM and noon (Spanish), and 10 AM (French).

VALLADOLID

Much slower-paced than Mérida or Cancún, Valladolid (which lies inland, precisely halfway between the two) is also less frequented by crowds of picture-snapping tourists. Scratch its calm exterior, however, to find a history of conflict that dates back to Valladolid's origins as the Maya ceremonial site of Zací. In 1543, the indomitable Maya drove off Spanish conquistador Francisco de Montejo, but Montejo's aptly named son, Montejo the Younger, succeeded where his father failed. He laid out Valladolid in the classic Spanish colonial style and built six grand churches. The Maya, who had been banned from the city, constantly raided Valladolid, sending many a Mexican fleeing back to Mérida.

Valladolid's colonial past is blended more or less successfully with its ultra-commercial present; at the heart of town is a daily **market** (Calles 37 and 34) where people come from miles around to sell their produce and wares. Aside from that—and a few cooling cenotes within walking distance of town—there isn't much to see in Valladolid, but the town is a convenient base from which to explore Chichén Itzá. A stop here can also be a welcome break from the six-hour bus ride between Mérida and Cancún. Each year beginning January 22 and ending February 3, Valladolid celebrates **La Fiesta de la Candelaria** in honor of the Virgin of the Candelaria, the city's patron saint. This religious and cultural celebration features parades, masses, *corridas* (bullfights), food, and *artesanía* (handicrafts).

BASICS

CASAS DE CAMBIO
Bancomer (Calle 40, facing the zócalo, tel. 985/6–21–50; open weekdays 9–2) exchanges currency and has an ATM that accepts Visa.

EMERGENCIES
For 24-hour emergency assistance, contact the **police** (Calle 41 No. 156-A, between Calles 20 and 22, tel. 985/6–21–00). For **ambulance** service call 985/6–24–13).

MEDICAL AID
Clínica Santa Anita (Calle 40 No. 221, at Calle 47, tel. 985/6–28–11) is open 24 hours for medical assistance. The **Farmacia El Descuento** (corner of Calles 39 and 42, across from zócalo, no phone) is a 24-hour pharmacy.

PHONES AND MAIL
The **post office** (Calle 40, facing the zócalo, tel. 985/6–26–23; open weekdays 8–3) will hold mail sent to you at the following address for up to 10 days: Lista de Correos, Valladolid, Yucatán, CP 97780, México. Card- and coin-operated **phones** are just outside the bus terminal and near the zócalo. To place a call in air-conditioned privacy, try the **Computel** office (Calle 42, at Calle 41, tel. and fax 985/6–39–77; open daily 7 AM–10 PM) next door to Hotel San Clemente.

VISITOR INFORMATION
A *módulo de turismo* (tourist information booth; open Mon.–Sat. 9–2 and 5–7) is just inside the doors of the *ayuntamiento* (city hall; SE corner of zócalo). The English spoken here is shaky, but you can get free maps and copies of the free magazine *Yucatán Today.* For thorough information on local fiestas, tours, and historical sites, call Emma Montes at **Hotel Mesón del Marqués** (tel. 985/6–20–73).

COMING AND GOING

Valladolid is an easy city to become familiar with, and everything is within walking distance. Like many other Yucatecan cities, the streets here are numbered, with even-numbered calles running north–south, and odd-numbered calles running east–west. The **zócalo** is bordered by Calles 39, 40, 41, and 42.

Valladolid is a major crossroads for buses headed almost anywhere on the peninsula. The small, clean 24-hour **bus terminal** (Calle 37, at Calle 54, tel. 985/6–34–49) is six long blocks from downtown. The two major bus lines here are **Autobuses del Norte** and **Autobuses del Centro del Estado de Yucatán,** which offer second-class service to Cancún (3 hrs, $3) hourly 7 AM–8 PM and to Mérida (3 hrs, $3.25) hourly 6 AM–8 PM. There is also service to Cobá (3½ hrs, $4.20), Tulum (2½ hrs, $4), Playa del Carmen (5 hrs, $4.75), and Tizimín (hourly; 1 hr, $1). Two buses leave for Izamal (1½ hrs, $2), though all of the Mérida-bound buses stop there, too.

WHERE TO SLEEP

The few budget hotels in Valladolid are conveniently located between the bus station and the zócalo. Nearest to the bus station, **Hotel Maya** (Calle 41 No. 231, between Calles 48 and 50, tel. 985/6–20–69) is clean and quiet and has an inner patio blossoming with exotic flowers and palms. Doubles with private bath and hot water go for $6, with air-conditioning $10. The deluxe **Hotel Zací** (Calle 44 No. 191, between Calles 37 and 39, tel. 985/6–21–67) has a clean pool that is big enough to swim laps in. Rooms have cable TVs and bathrooms with plenty of hot water, at $13.25 a double, plus $2 for air-conditioning. Both hotels accept cash only.

FOOD

Valladolid's restaurants don't offer a wide variety, but you can still sample Yucatecan food at reasonable prices. The local hangout is **El Bazar** (Calle 39, at Calle 40, NE corner of zócalo), a small plaza shared by many *comedores* (sit-down food stands). Great *comidas corridas* (preprepared lunch specials) with soup, a meat dish, tortillas, and a drink will run you about $3.25. Tacos and panuchos are readily available for about 40¢ each. At **Restaurant del Parque** (Calle 42, at Calle 41, tel. 985/6–23–65) try the specialty, *pollo a la yucateca* (chicken baked in a tasty red sauce and served with potatoes, rice, and beans). At **El Jacal de los Dzeles** (Calle 40 No. 211, between Calles 41 and 43, no phone; no breakfast) groups of tired-looking men sit around drinking beer and eating large plates of beef filetes ($2.50). A heaping pile of beans, rice, and tortillas goes for $1.50. **Paletería La Flor de Michoacán** (Calle 41, between Calles 42 and 44, no phone) serves something you've probably never tried before: corn ice cream, costing 65¢ a cone. All of the above are cash only.

The Maya have few female deities. Ix Chel is the goddess of fertility and childbirth, and midwives are her human representatives. Ix Tap, the goddess of suicide, is often depicted with a noose wrapped around her neck.

WORTH SEEING

CHURCHES

Valladolid's churches are more impressive from the exterior, since the interiors were looted during the Caste War (*see box, above*). Nonetheless, for anyone interested in colonial architecture or exploring old buildings, the complex containing **Iglesia de San Bernardino de Siena** and the **Convento de Sisal** (Calle 41-A, at Calle 49) are definitely worth a visit. The buildings are flanked on one side by an overgrown garden containing a grill-covered cenote. To enter the garden, you must ask permission from the resident priest or his secretary. Their office is across the driveway from the garden. *From zócalo, walk west on Calle 41 to intersection of Calles 41 and 46; from here, take diagonal road (Calle 41-A) SW 4 blocks. Admission free. Complex open Tues.–Sun. 8–noon and 5–8.*

CENOTES

Within walking distance of town, the **Cenote Zací** (Calle 36, between Calles 37 and 39; open for swimming daily 8–6) is well worth a visit on a hot afternoon. Though it glows an eerie green, the water is cool and fresh. Admission ($2) includes access to the cenote and entrance to a museum (complete with historical photographs of Valladolid), plus a peek at a few unhappily caged animals in a makeshift zoo. A visit to the beautiful **Cenote Dzitnup,** though not as convenient as Cenote Zací, will help you to realize why the Maya regarded these pools as sacred. If you haven't been paralyzed by awe, have a swim with the small catfish that live in its brilliant blue water. Don't let the rain dissuade you from coming here—the cenote is underground. Admission is $3, and it's open daily 7–5 (there are also changing rooms and a shower). To reach Cenote Dzitnup from Valladolid, take a combi from Hotel María Guadalupe (Calle 44, between Calles 39 and 41), which will let you off right at the cenote. You shouldn't pay more than 80¢ per person for the ride. Ask the driver when he is taking passengers back to Valladolid. You can also take a westbound bus on the highway; ask to be let off at the crossroads for the cenote, and walk 2 km (1 mi) along the pleasant country road. Yet another option is to rent a bicycle ($1 per hr) from Antonio "Negro" Águilar, whose shop (Calle 44, between Calles 39 and 41) is open 6 AM–7 PM daily. The cenote is only about 6 km (3¾ mi) from Valladolid.

NEAR VALLADOLID

RIO LAGARTOS

The creatures that gave "Alligator River" its name have long since disappeared—flamingos steal the show here now. The people of this small fishing village, 103 km (64 mi) north of Valladolid, are especially friendly and appreciate the peace and tranquility of their home. You won't find much in the way of nightlife here, but Río Lagartos outdoes itself during the annual **Festival of Apostle Santiago** (July 20–26), with folk dances, bullfights, and processions. On the first of June, all the boats get decked out and parade in the lagoon in celebration of **Día de Marina.**

Río Lagartos is a bird-watcher's heaven. Pelicans stand by the side of the road like old men, looking as if they'd strike up a conversation at any moment. You're also likely to see snowy egrets, red egrets, snowy white ibis, and great white herons, among other winged creatures. Flamingos supposedly inhabit the area throughout the year, but May through August is the time to watch them in large flocks. March and April, they're busy laying eggs, and the nesting sites are a three- to four-hour boat ride away. Arrangements for a boat trip to the flamingos' favorite hangout can be made with any of the motorboat owners along the malecón (usually about $32–$38 for up to six people). Note that laws prohibit approaching the flamingos' nesting areas too closely, for fear the birds will suddenly take flight and disturb the eggs. If you're traveling alone or in a pair, talk to Diego at **Restaurant Isla Contoy** (see below), who might be able to hook you up with some other visitors to cut the cost of a boat trip. You can also take a shortened ride to see the flamingos (which doesn't include the mangroves, salt flats, or their nesting sites) with an added stop at the beach for a flat rate of $15. If you're only interested in swimming, paddle around in the gulf off the Río Lagartos Peninsula, or get a boat to take you across to the beach for about $5. **Chiquilá,** a natural ojo de agua dulce is 1 km (½ mi) east of town; walk along the eastern shore from the malecón.

COMING AND GOING

The 2½-hour excursion from Valladolid could be staged as a day trip if you live by a rigid itinerary. Otherwise, plan to spend at least one night. Buses leave Valladolid hourly for Tizimín (1 hr, $1) until 5 PM; combis to Tizimín ($1.25) leave Valladolid from in front of the liquor store (Calle 40, at Calle 37). From Tizimín, you'll have to transfer to a second-class bus to Río Lagartos (8 per day, 1 hr, $1), which leaves roughly every two hours between 5:15 AM and 7 PM. The last bus back to Tizimín from Río Lagartos leaves at 5:30 PM.

WHERE TO SLEEP AND EAT

The only formal lodging in town, **Cabañas Los Dos Hermanos** (Calle 19, about 50 yds from bus station, tel. 986/3–26–68 ext. 183) rents four cabins, all with cold-water private bath, a large bed, and hammock hooks. The two less expensive cabins cost $8.75. The other two cabins, complete with mosquito netting and cable TV, cost $10. The inn accepts cash only. If all the cabins are full, you can rent a room in someone's home, hang a hammock at Restaurant Isla Contoy, or camp for free on the vast and unpeopled beaches along the gulf. To camp, bring all the supplies you'll need, including antimosquito paraphernalia. Bargain with a fisherman to take you across the lagoon to the gulf—the trip should cost around $5.

Food at Río Lagartos is amazingly fresh and cheap, especially the seafood. **Restaurant Los Negritos** (2 blocks from bus station, no phone) serves fried manta ray in tomato sauce for $5 as well as a tasty fish soup. They also serve $2 egg breakfasts. At 10 PM on Saturday Los Negritos becomes a disco. **Restaurant Isla Contoy** (Calle 19, tel. 986/3–26–68, ext. 100) is owned by a friendly family that enjoys helping foreign travelers. Hearty seafood dishes cost around $5. Visit **La Cueva de Macumba** (Calle 16, at Calle 11, just west of gazebo on malecón, no phone) for enchiladas de mole and excellent flautas ($2.50) in a festive palapa filled with the owner's artistic shell creations. If the gate is closed, just knock anytime between 6 AM and 2 AM.

SPANISH GLOSSARY

In Spanish, what you see is what you get: Every letter is pronounced and the accent usually falls on the second-to-last syllable, unless there is an accent mark. Of course, there are exceptions to both rules. And, to confound matters, you'd be hard pressed to find a Mexican who actually pronounces everything clearly. Still, if you learn a few rules, you should be able to pronounce almost any Spanish word; figuring out what it means may take a little more effort. The following letters are pronounced as follows:

a like the **a** in ah
i like the **ee** in beet
u like the **oo** in loot
ñ like the **ni** in senior

e like the **e** in deck
o like the **o** in cold
y like the **ea** in eat
ll like the **y** in kayak

The h is silent in Spanish, and the Spanish j is pronounced like the h in horse. G before a, o, u, or a consonant is hard (like in gate); when before e or i, it's soft, sounding just slightly harder than the h in hay. However, when g is paired with u (gu), the u sounds like the English w. For all practical purposes, b and v sound the same—roughly like a b in English. C before a, o, and u is hard like the English k; before e and i it's soft like the English s.

English	Spanish
BASICS	
Yes/no	Sí/no
Hello/goodbye	Hola/adiós
Good morning	Buenos días
Good afternoon	Buenas tardes
Good night	Buenas noches
How are you?	¿Cómo está?
I'm fine, thanks	Estoy bien, gracias
Pardon me	Perdóneme
Excuse me	Con permiso
What's your name?	¿Cómo se llama?
My name is. . .	Me llamo. . .
I'm from the United States	Soy estadounidense
I'm Australian	Soy australiano(a)
I'm Canadian	Soy canadiense
I'm English	Soy inglés(a)
I'm Scottish	Soy escocés(a)
Kiss me, I'm Irish	Bésame, soy irlandés
Do you speak English?	¿Habla inglés?
I don't speak Spanish	No hablo español
I don't understand	No entiendo

How do you say. . .	¿Cómo se dice. . . ?
More slowly, please	Más despacio, por favor
Could you please repeat that?	¿Podría repetir, por favor?
I don't know	No sé
Please	Por favor
Thank you	Gracias
You're welcome	De nada
Where is (are). . . ?	¿Dónde está(n). . . ?
Are there. . . ?	¿Hay. . . ?
Bathroom	Baño, sanitario
Backpack	Mochila
Post office	Oficina de correos
Long-distance telephone office	Caseta de larga distancia
Collect call	Llamada al cobrar
Laundromat	Lavandería
Bank/money exchange place	Banco/casa de cambio
Open	Abierto(a)
Closed	Cerrado(a)
Yesterday	Ayer
Today	Hoy
Tomorrow	Mañana
This morning	Esta mañana
This evening	Esta tarde
Tonight	Esta noche
What time is it?	¿Qué hora es?
Entrance	Entrada
Exit	Salida
Floor/story	Piso
Neighborhood	Colonia/barrio
How much is this/it?	¿Cuánto es?
Cheap	Barato
Expensive	Caro

EMERGENCIES AND MEDICAL AID

Help!	¡Socorro!
Leave me alone!	¡Déjame en paz!
Call the police	Llame la policía
Call a doctor	Llame un médico
Hospital	Hospital
I'm sick	Estoy enfermo(a)
I need a doctor	Necesito un médico
I have a headache	Me duele la cabeza
I have a stomachache	Me duele el estómago
Fever	Fiebre
Prescription	Receta
Medicine	Remedio
Aspirin	Aspirina
Condom	Preservativo
AIDS	SIDA

COMING AND GOING

Right	Derecha
Left	Izquierda
Straight	Derecho/recto
On foot	A pie
Hitchhike	Hacer dedo

Ride	Aventón
Ticket window	Taquilla
A ticket for. . .	Un boleto para. . .
One-way	Ida
Round-trip	Ida y vuelta
First/second class	Primera/segunda clase
Where are you going?	¿A dónde va?
How many kilometers?	¿Cuántos kilometros?
How long is the trip?	¿Cuánto tiempo dura el viaje?
I'm going to. . .	Me voy a. . .
I want to get off at. . .	Quiero bajar en. . .
Map	Mapa
Arrival	Llegada
Departure	Salida
Airport	Aeropuerto
Train station	Estación de ferrocarril
Bus	Autobús/camión
Bus station	Terminal de autobuses
Bus stop	Parada
Car	Carro
I'd like to rent a car	Me gustaría alquilar un carro
Insurance	Seguros
Gas	Gasolina
Tire	Llanta
Stoplight	Semáforo
Motorcycle	Motocicleta
Highway	Carretera
The road to. . .	El camino a. . .
Bridge	Puente
Metro stop	Estación de Metro
Fare	Tarifa
To cross	Cruzar
Bicycle	Bicicleta

WHERE TO SLEEP

Guest house	Casa de huéspedes
Key	Llave
Manager	Gerente
Room	Habitación/cuarto
For two people	Para dos personas
With/without	Con/sin
Shower	Ducha
Hot/cold water	Agua caliente/fría
Fan	Ventilador
Air-conditioning	Aire acondicionado
Double bed	Cama matrimonial
Sheets	Sábanas
Toilet paper	Papel de baño/papel higénico
Included	Incluido
Camping	Campground
Hammock	Hamaca
I would like to make a reservation	Me gustaría hacer una reservación
Is there a private bathroom?	¿Hay un baño privado?
Can I leave my bags here?	¿Puedo dejar mi equipaje aquí?

FOOD

Food	Comida
Bakery	Panadería
Supermarket	Supermercado
Groceries	Abarrotes
I'm hungry/thirsty	Tengo hambre/sed
I'm a vegetarian	Soy vegetariano(a)
I'm diabetic	Soy diabético(a)
Waiter/waitress	Mesero(a)
Breakfast	Desayuno
Lunch	Almuerzo
Dinner	Cena
Daily special	Menú del día
Preprepared lunch special	Comida corrida
Bill/check	Cuenta
(Wheat) bread	Pan (integral)
Toast	Pan tostado
(Purified) water	Agua (purificada)
Ice	Hielo
Cocktail	Trago
Tea/coffee	Té/café
Soda	Refresco
Milk	Leche
Juice	Jugo
Vegetables	Verduras
Fruit	Fruta
Apple	Manzana
Orange	Naranja
Pineapple	Piña
Lemon/Lime	Limón/Lima
Coconut	Coco
Strawberry	Fresa
Potato	Papa
French fries	Papas fritas
Rice	Arroz
Egg	Huevo
Salt/Pepper	Sal/Pimienta
Sugar	Azúcar
Meat	Carne
Steak	Bistec
Chicken	Pollo
Pork	Puerco
Fish	Pescado
Shellfish	Mariscos
Fork	Tenedor
Spoon	Cuchara
Knife	Cuchillo
Napkin	Servilleta
Ice cream	Helado

NUMBERS

One	Uno/una
Two	Dos
Three	Tres
Four	Cuatro
Five	Cinco

Six	Seis
Seven	Siete
Eight	Ocho
Nine	Nueve
Ten	Diez
Eleven	Once
Twelve	Doce
Thirteen	Trece
Fourteen	Catorce
Fifteen	Quince
Sixteen	Dieciséis/diez y seis
Seventeen	Diecisiete/diez y siete
Eighteen	Dieciocho
Nineteen	Diecinueve/diez y nueve
Twenty	Veinte
Thirty	Treinta
Forty	Cuarenta
Fifty	Cincuenta
Sixty	Sesenta
Seventy	Setenta
Eighty	Ochenta
Ninety	Noventa
One hundred	Cien
One thousand	Mil

DAYS AND MONTHS

day	día
month	mes
Sunday	Domingo
Monday	Lunes
Tuesday	Martes
Wednesday	Miércoles
Thursday	Jueves
Friday	Viernes
Saturday	Sábado
January	Enero
February	Febrero
March	Marzo
April	Abril
May	Mayo
June	Junio
July	Julio
August	Agosto
September	Septiembre
October	Octubre
November	Noviembre
December	Diciembre

INDEX

WHEREVER YOU TRAVEL, HELP IS NEVER FAR AWAY.

From planning your trip to providing travel assistance along the way, American Express® Travel Service Offices are always there to help you do more.

Mexico

Acapulco
American Express Travel Service
Centro Comercial—La Gran Plaza
Costera Miguel Aleman 1628
74/69-11-33

Cancun
American Express Travel Service
Av. Tulum 208 Esq. Agua
Supermanzana 4
98/84-19-00

Cozumel
Fiesta Cozumel S.A. De C.V. (R)
Calle II
Av. Pedro Joaquin Coldwell #385
98/72-13-89

Mexico City
American Express Travel Service
Hotel Camino Real
Mariano Escobedo 700
5/203-2355

Touracabos (R)
Hotel Pueblo Bonito Local I
Av. Playa Del Medano
Cabo San Lucas
11/43-27-87

Guadalajara
American Express Travel Service
Plaza Los Arcos Local 1A
Ave. Vallarta 2440
3/630-0200

Ixtapa
American Express Travel Service
Hotel Krystal
Boulevard Ixtapa S/N
75/33-08-53

Puerto Vallarta
American Express Travel Service
Lobby Hotel Camino Real
Playa Las Estacas, S/N
32/21-50-00

do more

Travel

http://www.americanexpress.com/travel

American Express Travel Service Offices are found in central locations throughout Mexico.